This Missal belongs to

......................

New *Saint Joseph*
WEEKDAY MISSAL
Complete Edition

Vol. II — Pentecost to Advent

This new Missal has been especially
designed to help you participate
at Mass . . . in the fullest and most
active way possible.

HOW EASY IT IS TO USE THIS MISSAL

- Refer to the Calendars (pp. [20]-[30] and
  [32]-[37] or use the **St. Joseph Missal Guide**
  (No. 921-G).

- This arrow (**↓**) means **continue to read.** This
  arrow (**➔**) indicates a **reference** back to the
  Order of Mass ("Ordinary") or to another part
  of the "Proper."

- **Boldface** type always indicates the **people's
  parts** that are to be recited aloud.

*The People of God together with Christ
worship the Father*

New ... Saint Joseph

WEEKDAY MISSAL

COMPLETE EDITION

Vol. II — Pentecost to Advent

**With the Proper Mass Texts
for Every Weekday and Feast Day
in a Continuous and Easy-to-Use Arrangement**

**ALL READINGS FOR LITURGICAL YEARS I and II
IN THE "NEW AMERICAN BIBLE" TEXT**

**With the People's Parts
Printed in Boldface Type**

In accordance with the New Liturgy
as decreed by Vatican II

Dedicated to ST. JOSEPH
Patron of the Universal Church

CATHOLIC BOOK PUBLISHING CO.
New York, N.Y.

NIHIL OBSTAT: Daniel V. Flynn, J.C.D.
Censor Librorum

IMPRIMATUR: ✠ James P. Mahoney, D.D.
Vicar General, Archdiocese of New York

The St. Joseph Missals have been diligently prepared with the invaluable assistance of a special Board of Editors, including specialists in Liturgy, Sacred Scripture, Catechetics, Sacred Music and Art.

In this Weekday Missal, the Scriptural commentaries have been prepared by a staff under the direction of Most Reverend James Sullivan.

The Scriptural Readings and Responsorial Psalms are taken from the *Lectionary for Mass*, © 1970 by Confraternity of Christian Doctrine, Washington, D.C. All rights reserved.

The prose English translations of the Sequence are taken from Joseph Connolly, *Hymns of the Roman Liturgy* (London: Longmans, Green.

English translation of the Roman Missal, original texts of The Alternative Opening Prayers, Invitatories and the Penitential Rites; titles, responsorial psalms and alleluia verses of the Lectionary for Mass, Copyright © 1969, 1970, 1973, International Committee on English in the Liturgy, Inc. All rights reserved.

(T-921)

PREFACE

Content

This new **St. Joseph Weekday Missal** is a necessary companion to the **St. Joseph Sunday Missal**. It contains the Mass texts for all weekdays of the year. In doing so, it combines the Antiphons and Prayers found in the new **Sacramentary** together with the Readings and Intervenient Chants contained in the **Lectionary for Mass**. The faithful are thus given access to the biblical and liturgical riches that make up the treasury of the Church.

So great is the amount of this treasury that a complete Weekday Missal is not possible in one manageable volume. The present volume contains the texts for the weekday Masses from Pentecost to Advent. It also includes the most commonly used texts for Masses and Prayers for Various Needs and Occasions and Votive Masses (such as those for First Fridays and Saturdays).

Simplified Arrangement

All the texts in this Missal are clearly printed in large type, in an attractive and legible arrangement. All references are immediately visible and one always knows what comes next, and whose part it is. Succinct rubrics inform the reader of the options available and running heads identify the Masses on each page.

Participation Format

A simple, easy-to-understand method of instant identification of the parts of Mass ensures that everyone will do all of, but only, those parts of the Mass which pertain to his office. **Boldface** type is used for all people's parts; lightface type indicates the priest's or lector's parts. All the people's texts are arranged for congregational recitation.

Order (Ordinary) of the Mass

The complete text of the Order of Mass with all its options is printed in the center of the book and clearly marked for easy use. Each part is numbered to facilitate finding one's place quickly when turning from the Proper to the Ordinary. All the options are given and conveniently arranged. A valuable Introduction to the Order of Mass contains much useful information.

General Introduction

An extensive General Introduction provides a complete view of the liturgical year, the different liturgical days, the various classifications of celebrations and their make-up, the readings and chants, the color of vestments, and an important note on the type of participation to be attained.

Seasonal Introductions and Mass Themes

Every season of the liturgical year is prefixed by a useful Introduction providing necessary background for the better understanding of the liturgy and the easier use of the Missal. Each weekday Mass is prefaced by a short note focusing on one of the themes of the day's texts and inculcating some particular Christian attitude that may be found in them.

Concise Scriptural Commentaries

A completely original, especially written and very helpful series of commentaries gives the setting for the scripture readings and the lessons to be drawn from them, leading to a more fruitful hearing on the part of the people when they are proclaimed.

Calendars for Quick Reference

Two sets of Calendars are provided to help the reader find the Mass as quickly as possible. One is the General Calendar of feasts that may occur month

by month. The second is the Calendar of Sundays
and Feasts that gives the precise date for every Sunday and hence week of the year. There is also a more
general Table of Principal Celebrations of the Liturgical Year which provides the dates for the two cycles
of scripture readings until 1999.

Tables of Choices of Masses and Texts

Two handy tables give a bird's-eye view of the
choices of Masses and texts available on any given
day.

Aids to Prayer and Study

A popular selection of private prayers and devo-
tions offers a fine starting point for a better prayer
life. An invaluable Index section facilitates a deeper
study of the Liturgy by listing all the Masses, Saints,
Biblical Readings, Responsorial Psalms, and Prefaces.

In the Spirit of Vatican II

We trust that this Missal with its many outstanding
features will enable all those who attend weekday
Mass, in keeping with the desire of the Church, to
"be led to that full, conscious, and active participation in liturgical celebrations which is demanded by
the very nature of the liturgy" (Vatican II, **On the
Sacred Liturgy,** no. 14).

CONTENTS

GENERAL INTRODUCTION

THE LITURGICAL YEAR

The Church celebrates the memory of Christ's saving work on appointed days in the course of the year. Every week the Church celebrates the memorial of the resurrection on Sunday, which is called the Lord's Day. This is also celebrated, together with the passion of Jesus, on the great feast of Easter once a year. Throughout the year the entire mystery of Christ is unfolded, and the birthdays (days of death) of the saints are commemorated.

By means of devotional exercises, instruction, prayer, and works of penance and mercy, the Church, according to traditional practices, completes the formation of the faithful during the various seasons of the liturgical year.

1. The Liturgical Day in General

Each day is made holy through liturgical celebrations of God's people, especially the eucharistic sacrifice and the divine office.

The liturgical day runs from midnight to midnight, but the observance of Sunday and of solemnities begins with the evening of the preceding day.

2. Sunday

The Church celebrates the paschal mystery on the first day of the week, known as the Lord's Day or Sunday. This follows a tradition handed down from the Apostles, which took its origin from the day of Christ's resurrection. Thus Sunday should be considered the original feast day.

Because of its special importance, the celebration of Sunday is replaced only by solemnities or by feasts of the Lord. The Sundays of Advent, Lent, and the Easter season, however, take precedence over all solemnities and feasts of the Lord. Solemnities that occur on these Sundays are observed on the preceding Saturday.

3. Solemnities, Feasts, and Memorials

In the course of the year, as the Church celebrates the mystery of Christ, Mary the Mother of God is especially honored, and the martyrs and other saints are proposed as examples for the faithful.

The celebration of the days of saints who have universal significance is required throughout the entire Church. The days of other saints are listed in the calendar as optional or are left to the veneration of particular churches, countries, or religious communities.

The different types of celebrations are distinguished from each other by their importance and are accordingly called solemnities, feasts, and memorials.

a) Solemnities are the days of greatest importance and begin with first vespers of the preceding day. Several solemnities have their own vigil Mass, to be used when Mass is celebrated in the evening of the preceding day.

The celebration of Easter and Christmas continues for eight days. Each octave is governed by its own rules.

b) Feasts are celebrated within the limits of a natural day. They do not have first vespers, with the exception of feasts of the Lord which fall on Sundays in ordinary time and Sundays of the Christmas season and which are substituted for the Sunday office.

c) Memorials are either obligatory or optional. Their observance is combined with the celebration of the occurring weekday according to norms given in the body of the Missal and seen at a glance in the Table of Choices of Masses and Texts, pp [18]-[19].

Obligatory memorials which occur on Lenten weekdays may be celebrated only as optional memorials.

Should more than one optional memorial fall on the same day, only one is celebrated; the others are omitted.

d) On Saturdays in ordinary time when there is no obligatory memorial, an optional memorial of the Blessed Virgin Mary may be observed.

4. Weekdays

The days following Sunday are called weekdays. They are celebrated in various ways according to the importance each one has:

a) Ash Wednesday and the days of Holy Week, from Monday to Thursday inclusive, are preferred to all other celebrations.

b) The weekdays of Advent from December 17 to December 24 inclusive and all the weekdays of Lent take precedence over obligatory memorials.

c) All other weekdays yield to solemnities and feasts and are combined with memorials.

d) Each weekday has its own special liturgical texts—at least, insofar as the Readings and Intervenient Chants are concerned.

e) The weekdays of the major seasons have their own Antiphons and Prayers. The weekdays of Ordinary Time make use of the Antiphons and Prayers of the preceding Sunday or any of the thirty-four Sundays or those of Masses for Various Needs and Occasions as well as Votive Masses or even Masses for the Dead, as noted in the Tables of Choices of Masses and Texts, pp. [18]-[19].

5. Liturgical Seasons

a) The **Advent Season** begins with first vespers of the Sunday which falls on or closest to November 30 and ends before first vespers of Christmas.

b) The **Christmas season** runs from first vespers of Christmas until Sunday after Epiphany, or after January 6, inclusive.

c) **Lent** lasts from Ash Wednesday to the Mass of the Lord's Supper exclusive.

d) The **Easter Triduum** begins with the evening Mass of the Lord's Supper, reaches its high point in the Easter vigil, and closes with vespers on Easter Sunday.

e) The **Easter Season** comprises the fifty days from Easter Sunday to Pentecost which are celebrated as one feast day, sometimes called "the great Sunday."

f) **Ordinary Time** comprises the thirty-three or thirty-four weeks in the course of the year which celebrate no particular aspect of the mystery of Christ. Instead, especially on the last Sundays, the mystery of Christ in all its fullness is celebrated. This period is known as ordinary time.

Ordinary time begins on Monday after the Sunday following January 6 and continues until Tuesday before Ash Wednesday inclusive. (See p. 1.) It begins again on Monday after Pentecost and ends before first vespers of the First Sunday of Advent.

6. Readings and Intervenient Chants

a) On the weekdays of Advent, Christmas, Lent, and Easter there is a one-year cycle of Readings. These do not change from year to year.

b) On the weekdays of Ordinary Time, however, there is a two-year cycle for the First Readings and Responsorial Psalms. Those designated "Year I" are read on odd numbered years and those designated "Year II" are read on even numbered years.

c) This Missal has been arranged as follows: The Masses with invariable Readings (for example, those of Advent) are arranged in the traditional order of Antiphons, Prayers and Readings.

The Masses with variable Readings (for example, the weekdays in Ordinary Time or the Masses of the Commons) are arranged in two separate sections. One section contains the Antiphons and Prayers (Entrance Antiphon, Opening Prayer, Prayer over the Gifts,

Communion Antiphon, and Prayer after Communion) and the other Readings and Intervenient Chants. (Year I and Year II are also found in different sections: see pp. 70 and 781.)

COLOR OF VESTMENTS

Colors in vestments give an effective expression to the celebration of the mysteries of the faith and, in the course of the year, a sense of progress in the Christian life.

1. White is used in Masses of the Easter and Christmas Seasons; on feasts and commemorations of the Lord, other than of his passion; on feasts and memorials of Mary, the angels, saints who were not martyrs.

2. Red is used on Passion Sunday (Palm Sunday) and Good Friday, Pentecost, celebrations of the passion, birthday feasts of the apostles and evangelists, and feasts of martyrs.

3. Green is used in the offices and Masses of ordinary time.

4. Violet is used in Lent and Advent. It may also be used in offices and Masses for the dead.

5. Black may be used in Masses for the dead.

6. Rose may be used on Gaudete Sunday (Third Sunday of Advent) and Laetare Sunday (Fourth Sunday of Lent).

7. On more solemn days it is permitted to use more precious vestments even if not of the color of day.

8. Votive Masses of the Lord, the Blessed Virgin Mary, and the Saints may be said either with the color proper to the Mass, or with the color proper to the day or Season.

9. Masses for various needs may be said in the color proper either to the day or to the Season.

10. Ritual Masses are said in the color indicated in rubrics of the rite.

11. Adaptations to needs and culture of various regions may be proposed to the Holy See by Episcopal Conferences.

PARTICIPATION AT MASS

1.   External and Internal Participation

a) The basic norm is that each one present at Mass has the right and duty to participate externally in the celebration—each one, however, doing wholly but solely what pertains to him by reason of the order to which he belongs or of the role assigned him.

b) In preparing liturgical celebrations, all concerned—whether of clergy or laity and whether directly interested in ritual or musical or pastoral aspects—should be consulted and should cooperate harmoniously under the leadership of the rector of the church.

c) In order that external participation may produce its full effects, something more is required than mere observance of laws governing valid and licit celebration. Participation should be **internal** also. This consists in right dispositions of faith and charity, cooperation with divine grace and effects.

d) Both internal and external participation is perfected by **spiritual,** and especially (when the law of Church permits) **sacramental**, Communion.

2.   Participation of the Faithful

a) Every Mass is an action not only of Christ but of the Church. This is true even if none of the faithful is present; nor is the efficacy or value of the Mass as an action of the Church thereby nullified or essentially impaired. Yet by their presence and association with the celebrant and by the sacramental or at least spiritual Communion the faithful participate in the mystical communion of the Church with Christ in the Paschal Mystery. For it is the Church which is here and now acting in them.

b) Participation of the faithful is not a ministry but an office. This prerogative is theirs, not as individuals but insofar as they unite to form one assembly or congregation. For it is as a community that they are the sacramental sign of the Church. Hence, it is through incorporation into the community, just as it is through incorporation into the Church, that individuals are associated with Christ in the Easter Mystery of his dying and rising in glory.

c) It is of the highest importance, that, whether few or many, the faithful participate in the Mass as one body, united in faith and charity and avoiding every appearance of singularity or division. It is as a group that the Word of God is addressed to them and the body of the Lord is offered to them and that they are invited to pray, to sing, to perform certain actions and take certain positions. It is, therefore, as a group that they should respond. This common participation, lest it degenerate into more outward conformity for the sake of good order, should be motivated by a deep religious sense of their relation to one another and to God in Christ and of their office to be a sign of the mystery of the Church.

d) Special importance attaches to acclamations and responses of the faithful. These are not merely external signs of common celebration but effect and foster communion with the celebrant as a sacramental sign of Christ. This degree of active participation is the requisite minimum, in whatever form Mass is celebrated.

e) Next in importance are: the Penitential Rite; Profession of Faith; responses in the Prayer of the Faithful; the Lord's Prayer.

f) Other parts pertaining to the faithful—either alone, or together with celebrant or choir or chanter —are either rites in themselves or accompaniments of rites. To the **former** belong: the **Gloria;** Responsorial Psalm; **Sanctus;** anamnetic acclamation: hymn or silent prayer after Communion. To the **latter** belong: various processional chants (Entrance and Communion Antiphons); chant during preparations for a Gospel; **the Lamb of God** during the rite of the breaking of the bread.

HANDY TABLE OF CHOICES OF MASSES

MASS NOT OF DAY ON →	Funeral Requiem	Requiem of Notification of a Death and on First Anniversary	"Daily" or Ordinary Requiem (1)	Nuptial Mass	For Grave Cause (2) with leave of Local Ordinary in Public Mass	For Just Cause (3) in judgment of Celebrant or Rector of church in Public Mass	Saint in Calendar or Martyrology of day	Votive, Public or Private
Easter Triduum — Sundays of Advent, Lent, Easter — Solemnities — Mon., Tues., Wed. of Holy Week	No (4)	No	No	No	No	No	No	No
Ash Wed., — Mon., Tues., Wed. of Holy Week	Yes	No	No	Yes	No	No	No	No
Mon. to Sat. of Octave of Easter	Yes	No	No (5)	No (5)	No	No	No	No
Sundays in Seasons of Christmas and "of the year"	Yes	No	No (6)	No (6)	Yes	No	No	No
Ferias of Advent from Dec 17 and octave of Christmas	Yes	No	No	Yes	Yes	Yes	No (7)	No
Ferias of Lent (exc. Ash Wed. and Holy Week)	Yes	Yes	No	Yes	Yes	Yes	No (7)	No
Ferias of Seasons of Advent to Dec. 16, of Christmas from Jan. 2, and of Easter	Yes	Yes	No	Yes	Yes	Yes	Yes (8)	No
Feasts	Yes	No	No	Yes	No	No	Yes	No
Obligatory Memorial	Yes	Yes	Yes	Yes	Yes	Yes	Yes	Yes
Optional Memorial	Yes	Yes	Yes	Yes	Yes	Yes	Yes	Yes
Ferias in Season "of the year"	Yes	Yes	Yes	Yes	Yes	Yes	Yes	Yes

(1) Mass must be applied for deceased — (2) Reference is to Masses for special intentions, including votive Masses, if common good is involved in a serious way — (3) Reference is to same Masses as in (2), if common good is involved in a real, though not necessarily serious, way — (4) Funeral Requiem is permitted on a Solemnity, that is not a Holyday in place — (5) Mass of day is said instead, with marriage rite included. One of readings of nuptial Mass can be used in place of corresponding reading in Mass of Day, exc. in Easter Triduum, on Solemnity if a Holyday in place, and on Solemnities of Christmas, Epiphany, Ascension, Pentecost, and Corpus Christi — (6) Not forbidden, if Mass is not a parish Mass — (7) If Saint is in general calendar, opening prayer in honor of the Saint may be said instead of opening prayer of Mass of the day — (8) Applies only to Saint in general or proper calendar.

Composed by: William T. Barry, C.SS.R.

[18]

HANDY TABLE OF CHOICES OF TEXTS

CHOICE OF TEXTS for → in ↓	ENTRANCE SONG	OPENING PRAYER	READING AND INTERVENIENT CHANTS	OFFERTORY SONG	PRAYER OVER GIFTS	COMMUNION SONG	PRAYER AFTER COMMUNION
Mass of Sunday	If sung: proper, as in Roman or Simple Graduals; or song approved by Bishops' Conference. — If not sung: antiphon in Missal (1)	Proper	Proper, as in Lectionary (2)	If sung: proper, as in Roman or Simple Graduals; or song approved by Bishops' Conference. — If not sung: it is omitted	Proper	If sung: proper, as in Roman or Simple Graduals; or song approved by Bishops' Conference. — If not sung: antiphon in Missal	Proper
Mass of Feria in Advent, Christmas, Lent, Easter Seasons	Same as above	Same as above (3)	Same as above (2)	Same as above	Same as above	Same as above	Same as above
Mass of Solemnity or Feast	Same as above. If no proper in Missal or Gradual: from Common	If no proper: from Common	If no proper: from Common (2)	If no proper in Graduals: from Common	Same as above. If no proper: from Common	Same as above. If no proper in Missal or Graduals: from Common	Same as above. If no proper: from Common or current Feria
Mass of Memorial	Same as above	Same as above	Same as above (2)	Same as above	If no proper, from Common or current Feria	Same as above	If no proper: from Common or current Feria
Mass of Feria in Season "of year"	As for Mass of preceding Sunday or of any Sunday "of year"	As for Mass of preceding Sunday or of any Sunday "of year" or any Mass for Various Occasions or Various Prayers	Proper, as in Lectionary (2)	As for Mass of preceding Sunday or of any Sunday "of year"	Same as for Opening Prayer	As for Mass of preceding Sunday or of any Sunday "of year"	As for Mass of preceding Sunday or of any Sunday "of year" or any Mass for Various Occasions or Various Prayers
Mass of Dead	If sung: proper, as in Roman or Simple Gradual; or an approved song. — If not sung: antiphon in Missal (1)	Any appropriate prayer for the dead in Missal	Any appropriate readings for the dead in Lectionary (2)	If sung: as in Roman or Simple Gradual; or an approved song. If not sung it is omitted	Any appropriate prayer for dead in Missal	If sung: as in Roman or Simple Gradual; or approved song — if not sung: antiphon in Missal	Any appropriate prayer for dead in Missal

(1) If current Missal is used, only antiphon after 1st reading is recited, psalm assigned to reading in Lectionary is used. If it is sung, it is permitted to use any of following: psalm assigned to reading in Lectionary; any psalm & response from common texts given in Lectionary for the season or class to which (in the case of a Solemnity, Feast, or Memorial) a Saint belongs; Gradual for the Mass given in Roman Gradual; the responsorial or alleluiatic psalm for the Mass given in Simple Gradual. If Alleluia or other chant before Gospel is not sung, it may be omitted — (3) If Alleluia or other chant before Gospel occurs on Feria from Dec. 17 to 24 or on Feria within octave of Christmas or Feria (exc. Ash Wed. & Holy Week) on Feria of Lent, opening prayer of Memorial may be used in ferial Mass, instead of opening prayer proper to Mass.

Composed by: William T. Barry, C.SS.R.

GENERAL CALENDAR

JANUARY

1.	Octave of Christmas SOLEMNITY OF MARY, MOTHER OF GOD	Solemnity
2.	Basil the Great and Gregory Nazianzen, bishops and doctors	Memorial
3.		
4.	Blessed Elizabeth Ann Seton	Memorial
5.	Blessed John Neumann, bishop	Memorial
6.	EPIPHANY	Solemnity
7.	*Raymond of Penyafort, priest**	
8.		
9.		
10.		
11.		
12.		
13.	*Hilary, bishop and doctor*	
14.		
15.		
16.		
17.	Anthony, abbot	Memorial
18.		
19.		
20.	*Fabian, pope and martyr* *Sebastian, martyr*	
21.	Agnes, virgin and martyr	Memorial
22.	*Vincent, deacon and martyr*	
23.		
24.	Francis de Sales, bishop and doctor	Memorial
25.	CONVERSION OF PAUL, APOSTLE	Feast
26.	Timothy and Titus, bishops	Memorial
27.	*Angela Merici, virgin*	
28.	Thomas Aquinas, priest and doctor	Memorial
29.		
30.		
31.	John Bosco, priest	Memorial

Sunday after January 6: BAPTISM OF THE LORD   Feast

*When no rank is given, it is an optional memorial.

FEBRUARY

1.		
2.	PRESENTATION OF THE LORD	Feast
3.	*Blase, bishop and martyr*	
	Ansgar, bishop	
4.		
5.	Agatha, virgin and martyr	Memorial
6.	Paul Miki and companions, martyrs	Memorial
7.		
8.	*Jerome Emiliani*	
9.		
10.	Scholastica, virgin	Memorial
11.	*Our Lady of Lourdes*	
12.		
13.		
14.	Cyril, monk, and Methodius, bishop	Memorial
15.		
16.		
17.	*Seven Founders of the Order of Servites*	
18.		
19.		
20.		
21.	*Peter Damian, bishop and doctor*	
22.	CHAIR OF PETER, APOSTLE	Feast
23.	Polycarp, bishop and martyr	Memorial
24.		
25.		
26.		
27.		
28.		

MARCH

1.		
2.		
3.		
4.	*Casimir*	
5.		
6.		
7.	Perpetua and Felicity, martyrs	Memorial
8.	*John of God, religious*	
9.	*Frances of Rome, religious*	

10.
11.
12.
13.
14.
15.
16.
17. *Patrick, bishop*
18. *Cyril of Jerusalem, bishop and doctor*
19. JOSEPH, HUSBAND OF MARY   Solemnity
20.
21.
22.
23. *Turibius de Mongrovejo, bishop*
24.
25. ANNUNCIATION   Solemnity
26.
27.
28.
29.
30.
31.

APRIL

1.
2. *Francis of Paola, hermit*
3.
4. *Isidore, bishop and doctor*
5. *Vincent Ferrer, priest*
6.
7. John Baptist de la Salle, priest   Memorial
8.
9.
10.
11. *Stanislaus, bishop and martyr*
12.
13. *Martin I, pope and martyr*
14.
15.
16.
17.
18.
19.

20.
21. *Anselm, bishop and doctor*
22.
23. *George, martyr*
24. *Fidelis of Sigmaringen, priest and martyr*
25. MARK, EVANGELIST   Feast
26.
27.
28. *Peter Chanel, priest and martyr*
29. Catherine of Siena, virgin and doctor   Memorial
30. *Pius V, pope*

MAY

1. *Joseph the Worker*
2. Athanasius, bishop and doctor   Memorial
3. PHILIP AND JAMES, APOSTLES   Feast
4.
5.
6.
7.
8.
9.
10.
11.
12. *Nereus and Achilleus, martyrs*
    Pancras, martyr
13.
14. MATTHIAS, APOSTLE   Feast
15. *Isidore*
16.
17.
18. *John I, pope and martyr*
19.
20. *Bernardine of Siena, priest*
21.
22.
23.
24.
25. *Venerable Bede, priest and doctor*
    Gregory VII, pope
    Mary Magdalene de Pazzi, virgin
26. Philip Neri, priest   Memorial

27. *Augustine of Canterbury, bishop*
28.
29.
30.
31. VISITATION   Feast

First Sunday after Pentecost: HOLY TRINITY   Sol.
Thursday after Holy Trinity: CORPUS CHRISTI   Sol.
Friday following Second Sunday after Pentecost:
    SACRED HEART   Solemnity
Saturday following Second Sunday after Pentecost:
    IMMACULATE HEART OF MARY

JUNE

1. Justin, martyr   Memorial
2. *Marcellinus and Peter, martyrs*
3. Charles Lwanga and companions, martyrs
                                               Memorial
4.
5. Boniface, bishop and martyr   Memorial
6. *Norbert, bishop*
7.
8.
9. *Ephrem, deacon and doctor*
10.
11. Barnabas, apostle   Memorial
12.
13. Anthony of Padua, priest and doctor   Memorial
14.
15.
16.
17.
18.
19. *Romuald, abbot*
20.
21. Aloysius Gonzaga, religious   Memorial
22. *Paulinus of Nola, bishop*
    John Fisher, bishop and martyr, and
      Thomas More, martyr
23.
24. BIRTH OF JOHN THE BAPTIST   Solemnity

25.
26.
27. *Cyril of Alexandria, bishop and doctor*
28. Irenaeus, bishop and martyr   Memorial
29. PETER AND PAUL, APOSTLES   Solemnity
30. *First Martyrs of the Church of Rome*

JULY

1.
2.
3. THOMAS, APOSTLE   Feast
4. *Elizabeth of Portugal*
   Independence Day
5. *Anthony Zaccaria, priest*
6. *Maria Goretti, virgin and martyr*
7.
8.
9.
10.
11. Benedict, abbot   Memorial
12.
13. *Henry*
14. *Camillus de Lellis, priest*
15. Bonaventure, bishop and doctor   Memorial
16. *Our Lady of Mount Carmel*
17.
18.
19.
20.
21. *Lawrence of Brindisi, priest and doctor*
22. Mary Magdalene   Memorial
23. *Bridget, religious*
24.
25. JAMES, APOSTLE   Feast
26. Joachim and Ann, parents of Mary   Memorial
27.
28.
29. Martha   Memorial
30. *Peter Chrysologus, bishop and doctor*
31. Ignatius of Loyola, priest   Memorial

AUGUST

1. Alphonsus Liguori, bishop and doctor   Memorial
2. *Eusebius of Vercelli, bishop*
3.
4. John Vianney, priest   Memorial
5. *Dedication of St. Mary Major*
6. TRANSFIGURATION   Feast
7. *Sixtus II, pope and martyr, and companions,*
    martyrs
    Cajetan, priest
8. Dominic, priest   Memorial
9.
10. LAWRENCE, DEACON AND MARTYR   Feast
11. Clare, virgin   Memorial
12.
13. *Pontian, pope and martyr, and Hippolytus,*
    priest and martyr
14.
15. ASSUMPTION   Solemnity
16. *Stephen of Hungary*
17.
18.
19. *John Eudes, priest*
20. Bernard, abbot and doctor   Memorial
21. Pius X, pope   Memorial
22. Queenship of Mary   Memorial
23. *Rose of Lima, virgin*
24. BARTHOLOMEW, APOSTLE   Feast
25. *Louis*
    Joseph Calasanz, priest
26.
27. Monica   Memorial
28. Augustine, bishop and doctor   Memorial
29. Beheading of John the Baptist, martyr   Memorial
30.
31.

SEPTEMBER

First Monday in September: LABOR DAY

1.
2.
3. Gregory the Great, pope and doctor   Memorial
4.

5.
6.
7.
8. BIRTH OF MARY   Feast
9. Peter Claver, priest   Memorial
10.
11.
12.
13. John Chrysostom, bishop and doctor   Memorial
14. TRIUMPH OF THE CROSS   Feast
15. Our Lady of Sorrows   Memorial
16. Cornelius, pope and martyr, and
      Cyprian, bishop and martyr   Memorial
17. *Robert Bellarmine, bishop and doctor*
18.
19. *Januarius, bishop and martyr*
20.
21. MATTHEW, APOSTLE AND EVANGELIST   Feast
22.
23.
24.
25.
26. *Cosmas and Damian, martyrs*   Memorial
27. Vincent de Paul, priest   Memorial
28. *Wenceslaus, martyr*
29. MICHAEL, GABRIEL, AND RAPHAEL,
      ARCHANGELS   Feast
30. Jerome, priest and doctor   Memorial

OCTOBER

1. Theresa of the Child Jesus, virgin   Memorial
2. Guardian Angels   Memorial
3.
4. Francis of Assisi   Memorial
5.
6. *Bruno, priest*
7. Our Lady of the Rosary   Memorial
8.
9. *Denis, bishop and martyr, and companions,*
      martyrs
   John Leonardi, priest
10.

11.
12.
13.
14. *Callistus I, pope and martyr*
15. Teresa of Avila, virgin and doctor   Memorial
16. *Hedwig, religious*
    Margaret Mary Alacoque, virgin
17. Ignatius of Antioch, bishop and martyr   Memorial
18. LUKE, EVANGELIST   Feast
19. Isaac Jogues and John de Brébeuf, priests and
        martyrs, and companions, martyrs   Memorial
    Paul of the Cross, priest
20.
21.
22.
23. *John of Capistrano, priest*
24. *Anthony Claret, bishop*
25.
26.
27.
28. SIMON AND JUDE, APOSTLES   Feast
29.
30.
31.

NOVEMBER

1. ALL SAINTS   Solemnity
2. ALL SOULS
3. *Martin de Porres, religious*
4. Charles Borromeo, bishop   Memorial
5.
6.
7.
8.
9. DEDICATION OF ST. JOHN LATERAN   Feast
10. Leo the Great, pope and doctor   Memorial
11. Martin of Tours, bishop   Memorial
12. Josaphat, bishop and martyr   Memorial
13. Frances Xavier Cabrini, virgin   Memorial
14.
15. *Albert the Great, bishop and doctor*

16. *Margaret of Scotland*
    Gertrude, virgin
17. Elizabeth of Hungary, religious — Memorial
18. *Dedication of the churches of Peter and*
    Paul, apostles
19.
20.
21. Presentation of Mary — Memorial
22. Cecilia, virgin and martyr — Memorial
23. *Clement I, pope and martyr*
    Columban, abbot
24.
25.
26.
27.
28.
29.
30. ANDREW, APOSTLE — Feast
Fourth Thursday *Thanksgiving Day*
Last Sunday in Ordinary Time:
    CHRIST THE KING — Solemnity

DECEMBER

1.
2.
3. Francis Xavier, priest — Memorial
4. *John Damascene, priest and doctor*
5.
6. *Nicholas, bishop*
7. Ambrose, bishop and doctor — Memorial
8. IMMACULATE CONCEPTION — Solemnity
9.
10.
11. *Damasus I, pope*
12. Our Lady of Guadalupe — Memorial
    Jane Frances de Chantal, religious
13. Lucy, virgin and martyr — Memorial
14. John of the Cross, priest and doctor — Memorial
15.
16.
17.
18.

19.
20.
21. *Peter Canisius, priest and doctor*
22.
23. *John of Kanty, priest*
24.
25. CHRISTMAS   Solemnity
26. STEPHEN, FIRST MARTYR   Feast
27. JOHN, APOSTLE AND EVANGELIST   Feast
28. HOLY INNOCENTS, MARTYRS   Feast
29. *Thomas Becket, bishop and martyr*
30.
31. *Sylvester I, pope*

Sunday within the octave of Christmas or
if there is no Sunday within the octave,
December 30: HOLY FAMILY   Feast

PRINCIPAL CELEBRATIONS OF LITURGICAL YEAR

Year	Lectionary Weekday Cycle	Ash Wednes.	Easter	Ascension	Pentecost	Corpus Christi	First Sun. of Advent
1974	II	27 Feb.	14 Apr.	23 May	2 June	13 June	1 Dec.
1975	I	12 Feb.	30 Mar.	8 May	18 May	29 May	30 Nov.
1976	II	3 Mar.	18 Apr.	27 May	6 June	17 June	28 Nov.
1977	I	23 Feb.	10 Apr.	19 May	29 May	9 June	27 Nov.
1978	II	8 Feb.	26 Mar.	4 May	14 May	25 May	3 Dec.
1979	I	28 Feb.	15 Apr.	24 May	3 June	14 June	2 Dec.
1980	II	20 Feb.	6 Apr.	15 May	25 May	5 June	30 Nov.
1981	I	4 Mar.	19 Apr.	28 May	7 June	18 June	29 Nov.
1982	II	24 Feb.	11 Apr.	20 May	30 May	10 June	28 Nov.
1983	I	16 Feb.	3 Apr.	12 May	22 May	2 June	27 Nov.
1984	II	7 Mar.	22 Apr.	31 May	10 June	21 June	2 Dec.
1985	I	20 Feb.	7 Apr.	16 May	26 May	6 June	1 Dec.
1986	II	12 Feb.	30 Mar.	8 May	18 May	29 May	30 Nov.
1987	I	4 Mar.	19 Apr.	28 May	7 June	18 June	29 Nov.
1988	II	17 Feb.	3 Apr.	12 May	22 May	2 June	27 Nov.
1989	I	8 Feb.	26 Mar.	4 May	14 May	25 May	3 Dec.
1990	II	28 Feb.	15 Apr.	24 May	3 June	14 June	2 Dec.
1991	I	13 Feb.	31 Mar.	9 May	19 May	30 May	1 Dec.
1992	II	4 Mar.	19 Apr.	28 May	7 June	18 June	29 Nov.
1993	I	24 Feb.	11 Apr.	20 May	30 May	10 June	28 Nov.
1994	II	16 Feb.	3 Apr.	12 May	22 May	2 June	27 Nov.
1995	I	1 Mar.	16 Apr.	25 May	4 June	15 June	3 Dec.
1996	II	21 Feb.	7 Apr.	16 May	26 May	6 June	1 Dec.
1997	I	12 Feb.	30 Mar.	8 May	18 May	29 May	30 Nov.
1998	II	25 Feb.	12 Apr.	21 May	31 May	11 June	29 Nov.
1999	I	17 Feb.	4 Apr.	13 May	23 May	3 June	28 Nov.

YEAR A

Sunday or Feast	1986	1989	1992	1995	1998	2001
1st Sun. Advent	30 Nov.	3 Dec.	29 Nov.	3 Dec.	29 Nov.	2 Dec.
Immac. Concep.	8 Dec.	8 Dec.	8 Dec.	8 Dec.	8 Dec.	8 Dec.
2nd Sun. Advent	7 Dec.	10 Dec.	6 Dec.	10 Dec.	6 Dec.	9 Dec.
3rd Sun. Advent	14 Dec.	17 Dec.	13 Dec.	17 Dec.	13 Dec.	16 Dec.
4th Sun. Advent	21 Dec.	24 Dec.	20 Dec.	24 Dec.	20 Dec.	23 Dec.
Christmas	25 Dec.	25 Dec.	25 Dec.	25 Dec.	25 Dec.	25 Dec.
Holy Family	28 Dec.	31 Dec.	27 Dec.	31 Dec.	27 Dec.	30 Dec.

Sunday or Feast	1987	1990	1993	1996	1999	2002
Oct. of Christ.	1 Jan.	1 Jan.	1 Jan.	1 Jan.	1 Jan.	1 Jan.
Epiphany	4 Jan.	7 Jan.	3 Jan.	7 Jan.	3 Jan.	6 Jan.
Baptism of Lord	11 Jan.	—	10 Jan.	—	10 Jan.	13 Jan.
2nd Ord. Sun.	18 Jan.	14 Jan.	17 Jan.	14 Jan.	17 Jan.	20 Jan.
3rd Ord. Sun.	25 Jan.	21 Jan.	24 Jan.	21 Jan.	24 Jan.	27 Jan.
4th Ord. Sun.	1 Feb.	28 Jan.	31 Jan.	28 Jan.	31 Jan.	3 Feb.
5th Ord. Sun.	8 Feb.	4 Feb.	7 Feb.	4 Feb.	7 Feb.	10 Feb.
6th Ord. Sun.	15 Feb.	11 Feb.	14 Feb.	11 Feb.	14 Feb.	—
7th Ord. Sun.	22 Feb.	18 Feb.	21 Feb.	18 Feb.	—	—
8th Ord. Sun.	1 Mar.	25 Feb.	—	—	—	—
9th Ord. Sun.	—	—	—	—	—	—
1st Sun. of Lent	8 Mar.	4 Mar.	28 Feb.	25 Feb.	21 Feb.	17 Feb.
2nd Sun. of Lent	15 Mar.	11 Mar.	7 Mar.	3 Mar.	28 Feb.	24 Feb.
3rd Sun. of Lent	22 Mar.	18 Mar.	14 Mar.	10 Mar.	7 Mar.	3 Mar.
4th Sun. of Lent	29 Mar.	25 Mar.	21 Mar.	17 Mar.	14 Mar.	10 Mar.
5th Sun. of Lent	5 Apr.	1 Apr.	28 Mar.	24 Mar.	21 Mar.	17 Mar.
Palm Sun.	12 Apr.	8 Apr.	4 Apr.	31 Mar.	28 Mar.	24 Mar.
Holy Thurs.	16 Apr.	12 Apr.	8 Apr.	4 Apr.	1 Apr.	28 Mar.
Holy Thurs.	16 Apr.	12 Apr.	8 Apr.	4 Apr.	1 Apr.	28 Mar.
Good Friday	17 Apr.	13 Apr.	9 Apr.	5 Apr.	2 Apr.	29 Mar.
Easter Vigil	18 Apr.	14 Apr.	10 Apr.	6 Apr.	3 Apr.	30 Mar.
Easter Sunday	19 Apr.	15 Apr.	11 Apr.	7 Apr.	4 Apr.	31 Mar.
2nd Sun. Easter	26 Apr.	22 Apr.	18 Apr.	14 Apr.	11 Apr.	7 Apr.
3rd Sun. Easter	3 May	29 Apr.	25 Apr.	21 Apr.	18 Apr.	14 Apr.
4th Sun. Easter	10 May	6 May	2 May	28 Apr.	25 Apr.	21 Apr.
5th Sun. Easter	17 May	13 May	9 May	5 May	2 May	28 Apr.

YEAR A

Sunday or Feast	1987	1990	1993	1996	1999	2002
6th Sun. Easter	24 May	20 May	16 May	12 May	9 May	5 May
Ascension	28 May	24 May	20 May	16 May	13 May	9 May
7th Sun. Easter	31 May	27 May	23 May	19 May	16 May	12 May
Pentecost Sun.	7 June	3 June	30 May	26 May	23 May	19 May
Trinity Sun.	14 June	10 June	6 June	2 June	30 May	26 May
Body and Blood	21 June	17 June	13 June	9 June	6 June	2 June
9th Ord. Sun.	—	—	—	—	—	—
10th Ord. Sun.	—	—	—	—	—	9 June
11th Ord. Sun.	—	—	—	16 June	13 June	16 June
12th Ord. Sun.	—	24 June	20 June	23 June	20 June	23 June
13th Ord. Sun.	28 June	1 July	27 June	30 June	27 June	30 June
14th Ord. Sun.	5 July	8 July	4 July	7 July	4 July	7 July
15th Ord. Sun.	12 July	15 July	11 July	14 July	11 July	14 July
16th Ord. Sun.	19 July	22 July	18 July	21 July	18 July	21 July
17th Ord. Sun.	26 July	29 July	25 July	28 July	25 July	28 July
18th Ord. Sun.	2 Aug.	5 Aug.	1 Aug.	4 Aug.	1 Aug.	4 Aug.
19th Ord. Sun.	9 Aug.	12 Aug.	8 Aug.	11 Aug.	8 Aug.	11 Aug.
Assumption	15 Aug.	15 Aug.	15 Aug.	15 Aug.	15 Aug.	15 Aug.
20th Ord. Sun.	16 Aug.	19 Aug.	—	18 Aug.	—	18 Aug.
21st Ord. Sun.	23 Aug.	26 Aug.	22 Aug.	25 Aug.	22 Aug.	25 Aug.
22nd Ord. Sun.	30 Aug.	2 Sept.	29 Aug.	1 Sept.	29 Aug.	1 Sept.
23rd Ord. Sun.	6 Sept.	9 Sept.	5 Sept.	8 Sept.	5 Sept.	8 Sept.
24th Ord. Sun.	13 Sept.	16 Sept.	12 Sept.	15 Sept.	12 Sept.	15 Sept.
25th Ord. Sun.	20 Sept.	23 Sept.	19 Sept.	22 Sept.	19 Sept.	22 Sept.
26th Ord. Sun.	27 Sept.	30 Sept.	26 Sept.	29 Sept.	26 Sept.	29 Sept.
27th Ord. Sun.	4 Oct.	7 Oct.	3 Oct.	6 Oct.	3 Oct.	6 Oct.
28th Ord. Sun.	11 Oct.	14 Oct.	10 Oct.	13 Oct.	10 Oct.	13 Oct.
29th Ord. Sun.	18 Oct.	21 Oct.	17 Oct.	20 Oct.	17 Oct.	20 Oct.
30th Ord. Sun.	25 Oct.	28 Oct.	24 Oct.	27 Oct.	24 Oct.	27 Oct.
All Saints	1 Nov.	1 Nov.	1 Nov.	1 Nov.	1 Nov.	1 Nov.
31st Ord. Sun.	—	4 Nov.	31 Oct.	3 Nov.	31 Oct.	3 Nov.
32nd Ord. Sun.	8 Nov.	11 Nov.	7 Nov.	10 Nov.	7 Nov.	10 Nov.
33rd Ord. Sun.	15 Nov.	18 Nov.	14 Nov.	17 Nov.	14 Nov.	17 Nov.
34th Ord. Sun.	22 Nov.	25 Nov.	21 Nov.	24 Nov.	21 Nov.	24 Nov.

YEAR B

Sunday or Feast	1984	1987	1990	1993	1996	1999
1st Sun. Advent	2 Dec.	29 Nov.	2 Dec.	28 Nov.	1 Dec.	28 Nov.
Immac. Concep.	8 Dec.	8 Dec.	8 Dec.	8 Dec.	8 Dec.	8 Dec.
2nd Sun. Advent	9 Dec.	6 Dec.	9 Dec.	5 Dec.	8 Dec.	5 Dec.
3rd Sun. Advent	16 Dec.	13 Dec.	16 Dec.	12 Dec.	15 Dec.	12 Dec.
4th Sun. Advent	23 Dec.	20 Dec.	23 Dec.	19 Dec.	22 Dec.	19 Dec.
Christmas	25 Dec.	25 Dec.	25 Dec.	25 Dec.	25 Dec.	25 Dec.
Holy Family	30 Dec.	27 Dec.	30 Dec	26 Dec.	29 Dec.	26 Dec.

Sunday or Feast	1985	1988	1991	1994	1997	2000
Oct. of Christ.	1 Jan.	1 Jan.	1 Jan.	1 Jan.	1 Jan.	1 Jan.
Epiphany	6 Jan.	3 Jan.	6 Jan.	2 Jan.	5 Jan.	2 Jan.
Baptism of Lord	13 Jan.	10 Jan.	13 Jan.	9 Jan.	12 Jan.	9 Jan.
2nd Ord. Sun.	20 Jan.	17 Jan.	20 Jan.	16 Jan.	19 Jan.	16 Jan.
3rd Ord. Sun.	27 Jan.	24 Jan.	27 Jan.	23 Jan.	26 Jan.	23 Jan.
4th Ord. Sun.	3 Feb.	31 Jan.	3 Feb.	30 Jan.	2 Feb.	30 Jan.
5th Ord. Sun.	10 Feb.	7 Feb.	10 Feb.	6 Feb.	9 Feb.	6 Feb.
6th Ord. Sun.	17 Feb.	14 Feb.	—	13 Feb.	—	13 Feb.
7th Ord. Sun.	—	—	—	—	—	20 Feb.
8th Ord. Sun.	—	—	—	—	—	27 Feb.
9th Ord. Sun.	—	—	—	—	—	5 Mar.
1st Sun. of Lent	24 Feb.	21 Feb.	17 Feb.	20 Feb.	16 Feb.	12 Mar.
2nd Sun. of Lent	3 Mar.	28 Feb.	24 Feb.	27 Feb.	23 Feb.	19 Mar.
3rd Sun. of Lent	10 Mar.	6 Mar	3 Mar.	6 Mar.	2 Mar.	26 Mar.
4th Sun. of Lent	17 Mar.	13 Mar.	10 Mar	13 Mar.	9 Mar.	2 Apr.
5th Sun. of Lent	24 Mar.	20 Mar	17 Mar	20 Mar.	16 Mar	9 Apr.
Palm Sun.	31 Mar.	27 Mar.	24 Mar.	27 Mar.	23 Mar.	16 Apr.
Holy Thurs.	4 Apr.	31 Mar.	28 Mar.	31 Mar.	27 Mar.	20 Apr.
Holy Thurs.	4 Apr.	31 Mar.	28 Mar.	31 Mar.	27 Mar.	20 Apr.
Good Friday	5 Apr.	1 Apr.	29 Mar.	1 Apr.	28 Mar.	21 Apr.
Easter Vigil	6 Apr.	2 Apr.	30 Mar.	2 Apr.	29 Mar.	22 Apr.
Easter Sunday	7 Apr.	3 Apr.	31 Mar.	3 Apr.	30 Mar.	23 Apr.
2nd Sun. Easter	14 Apr.	10 Apr.	7 Apr.	10 Apr.	6 Apr.	30 Apr.
3rd Sun. Easter	21 Apr.	17 Apr.	14 Apr.	17 Apr.	13 Apr.	7 May
4th Sun. Easter	28 Apr.	24 Apr.	21 Apr.	24 Apr.	20 Apr.	14 May
5th Sun. Easter	5 May	1 May	28 Apr.	1 May	27 Apr.	21 May

YEAR B

Sunday or Feast	1985	1988	1991	1994	1997	2000
6th Sun. Easter	12 May	8 May	5 May	8 May	4 May	28 May
Ascension	16 May	12 May	9 May	12 May	8 May	1 June
7th Sun. Easter	19 May	15 May	12 May	15 May	11 May	4 June
Pentecost Sun.	26 May	22 May	19 May	22 May	18 May	11 June
Trinity Sun.	2 June	29 May	26 May	29 May	25 May	18 June
Body and Blood	9 June	5 June	2 June	5 June	1 June	25 June
9th Ord. Sun.	—	—	—	—	—	—
10th Ord. Sun.	—	—	9 June	—	8 June	—
11th Ord. Sun.	16 June	12 June	16 June	12 June	15 June	—
12th Ord. Sun.	23 June	19 June	23 June	19 June	22 June	—
13th Ord. Sun.	30 June	26 June	30 June	26 June	29 June	2 July
14th Ord. Sun.	7 July	3 July	7 July	3 July	6 July	9 July
15th Ord. Sun.	14 July	10 July	14 July	10 July	13 July	16 July
16th Ord. Sun.	21 July	17 July	21 July	17 July	20 July	23 July
17th Ord. Sun.	28 July	24 July	28 July	24 July	27 July	30 July
18th Ord. Sun.	4 Aug.	31 July	4 Aug.	31 July	3 Aug.	6 Aug.
19th Ord. Sun.	11 Aug.	7 Aug.	11 Aug.	7 Aug.	10 Aug.	13 Aug.
Assumption	15 Aug.	15 Aug.	15 Aug.	15 Aug.	15 Aug.	15 Aug.
20th Ord. Sun.	18 Aug.	14 Aug.	18 Aug.	14 Aug.	17 Aug.	20 Aug.
21st Ord. Sun.	25 Aug.	21 Aug.	25 Aug.	21 Aug.	24 Aug.	27 Aug.
22nd Ord. Sun.	1 Sept.	28 Aug.	1 Sept.	28 Aug.	31 Aug.	3 Sept.
23rd Ord. Sun.	8 Sept.	4 Sept.	8 Sept.	4 Sept.	7 Sept.	10 Sept.
24th Ord. Sun.	15 Sept.	11 Sept.	15 Sept.	11 Sept.	14 Sept.	17 Sept.
25th Ord. Sun.	22 Sept.	18 Sept.	22 Sept.	18 Sept.	21 Sept.	24 Sept.
26th Ord. Sun.	29 Sept.	25 Sept.	29 Sept.	25 Sept.	28 Sept.	1 Oct.
27th Ord. Sun.	6 Oct.	2 Oct.	6 Oct.	2 Oct.	5 Oct.	8 Oct.
28th Ord. Sun.	13 Oct.	9 Oct.	13 Oct.	9 Oct.	12 Oct.	15 Oct.
29th Ord. Sun.	20 Oct.	16 Oct.	20 Oct.	16 Oct.	19 Oct.	22 Oct.
30th Ord. Sun.	27 Oct.	23 Oct.	27 Oct.	23 Oct.	26 Oct.	29 Oct.
All Saints	1 Nov.	1 Nov.	1 Nov.	1 Nov.	1 Nov.	1 Nov.
31st Ord. Sun.	3 Nov.	30 Oct.	3 Nov.	30 Oct.	2 Nov.	5 Nov.
32nd Ord. Sun.	10 Nov.	6 Nov.	10 Nov.	6 Nov.	9 Nov.	12 Nov.
33rd Ord. Sun.	17 Nov.	13 Nov.	17 Nov.	13 Nov.	16 Nov.	19 Nov.
34th Ord. Sun.	24 Nov.	20 Nov.	24 Nov.	20 Nov.	23 Nov.	26 Nov.

YEAR C

Sunday or Feast	1985	1988	1991	1994	1997	2000
1st. Sun. Advent	1 Dec.	27 Nov.	1 Dec.	27 Nov.	30 Nov.	3 Dec.
Immac. Concep.	8 Dec.	8 Dec.	8 Dec.	8 Dec.	8 Dec.	8 Dec.
2nd Sun. Advent	8 Dec.	4 Dec.	8 Dec.	4 Dec.	7 Dec.	10 Dec.
3rd Sun. Advent	15 Dec.	11 Dec.	15 Dec.	11 Dec.	14 Dec.	17 Dec.
4th Sun. Advent	22 Dec.	18 Dec.	22 Dec.	18 Dec.	21 Dec.	24 Dec.
Christmas	25 Dec.	25 Dec.	25 Dec.	25 Dec.	25 Dec.	25 Dec.
Holy Family	29 Dec.	—	29 Dec.	—	28 Dec.	31 Dec.

Sunday or Feast	1986	1989	1992	1995	1998	2001
Oct. of Christ.	1 Jan.	1 Jan.	1 Jan.	1 Jan.	1 Jan.	1 Jan.
Epiphany	5 Jan.	8 Jan.	5 Jan.	8 Jan.	4 Jan.	—
Baptism of Lord	12 Jan.	—	12 Jan.	—	11 Jan.	7 Jan.
2nd Ord. Sun.	19 Jan.	15 Jan.	19 Jan.	15 Jan.	18 Jan.	14 Jan.
3rd Ord. Sun.	26 Jan.	22 Jan.	26 Jan.	22 Jan.	25 Jan.	21 Jan.
4th Ord. Sun.	2 Feb.	29 Jan.	2 Feb.	29 Jan.	1 Feb.	28 Jan.
5th Ord. Sun.	9 Feb.	5 Feb.	9 Feb.	5 Feb.	8 Feb.	4 Feb.
6th Ord. Sun.	—	—	16 Feb.	12 Feb.	15 Feb.	11 Feb.
7th Ord. Sun.	—	—	23 Feb.	19 Feb.	22 Feb.	18 Feb.
8th Ord. Sun.	—	—	1 Mar.	26 Feb.	—	25 Feb.
9th Ord. Sun.	—	—	—	—	—	—
1st Sun. of Lent	16 Feb.	12 Feb.	8 Mar.	5 Mar.	1 Mar.	4 Mar.
2nd Sun. of Lent	23 Feb.	19 Feb.	15 Mar.	12 Mar.	8 Mar.	11 Mar.
3rd Sun. of Lent	2 Mar.	26 Feb.	22 Mar.	19 Mar.	15 Mar.	18 Mar.
4th Sun. of Lent	9 Mar.	5 Mar.	29 Mar.	26 Mar.	22 Mar.	25 Mar.
5th Sun. of Lent	16 Mar.	12 Mar.	5 Apr.	2 Apr.	29 Mar.	1 Apr.
Palm Sun.	23 Mar.	19 Mar.	12 Apr.	9 Apr.	5 Apr.	8 Apr.
Holy Thurs.	27 Mar.	23 Mar.	16 Apr.	13 Apr.	9 Apr.	12 Apr.
Holy Thurs.	27 Mar.	23 Mar.	16 Apr.	13 Apr.	9 Apr.	12 Apr.
Good Friday	28 Mar.	24 Mar.	17 Apr.	14 Apr.	10 Apr.	13 Apr.
Easter Vigil	29 Mar.	25 Mar.	18 Apr.	15 Apr.	11 Apr.	14 Apr.
Easter Sunday	30 Mar.	26 Mar.	19 Apr.	16 Apr.	12 Apr.	15 Apr.
2nd Sun. Easter	6 Apr.	2 Apr.	26 Apr.	23 Apr.	19 Apr.	22 Apr.
3rd Sun. Easter	13 Apr.	9 Apr.	3 May	30 Apr.	26 Apr.	29 Apr.
4th Sun. Easter	20 Apr.	16 Apr.	10 May	7 May	3 May	6 May
5th Sun. Easter	27 Apr.	23 Apr.	17 May	14 May	10 May	13 May

YEAR C

Sunday or Feast	1986	1989	1992	1995	1998	2001
6th Sun. Easter	4 May	30 Apr.	24 May	21 May	17 May	20 May
Ascension	8 May	4 May	28 May	25 May	21 May	24 May
7th Sun. Easter	11 May	7 May	31 May	28 May	24 May	27 May
Pentecost Sun.	18 May	14 May	7 June	4 June	31 May	3 June
Trinity Sun.	25 May	21 May	14 June	11 June	7 June	10 June
Body and Blood	1 June	28 May	21 June	18 June	14 June	17 June
9th Ord. Sun.	—	4 June	—	—	—	—
10th Ord. Sun.	8 June	11 June	—	—	—	—
11th Ord. Sun.	15 June	18 June	—	—	—	—
12th Ord. Sun.	22 June	25 June	—	25 June	21 June	24 June
13th Ord. Sun.	29 June	2 July	28 June	2 July	28 June	1 July
14th Ord. Sun.	6 July	9 July	5 July	9 July	5 July	8 July
15th Ord. Sun	13 July	16 July	12 July	16 July	12 July	15 July
16th Ord. Sun	20 July	23 July	19 July	23 July	19 July	22 July
17th Ord. Sun.	27 July	30 July	26 July	30 July	26 July	29 July
18th Ord. Sun.	3 Aug.	6 Aug.	2 Aug.	6 Aug.	2 Aug.	5 Aug.
19th Ord. Sun.	10 Aug.	13 Aug.	9 Aug.	13 Aug.	9 Aug.	12 Aug.
Assumption	15 Aug.	15 Aug.	15 Aug.	15 Aug.	15 Aug.	15 Aug.
20th Ord. Sun.	17 Aug.	20 Aug.	16 Aug.	20 Aug.	16 Aug.	19 Aug.
21st Ord.Sun.	24 Aug.	27 Aug.	23 Aug.	27 Aug.	23 Aug.	26 Aug.
22nd Ord. Sun.	31 Aug.	3 Sept.	30 Aug.	3 Sept.	30 Aug.	2 Sept.
23rd Ord. Sun.	7 Sept.	10 Sept.	6 Sept.	10 Sept.	6 Sept.	9 Sept.
24th Ord. Sun.	14 Sept.	17 Sept.	13 Sept.	17 Sept.	13 Sept.	16 Sept.
25th Ord. Sun.	21 Sept.	24 Sept.	20 Sept.	24 Sept.	20 Sept.	23 Sept.
26th Ord. Sun.	28 Sept.	1 Oct.	27 Sept.	1 Oct.	27 Sept.	30 Sept.
27th Ord. Sun.	5 Oct.	8 Oct.	4 Oct.	8 Oct.	4 Oct.	7 Oct.
28th Ord. Sun.	12 Oct.	15 Oct.	11 Oct.	15 Oct.	11 Oct.	14 Oct.
29th Ord. Sun.	19 Oct.	22 Oct.	18 Oct.	22 Oct.	18 Oct.	21 Oct.
30th Ord. Sun.	26 Oct.	29 Oct.	25 Oct.	29 Oct.	25 Oct.	28 Oct.
All Saints	1 Nov.	1 Nov.	1 Nov.	1 Nov.	1 Nov.	1 Nov.
31st Ord. Sun.	2 Nov.	5 Nov.	—	5 Nov.	—	4 Nov.
32nd Ord. Sun.	9 Nov.	12 Nov.	8 Nov.	12 Nov.	8 Nov.	11 Nov.
33rd Ord. Sun.	16 Nov.	19 Nov.	15 Nov.	19 Nov.	15 Nov.	18 Nov.
34th Ord. Sun.	23 Nov.	26 Nov.	22 Nov.	26 Nov.	22 Nov.	25 Nov.

CHRISTMAS
EASTER
ORDINARY TIME
ADVENT
LENT

VIRGINIA BRODERICK

PROPER OF SEASONS
ORDINARY TIME

The Sundays and Weekdays of the major seasons of the year are distinguished by their relationship to the Solemnities of Christmas (Advent, Christmas) and Easter (Lent, Easter). On the other hand, Ordinary Time refers to all the other Sundays and Weekdays under the all-embracing heading of celebrations of the "Day of the Lord." These weeks number thirty-three or thirty-four according to the particular character of each year and are assigned to two parts of the liturgical year.

The first part begins with the Sunday after Epiphany (although this First Sunday is perpetually impeded by the Feast of the Baptism of the Lord) and continues until Ash Wednesday. Since the date of Easter varies each year, this part may include as few as four and as many as nine weeks.

The second part of Ordinary Time begins with the day after Pentecost and runs to the Saturday before the First Sunday of Advent. If the number of ordinary weeks is thirty-four, the week after Pentecost is the one which follows immediately the last week celebrated before Lent. The Masses of Pentecost, Trinity Sunday and (in countries where Corpus Christi is not observed as a holyday of obligation and is therefore celebrated on the following Sunday) Corpus Christi replace the Sunday Masses in these weeks. If the number of ordinary weeks is thirty-three, the first week which would otherwise follow Pentecost is omitted.

Some of the unique features of these weeks are:

The Gloria and the Profession of Faith are sung or said on Sundays; they are omitted on weekdays.

On Sundays one of the Prefaces for Sundays in Ordinary Time is sung or said; on Weekdays, a Weekday Preface.

Two Antiphons are given for Communion, the first from the Psalms, the second for the most part from the Gospel. Either one may be selected, but preference should be given to the Antiphon which may happen to come from the Gospel of the Mass.

The most important characteristic of this Ordinary Time is that, in accord with the pastoral needs of the people, any of the thirty-four Sunday Masses may be celebrated on any weekday, regardless of the particular week in which it falls. This does not refer to the readings and intervenient chants which form the "Lectionary texts" and should be taken from the Weekday Lectionary for this period but to the processional chants (Entrance and Communion Antiphons) and presidential prayers (Opening Prayer, Prayer over the Gifts, and Prayer after Communion) which form the "Sacramentary texts."

Because of this fact, for this period of the year only, Lectionary texts will not be integrated into the Sacramentary texts in this Missal. The Sacramentary texts will be given first and the Lectionary texts will be given in another section. (Solely for the sake of convenience, cross-references according to weeks will be included.)

As mentioned on p. [14], there is a two-year cycle for the First Readings and Responsorial Psalms during Ordinary Time. Since this Missal is concerned only with Ordinary Time, the Readings have been arranged in two separate sections for easy use. The Readings for Year I (odd numbered years) are given before the Ordinary and those for Year II (even numbered years) are given after the Ordinary.

Friday After the Second Sunday After Pentecost
SACRED HEART
Solemnity

The heart is the pulsing center of a man, source of the amazing life-stream within us. It is a good symbol for love. This feast celebrates the truth that God is love, and his desire is for all generations to discover him through Christ, and respond to his love.

YEAR A
(1975, 1978, 1981, 1984, 1987, 1990, 1993, 1996)

ENTRANCE ANT. Ps 33, 11. 19

The thoughts of his heart last through every generation, that he will rescue them from death and feed them in time of famine. ➔ No. 2, p. 614

OPENING PRAYER
Let us pray
[that we will respond to the love of Christ]
Father,
we rejoice in the gifts of love
we have received from the heart of Jesus your Son.
Open our hearts to share his life
and continue to bless us with his love.
We ask this through our Lord Jesus Christ, your Son,
who lives and reigns with you and the Holy Spirit,
one God, for ever and ever. ℞. **Amen.** ℣

OR
Father,
we have wounded the heart of Jesus your Son,
but he brings us forgiveness and grace.
Help us to prove our grateful love
and make amends for our sins.
We ask this through our Lord Jesus Christ, your Son,
who lives and reigns with you and the Holy Spirit,
one God, for ever and ever. ℞. **Amen.** ℣

3

ALTERNATIVE OPENING PRAYER

Let us pray

[that the love of Christ's heart

may touch the world with healing and peace]

Father,

we honor the heart of your Son

broken by man's cruelty,

yet symbol of love's triumph,

pledge of all that man is called to be.

Teach us to see Christ in the lives we touch,

to offer him living worship

by love-filled service to our brothers and sisters.

We ask this through Christ our Lord. ℞. **Amen.** ℣

READING I   Dt 7, 6-11

Christians are the new people of God, chosen by him and sacred to
him. God always keeps his part of the bargain to show mercy to those
who love him. If we observe his commandments, we will enjoy his
love and mercy forever.

A reading from the book of Deuteronomy

Moses said to the people: "You are a people sacred
to the Lord, your God; he has chosen you from all
the nations on the face of the earth to be a people
peculiarly his own. It was not because you are the
largest of all nations that the Lord set his heart on
you and chose you, for you are really the smallest
of all nations. It was because the Lord loved you
and because of his fidelity to the oath he had sworn
to your fathers, that he brought you out with his
strong hand from the place of slavery, and ransomed
you from the hand of Pharaoh, king of Egypt. Understand, then, that the Lord, your God, is God indeed,
the faithful God who keeps his merciful covenant
down to the thousandth generation toward those
who love him and keep his commandments, but who
repays with destruction the person who hates him;
he does not dally with such a one, but makes him
personally pay for it. You shall therefore carefully

observe the commandments, the statutes and the decrees which I enjoin on you today."—This is the Word of the Lord. ℟. **Thanks be to God.** ✣

Responsorial Psalm Ps 103, 1-2. 3-4. 6-7. 8. 10

℟. (17) **The Lord's kindness is everlasting to those who fear him.**

Bless the Lord, O my soul;
    and all my being, bless his holy name.
Bless the Lord, O my soul,
    and forget not all his benefits. — ℟

He pardons all your iniquities,
    he heals all your ills.
He redeems your life from destruction,
    he crowns you with kindness and compassion.—℟

Merciful and gracious is the Lord,
    slow to anger and abounding in kindness.
Not according to our sins does he deal with us,
    nor does he requite us according to our crimes.—℟

READING II 1 Jn 4, 7-16

The key to our true relationship with God is whether we have love for our fellow man. If we refuse to love others, how can we love God who has demonstrated his real love for all men?

Beloved,
let us love one another
because love is of God;
everyone who loves is begotten of God
and has knowledge of God.
The man without love has known nothing of God,
for God is love.
God's love was revealed in our midst in this way:
he sent his only Son to the world
that we might have life through him.
Love, then, consists in this:
not that we have loved God,
but that he has loved us

and has sent his Son as an offering for our sins.
God dwells in us,
Beloved,
if God has loved us so,
we must have the same love for one another.
No one has ever seen God.
Yet if we love one another
God dwells in us
and his love is brought to perfection in us.
The way we know we remain in him
and he in us
is that he has given us of his Spirit,
We have seen for ourselves, and can testify,
that the Father has sent the Son as savior of the
   world.
When anyone acknowledges that Jesus is the Son
   of God,
God dwells in him
and he in God.
We have come to know and to believe in the love
   God has for us.
This is the Word of the Lord. ℟. **Thanks be to God. ℣**

GOSPEL   Mt 11, 25-30
Alleluia (Mt 11, 29)
℟. **Alleluia.** Take my yoke upon you;
learn from me, for I am gentle and lowly in heart.
   ℟. **Alleluia.**

The heart of Jesus constitutes a refuge for all who are overcome by
life's troubles and tribulations. This fact enables us to find ever renewed courage on our journey toward the everlasting joys of heaven.

℣. The Lord be with you. ℟. **And also with you.**
✠ A reading from the holy gospel according to Matthew. ℟. **Glory to you, Lord.**

At that time Jesus said: "Father, Lord, of heaven and
earth, to you I offer praise; for what you have hidden
from the learned and the clever you have revealed
to the merest children. Father, it is true. You have

graciously willed it so. Everything has been given over to me by my Father. No one knows the Son but the Father, and no one knows the Father but the Son —and anyone to whom the Son wishes to reveal him.

"Come to me, all you who are weary and find life burdensome, and I will refresh you. Take my yoke upon your shoulders and learn from me, for I am gentle and humble of heart. Your souls will find rest, for my yoke is easy and my burden light."—This is the gospel of the Lord. ℞. **Praise to you, Lord Jesus Christ.**

➤ No. 14, p. 622

PRAYER OVER THE GIFTS

Lord,
look on the heart of Christ your Son
filled with love for us.
Because of his love
accept our eucharist and forgive our sins.
Grant this through Christ our Lord. ℞. **Amen.** ▼

PREFACE (P 45)

℣. The Lord be with you. ℞. **And also with you.**
℣. Lift up your hearts. ℞. **We lift them up to the Lord.** ℣. Let us give thanks to the Lord our God.
℞. **It is right to give him thanks and praise.**

Father, all-powerful and ever-living God,
we do well always and everywhere to give you thanks
through Jesus Christ our Lord.

Lifted high on the cross,
Christ gave his life for us,
so much did he love us.
From his wounded side flowed blood and water,
the fountain of sacramental life in the Church.
To his open heart the Savior invites all men,
to draw water in joy from the springs of salvation.

Now, with all the saints and angels,
we praise you for ever:

➤ No. 23, p. 627

COMMUNION ANT.   Jn 7, 37-38

The Lord says: If anyone is thirsty, let him come to me; whoever believes in me, let him drink. Streams of living water shall flow out from within him. ℣

OR   Jn 19, 34

One of the soldiers pierced Jesus' side with a lance, and at once there flowed out blood and water. ℣

PRAYER AFTER COMMUNION

Father,
may this sacrament fill us with love.
Draw us closer to Christ your Son
and help us to recognize him in others.
We ask this in the name of Jesus the Lord.
℟. **Amen.**   ➔ No. 32, p. 650

YEAR B

(1976, 1979, 1982, 1985, 1988, 1991, 1994, 1997)

ENTRANCE ANT.   Ps 33, 11. 19

The thoughts of his heart last through every generation, that he will rescue them from death and feed them in time of famine.   ➔ No. 2, p. 614

OPENING PRAYER

Let us pray

[that we will respond to the love of Christ]

Father,
we rejoice in the gifts of love
we have received from the heart of Jesus your Son.
Open our hearts to share his life
and continue to bless us with his love.
We ask this through our Lord Jesus Christ, your Son,
who lives and reigns with you and the Holy Spirit,
one God, for ever and ever. ℟. **Amen.** ℣

OR

Father,
we have wounded the heart of Jesus your Son,
but he brings us forgiveness and grace.
Help us to prove our grateful love
and make amends for our sins.
We ask this through our Lord Jesus Christ, your Son,
who lives and reigns with you and the Holy Spirit,
one God, for ever and ever. R̅. **Amen.** ✠

ALTERNATIVE OPENING PRAYER

Let us pray
  [that the love of Christ's heart
    may touch the world with healing and peace]

Father,
we honor the heart of your Son
broken by man's cruelty,
yet symbol of love's triumph,
pledge of all that man is called to be.
Teach us to see Christ in the lives we touch,
  to offer him living worship
by love-filled service to our brothers and sisters.
We ask this through Christ our Lord. R̅. **Amen.** ✠

READING I   Hos 11, 1. 3-4. 8-9

God's love for his people is the love of a father for his child. The
prophet Hosea, in describing this divine tenderness for the prodigal
child, proclaims the divine tenderness of the only Son for all sinners.

A reading from the book of prophet Hosea
When Israel was a child I loved him,
  out of Egypt I called my son.
Yet it was I who taught Ephraim to walk,
  who took them in my arms;
I drew them with human cords,
  with bands of love;
I fostered them like one
  who raises an infant to his cheeks;

Yet, though I stooped to feed my child,
  they did not know that I was their healer.
My heart is overwhelmed,
  my pity is stirred.
I will not give vent to my blazing anger,
  I will not destroy Ephraim again;
For I am God and not man,
  the Holy One present among you;
  I will not let the flames consume you.
This is the Word of the Lord. ℟. **Thanks be to God.** ℣

Responsorial Psalm   Is 12, 2-3. 4. 5-6

℟. (3) **You will draw water joyfully from the springs
of salvation.**

God indeed is my savior;
  I am confident and unafraid.
My strength and my courage is the Lord,
  and he has been my savior.
With joy you will draw water
  at the fountain of salvation. — ℟

Give thanks to the Lord, acclaim his name;
  among the nations make known his deeds,
  proclaim how exalted is his name. — ℟

Sing praise to the Lord for his glorious achievement;
  let this be known throughout all the earth.
Shout with exultation, O city of Zion,
  for great in your midst
  is the Holy One of Israel! — ℟ ℣

READING II   Eph 3, 8-12. 14-19

Paul shouts his joy at having been chosen to proclaim the mystery
of God's love, manifested in Christ and in the Church. The Holy Spirit
can give us a glimpse of this mystery; but we must live it in order
to understand it well.

A reading from the letter of Paul to the Ephesians
To me, the least of all believers, was given the grace
to preach to the Gentiles the unfathomable riches of

Christ and to enlighten all men on the mysterious
design which for ages was hidden in God, the Creator
of all. Now, therefore, through the church, God's
manifold wisdom is made known to the principalities
and powers of heaven, in accord with his age-old
purpose, carried out in Christ Jesus our Lord. In
Christ and through faith in him we can speak freely
to God, drawing near him with confidence.

That is why I kneel before the Father from whom
every family in heaven and on earth takes its name;
and I pray that he will bestow on you gifts in keeping with the riches of his glory. May he strengthen
you inwardly through the working of his Spirit. May
Christ dwell in your hearts through faith, and may
charity be the root and foundation of your life. Thus
you will be able to grasp fully, with all the holy ones,
the breadth and length and height and depth of
Christ's love, and experience this love which surpasses all knowledge, so that you may attain to the
fullness of God himself.—This is the Word of the
Lord. ℟. **Thanks be to God.** ✠

GOSPEL   Jn 19, 31-37
Alleluia (Mt 11, 29)

℟. **Alleluia.** Take my yoke upon you;
for I am gentle and lowly in heart. ℟. **Alleluia.**

OR

Alleluia (Jn 1, 4-10)

℟. **Alleluia.** God first loved us
and sent his Son to take away our sins. ℟. **Alleluia.**

On the cross Christ loves us to the end: he accomplishes his mission
of Savior by shedding his blood for the salvation of all men. The
cross is thus the sign and the summit of love.

℣. The Lord be with you. ℟. **And also with you.**
✠ A reading from the holy gospel according to John
℟. **Glory to you, Lord.**

Since it was the Preparation Day the Jews did not want to have the bodies left on the cross during the sabbath, for that sabbath was a solemn feast day. They asked Pilate that the legs be broken and that the bodies be taken away. Accordingly, the soldiers came and broke the legs of the men crucified with Jesus, first of the one, then of the other. When they came to Jesus and saw that he was already dead, they did not break his legs. One of the soldiers thrust a lance into his side, and immediately blood and water flowed out. (This testimony has been given by an eyewitness, and his testimony is true. He tells what he knows is true, so that you may believe.) These events took place for the fulfillment of Scripture:

"Break none of his bones."

There is still another Scripture passage which says:

"They shall look on him whom they have pierced." This is the gospel of the Lord. ℟. **Praise to you, Lord Jesus Christ.**
➔ No. 14, p. 622

PRAYER OVER THE GIFTS
Lord,
look on the heart of Christ your Son
filled with love for us.
Because of his love
accept our eucharist and forgive our sins.
Grant this through Christ our Lord. ℟. **Amen.**
➔ Pref. (P 45), p. 7

COMMUNION ANT.   Jn 7, 37-38
The Lord says: If anyone is thirsty, let him come to me; whoever believes in me, let him drink. Streams of living water shall flow out from within him. ⱽ

OR   Jn 19, 34
One of the soldiers pierced Jesus' side with a lance, and at once there flowed out blood and water. ⱽ

PRAYER AFTER COMMUNION

Father,
may this sacrament fill us with love.
Draw us closer to Christ your Son
and help us to recognize him in others.
We ask this in the name of Jesus the Lord.
℟. **Amen.**   ➜ No. 32, p. 650

YEAR C

(1977, 1980, 1983, 1986, 1989, 1992, 1995, 1998)

ENTRANCE ANT.   Ps 33, 11. 19

The thoughts of his heart last through every generation, that he will rescue them from death and feed them in time of famine.   ➜ No. 2, p. 614

OPENING PRAYER

Let us pray
  [that we will respond to the love of Christ]
Father,
we rejoice in the gifts of love
we have received from the heart of Jesus your Son.
Open our hearts to share his life
and continue to bless us with his love.
We ask this through our Lord Jesus Christ, your Son,
who lives and reigns with you and the Holy Spirit,
one God, for ever and ever. ℟. **Amen.** ℣

OR

Father,
we have wounded the heart of Jesus your Son,
but he brings us forgiveness and grace.
Help us to prove our grateful love
and make amends for our sins.
We ask this through our Lord Jesus Christ, your Son,
who lives and reigns with you and the Holy Spirit,
one God, for ever and ever. ℟. **Amen.** ℣

ALTERNATIVE OPENING PRAYER

Let us pray
   [that the love of Christ's heart
   may touch the world with healing and peace]
Father,
we honor the heart of your Son
broken by man's cruelty,
yet symbol of love's triumph,
pledge of all that man is called to be.
Teach us to see Christ in the lives we touch,
to offer him living worship
by love-filled service to our brothers and sisters.
We ask this through Christ our Lord. ℟. **Amen.** ✠

READING I   Ez 34, 11-16

The Bible uses countless images to try and express the inexpressible
—how much God loves us. This passage uses the image of the Good
Shepherd.

   A reading from the book of the prophet Ezekiel

Thus says the Lord God: I myself will look after and
tend my sheep. **As** a shepherd tends his flock when
he finds himself among his scattered sheep, so will
I tend my sheep. I will rescue them from every place
where they were scattered when it was cloudy and
dark. I will lead them out from among the peoples
and gather them from the foreign lands; I will bring
them back to their own country and pasture them
upon the mountains of Israel [in the land's ravines
and all its inhabited places]. In good pastures will I
pasture them, and on the mountain heights of Israel
shall be their grazing ground. There they shall lie
down on good grazing ground, and in rich pastures
shall they be pastured on the mountains of Israel. I
myself will pasture my sheep; I myself will give them
rest, says the Lord God. The lost I will seek out, the
strayed I will bring back, the injured I will bind up,
the sick I will heal [but the sleek and the strong I

will destroy], shepherding them rightly.—This is the
Word of the Lord. ℟. **Thanks be to God.** ℣

Responsorial Psalm   Ps 23, 1-3. 3-4. 5. 6

℟. (1) **The Lord is my shepherd;**
   there is nothing I shall want.

The Lord is my shepherd; I shall not want.
   In verdant pastures he gives me repose;
Beside restful waters he leads me;
   he refreshes my soul. — ℟

He guides me in right paths
   for his name's sake.
Even though I walk in the dark valley
   I fear no evil; for you are at my side
With your rod and your staff
   that give me courage. — ℟

You spread the table before me
   in the sight of my foes;
You anoint my head with oil;
   my cup overflows. — ℟

Only goodness and kindness follow me
   all the days of my life;
And I shall dwell in the house of the Lord
   for years to come. — ℟ ℣

READING II   Rom 5, 5-11

The Spirit of Truth is also the Spirit of Love. Christ's love led him
to die for us and transmit to men the gift of his Spirit.

   A reading from the letter of Paul to the Romans
The love of God has been poured out in our hearts
through the Holy Spirit who has been given to us.
At the appointed time, when we were still powerless,
Christ died for us godless men. It is rare that anyone
should lay down his life for a just man, though it is
barely possible that for a good man someone may
have the courage to die. It is precisely in this that

God proves his love for us: that while we were still
sinners, Christ died for us. Now that we have been
justified by his blood, it is all the more certain that
we shall be saved by him from God's wrath. For if,
when we were God's enemies, we were reconciled
to him by the death of his Son, it is all the more
certain that we who have been reconciled will be
saved by his life. Not only that; we go so far as to
make God our boast through our Lord Jesus Christ,
through whom we have now received reconciliation.
This is the Word of the Lord. ℟. **Thanks be to God.** ℣

GOSPEL　　　　　　　　　　　　　　　　Lk 15, 3-7

Alleluia (Mt 11, 29)

℟. **Alleluia.** Take my yoke upon you;
for I am gentle and lowly in heart. ℟. **Alleluia.**

OR

Alleluia (Jn 1, 4-10)

℟. **Alleluia.** God first loved us
and sent his Son t otake away our sins. ℟. **Alleluia.**

Here is a picture of God's healing love, and the sacrament of reconciliation (Penance), which invites us to rejoice and gives cause for
our joy.

℣. The Lord be with you. ℟. **And also with you.**
✠ A reading from the holy gospel according to Luke
℟. **Glory to you, Lord.**

Jesus addressed this parable to the Pharisees and
the scribes: "Who among you, if he has a hundred
sheep and loses one of them, does not leave the
ninety-nine in the wasteland and follow the lost
one until he finds it? And when he finds it, he puts it on
his shoulders in jubilation. Once arrived home, he
invites friends and neighbors in and says to them,
'Rejoice with me because I have found my lost
sheep.' I tell you, there will likewise be more joy in
heaven over one repentant sinner than over ninety-

nine righteous people who have no need to repent."
This is the gospel of the Lord. ℞. **Praise to you, Lord
Jesus Christ.**   ➔ No. 14, p. 622

PRAYER OVER THE GIFTS

Lord,
look on the heart of Christ your Son
filled with love for us.
Because of his love
accept our eucharist and forgive our sins.
Grant this through Christ our Lord,
℞. **Amen.**   ➔ Pref. (P 45), p. 7

COMMUNION ANT.   Jn 7, 37-38

**The Lord says: If anyone is thirsty, let him come to
me; whoever believes in me, let him drink. Streams
of living water shall flow out from within him.** ⱽ

OR   Jn 19, 34

**One of the soldiers pierced Jesus side with a lance;
and at once there flowed out blood and water.** ⱽ

PRAYER AFTER COMMUNION

Father,
may this sacrament fill us with love.
Draw us closer to Christ your Son
and help us to recognize him in others.
We ask this in the name of Jesus the Lord.
℞. **Amen.**   ➔ No. 32, p. 650

ANTIPHONS AND PRAYERS
FOR ORDINARY TIME

1st WEEK

Our heavenly Father knows all things. He has made us for himself. In him we live and move and are. Let us pray that all we do will be pleasing to him.

ENTRANCE ANT.

I saw a man sitting on a high throne, being worshiped by a great number of angels who were singing together: This is he whose kingdom will last for ever.

➤ No. 2, p. 614

OPENING PRAYER

Father of love,
hear our prayers.
Help us to know your will
and to do it with courage and faith.
Grant this through our Lord Jesus Christ, your Son,
who lives and reigns with you and the Holy Spirit,
one God, for ever and ever. ℟. **Amen.** ✠

READINGS AND INTERVENIENT CHANTS

The *weekday* readings and intervenient chants for the 10th to 34th Weeks in Ordinary Time are found on pp. 70-432 (Year I) and 781-1033 (Year II).

PRAYER OVER THE GIFTS

Lord,
accept our offering.
Make us grow in holiness
and grant what we ask you in faith.
We ask this in the name of Jesus the Lord.
℟. **Amen.**   ➤ No. 21, p. 626 (Pref. P 37-42)

COMMUNION ANT.   Ps 36, 10

Lord, you are the source of life, and in the light of your glory we find happiness. ✠

OR Jn 10, 10

I came that men may have life, and have it to the full, says the Lord. ℣

PRAYER AFTER COMMUNION

All-powerful God,
you renew us with your sacraments.
Help us to thank you by lives of faithful service.
We ask this through Christ our Lord.
℟. **Amen.** ➜ No. 32, p. 650

2nd WEEK

God has made heaven and earth. He made the stars in the heavens and the seasons of the year. He has ordered them all well. Today we pray that his peace and order may abound in the lives of all men.

ENTRANCE ANT. Ps 66, 4

May all the earth give you worship and praise, and break into song to your name, O God, Most High.
➜ No. 2, p. 614

OPENING PRAYER

Father of heaven and earth,
hear our prayers,
and show us the way to peace in the world.
Grant this through our Lord Jesus Christ, your Son,
who lives and reigns with you and the Holy Spirit,
one God, for ever and ever. ℟. **Amen.** ℣

ALTERNATIVE OPENING PRAYER

Almighty and ever-present Father,
your watchful care reaches from end to end
and orders all things in such power
that even the tensions and the tragedies of sin
cannot frustrate your loving plans.
Help us to embrace your will,
give us the strength to follow your call,
so that your truth may live in our hearts
and reflect peace to those who believe in your love.
We ask this in the name of Jesus the Lord.
℟. **Amen.** ℣

READINGS AND INTERVENIENT CHANTS

The *weekday* readings and intervenient chants for the 10th to 34th Weeks in Ordinary Time are found on pp. 70-432 (Year I) and 781-1033 (Year II).

PRAYER OVER THE GIFTS

Father,
may we celebrate the eucharist
with reverence and love,
for when we proclaim the death of the Lord
you continue the work of his redemption,
who is Lord for ever and ever.
℞. **Amen.**   ➔ No. 21, p. 626 (Pref. P 37-42)

COMMUNION ANT.   Ps 23, 5

The Lord has prepared a feast for me: given wine in plenty for me to drink. ❯

OR   1 Jn 4, 16

We know and believe in God's love for us. ❯

PRAYER AFTER COMMUNION

Lord,
you have nourished us with bread from heaven.
Fill us with your Spirit,
and make us one in peace and love.
We ask this through Christ our Lord.
℞. **Amen**   ➔ No. 32, p. 650

3rd WEEK

St. Paul reminds us that what we do, whether we eat, work or sleep, all must be done for God. Out of love Jesus came into the world. In return he asks our love.

ENTRANCE ANT.   Ps 96, 1. 6

Sing a new song to the Lord! Sing to the Lord, all the earth. Truth and beauty surround him, he lives in holiness and glory.   ➔ No. 2, p. 614

OPENING PRAYER

All-powerful and ever-living God,
direct your love that is within us,
that our efforts in the name of your Son
may bring mankind to unity and peace.
We ask this through our Lord Jesus Christ, your Son,
who lives and reigns with you and the Holy Spirit,
one God, for ever and ever.
℟. **Amen.** ⍒

ALTERNATIVE OPENING PRAYER

Almighty Father,
the love you offer
always exceeds the furthest expression of our human
   longing,
for you are greater than the human heart.
Direct each thought, each effort of our life,
so that the limits of our faults and weaknesses
may not obscure the vision of your glory
or keep us from the peace you have promised.
We ask this through Christ our Lord.
℟. **Amen.** ⍒

READINGS AND INTERVENIENT CHANTS

The *weekday* readings and intervenient chants for the
10th to 34th Weeks in Ordinary Time are found on pp.
70-432 (Year I) and 781-1033 (Year II).

PRAYER OVER THE GIFTS

Lord,
receive our gifts.
Let our offerings make us holy
and bring us salvation.
Grant this through Christ our Lord.
℟. **Amen.**   ➔ No. 21, p. 626 (Pref. P 37-42)

COMMUNION ANT.   Ps 34, 6

**Look up at the Lord with gladness and smile; your
face will never be ashamed.** ⍒

OR   Jn 8, 12

I am the light of the world, says the Lord; the man who follows me will have the light of life. ℣

PRAYER AFTER COMMUNION

God, all-powerful Father,
may the new life you give us increase our love
and keep us in the joy of your kingdom.
We ask this in the name of Jesus the Lord.
℞. **Amen.**   ➔ No. 32, p. 650

4th WEEK

When Jesus came into the world, he left his place in heaven knowing that he was to suffer and die for all men. Greater love than this no man has: that he would lay down his life for his friend. Let us pray that we may love one another without reserve.

ENTRANCE ANT.   Ps 106, 47

Save us, Lord our God, and gather us together from the nations, that we may proclaim your holy name and glory in your praise.   ➔ No. 2, p. 614

OPENING PRAYER

Lord our God,
help us to love you with all our hearts
and to love all men as you love them.
Grant this through our Lord Jesus Christ, your Son,
who lives and reigns with you and the Holy Spirit,
one God, for ever and ever.
℞. **Amen.** ℣

ALTERNATIVE OPENING PRAYER

Father in heaven,
from the days of Abraham and Moses
until this gathering of your Church in prayer,
you have formed a people in the image of your Son.
Bless this people with the gift of your kingdom.
May we serve you with our every desire

and show love for one another
even as you have loved us.
Grant this through Christ our Lord. ℞. **Amen.** ✟

READINGS AND INTERVENIENT CHANTS

The *weekday* readings and intervenient chants for the 10th to 34th Weeks in Ordinary Time are found on pp. 70-432 (Year I) and 781-1033 (Year II).

PRAYER OVER THE GIFTS

Lord,
be pleased with the gifts we bring to your altar,
and make them the sacrament of our salvation.
We ask this through Christ our Lord.
℞. **Amen.**   ➤ No. 21, p. 626 (Pref. P 37-42)

COMMUNION ANT.   Ps 31, 17-18

Let your face shine on your servant, and save me by your love. Lord, keep me from shame, for I have called to you. ✟

OR   Mt 5, 3-4

Happy are the poor in spirit; the kingdom of heaven is theirs! Happy are the lowly; they shall inherit the land. ✟

PRAYER AFTER COMMUNION

Lord,
you invigorate us with this help to our salvation.
By this eucharist give the true faith continued growth throughout the world.
We ask this in the name of Jesus the Lord.
℞. **Amen.**   ➤ No. 32, p. 650

5th WEEK

In Old Testament days God led his people out of bondage. He guided them with a pillar of fire at night and a cloud during the day. He fed them with manna in the desert. May God continue to watch over and care for his people of today.

ENTRANCE ANT. Ps 95, 6-7

Come, let us worship the Lord. Let us bow down in the presence of our maker, for he is the Lord our God. ➔ No. 2, p. 614

OPENING PRAYER

Father,
watch over your family
and keep us safe in your care,
for all our hope is in you.
Grant this through our Lord Jesus Christ, your Son,
who lives and reigns with you and the Holy Spirit,
one God, for ever and ever. ℟. **Amen.** ↓

ALTERNATIVE OPENING PRAYER

In faith and love we ask you, Father,
to watch over your family gathered here.
In your mercy and loving kindness
no thought of ours is left unguarded,
no tear unheeded, no joy unnoticed.
Through the prayer of Jesus
may the blessings promised to the poor in spirit
lead us to the treasures of your heavenly kingdom.
We ask this in the name of Jesus the Lord.
℟. **Amen.** ↓

READINGS AND INTERVENIENT CHANTS

The *weekday* readings and intervenient chants for the 10th to 34th Weeks in Ordinary Time are found on pp. 70-432 (Year I) and 781-1033 (Year II).

PRAYER OVER THE GIFTS

Lord our God,
may the bread and wine
you give us for our nourishment on earth
become the sacrament of our eternal life.
We ask this through Christ our Lord.
℟. **Amen.** ➔ No. 21, p. 626 (Pref. P 37-42)

COMMUNION ANT. Ps 107, 8-9

Give praise to the Lord for his kindness, for his wonderful deeds toward men. He has filled the hungry with good things, he has satisfied the thirsty. ℣

OR Mt 5, 5-6

Happy are the sorrowing; they shall be consoled. Happy those who hunger and thirst for what is right; they shall be satisfied. ℣

PRAYER AFTER COMMUNION

God our Father,
you give us a share in the one bread and the one cup
and make us one in Christ.
Help us to bring your salvation and joy
to all the world.
We ask this through Christ our Lord.
℞. **Amen.** ➔ No. 32, p. 650

6th WEEK

God made a covenant with the Israelites that he would be their God and they would be his people. We pray today that he will look after us and keep us safe from all harm.

ENTRANCE ANT Ps 31, 3-4

Lord, be my rock of safety, the stronghold that saves me. For the honor of your name, lead me and guide me. ➔ No. 2, p. 614

OPENING PRAYER

God our Father,
you have promised to remain for ever
with those who do what is just and right.
Help us to live in your presence.
We ask this through our Lord Jesus Christ, your Son,
who lives and reigns with you and the Holy Spirit,
one God, for ever and ever. ℞. **Amen.** ℣

ALTERNATIVE OPENING PRAYER

Father in heaven,
the loving plan of your wisdom took flesh in Jesus
    Christ,
and changed mankind's history
by his command of perfect love.
May our fulfillment of his command reflect your
    wisdom
and bring your salvation to the ends of the earth.
We ask this through Christ our Lord. ℞. **Amen.** ℣

READINGS AND INTERVENIENT CHANTS

The *weekday* readings and intervenient chants for the
10th to 34th Weeks in Ordinary Time are found on pp.
70-432 (Year I) and 781-1033 (Year II).

PRAYER OVER THE GIFTS

Lord,
we make this offering in obedience to your word.
May it cleanse and renew us,
and lead us to our eternal reward.
We ask this in the name of Jesus the Lord
℞. **Amen.**   ➔ No. 21, p. 626 (Pref. P 37-42)

COMMUNION ANT.   Ps 78, 29-30

They ate and were filled; the Lord gave them what
they wanted: they were not deprived of their desire. ℣

OR   Jn 3, 16

God loved the world so much, he gave his only Son,
that all who believe in him might not perish, but
might have eternal life. ℣

PRAYER AFTER COMMUNION

Lord,
you give us food from heaven.
May we always hunger
for the bread of life.

Grant this through Christ our Lord.
℟. **Amen.**   ➔ No. 32, p. 650

_____

7th WEEK

Solomon was renowned for his wisdom. Jesus confounded the scribes and Pharisees who tried to trick him. "Give to Caesar what is Caesar's and to God what is God's." May we abide by the revealed word of God and live always according to his commandments.

ENTRANCE ANT.   Ps 13, 6

Lord, your mercy is my hope, my heart rejoices in your saving power. I will sing to the Lord for his goodness to me.   ➔ No. 2, p. 614

OPENING PRAYER

Father,
keep before us the wisdom and love
you have revealed in your Son.
Help us to be like him
in word and deed,
for he lives and reigns with you and the Holy Spirit,
one God, for ever and ever. ℟. **Amen.** ℣

ALTERNATIVE OPENING PRAYER

Almighty God,
Father of our Lord Jesus Christ,
faith in your word is the way to wisdom,
and to ponder your divine plan is to grow in the
    truth.
Open our eyes to your deeds,
our ears to the sound of your call,
so that our every act may increase our sharing
in the life you have offered us.
Grant this through Christ our Lord. ℟. **Amen.** ℣

READINGS AND INTERVENIENT CHANTS

The _weekday_ readings and intervenient chants for the 10th to 34th Weeks in Ordinary Time are found on pp. 70-432 (Year I) and 781-1033 (Year II).

PRAYER OVER THE GIFTS

Lord,
as we make this offering,
may our worship in Spirit and truth
bring us salvation.
We ask this in the name of Jesus the Lord.
℟. **Amen.**   ➔ No. 21, p. 626 (Pref. P 37-42)

COMMUNION ANT.   Ps 9, 2-3

**I will tell all your marvelous works. I will rejoice and
be glad in you, and sing to your name, Most High. ℣**

OR   Jn 11, 27

**Lord, I believe that you are the Christ, the Son of
God, who was to come into this world. ℣**

PRAYER AFTER COMMUNION

Almighty God,
help us to live the example of love
we celebrate in this eucharist,
that we may come to its fulfillment in your presence.
We ask this through Christ our Lord.
℟. **Amen.**   ➔ No. 32, p. 650

8th WEEK

Everything lives in the ever-present "now" in the mind of God. We are
born only to live for a time wherein we are to serve God. We pray
that we may live lives pleasing to God, that we may live in joy and
peace.

ENTRANCE ANT.   Ps 18, 19-20

**The Lord has been my strength; he has led me into
freedom. He saved me because he loves me.**

                                          ➔ No. 2, p. 614

OPENING PRAYER

Lord,
guide the course of world events

and give your Church the joy and peace
of serving you in freedom.
We ask this through our Lord Jesus Christ, your Son,
who lives and reigns with you and the Holy Spirit,
one God, for ever and ever. ℟. **Amen.** ♥

ALTERNATIVE OPENING PRAYER

Father in heaven,
form in us the likeness of your Son
and deepen his life within us.
Send us as witnesses of gospel joy
into a world of fragile peace and broken promises.
Touch the hearts of all men with your love
that they in turn may love one another.
We ask this through Christ our Lord.
℟. **Amen.** ♥

READINGS AND INTERVENIENT CHANTS

The *weekday* readings and intervenient chants for the
10th to 34th Weeks in Ordinary Time are found on pp.
70-432 (Year I) and 781-1033 (Year II).

PRAYER OVER THE GIFTS

God our Creator,
may this bread and wine we offer
as a sign of our love and worship
lead us to salvation.
Grant this through Christ our Lord.
℟. **Amen.** ➤ No. 21, p. 626 (Pref. P 37-42)

COMMUNION ANT. Ps 13, 6
I will sing to the Lord for his goodness to me, I will
sing the name of the Lord, Most High. ♥

OR Mt 28, 20
I, the Lord, am with you always, until the end of the
world. ♥

PRAYER AFTER COMMUNION

God of salvation,
may this sacrament which strengthens us here on
    earth
bring us to eternal life.
We ask this in the name of Jesus the Lord.
℟. **Amen.**   → No. 32, p. 650

9th WEEK

How much we take for granted as we live in a world of advanced
progress. It is easy to become immersed in the affairs around us and
they may easily ensnare us. May God who cares for us shield us
from all dangers as he provides for our needs.

ENTRANCE ANT.   Ps 25, 16. 18

O look at me and be merciful, for I am wretched and
alone. See my hardship and my poverty, and pardon
all my sins.   → No. 2, p. 614

OPENING PRAYER

Father,
your love never fails.
Hear our call.
Keep us from danger
and provide for all our needs.
Grant this through our Lord Jesus Christ, your Son,
who lives and reigns with you and the Holy Spirit,
one God, for ever and ever. ℟. **Amen.** ✟

ALTERNATIVE OPENING PRAYER

God our Father,
teach us to cherish the gifts that surround us.
Increase our faith in you
and bring our trust to its promised fulfillment
in the joy of your kingdom.
Grant this through Christ our Lord. ℟. **Amen.** ✟

READINGS AND INTERVENIENT CHANTS

The *weekday* readings and intervenient chants for the 10th to 34th Weeks in Ordinary Time are found on pp. 70-432 (Year I) and 781-1033 (Year II).

PRAYER OVER THE GIFTS

Lord,
as we gather to offer our gifts
confident in your love,
make us holy by sharing your life with us
and by this eucharist forgive our sins.
We ask this through Christ our Lord.
Ry. **Amen.**   ➜ No. 21, p. 626 (Pref. P 37-42)

COMMUNION ANT.   Ps 17, 6

I call upon you, God, for you will answer me; bend your ear and hear my prayer. ▼

OR   Mk 11, 23-24

I tell you solemnly, whatever you ask for in prayer, believe that you have received it, and it will be yours, says the Lord. ▼

PRAYER AFTER COMMUNION

Lord,
as you give us the body and blood of your Son,
guide us with your Spirit
that we may honor you
not only with our lips,
but also with the lives we lead,
and so enter your kingdom.
We ask this in the name of Jesus the Lord.
Ry. **Amen.**   ➜ No. 32, p. 650

10th WEEK

The life of the Holy Spirit dwells in those chosen by Jesus to carry on his work on earth. The openness of Christ to us through his Spirit is one of love and eternal presence. We are all called upon to be the means by which Christ may reach out to all mankind.

ENTRANCE ANT. Ps 27, 1-2

The Lord is my light and my salvation. Who shall frighten me? The Lord is the defender of my life. Who shall make me tremble? ➔ No. 2, p. 614

OPENING PRAYER

God of wisdom and love,
source of all good,
send your Spirit to teach us your truth
and guide our actions
in your way of peace.
We ask this through our Lord Jesus Christ, your Son,
who lives and reigns with you and the Holy Spirit,
one God, for ever and ever. ℟. **Amen.** ▼

ALTERNATIVE OPENING PRAYER

Father in heaven,
words cannot measure the boundaries of love
for those born to new life in Christ Jesus.
Raise us beyond the limits this world imposes,
so that we may be free to love as Christ teaches
and find our joy in your glory.
We ask this through Christ our Lord. ℟. **Amen.** ▼

READINGS AND INTERVENIENT CHANTS

The *weekday* readings and intervenient chants for each day of the 10th Week in Ordinary Time are found on pp. 72-84 (Year I) and 785-794 (Year II).

PRAYER OVER THE GIFTS

Lord, look with love on our service.
Accept the gifts we bring
and help us grow in Christian love.
Grant this through Christ our Lord.
℟. **Amen.** ➔ No. 21, p. 626 (Pref. P 37-42)

COMMUNION ANT. Ps 18, 3

I can rely on the Lord; I can always turn to him for shelter. It was he who gave me my freedom. My God, you are always there to help me! ℣

OR 1 Jn 4, 16

God is love, and he who lives in love, lives in God, and God in him. ℣

PRAYER AFTER COMMUNION

Lord,
may your healing love
turn us from sin
and keep us on the way that leads to you.
We ask this in the name of Jesus the Lord.
℟. **Amen.** ➔ No. 32, p. 650

11th WEEK

As Christians, we should remember that God's love as exemplified in Christ's dying for all of mankind should bring us to a stronger and more confident abandonment of ourselves in return to God and others. May this Eucharistic liturgy strengthen our confidence in ourselves as receivers and givers of God's love.

ENTRANCE ANT. Ps 27, 7. 9.

Lord, hear my voice when I call to you. You are my help; do not cast me off, do not desert me, my Savior God. ➔ No. 2, p. 614

OPENING PRAYER

Almighty God,
our hope and our strength,
without you we falter.
Help us to follow Christ
and to live according to your will.
We ask this through our Lord Jesus Christ, your Son,
who lives and reigns with you and the Holy Spirit,
one God, for ever and ever. ℟. **Amen.** ℣

ALTERNATIVE OPENING PRAYER

God our Father,
we rejoice in the faith that draws us together,
aware that selfishness can drive us apart.
Let your encouragement be our constant strength.
Keep us one in the love that has sealed our lives,
help us to live as one family
the gospel we profess.
We ask this through Christ our Lord. ℟. **Amen.** ✠

READINGS AND INTERVENIENT CHANTS

The *weekday* readings and intervenient chants for each
day of the 11th Week in Ordinary Time are found on
pp. 84-97 (Year I) and 794-805 (Year II).

PRAYER OVER THE GIFTS

Lord God,
in this bread and wine
you give us food for body and spirit.
May the eucharist renew our strength
and bring us health of mind and body.
We ask this in the name of Jesus the Lord.
℟. **Amen.**   ➤ No. 21, p. 626 (Pref. P 37-42)

COMMUNION ANT.   Ps 27, 4

**One thing I seek: to dwell in the house of the Lord
all the days of my life.** ✠

OR   Jn 17, 11

**Father, keep in your name those you have given me,
that they may be one as we are one, says the Lord.** ✠

PRAYER AFTER COMMUNION

Lord,
may this eucharist
accomplish in your Church
the unity and peace it signifies.
Grant this through Christ our Lord.
℟. **Amen.**   ➤ No. 32, p. 650

_____

12th WEEK

Jesus Christ is the Good Shepherd who protects us, his sheep. The sheep of his fold come first, and he will do all in his power to save them from harm. Christ our Shepherd laid down his life for us. How he has proved his love for us!

ENTRANCE ANT.   Ps 28, 8-9

God is the strength of his people. In him, we his chosen live in safety. Save us, Lord, who share in your life, and give us your blessings; be our shepherd for ever.   ➔ No. 2, p. 614

OPENING PRAYER

Father,
guide and protector of your people,
grant us an unfailing respect for your name,
and keep us always in your love.
Grant this through our Lord Jesus Christ, your Son,
who lives and reigns with you and the Holy Spirit,
one God, for ever and ever. ℟. **Amen.** ℣

ALTERNATIVE OPENING PRAYER

God of the universe,
we worship you as Lord.
God, ever close to us,
we rejoice to call you Father.
From this world's uncertainty we look to your covenant.
Keep us one in your peace, secure in your love.
We ask this through Christ our Lord. ℟. **Amen.** ℣

READINGS AND INTERVENIENT CHANTS

The *weekday* readings and intervenient chants for each day of the 12th Week in Ordinary Time are found on pp. 98-112 (Year I) and 806-817 (Year II).

PRAYER OVER THE GIFTS

Lord,
receive our offering,
and may this sacrifice of praise
purify us in mind and heart

and make us always eager to serve you.
We ask this in the name of Jesus the Lord.
℟. **Amen.**   ➔ No. 21, p. 626 (Pref. P 37-42)

COMMUNION ANT.   Ps 145, 15

**The eyes of all look to you, O Lord, and you give
them food in due season.** ℣

OR   Jn 10, 11. 15

**I am the Good Shepherd; I give my life for my sheep,
says the Lord.** ℣

PRAYER AFTER COMMUNION

Lord,
you give us the body and blood of your Son
to renew your life within us.
In your mercy, assure our redemption
and bring us to the eternal life
we celebrate in this eucharist.
We ask this through Christ our Lord. ℟. **Amen.**

➔ No. 32, p. 650

13th WEEK

Jesus Christ, the Light of the World, gives us hope. He lights the
way and guides us in the truth. Each day, his light comes to us to
help us overcome the darkness. As children of light and followers
of Christ, may we support each other and rely on the authority and
power of Jesus to live a life of faith.

ENTRANCE ANT.   Ps 47, 2

**All nations, clap your hands. Shout with a voice of
joy to God.**   ➔ No. 2, p. 614

OPENING PRAYER

Father,
you call your children
to walk in the light of Christ.
Free us from darkness
and keep us in the radiance of your truth.
We ask this through our Lord Jesus Christ, your Son,
who lives and reigns with you and the Holy Spirit,
one God, for ever and ever. ℟. **Amen.** ℣

ALTERNATIVE OPENING PRAYER

Father in heaven,
the light of Jesus
has scattered the darkness of hatred and sin.
Called to that light
we ask for your guidance.
Form our lives in your truth, our hearts in your
    love.
We ask this through Christ our Lord. ℟. **Amen.** ℣

READINGS AND INTERVENIENT CHANTS

The *weekday* readings and intervenient chants for each
day of the 13th Week in Ordinary Time are found on
pp. 113-129 (Year I) and 818-828 (Year II).

PRAYER OVER THE GIFTS

Lord God,
through your sacraments
you give us the power of your grace.
May this eucharist
help us to serve you faithfully.
We ask this in the name of Jesus the Lord.
℟. **Amen.**   → No. 21, p. 626 (Pref. P 37-42)

COMMUNION ANT.   Ps 103, 1

**O, bless the Lord, my soul, and all that is within me
bless his holy name.** ℣

OR   Jn 17, 20-21

**Father, I pray for them: may they be one in us, so
that the world may believe it was you who sent me.** ℣

PRAYER AFTER COMMUNION

Lord,
may this sacrifice and communion
give us a share in your life
and help us bring your love to the world.
Grant this through Christ our Lord.
℟. **Amen.**   → No. 32, p. 650

14th WEEK

Each day we are witness to God's dominion over all things. He is the Master of the universe, the Ruler over life and death. All laws of nature are subject to him. We cannot merely recognize that God is all-powerful but must acknowledge that truth in a practical way by conducting our lives in obedience to his Divine Will.

ENTRANCE ANT.   Ps 48, 10-11

Within your temple, we ponder your loving kindness, O God. As your name, so also your praise reaches to the ends of the earth; your right hand is filled with justice.   ➔ No. 2, p. 614

OPENING PRAYER

Father,
through the obedience of Jesus,
your servant and your Son,
you raised a fallen world.
Free us from sin
and bring us the joy that lasts for ever.
We ask this through our Lord Jesus Christ, your Son,
who lives and reigns with you and the Holy Spirit,
one God, for ever and ever. ℞. **Amen.** ℣

ALTERNATIVE OPENING PRAYER

Father,
in the rising of your Son
death gives birth to new life.
The sufferings he endured restored hope to a fallen
    world.
Let sin never ensnare us
with empty promises of passing joy.
Make us one with you always,
so that our joy may be holy,
and our love may give life.
We ask this through Christ our Lord. ℞. **Amen.** ℣

READINGS AND INTERVENIENT CHANTS

The *weekday* readings and intervenient chants for each day of the 14th Week in Ordinary Time are found on pp. 129-144 (Year I) and 826-836 (Year II).

PRAYER OVER THE GIFTS

Lord,
let this offering to the glory of your name
purify us and bring us closer to eternal life.
We ask this in the name of Jesus the Lord.
℟. **Amen.** ➔ No. 21, p. 626 (Pref. P 37-42)

COMMUNION ANT. Ps 34, 9

Taste and see the goodness of the Lord; blessed is he who hopes in God. ℣

OR Mt 11, 28

Come to me, all you that labor and are burdened, and I will give you rest, says the Lord. ℣

PRAYER AFTER COMMUNION

Lord,
may we never fail to praise you
for the fullness of life and salvation
you give us in this eucharist.
We ask this through Christ our Lord.
℟. **Amen.** ➔ No. 32, p. 650

15th WEEK

Jesus showed us that our God is a personal Father who knows the sound of our voice and who always hears the prayers of those who call on him. Jesus himself often prayed to his Father, remembering all of God's goodness and giving him praise. Let us join Jesus in praising the Father and thanking him for all that he has given us.

ENTRANCE ANT. Ps 17, 15

In my justice I shall see your face, O Lord; when your glory appears, my joy will be full.

➔ No. 2, p. 614

OPENING PRAYER

God our Father,
your light of truth
guides us to the way of Christ.
May all who follow him
reject what is contrary to the gospel.

We ask this through our Lord Jesus Christ, your Son,
who lives and reigns with you and the Holy Spirit,
one God, for ever and ever. R̶. **Amen.** ℣

ALTERNATIVE OPENING PRAYER

Father,
let the light of your truth
guide us to your kingdom
through a world filled with lights contrary to your
    own.
Christian is the name and the gospel we glory in.
May your love make us what you have called us to be.
We ask this through Christ our Lord. R̶. **Amen.** ℣

READINGS AND INTERVENIENT CHANTS

The *weekday* readings and intervenient chants for each
day of the 15th Week in Ordinary Time are found on
pp. 147-161 (Year I) and 839-849 (Year II).

PRAYER OVER THE GIFTS

Lord,
accept the gifts of your Church.
May this eucharist
help us grow in holiness and faith.
We ask this in the name of Jesus the Lord.
R̶. **Amen.** ➔ No. 21, p. 626 (Pref. P 37-42)

COMMUNION ANT.   Ps 84, 4-5

**The sparrow even finds a home, the swallow finds a
nest wherein to place her young, near to your altars,
Lord of hosts, my King, my God! How happy they
who dwell in your house! For ever they are praising
you.** ℣

OR   Jn 6, 57

**Whoever eats my flesh and drinks my blood will live
in me and I in him, says the Lord.** ℣

PRAYER AFTER COMMUNION

Lord,
by our sharing in the mystery of this eucharist,

let your saving love grow within us.
Grant this through Christ our Lord.
℟. **Amen.** _____ ➤ No. 32, p. 650

16th WEEK

In his goodness and mercy, God has given to men the power to forgive
our sins and thereby restore us to friendship with him. He has given
to men the power to change bread and wine into his own Body and
Blood so that we may have the spiritual strength to meet the problems
and trials of life. May we thus serve God in faith, hope, and love!

ENTRANCE ANT.   Ps 54, 6. 8
**God himself is my help. The Lord upholds my life. I
will offer you a willing sacrifice; I will praise your
name, O Lord, for its goodness.** ➤ No. 2, p. 614

OPENING PRAYER
Lord,
be merciful to your people.
Fill us with your gifts
and make us always eager to serve you
in faith, hope, and love.
Grant this through our Lord Jesus Christ, your Son,
who lives and reigns with you and the Holy Spirit,
one God, for ever and ever. ℟. **Amen.** ⍖

ALTERNATIVE OPENING PRAYER
Father,
let the gift of your life
continue to grow in us,
drawing us from death to faith, hope, and love.
Keep us alive in Christ Jesus.
Keep us watchful in prayers,
and true to his teaching
till your glory is revealed in us.
Grant this through Christ our Lord. ℟. **Amen.** ⍖

READINGS AND INTERVENIENT CHANTS
The *weekday* readings and intervenient chants for each
day of the 16th Week in Ordinary Time are found on
pp. 161-176 (Year I) and 849-858 (Year II).

PRAYER OVER THE GIFTS

Lord,
bring us closer to salvation
through these gifts which we bring in your honor.
Accept the perfect sacrifice you have given us,
bless it as you blessed the gifts of Abel.
We ask this through Christ our Lord.
℞. **Amen.**   ➤ No. 21, p. 626 (Pref. P 37-42)

COMMUNION ANT.   Ps 111, 4-5

**The Lord keeps in our minds the wonderful things he
has done. He is compassion and love; he always provides for his faithful.** ℣

OR   Rv 3, 20

**I stand at the door and knock, says the Lord. If any-
one hears my voice and opens the door, I will come
in and sit down to supper with him, and he with
me.** ℣

PRAYER AFTER COMMUNION

Merciful Father,
may these mysteries
give us new purpose
and bring us to a new life in you.
We ask this in the name of Jesus the Lord.
℞. **Amen.**   ➤ No. 32, p. 650

17th WEEK

If we have faith in God, we can be assured that he will provide us with
all that we need. God's call is extended to all people, and we have
only to accept the invitation to share in his bountiful gifts.

ENTRANCE ANT.   Ps 68, 6-7. 36

**God is in his holy dwelling; he will give a home to
the lonely, he gives power and strength to his people.**
                                        ➤ No. 2, p. 614

OPENING PRAYER

God our Father and protector,
without you nothing is holy,
nothing has value.
Guide us to everlasting life
by helping us to use wisely
the blessings you have given to the world.
We ask this through our Lord Jesus Christ, your Son,
who lives and reigns with you and the Holy Spirit,
one God, for ever and ever. ℞. **Amen.** ⅴ

ALTERNATIVE OPENING PRAYER

God our Father,
open our eyes to see your hand at work
in the splendor of creation,
in the beauty of human life.
Touched by your hand our world is holy.
Help us to cherish the gifts that surround us,
to share your blessings with our brothers and sisters,
and to experience the joy of life in your presence.
We ask this through Christ our Lord. ℞. **Amen.** ⅴ

READINGS AND INTERVENIENT CHANTS

The *weekday* readings and intervenient chants for each
day of the 17th Week in Ordinary Time are found on
pp. 176-191 (Year I) and 858-867 (Year II).

PRAYER OVER THE GIFTS

Lord,
receive these offerings
chosen from your many gifts.
May these mysteries make us holy
and lead us to eternal joy.
Grant this through Christ our Lord.
℞. **Amen.**   ➔ No. 21, p. 626 (Pref. P 37-42)

COMMUNION ANT.   Ps 103, 2

**O, bless the Lord, my soul, and remember all his
kindness.** ⅴ

OR   Mt 5, 7-8
**Happy are those who show mercy; mercy shall be
theirs. Happy are the poor of heart, for they shall
see God.** ℣

PRAYER AFTER COMMUNION

Lord,
we receive the sacrament
which celebrates the memory
of the death and resurrection of Christ your Son.
May this gift bring us closer to our eternal salvation.
We ask this through Christ our Lord.
℟. **Amen.**   ➜ No. 32, p. 650

18th WEEK

The soul of man requires spiritual food. Jesus offers us himself as
the Bread of Life which will fill our spiritual appetite so that we will
never hunger again. All things of this world are as nothing to us in
the presence of our Lord and Savior whom we receive in the Eucharist.

ENTRANCE ANT.   Ps 70, 2. 6

**God, come to my help. Lord, quickly give me assis-
tance. You are the one who helps me and sets me free:
Lord, do not be long in coming.**   ➜ No. 2, p. 614

OPENING PRAYER

Father of everlasting goodness,
our origin and guide,
be close to us
and hear the prayers of all who praise you.
Forgive our sins and restore us to life.
Keep us safe in your love.
Grant this through our Lord Jesus Christ, your Son,
who lives and reigns with you and the Holy Spirit,
one God, for ever and ever. ℟. **Amen.** ℣

ALTERNATIVE OPENING PRAYER

God our Father,
gifts without measure flow from your goodness

to bring us your peace.
Our life is your gift.
Guide our life's journey,
for only your love makes us whole.
Keep us strong in your love.
We ask this through Christ our Lord. ℟. **Amen.** ✝

READINGS AND INTERVENIENT CHANTS

The *weekday* readings and intervenient chants for each
day of the 18th Week in Ordinary Time are found on
pp. 191-208 (Year I) and 868-878 (Year II).

PRAYER OVER THE GIFTS

Merciful Lord,
make holy these gifts,
and let our spiritual sacrifice
make us an everlasting gift to you.
We ask this in the name of Jesus the Lord.
℟. **Amen.**   ➔ No. 21, p. 626 (Pref. P 37-42)

COMMUNION ANT.   Wis 16, 20

**You gave us bread from heaven, Lord: a sweet-tasting
bread that was very good to eat.** ✝

OR   Jn 6, 35

**The Lord says: I am the bread of life. A man who
comes to me will not go away hungry, and no one
who believes in me will thirst.** ✝

PRAYER AFTER COMMUNION

Lord,
you give us the strength of new life
by the gift of the eucharist.
Protect us with your love
and prepare us for eternal redemption.
We ask this through Christ our Lord.
℟. **Amen.**   ➔ No. 32, p. 650

19th WEEK

We have been chosen to be the people of God and to hear the Good News of salvation. We have been reborn in the waters of baptism and we have received the gift of the Holy Spirit, our guide and our protector. We have nothing to fear.

ENTRANCE ANT.   Ps 74, 20. 19. 22. 23

Lord, be true to your covenant, forget not the life of your poor ones for ever. Rise up, O God, and defend your cause; do not ignore the shouts of your enemies.

➤ No. 2, p. 614

OPENING PRAYER

Almighty and ever-living God,
your Spirit made us your children,
confident to call you Father.
Increase your Spirit within us
and bring us to our promised inheritance.
Grant this through our Lord Jesus Christ, your Son,
who lives and reigns with you and the Holy Spirit,
one God, for ever and ever. ℟. **Amen.** ✙

ALTERNATIVE OPENING PRAYER

Father,
we come, reborn in the Spirit,
to celebrate our sonship in the Lord Jesus Christ.
Touch our hearts,
help them grow toward the life you have promised.
Touch our lives,
make them signs of your love for all men.
Grant this through Christ our Lord. ℟. **Amen.** ✙

READINGS AND INTERVENIENT CHANTS

The *weekday* readings and intervenient chants for each day of the 19th Week in Ordinary Time are found on pp. 208-224 (Year I) and 878-888 (Year II).

PRAYER OVER THE GIFTS

God of power,
giver of the gifts we bring,

accept the offering of your Church
and make it the sacrament of our salvation.
We ask this through Christ our Lord.
℟. **Amen.**   ➔ No. 21, p. 626 (Pref. P 37-42)

COMMUNION ANT.   Ps 147, 12-14

Praise the Lord, Jerusalem; he feeds you with the finest wheat. ℣

OR   Jn 6, 52

The bread I shall give is my flesh for the life of the world, says the Lord. ℣

PRAYER AFTER COMMUNION

Lord,
may the eucharist you give us
bring us to salvation
and keep us faithful to the light of your truth.
We ask this in the name of Jesus the Lord.
℟. **Amen.**   ➔ No. 32, p. 650

20th WEEK

The Lord's call is universal, meant for all mankind. We are all brothers
and sisters in Christ. Each of us must support one another through
our concern, and in this way we witness Jesus and his message.

ENTRANCE ANT.   Ps 84, 10-11

God, our protector, keep us in mind; always give strength to your people. For if we can be with you even one day, it is better than a thousand without you.   ➔ No. 2, p. 614

OPENING PRAYER

God our Father,
may we love you in all things and above all things
and reach the joy you have prepared for us
beyond all our imagining.
We ask this through our Lord, Jesus Christ, your Son,
who lives and reigns with you and the Holy Spirit,
one God, for ever and ever. ℟. **Amen.** ℣

ALTERNATIVE OPENING PRAYER

Almighty God, ever-loving Father,
your care extends beyond the boundaries of race and nation
to the hearts of all who live.
May the walls, which prejudice raises between us,
crumble beneath the shadow of your outstretched arm.
We ask this through Christ our Lord. ℟. **Amen.** ↓

READINGS AND INTERVENIENT CHANTS

The *weekday* readings and intervenient chants for each day of the 20th Week in Ordinary Time are found on pp. 227-242 (Year I) and 893-902 (Year II)

PRAYER OVER THE GIFTS

Lord,
accept our sacrifice
as a holy exchange of gifts.
By offering what you have given us
may we receive the gift of yourself.
We ask this in the name of Jesus the Lord.
℟. **Amen.** ➔ No. 21, p. 626 (Pref. P 37-42)

COMMUNION ANT. Ps 130, 7

With the Lord there is mercy, and fullness of redemption. ↓

OR Jn 6, 51-52

I am the living bread from heaven, says the Lord; if anyone eats this bread he will live for ever. ↓

PRAYER AFTER COMMUNION

God of mercy,
by this sacrament you make us one with Christ.
By becoming more like him on earth,
may we come to share his glory in heaven,
where he lives and reigns for ever and ever.
℟. **Amen.** ➔ No. 32, p. 650

21st WEEK

Jesus alone can lead us to his Father, but we owe him service in order for him to give us this life. We find this life in loving one another, the same way Christ loved his Church. He was willing to give up his life to save his Church.

ENTRANCE ANT. Ps 86, 1-3

Listen, Lord, and answer me. Save your servant who trusts in you. I call to you all day long, have mercy on me, O Lord. ➔ No. 2, p. 614

OPENING PRAYER

Father,
help us to seek the values
that will bring us lasting joy in this changing world.
In our desire for what you promise
make us one in mind and heart.
Grant this through our Lord Jesus Christ, your Son,
who lives and reigns with you and the Holy Spirit,
one God, for ever and ever. ℟. **Amen.** ℣

ALTERNATIVE OPENING PRAYER

Lord our God,
all truth is from you,
and you alone bring oneness of heart.
Give your people the joy
of hearing your word in every sound
and of longing for your presence more than for life
itself.
May all the attractions of a changing world
serve only to bring us
the peace of your kingdom which this world does
not give.
Grant this through Christ our Lord. ℟. **Amen.** ℣

READINGS AND INTERVENIENT CHANTS

The *weekday* readings and intervenient chants for each day of the 21st Week in Ordinary Time are found on pp. 243-255 (Year I) and 902-910 (Year II).

PRAYER OVER THE GIFTS

Merciful God,
the perfect sacrifice of Jesus Christ
made us your people.
In your love,
grant peace and unity to your Church.
We ask this through Christ our Lord.
℟. **Amen.**   ➔ No. 21, p. 626 (Pref. P 37-42)

COMMUNION ANT.   Ps 104, 13-15

Lord, the earth is filled with your gift from heaven; man grows bread from earth, and wine to cheer his heart. ℣

OR   Jn 6, 55

The Lord says: The man who eats my flesh and drinks my blood will live for ever; I shall raise him to life on the last day. ℣

PRAYER AFTER COMMUNION

Lord,
may this eucharist increase within us
the healing power of your love.
May it guide and direct our efforts
to please you in all things.
We ask this in the name of Jesus the Lord.
℟. **Amen.**   ➔ No. 32, p. 650

─────────────

22nd WEEK

Christ calls all men to him, for all are sinners who need him. He calls us to come to him with repentance and he will not reject us. It is precisely because of our weakness that Christ holds out his hand of mercy and forgiveness to us.

ENTRANCE ANT.   Ps 86, 3. 5

I call to you all day long, have mercy on me, O Lord. You are good and forgiving, full of love for all who call to you.   ➔ No. 2, p. 614

OPENING PRAYER

Almighty God,
every good thing comes from you.
Fill our hearts with love for you,
increase our faith,
and by your constant care
protect the good you have given us.
We ask this through our Lord Jesus, your Son,
who lives and reigns with you and the Holy Spirit,
one God, for ever and ever. ℟. **Amen.** ♥

ALTERNATIVE OPENING PRAYER

Lord God of power and might,
nothing is good which is against your will,
and all is of value which comes from your hand.
Place in our hearts a desire to please you
and fill our minds with insight into love,
so that every thought may grow in wisdom
and all our efforts may be filled with your peace.
We ask this through Christ our Lord. ℟. **Amen.** ♥

READINGS AND INTERVENIENT CHANTS

The *weekday* readings and intervenient chants for each
day of the 22nd Week in Ordinary Time are found on
pp. 255-268 (Year I) and 910-918 (Year II).

PRAYER OVER THE GIFTS

Lord,
may this holy offering
bring us your blessing
and accomplish within us
its promise of salvation.
Grant this through Christ our Lord.
℟. **Amen.**   ➤ No. 21, p. 626 (Pref. P 37-42)

COMMUNION ANT.   Mt 5, 9-10

Happy are the peacemakers; they shall be called sons
of God. Happy are they who suffer persecution for
justice' sake; the kingdom of heaven is theirs. ♥

OR   Ps 31, 20

O Lord, how great is the depth of the kindness which
you have shown to those who love you. ℣

PRAYER AFTER COMMUNION
Lord,
you renew us at your table with the bread of life.
May this food strengthen us in love
and help us to serve you in each other.
We ask this in the name of Jesus the Lord.
℟. **Amen.**   → No. 32, p. 650

23rd WEEK

In every age and in every place, God makes his presence known to
man. We have come to know God through his Son, Jesus. It is our task
to share our knowledge of Christ with others.

ENTRANCE ANT.   Ps 119, 137. 124

Lord, you are just, and the judgments you make are
right. Show mercy when you judge me, your servant.
                              → No. 2, p. 614

OPENING PRAYER
God our Father,
you redeem us
and make us your children in Christ.
Look upon us,
give us true freedom
and bring us to the inheritance you promised.
Grant this through our Lord Jesus Christ, your Son,
who lives and reigns with you and the Holy Spirit,
one God, for ever and ever. ℟. **Amen.** ℣

ALTERNATIVE OPENING PRAYER
Lord our God,
in you justice and mercy meet.
With unparalleled love you have saved us from death

and drawn us into the circle of your life.
Open our eyes to the wonders this life sets before us,
that we may serve you free from fear
and address you as God our Father.
We ask this in the name of Jesus the Lord.
℞. **Amen.** ✔

READINGS AND INTERVENIENT CHANTS

The *weekday* readings and intervenient chants for each
day of the 23rd Week in Ordinary Time are found on
pp. 268-280 (Year I) and 919-927 (Year II).

PRAYER OVER THE GIFTS

God of peace and love,
may our offering bring you true worship
and make us one with you.
Grant this through Christ our Lord.
℞. **Amen.**   ➜ No. 21, p. 626 (Pref. P 37-42)

COMMUNION ANT.   Ps 42, 2-3

**Like a deer that longs for running streams, my soul
longs for you, my God. My soul is thirsting for the
living God.** ✔

OR   Jn 8, 12

**I am the light of the world, says the Lord; the man
who follows me will have the light of life.** ✔

PRAYER AFTER COMMUNION

Lord,
your word and your sacrament
give us food and life.
May this gift of your Son
lead us to share his life for ever.
We ask this through Christ our Lord.
℞. **Amen.**   ➜ No. 32, p. 650

————————

24th WEEK

All of us are called to serve our heavenly Father in some unique way. We must not bury or hide the talents he has given us; we must use those talents by giving good example to others and living at peace.

ENTRANCE ANT.   See Sir 36, 18

Give peace, Lord, to those who wait for you and your prophets will proclaim you as you deserve. Hear the prayers of your servant and of your people Israel.

OPENING PRAYER

Almighty God,
our creator and guide,
may we serve you with all our heart
and know your forgiveness in our lives.
We ask this through our Lord Jesus Christ, your Son,
who lives and reigns with you and the Holy Spirit,
one God, for ever and ever. ℟. **Amen.** ▼

ALTERNATIVE OPENING PRAYER

Father in heaven, Creator of all,
look down upon your people in their moments of
    need,
for you alone are the source of our peace.
Bring us to the dignity which distinguishes the poor
    in spirit
and show us how great is the call to serve,
that we may share in the peace of Christ
who offered his life in the service of all.
We ask this through Christ our Lord. ℟. **Amen.** ▼

READINGS AND INTERVENIENT CHANTS

The *weekday* readings and intervenient chants for each day of the 24th Week in Ordinary Time are found on pp. 280-293 (Year I) and 928-936 (Year II).

PRAYER OVER THE GIFTS

Lord,
hear the prayers of your people
and receive our gifts.
May the worship of each one here

bring salvation to all.
Grant this through Christ our Lord.
℟. **Amen.**   ➔ No. 21, p. 626 (Pref. P 37-42)

COMMUNION ANT.   Ps 36, 8
O God, how much we value your mercy! All mankind can gather under your protection. ℣

OR   See 1 Cor 10, 16
The cup that we bless is a communion with the blood of Christ; and the bread that we break is a communion with the body of the Lord. ℣

PRAYER AFTER COMMUNION
Lord,
may the eucharist you have given us
influence our thoughts and actions.
May your Spirit guide and direct us in your way.
We ask this in the name of Jesus the Lord.
℟. **Amen.**   ─────── ➔ No. 32, p. 650

25th WEEK

Love is a movement of the mind and heart. It is one of man's greatest and most powerful emotions. The world has many definitions for the word and places various interpretations upon it. The gospels tell us love is patient, kind, and never fails.

ENTRANCE ANT.

I am the Savior of all people, says the Lord. Whatever their troubles, I will answer their cry, and I will always be their Lord.   ➔ No. 2, p. 614

OPENING PRAYER
Father, guide us, as you guide creation
according to your law of love.
May we love one another
and come to perfection
in the eternal life prepared for us.
Grant this through our Lord Jesus Christ, your Son,
who lives and reigns with you and the Holy Spirit,
one God, for ever and ever. ℟. **Amen.** ℣

ALTERNATIVE OPENING PRAYER

Father in heaven,
the perfection of justice is found in your love
and all mankind is in need of your law.
Help us to find this love in each other
that justice may be attained
through obedience to your law.
We ask this through Christ our Lord. ℟. **Amen.** ↓

READINGS AND INTERVENIENT CHANTS

The *weekday* readings and intervenient chants for each
day of the 25th Week in Ordinary Time are found on
pp. 296-308 (Year I) and 939-948 (Year II).

PRAYER OVER THE GIFTS

Lord,
may these gifts which we now offer
to show our belief and our love
be pleasing to you.
May they become for us
the eucharist of Jesus Christ your Son,
who is Lord for ever and ever.
℟. **Amen.**   → No. 21, p. 626 (Pref. P 37-42)

COMMUNION ANT.   Ps 119, 4-5

**You have laid down your precepts to be faithfully
kept. May my footsteps be firm in keeping your commands.** ↓

OR   Jn 10, 14

**I am the Good Shepherd, says the Lord; I know my
sheep, and mine know me.** ↓

PRAYER AFTER COMMUNION

Lord, help us with your kindness.
Make us strong through the eucharist.
May we put into action
the saving mystery we celebrate.
We ask this in the name of Jesus the Lord.
℟. **Amen.**   → No. 32, p. 650

26th WEEK

When we are disobedient to the commandments given by God, we bring sorrow to others, to God, and, in the end, to ourselves. The people of God who shall live forever are those who do his will. Through obedience to God's word, men are enabled to enter into a close personal relationship with our Divine Savior.

ENTRANCE ANT. Dan 3, 31. 29. 30. 43. 42

O Lord, you had just cause to judge men as you did: because we sinned against you and disobeyed your will. But now show us your greatness of heart, and treat us with your unbounded kindness.

OPENING PRAYER ➤ No. 2, p. 614

Father,
you show your almighty power
in your mercy and forgiveness.
Continue to fill us with your gifts of love.
Help us to hurry toward the eternal life you promise
and come to share in the joys of your kingdom.
Grant this through our Lord Jesus Christ, your Son,
who lives and reigns with you and the Holy Spirit,
one God, for ever and ever. ℞. **Amen.**

ALTERNATIVE OPENING PRAYER

Father of our Lord Jesus Christ,
in your unbounded mercy
you have revealed the beauty of your power
through your constant forgiveness of our sins.
May the power of this love be in our hearts
to bring your pardon and your kingdom to all we
meet.
We ask this through Christ our Lord. ℞. **Amen.** ℣

READINGS AND INTERVENIENT CHANTS

The *weekday* readings and intervenient chants for each day of the 26th Week in Ordinary Time are found on pp. 308-322 (Year I) and 948- 958 (Year II).

PRAYER OVER THE GIFTS

God of mercy,
accept our offering

and make it a source of blessing for us.
We ask this in the name of Jesus the Lord.
R̸. **Amen.** ➤ No. 21, p. 626 (Pref. P 37-42)

COMMUNION ANT. Ps 119, 49-50

O Lord, remember the words you spoke to me, your servant, which made me live in hope and consoled me when I was downcast. ▼

OR 1 Jn 3, 16

This is how we know what love is: Christ gave up his life for us; and we too must give up our lives for our brothers. ▼

PRAYER AFTER COMMUNION

Lord, may this eucharist
in which we proclaim the death of Christ
bring us salvation
and make us one with him in glory,
for he is Lord for ever and ever.
R̸. **Amen.** ➤ No. 32, p. 650

27th WEEK

A just God is present. If we wish to find him, we must seek him. We must not be misled by a world where just men suffer and unjust men prosper. God has given us his Son to remain with us and to show us the way to the Father.

ENTRANCE ANT. Est 13, 9. 10-11

O Lord, you have given everything its place in the world, and no one can make it otherwise. For it is your creation, the heavens and the earth and the stars: you are the Lord of all.

OPENING PRAYER

Father,
your love for us
surpasses all our hopes and desires.
Forgive our failings,
keep us in your peace
and lead us in the way of salvation.

We ask this through our Lord Jesus Christ, your Son,
who lives and reigns with you and the Holy Spirit,
one God, for ever and ever. ℟. **Amen.** ✣

ALTERNATIVE OPENING PRAYER

Almighty and eternal God,
Father of the world to come,
your goodness is beyond what our spirit can touch
and your strength is more than the mind can bear.
Lead us to seek beyond our reach
and give us the courage to stand before your truth.
We ask this through Christ our Lord. ℟. **Amen.** ✣

READINGS AND INTERVENIENT CHANTS

The *weekday* readings and intervenient chants for each
day of the 27th Week in Ordinary Time are found on
pp. 322-337 (Year I) and 958-966 (Year II).

PRAYER OVER THE GIFTS

Father,
receive these gifts
which our Lord Jesus Christ
has asked us to offer in his memory.
May our obedient service
bring us to the fullness of your redemption.
We ask this in the name of Jesus the Lord.
℟. **Amen.**   ➔ No. 21, p. 626 (Pref. P 37-42)

COMMUNION ANT.   Lam 3, 25

**The Lord is good to those who hope in him, to those
who are searching for his love.** ✣

OR   See 1 Cor 10, 17

**Because there is one bread, we, though many, are
one body, for we all share in the one loaf and in the
one cup.** ✣

PRAYER AFTER COMMUNION

Almighty God,
let the eucharist we share
fill us with your life.

May the love of Christ
which we celebrate here
touch our lives and lead us to you.
We ask this in the name of Jesus the Lord.
℟. **Amen.** ➔ No. 32, p. 650

28th WEEK

Jesus warns us against being overly concerned about the riches of the world which can blind us to the spiritual wealth of the Father. In our need to overcome spiritual poverty, we must pray for a healthy detachment from material riches and a realization of the true riches of God.

ENTRANCE ANT.   Ps 130, 3-4

If you, O Lord, laid bare our guilt, who could endure it? But you are forgiving, God of Israel.

➔ No. 2, p. 614

OPENING PRAYER

Lord, our help and guide,
make your love the foundation of our lives.
May our love for you express itself
in our eagerness to do good for others.
Grant this through our Lord Jesus Christ, your Son,
who lives and reigns with you and the Holy Spirit,
one God, for ever and ever. ℟. **Amen.** ⍩

ALTERNATIVE OPENING PRAYER

Father in heaven,
the hand of your loving kindness
powerfully yet gently guides all the moments of our
    day.
Go before us in our pilgrimage of life,
anticipate our needs and prevent our falling.
Send your Spirit to unite us in faith,
that sharing in your service,
we may rejoice in your presence.
We ask this through Christ our Lord. ℟. **Amen.** ⍩

READINGS AND INTERVENIENT CHANTS

The *weekday* readings and intervenient chants for each day of the 28th Week in Ordinary Time are found on pp. 337-348 (Year I) and 966-974 (Year II).

PRAYER OVER THE GIFTS

Lord,
accept the prayers and gifts
we offer in faith and love.
May this eucharist bring us to your glory.
We ask this in the name of Jesus the Lord.
℟. **Amen.**   ➔ No. 21, p. 626 (Pref. P 37-42)

COMMUNION ANT.   Ps 34, 11

**The rich suffer want and go hungry, but nothing
shall be lacking to those who fear the Lord.** ℣

OR   1 Jn 3, 2

**When the Lord is revealed we shall be like him, for
we shall see him as he is.** ℣

PRAYER AFTER COMMUNION

Almighty Father,
may the body and blood of your Son
give us a share in his life,
for he is Lord for ever and ever.
℟. **Amen.**   ➔ No. 32, p. 650

29th WEEK

Carelessness and indifference may dim our vision; indeed, we may
be spiritually blind. Let us pray that we may see Jesus Christ as the
true spiritual guide of our lives and that we may see the light of
truth in what God has revealed.

ENTRANCE ANT.   Ps 17, 6. 8

**I call upon you, God, for you will answer me; bend
your ear and hear my prayer. Guard me as the pupil
of your eye; hide me in the shade of your wings.**
➔ No. 2, p. 614

OPENING PRAYER

Almighty and ever-living God,
our source of power and inspiration,
give us strength and joy
in serving you as followers of Christ,

who lives and reigns with you and the Holy Spirit,
one God, for ever and ever. ℟. **Amen.** ↓

ALTERNATIVE OPENING PRAYER

Lord our God, Father of all,
you guard us under the shadow of your wings
and search into the depths of our hearts.
Remove the blindness that cannot know you
and relieve the fear that would hide us from your
    sight.
We ask this through Christ our Lord. ℟. **Amen.** ↓

READINGS AND INTERVENIENT CHANTS

The *weekday* readings and intervenient chants for each
day of the 29th Week in Ordinary Time are found on
pp. 348-360 (Year I) and 974-983 (Year II).

PRAYER OVER THE GIFTS

Lord God,
may the gifts we offer
bring us your love and forgiveness
and give us freedom to serve you with our lives.
We ask this in the name of Jesus the Lord.
℟. **Amen.**   → No. 21, p. 626 (Pref. P 37-42)

COMMUNION ANT.   Ps 33, 18-19

**See how the eyes of the Lord are on those who fear
him, on those who hope in his love, that he may
rescue them from death and feed them in time of
famine.** ↓

OR   Mk 10, 45

**The Son of Man came to give his life as a ransom
for many.** ↓

PRAYER AFTER COMMUNION

Lord,
may this eucharist help us to remain faithful.
May it teach us the way to eternal life.
Grant this through Christ our Lord.
℟. **Amen.**   → No. 32, p. 650

30th WEEK

The reign of God does not begin at the moment of our death. Rather, it begins in each of us at our baptism and continues to grow and flourish throughout our entire life. Let us celebrate and rejoice in the great riches we have as God's people through Christ.

ENTRANCE ANT.   Ps 105, 3-4

Let hearts rejoice who search for the Lord. Seek the Lord and his strength, seek always the face of the Lord.   ➤ No. 2, p. 614

OPENING PRAYER

Almighty and ever-living God,
strengthen our faith, hope, and love.
May we do with loving hearts
what you ask of us
and come to share the life you promise.
We ask this through our Lord Jesus Christ, your Son,
who lives and reigns with you and the Holy Spirit,
one God, for ever and ever. ℞. **Amen.** ⩴

ALTERNATIVE OPENING PRAYER

Praised be you, God and Father of our Lord Jesus
    Christ.
There is no power for good
    which does not come from your covenant,
and no promise to hope in,
that your love has not offered.
Strengthen our faith to accept your covenant
and give us the love to carry out your command.
We ask this through Christ our Lord. ℞. **Amen.** ⩴

READINGS AND INTERVENIENT CHANTS

The *weekday* readings and intervenient chants for each day of the 30th Week in Ordinary Time are found on pp. 362-374 (Year I) and 987-994 (Year II).

PRAYER OVER THE GIFTS

Lord God of power and might,
receive the gifts we offer
and let our service give you glory.
Grant this through Christ our Lord.
℞. **Amen.**   ➤ No. 21, p. 626 (Pref. P 37-42)

COMMUNION ANT.   Ps 20, 6

We will rejoice at the victory of God and make our boast in his great name. ℣

OR   Eph 5, 2

Christ loved us and gave himself up for us as a fragrant offering to God. ℣

PRAYER AFTER COMMUNION

Lord,
bring to perfection within us
the communion we share in this sacrament.
May our celebration have an effect in our lives.
We ask this in the name of Jesus the Lord.
℟. **Amen.**   ➤ No. 32, p. 650

31st WEEK

The Church is the sacrament of Christ's presence in the world. The people of God constitute the Church, and to the extent that we follow Christ's teachings and have an effect on the world, Christ will be present in the world. Let us thank the Lord for his continued presence and love.

ENTRANCE ANT.   Ps 38, 22-23

Do not abandon me, Lord. My God, do not go away from me! Hurry to help me, Lord, my Savior.
                              ➤ No. 2, p. 614

OPENING PRAYER

God of power and mercy,
only with your help
can we offer you fitting service and praise.
May we live the faith we profess
and trust your promise of eternal life.
Grant this through our Lord Jesus Christ, your Son,
who lives and reigns with you and the Holy Spirit,
one God, for ever and ever. ℟. **Amen.** ℣

ALTERNATIVE OPENING PRAYER

Father in heaven, God of power and Lord of mercy,
from whose fullness we have received,

direct our steps in our everyday efforts.
May the changing moods of the human heart
and the limits which our failings impose on hope
never blind us to you, source of every good.
Faith gives us the promise of peace
and makes known the demands of love.
Remove the selfishness that blurs the vision of faith.
Grant this through Christ our Lord. ℟. **Amen.** ℣

READINGS AND INTERVENIENT CHANTS

The *weekday* readings and intervenient chants for each
day of the 31st Week in Ordinary Time are found on
pp. 374-386 (Year I) and 996-1004 (Year II).

PRAYER OVER THE GIFTS

God of mercy,
may we offer a pure sacrifice
for the forgiveness of our sins.
We ask this through Christ our Lord.
℟. **Amen.**   ➜ No. 21, p. 626, (Pref. P 37-42)

COMMUNION ANT.   Ps 16, 11

**Lord, you will show me the path of life and fill me
with joy in your presence.** ℣

OR   Jn 6, 58

**As the living Father sent me, and I live because of
the Father, so he who eats my flesh and drinks my
blood will live because of me.** ℣

PRAYER AFTER COMMUNION

Lord,
you give us new hope in this eucharist.
May the power of your love
continue its saving work among us
and bring us to the joy you promise.
We ask this in the name of Jesus the Lord.
℟. **Amen.**   ➜ No. 32, p. 650

32nd WEEK

Jesus inspired the people of his day because his authority was from a source beyond this world, and the people were in awe as the Spirit worked in him. So, too, for us. We should be in awe as we look about us at all God's creation, at all that has been given to us.

ENTRANCE ANT.   Ps 88, 3

Let my prayer come before you, Lord; listen, and answer me.   ➔ No. 2, p. 614

OPENING PRAYER

God of power and mercy,
protect us from all harm.
Give us freedom of spirit
and health in mind and body
to do your work on earth.
We ask this through our Lord Jesus Christ, your Son,
who lives and reigns with you and the Holy Spirit,
one God, for ever and ever. ℟. **Amen.** ↓

ALTERNATIVE OPENING PRAYER

Almighty Father,
strong is your justice and great is your mercy.
Protect us in the burdens and challenges of life.
Shield our minds from the distortion of pride
and enfold our desire with the beauty of truth.
Help us to become more aware of your loving design
so that we may more willingly give our lives in service to all.
We ask this through Christ our Lord. ℟. **Amen.** ↓

READINGS AND INTERVENIENT CHANTS

The *weekday* readings and intervenient chants for each day of the 32nd Week in Ordinary Time are found on pp. 387-400 (Year I) and 1004-1012 (Year II).

PRAYER OVER THE GIFTS

God of mercy,
in this eucharist we proclaim the death of the Lord.
Accept the gifts we present
and help us follow him with love,
for he is Lord for ever and ever.
℟. **Amen.**   ➔ No. 21, p. 626, (Pref. P 37-42)

COMMUNION ANT. Ps 23, 1-2

The Lord is my shepherd; there is nothing I shall want. In green pastures he gives me rest, he leads me beside the waters of peace. ℣

OR Lk 24, 35

The disciples recognized the Lord Jesus in the breaking of bread. ℣

PRAYER AFTER COMMUNION

Lord,
we thank you for the nourishment you give us
through your holy gift.
Pour out your Spirit upon us
and in the strength of this food from heaven
keep us single-minded in your service.
We ask this in the name of Jesus the Lord.
℟. **Amen.** ━━━━━━━━━ ➔ No. 32, p. 650

33rd WEEK

Faith is our instrument of peace, and if it is sincere and good, we do not need miracles to keep it alive. We know that God is with us always, in times of trouble as well as in times of joy. Look about you and believe!

ENTRANCE ANT. Jer 29, 11. 12. 14

The Lord says: my plans for you are peace and not disaster; when you call to me, I will listen to you, and I will bring you back to the place from which I exiled you.

OPENING PRAYER

Father of all that is good,
keep us faithful in serving you,
for to serve you is our lasting joy.
We ask this through our Lord Jesus Christ, your Son,
who lives and reigns with you and the Holy Spirit,
one God, for ever and ever. ℟. **Amen.** ℣

ALTERNATIVE OPENING PRAYER

Father in heaven,
ever-living source of all that is good,

from the beginning of time you promised man salvation
through the future coming of your Son, our Lord Jesus Christ.
Help us to drink of his truth
and expand our hearts with the joy of his promises,
so that we may serve you in faith and in love
and know for ever the joy of your presence.
We ask this through Christ our Lord. ℟. **Amen.** ↓

READINGS AND INTERVENIENT CHANTS

The *weekday* readings and intervenient chants for each day of the 33rd Week in Ordinary Time are found on pp. 400-416 (Year I) and 1013-1023 (Year II).

PRAYER OVER THE GIFTS

Lord God,
may the gifts we offer
increase our love for you
and bring us to eternal life.
We ask this in the name of Jesus the Lord.
℟. **Amen.**   ➔ No. 21, p. 626 (Pref. P 37-42)

COMMUNION ANT.   Ps 72, 28

It is good for me to be with the Lord and to put my hope in him. ↓

OR   Mk 11, 23. 24

I tell you solemnly, whatever you ask for in prayer, believe that you have received it, and it will be yours, says the Lord. ↓

PRAYER AFTER COMMUNION

Father,
may we grow in love
by the eucharist we have celebrated
in memory of the Lord Jesus,
who is Lord for ever and ever.
℟. **Amen.**

➔ No. 32, p. 650

34th WEEK

ENTRANCE ANT. Ps 85, 9

The Lord speaks of peace to his holy people, to those who turn to him with all their heart. ➔ No. 2, p. 614

OPENING PRAYER

Lord, increase our eagerness to do your will
and help us to know the saving power of your love.
Grant this through our Lord Jesus Christ, your Son,
who lives and reigns with you and the Holy Spirit,
one God, for ever and ever. ℟. **Amen.** ❢

READINGS AND INTERVENIENT CHANTS

The *weekday* readings and intervenient chants for each day of the 34th Week in Ordinary Time are found on pp. 416-432 (Year I) and 1023-1033 (Year II).

PRAYER OVER THE GIFTS

God of love,
may the sacrifice we offer
in obedience to your command
renew our resolution to be faithful to your word.
We ask this through Christ our Lord.
℟. **Amen.** ➔ No. 21, p. 626 (Pref. P 37-42)

COMMUNION ANT. Ps 117, 1-2

All you nations, praise the Lord, for steadfast is his kindly mercy to us. ❢

OR Mt 28, 20

I, the Lord, am with you always, until the end of the world.

PRAYER AFTER COMMUNION

Almighty God, in this eucharist
you give us the joy of sharing your life.
Keep us in your presence.
Let us never be separated from you.
We ask this in the name of Jesus the Lord.
℟. **Amen.** ➔ No. 32, p. 650

READINGS AND INTERVENIENT CHANTS FOR ORDINARY TIME
(YEAR I)
INTRODUCTION FOR 10th TO 14th WEEK

The Second Epistle to the Corinthians — *St. Paul wrote this Epistle from Macedonia toward the close of his third missionary journey, about 57 A.D. In it he defends his life and ministry, urges that the collection—already requested and begun— be made for the poor Christians in Jerusalem, and replies to his bitter opponents. The Epistle ranks with those to Timothy and the Galatians as the most intensely personal of Paul's writings. But unlike the letters to Timothy, which are calmly pastoral and directive, this Epistle is vehement and hotly polemical. Paul stresses that he is a true apostle of Jesus, and that his sincerity and authority have been amply attested by extraordinary visitations from heaven and unparalleled labors and sufferings in behalf of the Gospel.*

The Book of Genesis — *The second part of this book is read, dealing with the prehistory of the chosen people through the great patriarchs Abraham, Isaac, and Jacob and his twelve sons. They illustrate the fact that the God of the chosen people is not a far-off deity conceived by some philosopher. He is the God of Abraham, Isaac, and Jacob, the God who made a covenant with them and made promises to them, among which is the promise of the Messiah. Through the mystery of Christ and the Church, however, all peoples will be called to share the dignity of Abraham's children and members of the chosen people. (See also vol. I, p. 303.)*

The Gospel of Matthew — *Of all the Gospels that of Matthew gives the most faithful and distinct image of Christ's teaching. However, it would seem that it is not the oldest, for in its present form it uses almost all the material contained in the Gospel of Mark, although inserting a few changes and additions. Scholars today tend to place the definitive date of its composition during the years 80-85, or perhaps even 90.*

Even today readers are struck by its clearness, its pedagogical direction, and the remarkable balance kept between the narrative sections and the five magnificent discourses in ch. 6-7, 10, 13, 18, and 24-25.

While Mark probably addresses himself to the Romans and Luke to the Greeks, Matthew, who is a Jew, writes for the Jews. It is the most Jewish of the Gospels, in its style, its methods of composition, and its way of arguing. Matthew wants to convince his brethren that Jesus is indeed the Messiah who was expected by the Prophets, and thus he tries to show that Jesus has fulfilled the Scriptures.

For Matthew, Israel is the People of God, for it is to Israel that Jesus was sent and to Israel that Jesus announced the Kingdom of God, that reign which already with Jesus is secretly present among men. But Israel refuses to recognize Jesus. The hostility between Jesus and the scribes, the Pharisees and the high priests increases. Jesus himself hardens his position. He announces that the Kingdom destined for Israel will be taken away and entrusted to a people who will be fruitful, the new Israel, the Church. (Mt 21, 43.) Henceforth the drama hastens its course and quickly comes to its end with the Crucifixion.

Matthew's Gospel has been called the Gospel of the Church. However, it is even more the Gospel of Jesus. Matthew constantly seeks to bring out the majesty of Jesus, his superhuman greatness, and his power. For Matthew, Jesus is the Lord. This title recurs eighty times in his Gospel, while it appears only eighteen times in the Gospel of Mark. The term itself designates Jesus risen, working mightily, and always present in his Church.

For Matthew, Jesus is also the Christ, the Messiah, a title he gives him as early as in the genealogy (Mt 1, 16-18). But he is above all the Son of God (Mt 3, 17; 8, 29; 17, 5; 26, 63; 27, 34, etc.). In a word, Matthew professes the divinity of Jesus.

MONDAY OF THE TENTH WEEK
IN ORDINARY TIME

READING I   2 Cor 1, 1-7

St. Paul's letter begins with his usual wish for God's blessings upon those to whom he writes. He encourages his readers to bear patiently their troubles and opposition. Christ has shown that the cross leads to the resurrection.

The beginning of the second letter of Paul

Paul, by God's will an apostle of Jesus Christ, and Timothy his brother, to the church of God that is at Corinth and to all the holy ones of the church who live in Achaia. Grace and peace from God our Father and the Lord Jesus Christ.

Praised be God, the Father of our Lord Jesus Christ, the Father of mercies and the God of all consolation! He comforts us in all our afflictions and thus enables us to comfort those who are in any trouble, with the same consolation we have received from him. As we have shared much in the suffering of Christ, so through Christ do we share abundantly in his consolation. If we are afflicted it is for your encouragement and salvation, and when we are consoled it is for your consolation, so that you may endure patiently the same sufferings we endure. Our hope for you is firm because we know that just as you share in the sufferings, so you will share in the consolation.—This is the Word of the Lord. ℟. **Thanks be to God.** ℣

Responsorial Psalm   Ps 34, 2-3. 4-5. 6-7. 8-9

℟. (9) **Taste and see the goodness of the Lord.**

I will bless the Lord at all times;
   his praise shall be ever in my mouth.
Let my soul glory in the Lord;
   the lowly will hear me and be glad. — ℟

Glorify the Lord with me,
   let us together extol his name.

I sought the Lord, and he answered me
  and delivered me from all my fears. — ℟

Look to him that you may be radiant with joy,
  and your faces may not blush with shame.
When the afflicted man called out, the Lord heard,
  and from all his distress he saved him. — ℟

The angel of the Lord encamps
  around those who fear him, and delivers them.
Taste and see how good the Lord is;
  happy the man who takes refuge in him. — ℟ ℣

GOSPEL   Mt 5, 1-12
Alleluia (Mt 11, 25)

℟. **Alleluia.** Blessed are you, Father, Lord of heaven
  and earth;
you have revealed to little ones the mysteries of the
  kingdom. ℟. **Alleluia.**

In place of the Alleluia given for each Weekday Mass.
another may be selected from pp. 1267 and following.

In the Sermon on the Mount, Jesus presents the Beatitudes. He shows
that true happiness is to be found in directions that men often shun.
This text summarizes Christ's spiritual program.

℣. The Lord be with you. ℟. **And also with you.**
✠ A reading from the holy gospel according to Matthew. ℟. **Glory to you, Lord.**

When Jesus saw the crowds he went up on the
mountainside. After he had sat down his disciples
gathered around him, and he began to teach them:

  "How blest are the poor in spirit: the reign of
    God is theirs.
  Blest too are the sorrowing; they shall be con-
    soled.
  [Blest are the lowly; they shall inherit the land.]
  Blest are they who hunger and thirst for holi-
    ness;
  they shall have their fill.
  Blest are they who show mercy; mercy shall be
    theirs.

Blest are the single-hearted for they shall see God.

Blest too the peacemakers; they shall be called sons of God.

Blest are those persecuted for holiness' sake; the reign of God is theirs.

Blest are you when they insult you and persecute you and utter every kind of slander against you because of me.

Be glad and rejoice, for your reward in heaven is great;

they persecuted the prophets before you in the very same way."

This is the gospel of the Lord. ℟. **Praise to you, Lord Jesus Christ.**   ➤ No. 15, p. 623

TUESDAY OF THE TENTH WEEK IN ORDINARY TIME

READING I   2 Cor 1, 18-22

In his lifetime upon this earth, everything Jesus did was pleasing to God. He always did the work of his Father. Although men are human and weak, they must always try to love and obey God, without switching between "yes" and "no." God, in his love, is always faithful.

A reading from the second letter of Paul to the Corinthians

As God keeps his word, I declare that my word to you is not "yes" one minute and "no" the next. Jesus Christ, whom Silvanus, Timothy, and I preached to you as Son of God, was not alternately "yes" and "no"; he was never anything but "yes." Whatever promises God has made have been fulfilled in him; therefore it is through him that we address our Amen to God when we worship together. God is the one who firmly establishes us along with you in Christ; it is he who anointed us and has sealed us, thereby depositing the first payment, the Spirit in our hearts.—This is the Word of the Lord. ℟. **Thanks be to God.** ⍖

Responsorial Psalm

Ps 119, 129. 130. 131. 132. 133. 135

℟. (135) **Lord, let your face shine on me.**

Wonderful are your decrees;
> therefore I observe them. — ℟

The revelation of your words sheds light,
> giving understanding to the simple. — ℟

I gasp with open mouth
> in my yearning for your commands. — ℟

Turn to me in pity
> as you turn to those who love your name. — ℟

Steady my footsteps according to your promise,
> and let no iniquity rule over me. — ℟

Let your countenance shine upon your servant,
> and teach me your statutes. — ℟ ⍖

GOSPEL   Mt 5, 13-16

Alleluia (Mt 5, 16)

℟. **Alleluia.** Let your light shine before men,
that they may see your good works and glorify your
> Father. ℟. **Alleluia.**

Jesus reminds his followers that they are to be the salt of the earth
and the light of the world. Christ bearers are to let their good works
be seen by others. In this way praise and glory may be given to God.

℣. The Lord be with you. ℟. **And also with you.**
✠ A reading from the holy gospel according to Matthew. ℟. **Glory to you, Lord.**

Jesus said to his disciples: "You are the salt of the
earth. But what if salt goes flat? How can you restore
its flavor? Then it is good for nothing but to be
thrown out and trampled underfoot.

"You are the light of the world. A city set on a
hill cannot be hidden. Men do not light a lamp and
then put it under a bushel basket. They set it on a

stand where it gives light to all in the house. In the same way, your light must shine before men so that they may see goodness in your acts and give praise to your heavenly Father."—This is the gospel of the Lord. ℟. **Praise to you, Lord Jesus Christ.**

➤ No. 15, p. 623

WEDNESDAY OF THE TENTH WEEK IN ORDINARY TIME

READING I   2 Cor 3, 4-11

Jesus came to seal a new covenant which truly gives life and forgiveness of sins. A covenant is a solemn agreement between God and his people. The old covenant was a shadow and a preparation for the new. This new covenant is sealed in the blood of Christ.

A reading from the second letter of Paul to the Corinthians

This great confidence in God is ours, through Christ. It is not that we are entitled of ourselves to take credit for anything. Our sole credit is from God, who has made us qualified ministers of a new covenant, a covenant not of a written law but of spirit. The written law kills, but the Spirit gives life.

If the ministry of death, carved in writing on stone, was inaugurated with such glory that the Israelites could not look on Moses' face because of the glory that shone on it (even though it was a fading glory), how much greater will be the glory of the ministry of the Spirit? If the ministry of the covenant that condemned had glory, greater by far is the glory of the ministry that justifies. Indeed, when you compare that limited glory with this surpassing glory, the former should be declared no glory at all. If what was destined to pass away was given in glory, greater by far is the glory that endures.— This is the Word of the Lord. ℟. **Thanks be to God.** ⅴ

Responsorial Psalm Ps 99, 5. 6. 7. 8. 9

℟. (9) **Holy is the Lord our God.**

Extol the Lord, our God,
  and worship at his footstool;
  holy is he! — ℟

Moses and Aaron were among his priests,
  and Samuel, among those who called upon his
    name;
  they called upon the Lord, and he answered
    them. — ℟

From the pillar of cloud he spoke to them;
  they heard his decrees and the law he gave
    them. — ℟

O Lord, our God, you answered them;
  a forgiving God you were to them,
  though requiting their misdeeds. — ℟

Extol the Lord, our God,
  and worship at his holy mountain;
  for holy is the Lord, our God. — ℟ ⍒

GOSPEL Mt 5, 17-19

Alleluia. (Ps 25, 4. 5)

℟. **Alleluia.** Teach me your paths, my God,
and lead me in your truth. ℟. **Alleluia.**

Jesus speaks of the first covenant. He declares that God's actions
in the Old Testament prepared the Jews for his coming. All who hear
Jesus must advance by accepting the new law which he proclaimed
in the Sermon on the Mount.

℣. The Lord be with you. ℟. **And also with you.**

✠ A reading from the holy gospel according to Matthew. ℟. **Glory to you, Lord.**

Jesus said to his disciples: "Do not think that I have
come to abolish the law and the prophets. I have
come, not to abolish them, but to fulfill them. Of
this much I assure you: until heaven and earth pass
away, not the smallest letter of the law, not the
smallest part of a letter, shall be done away with

until it all comes true. That is why whoever breaks the least significant of these commands and teaches others to do so shall be called least in the kingdom of God. Whoever fulfills and teaches these commands shall be great in the kingdom of God."—This is the gospel of the Lord. ℟. **Praise to you, Lord Jesus Christ.**   ➤ No. 15, p. 623

THURSDAY OF THE TENTH WEEK
IN ORDINARY TIME

READING I   2 Cor 3, 15—4, 1. 3-6

Not everyone recognizes Jesus as the Son of God and the Savior. Faith is a gift of God. Men must prepare themselves for that gift by honesty, humility, and a good moral life, allowing their light to shine forth. An unbelieving mind is blinded by idols of the present day.

A reading from the second letter of Paul to the
Corinthians

Even now, when Moses is read a veil covers the understanding of the Israelites. "But whenever Israel turns to the Lord, the veil will be removed." The Lord is the Spirit, and where the Spirit of the Lord is, there is freedom. All of us, gazing on the Lord's glory with unveiled faces, are being transformed from glory to glory into his very image by the Lord who is the Spirit.

Because we possess this ministry through God's mercy, we do not give in to discouragement. If our gospel can be called "veiled" in any sense, it is such only for those who are headed toward destruction. Their unbelieving minds have been blinded by the god of the present age so that they do not see the splendor of the gospel showing forth the glory of Christ, the image of God. It is not ourselves we preach but Christ Jesus as Lord, and ourselves as your servants for Jesus' sake. For God, who said, "Let light shine out of darkness," has shone in our hearts, that we in turn might make known the glory of God shining on the face of Christ.—This is the Word of the Lord. ℟. **Thanks be to God.** ✣

Responsorial Psalm   Ps 85, 9-10. 11-12. 13-14

℟. (10) **The glory of the Lord will dwell in our land.**

I will hear what God proclaims:
    the Lord—for he proclaims peace to his people.
Near indeed is his salvation to those who fear him,
    glory dwelling in our land. — ℟

Kindness and truth shall meet;
    justice and peace shall kiss.
Truth shall spring out of the earth,
    and justice shall look down from heaven. — ℟

The Lord himself will give his benefits;
    our land shall yield its increase.
Justice shall walk before him,
    and salvation, along the way of his steps. — ℟ ✣

GOSPEL   Mt 5, 20-26

Alleluia (Jn 13, 34)

℟. **Alleluia.** I give you a new commandment:
love one another as I have loved you. ℟. **Alleluia.**

True holiness is much more than obeying laws and rules; even inner thoughts and attitudes must be corrected. In preparing to offer sacrifice to God, a man must be fully reconciled with all his brothers.

℣. The Lord be with you. ℟. **And also with you.**
✠ A reading from the holy gospel according to Matthew. ℟. **Glory to you, Lord.**

Jesus said to his disciples: "I tell you, unless your holiness surpasses that of the scribes and Pharisees you shall not enter the kingdom of God.

    "You have heard the commandment imposed on your forefathers, 'You shall not commit murder; every murderer shall be liable to judgment.' What I say to you is: everyone who grows angry with his brother shall be liable to judgment; any man who uses abusive language toward his brother shall be answerable to the Sanhedrin, and if he holds him in contempt he risks the fires of Gehenna. If you bring your gift to the altar and there recall that your brother has anything against you, leave your gift at the altar, go first to be reconciled with your brother, and then come and offer your gift. Lose no time; settle with your opponent while on your way to court with him. Otherwise your opponent may hand you over to the judge, who will hand you over to the guard, who will throw you into prison. I warn you, you will not be released until you have paid the last penny."—This is the gospel of the Lord. ℟. **Praise to you, Lord Jesus Christ.**   ➤ No. 15, p. 623

FRIDAY OF THE TENTH WEEK
IN ORDINARY TIME

READING I   2 Cor 4, 7-15

Life is frail; spiritual strength is small. However, regardless of persecution, strength and endurance come from the grace of Jesus Christ. God raised up Jesus, and he too will bring the believer into his presence.

A reading from the second letter of Paul to the Corinthians

The treasure [of the knowledge of the glory of God] we possess in earthen vessels to make it clear that its surpassing power comes from God and not from us. We are afflicted in every way possible, but we are not crushed; full of doubts, we never despair. We are persecuted but never abandoned; we are struck down but never destroyed. Continually we carry about in our bodies the dying of Jesus, so that in our bodies the life of Jesus also may be revealed. While we live we are constantly being delivered to death for Jesus' sake, so that the life of Jesus may be revealed in our mortal flesh. Death is at work in us, but life in you. We have the spirit of faith of which the Scripture says, "Because I believed, I spoke out." We believe and so we speak, knowing that he who raised up the Lord Jesus will raise us up along with Jesus and place both us and you in his presence. Indeed, everything is ordered to your benefit, so that the grace bestowed in abundance may bring greater glory to God because they who give thanks are many.—This is the Word of the Lord. ℟. **Thanks be to God.** ↓

Responsorial Psalm   Ps 116, 10-11. 15-16. 17-18

℟. (17) **To you, Lord, I will offer a sacrifice of praise.**

I believed, even when I said,
  "I am greatly afflicted";
I said in my alarm,
  "No man is dependable." — ℟

Precious in the eyes of the Lord
  is the death of his faithful ones.
O Lord, I am your servant;
  I am your servant, the son of your handmaid;
  you have loosed my bonds. — ℟

To you will I offer sacrifice of thanksgiving,
  and I will call upon the name of the Lord.
My vows to the Lord I will pay
  in the presence of all his people. — ℟ ↓

℟. Or: **Alleluia.** ↓

GOSPEL   Mt 5, 27-32

Alleluia (Phil 2, 15-16)

℟. **Alleluia.** Shine on the world like bright stars; you are offering it the word of life. ℟. **Alleluia.**

Sin is a matter of choosing the wrong things in life. The self-denial that is required to choose Christ is only a very small sacrifice, compared to heaven. Jesus describes the choice that must be made and the responsibility of a sinful choice.

℣. The Lord be with you. ℟. **And also with you.**
✠ A reading from the holy gospel according to Matthew. ℟. **Glory to you, Lord.**

Jesus said to his disciples: "You have heard the commandment, 'You shall not commit adultery.' What I say to you is: anyone who looks lustfully at a woman has already committed adultery with her in his thoughts. If your right eye is your trouble, gouge it out and throw it away! Better to lose part of your body than to have it all cast into Gehenna. Again, if your right hand is your trouble, cut it off and throw it away! Better to lose part of your body than to have it all cast into Gehenna.

"It was also said, 'Whenever a man divorces his wife, he must give her a decree of divorce.' What I say to you is: everyone who divorces his wife—lewd conduct is a separate case—forces her to commit adultery. The man who marries a divorced woman likewise commits adultery."—This is the gospel of the Lord. ℟. **Praise to you, Lord Jesus Christ.**

➤ No. 15, p. 623

SATURDAY OF THE TENTH WEEK IN ORDINARY TIME

READING I   2 Cor 5, 14-21

St. Paul explains why the Son of God became man and why he died upon the cross. Jesus offered his humanity as one of mankind. For the first time, there was someone human who was totally pleasing to God and who entered into heaven. A follower of Jesus becomes his ambassador.

A reading from the second letter of Paul to the Corinthians

The love of Christ impels us who have reached the conviction that since one died for all, all died. He died for all so that those who live might live no longer for themselves, but for him who for their sakes died and was raised up.

Because of this we no longer look on anyone in terms of mere human judgment. If at one time we so regarded Christ, we no longer know him by this standard. This means that if anyone is in Christ, he is a new creation. The old order has passed away; now all is new! All this has been done by God, who has reconciled us to himself through Christ and has given us the ministry of reconciliation. I mean that God, in Christ, was reconciling the world to himself, not counting men's transgressions against them, and that he has entrusted the message of reconciliation to us. This makes us ambassadors for Christ, God as it were appealing through us. We implore you, in Christ's name: be reconciled to God! For our sakes God made him who did not know sin to be sin, so that in him we might become the very holiness of God.—This is the Word of the Lord. ℟. **Thanks be to God.** ℣

Responsorial Psalm   Ps 103, 1-2. 3-4. 8-9. 11-12

℟. (8) **The Lord is kind and merciful.**

Bless the Lord, O my soul;
    and all my being, bless his holy name.
Bless the Lord, O my soul,
    and forget not all his benefits. — ℟

He pardons all your iniquities,
    he heals all your ills.
He redeems your life from destruction,
    he crowns you with kindness and compassion.—℟

Merciful and gracious is the Lord,
    slow to anger and abounding in kindness.
He will not always chide,
    nor does he keep his wrath forever. — ℟

For as the heavens are high above the earth,
    so surpassing is his kindness toward those who fear him.
As far as the east is from the west,
    so far has he put our transgressions from us.—℟ ℣

GOSPEL   Mt 5, 33-37

Alleluia (Ps 119, 35. 29)

℟. **Alleluia.** Turn my heart to do your will;
teach me your law, O God. ℟. **Alleluia.**

Jesus speaks against trivial and overly frequent oath-taking, not against swearing to the truth. Jesus testified under oath at his trial. The word of a Christian should be trustworthy and straightforward, without any kind of devious tricks, used to deceive.

℣. The Lord be with you. ℟. **And also with you.**
✠ A reading from the holy gospel according to Matthew. ℟. **Glory to you, Lord.**

Jesus said to his disciples: "You have heard the commandment imposed on your forefathers, 'Do not take a false oath; rather, make good to the Lord all your pledges.' What I tell you is: do not swear at all. Do not swear by heaven (it is God's throne), nor by the earth (it is his footstool), nor by Jerusalem (it is the city of the great King); do not swear by your head (you cannot make a single hair white or black). Say, 'Yes' when you mean 'Yes' and 'No' when you mean 'No.' Anything beyond that is from the evil one."—This is the gospel of the Lord. ℟. **Praise to you, Lord Jesus Christ.**   ➤ No. 15, p. 623

MONDAY OF THE ELEVENTH WEEK
IN ORDINARY TIME

READING I   2 Cor 6, 1-10

The grace of God is a gift that no one deserves. A man must ask for it and must accept it when it is given. A Christian must be a minister of God, patient, fasting, innocent, offering the message of truth, so that he will give honor to the name of Christ.

A reading from the second letter of Paul to the Corinthians

As your fellow workers we beg you not to receive the grace of God in vain. For he says, "In an acceptable time I have heard you; on a day of salvation I have helped you." Now is the acceptable time! Now is the day of salvation!

We avoid giving anyone offense so that our ministry may not be blamed. On the contrary, in all that

we do we strive to present ourselves as ministers of
God, acting with patient endurance amid trials, difficulties, distresses, beatings, imprisonments, and riots;
as men familiar with hard work, sleepless nights,
and fastings; conducting ourselves with innocence,
knowledge, and patience in the Holy Spirit, in sincere
love; as men with the message of truth and the power
of God, wielding the weapons of righteousness with
right hand and left, whether honored or dishonored,
spoken of well or ill. We are called imposters, yet
we are truthful; nobodies who in fact are well known;
dead, yet here we are alive; punished, but not put to
death; sorrowful, though we are always rejoicing;
poor, yet we enrich many. We seem to have nothing,
yet everything is ours!—This is the Word of the
Lord. ℟. **Thanks be to God.** ℣

Responsorial Psalm   Ps 98, 1. 2-3. 3-4

℟. (2) **The Lord has made known his salvation.**

Sing to the Lord a new song,
   for he has done wondrous deeds;
His right hand has won victory for him,
   his holy arm. — ℟

The Lord has made his salvation known:
   in the sight of the nations he has revealed his jus-
      tice.
He has remembered his kindness and his faithfulness
   toward the house of Israel. — ℟

All the ends of the earth have seen
   the salvation by our God.
Sing joyfully to the Lord, all you lands;
   break into song; sing praise. — ℟ ℣

GOSPEL   Mt 5, 38-42

Alleluia (Ps 119, 105)

℟. **Alleluia.** Your word is a lamp for my feet,
and a light on my path. ℟. **Alleluia.**

In the Old Testament, God brought his people to accept an equality in avenging an offense instead of inflicting a far greater injury. Jesus compares this old law with his new teaching of charity and love at all times, but especially for those in need.

℣. The Lord be with you. ℟. **And also with you.**
✠ A reading from the holy gospel according to Matthew. ℟. **Glory to you, Lord.**

Jesus said to his disciples: "You have heard the commandment, 'An eye for an eye, a tooth for a tooth.' But what I say to you is: offer no resistance to injury. When a person strikes you on the right cheek, turn and offer him the other. If anyone wants to go to law over your shirt, hand him your coat as well. Should anyone press you into service for one mile, go with him two miles. Give to the man who begs from you. Do not turn your back on the borrower."—This is the gospel of the Lord. ℟. **Praise to you, Lord Jesus Christ.**   ➔ No. 15, p. 623

TUESDAY OF THE ELEVENTH WEEK IN ORDINARY TIME

READING I   2 Cor 8, 1-9

The gift of faith, which is a sharing in the life of God, is not only for self. The Israelites were God's people and, as a family, they cared for one another. Therefore, Christians should care about one another and help each other, especially the poor, and this should be a mark of love.

A reading from the second letter of Paul to the Corinthians

Brothers, I should like you to know of the grace of God conferred on the churches of Macedonia. In the midst of severe trial their overflowing joy and deep poverty have produced an abundant generosity. According to their means—indeed I can testify even beyond their means—and voluntarily, they begged us insistently for the favor of sharing in this service to members of the church. Beyond our hopes they first gave themselves to God and then to us by the will of God. That is why I have exhorted Titus, who had already begun this work of charity among you, to bring it to successful completion: that just as you are rich in every respect, in faith and discourse, in knowledge, in total concern, and in our love for you, you may also abound in this charity.

I am not giving an order but simply testing your generous love against the concern which others show. You are well acquainted with the favor shown you by our Lord Jesus Christ: how for your sake he made himself poor though he was rich, so that you might become rich by his poverty.—This is the Word of the Lord. ℟. **Thanks be to God.** ℣

Responsorial Psalm   Ps 146, 2. 5-6. 7. 8-9

℟. (2) **Praise the Lord, my soul!**
I will praise the Lord all my life;
   I will sing praise to my God while I live. — ℟

Happy he whose help is the God of Jacob,
   whose hope is in the Lord, his God,
Who made heaven and earth,
   the sea and all that is in them. — ℟

Who keeps faith forever,
   secures justice for the oppressed,
   gives food to the hungry.
The Lord sets captives free. — ℟

The Lord gives sight to the blind.
   The Lord raises up those that were bowed down;
The Lord loves the just.
   The Lord protects strangers. — ℟ ℣

℟. Or: **Alleluia.** ℣

GOSPEL   Mt 5, 43-48
Alleluia (Jn 13, 34)

℟. **Alleluia.** I give you a new commandment:
love one another as I have loved you. ℟. **Alleluia.**

The Christian is called to have the same mind and the same attitudes as God himself. God is generous and forgiving to sinners. Jesus gives the command that all men must love one another, even their enemies, and pray for their persecutors.

℣. The Lord be with you. ℟. **And also with you.**

✠ A reading from the holy gospel according to Matthew. ℟. **Glory to you, Lord.**

Jesus said to his disciples: "You have heard the commandment, 'You shall love your countryman but hate your enemy.' My command to you is: love your enemies, pray for your persecutors. This will prove that you are sons of your heavenly Father, for his sun rises on the bad and the good, he rains on the just and the unjust. If you love those who love you, what merit is there in that? Do not tax collectors do as much? And if you greet your brothers only, what is so praiseworthy about that? Do not pagans do as much? In a word, you must be perfected as your heavenly Father is perfect.''—This is the gospel of the Lord. ℟. **Praise to you, Lord Jesus Christ.**

➤ No. 15, p. 623

WEDNESDAY OF THE ELEVENTH WEEK IN ORDINARY TIME

READING I   2 Cor 9, 6-11

In his insecurity and worry, a man may hoard more money and more possessions than he needs. St. Paul encourages the follower of Christ to be generous as an expression of confidence in God's watchful care. He who sows bountifully will reap bountifully.

A reading from the second letter of Paul to the Corinthians

Let me say this much: He who sows sparingly will reap sparingly, and he who sows bountifully will reap bountifully. Everyone must give according to

what he has inwardly decided; not sadly, not grudgingly, for God loves a cheerful giver. God can multiply his favors among you so that you may always
have enough of everything and even a surplus for
good works, as it is writtten:

"He scattered abroad and gave to the poor,
his justice endures forever."

He who supplies seed for the sower and bread for
the eater will provide in abundance; he will multiply
the seed you sow and increase your generous yield.
In every way your liberality is enriched; through us
it results in thanks offered to God.—This is the Word
of the Lord. ℟. **Thanks be to God.** ℣

Responsorial Psalm   Ps 112, 1-2. 3-4. 9

℟. (1) **Happy the man who fears the Lord.**

Happy the man who fears the Lord,
who greatly delights in his commands.
His posterity shall be mighty upon the earth;
the upright generation shall be blessed. — ℟

Wealth and riches shall be in his house;
his generosity shall endure forever.
The Lord dawns through the darkness, a light for the
upright;
he is gracious and merciful and just. — ℟

Lavishly he gives to the poor;
his generosity shall endure forever;
his horn shall be exalted in glory. — ℟ ℣

℟. Or: **Alleluia.** ℣

GOSPEL   Mt 6, 1-6. 16-18

Alleluia (Jn 14, 23)

℟. **Alleluia.** If anyone loves me, he will hold to my
words,
and my Father will love him, and we will come to
him. ℟. **Alleluia.**

In fasting, praying, and giving to charity, it is important to keep watch over one's motives. Jesus teaches that a man must be generous and devout, not because these things bring social approval and a good reputation, but because of his love of God and because he shares in God's love for his fellowmen. What God knows is important.

℣. The Lord be with you. ℟. **And also with you.**
✠ A reading from the holy gospel according to Matthew. ℟. **Glory to you, Lord.**

Jesus said to his disciples: "Be on guard against performing religious acts for people to see. Otherwise expect no recompense from your heavenly Father. When you give alms, for example, do not blow a horn before you in synagogues and streets like hypocrites looking for applause. You can be sure of this much, they are already repaid. In giving alms you are not to let your left hand know what your right hand is doing. Keep your deeds of mercy secret, and your Father who sees in secret will repay you.

"When you are praying, do not behave like the hypocrites who love to stand and pray in synagogues or on street corners in order to be noticed. I give you my word, they are already repaid. Whenever you pray, go to your room, close your door, and pray to your Father in private.

"When you fast, you are not to look glum as the hypocrites do. They change the appearance of their faces so that others may see they are fasting. I assure you, they are already repaid. When you fast, see to it that you groom your hair and wash your face. In that way no one can see you are fasting but your Father who is hidden; and your Father who sees what is hidden will repay you."—This is the gospel of the Lord. ℟. **Praise to you, Lord Jesus Christ.**

THURSDAY OF THE ELEVENTH WEEK
IN ORDINARY TIME

READING I   2 Cor 11, 1-11

St. Paul makes it clear that God guides him in the doctrine that he teaches. He wants the people of the Church to remain faithful to the teaching of the apostles. Faith is not decided by personal ideas or theories, but by what God has taught through his Church.

A reading from the second letter of Paul to the Corinthians

You must endure a little of my folly. Put up with me, I beg you! I am jealous of you with the jealousy of God himself, since I have given you in marriage to one husband, presenting you as a chaste virgin to Christ. My fear is that, just as the serpent seduced Eve by his cunning, your thoughts may be corrupted and you may fall away from your sincere and complete devotion to Christ. I say this because when someone comes preaching another Jesus than the one we preached, or when you receive a different spirit than the one you have received, or a gospel other than the gospel you accepted, you seem to endure it quite well. I consider myself inferior to the "super-apostles" in nothing. I may be unskilled in speech but I know that I am not lacking in knowledge. We have made this evident to you in every conceivable way.

Could I have done wrong when I preached the gospel of God to you free of charge, humbling myself with a view to exalting you? I robbed other churches, I accepted support from them in order to minister to you. When I was with you and in want I was a burden to none of you, for the brothers who came from Macedonia supplied my needs. In every way possible I kept myself from being burdensome to you, and I shall continue to do so. I swear by the Christ who is in me that this boast of mine will not cease in the regions of Achaia! Why? Because I do not love you? God knows I do.—This is the Word of the Lord. ℟. **Thanks be to God.** ℣

Responsorial Psalm   Ps 111, 1-2. 3-4. 7-8

℟. (7) **Your works, O Lord, are justice and truth.**

I will give thanks to the Lord with all my heart
   in the company and assembly of the just.
Great are the works of the Lord,
   exquisite in all their delights. — ℟

Majesty and glory are his work,
   and his justice endures forever.
He has won renown for his wondrous deeds;
   gracious and merciful is the Lord. — ℟

The works of his hands are faithful and just;
   sure are all his precepts,
Reliable forever and ever,
   wrought in truth and equity. — ℟ ℣

℟. Or: **Alleluia.** ℣

GOSPEL   Mt 6, 7-15

Alleluia (Rom 8, 15)

℟. **Alleluia.** You have received the Spirit which
    makes us God's children,
and in that Spirit we call God our Father. ℟. **Alleluia.**

Jesus teaches his disciples how to pray. The "Our Father" is not the only prayer, but its thoughts and its spirit are the standard for all prayer. Although God knows the needs of his people, still he wants them to pray.

℣. The Lord be with you. ℟. **And also with you.**
✠ A reading from the holy gospel according to Matthew. ℟. **Glory to you, Lord.**

Jesus said to his disciples: "In your prayer do not rattle on like the pagans. They think they will win a hearing by the sheer multiplication of words. Do not imitate them. Your Father knows what you need before you ask him. This is how you are to pray:
    'Our Father in heaven,

hallowed be your name,
your kingdom come,
your will be done
on earth as it is in heaven.
Give us today our daily bread,
and forgive us the wrong we have done
as we forgive those who wrong us.
Subject us not to the trial
but deliver us from the evil one.'

"If you forgive the faults of others, your heavenly
Father will forgive you yours. If you do not forgive
others, neither will your Father forgive you."—This
is the gospel of the Lord. ℟. **Praise to you, Lord Jesus
Christ.** ➤ No. 15, p. 623

FRIDAY OF THE ELEVENTH WEEK
IN ORDINARY TIME

READING I   2 Cor 11, 18. 21-30

St. Paul reacts to the "super-apostles" who have been downgrading
him and leading the people into error. His great sufferings do not
stop him; indeed, they count for little because he is driven by love
for Christ.

A reading from the second letter of Paul to the
Corinthians

Since many are bragging about their human distinc-
tions, I too will boast. To my shame I must confess
that we have been too weak to do such things. But
what anyone else dares to claim—I speak with absolute foolishness now—I, too, will dare. Are they Hebrews? So am I! Are they Israelites? So am I! Are they
the seed of Abraham? So am I! Are they ministers of
Christ? Now I am really talking like a fool—I am
more: with my many more labors and imprisonments, with far worse beatings and frequent brushes
with death. Five times at the hands of the Jews I
received forty lashes less one; three times I was

beaten with rods; I was stoned once, shipwrecked three times; I passed a day and a night on the sea. I traveled continually, endangered by floods, robbers, my own people, the Gentiles; imperiled in the city, in the desert, at sea, by false brothers; enduring labor, hardship, many sleepless nights; in hunger and thirst and frequent fastings, in cold and nakedness. Leaving other sufferings unmentioned, there is that daily tension pressing on me, my anxiety for all the churches. Who is weak that I am not affected by it? Who is scandalized that I am not aflame with indignation?—This is the Word of the Lord. ℟. **Thanks be to God.** ℣

Responsorial Psalm   Ps 34, 2-3. 4-5. 6-7

℟. (18) **From all their afflictions God will deliver the just.**

I will bless the Lord at all times;
  his praise shall be ever in my mouth.
Let my soul glory in the Lord;
  the lowly will hear me and be glad. — ℟

Glorify the Lord with me,
  let us together extol his name.
I sought the Lord, and he answered me
  and delivered me from all my fears. — ℟

Look to him that you may be radiant with joy,
  and your faces may not blush with shame.
When the afflicted man called out, the Lord heard,
  and from all his distress he saved him. — ℟ ℣

GOSPEL   Mt 6, 19-23
Alleluia (Mt 5, 3)

℟. **Alleluia.** Happy the poor in spirit;
  the kingdom of heaven is theirs. ℟. **Alleluia.**

Men often choose something to be the great driving value in their lives. Sometimes they choose riches and material comfort. These things will pass away and do not bring full happiness even now. One true treasure is to know, love, and serve the Lord, and to be with him in heaven.

℣. The Lord be with you. ℟. **And also with you.**

✠ A reading from the holy gospel according to Matthew. ℟. **Glory to you, Lord.**

Jesus said to his disciples: "Do not lay up for yourselves an earthly treasure. Moths and rust corrode; thieves break in and steal. Make it your practice instead to store up heavenly treasure, which neither moths nor rust corrode nor thieves break in and steal. Remember, where your treasure is, there your heart is also. The eye is the body's lamp. If your eyes are good, your body will be filled with light; if your eyes are bad, your body will be in darkness. And if your light is darkness, how deep the darkness will be!"—This is the gospel of the Lord. ℟. **Praise to you, Lord Jesus Christ.**   ➤ No. 15, p. 623

SATURDAY OF THE ELEVENTH WEEK IN ORDINARY TIME

READING I   2 Cor 12, 1-10

St. Paul humbly and openly tells of his mystical experiences with God. He achieved such close personal contact with God by accepting his vocation and serving the Lord with his whole heart. God will become a real person for those who serve him and do not ignore his requests.

A reading from the second letter of Paul to the Corinthians

I must go on boasting, however useless it may be, and speak of visions and revelations of the Lord. I know a man in Christ who, fourteen years ago—whether he was in or outside his body I cannot say, only God can say—a man who was snatched up to the third heaven. I know that this man—whether in or outside his body I do not know, God knows—was snatched up to Paradise to hear words which cannot be uttered, words which no man may speak. About this man I will boast; but I will do no boasting about myself unless it be about my weaknesses. And even if I were to boast it would not be folly in me because I would only be telling the truth.

But I refrain, lest anyone think more of me than what he sees in me or hears from my lips. As to the extraordinary revelations, in order that I might not become conceited I was given a thorn in the flesh, an angel of Satan to beat me and keep me from getting proud. Three times I begged the Lord that this might leave me. He said to me, "My grace is enough for you, for in weakness power reaches perfection." And so I willingly boast of my weaknesses instead, that the power of Christ may rest upon me.

Therefore I am content with weakness, with mistreatment, with distress, with persecutions and difficulties for the sake of Christ; for when I am powerless, it is then that I am strong.—This is the Word of the Lord. ℟. **Thanks be to God.** ⍒

Responsorial Psalm   Ps 34, 8-9. 10-11. 12-13

℟. (9) **Taste and see the goodness of the Lord.**

The angel of the Lord encamps
    around those who fear him, and delivers them.
Taste and see how good the Lord is;
    happy the man who takes refuge in him. — ℟

Fear the Lord, you his holy ones,
    for nought is lacking to those who fear him.
The great grow poor and hungry;
    but those who seek the Lord want for no good
        thing. — ℟

Come, children, hear me;
    I will teach you the fear of the Lord.
Which of you desires life,
    and takes delight in prosperous days? — ℟ ⍒

GOSPEL   Mt 6, 24-34

Alleluia (2 Cor 8, 9)

℟. **Alleluia.** Jesus Christ was rich but he became
    poor,

to make you rich out of his poverty. ℟. **Alleluia.**

Jesus warns that it is impossible to serve two masters. God really cares about his people. He cares about the birds of the air and the flowers, and man is of far more value. Man must learn to trust God who knows his every need.

℣. The Lord be with you. ℟. **And also with you.**

✠ A reading from the holy gospel according to Matthew. ℟. **Glory to you, Lord.**

Jesus said to his disciples: "No man can serve two masters. He will either hate one and love the other or be attentive to one and despise the other. You cannot give yourself to God and money. I warn you, then: do not worry about your livelihood, what you are to eat or drink or use for clothing. Is life not more than food? Is not the body more valuable than clothes?

"Look at the birds in the sky. They do not sow or reap, they gather nothing into barns; yet your heavenly Father feeds them. Are not you more important than they? Which of you by worrying can add a moment to his life-span? As for clothes, why be concerned? Learn a lesson from the way the wild flowers grow. They do not work; they do not spin. Yet I assure you, not even Solomon in all his splendor was arrayed like one of these. If God can clothe in such splendor the grass of the field, which blooms today and is thrown on the fire tomorrow, will he not provide much more for you, O weak in faith! Stop worrying, then, over questions like, 'What are we to eat, or what are we to drink, or what are we to wear?' The unbelievers are always running after these things. Your heavenly Father knows all that you need. Seek first his kingship over you, his way of holiness, and all these things will be given you besides. Enough, then, of worrying about tomorrow. Let tomorrow take care of itself. Today has troubles enough of its own."—This is the gospel of the Lord. ℟. **Praise to you, Lord Jesus Christ.** ➔ No. 15, p. 623

MONDAY OF THE TWELFTH WEEK
IN ORDINARY TIME

READING I   Gn 12, 1-9

Abraham leaves his own land and journeys toward the land that God promised to give to Abraham's descendants, and not to Abraham himself. God takes care of Abraham and all his descendants. Abraham responds to the Lord.

A reading from the book of Genesis

The Lord said to Abram: "Go forth from the land of your kinsfolk and from your father's house to a land that I will show you.

"I will make of you a great nation,
    and I will bless you;
I will make your name great,
    so that you will be a blessing.
I will bless those who bless you
    and curse those who curse you.
All the communities of the earth
    shall find blessing in you."

Abram went as the Lord directed him, and Lot went with him. Abram was seventy-five years old when he left Haran. Abram took his wife Sarai, his brother's son Lot, all the possessions that they had accumulated, and the persons they had acquired in Haran, and they set out for the land of Canaan. When they came to the land of Canaan, Abram passed through the land as far as the sacred place at She-chem, by the terebinth of Moreh. (The Canaanites were then in the land.)

The Lord appeared to Abram and said, "To your descendants I will give this land." So Abram built an altar there to the Lord who had appeared to him. From there he moved on to the hill country east of Bethel, pitching his tent with Bethel to the west and Ai to the east. He built an altar there to the Lord and invoked the Lord by name. Then Abram journeyed on by stages to the Negeb.—This is the Word of the Lord. ℟. **Thanks be to God.** ℣

Responsorial Psalm   Ps 33, 12-13. 18-19. 20. 22

℟. (12) **Happy the people the Lord has chosen to be his own.**

Happy the nation whose God is the Lord,
   the people he has chosen for his own inheritance.
From heaven the Lord looks down;
   he sees all mankind. — ℟

See, the eyes of the Lord are upon those who fear
      him,
   upon those who hope for his kindness,
To deliver them from death
   and preserve them in spite of famine. — ℟

Our soul waits for the Lord,
   who is our help and our shield.
May your kindness, O Lord, be upon us
   who have put our hope in you. — ℟ ℣

GOSPEL   Mt 7, 1-5

Alleluia (Heb 4, 12)

℟. **Alleluia.** The word of God is living and active;
it probes the thoughts and motives of our heart.
          ℟. **Alleluia.**

Jesus exposes the weakness of the human spirit. A man who judges
will be judged. How often, however, a man is blinded by his own
shortsightedness.

℣. The Lord be with you. ℟. **And also with you.**
✠ A reading from the holy gospel according to Matthew. ℟. **Glory to you, Lord.**

Jesus said to his disciples "If you want to avoid
judgment, stop passing judgment. Your verdict on
others will be the verdict passed on you. The measure
with which you measure will be used to measure
you. Why look at the speck in your brother's
eye when you miss the plank in your own? How can
you say to your brother, 'Let me take that speck out
of your eye,' while all the time the plank remains
in your own? You hypocrite! Remove the plank from

your own eye first; then you will see clearly to take the speck from your brother's eye." This is the gospel of the Lord. ℟. **Praise to you, Lord Jesus Christ.**

➜ No. 15, p. 623

TUESDAY OF THE TWELFTH WEEK
IN ORDINARY TIME

READING I   Gn 13, 2. 5-18

The sacred writer shows the generosity of Abraham, the ancestor of the chosen people. As the elder member of the group, he could have chosen the better land for himself. His generosity brings another promise of blessings from God.

A reading from the book of Genesis

Abram was very rich in livestock, silver and gold.

Lot, who went with Abram, also had flocks and herds and tents, so that the land could not support them if they stayed together; their possessions were so great that they could not dwell together. There were quarrels between the herdsmen of Abram's livestock and those of Lot's. (At this time the Canaanites and the Perizzites were occupying the land).

So Abram said to Lot: "Let there be no strife between you and me, or between your herdsmen and mine, for we are kinsmen. Is not the whole land at your disposal? Please separate from me. If you prefer the left, I will go to the right; if you prefer the right, I will go to the left." Lot looked about and saw how well watered the whole Jordan Plain was as far as Zoar, like the Lord's own garden, or like Egypt. (This was before the Lord had destroyed Sodom and Gomorrah.) Lot, therefore, chose for himself the whole Jordan Plain and set out eastward. Thus they separated from each other; Abram stayed in the land of Canaan, while Lot settled among the cities of the Plain, pitching his tents near Sodom. Now the inhabitants of Sodom were very wicked in the sins they committed against the Lord.

After Lot had left, the Lord said to Abram: "Look about you, and from where you are, gaze to the north and south, east and west; all the land that you see I will give to you and your descendants forever. I will make your descendants like the dust of the earth; if anyone could count the dust of the earth, your descendants too might be counted. Set forth and walk about in the land, through its length and breadth, for to you I will give it." Abram moved his tents and went on to settle near the terebinth of Mamre, which is at Hebron. There he built an altar to the Lord.—This is the Word of the Lord. ℟. **Thanks be to God.** ℣

Responsorial Psalm   Ps 15, 2-3. 3-4. 5

℟. (1) **He who does justice will live in the presence of the Lord.**

He who walks blamelessly and does justice;
   who thinks the truth in his heart
   and slanders not with his tongue. — ℟

Who harms not his fellow man,
   nor takes up a reproach against his neighbor;
By whom the reprobate is despised,
   while he honors those who fear the Lord. — ℟

Who lends not his money at usury
   and accepts no bribe against the innocent.
He who does these things
   shall never be disturbed. — ℟ ℣

GOSPEL   Mt 7, 6. 12-14

Alleluia (Jn 8, 12)

℟. **Alleluia.** I am the light of the world, says the Lord;
the man who follows me will have the light of life.
℟. **Alleluia.**

Jesus' command is simply stated: treat others as you would want them to treat you. However, Jesus warns that it is easy to be weak and selfish and full of revenge. The gate to salvation is open, but it is narrow. By charity and self-control, the gate is opened.

℣. The Lord be with you. ℟. **And also with you.**
✠ A reading from the holy gospel according to Matthew. ℟. **Glory to you, Lord.**

Jesus said to the disciples: "Do not give what is holy to dogs or toss your pearls before swine. They will trample them under foot, at best, and perhaps even tear you to shreds.

"Treat others the way you would have them treat you: this sums up the law and the prophets.

"Enter through the narrow gate. The gate that leads to damnation is wide, the road is clear, and many choose to travel it. But how narrow is the gate that leads to life, how rough the road, and how few there are who find it!"—This is the gospel of the Lord. ℟. **Praise to you, Lord Jesus Christ.**

➤ No. 15, p. 623

WEDNESDAY OF THE TWELFTH WEEK IN ORDINARY TIME

READING I   Gn 15, 1-12. 17-18

Abraham becomes just in the sight of God because of his faith, not because of the regulations of the law of Moses. He obeys the law in a spirit of faith and love. For his faith, God makes a solemn promise to Abraham.

A reading from the book of Genesis

The word of the Lord came to Abram in a vision:
        "Fear not, Abram!
        I am your shield;
        I will make your reward very great."
But Abram said, "O Lord God, what good will your gifts be, if I keep on being childless and have as my heir the steward of my house, Eliezer?" Abram continued, "See, you have given me no offspring, and so one of my servants will be my heir." Then the word of the Lord came to him: "No, that one shall not be your heir; your own issue shall be your heir." He

took him outside and said: "Look up at the sky and count the stars, if you can. Just so," he added, "shall your descendants be." Abram put his faith in the Lord, who credited it to him as an act of righteousness.

He then said to him, "I am the Lord who brought you from Ur of the Chaldeans to give you this land as a possession." "O Lord God," he asked, "how am I to know that I shall possess it?" He answered him, "Bring me a three-year-old heifer, a three-year-old she-goat, a three-year-old ram, a turtledove, and a young pigeon." He brought him all these, split them in two, and placed each half opposite the other; but the birds he did not cut up. Birds of prey swooped down on the carcasses, but Abram stayed with them. As the sun was about to set, a trance fell upon Abram, and a deep, terrifying darkness enveloped him.

When the sun had set and it was dark, there appeared a smoking brazier and a flaming torch, which passed between those pieces. It was on that occasion that the Lord made a covenant with Abram, saying: "To your descendants I give this land, from the Wadi of Egypt to the Great River [the Euphrates]."—This is the Word of the Lord. ℟. **Thanks be to God.** ✟

Responsorial Psalm   Ps 105, 1-2. 3-4. 6-7. 8-9

℟. (8) **The Lord remembers his covenant for ever.**

Give thanks to the Lord, invoke his name;
    make known among the nations his deeds.
Sing to him, sing his praise,
    proclaim all his wondrous deeds. — ℟

Glory in his holy name;
    rejoice, O hearts that seek the Lord!
Look to the Lord in his strength;
    seek to serve him constantly. — ℟

You descendants of Abraham, his servants,
    sons of Jacob, his chosen ones!

He, the Lord, is our God;
  throughout the earth his judgments prevail. — ℟

He remembers forever his covenant
  which he made binding for a thousand generations—
Which he entered into with Abraham
  and by his oath to Isaac. — ℟ ℣

℟. Or: **Alleluia.** ℣

GOSPEL Mt 7, 15-20

Alleluia (Jn 8, 31-32)

℟. **Alleluia.** If you stay in my word, you will indeed
  be my disciples,
and you will know the truth, says the Lord. ℟. **Alleluia.**

The true character of a person may be detected by how he acts, especially in the face of trouble or disappointment. Jesus points out that good trees produce good fruit. This requires following the law and the spirit of Christ sincerely.

℣. The Lord be with you. ℟. **And also with you.**
✠ A reading from the holy gospel according to Matthew. ℟. **Glory to you, Lord.**

Jesus said to his disciples: "Be on your guard against false prophets, who come to you in sheep s clothing but underneath are wolves on the prowl. You will know them by their deeds. Do you ever pick grapes from thornbushes, or figs from prickly plants? Never! Any sound tree bears good fruit, while a decayed tree bears bad fruit. A sound tree cannot bear bad fruit any more than a decayed tree can bear good fruit. Every tree that does not bear good fruit is cut down and thrown into the fire. You can tell a tree by its fruit."—This is the gospel of the Lord. ℟.
Praise to you, Lord Jesus Christ.

THURSDAY OF THE TWELFTH WEEK
IN ORDINARY TIME

READING I   Gn 16, 1-12. 15-16 or 16, 6-12. 15-16

This section of Genesis shows the marriage customs of the day. God would gradually lead his people to appreciate the exclusiveness of the marriage bond. In the meantime, God creates a new nation from the union of Abraham and the slave Hagar.

[*If the "Short Form" is used, the indented text in brackets is omitted.*]

A reading from the book of Genesis

[Abram's wife Sarai had borne him no children. She had, however, an Egyptian maid-servant named Hagar. Sarai said to Abram: "The Lord has kept me from bearing children. Have intercourse, then, with my maid; perhaps I shall have sons through her." Abram heeded Sarai's request. Thus, after Abram had lived ten years in the land of Canaan, his wife Sarai took her maid, Hagar the Egyptian, and gave her to her husband Abram to be his concubine. He had intercourse with her, and she became pregnant. When she became aware of her pregnancy, she looked on her mistress with disdain. So Sarai said to Abram: "You are responsible for this outrage against me. I myself gave my maid to your embrace; but ever since she became aware of her pregnancy, she has been looking on me with disdain. May the Lord decide between you and me!"]

Abram told Sarai: "Your maid is in your power. Do to her whatever you please." Sarai then abused her so much that Hagar ran away from her.

The Lord's messenger found her by a spring in the wilderness, the spring on the road to Shur, and he asked, "Hagar, maid of Sarai, where have you come from and where are you going?" She answered, "I am running away from my mistress, Sarai." But the

Lord's messenger told her: "Go back to your mistress and submit to her abusive treatment. I will make your descendants so numerous," added the Lord's messenger, "that they will be too many to count. Besides," the Lord's messenger said to her:

"You are now pregnant and shall bear a son;
　　you shall name him Ishmael,
For the Lord has heard you,
　　God has answered you.
He shall be a wild ass of a man,
　　his hand against everyone,
　　and everyone's hand against him;
In opposition to all his kin
　　shall he encamp."

Hagar bore Abram a son, and Abram named the son whom Hagar bore him Ishmael. Abram was eighty-six years old when Hagar bore him Ishmael.
—This is the Word of the Lord. ℟. **Thanks be to God.** ⱱ

Responsorial Psalm　　　　　　Ps 106, 1-2. 3-4. 4-5

℟. (1) **Give thanks to the Lord for he is good.**

Give thanks to the Lord, for he is good,
　　for his kindness endures forever.
Who can tell the mighty deeds of the Lord,
　　or proclaim his praises? — ℟

Who can tell the mighty deeds of the Lord,
　　or proclaim all his praises?
Happy are they who observe what is right,
　　who do always what is just.
Remember us, O Lord, as you favor your people. — ℟

Visit me with your saving help,
　　that I may see the prosperity of your chosen ones,
Rejoice in the joy of your people,
　　and glory with your inheritance. — ℟ ⱱ

℟. Or: **Alleluia.** ⱱ

GOSPEL   Mt 7, 21-29

Alleluia. (Jn 14, 23)

℟. **Alleluia.** If anyone loves me, he will hold to my
    words,
and my Father will love him, and we will come to
    him. ℟. **Alleluia.**

Jesus makes very clear what he expects of his followers. The Christian
name is not enough; Christ wants everyone to come to know him. This
requires faith, prayer, obedience, and service. The result is a union
with Christ that nothing can destroy.

℣. The Lord be with you. ℟. **And also with you.**

✠ A reading from the holy gospel according to Matthew. ℟. **Glory to you, Lord.**

Jesus said to his disciples: "None of those who cry
out, 'Lord, Lord,' will enter the kingdom of God but
only the one who does the will of my Father in
heaven. When that day comes, many will plead with
me, 'Lord, Lord, have we not prophesied in your
name? Have we not exorcised demons by its power?
Did we not do many miracles in your name as well?'
Then I will declare to them solemnly, 'I never knew
you. Out of my sight, you evildoers!'

"Anyone who hears my words and puts them into
practice is like the wise man who built his house on
rock. When the rainy season set in, the torrents came
and the winds blew and buffeted his house. It did not
collapse; it had been solidly set on rock. Anyone
who hears my words but does not put them into
practice is like the foolish man who built his house
on sandy ground. The rains fell, the torrents came,
the winds blew and lashed against his house. It collapsed under all this and was completely ruined."

    Jesus finished his discourse and left the crowds
spellbound at his teaching. The reason was that he
taught with authority and not like their scribes.—
This is the gospel of the Lord. ℟. **Praise to you, Lord
Jesus Christ.**   ➔ No. 15, p. 623

FRIDAY OF THE TWELFTH WEEK
IN ORDINARY TIME

READING I   Gn 17, 1. 9-10. 15-22

God imposes the Eastern practice of circumcision upon the Hebrews as a sign that they are his people. The act of begetting children is marked as being sacred to God. One day, a child would be born who would be the Messiah. The process begins with the birth of Isaac.

A reading from the book of Genesis

When Abram was ninety-nine years old, the Lord appeared to him and said: "I am God the Almighty. Walk in my presence and be blameless."

God also said to Abraham: "On your part, you and your descendants after you must keep my covenant throughout the ages. This is my covenant with you and your descendants after you that you must keep: every male among you shall be circumcised."

God further said to Abraham: "As for your wife Sarai, do not call her Sarai; her name shall be Sarah. I will bless her, and I will give you a son by her. Him also will I bless; he shall give rise to nations, and rulers of peoples shall issue from him." Abraham prostrated himself and laughed as he said to himself, "Can a child be born to a man who is a hundred years old? Or can Sarah give birth at ninety!" Then Abraham said to God, "Let but Ishmael live on by your favor!" God replied: "Nevertheless, your wife Sarah is to bear you a son, and you shall call him Isaac. I will maintain my covenant with him as an everlasting pact, to be his God and the God of his descendants after him. As for Ishmael, I am heeding you: I hereby bless him. I will make him fertile and will multiply him exceedingly. He shall become the father of twelve chieftains, and I will make of him a great nation. But my covenant I will maintain with Isaac, whom Sarah shall bear to you by this time next year." When he had finished speaking with him, God departed from Abraham.—This is the Word of the Lord. ℟. **Thanks be to God.** ℣

Responsorial Psalm Ps 128, 1-2. 3. 4-5

℟. (4) **See how the Lord blesses those who fear him.**

Happy are you who fear the Lord,
  who walk in his ways!
For you shall eat the fruit of your handiwork;
  happy shall you be, and favored. — ℟

Your wife shall be like a fruitful vine
  in the recesses of your home;
Your children like olive plants
  around your table. — ℟

Behold, thus is the man blessed
  who fears the Lord.
The Lord bless you from Zion:
  may you see the prosperity of Jerusalem
  all the days of your life. — ℟ ♥

GOSPEL Mt 8, 1-4

Alleluia (Mt 8, 17)

℟. **Alleluia.** He took our sicknesses away,
and carried our diseases for us. ℟. **Alleluia.**

This reading follows the Sermon on the Mount. Jesus gives his teaching, in which he demands obedience to his words as the path to salvation. He then works miracles to prove the authority of his teaching.

℣. The Lord be with you. ℟. **And also with you.**
✠ A reading from the holy gospel according to Matthew. ℟. **Glory to you, Lord.**

When Jesus came down from the mountain, great crowds followed him. Suddenly a leper came forward and did him homage, saying to him, "Sir, if you will to do so, you can cure me." Jesus stretched out his hand and touched him and said. "I do will it. Be cured." Immediately the man's leprosy disappeared. Then Jesus said to him: "See to it that you tell no one. Go and show yourself to the priest and offer the gift Moses prescribed. That should be the proof they need."—This is the gospel of the Lord. ℟. **Praise to you, Lord Jesus Christ.** ➜ No. 15, p. 623

SATURDAY OF THE TWELFTH WEEK
IN ORDINARY TIME

READING I   Gn 18, 1-15

God makes another promise to Abraham that he will have a son and that he will become the father of a great nation. Abraham is portrayed in a good light; he welcomes the strangers and provides food in the best tradition of Near Eastern hospitality.

A reading from the book of Genesis

The Lord appeared to Abraham by the terebinth of Mamre, as he sat in the entrance of his tent, while the day was growing hot. Looking up, he saw three men standing nearby. When he saw them, he ran from the entrance of the tent to greet them; and bowing to the ground, he said: "Sir, if I may ask you this favor, please do not go on past your servant. Let some water be brought, that you may bathe your feet, and then rest yourselves under the tree. Now that you have come this close to your servant, let me bring you a little food, that you may refresh yourselves; and afterward you may go on your way." "Very well," they replied, "do as you have said."

Abraham hastened into the tent and told Sarah, "Quick, three seahs of fine flour! Knead it and make rolls." He ran to the herd, picked out a tender, choice steer, and gave it to a servant, who quickly prepared it. Then he got some curds and milk, as well as the steer that had been prepared, and set these before them; and he waited on them under the tree while they ate.

"Where is your wife Sarah?" they asked him. "There in the tent," he replied. One of them said, "I will surely return to you about this time next year, and Sarah will then have a son." Sarah was listening at the entrance of the tent, just behind him. Now Abraham and Sarah were old, advanced in years, and Sarah had stopped having her womanly periods. So Sarah laughed to herself and said, "Now that I am so withered and my husband is so old, am I still to have sexual pleasure?" But the Lord said to Abraham: "Why did Sarah laugh and say, 'Shall I really bear a child, old as I am?" Is anything too marvelous for the Lord to do? At the appointed time, about this time next year, I will return to you, and Sarah will have a son." Because she was afraid, Sarah dissembled, saying, "I didn't laugh." But he said, "Yes you did."—This is the Word of the Lord. ℟. **Thanks be to God.** ℣

Responsorial Psalm Lk 1, 46-47. 48-49. 50. 53. 54-55

℟. (54) **The Lord has remembered his mercy.**

My being proclaims the greatness of the Lord,
  my spirit finds joy in God my savior. — ℟

For he has looked upon his servant in her lowliness;
  all ages to come shall call me blessed.
God who is mighty has done great things for me,
  holy is his name. — ℟

His mercy is from age to age
  on those who fear him.
The hungry he has given every good thing,
  while the rich he has sent away empty. — ℟

He has upheld Israel his servant,
  ever mindful of his mercy;
Even as he promised our fathers,
  promised Abraham and his descendants for-
    ever. — ℟ ℣

GOSPEL   Mt 8, 5-17

Alleluia (Mt 8, 17)

℟. **Alleluia.** He took our sicknesses away,
and carried our diseases for us. ℟. **Alleluia.**

Jesus cures the servant boy of the Roman centurion and the mother-in-law of Peter. These miracles are worked because the centurion and the woman have faith in Jesus. He shows his goodness to all—of every age, condition, and nation.

℣. The Lord be with you. ℟. **And also with you.**

✠ A reading from the holy gospel according to Matthew. ℟. **Glory to you, Lord.**

As Jesus entered Capernaum, a centurion approached him with this request: "Sir, my serving boy is at home in bed paralyzed, suffering painfully." He said to him, "I will come and cure him." "Sir," the centurion said in reply, "I am not worthy to have you under my roof. Just give an order and my boy will get better. I am a man under authority myself and I have troops assigned to me. If I give one man the order, 'Dismissed,' off he goes. If I say to another, 'Come here,' he comes. If I tell my slave, 'Do this,' he does it." Jesus showed amazement on hearing this and remarked to his followers, "I assure you, I have never found this much faith in Israel. Mark what I say! Many will come from the east and the west and will find a place at the banquet in the kingdom of God with Abraham, Isaac, and Jacob, while the natural heirs of the kingdom will be driven out into the dark. Wailing will be heard there, and the grinding of teeth." To the centurion Jesus said, "Go home. It shall be done because you trusted." That very moment the boy got better.

Jesus entered Peter's house and found Peter's mother-in-law in bed with a fever. He took her by the hand and the fever left her. She got up at once and began to wait on him.

As evening drew on, they brought him many who were possessed. He expelled the spirits by a simple command and cured all who were afflicted, thereby fulfilling what had been said through Isaiah the prophet:

"It was our infirmities he bore,
    our sufferings he endured."

This is the gospel of the Lord. ℟. **Praise to you, Lord Jesus Christ.**

➤ No. 15, p. 623

MONDAY OF THE THIRTEENTH WEEK
IN ORDINARY TIME

READING I   Gn 18, 16-33

God tells Abraham that he will destroy the evil city of Sodom so that
the children of Abraham will realize that God is a just judge. In speaking to Abraham, God shows how he listens to the prayers of his people.

A reading from the book of Genesis

The men set out from the valley of Mamre and
looked down toward Sodom; Abraham was walking
with them, to see them on their way. The Lord reflected: "Shall I hide from Abraham what I am
about to do, now that he is to become a great and
populous nation, and all the nations of the earth are
to find blessing in him? Indeed, I have singled him
out that he may direct his sons and his posterity to
keep the way of the Lord by doing what is right and
just, so that the Lord may carry into effect for
Abraham the promises he made about him." Then
the Lord said: "The outcry against Sodom and Gomorrah is so great, and their sin so grave, that I must
go down and see whether or not their actions fully
correspond to the cry against them that comes to me.
I mean to find out."

While the two men walked on farther toward Sodom, the Lord remained standing before Abraham.
Then Abraham drew nearer to him and said: "Will
you sweep away the innocent with the guilty? Suppose there were fifty innocent people in the city;
would you wipe out the place, rather than spare it for
the sake of the fifty innocent people within it? Far
be it from you to do such a thing, to make the innocent die with the guilty, so that the innocent and
the guilty would be treated alike! Should not the
judge of all the world act with justice?" The Lord
replied, "If I find fifty innocent people in the city of
Sodom, I will spare the whole place for their sake."
Abraham spoke up again: "See how I am presuming

to speak to my Lord, though I am but dust and ashes! What if there are five less than fifty innocent people? Will you destroy the whole city because of those five?" "I will not destroy it," he answered, "if I find forty-five there." But Abraham persisted, saying, "What if only forty are found there?" He replied, "I will forbear doing it for the sake of the forty." Then he said, "Let not my Lord grow impatient if I go on. What if only thirty are found there?" He replied, "I will forbear doing it if I can find but thirty there." Still he went on, "Since I have thus dared to speak to my Lord, what if there are no more than twenty?" "I will not destroy it," he answered, "for the sake of the twenty." But he still persisted: "Please, let not my Lord grow angry if I speak up this last time. What if there are at least ten there?" "For the sake of those ten," he replied, "I will not destroy it."

The Lord departed as soon as he had finished speaking with Abraham, and Abraham returned home.—This is the Word of the Lord. ℟. **Thanks be to God.** ▾

Responsorial Psalm Ps 103, 1-2. 3-4. 8-9. 10-11
℟. (8) **The Lord is kind and merciful.**

Bless the Lord, O my soul;
  and all my being, bless his holy name.
Bless the Lord, O my soul,
  and forget not all his benefits. — ℟

He pardons all your iniquities,
  he heals all your ills.
He redeems your life from destruction,
  he crowns you with kindness and compassion.—℟

Merciful and gracious is the Lord,
  slow to anger and abounding in kindness.
He will not always chide,
  nor does he keep his wrath forever. — ℟

Not according to our sins does he deal with us,
  nor does he requite us according to our crimes.
For as the heavens are high above the earth,
  so surpassing is his kindness toward those who
    fear him. — ℟ ❦

GOSPEL   Mt 8, 18-22
Alleluia (Ps 95, 8)
℟. **Alleluia.** If today you hear his voice,
harden not your hearts. ℟. **Alleluia.**

Jesus tells the scribe that following him requires a generous commitment. He points out how much even the Son of Man gives. To
another Jesus gives the invitation to follow him.

℣. The Lord be with you. ℟. **And also with you.**
✠ A reading from the holy gospel according to Matthew. ℟. **Glory to you, Lord.**

Jesus, seeing the people crowd around him, gave
orders to cross the lake to the other shore. A scribe
approached him and said, "Teacher, wherever you
go I will come after you." Jesus said to him, "The
foxes have lairs, the birds in the sky have nests, but
the Son of Man has nowhere to lay his head." Another, a disciple, said to him, "Lord, let me go and
bury my father first." But Jesus told him, "Follow
me, and let the dead bury their dead."—This is the
gospel of the Lord. ℟. **Praise to you, Lord Jesus
Christ.**
                                  ➜ No. 15, p. 623

TUESDAY OF THE THIRTEENTH WEEK
IN ORDINARY TIME

READING I   Gn 19, 15-29
Since Abraham cannot point out any just men, God destroys the evil
city of Sodom. The Lord is indeed the Master, and he will judge the
sinner. Yet, he is merciful by sparing Abraham and Lot, and he will
be merciful to those who repent.

A reading from the book of Genesis
As dawn was breaking, the angels urged Lot on, say-

ing, "On your way! Take with you your wife and your two daughters who are here, or you will be swept away in the punishment of Sodom." When he hesitated, the men, by the Lord's mercy, seized his hand and the hands of his wife and his two daughters and led them to safety outside the city. As soon as they had been brought outside, he was told: "Flee for your life! Don't look back or stop anywhere on the Plain. Get off to the hills at once, or you will be swept away." "Oh, no, my lord!" replied Lot. "You have already thought enough of your servant to do me the great kindness of intervening to save my life. But I cannot flee to the hills to keep the disaster from overtaking me, and so I shall die. Look, this town ahead is near enough to escape to. It's only a small place. Let me flee there—it's a small place, isn't it?— that my life may be saved." "Well, then," he replied, "I will also grant you the favor you now ask. I will not overthrow the town you speak of. Hurry, escape there! I cannot do anything until you arrive there." That is why the town is called Zoar.

The sun was just rising over the earth as Lot arrived in Zoar; at the same time the Lord rained down sulphurous fire upon Sodom and Gomorrah [from the Lord out of heaven]. He overthrew those cities and the whole Plain, together with the inhabitants of the cities and the produce of the soil. But Lot's wife looked back, and she was turned into a pillar of salt.

Early the next morning Abraham went to the place where he had stood in the Lord's presence. As he looked down toward Sodom and Gomorrah and the whole region of the Plain, he saw dense smoke over the land rising like fumes from a furnace.

Thus it came to pass: when God destroyed the Cities of the Plain, he was mindful of Abraham by sending Lot away from the upheaval by which God overthrew the cities where Lot had been living.— This is the Word of the Lord. ℟. **Thanks be to God.** ℣

Responsorial Psalm   Ps 26, 2-3. 9-10. 11-12

℞. (3) **O Lord, your kindness is before my eyes.**

Search me, O Lord, and try me;
    test my soul and my heart.
For your kindness is before my eyes,
    and I walk in your truth. — ℞

Gather not my soul with those of sinners,
    nor with men of blood my life.
On their hands are crimes,
    and their right hands are full of bribes. — ℞

But I walk in integrity;
    redeem me, and have pity on me.
My foot stands on level ground;
    in the assemblies I will bless the Lord. — ℞ ✟

GOSPEL   Mt 8, 23-27

Alleluia (Ps 130, 5)

℞. **Alleluia.** I hope in the Lord,
I trust in his word. ℞. **Alleluia.**

The lakes and seas inspired a healthy fear in the ancients, who did
not have strong boats or navigational instruments. Jesus shows his
power by subduing even the wind and the sea. The disciples simply
ask who he is.

℣. The Lord be with you. ℞. **And also with you.**
✠A reading from the holy gospel according to Matthew. ℞. **Glory to you, Lord.**

Jesus got into a boat and his disciples followed him.
Without warning a violent storm came up on the
lake, and the boat began to be swamped by the
waves. Jesus was sleeping soundly, so they made
their way toward him and woke him: "Lord, save us!
We are lost!" He said to them: "Where is your courage? How little faith you have!" Then he stood up
and took the winds and the sea to task. Complete
calm ensued; the men were dumbfounded. "What
sort of man is this," they said, "that even the winds

and the sea obey him?"—This is the gospel of the Lord. ℟. **Praise to you, Lord Jesus Christ.**

➤ No. 15, p. 623

WEDNESDAY OF THE THIRTEENTH WEEK IN ORDINARY TIME

READING I   Gn 21, 5. 8-20

Abraham sends away Ishmael, his son by the slave girl Hagar. His son Isaac would be the child of God's promise, leading to the formation of the Hebrew nation. God responds to Ishmael's cries, and he remains with him as he grows up.

A reading from the book of Genesis

Abraham was a hundred years old when his son Isaac was born to him. Isaac grew, and on the day of the child's weaning, Abraham held a great feast.

Sarah noticed the son whom Hagar the Egyptian had borne to Abraham playing with her son Isaac; so she demanded of Abraham: "Drive out that slave and her son! No son of that slave is going to share the inheritance with my son Isaac!' Abraham was greatly distressed, especially on account of his son Ishmael. But God said to Abraham: "Do not be distressed about the boy or about your slave woman. Heed the demands of Sarah, no matter what she is asking of you; for it is through Isaac that descendants shall bear your name. As for the son of the slave woman, I will make a great nation of him also, since he too is your offspring."

Early the next morning Abraham got some bread and a skin of water and gave them to Hagar. Then, placing the child on her back, he sent her away. As she roamed aimlessly in the wilderness of Beer-sheba, the water in the skin was used up. So she put the child down under a shrub, and then went and sat down opposite him, about a bowshot away; for she said to herself, "Let me not watch the child die." As she sat opposite him, he began to cry. God heard the boy's cry, and God's messenger called to Hagar from heaven: "What is the matter, Hagar? Don't be afraid; God has heard the boy's cry in this plight of his. Arise, lift up the boy and hold him by the hand; for I will make of him a great nation." Then God opened her eyes, and she saw a well of water. She went and filled the skin with water, and then let the boy drink.

God was with the boy as he grew up.—This is the Word of the Lord. ℟. **Thanks be to God.** ✔

Responsorial Psalm   Ps 34, 7-8. 10-11. 12-13

℟. (7) **The Lord hears the cry of the poor.**

When the afflicted man called out, the Lord heard,
   and from all his distress he saved him.
The angel of the Lord encamps
   around those who fear him, and delivers them.—℟

Fear the Lord, you his holy ones,
   for nought is lacking to those who fear him.
The great grow poor and hungry;
   but those who seek the Lord want for no good
   thing. — ℟

Come, children, hear me;
   I will teach you the fear of the Lord.
Which of you desires life,
   and takes delight in prosperous days? — ℟ ✔

GOSPEL   Mt 8, 28-34

Alleluia (Jas 1, 18)

℟. **Alleluia.** The Father gave us birth by his message
   of truth,
that we might be as the first fruits of his creation.
      ℟. **Alleluia.**

By driving the demons into the herd of swine, Jesus shows the horror and power of evil and of sin. However, the power of Christ is great, indeed absolute. The entire town comes out to see Jesus.

℣. The Lord be with you. ℟. **And also with you.**
✠ A reading from the holy gospel according to Matthew. ℟. **Glory to you, Lord.**

As Jesus approached the Gadarene boundary, he encountered two men coming out of the tombs. They were possessed by demons and were so savage that no one could travel along the road. With a sudden shriek they cried: "Why meddle with us, Son of God? Have you come to torture us before the appointed time?" Some distance away a large herd of swine was feeding. The demons kept appealing to him, "If you expel us, send us into the herd of swine." He answered, "Out with you!" At that they came forth and entered the swine. The whole herd went rushing down the bluff into the sea and were drowned.

The swineherds took to their heels, and upon their arrival in the town related everything that had happened, including the story about the two possessed men. The upshot was that the entire town came out to meet Jesus. When they caught sight of him, they begged him to leave their neighborhood.—This is the gospel of the Lord. ℟. **Praise to you, Lord Jesus Christ.**

➔ No. 15, p. 623

THURSDAY OF THE THIRTEENTH WEEK IN ORDINARY TIME

READING I   Gn 22, 1-19

The words "All this because you obeyed my command" convey the unlimited promises of abundance from the Lord's messenger to Abraham, after Abraham unfalteringly follows the details of God's command to offer his only son, Isaac, as a holocaust. This shows the great faith Abraham had.

A reading from the book of Genesis

God put Abraham to the test. He called to him, "Abraham!" "Ready!" he replied. Then God said: "Take you son Isaac, your only one, whom you love, and go to the land of Moriah. There you shall offer him up as a holocaust on a height that I will point out to you." Early the next morning Abraham saddled his donkey, took with him his son Isaac, and two of his servants as well, and with the wood that he had cut for the holocaust, set out for the place of which God had told him.

On the third day Abraham got sight of the place from afar. Then he said to his servants: "Both of you stay here with the donkey, while the boy and I go on over yonder. We will worship and then come back to you." Thereupon Abraham took the wood for the holocaust and laid it on his son Isaac's shoulders, while he himself carried the fire and the knife. As the two walked on together, Isaac spoke to his father Abraham. "Father!" he said. "Yes, son," he replied. Isaac continued, "Here are the fire and the wood, but where is the sheep for the holocaust?" "Son," Abraham answered, "God himself will provide the sheep for the holocaust." Then the two continued going forward.

When they came to the place of which God had told him, Abraham built an altar there and arranged the wood on it. Next he tied up his son Isaac, and put him on top of the wood on the altar. Then he reached out and took the knife to slaughter his son. But the Lord's messenger called to him from heaven, "Abraham, Abraham!" "Yes, Lord," he answered. "Do not lay your hand on the boy," said the messenger. "Do not do the least thing to him. I know now how devoted you are to God, since you did not withhold from me your own beloved son." As Abraham looked about, he spied a ram caught by its horns in the thicket. So he went and took the ram and offered it up as a holocaust in place of his son. Abraham named the site Yahweh-yireh; hence people now say, "On the mountain the Lord will see."

Again the Lord's messenger called to Abraham from heaven and said: "I swear by myself, declares the Lord, that because you acted as you did in not withholding from me your beloved son, I will bless

you abundantly and make your descendants as countless as the stars of the sky and the sands of the seashore; your descendants shall take possession of the
gates of their enemies, and in your descendants all
the nations of the earth shall find blessing—all this
because you obeyed my command."

Abraham then returned to his servants, and they
set out together for Beer-sheba, where Abraham made
his home.—This is the Word of the Lord. ℟. **Thanks
be to God.** ℣

Responsorial Psalm   Ps 115, 1-2. 3-4. 5-6. 8-9

℟. (9) **I will walk in the presence of the Lord,
      in the land of the living.**

Not to us, O Lord, not to us
   but to your name give glory
      because of your kindness, because of your truth.
Why should the pagans say,
   "Where is their God?" — ℟

Our God is in heaven;
   whatever he wills, he does.
Their idols are silver and gold,
   the handiwork of men. — ℟

They have mouths but speak not;
   they have eyes but see not;
They have ears but hear not;
   they have noses but smell not. — ℟

Their makers shall be like them,
   everyone that trusts in them.
The house of Israel trusts in the Lord;
   he is their help and their shield. — ℟ ℣

℟. Or: **Alleluia.** ℣

GOSPEL   Mt 9, 1-8
Alleluia (2 Cor 5, 19)
℟. **Alleluia.** God was in Christ, to reconcile the world
      to himself;

and the Good News of reconciliation he has entrust-
to us. ℟. **Alleluia.**

Struck by the people's faith as he gets out of the boat in his home
town, Jesus performs two miracles for the paralyzed man brought
to him. He shows he has the power and authority to effect spiritual
cures, as well as physical. The people around are amazed.

℣. The Lord be with you. ℟. **And also with you.**
✠ A reading from the holy gospel according to Matthew. ℟. **Glory to you, Lord.**

Jesus entered a boat, made the crossing, and came
back to his own town. There the people at once
brought to him a paralyzed man lying on a mat.
When Jesus saw their faith he said to the paralytic,
"Have courage, son, your sins are forgiven." At that
some of the scribes said to themselves, "The man
blasphemes." Jesus was aware of what they were
thinking and said: "Why do you harbor evil thoughts?
Which is less trouble to say, 'Your sins are forgiven'
or 'Stand up and walk'? To help you realize that the
Son of Man has authority on earth to forgive sins"—
he then said to the paralyzed man—"Stand up! Roll
up your mat, and go home." The man stood up and
went toward his home. At the sight, a feeling of awe
came over the crowd, and they praised God for giving
such authority to men.—This is the gospel of the
Lord. ℟. **Praise to you, Lord Jesus Christ.**

➔ No. 15, p. 623

FRIDAY OF THE THIRTEENTH WEEK
IN ORDINARY TIME

READING I   Gn 23, 1-4. 19; 24, 1-8. 62-67

Living his life of complete dependence on God's commands, Abraham
buries his wife, Sarah, then sends to his own land for a wife for Isaac.
The son was not to go back, as the Lord had said, "I will give this land
to your descendants." Rebekah comes with the servant and is loved
by Isaac.

A reading from the book of Genesis
The span of Sarah's life was one hundred and twenty-

seven years. She died in Kiriath-arba (that is, Hebron) in the land of Canaan, and Abraham performed the customary mourning rites for her. Then he left the side of his dead one and addressed the Hittites: "Although I am a resident alien among you, sell me from your holdings a piece of property for a burial ground, that I may bury my dead wife."

After this transaction, Abraham buried his wife Sarah in the cave of the field of Mach-pelah, facing Mamre (that is, Hebron) in the land of Canaan.

Abraham had now reached a ripe old age, and the Lord had blessed him in every way. Abraham said to the senior servant of his household, who had charge of all his possessions: "Put your hand under my thigh, and I will make you swear by the Lord, the God of heaven and the God of earth, that you will not procure a wife for my son from the daughters of the Canaanites among whom I live, but that you will go to my own land and to my kindred to get a wife for my son Isaac." The servant asked him: "What if the woman is unwilling to follow me to this land? Should I then take your son back to the land from which you migrated?" "Never take my son back there for any reason," Abraham told him. "The Lord, the God of heaven, who took me from my father's house and the land of my kin, and who confirmed by oath the promise he then made to me, 'I will give this land to your descendants'—he will send his messenger before you, and you will obtain a wife for my son there. If the woman is unwilling to follow you, you will be released from this oath. But never take my son back there!"

[A long time later, Isaac went] to live in the region of the Negeb. One day toward evening he went out . . . in the field, and as he looked around, he noticed that camels were approaching. Rebekah, too, was looking about, and when she saw him, she alighted from her camel and asked the servant, "Who is the man out there, walking through the fields toward us?" "That is my master," replied the servant. Then she covered herself with her veil.

The servant recounted to Isaac all the things he had done. Then Isaac took Rebekah into his tent; he married her, and thus she became his wife. In his love for her Isaac found solace after the death of his mother Sarah.—This is the Word of the Lord. ℟. **Thanks be to God.** ✟

Responsorial Psalm   Ps 106, 1-2. 3-4. 4-5

℟ (1) **Give thanks to the Lord for he is good.**

Give thanks to the Lord, for he is good,
    for his kindness endures forever.
Who can tell the mighty deeds of the Lord,
    or proclaim all his praises? — ℟

Happy are they who observe what is right,
    who do always what is just.
Remember me, O Lord, as you favor your people. —℟

Visit me with your saving help,
    that I may see the prosperity of your chosen ones,
Rejoice in the joy of your people,
    and glory with your inheritance. — ℟ ✟

℟. Or: **Alleluia.** ✟

GOSPEL   Mt 9, 9-13

Alleluia (Mt 11, 28)

℟. **Alleluia.** Come to me, all you that labor and are burdened,
and I will give you rest, says the Lord. ℟. **Alleluia.**

Jesus' love overflows to misguided people, such as sinners and those who disregard the law. He chooses to eat with them and mingle with them. Jesus does not follow the Pharisees' line of thinking in self-righteous judgment. He goes to those who need him.

℣. The Lord be with you. ℟. **And also with you.**
✠ A reading from the holy gospel according to Matthew. ℟. **Glory to you, Lord.**

As Jesus moved about, he saw a man named Matthew at his post where taxes were collected. He said to him, "Follow me." Matthew got up and followed him. Now it happened that, while Jesus was at table in Matthew's home, many tax collectors and those known as sinners came to join Jesus and his disciples at dinner. The Pharisees saw this and complained to his disciples, "What reason can the Teacher have for eating with tax collectors and those who disregard the law?" Overhearing the remark, he said: "People who are in good health do not need a doctor; sick people do. Go and learn the meaning of the words, 'It is mercy I desire and not sacrifice.' I have come to call, not the self-righteous, but sinners."— This is the gospel of the Lord. ℟. **Praise to you, Lord Jesus Christ.**   → No. 15, p. 623

SATURDAY OF THE THIRTEENTH WEEK IN ORDINARY TIME

READING I   Gn 27, 1-5. 15-29

Isaac, feeling the imminence of death, chooses to give his oldest son, Esau, his blessing. Jacobs takes advantage of his father's blindness and puts himself in his brother's place, thereby receiving this special blessing.

A reading from the book of Genesis

When Isaac was so old that his eyesight had failed him, he called his older son Esau and said to him, "Son!" "Yes, father!" he replied. Isaac then said, "As you can see, I am so old that I may now die at any time. Take your gear, therefore—your quiver and bow—and go out into the country to hunt some game for me. With your catch prepare an appetizing dish for me, such as I like, and bring it to me to eat, so that I may give you my special blessing before I die."

Rebekah had been listening while Isaac was speaking to his son Esau, who went out into the country to carry out his father's orders.

Rebekah then took the best clothes of her older son Esau that she had in the house, and gave them to her younger son Jacob to wear; and with the skins of the kids she covered up his hands and the hairless parts of his neck. Then she handed her son Jacob the appetizing dish and the bread she had prepared.

Bringing them to his father, Jacob said, "Father!" "Yes?" replied Isaac. "Which of my sons are you?" Jacob answered his father: "I am Esau, your first-born. I did as you told me. Please sit up and eat some of my game, so that you may give me your special blessing." But Isaac asked, "How did you succeed so quickly, son?" He answered, "The Lord, your God, let things turn out well with me." Isaac then said to Jacob, "Come closer, son, that I may feel you, to learn whether you really are my son Esau or not." So Jacob moved up closer to his father. When Isaac felt him, he said, "Although the voice is Jacob's, the hands are Esau's." (He failed to iden-tify him because his hands were hairy, like those of his brother Esau; so in the end he gave him his bless-ing.) Again he asked him, "Are you really my son Esau?" "Certainly," he replied. Then Isaac said, "Serve me your game, son, that I may eat of it and then give you my blessing." Jacob served it to him, and Isaac ate; he brought him wine, and he drank. Finally his father Isaac said to him, "Come closer, son, and kiss me." As Jacob went up and kissed him, Isaac smelled the fragance of his clothes. With that, he blessed him, saying,

"Ah, the fragrance of my son
is the fragrance of a field
that the Lord has blessed!"
"May God give to you
of the dew of the heavens

And of the fertility of the earth
abundance of grain and wine.
Let peoples serve you,
and nations pay you homage;
Be master of your brothers,
and may your mother's sons bow down to you.
Cursed be those who curse you,
and blessed be those who bless you."
This is the Word of the Lord. ℟. **Thanks be to God.** ⍦

Responsorial Psalm   Ps 135, 1-2. 3-4. 5-6

℟. (3) **Praise the Lord for he is good!**

Praise the name of the Lord;
praise, you servants of the Lord,
Who stand in the house of the Lord,
in the courts of the house of our God. — ℟

Praise the Lord, for the Lord is good;
sing praise to his name, which we love;
For the Lord has chosen Jacob for himself,
Israel for his own possession. — ℟

For I know that the Lord is great;
our Lord is greater than all gods.
All that the Lord wills he does
in heaven and on earth,
in the seas and in all the deeps. — ℟ ⍦

℟. Or: **Alleluia.** ⍦

GOSPEL   Mt 9, 14-17

Alleluia (Jn 10, 27)

℟. **Alleluia.** My sheep listen to my voice, says the
Lord;
I know them, and they follow me. ℟. **Alleluia.**

Jesus speaks of himself as the groom. While he is with his disciples,
at the wedding feast uniting him with his followers, they will not fast.
When the groom is taken away, then they will fast and do penance.

℣. The Lord be with you. ℟. **And also with you.**

✠ A reading from the holy gospel according to Matthew. ℟. **Glory to you, Lord.**

John's disciples came to Jesus with the objection, "Why is it that while we and the Pharisees fast, your disciples do not?" Jesus said to them: "How can wedding guests go in mourning so long as the groom is with them? When the day comes that the groom is taken away, then they will fast. Nobody sews a piece of unshrunken cloth on an old cloak; the very thing he has used to cover the hole will pull, and the rip only get worse. People do not pour new wine into old wineskins. If they do, the skins burst, the wine spills out, and the skins are ruined. No, they pour new wine into new wineskins, and in that way both are preserved."—This is the gospel of the Lord. ℟. **Praise to you, Lord Jesus Christ.**

➔ No. 15, p. 623

MONDAY OF THE FOURTEENTH WEEK IN ORDINARY TIME

READING I   Gn 28, 10-22

The Lord appears to Jacob in a dream as he is on a journey. It is at a shrine, and Jacob has taken a stone from it to put under his head. In the dream he hears the Lord promise him blessings and protection. He vows to set up a memorial as God's abode.

A reading from the book of Genesis

Jacob departed from Beer-sheba and proceeded toward Haran. When he came upon a certain shrine, as the sun had already set, he stopped there for the night. Taking one of the stones at the shrine, he put it under his head and lay down to sleep at that spot. Then he had a dream: a stairway rested on the ground, with its top reaching to the heavens; and God's messengers were going up and down on it. And there was the Lord standing beside him and saying:

"I, the Lord, am the God of your forefather Abraham and the God of Isaac; the land on which you are lying I will give to you and your descendants. These shall be plentiful as the dust of the earth, and through them you shall spread out east and west, north and south. In you and your descendants all the nations of the earth shall find blessing. Know that I am with you; I will protect you wherever you go, and bring you back to this land. I will never leave you until I have done what I promised you."

When Jacob awoke from his sleep, he exclaimed, "Truly, the Lord is in this spot, although I did not know it!" In solemn wonder he cried out: "How awesome is this shrine! This is nothing else but an abode of God, and that is the gateway to heaven!" Early the next morning Jacob took the stone that he had put under his head, set it up as a memorial stone, and poured oil on top of it. He called that site Bethel, whereas the former name of the town had been Luz.

Jacob then made this vow: "If God remains with me, to protect me on this journey I am making and to give me enough bread to eat and clothing to wear, and I come back safe to my father's house, the Lord shall be my God. This stone that I have set up as a memorial stone shall be God's abode.—This is the Word of the Lord. ℟. **Thanks be to God.** ℣

Responsorial Psalm   Ps 91, 1-2. 3-4. 14-15

℟. (2) **In you, my God, I place my trust.**

You who dwell in the shelter of the Most High,
    who abide in the shadow of the Almighty,
Say to the Lord, "My refuge and my fortress,
    my God, in whom I trust." — ℟

For he will rescue you from the snare of the fowler,
    from the destroying pestilence.
With his pinions he will cover you,
    and under his wings you shall take refuge. — ℟

Because he clings to me, I will deliver him;
  I will set him on high because he acknowledges
    my name.
He shall call upon me, and I will answer him;
  I will be with him in distress. — ℟ ✔

GOSPEL   Mt 9, 18-26
Alleluia (2 Tm 1, 10)
℟. **Alleluia.** Our Savior Jesus Christ has done away
    with death,
and brought us life through his gospel. ℟. **Alleluia.**

"Your faith has restored you to health." Two instances of unquestion-
ing faith are rewarded with miracles. The synagogue leader asks Jesus
to bring his daughter back to life; the woman with a hemorrhage knows
she will be cured if only she can touch his garment.

℣. The Lord be with you. ℟ .**And also with you.**
✠ A reading from the holy gospel according to Matthew. ℟. **Glory to you, Lord.**

As Jesus was speaking, a synagogue leader came up,
did him reverence and said: "My daughter has just
died. Please come and lay your hand on her and she
will come back to life." Jesus stood up and followed
him, and his disciples did the same. As they were
going, a woman who had suffered from hemorrhages
for twelve years came up behind him and touched
the tassel on his cloak. "If only I can touch his
cloak," she thought, "I shall get well." Jesus turned
around and saw her and said, "Courage, daughter!
Your faith has restored you to health." That very
moment the woman got well.

  When Jesus arrived at the synagogue leader's
house and saw the flute players and the crowd who
were making a din, he said, "Leave, all of you! The
little girl is not dead. She is asleep." At this they began to ridicule him. When the crowd had been put
out he entered and took her by the hand, and the little
girl got up. News of this circulated throughout the

district.—This is the gospel of the Lord. ℟. **Praise to you, Lord Jesus Christ.** ➤ No. 15, p. 623

TUESDAY OF THE FOURTEENTH WEEK IN ORDINARY TIME

READING I   Gn 32, 23-33

In the course of a journey, Jacob is engaged in a mortal fight. At its end, Jacob says, "I will not let you go until you bless me." His adversary replies, "You shall no longer be known as Jacob, but as Israel."

A reading from the book of Genesis

In the course of the night, Jacob arose, took his two wives, with the two maidservants and his eleven children, and crossed the ford of the Jabbok. After he had taken them across the stream and had brought over all his possessions, Jacob was left there alone. Then some man wrestled with him until the break of dawn. When the man saw that he could not prevail over him, he struck Jacob's hip at its socket, so that the hip socket was wrenched as they wrestled. The man then said, "Let me go, for it is daybreak." But Jacob said, "I will not let you go until you bless me." "What is your name?" the man asked. He answered, "Jacob." Then the man said, "You shall no longer be spoken of as Jacob, but as Israel, because you have contended with divine and human beings and have prevailed." Jacob then asked him, "Do tell me your name, please." He answered, "Why should you want to know my name?" With that, he bade him farewell. Jacob named the place Peniel, "Because I have seen God face to face," he said, "yet my life has been spared."

At sunrise, as he left Peniel, Jacob limped along because of his hip. That is why, to this day, the Israelites do not eat the sciatic muscle that is on the hip socket, inasmuch as Jacob's hip socket was struck at the sciatic muscle.—This is the Word of the Lord. ℟. **Thanks be to God.** ▼

Responsorial Psalm   Ps 17, 1. 2-3. 6-7. 8. 15

℟. (15) **In my justice, I shall see your face, O Lord.**

Hear, O Lord, a just suit;
  attend to my outcry;
    hearken to my prayer from lips without de-
      ceit. — ℟

From you let my judgment come;
  your eyes behold what is right.
Though you test my heart, searching it in the night,
  though you try me with fire, you shall find no
    malice in me. — ℟

I call upon you, for you will answer me, O God;
  incline your ear to me; hear my word.
Show your wondrous kindness,
  O savior of those who flee. — ℟ ⩔

GOSPEL   Mt 9, 32-38

Alleluia (Jn 10, 14)

℟. **Alleluia.** I am the good shepherd, says the Lord;
I know my sheep, and mine know me. ℟. **Alleluia.**

Jesus performs different kinds of miracles and cures, and he continues
in Galilee as an itinerant preacher. The new element is the compassion our Lord feels for the multitude. In understanding sympathy, he
says, "Beg the harvest master to send out laborers to gather his
harvest."

℣. The Lord be with you. ℟. **And also with you.**
✠ A reading from the holy gospel according to Matthew. ℟. **Glory to you, Lord.**

Some people brought Jesus a mute who was possessed by a demon. Once the demon was expelled the
mute began to speak, to the great surprise of the
crowds. "Nothing like this has ever been seen in
Israel!" they exclaimed. But the Pharisees were saying, "He casts out demons through the prince of demons."

  Jesus continued his tour of all the towns and villages. He taught in their synagogues, he proclaimed

the good news of God's reign, and he cured every sickness and disease. At the sight of the crowds, his heart was moved with pity. They were lying prostrate from exhaustion, like sheep without a shepherd. He said to his disciples: "The harvest is good but laborers are scarce. Beg the harvest master to send out laborers to gather his harvest."—This is the gospel of the Lord. ℟. **Praise to you, Lord Jesus Christ.**

→ No. 15, p. 623

WEDNESDAY OF THE FOURTEENTH WEEK IN ORDINARY TIME

READING I   Gn 41, 55-57; 42, 5-7. 17-24

Joseph, as governor of Egypt, dispenses rations of grain to those suffering from famine. His brothers come and he has them imprisoned for three days. Then he asks them to come back with their youngest brother. Their guilt overcomes them.

A reading from the book of Genesis

When hunger came to be felt throughout the land of Egypt and the people cried to Pharaoh for bread, Pharaoh directed all the Egyptians to go to Joseph and do whatever he told them. When the famine had spread throughout the land, Joseph opened all the cities that had grain and rationed it to the Egyptians, since the famine had gripped the land of Egypt. In fact, all the world came to Joseph to obtain rations of grain, for famine had gripped the whole world.

The sons of Israel were among those who came to Egypt to procure rations. It was Joseph, as governor of the country, who dispensed the rations to all the people. When Joseph's brothers came and knelt down before him with their faces to the ground, he recognized them as soon as he saw them. But he concealed his own identity from them and spoke sternly to them.

With that, he locked them up in the guardhouse for three days.

On the third day Joseph said to them: "Do this, and you shall live; for I am a God-fearing man. If you have been honest, only one of your brothers need be confined in this prison, while the rest of you may go and take home provisions for your starving families. But you must come back to me with your youngest brother. Your words will thus be verified, and you will not die." To this they agreed.

To one another, however, they said: "Alas, we are being punished because of our brother. We saw the anguish of his heart when he pleaded with us, yet we paid no heed; that is why this anguish has now come upon us." "Didn't I tell you," broke in Reuben, "not to do wrong to the boy? But you wouldn't listen! Now comes the reckoning for his blood." They did not know, of course, that Joseph understood what they said, since he spoke with them through an interpreter. But turning away from them, he wept.—This is the Word of the Lord. ℞. **Thanks be to God.** ℣

Responsorial Psalm   Ps 33, 2-3. 10-11. 18-19

℞. (22) **Lord, let your mercy be on us.**
    as we place our trust in you.

Give thanks to the Lord on the harp;
    with the ten-stringed lyre chant his praises.
Sing to him a new song;
    pluck the strings skillfully, with shouts of gladness. — ℞

The Lord brings to nought the plans of nations;
    he foils the designs of peoples.
But the plan of the Lord stands forever;
    the design of his heart, through all generations. — ℞

But see, the eyes of the Lord are upon those who fear him,
    upon those who hope for his kindness,
To deliver them from death
    and preserve them in spite of famine. — ℞ ℣

GOSPEL Mt 10, 1-7

Alleluia (Mk 1, 15)

℟. **Alleluia.** The kingdom of God is near; repent and believe the Good News! ℟. **Alleluia.**

Jesus summons his twelve disciples and, giving them authority over unclean spirits and disease, he tells them to go after the lost sheep of Israel announcing to them, "The reign of God is at hand."

℣. The Lord be with you. ℟. **And also with you.**
✠ A reading from the holy gospel according to Matthew. ℟. **Glory to you, Lord.**

Jesus summoned his twelve disciples and gave them authority to expel unclean spirits and to cure sickness and disease of every kind.

The names of the twelve apostles are these: first Simon, now known as Peter, and his brother Andrew; James, Zebedee's son, and his brother John; Philip and Bartholomew, Thomas and Matthew the tax collector; James, son of Alphaeus, and Thaddaeus; Simon the Zealot Party member, and Judas Iscariot, who betrayed him. Jesus sent these men on mission as the Twelve, after giving them the following instructions:

"Do not visit pagan territory and do not enter a Samaritan town. Go instead after the lost sheep of the house of Israel. As you go, make this announcement: 'The reign of God is at hand!' "—This is the gospel of the Lord. ℟. **Praise to you, Lord Jesus Christ.** → No. 15, p. 623

THURSDAY OF THE FOURTEENTH WEEK IN ORDINARY TIME

READING I Gn 44, 18-21. 23-29; 45, 1-5

Joseph's brothers come back for more food. At the news of his father and home, he tells them, "I am Joseph, your brother. Be not distressed. It was really for saving lives that God sent me here ahead of you."

A reading from the book of Genesis

Judah approached Joseph and said: "I beg you, my lord, let your servant speak earnestly to my lord, and do not become angry with your servant, for you are the equal of Pharaoh. My lord asked your servants, 'Have you a father, or another brother?' So we said to my lord, 'We have an aged father, and a young brother, the child of his old age. This one's full brother is dead, and since he is the only one by that mother who is left, his father dotes on him.' Then you told your servants, 'Bring him down to me that my eyes may look on him. Unless your youngest brother comes back with you, you shall not come into my presence again.' When we returned to your servant our father, we reported to him the words of my lord.

"Later, our father told us to come back and buy some food for the family. So we reminded him, 'We cannot go down there; only if our youngest brother is with us can we go, for we may not see the man if our youngest brother is not with us.' Then your servant our father said to us, 'As you know, my wife bore me two sons. One of them, however, disappeared, and I had to conclude that he must have been torn to pieces by wild beasts; I have not seen him since. If you now take this one away from me too, and some disaster befalls him, you will send my white head down to the nether world in grief.'"

Joseph could no longer control himself in the presence of all his attendants, so he cried out, "Have everyone withdraw from me!" Thus no one else was about when he made himself known to his brothers. But his sobs were so loud that the Egyptians heard him, and so the news reached Pharaoh's palace. "I am Joseph," he said to his brothers. "Is my father still in good health?" But his brothers could give him no answer, so dumbfounded were they at him.

"Come closer to me," he told his brothers. When

they had done so, he said: "I am your brother Joseph, whom you once sold into Egypt. But now do not be distressed, and do not reproach yourselves for having sold me here. It was really for the sake of saving lives that God sent me here ahead of you."—This is the Word of the Lord. ℟. **Thanks be to God.** ✣

Responsorial Psalm   Ps 105, 16-17. 18-19. 20-21

℟. (5) **Remember the marvels the Lord has done.**

When he called down a famine on the land
    and ruined the crop that sustained them,
He sent a man before them,
    Joseph, sold as a slave. — ℟

They had weighed him down with fetters,
    and he was bound with chains,
Till his prediction came to pass
    and the word of the Lord proved him true. — ℟

The king sent and released him,
    the ruler of the peoples set him free.
He made him lord of his house
    and ruler of all his possessions. — ℟ ✣

℟. Or: **Alleluia.** ✣

GOSPEL   Mt 10, 7-15

Alleluia (Mk 1, 15)

℟. **Alleluia.** The kingdom of God is near;
repent and believe the Good News! ℟. **Alleluia.**

Jesus gives his disciples practical points regarding their ministry. They should announce the reign of God and perform miracles, but should not expect money or material returns. "The gift you have received, give as a gift."

℣. The Lord be with you. ℟. **And also with you.**
✠ A reading from the holy gospel according to Matthew. ℟. **Glory to you, Lord.**

Jesus said to his disciples: "As you go, make this announcement: 'The reign of God is at hand!' Cure the sick, raise the dead, heal the leprous, expel demons.

The gift you have received, give as a gift. Provide yourselves with neither gold nor silver nor copper in your belts; no traveling bag, no change of shirt, no sandals, no walking staff. The workman, after all, is worth his keep.

"Look for a worthy citizen in every town or village you come to and stay with him until you leave. As you enter his home bless it. If the home is deserving, your blessing will descend on it. If it is not, your blessing will return to you. If anyone does not receive you or listen to what you have to say, leave that house or town, and once outside it shake its dust from your feet. I assure you, it will go easier for the region of Sodom and Gomorrah on the day of judgment than it will for that town."—This is the gospel of the Lord. ℟. **Praise to you, Lord Jesus Christ.**

➤ No. 15, p. 623

FRIDAY OF THE FOURTEENTH WEEK IN ORDINARY TIME

READING I   Gn 46, 1-7. 28-30

Jacob, named Israel, obeys God's bidding and takes his family into Egypt to meet Joseph. Joseph weeps on seeing his father. Israel can now die a happy death, knowing that Joseph is alive.

A reading from the book of Genesis

Israel set out with all that was his. When he arrived at Beer-sheba, he offered sacrifices to the God of his father Isaac. There God, speaking to Israel in a vision by night, called, "Jacob! Jacob!" "Here I am," he answered. Then he said: "I am God, the God of your father. Do not be afraid to go down to Egypt, for there I will make you a great nation. Not only will I go down to Egypt with you; I will also bring you back here, after Joseph has closed your eyes."

So Jacob departed from Beer-sheba, and the sons of Israel put their father and their wives and children on the wagons that Pharaoh had sent for his transport. They took with them their livestock and the possessions they had acquired in the land of Canaan. Thus Jacob and all his descendants migrated to Egypt. His sons and his grandsons, his daughters and his granddaughters—all his descendants—he took with him to Egypt.

Israel had sent Judah ahead to Joseph, so that he might meet him in Goshen. On his arrival in the region of Goshen, Joseph hitched the horses to his chariot and rode to meet his father Israel in Goshen. As soon as he saw him, he flung himself on his neck and wept a long time in his arms. And Israel said to Joseph, "At last I can die, now that I have seen for myself that Joseph is still alive."—This is the Word of the Lord. ℞. **Thanks be to God.** ℣

Responsorial Psalm   Ps 37, 3-4. 18-19. 27-28. 39-40

℞. (39) **The salvation of the just comes from the Lord.**

Trust in the Lord and do good,
    that you may dwell in the land and enjoy security.
Take delight in the Lord,
    and he will grant you your heart's requests. — ℞

The Lord watches over the lives of the wholehearted;
    their inheritance lasts forever.
They are not put to shame in an evil time;
    in days of famine they have plenty. — ℞

Turn from evil and do good,
    that you may abide forever;
For the Lord loves what is right,
    and forsakes not his faithful ones.
Criminals are destroyed,
    and the posterity of the wicked is cut off. — ℞

The salvation of the just is from the Lord;
    he is their refuge in time of distress.
And the Lord helps them and delivers them;

he delivers them from the wicked and saves them, because they take refuge in him. — ℟ ⍒

GOSPEL Mt 10, 16-23

Alleluia (Jn 16, 13; 14, 26)

℟. **Alleluia.** When the Spirit of truth comes, he will teach you all truth
and bring to your mind all I have told you. ℟. **Alleluia.**

In instructing his disciples, Jesus says, "Be on your guard with respect to others." He tells them not to worry about what to say if they are brought to trial, for "you yourselves will not be the speakers; the Spirit of your Father will be speaking in you."

℣. The Lord be with you. ℟. **And also with you.**
✠ A reading from the holy gospel according to Matthew. ℟. **Glory to you, Lord.**

Jesus said to his disciples: "I am sending you out like sheep among wolves. You must be clever as snakes and innocent as doves. Be on your guard with respect to others. They will hale you into court, they will flog you in their synagogues. You will be brought to trial before rulers and kings, to give witness before them and the Gentiles on my account. When they hand you over, do not worry about what you will say or how you will say it. When the hour comes, you will be given what you are to say. You yourselves will not be the speakers; the Spirit of your Father will be speaking in you.

"Brother will hand over brother to death, and the father his child; children will turn against parents and have them put to death. You will be hated by all on account of me. But whoever holds out till the end will escape death. When they persecute you in one town, flee to the next. I solemnly assure you, you will not have covered the towns of Israel before the Son of Man comes."—This is the gospel of the Lord. ℟. **Praise to you, Lord Jesus Christ.**

➤ No. 15, p. 623

SATURDAY OF THE FOURTEENTH WEEK
IN ORDINARY TIME

READING I   Gn 49, 29-33; 50, 15-24

Jacob asks to be buried with his father in the land of Canaan. Joseph's brothers worry that he will take vengeance on them for their cruelty to him, but Joseph kindly reassures them. Before he dies, he tells them God will lead them to the promised land.

A reading from the book of Genesis

Jacob gave this charge to his sons: "Since I am about to be taken to my kindred, bury me with my fathers in the cave that lies in the field of Ephron the Hittite, the cave in the field of Machpelah, facing on Mamre, in the land of Canaan, the field that Abraham bought from Ephron the Hittite for a burial ground. There Abraham and his wife Sarah are buried, and so are Isaac and his wife Rebekah, and there, too, I buried Leah—the field and the cave in it that had been purchased from the Hittites."

When Jacob had finished giving these instructions to his sons, he drew his feet into the bed, breathed his last, and was taken to his kindred.

Now that their father was dead, Joseph's brothers became fearful and thought, "Suppose Joseph has been nursing a grudge against us and now plans to pay us back in full for all the wrong we did him!" So they approached Joseph and said: "Before your father died, he gave us these instructions: 'You shall say to Joseph, Jacob begs you to forgive the criminal wrongdoing of your brothers, who treated you so cruelly.' Please, therefore, forgive the crime that we, the servants of your father's God, committed." When they spoke these words to him, Joseph broke into tears. Then his brothers proceeded to fling themselves down before him and said, "Let us be your slaves!" But Joseph replied to them: "Have no fear. Can I take the place of God? Even though you meant harm to me, God meant it for good, to achieve his present end, the survival of many people. Therefore have no fear. I will provide for you and for your children." By thus speaking kindly to them, he reassured them.

Joseph remained in Egypt, together with his father's family. He lived a hundred and ten years. He saw Ephraim's children to the third generation, and the children of Manasseh's son Machir were also born on Joseph's knees.

Joseph said to his brothers: "I am about to die. God will surely take care of you and lead you out of this land to the land that he promised on oath to Abraham, Isaac and Jacob."—This is the Word of the Lord. ℞. **Thanks be to God.** ℣

Responsorial Psalm   Ps 105, 1-2. 3-4. 6-7

℞. (33) **Turn to the Lord in your need and you will live.**

Give thanks to the Lord, invoke his name;
    make known among the nations his deeds.
Sing to him, sing his praise,
    proclaim all his wondrous deeds. — ℞

Glory in his holy name;
    rejoice, O hearts that seek the Lord!
Look to the Lord in his strength;
    seek to serve him constantly. — ℞

You descendants of Abraham, his servants,
    sons of Jacob, his chosen ones!
He, the Lord, is our God;
    throughout the earth his judgments prevail.—℞ ℣

GOSPEL   Mt 10, 24-33

Alleluia (1 Pt 4, 14)

℞. **Alleluia.** If you are insulted for the name of Christ, blessed are you,
for the Spirit of God rests upon you. ℞. **Alleluia.**

In speaking to his apostles, Jesus tells them not to fear those who can destroy only the body, but rather to fear him who can destroy both body and soul. Then he says, "Whoever acknowledges me before men I will acknowledge before my Father in heaven."

℣. The Lord be with you. ℟. **And also with you.**

✠ A reading from the holy gospel according to Matthew. ℟. **Glory to you, Lord.**

Jesus said to his apostles: "No pupil outranks his teacher, no slave his master. The pupil should be glad to become like his teacher, the slave like his master. If they call the head of the house Beelzebul, how much more the members of his household! Do not let them intimidate you. Nothing is concealed that will not be revealed, and nothing hidden that will not became known. What I tell you in darkness, speak in the light. What you hear in private, proclaim from the housetops.

"Do not fear those who deprive the body of life but cannot destroy the soul. Rather, fear him who can destroy both body and soul in Gehenna. Are not two sparrows sold for next to nothing? Yet not a single sparrow falls to the ground without your Father's consent. As for you, every hair of your head has been counted; so do not be afraid of anything. You are worth more than an entire flock of sparrows. Whoever acknowledges me before men I will acknowledge before my Father in heaven. Whoever disowns me before men I will disown before my Father in heaven."—This is the gospel of the Lord. ℟. **Praise to you, Lord Jesus Christ.** ➤ No. 15, p. 623

welcomes me welcomes him who sent me. He who welcomes a prophet because he bears the name of prophet receives a prophet's reward; he who welcomes a holy man because he is known as holy receives a holy man's reward. And I promise you that whoever gives a cup of cold water to one of these lowly ones because he is a disciple will not want for his reward."

When Jesus had finished instructing his twelve disciples, he left that locality to teach and preach in their towns.—This is the gospel of the Lord. ℟. **Praise to you, Lord Jesus Christ.**   ➔ No. 15, p. 623

TUESDAY OF THE FIFTEENTH WEEK IN ORDINARY TIME

READING I   Ex 2, 1-15

In order to save her baby boy, a Levite woman puts him in a basket among the reeds in the river. The Pharaoh's daughter sees it and asks the mother to nurse him for her. Later she adopts him and calls him Moses.

A reading from the book of Exodus

A certain man of the house of Levi married a Levite woman, who conceived and bore a son. Seeing that he was a goodly child, she hid him for three months. When she could hide him no longer, she took a papyrus basket, daubed it with bituman and pitch, and putting the child in it, placed it among the reeds on the river bank. His sister stationed herself at a distance to find out what would happen to him.

Pharaoh's daughter came down to the river to bathe, while her maids walked along the river bank. Noticing the basket among the reeds, she sent her handmaid to fetch it. On opening it, she looked and lo, there was a baby boy, crying! She was moved with pity for him and said, "It is one of the Hebrews' children." Then his sister asked Pharaoh's daughter,

"Shall I go and call one of the Hebrew women to nurse the child for you?" "Yes, do so," she answered. So the maiden went and called the child's own mother. Pharaoh's daughter said to her, "Take this child and nurse it for me, and I will repay you." The woman therefore took the child and nursed it. When the child grew, she brought him to Pharaoh's daughter, who adopted him as her own son and called him Moses; for she said, "I drew him out of the water."

On one occasion, after Moses had grown up, when he visited his kinsmen and witnessed their forced labor, he saw an Egyptian striking a Hebrew, one of his own kinsmen. Looking about and seeing no one, he slew the Egyptian and hid him in the sand. The next day he went out again, and now two Hebrews were fighting! So he asked the culprit, "Why are you striking your fellow Hebrew?" But he replied, "Who has appointed you ruler and judge over us? Are you thinking of killing me as you killed the Egyptian?" Then Moses became afraid and thought, "The affair must certainly be known."

Pharaoh, too, heard of the affair and sought to put him to death. But Moses fled from him and stayed in the land of Midian.—This is the Word of the Lord.
℟. **Thanks be to God.** ℣

Responsorial Psalm   Ps 69, 3. 14. 30-31. 33-34

℟. (33) **Turn to the Lord in your need, and you will live.**

I am sunk in the abysmal swamp
    where there is no foothold;
I have reached the watery depths;
    the flood overwhelms me. — ℟

But I pray to you, O Lord,
    for the time of your favor, O God!
In your great kindness answer me
    with your constant help. — ℟

But I am afflicted and in pain;
  let your saving help, O God, protect me.
I will praise the name of God in song,
  and I will glorify him with thanksgiving. — ℟

See, you lowly ones, and be glad;
  you who seek God, may your hearts be merry!
For the Lord hears the poor,
  and his own who are in bonds he spurns not.—℟ ℣

GOSPEL   Mt 11, 20-24

Alleluia (Ps 95, 8)

℟. **Alleluia.** If today you hear his voice,
harden not your hearts. ℟. **Alleluia.**

Jesus reproaches the people of the towns where most of his miracles
have been worked for they have not reformed. He tells them Sodom
would still be standing if such miracles had been worked there. Therefore, he says, judgment will be hard on them.

℣. The Lord be with you. ℟. **And also with you.**

✠ A reading from the holy gospel according to Matthew. ℟. **Glory to you, Lord.**

Jesus began to reproach the towns where most of
his miracles had been worked, with their failure to
reform: "It will go ill with you, Chorazin! And just
as ill with you, Bethsaida! If the miracles worked in
you had taken place in Tyre and Sidon, they would
have reformed in sackcloth and ashes long ago. I assure you, it will go easier for Tyre and Sidon than
for you on the day of judgment. As for you, Capernaum.
      'Are you to be exalted to the skies?
      You shall go down to the realm of death!'
If the miracles worked in you had taken place in
Sodom, it would be standing today. I assure you, it
will go easier for Sodom than for you on the day of
judgment."—This is the gospel of the Lord. ℟. **Praise
to you, Lord Jesus Christ.**   ➤ No. 15, p. 623

WEDNESDAY OF THE FIFTEENTH WEEK
IN ORDINARY TIME

READING I   Ex 3, 1-6. 9-12

While Moses is tending the flock, the Lord appears to him in a flaming
bush. He tells Moses that he is to go to the Pharoah and lead his
people, the Israelites, out of Egypt. He says, "I will be with you."

A reading from the book of Exodus

Moses was tending the flock of his father-in-law
Jethro, the priest of Midian. Leading the flock across
the desert, he came to Horeb, the mountain of God.
There an angel of the Lord appeared to him in fire
flaming out of a bush. As he looked on, he was surprised to see that the bush, though on fire, was
not consumed. So Moses decided, "I must go over
to look at this remarkable sight, and see why the
bush is not burned."

When the Lord saw him coming over to look at
it more closely, God called out to him from the bush,
"Moses! Moses!" He answered, "Here I am." God
said, "Come no nearer! Remove the sandals from your
feet, for the place where you stand is holy ground.
I am the God of your father," he continued, "the
God of Abraham, the God of Isaac, the God of Jacob." Moses hid his face, for he was afraid to look
at God.

The Lord said, "So indeed the cry of the Israelites
has reached me, and I have truly noted that the
Egyptians are oppressing them. Come, now! I will
send you to Pharaoh to lead my people, the Israelites,
out of Egypt."

But Moses said to God, "Who am I that I should
go to Pharaoh and lead the Israelites out of Egypt?"
He answered, "I will be with you; and this shall be
your proof that it is I who have sent you: when you
bring my people out of Egypt, you will worship God

on this very mountain."—This is the Word of the
Lord. ℟. **Thanks be to God.** ↓

Responsorial Psalm   Ps 103, 1-2. 3-4. 6-7

℟. (8) **The Lord is kind and merciful.**

Bless the Lord, O my soul;
   and all my being, bless his holy name.
Bless the Lord, O my soul,
   and forget not all his benefits. — ℟

He pardons all your iniquities,
   he heals all your ills.
He redeems your life from destruction,
   he crowns you with kindness and compassion.—℟

The Lord secures justice
   and the rights of all the oppressed.
He has made known his ways to Moses,
   and his deeds to the children of Israel. — ℟ ↓

GOSPEL   Mt 11, 25-27

Alleluia (Mt 11, 25)

℟. **Alleluia.** Blessed are you, Father, Lord of heaven
      and earth;
you have revealed to little ones the mysteries of the
      kingdom. ℟. **Alleluia.**

Jesus prays to his Father and offers him praise "for what you have
hidden from the learned and the clever you have revealed to the
merest children." The message of Jesus is not grasped by wisdom and
understanding; it is known only by revelation.

℣. The Lord be with you. ℟. **And also with you.**
✠ A reading from the holy gospel according to Matthew. ℟. **Glory to you, Lord.**

On one occasion Jesus spoke thus: "Father, Lord of
heaven and earth, to you I offer praise; for what you
have hidden from the learned and the clever you
have revealed to the merest children. Father, it is
true. You have graciously willed it so. Everything
has been given over to me by my Father. No one
knows the Son but the Father, and no one knows

the Father but the Son—and anyone to whom the Son wishes to reveal him."—This is the gospel of the Lord. ℟. **Praise to you, Lord Jesus Christ.**

➔ No. 15, p. 623

THURSDAY OF THE FIFTEENTH WEEK IN ORDINARY TIME

READING I   Ex 3, 11-20

God speaks to Moses in the burning bush, directing him to tell his people that he is concerned about them and the way they are being treated in Egypt. He will guide Moses to lead them out into the land flowing with milk and honey.

A reading from the book of Exodus

Moses, hearing the voice from the burning bush, said to God, "Who am I that I should go to Pharaoh and lead the Israelites out of Egypt?" He answered, "I will be with you; and this shall be your proof that it is I who have sent you: when you bring my people out of Egypt, you will worship God on this very mountain."

"But," said Moses to God, "when I go to the Israelites and say to them, 'The God of your fathers has sent me to you,' if they ask me, 'What is his name?' what am I to tell them?" God replied, "I am who am." Then he added, "This is what you shall tell the Israelites: I AM sent me to you."

God spoke further to Moses, "Thus shall you say to the Israelites: The Lord, the God of your fathers, the God of Abraham, the God of Isaac, the God of Jacob, has sent me to you.

"This is my name forever;
    this is my title for all generations.

"Go and assemble the elders of the Israelites, and tell them: The Lord, the God of your fathers, the God of Abraham, Isaac and Jacob, has appeared to me and said: I am concerned about you and about the way you are being treated in Egypt; so I have decided to lead you up out of the misery of Egypt into the land of the Canaanites, Hittites, Amorites, Perizzites, Hivites and Jebusites, a land flowing with milk and honey.

"Thus they will heed your message. Then you and the elders of Israel shall go to the king of Egypt and say to him: The Lord, the God of the Hebrews, has sent us word. Permit us, then, to go a three days' journey in the desert, that we may offer sacrifice to the Lord, our God.

"Yet I know that the king of Egypt will not allow you to go unless he is forced. I will stretch out my hand, therefore, and smite Egypt by doing all kinds of wondrous deeds there. After that he will send you away."—This is the Word of the Lord. ℞. **Thanks be to God.** ℣

Responsorial Psalm   Ps 105, 1. 5. 8-9. 24-25. 26-27

℞. (8) **The Lord remembers his covenant for ever.**

Give thanks to the Lord, invoke his name;
    make known among the nations his deeds.
Recall the wondrous deeds that he has wrought,
    his portents, and the judgments he has utter-
        ed. — ℞

He remembers forever his covenant
    which he made binding for a thousand genera-
        tions—
Which he entered into with Abraham
    and by his oath to Isaac. — ℞

He greatly increased his people
    and made them stronger than their foes,
Whose hearts he changed, so that they hated his
        people,
    and dealt deceitfully with his servants. — ℞

He sent Moses his servant;
    Aaron, whom he had chosen.

They wrought his signs among them,
  and wonders in the land of Ham. — ℟ ℣

℟. Or: **Alleluia.** ℣

GOSPEL   Mt 11, 28-30

Alleluia (Mt 11, 28)

℟. **Alleluia.** Come to me, all you that labor and are
   burdened,

and I will give you rest, says the Lord. ℟. **Alleluia.**

Jesus says, "Come to me, all you who are weary and find life burdensome." The yoke and the burden of Jesus are submission to the reign
of God. Jesus' yoke is easy and his burden light, for he is gentle
and humble of heart.

℣. The Lord be with you. ℟. **And also with you.**
✠ A reading from the holy gospel according to Matthew. ℟. **Glory to you, Lord.**

Jesus spoke thus: "Come to me, all you who are
weary and find life burdensome, and I will refresh
you. Take my yoke upon your shoulders and learn
from me, for I am gentle and humble of heart. Your
souls will find rest, for my yoke is easy and my
burden light."—This is the gospel of the Lord. ℟.
Praise to you, Lord Jesus Christ.   ➔ No. 15, p. 623

FRIDAY OF THE FIFTEENTH WEEK
IN ORDINARY TIME

READING I   Ex 11, 10—12, 14

The Lord gives Moses and Aaron detailed instructions as to the sacrifice for the Passover, specifying that the lamb's blood should be on
their door so the Lord's judgment will pass over their homes. This
will be a memorial for all generations.

A reading from the book of Exodus

Moses and Aaron performed various wonders in
Pharaoh's presence, but the Lord made Pharaoh obstinate, and he would not let the Israelites leave his
land.

The Lord said to Moses and Aaron in the land of

Egypt, "This month shall stand at the head of your calendar; you shall reckon it the first month of the year. Tell the whole community of Israel: On the tenth of this month every one of your families must procure for itself a lamb, one apiece for each household. If a family is too small for a whole lamb, it shall join the nearest household in procuring one and shall share in the lamb in proportion to the number of persons who partake of it. The lamb must be a year-old male and without blemish. You may take it from either the sheep or the goats. You shall keep it until the fourteenth day of this month, and then, with the whole assembly of Israel present, it shall be slaughtered during the evening twilight. They shall take some of its blood and apply it to the two doorposts and the lintel of every house in which they partake of the lamb. That same night they shall eat its roasted flesh with unleavened bread and bitter herbs. It shall not be eaten raw or boiled, but roasted whole, with its head and shanks and inner organs. None of it must be kept beyond the next morning; whatever is left over in the morning shall be burned up.

"This is how you are to eat it: with your loins girt, sandals on your feet and your staff in hand, you shall eat like those who are in flight. It is the Passover of the Lord. For on this same night I will go through Egypt, striking down every first-born of the land, both man and beast, and executing judgment on all the gods of Egypt—I, the Lord! But the blood will mark the houses where you are. Seeing the blood, I will pass over you; thus, when I strike the land of Egypt, no destructive blow will come upon you.

"This day shall be a memorial feast for you, which all your generations shall celebrate with pilgrimage to the Lord, as a perpetual institution."—This is the Word of the Lord. ℟. **Thanks be to God.** ❥

Responsorial Psalm   Ps 116, 12-13. 15-16. 17-18

℟. (13) **I will take the cup of salvation,
and call on the name of the Lord.**

How shall I make a return to the Lord
for all the good he has done for me?
The cup of salvation I will take up,
and I will call upon the name of the Lord. — ℟

Precious in the eyes of the Lord
is the death of his faithful ones.
I am your servant, the son of your handmaid;
you have loosed my bonds. — ℟

To you will I offer sacrifice of thanksgiving,
and I will call upon the name of the Lord.
My vows to the Lord I will pay
in the presence of all his people. — ℟ ✟

℟. Or: **Alleluia.** ✟

GOSPEL   Mt 12, 1-8

Alleluia (Jn 10, 27)

℟. **Alleluia.** My sheep listen to my voice, says the
Lord;
I know them, and they follow me. ℟. **Alleluia.**

Jesus and his disciples appear to break the law by being hungry and
taking some grain on the sabbath. He explains the practical meaning
of the law and that he, the Lord of the sabbath, desires mercy and
not sacrifice.

℣. The Lord be with you. ℟. **And also with you.**

✠ A reading from the holy gospel according to Matthew. ℟. **Glory to you, Lord.**

Once on a sabbath Jesus walked through the standing grain. His disciples felt hungry, so they began to
pull off the heads of grain and eat them. When the
Pharisees spied this, they protested: "See here! Your
disciples are doing what is not permitted on the sabbath." He replied: "Have you not read what David
did when he and his men were hungry, how he entered God's house and ate the holy bread, a thing

forbidden to him and his men or anyone other than priests? Have you not read in the law how the priests on temple duty can break the sabbath rest without incurring guilt? I assure you, there is something greater than the temple here. If you understood the meaning of the text, 'It is mercy I desire and not sacrifice,' you would not have condemned these innocent men. The Son of Man is indeed the Lord of the sabbath."—This is the gospel of the Lord. ℟. **Praise to you, Lord Jesus Christ.**

➤ No. 15, p. 623

SATURDAY OF THE FIFTEENTH WEEK IN ORDINARY TIME

READING I   Ex 12, 37-42

After some 430 years in Egypt, the time suddenly comes to flee for the Israelites, their children, and their herds. The dough is not leavened so they have to bake it into unleavened loaves. This exodus is to be kept as a vigil to the Lord throughout all generations.

A reading from the book of Exodus

The Israelites set out from Rameses for Succoth, about six hundred thousand men on foot, not counting the children. A crowd of mixed ancestry also went up with them, besides their livestock, very numerous flocks and herds. Since the dough they had brought out of Egypt was not leavened, they baked it into unleavened loaves. They had been rushed out of Egypt and had no opportunity even to prepare food for the journey.

The time the Israelites had stayed in Egypt was four hundred and thirty years. At the end of four hundred and thirty years, all the hosts of the Lord left the land of Egypt on this very date. This was a night of vigil for the Lord, as he led them out of the land of Egypt; so on this same night all the Israelites must keep a vigil for the Lord throughout

their generations.—This is the Word of the Lord.
℞. **Thanks be to God.** ✠

Responsorial Psalm   Ps 136, 1. 23-24. 10-12. 13-15

℞. **His love is everlasting.**

Give thanks to the Lord, for he is good,
    for his mercy endures forever;
Who remembered us in our abjection,
    for his mercy endures forever;
And freed us from our foes,
    for his mercy endures forever. — ℞

Who smote the Egyptians in their first-born,
    for his mercy endures forever;
And brought out Israel from their midst,
    for his mercy endures forever;
With a mighty hand and an outstretched arm,
    for his mercy endures forever. — ℞

Who split the Red Sea in twain,
    for his mercy endures forever;
And led Israel through its midst,
    for his mercy endures forever;
But swept Pharaoh and his army into the Red Sea,
    for his mercy endures forever. — ℞ ✠

℞. Or: **Alleluia.** ✠

GOSPEL   Mt 12, 14-21

Alleluia (2 Cor 5, 19)

℞. **Alleluia.** God was in Christ, to reconcile the
    world to himself;
and the Good News of reconciliation he has entrust-
    ed to us. ℞. **Alleluia.**

Because of the evil designs of the Pharisees, Jesus withdraws. He
cures the many who follow him but bids them to tell no one, as Isaiah
prophesied. He will bring hope and justice, with which will come mis-
judgments until victory.

℣. The Lord be with you. ℞. **And also with you.**
✠ A reading from the holy gospel according to Matthew. ℞. **Glory to you, Lord.**

When the Pharisees were outside they began to plot against Jesus to find a way to destroy him. Jesus was aware of this, and so he withdrew from that place.

Many people followed him and he cured them all, though he sternly ordered them not to make public what he had done. This was to fulfill what had been said through Isaiah the prophet:

"Here is my servant whom I have chosen,
my loved one in whom I delight.
I will endow him with my spirit
and he will proclaim justice to the Gentiles.
He will not contend or cry out,
nor will his voice be heard in the streets.
The bruised reed he will not crush;
the smoldering wick he will not quench
until judgment is made victorious.
In his name, the Gentiles will find hope."

This is the gospel of the Lord. ℟. **Praise to you, Lord Jesus Christ.** _____ ➤ No. 15, p. 623

MONDAY OF THE SIXTEENTH WEEK
IN ORDINARY TIME

READING I   Ex 14, 5-18

Pharoah pursues the Israelites, sending chariots with his soldiers and others from all over Egypt to give chase to the Israelites. Seeing this, the Israelites are afraid and cry out against Moses. They are in a desert beside a sea, and here the Lord promises safe passage to his people.

A reading from the book of Exodus

When it was reported to the king of Egypt that the people had fled, Pharaoh and his servants changed their minds about them. "What have we done!" they exclaimed. "Why, we have released Israel from our service!" So Pharaoh made his chariots ready and mustered his soldiers—six hundred first-class chariots and all the other chariots of Egypt, with warriors on them all. So obstinate had the Lord made

Pharaoh that he pursued the Israelites even while they were marching away in triumph. The Egyptians, then, pursued them; Pharaoh's whole army, his horses, chariots and charioteers, caught up with them as they lay encamped by the sea, at Pi-hahiroth, in front of Baal-zephon.

Pharaoh was already near when the Israelites looked up and saw that the Egyptians were on the march in pursuit of them. In great fright they cried out to the Lord. And they complained to Moses, "Were there no burial places in Egypt that you had to bring us out here to die in the desert? Why did you do this to us? Why did you bring us out of Egypt? Did we not tell you this in Egypt, when we said, 'Leave us alone. Let us serve the Egyptians'? Far better for us to be the slaves of the Egyptians than to die in the desert." But Moses answered the people, "Fear not! Stand your ground, and you will see the victory the Lord will win for you today. These Egyptians whom you see today you will never see again. The Lord himself will fight for you; you have only to keep still."

Then the Lord said to Moses, "Why are you crying out to me? Tell the Israelites to go forward. And you, lift up your staff and, with hand outstretched over the sea, split the sea in two, that the Israelites may pass through it on dry land. But I will make the Egyptians so obstinate that they will go in after them. Then I will receive glory through Pharaoh and all his army, his chariots and charioteers. The Egyptians shall know that I am the Lord, when I receive glory through Pharaoh and his chariots and charioteers."—This is the Word of the Lord. ℟. **Thanks be to God.** ⅴ

Responsorial Psalm   Ex 15, 1-2. 3-4. 5-6

℟. (1) **Let us sing to the Lord;**
   he has covered himself in glory.

I will sing to the Lord, for he is gloriously trium-
    phant;
    horse and chariot he has cast into the sea.
My strength and my courage is the Lord,
    and he has been my savior.
He is my God, I praise him;
    the God of my father, I extol him. — ℟

The Lord is a warrior,
    Lord is his name!
Pharaoh's chariots and army he hurled into the sea;
    the elite of his officers were submerged in the
    Red Sea. — ℟

The flood waters covered them,
    they sank into the depths like a stone.
Your right hand, O Lord, magnificent in power,
    your right hand, O Lord, has shattered the ene-
    my. — ℟ ℣

GOSPEL   Mt 12, 38-42
Alleluia (Ps 95, 8)
℟. **Alleluia.** If today you hear his voice,
harden not your hearts. ℟. **Alleluia.**

The scribes and Pharisees ask Jesus for a visible sign. Jesus answers,
"An evil and unfaithful age is eager for a sign." Jonah's three days
and nights in the whale prefigure the Son of Man's three days and
nights before his resurrection.

℣. The Lord be with you. ℟. **And also with you.**
✠ A reading from the holy gospel according to Matthew. ℟. **Glory to you, Lord.**

Some of the scribes and Pharisees then spoke up,
saying, "Teacher, we want to see you work some
signs." Jesus answered: "An evil and unfaithful age
is eager for a sign! No sign will be given it but that
of the prophet Jonah. Just as Jonah spent three days
and three nights in the belly of the whale, so will the
Son of Man spend three days and three nights in the
bowels of the earth. At the judgment, the citizens of
Nineveh will rise with the present generation and be

the ones to condemn it. At the preaching of Jonah they reformed their lives; but you have a greater than Jonah here. At the judgment, the queen of the South will rise with the present generation and be the one to condemn it. She came from the farthest corner of the earth to listen to the wisdom of Solomon; but you have a greater than Solomon here."— This is the gospel of the Lord. ℟. **Praise to you, Lord Jesus Christ.**   ⟶ No. 15, p. 623

TUESDAY OF THE SIXTEENTH WEEK
IN ORDINARY TIME

READING I   Ex 14, 21—15, 1

As Moses stretches out his hand, a strong wind dries the sea and allows the Israelites to pass through it. The Lord again tells Moses to extend his arm over the sea, which then flows normally and catches every Egyptian, thus demonstrating God's great power, love, and protection for his chosen people.

A reading from the book of Exodus

Moses stretched out his hand over the sea, and the Lord swept the sea with a strong east wind throughout the night and so turned it into dry land. When the water was thus divided, the Israelites marched into the midst of the sea on dry land, with the water like a wall to their right and to their left.

The Egyptians followed in pursuit; all Pharaoh's horses and chariots and charioteers went after them right into the midst of the sea. In the night watch just before dawn the Lord cast through the column of the fiery cloud upon the Egyptian force a glance that threw it into a panic; and he so clogged their chariot wheels that they could hardly drive. With that the Egyptians sounded the retreat before Israel, because the Lord was fighting for them against the Egyptians.

Then the Lord told Moses, "Stretch out your hand over the sea, that the water may flow back upon the Egyptians, upon their chariots and their charioteers."

So Moses stretched out his hand over the sea, and at dawn the sea flowed back to its normal depth. The Egyptians were fleeing head on toward the sea, when the Lord hurled them into its midst. As the water flowed back, it covered the chariots and the charioteers of Pharaoh's whole army which had followed the Israelites into the sea. Not a single one of them escaped. But the Israelites had marched on dry land through the midst of the sea, with the water like a wall to their right and to their left. Thus the Lord saved Israel on that day from the power of the Egyptians. When Israel saw the Egyptians lying dead on the seashore and beheld the great power that the Lord had shown against the Egyptians, they feared the Lord and believed in him and in his servant Moses.

Then Moses and the Israelites sang this song to the Lord:

> I will sing to the Lord, for he is gloriously triumphant;
>> horse and chariot he has cast into the sea.

This is the Word of the Lord. ℟. **Thanks be to God.** ℣

Responsorial Psalm   Ex 15, 8-9. 10. 12. 17

℟. (1) **Let us sing to the Lord;
he has covered himself in glory.**

At the breath of your anger the waters piled up,
    the flowing waters stood like a mound,
    the flood waters congealed in the midst of the sea.
The enemy boasted, "I will pursue and overtake them;
    I will divide the spoils and have my fill of them;
    I will draw my sword; my hand shall despoil them!" — ℟

When your wind blew, the sea covered them;
    like lead they sank in the mighty waters.
When you stretched out your right hand,
    the earth swallowed them! — ℟

And you brought them in and planted them on the
mountain of your inheritance—
the place where you made your seat, O Lord,
the sanctuary, O Lord, which your hands established. — ℟ ℣

GOSPEL Mt 12, 46-50

Alleluia (Jn 14, 23)

℟. **Alleluia.** If anyone loves me, he will hold to my
words,
and my Father will love him, and we will come to
him. ℟. **Alleluia.**

When Jesus is addressing the crowd around him, someone tells him
that his mother and brothers are there. He uses this occasion to show
that his ministry is to all mankind: "Whoever does the will of my
heavenly Father is brother, sister, and mother to me."

℣. The Lord be with you. ℟. **And also with you.**
✠ A reading from the holy gospel according to Matthew. ℟. **Glory to you, Lord.**

Jesus was addressing the crowds when his mother
and his brothers appeared outside to speak with
him. Someone said to him, "Your mother and your
brothers are standing out there and they wish to
speak to you." He said to the one who had told him,
"Who is my mother? Who are my brothers?" Then
extending his hands to his disciples, he said, "There
are my mother and my brothers. Whoever does the
will of my heavenly Father is brother and sister and
mother to me."—This is the gospel of the Lord. ℟.
Praise to you, Lord Jesus Christ. ➤ No. 15, p. 623

WEDNESDAY OF THE SIXTEENTH WEEK
IN ORDINARY TIME

READING I Ex 16, 1-5. 9-15

Within a couple of months after escaping from Egypt, food is low and
the Israelites fear famine. Again they grumble against Moses and
Aaron, who appeal to the Lord. God makes a promise and sends quail
and manna for their needs.

A reading from the book of Exodus

The whole Israelite community, having set out from Elim, came into the desert of Sin, which is between Elim and Sinai, on the fifteenth day of the second month after their departure from the land of Egypt. Here in the desert the whole Israelite community grumbled against Moses and Aaron. The Israelites said to them, "Would that we had died at the Lord's hand in the land of Egypt, as we sat by our fleshpots and ate our fill of bread! But you had to lead us into this desert to make the whole community die of famine!"

Then the Lord said to Moses, "I will now rain down bread from heaven for you. Each day the people are to go out and gather their daily portion; thus will I test them, to see whether they follow my instructions or not. On the sixth day, however, when they prepare what they bring in, let it be twice as much as they gather on the other days."

Then Moses said to Aaron, "Tell the whole Israelite community: Present yourselves before the Lord, for he has heard your grumbling." When Aaron announced this to the whole Israelite community, they turned toward the desert and lo, the glory of the Lord appeared in the cloud! The Lord spoke to Moses and said, "I have heard the grumbling of the Israelites. Tell them: In the evening twilight you shall eat flesh, and in the morning you shall have your fill of bread, so that you may know that I, the Lord, am your God."

In the evening quail came up and covered the camp. In the morning a dew lay all about the camp, and when the dew evaporated, there on the surface of the desert were fine flakes like hoarfrost on the ground. On seeing it, the Israelites asked one another, "What is this?" for they did not know what it was. But Moses told them, "This is the bread which the Lord has given you to eat."—This is the Word of the Lord. ℟. **Thanks be to God.** ℣

Responsorial Psalm Ps 78, 18-19. 23-24. 25-26. 27-28

℟. (24) **The Lord gave them bread from heaven.**

They tempted God in their hearts
  by demanding the food they craved.
Yes, they spoke against God, saying,
  "Can God spread a table in the desert?" — ℟

Yet he commanded the skies above
  and the doors of heaven he opened;
He rained manna upon them for food
  and gave them heavenly bread. — ℟

The bread of the mighty was eaten by men;
  even a surfeit of provisions he sent them.
He stirred up the east wind in the heavens,
  and by his power brought on the south wind.—℟

And he rained meat upon them like dust,
  and, like the sand of the sea, winged fowl,
Which fell in the midst of their camp
  round about their tents. — ℟ ⍗

GOSPEL Mt 13, 1-9

Alleluia

℟. **Alleluia.** The seed is the word of God, Christ is
    the sower;
all who come to him will live for ever. ℟. **Alleluia.**

As Jesus rests by the lakeshore, crowds follow him. He speaks in parables,
one being about the farmer who sows seeds. The seeds fall on various kinds
of unproductive soil, but some land on good soil and yield a hundred- or
sixty- or thirty-fold.

℣. **The Lord be with you.** ℟. **And also with you.**
✠ A reading from the holy gospel according to Mat-
them. ℟. **Glory to you, Lord.**

On leaving the house, Jesus sat down by the lakeshore. Such great crowds gathered around him that
he went and took his seat in a boat while the crowd
stood along the shore. **He addressed them at length**
in parables, speaking in this fashion:

  "One day a farmer went out sowing. Part of what

he sowed landed on a footpath, where birds came and ate it up. Part of it fell on rocky ground, where it had little soil. It sprouted at once since the soil had no depth, but when the **sun rose and scorched** it, it began to wither for lack of roots. Again, part of the seed fell among thorns, which grew up and choked it. Part of it, finally, landed on good soil **and yielded grain a hundred- or sixty- or thirty-fold.** Let everyone heed what he hears!"—This is the gospel of the Lord. ℞. **Praise to you, Lord Jesus Christ.**

→ No. 15, p. 623

THURSDAY OF THE SIXTEENTH WEEK IN ORDINARY TIME

READING I   Ex 19, 1-2. 9-11. 16-20

God's personal guidance for his chosen people is again evident in his contact with Moses. He directs Moses to prepare the people for his appearance. Unmistakable displays of nature in the mountain and atmosphere herald the meeting.

A reading from the book of Exodus

In the third month after their departure from the land of Egypt, on its first day, the Israelites came to the desert of Sinai. After the journey from Rephidim to the desert of Sinai, they pitched camp. While Israel was encamped here in front of the mountain, the Lord told Moses, "I am coming to you in a dense cloud, so that when the people hear me speaking with you, they may always have faith in you also." When Moses, then, had reported to the Lord the response of the people, the Lord added, "Go to the people and have them sanctify themselves today and tomorrow. Make them wash their garments and be ready for the third day; for on the third day the Lord will come down on Mount Sinai before the eyes of all the people."

On the morning of the third day there were peals of thunder and lightning, and a heavy cloud over the mountain, and a very loud trumpet blast, so that all the people in the camp trembled. But Moses led the people out of the camp to meet God, and they stationed themselves at the foot of the mountain. Mount Sinai was all wrapped in smoke, for the Lord came down upon it in fire. The smoke rose from it as though from a furnace, and the whole mountain trembled violently. The trumpet blast grew louder and louder, while Moses was speaking and God answering him with thunder.

When the Lord came down to the top of Mount Sinai, he summoned Moses to the top of the mountain.—This is the Word of the Lord. R̃. **Thanks be to God.** ℣

Responsorial Psalm   Dn 3, 52. 53. 54. 55. 56

R̃. (52) **Glory and praise for ever!**

Blessed are you, O Lord, the God of our fathers,
    praiseworthy and exalted above all forever;
And blessed is your holy and glorious name,
    praiseworthy and **exalted above all for all**
    ages. — R̃

Blessed are you in the temple of your holy glory,
    praiseworthy and glorious above all forever. — R̃

Blessed are you on the throne of your kingdom,
    praiseworthy and exalted above all forever. — R̃

Blessed are you who look into the depths
    from your throne upon the cherubim,
    praiseworthy and exalted above all forever. — R̃

Blessed are you in the firmanent of heaven,
    praiseworthy and glorious forever. — R̃ ℣

GOSPEL   Mt 13, 10-17

Alleluia (Mt 11, 25)

R̃. **Alleluia.** Blessed are you, Father, Lord of heaven
    and earth;
you have revealed to little ones the mysteries of the
    kingdom. R̃. **Alleluia.**

The loving example of Christ in teaching is given when he responds to his disciples' question about his using parables. He explains that this is the way to reach some who cannot understand his words since they have not been as blessed as the disciples.

℣. The Lord be with you. ℟. **And also with you.**

✠ A reading from the holy gospel according to Matthew. ℟. **Glory to you, Lord.**

When the disciples approached Jesus, they asked him, "Why do you speak to them in parables?" He answered: "To you has been given a knowledge of the mysteries of the reign of God, but it has not been given to the others. To the man who has, more will be given until he grows rich; the man who has not, will lose what little he has.

"I use parables when I speak to them because they look but do not see, they listen but do not hear or understand. Isaiah's prophecy is fulfilled in them which says:

'Listen as you will, you will not understand,
look intently as you will, you shall not see.
Sluggish indeed is this people's heart.
They have scarcely heard with their ears,
they have firmly closed their eyes;
otherwise they might see with their eyes,
and hear with their ears,
and understand with their hearts,
and turn back to me,
and I should hear **them.**'

"But blest are your eyes because they see and blest are your ears because they hear. I assure you, many a prophet and many a saint longed to see what you see but did not see it, to hear what you hear but did not hear it."—This is the gospel of the Lord. ℟. **Praise to you, Lord Jesus Christ.**   ➔ No. 15, p. 623

FRIDAY OF THE SIXTEENTH WEEK
IN ORDINARY TIME

READING I   Ex 20, 1-17

God delivers the commandments. In the first, he makes it clear he is the one who brought them out of slavery and he is a jealous God, inflicting punishment on the children of those who hate him, but mercy down to the thousandth generation on children of those who love him and keep his commandments.

A reading from the book of Exodus

God delivered all these commandments:

"I, the Lord, am your God, who brought you out of the land of Egypt, that place of slavery. You shall not have other gods besides me. You shall not carve idols for yourselves in the shape of anything in the sky above or on the earth below or in the waters beneath the earth; you shall not bow down before them or worship them. For I, the Lord, your God, am a jealous God, inflicting punishment for their fathers' wickedness on the children of those who hate me, down to the third and fourth generation; but bestowing mercy down to the thousandth generation, on the children of those who love me and keep my commandments.

"You shall not take the name of the Lord, your God, in vain. For the Lord will not leave unpunished him who takes his name in vain.

"Remember to keep holy the sabbath day. Six days you may labor and do all your work, but the seventh day is the sabbath of the Lord, your God. No work may be done then either by you, or your son or daughter, or your male or female slave, or your beast, or by the alien who lives with you. In six days the Lord made the heavens and the earth, the sea and all that is in them; but on the seventh day he rested. That is why the Lord has blessed the sabbath day and made it holy.

"Honor your father and your mother, that you may have a long life in the land which the Lord, your

God, is giving you.

"You shall not kill.

"You shall not commit adultery.

"You shall not steal.

"You shall not bear false witness against your neighbor.

"You shall not covet your neighbor's house. You shall not covet your neighbor's wife, nor his male or female slave, nor his ox or ass, nor anything else that belongs to him."—This is the Word of the Lord. ℞. **Thanks be to God.** ℣

Responsorial Psalm   Ps 19, 8. 9. 10. 11

℞. (Jn 6, 69) **Lord, you have the words of everlasting life.**

The law of the Lord is perfect,
    refreshing the soul;
The decree of the Lord is trustworthy,
    giving wisdom to the simple. — ℞

The precepts of the Lord are right,
    rejoicing the heart;
The command of the Lord is clear,
    enlightening the eye; — ℞

The fear of the Lord is pure,
    enduring forever;
The ordinances of the Lord are true,
    all of them just. — ℞

They are more precious than gold,
    than a heap of purest gold;
Sweeter also than syrup
    or honey from the comb. — ℞ ℣

GOSPEL   Mt 13, 18-23

Alleluia (See Lk 8, 15)

℞. **Alleluia.** Happy are they who have kept the word with a generous heart,
and yield a harvest through perseverance. ℞. **Alleluia.**

Jesus speaks in the parable of the sower. It takes good soil to receive the word of God and produce a yield. The seed that falls on rocky soil or has no roots or is among weeds will not produce. In like manner, the message of God is planted.

℣. The Lord be with you. ℟. **And also with you.**
✠ A reading from the holy gospel according to Matthew. ℟. **Glory to you, Lord.**

Jesus said to his disciples, "Mark well the parable of the sower. The seed along the path is the man who hears the message about God's reign without understanding it. The evil one approaches him to steal away what was sown in his mind. The seed that fell on patches of rock is the man who hears the message and at first receives it with joy. But he has no roots, so he lasts only for a time. When some setback or persecution involving the message occurs, he soon falters. What was sown among briers is the man who hears the message, but then worldly anxiety and the lure of money choke it off. Such a one produces no yield. But what was sown on good soil is the man who hears the message and takes it in. He it is who bears a yield of a hundred- or sixty- or thirty-fold."—This is the gospel of the Lord. ℟. **Praise to you, Lord Jesus Christ.** ➔ No. 15, p. 623

SATURDAY OF THE SIXTEENTH WEEK IN ORDINARY TIME

READING I   Ex 24, 3-8

Moses relates to the people all the words and ordinances of the Lord, and they unanimously agree to heed them. He then ceremoniously prepares the sacrifices as peace offerings to the Lord and seals the covenant with blood on the altar and on the people.

A reading from the book of Exodus

When Moses came to the people and related all the words and ordinances of the Lord, they all answered with one voice, "We will do everything that the Lord has told us." Moses then wrote down all the words of the Lord and, rising early the next day, he erected at the foot of the mountain an altar and twelve pillars for the twelve tribes of Israel. Then, having sent certain young men of the Israelites to offer holocausts and sacrifice young bulls as peace offerings to the Lord, Moses took half of the blood and put it in large bowls; the other half he splashed on the altar. Taking the book of the covenant, he read it aloud to the people, who answered, "All that the Lord has said, we will heed and do." Then he took the blood and sprinkled it on the people, saying, "This is the blood of the covenant which the Lord has made with you in accordance with all these words of his."—This is the Word of the Lord. ℟. **Thanks be to God.** ℣

Responsorial Psalm   Ps 50, 1-2. 5-6. 14-15

℟. (14) **Offer to God a sacrifice of praise.**

God the Lord has spoken and summoned the earth,
  from the rising of the sun to its setting.
From Zion, perfect in beauty,
  God shines forth. — ℟

"Gather my faithful ones before me,
  those who have made a covenant with me by
    sacrifice."
And the heavens proclaim his justice;
  for God himself is the judge. — ℟

"Offer to God praise as your sacrifice
  and fulfill your vows to the Most High;
Then call upon me in time of distress;
  I will rescue you, and you shall glorify me."—℟ ℣

GOSPEL   Mt 13, 24-30

Alleluia (Jas 1, 18)

℟. **Alleluia.** The Father gave us birth by his message
    of truth,
that we might be as the first fruits of his creation.
  ℟. **Alleluia.**

Jesus proposes another parable regarding an enemy sowing weeds in a field of good wheat. The owner advises his workers to let them grow together; then at harvest time, they will be separated.

℣. The Lord be with you. ℟. **And also with you.**

✠ A reading from the holy gospel according to Matthew. ℟. **Glory to you, Lord.**

Jesus proposed to the crowds another parable: "The reign of God may be likened to a man who sowed good seed in his field. While everyone was asleep, his enemy came and sowed weeds through his wheat, and then made off. When the crop began to mature and yield grain, the weeds made their appearance as well. The owner's slaves came to him and said, 'Sir, did you not sow good seed in your field? Where are the weeds coming from?' He answered, 'I see an enemy's hand in this.' His slaves said to him, 'Do you want us to go out and pull them up?' 'No,' he replied, 'pull up the weeds and you might take the wheat along with them. Let them grow together until harvest; then at harvest time I will order the harvesters, first collect the weeds and bundle them up to burn, then gather the wheat into my barn.' "— This is the gospel of the Lord. ℟. **Praise to you, Lord Jesus Christ.**   ➔ No. 15, p. 623

MONDAY OF THE SEVENTEENTH WEEK IN ORDINARY TIME

READING I   Ex 32, 15-24. 30-34

By the times Moses comes back from the mountain with the tablets inscribed by God, he sees his people reveling around a golden calf. Enraged, he throws the tablets down and they break. Next he melts the calf down and makes the people drink water with its ashes. He then pleads wth God to forgive them.

A reading from the book of Exodus

Moses turned and came down the mountain with the two tablets of the commandments in his hands, tablets that were written on both sides, front and back; tablets that were made by God, having inscriptions on them that were engraved by God himself. Now, when Joshua heard the noise of the people shouting, he said to Moses, "That sounds like a battle in the camp." But Moses answered, "It does not sound like cries of victory, nor does it sound like cries of defeat; the sounds that I hear are cries of revelry." As he drew near the camp, he saw the calf and the dancing. With that Moses' wrath flared up, so that he threw the tablets down and broke them on the base of the mountain. Taking the calf they had made, he fused it in the fire and then ground it down to powder, which he scattered on the water and made the Israelites drink.

Moses asked Aaron, "What did this people ever do to you that you should lead them into so grave a sin?" Aaron replied, "Let not my lord be angry. You know well enough how prone the people are to evil. They said to me, 'Make us a god to be our leader; as for the man Moses who brought us out of the land of Egypt, we do not know what has happened to him.' So I told them, 'Let anyone who has gold jewelry take it off.' They gave it to me, and I threw it into the fire, and this calf came out."

On the next day Moses said to the people, "You have committed a grave sin. I will go up to the Lord, then; perhaps I may be able to make atonement for your sin." So Moses went back to the Lord and said, "Ah, this people has indeed committed a grave sin in making a god of gold for themselves! If you would only forgive their sin! If you will not, then strike me out of the book that you have written." The Lord answered, "Him only who has sinned against me will I strike out of my book. Now, go and lead the people whither I have told you. My angel will go before you. When it is time for me to punish, I will punish them for their sin."—This is the Word of the Lord. ℞. **Thanks be to God.** ℣

Responsorial Psalm   Ps 106, 19-20. 21-22. 23

℟. (1) **Give thanks to the Lord for he is good.**

They made a calf in Horeb
    and adored a molten image;
They exchanged their glory
    for the image of a grass-eating bullock. — ℟

They forgot the God who had saved them,
    who had done great deeds in Egypt,
Wondrous deeds in the land of Ham,
    terrible things at the Red Sea. — ℟

Then he spoke of exterminating them,
    but Moses, his chosen one,
Withstood him in the breach
    to turn back his destructive wrath. — ℟ ℣

℟. Or: **Alleluia.** ℣

GOSPEL   Mt 13, 31-35

Alleluia (Jas 1, 18)

℟. **Alleluia.** The Father gave us birth by his message
    of truth,
that we might be as the first fruits of his creation.
    ℟. **Alleluia.**

Using the parables of the tiny mustard seed and the bit of yeast in
flour, Jesus teaches what big and great things may come from small
beginnings. As the prophet predicted, these thoughts have laid hidden
since the creation of the world.

℣. The Lord be with you. ℟. **And also with you.**
✠ A reading from the holy gospel according to Matthew. ℟. **Glory to you, Lord.**

Jesus proposed to the crowds another parable: "The
reign of God is like a mustard seed which someone
took and sowed in his field. It is the smallest seed of
all, yet when full-grown it is the largest of plants. It
becomes so big a shrub that the birds of the sky
come and build their nests in its branches."

    He offered them still another image: "The reign
of God is like yeast which a woman took and knead-

ed into three measures of flour. Eventually the whole mass of dough began to rise." All these lessons Jesus taught the crowds in the form of parables. He spoke to them in parables only, to fulfill what had been said through the prophet:

"I will open my mouth in parables,
I will announce what has lain hidden since the creation of the world."

This is the gospel of the Lord. ℟. **Praise to you, Lord Jesus Christ.** ➔ No. 15, p. 623

TUESDAY OF THE SEVENTEENTH WEEK
IN ORDINARY TIME

READING I Ex 33, 7-11; 34, 5-9. 28

Moses has a meeting tent outside the camp. As he enters this, the Lord comes in a cloud and communicates with him face to face. The Lord declares himself as slow to anger, yet just. Moses is with the Lord for forty days and forty nights.

A reading from the book of Exodus

The tent, which was called the meeting tent, Moses used to pitch at some distance away, outside the camp. Anyone who wished to consult the Lord would go to this meeting tent outside the camp. Whenever Moses went out to the tent, the people would all rise and stand at the entrance of their own tents, watching Moses until he entered the tent. As Moses entered the tent, the column of cloud would come down and stand at its entrance while the Lord spoke with Moses. On seeing the column of cloud stand at the entrance of the tent, all the people would rise and worship at the entrance of their own tents. The Lord used to speak to Moses face to face, as one man speaks to another. Moses would then return to the camp, but his young assistant, Joshua, son of Nun, would not move out of the tent.

Moses invoked the name of the Lord who stood with him there and proclaimed his name, "Lord."

Thus the Lord passed before him and cried out, "The Lord, the Lord, a merciful and gracious God, slow to anger and rich in kindness and fidelity, continuing his kindness for a thousand generations, and forgiving wickedness and crime and sin; yet not declaring the guilty guiltless, but punishing children and grandchildren to the third and fourth generation for their fathers' wickedness!" Moses at once bowed down to the ground in worship. Then he said, "If I find favor with you, O Lord, do come along in our company. This is indeed a stiff-necked people; yet pardon our wickedness and sins, and receive us as your own."

So Moses stayed there with the Lord for forty days and forty nights, without eating any food or drinking any water, and he wrote on the tablets the words of the covenant, the ten commandments.— This is the Word of the Lord. ℟. **Thanks be to God. ℣**

Responsorial Psalm   Ps 103, 6-7. 8-9. 10-11. 12-13

℟. (8) **The Lord is kind and merciful.**

The Lord secures justice
    and the rights of all the oppressed.
He has made known his ways to Moses,
    and his deeds to the children of Israel. — ℟

Merciful and gracious is the Lord,
    slow to anger and abounding in kindness.
He will not always chide,
    nor does he keep his wrath forever. — ℟

Not according to our sins does he deal with us,
    nor does he requite us according to our crimes.
For as the heavens are high above the earth,
    so surpassing is his kindness toward those who
        fear him. — ℟

As far as the east is from the west,
    so far has he put our transgressions from us.

As a father has compassion on his children,
  so the Lord has compassion on those who fear
    him. — ℟ ♥

GOSPEL   Mt 13, 35-43
Alleluia

℟. **Alleluia.** The seed is the word of God, Christ is
    the sower;
all who come to him will live for ever. ℟. **Alleluia.**

Jesus responds to his disciples' question about the good seed parable.
The Son of Man is the farmer, the devil the weed-sower. At the end
of the world, the Son of Man will dispatch angels to hurl evildoers
into a furnace and the saints will shine like the sun.

℣. The Lord be with you. ℟. **And also with you.**
✠ A reading from the holy gospel according to Matthew. ℟. **Glory to you, Lord.**

Jesus dismissed the crowds and went home. His
disciples came to him with the request, "Explain to
us the parable of the weeds in the field." He said in
answer: "The farmer sowing good seed is the Son
of Man; the field is the world, the good seed the citizens of the kingdom. The weeds are the followers
of the evil one and the enemy who sowed them is
the devil. The harvest is the end of the world, while
the harvesters are the angels. Just as weeds are collected and burned, so it will be at the end of the
world. The Son of Man will dispatch his angels to
collect from his kingdom all who draw others to
apostasy, and all evildoers. The angels will hurl
them into the fiery furnace where they will wail and
grind their teeth. Then the saints will shine like the
sun in their Father's kingdom. Let everyone heed
what he hears!"—This is the gospel of the Lord. ℟.
Praise to you, Lord Jesus Christ.   → No. 15, p. 623

WEDNESDAY OF THE SEVENTEENTH WEEK
IN ORDINARY TIME

READING I   Ex 34, 29-35

Coming down from Mount Sinai, Moses' face is so radiant that the
Israelites are frightened. He appears this way when he converses with
the Lord, so he wears a veil over his face when he is not with the Lord.

A reading from the book of Exodus

As Moses came down from Mount Sinai with the
two tablets of the commandments in his hands, he
did not know that the skin of his face had become
radiant while he conversed with the Lord. When
Aaron, then, and the other Israelites saw Moses and
noticed how radiant the skin of his face had become,
they were afraid to come near him. Only after Moses
called to them did Aaron and all the rulers of the
community come back to him. Moses then spoke to
them. Later on, all the Israelites came up to him,
and he enjoined on them all that the Lord had told
him on Mount Sinai. When he finished speaking
with them, he put a veil over his face. Whenever
Moses entered the presence of the Lord to converse
with him, he removed the veil until he came out
again. On coming out, he would tell the Israelites
all that had been commanded. Then the Israelites
would see that the skin of Moses' face was radiant;
so he would again put the veil over his face until he
went in to converse with the Lord.—This is the Word
of the Lord. ℟. **Thanks be to God.** ℣

Responsorial Psalm   Ps 99, 5. 6. 7. 9

℟. (9) **Holy is the Lord our God.**

Extol the Lord, our God,
    and worship at his footstool;
    holy is he! — ℟

Moses and Aaron were among his priests,

and Samuel, among those who called upon his
   name;
they called upon the Lord, and he answered
   them. — ℟

From the pillar of cloud he spoke to them;
   they heard his decrees and the law he gave
   them. — ℟

Extol the Lord, our God,
   and worship at his holy mountain;
   for holy is the Lord, our God. — ℟ ▼

GOSPEL   Mt 13, 44-46
Alleluia (Jn 15, 15)
℟. **Alleluia.** I call you my friends, says the Lord,
for I have made known to you all that the Father
   has told me. ℟. **Alleluia.**

Jesus compares the reign of God to a buried treasure for which a
man would sell everything, and the kingdom of heaven to a valuable
pearl for which a merchant would give up all.

℣. The Lord be with you. ℟. **And also with you.**
✠ A reading from the holy gospel according to Matthew. ℟. **Glory to you, Lord.**
Jesus said to the crowds: "The reign of God is like
a buried treasure which a man found in a field. He
hid it again, and rejoicing at his find went and sold
all he had and bought that field. Or again, the kingdom of heaven is like a merchant's search for fine
pearls. When he found one really valuable pearl, he
went back and put up for sale all that he had and
bought it."—This is the gospel of the Lord. ℟. **Praise
to you, Lord Jesus Christ.**   ➤ No. 15, p. 623

THURSDAY OF THE SEVENTEENTH WEEK
IN ORDINARY TIME

READING I   Ex 40, 16-21. 34-38

The Lord directs Moses on details of a Dwelling, with the tent covering it. He puts the commandments in an ark, places them in the Dwelling, and hangs the veil, thus screening off the ark of the commandments. A cloud covers the tent and is a sign; only if it lifts do they go forward on their journey.

A reading from the book of Exodus

Moses did all that the Lord had commanded him. On the first day of the first month of the second year the Dwelling was erected. It was Moses who erected the Dwelling. He placed its pedestals, set up its boards, put in its bars, and set up its columns. He spread the tent over the Dwelling and put the covering on top of the tent, as the Lord had commanded him. He took the commandments and put them in the ark; he placed poles alongside the ark and set the propitiatory upon it. He brought the ark into the Dwelling and hung the curtain veil, thus screening off the ark of the commandments, as the Lord had commanded him.

Then the cloud covered the meeting tent, and the glory of the Lord filled the Dwelling. Moses could not enter the meeting tent, because the cloud settled down upon it and the glory of the Lord filled the Dwelling. Whenever the cloud rose from the Dwelling, the Israelites would set out on their journey. But if the cloud did not lift, they would not go forward; only when it lifted did they go forward. In the daytime the cloud of the Lord was seen over the Dwelling; whereas at night, fire was seen in the cloud by the whole house of Israel in all the stages of their journey.—This is the Word of the Lord. ℞. **Thanks be to God. ℣**

Responsorial Psalm   Ps 84, 3. 4. 5-6. 8. 11

℞. (2) **How lovely is your dwelling-place, Lord, mighty God!**

My soul yearns and pines
    for the courts of the Lord.
My heart and my flesh
    cry out for the living God. — ℟

Even the sparrow finds a home,
    and the swallow a nest
    in which she puts her young—
Your altars, O Lord of hosts,
    my king and my God! — ℟

Happy they who dwell in your house!
    continually they praise you.
Happy the men whose strength you are!
    They go from strength to strength; — ℟

I had rather one day in your courts
    than a thousand elsewhere;
I had rather lie at the threshold of the house of my
    God
    than dwell in the tents of the wicked. — ℟ ℣

GOSPEL   Mt 13, 47-53

Alleluia (See Acts 16, 14)

℟. **Alleluia.** Open our hearts, O Lord,
to listen to the words of your Son. ℟. **Alleluia.**

Jesus says the reign of God is like a fisherman's dragnet which collects all sorts of things. At the end of the world, angels will go out and separate the wicked from the just.

℣. The Lord be with you. ℟. **And also with you.**
✠ A reading from the holy gospel according to Matthew. ℟. **Glory to you, Lord.**

Jesus said to the crowds: "The reign of God is also like a dragnet thrown into the lake, which collected all sorts of things. When it was full they hauled it ashore and sat down to put what was worthwhile into containers. What was useless they threw away. That is how it will be at the end of the world. Angels will go out and separate the wicked from the just and hurl the wicked into the fiery furnace, where they will wail and grind their teeth.

"Have you understood all this?" "Yes," they answered; to which he replied, "Every scribe who is learned in the reign of God is like the head of a household who can bring from his storeroom both the new and the old." When Jesus had finished this parable he moved on from that district.—This is the gospel of the Lord. ℟. **Praise to you, Lord Jesus Christ.** ➔ No. 15, p. 623

FRIDAY OF THE SEVENTEENTH WEEK IN ORDINARY TIME

READING I   Lv 23, 1. 4-11. 15-16. 27. 34-37

The Hebrews celebrate a number of feasts, commemorating events in their salvation history. God gives details as to how and when these feasts will take place.

A reading from the book of Leviticus

The Lord said to Moses, "These are the festivals of the Lord which you shall celebrate at their proper time with a sacred assembly. The Passover of the Lord falls on the fourteenth day of the first month, at the evening twilight. The fifteenth day of this month is the Lord's feast of Unleavened Bread. For seven days you shall eat unleavened bread. On the first of these days you shall hold a sacred assembly and do no sort of work. On each of the seven days you shall offer an oblation to the Lord. Then on the seventh day you shall again hold a sacred assembly and do no sort of work."

The Lord said to Moses, "Speak to the Israelites and tell them: When you come into the land which I am giving you, and reap your harvest, you shall bring a sheaf of the first fruits of your harvest to the priest, who shall wave the sheaf before the Lord that it may be acceptable for you.

"Beginning with the day after the sabbath, the day on which you bring the wave-offering sheaf, you shall count seven full weeks, and then on the day after the seventh week, the fiftieth day, you shall present the new cereal offering to the Lord. The tenth of this seventh month is the Day of Atonement, when you shall hold a sacred assembly and mortify yourselves and offer an oblation to the Lord. The fifteenth day of this seventh month is the Lord's feast of Booths, which shall continue for seven days. On the first day there shall be a sacred assembly, and you shall do no sort of work. For seven days you shall offer an oblation to the Lord, and on the eighth day you shall again hold a sacred assembly and offer an oblation to the Lord. On that solemn closing you shall do no sort of work.

"These, therefore, are the festivals of the Lord on which you shall proclaim a sacred assembly, and offer as an oblation to the Lord holocausts and cereal offerings, sacrifices and libations, as prescribed for each day."—This is the Word of the Lord. ℟. **Thanks be to God.** ✣

Responsorial Psalm   Ps 81, 3-4. 5-6. 10-11

℟. (2) **Sing with joy to God our help.**

Take up a melody, and sound the timbrel,
    the pleasant harp and the lyre.
Blow the trumpet at the new moon,
    at the full moon, on our solemn feast; — ℟

For it is a statute in Israel,
    an ordinance of the God of Jacob,
Who made it a decree for Joseph
    when he came forth from the land of Egypt. — ℟

There shall be no strange god among you
    nor shall you worship an alien god.
I, the Lord, am your God
    who led you forth from the land of Egypt. — ℟ ✣

GOSPEL   Mt 13, 54-58
Alleluia (1 Pt 1, 25)

℟. **Alleluia.** The word of the Lord stands for ever; it is the word given to you, the Good News. ℟. **Alleluia.**

Jesus goes to his native place and teaches in the synagogue, but since the people feel they know his family, they cannot accept his wisdom and miraculous powers. He says, "No prophet is without honor except in his own house."

℣. The Lord be with you. ℟. **And also with you.**
✠ A reading from the holy gospel according to Matthew. ℟. **Glory to you, Lord.**

Jesus went to his native place and spent his time teaching the people in their synagogue. They were filled with amazement, and said to one another, "Where did this man get such wisdom and miraculous powers? Isn't this the carpenter's son? Isn't Mary known to be his mother and James, Joseph, Simon, and Judas his brothers? Aren't his sisters our neighbors? Where did he get all this?" They found him altogether too much for them. Jesus said to them, "No prophet is without honor except in his native place, indeed in his own house." And he did not work many miracles there because of their lack of faith.—This is the gospel of the Lord. ℟. **Praise to you, Lord Jesus Christ.**   → No. 15, p. 623

SATURDAY OF THE SEVENTEENTH WEEK IN ORDINARY TIME

READING I   Lv 25, 1. 8-17

The Lord tells Moses on Mount Sinai: "In the fiftieth year you shall celebrate a jubilee, which shall be sacred. Each one shall return to his own property; do not deal unfairly; stand in fear of your God."

A reading from the book of Leviticus
The Lord said to Moses on Mount Sinai, "Seven

weeks of years shall you count—seven times seven years—so that the seven cycles amount to forty-nine years. Then, on the tenth day of the seventh month let the trumpet resound; on this, the Day of Atonement, the trumpet blast shall re-echo throughout your land. This fiftieth year you shall make sacred by proclaiming liberty in the land for all its inhabitants. It shall be a jubilee for you, when every one of you shall return to his own property, every one to his own family estate. In this fiftieth year, your year of jubilee, you shall not sow, nor shall you reap the aftergrowth or pick the grapes from the untrimmed vines. Since this is the jubilee, which shall be sacred for you, you may not eat of its produce, except as taken directly from the field.

"In this year of jubilee, then, every one of you shall return to his own property. Therefore, when you sell any land to your neighbor or buy any from him, do not deal unfairly. On the basis of the number of years since the last jubilee shall you purchase the land from him; and so also, on the basis of the number of years for crops, shall he sell it to you. When the years are many, the price shall be so much the more; when the years are few, the price shall be so much the less. For it is really the number of crops that he sells you. Do not deal unfairly, then; but stand in fear of your God. I, the Lord, am your God."—This is the Word of the Lord. ℞. **Thanks be to God.** ⱽ

Responsorial Psalm   Ps 67, 2-3. 5. 7-8

℞. (4) **O God, let all the nations praise you!**

May God have pity on us and bless us;
    may he let his face shine upon us.
So may your way be known upon the earth;
    among all nations, your salvation. — ℞

May the nations be glad and exult
    because you rule the peoples in equity;

the nations on the earth you guide. — ℟
The earth has yielded its fruits;
    God, our God, has blessed us.
May God bless us,
    and may all the ends of the earth fear him! — ℟ ℣

GOSPEL   Mt 14, 1-12
Alleluia (Mt 5, 10)
℟. **Alleluia.** Happy are they who suffer persecution
    for justice' sake;
the kingdom of heaven is theirs. ℟. **Alleluia.**

Herod thinks that Jesus is John the Baptizer, raised from the dead.
The Baptist had condemned Herod for having married Herodias, his
brother's wife, and for this he had been beheaded at the request of
Herodias' daughter.

℣. The Lord be with you. ℟. **And also with you.**
✠ A reading from the holy gospel according to Matthew. ℟. **Glory to you, Lord.**

On one occasion Herod the tetrarch, having heard of
Jesus' reputation, exclaimed to his courtiers, "This
man is John the Baptizer—it is he in person, raised
from the dead; that is why such miraculous powers
are at work in him!" Recall that Herod had had John
arrested, put in chains, and imprisoned on account
of Herodias, the wife of his brother Philip. That was
because John had told him, "It is not right for you
to live with her." Herod wanted to kill John but was
afraid of the people, who regarded him as a prophet.
Then on Herod's birthday Herodias' daughter performed a dance before the court which delighted
Herod so much that he swore he would grant her
anything she asked for. Prompted by her mother she
said, "Bring me the head of John the Baptizer on
a platter." The king immediately had his misgivings,
but because of his oath and the guests who were
present he gave orders that the request be granted.
He sent the order to have John beheaded in prison.
John's head was brought in on a platter and given

he withdrew by boat from there to a deserted place by himself. The crowds heard of it and followed him on foot from the towns. When he **disembarked** and saw the vast throng, his heart was moved with pity, and he cured their sick. As evening drew on, his disciples came to him with the suggestion: "This is a deserted place and it is already late. Dismiss the crowds so that they may go to the villages and buy some food for themselves." Jesus said to them: "There is no need for them to disperse. Give them something to eat yourselves." "We have nothing here," they replied, "but five loaves and a couple of fish." "Bring them here," he said. Then he ordered the crowds to sit down on the grass. He took the five loaves and two fish, looked up to heaven, blessed and broke them and gave the loaves to the disciples, who in turn gave them to **people**. All those present ate their fill. The fragments which **remained,** when gathered up, filled twelve baskets. Those who ate were about five thousand, not counting women and children.—This is the gospel of the Lord. ℟. **Praise to you, Lord Jesus Christ.** ➔ No. 15, p. 623

OR

In Year A, when the above Gospel is read on the preceding Sunday, the following Gospel (from Tuesday) is substituted:

GOSPEL Mt 14, 22-36

Alleluia (Jn 1, 49)

℟. **Alleluia.** Master, you are the Son of God, you are the king of Israel. ℟. **Alleluia.**

The disciples become frightened by the storm. Jesus appears, and Peter walks on the water at the invitation of the Lord, until his faith falters. Jesus performs more cures.

℣. The Lord be with you. ℟. **And also with you.**
✠ A reading from the holy gospel according to Matthew. ℟. **Glory to you, Lord.**

After the crowds had eaten their fill Jesus insisted that his disciples get into a boat and precede him to the other side. When he had sent them away, he went up on the mountain by himself to pray, remaining there alone as evening drew on. Meanwhile the boat, already several hundred yards out from shore, was being tossed about in the waves raised by strong headwinds. At about three in the morning, he came walking toward them on the lake. When the disciples saw him walking on the water, they were terrified. "It is a ghost!" they said, and in their fear they began to cry out. Jesus hastened to reassure them: "Get hold of yourselves! It is I. Do not be afraid!" Peter spoke up and said, "Lord, if it is really you, tell me to come to you across the water." "Come!" he said. So Peter got out of the boat and began to walk on the water, moving toward Jesus. But when he perceived how strong the wind was, becoming frightened, he began to sink and cried out, "Lord, save me!" Jesus at once stretched out his hand and caught him. "How little faith you have!" he exclaimed. "Why did you falter?" Once they had climbed into the boat, the wind died down. Those who were in the boat showed him reverence, declaring, "Undoubtedly you are the Son of God!"

After making the crossing they reached the shore at Gennesaret; and when the men of that place recognized him they spread the word throughout the region. People brought him all the afflicted, with the plea that he let them do no more than touch the tassel of his cloak. As many as touched it were fully restored to health.—This is the gospel of the Lord.
℟. **Praise to you, Lord Jesus Christ.** ➔ No. 15, p. 623

TUESDAY OF THE EIGHTEENTH WEEK
IN ORDINARY TIME

READING I   Nm 12, 1-13

Miriam and Aaron, good people though they are, make the foolish mistake of speaking against Moses, God's chosen one. The Lord is angry at their boldness until Moses himself joins Aaron in pleading for their forgiveness.

A reading from the book of Numbers

Miriam and Aaron spoke against Moses on the pretext of the marriage he had contracted with a Cushite woman. They complained, "Is it through Moses alone that the Lord speaks? Does he not speak through us also?" And the Lord heard this. Now, Moses himself was by far the meekest man on the face of the earth. So at once the Lord said to Moses and Aaron and Miriam, "Come out, you three, to the meeting tent." And the three of them went. Then the Lord came down in the column of cloud, and standing at the entrance of the tent, called Aaron and Miriam. When both came forward, he said, "Now listen to the words of the Lord:

Should there be a prophet among you,
    in visions will I reveal myself to him,
    in dreams will I speak to him;
Not so with my servant Moses!
Throughout my house he bears my trust:
    face to face I speak to him,
    plainly and not in riddles.
The presence of the Lord he beholds.

Why, then, did you not fear to speak against my servant Moses?"

So angry was the Lord against them that when he departed, and the cloud withdrew from the tent, there was Miriam, a snow-white leper! When Aaron turned and saw her a leper, "Ah, my lord!" he said to Moses, "please do not charge us with the sin that we have foolishly committed! Let her not thus be like the stillborn babe that comes forth from its mother's womb with its flesh half consumed." Then Moses cried to the Lord, "Please, not this! Pray, heal her!"—This is the Word of the Lord. ℟. **Thanks be to God.** ℣

Responsorial Psalm   Ps 51, 3-4. 5-6. 6-7. 12-13

℟. (3) **Be merciful, O Lord, for we have sinned.**

Have mercy on me, O God, in your goodness;
   in the greatness of your compassion wipe out my
      offense.
Thoroughly wash me from my guilt
   and of my sin cleanse me. — ℟

For I acknowledge my offense,
   and my sin is before me always:
"Against you only have I sinned
   and done what is evil in your sight" — ℟

That you may be justified in your sentence,
   vindicated when you condemn.
Indeed, in guilt was I born,
   and in sin my mother conceived me. — ℟

A clean heart create for me, O God,
   and a steadfast spirit renew within me.
Cast me not out from your presence,
   and your holy spirit take not from me. — ℟ ℣

GOSPEL   Mt 14, 22-36

Alleluia (Jn 1, 49)

℟. **Alleluia.** Master, you are the Son of God,
you are the king of Israel. ℟. **Alleluia.**

The disciples become frightened by the storm. Jesus appears, and Peter walks on the water at the invitation of the Lord, until his faith falters. Jesus performs more cures.

℣. The Lord be with you. ℟. **And also with you.**
✠ A reading from the holy gospel according to Matthew. ℟. **Glory to you, Lord.**

After the crowds had eaten their fill Jesus insisted that his disciples get into a boat and precede him to the other side. When he had sent them away, he went up on the mountain by himself to pray, remaining there alone as evening drew on. Meanwhile the boat, already several hundred yards out from shore, was being tossed about in the waves raised by strong headwinds. At about three in the morning, he came walking toward them on the lake. When the disciples saw him walking on the water, they were terrified. "It is a ghost!" they said, and in their fear they began to cry out. Jesus hastened to reassure them: "Get hold of yourselves! It is I. Do not be afraid!" Peter spoke up and said, "Lord, if it is really you, tell me to come to you across the water." "Come!" he said. So Peter got out of the boat and began to walk on the water, moving toward Jesus. But when he perceived how strong the wind was, becoming frightened, he began to sink and cried out, "Lord, save me!" Jesus at once stretched out his hand and caught him. "How little faith you have!" he exclaimed. "Why did you falter?" Once they had climbed into the boat, the wind died down. Those who were in the boat showed him reverence, declaring, "Undoubtedly you are the Son of God!"

After making the crossing they reached the shore at Gennesaret; and when the men of that place recognized him they spread the word throughout the region. People brought him all the afflicted, with the plea that he let them do no more than touch the tassel of his cloak. As many as touched it were fully restored to health.—This is the gospel of the Lord.
℟. **Praise to you, Lord Jesus Christ.** ➤ No. 15, p. 623

OR

The following text may be substituted especially in year A when the above gospel is read on Monday.

GOSPEL Mt 15, 1-2. 10-14
Alleluia (Jn 1, 49)
℟. **Alleluia.** Master, you are the Son of God, you are the king of Israel. ℟. **Alleluia.**

Jesus answer the scribes about their tradition of washing. A man is defiled by his inner thoughts. Jesus reminds them that only the teaching of his Father will last.

℣. The Lord be with you. ℟. **And also with you.**
✠ A reading from the holy gospel according to Matthew. ℟. **Glory to you, Lord.**

The scribes from Jerusalem approached Jesus with the question: "Why do your disciples act contrary to the tradition of our ancestors? They do not wash their hands, for example, before eating a meal."

Jesus summoned the crowd and said to them: "Give ear and try to understand. It is not what goes into a man's mouth that makes him impure; it is what comes out of his mouth." His disciples approached him and said, "Do you realize the Pharisees were scandalized when they heard your pronouncement?" "Every planting not put down by my heavenly Father will be uprooted," he replied. "Let them go their way; they are blind leaders of the blind. If one blind man leads another, both will end in a pit." —This is the gospel of the Lord. ℟. **Praise to you, Lord Jesus Christ.** ➤ No. 15, p. 623

WEDNESDAY OF THE EIGHTEENTH WEEK IN ORDINARY TIME

READING I   Nm 13, 1-2. 25—14, 1. 26-29. 34-35

The Israelites have every reason to trust in the Lord no matter how powerful the foe, and yet they doubt him. He punishes them by letting their worst fears become realities. Only Joshua and Caleb will survive the long wilderness wanderings, and they will lead the people into the land.

A reading from the book of Numbers

The Lord said to Moses in the desert of Paran, "Send men to reconnoiter the land of Canaan, which I am giving the Israelites." After reconnoitering the land for forty days they returned, met Moses and

Aaron and the whole community of the Israelites in the desert of Paran at Kadesh, made a report to them all, and showed them the fruit of the country. They told Moses: "We went into the land to which you sent us. It does indeed flow with milk and honey, and here is its fruit. However, the people who are living in the land are fierce, and the towns are fortified and very strong. Besides, we saw descendants of the Anakim there. Amalekites live in the region of the Negeb; Hittites, Jebusites and Amorites dwell in the highlands, and Canaanites along the seacoast and the banks of the Jordan."

Caleb, however, to quiet the people toward Moses, said, "We ought to go up and seize the land, for we can certainly do so." But the men who had gone up with him said, "We cannot attack these people; they are too strong for us." So they spread discouraging reports among the Israelites about the land they had scouted, saying, "The land that we explored is a country that consumes its inhabitants. And all the people we saw there are huge men, veritable giants [the Anakim were a race of giants]; we felt like mere grasshoppers, and so we must have seemed to them."

At this, the whole community broke out with loud cries, and even in the night the people wailed.

The Lord said to Moses and Aaron: "How long will this wicked community grumble against me? I have heard the grumblings of the Israelites against me. Tell them: By my life, says the Lord, I will do to you just what I have heard you say. Here in the desert shall your dead bodies fall. Forty days you spent in scouting the land; forty years shall you suffer for your crimes: one year for each day. Thus you will realize what it means to oppose me. I, the Lord, have sworn to do this to all this wicked community that conspired against me: here in the desert they shall die to the last man."—This is the Word of the Lord. ℟. **Thanks be to God.** ℣

Responsorial Psalm   Ps 106, 6-7. 13-14. 21-22. 23

℟. (4) **Lord, remember us,**
   for the love you bear your people.

We have sinned, we and our fathers;
   we have committed crimes; we have done wrong.
Our fathers in Egypt
   considered not your wonders. — ℟

But soon they forgot his works;
   they waited not for his counsel.
They gave way to craving in the desert
   and tempted God in the wilderness. — ℟

They forgot the God who had saved them,
   who had done great deeds in Egypt,
Wondrous deeds in the land of Ham,
   terrible things at the Red Sea. — ℟

Then he spoke of exterminating them,
   but Moses, his chosen one,
Withstood him in the breach
   to turn back his destructive wrath. — ℟ ❧

℟. Or: **Alleluia.** ❧

GOSPEL   Mt 15, 21-28

Alleluia (Lk 7, 16)

℟. **Alleluia.** A great prophet has risen among us;
God has visited his people. ℟. **Alleluia.**

Faith and persistence find the Lord's favor even when his first response seems to be rejection. The Canaanite woman's faith overcomes
Jesus' test and wins health for her daughter.

℣. The Lord be with you. ℟. **And also with you.**
✠ A reading from the holy gospel according to Matthew. ℟. **Glory to you, Lord.**

Jesus withdrew to the district of Tyre and Sidon. It
happened that a Canaanite woman living in that locality presented herself, crying out to him, "Lord,
Son of David, have pity on me! My daughter is terribly troubled by a demon." He gave her no word

of response. His disciples came up and began to entreat him, "Get rid of her. She keeps shouting after us." "My mission is only to the lost sheep of the house of Israel," Jesus replied. She came forward then and did him homage with the plea, "Help me, Lord!" But he answered, "It is not right to take the food of sons and daughters and throw it to the dogs." "Please, Lord," she insisted, "even the dogs eat the leavings that fall from their masters' tables." Jesus then said in reply, "Woman, you have great faith! Your wish will come to pass." That very moment her daughter got better.—This is the gospel of the Lord. ℟. **Praise to you, Lord Jesus Christ.**

➤ No. 15, p. 623

THURSDAY OF THE EIGHTEENTH WEEK IN ORDINARY TIME

READING I Nm 20, 1-13

The Israelites lose their faith-vision and complain against the good the Lord has done for them. Even Moses and Aaron are doubtful. It takes a miracle to move them on toward the promised land.

A reading from the book of Numbers

The whole Israelite community arrived in the desert of Zin in the first month, and the people settled at Kadesh. It was here that Miriam died, and here that she was buried.

As the community had no water, they held a council against Moses and Aaron. The people contended with Moses, exclaiming, "Would that we too had perished with our kinsmen in the Lord's presence! Why have you brought the Lord's community into this desert where we and our livestock are dying? Why did you lead us out of Egypt, only to bring us to this wretched place which has neither grain nor figs nor vines nor pomegranates? Here there is not even water to drink!" But Moses and Aaron went away from the assembly to the entrance of the meeting tent, where they fell prostrate.

Then the glory of the Lord appeared to them, and the Lord said to Moses, "Take the staff and assemble the community, you and your brother Aaron, and in their presence order the rock to yield its waters. From the rock you shall bring forth water for the community and their livestock to drink." So Moses took the staff from its place before the Lord, as he was ordered. He and Aaron assembled the community in front of the rock, where he said to them, "Listen to me, you rebels! Are we to bring water for you out of this rock?" Then, raising his hand, Moses struck the rock twice with his staff, and water gushed out in abundance for the community and their livestock to drink. But the Lord said to Moses and Aaron, "Because you were not faithful to me in showing forth my sanctity before the Israelites, you shall not lead this community into the land I will give them."

These are the waters of Meribah, where the Israelites contended against the Lord, and where he revealed his sanctity among them.—This is the Word of the Lord. ℟. **Thanks be to God.** ℣

Responsorial Psalm   Ps 95, 1-2. 6-7. 8-9

℟. (8) **If today you hear his voice,**
  harden not your hearts.

Come, let us sing joyfully to the Lord;
  let us acclaim the Rock of our salvation.
Let us greet him with thanksgiving;
  let us joyfully sing psalms to him. — ℟

Come, let us bow down in worship;
  let us kneel before the Lord who made us.
For he is our God,
  and we are the people he shepherds, the flock he
    guides. — ℟

Oh, that today you would hear his voice:
"Harden not your hearts as at Meribah,
   as in the day of Massah in the desert,
Where your fathers tempted me;
   they tested me though they had seen my
      works." — ℟ ℣

GOSPEL   Mt 16, 13-23

Alleluia (Mt 16, 18)

℟. **Alleluia.** You are Peter, the rock on which I will
      build my Church;
the gates of hell will not hold out against it. ℟. **Alleluia.**

When Peter speaks the truth the Father has revealed to him, Jesus
endows him with power. When Peter clouds the issue by introducing
his own distorted notions, Jesus reprimands him for abandoning God's
viewpoint in favor of his own.

℣. The Lord be with you. ℟. **And also with you.**
✠ A reading from the holy gospel according to Matthew. ℟. **Glory to you, Lord.**

When Jesus came to the neighborhood of Caesarea
Philippi, he asked his disciples this question: "Who
do people say that the Son of Man is?" They replied,
"Some say John the Baptizer, others Elijah, still
others Jeremiah or one of the prophets." "And you,"
he said to them, "who do you say that I am?" "You
are the Messiah," Simon Peter answered, "the Son
of the living God!" Jesus replied, "Blest are you,
Simon son of John! No mere man has revealed this
to you, but my heavenly Father. I for my part declare to you, you are 'Rock,' and on this rock I will
build my church, and the jaws of death shall not
prevail against it. I will entrust to you the keys of
the kingdom of heaven. Whatever you declare bound
on earth shall be bound in heaven; whatever you declare loosed on earth shall be loosed in heaven."
Then he strictly ordered his disciples not to tell anyone that he was the Messiah.

From then on Jesus [the Messiah] started to indicate to his disciples that he must go to Jerusalem to suffer greatly there at the hands of the elders. the chief priests, and the scribes, and to be put to death, and raised up on the third day. At this, Peter took him aside and began to remonstrate with him. "May you be spared, Master! God forbid that any such thing ever happen to you!" Jesus turned on Peter and said, "Get out of my sight, you satan! You are trying to make me trip and fall. You are not judging by God's standards but by man's."—This is the gospel of the Lord. ℟. **Praise to you, Lord Jesus Christ.**

➤ No. 15, p. 623

FRIDAY OF THE EIGHTEENTH WEEK
IN ORDINARY TIME

READING I Dt 4, 32-40

Because of the constant wonders God works among his people Israel, they have to acknowledge him as their God. They have to keep his commandments if they are to continue to receive his blessings.

A reading from the book of Deuteronomy

Moses said to the people: "Ask now of the days of old, before your time, ever since God created man upon the earth; ask from one end of the sky to the other: Did anything so great ever happen before? Was it ever heard of? Did a people ever hear the voice of God speaking from the midst of fire, as you did, and live? Or did any God venture to go and take a nation for himself from the midst of another nation, by testings, by signs and wonders, by war, with his strong hand and outstretched arm, and by great terrors, all of which the Lord, your God, did for you in Egypt before your very eyes? All this you were allowed to see that you might know the Lord is God and there is no other. Out of the heavens he

let you hear his voice to discipline you; on earth he let you see his great fire, and you heard him speaking out of the fire. For love of your fathers he chose their descendants and personally led you out of Egypt by his great power, driving out of your way nations greater and mightier than you, so as to bring you in and to make their land your heritage, as it is today. This is why you must now know, and fix in your heart, that the Lord is God in the heavens above and on earth below, and that there is no other. You must keep his statutes and commandments which I enjoin on you today, that you and your children after you may prosper, and that you may have long life on the land which the Lord, your God, is giving you forever."—This is the Word of the Lord.
℟. **Thanks be to God.** ℣

Responsorial Psalm   Ps 77, 12-13. 14-15. 16. 21

℟. (12) **I remember the deeds of the Lord.**

I remember the deeds of the Lord;
　　yes, I remember your wonders of old.
And I meditate on your works;
　　your exploits I ponder. — ℟

O God, your way is holy;
　　what great god is there like our God?
You are the God who works wonders;
　　among the peoples you have made known your
　　　　power. — ℟

With your strong arm you redeemed your people,
　　the sons of Jacob and Joseph.
You led your people like a flock
　　under the care of Moses and Aaron. — ℟ ℣

GOSPEL   Mt 16, 24-28

Alleluia (Mt 5, 10)

℟. **Alleluia.** Happy are they who suffer for justice'
　　sake;
the kingdom of heaven is theirs. ℟. **Alleluia.**

The cost of discipleship is great, but its rewards are greater still. What can be more valuable than salvation? To follow Jesus a man must be willing to take up his cross. This is the way to salvation.

℣. The Lord be with you. ℟. **And also with you.**

✠ A reading from the holy gospel according to Matthew. ℟. **Glory to you, Lord.**

Jesus said to his disciples: "If a man wishes to come after me, he must deny his very self, take up his cross, and begin to follow in my footsteps. Whoever would save his life will lose it, but whoever loses his life for my sake will find it. What profit would a man show if he were to gain the whole world and ruin himself in the process? What can a man offer in exchange for his very self? The Son of Man will come with his Father's glory accompanied by his angels. When he does, he will repay each man according to his conduct. I assure you, among those standing here there are some who will not experience death before they see the Son of Man come in his kingship."—This is the gospel of the Lord. ℟. **Praise to you, Lord Jesus Christ.**   ➤ No. 15, p. 623

SATURDAY OF THE EIGHTEENTH WEEK IN ORDINARY TIME

READING I   Dt 6, 4-13

Moses sums up here the whole covenant of the Lord and his people: "The Lord is our God, the Lord alone." He has made them his special people. In return, they are to love and serve him with all they are and all they have.

A reading from the book of Deuteronomy
Moses said to the people: "Hear, O Israel! The Lord is our God, the Lord alone! Therefore, you shall love the Lord, your God, with all your heart, and with all your soul, and with all your strength. Take to heart these words which I enjoin on you today. Drill them into your children. Speak of them at home and abroad, whether you are busy or at rest. Bind them

at your wrist as a sign and let them be as a pendant on your forehead. Write them on the doorposts of your houses and on your gates.

"When the Lord, your God, brings you into the land which he swore to your fathers, Abraham, Isaac and Jacob, that he would give you, a land with fine, large cities that you did not build, with houses full of goods of all sorts that you did not garner, with cisterns that you did not dig, with vineyards and olive groves that you did not plant; and when, therefore, you eat your fill, take care not to forget the Lord, who brought you out of the land of Egypt, that place of slavery. The Lord, your God, shall you fear; him shall you serve, and by his name shall you swear."—This is the Word of the Lord. ℞. **Thanks be to God.** ℣

Responsorial Psalm   Ps 18, 2-3. 3-4. 47. 51

℞. (2) **I love you, Lord, my strength.**

I love you, O Lord, my strength,
    O Lord, my rock, my fortress, my deliverer. — ℞
My God, my rock of refuge,
    my shield, the horn of my salvation, my strong-
        hold!
Praised be the Lord, I exclaim,
    and I am safe from my enemies. — ℞

The Lord live! And blessed be my rock!
    Extolled be God my savior.
You who gave great victories to your king
    and showed kindness to your anointed,
        to David and his posterity forever. — ℞ ℣

GOSPEL   Mt 17, 14-20

Alleluia (2 Tm 1, 10)

℞. **Alleluia.** Our Savior Jesus Christ has done away
        with death,
and brought us life through his gospel. ℞. **Alleluia.**

Good intentions are not enough. It is faith and faith alone which makes all things possible. Nothing is impossible to God and to the man who has real faith in him. Jesus expels the demon.

℣. The Lord be with you. ℟. **And also with you.**

✠ A reading from the holy gospel according to Matthew. ℟. **Glory to you, Lord.**

A man came up to Jesus and knelt before him. "Lord," he said, "take pity on my son, who is demented and in a serious condition. For example, he often falls into the fire and frequently into the water. I have brought him to your disciples but they could not cure him." In reply Jesus said: "What an unbelieving and perverse lot you are! How long must I remain with you? How long can I endure you? Bring him here to me!" Then Jesus reprimanded him, and the demon came out of him. That very moment the boy was cured.

The disciples approached Jesus at that point and asked him privately, "Why could we not expel it?" "Because you have so little trust," he told them. "I assure you, if you had faith the size of a mustard seed, you would be able to say to this mountain, 'Move from here to there,' and it would move. Nothing would be impossible for you."—This is the gospel of the Lord. ℟. **Praise to you, Lord Jesus Christ.**

MONDAY OF THE NINETEENTH WEEK
IN ORDINARY TIME

READING I   Dt 10, 12-22

Moses inspires his people to action by recalling the great works the Lord has done for them and the great love with which he has done it all. The people chosen by such a God must treat others as their God has treated them.

A reading from the book of Deuteronomy

Moses said to the people: "And now, Israel, what does the Lord, your God, ask of you but to fear the

Lord, your God, and follow his ways exactly, to love and serve the Lord, your God, with all your heart and all your soul, to keep the commandments and statutes of the Lord which I enjoin on you today for your own good? Think! The heavens, even the highest heavens, belong to the Lord, your God, as well as the earth and everything on it. Yet in his love for your fathers the Lord was so attached to them as to choose you, their descendants, in preference to all other peoples, as indeed he has now done. Circumcise your hearts, therefore, and be no longer stiff-necked. For the Lord, your God, is the God of gods, the Lord of lords, the great God, mighty and awesome, who has no favorites, accepts no bribes; who executes justice for the orphan and the widow, and befriends the alien, feeding and clothing him. So you too must befriend the alien, for you were once aliens yourselves in the land of Egypt. The Lord, your God, shall you fear, and him shall you serve; hold fast to him and swear by his name. He is your glory, he, your God, who has done for you those great and terrible things which your own eyes have seen. Your ancestors went down to Egypt seventy strong, and now the Lord, your God, has made you as numerous as the stars of the sky."— This is the Word of the Lord. ℞. **Thanks be to God.** ℣

Responsorial Psalm　　Ps 147, 12-13. 14-15. 19-20

℞. (12) **Praise the Lord, Jerusalem.**

Glorify the Lord, O Jerusalem;
　praise your God, O Zion.
For he has strengthened the bars of your gates;
　he has blessed your children within you. — ℞

He has granted peace in your borders;
　with the best of wheat he fills you.
He sends forth his command to the earth;
　swiftly runs his word! — ℞

He has proclaimed his word to Jacob,

his statutes and his ordinances to Israel.
He has not done thus for any other nation;
his ordinances he has not made known to them.
Alleluia. — ℟ ℣

℟. Or: **Alleluia.** ℣

GOSPEL   Mt 17, 22-27

Alleluia (2 Thes 2, 14)
℟. **Alleluia.** God has called us with the gospel;
the people won for him by Jesus Christ our Lord.
℟. **Alleluia.**

Jesus reveals his coming death and resurrection. He uses the practical
question of a temple tax to teach a lesson about freedom as sons of
the Father. He observes this particular law, but shows that in spirit
it does not really bind him who created heaven and earth.

℣. The Lord be with you. ℟. **And also with you.**
✠ A reading from the holy gospel according to Matthew. ℟. **Glory to you, Lord.**

When Jesus and the disciples met in Galilee, he said
to them, "The Son of Man is going to be delivered
into the hands of men who will put him to death,
and he will be raised up on the third day." At these
words they were overwhelmed with grief.

When they entered Capernaum, the collectors of
the temple tax approached Peter and said, "Does
your master not pay the temple tax?" "Of course he
does," Peter replied. Then Jesus on entering the
house asked, without giving him time to speak:
"What is your opinion, Simon? Do the kings of the
world take tax or toll from their sons, or from
foreigners?" When he replied, "From foreigners,"
Jesus observed: "Then their sons are exempt. But
for fear of disedifying them go to the lake, throw
in a line, and take out the first fish you catch. Open
its mouth and you will discover there a coin worth
twice the temple tax. Take it and give it to them for
you and me."—This is the gospel of the Lord. ℟.
Praise to you, Lord Jesus Christ.   ➔ No. 15, p. 623

TUESDAY OF THE NINETEENTH WEEK
IN ORDINARY TIME

READING I   Dt 31, 1-8

Moses has led his people to the promised land; he now passes the
command to Joshua for the actual entry. Each had his specific calling,
but both from the same Lord and united in him with each other.

A reading from the book of Deuteronomy

When Moses finished speaking to all Israel, he said
to them, "I am now one hundred and twenty years
old and am no longer able to move about freely;
besides, the Lord has told me that I shall not cross
this Jordan. It is the Lord, your God, who will cross
before you; he will destroy these nations before you,
that you may supplant them. [It is Joshua who will
cross before you, as the Lord promised.] The Lord
will deal with them just as he dealt with Sihon and
Og, the kings of the Amorites whom he destroyed,
and with their country. When, therefore, the Lord
delivers them up to you, you must deal with them
exactly as I have ordered you. Be brave and steadfast; have no fear or dread of them, for it is the
Lord, your God, who marches with you; he will never
fail you or forsake you."

Then Moses summoned Joshua and in the presence
of all Israel said to him, "Be brave and steadfast, for
you must bring this people into the land which the
Lord swore to their fathers he would give them;
you must put them in possession of their heritage.
It is the Lord who marches before you; he will be
with you and will never fail you or forsake you. So
do not fear or be dismayed."—This is the Word of
the Lord. ℟. **Thanks be to God.** ↓

Responsorial Psalm   Dt 32, 3-4. 7. 8. 9. 12

℟. (9) **The portion of the Lord is his people.**

For I will sing the Lord's renown.
   Oh, proclaim the greatness of our God!

The Rock—how faultless are his deeds,
  how right all his ways! — ℟

Think back on the days of old,
  reflect on the years of age upon age.
Ask your father and he will inform you,
  ask your elders and they will tell you. — ℟

When the Most High assigned the nations their heri-
    tage,
  when he parceled out the descendants of Adam,
He set up the boundaries of the peoples
  after the number of the sons of God. — ℟

While the Lord's own portion was Jacob,
  his hereditary share was Israel.
The Lord alone was their leader,
  no strange god was with him. — ℟ ℣

GOSPEL   Mt 18, 1-5. 10. 12-14
Alleluia (Mt 11, 29)
℟. **Alleluia.** Take my yoke upon you;
learn from me, for I am gentle and lowly in heart.
        ℟. **Alleluia.**

God is greatly concerned about his little ones. Little children, the
lowly, the childlike, the wandering sinner are all objects of the Lord's
special love and interest. Followers of Jesus should reflect the same
hierarchy of values.

℣. The Lord be with you. ℟. **And also with you.**
✠ A reading from the holy gospel according to Matthew. ℟. **Glory to you, Lord.**

The disciples came up to Jesus with the question,
"Who is of greatest importance in the kingdom of
God?" He called a little child over and stood him in
their midst and said: "I assure you, unless you
change and become like little children, you will not
enter the kingdom of God. Whoever makes himself
lowly, becoming like this child, is of greatest importance in that heavenly reign.

  "Whoever welcomes one such child for my sake
welcomes me. See that you never despise one of

these little ones. I assure you, their angels in heaven constantly behold my heavenly Father's face.

"What is your thought on this: A man owns a hundred sheep and one of them wanders away; will he not leave the ninety-nine out on the hills and go in search of the stray? If he succeeds in finding it, believe me he is happier about this one than about the ninety-nine that did not wander away. Just so, it is no part of your heavenly Father's plan that a single one of these little ones shall ever come to grief."—This is the gospel of the Lord. ℟. **Praise to you, Lord Jesus Christ.**   ➔ No. 15, p. 623

WEDNESDAY OF THE NINETEENTH WEEK IN ORDINARY TIME

READING I   Dt 34, 1-12

Moses was the greatest prophet and leader of all Israelite history. God worked fully through him. Though unable to enter the promised land, he dies praising the Lord. His death is mourned by the whole nation.

A reading from the book of Deuteronomy

Moses went up from the plains of Moab to Mount Nebo, the headland of Pisgah which faces Jericho, and the Lord showed him all the land—Gilead, and as far as Dan, all Naphtali, the land of Ephraim and Manasseh, all the land of Judah as far as the Western Sea, the Negeb, the circuit of the Jordan with the lowlands at Jericho, city of palms, and as far as Zoar. The Lord then said to him, "This is the land which I swore to Abraham, Isaac and Jacob that I would give to their descendants. I have let you feast your eyes upon it, but you shall not cross over." So there, in the land of Moab, Moses, the servant of the Lord, died as the Lord had said; and he was buried in the ravine opposite Beth-peor in the land of Moab, but to this day no one knows the place of his burial.

Moses was one hundred and twenty years old when he died, yet his eyes were undimmed and his vigor unabated. For thirty days the Israelites wept for Moses in the plains of Moab, till they had completed the period of grief and mourning for Moses.

Now Joshua, son of Nun, was filled with the spirit of wisdom, since Moses had laid his hands upon him; and so the Israelites gave him their obedience, thus carrying out the Lord's command to Moses.

Since then no prophet has arisen in Israel like Moses, whom the Lord knew face to face. He had no equal in all the signs and wonders the Lord sent him to perform in the land of Egypt against Pharaoh and all his servants and against all his land, and for the might and the terrifying power that Moses exhibited in the sight of all Israel.—This is the Word of the Lord. ℟. **Thanks be to God.** ℣

Responsorial Psalm   Ps 66, 1-3. 5. 8. 16-17

℟. (20. 9) **Blessed be God who filled my soul with fire!**

Shout joyfully to God, all you on earth,
  sing praise to the glory of his name;
  proclaim his glorious praise.
Say to God, "How tremendous are your deeds!"—℟

Come and see the works of God,
  his tremendous deeds among men.
Bless our God, you peoples,
  loudly sound his praise. — ℟

Hear now, all you who fear God, while I declare
  what he has done for me.
When I appealed to him in words,
  praise was on the tip of my tongue. — ℟ ℣

GOSPEL   Mt 18, 15-20

Alleluia (2 Cor 5, 19)

℟. **Alleluia.** God was in Christ, to reconcile the world
  to himself;

and the Good News of reconciliation he has entrusted to us. ℟. **Alleluia.**

Jesus encourages fraternal correction, privately if possible, but failing that, along with others or with the assistance of the Church. There is something special about groups gathered in Christ's name; he is there in the midst of them.

℣. The Lord be with you. ℟. **And also with you.**
✠ A reading from the holy gospel according to Matthew. ℟. **Glory to you, Lord.**

Jesus said to his disciples: "If your brother should commit some wrong against you, go and point out his fault, but keep it between the two of you. If he listens to you, you have won your brother over. If he does not listen, however, summon another, so that every case may stand on the word of two or three witnesses. If he ignores them refer it to the church. If he ignores even the church, then treat him as you would a Gentile or a tax collector. I assure you, whatever you declare bound on earth shall be held bound in heaven, and whatever you declare loosed on earth shall be held loosed in heaven.

"Again I tell you, if two of you join your voices on earth to pray for anything whatever, it shall be granted you by my Father in heaven. Where two or three are gathered in my name, there am I in their midst."—This is the gospel of the Lord. ℟. **Praise to you, Lord Jesus Christ.**   ➨ No. 15, p. 623

THURSDAY OF THE NINETEENTH WEEK IN ORDINARY TIME

READING I   Jos 3, 7-10. 11. 13-17

Joshua is the great leader who carries on the work of Moses. As Moses led them through the Red Sea out of Egypt, Joshua leads them through the Jordan into the promised land.

A reading from the book of Joshua
The Lord said to Joshua, "Today I will begin to exalt

you in the sight of all Israel, that they may know I am with you, as I was with Moses. Now command the priests carrying the ark of the covenant to come to a halt in the Jordan when they reach the edge of the waters."

So Joshua said to the Israelites, "Come here and listen to the words of the Lord, your God." He continued: "This is how you will know that there is a living God in your midst, who at your approach will dispossess the Canaanites. The ark of the covenant of the Lord of the whole earth will precede you into the Jordan. When the soles of the feet of the priests carrying the ark of the Lord, the Lord of the whole earth, touch the water of the Jordan, it will cease to flow; for the water flowing down from upstream will halt in a solid bank."

The people struck their tents to cross the Jordan, with the priests carrying the ark of the covenant ahead of them. No sooner had these priestly bearers of the ark waded into the waters at the edge of the Jordan, which overflows all its banks during the entire season of the harvest, than the waters flowing from upstream halted, backing up in a solid mass for a very great distance indeed, from Adam, a city in the direction of Zarethan; while those flowing downstream toward the Salt Sea of the Arabah disappeared entirely. Thus the people crossed over opposite Jericho. While all Israel crossed over on dry ground, the priests carrying the ark of the covenant of the Lord remained motionless on dry ground in the bed of the Jordan until the whole nation had completed the passage.—This is the Word of the Lord. ℟. **Thanks be to God.** ℣

Responsorial Psalm   Ps 114, 1-2. 3-4. 5-6
℟. **Alleluia.**

When Israel came forth from Egypt,
   the house of Jacob from a people of alien tongue,

Judah became his sanctuary,
　　Israel his domain. — ℟
The sea beheld and fled;
　　Jordan turned back.
The mountains skipped like rams,
　　the hills like the lambs of the flock. — ℟
Why is it, O sea, that you flee?
　　O Jordan, that you turn back?
You mountains, that you skip like rams?
　　You hills, like the lambs of the flock? — ℟ ℣

GOSPEL Mt 18, 21—19, 1
Alleluia (Ps 119, 135)
℟. **Alleluia.** Let your face shine on your servant,
and teach me your laws. ℟. **Alleluia.**

God's forgiveness knows no limit, and men should forgive each other
just as readily. Jesus teaches the lesson of forgiveness by the parable
of the debtor.

℣. The Lord be with you. ℟. **And also with you.**
✠ A reading from the holy gospel according to Matthew. ℟. **Glory to you, Lord.**

Peter came up to Jesus and asked him, "Lord, when
my brother wrongs me, how often must I forgive
him? Seven times?" "No," Jesus replied, "not seven
times; I say, seventy times seven times. That is why
the reign of God may be said to be like a king who
decided to settle accounts with his officials. When
he began his auditing, one was brought in who owed
him a huge amount. As he had no way of paying it,
his master ordered him to be sold, along with his
wife, his children, and all his property, in payment
of the debt. At that the official prostrated himself
in homage and said, 'My lord, be patient with me
and I will pay you back in full.' Moved with pity,
the master let the official go and wrote off the debt.
But when that same official went out he met a fellow servant who owed him a mere fraction of what

he himself owed. He seized him and throttled him. 'Pay back what you owe,' he demanded. His fellow servant dropped to his knees and began to plead with him, 'Just give me time and I will pay you back in full.' But he would hear none of it. Instead, he had him put in jail until he paid back what he owed. When his fellow servants saw what had happened they were badly shaken, and went to their master to report the whole incident. His master sent for him and said, 'You worthless wretch! I canceled your entire debt when you pleaded with me. Should you not have dealt mercifully with your fellow servant, as I dealt with you?' Then in anger the master handed him over to the torturers until he paid back all that he owed. My heavenly Father will treat you in exactly the same way unless each of you forgives his brother from his heart."

When Jesus had finished this discourse, he left Galilee and came to the district of Judea across the Jordan.—This is the gospel of the Lord. ℟. **Praise to you, Lord Jesus Christ.**   ➔ No. 15, p. 623

FRIDAY OF THE NINETEENTH WEEK
IN ORDINARY TIME

READING I   Jos 24, 1-13

The Lord had formed Israel into a people, led them out of bondage, and brought them to the promised land. Joshua here reviews for them all the Lord has done on their behalf.

A reading from the book of Joshua

Joshua gathered together all the tribes of Israel at Shechem, summoning their elders, their leaders, their judges and their officers. When they stood in ranks before God, Joshua addressed all the people: "Thus says the Lord, the God of Israel: In times past your fathers, down to Terah, father of Abraham and Nahor, dwelt beyond the River and served other gods. But I brought your father Abraham from the region beyond the River and led him through the entire land of Canaan. I made his descendants numerous, and gave him Isaac. To Isaac I gave Jacob and Esau. To Esau I assigned the mountain region of Seir in which to settle, while Jacob and his children went down to Egypt.

"Then I sent Moses and Aaron, and smote Egypt with the prodigies which I wrought in her midst. Afterward I led you out of Egypt, and when you reached the sea, the Egyptians pursued your fathers to the Red Sea with chariots and horsemen. Because they cried out to the Lord, he put darkness between your people and the Egyptians, upon whom he brought the sea so that it engulfed them. After you witnessed what I did to Egypt, and dwelt a long time in the desert, I brought you into the land of the Amorites who lived east of the Jordan. They fought against you, but I delivered them into your power. You took possession of their land, and I destroyed them [the two kings of the Amorites] before you. Then Balak, son of Zippor, king of Moab, prepared to war against Israel. He summoned Balaam, son of Beor, to curse you; but I would not listen to Balaam. On the contrary, he had to bless you, and I saved you from him. Once you crossed the Jordan and came to Jericho, the men of Jericho fought against you, but I delivered them also into your power. And I sent the hornets ahead of you which drove them [the Amorites, Perizzites, Canaanites, Hittites, Girgashites, Hivites and Jebusites] out of your way; it was not your sword or your bow.

"I gave you a land which you had not tilled and cities which you had not built, to dwell in; you have eaten of vineyards and olive groves which you did not plant."—This is the Word of the Lord. ℟. **Thanks be to God.** ℣

Responsorial Psalm   Ps 136, 1-3. 16-18. 21-22. 24

℟. **His love is everlasting.**

Give thanks to the Lord, for he is good,
  for his mercy endures forever;
Give thanks to the God of gods,
  for his mercy endures forever;
Give thanks to the Lord of lords,
  for his mercy endures forever. — ℟

Who led his people through the wilderness,
  for his mercy endures forever;
Who smote great kings,
  for his mercy endures forever;
And slew powerful kings,
  for his mercy endures forever. — ℟

And made their land a heritage,
  for his mercy endures forever;
The heritage of Israel his servant,
  for his mercy endures forever;
And freed us from our foes,
  for his mercy endures forever. — ℟ ∀

℟. Or: **Alleluia.** ∀

GOSPEL   Mt 19, 3-12
Alleluia (1 Thes 2, 13)

℟. **Alleluia.** Receive this message not as the words
  of man,
but as truly the word of God. ℟. **Alleluia.**

From the beginning God made them male and female. Even if for a
time divorce was permitted because of the hardness of men's hearts, this
was not the Creator's intention. Let those who can accept this teaching
do so.

℣. The Lord be with you. ℟. **And also with you.**
✠ A reading from the holy gospel according to Matthew. ℟. **Glory to you, Lord.**

Some Pharisees came up to Jesus and said, to test
him, "May a man divorce his wife for any reason
whatever?" He replied, "Have you not read that at

the beginning the Creator made them male and female and declared, 'For this reason a man shall
leave his father and mother and cling to his wife,
and the two shall become as one'? Thus they are no
longer two but one flesh. Therefore, let no man
separate what God has joined." They said to him,
"Then why did Moses command divorce and the promulgation of a divorce decree?" "Because of your
stubbornness Moses let you divorce your wives," he
replied; "but at the beginning it was not that way.
I now say to you, whoever divorces his wife (lewd
conduct is a separate case) and marries another commits adultery, and the man who marries a divorced
woman commits adultery."

His disciples said to him, "If that is the case between man and wife, it is better not to marry." He
said, "Not everyone can accept this teaching, only
those to whom it is given to do so. Some men are
incapable of sexual activity from birth; some have
been deliberately made so; and some there are who
have freely renounced sex for the sake of God's
reign. Let him accept this teaching who can."—This
is the gospel of the Lord. ℟. **Praise to you, Lord
Jesus Christ.**   ➔ No. 15, p. 623

SATURDAY OF THE NINETEENTH WEEK
IN ORDINARY TIME

READING I   Jos 24, 14-29

Near the end of his life, Joshua moves his people to profess their
choice of the Lord as their God. They renounce false gods and set
up a large stone in the sanctuary as a sign of their covenant.

A reading from the book of Joshua

Joshua said to the people, "Fear the Lord and serve
him completely and sincerely. Cast out the gods your
fathers served beyond the River and in Egypt, and

serve the Lord. If it does not please you to serve the Lord, decide today whom you will serve, the gods your fathers served beyond the River or the gods of the Amorites in whose country you are dwelling. As for me and my household, we will serve the Lord."

But the people answered, "Far be it from us to forsake the Lord for the service of other gods. For it was the Lord, our God, who brought us and our fathers up out of the land of Egypt, out of a state of slavery. He performed those great miracles before our very eyes and protected us along our entire journey and among all the peoples through whom we passed. At our approach the Lord drove out [all the peoples, including] the Amorites who dwelt in the land. Therefore we also will serve the Lord, for he is our God."

Joshua in turn said to the people, "You may not be able to serve the Lord, for he is a holy God; he is a jealous God who will not forgive your transgressions or your sins. If, after the good he has done for you, you forsake the Lord and serve strange gods, he will do evil to you and destroy you."

But the people answered Joshua, "We will still serve the Lord." Joshua therefore said to the people, "You are your own witnesses that you have chosen to serve the Lord." They replied, "We are, indeed!" [Joshua continued:] "Now, therefore, put away the strange gods that are among you and turn your hearts to the Lord, the God of Israel." Then the people promised Joshua, "We will serve the Lord, our God, and obey his voice."

So Joshua made a covenant with the people that day and made statutes and ordinances for them at Shechem, which he recorded in the book of the law of God. Then he took a large stone and set it up there under the oak that was in the sanctuary of the Lord. And Joshua said to all the people, "This stone shall be our witness, for it has heard all the words which the Lord spoke to us. It shall be a witness against you, should you wish to deny your God" Then Joshua dismissed the people, each to his own heritage.

After these events, Joshua, son of Nun, servant of the Lord, died at the age of a hundred and ten.— This is the Word of the Lord. ℟. **Thanks be to God.** ℣

Responsorial Psalm   Ps 16, 1-2. 5. 7-8. 11

℟. **You are my inheritance, O Lord.**

Keep me, O God, for in you I take refuge;
    I say to the Lord, "My Lord are you.
    Apart from you I have no good."
O Lord, my allotted portion and my cup,
    you it is who hold fast my lot. — ℟

I bless the Lord who counsels me;
    even in the night my heart exhorts me.
I set the Lord ever before me;
    with him at my right hand I shall not be disturbed. — ℟

You will show me the path to life,
    fullness of joys in your presence,
    the delights at your right hand forever. — ℟ ℣

GOSPEL   Mt 19, 13-15

Alleluia (Mt 11, 25)

℟. **Alleluia.** Blessed are you, Father, Lord of heaven
    and earth;
you have revealed to little ones the mysteries of the
    kingdom. ℟. **Alleluia.**

Jesus' special concern for his little ones is shown when he welcomes the children despite the disciples' protest. He sees in them the simplicity and humility that characterizes the kingdom of God.

℣. The Lord be with you. ℟. **And also with you.**
✠ A reading from the holy gospel according to Matthew. ℟. **Glory to you, Lord.**

Children were brought to Jesus so that he could place his hands on them in prayer. The disciples began to scold them, but Jesus said, "Let the children come to me. Do not hinder them. The kingdom of God belongs to such as these." And he laid his hands on their heads before he left that place.—This is the gospel of the Lord. ℟. **Praise to you, Lord Jesus Christ.**   ➔ No. 15, p. 623

INTRODUCTION FOR 20th TO 24th WEEK

The Book of Joshua—*Like the books which precede it in the Bible, this book was built up by a long and complex process of editing traditional materials. It derives its name from the successor of Moses, with whose deeds it is principally concerned. The purpose of the book is to demonstrate God's fidelity in giving to the Israelites the land he had promised them for an inheritance. The entire history of the conquest of the Promised Land is a prophecy of the spiritual conquest of the world through the Church under the leadership of Jesus the Messiah.*

The Book of Judges—*Its title stems from the twelve heroes of Israel whose deeds it records. They were not magistrates, but military leaders sent by God to aid and to relieve his people in time of external danger. They exercised their activities in the interval of time between the death of Joshua and the institution of the monarchy in Israel. The purpose of the book is to show that the fortunes of Israel de-*

pended upon the obedience of the people to God's law. Whenever they rebelled against him, they were oppressed by pagan nations; when they repented, he raised up judges to deliver them (cf Jgs 2, 10-23).

The Book of Ruth—*This book is named after the Moabite woman who was joined to the Israelite people by her marriage with the influential Boaz of Bethlehem. Its aim is to demonstrate the divine reward for such piety even when practiced by a stranger. Ruth's piety, her spirit of self-sacrifice, and her moral integrity were favored by God with the gift of faith and an illustrious marriage whereby she became the ancestress of David and of Christ. In this, the universality of the messianic salvation is foreshadowed.*

The First Epistle to the Thessalonians—*Written in 51 or 52 A.D., this is regarded as the earliest of Paul's works. After reminding the Thessalonians of his work among them and of his affection for them, Paul urges them to preserve purity and charity, in expectation of the resurrection which will happen when least expected. The Epistle is of great doctrinal value, revealing as it does the faith of the community. It also manifests the care and labor which were expended in instructing the Christian communities in New Testament times.*

The Gospel of Luke—*Many scholars discern in the Lucan Gospel and Acts of the Apostles an apologetic strain presumably directed against unfounded criticisms of Christian teaching. Written after the persecution of Nero that began in 64 A.D. and caused hostility toward Christians throughout the empire, Luke-Acts reveal that Jesus himself was accounted innocent by the Roman governor Pontius Pilate (Lk 23, 4. 15. 22), and that St. Paul, founder of many Christian communities in the empire, was often acquitted by the Roman magistrates of charges against him (Acts 16, 36; 18, 12-17; 25, 26; 26, 32).*

The evangelist portrays Christianity, not as a political movement, nor as a sect organized for an initiated few, but as a religious faith open to all men. His portrait of Jesus, drawn from the Gospel tradition, manifests the Savior's concern for humanity, and his identification with the poor, the outcast, and the criminal. Although the apologetic thought in Luke's writings must be acknowledged, it was nevertheless not his chief purpose to produce an apology for Christianity.

Luke wants to present the history of salvation from the beginnings of the world until the return of Christ. For Luke, this history comprises three great periods which he clearly distinguishes: "The Law and the Prophets were in force until John" (16, 16); the time of Christ, from his coming on earth until his Ascension; finally, the time of the Church whose foundations were laid in the preceding period, and which is unfolding fully from that time on.

In this history it is the coming of Christ that marks the truly decisive turning point; it constitutes the "middle of the times." During the time of expectation men had fixed their eyes on the "middle of the times" that was to come. During the time of the Church, men look backward with their eyes on Jesus. The life of Jesus becomes for the Church a sort of prototype of her own life and a model for every member. It is a question of realizing, of fulfilling from day to day, what Jesus has lived and what he has taught (9, 23), until his final return.

The Epistle to the Colossians—*Written by Paul during his first Roman captivity (61-63 A.D.), this Epistle has as its theme the preeminence of Christ. To counter errors that have been spread about, Paul sets forth in clear terms the true doctrine concerning Christ, our Redeemer, head of the mystical body, the Church, and draws up rules for an ideal Christian life. Between these two positive sections he inserts a vigorous condemnation of the false teachings.*

The First Epistle to Timothy—*The two Epistles to Timothy and the one to Titus are called the Pastoral Epistles because they are addressed directly, not to any church as a group, but to its head or pastor for his guidance in the rule of the Church. This first Epistle was written between Paul's liberation from the first imprisonment (63 A.D.) and his death (67 A.D.) and has a twofold purpose: to provide guidance in the problems of Church administration and to oppose false teaching of a speculative and moralistic type.*

MONDAY OF THE TWENTIETH WEEK
IN ORDINARY TIME

READING I   Jgs 2, 11-19

Despite their previous promises of fidelity, the Israelites lapse into the worship of false gods. Over and over the same cycle occurs: the people abandon the Lord, he punishes them, they repent, he forgives them, and then they abandon him again.

A reading from the book of Judges

The Israelites offended the Lord by serving the Baals. Abandoning the Lord, the God of their fathers, who had led them out of the land of Egypt, they followed the other gods of the various nations around them, and by their worship of these gods provoked the Lord.

Because they had thus abandoned him and served Baal and the Ashtaroth, the anger of the Lord flared up against Israel, and he delivered them over to plunderers who despoiled them. He allowed them to fall into the power of their enemies round about whom they were no longer able to withstand. Whatever they undertook, the Lord turned into disaster for them, as in his warning he had sworn he would do, till they were in great distress. Even when the Lord raised up judges to deliver them from the power of their despoilers, they did not listen to their judges, but abandoned themselves to the worship of other gods. They were quick to stray from the way their fathers had taken, and did not follow their example of obedience to the commandments of the Lord. Whenever the Lord raised up judges for them, he would be with the judge and save them from the power of their enemies as long as the judge lived; it was thus the Lord took pity on their distressful cries of affliction under their oppressors. But when the judge died, they would relapse and do worse than their fathers, following other gods in service and worship, relinquishing none of their evil practices or stubborn conduct.—This is the Word of the Lord. ℞. **Thanks be to God.** ℣

Responsorial Psalm Ps 106, 34-35. 36-37. 39-40. 43. 44

℞. (4) **Lord, remember us,**
for the love you bear your people.

They did not exterminate the peoples,
as the Lord had commanded them,
But mingled with the nations
and learned their works. — ℞

They served their idols,
which became a snare for them.
They sacrificed their sons
and their daughters to demons. — ℞

They became defiled by their works,
and wanton in their crimes.

And the Lord grew angry with his people,
  and abhorred his inheritance. — ℟

Many times did he rescue them,
  but they embittered him with their counsels.
Yet he had regard for their affliction
  when he heard their cry. — ℟ ✟

GOSPEL   Mt 19, 16-22

Alleluia (Mt 5, 3)

℟. **Alleluia.** Happy the poor in spirit;
the kingdom of heaven is theirs. ℟. **Alleluia.**

The rich young man sincerely seeks perfection. He keeps all the commandments, but his possessions block him from taking the further step of full renunciation. He departs in sadness.

℣. The Lord be with you. ℟. **And also with you.**

✠ A reading from the holy gospel according to Matthew. ℟. **Glory to you, Lord.**

A man came up to Jesus and said, "Teacher, what good must I do to possess everlasting life?" He answered, "Why do you question me about what is good? There is One who is good. If you wish to enter into life, keep the commandments." "Which ones?" he asked. Jesus replied, " 'You shall not kill'; 'You shall not commit adultery'; 'You shall not steal'; 'You shall not bear false witness'; 'Honor your father and your mother'; and 'Love your neighbor as yourself.' " The young man said to him, "I have kept all these; what do I need to do further?" Jesus told him, "If you seek perfection, go, sell your possessions, and give to the poor. You will then have treasure in heaven. After that, come back and follow me." Hearing these words, the young man went away sad, for his possessions were many.—This is the gospel of the Lord. ℟. **Praise to you, Lord Jesus Christ.**

➤ No. 15, p. 623

TUESDAY OF THE TWENTIETH WEEK
IN ORDINARY TIME

READING I   Jgs 6, 11-24

The Lord chooses a weak, insignificant man like Gideon to be an instrument of deliverance for his people. Gideon, unsure, receives a sign of his election and becomes strong with the strength of the Lord.

A reading from the book of Judges

The angel of the Lord came and sat under the terebinth in Ophrah that belonged to Joash the Abiezrite. While his son Gideon was beating out wheat in the wine press to save it from the Midianites, the angel of the Lord appeared to him and said, "The Lord is with you, O champion!" "My lord," Gideon said to him, "if the Lord is with us, why has all this happened to us? Where are his wondrous deeds of which our fathers told us when they said, 'Did not the Lord bring us up from Egypt?' For now the Lord has abandoned us and has delivered us into the power of Midian." The Lord turned to him and said, "Go with the strength you have and save Israel from the power of Midian. It is I who send you." But he answered him, "Please, my lord, how can I save Israel? My family is the meanest in Manasseh, and I am the most insignificant in my father's house." "I shall be with you," the Lord said to him, "and you will cut down Midian to the last man." He answered him, "If I find favor with you, give me a sign that you are speaking with me. Do not depart from here, I pray you, until I come back to you and bring out my offering and set it before you." He answered, "I will await your return."

So Gideon went off and prepared a kid and an ephah of flour in the form of unleavened cakes. Putting the meat in a basket and the broth in a pot, he brought them out to him under the terebinth and presented them. The angel of God said to him, "Take the meat and unleavened cakes and lay them on this rock; then pour out the broth." When he had done so, the angel of the Lord stretched out the tip of the staff he held, and touched the meat and unleavened cakes. Thereupon a fire came up from the rock which consumed the meat and unleavened cakes, and the angel of the Lord disappeared from sight. Gideon, now aware that it had been the angel of the Lord, said, "Alas, Lord God, that I have seen the angel of the Lord face to face!" The Lord answered him, "Be calm, do not fear. You shall not die." So Gideon built there an altar to the Lord and called it Yahweh-shalom.—This is the Word of the Lord. ℟. **Thanks be to God.** ℣

Responsorial Psalm   Ps 85, 9. 11-12. 13-14

℟. (9) **The Lord speaks of peace to his people.**

I will hear what God proclaims;
    the Lord—for he proclaims peace
To his people, and to his faithful ones,
    and to those who put in him their hope. — ℟

Kindness and truth shall meet;
    justice and peace shall kiss.
Truth shall spring out of the earth,
    and justice shall look down from heaven. — ℟

The Lord himself will give his benefits;
    our land shall yield its increase.
Justice shall walk before him,
    and salvation, along the way of his steps. — ℟ ℣

GOSPEL   Mt 19, 23-30

Alleluia (2 Cor 8, 9)

℟. **Alleluia.** Jesus Christ was rich but he became poor,
to make you rich out of his poverty. ℟. **Alleluia.**

It is difficult for the rich to enter the kingdom of heaven, though for God nothing is impossible. God's values are different from man's. Jesus teaches that it is the poor in spirit who will be exalted and the last who will come first.

℣. The Lord be with you. ℟. **And also with you.**
✠ A reading from the holy gospel according to Matthew. ℟. **Glory to you, Lord.**

Jesus said to his disciples: "I assure you, only with difficulty will a rich man enter into the kingdom of God. I repeat what I said: it is easier for a camel to pass through a needle's eye than for a rich man to enter the kingdom of God." When the disciples heard this they were completely overwhelmed, and exclaimed, "Then who can be saved?" Jesus looked at them and said, "For man it is impossible; but for God all things are possible." Then it was Peter's turn to say to him: "Here we have put everything aside to follow you. What can we expect from it?" Jesus said to them: "I give you my solemn word, in the new age when the Son of Man takes his seat upon a throne befitting his glory, you who have followed me shall likewise take your places on twelve thrones to judge the twelve tribes of Israel. Moreover, everyone who has given up home, brothers or sisters, father or mother, wife or children or property for my sake will receive many times as much and inherit everlasting life. Many who are first shall come last, and the last shall come first."—This is the gospel of the Lord. ℟. **Praise to you, Lord Jesus Christ.** ➤ No. 15, p. 623

WEDNESDAY OF THE TWENTIETH WEEK IN ORDINARY TIME

READING I Jgs 9, 6-15

Jotham, inspired by the Lord, protests the election of Abimelech as king. Jotham's fable of the trees seeking a king likens Abimelech to a thornbush and forebodes evil times for those over whom he would reign.

A reading from the book of Judges

All the citizens of Shechem and all Beth-millo came together and proceeded to make Abimelech king by the terebinth at the memorial pillar in Shechem.

When this was reported to him, Jotham went to the top of Mount Gerizim, and standing there, cried out to them in a loud voice: "Hear me, citizens of Shechem, that God may then hear you! Once the trees went to anoint a king over themselves. So they said to the olive tree, 'Reign over us.' But the olive tree answered them, 'Must I give up my rich oil, whereby men and gods are honored, and go to wave over the trees?' Then the trees said to the fig tree, 'Come; you reign over us!' But the fig tree answered them, 'Must I give up my sweetness and my good fruit, and go to wave over the trees?' Then the trees said to the vine, 'Come you, and reign over us.' But the vine answered them, 'Must I give up my wine that cheers gods and men, and go to wave over the trees?' Then all the trees said to the buckthorn, 'Come; you reign over us!' But the buckthorn replied to the trees, 'If you wish to anoint me king over you in good faith, come and take refuge in my shadow. Otherwise, let fire come from the buckthorn and devour the cedars of Lebanon.'"—This is the Word of the Lord. ℟. **Thanks be to God.** ℣

Responsorial Psalm   Ps 21, 2-3. 4-5. 6-7

℟. (2) **Lord, your strength gives joy to the king.**

O Lord, in your strength the king is glad;
   in your victory how greatly he rejoices!
You have granted him his heart's desire;
   you refused not the wish of his lips. — ℟

For you welcomed him with goodly blessings,
   you placed on his head a crown of pure gold.
He asked life of you: you gave him
   length of days forever and ever. — ℟

Great is his glory in your victory;
   majesty and splendor you conferred upon him.
For you made him a blessing forever;
   you gladdened him with the joy of your presence. — ℟ ℣

GOSPEL Mt 20, 1-16

Alleluia (Heb 4, 12)

℞. **Alleluia.** The word of God is living and active; it probes the thoughts and motives of our heart. ℞. **Alleluia.**

Jesus uses the parable of the owner of an estate and how he hires his workers. The master chooses to pay equally all whom he has hired to work in his vineyard, regardless of the length of their service. Jesus emphasizes the rights of the owner and how the first shall be last and the last first.

℣. The Lord be with you. ℞. **And also with you.**

✠ A reading from the holy gospel according to Matthew. ℞. **Glory to you, Lord.**

Jesus told his disciples this parable: "The reign of God is like the case of the owner of an estate who went out at dawn to hire workmen for his vineyard. After reaching an agreement with them for the usual daily wage, he sent them out to his vineyard. He came out about midmorning and saw other men standing around the marketplace without work, so he said to them, 'You too go along to my vineyard and I will pay you whatever is fair.' At that they went away. He came out again around noon and midafternoon and did the same. Finally, going out in late afternoon he found still others standing around. To these he said, 'Why have you been standing here idle all day?' 'No one has hired us,' they told him. He said, 'You go to the vineyard too.' When evening came the owner of the vineyard said to his foreman, 'Call the workmen and give them their pay, but begin with the last group and end with the first.' When those hired late in the afternoon came up they received a full day's pay, and when the first group appeared they supposed they would get more; yet they received the same daily wage. Thereupon they complained to the owner, 'This last group did only an hour's work, but you have put them on the same basis as us who have worked a full day in the scorching heat.' 'My friend,' he said to one in reply, 'I do you no injustice. You agreed on the usual wage, did you not? Take your pay and go home. I intend to give this man who was hired last the same pay as you. I am free to do as I please with my money, am I not? Or are you envious because I am generous?' Thus the last shall be the first and the first shall be last."— This is the gospel of the Lord. ℞. **Praise to you, Lord Jesus Christ.** ➔ No. 15, p. 623

THURSDAY OF THE TWENTIETH WEEK IN ORDINARY TIME

READING I Jgs 11, 29-39

Jephthah is another chosen instrument of the Lord. With the Lord's help, he defeats the Ammonites. In his fidelity he fulfills a strange and very difficult vow, even though it means the sacrifice of his only child.

A reading from the book of Judges

The spirit of the Lord came upon Jephthah. He passed through Gilead and Manasseh, and through Mizpah-Gilead as well, and from there he went on to the Ammonites. Jephthah made a vow to the Lord. "If you deliver the Ammonites into my power," he said, "whoever comes out of the doors of my house to meet me when I return in triumph from the Ammonites shall belong to the Lord. I shall offer him up as a holocaust."

Jephthah then went on to the Ammonites to fight against them, and the Lord delivered them into his power, so that he inflicted a severe defeat on them, from Aroer to the approach of Minnith (twenty cities in all) and as far as Abel-keramin. Thus were the Ammonites brought into subjection by the Israelites. When Jephthah returned to his house in Mizpah, it was his daughter who came forth, playing the tambourines and dancing. She was an only child: he had neither son nor daughter besides her. When he saw her, he rent his garments and said, "Alas, daughter,

you have struck me down and brought calamity upon me. For I have made a vow to the Lord and I cannot retract." "Father," she replied, "you have made a vow to the Lord. Do with me as you have vowed, because the Lord has wrought vengeance for you on your enemies the Ammonites." Then she said to her father, "Let me have this favor. Spare me for two months, that I may go off down the mountains to mourn my virginity with my companions." "Go," he replied, and sent her away for two months. So she departed with her companions and mourned her virginity on the mountains. At the end of the two months she returned to her father, who did to her as he had vowed.—This is the Word of the Lord. ℟.
Thanks be to God. ℣

Responsorial Psalm   Ps 40, 5. 7-8. 8-9. 10
℟. (8. 9) **Here am I, Lord;**
  I come to do your will.

Happy the man who makes the Lord his trust;
  who turns not to idolatry
  or to those who stray after falsehood. — ℟
Sacrifice or oblation you wished not,
  but ears open to obedience you gave me.
Holocausts or sin-offerings you sought not;
  then said I, "Behold I come"; — ℟
"In the written scroll it is prescribed for me.
  To do your will, O my God, is my delight,
  and your law is within my heart!" — ℟
I announced your justice in the vast assembly;
  I did not restrain my lips, as you, O Lord,
    know. — ℟ ℣

GOSPEL   Mt 22, 1-14
Alleluia (Ps 95, 8)
℟. **Alleluia.** If today you hear his voice,
harden not your hearts. ℟. **Alleluia.**

Jesus explains the reign of God. When the invited guests make excuses and do not come to the banquet, the king destroys them and invites the poor and the simple. Yet even the man who accepts his generosity must put on the necessary wedding garment of sanctifying grace or he will be punished while the others feast.

℣. The Lord be with you. ℟. **And also with you.**

✠ A reading from the holy gospel according to Matthew. ℟. **Glory to you, Lord.**

Jesus began to address the chief priests and elders of the people, once more using parables. "The reign of God may be likened to a king who gave a wedding banquet for his son. He dispatched his servants to summon the invited guests to the wedding, but they refused to come. A second time he sent other servants, saying: 'Tell those who are invited, See, I have my dinner prepared! My bullocks and corn-fed cattle are killed; everything is ready. Come to the feast.' Some ignored the invitation and went their way, one to his farm, another to his business. The rest laid hold of his servants, insulted them, and killed them. At this the king grew furious and sent his army to destroy those murderers and burn their city. Then he said to his servants: 'The banquet is ready, but those who were invited were unfit to come. That is why you must go out into the byroads and invite to the wedding anyone you come upon.' The servants then went out into the byroads and rounded up everyone they met, bad as well as good. This filled the wedding hall with banqueters.

"When the king came in to meet the guests, however, he caught sight of a man not properly dressed for a wedding feast. 'My friend,' he said, 'how is it you came in here not properly dressed?' The man had nothing to say. The king then said to the attendants, 'Bind him hand and foot and throw him out into the night to wail and grind his teeth.' The invited are many, the elect are few."—This is the gospel of the Lord. ℟. **Praise to you, Lord Jesus Christ.**   ➔ No. 15, p. 623

FRIDAY OF THE TWENTIETH WEEK
IN ORDINARY TIME

READING I   Ru 1, 1. 3-6. 14-16. 22

Ruth is an exceptionally faithful woman who remains with her mother-in-law through all difficulties. She is a model of devotion to a loved one even when it means great personal sacrifice.

The beginning of the book of Ruth

Once in the time of the judges there was a famine in the land; so a man from Bethlehem of Judah departed with his wife and two sons to reside on the plateau of Moab. Elimelech, the husband of Naomi, died, and she was left with her two sons, who married Moabite women, one named Orpah, the other Ruth. When they had lived there about ten years, both Mahlon and Chilion died also, and the woman was left with neither her two sons nor her husband. She then made ready to go back from the plateau of Moab because word reached her there that the Lord had visited his people and given them food.

Orpah kissed her mother-in-law good-bye, but Ruth stayed with her.

"See now!" she said, "your sister-in-law has gone back to her people and her god. Go back after your sister-in-law!" But Ruth said, "Do not ask me to abandon or forsake you! for wherever you go I will go, wherever you lodge I will lodge, your people shall be my people, and your God my God."

Thus it was that Naomi returned with the Moabite daughter-in-law, Ruth, who accompanied her back from the plateau of Moab. They arrived in Bethlehem at the beginning of the barley harvest.—This is the Word of the Lord. ℟. **Thanks be to God.** ↓

Responsorial Psalm   Ps 146, 5-6. 7. 8-9. 9-10

℟. (2) **Praise the Lord, my soul!**

Happy he whose help is the God of Jacob,
  whose hope is in the Lord, his God,
Who made heaven and earth,
  the sea and all that is in them; — ℟

Who keeps faith forever,
  secures justice for the oppressed,
  gives food to the hungry.
The Lord sets captives free; — ℟

The Lord gives sight to the blind.
  The Lord raises up those that were bowed down;
  the Lord loves the just.
The Lord protects strangers; — ℟

The fatherless and the widow he sustains,
  but the way of the wicked he thwarts.
The Lord shall reign forever;
  your God, O Zion, through all generations. Alle-
    luia. — ℟ ℣

℟. Or: **Alleluia.** ℣

GOSPEL   Mt 22, 34-40

Alleluia (Ps 25, 4. 5)

℟. **Alleluia.** Teach me your paths, my God,
and lead me in your truth. ℟. **Alleluia.**

Jesus turns an attempt by the Pharisees to trap him into an occasion
to state a sublime truth; the two great commandments of love of God
and love of neighbor are the basis of the whole law.

℣. The Lord be with you. ℟. **And also with you.**
✠ A reading from the holy gospel according to Matthew. ℟. **Glory to you, Lord.**

When the Pharisees heard that Jesus had silenced
the Sadducees, they assembled in a body; and one
of them, a lawyer, in an attempt to trip him up, asked
him, "Teacher, which commandment of the law is
the greatest?" Jesus said to him:
    " 'You shall love the Lord your God
      with your whole heart,

with your whole soul,
and with all your mind.'
This is the greatest and first commandment. The second is like it:

'You shall love your neighbor as yourself.'

On these two commandments the whole law is based, and the prophets as well."—This is the gospel of the Lord. ℟. **Praise to you, Lord Jesus Christ.**

➤ No. 15, p. 623

SATURDAY OF THE TWENTIETH WEEK IN ORDINARY TIME

READING I   Ru 2, 1-3. 8-11; 4, 13-17

Boaz is impressed with what he has heard of Ruth's fidelity, and he takes her as his wife. Thus she who was originally a Moabitess becomes part of the line which will produce David and eventually the Messiah.

A reading from the book of Ruth

Naomi had a prominent kinsman named Boaz, of the clan of her husband Elimelech. Ruth the Moabite said to Naomi, "Let me go and glean ears of grain in the field of anyone who will allow me that favor." Naomi said to her, "Go, my daughter," and she went. The field she entered to glean after the harvesters happened to be the section belonging to Boaz of the clan of Elimelech.

Boaz said to Ruth, "Listen, my daughter! Do not go to glean in anyone else's field; you are not to leave here. Stay here with my woman servants. Watch to see which field is to be harvested, and follow them; I have commanded the young men to do you no harm. When you are thirsty, you may go and drink from the vessels the young men have filled." Casting herself prostrate upon the ground, she said to him, "Why should I, a foreigner, be favored with your notice?" Boaz answered her: "I have had a complete account of what you have done for your mother-in-law after your husband's death; you have left your father and your mother and the land of your birth, and have come to a people whom you did not know previously."

Boaz took Ruth. When they came together as man and wife, the Lord enabled her to conceive and she bore a son. Then the women said to Naomi, "Blessed is the Lord who has not failed to provide you today with an heir! May he become famous in Israel! He will be your comfort and the support of your old age, for his mother is the daughter-in-law who loves you. She is worth more to you than seven sons!" Naomi took the child, placed him on her lap, and became his nurse. And the neighbor women gave him his name, at the news that a grandson had been born to Naomi. They called him Obed. He was the father of Jesse, the father of David.—This is the Word of the Lord. Ry. **Thanks be to God.** ℣

Responsorial Psalm   Ps 128, 1-2. 3. 4. 5

Ry. (4) **See how the Lord blesses those who fear him.**

Happy are you who fear the Lord,
    who walk in his ways!
For you shall eat the fruit of your handiwork;
    happy shall you be, and favored. — Ry

Your wife shall be like a fruitful vine
    in the recesses of your home;
Your children like olive plants
    around your table. — Ry

Behold, thus is the man blessed
    who fears the Lord. — Ry

The Lord bless you from Zion:
    may you see the prosperity of Jerusalem
    all the days of your life. — Ry ℣

GOSPEL   Mt 23, 1-12

Alleluia (Mt 23, 9. 10)

℟. **Alleluia.** You have one Father, your Father in heaven;

you have one teacher: the Lord Jesus Christ! ℟. **Alleluia.**

Jesus identifies the scribes and Pharisees as men who say the right things but do not live them out in their lives. They should practice what they preach. Those who seek honor and high positions at times even want to usurp the worship and respect due to God alone. There is only one Lord, one God.

℣. The Lord be with you. ℟. **And also with you.**

✠ A reading from the holy gospel according to Matthew. ℟. **Glory to you, Lord.**

Jesus told the crowds and his disciples: "The scribes and the Pharisees have succeeded Moses as teachers; therefore, do everything and observe everything they tell you. But do not follow their example. Their words are bold but their deeds are few. They bind up heavy loads, hard to carry, to lay on other men's shoulders, while they themselves will not lift a finger to budge them. All their works are performed to be seen. They widen their phylacteries and wear huge tassels. They are fond of places of honor at banquets and the front seats in synagogues, of marks of respect in public and of being called 'Rabbi.' As to you, avoid the title 'Rabbi.' One among you is your teacher, the rest are learners. Do not call anyone on earth your father. Only one is your father, the One in heaven. Avoid being called teachers. Only one is your teacher, the Messiah. The greatest among you will be the one who serves the rest. Whoever exalts himself shall be humbled, but whoever humbles himself shall be exalted."—This is the gospel of the Lord. ℟. **Praise to you, Lord Jesus Christ.**

➤ No. 15, p. 623

MONDAY OF THE TWENTY-FIRST WEEK
IN ORDINARY TIME

READING I 1 Thes 1, 2-5. 8-10

Paul has preached the good news of Jesus Christ to the Thessalonians, and the Holy Spirit is very much at work among them. Paul's selfless efforts have nurtured a growth among these people which continues even when he is away from them.

A reading from the first letter of Paul to the Thessalonians

We constantly remember you in our prayers, for we are mindful before our God and Father of the way you are proving your faith, laboring in love, and showing constancy in hope in our Lord Jesus Christ. We know, too, brothers beloved of God, how you were chosen. Our preaching of the gospel proved not a mere matter of words for you but one of power; it was carried on in the Holy Spirit and out of complete conviction. You know as well as we do what we proved to be like when, while still among you, we acted on your behalf.

This is true not only in Macedonia and Achaia; throughout every region your faith in God is celebrated, which makes it needless for us to say anything more. The people of those parts are reporting what kind of reception we had from you and how you turned to God from idols, to serve him who is the living and true God and to await from heaven the Son he raised from the dead—Jesus, who delivers us from the wrath to come.—This is the Word of the Lord. ℞. **Thanks be to God.** ℣

Responsorial Psalm Ps 149, 1-2. 3-4. 5-6. 9

℞. (4) **The Lord takes delight in his people.**

Sing to the Lord a new song
of praise in the assembly of the faithful.
Let Israel be glad in their maker,
let the children of Zion rejoice in their king. — ℞

Let them praise his name in the festive dance,
    let them sing praise to him with timbrel and harp.
For the Lord loves his people,
    and he adorns the lowly with victory. — ℟

Let the faithful exult in glory;
    let them sing for joy upon their couches;
    let the high praises of God be in their throats.
    This is the glory of all his faithful. Alleluia.—℟ ℣

℟. Or: **Alleluia.** ℣

GOSPEL   **Alleluia** (Jn 10, 27)   Mt 23, 13-22

℟. **Alleluia.** My sheep listen to my voice, says the
    Lord;
I know them, and they follow me. ℟. **Alleluia.**

The one group of people Jesus confronts again and again are the
scribes and Pharisees. He cannot stand their hypocrisy, and he denounces them in no uncertain terms, especially attacking their
emphasis on the external to the neglect of the internal.

℣. The Lord be with you. ℟. **And also with you.**
✠ A reading from the holy gospel according to Matthew. ℟. **Glory to you, Lord.**

Jesus said, "Woe to you scribes and Pharisees, you
frauds! You shut the doors of the kingdom of God
in men's faces, neither entering yourselves nor ad-
mitting those who are trying to enter. Woe to you
scribes and Pharisees, you frauds! You travel over
sea and land to make a single convert, but once he
is converted you make a devil of him twice as wicked
as yourselves. It is an evil day for you, blind guides!
You declare, 'If a man swears by the temple it means
nothing, but if he swears by the gold of the temple
he is obligated.' Blind fools! Which is more important, the gold or the temple which makes it sacred? Again you declare, 'If a man swears by the
altar it means nothing, but if he swears by the gift
on the altar he is obligated.' How blind you are!
Which is more important, the offering or the altar
which makes the offering sacred? The man who

swears by the altar is swearing by it and by everything on it. The man who swears by the temple is swearing by it and by him who dwells there. The man who swears by heaven is swearing by God's throne and by him who is seated on that throne."— This is the gospel of the Lord. ℟. **Praise to you, Lord Jesus Christ.** ➤ No. 15, p. 623

TUESDAY OF THE TWENTY-FIRST WEEK IN ORDINARY TIME

READING I   1 Thes 2, 1-8

Paul was the kind of man who could bounce back from failure and come on strong. This was because his strength was from the Lord He always preached Jesus Christ, not himself, and that is why his preaching had such far-reaching effects.

A reading from the first letter of Paul to the Thessalonians

You know well enough, brothers, that our coming among you was not without effect. Fresh from the humiliation we had suffered at Philippi—about which you know—we drew courage from our God to preach his good tidings to you in the face of great opposition. The exhortation we deliver does not spring from deceit or impure motives or any sort of trickery; rather, having met the test imposed on us by God, as men entrusted with the good tidings we speak like those who strive to please God, "the tester of our hearts," rather than men.

We were not guilty, as you well know, of flattering words or greed under any pretext, as God is our witness! Neither did we seek glory from men, you or any others, even though we could have insisted on our own importance as apostles of Christ.

On the contrary, while we were among you we were as gentle as any nursing mother fondling her little ones. So well disposed were we to you, in fact, that we wanted to share with you not only God's tidings but our very lives, so dear had you become to us.—This is the Word of the Lord. ℟. **Thanks be to God.** ℣

Responsorial Psalm   Ps 139, 1-3. 4-6

℟. (1) **You have searched me and you know me, Lord.**

O Lord, you have probed me and you know me;
  you know when I sit and when I stand;
  you understand my thoughts from afar.
My journeys and my rest you scrutinize,
  with all my ways you are familiar. — ℟

Even before a word is on my tongue,
  behold, O Lord, you know the whole of it.
Behind me and before, you hem me in
  and rest your hand upon me.
Such knowledge is too wonderful for me;
  too lofty for me to attain. — ℟ ℣

GOSPEL   Mt 23, 23-26

Alleluia (Heb 4, 12)

℟. **Alleluia.** The word of God is living and active;
it probes the thoughts and motives of our heart.
    ℟. **Alleluia.**

Jesus upbraids the scribes and Pharisees for having such a twisted set of values, especially for not being able to distinguish what is of primary importance and what is peripheral. Their double standard not only is their own downfall, but it also leads others to destruction.

℣. The Lord be with you. ℟. **And also with you.**
✠ A reading from the holy gospel according to Matthew. ℟. **Glory to you, Lord.**

Jesus said: "Woe to you scribes and Pharisees, you frauds! You pay tithes on mint and herbs and seeds while neglecting the weightier matters of the law, justice and mercy and good faith. It is these you should have practiced, without neglecting the others.

  "Blind guides! You strain out the gnat and swallow the camel! Woe to you scribes and Pharisees, you frauds! You cleanse the outside of cup and dish, and leave the inside filled with loot and lust! Blind Pharisee! First cleanse the inside of the cup so that its outside may be clean."—This is the gospel of the Lord. ℟. **Praise to you, Lord Jesus Christ.**

➤ No. 15, p. 623

WEDNESDAY OF THE TWENTY-FIRST WEEK IN ORDINARY TIME

READING I   1 Thes 2, 9-13

Paul recalls his good efforts among the Thessalonians, not in a boastful way, but justly proud that he has done well the work of the Lord. He is thankful that the people could see it was not his own word he was preaching, but that of God.

A reading from the first letter of Paul to the Thessalonians

You must recall, brothers, our efforts and our toil: how we worked day and night all the time we preached God's good tidings to you in order not to impose on you in any way. You are witnesses, as is God himself, of how upright, just, and irreproachable our conduct was toward you who are believers. You likewise know how we exhorted every one of you, as a father does his children—how we encouraged and pleaded with you to make your lives worthy of the God who calls you to his kingship and glory. That is why we thank God constantly that in receiving his message from us you took it, not as the word of men, but as it truly is, the word of God at work within you who believe.—This is the Word of the Lord. ℟. **Thanks be to God. ℣**

Responsorial Psalm   Ps 139, 7-8. 9-10. 11-12

℟. (1) **You have searched me and you know me, Lord.**

Where can I go from your spirit?
    from your presence where can I flee?

If I go up to the heavens, you are there;
 if I sink to the nether world, you are present
  there. — ℟

If I take the wings of the dawn,
 if I settle at the farthest limits of the sea,
Even there your hand shall guide me,
 and your right hand hold me fast. — ℟

If I say, "Surely the darkness shall hide me,
 and night shall be my light"—
For you darkness itself is not dark,
 and night shines as the day. — ℟ ℣

GOSPEL   Mt 23, 27-32
Alleluia (1 Jn 2, 5)

℟. **Alleluia.** He who keeps the word of Christ,
grows perfect in the love of God. ℟. **Alleluia.**

The scribes and Pharisees in their hypocrisy claim that they never
would have done some of the fearful deeds their ancestors committed.
And yet it will be these same hypocrites who will be responsible for
putting the Son of God himself to death.

℣. The Lord be with you. ℟. **And also with you.**
✠ A reading from the holy gospel according to Matthew. ℟. **Glory to you, Lord.**

Jesus said: "Woe to you scribes and Pharisees, you
frauds! You are like whitewashed tombs, beautiful
to look at on the outside but inside full of filth and
dead men's bones. Thus you present to view a holy
exterior while hypocrisy and evil fill you within.
Woe to you scribes and Pharisees, you frauds! You
erect tombs for the prophets and decorate the monu-
ments of the saints. You say, 'Had we lived in our
forefathers' time we would not have joined them in
shedding the prophets' blood.' Thus you show that
you are the sons of the prophets' murderers. Now it
is your turn: fill up the vessel measured off by your
forefathers."—This is the gospel of the Lord. ℟.
Praise to you, Lord Jesus Christ. ➤ No. 15, p. 623

THURSDAY OF THE TWENTY-FIRST WEEK
IN ORDINARY TIME

READING I   1 Thes 3, 7-13

The missionary's greatest joy and consolation is the growing faith of the people to whom he has preached. Paul tells the Thessalonians how joyful he is on their account. He yearns to be with them and prays for their continued growth in the faith.

A reading from the first letter of Paul to the Thessalonians

We have been much consoled by your faith throughout our distress and trial—so much so that we shall continue to flourish only if you stand firm in the Lord!

What thanks can we give to God for all the joy we feel in his presence because of you, as we ask him fervently night and day that we may see you face to face and remedy any shortcomings in your faith? May God himself, who is our Father, and our Lord Jesus make our path to you a straight one! And may the Lord increase you and make you overflow with love for one another and for all, even as our love does for you. May he strengthen your hearts, making them blameless and holy before our God and Father at the coming of our Lord Jesus with all his holy ones.—This is the Word of the Lord. ℟. **Thanks be to God.** ℣

Responsorial Psalm   Ps 90, 3-4. 12-13. 14. 17

℟. (14) **Fill us with your love, O Lord,
    and we will sing for joy!**

You turn man back to dust,
    saying, "Return, O children of men."
For a thousand years in your sight
    are as yesterday, now that it is past,
    or as a watch of the night. — ℟

Teach us to number our days aright,
    that we may gain wisdom of heart.

Return, O Lord! How long?
  Have pity on your servants! — ℟
Fill us at daybreak with your kindness,
  that we may shout for joy and gladness all our
    days.
And may the gracious care of the Lord our God be
    ours;
  prosper the work of our hands for us!
  [Prosper the work of our hands!] — ℟ ↓

GOSPEL   Mt 24, 42-51
Alleluia (Mt 24, 42. 44)
℟. **Alleluia.** Be watchful and ready:
you know not when the Son of Man is coming. ℟.
    Alleluia.

Jesus teaches that constant watchfulness must be the attitude of
his followers, for they do not know when and how the Lord is coming.
The far-sighted man will be prepared by always being about the
master's work and never running the risk of being caught idle.

℣. The Lord be with you. ℟. **And also with you.**
✠ A reading from the holy gospel according to Matthew. ℟. **Glory to you, Lord.**

Jesus said to his disciples: "Stay awake, therefore!
You cannot know the day your Lord is coming.

  "Be sure of this: if the owner of the house knew
when the thief was coming he would keep a watchful eye and not allow his house to be broken into.
You must be prepared in the same way. The Son of
Man is coming at the time you least expect. Who is
the faithful, farsighted servant whom the master has
put in charge of his household to dispense food at
need? Happy that servant whom his master discovers
at work on his return! I assure you, he will put him
in charge of all his property. But if the servant is
worthless and tells himself, 'My master is a long
time in coming,' and begins to beat his fellow servants, to eat and drink with drunkards, that man's
master will return when he is not ready and least

expects him. He will punish him severely and settle with him as is done with hypocrites. There will be wailing then and grinding of teeth."—This is the gospel of the Lord. ℟. **Praise to you, Lord Jesus Christ.** ➔ No. 15, p. 623

FRIDAY OF THE TWENTY-FIRST WEEK IN ORDINARY TIME

READING I   1 Thes 4, 1-8

The message of Christ bears repeating, and so Paul reminds the Thessalonians again of the kind of life to which they have been called in Christ. It is God's will that they grow in holiness, and no man can reject such growth without rejecting God himself.

A reading from the first letter of Paul to the Thessalonians

Now, my brothers, we beg and exhort you in the Lord Jesus that, even as you learned from us how to conduct yourselves in a way pleasing to God—which you are indeed doing—so you must learn to make still greater progress. You know the instructions we gave you in the Lord Jesus. It is God's will that you grow in holiness: that you abstain from immorality, each of you guarding his member in sanctity and honor, not in passionate desire as do the Gentiles who know not God; and that each refrain from overreaching or cheating his brother in the matter at hand; for the Lord is an avenger of all such things, as we once indicated to you by our testimony. God has not called us to immorality but to holiness; hence, whoever rejects these instructions rejects, not man, but God "who sends his holy Spirit upon you."—This is the Word of the Lord. ℟. **Thanks be to God.** ▼

Responsorial Psalm   Ps 97, 1. 2. 5-6. 10. 11-12
℟. (12) **Let good men rejoice in the Lord.**

The Lord is king; let the earth rejoice;
let the many isles be glad.
Justice and judgment are the foundation of his
throne. — ℟

The mountains melt like wax before the Lord,
before the Lord of all the earth.
The heavens proclaim his justice,
and all peoples see his glory. — ℟

The Lord loves those that hate evil;
he guards the lives of his faithful ones;
from the hand of the wicked he delivers them.—℟

Light dawns for the just;
and gladness, for the upright of heart.
Be glad in the Lord, you just,
and give thanks to his holy name. — ℟ ℣

GOSPEL

Mt 25, 1-13

Alleluia (Lk 21, 36)

℟. **Alleluia.** Be watchful, pray constantly,
that you may be worthy to stand before the Son of
Man. ℟. **Alleluia.**

The foolish bridesmaids are caught unprepared when the bridegroom
makes his appearance. By then it is too late to turn to others for
assistance, and their last-minute preparations are too little and too
late. Jesus teaches how important it is at all times to be ready for
the coming of God.

℣. The Lord be with you. ℟. **And also with you.**
✠ A reading from the holy gospel according to Matthew. ℟. **Glory to you, Lord.**

Jesus told this parable to his disciples: "The reign
of God can be likened to ten bridesmaids who took
their torches and went out to welcome the groom.
Five of them were foolish, while the other five were
sensible. The foolish ones, in taking their torches,
brought no oil along, but the sensible ones took
flasks of oil as well as their torches. The groom delayed his coming, so they all began to nod, then to
fall asleep. At midnight someone shouted, 'The groom
is here! Come out and greet him!' At the outcry
all the virgins woke up and got their torches ready.

The foolish ones said to the sensible, 'Give us some of your oil. Our torches are going out.' But the sensible ones replied, 'No, there may not be enough for you and us. You had better go to the dealers and buy yourselves some.' While they went off to buy it the groom arrived, and the ones who were ready went in to the wedding with him. Then the door was barred. Later the other bridesmaids came back. 'Master, master!' they cried. 'Open the door for us.' But he answered, 'I tell you, I do not know you.' The moral is: keep your eyes open, for you know not the day or the hour.'—This is the gospel of the Lord. ℟. **Praise to you, Lord Jesus Christ.** ✠ No. 15, p. 623

SATURDAY OF THE TWENTY-FIRST WEEK IN ORDINARY TIME

READING I   1 Thes 4, 9-12

Paul commends the Thessalonians on the way they have learned brotherly love from the Lord and the way they are living it out. But he urges a healthy restlessness which will push them to still greater progress.

A reading from the first letter of Paul to the Thessalonians

As regards brotherly love, there is no need for me to write you. God himself has taught you to love one another, and this you are doing with respect to all the brothers throughout Macedonia. Yet we exhort you to even greater progress, brothers. Make it a point of honor to remain at peace and attend to your own affairs. Work with your hands as we directed you to do, so that you will give good example to outsiders and want for nothing.—This is the Word of the Lord. ℟. **Thanks be to God.** ℣

Responsorial Psalm   Ps 98, 1. 7-8. 9

℟. (9) **The Lord comes to rule the earth with justice.**

Sing to the Lord a new song,
  for he has done wondrous deeds;

His right hand has won victory for him,
    his holy arm. — ℞

Let the sea and what fills it resound,
    the world and those who dwell in it;
Let the rivers clap their hands,
    the mountains shout with them for joy. — ℞

Before the Lord, for he comes,
    for he comes to rule the earth;
He will rule the world with justice
    and the peoples with equity. — ℞

GOSPEL   Mt 25, 14-30

Alleluia (Jn 13, 34)

℞. **Alleluia.** I give you a new commandment:
love one another as I have loved you. ℞. **Alleluia.**

In the parable of the talents Jesus shows how God's values work.
Service is measured not by the sheer quantity of net result but by
the degree to which a man can increase his God-given share. The
third servant is condemned not for having only a thousand but for
having done nothing with it.

℣. The Lord be with you. ℞. **And also with you.**

✠ A reading from the holy gospel according to Matthew. ℞. **Glory to you, Lord,**

Jesus told this parable to his disciples: "A certain
man was going on a journey. He called in his servants and handed his funds over to them according to
each man's abilities. To one he disbursed five thousand silver pieces, to a second two thousand, and to
a third a thousand. Then he went away. Immediately
the man who received the five thousand went to invest it and made another five. In the same way, the
man who received the two thousand doubled his
figure. The man who received the thousand went off
instead and dug a hole in the ground, where he
buried his master's money. After a long absence, the
master of those servants came home and settled accounts with them. The man who had received the
five thousand came forward bringing the additional
five. 'My lord,' he said, 'you let me have five thou-

sand. See, I have made five thousand more.' His master said to him, 'Well done! You are an industrious and reliable servant. Since you were dependable in a small matter I will put you in charge of larger affairs. Come, share your master's joy!' The man who had received the two thousand then stepped forward. 'My lord,' he said, 'you entrusted me with two thousand and I have made two thousand more.' His master said to him, 'Cleverly done! You too are an industrious and reliable servant. Since you were dependable in a small matter I will put you in charge of larger affairs. Come, share your master's joy!'

"Finally the man who had received the thousand stepped forward. 'My lord,' he said, 'I knew you were a hard man. You reap where you did not sow and gather where you did not scatter, so out of fear I went off and buried your thousand silver pieces in the ground. Here is your money back.' His master exclaimed: 'You worthless, lazy lout! You know I reap where I did not sow and gather where I did not scatter. All the more reason to deposit my money with the bankers, so that on my return I could have had it back with interest. You, there! Take the thousand away from him and give it to the man with the ten thousand. Those who have, will get more until they grow rich, while those who have not, will lose even the little they have. Throw this worthless servant into the darkness outside, where he can wail and grind his teeth.' "—This is the gospel of the Lord. ℟. **Praise to you, Lord Jesus Christ.** ➔ No. 15, p. 623

MONDAY OF THE TWENTY-SECOND WEEK IN ORDINARY TIME

READING I   1 Thes 4, 13-18

The Thessalonians, thinking Christ's final coming was just around the corner, were concerned about those who were dying before the awaited day. Paul consoles them with the message that neither the living nor the deceased have an advantage; both can be saved by believing in Christ's death and resurrection.

A reading from the first letter of Paul to the Thessalonians

We would have you be clear about those who sleep in death, brothers; otherwise you might yield to grief, like those who have no hope. For if we believe that Jesus died and rose, God will bring forth with him from the dead those also who have fallen asleep believing in him. We say to you, as if the Lord himself had said it, that we who live, who survive until his coming, will in no way have an advantage over those who have fallen asleep. No, the Lord himself will come down from heaven at the word of command, at the sound of the archangel's voice and God's trumpet; and those who have died in Christ will rise first. Then we, the living, the survivors, will be caught up with them in the clouds to meet the Lord in the air. Thenceforth we shall be with the Lord unceasingly. Console one another with this message.—This is the Word of the Lord. ℞. **Thanks be to God.** ↓

Responsorial Psalm   Ps 96, 1. 3. 4-5. 11-12. 13

℞. (13) **The Lord comes to judge the earth.**

Sing to the Lord a new song;
    sing to the Lord, all you lands.
Tell his glory among the nations;
    among all peoples, his wondrous deeds. — ℞

For great is the Lord and highly to be praised;
    awesome is he, beyond all gods.
For all the gods of the nations are things of nought,
    but the Lord made the heavens. — ℞

Let the heavens be glad and the earth rejoice;
    let the sea and what fills it resound;
    let the plains be joyful and all that is in them!
Then shall all the trees of the forest exult. — ℞

Before the Lord, for he comes;
    for he comes to rule the earth.

He shall rule the world with justice
   and the peoples with his constancy. — ℟ ℣

GOSPEL   Lk 4, 16-30

Alleluia (Is 61, 1: cited in Lk 4, 18)

℟. **Alleluia.** The spirit of the Lord is upon me;
he sent me to bring Good News to the poor. ℟. **Alleluia.**

Jesus returns to his home town of Nazareth to preach his message
to his townsfolk. His contention that no prophet is ever accepted in
his own country both anticipates and precipitates their rejection of
him.

℣. The Lord be with you. ℟. **And also with you.**
✠ A reading from the holy gospel according to Luke
℟. **Glory to you, Lord.**

Jesus came to Nazareth where he had been reared,
and entering the synagogue on the sabbath as he
was in the habit of doing, he stood up to do the
reading. When the book of the prophet Isaiah was
handed him, he unrolled the scroll and found the
passage where it was written:
   "The spirit of the Lord is upon me;
      therefore he has anointed me.
   He has sent me to bring glad tidings to the poor,
      to proclaim liberty to captives,
   Recovery of sight to the blind
      and release to prisoners,
   To announce a year of favor from the Lord."
Rolling up the scroll, he gave it back to the assistant and sat down. All in the synagogue had their
eyes fixed on him. Then he began by saying to them,
"Today this Scripture passage is fulfilled in your
hearing." All who were present spoke favorably of
him; they marveled at the appealing discourse which
came from his lips. They also asked, "Is not this
Joseph's son?"
   He said to them, "You will doubtless quote me the
proverb, 'Physician, heal yourself,' and say, 'Do here

in your own country the things we have heard you have done in Capernaum.' But in fact," he went on, "no prophet gains acceptance in his native place. Indeed, let me remind you, there were many widows in Israel in the days of Elijah when the heavens remained closed for three and a half years and a great famine spread over the land. It was to none of these that Elijah was sent, but to a widow of Zarephath near Sidon. Recall, too, the many lepers in Israel in the time of Elisha the prophet; yet not one was cured except Naaman the Syrian."

At these words the whole audience in the synagogue was filled with indignation. They rose up and expelled him from the town, leading him to the brow of the hill on which it was built and intending to hurl him over the edge. But he went straight through their midst and walked away.—This is the gospel of the Lord. ℟. **Praise to you, Lord Jesus Christ.**

➤ No. 15, p. 623

TUESDAY OF THE TWENTY-SECOND WEEK IN ORDINARY TIME

READING I   1 Thes 5, 1-6. 9-11

No one knows when the day of the Lord is coming, but Paul seems to indicate a time when people become comfortable and complacent. As children of the light, Christians must not live in such darkness. The Lord wishes the salvation of all.

A reading from the first letter of Paul to the Thessalonians

As regards specific times and moments, brothers, we do not need to write you; you know very well that the day of the Lord is coming like a thief in the night. Just when people are saying, "Peace and security," ruin will fall on them with the suddenness of pains overtaking a woman in labor, and there will be no escape. You are not in the dark, brothers, so that the day might catch you off guard, like a thief. No, all of you are children of light and of the day. We belong neither to darkness nor to night; therefore let us not be asleep like the rest, but awake and sober!

God has not destined us for wrath but for acquiring salvation through our Lord Jesus Christ. He died for us that all of us, whether awake or asleep, together might live with him. Therefore, comfort and upbuild one another, as indeed you are doing.—This is the Word of the Lord. ℟. **Thanks be to God. ✟**

Responsorial Psalm   Ps 27, 1. 4. 13-14

℟. (13) **I believe that I shall see the good things of the Lord in the land of the living.**

The Lord is my light and my salvation;
  whom should I fear?
The Lord is my life's refuge;
  of whom should I be afraid? — ℟

One thing I ask of the Lord;
  this I seek:
To dwell in the house of the Lord
  all the days of my life,
That I may gaze on the loveliness of the Lord
  and contemplate his temple. — ℟

I believe that I shall see the bounty of the Lord
  in the land of the living.
Wait for the Lord with courage;
  be stouthearted, and wait for the Lord. — ℟ ✟

GOSPEL   Lk 4, 31-37

Alleluia (Lk 7, 16)

℟. **Alleluia.** A great prophet has risen among us;
God has visited his people. ℟. **Alleluia.**

The authority Jesus shows inspires people to believe in him. Both his teaching and his actions are all marked by power, and people respond with amazement, spreading his fame far and wide.

℣. The Lord be with you. ℟. **And also with you.**

✠ A reading from the holy gospel according to Luke
℟. **Glory to you, Lord.**

Jesus went down to Capernaum, a town of Galilee,
where he began instructing the people on the sabbath day. They were spellbound by his teaching, for
his words had authority.

In the synagogue there was a man with an unclean
spirit, who shrieked in a loud voice: "Leave us alone!
What do you want of us, Jesus of Nazareth? Have
you come to destroy us? I know who you are: the
Holy One of God." Jesus said to him sharply, "Be
quiet! Come out of him." At that, the demon threw
him to the ground before everyone's eyes and came
out of him without doing him any harm. All were
struck with astonishment, and they began saying
to one another: "What is there about his speech? He
commands the unclean spirits with authority and
power, and they leave." His renown kept spreading
through the surrounding country.—This is the gospel
of the Lord. ℟. **Praise to you, Lord Jesus Christ.**

➔ No. 15, p. 623

WEDNESDAY OF THE TWENTY-SECOND WEEK IN ORDINARY TIME

READING I   Col 1, 1-8

Paul has received word that the Colossians are responding well to
the Gospel which has been preached to them. He writes to congratulate
them, to encourage them, and to pray that their faithful growth may
continue and increase.

The beginning of the letter of Paul to the Colossians

Paul, an apostle of Christ Jesus by the will of God,
and Timothy our brother, to the holy ones at Colossae, faithful brothers in Christ. May God our Father
give you grace and peace.

We always give thanks to God, the Father of our
Lord Jesus Christ, in our prayers for you because

we have heard of your faith in Christ Jesus and the love you bear toward all the saints—moved as you are by the hope held in store for you in heaven. You heard of this hope through the message of truth, the gospel, which has come to you, has borne fruit, and has continued to grow in your midst as it has everywhere in the world. This has been the case from the day you first heard it and comprehended God's gracious intention through the instructions of Epaphras, our dear fellow slave, who represents us as a faithful minister of Christ. He it was who told us of your love in the Spirit.—This is the Word of the Lord. ℞. **Thanks be to God.** ℣

Responsorial Psalm   Ps 52, 10. 11

℞. (10) **I trust in the kindness of God for ever.**

I, like a green olive tree
    in the house of God,
Trust in the kindness of God
    forever and ever. — ℞

I will thank you always for what you have done,
    and proclaim the goodness of your name
    before your faithful ones. — ℞ ℣

GOSPEL   Lk 4, 38-44

Alleluia (Lk 4, 18-19)

℞. **Alleluia.** The Lord sent me to bring Good News
    to the poor.
and freedom to prisoners. ℞. **Alleluia.**

Jesus wins people to him everywhere by his teaching and his miracles, but he never will settle in one place. He is driven ever onward to announce the good news of salvation to many people and many places in accord with the will of his Father.

℣. The Lord be with you. ℞. **And also with you.**
✠ A reading from the holy gospel according to Luke
℞. **Glory to you, Lord.**

On leaving the synagogue, Jesus entered the house of Simon. Simon's mother-in-law was in the grip of a severe fever, and they interceded with him for her. He stood over her and addressed himself to the fever, and it left her. She got up immediately and waited on them.

At sunset, all who had people sick with a variety of diseases took them to him, and he laid hands on each of them and cured them. Demons departed from many, crying out as they did so, "You are the Son of God!" He rebuked them and did not allow them to speak because they knew that he was the Messiah.

The next morning he left the town and set out into the open country. The crowds went in search of him, and when they found him they tried to keep him from leaving them. But he said to them, "To other towns I must announce the good news of the reign of God, because that is why I was sent." And he continued to preach in the synagogues of Judea.
—This is the gospel of the Lord. ℟. **Praise to you, Lord Jesus Christ.**　　　　　　　➤ No. 15, p. 623

———————————

THURSDAY OF THE TWENTY-SECOND WEEK IN ORDINARY TIME

READING I　　　　　　　　　　　　Col 1, 9-14

It is by becoming more deeply and more intensely aware of all that God has done that Christians are moved to progress in his love. The continuing and increasing goodness of God should produce continuing and increasing growth in his love.

A reading from the letter of Paul to the Colossians

Ever since we heard this we have been praying for you unceasingly and asking that you may attain full knowledge of his will through perfect wisdom and spiritual insight. Then you will lead a life worthy of the Lord and pleasing to him in every way. You will multiply good works of every sort and grow in the knowledge of God. By the might of his glory you will be endowed with the strength needed to stand fast, even to endure joyfully whatever may come, giving thanks to the Father for having made you worthy to share the lot of the saints in light. He rescued us from the power of darkness and brought us into the kingdom of his beloved Son. Through him we have redemption, the forgiveness of our sins.— This is the Word of the Lord. ℟. **Thanks be to God.** ℣

Responsorial Psalm   Ps 98, 2-3. 3-4. 5-6

℟. (2) **The Lord has made known his salvation.**

The Lord has made his salvation known:
  in the sight of the nations he has revealed his justice.
He has remembered his kindness and his faithfulness
  toward the house of Israel. — ℟

All the ends of the earth have seen
  the salvation by our God.
Sing joyfully to the Lord, all you lands;
  break into song; sing praise. — ℟

Sing praise to the Lord with the harp,
  with the harp and melodious song.
With trumpets and the sound of the horn
  sing joyfully before the King, the Lord. — ℟ ℣

GOSPEL   Lk 5, 1-11

Alleluia (Mt 4, 19)

℟. **Alleluia.** Come follow me, says the Lord,
and I will make you fishers of men. ℟. **Alleluia.**

God's wisdom is so much fuller than man's. Why do men trust themselves so much and him so little? Once the disciples make the small step of following a particular command of Jesus, he carries them beyond that to being his full followers and fishers of men.

℣. The Lord be with you. ℟. **And also with you.**
✠ A reading from the holy gospel according to Luke
℟. **Glory to you, Lord.**

As the crowd pressed in on Jesus to hear the word of God, he saw two boats moored by the side of the lake; the fishermen had disembarked and were washing their nets. He got into one of the boats, the one belonging to Simon, and asked him to pull out a short distance from the shore; then, remaining seated, he continued to teach the crowds from the boat. When he had finished speaking he said to Simon, "Put out into deep water and lower your nets for a catch." Simon answered, "Master, we have been hard at it all night long and have caught nothing; but if you say so, I will lower the nets." Upon doing this they caught such a great number of fish that their nets were at the breaking point. They signaled to their mates in the other boat to come and help them. These came, and together they filled the two boats until they nearly sank.

At the sight of this, Simon Peter fell at the knees of Jesus saying, "Leave me, Lord. I am a sinful man." For indeed, amazement at the catch they had made seized him and all his shipmates, as well as James and John, Zebedee's sons, who were partners with Simon. Jesus said to Simon, "Do not be afraid. From now on you will be catching men." With that they brought their boats to land, left everything, and became his followers.—This is the gospel of the Lord. ℟. **Praise to you, Lord Jesus Christ.** ➔ No. 15, p. 623

FRIDAY OF THE TWENTY-SECOND WEEK IN ORDINARY TIME

READING I   Col 1, 15-20

Christ is the head of creation; he is the first-born of the new creation, of redemption. It is through him and in him that all things are reconciled and brought together. Through his death the world is offered the possibility of peace.

A reading from the letter of Paul to the Colossians

Christ is the image of the invisible God, the first-born of all creatures. In him everything in heaven and on earth was created, things visible and invisible, whether thrones or dominations, principalities or powers; all were created through him and for him. He is before all else that is. In him everything continues in being. It is he who is head of the body, the church; he who is the beginning, the first-born of the dead, so that primacy may be his in everything. It pleased God to make absolute fullness reside in him and, by means of him, to reconcile everything in his person, everything, I say, both on earth and in the heavens, making peace through the blood of his cross.—This is the Word of the Lord. ℟. **Thanks be to God.** ⩊

Responsorial Psalm   Ps 100, 1. 2. 3. 4. 5

℟. (2) **Come with joy into the presence of the Lord.**

Sing joyfully to the Lord, all you lands;
    serve the Lord with gladness;
    come before him with joyful song. — ℟

Know that the Lord is God;
    he made us, his we are;
    his people, the flock he tends. — ℟

Enter his gates with thanksgiving,
    his courts with praise;
Give thanks to him; bless his name. — ℟

The Lord is good,
    the Lord, whose kindness endures forever,
    and his faithfulness, to all generations. — ℟ ⩊

GOSPEL   Lk 5, 33-39

Alleluia (Jn 8, 12)

℟. **Alleluia.** I am the light of the world, says the Lord;
the man who follows me will have the light of life.
    ℟. **Alleluia.**

It is customary to rejoice at times when the master is present; it is in times of his absence that his followers fast and sacrifice. Mixing the old and the new is difficult, sometimes harmful to both. Jesus warns that it is necessary to be careful how they are blended.

℣. The Lord be with you. ℟. **And also with you.**

✠ A reading from the holy gospel according to Luke
℟. **Glory to you, Lord.**

The scribes and Pharisees said to Jesus: "John's disciples fast frequently and offer prayers; the disciples of the Pharisees do the same. Yours, on the contrary, eat and drink freely." Jesus replied: "Can you make guests of the groom fast while the groom is still with them? But when the days come that the groom is removed from their midst, they will surely fast in those days."

He then proposed to them this figure: "No one tears a piece from a new coat to patch an old one. If he does he will only tear the new coat, and the piece taken from it will not match the old. Moreover, no one pours new wine into old wineskins. Should he do so, the new wine will burst the old skins, the wine will spill out, and the skins will be lost. New wine should be poured into fresh skins. No one, after drinking old wine, wants new. He says, 'I find the old wine better.' "—This is the gospel of the Lord. ℟. **Praise to you, Lord Jesus Christ.**

➤ No. 15, p. 623

SATURDAY OF THE TWENTY-SECOND WEEK IN ORDINARY TIME

READING I   Col 1, 21-23

Paul, the servant of the Lord's Gospel, proclaims that Christ has won reconciliation for men who were once alienated from God. How important it is to hold on to what Jesus has taught.

A reading from the letter of Paul to the Colossians
You yourselves were once alienated from him; you nourished hostility in your hearts because of your evil deeds. But now Christ has achieved reconciliation for you in his mortal body by dying, so as to present you to God holy, free of reproach and blame.

But you must hold fast to faith, be firmly grounded and steadfast in it, unshaken in the hope promised you by the gospel you have heard. It is the gospel which has been announced to every creature under heaven, and I, Paul, am its servant.—This is the Word of the Lord. ℟. **Thanks be to God.** ℣

Responsorial Psalm   Ps 54, 3-4. 6. 8

℟. (6) **God himself is my help.**

O God, by your name save me,
    and by your might defend my cause.
O God, hear my prayer;
    hearken to the words of my mouth. — ℟

Behold, God is my helper;
    the Lord sustains my life.
Freely will I offer you sacrifice;
    I will praise your name, O Lord, for its goodness. — ℟ ℣

GOSPEL   Lk 6, 1-5

Alleluia (Jn 14, 5)

℟. **Alleluia.** I am the way, the truth, and the life, says the Lord;
no one comes to the Father, except through me.
    ℟. **Alleluia.**

The Lord's dominion is over all, and in his plan of values, human needs are more important than laws and rules, no matter how good they are. The disciples, as David before them, "break the law" but in no way displease the Lord; their need is real.

℣. The Lord be with you. ℟. **And also with you.**
✠ A reading from the holy gospel according to Luke
℟. **Glory to you, Lord.**

Once on a sabbath Jesus was walking through the standing grain. His disciples were pulling off grain-heads, shelling them with their hands, and eating them. Some of the Pharisees asked, "Why are you doing what is prohibited on the sabbath?" Jesus said to them: "Have you not read what David did when he and his men were hungry—how he entered God's house and took and ate the holy bread and gave it to his men, even though only priests are allowed to eat it?" Then he said to them, "The Son of Man is Lord even of the sabbath."—This is the gospel of the Lord. ℟. **Praise to you, Lord Jesus Christ.**

MONDAY OF THE TWENTY-THIRD WEEK IN ORDINARY TIME

READING I   Col 1, 24—2, 3

Paul gives his all, including suffering hardships beyond description, to preach Christ to people who have heard of him. In preaching his word in its fullness, he wishes to reveal to all men the **mystery of Christ.**

A reading from the letter of Paul to the Colossians

Even now I find my joy in the suffering I endure for you. In my own flesh I fill up what is lacking in the sufferings of Christ for the sake of his body, the church. I became a minister of this church through the commission God gave me to preach among you his word in its fullness, that mystery hidden from ages and generations past but now revealed to his holy ones. God has willed to make known to them the glory beyond price which this mystery brings to the Gentiles—the mystery of Christ in you, your hope of glory. This is the Christ we proclaim while we admonish all men and teach them in the full measure of wisdom, hoping to make every man complete in Christ. For this I work and struggle, impelled by that energy of his which is so powerful a force within me.

I want you to know how hard I am struggling for you and for the Laodiceans and the many others who have never seen me in the flesh. I wish their hearts to be strengthened and themselves to be close-ly united in love, enriched with full assurance by their knowledge of the mystery of God—namely Christ—in whom every treasure of wisdom and knowledge is hidden.—This is the Word of the Lord. ℟. **Thanks be to God.** ⅴ

Responsorial Psalm   Ps 62, 6-7. 9

℟. (8) **In God is my safety and my glory.**

Only in God be at rest, my soul,
   for from him comes my hope.
He only is my rock and my salvation,
   my stronghold; I shall not be disturbed. — ℟

Trust in him at all times, O my people!
   Pour out your hearts before him;
   God is our refuge! — ℟ ⅴ

GOSPEL   Lk 6, 6-11

Alleluia (Jn 10, 27)

℟. **Alleluia.** My sheep listen to my voice, says the Lord;
I know them, and they follow me. ℟. **Alleluia.**

The sabbath rest was no reason to refrain from a good work like healing. Knowing that, Jesus cures the man with the withered hand in response to the man's faith. Yet the scribes and Pharisees react not with faith but with vengeance.

ⅴ. The Lord be with you. ℟. **And also with you.**
✠ A reading from the holy gospel according to Luke
℟. **Glory to you, Lord.**

On a sabbath Jesus came to teach in a synagogue where there was a man whose right hand was withered. The scribes and Pharisees were on the watch to see if he would perform a cure on the sabbath so that they could find a charge against him. He knew their thoughts, however, and said to the man whose hand was withered, "Get up and stand here in front." The man rose and remained standing. Jesus said to them, "I ask you, is it lawful to do good on the sabbath—or evil? To preserve life—or destroy it?" He looked around at them all and said to the man,

"Stretch out your hand." The man did so and his hand was perfectly restored.

At this they became frenzied and began asking one another what could be done to Jesus.—This is the gospel of the Lord. ℟. **Praise to you, Lord Jesus Christ.**

➤ No. 15, p. 623

TUESDAY OF THE TWENTY-THIRD WEEK IN ORDINARY TIME

READING I Col 2, 6-15

Paul tells the Colossians that they have begun to live in Christ Jesus and must continue. Those who have been baptized into him must live his life, his death, his resurrection and final victory. Anything less is to turn backward.

A reading from the letter of Paul to the Colossians

Continue to live in Christ Jesus the Lord, in the spirit in which you received him. Be rooted in him and built up in him, growing ever stronger in faith as you were taught, and overflowing with gratitude. See to it that no one deceives you through any empty, seductive philosophy that follows mere human traditions, a philosophy based on cosmic powers rather than on Christ.

In Christ the fullness of deity resides in bodily form. Yours is a share of this fullness, in him who is the head of every principality and power. You were also circumcised in him, not with the circumcision administered by hand but with Christ's circumcision which strips off the carnal body completely. In baptism you were not only buried with him but also raised to life with him because you believed in the power of God who raised him from the dead. Even when you were dead in sin and your flesh was uncircumcised, God gave you new life in company with Christ. He pardoned all our sins. He canceled the bond that stood against us with all its claims, snatching it up and nailing it to the cross. Thus did God disarm the principalities and powers. He made a public show of them and, leading them off captive, he triumphed in the person of Christ.—This is the Word of the Lord. ℟. **Thanks be to God.** ℣

Responsorial Psalm   Ps 145, 1-2. 8-9. 10-11

℟. (9) **The Lord is compassionate to all his creatures.**

I will extol you, O my God and King,
    and I will bless your name forever and ever.
Every day will I bless you,
    and I will praise your name forever and ever. — ℟

The Lord is gracious and merciful,
    slow to anger and of great kindness.
The Lord is good to all
    and compassionate toward all his works. — ℟

Let all your works give you thanks, O Lord,
    and let your faithful ones bless you.
Let them discourse of the glory of your kingdom
    and speak of your might. — ℟ ℣

GOSPEL   Lk 6, 12-19

Alleluia (Jn 15, 16)

℟. **Alleluia.** I have chosen you from the world,
    says the Lord,
to go and bear fruit that will last. ℟. **Alleluia.**

Jesus invariably spent long periods in prayer at different crucial junctures of his life. Here, after a night in prayer, he chooses from his disciples twelve to be apostles, the special bearers of his message to all men.

℣. The Lord be with you. ℟. **And also with you.**

✠ A reading from the holy gospel according to Luke
℟. **Glory to you, Lord.**

Jesus went out to the mountain to pray, spending the night in communion with God. At daybreak he called his disciples and selected twelve of them to be his apostles: Simon, to whom he gave the name Peter, and Andrew his brother, James and John, Philip and

Bartholomew, Matthew and Thomas, James son of Alphaeus, and Simon called the Zealot, Judas son of James, and Judas Iscariot, who turned traitor.

Coming down the mountain with them, he stopped at a level stretch where there were many of his disciples; a large crowd of people was with them from all Judea and Jerusalem and the coast of Tyre and Sidon, people who came to hear him and be healed of their diseases. Those who were troubled with unclean spirits were cured; indeed, the whole crowd was trying to touch him because power went out from him which cured all.—This is the gospel of the Lord. ℟. **Praise to you, Lord Jesus Christ.**

➤ No. 15, p. 623

WEDNESDAY OF THE TWENTY-THIRD WEEK IN ORDINARY TIME

READING I   Col 3, 1-11

In baptism the Christian is to die to his old self and to sin. All must be put aside in order to live with Christ. When he appears, all who have been faithful will appear with him in glory.

A reading from the letter of Paul to the Colossians

Since you have been raised up in company with Christ, set your heart on what pertains to higher realms where Christ is seated at God's right hand. Be intent on things above rather than on things of earth. After all, you have died! Your life is hidden now with Christ in God. When Christ our life appears, then you shall appear with him in glory.

Put to death whatever in your nature is rooted in earth: fornication, uncleanness, passion, evil desires, and that lust which is idolatry. These are the sins which provoke God's wrath. Your own conduct was once of this sort, when these sins were your very life. You must put that aside now: all the anger and quick temper, the malice, the insults, the foul language. Stop lying to one another. What you have

done is put aside your old self with its past deeds
and put on a new man, one who grows in knowledge
as he is formed anew in the image of his Creator.
There is no Greek or Jew here, circumcised or uncircumcised, foreigner, Scythian, slave or freeman.
Rather Christ is everything in all of you.—This is
the Word of the Lord. ℟. **Thanks be to God.** ✝

Responsorial Psalm   Ps 145, 2-3. 10-11. 12-13

℟. (9) **The Lord is compassionate to all his creatures.**

Every day will I bless you,
   and I will praise your name forever and ever.
Great is the Lord and highly to be praised;
   his greatness is unsearchable. — ℟

Let all your works give you thanks, O Lord,
   and let your faithful ones bless you.
Let them discourse of the glory of your kingdom
   and speak of your might. — ℟

Making known to men your might
   and the glorious splendor of your kingdom.
Your kingdom is a kingdom of all ages,
   and your dominion endures through all generations. — ℟ ✝

GOSPEL   Lk 6, 20-26

Alleluia (Lk 7, 16)

℟. **Alleluia.** A great prophet has risen among us;
God has visited his people. ℟. **Alleluia.**

The values Jesus teaches are so different from those to which human
nature is inclined: the poor and hungry are blest; the rich and satisfied
are to be pitied. The criterion of true and lasting happiness is not
found in this world.

℣. The Lord be with you. ℟. **And also with you.**
✠ A reading from the holy gospel according to Luke
℟. **Glory to you, Lord.**

Jesus raised his eyes to his disciples and said:
   "Blest are you poor; the reign of God is yours.
   Blest are you who hunger; you shall be filled.

Blest are you who are weeping; you shall laugh.

Blest shall you be when men hate you, when they ostracize you and insult you and proscribe your name as evil because of the Son of Man. On the day they do so, rejoice and exult, for your reward shall be great in heaven. Thus it was that their fathers treated the prophets.

"But woe to you rich, for your consolation is now.

Woe to you who are full; you shall go hungry.

Woe to you who laugh now; you shall weep in your grief.

Woe to you when all speak well of you. Their fathers treated the false prophets in just this way."—This is the gospel of the Lord. ℟. **Praise to you, Lord Jesus Christ.** ➔ No. 15, p. 623

THURSDAY OF THE TWENTY-THIRD WEEK IN ORDINARY TIME

READING I Col 3, 12-17

Being God's chosen ones demands a special way of life. Among the characteristic virtues of such a life, love must be predominant; it summarizes and perfects all the others. All that is done must be done in the name of Jesus.

A reading from the letter of Paul to the Colossians

Because you are God's chosen ones, holy and beloved, clothe yourselves with heartfelt mercy, with kindness, humility, meekness, and patience. Bear with one another; forgive whatever grievances you have against one another. Forgive as the Lord has forgiven you. Over all these virtues put on love, which binds the rest together and makes them perfect. Christ's peace must reign in your hearts, since as members of the one body you have been called to that peace. Dedicate yourselves to thankfulness. Let the word of Christ, rich as it is, dwell in you. In wisdom made perfect, instruct and admonish one another. Sing gratefully to God from your hearts in psalms, hymns, and inspired songs. Whatever you do, whether in speech or in action, do it in the name of the Lord Jesus. Give thanks to God the Father through him.—This is the Word of the Lord. ℟. **Thanks be to God.** ℣

Responsorial Psalm   Ps 150, 1-2. 3-4. 5-6

℟. (6) **Let everything that breathes praise the Lord!**

Praise the Lord in his sanctuary,
    praise him in the firmament of his strength.
Praise him for his mighty deeds,
    praise him for his sovereign majesty. — ℟

Praise him with the blast of the trumpet,
    praise him with lyre and harp,
Praise him with timbrel and dance,
    praise him with strings and pipe. — ℟

Praise him with sounding cymbals,
    praise him with clanging cymbals.
Let everything that has breath
    praise the Lord! Alleluia. — ℟ ℣

℟. Or: **Alleluia.** ℣

GOSPEL   Lk 6, 27-38

Alleluia (1 Jn 4, 12)

℟. **Alleluia.** If we love one another,
God will live in us in perfect love. ℟. **Alleluia.**

The follower of Christ must love, be merciful, be compassionate even when he finds no return from his goodness. A follower of Jesus will not be judged according to how others treat him, but according to how he treats others.

℣. The Lord be with you. ℟. **And also with you.**
✠ A reading from the holy gospel according to Luke
℟. **Glory to you, Lord.**

Jesus said to his disciples: "To you who hear me, I say: Love your enemies, do good to those who hate you; bless those who curse you and pray for those who maltreat you. When someone slaps you on one cheek, turn and give him the other; when someone takes your coat, let him have your shirt as well. Give to all who beg from you. When a man takes what is yours, do not demand it back. Do to others what you would have them do to you. If you love those who love you, what credit is that to you? Even sinners love those who love them. If you do good to those who do good to you, how can you claim any credit? Sinners do as much. If you lend to those from whom you expect repayment, what merit is there in it for you? Even sinners lend to sinners, expecting to be repaid in full.

"Love your enemy and do good; lend without expecting repayment. Then will your recompense be great. You will rightly be called sons of the Most High, since he himself is good to the ungrateful and the wicked.

"Be compassionate, as your Father is compassionate. Do not judge, and you will not be judged. Do not condemn, and you will not be condemned. Pardon, and you shall be pardoned. Give, and it shall be given to you. Good measure pressed down, shaken together, running over, will they pour into the fold of your garment. For the measure you measure with will be measured back to you."—This is the gospel of the Lord. ℟. **Praise to you, Lord Jesus Christ.**

➔ No. 15, p. 623

_____

FRIDAY OF THE TWENTY-THIRD WEEK
IN ORDINARY TIME

READING I   1 Tm 1, 1-2. 12-14

Paul is intensely aware of what kind of man he used to be, and how totally what he has become is due to the grace of God. The only possible response to such an acute awareness of God's power and goodness is an overwhelming feeling of gratitude.

The beginning of the first letter of Paul to
Timothy

Paul, an apostle of Christ Jesus by command of God

our savior and Christ Jesus our hope, to Timothy, my own true child in faith. May grace, mercy and peace be yours from God the Father and Christ Jesus our Lord.

I thank Christ Jesus our Lord, who has strengthened me, that he has made me his servant and judged me faithful. I was once a blasphemer, a persecutor, a man filled with arrogance but because I did not know what I was doing in my unbelief, I have been treated mercifully, and the grace of our Lord has been granted me in overflowing measure, along with the faith and love which are in Christ Jesus.—This is the Word of the Lord. ℞. **Thanks be to God.** ℣

Responsorial Psalm   Ps 16, 1-2. 5. 7-8. 11

℞. (5) **You are my inheritance, O Lord.**

Keep me, O God, for in you I take refuge;
  I say to the Lord, "My Lord are you."
O Lord, my allotted portion and my cup,
  you it is who hold fast my lot. — ℞

I bless the Lord who counsels me;
  even in the night my heart exhorts me.
I set the Lord ever before me;
  with him at my right hand I shall not be disturbed. — ℞

You will show me the path to life,
  fullness of joys in your presence,
    the delights at your right hand forever. — ℞ ℣

GOSPEL   Lk 6, 39-42

Alleluia (Jn 17, 17)

℞. **Alleluia.** Your word, O Lord, is truth;
make us holy in the truth. ℞. **Alleluia.**

A blind man cannot serve as a guide to another blind man. If anyone wishes to be a leader of men, he must clear his own vision before calling others to follow or imitate him.

℣. The Lord be with you. ℞. **And also with you.**

✠ A reading from the holy gospel according to Luke
℟. **Glory to you, Lord.**

Jesus used images in speaking to his disciples: "Can a blind man act as guide to a blind man? Will they not both fall into a ditch? A student is not above his teacher; but every student when he has finished his studies will be on a par with his teacher.

"Why look at the speck in your brother's eye when you miss the plank in your own? How can you say to your brother, 'Brother, let me remove the speck from your eye,' yet fail yourself to see the plank lodged in your own? Hypocrite, remove the plank from your own eye first; then you will see clearly enough to remove the speck from your brother's eye."—This is the gospel of the Lord. ℟. **Praise to you, Lord Jesus Christ.**

➤ No. 15, p. 623

SATURDAY OF THE TWENTY-THIRD WEEK IN ORDINARY TIME

READING I
1 Tm 1, 15-17

Paul feels that God has turned him, the worst of sinners, into an example of faith. He delights that God has worked so powerfully in him, for this is a sign to other men of what a great effect the Lord can have on their lives.

A reading from the first letter of Paul to
Timothy

You can depend on this as worthy of full acceptance: that Christ Jesus came into the world to save sinners. Of these I myself am the worst. But on that very account I was dealt with more mercifully, so that in me, as an extreme case, Jesus Christ might display all his patience, and that I might become an example to those who would later have faith in him and gain everlasting life. To the King of ages, the immortal, the invisible, the only God, be honor and glory forever and ever! Amen. —This is the Word of the Lord. ℟. **Thanks be to God.** ℣

Responsorial Psalm   Ps 113, 1-2. 3-4. 5. 6-7

℟. (2) **Blessed be the name of the Lord for ever.**

Praise, you servants of the Lord,
  praise the name of the Lord.
Blessed be the name of the Lord
  both now and forever. — ℟

From the rising to the setting of the sun
  is the name of the Lord to be praised.
High above all nations is the Lord;
  above the heavens is his glory. — ℟

Who is like the Lord, our God, who is enthroned on
    high
  and looks upon the heavens and the earth below?
He raises up the lowly from the dust;
  from the dunghill he lifts up the poor. — ℟ ❖

℟. Or: **Alleluia.** ❖

GOSPEL   Lk 6, 43-49

Alleluia (Jn 14, 23)

℟. **Alleluia.** If anyone loves me, he will hold to my
        words,
and my Father will love him, and we will come to
        him. ℟. **Alleluia.**

Good tends to produce good, and evil inclines to further evil. Anyone
wishing to follow the Lord in his goodness must be a doer of his word,
not one who mouths platitudes. A solid foundation is essential.

℣. The Lord be with you. ℟. **And also with you.**
✠ A reading from the holy gospel according to Luke
℟. **Glory to you, Lord.**

Jesus said to his disciples: "A good tree does not
produce decayed fruit any more than a decayed tree
produces good fruit. Each tree is known by its yield.
Figs are not taken from thornbushes, nor grapes
picked from brambles. A good man produces goodness from the good in his heart; an evil man produces evil out of his store of evil. Each man speaks
from his heart's abundance. Why do you call me

'Lord, Lord,' and not put into practice what I teach you? Any man who desires to come to me will hear my words and put them into practice. I will show you with whom he is to be compared. He may be likened to the man who, in building a house, dug deeply and laid the foundation on a rock. When the floods came the torrent rushed in on that house, but failed to shake it because of its solid foundation. On the other hand, anyone who has heard my words but not put them into practice is like the man who built his house on the ground without any foundation. When the torrent rushed upon it, it immediately fell in and was completely destroyed."—This is the gospel of the Lord. ℟. **Praise to you, Lord Jesus Christ.**

➤ No. 15, p. 623

MONDAY OF THE TWENTY-FOURTH WEEK IN ORDINARY TIME

READING I   1 Tm 2, 1-8

The prayer which Paul urges is the key to the message that he preaches. He is the chosen herald of that truth, and he wants all those to whom he proclaims that truth to further their growth and his efforts by their prayer.

A reading from the first letter of Paul to
Timothy

First of all, I urge that petitions, prayers, intercessions, and thanksgivings be offered for all men, especially for kings and those in authority, that we may be able to lead undisturbed and tranquil lives in perfect piety and dignity. Prayer of this kind is good, and God our savior is pleased with it, for he wants all men to be saved and come to know the truth. And the truth is this:

"God is one.
One also is the mediator between God and men,
the man Christ Jesus,
who gave himself as a ransom for all."

This truth was attested at the fitting time. I have been made its herald and apostle (believe me, I am not lying but speak the truth), the teacher of the nations in the true faith.

It is my wish, then, that in every place the men shall offer prayers with blameless hands held aloft, and be free from anger and dissension.—This is the Word of the Lord. ℟. **Thanks be to God.** ⱽ

Responsorial Psalm   Ps 28, 2. 7. 8-9

℟. (6) **Blest be the Lord for he has heard my prayer.**

Hear the sound of my pleading, when I cry to you,
  lifting up my hands toward your holy shrine. — ℟

The Lord is my strength and my shield.
  In him my heart trusts, and I find help;
Then my heart exults, and with my song I give him
  thanks. — ℟

The Lord is the strength of his people,
  the saving refuge of his anointed.
Save your people, and bless your inheritance;
  feed them, and carry them forever! — ℟ ⱽ

GOSPEL   Lk 7, 1-10

Alleluia (Jn 3, 16)

℟. **Alleluia.** God loved the world so much, he gave
    us his only Son,
that all who believe in him might have eternal life.
    ℟. **Alleluia.**

A difference in nationality means nothing, but the depth of the centurion's faith wins the cure of his servant along with the amazement and praise of Jesus. Often the strongest faith is found where it would least be expected.

℣. The Lord be with you. ℟. **And also with you.**
✠ A reading from the holy gospel according to Luke
℟. **Glory to you, Lord.**

When Jesus had finished his discourse in the hearing of the people, he entered Capernaum. A centurion had a servant he held in high regard, who was at that moment sick to the point of death. When he heard about Jesus he sent some Jewish elders to him, asking him to come and save the life of his servant. Upon approaching Jesus they petitioned him earnestly. "He deserves this favor from you," they said, "because he loves our people, and even built our synagogue for us." Jesus set out with them. When he was only a short distance from the house, the centurion sent friends to tell him: "Sir, do not trouble yourself, for I am not worthy to have you enter my house. That is why I did not presume to come to you myself. Just give the order and my servant will be cured. I too am a man who knows the meaning of an order, having soldiers under my command. I say to one, 'On your way,' and off he goes; to another, 'Come here,' and he comes; to my slave, 'Do this,' and he does it." Jesus showed amazement on hearing this, and turned to the crowd which was following him to say, "I tell you, I have never found so much faith among the Israelites." When the deputation returned to the house, they found the servant in perfect health.—This is the gospel of the Lord. ℟. **Praise to you, Lord Jesus Christ.**

➤ No. 15, p. 623

_____

TUESDAY OF THE TWENTY-FOURTH WEEK IN ORDINARY TIME

READING I 1 Tm 3, 1-13

Paul sets down for Timothy the many positive characteristics required in a bishop who is to be a leader of his people. Deacons too must be distinguished by noble qualities. Anyone engaged in the ministry must live a life worthy of his calling.

A reading from the first letter of Paul to
Timothy

You can depend on this: whoever wants to be a bishop aspires to a noble task. A bishop must be irreproachable, married only once, of even temper, self-controlled, modest, and hospitable. He should be a good teacher. He must not be addicted to drink. He ought not to be contentious but, rather, gentle, a man of peace. Nor can he be someone who loves money. He must be a good manager of his own household, keeping his children under control without sacrificing his dignity; for if a man does not know how to manage his own house, how can he take care of the church of God? He should not be a new convert, lest he become conceited and thus incur the punishment once meted out to the devil. He must also be well thought of by those outside the church, to ensure that he not fall into disgrace and the devil's trap. In the same way, deacons must be serious, straightforward, and truthful. They may not overindulge in drink, or give in to greed. They must hold fast to the divinely revealed faith with a clear conscience. They should be put on probation first; then, if there is nothing against them, they may serve as deacons. The women, similarly, should be serious, not slanderous gossips. They should be temperate and entirely trustworthy. Deacons may be married but once and must be good managers of their children and their households. Those who serve well as deacons gain a worthy place for themselves and much assurance in their faith in Christ Jesus.—This is the Word of the Lord. ℟. **Thanks be to God.** ℣

Responsorial Psalm Ps 101, 1-2. 2-3. 5. 6

℟. (2) **I will walk with blameless heart.**

Of kindness and judgment I will sing;
  to you, O Lord, I will sing praise.
I will persevere in the way of integrity;
  when will you come to me? — ℟

I will walk in the integrity of my heart,
  within my house;
I will not set before my eyes
  any base thing. — ℟

Whoever slanders his neighbor in secret,
  him will I destroy.
The man of haughty eyes and puffed-up heart
  I will not endure. — ℟

My eyes are upon the faithful of the land,
  that they may dwell with me.
He who walks in the way of integrity
  shall be in my service. — ℟ ⍦

GOSPEL   Lk 7, 11-17
Alleluia (Lk 7, 16)

℟. **Alleluia.** A great prophet has risen among us;
God has visited his people. ℟. **Alleluia.**

Moved by the tears of the widowed mother, Jesus intervenes to restore
her son to life. She makes no direct request; her grief alone is enough
to move Jesus to action.

℣. The Lord be with you. ℟. **And also with you.**
✠ A reading from the holy gospel according to Luke
℟. **Glory to you, Lord.**

Jesus went to a town called Naim, and his disciples
and a large crowd accompanied him. As he approached the gate of the town a dead man was being carried out, the only son of a widowed mother. A con-
siderable crowd of townsfolk were with her. The
Lord was moved with pity upon seeing her and said
to her, "Do not cry." Then he stepped forward and
touched the litter; at this, the bearers halted. He
said, "Young man, I bid you get up." The dead man
sat up and began to speak. Then Jesus gave him
back to his mother. Fear seized them all and they
began to praise God. "A great prophet has risen
among us," they said; and, "God has visited his people." This was the report that spread about him
throughout Judea and the surrounding country.—
This is the gospel of the Lord. ℟. **Praise to you, Lord
Jesus Christ.**
➤ No. 15, p. 623

WEDNESDAY OF THE TWENTY-FOURTH WEEK
IN ORDINARY TIME

READING I   1 Tm 3, 14-16

At the heart of all belief is Jesus Christ. Paul notes the conduct that befits a Christian.

A reading from the first letter of Paul to
Timothy

Although I hope to visit you soon, I am writing you about these matters so that if I should be delayed you will know what kind of conduct befits a member of God's household, the church of the living God, the pillar and bulwark of truth. Wonderful, indeed, is the mystery of our faith, as we say in professing it:

"He was manifested in the flesh,
    vindicated in the Spirit;
Seen by the angels;
    preached among the Gentiles,
Believed in throughout the world,
    taken up into glory."

This is the Word of the Lord. ℟. **Thanks be to God.** ℣

Responsorial Psalm   Ps 111, 1-2. 3-4. 5-6

℟. (2) **How great are the works of the Lord!**

I will give thanks to the Lord with all my heart
    in the company and assembly of the just.
Great are the works of the Lord,
    exquisite in all their delights. — ℟

Majesty and glory are his work,
    and his justice endures forever.
He has won renown for his wondrous deeds,
    gracious and merciful is the Lord. — ℟

He has given food to those who fear him;
    he will forever be mindful of his covenant.
He has made known to his people the power of his
    works,

giving them the inheritance of the nations. — ℟ ❣

℟. Or: **Alleluia.** ❣

GOSPEL   Lk 7, 31-35

Alleluia (Jn 6, 64. 69)

℟. **Alleluia.** Your words, Lord, are spirit and life,
you have the words of everlasting life. ℟. **Alleluia.**

Jesus denounces his listeners for being so deaf, so hard-hearted and
unresponsive. God tried to break through to them in various ways,
but they spurned all his initiatives.

℣. The Lord be with you. ℟. **And also with you.**
✠ A reading from the holy gospel according to Luke
℟. **Glory to you, Lord.**

Jesus said: "What comparison can I use for the men
of today? What are they like? They are like children
squatting in the city squares and calling to their
playmates,

'We piped you a tune but you did not dance,
we sang you a dirge but you did not wail.'

I mean that John the Baptizer came neither eating
bread nor drinking wine, and you say, 'He is mad!'
The Son of Man came and he both ate and drank,
and you say, 'Here is a glutton and a drunkard, a
friend of tax collectors and sinners!' God's wisdom
is vindicated by all who accept it."—This is the gospel of the Lord. ℟. **Praise to you, Lord Jesus Christ.**

➙ No. 15, p. 623

THURSDAY OF THE TWENTY-FOURTH WEEK IN ORDINARY TIME

READING I   1 Tm 4, 12-16

Paul urges those called to the ministry to concentrate on the Scriptures, on preaching and teaching. Such devotion to duty will win
salvation both for themselves and for their hearers.

A reading from the first letter of Paul to
Timothy

Let no one look down on you because of your youth,
but be a continuing example of love, faith and purity
to believers. Until I arrive, devote yourself to the
reading of Scripture, to preaching and teaching. Do
not neglect the gift you received when, as a result of
prophecy, the presbyters laid their hands on you.
Attend to your duties; let them absorb you, so that
everyone may see your progress. Watch yourself
and watch your teaching. Persevere at both tasks.
By doing so you will bring to salvation **yourself**
and all who hear you.—This is the Word of the
Lord. ℟. **Thanks be to God.** ℣

Responsorial Psalm   Ps 111, 7-8. 9. 10

℟. (2) **How great are the works of the Lord!**

The works of his hand are faithful and just;
  sure are all his precepts,
Reliable for ever and ever,
  wrought in truth and equity. — ℟

He has sent deliverance to his people;
  he has ratifed his covenant forever;
  holy and awesome is his name. — ℟

The fear of the Lord is the beginning of wisdom;
  prudent are all who live by it.
  His praise endures forever. — ℟ ℣

℟. Or: **Alleluia.** ℣

GOSPEL   Lk 7, 36-50

Alleluia (Mt 11, 28)

℟. **Alleluia.** Come to me, all you that labor and are
    burdened,
and I will give you rest, says the Lord. ℟. **Alleluia.**

Jesus not only accepts the sinful woman, but holds her up as an
example to those who criticized her. Her faith and sorrow win her
salvation; their self-righteousness has no such effect. Who is better
off?

℣. The Lord be with you. ℟. **And also with you.**

✠ A reading from the holy gospel according to Luke

℟. **Glory to you, Lord.**

There was a certain Pharisee who invited Jesus to dine with him. Jesus went to the Pharisee's home and reclined to eat. A woman known in the town to be a sinner learned that he was dining in the Pharisee's home. She brought in a vase of perfumed oil and stood behind him at his feet, weeping so that her tears fell upon his feet. Then she wiped them with her hair, kissing them and perfuming them with the oil. When his host, the Pharisee, saw this, he said to himself, "If this man were a prophet, he would know who and what sort of woman this is that touches him—that she is a sinner." In answer to his thoughts, Jesus said to him, "Simon, I have something to propose to you." "Teacher," he said, "speak."

"Two men owed money to a certain moneylender; one owed a total of five hundred coins, the other fifty. Since neither was able to repay, he wrote off both debts. Which of them was more grateful to him?" Simon answered, "He, I presume, to whom he remitted the larger sum." Jesus said to him, "You are right."

Turning then to the woman, he said to Simon: "You see this woman? I came to your home and you provided me with no water for my feet. She has washed my feet with her tears and wiped them with her hair. You gave me no kiss, but she has not ceased kissing my feet since I entered. You did not anoint my head with oil, but she has anointed my feet with perfume. I tell you, that is why her many sins are forgiven—because of her great love. Little is forgiven the one whose love is small."

He said to her then, "Your sins are forgiven," at which his fellow guests began to ask among themselves, "Who is this that he even forgives sin?"

Meanwhile he said to the woman, "Your faith has been your salvation. Now go in peace."—This is the gospel of the Lord. ℟. **Praise to you, Lord Jesus Christ.** ➤ No. 15, p. 623

FRIDAY OF THE TWENTY-FOURTH WEEK IN ORDINARY TIME

READING I 1 Tm 6, 2-12

Accepting Jesus as Lord puts tremendous demands on a man. Sound teaching must be treasured; all evil avoided; all virtues sought with faith and perseverance. It is to such a life that a follower of Jesus is called.

A reading from the first letter of Paul to Timothy

These are the things you must teach and preach. Whoever teaches in any other way, not holding to the sound doctrines of our Lord Jesus Christ and the teaching proper to true religion, should be recognized as both conceited and ignorant, a sick man in his passion for polemics and controversy. From these come envy, dissension, slander, evil suspicions —in a word, the bickering of men with twisted minds who have lost all sense of truth. Such men value religion only as a means of personal gain. There is, of course, great gain in religion—provided one is content with a sufficiency. We brought nothing into this world, nor have we the power to take anything out. If we have food and clothing we have all that we need. Those who want to be rich are falling into temptation, and a trap. They are letting themselves be captured by foolish and harmful desires which draw men down to ruin and destruction. The love of money is the root of all evil. Some men in their passion for it have strayed from the faith and have come to grief amid great pain.

Man of God that you are, flee from all this. Instead, seek after integrity, piety, faith, love, steadfastness, and a gentle spirit. Fight the good fight of faith. Take firm hold on the everlasting life to which you were called when, in the presence of many witnesses, you made your profession of faith.—This is the Word of the Lord. ℟. **Thanks be to God.** ∀

Responsorial Psalm   Ps 49, 6-7. 8-10. 17-18. 19-20

℟. (Mt 5, 3) **Happy the poor in spirit;**
  the kingdom of heaven is theirs!

Why should I fear in evil days
  when my wicked ensnarers ring me round?
They trust in their wealth;
  the abundance of their riches is their boast. — ℟

Yet in no way can a man redeem himself,
  or pay his own ransom to God;
Too high is the price to redeem one's life; he would
    never have enough
  to remain alive always and not see destruction.—℟

Fear not when a man grows rich,
  when the wealth of his house becomes great,
For when he dies, he shall take none of it;
  his wealth shall not follow him down. — ℟

Though in his lifetime he counted himself blessed,
  "They will praise you for doing well for yourself,"
He shall join the circle of his forebears
  who shall never more see light. — ℟ ∀

GOSPEL   Lk 8, 1-3

Alleluia (Mt 11, 25)

℟. **Alleluia.** Blessed are you, Father, Lord of heaven
    and earth;
you have revealed to little ones the mysteries of the
    kingdom. ℟. **Alleluia.**

Jesus acquires a small but devoted band of followers. Prominent among them are several women who minister to him and to the disciples, providing for them out of their own resources.

℣. The Lord be with you. ℟. **And also with you.**
✠ A reading from the holy gospel according to Luke
℟. **Glory to you, Lord.**

Jesus journeyed through towns and villages preaching and proclaiming the good news of the kingdom of God. The Twelve accompanied him, and also some women who had been cured of evil spirits and maladies: Mary called the Magdalene, from whom seven devils had gone out, Joanna, the wife of Herod's steward Chuza, Susanna, and many others who were assisting them out of their means.—This is the gospel of the Lord. ℟. **Praise to you, Lord Jesus Christ.**

➔ No. 15, p. 623

_____

SATURDAY OF THE TWENTY-FOURTH WEEK IN ORDINARY TIME

READING I   1 Tm 6, 13-16

Paul has preached to Timothy about Christ's coming. He urges him to hold on to such truths and to live accordingly until Christ comes again.

A reading from the first letter of Paul to Timothy

Before God, who gives life to all, and before Christ Jesus, who in bearing witness made his noble profession before Pontius Pilate, I charge you to keep God's command without blame or reproach until our Lord Jesus Christ shall appear. This appearance God will bring to pass at his chosen time. He is the blessed and only ruler, the King of kings and Lord of lords who alone has immortality and who dwells in inapproachable light, whom no human being has ever seen or can see. To him be honor and everlasting rule! Amen.—This is the Word of the Lord. ℟. **Thanks be to God.** ℣

Responsorial Psalm   Ps 100, 2. 3. 4. 5
℟. (2) **Come with joy into the presence of the Lord.**

Serve the Lord with gladness;
   come before him with joyful song. — ℟

Know that the Lord is God;
   he made us, his we are;
   his people, the flock he tends. — ℟

Enter his gates with thanksgiving,
   his courts with praise;
Give thanks to him; bless his name. — ℟

For he is good:
   the Lord, whose kindness endures forever,
   and his faithfulness, to all generations. — ℟ ℣

GOSPEL   Lk 8, 4-15

Alleluia (See Lk 8, 15)

℟. **Alleluia.** Happy are they who have kept the word
          with a generous heart,
and yield a harvest through perseverance. ℟. **Alleluia.**

In the veiled images of a parable, Jesus speaks of the way the word
of God is accepted by various types of people. Most are left on their
own to accept his meaning; only to the disciples, those who care
enough to seek deeper, does Jesus reveal the interpretation of his
teaching.

℣. The Lord be with you. ℟. **And also with you.**
✠ A reading from the holy gospel according to Luke
℟. **Glory to you, Lord.**

A large crowd was gathering, with people resorting
to Jesus from one town after another. He spoke to
them in a parable: "A farmer went out to sow some
seed. In the sowing, some fell on the footpath where
it was walked on and the birds of the air ate it up.
Some fell on rocky ground, sprouted up, then withered through lack of moisture. Some fell among briers,
and the thorns growing up with it stifled it. But some
fell on good soil, grew up, and yielded grain a hundred-fold."

   As he said this he exclaimed: "Let everyone who
has ears attend to what he has heard." His **disciples**
began asking him what the meaning of this parable

might be. He replied, "To you the mysteries of the reign of God have been confided, but to the rest in parables that,

'Seeing they may not perceive,
and hearing they may not understand.'

This is the meaning of the parable. The seed is the word of God. Those on the footpath are people who hear, but the devil comes and takes the word out of their hearts lest they believe and be saved. Those on the rocky ground are the ones who, when they hear the word, receive it with joy. They have no root; they believe for a while, but fall away in time of temptation. The seed fallen among briers are those who hear, but their progress is stifled by the cares and riches and pleasures of life and they do not mature. The seed on good ground are those who hear the word in a spirit of openness, retain it, and bear fruit through perseverance."—This is the gospel of the Lord. ℟. **Praise to you, Lord Jesus Christ.**

→ No. 15, p. 623

INTRODUCTION FOR 25th TO 29th WEEK

The Books of Ezra and Nehemiah—*The last four books of the Hebrew canon are Ezra, Nehemiah, 1 and 2 Chronicles, in that order. Originally, however, Ezra and Nehemiah followed the Books of Chronicles, and formed with them a unified historical work so homogeneous in spirit that one usually speaks of a single author for the four books. He is called "the Chronicler." The treatment of Ezra-Nehemiah as a single book by the earliest chroniclers was undoubtedly due to the fact that in ancient times the two books were put under the one name—Ezra. The combined work Ezra-Nehemiah is our most important literary source for the formation of the Jewish religious community after the Babylonian exile. This is known as the period of the Restoration, and the two men most responsible for the reorganization of Jewish life at this time were Ezra and Nehemiah.*

The achievements of the two men were complementary; each helped to make it possible for Judaism to maintain its identity during the difficult days of the Restoration. Nehemiah was the man of action who rebuilt the walls of Jerusalem and introduced necessary administrative reforms. Ezra in turn was the great religious reformer who succeeded in establishing the Torah as the constitution of the returned community.

The Book of Haggai—*Postexilic prophecy begins with Haggai who received the word of the Lord in the second year of Darius (520 B.C.). The Jews who returned from the Exile in Babylonia had encountered formidable obstacles in their efforts to reestablish Jewish life in Judah. The Samaritans had succeeded in blocking the rebuilding of the temple; but after Darius acceded to the throne (522), permission was given to resume the work. At this critical moment, when defeatism and a certain lethargy had overtaken his repatriated countrymen, Haggai came forward with his exhortations to them to complete the great task.*

The Book of Zechariah—*Zechariah's initial prophecy is dated to 520 B.C., the same year in which Haggai received the prophetic call. His prophecies promote the work of rebuilding the temple and encourage the returned exiles, especially their leaders, Joshua and Zerubbabel. They also portray the Messiah and the triumphant Messianic Age.*

The Book of Baruch—*This book is ascribed to the secretary of Jeremiah but is more probably the pious reflection of a later Jewish writer upon the circumstances of the exiles in Babylon as he knew them* from the Book of Jeremiah with the purpose of portraying for his own and later generations the spirit of repentance which prompted God to bring the Exile to an end. It is thought that the five compositions which it comprises were used in the liturgy during the 2nd century B.C. by Jewish communities dispersed in the pagan world.

The Book of Jonah—Written in the postexilic era, probably in the fifth century B.C., this book is a didactic story with an important theological message. It is a parable of mercy, showing that God's threatened punishments are but the expression of a merciful will which moves all men to repent and seek forgiveness. The universality of the story contrasts sharply with the particularistic spirit of many in the postexilic community. The book has also prepared the way for the Gospel with its message of redemption for all, both Jew and Gentile.

The Epistle to the Romans—This is unquestionably Paul's most important Epistle, written about 57 A.D. to the Church of Rome which was deeply divided, broken up into communities, one made up of converts from paganism and the other made up of converts from Judaism. It contains a powerful exposition of the doctrine of the supremacy of Christ and of faith in him as the source of salvation. It is an implicit plea to the Christians of Rome to hold fast to that faith. They are to resist any pressure put on them to accept a doctrine of salvation through works of the law. At the same time they are not to exaggerate Christian freedom through repudiation of law itself.

The implication of Paul's exposition by faith rather than by the law is that the divine plan of salvation works itself out on a broad theological plane to include the whole of humanity despite the differences in the content of the given religious system to which a human culture is heir.

MONDAY OF THE TWENTY-FIFTH WEEK
IN ORDINARY TIME

READING I   Ezr 1, 1-6

God works in strange ways. It is Cyrus of Persia whom he inspires to build his temple in Jerusalem. Many others are inspired to help, and the enthusiasm and generosity of their efforts seem a solid guarantee that God is behind their quest.

The beginning of the book of Ezra

In the first year of Cyrus, king of Persia, in order to fulfill the word of the Lord spoken by Jeremiah, the Lord inspired King Cyrus of Persia to issue this proclamation throughout his kingdom, both by word of mouth and in writing: "Thus says Cyrus, king of Persia: 'All the kingdoms of the earth the Lord, the God of heaven, has given to me, and he has also charged me to build him a house in Jerusalem, which is in Judah. Whoever, therefore, among you belongs to any part of his people, let him go up, and may his God be with him! Let everyone who has survived, in whatever place he may have dwelt, be assisted by the people of that place with silver, gold, goods, and cattle, together with free-will offerings for the house of God in Jerusalem.' "

Then the family heads of Judah and Benjamin and the priests and Levites—everyone, that is, whom God had inspired to do so—prepared to go up to build the house of the Lord in Jerusalem. All their neighbors gave them help in every way, with silver, gold, goods, and cattle, and with many precious gifts besides all their free-will offerings.—This is the Word of the Lord. ℟. **Thanks be to God.** ℣

Responsorial Psalm   Ps 126, 1-2. 2-3. 4-5. 6
℟. (3) **The Lord has done marvels for us.**

When the Lord brought back the captives of Zion,
  we were like men dreaming,

Then our mouth was filled with laughter,
and our tongue with rejoicing. — ℟

Then they said among the nations,
"The Lord has done great things for them."
The Lord has done great things for us;
we are glad indeed. — ℟

Restore our fortunes, O Lord,
like the torrents in the southern desert.
Those that sow in tears
shall reap rejoicing. — ℟

Although they go forth weeping,
carrying the seed to be sown,
They shall come back rejoicing,
carrying their sheaves. — ℟ ⱱ

GOSPEL   Lk 8, 16-18

Alleluia (Mt 5, 16)

℟. **Alleluia.** Let your light shine before men,
that they may see your good works and glorify
your Father. ℟. **Alleluia.**

Jesus teaches that no one covers the light from a lamp under a bushel
basket. Everything will come to light and all deeds will be manifest.
Justice will be administered accordingly.

℣. The Lord be with you. ℟. **And also with you.**
✠ A reading from the holy gospel according to Luke
℟. **Glory to you, Lord.**
Jesus said to the crowds: "No one lights a lamp and
puts it under a bushel basket or under a bed; he
puts it on a lampstand so that whoever comes in
can see it. There is nothing hidden that will not be
exposed, nothing concealed that will not be known
and brought to light. Take heed, therefore, how you
hear: to the man who has, more will be given; and
he who has not, will lose even the little he thinks he
has."—This is the gospel of the Lord. ℟. **Praise to
you, Lord Jesus Christ.**   ➙ No. 15, p. 623

TUESDAY OF THE TWENTY-FIFTH WEEK IN ORDINARY TIME

READING I   Ezr 6, 7-8. 12. 14-20

The completion of the temple is an occasion for great rejoicing among all the Israelites. The culmination of their celebration is the observance of the Passover, the memorial meal of their deliverance from slavery.

A reading from the book of Ezra

King Darius issued an order to the officials of West-of-Euphrates: "Let the governor and the elders of the Jews continue the work on that house of God; they are to rebuild it on its former site. I also issue this decree concerning your dealing with these elders of the Jews in the rebuilding of that house of God: From the royal revenue, the taxes of West-of-Euphrates, let these men be repaid for their expenses, in full and without delay. I, Darius, have issued this decree; let it be carefully executed."

The elders of the Jews continued to make progress in the building, supported by the message of the prophets, Haggai and Zechariah, son of Iddo. They finished the building according to the command of the God of Israel and the decrees of Cyrus and Darius [and of Artaxerxes, king of Persia]. They completed this house on the third day of the month Adar, in the sixth year of the reign of King Darius. The Israelites —priests, Levites, and the other returned exiles— celebrated the dedication of this house of God with joy. For the dedication of this house of God, they offered one hundred bulls, two hundred rams, and four hundred lambs, together with twelve he-goats as a sin-offering for all Israel, in keeping with the number of the tribes of Israel. Finally, they set up the priests in their classes and the Levites in their divisions for the service of God in Jerusalem, as is prescribed in the book of Moses.

The exiles kept the Passover on the fourteenth

day of the first month. The Levites, every one of whom had purified himself for the occasion, sacrificed the Passover for the rest of the exiles, for their brethren the priests, and for themselves.—This is the Word of the Lord. ℞. **Thanks be to God.** ℣

Responsorial Psalm   Ps 122, 1-2. 3-4. 4-5

℞. (1) **I rejoiced when I heard them say:**
    let us go to the house of the Lord.

I rejoiced because they said to me,
    "We will go up to the house of the Lord."
And now we have set foot
    within your gates, O Jerusalem. — ℞

Jerusalem, built as a city
    with compact unity.
To it the tribes go up.
    the tribes of the Lord, — ℞

According to the decree of Israel,
    to give thanks to the name of the Lord.
In it are set up judgment seats,
    seats for the house of David. — ℞ ℣

GOSPEL   Lk 8, 19-21
Alleluia (Lk 11, 28)

℞. **Alleluia.** Blessed are they who hear the word of
    God
    and keep it. ℞. **Alleluia.**

The family of God is not determined by blood ties, but by the way a person adheres to the word of God and puts it into action. Mary, the mother of the Lord, excels in her adherence to his word and the way in which she lives it out.

℣. The Lord be with you. ℞. **And also with you.**
✠ A reading from the holy gospel according to Luke
℞. **Glory to you, Lord.**

The mother and brothers of Jesus came to be with him, but they could not reach him because of the crowd. He was informed, "Your mother and your brothers are standing outside and wish to see you."

He told them in reply, "My mother and my brothers are those who hear the word of God and act upon it."—This is the gospel of the Lord. ℟. **Praise to you, Lord Jesus Christ.**   ⇥ No. 15, p. 623

WEDNESDAY OF THE TWENTY-FIFTH WEEK IN ORDINARY TIME

READING I   Ezr 9, 5-9

Ezra prays to the Lord God in shame, conscious of his sins and the sins of his people. But he knows God has never abandoned them in the past, and he has every hope that God will remain faithful and give Israel new life once again.

A reading from the book of Ezra

At the time of the evening sacrifice, I Ezra rose in my wretchedness, and with cloak and mantle torn I fell on my knees, stretching out my hands to the Lord my God.

I said: "My God, I am too ashamed and confounded to raise my face to you, O my God, for our wicked deeds are heaped up above our heads and our guilt reaches up to heaven. From the time of our fathers even to this day great has been our guilt, and for our wicked deeds we have been delivered over, we and our kings and our priests, to the will of the kings of foreign lands, to the sword, to captivity, to pillage, and to disgrace, as is the case today.

"And now, but a short time ago, mercy came to us from the Lord our God, who left us a remnant and gave us a stake in his holy place; thus our God has brightened our eyes and given us relief in our servitude. For slaves we are, but in our servitude our God has not abandoned us; rather, he has turned the good will of the kings of Persia toward us. Thus he has given us new life to raise again the house of our God and restore its ruins, and has granted us a fence in Judah and Jerusalem."—This is the Word of the Lord. ℟. **Thanks be to God.** ↓

Responsorial Psalm   Tb 13, 2. 3-4. 6. 7-8. 6

℟. (1) **Blessed be God, who lives for ever.**

He scourges and then has mercy;
  he casts down to the depths of the nether world,
  and he brings up from the great abyss.
No one can escape his hand. — ℟

For though he has scattered you among the Gentiles,
  he has shown you his greatness even there.
Exalt him before every living being,
  because he is the Lord our God,
  our Father and God forever. — ℟

So now consider what he has done for you,
  and praise him with full voice.
Bless the Lord of righteousness,
  and exalt the King of ages. — ℟

As for me, I exalt my God,
  and my spirit rejoices in the King of heaven.
Let all men speak of his majesty,
  and sing his praises in Jerusalem. — ℟

Turn back, you sinners! do the right before him:
  perhaps he may look with favor upon you
  and show you mercy." — ℟ ℣

GOSPEL   Lk 9, 1-6

Alleluia (Mk 1, 15)

℟. **Alleluia.** The kingdom of God is near:
repent and believe the Good News! ℟. **Alleluia.**

Jesus sends the Twelve out to preach and to heal. They take nothing
with them and, humanly speaking, have little chance for success.
This only serves to make it clearer that the wonders they perform
result from the Lord at work in them.

℣. The Lord be with you. ℟. **And also with you.**
✠ A reading from the holy gospel according to Luke
℟. **Glory to you, Lord.**

Jesus called the twelve together and gave them
power and authority to overcome all demons and
to cure diseases. He sent them forth to proclaim the

reign of God and heal the afflicted. Jesus advised them: "Take nothing for the journey, neither walking staff nor traveling bag; no bread, no money. No one is to have two coats. Stay at whatever house you enter and proceed from there. When people will not receive you, leave that town and shake its dust from your feet as a testimony against them." So they set out and went from village to village, spreading the good news everywhere and curing diseases.
—This is the gospel of the Lord. ℟. **Praise to you, Lord Jesus Christ.** ➤ No. 15, p. 623

THURSDAY OF THE TWENTY-FIFTH WEEK IN ORDINARY TIME

READING I   Hg 1, 1-8

The prophet Haggai is the Lord's instrument to stir up the needed reconstruction of the temple. Men are living in luxury, yet sacrificing nothing to build a worthy dwelling-place for the Lord.

The beginning of the book of the prophet Haggai

In the second year of King Darius, the word of the Lord came through the prophet Haggai to the governor of Judah, Zerubbabel, son of Shealtiel, and to the high priest Joshua, son of Jehozadak:

Thus says the Lord of hosts: This people says: "Not now has the time come to rebuild the house of the Lord." (Then this word of the Lord came through Haggai, the prophet:) Is it time for you to dwell in your own paneled houses, while this house lies in ruins?

Now thus says the Lord of hosts:
Consider your ways!
You have sown much, but have brought in little;
    you have eaten, but have not been satisfied;
You have drunk, but have not been exhilarated;
    have clothed yourselves, but not been warmed;
And he who earned wages

earned them for a bag with holes in it.
Thus says the Lord of hosts:
Consider your ways!
Go up into the hill country;
bring timber, and build the house
That I may take pleasure in it
and receive my glory, says the Lord.

This is the Word of the Lord. ℞. **Thanks be to God.** ℣

Responsorial Psalm   Ps 149, 1-2. 3-4. 5-6. 9

℞. (4) **The Lord takes delight in his people.**

Sing to the Lord a new song
of praise in the assembly of the faithful.
Let Israel be glad in their maker,
let the children of Zion rejoice in their king. — ℞

Let them praise his name in the festive dance,
let them sing praise to him with timbrel and harp.
For the Lord loves his people,
and he adorns the lowly with victory. — ℞

Let the faithful exult in glory;
let them sing for joy upon their couches;
let the high praises of God be in their throats.
This is the glory of all his faithful. Alleluia. — ℞ ℣

GOSPEL   Lk 9, 7-9

Alleluia (Jn 14, 5)

℞. **Alleluia.** I am the way, the truth, and the life,
says the Lord;
no one comes to the Father, except through me.
℞. **Alleluia.**

The fame of Jesus spreads, and people wonder. Herod is among the perplexed, and he seeks to know more about Jesus.

℣. The Lord be with you. ℞. **And also with you.**
✠ A reading from the holy gospel according to Luke
℞. **Glory to you, Lord.**

Herod the tetrarch heard of all that Jesus was doing

and he was perplexed, for some were saying, "John has been raised from the dead"; others, "Elijah has appeared"; and still others, "One of the prophets of old has arisen." But Herod said, "John I beheaded. Who is this man about whom I hear all these reports?" He was very curious to see him.—This is the gospel of the Lord. ℞. **Praise to you, Lord Jesus Christ.** ➤ No. 15, p. 623

FRIDAY OF THE TWENTY-FIFTH WEEK IN ORDINARY TIME

READING I Hg 1, 15—2, 9

The Lord through Haggai promises that his temple will be a great place, a source of glory to God and peace to his people. Those who work to build it will be blessed by God who is ever conscious of the needs of his people.

A reading from the book of the prophet Haggai

In the second year of King Darius, on the twenty-first day of the seventh month, the word of the Lord came through the prophet Haggai: Tell this to the governor of Judah, Zerubbabel, son of Shealtiel, and to the high priest Joshua, son of Jehozadak, and to the remnant of the people:

Who is left among you
   that saw this house in its former glory?
And how do you see it now?
   Does it not seem like nothing in your eyes?
But now take courage, Zerubbabel, says the Lord,
   and take courage, Joshua, high priest, son of
      Jehozadak,
And take courage, all you people of the land,
   says the Lord, and work!
   For I am with you, says the Lord of hosts.
This is the pact that I made with you
   when you came out of Egypt,
And my spirit continues in your midst;
   do not fear!

For thus says the Lord of hosts:
One moment yet, a little while,
    and I will shake the heavens and the earth,
    the sea and the dry land.
I will shake all the nations,
    and the treasures of all the nations will come in,
And I will fill this house with glory,
    says the Lord of hosts.
Mine is the silver and mine the gold
    says the Lord of hosts.
Greater will be the future glory of this house
    than the former, says the Lord of hosts;
And in this place I will give peace,
    says the Lord of hosts!
This is the Word of the Lord. ℟. **Thanks be to God.** ℣

Responsorial Psalm   Ps 43, 1. 2. 3. 4

℟. (5) **Hope in God; I will praise him,
    my savior and my God.**

Do me justice, O God, and fight my fight
    against a faithless people;
        from the deceitful and impious man rescue me.—℟

For you, O God, are my strength.
    Why do you keep me so far away?
Why must I go about in mourning,
    with the enemy oppressing me? — ℟

Send forth your light and your fidelity;
    they shall lead me on
And bring me to your holy mountain,
    to your dwelling-place. — ℟

Then will I go to the altar of God,
    the God of my gladness and joy;
Then will I give you thanks upon the harp,
    O God, my God! — ℟ ℣

GOSPEL   Lk 9, 18-22
Alleluia (Mt 11, 25)

℟. **Alleluia.** Blessed are you, Father, Lord of heaven

and earth;
you have revealed to little ones the mysteries of the
kingdom. ℟. **Alleluia.**

Jesus asks a most central question: Who do you say that I am? Peter,
in faith, answers but hardly understands the implications. A suffering
Son of Man is a difficult Messiah for anyone to accept.

℣. The Lord be with you. ℟. **And also with you.**
✠ A reading from the holy gospel according to Luke
℟. **Glory to you, Lord.**

One day when Jesus was praying in seclusion and
his disciples were with him, he put the question to
them, "Who do the crowds say that I am?" "John
the Baptizer," they replied, "and some say Elijah,
while others claim that one of the prophets of old
has returned from the dead." "But you—who do you
say that I am?" he asked them. Peter said in reply,
"The Messiah of God." He strictly forbade them to
tell this to anyone. "The Son of Man," he said, "must
first endure many sufferings, be rejected by the
elders, the high priests and the scribes, and be put
to death, and then be raised up on the third day."—
This is the gospel of the Lord. ℟. **Praise to you, Lord
Jesus Christ.** → No. 15, p. 623

SATURDAY OF THE TWENTY-FIFTH WEEK
IN ORDINARY TIME

READING I Zec 2, 5-9. 14-15

Jerusalem is a blessed city, especially protected by the Lord. It is
there he is present to his people as the glory in their midst. All too
often it has been a place of division, but it is intended for peace
and unity.

A reading from the book of the prophet Zechariah

Again I raised my eyes and looked: there was a man
with a measuring line in his hand. "Where are you
going?" I asked. "To measure Jerusalem," he an-

swered; "to see how great is its width and how great
its length."

Then the angel who spoke with me advanced, and
another angel came out to meet him and said to him,
"Run, tell this to that young man: People will live in
Jerusalem as though in open country, because of the
multitude of men and beasts in her midst. But I will
be for her an encircling wall of fire, says the Lord,
and I will be the glory in her midst."

Sing and rejoice, O daughter Zion! See, I am coming to dwell among you, says the Lord. Many nations shall join themselves to the Lord on that day.
—This is the Word of the Lord. ℟. **Thanks be to
God.** ℣

Responsorial Psalm   Jer 31, 10, 11-12. 13

℟. (10) **The Lord will guard us,
like a shepherd guarding his flock.**

Hear the word of the Lord, O nations,
     proclaim it on distant coasts, and say:
He who scattered Israel, now gathers them together,
     he guards them as a shepherd his flock. — ℟

The Lord shall ransom Jacob,
     he shall redeem him from the hand of his con-
          queror.
Shouting, they shall mount the heights of Zion,
     they shall come streaming to the Lord's bless-
          ings. — ℟

Then the virgins shall make merry and dance,
     and young men and old as well.
I will turn their mourning into joy,
     I will console and gladden them after their sor-
          rows. — ℟ ℣

GOSPEL   Lk 9, 43-45
Alleluia (2 Tm 1, 10)

℟. **Alleluia.** Our Savior Jesus Christ has done away
     with death,
and brought us life through his gospel. ℟. **Alleluia.**

Jesus tries to convey to his disciples a correct view of his mission, but they simply do not comprehend. The **notion** of a suffering Messiah is just too much for them to grasp at first; they even hesitate to inquire more deeply about it.

℣. The Lord be with you. ℟. **And also with you.**
✠ A reading from the holy gospel according to Luke
℟. **Glory to you, Lord.**

In the midst of the disciples' amazement at all that Jesus was doing, he said to his disciples: "Pay close attention to what I tell you: The Son of Man must be delivered into the hands of men." They failed, however, to understand this warning; its meaning was so concealed from them they did not grasp it at all, and they were afraid to question him about the matter.—This is the gospel of the Lord. ℟. **Praise to you, Lord Jesus Christ.** ➔ No. 15, p. 623

MONDAY OF THE TWENTY-SIXTH WEEK IN ORDINARY TIME

READING I   Zec 8, 1-8

The Lord resolves to put an end to his people's exile and restore the privileged position of Jerusalem. The covenant still stands: they are his people, and he is their God.

A reading from the book of the prophet Zechariah
This word of the Lord of hosts came: Thus says the Lord of hosts:
I am intensely jealous for Zion,
    stirred to jealous wrath for her.
Thus says the Lord:
I will return to Zion,
    and I will dwell within Jerusalem;
Jerusalem shall be called the faithful city,
    and the mountain of the Lord of hosts,
    the holy mountain.
Thus says the Lord of hosts: Old men and old women, each with staff in hand because of old age, shall

again sit in the streets of Jerusalem. The city shall be filled with boys and girls playing in her streets. Thus says the Lord of hosts: Even if this should seem impossible in the eyes of the remnant of this people, shall it in those days be impossible in my eyes also, says the Lord of hosts? Thus says the Lord of hosts: Lo, I will rescue my people from the land of the rising sun, and from the land of the setting sun. I will bring them back to dwell within Jerusalem. They shall be my people, and I will be their God, with faithfulness and justice. — This is the Word of the Lord. ℟. **Thanks be to God.** ℣

Responsorial Psalm   Ps 102, 16-18. 19-21. 29. 22-23

℟. (17) **The Lord will build up Zion again,
    and appear in all his glory.**

And the nations shall revere your name, O Lord,
    and all the kings of the earth your glory,
When the Lord has rebuilt Zion
    and appeared in his glory;
When he has regarded the prayer of the destitute,
    and not despised their prayer. — ℟

Let this be written for the generation to come,
    and let his future creatures praise the Lord:
"The Lord looked down from his holy height,
    from heaven he beheld the earth,
To hear the groaning of the prisoners,
    to release those doomed to die." — ℟

The children of your servants shall abide,
    and their posterity shall continue in your presence.
That the name of the Lord may be declared in Zion;
    and his praise, in Jerusalem,
When the peoples gather together,
    and the kingdoms, to serve the Lord. — ℟ ℣

GOSPEL   Lk 9, 46-50

Alleluia (Mt 11, 25)

℟. **Alleluia.** Blessed are you, Father, Lord of heaven
    and earth;

you have revealed to little ones the mysteries of the kingdom. ℞. **Alleluia.**

The disciples quarrel over who is the greatest. Again and again the Lord tells them that in his hierarchy of values it is the least among them who is the greatest. But it seems they never quite understand.

℣. The Lord be with you. ℞. **And also with you.**

✠ A reading from the holy gospel according to Luke ℞. **Glory to you, Lord.**

A discussion arose among the disciples as to which of them was the greatest. Jesus, who knew their thoughts, took a little child and placed it beside him, after which he said to them, "Whoever welcomes this little child on my account welcomes me, and whoever welcomes me welcomes him who sent me; for the least one among you is the greatest."

It was John who said, "Master, we saw a man using your name to expel demons, and we tried to stop him because he is not of our company." Jesus told him in reply, "Do not stop him, for any man who is not against you is on your side."—This is the gospel of the Lord. ℞. **Praise to you, Lord Jesus Christ.** _____ No. 15, p. 623

TUESDAY OF THE TWENTY-SIXTH WEEK IN ORDINARY TIME

READING I Zec 8, 20-23

Once Jerusalem is established in power and wisdom, people will come from all over the world. All nations will seek the favor and assistance of the God of Israel.

A reading from the book of the prophet Zechariah

Thus says the Lord of hosts: There shall yet come peoples, the inhabitants of many cities; and the inhabitants of one city shall approach those of another, and say, "Come! let us go to implore the favor of the Lord"; and, "I too will go to seek the Lord."

Many peoples and strong nations shall come to seek the Lord of hosts in Jerusalem and to implore the favor of the Lord. Thus says the Lord of hosts: In those days ten men of every nationality, speaking different tongues, shall take hold, yes, take hold of every Jew by the edge of his garment and say, "Let us go with you, for we have heard that God is with you."—This is the Word of the Lord. ℞. **Thanks be to God.** ⩔

Responsorial Psalm   Ps 87, 1-3. 4-5. 6-7

℞. (Zec 8, 23) **God is with us.**

His foundation upon the holy mountains
   the Lord loves:
The gates of Zion,
   more than any dwelling of Jacob.
Glorious things are said of you,
   O city of God! — ℞

I tell of Egypt and Babylon
   among those that know the Lord;
Of Philistia, Tyre, Ethiopia:
   "This man was born there."
And of Zion they shall say:
   "One and all were born in her;
And he who has established her
   is the Most High Lord." — ℞

They shall note, when the peoples are enrolled:
   "This man was born there."
And all shall sing, in their festive dance:
   "My home is within you." — ℞ ⩔

GOSPEL   Lk 9, 51-56

Alleluia (Phil 2, 15-16)

℞. **Alleluia.** Shine on the world like bright stars; you are offering it the word of life. ℞. **Alleluia.**

The Samaritans rebuff Jesus on his way to Jerusalem, but he does not condemn them for their actions. In fact, he reprimands his disciples for their harsh judgment. Undaunted by opposition, he continues his journey.

℣. The Lord be with you. ℟. **And also with you.**
✠ A reading from the holy gospel according to Luke
℟. **Glory to you, Lord.**

As the time approached when Jesus was to be taken from this world, he firmly resolved to proceed toward Jerusalem, and sent messengers on ahead of him. These entered a Samaritan town to prepare for his passing through, but the Samaritans would not welcome him because he was on his way to Jerusalem. When his disciples James and John saw this, they said, "Lord, would you not have us call down fire from heaven to destroy them?" He turned toward them only to reprimand them. Then they set off for another town.—This is the gospel of the Lord. ℟. **Praise to you, Lord Jesus Christ.**

➔ No. 15, p. 623

_____

WEDNESDAY OF THE TWENTY-SIXTH WEEK IN ORDINARY TIME

READING I   Neh 2, 1-8

Nehemiah is in favor with King Artaxerxes, and the king wishes to solve the poor exile's sorrow. So he grants Nehemiah's request to be allowed to go to Judah and rebuild the city. The king also provides much support. The Lord is with Nehemiah in his efforts.

A reading from the book of Nehemiah

In the month Nisan of the twentieth year of King Artaxerxes, when the wine was in my charge, I Nehemiah took some and offered it to the king. As I had never before been sad in his presence, the king asked me, "Why do you look sad? If you are not sick, you must be sad at heart." Though I was seized with great fear, I answered the king: "May the king live forever! How could I not look sad when the city where my ancestors are buried lies in ruins, and its gates have been eaten out by fire?" The king asked me, "What is it, then, that you wish?" I prayed to the God of heaven and then answered the king: "If it please the king, and if your servant is deserving of your favor, send me to Judah, to the city of my ancestors' graves, to rebuild it." Then the king, and the queen seated beside him, asked me how long my journey would take and when I would return. I set a date that was acceptable to him, and the king agreed that I might go.

I asked the king further: "If it please the king, let letters be given to me for the governors of West-of-Euphrates, that they may afford me safe-conduct till I arrive in Judah; also a letter for Asaph, the keeper of the royal park, that he may give me wood for timbering the gates of the temple-citadel and for the city wall and the house that I shall occupy." The king granted my requests, for the favoring hand of my God was upon me.—This is the Word of the Lord.
℟. **Thanks be to God.** ℣

Responsorial Psalm　　　　　　Ps 137, 1-2. 3. 4-5. 6

℟. (6) **Let my tongue be silenced, if I ever forget you!**

By the streams of Babylon
　　we sat and wept
　　when we remembered Zion.
On the aspens of that land
　　we hung up our harps. — ℟

Though there our captors asked of us
　　the lyrics of our songs,
And our despoilers urged us to be joyous:
　　"Sing for us the songs of Zion!" — ℟

How could we sing a song of the Lord
　　in a foreign land?
If I forget you, Jerusalem,
　　may my right hand be forgotten! — ℟

May my tongue cleave to my palate
　　if I remember you not,

If I place not Jerusalem
  ahead of my joy. — ℟ ℣

GOSPEL Lk 9, 57-62

Alleluia (Phil 3, 8-9)

℟. **Alleluia.** I count all things worthless but this:
to gain Jesus Christ and to be found in him. ℟. **Alleluia.**

The man who professes to follow Jesus must accept the terms of
complete dedication. Jesus will not allow anyone to be looking backward or sideways. He must follow Jesus without any hesitation.

℣. The Lord be with you. ℟. **And also with you.**
✠ A reading from the holy gospel according to Luke
℟. **Glory to you, Lord.**

As Jesus and his disciples were making their way
along, someone said to Jesus, "I will be your follower wherever you go." Jesus said to him, "The
foxes have lairs, the birds of the sky have nests, but
the Son of Man has nowhere to lay his head." To
another he said, "Come after me." The man replied,
"Let me bury my father first." Jesus said to him,
"Let the dead bury their dead; come away and proclaim the kingdom of God." Yet another said to him,
"I will be your follower, Lord, but first let me take
leave of my people at home." Jesus answered him,
"Whoever puts his hand to the plow but keeps looking back is unfit for the reign of God."—This is the
gospel of the Lord. ℟. **Praise to you, Lord Jesus
Christ.** ⟶ No. 15, p. 623

THURSDAY OF THE TWENTY-SIXTH WEEK
IN ORDINARY TIME

READING I Neh 8, 1-4. 5-6. 7-12

Ezra the scribe reads to the people from the book of the law of Moses.
They understand that that day is holy to the Lord and an occasion for
rejoicing, and they celebrate as the Lord desires.

A reading from the book of Nehemiah

The whole people gathered as one man in the open space before the Water Gate, and they called upon Ezra the scribe to bring forth the book of the law of Moses which the Lord prescribed for Israel. On the first day of the seventh month, therefore, Ezra the priest brought the law before the assembly, which consisted of men, women, and those children old enough to understand. Standing at one end of the open place that was before the Water Gate, he read out of the book from daybreak until midday, in the presence of the men, the women, and those children old enough to understand; and all the people listened attentively to the book of the law. Ezra the scribe stood on a wooden platform that had been made for the occasion.

Ezra opened the scroll so that all the people might see it (for he was standing higher up than any of the people); and, as he opened it, all the people rose. Ezra blessed the Lord, the great God, and all the people, their hands raised high, answered, "Amen, amen!" Then they bowed down and prostrated themselves before the Lord, their faces to the ground. As the people remained in their places Ezra read plainly from the book of the law of God, interpreting it so that all could understand what was read. Then [Nehemiah, that is, His Excellency, and] Ezra the priest-scribe [and the Levites who were instructing the people] said to all the people: "Today is holy to the Lord your God. Do not be sad, and do not weep"— for all the people were weeping as they heard the words of the law. He said further: "Go, eat rich foods and drink sweet drinks, and allot portions to those who had nothing prepared; for today is holy to our Lord. Do not be saddened this day, for rejoicing in the Lord must be your strength!" [And the Levites quieted all the people, saying, "Hush, for today is holy, and you must not be saddened."] Then all the people went to eat and drink, to distribute portions, and to celebrate with great joy, for they understood the words that had been expounded to them.—This is the Word of the Lord. ℟. **Thanks be to God. ▼**

Responsorial Psalm   Ps 19, 8. 9. 10. 11

℟. (9) **The precepts of the Lord give joy to the heart.**

The law of the Lord is perfect,
   refreshing the soul;
The decree of the Lord is trustworthy,
   giving wisdom to the simple. — ℟

The precepts of the Lord are right,
   rejoicing the heart;
The command of the Lord is clear,
   enlightening the eye; — ℟

The fear of the Lord is pure,
   enduring forever;
The ordinances of the Lord are true,
   all of them just. — ℟

They are more precious than gold,
   than a heap of purest gold;
Sweeter also than syrup
   or honey from the comb. — ℟ ▼

GOSPEL   Lk 10, 1-12

Alleluia (Mk 1, 15)

℟. **Alleluia.** The kingdom of God is near: repent and believe the Good News! ℟. **Alleluia.**

Jesus sends his disciples out with very specific instructions. They are to go in poverty, bearing the Lord's peace and doing wonders for whoever accepts them. But a severe fate is in store for any town which rejects their message.

℣. The Lord be with you. ℟. **And also with you.**

✠ A reading from the holy gospel according to Luke

℟. **Glory to you, Lord.**

Jesus appointed a further seventy-two and sent them in pairs before him to every town and place he intended to visit. He said to them: "The harvest is rich but the workers are few; therefore ask the harvest-master to send workers to his harvest. Be on your way, and remember: I am sending you as lambs in the midst of wolves. Do not carry a walking staff or traveling bag; wear no sandals and greet no one along the way. On entering any house, first say, 'Peace to this house.' If there is a peaceable man there, your peace will rest on him; if not, it will come back to you. Stay in the one house eating and drinking what they have, for the laborer is worth his wage. Do not move from house to house.

"Into whatever city you go, after they welcome you, eat what they set before you, and cure the sick there. Say to them, 'The reign of God is at hand.' If the people of any town you enter do not welcome you, go into its streets and say, 'We shake the dust of this town from our feet as testimony against you. But know that the reign of God is near.' I assure you, on that day the fate of Sodom will be less severe than that of such a town."—This is the gospel of the Lord. ℟. **Praise to you, Lord Jesus Christ.**

➤ No. 15, p. 623

FRIDAY OF THE TWENTY-SIXTH WEEK IN ORDINARY TIME

READING I   Bar 1, 15-22

The Lord calls to his chosen ones. But because they are absorbed in their own interests, they do not listen. Time and again he gives them more opportunities to hear him; time and again they refuse. Now they are brought to shame.

A reading from the book of the prophet Baruch

Justice is with the Lord, our God; and we today are flushed with shame, we men of Judah and citizens of Jerusalem, that we, with our kings and rulers and priests and prophets, and with our fathers, have sinned in the Lord's sight and disobeyed him. We have neither heeded the voice of the Lord, our God, nor followed the precepts which the Lord set before us. From the time the Lord led our fathers out of the land of Egypt until the present day, we have been disobedient to the Lord, our God, and only too ready to disregard his voice. And the evils and the curse which the Lord enjoined upon Moses, his servant, at the time he led our fathers forth from the land of Egypt to give us the land flowing with milk and honey, cling to us even today. For we did not heed the voice of the Lord, our God, in all the words of the prophets whom he sent us, but each one of us went off after the devices of his own wicked heart, served other gods, and did evil in the sight of the Lord, our God. — This is the Word of the Lord. ℟. **Thanks be to God.** ⋎

Responsorial Psalm   Ps 79, 1-2. 3-5. 8. 9.

℟. (9) **For the glory of your name,**
  O Lord, deliver us.

O God, the nations have come into your inheritance;
  they have defiled your holy temple,
  they have laid Jerusalem in ruins.
They have given the corpses of your servants
    as food to the birds of heaven,
    the flesh of your faithful ones to the beasts of the
      earth. — ℟

They have poured out their blood like water
    round about Jerusalem,
    and there is no one to bury them.
We have become the reproach of our neighbors,
    the scorn and derision of those around us.
O Lord, how long? Will you be angry forever?
    Will your jealousy burn like fire? — ℟

Remember not against us the iniquities of the past;
    may your compassion quickly come to us,
    for we are brought very low. — ℟

Help us, O God our savior,
    because of the glory of your name;

Deliver us and pardon our sins
for your name's sake — ℟ ⍢

GOSPEL Lk 10, 13-16

Alleluia (Ps 95, 8)

℟. **Alleluia.** If today you hear his voice,
harden not your hearts. ℟. **Alleluia.**

Jesus speaks condemnation for Chorazin and Bethsaida. What they
would receive they brought down upon themselves because they looked
but refused to see, they listened but refused to hear.

℣. The Lord be with you. ℟. **And also with you.**
✠ A reading from the holy gospel according to Luke
℟. **Glory to you, Lord.**

Jesus said: "It will go ill with you, Chorazin! And
just as ill with you, Bethsaida! If the miracles worked
in your midst had occurred in Tyre and Sidon, they
would long ago have reformed in sackcloth and ashes.
It will go easier on the day of judgment for Tyre and
Sidon than for you. And as for you, Capernaum, 'Are
you to be exalted to the skies? You shall be hurled
down to the realm of death!'

   "He who hears you, hears me. He who rejects you,
rejects me. And he who rejects me, rejects him who
sent me."—This is the gospel of the Lord. ℟. **Praise
to you Lord Jesus Christ.** ➔ No. 15, p. 623

SATURDAY OF THE TWENTY-SIXTH WEEK
IN ORDINARY TIME

READING I Bar 4, 5-12. 27-29

The people develop a certain independence, so much so that they
turn from God. When this happens they are led into captivity. However,
their end is not despair but hope. That hope rests on their ability
to call to God for help.

   A reading from the book of the prophet Baruch

Fear not, my people!
   Remember, Israel,

You were sold to the nations
   not for your destruction;
It was because you angered God
   that you were handed over to your foes.
For you provoked your Maker
   with sacrifices to demons, to no-gods;
You forsook the Eternal God who nourished you,
   and you grieved Jerusalem who fostered you.
She indeed saw coming upon you
   the anger of God; and she said:
"Hear, you neighbors of Zion!
   God has brought great mourning upon me,
For I have seen the captivity
   that the Eternal God has brought
   upon my sons and daughters.
With joy I fostered them;
   but with mourning and lament I let them go.
Let no one gloat over me, a widow,
   bereft of many:
For the sins of my children I am left desolate,
   because they turned from the law of God.
Fear not, my children; call out to God!
   He who brought this upon you will remember you.
As your hearts have been disposed to stray from God,
   turn now ten times the more to seek him;
For he who has brought disaster upon you
   will, in saving you, bring you back enduring joy."
This is the Word of the Lord. ℟. **Thanks be to God.** ℣

Responsorial Psalm   Ps 69, 33-35. 36-37
℟. (34) **The Lord listens to the poor.**
"See, you lowly ones, and be glad;
   you who seek God, may your hearts be merry!
For the Lord hears the poor,
   and his own who are in bonds he spurns not.
Let the heavens and the earth praise him,
   the seas and whatever moves in them!" — ℟

For God will save Zion
and rebuild the cities of Judah.
They shall dwell in the land and own it,
and the descendants of his servants shall inherit it,
and those who love his name shall inhabit it.—℟ ↓

GOSPEL Lk 10, 17-24

Alleluia (Mt 11, 25)

℟. **Alleluia.** Blessed are you, Father, Lord of heaven and earth;
you have revealed to little ones the mysteries of the kingdom. ℟. **Alleluia.**

The disciples are enamored with the works they can do. Somehow they fail to see the distinction of their being called by the Father through his Son, Jesus Christ. It is because of him, and the call he put forth to the Seventy-Two, that the power to overcome the enemy is given.

℣. The Lord be with you. ℟. **And also with you.**
✠ A reading from the holy gospel according to Luke
℟. **Glory to you, Lord.**

The seventy-two disciples returned in jubilation, saying, "Master, even the demons are subject to us in your name." He said in reply: "I watched Satan fall from the sky like lightning. See what I have done; I have given you power to tread on snakes and scorpions and all the forces of the enemy, and nothing shall ever injure you. Nevertheless, do not rejoice so much in the fact that the devils are subject to you as that your names are inscribed in heaven."

At that moment Jesus rejoiced in the Holy Spirit and said: "I offer you grateful praise, O Father, Lord of heaven and earth, because what you have hidden from the learned and the clever you have revealed to the merest children.

"Yes, Father, you have graciously willed it so. Everything has been given over to me by my Father. No one knows the Son except the Father and no one knows the Father except the Son—and anyone to whom the Son wishes to reveal him.

Turning to his disciples he said to them privately: "Blest are the eyes that see what you see. I tell you, many prophets and kings wished to see what you see but did not see it, and to hear what you hear but did not hear it."—This is the gospel of the Lord. ℟. **Praise to you, Lord Jesus Christ.** → No. 15, p. 623

MONDAY OF THE TWENTY-SEVENTH WEEK IN ORDINARY TIME

READING I   Jon 1, 1—2, 1. 11

The request that the Lord makes of Jonah is not unusual. But because Jonah does not feel capable of responding, he runs away, seeking refuge on a ship. His running, however, does no good. A violent storm arises. Jonah knows the reason and asks to be thrown overboard. He is swallowed by a large fish and brought to shore.

The beginning of the book of the prophet Jonah

This is the word of the Lord that came to Jonah, son of Amitttai: "Set out for the great city of Nineveh, and preach against it; their wickedness has come up before me." But Jonah made ready to flee to Tarshish away from the Lord. He went down to Joppa, found a ship going to Tarshish, paid the fare, and went aboard to journey with them to Tarshish, away from the Lord.

The Lord, however, hurled a violent wind upon the sea, and in the furious tempest that arose the ship was on the point of breaking up. Then the mariners became frightened and each one cried to his god. To lighten the ship for themselves, they threw its cargo into the sea. Meanwhile, Jonah had gone down into the hold of the ship, and lay there fast asleep. The captain came to him and said, "What are you doing asleep? Rise up, call upon your God! Perhaps God will be mindful of us so that we may not perish."

Then they said to one another, "Come, let us cast lots to find out on whose account we have met with this misfortune." So they cast lots, and thus singled out Jonah. "Tell us," they said, "what is your business? Where do you come from? What is your country, and to what people do you belong?" "I am a Hebrew," Jonah answered them; "I worship the Lord, the God of heaven, who made the sea and the dry land."

Now the men were seized with great fear and said to him, "How could you do such a thing!"—They knew that he was fleeing from the Lord, because he had told them.—"What shall we do with you," they asked, "that the sea may quiet down for us?" For the sea was growing more and more turbulent. Jonah said to them, "Pick me up and throw me into the sea, that it may quiet down for you; since I know it is because of me that this violent storm has come upon you."

Still the men rowed hard to regain the land, but they could not, for the sea grew ever more turbulent. Then they cried to the Lord: "We beseech you, O Lord, let us not perish for taking this man's life; do not charge us with shedding innocent blood, for you, Lord, have done as you saw fit." Then they took Jonah and threw him into the sea, and the sea's raging abated. Struck with great fear of the Lord, the men offered sacrifice and made vows to him.

But the Lord sent a large fish, that swallowed Jonah; and he remained in the belly of the fish three days and three nights. Then the Lord commanded the fish to spew Jonah upon the shore.—This is the Word of the Lord. ℟. **Thanks be to God.** ℣

Responsorial Psalm   Jon 2, 2. 3. 4. 5. 8

℟. (7) **You will rescue my life from the pit, O Lord.**

From the belly of the fish Jonah said this prayer to the Lord, his God: — ℟

Out of my distress I called to the Lord,
  and he answered me;
From the midst of the nether world I cried for help,
  and you heard my voice. — ℟

For you cast me into the deep, into the heart of the
sea,
and the flood enveloped me;
All your breakers and your billows
passed over me. — ℟

Then I said, "I am banished from your sight!
yet would I again look upon your holy temple."—℟
When my soul fainted within me,
I remembered the Lord;
My prayer reached you
in your holy temple. — ℟ ✓

GOSPEL

Lk 10, 25-37

Alleluia (Jn 13, 34)

℟. **Alleluia.** I give you a new commandment:
love one another as I have loved you. ℟. **Alleluia.**

The lawyer asks Jesus, "Who is my neighbor, the person I must love
as myself?" The anwer that comes back is: "The man whom you would
least expect, or even want, to help you . . . this is your neighbor. Love
him as you do yourself."

℣. The Lord be with you. ℟. **And also with you.**
✠ A reading from the holy gospel according to Luke
℟. **Glory to you, Lord.**

On one occasion a lawyer stood up to pose to Jesus
this problem: "Teacher, what must I do to inherit
everlasting life?" Jesus answered him: "What is
written in the law? How do you read it?" He replied:
"You shall love the Lord your God
with all your heart,
with all your soul,
with all your strength,
and with all your mind;
and your neighbor as yourself."
Jesus said, "You have answered correctly. Do this
and you shall live." But because he wished to justify
himself he said to Jesus, "And who is my neighbor?"
Jesus replied: "There was a man going down from
Jerusalem to Jericho who fell in with robbers. They

stripped him, beat him, and then went off leaving him half-dead. A priest happened to be going down the same road; he saw him but continued on. Likewise there was a Levite who came the same way; he saw him and went on. But a Samaritan who was journeying along came on him and was moved to pity at the sight. He approached him and dressed his wounds, pouring in oil and wine. He then hoisted him on his own beast and brought him to an inn, where he cared for him. The next day he took out two silver pieces and gave them to the innkeeper with the request: 'Look after him, and if there is any further expense I will repay you on my way back.'

"Which of these three, in your opinion, was neighbor to the man who fell in with the robbers?" The answer came, "The one who treated him with compassion." Jesus said to him, "Then go and do the same."—This is the gospel of the Lord. ℟. **Praise to you, Lord Jesus Christ.** ➔ No. 15, p. 623

TUESDAY OF THE TWENTY-SEVENTH WEEK IN ORDINARY TIME

READING I Jon 3, 1-10

What the Lord God demands is more than pious resolutions. It is not until the people finally act, until they turn from their evil ways and their violence, that the Lord holds back the evil he has threatened.

A reading from the book of the prophet Jonah

The word of the Lord came to Jonah a second time: "Set out for the great city of Nineveh, and announce to it the message that I will tell you." So Jonah made ready and went to Nineveh, according to the Lord's bidding. Now Nineveh was an enormously large city; it took three days to go through it. Jonah began his journey through the city, and had gone but a single day's walk, announcing, "Forty days more and Nineveh shall be destroyed," when the people of Nineveh believed God; they proclaimed a fast and all of them, great and small, put on sackcloth.

When the news reached the king of Nineveh, he rose from his throne, laid aside his robe, covered himself with sackcloth, and sat in the ashes. Then he had this proclaimed throughout Nineveh, by decree of the king and his nobles: "Neither man nor beast, neither cattle nor sheep, shall taste anything; they shall not eat, nor shall they drink water. Man and beast shall be covered with sackcloth and call loudly to God; every man shall turn from his evil way and from the violence he has in hand. Who, knows, God may relent and forgive, and withhold his blazing wrath, so that we shall not perish." When God saw by their actions how they turned from their evil way, he repented of the evil that he had threatened to do to them; he did not carry it out.—This is the Word of the Lord. ℟. **Thanks be to God.** ℣

Responsorial Psalm   Ps 130, 1-2. 3-4. 7-8

℟. (3) **If you, O Lord, laid bare our guilt,**
   who could endure it?

Out of the depths I cry to you, O Lord;
   Lord, hear my voice!
Let your ears be attentive
   to my voice in supplication. — ℟

If you, O Lord, mark iniquities,
   Lord, who can stand?
But with you is forgiveness,
   that you may be revered. — ℟

   Let Israel wait for the Lord,
For with the Lord is kindness
   and with him is plenteous redemption;
And he will redeem Israel
   from all their iniquities. — ℟ ℣

GOSPEL   Lk 10, 38-42

Alleluia (Lk 11, 28)

℟. **Alleluia.** Blessed are they who hear the word of
    God
and keep it. ℟. **Alleluia.**

Jesus visits the home of Martha and Mary. Each of the sisters sees
where her responsibility is—one in observing the regular custom of
hospitality, the other in making the Lord feel personally welcome.
Neither is wrong, yet one benefits more.

℣. The Lord be with you. ℟. **And also with you.**

✠ A reading from the holy gospel according to Luke
℟. **Glory to you, Lord.**

Jesus entered a village where a woman named Martha welcomed him to her home. She had a sister
named Mary, who seated herself at the Lord's feet
and listened to his words. Martha, who was busy
with all the details of hospitality, came to him and
said, "Lord, are you not concerned that my sister
has left me all alone to do the household tasks? Tell
her to help me."

The Lord in reply said to her: "Martha, Martha,
you are anxious and upset about many things; one
thing only is required. Mary has chosen the better
portion and she shall not be deprived of it."—This is
the gospel of the Lord. ℟. **Praise to you, Lord Jesus
Christ.**   ➔ No. 15, p. 623

WEDNESDAY OF THE TWENTY-SEVENTH WEEK
IN ORDINARY TIME

READING I   Jon 4, 1-11

Jonah, pursued by the Lord, sees only his own personal needs and fails
to marvel at the wonder that God has not destroyed the city. Jonah
does not see that God worked through him and his preaching and
brought Nineveh to repentance.

A reading from the book of the prophet Jonah

Jonah was greatly displeased and became angry that
God did not carry out the evil he threatened [against

Nineveh]. "I beseech you, Lord," he prayed, "is not this what I said while I was still in my own country? This is why I fled at first to Tarshish. I knew that you are a gracious and merciful God, slow to anger, rich in clemency, loathe to punish. And now, Lord, please take my life from me; for it is better for me to die than to live." But the Lord asked, "Have you reason to be angry?"

Jonah then left the city for a place to the east of it, where he built himself a hut and waited under it in the shade, to see what would happen to the city. And when the Lord God provided a gourd plant, that grew up over Jonah's head, giving shade that relieved him of any discomfort, Jonah was very happy over the plant. But the next morning at dawn God sent a worm which attacked the plant, so that it withered. And when the sun arose, God sent a burning east wind; and the sun beat upon Jonah's head till he became faint. Then he asked for death, saying, "I would be better off dead than alive."

But God said to Jonah, "Have you reason to be angry over the plant?" "I have reason to be angry," Jonah answered, "angry enough to die." Then the Lord said, "You are concerned over the plant which cost you no labor and which you did not raise; it came up in one night and in one night it perished. And should I not be concerned over Nineveh, the great city, in which there are more than a hundred and twenty thousand persons who cannot distinguish their right hand from their left, not to mention the many cattle?"—This is the Word of the Lord. ℟. **Thanks be to God.** ⩔

Responsorial Psalm Ps 86, 3-4. 5-6. 9-10

℟. (15) **Lord, you are tender and full of love.**

You are my God; have pity on me, O Lord,
  for to you I call all the day.
Gladden the soul of your servant,
  for to you, O Lord, I lift up my soul. — ℟

For you, O Lord, are good and forgiving,
    abounding in kindness to all who call upon you.
Hearken, O Lord, to my prayer
    and attend to the sound of my pleading. — ℟

All the nations you have made shall come
    and worship you, O Lord,
    and glorify your name.
For you are great, and you do wondrous deeds;
    you alone are God. — ℟ ℣

GOSPEL   Lk 11, 1-4

Alleluia (Rom 8, 15)

℟. Alleluia. You have received the Spirit which
    makes us God's children,
and in that Spirit we call God our Father. ℟. **Alleluia.**

The disciples ask Jesus how they should pray. The prayer is a sign
of dependence on the Father and confidence in mankind. The two
are intimately connected. A sharing between them both allows us to
raise our voices in thanksgiving to the Father.

℣. The Lord be with you. ℟. **And also with you.**
✠ A reading from the holy gospel according to Luke
℟. **Glory to you, Lord.**

One day Jesus was praying in a certain place. When
he had finished, one of his disciples asked him, "Lord,
teach us to pray as John taught his disciples." He
said to them, "When you pray, say:
        " 'Father,
        hallowed be your name,
        your kingdom come.
        Give us each day our daily bread.
        Forgive us our sins,
        for we too forgive all who do us wrong;
        and subject us not to the trial.' "
This is the gospel of the Lord. ℟. **Praise to you, Lord
Jesus Christ.**   ➜ No. 15, p. 623

THURSDAY OF THE TWENTY-SEVENTH WEEK
IN ORDINARY TIME

READING I   Mal 3, 13-20

The Lord says to the prophet: I will have compassion on those who
serve those who are just, those who fear the Lord. They will experience
the sun of justice with its healing rays.

A reading from the book of the prophet Malachi

You have defied me in word, says the Lord,
　　yet you ask, "What have we spoken against you?"
You have said, "It is vain to serve God,
　　and what do we profit by keeping his command,
And going about in penitential dress
　　in awe of the Lord of hosts?
Rather must we call the proud blessed;
　　for indeed evildoers prosper,
　　and even tempt God with impunity."
Then they who fear the Lord spoke with one another,
　　and the Lord listened attentively;
And a record book was written before him
　　of those who fear the Lord and trust in his name.
And they shall be mine, says the Lord of hosts,
　　my own special possession, on the day I take ac-
　　tion.
And I will have compassion on them,
　　as a man has compassion on his son who serves
　　him.
Then you will again see the distinction
　　between the just and the wicked;
Between him who serves God
　　and him who does not serve him.
For lo, the day is coming, blazing like an oven,
　　when all the proud and all evildoers will be stub-
　　ble,
And the day that is coming will set them on fire,
　　leaving them neither root nor branch,
　　says the Lord of hosts.

But for you who fear my name, there will arise
   the sun of justice with its healing rays.
This is the Word of the Lord. ℟. **Thanks be to God.** ℣

Responsorial Psalm Ps 1, 1-2. 3. 4. 6

℟. (Ps 40, 5) **Happy are they who hope in the Lord.**

Happy the man who follows not
   the counsel of the wicked
Nor walks in the way of sinners,
   nor sits in the company of the insolent,
But delights in the law of the Lord
   and meditates on his law day and night. — ℟

He is like a tree
   planted near running water,
That yields its fruit in due season,
   and whose leaves never fade.
   [Whatever he does, prospers.] — ℟

Not so the wicked, not so;
   they are like chaff which the wind drives away.
For the Lord watches over the way of the just,
   but the way of the wicked vanishes. — ℟ ℣

GOSPEL Lk 11, 5-13

Alleluia (See Acts 16, 14)

℟. **Alleluia.** Open our hearts, O Lord,
to listen to the words of your Son. ℟. **Alleluia.**

Jesus uses the parable of a friend in need. The Lord is attentive to
the prayers of his people. A reply is given when the difference is
seen as to what the person wants and what he really needs.

℣. The Lord be with you. ℟. **And also with you.**
✠ A reading from the holy gospel according to Luke
℟. **Glory to you, Lord.**

Jesus said to his disciples: "If one of you knows
someone who comes to him in the middle of the
night and says to him, 'Friend, lend me three loaves,
for a friend of mine has come in from a journey and
I have nothing to offer him'; and he from inside

should reply, 'Leave me alone. The door is shut now and my children and I are in bed. I can't get up to look after your needs'—I tell you, even though he does not get up and take care of the man because of friendship, he will find himself doing so because of his persistence and give him as much as he needs.

"So I say to you, 'Ask and you shall receive; seek and you shall find; knock and it shall be opened to you.'

"For whoever asks, receives; whoever seeks, finds; whoever knocks, is admitted. What father among you will give his son a snake if he asks for a fish, or hand him a scorpion if he asks for an egg? If you, with all your sins, know how to give your children good things, how much more will the heavenly Father give the Holy Spirit to those who ask him."—This is the gospel of the Lord. ℟. **Praise to you, Lord Jesus Christ.**

➤ No. 15, p. 623

FRIDAY OF THE TWENTY-SEVENTH WEEK IN ORDINARY TIME

READING I   Jl 1, 13-15—2, 1-2

The prophet goes out to confront the people: "Where is your God? Have you forgotten the great things he has done for you? His day is near as long as you refuse to recognize his presence among you."

A reading from the book of the prophet Joel

Gird yourselves and weep, O priests!
    wail, O ministers of the altar!
Come, spend the night in sackcloth,
    O ministers of my God!
The house of your God is deprived
    of offering and libation.
Proclaim a fast,
    call an assembly;
Gather the elders,
    all who dwell in the land,
Into the house of the Lord, your God,
    and cry to the Lord!

Alas, the day!
for near is the day of the Lord,
and it comes as ruin from the Almighty.
Blow the trumpet in Zion,
sound the alarm on my holy mountain!
Let all who dwell in the land tremble,
for the day of the Lord is coming;
Yes, it is near, a day of darkness and of gloom,
a day of clouds and somberness!
Like dawn spreading over the mountains,
a people numerous and mighty!
Their like has **no**t been from of old,
nor will it be after them,
even to the years of distant generations.
This is the Word of the Lord. ℟. **Thanks be to God.** ℣

Responsorial Psalm   Ps 9, 2-3. 6. 16. 8-9

℟. (9) **The Lord will judge the world with justice.**

I will give thanks to you, O Lord, with all my heart;
I will declare all your wondrous deeds.
I will be glad and exult in you;
I will sing praise to your name, Most High. — ℟

You rebuked the nations and destroyed the wicked;
their names you blotted out forever and ever.
The nations are sunk in the pit they have made;
in the snare they set, their foot is caught. — ℟

But the Lord sits enthroned forever;
he has set up his throne for judgment.
He judges the world with justice;
he governs the peoples with equity. — ℟ ℣

GOSPEL   Lk 11, 15-26

Alleluia (Jn 1, 14. 12)

℟. **Alleluia.** The Word of God became a man and
lived among us.
He enabled those who accepted him to become the
children of God. ℟. **Alleluia.**

Jesus casts out a devil and teaches a lesson about his authority. The dissension that reigns must cease. Only one Spirit can dwell in the house, the man. And it is this Spirit which renews the man and makes him whole again.

℣. The Lord be with you. ℟. **And also with you.**
✠ A reading from the holy gospel according to Luke
℟. **Glory to you, Lord.**

As Jesus was casting out a devil, some of the crowd said, "It is by Beelzebul, the prince of devils, that he casts out devils." Others, to test him, were demanding of him a sign from heaven.

Because he knew their thoughts, he said to them: "Every kingdom divided against itself is laid waste. Any house torn by dissension falls. If Satan is divided against himself, how can his kingdom last?—since you say it is by Beelzebul that I cast out devils. If I cast out devils by Beelzebul, by whom do your people cast them out? In such a case, let them act as your judges. But if it is by the finger of God that I cast out devils, then the reign of God is upon you.

"When a strong man fully armed guards his courtyard, his possessions go undisturbed. But when someone stronger than he comes and overpowers him, such a one carries off the arms on which he was relying and divides the spoils. The man who is not with me is against me, and the man who does not gather with me scatters.

"When an unclean spirit has gone out of a man, it wanders through arid wastes, searching for a resting place; failing to find one, it says, 'I will go back where I came from.' It then returns, to find the house swept and tidied. Next it goes out and returns with seven other spirits far worse than itself, who enter in and dwell there. The result is that the last state of the man is worse than the first."—This is the gospel of the Lord. ℟. **Praise to you, Lord Jesus Christ.** ➤ No. 15, p. 623

SATURDAY OF THE TWENTY-SEVENTH WEEK
IN ORDINARY TIME

READING I Jl 4, 12-21

The Lord speaks another warning through the prophets. Violence has reigned too long now and the time has come for the people to know just where they stand. The faithless will be laid waste. The faithful will receive a coveted treasure: Judah will abide forever.

A reading from the book of the prophet Joel

The Lord said:
Let the nations bestir themselves and come up
    to the Valley of Jehoshaphat;
For there will I sit in judgment
    upon all the neighboring nations.
Apply the sickle,
    for the harvest is ripe;
Come and tread,
    for the wine press is full;
The vats overflow,
    for great is their malice.
Crowd upon crowd
    in the valley of decision;
For near is the day of the Lord
    in the valley of decision.
Sun and moon are darkened,
    and the stars withhold their brightness.
The Lord roars from Zion,
    and from Jerusalem raises his voice;
The heavens and the earth quake,
    but the Lord is a refuge to his people,
    a stronghold to the men of Israel.
Then shall you know that I, the Lord, am your God,
    dwelling on Zion, my holy mountain;
Jerusalem shall be holy,
    and strangers shall pass through her no more.
And then, on that day,
    the mountains shall drip new wine,
    and the hills shall flow with milk;

And the channels of Judah
  shall flow with water:
A fountain shall issue from the house of the Lord,
  to water the Valley of Shittim.
Egypt shall be a waste,
  and Edom a desert waste,
Because of violence done to the people of Judah,
  because they shed innocent blood in their land.
But Judah shall abide forever,
  and Jerusalem for all generations.
I will avenge their blood,
  and not leave it unpunished.
  The Lord dwells in Zion.
This is the Word of the Lord. ℞. **Thanks be to God.** ℣

Responsorial Psalm   Ps 97, 1-2. 5-6. 11-12

℞. (12) **Let good men rejoice in the Lord.**

The Lord is king; let the earth rejoice;
  let the many isles be glad.
Clouds and darkness are round about him,
  justice and judgment are the foundation of his
    throne. — ℞

The mountains melt like wax before the Lord,
  before the Lord of all the earth.
The heavens proclaim his justice,
  and all peoples see his glory. — ℞

Light dawns for the just;
  and gladdens, for the upright of heart.
Be glad in the Lord, you just,
  and give thanks to his holy name. — ℞ ℣

GOSPEL   Lk 11, 27-28

Alleluia (Lk 11, 28)

℞. **Alleluia.** Blessed are they who hear the word of
    God
and keep it. ℞. **Alleluia.**

Jesus teaches that those who keep the word of God are blessed. The
importance lies in the faith given to man, and in the way that faith is
lived out.

℣. The Lord be with you. ℟. **And also with you.**

✠ A reading from the holy gospel according to Luke
℟. **Glory to you, Lord.**

While Jesus was speaking, a woman from the crowd called out, "Blest is the womb that bore you and the breasts that nursed you!" "Rather," he replied, "blest are they who hear the word of God and keep it."— This is the gospel of the Lord. ℟. **Praise to you, Lord Jesus Christ.** _____ ➔ No. 15, p. 623

MONDAY OF THE TWENTY-EIGHTH WEEK
IN ORDINARY TIME

READING I   Rom 1, 1-7

Because of Christ's death and resurrection each is given the rank of apostle, set apart to proclaim the Gospel of God concerning his Son. This role of apostleship is not restricted to only a few, but is demanded of all.

The beginning of the letter of Paul to the Romans Greetings from Paul, a servant of Christ Jesus, called to be an apostle and set apart to proclaim the gospel of God which he promised long ago through his prophets, as the Holy Scriptures record—the gospel concerning his Son, who was descended from David according to the flesh but was made Son of God in power, according to the spirit of holiness, by his resurrection from the dead: Jesus Christ our Lord. Through him we have been favored with apostleship, that we may spread his name and bring to obedient faith all the Gentiles, among whom are you who have been called to belong to Jesus Christ.

To all in Rome, beloved of God and called to holiness, grace and peace from God our Father and the Lord Jesus Christ.—This is the Word of the Lord. ℟. **Thanks be to God.** ℣

Responsorial Psalm   Ps 98, 1. 2-3. 3-4
℟. (2) **The Lord has made known his salvation.**

Sing to the Lord a new song,
   for he has done wondrous deeds;
His right hand has won victory for him,
   his holy arm. — ℟

The Lord has made his salvation known:
   in the sight of the nations he has revealed his
   justice.
He has remembered his kindness and his faithfulness
   toward the house of Israel. — ℟

All the ends of the earth have seen
   the salvation by our God.
Sing joyfully to the Lord, all you lands;
   break into song; sing praise. — ℟ ℣

GOSPEL   Lk 11, 29-32
Alleluia (Ps 95, 8)
℟. **Alleluia.** If today you hear his voice,
harden not your hearts. ℟. **Alleluia.**

Every generation seeks signs of Christ's presence and every generation is presented with that same sign: Jesus the risen Lord. He is
a sign greater than Jonah.

℣. The Lord be with you. ℟. **And also with you.**
✠ A reading from the holy gospel according to Luke
℟. **Glory to you, Lord.**

While the crowds pressed around him Jesus began
to speak to them in these words: "This is an evil
age. It seeks a sign. But no sign will be given it
except the sign of Jonah. Just as Jonah was a sign
for the Ninevites, so will the Son of Man be a sign
for the present age. The queen of the south will rise
at the judgment along with the men of this generation, and she will condemn them. She came from the
farthest corner of the world to listen to the wisdom
of Solomon, but you have a greater than Solomon
here. At the judgment, the citizens of Nineveh will
rise along with the present generation, and they will

condemn it. For at the preaching of Jonah they reformed, but you have a greater than Jonah here."— This is the gospel of the Lord. ℞. **Praise to you, Lord Jesus Christ.** ──────────── ➔ No. 15, p. 623

TUESDAY OF THE TWENTY-EIGHTH WEEK IN ORDINARY TIME

READING I   Rom 1, 16-25

It does man no good to speculate about God because this waste of time cuts down the amount of effectiveness he would have if he lived the faith.

A reading from the letter of Paul to the Romans

I am not ashamed of the gospel. It is the power of God leading everyone who believes in it to salvation, the Jew first, then the Greek. For in the gospel is revealed the justice of God which begins and ends with faith; as Scripture says, "The just man shall live by faith."

The wrath of God is being revealed from heaven against the irreligious and perverse spirit of men who, in this perversity of theirs, hinder the truth. In fact, whatever can be known about God is clear to them; he himself made it so. Since the creation of the world, invisible realities, God's eternal power and divinity, have become visible, recognized through the things he has made. Therefore these men are inexcusable. They certainly had knowledge of God, yet they did not glorify him as God or give him thanks; they stultified themselves through speculating to no purpose, and their senseless hearts were darkened. They claimed to be wise, but turned into fools instead; they exchanged the glory of the immortal God for images representing mortal man, birds, beasts and snakes. In consequence, God delivered them up in their lusts to unclean practices; they engaged in the mutual degradation of their bodies, these men who exchanged the truth of God for a lie and worshiped and served the creature rather than the Creator—blessed be he forever, amen! —This is the Word of the Lord. ℟. **Thanks be to God.** ℣

Responsorial Psalm   Ps 19, 2-3. 4-5

℟. (2) **The heavens proclaim the glory of God.**

The heavens declare the glory of God,
  and the firmament proclaims his handiwork.
Day pours out the word to day,
  and night to night imparts knowledge. — ℟

Not a word nor a discourse
  whose voice is not heard;
Through all the earth their voice resounds,
  and to the ends of the world, their message.—℟ ℣

GOSPEL   Lk 11, 37-41

Alleluia (Heb 4, 12)

℟. **Alleluia.** The word of God is living and active; it probes the thoughts and motives of our heart. ℟.
  Alleluia.

The Pharisees are notorious for their strict observance of the law. What matters little to them is the person's reason for observing that law. Jesus brings a new law that goes down deep within the person.

℣. The Lord be with you. ℟. **And also with you.**
✠ A reading from the holy gospel according to Luke
℟. **Glory to you, Lord.**

As Jesus was speaking, a Pharisee invited him to dine at his house. He entered and reclined at table. Seeing this, the Pharisee was surprised that he had not first performed the ablutions prescribed before eating. The Lord said to him: "You Pharisees! You cleanse the outside of cup and dish, but within you are filled with rapaciousness. Fools! Did not he who made the outside make the inside too? But if you give what you have as alms, all will be wiped clean for you."—This is the gospel of the Lord. ℟. **Praise to you, Lord Jesus Christ.**   ➜ No. 15, p. 623

WEDNESDAY OF THE TWENTY-EIGHTH WEEK
IN ORDINARY TIME

READING I   Rom 2, 1-11

Paul speaks out against the man who condemns quickly without reflecting on his own condition. The judgment he receives will be as just as the one he gives to his fellowman.

A reading from the letter of Paul to the Romans

Every one of you who judges another is inexcusable. By your judgment you convict yourself, since you do the very same things. "We know that God's judgment on men who do such things is just." Do you suppose, then, that you will escape his judgment, you who condemn these things in others yet do them yourself? Or do you presume on his kindness and forbearance? Do you not know that God's kindness is an invitation to you to repent? In spite of this, your hard and impenitent heart is storing up retribution for that day of wrath when the just judgment of God will be revealed, when he will repay every man for what he has done: eternal life to those who strive for glory, honor, and immortality by patiently doing right; wrath and fury to those who selfishly disobey the truth and obey wickedness. Yes, affliction and anguish will come upon every man who has done evil, the Jew first, then the Greek. But there will be glory, honor, and peace for everyone who has done good, likewise the Jew first, then the Greek. With God there is no favoritism.—This is the Word of the Lord. ℞. **Thanks be to God.** ✟

Responsorial Psalm   Ps 62, 2-3. 6-7. 9

℞. (13) **Lord, you give back to every man according to his works.**

Only in God is my soul at rest;
  from him comes my salvation.

He only is my rock and my salvation,
 my stronghold; I shall not be disturbed at all. — ℟

Only in God be at rest, my soul,
 for from him comes my hope.
He only is my rock and my salvation,
 my stronghold; I shall not be disturbed. — ℟

Trust in him at all times, O my people!
 Pour out your hearts before him;
 God is our refuge! — ℟ ↓

GOSPEL
Lk 11, 42-46

Alleluia (Jn 10, 27)

℟. **Alleluia.** My sheep listen to my voice, says the
 Lord;
I know them, and they follow me. ℟. **Alleluia.**

The hypocritical lives of the Pharisees are beyond reproach by external standards. What is lacking is any notion of other-centered
motives. They love the respect the people show to them, but miss the
whole point of the laws of God.

℣. The Lord be with you. ℟. **And also with you.**
✠ A reading from the holy gospel according to Luke
℟. **Glory to you, Lord.**

The Lord said: "Woe to you Pharisees! You pay
tithes on mint and rue and all the garden plants,
while neglecting justice and the love of God. These
are the things you should practice, without omitting
the others. Woe to you Pharisees! You love the front
seats in synagogues and marks of respect in public.
Woe to you! You are like hidden tombs over which
men walk unawares."

In reply one of the lawyers said to him, "Teacher,
in speaking this way you insult us too." Jesus answered: "Woe to you lawyers also! You lay impossible burdens on men but will not lift a finger to
lighten them."—This is the gospel of the Lord. ℟.
Praise to you, Lord Jesus Christ. ➔ No. 15, p. 623

THURSDAY OF THE TWENTY-EIGHTH WEEK IN ORDINARY TIME

READING I Rom 3, 21-29

Paul tries to convince the people that it takes more than their obedience of the law to make them deserving of God's justice. Practicing that law is of little merit if the interior self does not express real faith.

A reading from the letter of Paul to the Romans

The justice of God has been manifested apart from the law, even though both law and prophets bear witness to it—that justice of God which works through faith in Jesus Christ for all who believe. All men have sinned and hence are deprived of the glory of God. All men are now undeservedly justified by the gift of God, through the redemption wrought in Christ Jesus. Through his blood, God made him the means of expiation for all who believe. He did so to manifest his own justice, for the sake of remitting sins committed in the past—to manifest his justice in the present, by way of forbearance, so that he might be just and might justify those who believe in Jesus.

What occasion is there then for boasting? It is ruled out. By what law, the law of works? Not at all! By the law of faith. For we hold that a man is justified by faith apart from observance of the law. Does God belong to the Jews alone? Is he not also the God of the Gentiles? Yes, of the Gentiles too. It is the same God.—This is the Word of the Lord. ℟. **Thanks be to God.** ℣

Responsorial Psalm Ps 130, 1-2. 3-4. 5-6

℟. (7) **With the Lord there is mercy, and fullness of redemption.**

Out of the depths I cry to you, O Lord;
    Lord, hear my voice!
Let your ears be attentive
    to my voice in supplication. — ℟

If you, O Lord, mark iniquities,
  Lord, who can stand?
But with you is forgiveness,
  that you may be revered. — ℟

I trust in the Lord;
  my soul trusts in his word.
My soul waits for the Lord
  more than sentinels wait for the dawn. — ℟ ℣

GOSPEL Lk 11, 47-54

Alleluia (Jn 14, 5)

℟. **Alleluia.** I am the way, the truth, and the life, says
    the Lord;
no one comes to the Father, except through me. ℟.
    Alleluia.

Jesus confronts the Pharisees again. This time he points to the fact
that they continue to bring the Lord's revenge down upon the people.
They set up stumbling blocks to the people which eventually direct
the people away from the Father.

℣. The Lord be with you. ℟. **And also with you.**
✠ A reading from the holy gospel according to Luke
℟. **Glory to you, Lord.**

The Lord said: "Woe to you! You build the tombs of
the prophets, but it was your fathers who murdered
them. You show that you stand behind the deeds of
your fathers: they did the murders and you erect
the tombs. That is why the wisdom of God has said,
'I will send them prophets and apostles, and some
of these they will persecute and kill'; so that this
generation will have to account for the blood of all
the prophets shed since the foundation of the world.
Their guilt stretches from the blood of Abel to the
blood of Zechariah, who met his death between the
altar and the sanctuary! Yes, I tell you, this generation will have to account for it. Woe to you lawyers.
You have taken away the key of knowledge. You
yourselves have not gained access, yet you have
stopped those who wish to enter!" After he had left

this gathering, the scribes and Pharisees began to manifest fierce hostility to him and to make him speak on a multitude of questions, setting traps to catch him in his speech.—This is the gospel of the Lord. ℞. **Praise to you, Lord Jesus Christ.**

———————————— ➤ No. 15, p. 623

FRIDAY OF THE TWENTY-EIGHTH WEEK
IN ORDINARY TIME

READING I   Rom 4, 1-8

What Paul is telling the Romans is that faith, with or without tremendous works, is what the Lord ask of each man. It is this same faith, this gift, that is offered to every man. His choice is one of response or no response.

A reading from the letter of Paul to the Romans

What shall we say of Abraham our ancestor according to the flesh? Certainly if Abraham was justified by his deeds he has grounds for boasting, but not in God's view, for what does Scripture say? "Abraham believed God, and it was credited to him as justice." Now, when a man works, his wages are not regarded as a favor but as his due. But when a man does nothing, yet believes in him who justifies the sinful, his faith is credited as justice. Thus David congratulates the man to whom God credits justice without requiring deeds:

"Blest are they whose iniquities are forgiven,
    whose sins are covered over.
Blest is the man to whom the Lord imputes no
    guilt."

This is the Word of the Lord. ℞. **Thanks be to God.** ⴸ

Responsorial Psalm   Ps 32, 1-2. 5. 11

℞. (7) **I turn to you, Lord, in time of trouble,
and you fill me with the joy of salvation.**

Happy is he whose fault is taken away,
    whose sin is covered.
Happy the man to whom the Lord imputes not guilt,
    in whose spirit there is no guile. — ℞

Then I acknowledged my sin to you,
  my guilt I covered not.
I said, "I confess my faults to the Lord,"
  and you took away the guilt of my sin. — ℟

Be glad in the Lord and rejoice, you just;
  exult, all you upright of heart. — ℟ ℣

GOSPEL
Lk 12, 1-7

Alleluia (Ps 33, 22)

℟. **Alleluia.** Lord, let your mercy be on us,
as we place our trust in you. ℟. **Alleluia.**

The mystery of the Father's love is revealed all around. Fear should
be had for him who can cast another into hellfire. But since God
knows all things, there is no real need for fear.

℣. The Lord be with you. ℟. **And also with you.**
✠ A reading from the holy gospel according to Luke
℟. **Glory to you, Lord.**

A crowd of thousands had gathered, so dense that
they were treading on one another. Jesus began to
speak first to his disciples: "Be on guard against the
yeast of the Pharisees, which is hypocrisy. There is
nothing hidden that will not be revealed, nothing
hidden that will not be made known. Everything
you have said in the dark will be heard in the day-
light; what you have whispered in locked rooms will
be proclaimed from the rooftops.

  "I say to you who are my friends: Do not be
afraid of those who kill the body and can do no
more. I will show you whom you ought to fear. Fear
him who has power to cast into Gehenna after he
has killed. Yes, I tell you, fear him. Are not five sparrows sold for a few pennies? Yet not one of them
is neglected by God. In very truth, even the hairs of
your head are counted! Fear nothing, then. You are
worth more than a flock of sparrows."—This is the
gospel of the Lord. ℟. **Praise to you, Lord Jesus
Christ.**
→ No. 15, p. 623

SATURDAY OF THE TWENTY-EIGHTH WEEK
IN ORDINARY TIME

READING I   Rom 4, 13. 16-18

Abraham's faith determines his long line of descendants. He hopes against hope, and his reward is long life. He is respected as the father of many nations.

A reading from the letter of Paul to the Romans

The promise made to Abraham and his descendants that they would inherit the world did not depend on the law; it was made in view of the justice that comes from faith. Hence all depends on faith, everything is a grace. Thus the promise holds true for all Abraham's descendants, not only for those who have the law but for all who have his faith. He is the father of us all, which is why Scripture says, "I have made you father of many nations." Yes, he is our father in the sight of God in whom he believed, the God who restores the dead to life and calls into being those things which had not been. Hoping against hope, Abraham believed and so became the father of many nations, just as it was once told him, "Numerous as this shall your descendants be."— This is the Word of the Lord. ℟. **Thanks be to God.** ℣

Responsorial Psalm   Ps 105, 6-7. 8-9. 42-43

℟. (8) **The Lord remembers his covenant for ever.**

You descendants of Abraham, his servants,
　　sons of Jacob, his chosen ones!
He, the Lord, is our God;
　　throughout the earth his judgments prevail. — ℟

He remembers forever his covenant
　　which he made binding for a thousand genera-
　　　　tions—
Which he entered into with Abraham
　　and by his oath to Isaac. — ℟

For he remembered his holy word
　　to his servant Abraham.

And he led forth his people with joy;
  with shouts of joy, his chosen ones. — ℟ ℣

℟. Or: **Alleluia.** ℣

GOSPEL   Lk 12, 8-12

Alleluia (Jn 15, 26. 27)

℟. **Alleluia.** The Spirit of truth will bear witness to
    me, says the Lord,
and you also will be my witnesses. ℟. **Alleluia.**

Jesus promises that whoever is faithful to him, especially in the face
of persecution, will be acknowledged before his Father in heaven.
Man expresses his faith with the aid of the Spirit.

℣. The Lord be with you. ℟. **And also with you.**
✠ A reading from the holy gospel according to Luke
℟. **Glory to you, Lord.**

Jesus said to his disciples: "I tell you, whoever
acknowledges me before men—the Son of Man will
acknowledge him before the angels of God. But the
man who has disowned me in the presence of men
will be disowned in the presence of the angels of
God. Anyone who speaks against the Son of Man
will be forgiven, but whoever blasphemes the Holy
Spirit will never be forgiven. When they bring you
before synagogues, rulers and authorities, do not
worry about how to defend yourselves or what to
say. The Holy Spirit will teach you at that moment
all that should be said."—This is the gospel of the
Lord. ℟. **Praise to you, Lord Jesus Christ.**

MONDAY OF THE TWENTY-NINTH WEEK
IN ORDINARY TIME

READING I   Rom 4, 20-25

Paul identifies Abraham as an example to be followed. His faith in
God was great. His belief was based on God's promise. How much
greater must that faith be now when that promise has been fulfilled
in Jesus, the risen Lord.

A reading from the letter of Paul to the Romans

Abraham never questioned or doubted God's promise; rather, he was strengthened in faith and gave glory to God, fully persuaded that God could do whatever he had promised. Thus his faith was credited to him as justice.

The words, "It was credited to him," were not written with him alone in view; they were intended for us too. For our faith will be credited to us also if we believe in him who raised Jesus our Lord from the dead, the Jesus who was handed over to death for our sins and raised up for our justification.— This is the Word of the Lord. ℟. **Thanks be to God.** ℣

Responsorial Psalm   Lk 1, 69-70. 71-72. 73-75

℟. (68) **Blessed be the Lord God of Israel,**
   for he has visited his people.

He has raised a horn of saving strength for us
   in the house of David his servant,
As he promised through the mouths of his holy ones,
   the prophets of ancient times. — ℟

Salvation from our enemies
   and from the hands of all our foes.
He has dealt mercifully with our fathers
   and remembered the holy covenant he made. — ℟

The oath he swore to Abraham our father he would
      grant us:
   that, rid of fear and delievered from the enemy,
We should serve him devoutly and through all our
      days
   be holy in his sight. — ℟ ℣

GOSPEL   Lk 12, 13-21

Alleluia (Mt 5, 3)

℟. **Alleluia.** Happy the poor in spirit;
   the kingdom of heaven is theirs! ℟. **Alleluia.**

Material prosperity counts for little today as it did in the time of Jesus. If a person has nothing within himself, no faith, then all that he has outside himself is worthless. Everyone will be asked to account for the response he makes to the gifts of life and faith that come from God.

℣. The Lord be with you. ℟. **And also with you.**
✠ A reading from the holy gospel according to Luke
℟. **Glory to you, Lord.**

Someone in the crowd said to Jesus, "Teacher, tell my brother to give me my share of our inheritance." He replied, "Friend, who has set me up as your judge or arbiter?" Then he said to the crowd, "Avoid greed in all its forms. A man may be wealthy, but his possessions do not guarantee him life."

He told them a parable in these words: "There was a rich man who had a good harvest. 'What shall I do?' he asked himself. 'I have no place to store my harvest. I know!' he said. 'I will pull down my grain bins and build larger ones. All my grain and my goods will go there. Then I will say to myself: You have blessings in reserve for years to come. Relax! Eat heartily, drink well. Enjoy yourself.'

"But God said to him, 'You fool! This very night your life shall be required of you. To whom will all this piled-up wealth of yours go?' That is the way it works with the man who grows rich for himself instead of growing rich in the sight of God."—This is the gospel of the Lord. ℟. **Praise to you, Lord Jesus Christ.** _____ ➔ No. 15, p. 623

TUESDAY OF THE TWENTY-NINTH WEEK IN ORDINARY TIME

READING I   Rom 5, 12. 15. 17-19. 20-21

The death and resurrection, as Paul sees them, are the two elements that bring the purging of sin and the hope of new life. But this is not simply a one-time event. It is only the beginning of a recurring event.

A reading from the letter of Paul to the Romans

Just as through one man sin entered the world and with sin death, so death came to all men inasmuch as all sinned. For if by the offense of the one man, all died, much more did the grace of God and the gracious gift of the one man, Jesus Christ, abound for all. If death began its reign through one man because of his offense, much more shall those who receive the overflowing grace and gift of justice live and reign through the one man, Jesus Christ.

To sum up, then: just as a single offense brought condemnation to all men, a single righteous act brought all men acquittal and life. Just as through one man's disobedience all became sinners, so through one man's obedience all shall become just.

Despite the increase of sin, grace has far surpassed it, so that, as sin reigned through death, grace may reign by way of justice leading to eternal life, through Jesus Christ our Lord.—This is the Word of the Lord. ℟. **Thanks be to God.** ℣

Responsorial Psalm   Ps 40, 7-8. 8-9. 10. 17

℟. (8. 9) **Here am I, Lord;**
   I come to do your will.

Sacrifice or oblation you wished not,
   but ears open to obedience you gave me.
Holocausts or sin-offerings you sought not;
   then said I, "Behold I come." — ℟

"In the written scroll it is prescribed for me.
To do your will, O my God, is my delight,
   and your law is within my heart!" — ℟

I announced your justice in the vast assembly;
   I did not restrain my lips, as you, O Lord,
     know. — ℟

But may all who seek you
   exult and be glad in you.
And may those who love your salvation
   say ever, "The Lord be glorified." — ℟ ℣

GOSPEL   Lk 12, 35-38

Alleluia (Lk 21, 36)

℟. **Alleluia.** Be watchful, pray constantly,

that you may be worthy to stand before the Son of Man. ℟. **Alleluia.**

Jesus is not saying "do not sleep," but he is saying, "be ready when you prepare to sleep." Make sure that all is in order. Each one must be prepared and ready to respond to the call to faith when it comes.

℣. The Lord be with you. ℟. **And also with you.**

✠ A reading from the holy gospel according to Luke ℟. **Glory to you, Lord.**

Jesus said to his disciples: "Let your belts be fastened around your waists and your lamps be burning ready. Be like men awaiting their master's return from a wedding, so that when he arrives and knocks, you will open for him without delay. It will go well with those servants whom the master finds wide-awake on his return. I tell you, he will put on an apron, seat them at table, and proceed to wait on them. Should he happen to come at midnight or before sunrise and find them prepared, it will go well with them."—This is the gospel of the Lord. ℟. **Praise to you, Lord Jesus Christ.** ➔ No. 15, p. 623

WEDNESDAY OF THE TWENTY-NINTH WEEK IN ORDINARY TIME

READING I Rom 6, 12-18

Paul contrasts death and life, sin and justice, to point out what has been given to men by God. The resurrection of Jesus has delivered men from sin and death and set them free for life and justice.

A reading from the letter of Paul to the Romans

Do not, therefore, let sin rule your mortal body and make you obey its lusts; no more shall you offer the members of your body to sin as weapons for evil. Rather, offer yourselves to God as men who have come back from the dead to life, and your bodies to God as weapons for justice. Sin will no longer have power over you; you are now under grace, not under the law.

What does all this lead to? Just because we are not under the law but under grace, are we free to sin? By no means! You must realize that, when you offer yourselves to someone as obedient slaves, you are the slave of the one you obey, whether yours is the slavery of sin, which leads to death, or of obedience, which leads to justice. Thanks be to God, though once you were slaves of sin, you sincerely obeyed that rule of teaching which was imparted to you; freed from your sin, you became slaves of justice.—This is the Word of the Lord. ℞. **Thanks be to God.** ℣

Responsorial Psalm   Ps 124, 1-3. 4-6. 7-8

℞. (8) **Our help is in the name of the Lord.**

Had not the Lord been with us,
     let Israel say,
     had not the Lord been with us—
When men rose up against us,
     then would they have swallowed us alive.
When their fury was inflamed against us. — ℞

Then would the waters have overwhelmed us;
The torrent would have swept over us;
     over us then would have swept
     the raging waters.
Blessed be the Lord, who did not leave us
     a prey to their teeth. — ℞

We were rescued like a bird
     from the fowlers' snare;
Broken was the snare,
     and we were freed.
Our help is in the name of the Lord,
     who made heaven and earth. — ℞ ℣

GOSPEL   Lk 12, 39-48

Alleluia (Mt 24, 42. 44)

℞. **Alleluia.** Be watchful and ready:
you know not when the Son of Man is coming. ℞.
     Alleluia.

The gifts that each one has been given will be the gifts that will have to be accounted for. If much has been given, much will be expected; if only a little, then only a little will be expected.

℣. The Lord be with you. ℟. **And also with you.**
✠ A reading from the holy gospel according to Luke
℟. **Glory to you, Lord.**

Jesus said to his disciples: "You know as well as I that if the head of the house knew when the thief was coming he would not let him break into his house. Be on guard, therefore. The Son of Man will come when you least expect him."

Peter said, "Do you intend this parable for us, Lord, or do you mean it for the whole world?" The Lord said, "Who in your opinion is that faithful, far-sighted steward whom the master will set over his servants to dispense their ration of grain in season? That servant is fortunate whom his master finds busy when he returns. Assuredly, his master will put him in charge of all his property. But if the servant says to himself, 'My master is taking his time about coming,' and begins to abuse the housemen and servant girls, to eat and drink and get drunk, that servant's master will come back on a day when he does not expect him, at a time he does not know. He will punish him severely and rank him among those undeserving of trust. The slave who knew his master's wishes but did not prepare to fulfill them will get a severe beating, whereas the one who did not know them and who nonetheless deserved to be flogged will get off with fewer stripes. When much has been given a man, much will be required of him. More will be asked of a man to whom more has been entrusted."—This is the gospel of the Lord. ℟. **Praise to you, Lord Jesus Christ.**

THURSDAY OF THE TWENTY-NINTH WEEK
IN ORDINARY TIME

READING I Rom 6, 19-23

Formerly men were slaves to degradation. Now they are freed from sin and have become slaves of God for their sanctification. God gives eternal life.

A reading from the letter of Paul to the Romans

I use the following example from human affairs because of your weak human nature. Just as formerly you enslaved your bodies to impurity and licentiousness for their degradation, make them now the servants of justice for their sanctification. When you were slaves of sin, you had freedom from justice. What benefit did you then enjoy? Things you are now ashamed of, all of them tending toward death. But now that you are freed from sin and have become slaves of God, your benefit is sanctification as you tend toward eternal life. The wages of sin is death, but the gift of God is eternal life in Christ Jesus our Lord.—This is the Word of the Lord. ℟.
Thanks be to God. ℣

Responsorial Psalm Ps 1, 1-2. 3. 4. 6

℟. (Ps 40, 5) **Happy are they who hope in the Lord.**

Happy the man who follows not
   the counsel of the wicked
Nor walks in the way of sinners,
   nor sits in the company of the insolent,
But delights in the law of the Lord
   and meditates on his law day and night. — ℟

He is like a tree
   planted near running water,
That yields its fruit in due season,
   and whose leaves never fade.
   [Whatever he does, prospers.] — ℟

Not so the wicked, not so;
   they are like chaff which the wind drives away.

For the Lord watches over the way of the just,
but the way of the wicked vanishes. — ℟ ℣

GOSPEL   Lk 12, 49-53

Alleluia (Phil 3, 8-9)

℟. **Alleluia.** I count all things worthless but this:
to gain Jesus Christ and to be found in him. ℟. **Alleluia.**

The division that Jesus speaks of is already present. It is the division
that comes from children growing up and becoming individuals. It
is the division that parents experience when their children grow up.

℣. The Lord be with you. ℟. **And also with you.**
✠ A reading from the holy gospel according to Luke
℟. **Glory to you, Lord.**

Jesus said to his disciples: "I have come to light a
fire on the earth. How I wish the blaze were ignited!
I have a baptism to receive. What anguish I feel till
it is over! Do you think I have come to establish
peace on the earth? I assure you, the contrary is
true; I have come for division. From now on, a
household of five will be divided three against two
and two against three; father will be split against
son and son against father, mother against daughter
and daughter against mother, mother-in-law against
daughter-in-law, daughter-in-law against mother-in-
law."—This is the gospel of the Lord. ℟. **Praise to
you, Lord Jesus Christ.**   ➔ No. 15, p. 623

FRIDAY OF THE TWENTY-NINTH WEEK IN ORDINARY TIME

READING I   Rom 7, 18-25

What Paul really wants to do he cannot, and what he does not want
to do he finds himself doing. The struggle within mankind is between
life and death. A war is waged within the body, and Paul asks who
can free him from the power of death.

A reading from the letter of Paul to the Romans
I know that no good dwells in me, that is, in my

flesh; the desire to do right is there but not the power. What happens is that I do, not the good I will to do, but the evil I do not intend. But if I do what is against my will, it is not I who do it, but sin which dwells in me. This means that even though I want to do what is right, a law that leads to wrong-doing is always ready to hand. My inner self agrees with the law of God, but I see in my body's members another law at war with the law of my mind; this makes me the prisoner of the law of sin in my members. What a wretched man I am! Who can free me from this body under the power of death? All praise to God, through Jesus Christ our Lord.—This is the Word of the Lord. ℟. **Thanks be to God. ℣**

Responsorial Psalm   Ps 119, 66. 68. 76. 77. 93. 94

℟. (68) **Teach me your laws, O Lord.**

Teach me wisdom and knowledge,
    for in your commands I trust. — ℟

You are good and bountiful;
    teach me your statutes. — ℟

Let your kindness comfort me
    according to your promise to your servants. — ℟

Let your compassion come to me that I may live,
    for your law is my delight. — ℟

Never will I forget your precepts,
    for through them you give me life. — ℟

I am yours; save me,
    for I have sought your precepts. — ℟ ℣

GOSPEL   Lk 12, 54-59

Alleluia (Mt 11, 25)

℟. **Alleluia.** Blessed are you, Father, Lord of heaven
        and earth;
you have revealed to little ones the mysteries of the
        kingdom. ℟. **Alleluia.**

Man is capable of predicting weather changes, the amount of snow, and the direction of the wind. Yet through it all he is incapable of bringing to an end the wars he fights. Jesus advises a peaceful settlement in disputes.

℣. The Lord be with you. ℟. **And also with you.**

✠ A reading from the holy gospel according to Luke ℟. **Glory to you, Lord.**

Jesus said to the crowds: "When you see a cloud rising in the west, you say immediately that rain is coming—and so it does. When the wind blows from the south, you say it is going to be hot—and so it is. You hypocrites! If you can interpret the portents of earth and sky, why can you not interpret the present time? Tell me, why do you not judge for yourselves what is just? When you are going with your opponent to appear before a magistrate, try to settle with him on the way lest he turn you over to the judge, and the judge deliver you up to the jailer, and the jailer throw you into prison. I warn you, you will not be released from there until you have paid the last penny."—This is the gospel of the Lord. ℟. **Praise to you, Lord Jesus Christ.** ➔ No. 15, p. 623

SATURDAY OF THE TWENTY-NINTH WEEK IN ORDINARY TIME

READING I Rom 8, 1-11

Paul expresses strength in the spirit which comes through the Spirit of Christ. The strength comes as an aid against the flesh which Paul calls sin. Those who have the spirit are dead to that sin and alive with Christ.

A reading from the letter of Paul to the Romans

There is no condemnation now for those who are in Christ Jesus. The law of the spirit, the spirit of life in Christ Jesus, has freed you from the law of sin and death. The law was powerless because of its weakening by the flesh. Then God sent his Son in the likeness of sinful flesh as a sin offering, thereby condemning sin in the flesh, so that the just demands of the law might be fulfilled in us who live, not according to the flesh, but according to the spirit.

Those who live according to the flesh are intent on the things of the flesh, those who live according to the spirit, on those of the spirit. The tendency of the flesh is toward death but that of the spirit toward life and peace. The flesh in its tendency is at enmity with God; it is not subject to God's law. Indeed, it cannot be; those who are in the flesh cannot please God. But you are not in the flesh; you are in the spirit, since the Spirit of God dwells in you. If anyone does not have the Spirit of Christ, he does not belong to Christ. If Christ is in you, the body is indeed dead because of sin, while the spirit lives because of justice. If the Spirit of him who raised Jesus from the dead dwells in you, then he who raised Christ from the dead will bring your mortal bodies to life also through his Spirit dwelling in you.—This is the Word of the Lord. R̂. **Thanks be to God.** ♦

Responsorial Psalm   Ps 24, 1-2. 3-4. 5-6

R̂. (6) **Lord, this is the people that longs to see your face.**

The Lord's are the earth and its fullness;
   the world and those who dwell in it.
For he founded it upon the seas
   and established it upon the rivers. — R̂

Who can ascend the mountain of the Lord?
   or who may stand in his holy place?
He whose hands are sinless, whose heart is clean,
   who desires not what is vain. — R̂

He shall receive a blessing from the Lord,
   a reward from God his savior.
Such is the race that seeks for him,
   that seeks the face of the God of Jacob. — R̂ ♦

GOSPEL   Lk 13, 1-9

Alleluia (Ez 33, 11)

R̂. **Alleluia.** I do not wish the sinner to die, says the Lord,
   but to turn to me and live. R̂. **Alleluia.**

Jesus teaches about reform and uses the example of the fig tree. God is willing to give this time; still, if there is no improvement, the tree will be cut down.

℣. The Lord be with you. ℟. **And also with you.**

✠ A reading from the holy gospel according to Luke

℟. **Glory to you, Lord.**

Persons were present who told Jesus about the Galileans whose blood Pilate had mixed with their sacrifices. He said in reply: "Do you thiink that these Galileans were the greatest sinners in Galilee just because they suffered this? By no means! But I tell you, you will all come to the same end unless you reform. Or take those eighteen who were killed by a falling tower in Siloam. Do you think they were more guilty than anyone else who lived in Jerusalem? Certainly not! But I tell you, you will all come to the same end unless you reform."

Jesus spoke this parable: "A man had a fig tree growing in his vineyard, and he came out looking for fruit on it but did not find any. He said to the vinedresser, 'Look here! For three years now I have come in search of fruit on this fig tree and found none. Cut it down. Why should it clutter up the ground?' In answer, the man said, 'Sir, leave it another year, while I hoe around it and manure it; then perhaps it will bear fruit. If not, it shall be cut down.' "—This is the gospel of the Lord. ℟. **Praise to you, Lord Jesus Christ.** ➤ No. 15, p. 623

INTRODUCTION FOR 30th TO 34th WEEK

The Book of Wisdom—*Written about 100 B.C. by an unknown member of the Jewish community at Alexandria, Egypt, whose primary purpose was the edification of his co-religionists in a time when they had experienced suffering and oppression, in part at least at the hands of apostate fellow Jews. To convey his message he made use of the most popular religious themes of his time, namely, the splendor and worth of divine wisdom, the glorious events of the Exodus, God's mercy, the folly of idolatry, and the manner in which God's justice is vindicated in rewarding or punishing the individual soul.*

The Books of Maccabees—*The two Books of Maccabees contain independent accounts of events in parts identical which accompanied the attempted suppression of Judaism in Palestine in the second century B.C. The vigorous reaction to this attempt established for a time the religious and political independence of the Jews.*

The first book was written about 100 B.C. and expresses the customary belief of Israel without the new elements that appear in 2 Maccabees and Daniel.

The second book has for its purpose to give a theological interpretation to the history of the period from 180 to 161 B.C. Of theological importance are the author's teaching on the resurrection of the just on the last day, the intercession of the saints in heaven for people living on earth, and the power of the living to offer prayers and sacrifices for the dead.

The Book of Daniel—*This book takes its name, not from the author, who is actually unknown, but from its hero, a young Jew taken early to Babylon, where he lived at least until 538 B.C. Strictly speaking, the book does not belong to the prophetic writings but rather to a distinctive type of literature known as "apocalyptic," of which it is an early specimen. Apoc-*

alptic writing enjoyed its greatest popularity from 200 B.C. to 100 A.D., a time of distress and persecution for Jews and, later, for Christians. Though subsequent in time to the prophetic, apocalyptic literature has its roots in the teaching of the prophets, who often pointed ahead to the day of the Lord, the consummation of history. For both prophet and apocalyptist Yahweh was the Lord of history, and he would ultimately vindicate his people.

This work was composed during the bitter persecution carried on by Antiochus IV Epiphanes (167-164) and was written to strengthen and comfort the Jewish people in their ordeal. It contains stories originating in and transmitted by popular traditions which tell of the trials and triumphs of the wise Daniel and his three companions. The moral is that men of faith can resist temptation and conquer adversity. The characters are not purely legendary but rest on older historical tradition.

MONDAY OF THE THIRTIETH WEEK
IN ORDINARY TIME

READING I   Rom 8, 12-17

Paul reminds the Romans that they cannot live according to the flesh. Through Jesus a new life has come—adoption by the Father and a promise to be heirs with Jesus.

A reading from the letter of Paul to the Romans

We are debtors, then, my brothers—but not to the flesh, so that we should live according to the flesh. If you live according to the flesh, you will die; but if by the spirit you put to death the evil deeds of the body, you will live.

All who are led by the Spirit of God are sons of God. You did not receive a spirit of slavery leading you back into fear, but a spirit of adoption through which we cry out, "Abba!" (that is, "Father"). The Spirit himself gives witness with our spirit that we are children of God. But if we are children, we are heirs as well: heirs of God, heirs with Christ, if only we suffer with him so as to be glorified with him.— This is the Word of the Lord. ℟. **Thanks be to God. ♥**

Responsorial Psalm   Ps 68, 2. 4. 6-7. 20-21

℟. (21) **Our God is the God of salvation.**

God arises; his enemies are scattered,
    and those who hate him flee before him.
But the just rejoice and exult before God;
    they are glad and rejoice. — ℟

The father of orphans and the defender of widows
    is God in his holy dwelling.
God gives a home to the forsaken;
    he leads forth prisoners to prosperity. — ℟

Blessed day by day be the Lord,
    who bears our burdens; God, who is our salvation.
God is a saving God for us;
    the Lord, my Lord, controls the passageways of
        death. — ℟ ♥

GOSPEL   Lk 13, 10-17

Alleluia (Jn 17, 17)

℟. **Alleluia.** Your word, O Lord is truth;
make us holy in the truth. ℟. **Alleluia.**

The Pharisees, considering the sabbath to be a day of rest and worship, cannot see what is before them. This man, this Jesus whom they are questioning, has just returned a woman's strength to her and in this action is worshiping the Father.

℣. The Lord be with you. ℟. **And also with you.**

✠ A reading from the holy gospel according to Luke

℟. **Glory to you, Lord.**

On a sabbath day Jesus was teaching in one of the synagogues. There was a woman there who for eighteen years had been possessed by a spirit which drained her strength. She was badly stooped—quite incapable of standing erect. When Jesus saw her, he called her to him and said, "Woman, you are free of your infirmity." He laid his hand on her, and immediately she stood up straight and began thanking God.

The chief of the synagogue, indignant that Jesus should have healed on the sabbath, said to the congregation, "There are six days for working. Come on those days to be cured, not on the sabbth." The Lord said in reply, "O you hypocrites! Which of you does not let his ox or ass out of the stall on the sabbath to water it? Should not this daughter of Abraham here who has been in the bondage of Satan for eighteen years have been released from her shackles on the sabbath?" At these words, his opponents were covered with confusion; meanwhile, everyone else rejoiced at the marvels Jesus was accomplishing.— This is the gospel of the Lord. ℟. **Praise to you, Lord Jesus Christ.**   ➔ No. 15, p. 623

TUESDAY OF THE THIRTIETH WEEK IN ORDINARY TIME

READING I   Rom 8, 18-25

In hope, all of creation eagerly awaits the revelation of the sons of God. The sufferings of the present life are as nothing compared with the glory that is to come.

A reading from the letter of Paul to the Romans

I consider the sufferings of the present to be as

nothing compared with the glory to be revealed in us. Indeed, the whole created world eagerly awaits the revelation of the sons of God. Creation was made subject to futility, not of its own accord but by him who once subjected it; yet not without hope, because the world itself will be freed from its slavery to corruption and share in the glorious freedom of the children of God. Yes, we know that all creation groans and is in agony even until now. Not only that, but we ourselves, although we have the Spirit as first fruits, groan inwardly while we await the redemption of our bodies. In hope we were saved. But hope is not hope if its object is seen; how is it possible for one to hope for what he sees? And hoping for what we cannot see means awaiting it with patient endurance.—This is the Word of the Lord. ℟. **Thanks be to God.** ✟

Responsorial Psalm   Ps 126, 1-2. 2-3. 4-5. 6

℟. (3) **The Lord has done marvels for us.**

When the Lord brought back the captives of Zion,
   we were like men dreaming.
Then our mouth was filled with laughter,
   and our tongue with rejoicing. — ℟

Then they said among the nations,
   "The Lord has done great things for them."
The Lord has done great things for us;
   we are glad indeed. — ℟

Restore our fortunes, O Lord,
   like the torrents in the southern desert.
Those that sow in tears
   shall reap rejoicing. — ℟

Although they go forth weeping,
   carrying the seed to be sown,
They shall come back rejoicing,
   carrying their sheaves. — ℟ ✟

GOSPEL   Lk 13, 18-21

Alleluia (Mt 11, 25)

℟. **Alleuia.** Blessed are you, Father, Lord of heaven
    and earth;
you have revealed to little ones the mysteries of the
    kingdom. ℟. **Alleluia.**

The reign, the kingdom of God, is like the tiny mustard seed which
grows into a mighty shrub or like the yeast that is kneaded in flour.

℣. The Lord be with you. ℟. **And also with you.**
✠ A reading from the holy gospel according to Luke
℟. **Glory to you, Lord.**

Jesus said: "What does the reign of God resemble?
To what shall I liken it? It is like mustard seed
which a man took and planted in his garden. It
grew and became a large shrub and the birds of the
air nested in its branches."

He went on: "To what shall I compare the reign
of God? It is like yeast which a woman took to knead
into three measures of flour until the whole mass
of dough began to rise."—This is the gospel of the
Lord. ℟. **Praise to you, Lord Jesus Christ.**

➔ No. 15, p. 623

────────────

WEDNESDAY OF THE THIRTIETH WEEK
IN ORDINARY TIME

READING I   Rom 8, 26-30

God knows man's weaknesses and how difficult it is to pray. But for
those who are anxious to serve God, the Spirit fills up the weakness
so that all may share the image of his Son.

A reading from the letter of Paul to the Romans
The Spirit too helps us in our weakness, for we do
not know how to pray as we ought; but the Spirit
himself makes intercession for us with groanings

which cannot be expressed in speech. He who search-es hearts knows what the Spirit means, for the Spirit intercedes for the saints as God himself wills.

We know that God makes all things work together for the good of those who have been called accord-ing to his decree. Those whom he foreknew he pre-destined to share the image of his Son, that the Son might be the first-born of many brothers. Those he predestined he likewise called; those he called he also justified; and those he justified he in turn glori-fied.—This is the Word of the Lord. ℞. **Thanks be to God.** ℣

Responsorial Psalm   Ps 13, 4-5. 6

℞. (6) **All my hope, O Lord,
is in your loving kindness.**

Look, answer me, O Lord, my God!
   Give light to my eyes that I may not sleep in death
Lest my enemy say, "I have overcome him";
   lest my foes rejoice at my downfall. — ℞

Though I trusted in your kindness,
   let my heart rejoice in your salvation;
   let me sing of the Lord, "He has been good to
   me." — ℞ ℣

GOSPEL   Lk 13, 22-30
Alleluia (2 Thes 2, 14)

℞. **Alleluia.** God has called us with the gospel;
the people won for him by Jesus Christ our Lord.
   ℞. **Alleluia.**

Many from the east and the west will come to take their places in the kingdom of God. Those who are evildoers, however, will be shut out from eternal joy. Some who are last will be first.

℣. The Lord be with you. ℞. **And also with you.**
✠ A reading from the holy gospel according to Luke
℞. **Glory to you, Lord.**

Jesus went through cities and towns teaching—all

the while making his way toward Jerusalem. Someone asked him, "Lord, are they few in number who are to be saved?" He replied: "Try to come in through the narrow door. Many, I tell you, will try to enter and be unable. When once the master of the house has risen to lock the door and you stand outside knocking and saying, 'Sir, open for us,' he will say in reply, 'I do not know where you come from.' Then you will begin to say, 'We ate and drank in your company. You taught in our streets.' But he will answer, 'I tell you, I do not know where you come from. Away from me, you evildoers!'

"There will be wailing and grinding of teeth when you see Abraham, Isaac, Jacob, and all the prophets safe in the kingdom of God, and you yourselves rejected. People will come from the east and the west, from the north and the south, and will take their place at the feast in the kingdom of God. Some who are last will be first and some who are first will be last."—This is the gospel of the Lord. ℟. **Praise to you, Lord Jesus Christ.** ➤ No. 15, p. 623

THURSDAY OF THE THIRTIETH WEEK IN ORDINARY TIME

READING I Rom 8, 31-39

God's love for his people was so intense that he did not spare his Son for their redemption. Who could separate them from the love of Jesus? No trial, nor distress, nor even death itself.

A reading from the letter of Paul to the Romans

If God is for us, who can be against us? Is it possible that he who did not spare his own Son but handed him over for the sake of us all will not grant us all things besides? Who shall bring a charge against God's chosen ones? God, who justifies? Who shall condemn them? Christ Jesus, who died or rather was raised up, who is at the right hand of God and who intercedes for us?

Who will separate us from the love of Christ? Trial, or distress, or persecution, or hunger, or nakedness, or danger, or the sword? As Scripture says: "For your sake we are being slain all the day long; we are looked upon as sheep to be slaughtered." Yet in all this we are more than conquerors because of him who has loved us. For I am certain that neither death nor life, neither angels nor principalities, nor powers, neither the present nor the future, neither height nor depth, nor any other creature, will be able to separate us from the love of God that comes to us in Christ Jesus, our Lord.—This is the Word of the Lord. ℟. **Thanks be to God.** ℣

Responsorial Psalm   Ps 109, 21-22. 26-27. 30-31

℟. (26) **Save me, O Lord,
 in your kindness.**

Do you, O God, my Lord, deal kindly with me for
    your name's sake;
    in your generous kindness rescue me;
For I am wretched and poor,
    and my heart is pierced within me. — ℟

Help me, O Lord, my God;
    save me, in your kindness,
And let them know that this is your hand;
    that you, O Lord, have done this. — ℟

I will speak my thanks earnestly to the Lord,
    and in the midst of the throng I will praise him,
For he stood at the right hand of the poor man,
    to save him from those who would condemn
    him. — ℟ ℣

GOSPEL   Lk 13, 31-35

Alleluia (Lk 19, 38)

℟. **Alleluia.** Blessed is the king who comes in the
    name of the Lord:
peace on earth, and glory in heaven! ℟. **Alleluia.**

Jesus is warned that Herod is trying to kill him. Jesus answers that already he performs miracles and cures, and on the third day his purpose for coming into the world will be accomplished.

℣. The Lord be with you. ℟. **And also with you.**
✠ A reading from the holy gospel according to Luke
℟. **Glory to you, Lord.**

Certain Pharisees came to Jesus. "Go on your way!" they said. "Leave this place! Herod is trying to kill you." His answer was: "Go tell that fox, 'Today and tomorrow I cast out devils and perform cures, and on the third day my purpose is accomplished. For all that, I must proceed on course today, tomorrow, and the day after, since no prophet can be allowed to die anywhere except in Jerusalem.'

"O Jerusalem, Jerusalem, you slay the prophets and stone those who are sent to you! How often have I wanted to gather your children together as a mother bird collects her young under her wings, and you refused me! Your temple will be abandoned. I say to you, you shall not see me until the time comes when you say, 'Blessed is he who comes in the name of the Lord.'"—This is the gospel of the Lord. ℟. **Praise to you, Lord Jesus Christ.** ➔ No. 15, p. 623

FRIDAY OF THE THIRTIETH WEEK IN ORDINARY TIME

READING I   Rom 9, 1-5

Paul claims grief and pain. He says that he would even be parted from Jesus for his brothers if this would help them. To them so many special promises were made; from them came the Messiah.

A reading from the letter of Paul to the Romans

I speak the truth in Christ: I do not lie. My conscience bears me witness in the Holy Spirit that there is great grief and constant pain in my heart. Indeed, I could even wish to be separated from

Christ for the sake of my brothers, my kinsmen the Israelites. Theirs were the adoption, the glory, the covenants, the law-giving, the worship, and the promises; theirs were the patriarchs, and from them came the Messiah (I speak of his human origins). Blessed forever be God who is over all! Amen.— This is the Word of the Lord. ℟. **Thanks be to God.** ✟

Responsorial Psalm   Ps 147, 12-13. 14-15. 19-20

℟. (12) **Praise the Lord, Jerusalem.**

Glorify the Lord, O Jerusalem;
  praise your God, O Zion.
For he has strengthened the bars of your gates;
  he has blessed your children within you. — ℟

He has granted peace in your borders;
  with the best of wheat he fills you.
He sends forth his command to the earth;
  swiftly runs his word! — ℟

He has proclaimed his word to Jacob,
  his statutes and his ordinances to Israel.
He has not done thus for any other nation;
  his ordinances he has not made known to them.
    Alleluia. — ℟ ✟

GOSPEL   Lk 14, 1-6

Alleluia (Jn 10, 27)

℟. **Alleluia.** My sheep listen to my voice, says the Lord;
I know them, and they follow me. ℟. **Alleluia.**

After curing the man from dropsy, Jesus asks the lawyers if it is lawful to heal a man on the sabbath. Jesus also asks if they would take their son or their ox out of a well on the sabbath. No answer comes.

℣. The Lord be with you. ℟. **And also with you.**
✠ A reading from the holy gospel according to Luke
℟. **Glory to you, Lord.**

When Jesus came on a sabbath to eat a meal in the house of one of the leading Pharisees, they observed him closely. Directly in front of him was a man who suffered from dropsy. Jesus asked the lawyers and the Pharisees, "Is it lawful to cure on the sabbath or not?" At this they kept silent. He took the man, healed him, and sent him on his way. Then he addressed himself to them: "If one of you has a son or an ox and he falls into a pit, will he not immediately rescue him on the sabbath day?" This they could not answer.—This is the gospel of the Lord. ℟. **Praise to you, Lord Jesus Christ.** ➤ No. 15, p. 623

SATURDAY OF THE THIRTIETH WEEK IN ORDINARY TIME

READING I   Rom 11, 1-2. 11-12. 25-29

Paul asks if God has rejected his own people. Because the Jews rejected Jesus, Paul has gone to the Gentiles to make the Jews envious. This faith is a rich treasure for the Gentiles.

A reading from the letter of Paul to the Romans

I ask, then, has God rejected his people? Of course not! I myself am an Israelite, descended from Abraham, of the tribe of Benjamin. No, God has not rejected his people whom he foreknew.

I further ask, does their stumbling mean that they are forever fallen? Not at all! Rather, by their transgressions salvation has come to the Gentiles to stir Israel to envy. But if their transgression and their diminishing have meant riches for the Gentile world, how much more their full number!

Brothers, I do not want you to be ignorant of this mystery lest you be conceited: blindness has come upon part of Israel until the full number of Gentiles enter in, and then all Israel will be saved. As Scripture says: "Out of Zion will come the deliverer who shall remove all impiety from Jacob; and this is the covenant I will make with them when I take away their sins." In respect to the gospel, the Jews are enemies of God for your sake; in respect to the election, they are beloved by him because of the patriarchs. God's gifts and his call are irrevocable.—This is the Word of the Lord. ℞. **Thanks be to God.** ℣

Responsorial Psalm   Ps 94, 12-13. 14-15. 17-18

℞. (14) **The Lord will not abandon his people.**

Happy the man whom you instruct, O Lord,
  whom by your law you teach,
Giving him rest from evil days. — ℞

For the Lord will not cast off his people,
  nor abandon his inheritance;
But judgment shall again be with justice,
  and all the upright of heart shall follow it. — ℞

Were not the Lord my help,
  I would soon dwell in the silent grave.
When I say, "My foot is slipping,"
  your kindness, O Lord, sustains me. — ℞ ℣

GOSPEL   Lk 14, 1. 7-11

Alleluia (Mt 11, 29)

℞. **Alleluia.** Take my yoke upon you;
learn from me, for I am gentle and lowly of heart.
      ℞. **Alleluia.**

Jesus teaches by the parable of the wedding feast. The Jews who are proud are anxious for recognition. Go to the last place, Jesus counsels. He who humbles himself shall be exalted.

℣. The Lord be with you. ℞. **And also with you.**
✠ A reading from the holy gospel according to Luke
℞. **Glory to you, Lord.**

When Jesus came on a sabbath to eat a meal in the house of one of the leading Pharisees, they observed him closely. He went on to address a parable to the guests, noticing how they were trying to get the places of honor at the table: "When you are invited by someone to a wedding party, do not sit in the place of honor in case some greater dignitary has been invited. Then the host might come and say to you, 'Make room for this man,' and you would have to proceed shamefacedly to the lowest place. What you should do when you have been invited is go and sit in the lowest place, so that when your host approaches you he will say, 'My friend, come up higher.' This will win you the esteem of your fellow guests. For everyone who exalts himself shall be humbled, and he who humbles himself shall be exalted."—This is the gospel of the Lord. ℞. **Praise to you, Lord Jesus Christ.**   ➜ No. 15, p. 623

MONDAY OF THE THIRTY-FIRST WEEK IN ORDINARY TIME

READING I   Rom 11, 29-36

All men were once disobedient to God; still, God shows them his mercy. Who can fathom the riches of the mind of God? Through him all creation has life.

A reading from the letter of Paul to the Romans

God's gifts and his call are irrevocable. Just as you were once disobedient to God and now have received mercy through their disobedience, so they have become disobedient—since God wished to show you mercy—that they too may receive mercy. God has imprisoned all in disobedience that he might have mercy on all.

How deep are the riches and the wisdom and the knowledge of God! How inscrutable his judgments, how unsearchable his ways! For "who has known the mind of the Lord? Or who has ever been his counselor? Who has given him anything so as to deserve return?" For from him and through him and for him all things are: To him be glory forever. Amen. —This is the Word of the Lord. ℞. **Thanks be to God.** ℣

Responsorial Psalm   Ps 69, 30-31. 33-34. 36-37

℞. (14) **Lord, in your great love, answer me.**

But I am afflicted and in pain;
  let your saving help, O God, protect me.
I will praise the name of God in song,
  and I will glorify him with thanksgiving. — ℟

"See, you lowly ones, and be glad;
  you who seek God, may your hearts be merry!
For the Lord hears the poor,
  and his own who are in bonds he spurns not." — ℟

For God will save Zion
  and rebuild the cities of Judah.
They shall dwell in the land and own it,
  and the descendants of his servants shall inherit it,
  and those who love his name shall inhabit it.—℟ ℣

GOSPEL   Lk 14, 12-14

Alleluia (Jn 8, 31-32)

℟. **Alleluia.** If you stay in my word, you will indeed
    be my disciples,
and you will know the truth, says the Lord. ℟. **Alleluia.**

Jesus teaches that it is better that good works will be rewarded
after the resurrection. Do good to those who cannot likely repay now,
especially the poor and crippled.

℣. The Lord be with you. ℟. **And also with you.**
✠ A reading from the holy gospel according to Luke
℟. **Glory to you, Lord.**

Jesus said to the chief of the Pharisees who had invited him to dinner: "Whenever you give a lunch or
dinner, do not invite your friends or brothers or
relatives or wealthy neighbors. They might invite
you in return and thus repay you. No, when you
have a reception, invite beggars and the crippled,
the lame and the blind. You should be pleased that
they cannot repay you, for you will be repaid in the
resurrection of the just."—This is the gospel of the
Lord. ℟. **Praise to you, Lord Jesus Christ.**

➔ No. 15, p. 623

TUESDAY OF THE THIRTY-FIRST WEEK
IN ORDINARY TIME

READING I   Rom 12, 5-16

In the body of Jesus Christ, the Church, there are many roles. Since each person has different talents, he has a corresponding responsibility. All are to love one another as brothers.

A reading from the letter of Paul to the Romans

We, though many, are one body in Christ and individually members one of another. We have gifts that differ according to the favor bestowed on each of us. One's gift may be prophecy; its use should be in proportion to his faith. It may be the gift of ministry; it should be used for service. One who is a teacher should use his gift for teaching; one with the power of exhortation should exhort. He who gives alms should do so generously; he who rules should exercise his authority with care; he who performs works of mercy should do so cheerfully.

Your love must be sincere. Detest what is evil, cling to what is good. Love one another with the affection of brothers. Anticipate each other in showing respect. Do not grow slack but be fervent in spirit; he whom you serve is the Lord. Rejoice in hope, be patient under trial, persevere in prayer. Look on the needs of the saints as your own; be generous in offering hospitality. Bless your persecutors; bless and do not curse them. Rejoice with those who rejoice, weep with those who weep. Have the same attitude toward all.—This is the Word of the Lord. ℟. **Thanks be to God.** ✝

Responsorial Psalm   Ps 131, 1. 2. 3

℟. **In you, Lord, I have found my peace.**

O Lord, my heart is not proud,
    nor are my eyes haughty;
I busy not myself with great things,
    nor with things too sublime for me. — ℟

Nay rather, I have stilled and quieted
  my soul like a weaned child.
Like a weaned child on its mother's lap,
  [so is my soul within me.] — ℟

O Israel, hope in the Lord,
  both now and forever. — ℟ ℣

GOSPEL   Lk 14, 15-24
Alleluia (Mt 11, 28)

℟. **Alleluia.** Come to me, all you that labor and are
    burdened,
and I will give you rest, says the Lord. ℟. **Alleluia.**

Happy will be those who eat with God. Many during life find excuses
to avoid God's table. Jesus warns that these will not taste a morsel
at the heavenly banquet.

℣. The Lord be with you. ℟. **And also with you.**
✠ A reading from the holy gospel according to Luke
℟. **Glory to you, Lord.**

One of the guests at a party said to Jesus, "Happy is
he who eats bread in the kingdom of God." Jesus responded: "A man was giving a large dinner and he
invited many. At dinner time he sent his servant to
say to those invited, 'Come along, everything is ready
now.' But they began to excuse themselves, one and
all. The first one said to the servant, 'I have bought
some land and must go out and inspect it. Please
excuse me.' Another said, 'I have bought five yoke
of oxen and I am going out to test them. Please
excuse me.' A third said, 'I am newly married and
so I cannot come.' The servant, returning, reported
all this to his master. The master of the house grew
angry at the account. He said to his servant, 'Go
out quickly into the streets and alleys of the town
and bring in the poor and crippled, the blind and the
lame.' The servant reported, after some time, 'Your
orders have been carried out, my lord, and there is
still room.' The master then said to the servant, 'Go
out into the highways and along the hedgerows

and force them to come in. I want my house to be full, but I tell you that not one of those invited shall taste a morsel of my dinner.' "—This is the gospel of the Lord. ℟. **Praise to you, Lord Jesus Christ.**

➔ No. 15, p. 623

WEDNESDAY OF THE THIRTY-FIRST WEEK IN ORDINARY TIME

READING I   Rom 13, 8-10

Love does not violate the rights of a neighbor; it is the fulfillment of the law. Everyone must love his neighbor as he loves himself.

A reading from the letter of Paul to the Romans

Owe no debt to anyone except the debt that binds us to love one another. He who loves his neighbor has fulfilled the law. The commandments, "You shall not commit adultery; you shall not murder; you shall not steal; you shall not covet," and any other commandment there may be are all summed up in this, "You shall love your neighbor as yourself." Love never does any wrong to the neighbor, hence love is the fulfillment of the law.—This is the Word of the Lord. ℟. **Thanks be to God.** ℣

Responsorial Psalm   Ps 112, 1-2. 4-5. 9

℟. (5) **Happy the man who is merciful and lends to those in need.**

Happy the man who fears the Lord,
    who greatly delights in his commands.
His posterity shall be mighty upon the earth;
    the upright generation shall be blessed. — ℟

He dawns through the darkness, a light for the upright;
    he is gracious and merciful and just.
Well for the man who is gracious and lends,
    who conducts his affairs with justice. — ℟

Lavishly he gives to the poor;
  his generosity shall endure forever;
  his horn shall be exalted in glory. — ℟ ✔

℟. Or: **Alleluia.** ✔

GOSPEL   Lk 14, 25-33

Alleluia (1 Pt 4, 14)

℟. **Alleluia.** If you are insulted for the name of
    Christ, blessed are you,
for the Spirit of God rests upon you. ℟. **Alleluia.**

To come to Jesus a decision has to be made. Christ must come before
all else. It takes careful thought. Only he who is willing to take up his
cross will rightfully follow Jesus.

℣. The Lord be with you. ℟. **And also with you.**
✠ A reading from the holy gospel according to Luke
℟. **Glory to you, Lord.**

On one occasion when a great crowd was with
Jesus, he turned to them and said, "If anyone comes
to me without turning his back on his father and
mother, his wife and his children, his brothers and
sisters, indeed his very self, he cannot be my follower. Anyone who does not take up his cross and
follow me cannot be my disciple. If one of you decides to build a tower, will he not first sit down and
calculate the outlay to see if he has enough money
to complete the project? He will do that for fear of
laying the foundation and then not being able to
complete the work; at which all who saw it would
then jeer at him, saying, 'That man began to build
what he could not finish.'

"Or if a king is about to march on another king
to do battle with him, will he not sit down first
and consider whether, with ten thousand men, he
can withstand an enemy coming against him with
twenty thousand? If he cannot, he will send a delegation while the enemy is still at a distance, asking
for terms of peace. In the same way, none of you

can be my disciple if he does not renounce all his possessions."—This is the gospel of the Lord. ℟. **Praise to you, Lord Jesus Christ.** ➔ No. 15, p. 623

THURSDAY OF THE THIRTY-FIRST WEEK IN ORDINARY TIME

READING I Rom 14, 7-12

Every man shall have to give an account of his life before God. No one is a master of his own life. Life comes to us from God.

A reading from the letter of Paul to the Romans

None of us lives as his own master and none of us dies as his own master. While we live we are responsible to the Lord, and when we die we die as his servants. Both in life and in death we are the Lord's. That is why Christ died and came to life again, that he might be Lord of both the dead and the living. But you, how can you sit in judgment on your brother? Or you, how can you look down on your brother? We shall all have to appear before the judgment seat of God. It is written, "As surely as I live, says the Lord, every knee shall bend before me and every tongue shall give praise to God."

Every one of us will have to give an account of himself before God.—This is the Word of the Lord. ℟. **Thanks be to God.** ✣

Responsorial Psalm Ps 27, 1. 4. 13-14

℟. (13) **I believe that I shall see the good things of the Lord in the land of the living.**

The Lord is my light and my salvation;
    whom should I fear?
The Lord is my life's refuge;
    of whom should I be afraid? — ℟

One thing I ask of the Lord;
    this I seek:

To dwell in the house of the Lord
  all the days of my life,
That I may gaze on the loveliness of the Lord
  and contemplate his temple. — ℟

I believe that I shall see the bounty of the Lord
  in the land of the living.
Wait for the Lord with courage;
  be stouthearted, and wait for the Lord. — ℟ ℣

GOSPEL   Lk 15, 1-10

Alleluia (Mt 11, 28)

℟. **Alleluia.** Come to me, all you that labor and are
  burdened,
and I will give you rest, says the Lord. ℟. **Alleluia.**

A shepherd who finds a sheep that was lost or a poor woman who
loses a silver piece and finds it will be happy and rejoice. So in
heaven a sinner who repents will cause great joy.

℣. The Lord be with you. ℟. **And also with you.**
✠ A reading from the holy gospel according to Luke
℟. **Glory to you, Lord.**

The tax collectors and sinners were all gathering
around to hear Jesus, at which the Pharisees and
the scribes murmured, "This man welcomes sinners
and eats with them." Then he addressed this parable
to them: "Who among you, if he has a hundred sheep
and loses one of them, does not leave the ninety-
nine in the wasteland and follow the lost one until
he finds it? And when he finds it, he puts it on his
shoulders in jubilation. Once arrived home, he invites
friends and neighbors in and says to them, 'Rejoice
with me because I have found my lost sheep.' I tell
you, there will likewise be more joy in heaven over
one repentant sinner than over ninety-nine righteous
people who have no need to repent.

"What woman, if she has ten silver pieces and
loses one, does not light a lamp and sweep the house
in a diligent search until she has retrieved what she

lost? And when she finds it, she calls in her friends and neighbors to say, 'Rejoice with me! I have found the silver piece I lost.' I tell you, there will be the same kind of joy before the angels of God over one repentant sinner."—This is the gospel of the Lord. ℟. **Praise to you, Lord Jesus Christ.**

➤ No. 15, p. 623

FRIDAY OF THE THIRTY-FIRST WEEK IN ORDINARY TIME

READING I   Rom 15, 14-21

Paul sees a need to give advice because he is a minister of Christ. His duty is to preach the gospel. He would not dare, however, to preach anything except what Christ has done through him to win the Gentiles.

A reading from the letter of Paul to the Romans

I am convinced, my brothers, that you are filled with goodness, that you have complete knowledge, and that you are able to give advice to one another. Yet I have written to you rather boldly in parts of this letter by way of reminder. I take this liberty because God has given me the grace to be a minister of Christ Jesus among the Gentiles, with the priestly duty of preaching the gospel of God so that the Gentiles may be offered up as a pleasing sacrifice, consecrated by the Holy Spirit. This means I can take glory in Christ Jesus for the work I have done for God. I will not dare to speak of anything except what Christ has done through me to win the Gentiles to obedience by word and deed, with mighty signs and marvels, by the power of God's Spirit. As a result, I have completed preaching the gospel of Christ from Jerusalem all the way around to Illyria. It has been a point of honor with me never to preach in places where Christ's name was already known, for I did not want to build on a foundation laid by

another but rather to fulfill the words of Scripture,
"They who received no word of him will see him,
and they who have never heard will understand."—
This is the Word of the Lord. ℟. **Thanks be to God.** ↓

Responsorial Psalm   Ps 98, 1. 2-3. 3-4

℟. (2) **The Lord has revealed to the nations his saving power.**

Sing to the Lord a new song,
  for he has done wondrous deeds;
His right hand has won victory for him,
  his holy arm. — ℟

The Lord has made his salvation known:
  in the sight of the nations he has revealed his
    justice.
He has remembered his kindness and his faithful-
    ness
  toward the house of Israel. — ℟

All the ends of the earth have seen
  the salvation by our God.
Sing joyfully to the Lord, all you lands;
  break into song; sing praise. — ℟ ↓

GOSPEL   Lk 16, 1-8

Alleluia (1 Jn 2, 5)

℟. **Alleluia.** He who keeps the word of Christ,
grows perfect in the love of God. ℟. **Alleluia.**

Jesus relates the parable of the enterprising manager who is about
to be dismissed. The manager cancels parts of his employer's debts
so that he will have friends to go to later. How ingenious people are
in the ways of the world.

℣. The Lord be with you. ℟. **And also with you.**
✠ A reading from the holy gospel according to Luke
℟. **Glory to you, Lord.**

Another time Jesus said to his disciples: "A rich
man had a manager who was reported to him for
dissipating his property. He summoned him and said,
'What is this I hear about you? Give me an account

of your service, for it is about to come to an end.' The manager thought to himself, 'What shall I do next? My employer is sure to dismiss me. I cannot dig ditches. I am ashamed to go begging. I have it! Here is a way to make sure that people will take me into their homes when I am let go.'

"So he called in each of his master's debtors, and said to the first, 'How much do you owe my master?' The man replied, 'A hundred jars of oil.' The manager said, 'Take your invoice, sit down quickly, and make it fifty.' Then he said to a second, 'How much do you owe?' The answer came, 'A hundred measures of wheat,' and the manager said, 'Take your invoice and make it eighty.'

"The owner then gave his devious employee credit for being enterprising! Why? Because the worldly take more initiative than the other-worldly when it comes to dealing with their own kind.—This is the gospel of the Lord. ℟. **Praise to you, Lord Jesus Christ.**

➔ No. 15, p. 623

SATURDAY OF THE THIRTY-FIRST WEEK IN ORDINARY TIME

READING I Rom 16, 3-9. 16. 22-27

In closing the letter to the Romans, Paul names many in his flock. He sends special Christ-like greetings and, in turn, he sets an example. Paul offers a prayer of praise to God through Jesus Christ.

A reading from the letter of Paul to the Romans

Give my greetings to Prisca and Aquila; they were my fellow workers in the service of Christ Jesus and even risked their lives for the sake of mine. Not only I but all the churches of the Gentiles are grateful to them. Remember me also to the congregation that meets in their house. Greetings to my beloved Epaenetus; he is the first offering that Asia made to

Christ. My greetings to Mary, who has worked hard for you, and to Andronicus and Junias, my kinsmen and fellow prisoners; they are outstanding apostles, and they were in Christ even before I was. Greetings to Ampliatus, who is dear to me in the Lord; to Urbanus, our fellow worker in the service of Christ; and to my beloved Stachys. Greet one another with a holy kiss. All the churches of Christ send you greetings.

I, Tertius, who have written this letter, send you my greetings in the Lord. Greetings also from Gaius, who is host to me and to the whole church. Erastus, the city treasurer, and our brother Quartus wish to be remembered to you.

Now to him who is able to strengthen you in the gospel which I proclaim when I preach Jesus Christ, the gospel which reveals the mystery hidden for many ages but now manifested through the writings of the prophets, and, at the command of the eternal God, made known to all the Gentiles that they may believe and obey—to him, the God who alone is wise, may glory be given through Jesus Christ unto endless ages. Amen.—This is the Word of the Lord.
℟. **Thanks be to God.** ℣

Responsorial Psalm   Ps 145, 2-3. 4-5. 10-11

℟ (1) **I will praise your name for ever, Lord.**

Every day will I bless you,
    and I will praise your name forever and ever.
Great is the Lord and highly to be praised;
    his greatness is unsearchable. — ℟

Generation after generation praises your works
    and proclaims your might.
They speak of the splendor of your glorious majesty
    and tell of your wondrous works. — ℟

Let all your works give you thanks, O Lord,
    and let your faithful ones bless you.
Let them discourse of the glory of your kingdom
    and speak of your might. — ℟ ℣

GOSPEL Lk 16, 9-15

Alleluia (2 Cor 8, 9)

℟. **Alleluia.** Jesus Christ was rich but he became poor,

to make you rich out of his poverty. ℟. **Alleluia.**

If a man can be trusted in little things, he proves his trustworthiness in greater matters. Still, no man can serve two masters. No one can serve God and money at the same time.

℣. The Lord be with you. ℟. **And also with you.**

✠ A reading from the holy gospel according to Luke
℟. **Glory to you, Lord.**

[Jesus said to his disciples:] "Make friends for yourselves through your use of this world's goods, so that when they fail you, a lasting reception will be yours. If you can trust a man in little things, you can also trust him in greater; while anyone unjust in a slight matter is also unjust in greater. If you cannot be trusted with elusive wealth, who will trust you with lasting? And if you have not been trustworthy with someone else's money, who will give you what is your own?

"No servant can serve two masters. Either he will hate the one and love the other or be attentive to the one and despise the other. You cannot give yourself to God and money." The Pharisees, who were avaricious men, heard all this and began to deride him. He said to them: "You justify yourselves in the eyes of men, but God reads your hearts. What man thinks important, God holds in contempt."—This is the gospel of the Lord. ℟. **Praise to you, Lord Jesus Christ.** ➔ No. 15, p. 623

MONDAY OF THE THIRTY-SECOND WEEK IN ORDINARY TIME

READING I Wis 1, 1-7

Justice should judge the earth. Perverse counsels separate a man from God. The Holy Spirit flees from deceit. The Spirit of the Lord fills the earth and knows what man says.

The beginning of the book of Wisdom

Love justice, you who judge the earth;
think of the Lord in goodness,
and seek him in integrity of heart;
Because he is found by those who test him not,
and he manifests himself to those who do not disbelieve him.
For perverse counsels separate a man from God,
and his power, put to the proof, rebukes the foolhardy;
Because into a soul that plots evil wisdom enters not,
nor dwells she in a body under debt of sin.
For the holy spirit of discipline flees deceit
and withdraws from senseless counsels;
and when injustice occurs it is rebuked.
For wisdom is a kindly spirit,
yet she acquits not the blasphemer of his guilty lips;
Because God is the witness of his inmost self
and the sure observer of his heart
and the listener to his tongue.
For the spirit of the Lord fills the world,
is all-embracing, and knows what man says.
This is the Word of the Lord. ℟. **Thanks be to God.** ↓

Responsorial Psalm Ps 139, 1-3. 4-6. 7-8. 9-10

℟. (24) **Guide me, Lord, along the everlasting way.**

O Lord, you have probed me and you know me;
you know when I sit and when I stand;
you understand my thoughts from afar.

My journeys and my rest you scrutinize,
  with all my ways you are familiar. — ℟

Even before a word is on my tongue,
  behold, O Lord, you know the whole of it.
Behind me and before, you hem me in
  and rest your hand upon me.
Such knowledge is too wonderful for me;
  too lofty for me to attain. — ℟

Where can I go from your spirit?
  from your presence where can I flee?
If I go up to the heavens, you are there;
  if I sink to the nether world, you are present
    there. — ℟

If I take the wings of the dawn,
  if I settle at the farthest limits of the sea,
Even there your hand shall guide me,
  and your right hand hold me fast. — ℟ ✇

GOSPEL Lk 17, 1-6

Alleluia (Phil 2, 15-16)

℟. **Alleluia.** Shine on the world like bright stars;
you are offering it the word of life. ℟. **Alleluia.**

To lead another into sin is serious. Forgiveness, however, is the mark
of a Christian. Jesus says that forgiveness should always be present
if a man is truly repentant.

℣. The Lord be with you. ℟. **And also with you.**
✠ A reading from the holy gospel according to Luke
℟. **Glory to you, Lord.**

Jesus said to his disciples: "Scandals will inevitably
arise, but woe to him through whom they come. He
would be better off thrown into the sea with a millstone around his neck than giving scandal to one
of these little ones.

  "Be on your guard. If your brother does wrong,
correct him; if he repents, forgive him. If he sins
against you seven times a day, and seven times a
day turns back to you saying, 'I am sorry,' forgive
him."

The apostles said to the Lord, "Increase our faith," and he answered: "If you had faith the size of a mustard seed, you could say to this sycamore, 'Be uprooted and transplanted into the sea,' and it would obey you."—This is the gospel of the Lord. ℟. **Praise to you, Lord Jesus Christ.**   ➔ No. 15, p. 623

TUESDAY OF THE THIRTY-SECOND WEEK IN ORDINARY TIME

READING I   Wis 2, 23—3, 9

Man is made to the image of God. The souls of the just belong to God. Man is to be tried like gold in a furnace. The Lord will be their king.

A reading from the book of Wisdom

For God formed man to be imperishable;
the image of his own nature he made him.
But by the envy of the devil, death entered the world,
and they who are in his possession experience it.
But the souls of the just are in the hands of God,
and no torment shall touch them.
They seemed, in the view of the foolish, to be dead;
and their passing away was thought an affliction
and their going forth from us, utter destruction.
But they are in peace.
For if before men, indeed, they be punished,
yet is their hope full of immortality;
Chastised a little, they shall be greatly blessed,
because God tried them
and found them worthy of himself.
As gold in the furnace, he proved them,
and as sacrificial offerings he took them to himself.
In the time of their visitation they shall shine,
and shall dart about as sparks through stubble;
They shall judge nations and rule over peoples,
and the Lord shall be their king forever.

Those who trust in him shall understand truth,
    and the faithful shall abide with him in love:
Because grace and mercy are with his holy ones,
    and his care is with his elect.
This is the Word of the Lord. ℟. **Thanks be to God.** ✟

Responsorial Psalm   Ps 34, 2-3. 16-17. 18-19

℟. (2) **I will bless the Lord at all times.**

I will bless the Lord at all times;
    his praise shall be ever in my mouth.
Let my soul glory in the Lord;
    the lowly will hear me and be glad. — ℟

The Lord has eyes for the just,
    and ears for their cry.
The Lord confronts the evildoers,
    to destroy remembrance of them from the
      earth. — ℟

When the just cry out, the Lord hears them,
    and from all their distress he rescues them.
The Lord is close to the brokenhearted;
    and those who are crushed in spirit he saves.—℟ ✟

GOSPEL   Lk 17, 7-10

Alleluia (Jn 14, 23)

℟. **Alleluia.** If anyone loves me, he will hold to my
    words,
and my Father will love him, and we will come to
    him. ℟. **Alleluia.**

If a man has a servant, what should he expect from that servant?
In serving God, all men are servants and they do no more than their
duty.

℣. The Lord be with you. ℟. **And also with you.**
✠ A reading from the holy gospel according to Luke
℟. **Glory to you, Lord.**

The Lord said: "If one of you had a servant plowing
or herding sheep and he came in from the fields,
would you say to him, 'Come and sit down at table'?

Would you not rather say, 'Prepare my supper. Put on your apron and wait on me while I eat and drink. You can eat and drink afterward'? Would he be grateful to the servant who was only carrying out his orders? It is quite the same with you who hear me. When you have done all you have been commanded to do, say, 'We are useless servants. We have done no more than our duty.' "—This is the gospel of the Lord. ℟. **Praise to you, Lord Jesus Christ.**

➤ No. 15, p. 623

WEDNESDAY OF THE THIRTY-SECOND WEEK IN ORDINARY TIME

READING I   Wisdom 6, 2-11

All authority is from God. Those in authority are responsible to God. The humble may be more easily pardoned. Those who keep the law shall become holy.

A reading from the book of Wisdom

Hear, therefore, kings, and understand;
   learn, you magistrates of the earth's expanse!
Hearken, you who are in power over the multitude
   and lord it over throngs of peoples!
Because authority was given you by the Lord
   and sovereignty by the Most High,
   who shall probe your works and scrutinize your
      counsels!
Because, though you were ministers of his kingdom,
      you judged not rightly,
   and did not keep the law,
   nor walk according to the will of God,
Terribly and swiftly shall he come against you,
   because judgment is stern for the exalted—
For the lowly may be pardoned out of mercy
   but the mighty shall be mightily put to the test.
For the Lord of all shows no partiality,
   nor does he fear greatness,

Because he himself made the great as well as the
small,
    and he provides for all alike;
    but for those in power a rigorous scrutiny im-
pends.
To you, therefore, O princes, are my words addressed
    that you may learn wisdom and that you may not
sin.
For those who keep the holy precepts hallowed shall
be found holy,
    and those learned in them will have ready a re-
sponse.
Desire therefore my words;
    long for them and you shall be instructed.
This is the Word of the Lord. ℞. **Thanks be to God.** ⍒

Responsorial Psalm   Ps 82, 3-4. 6-7

℞. (8) **Rise up, O God, bring judgment to the earth.**
Defend the lowly and the fatherless;
    render justice to the afflicted and the destitute.
Rescue the lowly and the poor;
    from the hand of the wicked deliver them. — ℞
"I said: You are gods,
    all of you sons of the Most High;
Yet like men you shall die,
    and fall like any prince." — ℞ ⍒

GOSPEL   Lk 17, 11-19

Alleluia (1 Thes 5, 18)

℞. **Alleluia.** For all things give thanks to God,
because this is what he expects of you in Christ
    Jesus. ℞. **Alleluia.**

Ten lepers come to Jesus and ask for pity. Jesus sends them to the
priests. On the way they are cleansed. One, a foreigner, returns to
give thanks to Jesus.

℣. The Lord be with you. ℞. **And also with you.**
✠ A reading from the holy gospel according to Luke
℞. **Glory to you, Lord.**

On his journey to Jerusalem Jesus passed along the borders of Samaria and Galilee. As he was entering a village, ten lepers met him. Keeping their distance, they raised their voices and said, "Jesus, Master, have pity on us!" When he saw them, he responded, "Go and show yourselves to the priests." On their way there they were cured. One of them, realizing that he had been cured, came back praising God in a loud voice. He threw himself on his face at the feet of Jesus and spoke his praises. This man was a Samaritan.

Jesus took the occasion to say, "Were not all ten made whole? Where are the other nine? Was there no one to return and give thanks to God except this foreigner?" He said to the man, "Stand up and go your way; your faith has been your salvation."— This is the gospel of the Lord. ℟. **Praise to you, Lord Jesus Christ.** ➔ No. 15, p. 623

_____

THURSDAY OF THE THIRTY-SECOND WEEK IN ORDINARY TIME

READING I   Wis 7, 22—8, 1

Wisdom is a reflection of eternal light. It pervades all things. It shows the goodness of God. Wisdom prevails showing the majesty of God.

A reading from the book of Wisdom

In Wisdom is a spirit
    intelligent, holy, unique,
Manifold, subtle, agile,
    clear, unstained, certain,
Not baneful, loving the good, keen,
    unhampered, beneficent, kindly,
Firm, secure, tranquil,
    all-powerful, all-seeing,
And pervading all spirits,
    though they be intelligent, pure, and very subtle.

For Wisdom is mobile beyond all motion,
  and she penetrates and pervades all things by
    reason of her purity.
For she is an aura of the might of God
  and a pure effusion of the glory of the Almighty;
    therefore nought that is sullied enters into her.
For she is the refulgence of eternal light,
  the spotless mirror of the power of God,
    the image of his goodness.
And she, who is one, can do all things,
  and renews everything while herself perduring;
And passing into holy souls from age to age,
  she produces friends of God and prophets.
For there is nought God loves, be it not one who
    dwells with Wisdom.
For she is fairer than the sun
  and surpasses every constellation of the stars.
Compared to light, she takes precedence;
  for that, indeed, night supplants,
  but wickedness prevails not over Wisdom.
Indeed, she reaches from end to end mightily
  and governs all things well.
This is the Word of the Lord. ℟. **Thanks be to God.** ℣

Responsorial Psalm Ps 119, 89. 90. 91. 130. 135. 175

℟. (89) **Your word is for ever, O Lord.**

Your word, O Lord, endures forever;
  it is firm as the heavens. — ℟

Through all generations your truth endures;
  you have established the earth, and it stands
    firm. — ℟

According to your ordinances they still stand firm:
  all things serve you. — ℟

The revelation of your words sheds light,
  giving understanding to the simple. — ℟

Let your countenance shine upon your servant,
  and teach me your statutes. — ℟

Let my soul live to praise you,
   and may your ordinances help me. — ℟ ❦

GOSPEL   Lk 17, 20-25

Alleluia (Jn 15, 5)

℟. **Alleluia.** I am the vine and you are the branches,
   says the Lord:
he who lives in me, and I in him, will bear much
   fruit. ℟. **Alleluia.**

The kingdom of God is already at hand. How often there will be
rumors of the Son of Man. First, the Son of Man must suffer and be
rejected by the present age.

℣. The Lord be with you. ℟. **And also with you.**
✠ A reading from the holy gospel according to Luke
℟. **Glory to you, Lord.**

Jesus, on being asked by the Pharisees when the
reign of God would come, replied: "You cannot tell
by careful watching when the reign of God will come.
Neither is it a matter of reporting that it is 'here'
or 'there.' The reign of God is already in your midst."

   He said to the disciples: "A time will come when
you will long to see one day of the Son of Man but
will not see it. They will tell you he is to be found
in this place or that. Do not go running about ex-
citedly. The Son of Man in his day will be like the
lightning that flashes from one end of the sky to
the other. First, however, he must suffer much and
be rejected by the present age."—This is the gospel
of the Lord. ℟. **Praise to you, Lord Jesus Christ.**

➤ No. 15, p. 623

FRIDAY OF THE THIRTY-SECOND WEEK
IN ORDINARY TIME

READING I   Wis 13, 1-9

The foolish, ignorant men did not know God. Some thought fire, wind,
or air were gods because of their might. Still they seek to find God.

A reading from the book of Wisdom

For all men were by nature foolish who were in
  ignorance of God,
    and who from the good things seen did not suc-
      ceed in knowing him who is,
    and from studying the works did not discern the
      artisan:
But either fire, or wind, or the swift air,
    or the circuit of the stars, or the mighty water,
    or the luminaries of heaven, the governors of the
      world, they considered gods.
Now if out of joy in their beauty they thought them
      gods,
    let them know how far more excellent is the Lord
      than these;
    for the original source of beauty fashioned them.
Or if they were struck by their might and energy,
    let them from these things realize how much more
      powerful is he who made them.
For from the greatness and the beauty of created
      things
    their original author, by analogy, is seen.
But yet, for these the blame is less;
For they indeed have gone astray perhaps,
    though they seek God and wish to find him.
For they search busily among his works,
    but are distracted by what they see, because the
      things seen are fair.
But again, not even these are pardonable.
For if they so far succeeded in knowledge
    that they could speculate about the world,
    how did they not more quickly find its Lord?
This is the Word of the Lord. ℟. **Thanks be to God.** ℣

Responsorial Psalm   Ps 19, 2-3. 4-5
℟. (2) **The heavens proclaim the glory of God.**
The heavens declare the glory of God,
    and the firmament proclaims his handiwork.

Day pours out the word to day,
  and night to night imparts knowledge. — ℟

Not a word nor a discourse
  whose voice is not heard;
Through all the earth their voice resounds,
  and to the ends of the world, their message. — ℟ ⩫

GOSPEL   Lk 17, 26-37

Alleluia (Lk 21, 28)

℟. **Alleluia.** Lift up your heads and see;
your redemption is near at hand. ℟. **Alleluia.**

In the days of Noah and Lot, people did not realize their faults or
the plight that was at hand. So will it be on the day the Son of Man
is revealed.

℣. The Lord be with you. ℟. **And also with you.**
✠ A reading from the holy gospel according to Luke
℟. **Glory to you, Lord.**

Jesus said to his disciples: "As it was in the days of
Noah, so will it be in the days of the Son of Man.
They ate and drank, they took husbands and wives,
right up to the day Noah entered the ark—and when
the flood came, it destroyed them all. It was much
the same in the days of Lot: they ate and drank, they
bought and sold, they built and planted. But on the
day Lot left Sodom, fire and brimstone rained down
from heaven and destroyed them all.

    "It will be like that on the day the Son of Man is
revealed. On that day, if a man is on the rooftop
and his belongings are in the house, he should not
go down to get them; neither should the man in the
field return home. Remember Lot's wife. Whoever
tries to spare his life will lose it; whoever seems to
forfeit it will keep it. I tell you, on that night there
will be two men in one bed; one will be taken and
the other left. Two women will be grinding grain
together; one will be taken and the other left."
"Where, Lord?" they asked him, and he answered,

"Wherever the carcass is, there will the vultures gather."—This is the gospel of the Lord. ℞. **Praise to you, Lord Jesus Christ.** ➔ No. 15, p. 623

SATURDAY OF THE THIRTY-SECOND WEEK IN ORDINARY TIME

READING I   Wis 18, 14-16; 19, 6-9

The powerful word comes from heaven into the doomed land. All creation is being made over. Out of the Red Sea emerges an open road. Men praise God, their deliverer.

A reading from the book of Wisdom

For when peaceful stillness compassed everything
  and the night in its swift course was half spent,
Your all-powerful word from heaven's royal throne
  bounded, a fierce warrior, into the doomed land,
    bearing the sharp sword of your inexorable decree.
And as he alighted, he filled every place with death;
  he still reached to heaven, while he stood upon the earth.
For all creation, in its several kinds, was being made over anew,
    serving its natural laws,
  that your children might be preserved unharmed.
The cloud overshadowed their camp;
  and out of what had before been water, dry land was seen emerging:
Out of the Red Sea an unimpeded road,
  and a grassy plain out of the mighty flood.
Over this crossed the whole nation sheltered by your hand,
  after they beheld stupendous wonders.
For they ranged about like horses,
  and bounded about like lambs,
    praising you, O Lord! their deliverer.
This is the Word of the Lord. ℞. **Thanks be to God.** ℣

Responsorial Psalm   Ps 105, 2-3. 36-37. 42-43

℟. (5) **Remember the marvels the Lord has done.**

Sing to him, sing his praise,
    proclaim all his wondrous deeds.
Glory in his holy name;
    rejoice, O hearts that seek the Lord! — ℟

Then he struck every first-born throughout their
    land,
    the firstfruits of all their manhood.
And he led them forth laden with silver and gold,
    with not a weakling among their tribes. — ℟

For he remembered his holy word
    to his servant Abraham.
And he led forth his people with joy;
    with shouts of joy, his chosen ones. — ℟ ℣

℟. Or: **Alleluia.** ℣

GOSPEL   Lk 18, 1-8

Alleluia (2 Thes 2, 14)

℟. **Alleluia.** God has called us with the gospel;
the people won for him by Jesus Christ our Lord.
    ℟. **Alleluia.**

Jesus tells his disciples about the value of praying always without
giving up. It is the parable of the widow. God will answer those who
pray to him.

℣. The Lord be with you. ℟. **And also with you.**

✠ A reading from the holy gospel according to Luke
℟. **Glory to you, Lord.**

Jesus told his disciples a parable on the necessity
of praying always and not losing heart: "Once there
was a judge in a certain city who respected neither
God nor man. A widow in that city kept coming to
him saying, 'Give me my rights against my opponent.' For a time he refused, but finally he thought,
'I care little for God or man, but this widow is wearing me out. I am going to settle in her favor or she
will end by doing me violence.'" The Lord said,

"Listen to what the corrupt judge has to say. Will not God then do justice to his chosen who call out to him day and night? Will he delay long over them, do you suppose? I tell you, he will give them swift justice. But when the Son of Man comes, will he find any faith on the earth?"—This is the gospel of the Lord. ℟. **Praise to you, Lord Jesus Christ.**

➜ No. 15, p. 623

MONDAY OF THE THIRTY-THIRD WEEK IN ORDINARY TIME

READING I   1 Mc 1, 10-15. 41-43. 54-57. 62-63

Some Israelites under King Antiochus seek to betray their heritage and identify with the Gentiles. They ignore their law and sacrifice to pagan idols. Other Israelites, however, are intent on pleasing God.

A reading from the first book of Maccabees

There sprang a sinful offshoot, Antiochus Epiphanes, son of King Antiochus, once a hostage at Rome. He became king in the year one hundred and thirty-seven of the kingdom of the Greeks.

In those days there appeared in Israel men who were breakers of the law, and they seduced many people, saying: "Let us go and make an alliance with the Gentiles all around us; since we separated from them, many evils have come upon us." The proposal was agreeable; some from among the people promptly went to the king, and he authorized them to introduce the way of living of the Gentiles. Thereupon they built a gymnasium in Jerusalem according to the Gentile custom. They covered over the mark of their circumcision and abandoned the holy covenant; they allied themselves with the Gentiles and sold themselves to wrongdoing.

Then the king wrote to his whole kingdom that all should be one people, each abandoning his particular customs. All the Gentiles conformed to the command of the king, and many Israelites were in favor of his religion; they sacrificed to idols and profaned the sabbath.

On the fifteenth day of the month Chislev, in the year one hundred and forty-five, the king erected the horrible abomination upon the altar of holocausts, and in the surrounding cities of Judah they built pagan altars. They also burnt incense at the doors of houses and in the streets. Any scrolls of the law which they found they tore up and burnt. Whoever was found with a scroll of the covenant, and whoever observed the law, was condemned to death by royal decree. But many in Israel were determined and resolved in their hearts not to eat anything unclean; they preferred to die rather than to be defiled with unclean food or to profane the holy covenant; and they did die. Terrible affliction was upon Israel.—This is the Word of the Lord. ℟. **Thanks be to God.** ℣

Responsorial Psalm Ps 119, 53. 61. 134. 150. 155. 158
℟. (88) **Give me life, O Lord,**
and I will do your commands.

Indignation seizes me because of the wicked
  who forsake your law. — ℟

Though the snares of the wicked are twined about
    me,
  your law I have not forgotten. — ℟

Redeem me from the oppression of men,
  that I may keep your precepts. — ℟

I am attacked by malicious persecutors
  who are far from your law. — ℟

Far from sinners is salvation,
  because they seek not your statutes. — ℟

I beheld the apostates with loathing,
  because they kept not to your promise. — ℟ ℣

GOSPEL   Lk 18, 35-43

Alleluia (Jn 8, 12)

℟. **Alleluia.** I am the light of the world, says the
   Lord:

he who follows me will have the light of life. ℟.
   Alleluia.

The blind man at Jericho shouts to Jesus, "Son of David, have pity on
me!" He asks Jesus to help him see. Because of the blind man's
faith, Jesus heals him. All those who see this praise God.

℣. The Lord be with you. ℟. **And also with you.**

✠ A reading from the holy gospel according to Luke
℟. **Glory to you, Lord.**

As Jesus drew near Jericho a blind man sat at the
side of the road begging. Hearing a crowd go by the
man asked, "What is that?" The answer came that
Jesus of Nazareth was passing by. He shouted out,
"Jesus, Son of David, have pity on me!" Those in
the lead sternly ordered him to be quiet, but he
cried out all the more, "Son of David, have pity on
me!" Jesus halted and ordered him to be brought to
him. When he had come close, Jesus asked him,
"What do you want me to do for you?" "Lord," he
answered, "I want to see." Jesus said to him, "Receive your sight. Your faith has healed you." At that
very moment he was given his sight and began to
follow him, giving God the glory. All the people
witnessed it and they too gave praise to God.—This
is the gospel of the Lord. ℟. **Praise to you, Lord
Jesus Christ.**   ➜ No. 15, p. 623

TUESDAY OF THE THIRTY-THIRD WEEK
IN ORDINARY TIME

READING I   2 Mc 6, 18-31

Eleazar, an aging scribe, is being forced to eat unclean meat. Not
even under pretense will he disobey the law. Courageously, he goes
to torture knowing that he will die. He becomes a model of courage,
not only for the young, but for all Israel.

A reading from the second book of Maccabees

Eleazar, one of the foremost scribes, a man of advanced age and noble appearance, was being forced to open his mouth to eat pork. But preferring a glorious death to a life of defilement, he spat out the meat, and went forward of his own accord to the instrument of torture, as men ought to do who have the courage to reject the food which it is unlawful to taste even for love of life. Those in charge of that unlawful ritual meal took the man aside privately, because of their long acquaintance with him, and urged him to bring meat of his own providing, such as he could legitimately eat, and to pretend to be eating some of the meat of the sacrifice prescribed by the king; in this way he would escape the death penalty, and be treated kindly because of their old friendship with him. But he made up his mind in a noble manner, worthy of his years, the dignity of his advanced age, the merited distinction of his gray hair, and the admirable life he had lived from childhood; and so he declared that above all he would be loyal to the holy laws given by God.

He told them to send him at once to the abode of the dead, explaining: "At our age it would be unbecoming to make such a pretense; many young men would think the ninety-year-old Eleazar had gone over to an alien religion. Should I thus dissimulate for the sake of a brief moment of life, they would be led astray by me, while I would bring shame and dishonor on my old age. Even if, for the time being, I avoid the punishment of men, I shall never, whether alive or dead, escape the hands of the Almighty. Therefore, by manfully giving up my life now, I will prove myself worthy of my old age, and I will leave to the young a noble example of how to die willingly and generously for the revered and holy laws."

He spoke thus, and went immediately to the instrument of torture. Those who shortly before had been kindly disposed, now became hostile toward him because what he had said seemed to them utter madness. When he was about to die under the blows, he groaned and said: "The Lord in his holy knowledge knows full well that, although I could have escaped death, I am not only enduring terrible pain in my body from this scourging, but also suffering it with joy in my soul because of my devotion to him." This is how he died, leaving in his death a model of courage and an unforgettable example of virtue not only for the young but for the whole nation.—This is the Word of the Lord. ℞. **Thanks be to God.** ℣

Responsorial Psalm   Ps 3, 2-3. 4-5. 6-8

℞ (6) **The Lord upholds me.**

O Lord, how many are my adversaries!
    Many rise up against me!
Many are saying of me,
    "There is no salvation for him in God." — ℞

But you, O Lord, are my shield;
    my glory, you lift up my head!
When I call out to the Lord,
    he answers me from his holy mountain. — ℞

When I lie down in sleep,
    I wake again, for the Lord sustains me.
I fear not the myriads of people
    arrayed against me on every side.
Rise up, O Lord!
    Save me, my God! — ℞ ℣

GOSPEL   Lk 19, 1-10

Alleluia (1 Jn 4, 10)

℞. **Alleluia.** God first loved us
and sent his Son to take away our sins. ℞. **Alleluia.**

Zacchaeus, the chief tax collector, is a man small in height. To see Jesus at Jericho, he climbs a tree. When Jesus sees Zacchaeus, he bids him come down, promising to spend the night at his house. Zacchaeus repents from all his past wrong-doing.

℣. The Lord be with you. ℟. **And also with you.**

✠ A reading from the holy gospel according to Luke ℟. **Glory to you, Lord.**

On entering Jericho, Jesus passed through the city. There was a man there named Zacchaeus, the chief tax collector and a wealthy man. He was trying to see what Jesus was like, but being small of stature, was unable to do so because of the crowd. He first ran on in front, then climbed a sycamore tree which was along Jesus' route, in order to see him. When Jesus came to the spot he looked up and said, "Zacchaeus, hurry down. I mean to stay at your house today." He quickly descended, and welcomed him with delight. When this was observed, everyone began to murmur, "He has gone to a sinner's house as a guest." Zacchaeus stood his ground and said to the Lord: "I give half my belongings, Lord, to the poor. If I have defrauded anyone in the least, I pay him back fourfold." Jesus said to him: "Today salvation has come to this house, for this is what it means to be a son of Abraham. The Son of Man has come to search out and save what was lost."—This is the gospel of the Lord. ℟. **Praise to you, Lord Jesus Christ.**

➤ No. 15, p. 623

WEDNESDAY OF THE THIRTY-THIRD WEEK IN ORDINARY TIME

READING I   2 Mc 7, 1. 20-31

The king orders seven brothers and their mother to be tortured to force them to disobey the law of God. All refuse, and six are killed. The mother encourages the seventh to persevere in the law. God who gives life will give it again. The boy holds fast to the law.

A reading from the second book of Maccabees

Seven brothers with their mother were arrested and tortured with whips and scourges by the king, to force them to eat pork in violation of God's law.

Most admirable and worthy of everlasting remembrance was the mother, who saw her seven sons perish in a single day, yet bore it courageously because of her hope in the Lord. Filled with a noble spirit that stirred her womanly heart with manly courage, she exhorted each of them in the language of their forefathers with these words: "I do not know how you came into existence in my womb; it was not I who gave you the breath of life, nor was it I who set in order the elements of which each of you is composed. Therefore, since it is the Creator of the universe who shapes each man's beginning, as he brings about the origin of everything, he, in his mercy, will give you back both breath and life, because you now disregard yourselves for the sake of his law."

Antiochus, suspecting insult in her words, thought he was being ridiculed. As the youngest brother was still alive, the king appealed to him, not with mere words, but with promises on oath, to make him rich and happy if he would abandon his ancestral customs: he would make him his Friend and entrust him with high office. When the youth paid no attention to him at all, the king appealed to the mother, urging her to advise her boy to save his life. After he had urged her for a long time, she went through the motions of persuading her son. In derision of the cruel tyrant, she leaned over close to her son and said in their native language: "Son, have pity on me, who carried you in my womb for nine months, nursed you for three years, brought you up, educated and supported you to your present age. I beg you, child, to look at the heavens and the earth and see all that is in them; then you will know that God did not make them out of existing things; and in the same way the human race came into existence. Do not be afraid of this executioner, but be worthy of your brothers and accept death, so that in the time of mercy I may receive you again with them."

She had scarcely finished speaking when the youth said: "What are you waiting for? I will not obey the king's command. I obey the command of the law given to our forefathers through Moses. But you, who have contrived every kind of affliction for the Hebrews, will not escape the hands of God."— This is the Word of the Lord. ℟. **Thanks be to God.** ℣

Responsorial Psalm   Ps 17, 1. 5-6. 8. 15

℟. (15) **Lord, when your glory appears,**
    my joy will be full.

Hear, O Lord, a just suit;
    attend to my outcry;
    hearken to my prayer from lips without deceit.—℟

My steps have been steadfast in your paths,
    my feet have not faltered.
I call upon you, for you will answer me, O God;
    incline your ear to me; hear my word. — ℟

Hide me in the shadow of your wings.
But I in justice shall behold your face;
    in waking, I shall be content in your pres-
        ence. — ℟ ℣

GOSPEL   Lk 19, 11-28

Alleluia (Jn 15, 16)

℟. **Alleluia.** I have chosen you from the world, says
    the Lord,
to go and bear fruit that will last. ℟. **Alleluia.**

A nobleman, upon leaving his domain, entrusts money to three servants. Then he returns as king and asks an accounting. Two servants doubled their treasure and are rewarded. The third buried his. The king takes the gift away and upbraids this servant's imprudence.

℣. The Lord be with you. ℟. **And also with you.**

✠ A reading from the holy gospel according to Luke

℟. **Glory to you, Lord.**

While the disciples were listening Jesus went on to tell a parable, because he was near Jerusalem where they thought that the reign of God was about to appear. He said: "A man of noble birth went to a faraway country to become its king, and then return. He summoned ten of his servants and gave them sums of ten units each, saying to them, 'Invest this until I get back.' But his fellow citizens despised him, and they immediately sent a deputation after him with instructions to say, 'We will not have this man rule over us.' He returned, however, crowned as king. Then he sent for the servants to whom he had given the money, to learn what profit each had made. The first presented himself and said, 'Lord, the sum you gave me has earned you another ten.' 'Good man!' he replied. 'You showed yourself capable in a small matter. For that you can take over ten villages.' The second came and said, 'Your investment, my lord, has netted you five.' His word to him was, 'Take over five villages.' The third came in and said: 'Here is your money, my lord, which I hid for safekeeping. You see, I was afraid of you because you are a hard man. You withdraw what you never deposited. You reap what you never sowed.' To him the king said: 'You worthless lout! I intend to judge you on your own evidence. You knew I was a hard man, withdrawing what I never deposited, reaping what I never sowed! Why, then, did you not put my money out on loan, so that on my return I could get it back with interest?' He said to those standing around, 'Take from him what he has, and give it to the man with the ten.' 'Yes, but he already has ten,' they said. He responded with, 'The moral is: whoever has will be given more, but the one who has not will lose the little he has. Now about those enemies of mine who did not want me to be king, bring them in and slay them in my presence.'"

Having spoken thus he went ahead with his ascent to Jerusalem.—This is the gospel of the Lord. ℟. **Praise to you, Lord Jesus Christ.**   ➤ No. 15, p. 623

THURSDAY OF THE THIRTY-THIRD WEEK IN ORDINARY TIME

READING I   1 Mc 2, 15-29

Mattathias and his sons will not be persuaded to become apostates from the religion of their forefathers. In spite of promises of great wealth, he will not depart from his religion in the slightest degree even in the face of death.

A reading from the first book of Maccabees

The officers of the king in charge of enforcing the apostasy came to the city of Modein to organize the sacrifices. Many of Israel joined them, but Mattathias and his sons gathered in a group apart. Then the officers of the king addressed Mattathias: "You are a leader, an honorable and great man in this city, supported by sons and kinsmen. Come now, be the first to obey the king's command, as all the Gentiles and the men of Judah and those who are left in Jerusalem have done. Then you and your sons shall be numbered among the King's Friends, and shall be enriched with silver and gold and many gifts." But Mattathias answered in a loud voice: "Although all the Gentiles in the king's realm obey him, so that each forsakes the religion of his fathers and consents to the king's orders, yet I and my sons and my kinsmen will keep to the covenant of our fathers. God forbid that we should forsake the law and the commandments. We will not obey the words of the king nor depart from our religion in the slightest degree."

As he finished saying these words, a certain Jew came forward in the sight of all to offer sacrifice on the altar in Modein according to the king's order. When Mattathias saw him, he was filled with zeal; his heart was moved and his just fury was aroused; he sprang forward and killed him upon the altar. At the same time, he also killed the messenger of the king who was forcing them to sacrifice, and he tore down the altar. Thus he showed his zeal for the law, just as Phinehas did with Zimri, son of Salu.

Then Mattathias went through the city shouting, "Let everyone who is zealous for the law and who stands by the covenant follow after me!" Thereupon he fled to the mountains with his sons, leaving behind in the city all their possessions. Many who sought to live according to righteousness and religious custom went out into the desert to settle there. —This is the Word of the Lord. ℟. **Thanks be to God.** ℣

Responsorial Psalm   Ps 50, 1-2. 5-6. 14-15

℟. (23) **To the upright I will show the saving power of God.**

God the Lord has spoken and summoned the earth,
    from the rising of the sun to its setting.
From Zion, perfect in beauty,
    God shines forth. — ℟

"Gather my faithful ones before me,
    those who have made a covenant with me by sacrifice."
And the heavens proclaim his justice;
    for God himself is the judge. — ℟

"Offer to God praise as your sacrifice
    and fulfill your vows to the Most High;
Then call upon me in time of distress;
    I will rescue you, and you shall glorify me."—℟ ℣

GOSPEL   Lk 19, 41-44
Alleluia (Ps 95, 8)

℟. **Alleluia.** If today you hear his voice, harden not your hearts. ℟. **Alleluia.**

Jesus comes to Jerusalem, He weeps over it, lamenting its future destruction. The people of Jerusalem fail to recognize the time of his coming.

℣. The Lord be with you. ℟. **And also with you.**

✠ A reading from the holy gospel according to Luke ℟. **Glory to you, Lord.**

Coming within sight of the city of Jerusalem, Jesus wept over it and said: "If only you had known the path to peace this day; but you have completely lost it from view! Days will come upon you when your enemies encircle you with a rampart, hem you in, and press you hard from every side. They will wipe you out, you and your children within your walls, and leave not a stone on a stone within you, because you failed to recognize the time of your visitation."—This is the gospel of the Lord. ℟. **Praise to you, Lord Jesus Christ.** ➤ No. 15, p. 623

FRIDAY OF THE THIRTY-THIRD WEEK IN ORDINARY TIME

READING I 1 Mc 4, 36-37. 52-59

Judas and his brothers reconstruct the altar of sacrifice. All the people adore and praise God. They offer holocausts and sacrifices of deliverance and praise.

A reading from the first book of Maccabees

Judas and his brothers said, "Now that our enemies have been crushed, let us go up to purify the sanctuary and rededicate it." So the whole army assembled, and went up to Mount Zion.

Early in the morning on the twenty-fifth day of the ninth month, that is, the month of Chislev, in the year one hundred and forty-eight, they arose and offered sacrifice according to the law on the new altar of holocausts that they had made. On the anni-

versary of the day on which the Gentiles had defiled
it, on that very day it was reconsecrated with songs,
harps, flutes, and cymbals. All the people prostrated
themselves and adored and praised Heaven, who had
given them success.

For eight days they celebrated the dedication of
the altar and joyfully offered holocausts and sacrifices of deliverance and praise. They ornamented
the facade of the temple with gold crowns and
shields; they repaired the gates and the priests'
chambers and furnished them with doors. There was
great joy among the people now that the disgrace of
the Gentiles was removed. Then Judas and his brothers and the entire congregation of Israel decreed
that the days of the dedication of the altar should
be observed with joy and gladness on the anniversary every year for eight days, from the twenty-fifth
day of the month Chislev.—This is the Word of the
Lord. ℞. **Thanks be to God.** ℣

Responsorial Psalm   1 Chr 29, 10. 11. 11-12. 12

℞. 13) **We praise your glorious name, O mighty God.**

Blessed may you be, O Lord,
　　God of Israel our father,
　　　from eternity to eternity. — ℞

Yours, O Lord, are grandeur and power,
　　majesty, splendor, and glory.
For all in heaven and on earth is yours; — ℞

Yours, O Lord, is the sovereignty;
　　you are exalted as head over all.
　　Riches and honor are from you. — ℞

And you have dominion over all,
　　in your hand are power and might;
　　it is yours to give grandeur and strength to
　　　all. — ℞ ℣

GOSPEL   Lk 19, 45-48
Alleluia (Jn 10, 27)

℟. **Alleluia.** My sheep listen to my voice, says the
   Lord;
I know them, and they follow me. ℟. **Alleluia.**

Jesus is becoming influential. Great crowds follow him. He enters the
temple and throws out those who have made it a bargaining center.

℣. The Lord be with you. ℟. **And also with you.**
✠ A reading from the holy gospel according to Luke
℟. **Glory to you, Lord.**

Jesus entered the temple and began ejecting the
traders saying: "Scripture has it,
   'My house is meant for a house of prayer'
but you have made it 'a den of thieves.'"

   He was teaching in the temple area from day to
day. The chief priests and scribes meanwhile were
looking for a way to destroy him, as were the leaders of the people, but they had no idea how to
achieve it, for indeed, the entire populace was listening to him and hanging on his words.—This is
the gospel of the Lord. ℟. **Praise to you, Lord Jesus
Christ.**   ➤ No. 15, p. 623

SATURDAY OF THE THIRTY-THIRD WEEK
IN ORDINARY TIME

READING I   1 Mc 6, 1-13

King Antiochus, anxious for great wealth, presses upon the temple
in the city of Elymais but is forced to retreat. His armies also are
overcome by the Israelites in Jerusalem. He hears the news and becomes grief-stricken with fright. He knows that he is about to die.

   A reading from the first book of Maccabees

As King Antiochus was traversing the inland provinces, he heard that in Persia there was a city called
Elymais, famous for its wealth in silver and gold,
and that its temple was very rich, containing gold
helmets, breastplates, and weapons left there by
Alexander, son of Philip, king of Macedon, the first
king of the Greeks. He went therefore and tried to

capture and pillage the city. But he could not do so, because his plan became known to the people of the city who rose up in battle against him. So he retreated and in great dismay withdrew from there to return to Babylon.

While he was in Persia, a messenger brought him news that the armies sent into the land of Judah had been put to flight; that Lysias had gone at first with a strong army and been driven back by the Israelites; that they had grown strong by reason of the arms, men, and abundant possessions taken from the armies they had destroyed; that they had pulled down the Abomination which he had built upon the altar in Jerusalem; and that they had surrounded with high walls both the sanctuary, as it had been before, and his city of Beth-zur.

When the king heard this news, he was struck with fear and very much shaken. Sick with grief because his designs had failed, he took to his bed. There he remained many days, overwhelmed with sorrow, for he knew he was going to die.

So he called in all his Friends and said to them: "Sleep has departed from my eyes, for my heart is sinking with anxiety. I said to myself: 'Into what tribulation have I come, and in what floods of sorrow am I now! Yet I was kindly and beloved in my rule.' But I now recall the evils I did in Jerusalem, when I carried away all the vessels of gold and silver that were in it, and for no cause gave orders that the inhabitants of Judah be destroyed. I know that this is why these evils have overtaken me; and now I am dying, in bitter grief, in a foreign land."— This is the Word of the Lord. ℟. **Thanks be to God.** ℣

Responsorial Psalm   Ps 9, 2-3. 4. 6. 16. 19

℟. (16) **I will rejoice in your salvation, O Lord.**

I will give thanks to you, O Lord, with all my heart;
   I will declare all your wondrous deeds.

I will be glad and exult in you;
    I will sing praise to your name, Most High. — ℟
Because my enemies are turned back,
    overthrown and destroyed before you.
You rebuked the nations and destroyed the wicked;
    their name you blotted out forever and ever. — ℟
In the snare they set, their foot is caught;
    for the needy shall not always be forgotten,
    nor shall the hope of the afflicted forever
      perish. — ℟ ℣

GOSPEL   Lk 20, 27-40
Alleluia (2 Tm 1, 10)
℟. **Alleluia.** Our Savior Jesus Christ has done away
    with death,
and brought us life through his gospel. ℟. **Alleluia.**

The Sadducees, trying to trick Jesus, pose the question of marriage. According to Mosaic law, a man was to marry his brother's widow. If this was done by a series of seven brothers, whose wife would she be in heaven? Jesus answers that God is the God of the living.

℣. The Lord be with you. ℟. **And also with you.**
✠ A reading from the holy gospel according to Luke
℟. **Glory to you, Lord.**

Some Sadducees came forward (the ones who claim there is no resurrection) to pose this problem to Jesus: "Master, Moses prescribed that if a man's brother dies leaving a wife and no child, the brother should marry the widow and raise posterity to his brother. Now, there were seven brothers. The first one married and died childless. Next, the second brother married the widow, then the third, and so on. All seven died without leaving her any children. Finally the widow herself died. At the resurrection, whose wife will she be? Remember, seven married her."

Jesus said to them: "The children of this age marry and are given in marriage, but those judged worthy of a place in the age to come and of resurrection from the dead do not. They become like angels and are no longer liable to death. Sons of the resurrection, they are sons of God. Moses in the passage about the bush showed that the dead rise again when he called the Lord the God of Abraham, and the God of Isaac, and the God of Jacob. God is not the God of the dead but of the living. All are alive for him."

Some of the scribes responded, "Well said, Teacher." They did not dare ask him anything else.—This is the gospel of the Lord. ℟. **Praise to you, Lord Jesus Christ.**

➤ No. 15, p. 623

MONDAY OF THE THIRTY-FOURTH WEEK IN ORDINARY TIME

READING I   Dn 1, 1-6. 8-20

King Nebuchadnezzar of Babylon conquers the Israelites. He chooses Daniel, Hananiah, Mishael and Azariah to become his followers. They will not betray their heritage. God gives exceptional wisdom to Daniel.

The beginning of the book of the prophet
Daniel

In the third year of the reign of Jehoiakim, king of Judah, King Nebuchadnezzar of Babylon came and laid siege to Jerusalem. The Lord handed over to him Jehoiakim, king of Judah, and some of the vessels of the temple of God, which he carried off to the land of Shinar, and placed in the temple treasury of his god.

The king told Ashpenaz, his chief chamberlain, to bring in some of the Israelites of royal blood and of the nobility, young men without any defect, handsome, intelligent and wise, quick to learn, and prudent in judgment, such as could take their place in the king's palace; they were to be taught the language and literature of the Chaldeans; after three years' training they were to enter the king's service. The king allotted them a daily portion of food and wine from the royal table. Among these were men of Judah: Daniel, Hananiah, Mishael, and Azariah.

But Daniel was resolved not to defile himself with the king's food or wine; so he begged the chief chamberlain to spare him this defilement. Though God had given Daniel the favor and sympathy of the chief chamberlain, he nevertheless said to Daniel, "I am afraid of my lord the king; it is he who allotted your food and drink. If he sees that you look wretched by comparison with the other young men of your age, you will endanger my life with the king." Then Daniel said to the steward whom the chief chamberlain had put in charge of Daniel, Hananiah, Mishael, and Azariah, "Please test your servants for ten days. Give us vegetables to eat and water to drink. Then see how we look in comparison with the other young men who eat from the royal table, and treat your servants according to what you see." He acceded to this request, and tested them for ten days; after ten days they looked healthier and better fed than any of the young men who ate from the royal table. So the steward continued to take away the food and wine they were to receive, and gave them vegetables.

To these four young men God gave knowledge and proficiency in all literature and science, and to Daniel the understanding of all visions and dreams. At the end of the time the king had specified for their preparation, the chief chamberlain brought them before Nebuchadnezzar. When the king had spoken with all of them, none was found equal to Daniel, Hananiah, Mishael, and Azariah; and so they entered the king's service. In any question of wisdom or prudence which the king put to them, he found them ten times better than all the magicians and enchanters in his kingdom.—This is the Word of the Lord. ℞. **Thanks be to God.** ℣

Responsorial Psalm   Dn 3, 52. 53. 54. 55. 56
℞. (52) **Glory and praise for ever!**

Blessed are you, O Lord, the God of our fathers,
      praiseworthy and exalted above all forever;
And blessed is your holy and glorious name,
      praiseworthy and exalted above all for all
          ages. — ℞

Blessed are you in the temple of your holy glory,
      praiseworthy and glorious above all forever.—℞

Blessed are you on the throne of your kingdom,
      praiseworthy and exalted above all forever. — ℞

Blessed are you who look into the depths
      from your throne upon the cherubim,
      praiseworthy and exalted above all forever. — ℞

Blessed are you in the firmament of heaven,
      praiseworthy and glorious forever. — ℞ ℣

GOSPEL   Lk 21, 1-4
Alleluia (Mt 24, 42. 44)
℞. **Alleluia.** Be watchful and ready:
you know not when the Son of Man is coming. ℞.
          Alleluia.

The poor widow, who makes a true sacrifice to the temple treasury, is pleasing to God. She gives from her want, not her surplus.

℣. The Lord be with you. ℞. **And also with you.**
✠ A reading from the holy gospel according to Luke
℞. **Glory to you, Lord.**

Jesus glanced up and saw the rich putting their offerings into the treasury, and also a poor widow putting in two copper coins. At that he said: "I assure you, this poor widow has put in more than all the rest. They make contributions out of their surplus, but she from her want has given what she could not afford—every penny she had to live on."—This is the gospel of the Lord. ℟. **Praise to you, Lord Jesus Christ.**

→ No. 15, p. 623

TUESDAY OF THE THIRTY-FOURTH WEEK IN ORDINARY TIME

READING I   Dn 2, 31-45

Daniel interprets Nebuchadnezzar's dream. There will be a succession of kingdoms, but God will raise up one which will not end. It shall destroy all these other kingdoms and absorb them.

A reading from the book of the prophet Daniel

Daniel said to Nebuchadnezzar: "In your vision, O king, you saw a statue, very large and exceedingly bright, terrifying in appearance as it stood before you. The head of the statue was pure gold, its chest and arms were silver, its belly and thighs bronze, the legs iron, its feet partly iron and partly tile. While you looked at the statue, a stone which was hewn from a mountain without a hand being put to it, struck its iron and tile feet, breaking them in pieces. The iron, tile, bronze, silver, and gold all crumbled at once, fine as the chaff on the threshing floor in summer, and the wind blew them away without leaving a trace. But the stone that struck the statue became a great mountain and filled the whole earth.

"This was the dream; the interpretation we shall also give in the king's presence. You, O king, are the king of kings; to you the God of heaven has given dominion and strength, power and glory; men, wild beasts, and birds of the air, wherever they may dwell, he has handed over to you, making you ruler over them all; you are the head of gold. Another kingdom shall take your place, inferior to yours, then a third kingdom, of bronze, which shall rule

over the whole earth. There shall be a fourth kingdom, strong as iron; it shall break in pieces and sub-
due all these others, just as iron breaks in pieces
and crushes everything else. The feet and toes you
saw, partly of potter's tile and partly of iron, mean
that it shall be a divided kingdom, but yet have
some of the hardness of iron. As you saw the iron
mixed with clay tile, and the toes partly iron and
partly tile, the kingdom shall be partly strong and
partly fragile. The iron mixed with clay tile means
that they shall seal their alliances by intermarriage,
but they shall not stay united, any more than iron
mixes with clay. In the lifetime of those kings the
God of heaven will set up a kingdom that shall
never be destroyed or delivered up to another people; rather, it shall break in pieces all these kingdoms and put an end to them, and it shall stand forever. That is the meaning of the stone you saw hewn
from the mountain without a hand being put to it,
which broke in pieces the tile, iron, bronze, silver,
and gold. The great God has revealed to the king
what shall be in the future; this is exactly what you
dreamed, and its meaning is sure."—This is the Word
of the Lord. ℟. **Thanks be to God.** ℣

Responsorial Psalm   Dn 3, 57. 58. 59. 60. 61

℟. (59) **Give glory and eternal praise to him.**
Bless the Lord, all you works of the Lord,
  praise and exalt him above all forever. — ℟
Angels of the Lord, bless the Lord,
  praise and exalt him above all forever. — ℟
You heavens, bless the Lord,
  praise and exalt him above all forever. — ℟
All you waters above the heavens, bless the Lord,
  praise and exalt him above all forever. — ℟
All you hosts of the Lord, bless the Lord;
  praise and exalt him above all forever. — ℟ ℣

GOSPEL   Lk 21, 5-11

Alleluia (Rv 2, 10)

℟. **Alleluia.** Be faithful until death, says the Lord, and I will give you the crown of life. ℟. **Alleluia.**

Jesus says that all the stones of the temple will be torn down. When will this happen? Jesus warns the people not to be misled. Wars, crimes, plagues, and fearful omens will all take place, but the end does not follow immediately.

℣. The Lord be with you. ℟. **And also with you.**

✠ A reading from the holy gospel according to Luke ℟. **Glory to you, Lord.**

People were speaking of how the temple was adorned with precious stones and votive offerings. Jesus said, "These things you are contemplating—the day will come when not one stone will be left on another, but it will all be torn down." They asked him, "When will this occur, Teacher? And what will be the sign it is going to happen?" He said, "Take care not to be misled. Many will come in my name saying, 'I am he' and 'The time is at hand.' Do not follow them. Neither must you be perturbed when you hear of wars and insurrections. These things are bound to happen first, but the end does not follow immediately."

He said to them further: "Nation will rise against nation and kingdom against kingdom. There will be great earthquakes, plagues and famines in various places, and in the sky fearful omens and great signs." —This is the gospel of the Lord. ℟. **Praise to you, Lord Jesus Christ.**   ➙ No. 15, p. 623

WEDNESDAY OF THE THIRTY-FOURTH WEEK IN ORDINARY TIME

READING I   Dn 5, 1-6. 13-14. 16-17. 23-28

At banquet, King Belshazzar profanes the vessels of the temple. A hand begins to write on the wall. Daniel interprets the words to mean that God will bring Belshazzar's rule to an end.

A reading from the book of the prophet Daniel

King Belshazzar gave a great banquet for a thousand of his lords, with whom he drank. Under the influence of the wine, he ordered the gold and silver vessels which Nebuchadnezzar, his father, had taken from the temple in Jerusalem, to be brought in so that the king, his lords, his wives and his entertainers might drink from them. When the gold and silver vessels taken from the house of God in Jerusalem had been brought in, and while the king, his lords, his wives and his entertainers were drinking wine from them, they praised their gods of gold and silver, bronze and iron, wood and stone.

Suddenly, opposite the lampstand, the fingers of a human hand appeared, writing on the plaster of the wall in the king's palace. When the king saw the wrist and hand that wrote, his face blanched; his thoughts terrified him, his hip joints shook, and his knees knocked.

Then Daniel was brought into the presence of the king. The king asked him, "Are you the Daniel, the Jewish exile, whom my father, the king, brought from Judah? I have heard that the spirit of God is in you, that you possess brilliant knowledge and extraordinary wisdom. But I have heard that you can interpret dreams and solve difficulties; if you are able to read the writing and tell me what it means, you shall be clothed in purple, wear a gold collar about your neck, and be third in the government of the kingdom."

Daniel answered the king: "You may keep your gifts, or give your presents to someone else; but the writing I will read for you, O king, and tell you what it means. You have rebelled against the Lord of heaven. You had the vessels of his temple brought before you, so that you and your nobles, your wives and your entertainers, might drink wine from them; and you praised the gods of silver and gold, bronze and iron, wood and stone, that neither see nor hear nor have intelligence. But the God in whose hand is your life breath and the whole course of your life, you did not glorify. By him were the wrist and hand sent, and the writing set down.

"This is the writing that was inscribed: MENE, TEKEL, and PERES. These words mean: MENE, God has numbered your kingdom and put an end to it; TEKEL, you have been weighed on the scales and found wanting; PERES, your kingdom has been divided and given to the Medes and Persians."—This is the Word of the Lord. ℟. **Thanks be to God.** ⍟

Responsorial Psalm   Dn 3, 62. 63. 64. 65. 66. 67

℟. (59) **Give glory and eternal praise to him.**

Sun and moon, bless the Lord;
    praise and exalt him above all forever. — ℟

Stars of heaven, bless the Lord;
    praise and exalt him above all forever. — ℟

Every shower and dew, bless the Lord;
    praise and exalt him above all forever. — ℟

All you winds, bless the Lord;
    praise and exalt him above all forever. — ℟

Fire and heat, bless the Lord;
    praise and exalt him above all forever. — ℟

[Cold and chill, bless the Lord;
    praise and exalt him above all forever.] — ℟

GOSPEL   Lk 21, 12-19

Alleluia (Rv 2, 10)

℟. **Alleluia.** Be faithful until death, says the Lord, and I will give you the crown of life. ℟. **Alleluia.**

Jesus tells his disciples that they will be arrested and persecuted, even delivered over by their families. They will be hated, but not a hair of their heads will be lost.

℣. The Lord be with you. ℟. **And also with you.**

✠ A reading from the holy gospel according to Luke
℟. **Glory to you, Lord.**

Jesus said to his disciples: "People will manhandle and persecute you, summoning you to synagogues and prisons, bringing you to trial before kings and governors, all because of my name. You will be brought to give witness on account of it. I bid you resolve not to worry about your defense beforehand, for I will give you words and a wisdom which none of your adversaries can take exception to or contradict. You will be delivered up even by your parents, brothers, relatives and friends, and some of you will be put to death. All will hate you because of me, yet not a hair of your head will be harmed. By patient endurance you will save your lives."— This is the gospel of the Lord. ℟. **Praise to you. Lord Jesus Christ.** ➜ No. 15, p. 623

THURSDAY OF THE THIRTY-FOURTH WEEK IN ORDINARY TIME

READING I Dn 6, 12-28

Daniel prays to the Lord, contrary to the order of the king. Under the Mede and Persian law, the punishment will be death. Daniel is cast to the lions, but he is saved by an angel.

A reading from the book of the prophet Daniel

Men rushed into the upper chamber of Daniel's home and found him praying and pleading before his God. Then they went to remind the king about the prohibition: "Did you not decree, O king, that no one is to address a petition to god or man for thirty days, except to you, O king; otherwise he shall be cast into a den of lions?" The king answered them, "The decree is absolute, irrevocable under the Mede and Persian law." To this they replied, "Daniel, the Jewish exile, has paid no attention to you, O king, or to the decree you issued; three times a day he offers his prayer." The king was deeply grieved at this news and he made up his mind to save Daniel; he worked till sunset to rescue him. But these men insisted. "Keep in mind, O king," they said, "that under the Mede and Persian law every royal prohibition or decree is irrevocable." So the king ordered Daniel to be brought and cast into the lions' den. To Daniel he said, "May your God, whom you serve so constantly, save you." To forestall any tampering, the king sealed with his own ring and the rings of the lords the stone that had been brought to block the opening of the den.

Then the king returned to his palace for the night; he refused to eat and he dismissed the entertainers. Since sleep was impossible for him, the king rose very early the next morning and hastened to the lions' den. As he drew near, he cried out to Daniel sorrowfully, "O Daniel, servant of the living God, has the God whom you serve so constantly been able to save you from the lions?" Daniel answered the king: "O king, live forever! My God has sent his angel and closed the lions' mouths so that they have not hurt me. For I have been found innocent before him; neither to you have I done any harm, O king!" This gave the king great joy. At his order Daniel was removed from the den, unhurt because he trusted in his God. The king then ordered the men who had accused Daniel, along with their children and their wives, to be cast into the lions' den. Before they reached the bottom of the den, the lions overpowered them and crushed all their bones.

Then King Darius wrote to the nations and peoples of every language, wherever they dwell on the earth: "All peace to you! I decree that throughout my royal domain the God of Daniel is to be reverenced and feared:

"For he is the living God, enduring forever;
    his kingdom shall not be destroyed,
    and his dominion shall be without end.

He is a deliverer and savior,
> working signs and wonders in heaven and on
> earth,
> and he delivered Daniel from the lions' power."

This is the Word of the Lord. ℟. **Thanks be to God.** ✟

Responsorial Psalm   Dn 3, 68, 69. 70. 71. 72. 73. 74

℟. (59) **Give glory and eternal praise to him.**

Dew and rain, bless the Lord;
> praise and exalt him above all forever. — ℟

Frost and chill, bless the Lord;
> praise and exalt him above all forever. — ℟

Ice and snow, bless the Lord;
> praise and exalt him above all forever. — ℟

Nights and days, bless the Lord;
> praise and exalt him above all forever. — ℟

Light and darkness, bless the Lord;
> praise and exalt him above all forever. — ℟

Lightnings and clouds, bless the Lord;
> praise and exalt him above all forever. — ℟

Let the earth bless the Lord,
> praise and exalt him above all forever. — ℟ ✟

GOSPEL   Lk 21, 20-28

Alleluia (Lk 21, 28)

℟. **Alleluia.** Lift up your heads and see;
your redemption is near at hand. ℟. **Alleluia.**

Jerusalem will be desolate and the people will be led away captive.
There will be days of tribulation. Men will die of fright. After all this,
the Son of Man will come in glory and ransom will be near.

℣. The Lord be with you. ℟. **And also with you.**
✠ A reading from the holy gospel according to Luke
℟. **Glory to you, Lord.**

Jesus said to his disciples: "When you see Jerusalem
encircled by soldiers, know that its devastation is
near. Those in Judea at the time must flee to the

mountains; those in the heart of the city must escape it; those in the country must not return. These indeed will be days of retribution, when all that is written must be fulfilled.

"The women who are pregnant or nursing at the breast will fare badly in those days! The distress in the land and the wrath against this people will be great. The people will fall before the sword; they will be led captive in the midst of the Gentiles. Jerusalem will be trampled by the Gentiles, until the times of the Gentiles are fulfilled.

"There will be signs in the sun, the moon and the stars. On the earth, nations will be in anguish, distraught at the roaring of the sea and the waves. Men will die of fright in anticipation of what is coming upon the earth. The powers in the heavens will be shaken. After that, men will see the Son of Man coming on a cloud with great power and glory. When these things begin to happen, stand up straight and raise your heads, for your ransom is near at hand."—This is the gospel of the Lord. ℟. **Praise to you, Lord Jesus Christ.** ➔ No. 15, p. 623

FRIDAY OF THE THIRTY-FOURTH WEEK IN ORDINARY TIME

READING I Dn 7, 2-14

Daniel has a vision: four winds of heaven, four beasts. Finally, thrones are set up, and the books are opened. The Son of Man receives dominion, glory, and kingship which shall not be destroyed.

A reading from the book of the prophet Daniel

In the vision I saw during the night, suddenly the four winds of heaven stirred up the great sea, from which emerged four immense beasts, each different from the others. The first was like a lion, but with eagle's wings. While I watched, the wings were plucked; it was raised from the ground to stand on two feet like a man, and given a human mind. The second was like a bear; it was raised up on one side, and among the teeth in its mouth were three tusks. It was given the order, "Up, devour much flesh." After this I looked and saw another beast, like a leopard; on its back were four wings like those of a bird, and it had four heads. To this beast dominion was given. After this, in the visions of the night I saw the fourth beast, different from all the others, terrifying, horrible, and of extraordinary strength; it had great iron teeth with which it devoured and crushed, and what was left it trampled with its feet. I was considering the ten horns it had, when suddenly another, a little horn, sprang out of their midst, and three of the previous horns were torn away to make room for it. This horn had eyes like a man, and a mouth that spoke arrogantly. As I watched,

Thrones were set up
and the Ancient One took his throne.
His clothing was snow bright,
and the hair on his head as white as wool;
His throne was flames of fire,
with wheels of burning fire.
A surging stream of fire
flowed out from where he sat;
Thousands upon thousands were ministering to
him,
and myriads upon myriads attended him.

The court was convened, and the books were opened. I watched, then, from the first of the arrogant words which the horn spoke, until the beast was slain and its body thrown into the fire to be burnt up. The other beasts, which also lost their dominion, were granted a prolongation of life for a time and a season. As the visions during the night continued, I saw

One like a son of man coming,
  on the clouds of heaven;
When he reached the Ancient One
  and was presented before him,
He received dominion, glory, and kingship;
  nations and peoples of every language serve
  him.
His dominion is an everlasting dominion
  that shall not be taken away,
  his kingship shall not be destroyed.
This is the Word of the Lord. ℟. **Thanks be to God.** ⩔

Responsorial Psalm   Dn 3, 75. 76. 77. 78. 79. 80. 81
℟. (59) **Give glory and eternal praise to him.**

Mountains and hills, bless the Lord;
  praise and exalt him above all forever. — ℟

Everything growing from the earth, bless the Lord;
  praise and exalt him above all forever. — ℟

You springs, bless the Lord;
  praise and exalt him above all forever. — ℟

Seas and rivers, bless the Lord;
  praise and exalt him above all forever. — ℟

You dolphins and all water creatures, bless the Lord;
  praise and exalt him above all forever. — ℟

All you birds of the air, bless the Lord;
  praise and exalt him above all forever. — ℟

All you beasts, wild and tame, bless the Lord;
  praise and exalt him above all forever. — ℟ ⩔

GOSPEL   Lk 21, 29-33
Alleluia (Lk 21, 28)

℟. **Alleluia.** Lift up your heads and see;
your redemption is near at hand. ℟. **Alleluia.**

By the signs of a budding fig tree, it is obvious that springtime is near.
All the signs about which Jesus spoke must come about. Heaven and
earth will pass away but not the word of God.

℣. The Lord be with you. ℟. **And also with you.**

✠ A reading from the holy gospel according to Luke

℟. **Glory to you, Lord.**

Jesus told his disciples a parable: "Notice the fig tree, or any other tree. You observe them when they are budding, and know for yourselves that summer is near. Likewise when you see all the things happening of which I speak, know that the reign of God is near. Let me tell you this: the present generation will not pass away until all this takes place. The heavens and the earth will pass away, but my words will not pass."—This is the gospel of the Lord. ℟. **Praise to you, Lord Jesus Christ.**   → No. 15, p. 623

SATURDAY OF THE THIRTY-FOURTH WEEK IN ORDINARY TIME

READING I   Dn 7, 15-27

Daniel is upset by his vision. The holy one shall receive the kingdom to last forever. These shall be the people of the Most High. All dominions shall obey and serve him.

A reading from the book of the prophet Daniel

I, Daniel, found my spirit anguished within its sheath of flesh, and I was terrified by the visions of my mind. I approached one of those present and asked him what all this meant in truth; in answer, he made known to me the meaning of the things: "These four great beasts stand for four kingdoms which shall arise on the earth. But the holy ones of the Most High shall receive the kingship, to possess it forever and ever."

But I wished to make certain about the fourth beast, so very terrible and different from the others, devouring and crushing with its iron teeth and bronze claws, and trampling with its feet what was left; about the ten horns on its head, and the other

cne that sprang up, before which three horns fell;
about the horn with the eyes and the mouth that
spoke arrogantly, which appeared greater than its
fellows. For, as I watched, that horn made war
against the holy ones and was victorious until the
Ancient One arrived; judgment was pronounced in
favor of the holy ones of the Most High, and the
time came when the holy ones possessed the kingdom. He answered me thus:

"The fourth beast shall be a fourth kingdom on
   earth,
   different from all the others;
It shall devour the whole earth,
   beat it down, and crush it.
The ten horns shall be ten kings
   rising out of that kingdom;
   another shall rise up after them,
Different from those before him,
   who shall lay low three kings.
He shall speak against the Most High
   and oppress the holy ones of the Most High,
   thinking to change the feast days and the law.
They shall be handed over to him
   for a year, two years, and a half-year.
But when the court is convened,
   and his power is taken away
   by final and absolute destruction,
Then the kingship and dominion and majesty
   of all the kingdoms under the heavens
   shall be given to the holy people of the Most
     High,
Whose kingdom shall be everlasting:
   all dominions shall serve and obey him."
This is the Word of the Lord. ℟. **Thanks be to God.** ℣

Responsorial Psalm   Dn 3, 82. 83. 84. 85. 86. 87
℟. (59) **Give glory and eternal praise to him.**
You sons of men, bless the Lord;

praise and exalt him above all forever. — ℟

O Israel, bless the Lord;
  praise and exalt him above all forever. — ℟

Priests of the Lord, bless the Lord;
  praise and exalt him above all forever. — ℟

Servants of the Lord, bless the Lord;
  praise and exalt him above all forever. — ℟

Spirits and souls of the just, bless the Lord;
  praise and exalt him above all forever. — ℟

Holy men of humble heart, bless the Lord;
  praise and exalt him above all forever. — ℟ ℣

GOSPEL   Lk 21, 34-36

Alleluia (Lk 21, 36)

℟. **Alleluia.** Be watchful, pray constantly,
that you may be worthy to stand before the Son of
  Man. ℟. **Alleluia.**

Jesus teaches his disciples not to be overcome by the wiles of this
world. The great day will spring like a trap. They should watch and
pray to stand secure before the Son of Man.

℣. The Lord be with you. ℟. **And also with you.**
✠ A reading from the holy gospel according to Luke
℟. **Glory to you, Lord.**

Jesus said to his disciples: "Be on guard lest your
spirits become bloated with indulgence and drunkenness and worldly cares. The great day will suddenly close in on you like a trap. The day I speak
of will come upon all who dwell on the face of the
earth. So be on the watch. Pray constantly for the
strength to escape whatever is in prospect, and to
stand secure before the Son of Man."—This is the
gospel of the Lord. ℟. **Praise to you, Lord Jesus
Christ.**   ➤ No. 15, p. 623

PROPER OF SAINTS

"In celebrating the annual cycle of Christ's mysteries, holy Church honors with special love the Blessed Mary, Mother of God, who is joined by an inseparable bond to the saving work of her Son. In her the Church holds up and admires the most excellent fruit of the redemption, and joyfully contemplates, as in a faultless model, that which she herself wholly desires and hopes to be.

"The Church has also included in the annual cycle days devoted to the memory of the martyrs and the other saints. Raised up to perfection by the manifold grace of God, and already in possession of eternal salvation, they sing God's perfect praise in heaven and offer prayers for us. By celebrating the passage of these saints from earth to heaven the Church proclaims the paschal mystery as achieved in the saints who have suffered and been glorified with Christ; she proposes them to the faithful as examples who draw all to the Father through Christ, and through their merits she pleads for God's favors" (Vatican II Constitution on the Sacred Liturgy, nos. 103-104).

Solemnities and Feasts

A proper Mass is provided in its entirety for each solemnity and feast. There is no substitute for the processional chants, presidential prayers, and special readings and intervenient chants given for these days.

Obligatory Memorials

1) Processional Chants and Presidential Prayers

a) Proper texts, given on some days, should always be used.

b) When there is a reference to a particular common, appropriate texts should be chosen according to the principles at the beginning of the Commons. The page reference in each case indicates only the beginning of the common to which reference is made.

c) If the reference is to more than one common, one or the other may be used, according to pastoral need. It is always permissible to interchange texts from several Masses within the same common.

For example, if a saint is both a martyr and a bishop, either the Common of Martyrs or the Common of Pastors (for bishops) may be used.

d) In addition to the commons which express a special characteristic holiness, (e.g., of martyrs, virgins, or pastors), the texts from the Common of Holy Men and Women, referring to holiness in general, may always be used.

For example, in the case of a saint who is both a virgin and a martyr, texts from the Common of Holy Men and Women in general may be used, in addition to texts from the Common of Martyrs or the Common of Virgins.

e) The Prayers over the Gifts and after Communion, unless there are proper prayers, may be taken either from the common or from the current liturgical season.

2) Readings and Intervenient Chants

a) The weekday readings and intervenient chants are to be preferred.

b) However, sometimes special readings are assigned, that is, readings which mention the saint or mystery being celebrated; these are to be said in place of the weekday readings. (Whenever this is the case, a clear indication is given in this Missal.)

c) In all other cases the readings found in the Proper of Saints are used only if special reasons (particularly of a pastoral nature) exist. Sometimes, these readings will be appropriate, that is, they will shed light on some outstanding trait of the saint's spiritual life. Others will be simply references to the general readings in the Commons so as to facilitate a selection. However, they are only suggestions; in place of these appropriate readings or suggested gen-

eral *readings, any other reading from the common indicated may be said.*

d) *Whenever there are compelling reasons for doing so, readings can always be chosen from the Common of Holy Men and Women.*

Optional Memorials

The category of Optional Memorials is like that of Obligatory Memorials as far as choice of texts is concerned but it allows many more options of Masses to be chosen. In place of the Mass of the Optional Memorial, the priest has the option to choose the Mass of the Weekday, or of one of the saints commemorated or mentioned in the martyrology on that day, or a Mass for Various Needs and Occasions or a Votive Mass. Masses of the saints from the martyrology can be taken from the Mass of a saint in the Missal who is in a similar category, e.g., a martyr, priest, etc.

Saturday following the Second Sunday
after Pentecost

IMMACULATE HEART OF MARY

Optional Memorial

Our Lady of Fatima is said to have asked for the Consecration of the world to her Immaculate Heart in order to obtain world peace and the conversion of Russia. To it must be added devout prayers, true repentance and penance for the sins of men. In 1942, Pope Pius XII consecrated the world to the Immaculate Heart of Mary. In 1945, the sovereign Pontiff established this new Feast to promote devotion to the Immaculate Heart of Mary and extended it to the Universal Church.

ENTRANCE ANT.   Ps 13, 6

My heart rejoices in your saving power. I will sing to the Lord for his goodness to me. ➔ No. 2, p. 614

OPENING PRAYER

Father,
you prepared the heart of the Virgin Mary
to be a fitting home for your Holy Spirit.
By her prayers
may we become a more worthy temple of your glory.
Grant this through our Lord Jesus Christ, your Son,
who lives and reigns with you and the Holy Spirit,
one God, for ever and ever. ℟. **Amen.**

Readings and Intervenient Chants from the Common of the Blessed Virgin Mary, p. 1118.

Reading I (Is 61, 9-11), p. 1123, no. 9.
Responsorial Psalm (1 Sm 2), p. 1125, no. 1.

The Gospel is special in this Optional Memorial:

GOSPEL   Lk 2, 41-51

Alleluia (See Lk 2, 19)

℟. **Alleluia.** Blessed is the Virgin Mary who kept the word of God,

and pondered it in her heart. ℟. **Alleluia.**

Jesus and his parents go to Jerusalem for the Passover. Upon returning, Jesus is separated from them. Mary and Joseph find him in the temple teaching. When Mary asks why, Jesus replies that he must be doing his Father's work. Jesus returns with Mary and Joseph to Nazareth.

℣. The Lord be with you. ℟. **And also with you.**

✠ A reading from the holy gospel according to Luke ℟. **Glory to you, Lord.**

The parents of Jesus used to go every year to Jerusalem for the feast of the Passover, and when he was twelve they went up for the celebration as was their custom. As they were returning at the end of the feast, the child Jesus remained behind unknown to his parents. Thinking he was in the party, they continued their journey for a day, looking for him among their relatives and acquaintances.

Not finding him, they returned to Jerusalem in search of him. On the third day they came upon him in the temple sitting in the midst of the teachers, listening to them and asking them questions. All who heard him were amazed at his intelligence and his answers.

When his parents saw him they were astonished, and his mother said to him: "Son, why have you done this to us? You see that your father and I have been searching for you in sorrow." He said to them: "Why did you search for me? Did you not know I had to be in my Father's house?" But they did not grasp what he said to them.

He went down with them then, and came to Nazareth, and was obedient to them. His mother meanwhile kept all these things in memory.—This is the gospel of the Lord. ℟. **Praise to you, Lord Jesus Christ.**   ➤ No. 15, p. 623

PRAYER OVER THE GIFTS

Lord,
accept the prayers and gifts we offer
in honor of Mary, the Mother of God.
May they please you
and bring us your help and forgiveness.
We ask this in the name of Jesus the Lord.
℟. **Amen.**   ➔ No. 21, p. 626 (P 56-57)

COMMUNION ANT.   Lk 2, 19

**Mary treasured all these words and pondered them
in her heart.** ⱽ

PRAYER AFTER COMMUNION

Lord,
you have given us the sacrament of eternal redemption.
May we who honor the mother of your Son
rejoice in the abundance of your blessings
and experience the deepening of your life within us.
We ask this through Christ our Lord.
℟. **Amen.**   ➔ No. 32, p. 650

─────────

— JUNE —

June 1 — ST. JUSTIN, Martyr

Memorial

St. Justin was converted from a pagan philosopher to
Christianity. He then became the most illustrious opponent of pagan philosophers. He addressed two Apolo-
gies to the Emperor Antoninus and the Roman Senate.
He died in 165.

ENTRANCE ANT.   See Ps 119, 85. 46

**The wicked tempted me with their fables against
your law, but I proclaimed your decrees before kings
without fear or shame.**   ➔ No. 2, p. 614

OPENING PRAYER

Father,
through the folly of the cross
you taught St. Justin the sublime wisdom of Jesus
    Christ.
May we too reject falsehood
and remain loyal to the faith.
We ask this through our Lord Jesus Christ, your Son,
who lives and reigns with you and the Holy Spirit,
one God, for ever and ever. ℟. **Amen.**

*Readings and Intervenient Chants from the Common of
Martyrs, p. 1138.*

READING I   1 Cor 1, 18-25

Paul says our wisdom is foolishness to the world. What does the world
know about the cross, or eternal life? "God's folly is wiser than men,
and his weakness more powerful."

A reading from the first letter of Paul to the
Corinthians

The message of the cross is complete absurdity to
those who are headed for ruin, but to us who are experiencing salvation it is the power of God. Scripture says,

"I will destroy the wisdom of the wise,
    and thwart the cleverness of the clever."

Where is the wise man to be found? Where is the
scribe? Where is the master of worldly argument?
Has not God turned the wisdom of this world into
folly? Since in God's wisdom the world did not come
to know him through wisdom, it pleased God to
save those who believe through the absurdity of the
preaching of the gospel. Yes, Jews demand "signs"
and Greeks look for "wisdom," but we preach Christ
crucified, a stumbling block to Jews and an absurdity
to Gentiles, but to those who are called, Jews and
Greeks alike, Christ the power of God and the wisdom of God. For God's folly is wiser than men, and
his weakness more powerful than men.—This is
the Word of the Lord. ℟. **Thanks be to God.**

Responsorial Psalm (Ps 34), p. 1144, no. 2.
Gospel (Mt 5, 13-16), p. 1186, no. 1.

PRAYER OVER THE GIFTS

Lord,
help us to worship you as we should
when we celebrate these mysteries
which St. Justin vigorously defended.
We ask this in the name of Jesus the Lord.
℟. **Amen.**   ➔ No. 21, p. 626

COMMUNION ANT.   1 Cor 2, 2

**I resolved that while I was with you I would think
of nothing but Jesus Christ and him crucified. ℣**

PRAYER AFTER COMMUNION

Lord,
hear the prayer of those you renew with spiritual
    food.
By following the teaching of St. Justin
may we offer constant thanks for the gifts we receive.
Grant this through Christ our Lord.
℟. **Amen.** _____ ➔ No. 32, p. 650

June 2 — STS. MARCELLINUS and PETER, Martyrs

Optional Memorial

The exorcist Peter succeeded in converting his jailer and
his family. All were baptized by St. Marcellinus. Both
were beheaded in 304.

Common of Martyrs, p. 1049 or 1059.

OPENING PRAYER

Father,
may we benefit from the example
of your martyrs Marcellinus and Peter,
and be supported by their prayers.
Grant this through our Lord Jesus Christ, your Son,
who lives and reigns with you and the Holy Spirit,
one God, for ever and ever. ℟. **Amen.**

Reading I (2 Cor 6, 4-10), p. 1147, no. 4.
Responsorial Psalm (Ps 124), p. 1145, no. 3.
Gospel (Jn 17, 11-19), p. 1153, no. 7.

June 3 — STS. CHARLES LWANGA and COMPANIONS, Martyrs

Memorial

St. Charles Lwanga and his Companions, martyrs of
Uganda, are the first martyrs of black Africa. St.
Charles was martyred with twelve companions near Ru-
baga on June 3, 1886; the others were killed between
May 26, 1886 and January 27, 1887. They were canonized
in 1964.

Common of Martyrs, p. 1049 or 1059.

OPENING PRAYER

Father,
you have made the blood of the martyrs
the seed of Christians.
May the witness of St. Charles and his companions
and their loyalty to Christ in the face of torture
inspire countless men and women
to live the Christian faith.
We ask this through our Lord Jesus Christ, your Son,
who lives and reigns with you and the Holy Spirit,
one God, for ever and ever. ℟. **Amen.**

Reading I (2 Mc 7, 1-2. 9-14), p. 1139, no. 3.
Responsorial Psalm (Ps 124), p. 1145, no. 3.
Gospel (Mt 5, 1-12), p. 1220, no. 1.

PRAYER OVER THE GIFTS

Lord,
accept the gifts we present at your altar.
As you gave your holy martyrs courage to die rather
    than sin,
help us to give ourselves completely to you.
We ask this in the name of Jesus the Lord.
℟. **Amen.**

➤ No. 21, p. 626

PRAYER AFTER COMMUNION

Lord,
at this celebration of the triumph of your martyrs,
we have received the sacraments
which helped them endure their sufferings.
In the midst of our own hardships
may this eucharist keep us steadfast in faith and love.
Grant this through Christ our Lord.
℟. **Amen.**   ➤ No. 32, p. 650

June 5 — ST. BONIFACE, Bishop and Martyr

Memorial

Born in England about 680, St. Boniface became a Benedictine monk. He preached in Germany and later was
consecrated first Bishop of Germany by Pope Gregory
II. He died a martyr together with thirty companions,
in 754.

*Common of Martyrs, p. 1056 or 1061; or Common of
Pastors: for Missionaries, p. 1077.*

OPENING PRAYER

Lord,
your martyr Boniface
spread the faith by his teaching
and witnessed to it with his blood.
By the help of his prayers
keep us loyal to our faith
and give us the courage to profess it in our lives.
Grant this through our Lord Jesus Christ, your Son,
who lives and reigns with you and the Holy Spirit,
one God, for ever and ever. ℟. **Amen.**

Reading I (Acts 26, 19-23), p. 1160, no. 3.
Responsorial Psalm (Ps 117), p. 1163, no. 6.
Gospel (Jn 10, 11-16), p. 1175, no. 9.

June 6 — ST. NORBERT, Bishop

Optional Memorial

St. Norbert was born at Xanten, Germany, in 1080. After a somewhat worldly and licentious life, he retired to Prémontre and there founded the Premonstratensians under the rule of St. Augustine. He died in 1134 while holding the exalted office of Archbishop of Magdeburg.

Common of Pastors: for Bishops, p, 1069; *or Common of Holy Men and Women: for Religious, p.* 1097.

OPENING PRAYER

Father,
you made the bishop Norbert
an outstanding minister of your Church,
renowned for his preaching and pastoral zeal.
Always grant to your Church faithful shepherds
to lead your people to eternal salvation.
We ask this through our Lord Jesus Christ, your Son,
who lives and reigns with you and the Holy Spirit,
one God, for ever and ever. ℟. **Amen.**

Reading I (Ez 34, 11-16), p. 1158, no. 9.
Responsorial Psalm (Ps 23), p. 1161, no. 2.
Gospel (Lk 14, 25-33), p. 1230, no. 19.

June 9 — ST. EPHREM, Deacon and Doctor

Optional Memorial

St. Ephrem, of Nisibis in Mesopotamia, was cast forth from his home by his father, a pagan priest. He lived as a hermit but was later ordained a Deacon of Edessa and became renowned as a poet, orator, and holy monk. He died in 373.

Common of Doctors of the Church, p. 1082.

OPENING PRAYER

Lord,
in your love fill our hearts with the Holy Spirit,
who inspired the deacon Ephrem to sing the praise
    of your mysteries

and gave him strength to serve you alone.
Grant this through our Lord Jesus Christ, your Son,
who lives and reigns with you and the Holy Spirit,
one God, for ever and ever. ℞. **Amen.**

Reading I (1 Pt 4, 7-11), p. 1216, no. 14.
Responsorial Psalm (Ps 37), p 1181, no. 2.
Gospel (Mk 3, 31-35), p. 1226, no. 11.

June 11 — ST. BARNABAS, Apostle

Memorial

St. Barnabas was the companion of St. Paul in the evan-
gelization of the pagans in Cyprus. After having conquered many souls for Christ, Barnabas died a martyr
at Cyprus during Nero's reign with the Gospel of St.
Matthew, written by his own hand, on his chest.

ENTRANCE ANT.　　　　　See Acts 11, 24

**Blessed are you, St. Barnabas: you were a man of
faith filled with the Holy Spirit and counted among
the apostles.**　　　　　➤ No. 2, p. 614

OPENING PRAYER

God our Father,
you filled St. Barnabas with faith and the Holy Spirit,
and sent him to convert the nations.
Help us to proclaim the gospel by word and deed.
We ask this through our Lord Jesus Christ, your Son,
who lives and reigns with you and the Holy Spirit,
one God, for ever and ever. ℞. **Amen.** ↓

Reading I is special in this Memorial.

READING I　　　　　Acts 11, 21-26; 13, 1-3

Today's saint, Barnabas, is commended as a man full of the Spirit of
faith. St. Barnabas introduced St. Paul to the Christian community.
Together, they were added to the number of the apostles and were
sent to the Gentiles.

A reading from the Acts of the Apostles

A great number believed and were converted to the
Lord. News of this eventually reached the ears of

the church in Jerusalem, resulting in Barnabas' being sent to Antioch. On his arrival he rejoiced to see the evidence of God's favor. He encouraged them all to remain firm in their commitment to the Lord, since he himself was a good man filled with the Holy Spirit and faith. Thereby large numbers were added to the Lord. Then Barnabas went off to Tarsus to look for Saul; once he had found him, he brought him back to Antioch. For a whole year they met with the church and instructed great numbers. It was in Antioch that the disciples were called Christians for the first time.

There were in the church at Antioch certain prophets and teachers: Barnabas, Symeon known as Niger, Lucius of Cyrene, Manaen (who had been brought up with Herod the tetrarch), and Saul. On one occasion, while they were engaged in the liturgy of the Lord and were fasting, the Holy Spirit spoke to them: "Set apart Barnabas and Saul for me to do the work for which I have called them." Then, after they had fasted and prayed, they imposed hands on them and sent them off.—This is the Word of the Lord. ℟. **Thanks be to God.** ℣

Responsorial Psalm   Ps 98, 1. 2-3. 3-4. 5-6
℟. (2) **The Lord has revealed to the nations his saving power.**

Sing to the Lord a new song,
 for he has done wondrous deeds;
His right hand has won victory for him,
 his holy arm. — ℟

The Lord has made his salvation known:
 in the sight of the nations he has revealed his justice.
He has remembered his kindness and his faithfulness
 toward the house of Israel. — ℟

All the ends of the earth have seen
 the salvation by our God.

Sing joyfully to the Lord, all you lands;
  break into song; sing praise. — ℟

Sing praise to the Lord with the harp,
  with the harp and melodious song.

With trumpets and the sound of the horn
  sing joyfully before the King, the Lord. — ℟ ℣

GOSPEL   Mt 10, 7-13

Alleluia

℟. **Alleluia.** We praise you, God; we acknowledge
  you as Lord;

your glorious band of apostles extols you. ℟. **Alleluia.**

Jesus empowered his apostles to work wonders and miracles, to
prove their teaching about Christ. The greater miracles are men who
still leave everything today, in order to preach the Good News.
Miracles of grace accompany such dedication.

℣. The Lord be with you. ℟. **And also with you.**

✠ A reading from the holy gospel according to Matthew. ℟. **Glory to you, Lord.**

Jesus said to his disciples: "As you go, make this
announcement: 'The reign of God is at hand!' Cure
the sick, raise the dead, heal the leprous, expel demons. The gift you have received, give as a gift.
Provide yourselves with neither gold nor silver nor
copper in your belts; no traveling bag, no change of
shirt, no sandals, no walking staff. The workman,
after all, is worth his keep.

  "Look for a worthy citizen in every town or village you come to and stay with him until you leave.
As you enter his home bless it. If the home is deserving, your blessing will descend on it. If it is not,
your blessing will return to you."—This is the gospel of the Lord. ℟. **Praise to you, Lord Jesus Christ.**

➤ No. 15, p. 623

PRAYER OVER THE GIFTS

Lord,
bless these gifts we present to you.
May they kindle in us the flame of love
by which St. Barnabas brought the light of the gospel
to the nations.
Grant this through Christ our Lord.
℟. **Amen.**   → No. 21, p. 626 (Pref. P 64-65)

COMMUNION ANT.   Jn 15, 15

No longer shall I call you servants, for a servant knows not what his master does. Now I shall call you friends, for I have revealed to you all that I have heard from my Father. ℣

PRAYER AFTER COMMUNION

Lord,
hear the prayers of those who receive the pledge of
   eternal life
on the feast of St. Barnabas.
May we come to share the salvation
we celebrate in this sacrament.
We ask this in the name of Jesus the Lord.
℟. **Amen.**   → No. 32, p. 650

June 13 — ST ANTHONY OF PADUA,
Priest and Doctor

Memorial

St. Anthony, called "St. Anthony of Padua" because of his long residence in that city, was a native of Lisbon, Portugal, where he was born in 1195. He is venerated as one of the greatest Franciscan Saints. St. Anthony was a profound theologian, a brilliant preacher, and a formidable foe of heresy, through the supernatural forces which seemed to be always at his command. He died in 1231.

Common of Pastors, p. 1071; or Common of Doctors of the Church, p. 1082; or Common of Holy Men and Women: for Religious, p. 1097.

OPENING PRAYER

Almighty God,
you have given St. Anthony to your people
as an outstanding preacher
and a ready helper in time of need.
With his assistance may we follow the gospel of
    Christ
and know the help of your grace in every difficulty.
Grant this through our Lord Jesus Christ, your Son,
who lives and reigns with you and the Holy Spirit,
one God, for ever and ever. ℟. **Amen.**

Reading I (Is 61, 1-3), p. 1157, no. 6.
Responsorial Psalm (Ps 89), p. 1161, no. 3.
Gospel (Lk 10, 1-9), p. 1174, no. 7.

June 19 — ST. ROMUALD, Abbot

Optional Memorial

St. Romuald, born at Ravenna, Italy, became the hero of penance and the angelic hermit of the Camaldolese forests. A follower of St. Benedict, he in turn founded the Camaldolese monks. He died in 1027 at 100 years of age.

Common of Holy Men and Women: for Religious, p. 1097.

OPENING PRAYER

Father,
through St. Romuald
you renewed the life of solitude and prayer in your
    Church.
By our self-denial as we follow Christ
bring us the joy of heaven.
We ask this through our Lord Jesus Christ, your Son,
who lives and reigns with you and the Holy Spirit,
one God, for ever and ever. ℟. **Amen.**

Reading I (Eph 6, 10-13. 18), p. 1213, no. 8.
Responsorial Psalm (Ps 131), p. 1210, no. 8.
Gospel (Lk 14, 25-33), p. 1230, no. 19.

June 21 — ST. ALOYSIUS GONZAGA, Religious

Memorial

Born at Castiglione in Lombardy in 1568, St. Aloysius is
hailed as a veritable angel in the flesh because of his
purity of life. He made a vow of virginity at nine years
of age. At sixteen, he entered the Jesuit Order, distin-
guishing himself by his mortifications and as a model of
purity and innocence. In 1591, at twenty-three years of
age, he died. Pope Benedict XIII proclaimed him "Patron of Youth."

ENTRANCE ANT.

See Ps 24, 4. 3

**Who shall climb the mountain of the Lord and stand
in his holy place? The innocent man, the pure of
heart.**
➤ No. 2, p. 614

OPENING PRAYER

Father of love,
giver of all good things,
in St. Aloysius you combined remarkable innocence
with the spirit of penance.
By the help of his prayers
may we who have not followed his innocence
follow his example of penance.

Grant this through our Lord Jesus Christ, your Son,
who lives and reigns with you and the Holy Spirit,
one God, for ever and ever. ℞. **Amen.**

Readings and Intervenient Chants are taken from the
Common of Holy Men and Women: for Religious, p.
1195.

Reading I (1 Jn 5, 1-5), p. 1218, no. 17.
Responsorial Psalm (Ps 16), p. 1207, no. 3.
Gospel (Mt 16, 24-27), p. 1222, no. 5.

PRAYER OVER THE GIFTS

Lord,
help us to follow the example of St. Aloysius
and always come to the eucharist
with hearts free from sin.
By our sharing in this mystery
make us rich in your blessings.
We ask this in the name of Jesus the Lord.
℞. **Amen.**   ➜ No. 21, p. 626

COMMUNION ANT.   Ps 78, 24-25

God gave them bread from heaven; men ate the bread
of angels. ℣

PRAYER AFTER COMMUNION

Lord,
you have nourished us with the bread of life.
Help us to serve you without sin.
By following the example of St. Aloysius
may we continue to spend our lives in thanksgiving.
We ask this through Christ our Lord.
℞. **Amen.**   ➜ No. 32, p. 650

_____

June 22 — ST. PAULINUS OF NOLA, Bishop

Optional Memorial

Born at Bordeaux, Paulinus was elected consul of Nola
near Naples. Touched by grace at the tomb of St. Felix,
he abandoned earthly goods and became a priest. He

was consecrated Bishop of Nola, and his life of asceticism and charity earned for him the title of Father of the Church. He died in 431.

Common of Pastors: for Bishops, p. 1069.

OPENING PRAYER

Lord,
you made St. Paulinus
renowned for his love of poverty
and concern for his people.
May we who celebrate his witness to the gospel
imitate his example of love for others.
We ask this through our Lord Jesus Christ, your Son,
who lives and reigns with you and the Holy Spirit,
one God, for ever and ever. R̷. **Amen.**

READING I   2 Cor 8, 9-15

Jesus first offered the example of giving himself for all men. Paul reminds the Corinthians that they should be anxious to willingly give and share all with those in need.

A reading from the second letter of Paul to the
Corinthians

You are well acquainted with the favor shown you by our Lord Jesus Christ: how for your sake he made himself poor though he was rich, so that you might become rich by his poverty. I am about to give you some advice on this matter of rich and poor. It will help you who began this good work last year, not only to carry it through but to do so willingly. Carry it through now to a successful completion, so that your ready resolve may be matched by giving according to your means. The willingness to give should accord with one's means, but not go beyond them. The relief of others ought not to impoverish you; there should be a certain equality. Your plenty at the present time should supply their need so that their surplus may one day supply your need, with equality as the result. It is written, "He who gathered much had no excess and he who gathered little had no lack."—This is the Word of the Lord. R̷. **Thanks be to God.** ⱱ

Responsorial Psalm   Ps 40, 2-5. 7-8. 8-9. 10

℞. (8. 9) **Here am I, Lord; I come to do your will.**

I have waited, waited for the Lord,
  and he stooped toward me.
Happy the man who makes the Lord his trust;
  who turns not to idolatry
  or to those who stray after falsehood. — ℞

Sacrifice or oblation you wished not,
  but ears open to obedience you gave me.
Holocausts or sin-offerings you sought not;
  then said I, "Behold I come." — ℞

"In the written scroll it is prescribed for me.
  To do your will, O my God, is my delight,
And your law is within my heart!" — ℞

I announced your justice in the vast assembly;
  I did not restrain my lips, as you, O Lord,
    know. — ℞

Gospel (Lk 12, 32-34), p. 1229, no. 17.

The Same Day, June 22
STS. JOHN FISHER, Bishop and Martyr
and THOMAS MORE, Martyr

Optional Memorial

St. John Fisher suffered martyrdom in London on June 22, 1535, and St. Thomas More on July 6 of that same year. These two illustrious martyrs, one a bishop and the other a layman, were canonized in 1935. It seemed quite fitting that their example of fidelity be set forth for Christians of our time.

Common of Martyrs, p. 1049.

OPENING PRAYER

Father,
you confirm the true faith
with the crown of martyrdom.
May the prayers of Saints John Fisher and Thomas
  More

on this feast of John the Baptist.
Help us put into action
the mystery we celebrate in this sacrament.
We ask this in the name of Jesus the Lord.
℟. **Amen.** ▼

PREFACE (P 61)

℣. The Lord be with you. ℟. **And also with you.**
℣. Lift up your hearts. ℟. **We lift them up to the Lord.** ℣. Let us give thanks to the Lord our God.
℟. **It is right to give him thanks and praise.**

Father, all-powerful and ever-living God,
we do well always and everywhere to give you thanks
through Jesus Christ our Lord.
We praise your greatness
as we honor the prophet
who prepared the way before your Son.
You set John the Baptist apart from other men,
marking him out with special favor.
His birth brought great rejoicing:
even in the womb he leapt for joy,
so near was man's salvation.
You chose John the Baptist from all the prophets
to show the world its redeemer,
the lamb of sacrifice.
He baptized Christ, the giver of baptism,
in waters made holy by the one who was baptized.
You found John worthy of a martyr's death,
his last and greatest act of witness to your Son.
In our unending joy we echo on earth
the song of the angels in heaven
as they praise your glory for ever: ➔ No. 23, p. 627

COMMUNION ANT.   Lk 1, 68
Blessed be the Lord God of Israel, for he has visited and redeemed his people. ▼

PRAYER AFTER COMMUNION
Father,
may the prayers of John the Baptist
lead us to the Lamb of God.
May this eucharist bring us the mercy of Christ,
who is Lord for ever and ever.
R̸. **Amen.** ———————— ➔ No. 32, p. 650

MASS DURING THE DAY

ENTRANCE ANT. Jn 1, 6-7; Lk 1, 17
**There was a man sent from God whose name was
John. He came to bear witness to the light, to pre-
pare an upright people for the Lord.** ➔ No. 2, p. 614

OPENING PRAYER
Let us pray
[that God will give us joy and peace]
God our Father,
you raised up John the Baptist
to prepare a perfect people for Christ the Lord.
Give your Church joy in spirit
and guide those who believe in you
into the way of salvation and peace.
We ask this through our Lord Jesus Christ, your Son,
who lives and reigns with you and the Holy Spirit,
one God, for ever and ever. R̸. **Amen.** ♥

ALTERNATE OPENING PRAYER
Let us pray
[as we honor John the Baptist
for the faith to recognize Christ in our midst]
God our Father,
the voice of John the Baptist challenges us to repentance
and points the way to Christ the Lord.
Open our ears to his message, and free our hearts
to turn from our sins and receive the life of the
gospel.
We ask this through Christ our Lord. R̸. **Amen.** ♥

READING I Is 49, 1-6

The Lord chose the people of Israel to be his servants and to make his name known to men. The words of Isaiah find their fulfillment in the nation, but especially in the Messiah, who will come from among the chosen people.

A reading from the book of the prophet Isaiah

Hear me, O coastlands,
 listen, O distant peoples.
The Lord called me from birth,
 from my mother's womb he gave me my name.
He made of me a sharp-edged sword
 and concealed me in the shadow of his arm.
He made me a polished arrow,
 in his quiver he hid me.
You are my servant, he said to me,
 Israel, through whom I show my glory.
Though I thought I had toiled in vain,
 and for nothing, uselessly, spent my strength,
Yet my reward is with the Lord,
 my recompense is with my God.
For now the Lord has spoken
 who formed me as his servant from the womb,
That Jacob may be brought back to him
 and Israel gathered to him;
And I am made glorious in the sight of the Lord,
 and my God is now my strength!
It is too little, he says, for you to be my servant,
 to raise up the tribes of Jacob,
 and restore the survivors of Israel;
I will make you a light to the nations,
 that my salvation may reach to the ends of the earth.
This is the Word of the Lord. ℟. **Thanks be to God.** ℣

Responsorial Psalm Ps 139, 1-3. 13-14. 14-15

℟. (4) **I praise you for I am wonderfully made.**

O Lord, you have probed me and you know me;
 you know when I sit and when I stand;
 you understand my thoughts from afar.

My journeys and my rest you scrutinize,
    with all my ways you are familiar. — ℟

Truly you have formed my inmost being;
    you knit me in my mother's womb.

I give you thanks that I am fearfully, wonderfully
    made;
    wonderful are your works. — ℟

My soul also you knew full well;
    nor was my frame unknown to you

When I was made in secret,
    when I was fashioned in the depths of the
       earth. — ℟ ❡

READING II   Acts 13, 22-26

Luke quotes Paul as applying the prophecies of the Old Testament to Jesus Christ, the son of David and the Savior of Israel. John the Baptizer proclaimed his coming to Jew and Gentile alike.

A reading from the Acts of the Apostles

Paul said: "God raised up David as their king; on his behalf God testified, 'I have found David son of Jesse to be a man after my own heart who will fulfill my every wish.'

"According to his promise, God has brought forth from this man's descendants Jesus, a savior for Israel. John heralded the coming of Jesus by proclaiming a baptism of repentance to all the people of Israel. As John's career was coming to an end, he would say, 'What you suppose me to be I am not. Rather, look for the one who comes after me. I am not worthy to unfasten the sandals on his feet.' My brothers, children of the family of Abraham and you others who reverence our God, it was to us that this message of salvation was sent forth."—This is the Word of the Lord. ℟. **Thanks be to God.** ❡

GOSPEL   Lk 1, 57-66. 80

Alleluia (Lk 1, 76)

℞. **Alleluia.** You, child, will be called the prophet of
the Most High;
you will go before the Lord to prepare his ways.
℞. **Alleluia.**

The birth of John and the birth of Jesus are alike in some details.
Both are chosen from their first moment of life; both receive names
assigned by an angel. Both come out of the desert—John to announce,
and Jesus to fulfill.

℣. The Lord be with you. ℞. **And also with you.**
✠ A reading from the holy gospel according to Luke
℞. **Glory to you, Lord.**

When Elizabeth's time for delivery arrived, she gave
birth to a son. Her neighbors and relatives, upon
hearing that the Lord had extended his mercy to
her, rejoiced with her. When they assembled for the
circumcision of the child on the eighth day, they
intended to name him after his father Zechariah.
At this his mother intervened, saying, "No, he is to
be called John."

They pointed out to her, "None of your relatives
has this name." Then, using signs, they asked the
father what he wished him to be called.

He signaled for a writing tablet and wrote the
words, "His name is John." This astonished them
all. At that moment his mouth was opened and his
tongue loosed, and he began to speak in praise of
God.

Fear descended on all in the neighborhood;
throughout the hill country of Judea these happening began to be recounted to the last detail. All
who heard stored these things up in their hearts,
saying, "What will this child be?" and, "Was not
the hand of the Lord upon him?"

The child grew up and matured in spirit. He lived
in the desert until the day when he made his public
appearance in Israel.—This is the gospel of the Lord.
℞. **Praise to you, Lord Jesus Christ.** ➔ No. 14, p. 622

PRAYER OVER THE GIFTS

Father,
accept the gifts we bring to your altar
to celebrate the birth of John the Baptist,
who foretold the coming of our Savior
and made him known when he came.
We ask this in the name of Jesus the Lord.
℟. **Amen.**   ➜ Pref. (P 61), p. 457

COMMUNION ANT.   Lk 1, 78

**Through the tender compassion of our God, the dawn
from on high shall break upon us.** ℣

PRAYER AFTER COMMUNION

Lord,
you have renewed us with this eucharist,
as we celebrate the feast of John the Baptist,
who foretold the coming of the Lamb of God.
May we welcome your Son as our Savior,
for he gives us new life,
and is Lord for ever and ever.
℟. **Amen.**   ➜ No. 32, p. 650

June 27 — ST. CYRIL OF ALEXANDRIA,
Bishop and Doctor

Optional Memorial

St. Cyril was born in Alexandria about 375. As a Bishop
and Doctor he became the glory of the Church in Egypt.
He is renowned principally for his strenuous defense of
the Divine Maternity of the Blessed Virgin Mary against
the heresy of Nestorius, Bishop of Constantinople. He
died in 444.

*Common of Pastors: for Bishops, p. 1069; or Common
of Doctors of the Church, p. 1082.*

OPENING PRAYER

Father,
the bishop Cyril courageously taught
that Mary was the Mother of God.
May we who cherish this belief

receive salvation through the incarnation of Christ
your Son,
who lives and reigns with you and the Holy Spirit,
one God, for ever and ever. ℞. **Amen.**

Reading I (2 Tm 4, 1-5), p. 1169, no. 12.
Responsorial Psalm (Ps 89), p. 1161, no. 3.
Gospel (Mt 5, 13-16), p. 1186, no. 1.

June 28 — ST. IRENAEUS, Bishop and Martyr

Memorial

St. Irenaeus was a disciple of St. Polycarp of Smyrna.
His treatises did much to stamp out the gnostic sects.
He succeeded St. Pothinus in the See of Lyons and died
during the persecution of Septimus Severus in 202.

*Common of Martyrs, p. 1056; or Common of Pastors:
for Bishops, p. 1069.*

OPENING PRAYER

Father,
you called St. Irenaeus to uphold your truth
and bring peace to your Church.
By his prayers renew us in faith and love
that we may always be intent
on fostering unity and peace.
Grant this through our Lord Jesus Christ, your Son,
who lives and reigns with you and the Holy Spirit,
one God, for ever and ever. ℞. **Amen.**

*Readings and Intervenient Chants may also be taken
from the Common of Doctors of the Church, p. 1082.*

READING I   2 Tm 2, 22-26

Paul instructs Timothy to pursue virtue, faith, love, peace, purity. He
is to be kindly and to be a teacher, doing the will of God.

A reading from the second letter of Paul to
Timothy

Pursue integrity, faith, love, and peace, along with
those who call on the Lord in purity of heart. Have

nothing to do with senseless, ignorant disputations. As you well know, they only breed quarrels, and the servant of the Lord must not be quarrelsome but must be kindly toward all. He must be an apt teacher, patiently and gently correcting those who contradict him, in the hope always that God will enable them to repent and know the truth. Thus, taken captive by God to do his will, they shall escape the devil's trap.—This is the Word of the Lord. R̰. **Thanks be to God.** ℣

Responsorial Psalm (Ps 37), p. 1181, no. 2.
Gospel (Jn 17, 20-26), p. 1233, no. 22.

PRAYER OVER THE GIFTS

Lord,
as we celebrate the feast of St. Irenaeus
may this eucharist bring you glory,
increase our love of truth,
and help your Church to remain firm in faith and
    unity.
We ask this in the name of Jesus the Lord.
R̰. **Amen.**   ➔ No. 21, p. 626

PRAYER AFTER COMMUNION

Lord,
by these holy mysteries increase our faith.
As the holy bishop Irenaeus reached eternal glory
by being faithful until death,
so may we be saved by living our faith.
We ask this through Christ our Lord.
R̰. **Amen.**   ➔ No. 32, p. 650

June 29 — STS. PETER AND PAUL, apostles

Solemnity

This feast is almost entirely devoted to St. Peter, the Bishop of Rome. After the Descent of the Holy Spirit, St. Peter preached the gospel in Judea and was cast into prison by the cruel Herod. He was miraculously delivered by an angel and established his See first at Antioch, and then finally at Rome. That Peter established himself at Rome, making it the center of the Church, is evident from tradition, his first Epistle, and from data found in the catacombs and ancient churches of Rome. Like St. Paul, he died at Rome during the persecution of Nero (64-68), by being crucified head downward.

VIGIL MASS

ENTRANCE ANT.

Peter the apostle and Paul the teacher of the Gentiles have brought us to know the law of the Lord.

➤ No. 2, p. 614

OPENING PRAYER

Let us pray
  [that the prayers of the apostles
  will lead us to salvation]
Lord our God,
encourage us through the prayers of Saints Peter
  and Paul.
May the apostles who strengthened the faith of the
  infant Church
help us on our way of salvation.
We ask this through our Lord Jesus Christ, your Son,
who lives and reigns with you and the Holy Spirit,
one God, for ever and ever. ℟. **Amen.** ↓

ALTERNATIVE OPENING PRAYER

Let us pray
  [to be true to the faith
  which has come to us through the
  apostles Peter and Paul]
Father in heaven,
the light of your revelation brought Peter and Paul
the gift of faith in Jesus your Son.
Through their prayers
may we always give thanks for your life

given us in Christ Jesus,
and for having been enriched by him
in all knowledge and love.
We ask this through Christ our Lord. ℟. **Amen.** ℣

READING I   Acts 3, 1-10

Peter cures the crippled man, not in his own name, but in the name
of Christ. Peter and John do not have money, but they share what
they have—the power of God.

A reading from the Acts of the Apostles

Once, when Peter and John were going up to the
temple for prayer at the three o'clock hour, a man
crippled from birth was being carried in. They would
bring him every day and put him at the temple gate
called "the Beautiful" to beg from the people as they
entered. When he saw Peter and John on their way
in, he begged them for an alms. Peter fixed his gaze
on the man; so did John. "Look at us!" Peter said.
The cripple gave them his whole attention, hoping
to get something. Then Peter said: "I have neither
silver nor gold, but what I have I give you! In the
name of Jesus Christ the Nazorean, walk!" Then
Peter took him by the right hand and pulled him up.
Immediately the beggar's feet and ankles became
strong; he jumped up, stood for a moment, then began
to walk around. He went into the temple with them—
walking, jumping about, and praising God. When the
people saw him moving and giving praise to God,
they recognized him as that beggar who used to
sit at the Beautiful Gate of the temple. They were
struck with astonishment—utterly stupefied at what
had happened to him.—This is the Word of the Lord.
℟. **Thanks be to God.** ℣

Responsorial Psalm   Ps 19, 2-3. 4-5
℟. (5) **Their message goes out through all the earth.**
The heavens declare the glory of God,
    and the firmament proclaims his handiwork.

Day pours out the word to day,
    and night to night imparts knowledge. — ℟

Not a word nor a discourse
    whose voice is not heard;

Through all the earth their voice resounds,
    and to the ends of the world, their message.—℟ ↯

READING II   Gal 1, 11-20

Paul explains how he and the other apostles can claim authority for
their teaching. The message comes from Christ and is delivered by
those whom the Lord has chosen. Paul is intent on associating himself
with his brother apostles in his work.

A reading from the letter of Paul to the Galatians

I assure you, brothers, the gospel I proclaimed to
you is no mere human invention. I did not receive
it from any man, nor was I schooled in it. It came
by revelation from Jesus Christ. You have heard, I
know, the story of my former way of life in Judaism. You know that I went to extremes in persecuting the church of God and tried to destroy it; I
made progress in Jewish observance far beyond most
of my contemporaries, in my excess of zeal to live
out all the traditions of my ancestors.

But the time came when he who had set me apart before I was born and called by his favor chose
to reveal his Son to me, that I might spread among
the Gentiles the good tidings concerning him. Immediately, without seeking human advisers or even
going to Jerusalem to see those who were apostles
before me, I went off to Arabia; later I returned to
Damascus. Three years after that I went up to Jerusalem to get to know Cephas, with whom I stayed
fifteen days. I did not meet any other apostles except James, the brother of the Lord. I declare before
God that what I have just written is true.—This is
the Word of the Lord. ℟. **Thanks be to God.** ↯

GOSPEL   Jn 21, 15-19

Alleluia (Jn 21, 17)

℟. **Alleluia.** Lord, you know all things: you know that I love you. ℟. **Alleluia.**

The words of Jesus to Peter indicate the dignity bestowed on him, and also the great responsibility. Peter must tend the flock of Christ, even to the point of sacrificing his life. Jesus foretells Peter's martyrdom.

℣. The Lord be with you. ℟. **And also with you.**

✠ A reading from the holy gospel according to John
℟. **Glory to you, Lord.**

When Jesus had appeared to his disciples and had eaten with them, he said to Simon Peter, "Simon, son of John, do you love me more than these?" "Yes, Lord," Peter said, "you know that I love you." At which Jesus said, "Feed my lambs."

A second time he put his question, "Simon, son of John, do you love me?" "Yes, Lord," Peter said, "you know, that I love you." Jesus replied, "Tend my sheep."

A third time Jesus asked him, "Simon, son of John, do you love me?" Peter was hurt because he had asked a third time, "Do you love me?" So he said to him: "Lord, you know everything. You know well that I love you." Jesus told him, "Feed my sheep.

"I tell you solemnly:
as a young man
you fastened your belt
and went about as you pleased;
but when you are older
you will stretch out your hands,
and another will tie you fast
and carry you off against your will."

(What he said indicated the sort of death by which Peter was to glorify God.) When Jesus had finished speaking he said to him, "Follow me."—This is the gospel of the Lord. ℟. **Praise to you, Lord Jesus Christ.** ➜ No. 14, p. 622

PRAYER OVER THE GIFTS

Lord,
we present these gifts
on this feast of the apostles Peter and Paul.
Help us to know our own weakness
and to rejoice in your saving power.
Grant this through Christ our Lord. ℟. **Amen.** ▼

PREFACE (P 63)

℣. The Lord be with you. ℟. **And also with you.**
℣. Lift up your hearts. ℟. **We lift them up to the
Lord.** ℣. Let us give thanks to the Lord our God.
℟. **It is right to give him thanks and praise.**

Father, all-powerful and ever-living God,
we do well always and everywhere to give you
    thanks.
You fill our hearts with joy
as we honor your great apostles:
Peter, our leader in the faith,
and Paul, its fearless preacher.
Peter raised up the Church
from the faithful flock of Israel.
Paul brought your call to the nations,
and became the teacher of the world.
Each in his chosen way gathered into unity
the one family of Christ.
Both shared a martyr's death
and are praised throughout the world.
Now, with the apostles and all the angels and saints,
we praise you for ever: ➔ No. 23, p. 627

COMMUNION ANT. Jn 21, 15-17

**Simon, son of John, do you love me more than these?
Lord, you know all things; you know that I love
you.** ▼

PRAYER AFTER COMMUNION

Father,

you give us light by the teaching of your apostles.
In this sacrament we have received
fill us with your strength.
We ask this in the name of Jesus the Lord.
R̸. **Amen.** _____ ➙ No. 32, p. 650

MASS DURING THE DAY

ENTRANCE ANT.

**These men, conquering all human frailty, shed their
blood and helped the Church to grow. By sharing the
cup of the Lord's suffering, they became the friends
of God.** ➙ No. 2, p. 614

OPENING PRAYER

Let us pray
[that we will remain true to
the faith of the apostles]

God our Father,
today you give us the joy
of celebrating the feast of the apostles Peter and
Paul.
Through them your Church first received the faith.
Keep us true to their teaching.
Grant this through our Lord Jesus Christ, your Son,
who lives and reigns with you and the Holy Spirit,
one God, for ever and ever. R̸. **Amen.** ⋎

ALTERNATIVE OPENING PRAYER

Let us pray
[one with Peter and Paul in our faith in
Christ the Son of the living God]

Praise to you, the God and Father of our Lord Jesus
Christ,
who in your great mercy
have given us new birth and hope
through the power of Christ's resurrection.
Through the prayers of the apostles Peter and Paul
may we who received this faith through their preaching

share their joy in following the Lord
to the unfading inheritance
reserved for us in heaven.
We ask this in the name of Jesus the Lord.
℞. **Amen.** ℣

READING I   Acts 12, 1-11

The apostles are not stopped by accusations and imprisonment. They
continue their witnessing to the Good News of Jesus Christ. The Lord
works with them and through them and often saves them from death.

A reading from the Acts of the Apostles

King Herod started to harass some of the members
of the church. He beheaded James the brother of
John, and when he saw that this pleased certain of
the Jews, he took Peter into custody too. During the
feast of Unleavened Bread he had him arrested and
thrown into prison, with four squads of soldiers to
guard him. Herod intended to bring him before the
people after the Passover. Peter was thus detained
in prison, while the church prayed fervently to God
in his behalf. During the night before Herod was to
bring him to trial, Peter was sleeping between two
soldiers, fastened with double chains, while guards
kept watch at the door. Suddenly an angel of the
Lord stood nearby and light shone in the cell. He
tapped Peter on the side and woke him. "Hurry, get
up!" he said. With that, the chains dropped from
Peter's wrists. The angel said, "Put on your belt and
your sandals!" This he did. Then the angel told him,
"Now put on your cloak and follow me."

Peter followed him out, but with no clear realization that this was taking place through the angel's
help. The whole thing seemed to him a mirage. They
passed the first guard, then the second, and finally
came to the iron gate leading out to the city, which
opened for them of itself. They emerged and made
their way down a narrow alley, when suddenly the
angel left him. Peter had recovered his senses by

this time, and said, "Now I know for certain that the Lord has sent his angel to rescue me from Herod's clutches and from all that the Jews hoped for."—This is the Word of the Lord. ℟. **Thanks be to God.** ⩒

Responsorial Psalm   Ps 34, 2-3. 4-5. 6-7. 8-9

℟. (8) **The angel of the Lord will rescue those who fear him.**

I will bless the Lord at all times;
    his praise shall be ever in my mouth.
Let my soul glory in the Lord;
    the lowly will hear me and be glad. — ℟

Glorify the Lord with me,
    let us together extol his name.
I sought the Lord, and he answered me
    and delivered me from all my fears. — ℟

Look to him that you may be radiant with joy,
    and your faces may not blush with shame.
When the afflicted man called out, the Lord heard,
    and from all his distress he saved him. — ℟

The angel of the Lord encamps
    around those who fear him, and delivers them.
Taste and see how good the Lord is;
    happy the man who takes refuge in him. — ℟ ⩒

READING II   2 Tm 4, 6-8. 17-18

Paul's trials are added to the description of the freeing of Peter. The apostles rely totally on God to guide them and to grant faith to those who hear their preaching. Their human weakness makes God's power more obvious.

A reading from the second letter of Paul to Timothy

I am already being poured out like a libation. The time of my dissolution is near. I have fought the good fight, I have finished the race, I have kept the faith. From now on a merited crown awaits me; on that Day the Lord, just judge that he is, will award it to me—and not only to me but to all who have looked for his appearing with eager longing. But the Lord stood by my side and gave me strength, so that through me the preaching task might be completed and all the nations might hear the gospel. That is how I was saved from the lion's jaws. The Lord will continue to rescue me from all attempts to do me harm and will bring me safe to his heavenly kingdom. To him be glory forever and ever. Amen..—This is the Word of the Lord. ℟. **Thanks be to God.** ℣

GOSPEL   Mt 16, 13-19

Alleluia (Mt 16, 18)

℟. **Alleluia.** You are Peter, the rock on which I will build my Church;

the gates of hell will not hold out against it. ℟. **Alleluia.**

To the Jews, a change of name means a change of the very person and of that person's life. Jesus changes the name of Simon to Peter, which means "rock." He will be the human rock of firmness that will protect the word of God and will guide the whole Church.

℣. The Lord be with you. ℟. **And also with you.**

✠ A reading from the holy gospel according to Matthew. ℟. **Glory to you, Lord.**

When Jesus came to the neighborhood of Caesarea Philippi, he asked his disciples this question: "Who do people say that the Son of Man is?" They replied, "Some say John the Baptizer, other Elijah, still others Jeremiah or one of the prophets." "And you," he said to them, "who do you say that I am?" "You are the Messiah," Simon Peter answered, "the Son of the living God!" Jesus replied, "Blest are you, Simon son of John! No mere man has revealed this to you, but my heavenly Father. I for my part declare to you, you are 'Rock,' and on this rock I will build my church, and the jaws of death shall not prevail against it. I will entrust to you the keys of the kingdom of heaven. Whatever you declare bound

on earth shall be bound in heaven; whatever you
declare loosed on earth shall be loosed in heaven."
—This is the gospel of the Lord. ℟. **Praise to you,
Lord Jesus Christ.** ➤ No. 14, p. 622

PRAYER OVER THE GIFTS

Lord,
may your apostles join their prayers to our offering
and help us to celebrate this sacrifice in love and
     unity.
We ask this through Christ our Lord.
℟. **Amen.** ➤ Pref. (P 63), p. 469

COMMUNION ANT. Mt 16, 16. 18

**Peter said: You are the Christ, the Son of the living
God. Jesus answered: You are Peter, the rock on
which I will build my Church.** ℣

PRAYER AFTER COMMUNION

Lord,
renew the life of your Church
with the power of this sacrament.
May the breaking of bread
and the teaching of the apostles
keep us united in your love.
We ask this in the name of Jesus the Lord.
℟. **Amen.** ➤ No. 32, p. 650

*Optional Solemn Blessings, p. 682, and Prayers over the
People, p. 689.*

June 30 — FIRST MARTYRS OF THE CHURCH OF ROME

Optional Memorial

Since the reformed Roman Calendar has suppressed
many names of ancient martyrs, this Memorial has been
inerted into the Calendar on the day following the
Solemnity of the holy apostles Peter and Paul in honor
of the first martyrs of the Church of Rome who were

put to death at the Vatican Circus at the time of the persecution under Nero (64 A.D.). Their feast had been celebrated on June 27 in Rome from 1923 onward.

Common of Martyrs, p. 1049.

OPENING PRAYER

Father,
you sanctified the Church of Rome
with the blood of its first martyrs.
May we find strength from their courage
and rejoice in their triumph.
We ask this through our Lord Jesus Christ, your Son,
who lives and reigns with you and the Holy Spirit,
one God, for ever and ever. R̥. **Amen.**

Reading I (Rom 8, 31-39), p. 1146, no. 2.
Responsorial Psalm (Ps 124), p. 1145, no. 3.

GOSPEL   Mt 24, 4-13

Alleluia (Mt 5, 10)

R̥. **Alleluia.** Happy are they who suffer persecution
        for justice' sake;
the kingdom of heaven is theirs. R̥. **Alleluia.**

Jesus warns his disciples that they are not to be misled by false teachers or hearsay. They will undergo trials and persecutions, but the loyal followers will be saved.

V̥. The Lord be with you. R̥. **And also with you.**
✠ A reading from the holy gospel according to Matthew. R̥. **Glory to you, Lord.**

Jesus said to his disciples: "Be on guard! Let no one mislead you. Many will come attempting to impersonate me. 'I am the Messiah!' they will claim, and they will deceive many. You will hear of wars and rumors of wars. Do not be alarmed. Such things are bound to happen, but that is not yet the end. Nation will rise against nation, one kingdom against another. There will be famine and pestilence and earthquakes in many places. These are the early stages of the birth pangs. They will hand you over to torture and kill you. Indeed, you will be hated by all nations on my account. Many will falter then, betraying and hating one another. False prophets will rise in great numbers to mislead many. Because of the increase of evil, the love of most will grow cold. The man who holds out to the end, however, is the one who will see salvation."—This is the gospel of the Lord. ℞. **Praise to you, Lord Jesus Christ.**

➤ No. 15, p. 623

— JULY —

July 3 — ST. THOMAS, Apostle

Feast

St. Thomas doubted the Lord's resurrection. He was invited by Jesus to place his fingers into his wounds. Suddenly from incredulity he passed to ardent faith, exclaiming: *"My Lord and my God!"* He became a great apostolic missionary and died in the 1st century.

ENTRANCE ANT.   Ps 118, 28

You are my God: I will give you praise, O my God, I will extol you, for you are my savior. ➤ No. 2, p. 614

OPENING PRAYER

Almighty Father,
as we honor Thomas the apostle,
let us always experience the help of his prayers.
May we have eternal life by believing in Jesus,
whom Thomas acknowledged as Lord,
for he lives and reigns with you and the Holy Spirit,
one God, for ever and ever. ℞. **Amen.** ⅴ

READING I   Eph 2, 19-22

Christ is the keystone of the building of the Church. Paul speaks of all Christians as a building rising upon the foundation of the apostles and prophets.

A reading from the letter of Paul to the Ephesians

You are strangers and aliens no longer. No, you are fellow citizens of the saints and members of the household of God. You form a building which rises on the foundation of the apostles and prophets, with Christ Jesus himself as the capstone. Through him the whole structure is fitted together and takes shape as a holy temple in the Lord; in him you are being built into this temple, to become a dwelling place for God in the Spirit.—This is the Word of the Lord. ℟. **Thanks be to God.** ℣

Responsorial Psalm   Ps 117, 1. 2

℟. (Mk 16, 15) **Go out to all the world,
    and tell the Good News.**

Praise the Lord, all you nations;
    glorify him, all you peoples! — ℟

For steadfast is his kindness toward us,
    and the fidelity of the Lord endures forever.—℟ ℣

GOSPEL   Jn 20, 24-29

Alleluia (Jn 20, 29)

℟. **Alleluia.** You believed in me, Thomas, because
    you have seen me;
happy those who have not seen me, but still believe.
    ℟. **Alleluia.**

Thomas, for all his doubts and possible obstinacy, has a point at which he will believe. Jesus calls on him to accept his proof, and Thomas answers with a profession of faith. Jesus says that blessed are those who have not seen and still believe.

℣. The Lord be with you. ℟. **And also with you.**
✠ A reading from the holy gospel according to John
℟. **Glory to you, Lord.**

Thomas (the name means "Twin"), one of the Twelve, was absent when Jesus came into the room. The other disciples kept telling him: "We have seen the Lord!" His answer was, "I'll never believe it without probing the nailprints in his hands, without putting my finger in the nailmarks and my hand into his side."

A week later, the disciples were once more in the room, and this time Thomas was with them. Despite the locked doors, Jesus came and stood before them. "Peace be with you," he said; then, to Thomas: "Take your finger and examine my hands. Put your hand into my side. Do not persist in your unbelief, but believe!" Thomas said in response, "My Lord and my God!" Jesus then said to him:

"You became a believer because you saw me.
Blest are they who have not seen and have believed."

This is the gospel of the Lord. ℟. **Praise to you, Lord Jesus Christ.**
➔ No. 15, p. 623

PRAYER OVER THE GIFTS

Lord,
we offer you our service and we pray:
protect the gifts you have given us
as we offer this sacrifice of praise
on the feast of your apostle Thomas.
We ask this in the name of Jesus the Lord.
℟. **Amen.**   ➔ No. 21 (Pref. P 64-65), p. 626

COMMUNION ANT.   See Jn 20, 27

Jesus spoke to Thomas: Put your hands here, and see the place of the nails. Doubt no longer, but believe. ↓

PRAYER AFTER COMMUNION

Father,
in this sacrament we have received
the body and blood of Christ.
With St. Thomas we acknowledge him to be our
    Lord and God.
May we show by our lives that our faith is real.
We ask this through Christ our Lord.
℟. **Amen.**   ➔ No. 32, p. 650

July 4 — ST. ELIZABETH OF PORTUGAL

Optional Memorial

Daughter of Peter II, King of Aragon, and grandniece of St. Elizabeth of Hungary, St. Elizabeth, Queen of Portugal, married Dionysius I, King of Portugal. When a widow, she became a Franciscan Tertiary, and died at Coimbra in 1336.

Common of Holy Men and Women: for Those Who Work for the Underprivileged, p. 1099.

OPENING PRAYER

Father of peace and love,
you gave St. Elizabeth the gift of reconciling enemies.
By the help of her prayers
give us the courage to work for peace among men,
that we may be called the sons of God.
We ask this through our Lord Jesus Christ, your Son,
who lives and reigns with you and the Holy Spirit,
one God, for ever and ever. ℟. **Amen.**

Reading I (1 Pt 4, 7-11), p. 1216, no. 14.
Responsorial Psalm (Ps 112), p. 1209, no. 6.
Gospel (Mt 25, 31-46), p. 1225, no. 10.

[In the dioceses of the United States]

July 4 — INDEPENDENCE DAY
(and for Other Civic Observances)

The Sacred Congregation for Divine Worship has confirmed the following English Mass for use on Independence Day and other civic observances.

ENTRANCE ANT. Sir 36, 18-19

Give peace, Lord to those who wait for you; listen to the prayers of your servants, and guide us in the way of justice. ➜ No. 2, p. 614

OPENING PRAYER

Let us pray
[for peace and justice and truth
here and in every land]

A

God of love, Father of us all,
in wisdom and goodness you guide creation
to fulfillment in Christ your Son.
Open our hearts to the truth of his gospel,
that your peace may rule in our hearts
and your justice guide our lives.
Grant this through our Lord Jesus Christ, your Son,
who lives and reigns with you and the Holy Spirit,
one God, for ever and ever. ℟. **Amen.**

B

Father of the family of man,
open our hearts to greater love of your Son.
Let national boundaries not set limits to our concern.
Ward off the pride that comes with worldly wealth
    and power.
Give us the courage to open ourselves in love
to the service of all your people.
Grant this through our Lord Jesus Christ, your Son,
who lives and reigns with you and the Holy Spirit,
one God, for ever and ever. ℟. **Amen.**

C

Father of the family of nations.
open our hearts to greater love of your Son.
Grant that the boundaries of nations
will not set limits to our love
and give us the courage to build a land
that serves you in truth and justice.
Grant this through our Lord Jesus Christ, your Son,
who lives and reigns with you and the Holy Spirit,
one God, for ever and ever. ℟. **Amen.**

The readings listed on p. 484 may also be used.

READING I   Nm 6, 22-27

God instructs Moses how he is to ask for a blessing and how the
Israelites should invoke his name.

A reading from the book of Numbers

The Lord said to Moses: "Speak to Aaron and his sons and tell them: This is how you shall bless the Israelites. Say to them:

The Lord bless you and keep you!

The Lord let his face shine upon you, and be gracious to you!

The Lord look upon you kindly and give you peace!

So shall they invoke my name upon the Israelites, and I will bless them."—This is the Word of the Lord. ℞. **Thanks be to God.** ℣

READING II   Jas 4, 13-15

The apostle James counsels us how to plan things with the proviso that it be God's will. Always there should be the condition, "If the Lord wills it."

A reading from the letter of James

Come now, you who say, "Today or tomorrow we shall go to such and such a town, spend a year there, trade, and come off with a profit!" You have no idea what kind of life will be yours tomorrow. You are a vapor that appears briefly and vanishes. You should say, "If the Lord wills it, we shall live to do this or that."—This is the Word of the Lord. ℞. **Thanks be to God.** ℣

Responsorial Psalm   Ps 90, 2. 3-4. 5-6. 12-13. 14-16
℞. (17) **Lord, give success to the work of our hands.**

Before the mountains were begotten
  and the earth and the world were brought forth,
    from everlasting to everlasting you are God. — ℞

You turn man back to dust,
  saying, "Return, O children of men."
For a thousand years in your sight
  are as yesterday, now that it is past,
    or as a watch of the night. — ℞

You make an end of them in their sleep;

the next morning they are like the changing grass,
Which at dawn springs up anew,
but by evening wilts and fades. — ℟

Teach us to number our days aright,
that we may gain wisdom of heart.
Return, O Lord! How long?
Have pity on your servants! — ℟

Fill us at daybreak with your kindness,
that we may shout for joy and gladness all our
days.
Let your work be seen by your servants
and your glory by their children. — ℟ ⍊

GOSPEL   Mt 6, 31-34

Alleluia (1 Chr 29, 10. 11)

℟. **Alleluia.** Blessed are you, O Lord our God;
all things in heaven and earth are yours. ℟. **Alleluia.**

Jesus instructs his disciples to avoid harmful anxieties. The Father
knows all their needs and will take care of them, but they must
acknowledge his kingship, his way of holiness.

℣. The Lord be with you. ℟. **And also with you.**
✠ A reading from the holy gospel according to Matthew. ℟. **Glory to you, Lord.**

Jesus said to his disciples: "Stop worrying over
questions like, 'What are we to eat, or what are we
to drink, or what are we to wear?' The unbelievers
are always running after these things. Your heavenly
Father knows all that you need. Seek first his kingship over you, his way of holiness, and all these
things will be given you besides. Enough, then, of
worrying about tomorrow. Let tomorrow take care
of itself. Today has troubles enough of its own."—
This is the gospel of the Lord. ℟. **Praise to you, Lord
Jesus Christ.**   ➔ No. 15, p. 623

PRAYER OVER THE GIFTS

A

God our Father,
you have given us in abundance
that we might give you praise
and serve all your people in love.
Accept these gifts we bring
for the salvation of all the world
and help us to live in love as you have commanded.
We ask this through Christ our Lord. ℟. **Amen.**

B

Lord God,
accept these gifts we bring to this altar
and teach us the wisdom of the gospel
which leads to true justice and lasting peace.
We ask this through Christ our Lord.
℟. **Amen.** ➔ No. 21, p. 626 (Pref. P 82-83)

COMMUNION ANT. Mt 5, 9

**Happy the peacemakers; they shall be called sons
of God. ℣**

PRAYER AFTER COMMUNION

A

Father,
now that we have shared the body and blood of
  Christ,
teach us the proper use of your gifts
and true love for our brothers and sisters.
We ask this through Christ our Lord. ℟. **Amen.**

B

God our Father,
through the power of this eucharist
keep us constant in the love of your Son.
Help us to play our part in the life of this nation.
that its thoughts may be directed
toward peace, justice,

and the loving service of all mankind.
We ask this through Christ our Lord. ℟. **Amen.**

C

God our Father
through the food we have received
you bless and sanctify us and the fruit of our toil.
Help us to serve each other in justice and mercy
and share what we have
for the welfare of all men and women.
We ask this through Christ our Lord.
℟. **Amen.**   ➔ No. 32, p. 650

OTHER POSSIBLE READINGS

Reading I: Is 9, 1-6; Is 32, 15-20; Is 57, 15-19.

Resp. Psalm: Ps 72, 1-2. 3-4. 7-8. 12-13. 17; Ps 85, 9-10.
                11-12. 13-14; Ps 122, 1-2. 3-4. 4-5. 6-7.
                8-9.

Reading II: Phil 4, 6-9; Col 3, 12-15; Jas 3, 13-18.

Gospel: Mt 5, 1-12; Mt 5, 38-48; Jn 14, 23-29; Jn
                20, 19-23.

July 5 — ST. ANTHONY ZACCARIA, Priest

Optional Memorial

Born in Cremona, Italy, St. Anthony gave up his practice of medicine to embrace the religious life. Later, he
founded the Order of Clerks Regular of St. Paul called
Barnabites. He died at 36 years of age, in 1539.

*Common of Pastors, p. 1071; or Common of Holy Men:
for Teachers, p. 1101, or for Religious, p. 1097.*

OPENING PRAYER

Lord,
enable us to grasp in the spirit of St. Paul,
the sublime wisdom of Jesus Christ,
the wisdom which inspired St. Anthony Zaccaria
to preach the message of salvation in your Church.

Grant this through our Lord Jesus Christ, your Son,
who lives and reigns with you and the Holy Spirit,
one God, for ever and ever. ℟. **Amen.**

Reading I (2 Tm 1, 13-14; 2, 1-3), p. 1168, no. 11.
Responsorial Psalm (Ps 1), p. 1206, no. 1.
Gospel (Mk 10, 13-16), p. 1227, no. 13.

July 6 — ST. MARIA GORETTI, Virgin and Martyr

Optional Memorial

St. Maria Goretti died as a virgin and martyr at Net-
tuno, not far from Rome, on July 16, 1906. She was
canonized in 1950.

Common of Martyrs, p. 1056; *or Common of Virgins, p.*
1085.

OPENING PRAYER

Father,
source of innocence and lover of chastity,
you gave St. Maria Goretti the privilege
of offering her life in witness to Christ.
As you gave her the crown of martyrdom,
let her prayers keep us faithful to your teaching.
We ask this through our Lord Jesus Christ, your Son,
who lives and reigns with you and the Holy Spirit,
one God, for ever and ever. ℟. **Amen.**

READING I   1 Cor 6, 13-15. 17-20

God is the creator of all. He made the body which is to be used as a
member of the Body of Christ. The body is the temple of the Holy
Spirit.

A reading from the first letter of Paul to the
Corinthians

The body is not for immorality; it is for the Lord, and
the Lord is for the body. God, who raised up the Lord,
will raise us also by his power.

Do you not see that your bodies are members of
Christ? But whoever is joined to the Lord becomes

one spirit with him. Shun lewd conduct. Every other
sin a man commits is outside his body, but the fornicator sins against his own body. You must know that
your body is a temple of the Holy Spirit, who is within—the Spirit you have received from God. You are
not your own. You have been purchased, and at
what a price! So glorify God in your body.—This is
the Word of the Lord. ℟. **Thanks be to God.**

Responsorial Psalm (Ps 31), p. 1144, no. 1.
Gospel (Jn 12, 24-26), p. 1152, no. 5.

July 11 — ST. BENEDICT, Abbot

Memorial

St. Benedict was born at Nursia, Italy, in the year 480.
He gave up his studies at Rome and retired to Subiaco
and lived as a hermit. He founded twelve monasteries,
the chief one being at Monte Cassino. He died in 543.

Common of Holy Men and Women: for Religious, p.
1097.

OPENING PRAYER

God our Father,
you made St. Benedict an outstanding guide
to teach men how to live in your service.
Grant that by preferring your love to everything else,
we may walk in the way of your commandments.
We ask this through our Lord Jesus Christ, your Son,
who lives and reigns with you and the Holy Spirit,
one God, for ever and ever. ℟. **Amen.**

READING I   Prv 2, 1-9

He who treasures the word of God should turn to understanding. The
Lord gives wisdom; he counsels the upright; he guards the way of the
pious.

A reading from the book of Proverbs

My son, if you receive my words
    and treasure my commands,

Turning your ear to wisdom,
  inclining your heart to understanding;
Yes, if you call to intelligence,
  and to understanding raise your voice;
If you seek her like silver,
  and like hidden treasures search her out:
Then will you understand the fear of the Lord;
  the knowledge of God you will find;
For the Lord gives wisdom,
  from his mouth come knowledge and understand-
    ing;
He has counsel in store for the upright,
  he is the shield of those who walk honestly,
Guarding the paths of justice,
  protecting the way of his pious ones.
Then you will understand rectitude and justice,
  honestly, every good path.
This is the Word of the Lord. ℟. **Thanks be to God.**

Responsorial Psalm (Ps 34), p. 1207, no. 4.
Gospel (Mk 10, 17-30), p. 1227, no. 14.

PRAYER OVER THE GIFTS

Lord,
look kindly on these gifts we present
on the feast of St. Benedict.
By following his example in seeking you,
may we know unity and peace in your service.
Grant this through Christ our Lord.
℟. **Amen.**   ➤ No. 21, p. 626

PRAYER AFTER COMMUNION

Lord,
hear the prayers of all
who have received this pledge of eternal life.
By following the teaching of St. Benedict,
may we be faithful in doing your work
and in loving our brothers and sisters in true charity.
We ask this in the name of Jesus the Lord.
℟. **Amen.**   ➤ No. 32, p. 650

July 13 — ST. HENRY

Optional Memorial

St. Henry, Duke of Bavaria, King of Germany and head of the Holy Roman Empire, used his power to extend the kingdom of God. By agreement with his spouse, he preserved virginity in marriage. He died in 1024.

Common of Holy Men and Women, p. 1090.

OPENING PRAYER

Lord,
you filled St. Henry with your love
and raised him from the cares of an earthly kingdom
to eternal happiness in heaven.
In the midst of the changes of this world,
may his prayers keep us free from sin
and help us on our way to you.
Grant this through our Lord Jesus Christ, your Son,
who lives and reigns with you and the Holy Spirit,
one God, for ever and ever. ℞. **Amen.**

Reading I (Mi 6, 6-8), p. 1203, no. 17.
Responsorial Psalm (Ps 1), p. 1206, no. 1.
Gospel (Mk 3, 31-35), p. 1226, no. 11.

July 14 — ST. CAMILLUS DE LELLIS, Priest

Optional Memorial

Of the noble family of Lellis, St. Camillus, when still a young priest, consecrated his life to the service of the sick, even those stricken with the plague. He founded the *Order of Hospitallers,* which bears his name, and died a victim of his charity in 1614.

Common of Holy Men and Women: for Those Who Work for the Underprivileged, p. 1099.

OPENING PRAYER

Father,
you gave St. Camillus a special love for the sick.
Through his prayers inspire us with your grace,
so that by serving you in our brothers and sisters
we may come safely to you at the end of our lives.

We ask this through our Lord Jesus Christ, your Son,
who lives and reigns with you and the Holy Spirit,
one God, for ever and ever. ℟. **Amen.**

Reading I (1 Jn 3, 14-18), p. 1217, no. 15.
Responsorial Psalm (Ps 112), p. 1209, no. 6.
Gospel (Jn 15, 9-17), p. 1232, no. 21.

July 15 — ST. BONAVENTURE, Bishop and Doctor

Memorial

St. Bonaventure entered the Franciscan Order. He lec-
tured at the University of Paris, where he was acquainted with St. Thomas Aquinas. Known as the Seraphic
Doctor, he became General of the Franciscan Order and
Cardinal of Albano. He is considered the greatest ex-
ponent of mystical theology in the Middle Ages. He
died in 1274.

Common of Pastors: for Bishops, p. 1069; *or Common of
Doctors of the Church, p.* 1082.

OPENING PRAYER

All-powerful Father,
may we who celebrate the feast of St. Bonaventure
always benefit from his wisdom
and follow the example of his love.
Grant this through our Lord Jesus Christ, your Son,
who lives and reigns with you and the Holy Spirit,
one God, for ever and ever. ℟. **Amen.**

Reading I (Eph 3, 14-19), p. 1213, no. 7.
Responsorial Psalm (Ps 119), p. 1181, no. 3.
Gospel (Mt 23, 8-12), p. 1171, no. 2.

July 16 — OUR LADY OF MOUNT CARMEL

Optional Memorial

This feast commemorates the favors granted by our
Lady on Mount Carmel and was extended to the Uni-
versal Church in 1726 by Benedict XIII. The Blessed
Virgin appeared to St. Simon Stock, General of the
Order of Carmelites, holding in her hand a scapular,

and directed him to found a Confraternity whose members should wear this scapular and consecrate themselves to her service.

Common of the Blessed Virgin, p. 1040.

OPENING PRAYER

Father,
may the prayers of the Virgin Mary protect us
and help us to reach Christ her Son
who lives and reigns with you and the Holy Spirit,
one God, for ever and ever. ℞. **Amen.**

Reading I (Zec 2, 14-17), p. 1124, no. 11.
Responsorial Psalm (Lk 1), p. 1128, no. 5.
Gospel (Mt 11, 27-28), p. 1136, no. 9.

July 21 — ST. LAWRENCE OF BRINDISI,
Priest and Doctor

Optional Memorial

Born at Brindisi, Italy, on July 22, 1559, St. Lawrence was famed as a pioneer of the Capuchin Order in Germany and for his writings both against the Moslems and against the Protestant Reformation. He was the leader in the repulse of the Turkish armies in Hungary. He died in 1619. On March 19, 1959, Pope John XXIII proclaimed him a Doctor and extended his feast to the Universal Church.

Common of Pastors, p. 1071; or Common of Doctors of the Church, p. 1082.

OPENING PRAYER

Lord,
for the glory of your name and the salvation of souls
you gave Lawrence of Brindisi
courage and right judgment.
By his prayers,
help us to know what we should do
and give us the courage to do it.
We ask this through our Lord Jesus Christ, your Son,

who lives and reigns with you and the Holy Spirit,
one God, for ever and ever. ℞. **Amen.**

Reading I (2 Cor 5, 1-2. 5-7), p. 1166, no. 6.
Responsorial Psalm (Ps 40), p. 236.
Gospel (Mk 4, 1-10. 13-20), p. 1186, no. 3.

___

July 22 — ST. MARY MAGDALENE

Memorial

Mary Magdalene was one of the few faithful souls who
remained with Christ during his agony on the Cross.
After our Lord's resurrection, he appeared to her and
told her to announce his resurrection to the apostles.

ENTRANCE ANT.   Jn 20, 17

**The Lord said to Mary Magdalene: Go and tell my
brothers that I shall ascend to my Father and your
Father, to my God and to your God.** ➤ No. 2, p. 614

OPENING PRAYER

Father,
your Son first entrusted to Mary Magdalene
the joyful news of his resurrection.
By her prayers and example
may we proclaim Christ as our living Lord
and one day see him in glory,
for he lives and reigns with you and the Holy Spirit,
one God, for ever and ever. ℞. **Amen.** ℣

READING I   Sg 3, 1-4

Solomon writes that he has searched in and out for him whom his
soul loves. He has asked everywhere; then he finds him whom his
heart loves.

A reading from the Song of Solomon

On my bed at night I sought him
    whom my heart loves—
I sought him but I did not find him.

I will rise then and go about the city;
　in the streets and crossings I will seek
Him whom my heart loves.
　I sought him but I did not find him.
The watchmen came upon me
　as they made their rounds of the city:
Have you seen him whom my heart loves?
I had hardly left them
　when I found him whom my heart loves.
This is the Word of the Lord. ℟. **Thanks be to God.** ℣

OR

READING I   2 Cor 5, 14-17

Paul writes that since one died, all died. He died that those who live, live not for themselves, but for him. This means that if anyone is in Christ, he is a new creation.

A reading from the second letter of Paul to the Corinthians

The love of Christ impels us who have reached the conviction that since one died for all, all died. He died for all so that those who live might live no longer for themselves, but for him who for their sakes died and was raised up.

　Because of this we no longer look on anyone in terms of mere human judgment. If at one time we so regarded Christ, we no longer know him by this standard. This means that if anyone is in Christ, he is a new creation. The old order has passed away; now all is new!—This is the Word of the Lord. ℟. **Thanks be to God.**

Responsorial Psalm   Ps 63, 2. 3-4. 5-6. 8-9

℟. (2) **My soul is thirsting for you, O Lord my God.**

O my God, you are my God whom I seek;
　for you my flesh pines and my soul thirsts
　like the earth, parched, lifeless and without
　　water. — ℟

Thus have I gazed toward you in the sanctuary
  to see your power and your glory,
For your kindness is a greater good than life;
  my lips shall glorify you. — ℟

Thus will I bless you while I live;
  lifting up my hands, I will call upon your name.
As with the riches of a banquet shall my soul be
    satisfied,
  and with exultant lips my mouth shall praise
    you. — ℟

That you are my help,
  and in the shadow of your wings I shout for joy.
My soul clings fast to you;
  your right hand upholds me. — ℟ ✟

The Gospel is special in this memorial.

GOSPEL   Jn 20, 1-2. 11-18
Alleluia

℟. **Alleluia.** Tell us, Mary, what did you see on the
  way?
I saw the glory of the risen Christ, I saw his empty
  tomb. ℟. **Alleluia.**

Mary Magdalene goes to the tomb where Jesus has been laid, and
his body is not there. She weeps. A man stands by her asking why.
She tells him, and he says, "Mary." She recognizes Jesus and carries
his message to the disciples.

℣. The Lord be with you. ℟. **And also with you.**
✠ A reading from the holy gospel according to John
℟. **Glory to you, Lord.**

Early in the morning on the first day of the week,
while it was still dark, Mary Magdalene came to the
tomb. She saw that the stone had been moved away,
so she ran off to Simon Peter and the other disciple
(the one Jesus loved) and told them, "The Lord has
been taken from the tomb! We do not know where
they have put him!"

    Mary stood weeping beside the tomb. Even as she
wept, she stooped to peer inside, and there she saw

two angels in dazzling robes. One was seated at the head and the other at the foot of the place where Jesus' body had lain. "Woman," they asked her, "why are you weeping?" She answered them, "Because the Lord has been taken away, and I do not know where they have put him." She had no sooner said this than she turned around and caught sight of Jesus standing there. But she did not know him. "Woman," he asked her, "why are you weeping? Who is it you are looking for?" She supposed he was the gardener, so she said, "Sir, if you are the one who carried him off, tell me where you have laid him and I will take him away." Jesus said to her, "Mary!" She turned to him and said [in Hebrew], **"Rabboni!"** (meaning "Teacher"). Jesus then said: "Do not cling to me, for I have not yet ascended to the Father. Rather, go to my brothers and tell them, 'I am ascending to my Father and your Father, to my God and your God!'" Mary Magdalene went to the disciples. "I have seen the Lord!" she announced. Then she reported what he had said to her.—This is the gospel of the Lord. ℟. **Praise to you, Lord Jesus Christ.**   ➔ No. 15, p. 623

PRAYER OVER THE GIFTS

Lord,
accept the gifts we present in memory of St. Mary
   Magdalene;
her loving worship was accepted by your Son,
who is Lord for ever and ever.
℟. **Amen.**   ➔ No. 21, p. 626

COMMUNION ANT.   2 Cor 5, 14-15

**The love of Christ compels us to live not for our-
selves but for him who died and rose for us.** ℣

PRAYER AFTER COMMUNION

Father,
may the sacrament we have received

fill us with the same faithful love
that kept Mary Magdalene close to Christ,
who is Lord for ever and ever.
Ry. **Amen.**   ➔ No. 32, p. 650

July 23 — ST. BRIDGET, Religious

Optional Memorial

Of the royal house of Sweden, Bridget married Prince
Ulfo, by whom she had eight children, one of whom was
St. Catherine of Sweden. St. Bridget founded the Order
of the Most Holy Savior. She died at Rome in 1373.

Common of Holy Men and Women, p. 1102.

OPENING PRAYER

Lord our God,
you revealed the secrets of heaven to St. Bridget
as she meditated on the suffering and death of your
    Son.
May your people rejoice in the revelation of your
    glory.
Grant this through our Lord Jesus Christ, your Son,
who lives and reigns with you and the Holy Spirit,
one God, for ever and ever. Ry. **Amen.**

Reading I (Gal 2, 19-20), p. 1212, no. 5.
Responsorial Psalm (Ps 34), p. 1207, no. 4.
Gospel (Jn 15, 1-8), p. 1231, no. 20.

July 25 — ST. JAMES, Apostle

Feast

St. James is called "Greater" because his vocation to
serve Christ preceded that of the other Apostle of the
same name. After preaching the Gospel in Samaria,
Judea and Spain, he was condemned to death by Herod
in the year 44.

ENTRANCE ANT.   See Mt 4, 18. 21

**Walking by the Sea of Galilee, Jesus saw James and
John, the sons of Zebedee, mending their nets, and
he called them to follow him.**   ➔ No. 2, p. 614

OPENING PRAYER

Almighty Father,
by the martyrdom of St. James
you blessed the work of the early Church.
May his profession of faith give us courage
and his prayers bring us strength.
We ask this through our Lord Jesus Christ, your Son,
who lives and reigns with you and the Holy Spirit,
one God, for ever and ever. ℟. **Amen.** ✝

READING I   2 Cor 4, 7-15

Paul's sufferings re-enact the life of Jesus, both as a sign and as an instrument of the divine life he ministers to men. Paul lives through faith in his own future resurrection and that of his fellow Christians.

A reading from the second letter of Paul to the
Corinthians

We possess a treasure in earthen vessels to make it clear that its surpassing power comes from God and not from us. We are afflicted in every way possible, but we are not crushed; full of doubts, we never despair. We are persecuted but never abandoned; we are struck down but never destroyed. Continually we carry about in our bodies the dying of Jesus, so that in our bodies the life of Jesus may also be revealed. While we live we are constantly being delivered to death for Jesus' sake, so that the life of Jesus may be revealed in our mortal flesh. Death is at work in us, but life in you. We have that spirit of faith of which the Scripture says, "Because I believed, I spoke out." We believe and so we speak, knowing that he who raised up the Lord Jesus will raise us up along with Jesus and place both us and you in his presence. Indeed, everything is ordered to your benefit, so that the grace bestowed in abundance may bring greater glory to God because they who give thanks are many.—This is the Word of the Lord.
℟. **Thanks be to God.** ✝

Responsorial Psalm   Ps 126, 1-2. 2-3. 4-5. 6

℟. (5) **Those who sow in tears, shall reap with shouts of joy.**

When the Lord brought back the captives of Zion,
 we were like men dreaming.
Then our mouth was filled with laughter,
 and our tongue with rejoicing. — ℟

Then they said among the nations,
 "The Lord has done great things for them."
The Lord has done great things for us;
 we are glad indeed. — ℟

Restore our fortunes, O Lord,
 like the torrents in the southern desert.
Those that sow in tears
 shall reap rejoicing. — ℟

Although they go forth weeping,
 carrying the seed to be sown,
They shall come back rejoicing,
 carrying their sheaves. — ℟ ℣

GOSPEL   Mt 20, 20-28

Alleluia (Jn 15, 16)

℟. **Alleluia.** I have chosen you from the world, says
 the Lord,
to go and bear fruit that will last. ℟. **Alleluia.**

The mother of James asks that Jesus place him by his side, together
with his brother John. Jesus promises that these two will indeed share
his sufferings, but only the Father can assign places of honor. The
real disciple must be a servant of all, as Jesus was.

℣. The Lord be with you. ℟. **And also with you.**
✠ A reading from the holy gospel according to Matthew. ℟. **Glory to you, Lord.**
The mother of Zebedee's sons came up to Jesus accompanied by her sons, to do him homage and ask
of him a favor. "What is it you want?" he said. She
answered, "Promise me that these sons of mine will
sit, one at your right hand and the other at your left,

in your kingdom." In reply Jesus said, "You do not know what you are asking. Can you drink of the cup I am to drink of?" "We can," they said. He told them, "From the cup I drink of you shall drink. Sitting at my right hand or my left is not mine to give. That is for those for whom it has been reserved by my Father." The other ten, on hearing this, became indignant at the two brothers. Jesus then called them together and said: "You know how those who exercise authority among the Gentiles lord it over them; their great ones make their importance felt. It cannot be like that with you. Anyone among you who aspires to greatness must serve the rest, and whoever wants to rank first among you must serve the needs of all. Such is the case with the Son of Man who has come, not to be served by others but to serve, to give his own life as a ransom for many."
—This is the gospel of the Lord. ℟. **Praise to you, Lord Jesus Christ.**   ➔ No. 15, p. 623

PRAYER OVER THE GIFTS
Lord,
as we honor St. James,
the first apostle to share the cup of suffering and death,
wash away our sins
by the saving passion of your Son,
and make our sacrifice pleasing to you.
We ask this through Christ our Lord.
℟. **Amen.**   ➔ No. 21, p. 626 (Pref. P 64-65)

COMMUNION ANT.   See Mt 20, 22-23
By sharing the cup of the Lord's suffering, they became the friends of God. ℣

PRAYER AFTER COMMUNION
Father,
we have received this holy eucharist with joy
as we celebrate the feast of the apostle James.

Hear his prayers
and bring us your help.
We ask this in the name of Jesus the Lord.
℟. **Amen.**   ➔ No. 32, p. 650

────────────────────

July 26 — STS. JOACHIM AND ANN, Parents of Mary

Memorial

Since early Christian times, churches were dedicated
in honor of St. Ann. The Fathers of the Church frequently extolled her virtues, sanctity and privileges. St.
Ann is the Patroness of Christian mothers. Her husband, St. Joachim, also had a feast dedicated to him
that became part of the Roman Calendar in 1584. Now
there is one feast for both.

ENTRANCE ANT.

**Praised be Joachim and Ann for the child they bore.
The Lord gave them the blessing of all the nations.**
                                      ➔ No. 2, p. 614

OPENING PRAYER

God of our fathers,
you gave Saints Joachim and Ann
the privilege of being the parents of Mary,
the mother of your incarnate Son.
May their prayers help us to attain
the salvation you have promised to your people.
Grant this through our Lord Jesus Christ, your Son,
who lives and reigns with you and the Holy Spirit,
one God, for ever and ever. ℟. **Amen.** ℣

READING I   Sir 44, 1. 10-15

Sirach extols the virtues of Israel's ancestors. Their heritage is handed
down through God's covenant.

A reading from the book of Sirach

Now will I praise those godly men,
    our ancestors, each in his own time:

These were godly men
  whose virtues have not been forgotten;
Their wealth remains in their families,
  their heritage with their descendants;
Through God's covenant with them their family en-
    dures,
  their posterity, for their sake.
And for all time their progeny will endure,
  their glory will never be blotted out;
Their bodies are peacefully laid away,
  but their name lives on and on.
At gatherings their wisdom is retold,
  and the assembly proclaims their praise.
This is the Word of the Lord. ℞. **Thanks be to God.** ⍅

Responsorial Psalm   Ps 132, 11. 13-14. 17-18
℞. (Lk 1, 32) **God will give him the throne of David,
his father.**

The Lord swore to David
  a firm promise from which he will not withdraw:
"Your own offspring
  I will set upon your throne." — ℞

For the Lord has chosen Zion;
  he prefers her for his dwelling.
"Zion is my resting place forever;
  in her will I dwell, for I prefer her. — ℞

"In her will I make a horn to sprout forth for David;
  I will place a lamp for my anointed.
His enemies I will clothe with shame,
  but upon him my crown shall shine." — ℞ ⍅

GOSPEL   Mt 13, 16-17
Alleluia (Lk 2, 25)
℞. **Alleluia.** They yearned for the comforting of Israel,
and the Holy Spirit dwelt in them. ℞. **Alleluia.**

Jesus tells the disciples that many holy people in the past wished to
see the Messiah and to hear the word of God from him, but they
did not.

℣. The Lord be with you. ℟. **And also with you.**
✠ A reading from the holy gospel according to Matthew. ℟. **Glory to you, Lord.**

Jesus said to his disciples: "Blest are your eyes because they see and blest are your ears because they hear. I assure you, many a prophet and many a saint longed to see what you see but did not see it, to hear what you hear but did not hear. it."—This is the gospel of the Lord. ℟. **Praise to you, Lord Jesus Christ.**

➔ No. 15, p. 623

PRAYER OVER THE GIFTS

Lord,
receive these gifts as signs of our love
and give us a share in the blessing you promised
to Abraham and his descendants.
We ask this in the name of Jesus the Lord.
℟. **Amen.**   ➔ No. 21, p. 626

COMMUNION ANT.   See Ps 24, 5

They received a blessing from the Lord, and kindness from God their Savior. ℣

PRAYER AFTER COMMUNION

Father,
your Son was born as a man
so that men could be born again in you.
As you nourish us with the bread of life,
given only to your sons and daughters,
fill us with the Spirit who makes us your children.
We ask this through Christ our Lord.
℟. **Amen.**   ➔ No. 32, p. 650

July 29 — ST MARTHA

Memorial

St. Martha was the sister of Mary and Lazarus. She too enjoyed the favored love which Jesus had for that family of Bethany.

ENTRANCE ANT.   Lk 10, 38

**As Jesus entered a certain village a woman called
Martha welcomed him into her house.** ➤ No. 2, p. 614

OPENING PRAYER

Father,
your Son honored St. Martha
by coming to her home as a guest.
By her prayers
may we serve Christ in our brothers and sisters
and be welcomed by you into heaven, our true home.
We ask this through our Lord Jesus Christ, your Son,
who lives and reigns with you and the Holy Spirit,
one God, for ever and ever. ℟. **Amen.**

*Readings and Intervenient Chants from the Common
of Holy Men and Women, p. 1195.*

Reading I (1 Jn 4, 7-16), p. 1217, no. 16.
Responsorial Psalm (Ps 34), p. 1207, no. 4.

The Gospel is special in this Memorial.

GOSPEL   Jn 11, 19-27

Alleluia (Jn 8, 12)

℟. **Alleluia.** I am the light of the world, says the
        Lord;
the man who follows me will have the light of life.
        ℟. **Alleluia.**

Martha meets Jesus and tells him of her brother's death. Jesus says,
"I am the resurrection and the life." Asked if she believes this, she
says, "Yes, Lord, I believe that you are the Messiah, the Son of God;
he who is come into the world."

℣. The Lord be with you. ℟. **And also with you.**
✠ A reading from the holy gospel according to John
℟. **Glory to you, Lord.**

Many Jewish people had come out to console Martha
and Mary over their brother. When Martha heard
that Jesus was coming she went to meet him, while
Mary sat at home. Martha said to Jesus, "Lord, if
you had been here, my brother would never have

died. Even now, I am sure that God will give you
whatever you ask of him." "Your brother will rise
again," Jesus assured her. "I know he will rise again,"
Martha replied, "in the resurrection on the last day."
Jesus told her:

> "I am the resurrection and the life:
> whoever believes in me,
> though he should die, will come to life;
> and whoever is alive and believes in me
> will never die.

Do you believe this?" "Yes Lord," she replied. "I
have come to believe that you are the Messiah, the
Son of God: he who is to come into the world."—
This is the gospel of the Lord. ℟. **Praise to you, Lord
Jesus Christ.**   ➜ No. 15, p. 623

OR

Gospel (Lk 10, 38-42), p. 1194, no. 3.

PRAYER OVER THE GIFTS

Father,
we praise you for your glory
on the feast of St. Martha.
Accept this service of our worship
as you accepted her love.
Grant this through Christ our Lord.
℟. **Amen.**   ➜ No. 21, p. 626

COMMUNION ANT.   Jn 11, 27

**Martha said to Jesus: You are the Christ, the Son
of God, who was to come into this world.** ℣

PRAYER AFTER COMMUNION

Lord,
you have given us the body and blood of your Son
to free us from undue attachment to this passing life.
By following the example of St. Martha,
may we grow in love for you on earth
and rejoice for ever in the vision of your glory in
    heaven.

We ask this in the name of Jesus the Lord.
℟. **Amen.**   ➔ No. 32, p. 650

July 30 — ST. PETER CHRYSOLOGUS, Bishop and Doctor

Optional Memorial

St. Peter merited being called "Chrysologus" (golden-worded) from his exceptional oratorical eloquence. Pope Sixtus III elevated him to the Archbishopric of Ravenna.

Common of Pastors: for Bishops, p. 1069; *or Common of Doctors of the Church, p.* 1082.

OPENING PRAYER

Father,
you made Peter Chrysologus
an outstanding preacher of your incarnate Word.
May the prayers of St. Peter help us to cherish
the mystery of our salvation
and make its meaning clear in our love for others.
Grant this through our Lord Jesus Christ, your Son,
who lives and reigns with you and the Holy Spirit,
one God, for ever and ever. ℟. **Amen.**

Reading I (Eph 3, 8-12), p. 1183, no. 4.
Responsorial Psalm (Ps 119), p. 1181, no. 3.
Gospel (Mt 5, 13-16), p. 1186, no. 1.

July 31 — ST. IGNATIUS OF LOYOLA, Priest

Memorial

St. Ignatius, born in 1491 at the regal Castle of Loyola, Spain, became a famous courtier and knight in the court of Ferdinand V. Wounded in the siege of Pampeluna, he retired to Manresa to lead a life of prayer and contemplation. After being ordained a priest, he founded the Society of Jesus to fight the forces of Satan.

ENTRANCE ANT.   Phil 2, 10-11

At the name of Jesus every knee must bend, in heaven, on earth, and under the earth; every tongue should proclaim to the glory of God the Father: Jesus Christ is Lord.   ➜ No. 2, p. 614

OPENING PRAYER

Father,
you gave St. Ignatius of Loyola to your Church
to bring greater glory to your name.
May we follow his example on earth
and share the crown of life in heaven.
We ask this through our Lord Jesus Christ, your Son,
who lives and reigns with you and the Holy Spirit,
one God, for ever and ever. ℟. **Amen.**

Readings and Intervenient Chants from the Common of Pastors, p. 1154, or Common of Holy Men and Women, p. 1195.

READING I   1 Cor 10, 31—11, 1

Everything that a Christian does is to be offered for the honor and glory of God. He is to imitate Jesus Christ.

A reading from the first letter of Paul to the
Corinthians

Whether you eat or drink—whatever you do—you should do all for the glory of God. Give no offense to Jew or Greek or to the church of God, just as I try to please all in any way I can by seeking, not my own advantage, but that of the many, that they may be saved. Imitate me as I imitate Christ.—This is the Word of the Lord. ℟. **Thanks be to God.**

Responsorial Psalm (Ps 34), p. 1207, no. 4.
Gospel (Lk 14, 25-33), p. 1230, no. 19.

PRAYER OVER THE GIFTS

Lord God,
be pleased with the gifts we present to you
at this celebration in honor of St. Ignatius.

Make us truly holy by this eucharist
which you give us as the source of all holiness.
We ask this in the name of Jesus the Lord.
℞. **Amen.** ➜ No. 21, p. 626

COMMUNION ANT. Lk 12, 49

I have come to bring fire to the earth. How I wish it were already blazing! ↓

PRAYER AFTER COMMUNION

Lord,
may the sacrifice of thanksgiving which we have
    offered
on the feast of St. Ignatius
lead us to the eternal praise of your glory.
Grant this through Christ our Lord.
℞. **Amen.** ➜ No. 32, p. 650

— AUGUST —

Aug. 1 — ST. ALPHONSUS DE LIGUORI, Bishop and Doctor

Memorial

St. Alphonsus was born in the village of Marianella, near
Naples, Italy, Sept. 27, 1696. At sixteen he earned his
degree of Doctor of Laws. In 1726 he was ordained to
the priesthood. After a few years he founded the *Congregation of the Most Holy Redeemer* (Redemptorists)
with the object of laboring for the salvation of the most
abandoned souls. He died in 1787.

*Common of Pastors: for Bishops, p. 1069; or Common
of Doctors of the Church, p. 1082.*

OPENING PRAYER

Father,
you constantly build up your Church
by the lives of your saints.
Give us grace to follow St. Alphonsus
in his loving concern for the salvation of men,

and so come to share his reward in heaven.
Grant this through our Lord Jesus Christ, your Son,
who lives and reigns with you and the Holy Spirit,
one God, for ever and ever. ℟. **Amen.**

*Readings and Intervenient Chants may also be taken
from the Common of Holy Men and Women: for Religious, p. 1195.*

READING I   Rom 8, 1-4

Jesus has freed his followers from sin and death. God sent Jesus as
a sin offering that the law might be fulfilled, not by the flesh but
by the spirit.

A reading from the letter of Paul to the Romans
There is no condemnation now for those who are
in Christ Jesus. The law of the spirit, the spirit of
life in Christ Jesus, has freed you from the law of
sin and death. The law was powerless because of
its weakening by the flesh. Then God sent his Son
in the likeness of sinful flesh as a sin offering, thereby condemning sin in the flesh, so that the just demands of the law might be fulfilled in us who live,
not according to the flesh, but according to the
spirit.—This is the Word of the Lord. ℟. **Thanks be
to God.**

Responsorial Psalm (Ps 119), p. 1181, no. 3.
Gospel (Mt 5, 13-16), p. 1186, no. 1.

PRAYER OVER THE GIFTS
Father,
inflame our hearts with the Spirit of your love
as we present these gifts on the feast of St. Alphon-
    sus,
who dedicated his life to you in the eucharist.
We ask this in the name of Jesus the Lord.
℟. **Amen.**   ➤ No. 21, p. 626 (Pref. P 37-42)

PRAYER AFTER COMMUNION
Lord,
you made St. Alphonsus

a faithful minister and preacher of this holy eucha-
rist.
May all who believe in you receive it often
and give you never-ending praise.
We ask this through Christ our Lord.
℟. **Amen.**　　　　　　　　　　　➔ No. 32, p. 650

Aug. 2 — ST. EUSEBIUS OF VERCELLI, Bishop

Optional Memorial

St. Eusebius fought with great valor against the Arian
heresy which denied the Divinity of Jesus Christ. He
suffered exiles, torment and privations of every kind at
the hands of the Arians and died at Vercelli, Italy, in
371.

Common of Pastors: for Bishops, p. 1069.

OPENING PRAYER

Lord God,
St. Eusebius affirmed the divinity of your Son.
By keeping the faith he taught,
may we come to share the eternal life of Christ,
who lives and reigns with you and the Holy Spirit,
one God, for ever and ever. ℟. **Amen.**

Reading I (1 Jn 5, 1-5), p. 1218, no. 17.
Responsorial Psalm (Ps 89), p. 1161, no. 3.
Gospel (Mt 5, 1-12), p. 1220, no. 1.

Aug. 4 — ST. JOHN VIANNEY, Priest

Memorial

Universally known as the "Curé of Ars," St. John Vianney was born at Dardilly in 1786. He heard confessions
of people from all over the world for sixteen hours each
day. His life was filled with works of charity and love.
He died on August 4, 1859 and was canonized on May
31, 1925.

Common of Pastors, p. 1071.

OPENING PRAYER

Father of mercy,
you made St. John Vianney outstanding
in his priestly zeal and concern for your people.
By his example and prayers,
enable us to win our brothers and sisters
to the love of Christ
and come with them to eternal glory.
We ask this through our Lord Jesus Christ, your Son,
who lives and reigns with you and the Holy Spirit,
one God, for ever and ever. ℟. **Amen.**

Reading I (Ez 3, 17-21), p. 1158, no. 8.
Responsorial Psalm (Ps 117), p. 1163, no. 6.

GOSPEL   Mt 9, 35—10, 1

Alleluia (Lk 4, 18-19)

℟. **Alleluia.** The Lord sent me to bring Good News
    to the poor
and freedom to prisoners. ℟. **Alleluia.**

Jesus goes about curing sickness and disease. As he has pity on the
crowds, he notes how the harvest is great but the workers are few.

℣. The Lord be with you. ℟. **And also with you.**
✠ A reading from the holy gospel according to Matthew. ℟. **Glory to you, Lord.**

Jesus continued his tour of all the towns and villages.
He taught in their synagogues, he proclaimed the
good news of God's reign, and he cured every sickness and disease. At the sight of the crowds, his
heart was moved with pity. They were lying prostrate from exhaustion, like sheep without a shepherd.
He said to his disciples: "The harvest is good but
laborers are scare. Beg the harvest master to send
out laborers to gather his harvest."

Then he summoned his twelve disciples and gave
them authority to expel unclean spirits and to cure
sickness and disease of every kind.—This is the

gospel of the Lord. ℟. **Praise to you, Lord Jesus Christ.**

➜ No. 15, p. 623

Aug. 5 — DEDICATION OF ST. MARY MAJOR

Optional Memorial

The *Hieronymian Martyrology* lists the dedication of the basilica of St. Mary on August 5, at the time of Pope Sixtus III. In the 13th century the legend of the founding of the basilica of St. Mary Major popularized this local memorial under the title of the "Dedication of the Blessed Virgin Mary of the Snows." The feast was introduced into the Roman calendar in 1568.

Common of the Blessed Virgin Mary, p. 1040.

OPENING PRAYER

Lord,
pardon the sins of your people.
May the prayers of Mary, the mother of your Son,
help to save us,
for by ourselves we cannot please you.
Grant this through our Lord Jesus Christ, your Son,
who lives and reigns with you and the Holy Spirit,
one God, for ever and ever. ℟. **Amen.**

Reading I (Rv 21, 1-5), p. 1125, no. 3.
Responsorial Psalm (Jdt 13), p. 1126, no. 2.
Gospel (Lk 11, 27-28), p. 1136, no. 9.

Aug. 6 — TRANSFIGURATION

Feast

The Transfiguration of the Lord is celebrated on August 6 in the Syrian (both Western and Eastern), Byzantine and Coptic Rites, and on the following Sunday in the Armenian Rite. This feast became widespread in the West in the 11th century and was introduced into the Roman calendar in 1457.

ENTRANCE ANT. See Mt 17, 5

In the shining cloud the Spirit is seen; from it the voice of the Father is heard: This is my Son, my beloved, in whom is all my delight. Listen to him.

➜ No. 2, p. 614

OPENING PRAYER

Let us pray

[that we may hear the Lord Jesus
and share his everlasting life]

God our Father,
in the transfigured glory of Christ your Son,
you strengthen our faith
by confirming the witness of your prophets,
and show us the splendor of your beloved sons and
daughters.

As we listen to the voice of your Son,
help us to become heirs to eternal life with him
who lives and reigns with you and the Holy Spirit,
one God, for ever and ever. ℞. **Amen.**

*When this feast occurs apart from Sunday, only one of
the first two Readings is read before the Gospel.*

READING I   Dn 7, 9-10. 13-14

Daniel's vision portrays the son of man who has power, glory and
dominion. Thousands minister to him. His dominion is everlasting.

A reading from the book of the prophet Daniel

As Daniel watched:
Thrones were set up
    and the Ancient One took his throne.
His clothing was snow bright,
    and the hair on his head as white as wool;
His throne was flames of fire,
    with wheels of burning fire.
A surging stream of fire
    flowed out from where he sat;
Thousands upon thousands were ministering to him,
    and myriads upon myriads attended him.
    The court was convened and the books were
opened. As the visions during the night continued,
I saw
One like a son of man coming,
    on the clouds of heaven;

When he reached the Ancient One
and was presented before him,
He received dominion, glory, and kingship;
nations and peoples of every language serve him.
His dominion is an everlasting dominion
that shall not be taken away,
his kingship shall not be destroyed.
This is the Word of the Lord. ℟. **Thanks be to God.** ℣

Responsorial Psalm   Ps 97, 1-2. 5-6. 9

℟. (1. 9) **The Lord is King, the most high over all the earth.**

The Lord is king; let the earth rejoice;
let the many isles be glad.
Clouds and darkness are round about him,
justice and judgment are the foundation of his
throne. — ℟

The mountains melt like wax before the Lord,
before the Lord of all the earth.
The heavens proclaim his justice,
and all peoples see his glory. — ℟

Because you, O Lord, are the Most High over all the
earth,
exalted far above all gods. — ℟ ℣

READING II   2 Pt 1, 16-19

Peter was an eyewitness of the Transfiguration of the Lord Jesus
Christ in power and glory. He proclaims Jesus' message with authority;
his teaching is trustworthy and reliable.

A reading from the second letter of Peter

It was not by way of cleverly concocted myths that
we taught you about the coming in power of our
Lord Jesus Christ, for we were eye-witnesses of his
sovereign majesty. He received glory and praise
from God the Father when that unique declaration
came to him out of the majestic splendor: "This is
my beloved Son on whom my favor rests." We our-

selves heard this said from heaven while we were in his company on the holy mountain. Besides, we possess the prophetic message as something altogether reliable. Keep your attention closely fixed on it, as you would on a lamp shining in a dark place until the first streaks of dawn appear and the morning star rises in your hearts.—This is the Word of the Lord. ℟. **Thanks be to God.** ℣

GOSPEL

Alleluia (Mt 17, 5)

℟. **Alleluia.** This is my Son, my beloved, in whom is all my delight:
listen to him. ℟. **Alleluia.**

— YEAR A — (Mt 17, 1-9)

Peter, James, and John witness the Transfiguration of Jesus. He becomes as dazzling as the sun. His Father in the heavens identifies Jesus as his Son.

℣. The Lord be with you. ℟. **And also with you.**
✠ A reading from the holy gospel according to Matthew. ℟. **Glory to you, Lord.**

Jesus took Peter, James, and his brother John and led them up on a high mountain by themselves. He was transfigured before their eyes. His face became as dazzling as the sun, his clothes as radiant as light. Suddenly Moses and Elijah appeared to them conversing with him. Upon this, Peter said to Jesus, "Lord, how good it is for us to be here! With your permission I will erect three booths here, one for you, one for Moses, and one for Elijah." He was still speaking when suddenly a bright cloud overshadowed them. Out of the cloud came a voice which said, "This is my beloved Son on whom my favor rests. Listen to him." When they heard this the disciples fell forward on the ground, overcome with fear. Jesus came toward them and laying his hand on them, said, "Get up! Do not be afraid." When they looked up they did not see anyone but Jesus.

As they were coming down the mountainside Jesus commanded them, "Do not tell anyone of the vision until the Son of Man rises from the dead."—This is the gospel of the Lord. ℟. **Praise to you, Lord Jesus Christ.**   ➤ No. 15, p. 623

— YEAR B —   (Mk 9, 2-10)

Peter, James, and John are awestruck when Jesus is transfigured before them. They want to build a memorial there. Jesus bids them to tell no one until he rises from the dead.

℣. The Lord be with you. ℟. **And also with you.**
✠ A reading from the holy gospel according to Mark
℟. **Glory to you, Lord.**

Jesus took Peter, James and John off by themselves with him and led them up a high mountain. He was transfigured before their eyes and his clothes became dazzlingly white—whiter than the work of any bleacher could make them. Elijah appeared to them along with Moses, the two were in conversation with Jesus. Then Peter spoke to Jesus: "Rabbi, how good it is for us to be here. Let us erect three booths on this site, one for you, one for Moses, and one for Elijah." He hardly knew what to say, for they were all overcome with awe. A cloud came, overshadowing them, and out of the cloud a voice: "This is my Son, my beloved. Listen to him." Suddenly looking around they no longer saw anyone with them—only Jesus.

As they were coming down the mountain, he strictly enjoined them not to tell anyone what they had seen before the Son of Man had risen from the dead. They kept this word of his to themselves, though they continued to discuss what "to rise from the dead" meant.—This is the gospel of the Lord. ℟. **Praise to you, Lord Jesus Christ.** ➤ No. 15, p. 623

— YEAR C — (Lk 9, 28-36)

As Jesus prays on the mountain, Moses and Elijah appear. The disciples had fallen asleep but, awakening, they see Jesus in all his splendor. God acknowledges Jesus as his Son.

℣. The Lord be with you. ℟. **And also with you.**
✠ A reading from the holy gospel according to Luke
℟. **Glory to you, Lord.**

Jesus took Peter, John and James, and went up onto a mountain to pray. While he was praying, his face changed in appearance and his clothes became dazzlingly white. Suddenly two men were talking with him—Moses and Elijah. They appeared in glory and spoke of his passage, which he was about to fulfill in Jerusalem. Peter and those with him had fallen into a deep sleep; but awakening, they saw his glory and likewise saw the two men who were standing with him. When these were leaving, Peter said to Jesus, "Master, how good it is for us to be here. Let us set up three booths, one for you, one for Moses, and one for Elijah." (He did not really know what he was saying.) While he was speaking, a cloud came and overshadowed them, and the disciples grew fearful as the others entered it. Then from the cloud came a voice which said, "This is my Son, my Chosen One. Listen to him." When the voice feel silent, Jesus was there alone. The disciples kept quiet, telling nothing of what they had seen at that time to anyone.
—This is the gospel of the Lord. ℟. **Praise to you, Lord Jesus Christ.**   ➤ No. 15, p. 623

PRAYER OVER THE GIFTS
Lord,
by the transfiguration of your Son
make our gifts holy,
and by his radiant glory free us from our sins.
We ask this in the name of Jesus the Lord.
℟. **Amen.** ℣

PREFACE (P 50)

℣. The Lord be with you. ℟. **And also with you.**
℣. Lift up your hearts. ℟. **We lift them up to the
Lord.** ℣ Let us give thanks to the Lord our God.
℟. **It is right to give him thanks and praise.**

Father, all-powerful and ever-living God,
we do well always and everywhere to give you thanks
through Jesus Christ our Lord.
He revealed his glory to the disciples
to strengthen them for the scandal of the cross.
His glory shone from a body like our own,
to show that the Church,
which is the body of Christ,
would one day share his glory.
In our unending joy we echo on earth
the song of the angels in heaven
as they praise your glory for ever: ➤ No. 23, p. 627

COMMUNION ANT.   1 Jn 3, 2

**When Christ is revealed we shall be like him, for we
shall see him as he is.** ℣

PRAYER AFTER COMMUNION

Lord,
you revealed the true radiance of Christ
in the glory of his transfiguration.
May the food we receive from heaven
change us into his image.
We ask this in the name of Jesus the Lord.
℟. **Amen.**   ➤ No. 32, p. 650

*Optional Solemn Blessings, p. 682, and Prayers over the
People, p. 689.*

Aug. 7 — STS. SIXTUS II, Pope and Martyr
AND COMPANIONS, Martyrs

Optional Memorial

During the persecution of Decius, Sixtus II, as well as his Deacons, Felicissimus and Agapitus, were martyred.

Common of Martyrs, p. 1049.

OPENING PRAYER

Father,
by the power of the Holy Spirit
you enabled St. Sixtus and his companions to lay
  down their lives
for your word in witness to Jesus.
Give us the grace to believe in you
and the courage to profess our faith.
We ask this through our Lord Jesus Christ, your Son,
who lives and reigns with you and the Holy Spirit,
one God, for ever and ever. ℟. **Amen.**

Reading I (Wis 3, 1-9), p. 1140, no. 5.
Responsorial Psalm (Ps 126), p. 1145, no. 4.
Gospel (Mt 10, 28-33), p. 1151, no. 2.

The Same Day, Aug. 7
ST. CAJETAN, Priest

Optional Memorial

St. Cajetan is the founder of the Theatines, the Order of the Congregation of Clerks Regular. He contributed greatly to the reform of morals in the 16th century. He died in 1547.

Common of Pastors, p. 1071; *or Common of Holy Men and Women: for Religious, p.* 1097.

OPENING PRAYER

Lord,
you helped St. Cajetan
to imitate the apostolic way of life.
By his example and prayers
may we trust in you always

and be faithful in seeking your kingdom.
Grant this through our Lord Jesus Christ, your Son,
who lives and reigns with you and the Holy Spirit,
one God, for ever and ever. ℞. **Amen.**

Reading I (1 Cor 2, 1-10), p. 1182, no. 2.
Responsorial Psalm (Ps 96), p. 1162, no. 4.
Gospel (Lk 9, 57-62), p. 1228, no. 15.

Aug. 8 — ST. DOMINIC, Priest

Memorial

St. Dominic, a native of Calaroga in old Castile, Spain,
was a member of the illustrious house of Guzman. Born
in 1170, he founded the *Order of Friars Preachers*, prop-
agated devotion to the Rosary, and saved the Western
Church from the growing power of the Albigensian
heresy. He led an extremely active life, preaching the
gospel, lecturing on theology and establishing houses
of his Order. He died at Bologna, Italy, in 1221.

*Common of Pastors, p. 1071; or Common of Holy Men
and Women: for Religious, p. 1097.*

OPENING PRAYER

Lord,
let the holiness and teaching of St. Dominic
come to the aid of your Church.
May he help us now with his prayers
as he once inspired people by his preaching.
We ask this through our Lord Jesus Christ, your Son,
who lives and reigns with you and the Holy Spirit,
one God, for ever and ever. ℞. **Amen.**

Reading I (1 Cor 2, 1-10), p. 1182, no. 2.
Responsorial Psalm (Ps 96), p. 1162, no. 4.
Gospel (Lk 9, 57-62), p. 1228, no. 15.

PRAYER OVER THE GIFTS

Lord of mercy,
at the intercession of St. Dominic
hear our prayers,
and by the power of this sacrifice

give us the grace to preach and defend our faith.
Grant this through Christ our Lord.
℟. **Amen.** ➔ No. 21, p. 626 (Pref. P 37-42)

PRAYER AFTER COMMUNION

Lord,
may your Church share with a living faith
the power of the sacrament we have received.
As the preaching of St. Dominic helped your Church to grow,
may his prayers help us to live for you.
We ask this in the name of Jesus the Lord.
℟. **Amen.** ➔ No. 32, p. 650

Aug. 10 — ST. LAWRENCE, Deacon and Martyr

Feast

In 257 Pope Sixtus II ordained St. Lawrence to the diaconate. Though St. Lawrence was still young, the same Pope appointed him as one of the seven deacons of the Roman Church. Summoned by the Prefect of Rome to surrender the treasury of the Church, St. Lawrence instead distributed it among the poor. According to tradition, St. Lawrence was roasted to death on a red-hot gridiron over a slow fire.

ENTRANCE ANT.

Today let us honor St. Lawrence, who spent himself for the poor of the Church. Thus he merited to suffer martyrdom and to ascend in joy to Jesus Christ the Lord. ➔ No. 2, p. 614

OPENING PRAYER

Father,
you called St. Lawrence to serve you by love
and crowned his life with glorious martyrdom.
Help us to be like him
in loving you and doing your work.
Grant this through our Lord Jesus Christ, your Son,
who lives and reigns with you and the Holy Spirit,
one God, for ever and ever. ℟. **Amen.** ↓

READING I   2 Cor 9, 6-10

The man who gives generously and cheerfully will be blessed far
beyond the bounds of his own generosity. The God who inspires such
generosity will also reward it abundantly.

A reading from the second letter of Paul to the
Corinthians

He who sows sparingly will reap sparingly, and he
who sows bountifully will reap bountifully. Everyone must give according to what he has inwardly
decided; not sadly, not grudgingly, for God loves a
cheerful giver. God can multiply his favors among
you so that you may always have enough of everything and even a surplus for good works, as it is
written:

"He scattered abroad and gave to the poor,
his justice endures forever."

He who supplies seed for the sower and bread for
the eater will provide in abundance; he will multiply
the seed you sow and increase your generous yield.
—This is the Word of the Lord. ℟. **Thanks be to
God. ℣**

Responsorial Psalm   Ps 112, 1-2. 5-6. 7-8. 9

℟. (5) **Happy the man who is merciful
and lends to those in need.**

Happy the man who fears the Lord,
who greatly delights in his commands.
His posterity shall be mighty upon the earth;
the upright generation shall be blessed. — ℟

Well for the man who is gracious and lends,
who conducts his affairs with justice;
He shall never be moved;
the just man shall be in everlasting remembrance. — ℟

An evil report he shall not fear;
his heart is firm, trusting in the Lord.
His heart is steadfast; he shall not fear

till he looks down upon his foes. — ℞

Lavishly he gives to the poor;
   his generosity shall endure forever;
   his horn shall be exalted in glory. — ℞ ℣

GOSPEL   Jn 12, 24-26
Alleluia (Jn 8, 12)

℞. **Alleluia.** I am the light of the world, says the
   Lord;
the man who follows me will have the light of life.
   ℞. **Alleluia.**

Through death to life is the paschal mystery which forms the heart
of redemption. Jesus is the model; it is he who has given the example
and will lead his followers to life with the Father.

℣. The Lord be with you. ℞. **And also with you.**
✠ A reading from the holy gospel according to John
℞. **Glory to you, Lord.**

Jesus said to his disciples:
   "I solemnly assure you,
     unless the grain of wheat falls to the earth and
       dies,
     it remains just a grain of wheat.
     But if it dies,
     it produces much fruit.
     The man who loves his life
     loses it,
     while the man who hates his life in this world
     preserves it to life eternal.
     If anyone would serve me,
     let him follow me;
     where I am,
     there will my servant be.
     Anyone who serves me,
     the Father will honor."

This is the gospel of the Lord. ℞. **Praise to you, Lord
Jesus Christ.**
➤ No. 15, p. 623

PRAYER OVER THE GIFTS

Lord,
at this celebration in honor of St. Lawrence,
accept the gifts we offer
and let them become a help to our salvation.
We ask this in the name of Jesus the Lord.
℟. **Amen.**   ➔ No. 21, p. 626 (Pref. P 37-42)

COMMUNION ANT.   Jn 12, 26

**He who serves me, follows me, says the Lord; and
where I am, my servant will also be.** ℣

PRAYER AFTER COMMUNION

Lord,
we have received your gifts
on this feast of St. Lawrence.
As we offer you our worship in this eucharist,
may we experience the increase of your saving grace.
We ask this through Christ our Lord.
℟. **Amen.**   ➔ No. 32, p. 650

Aug. 11 — ST. CLARE, Virgin

Memorial

St. Clare renounced all her worldly goods, in spite of the
opposition of her family; she received the penitential
habit from the hands of Francis of Assisi, and founded
the Second Franciscan Order ("Poor Clares"). She died
in 1253.

*Common of Virgins, p. 1085; or Common of Holy Men
and Women: for Religious, p. 1097.*

OPENING PRAYER

God of mercy,
you inspired St. Clare with the love of poverty.
By the help of her prayers
may we follow Christ in poverty of spirit
and come to the joyful vision of your glory
in the kingdom of heaven.
We ask this through our Lord Jesus Christ, your Son,

who lives and reigns with you and the Holy Spirit, one God, for ever and ever. ℞. **Amen.**

Reading I (Phil 3, 8-14), p. 1214, no. 9.
Responsorial Psalm (Ps 16), p. 1207, no. 3.
Gospel (Mt 16, 24-27), p. 1222, no. 5.

Aug. 13 — STS. PONTIAN, Pope and Martyr, AND HIPPOLYTUS, Priest and Martyr

Optional Memorial

St. Hippolytus was baptized by St. Lawrence and suffered martyrdom during the reign of Valerian. St. Pontian was deported to the island of Sardina and subsequently beaten to death while in exile in 235.

Common of Martyrs, p. 1049; or Common of Pastors, p 1071.

OPENING PRAYER

Lord,
may the loyal suffering of your saints, Pontian and Hippolytus,
fill us with your love
and make our hearts steadfast in faith.
Grant this through our Lord Jesus Christ, your Son, who lives and reigns with you and the Holy Spirit, one God, for ever and ever. ℞. **Amen.**

Reading I (1 Pt 4, 12-19), p. 1149, no. 9.
Responsorial Psalm (Ps 124), p. 1145, no. 3.
Gospel (Jn 15, 18-21), p. 1153, no. 6.

Aug. 15 — ASSUMPTION

See Vol. I (Sunday Missal), p. 1287.

Aug. 16 — ST. STEPHEN OF HUNGARY

Optional Memorial

This first Catholic King of Hungary, rightly called its "apostle," was a model of humility and charity toward the poor. He declared our Lady Patroness of Hungary. He died in 1038.

Common of Holy Men and Women, p. 1090.

OPENING PRAYER

Almighty Father,
grant that St. Stephen of Hungary,
who fostered the growth of your Church on earth,
may continue to be our powerful helper in heaven.
We ask this through our Lord Jesus Christ, your Son,
who lives and reigns with you and the Holy Spirit,
one God, for ever and ever. ℞. **Amen.**

Reading I (Dt 6, 3-9), p. 1195, no. 3.
Responsorial Psalm (Ps 112), p. 1209, no. 6.
Gospel (Mt 25, 14-30), p. 1224, no. 9.

Aug. 19 — ST. JOHN EUDES, Priest

Optional Memorial

Born in France, Nov. 14, 1601, St. John Eudes founded
the Congregation of the "Priests of Jesus and Mary"
and the Congregation of "Sisters of Our Lady of Charity." He died in 1680.

*Common of Pastors, p. 1071; or Common of Holy Men
and Women: for Religious, p. 1097.*

OPENING PRAYER

Father,
you chose the priest John Eudes
to preach the infinite riches of Christ.
By his teaching and example
help us to know you better
and live faithfully in the light of the gospel.
Grant this through our Lord Jesus Christ, your Son,
who lives and reigns with you and the Holy Spirit,
one God, for ever and ever. ℞. **Amen.**

Reading I (Eph 3, 14-19), p. 1213, no. 7.
Responsorial Psalm (Ps 131), p. 1210, no. 8.
Gospel (Mt 11, 25-30), p. 1221, no. 3.

Aug. 20 — ST. BERNARD, Abbot and Doctor

Memorial

Confessor, Abbot, and Doctor of the Church, St. Bernard was the guiding light of the Church in the 12th century. At 22 years of age, he became a Cistercian Monk. Appointed Abbot of the Monastery of Clairvaux, he was the arbiter of his century. Preacher of the second crusade, he wrote many pages on the Blessed Virgin and Jesus Christ. He died in 1153.

Common of Doctors of the Church, p. 1082; *or Common of Holy Men and Women: for Religious, p.* 1097.

OPENING PRAYER

Heavenly Father,
St. Bernard was filled with zeal for your house
and was a radiant light in your Church.
By his prayers
may we be filled with this spirit of zeal
and walk always as children of light.
We ask this through our Lord Jesus Christ, your Son,
who lives and reigns with you and the Holy Spirit,
one God, for ever and ever. ℟. **Amen.**

Reading I (Sir 15, 1-6), p. 1178, no. 3.
Responsorial Psalm (Ps 119), p. 1181, no. 3.
Gospel (Jn 17, 20-26), p. 1233, no. 22.

PRAYER OVER THE GIFTS

Lord our God,
may the eucharist we offer
be a sign of unity and peace
as we celebrate the memory of St. Bernard,
who strove in word and deed
to bring harmony to your Church.
We ask this through Christ our Lord.
℟. **Amen.** → No. 21, p. 626 (Pref. P 37-42)

PRAYER AFTER COMMUNION

Father,
may the holy food we have received

at this celebration of the feast of St. Bernard
continue your work of salvation in us.
By his example, give us courage,
by his teachings, make us wise,
so that we too may burn with love for your Word,
    Jesus Christ,
who is Lord for ever and ever.
℟. **Amen.**   ➤ No. 32, p. 650

Aug. 21 — ST. PIUS X, Pope

Memorial

On June 2, 1835, Giuseppe Melchoire Sarto saw the light
of earth at Riesi, Province of Treviso, in Venice; on
August 20, 1914, he saw the light of heaven; and on May
29, 1954, he who had become the 259th Pope was canonized St. Pius X. From St. Pius X we learn again that "the
folly of the cross," simplicity of life, and humility of
heart are still the indispensable conditions of a perfect
Christian life.

Common of Pastors: for Popes, p. 1066.

OPENING PRAYER

Father,
to defend the Catholic faith
and to make all things new in Christ,
you filled St. Pius X
with heavenly wisdom and apostolic courage.
May his example and teaching
lead us to the reward of eternal life.
Grant this through our Lord Jesus Christ, your Son,
who lives and reigns with you and the Holy Spirit,
one God, for ever and ever. ℟. **Amen.**

Reading I (1 Thes 2, 2-8), p. 1168, no. 10.
Responsorial Psalm (Ps 89), p. 1161, no. 3.
Gospel (Jn 21, 15-17), p. 1176, no. 11.

PRAYER OVER THE GIFTS

Lord,
be pleased to accept our offerings.

May we follow the teaching of St. Pius X,
and so come to these mysteries with reverence
and receive them with faith.
We ask this through Christ our Lord.
℟. **Amen.**   ➤ No. 21, p. 626 (Pref. P 37-42)

PRAYER AFTER COMMUNION

Lord our God,
we honor the memory of St. Pius X
by sharing the bread of heaven.
May it strengthen our faith and unite us in your love.
We ask this in the name of Jesus the Lord.
℟. **Amen.**   ➤ No. 32, p. 650

Aug. 22 — QUEENSHIP OF MARY

Memorial

On October 11, 1954, His Holiness, Pope Pius XII, in his encyclical letter, "Ad Caeli Reginam," decreed and instituted the feast of the Queenship of Mary to be celebrated throughout the world every year. Likewise, he decreed that on that feast "there be renewed the consecration of the human race to the Immaculate Heart of the Blessed Virgin Mary."

ENTRANCE ANT.   Ps 45, 10

The queen stands at your right hand arrayed in cloth of gold.   ➤ No. 2, p. 614

OPENING PRAYER

Father,
you have given us the mother of your Son
to be our queen and mother.
With the support of her prayers
may we come to share the glory of your children
in the kingdom of heaven.
We ask this through our Lord Jesus Christ, your Son,
who lives and reigns with you and the Holy Spirit,
one God, for ever and ever. ℟. **Amen.**

Readings and Intervenient Chants are taken from the Common of the Blessed Virgin Mary, p. 1118.

Reading I (Is 9, 1-6), p. 1122, no. 8.
Responsorial Psalm (Ps 113), p. 1127, no. 4.
Gospel (Lk 1, 26-38), p. 1133, no. 3.

PRAYER OVER THE GIFTS

Lord,
celebrating the feast of the Virgin Mary,
we offer you our gifts and prayers:
may Christ, who offered himself as a perfect sacrifice,
bring mankind the peace and love of your kingdom,
where he lives and reigns for ever and ever.
R̲. **Amen.**   → No. 21, p. 626 (Pref. P 56-57)

COMMUNION ANT.   Lk 1, 45

**Blessed are you for your firm believing, that the
promises of the Lord would be fulfilled.** ℣

PRAYER AFTER COMMUNION

Lord,
we have eaten the bread of heaven.
May we who honor the memory of the Virgin Mary
share one day in your banquet of eternal life.
We ask this in the name of Jesus the Lord.
R̲. **Amen.**   → No. 32, p. 650

_____

Aug. 23 — ST. ROSE OF LIMA, Virgin

Optional Memorial

Born in Lima, Peru, St. Rose is the first American
Saint. At five years of age she is said to have taken a
vow of virginity and modeled her life on that of St.
Catherine of Siena. At fifteen years of age she received
the habit of the Third Order of St. Dominic, and for
16 years lived a life of mortification and penance. She
died in 1617 at thirty-one years of age.

*Common of Virgins, p. 1085; or Common of Holy Men
and Women: for Religious, p. 1097.*

OPENING PRAYER

God our Father,
for love of you

St. Rose gave up everything
to devote herself to a life of penance.
By the help of her prayers
may we imitate her selfless way of life on earth
and enjoy the fullness of your blessings in heaven.
Grant this through our Lord Jesus Christ, your Son,
who lives and reigns with you and the Holy Spirit,
one God, for ever and ever. ℟. **Amen.**

Reading I (2 Cor 10, 17—11, 2), p. 1192, no. 2.
Responsorial Psalm (Ps 148), p. 1191, no. 2.
Gospel (Mt 13, 44-46), p. 1221, no. 4.

Aug. 24 — ST. BARTHOLOMEW, Apostle

Feast

In the Gospel of St. John, Bartholomew is not mentioned among the apostles; but it describes an incident
when Philip and Nathanael came to Jesus who char-
acterized Nathanael as an Israelite without guile. In
the list of the apostles in the other Gospels, Nathanael
is not mentioned but the place after Philip is accorded
to Bartholomew. Hence, many Scripture scholars believe Bartholomew is the Nathanael in question. He
preached the gospel in Arabia and tradition tells us that
he was flayed alive.

ENTRANCE ANT.   Ps 96, 2. 3

**Day after day proclaim the salvation of the Lord.
Proclaim his glory to all nations.**   → No. 2, p. 614

OPENING PRAYER

Lord,
sustain within us the faith
which made St. Bartholomew ever loyal to Christ.
Let your Church be the sign of salvation
for all the nations of the world.
We ask this through our Lord Jesus Christ, your Son,
who lives and reigns with you and the Holy Spirit,
one God, for ever and ever. ℟. **Amen.** ℣

READING I   Rv 21, 9-14

Jerusalem was the holy city, specially favored by God, particularly
blessed by him. Here John sees the city in a vision and gives a
poetic description of what he saw. The holy city is the bride of the
Lamb.

A reading from the book of Revelation

An angel said to me, "Come, I will show you the
woman who is bride of the Lamb." He carried me
away in spirit to the top of a very high mountain
and showed me the holy city Jerusalem coming down
out of heaven from God. It gleamed with the splendor
of God. The city had the radiance of a precious jewel
that sparkled like a diamond. Its wall, massive and
high, had twelve gates at which twelve angels were
stationed. Twelve names were written on the gates,
the names of the twelve tribes of Israel. There were
three gates facing east, three north, three south,
and three west. The wall of the city had twelve
courses of stones as its foundation, on which were
written the names of the twelve apostles of the
Lamb.—This is the Word of the Lord. ℟. **Thanks
to be God.** ℣

Responsorial Psalm   Ps 145, 10-11. 12-13. 17-18

℟. (12) **Your friends tell the glory of your kingship,
     Lord.**

Let all your works give you thanks, O Lord,
    and let your faithful ones bless you.
Let them discourse of the glory of your kingdom
    and speak of your might. — ℟

Making known to men your might
    and the glorious splendor of your kingdom.
Your kingdom is a kingdom for all ages,
    and your dominion endures through all genera-
        tions — ℟

The Lord is just in all his ways
    and holy in all his works.
The Lord is near to all who call upon him,
    to all who call upon him in truth. — ℟ ℣

GOSPEL   Jn 1, 45-51

Alleluia (Jn 1, 49)

℟. **Alleluia.** Master you are the Son of God
you are the king of Israel. ℟. **Alleluia.**

Nathanael is won over to the Master by the very simple insights into
his life and character which Jesus reveals to him. Jesus take the
occasion to tell his disciples that there are much greater things in
store for them to see and hear.

℣. The Lord be with you. ℟. **And also with you.**

✠ A reading from the holy gospel according to John
℟. **Glory to you, Lord.**

Philip sought out Nathanael and told him, "We
have found the one Moses spoke of in the law—the
prophets too—Jesus, son of Joseph, from Nazareth."
Nathanael's response to that was, "Can anything
good come from Nazareth?" and Philip replied,
"Come, see for yourself." When Jesus saw Nathanael
coming toward him, he remarked: "This man is a
real Israelite. There is no guile in him." "How do you
know me?" Nathanael asked him. "Before Philip
called you," Jesus answered, "I saw you under the
fig tree." "Rabbi,'" said Nathanael, "you are the Son
of God; you are the king of Israel." Jesus responded:
"Do you believe just because I told you I saw you
under the fig tree? You will see much greater things
than that."

He went on to tell them, "I solemnly assure you,
you shall see the sky opened and the angels of God
ascending and descending on the Son of Man."—
This is the gospel of the Lord. ℟. **Praise to you, Lord
Jesus Christ.**
➤ No. 15, p. 623

PRAYER OVER THE GIFTS
Lord,
we offer you this sacrifice of praise
on this feast of St. Bartholomew.
May his prayers win us your help.
We ask this in the name of Jesus the Lord.
℟. **Amen.**   ➤ No. 21, p. 626 (Pref. P 64-65)

COMMUNION ANT.   Lk 22, 29-30

I will give you the kingdom that my Father gave to me; and in that kingdom you will eat and drink at my table. ℣

PRAYER AFTER COMMUNION
Lord,
as we celebrate the feast of St. Bartholomew,
we receive the pledge of eternal salvation.
May it help us in this life
and in the life to come.
Grant this through Christ our Lord.
℞. **Amen.**   ➔ No. 32, p. 650

Aug. 25 — ST. LOUIS

Optional Memorial

Born in 1215, Louis IX became King of France at 15 years of age. Educated as a Christian King by his saintly mother, St. Louis undertook two Crusades to the Holy Land. He died at Tunis in 1270.

Common of Holy Men and Women, p. 1090.

OPENING PRAYER
Father,
you raised St. Louis
from the cares of earthly rule
to the glory of your heavenly kingdom.
By the help of his prayers
may we come to your eternal kingdom
by our work here on earth.
Grant this through our Lord Jesus Christ, your Son,
who lives and reigns with you and the Holy Spirit,
one God, for ever and ever. ℞. **Amen.**

Reading I (Is 58, 6-11), p. 1202, no. 15.
Responsorial Psalm (Ps 112), p. 1209, no. 6.
Gospel (Mt 16, 24-27), p. 1222, no. 5.

The Same Day, Aug. 25
ST. JOSEPH CALASANZ, Priest

Optional Memorial

This holy priest was born in Spain in 1556. For 52 years he instructed children in the faith and founded "The Order of Clerks Regular of the Poor Schools of the Mother of God." He died in 1648 and was canonized by Pope Clement XIII in 1767.

Common of Holy Men and Women: for Teachers, p. 1101; or Common of Pastors, p. 1071.

OPENING PRAYER

Lord,
you blessed St. Joseph Calasanz
with such charity and patience
that he dedicated himself
to the formation of Christian youth.
As we honor this teacher of wisdom
may we follow his example in working for truth.
We ask this through our Lord Jesus Christ, your Son,
who lives and reigns with you and the Holy Spirit,
one God, for ever and ever. ℟. **Amen.**

Reading I (1 Cor 12, 31—13, 13), p. 1211, no. 3.
Responsorial Psalm (Ps 34), p. 1207, no. 4.
Gospel (Mt 18, 1-4), p. 1222, no. 6.

Aug. 27 — ST. MONICA

Memorial

St. Monica was born in Africa. She first converted her pagan husband, and then, by her tears and unceasing prayers, her son St. Augustine, who is regarded as one of the greatest Doctors of the Western Church. She died at Ostia in 387.

Common of Holy Men and Women, p. 1102.

OPENING PRAYER

God of mercy,
comfort of those in sorrow,
the tears of St. Monica moved you

to convert her son St. Augustine to the faith of
  Christ.
By their prayers, help us to turn from our sins
and to find your loving forgiveness.
Grant this through our Lord Jesus Christ, your Son,
who lives and reigns with you and the Holy Spirit,
one God, for ever and ever. ℟. **Amen.**

Reading I (Sir 26, 1-4. 13-16), p. 1201, no. 14.
Responsorial Psalm (Ps 131), p. 1210, no. 8.

GOSPEL   Lk 7, 11-17

Alleluia (Jn 8, 12)

℟. **Alleluia.** I am the light of the world, says the Lord;
the man who follows me will have the light of life.
        ℟. **Alleluia.**

At Naim Jesus meets a funeral in which an only son of a widow is
being buried. Jesus is moved with pity and restores the boy back to
life and gives him to his mother.

℣. The Lord be with you. ℟. **And also with you.**
✠ A reading from the holy gospel according to Luke
℟. **Glory to you, Lord.**

Jesus went to a town called Naim, and his disciples
and a large crowd accompanied him. As he approached the gate of the town a dead man was being carried
out, the only son of a widowed mother. A consider-
able crowd of townsfolk were with her. The Lord
was moved with pity upon seeing her and said to her,
"Do not cry." Then he stepped forward and touched
the litter; at this, the bearers halted. He said, "Young
man, I bid you get up." The dead man sat up and
began to speak. Then Jesus gave him back to his
mother. Fear seized them all and they began to
praise God. "A great prophet has risen among us,"
they said; and, "God has visited his people." This
was the report that spread about him throughout
Judea and the surrounding country.—This is the
gospel of the Lord. ℟. **Praise to you, Lord Jesus
Christ.**   ➔ No. 15, p. 622

Aug. 28 — ST. AUGUSTINE, Bishop and Doctor

Memorial

St. Augustine was born at Tagaste, Africa, in 354. Monica, his mother, constantly prayed for his conversion. At thirty-five years of age, St. Augustine finally received Baptism. At forty-one, he became Bishop of Hippo. From this time until his death, he wrote voluminous works that have been the admiration of the ages. His sublime knowledge merited for him the title of one of the greatest Doctors of the Western Church.

ENTRANCE ANT. Sir 15, 5

The Lord opened his mouth in the assembly, and filled him with the spirit of wisdom and understanding, and clothed him in a robe of glory. ➤ No. 2, p. 614

OPENING PRAYER

Lord,
renew in your Church
the spirit you gave St. Augustine.
Filled with this spirit,
may we thirst for you alone as the fountain of wisdom
and seek you as the source of eternal love.
We ask this through our Lord Jesus Christ, your Son,
who lives and reigns with you and the Holy Spirit,
one God, for ever and ever. ℟. **Amen.**

Readings and Intervenient Chants are taken from the Common of Pastors, p. 1154, or the Common of Doctors of the Church, p. 1177.

Reading I (1 Jn 4, 7-16), p. 1217, no. 16.
Responsorial Psalm (Ps 37), p. 1181, no. 2.
Gospel (Mt 23, 8-12), p. 1171, no. 2.

PRAYER OVER THE GIFTS

Lord,
as we celebrate the memorial of our salvation,
we pray that this sacrament may be for us
a sign of unity and a bond of love.
We ask this in the name of Jesus the Lord.
℟. **Amen.** ➤ No. 21, p. 626 (Pref. P 37-42)

COMMUNION ANT.   Mt 23, 10. 8

**Christ is your only teacher: and all of you are bro-
thers.** ✟

PRAYER AFTER COMMUNION

Lord,
make us holy by our sharing at the table of Christ.
As members of his body,
help us to become what we have received.
Grant this through Christ our Lord.
℟. **Amen.**   ➔ No. 32, p. 650

_____

Aug. 29 — BEHEADING OF ST. JOHN THE BAPTIST, Martyr

Memorial

Although the feast of a saint is usually the date of his
death, the Church commemorates both the nativity of
St. John the Baptist, or Baptizer (June 24), and his
martyrdom on this day. The saint's fearless condemnation of Herod's incestuous marriage incurred the hatred
of the king's bride, Herodias, who brought about his
imprisonment and (through her daughter) his eventual
death.

ENTRANCE ANT.   Ps 119, 46-47

**Lord, I shall expound your law before kings and not
fear disgrace; I shall ponder your decrees, which I
have always loved.**   ➔ No. 2, p. 614

OPENING PRAYER

God our Father,
you called John the Baptist
to be the herald of your Son's birth and death.
As he gave his life in witness to truth and justice,
so may we strive to profess our faith in your gospel.
Grant this through our Lord Jesus Christ, your Son,
who lives and reigns with you and the Holy Spirit,
one God, for ever and ever. ℟. **Amen.** ✟

READING I Jer 1, 17-19

These words of the Lord come to Jeremiah. He stands up to the wicked leaders of the people in the name of the Lord who sent him. The Lord promises that they will not prevail.

A reading from the book of the prophet Jeremiah

The word of the Lord said to me:
Do you gird your loins;
    stand up and tell them
    all that I command you.
Be not crushed on their account,
    as though, I would leave you crushed before them;
For it is I this day
    who have made you a fortified city,
A pillar of iron, a wall of brass,
    against the whole land:
Against Judah's kings and princes,
    against its priests and people.
They will fight against you, but not prevail over you,
    for I am with you to deliver you, says the Lord.
This is the Word of the Lord. ℟. **Thanks be to God.** ℣

Responsorial Psalm Ps 71, 1-2. 3-4. 5-6. 15. 17

℟. (15) **I will sing of your salvation.**

In you, O Lord, I take refuge;
    let me never be put to shame.
In your justice rescue me, and deliver me;
    incline your ear to me, and save me. — ℟

Be my rock of refuge,
    a stronghold to give me safety,
    for you are my rock and my fortress.
O my God, rescue me from the hand of the wick-
    ed. — ℟

For you are my hope, O Lord:
    my trust, O God, from my youth.
On you I depend from birth;
    from my mother's womb you are my strength.—℟

My mouth shall declare your justice,

day by day your salvation.
O God, you have taught me from my youth,
    and till the present I proclaim your wondrous
      deeds. — ℟ ℣

The Gospel is special *in this Memorial.*

GOSPEL   Mk 6, 17-29

Alleluia (Mt 5, 10)

℟. **Alleluia.** Happy are they who suffer persecution
    for justice' sake;
the kingdom of heaven is theirs. ℟. **Alleluia.**

Mark records the martyrdom of John the Baptizer occasioned by
Herod's pleasure at seeing his stepdaughter's dance. After faithfully
preparing the way for the Messiah, John is taken to his heavenly
reward.

℣. The Lord be with you. ℟. **And also with you.**

✠ A reading from the holy gospel according to Mark
℟. **Glory to you, Lord.**

Herod was the one who had ordered John arrested,
chained, and imprisoned on account of Herodias, the
wife of his brother Philip, whom he had married.
That was because John had told Herod, "It is not
right for you to live with your brother's wife." Herodias harbored a grudge against him for this and
wanted to kill him but was unable to do so. Herod
feared John, knowing him to be an upright and holy
man, and kept him in custody. When he heard him
speak he was very much disturbed; yet he felt the
attraction of his words. Herodias had her chance
one day when Herod held a birthday dinner for his
court circle, military officers, and the leading men
of Galilee. Herodias' own daughter came in at one
point and performed a dance which delighted Herod
and his guests. The king told the girl, "Ask for anything you want and I will give it to you." He went
so far as to swear to her: "I will grant you whatever
you ask, even to half my kingdom!" She went out
and said to her mother, "What shall I ask for?" The

mother answered, "The head of John the Baptizer."
At that the girl hurried back to the king's presence
and made her request: "I want you to give me, at
once, the head of John the Baptizer on a platter." The
king bitterly regretted the request; yet because of
his oath and the presence of the guests, he did not
want to refuse her. He promptly dispatched an executioner, ordering him to bring back the Baptizer's
head. The man went and beheaded John in the prison.
He brought in the head on a platter and gave it to
the girl, and the girl gave it to her mother. Later,
when the disciples heard about this, they came and
carried his body away and laid it in a tomb.—This is
the gospel of the Lord. ℞. **Praise to you, Lord Jesus
Christ.**

→ No. 15, p. 623

PRAYER OVER THE GIFTS

Lord,
by these gifts we offer,
keep us faithful to your way of life,
which John the Baptist preached in the wilderness,
and to which he courageously witnessed
by shedding his blood.
We ask this through Christ our Lord.
℞. **Amen.**

→ Pref. (P 61), p. 000

COMMUNION ANT.

Jn 3, 27. 30

**John's answer was: He must grow greater and I must
grow less.** ↓

PRAYER AFTER COMMUNION

Lord,
may we who celebrate the martyrdom of John the
Baptist
honor this sacrament of our salvation
and rejoice in the life it brings us.
We ask this in the name of Jesus the Lord.
℞. **Amen.**

→ No. 32, p. 650

— SEPTEMBER —

[In the dioceses of the United States]

First Monday of September

LABOR DAY

In line with the latest liturgical thinking whereby it is good to have specific texts for major secular events that affect the life of an entire people, such as Thanksgiving Day and Independence Day in the United States, the following formularies may be used on Labor Day.

ENTRANCE ANT. Ps 90, 17

May the goodness of the Lord be upon us, and give success to the work of our hands. ➔ No. 2, p. 614

OPENING PRAYER

A

God our Creator,
it is your will that man accept the duty of work.
In your kindness may the work we begin
bring us growth in this life
and help to extend the kingdom of Christ.
We ask this through our Lord Jesus Christ, your Son,
who lives and reigns with you and the Holy Spirit,
one God, for ever and ever. ℟. **Amen.** ↓

OR

God our Father,
by the labor of man you govern and guide to perfection
    tion
the work of creation.
Hear the prayers of your people
and give all men work that enhances their human
    dignity
and draws them closer to each other
in the service of their brothers.
We ask this through our Lord Jesus Christ, your Son,
who lives and reigns with you and the Holy Spirit,
one God, for ever and ever. ℟. **Amen.**

B

God our Father,
you have placed all the powers of nature
under the control of man and his work.
May we bring the spirit of Christ to all our efforts
and work with our brothers and sisters at our common task,
establishing true love and guiding your creation to
perfect fulfillment.
We ask this through our Lord Jesus Christ, your Son,
who lives and reigns with you and the Holy Spirit,
one God, for ever and ever. ℟. **Amen.** ⩔

The readings listed at the end of this Mass may also be chosen.

READING I   Gn 2, 4-9. 15

Genesis shows God settling Adam in the Garden of Eden to cultivate
and take care of it. God created the world and all that is in it.

A reading from the book of Genesis

At the time when the Lord God made the earth and
the heavens—while as yet there was no field shrub on
earth and no grass of the field had sprouted, for the
Lord God had sent no rain upon the earth and there
was no man to till the soil, but a stream was welling
up out of the earth and was watering all the surface of
the ground—the Lord God formed man out of the clay
of the ground and blew into his nostrils the breath of
life, and so man became a living being.

Then the Lord planted a garden in Eden, in the east,
and he placed there the man whom he had formed.
Out of the ground the Lord God made various trees
grow that were delightful to look at and good for
food, with the tree of life in the middle of the garden
and the tree of the knowledge of good and bad.

The Lord God then took the man and settled him in
the garden of Eden, to cultivate and care for it.—
This is the Word of the Lord. ℟. **Thanks be to God.** ⩔

Responsorial Psalm   Ps 90, 2. 3-4. 12-13. 14. 26

℟. (17) **Lord, give success to the work of our hands.**

Before the mountains were begotten
     and the earth and the world were brought forth,
     from everlasting to everlasting you are God. — ℟

You turn man back to dust,
     saying, "Return, O children of men."
For a thousand years in your sight
     are as yesterday, now that it is past,
     or as a watch of the night. — ℟

Teach us to number our days aright,
     that we may gain wisdom of heart.
Return, O Lord! How long?
     Have pity on your servants! — ℟

Fill us at daybreak with your kindness,
     that we may shout for joy and gladness all our
     days.
Let your work be seen by your servants
     and your glory by their children. — ℟ ℣

READING II   2 Thes 3, 6-12. 16

Paul exhorts all Christians to follow his example and work diligently
for their livelihood. They should live in peace with one another, but
if anyone will not work, he should not eat.

A reading from the second letter of Paul to the
Thessalonians

We command you, brothers, in the name of the Lord
Jesus Christ, to avoid any brother who wanders from
the straight path and does not follow the tradition
you received from us. You know how you ought to
imitate us. We did not live lives of disorder when
we were among you, nor depend on anyone for food.
Rather, we worked day and night, laboring to the
point of exhaustion so as not to impose on any of
you. Not that we had no claim on you, but that we
might present ourselves as an example for you to
imitate. Indeed, when we were with you we used to

lay down the rule that anyone who would not work should not eat.

We hear that some of you are unruly, not keeping busy but acting like busybodies. We enjoin all and we urge them strongly in the Lord Jesus Christ to earn the food they eat by working quietly.

May he who is the Lord of peace give you continued peace in every possible way. The Lord be with you all.—This is the Word of the Lord. ℟. **Thanks be to God.** ℣

GOSPEL   Mt 6, 31-34

Alleluia (Mt 11, 28)

℟. **Alleluia.** Come to me, all you that labor and are burdened,

and I will give you rest, says the Lord. ℟. **Alleluia.**

Jesus cautions his disciples not to worry about eating and drinking. God knows the needs of his children. They are to seek first after holiness.

℣. The Lord be with you. ℟. **And also with you.**

✠ A reading from the holy gospel according to Matthew. ℟. **Glory to you, Lord.**

Jesus said to his disciples: "Stop worrying over questions like, 'What are we to eat, or what are we to drink, or what are we to wear?' The unbelievers are always running after these things. Your heavenly Father knows all that you need. Seek first his kingship over you, his way of holiness, and all these things will be given you besides. Enough, then, of worrying about tomorrow. Let tomorrow take care of itself. Today has troubles enough of its own." —This is the gospel of the Lord. ℟. **Praise to you, Lord Jesus Christ.**

➔ No. 15, p. 623

PRAYER OVER THE GIFTS

A

God our Father,
you provide the human race with food for strength

and with the eucharist for its renewal;
may these gifts which we offer
always bring us health of mind and body.
Grant this through Christ our Lord. ℟. **Amen.**

B

Lord,
receive the gifts of your Church,
and by the human labor we offer you
join us to the saving work of Christ,
who is Lord for ever and ever.
℟. **Amen.**   ➔ No. 21, p. 626 (Pref. P 82-83

COMMUNION ANT.   Col 3, 17
**Let everything you do or say be in the name of the
Lord with thanksgiving to God.** ℣

PRAYER AFTER COMMUNION

A

Lord,
hear the prayers
of those who gather at your table of unity and love.
By doing the work you have entrusted to us
may we sustain our life on earth
and build up your kingdom in faith.
Grant this through Christ our Lord.
℟. **Amen.**

B

Lord,
guide and govern us by your help in this life
as you have renewed us by the mysteries of eternal
    life.
We ask this through Christ our Lord.
℟. **Amen.**   ➔ No. 32, p. 650

OTHER POSSIBLE READINGS

Reading I: Gn 1, 26—2, 3
Resp. Psalm: Ps 127, 1. 2.
Gospel: Mt 25, 14-30

Sept. 3 — ST. GREGORY THE GREAT,
Pope and Doctor

Memorial

This Benedictine who was elected Pope by the unanimous voice of priests and people is "Great" above all because of his magnificent contributions to the Liturgy of the Mass and Office. Plain chant which in holy humility accompanies our most sacred functions will for all time be named after him "Gregorian Chant." He is one of the four great Doctors of the Latin Church. He died in the year 604.

Common of Pastors: for Popes, p. 1066; or Common of Doctors of the Church, p. 1082.

OPENING PRAYER

Father,
you guide your people with kindness
and govern us with love.
By the prayers of St. Gregory
give the spirit of wisdom
to those you have called to lead your Church.
May the growth of your people in holiness
be the eternal joy of our shepherds.
We ask this through our Lord Jesus Christ, your Son,
who lives and reigns with you and the Holy Spirit,
one God, for ever and ever. ℟. **Amen.**

Reading I (2 Cor 4, 1-2. 5-7), p. 1166, no. 6.
Responsorial Psalm (Ps 96), p. 1162, no. 4.
Gospel (Lk 22, 24-30), p. 1174, no. 8.

PRAYER OVER THE GIFTS

Lord,
by this sacrifice you free the world from sin.
As we offer it in memory of St. Gregory,
may it bring us closer to eternal salvation.
Grant this through Christ our Lord.
℟. **Amen.**
→ No. 21, p. 626 (Pref. P 37-42)

PRAYER AFTER COMMUNION

Lord,
at this eucharist you give us Christ to be our living
  bread.
As we celebrate the feast of St. Gregory,
may we also come to know your truth
and live it in love for others.
We ask this in the name of Jesus the Lord.
℟. **Amen.**   ➔ No. 32, p. 650

Sept. 8 — BIRTH OF MARY

Feast

The Feast of September 8 in honor of the Blessed Virgin
Mary originated at Jerusalem, as did the Solemnity of
August 15. It is a question of the Feast of the basilica
known at the end of the 5th century as the basilica "of
holy Mary where she was born," and now known as the
basilica of St. Anne. In the 7th century there was celebrated on this day, in the Byzantine Rite and at Rome,
the Birth of the Blessed Virgin. The feast is also celebrated on September 8 in the Syriac Rite and on September 7 in the Coptic Rite.

ENTRANCE ANT.

**Let us celebrate with joyful hearts the birth of the
Virgin Mary, of whom was born the sun of justice,
Christ our Lord.**   ➔ No. 2, p. 614

OPENING PRAYER

Father of mercy,
give your people help and strength from heaven.
The birth of the Virgin Mary's Son
was the dawn of our salvation.
May this celebration of her birthday
bring us closer to lasting peace.
Grant this through our Lord Jesus Christ, your Son,
who lives and reigns with you and the Holy Spirit,
one God, for ever and ever. ℟. **Amen.**

READING I   Mi 5, 1-4

From simple origins, from a town as lowly as Bethlehem, came the Messiah. Micah makes reference to the prophecy of his contemporary, Isaiah, that a humble maiden will give birth to him who is to be the shepherd of all and bring peace to men.

A reading from the book of the prophet Micah

You, Bethlehem-Ephrathah,
  too small to be among the clans of Judah,
From you shall come forth for me
  one who is to be ruler in Israel:
Whose origin is from of old,
  from ancient times.
(Therefore the Lord will give them up, until the time
  when she who is to give birth has borne,
And the rest of his brethren shall return
  to the children of Israel.)
He shall stand firm and shepherd his flock
  by the strength of the Lord,
  in the majestic name of the Lord, his God;
And they shall remain, for now his greatness
  shall reach to the ends of the earth;
  he shall be peace.
This is the Word of the Lord. ℟. **Thanks be to God.** ℣

OR

READING I   Rom 8, 28-30

God knows from all eternity those whom he has predestined to greatness. Mary's special privileges he foreknew; thus he also predestined, called, justified, and glorified her.

A reading from the letter of Paul to the Romans

We know that God makes all things work together for the good of those who have been called according to his decree. Those whom he foreknew he predestined to share the image of his Son, that the Son might be the first-born of many brothers. Those he predestined he likewise called; those he called he also justified, and those he justified he in turn glorified.—This is the Word of the Lord. ℟. **Thanks be to God.** ℣

Responsorial Psalm   Ps 13, 6. 6

℟. (Is 61, 9) **With delight I rejoice in the Lord.**

Though I trusted in your kindness,
  let my heart rejoice in your salvation. — ℟

Let me sing of the Lord, "He has been good to
  me." — ℟

GOSPEL   Mt 1, 1-16. 18-23 or 1, 18-23
Alleluia

℟. **Alleluia.** Happy are you, holy Virgin Mary, deserving of all praise;
from you arose the sun of justice, Christ the Lord.
  ℟. **Alleluia.**

In a genealogy some few are men of renown; most are figures long
forgotten. But each plays his part in carrying on the line. From such
a line came Joseph, the husband of Mary, the virgin from whom
was born Emmanuel, "God-with-us."

[*If the "Short Form" is used, the indented text in
brackets is omitted.*]

℣. The Lord be with you. ℟. **And also with you.**
✠ The beginning of the holy gospel according to Matthew. ℟. **Glory to you, Lord.**

[A family record of Jesus Christ, son of David,
son of Abraham. Abraham was the father of Isaac,
Isaac the father of Jacob, Jacob the father of
Judah and his brothers.
    Judah was the father of Perez and Zerah, whose
        mother was Tamar.
    Perez was the father of Hezron,
    Hezron the father of Ram.
    Ram was the father of Amminadab,
    Amminadab the father of Nahshon,
    Nahshon the father of Salmon.
    Salmon was the father of Boaz, whose mother
        was Rahab,
    Boaz was the father of Obed, whose mother
        was Ruth.
    Obed was the father of Jesse,

Jesse the father of King David.

David was the father of Solomon, whose mother had been the wife of Uriah.

Solomon was the father of Rehoboam,

Rehoboam the father of Abijah,

Abijah the father of Asa.

Asa was the father of Jehoshaphat,

Jehoshaphat the father of Joram,

Joram the father of Uzziah.

Uzziah was the father of Jotham,

Jotham the father of Ahaz,

Ahaz the father of Hezekiah.

Hezekiah was the father of Manasseh,

Manasseh the father of Amos,

Amos the father of Josiah.

Josiah became the father of Jechoniah and his brothers at the time of the Babylonian exile.

After the Babylonian exile

Jechoniah was the father of Shealtiel,

Shealtiel the father of Zerubbabel.

Zerubbabel was the father of Abiud,

Abiud the father of Eliakim,

Eliakim the father of Azor.

Azor was the father of Zadok,

Zadok the father of Achim,

Achim the father of Eliud.

Eliud was the father of Eleazar,

Eleazar the father of Matthan,

Matthan the father of Jacob.

Jacob was the father of Joseph the husband of Mary.

It was of her that Jesus who is called the Messiah was born.]

Now this is how the birth of Jesus Christ came about. When his mother Mary was engaged to Joseph, but before they lived together, she was found with child through the power of the Holy Spirit. Joseph her husband, an upright man unwilling to expose her to the law, decided to divorce her quietly. Such was his intention when suddenly the angel of the Lord appeared in a dream and said to him: "Joseph, son of David, have no fear about taking Mary as your wife. It is by the Holy Spirit that she has conceived this child. She is to have a son and you are to name him Jesus because he will save his people from their sins." All this happened to fulfill what the Lord had said through the prophet:

"The virgin shall be with child
and give birth to a son,
and they shall call him Emmanuel,"

a name which means "God is with us."—This is the gospel of the Lord. ℟. **Praise to you, Lord Jesus Christ.**

➜ No. 15, p. 623

PRAYER OVER THE GIFTS

Father,
the birth of Christ your Son
increased the virgin mother's love for you.
May his sharing in our human nature
give us courage in our weakness,
free us from our sins,
and make our offering acceptable.
We ask this in the name of Jesus the Lord.
℟. **Amen.**

➜ No. 21, p. 626 (Pref. P 56-57)

COMMUNION ANT.
Is 7, 14; Mt 1, 21

The Virgin shall bear a son, who will save his people from their sins. ℣

PRAYER AFTER COMMUNION

Lord,
may your Church, renewed in this holy eucharist,
be filled with joy at the birth of the Virgin Mary,
who brought the dawn of hope and salvation to the world.
We ask this through Christ our Lord.
℟. **Amen.**

➜ No. 32, p. 650

[In the dioceses of the United States]

Sept. 9 — ST. PETER CLAVER, Priest

Memorial

While a student at Majorca, St. Peter Claver was influenced by St. Alphonsus Rodriguez to become a missionary in America. When he was ordained at Cartagena in 1616, he dedicated himself by a special vow to the service of the Negro slaves. Boarding the slave ships as they entered the harbor, he would hurry to the revolting inferno of the hold, and offer whatever poor refreshments he could afford; he would care for the sick and dying, and instruct the slaves through Negro catechists, before administering the sacraments. Through his efforts three hundred thousand souls entered the Church. Furthermore, he did not lose sight of his converts when they left the ships, but followed them to the plantations to which they were sent, encouraged them to live as Christians, and prevailed on their masters to treat them humanely. He died in 1654.

Common of Pastors: for Missionaries, p. 1077.

OPENING PRAYER

God of mercy and love,
you offer all peoples
the dignity of sharing in your life.
By the example and prayers of St. Peter Claver,
strengthen us to overcome all racial hatreds
and to love each other as brothers and sisters.
We ask this through our Lord Jesus Christ, your Son,
who lives and reigns with you and the Holy Spirit,
one God, for ever and ever. ℟. **Amen.**

Reading I (Is 52, 7-10), p. 1156, no. 5.
Responsorial Psalm (Ps 96), p. 1162, no. 4.
Gospel (Mt 28, 16-20), p. 1171, no. 3.

Sept. 13 — ST. JOHN CHRYSOSTOM,
Bishop and Doctor

Memorial

St. John, named Chrysostom (golden-mouthed) for his sublime eloquence, was born in Antioch and became

Patriarch of Constantinople. The envy and calumny of his persecutors followed his every step until he died in 407.

Common of Pastors: for Bishops, p. 1069; or Common of Doctors of the Church, p. 1082.

OPENING PRAYER

Father,
the strength of all who trust in you,
you made John Chrysostom
renowned for his eloquence
and heroic in his sufferings.
May we learn from his teaching
and gain courage from his patient endurance.
We ask this through our Lord Jesus Christ, your Son,
who lives and reigns with you and the Holy Spirit,
one God, for ever and ever. ℟. **Amen.**

Reading I (Eph 4, 1-7. 11-13), p. 1167, no. 8.
Responsorial Psalm (Ps 40), p. 236.
Gospel (Mk 4, 1-10. 13-20), p. 1186, no. 3.

PRAYER OVER THE GIFTS

Lord,
be pleased with this sacrifice we present
in honor of John Chrysostom,
for we gather to praise you as he taught us.
Grant this through Christ our Lord.
℟. **Amen.**   ➔ No. 21, p. 626 (Pref. P 37-42)

PRAYER AFTER COMMUNION

God of mercy,
may the sacrament we receive
in memory of John Chrysostom
make us strong in your love
and faithful in our witness to your truth.
We ask this in the name of Jesus the Lord.
℟. **Amen.**   ➔ No. 32, p. 650

Sept. 14 — TRIUMPH OF THE CROSS

Feast

At Jerusalem, already in the 5th century, on the day after the feast of the dedication of the basilica of the Resurrection (Sept. 13, 335) the wood of the Holy Cross was shown to the people. This rite gave rise to today's feast, celebrated with great solemnity in all the Eastern Rites and accepted at Rome in the 7th century.

ENTRANCE ANT.   See Gal 6, 14

We should glory in the cross of our Lord Jesus Christ, for he is our salvation, our life and our resurrection; through him we are saved and made free.

➔ No. 2, p. 614

OPENING PRAYER

Let us pray

[that the death of Christ on the cross
    will bring us to the glory of the resurrection]

God our Father,
in obedience to you
your only Son accepted death on the cross
for the salvation of mankind.
We acknowledge the mystery of the cross on earth.
May we receive the gift of redemption in heaven.
We ask this through our Lord Jesus Christ, your Son,
who lives and reigns with you and the Holy Spirit,
one God, for ever and ever. ℟. **Amen.** ▾

When this feast occurs apart from Sunday, only one of the first two readings is read before the Gospel.

READING I   Nm 21, 4-9

To people who are discouraged and full of complaints, the Lord gives a sign. The bronze serpent on a pole, raised on high, is a healing force for all the afflicted who look upon it.

A reading from the book of Numbers

With their patience worn out by the journey, the people complained against God and Moses, "Why have you brought us up from Egypt to die in this desert, where there is no food or water? We are disgusted with this wretched food!"

In punishment the Lord sent among the people saraph serpents, which bit the people so that many of them died. Then the people came to Moses and said, "We have sinned in complaining against the Lord and you. Pray the Lord to take the serpents from us." So Moses prayed for the people, and the Lord said to Moses, "Make a saraph and mount it on a pole, and if anyone who has been bitten looks at it, he will recover." Moses accordingly made a bronze serpent and mounted it on a pole, and whenever anyone who had been bitten by a serpent looked at the bronze serpent, he recovered.—This is the Word of the Lord. ℟. **Thanks be to God.** ℣

Responsorial Psalm   Ps 78, 1-2. 34-35. 36-37. 38

℟. (7) **Do not forget the works of the Lord!**

Hearken, my people, to my teaching;
    incline your ears to the words of my mouth.
I will open my mouth in a parable,
    I will utter mysteries from of old. — ℟

While he slew them they sought him
    and inquired after God again,
Remembering that God was their rock
    and the Most High God, their redeemer. — ℟

But they flattered him with their mouths
    and lied to him with their tongues,
Though their hearts were not steadfast toward him,
    nor were they faithful to his covenant. — ℟

Yet he, being merciful, forgave their sin
    and destroyed them not;
Often he turned back his anger
    and let none of his wrath be roused. — ℟ ℣

READING II   Phil 2, 6-11

Jesus' emptying of himself to be born in the likeness of men reached its ultimate point in his death on the cross. Yet there at the depth of degradation began his rise to exaltation: Jesus Christ is Lord!

A reading from the letter of Paul to the
Philippians

Christ Jesus, though he was in the form of God,
    did not deem equality with God
    something to be grasped at.
Rather, he emptied himself
    and took the form of a slave,
    being born in the likeness of men.
He was known to be of human estate
    and it was thus that he humbled himself,
    obediently accepting even death,
    death on a cross!
Because of this,
    God highly exalted him
    and bestowed on him the name
    above every other name,
So that at Jesus' name
    every knee must bend
    in the heavens, on the earth,
    and under the earth,
    and every tongue proclaim
    to the glory of God the Father:
    JESUS CHRIST IS LORD!
This is the Word of the Lord. ℟. **Thanks be to God.** ℣

GOSPEL   Jn 3, 13-17
Alleluia

℟. **Alleluia.** We adore you, O Christ, and we praise
    you,
because by your cross you have redeemed the world.
    ℟. **Alleluia.**

Moses' lifting up of the serpent in the desert had the salutary effect
of healing. The lifting up of the Son of Man on the cross has the
saving effect of redemption, winning eternal life for all who believe.

℣. The Lord be with you. ℟. **And also with you.**
✠ A reading from the holy gospel according to John
℟. **Glory to you, Lord.**

Jesus said to Nicodemus:

"No one has gone up to heaven
except the One who came down from there—
the Son of Man [who is in heaven].
Just as Moses lifted up the serpent in the desert,
so must the Son of Man be lifted up,
that all who believe
may have eternal life in him.
Yes, God so loved the world
that he gave his only Son,
that whoever believes in him may not die
but may have eternal life.
God did not send the Son into the world
to condemn the world,
but that the world might be saved through him."

This is the gospel of the Lord. ℟. **Praise to you, Lord Jesus Christ.** ➜ No. 15, p. 623

PRAYER OVER THE GIFTS

Lord,
may this sacrifice once offered on the cross
to take away the sins of the world
now free us from our sins.
We ask this through Christ our Lord. ℟. **Amen.** ℣

PREFACE (P 46)

℣. The Lord be with you. ℟. **And also with you.**
℣. Lift up your hearts. ℟. **We lift them up to the Lord.** ℣. Let us give thanks to the Lord our God.
℟. **It is right to give him thanks and praise.**

(Pref. P 17, p. 662, may also be said)

Father, all-powerful and ever-living God,
we do well always and everywhere to give you thanks.
You decreed that man should be saved through the wood of the cross.
The tree of man's defeat became his tree of victory;
where life was lost, there life has been restored through Christ our Lord.

Through him the choirs of angels
and all the powers of heaven
praise and worship your glory.
May our voices blend with theirs
as we join in their unending hymn: ➔ No. 23, p. 627

COMMUNION ANT. Jn 12, 32

**When I am lifted up from the earth, I will draw all
men to myself, says the Lord.** ⍦

PRAYER AFTER COMMUNION

Lord Jesus Christ,
you are the holy bread of life.
Bring to the glory of the resurrection
the people you have redeemed by the wood of the
    cross.
We ask this through Christ our Lord.
℞. **Amen.** ➔ No. 32, p. 650

*Optional Solemn Blessings, p. 682, and Prayers over the
People, p. 689.*

Sept. 15 — OUR LADY OF SORROWS

Memorial

The Feast of Our Lady of Sorrows was originally granted to the Order of the Servants of Mary in 1667; it was
introduced into the Roman Calendar in 1814 and assigned to the third Sunday in September. In 1913 the
date of the feast was assigned to September 15.

ENTRANCE ANT. Lk 2, 34-35

**Simeon said to Mary: This child is destined to be a
sign which men will reject; he is set for the fall and
the rising of many in Israel; and your own soul a
sword shall pierce.** ➔ No. 2, p. 614

OPENING PRAYER

Father,
as your Son was raised on the cross,
his mother Mary stood by him, sharing his sufferings.

May your Church be united with Christ
in his suffering and death
and so come to share in his rising to new life,
where he lives and reigns with you and the Holy
    Spirit,
one God, for ever and ever. ℟. **Amen.** ℣

READING I   Heb 5, 7-9
Reverence was the reason why God heard the prayers of Christ in his
anguish. And obedience was what the Son learned through his suffering. In this he became perfect.

    A reading from the letter to the Hebrews
In the days when Christ was in the flesh, he offered
prayers and supplications with loud cries and tears
to God, who was able to save him from death, and
he was heard because of his reverence. Son though
he was, he learned obedience from what he suffered;
and when perfected, he became the source of eternal
salvation for all who obey him.—This is the Word
of the Lord. ℟. **Thanks be to God.** ℣

Responsorial Psalm   Ps 31, 2-3. 3-4. 5-6. 15-16. 20
℟. (17) **Save me, O Lord, in your steadfast love.**
In you, O Lord, I take refuge;
    let me never be put to shame.
In your justice rescue me,
    incline your ear to me,
    make haste to deliver me! — ℟

Be my rock of refuge,
    a stronghold to give me safety.
You are my rock and my fortress;
    for your name's sake you will lead and guide
    me. — ℟
You will free me from the snare they set for me,
    for you are my refuge.
Into your hands I commend my spirit;
    you will redeem me, O Lord, O faithful God. — ℟

But my trust is in you, O Lord;
   I say, "You are my God."
In your hands is my destiny; rescue me
  from the clutches of my enemies and my persecu-
    tors. — ℟

How great is the goodness, O Lord,
  which you have in store for those who fear you,
And which, toward those who take refuge in you,
  you show in the sight of men. — ℟ ℣

SEQUENCE (OPTIONAL) (Prose Text)

The sorrowful mother was standing in tears beside the cross on which her Son was hanging. Her soul was full of grief and anguish and sorrow, for the sword of prophecy pierced it.

How sad now and how unhappy at the fate of her only Son was that mother, once called blessed; how the faithful mother grieved and lamented as she saw her glorious Son so shamefully treated.

Who is there who would not weep, were he to see Christ's mother in such great suffering? Or who could help feeling sympathy with the mother, were he to think of her sorrowing with her Son?

Yet she actually saw Jesus in agony and broken by the scourging—and this because of the sins of her own people. She saw her dear Son all the time he was dying and abandoned until he yielded up his soul.

Come then, mother, from whom all love springs, make me understand the meaning of your sorrow that I may mourn with you. Make my heart burn with love of Christ, my God, that he may look on me with favor.

Holy mother, do this for me. Pierce my heart once and forever with the wounds of your crucified Son. Let me share with you the pain of your Son's wounds, for he thought it right to bear such sufferings for me.

Grant that my tears of love may mingle with yours

and that, as long as I live, I may feel the pains of my crucified Lord. To stand with you beside the cross and be your companion in grief is my own wish.

Virgin without equal among virgins, do not now turn down my request; grant that I may mourn with you. Grant that I carry about the dying state of Christ; grant that I be a sharer of his passion; grant that I relive his wounds.

Grant that I be wounded with his wounds; grant that I drink to my soul's content of the chalice of his cross and blood. Be a defense to me, virgin Mary, on the judgment day, and I will not burn and be consumed in the fires of hell.

When it is time, Lord Christ, for me to leave this world, give me through your mother's prayers the palm of victory. When my body is dead, grant that my soul be given the glory of paradise. Amen. (Alleluia.) ℣

OR   (Poetic Text)

At the cross her station keeping, * Stood the mournful Mother weeping, * Close to Jesus to the last. * Through her heart, his sorrow sharing, * All his bitter anguish bearing, * Now at length the sword had passed. * Oh, how sad and sore distressed * Was that Mother highly blessed * Of the sole begotten One! * Christ above in torment hangs, * She beneath beholds the pangs * Of her dying, glorious Son.

Is there one who would not weep, * 'Whelmed in miseries so deep, * Christ's dear Mother to behold? * Can the human heart refrain * From partaking in her pain, * In that mother's pain untold? * Bruised, derided, cursed, defiled, * She beheld her tender Child, * All with bloody scourges rent. * For the sins of his own nation * Saw him hang in desolation * Till his spirit forth he sent.

O sweet Mother! font of love, * Touch my spirit from above, * Make my heart with yours accord. *

Make me feel as you have felt; * **Make my soul to
glow and melt** * **With the love of Christ, my Lord.** *
Holy Mother, pierce me through, * **In my heart each
wound renew** * **Of my Savior crucified.** * **Let me
share with you his pain,** * **Who for all our sins was
slain.** * **Who for me in torments died.**

Let me mingle tears with you, * **Mourning him who
mourned for me,** * **All the days that I may live.** *
By the cross with you to stay, * **There with you to
weep and pray,** * **Is all I ask of you to give.** * **Virgin
of all virgins blest!** * **Listen to my fond request:** *
Let me share your grief divine. * **Let me to my latest
breath,** * **In my body bear the death** * **Of that dying
Son of yours.**

Wounded with his every wound, * **Steep my soul
till it has swooned** * **In his very blood away.** * **Be
to me, O Virgin, nigh,** * **Lest in flames I burn and
die,** * **In his awful judgment day.** * **Christ, when
you shall call me hence,** * **Be your Mother my defense,** * **Be your cross my victory.** * **While my body
here decays,** * **May my soul your goodness praise,** *
Safe in heaven eternally. * **Amen. (Alleluia.)** ℣

The Gospel is special in this Memorial.

GOSPEL   Jn 19, 25-27
Alleluia

℞. **Alleluia.** Happy are you, O Blessed Virgin Mary;
without dying you won the martyr's crown beside
the cross of the Lord. ℞. **Alleluia.**

The love Jesus shows even in his suffering provides care for his
sorrowful mother and his beloved disciple. They are with him till the
end; no sorrow can separate them from his love.

℣. The Lord be with you. ℞. **And also with you.**
✠ A reading from the holy gospel according to John
℞. **Glory to you, Lord.**

Near the cross of Jesus there stood his mother, his
mother's sister, Mary the wife of Clopas, and Mary

Magdalene. Seeing his mother there with the disciple whom he loved, Jesus said to his mother, "Woman, there is your son." In turn he said to the disciple, "There is your mother." From that hour onward, the disciple took her into his care.—This is the gospel of the Lord. ℟. **Praise to you, Lord Jesus Christ.**

➤ No. 15, p. 623

OR

GOSPEL   Lk 2, 33-35

Alleluia

℟. **Alleluia.** Happy are you, O Blessed Virgin Mary; without dying you won the martyr's crown beside the cross of the Lord. ℟. **Alleluia.**

Mary knows early in her motherhood that her Son is destined for great things. She also knows that she will suffer, but that through her suffering good will come to many.

℣. The Lord be with you. ℟. **And also with you.**
✠ A reading from the holy gospel according to Luke
℟. **Glory to you, Lord.**

Mary and Joseph were marveling at what was being said about Jesus. Simeon blessed them and said to Mary his mother: "This child is destined to be the downfall and the rise of many in Israel, a sign that will be opposed—and you yourself shall be pierced with a sword—so that the thoughts of many hearts may be laid bare."—This is the gospel of the Lord. ℟. **Praise to you, Lord Jesus Christ.** ➤ No. 15, p. 623

PRAYER OVER THE GIFTS

God of mercy,
receive the prayers and gifts we offer
in praise of your name
on this feast of the Virgin Mary.
While she stood beside the cross of Jesus
you gave her to us as our loving mother.
Grant this through Christ our Lord.
℟. **Amen.**   ➤ No. 21, p. 626 (Pref. P 56-57)

COMMUNION ANT. 1 Pt 4, 13

Be glad to share in the sufferings of Christ! When he comes in glory, you will be filled with joy. ℣

PRAYER AFTER COMMUNION

Lord,
hear the prayers
of those who receive the sacraments of eternal salvation.
As we honor the compassionate love of the Virgin Mary,
may we make up in our own lives
whatever is lacking in the sufferings of Christ
for the good of the Church.
We ask this in the name of Jesus the Lord.
℟. **Amen.** ➔ No. 32, p. 650

Sept. 16 — STS. CORNELIUS, Pope and Martyr AND CYPRIAN, Bishop and Martyr

Memorial

Pope Cornelius (251-253) and Cyprian, Archbishop of Carthage, worked together to maintain unity in the Church in a time of schism and apostasy. Cornelius died in exile at Centum-Cellae, near Rome, driven from his see in reprisal against the Christians, who were said to have provoked the gods to send the plague ravaging Rome. Cyprian was martyred in the presence of his flock in 258.

Common of Martyrs, p. 1049; or Common of Pastors: for Bishops, p. 1069.

OPENING PRAYER

God our Father,
in Saints Cornelius and Cyprian
you have given your people an inspiring example
of dedication to the pastoral ministry
and constant witness to Christ in their suffering.
May their prayers and faith give us courage
to work for the unity of your Church.

Grant this through our Lord Jesus Christ, your Son,
who lives and reigns with you and the Holy Spirit,
one God, for ever and ever. ℟. **Amen.**

Reading I (2 Cor 4, 7-15), p. 1147, no. 3.
Responsorial Psalm (Ps 126), p. 1145, no. 4.
Gospel (Jn 17, 11-19), p. 1153, no. 7.

PRAYER OVER THE GIFTS

Lord,
accept the gifts of your people
as we honor the suffering and death
of Saints Cornelius and Cyprian.
The eucharist gave them courage
to offer their lives for Christ.
May it keep us faithful in all our trials.
We ask this through Christ our Lord.
℟. **Amen.**   ➤ No. 21, p. 626 (Pref. P 37-42)

PRAYER AFTER COMMUNION

Lord,
by the example of your martyrs Cornelius and
  Cyprian
and by the sacrament we have received,
make us strong in the Spirit
so that we may offer faithful witness
to the truth of your gospel.
We ask this in the name of Jesus the Lord.
℟. **Amen.**   ➤ No. 32, p. 650

Sept. 17 — ST. ROBERT BELLARMINE,
Bishop and Doctor

Optional Memorial

St. Robert Bellarmine was born at Montepulciano, Italy,
on October 4, 1542. He joined the Society of Jesus, and
was later made Cardinal and Archbishop of Capua. He
was famous throughout Europe as a theologian and as
a strenuous defender of the faith. His numerous writings
include works of devotion and instruction, as well as
of controversy. He died in 1621.

Common of Pastors: for Bishops, p. 1069; *or Common of Doctors of the Church, p.* 1082.

OPENING PRAYER

God our Father,
you gave Robert Bellarmine wisdom and goodness
to defend the faith of your Church.
By his prayers
may we always rejoice in the profession of our faith.
We ask this through our Lord Jesus Christ, your Son,
who lives and reigns with you and the Holy Spirit,
one God, for ever and ever. ℞. **Amen.**

Reading I (Wis 7, 7-10. 15-16), p. 1177, no. 2.
Responsorial Psalm (Ps 19), p. 1180, no. 1.
Gospel (Mk 4, 1-10. 13-20), p. 1186, no. 3.

Sept. 19 — ST. JANUARIUS, Bishop and Martyr

Optional Memorial

St. Januarius, Bishop of Benevento, was beheaded during the reign of Diocletian. He is the patron of Naples where the liquefaction of his blood takes place annually when it is placed near the head of the holy martyr.

Common of Martyrs, p. 1056; *or Common of Pastors: for Bishops, p.* 1069.

OPENING PRAYER

God our Father,
enable us who honor the memory of St. Januarius
to share with him the joy of eternal life.
Grant this through our Lord Jesus Christ, your Son,
who lives and reigns with you and the Holy Spirit,
one God, for ever and ever. ℞. **Amen.**

Reading I (Heb 10, 32-36), p. 1148, no. 6.
Responsorial Psalm (Ps 126), p. 1145, no. 4.
Gospel (Mt 12, 24-26), p. 1152, no. 5.

Sept. 21 — ST. MATTHEW, Apostle and Evangelist

Feast

St. Matthew, one of the twelve apostles, is the author of the first gospel. When our Lord passed by the toll station of Matthew, the Publican, he merely said, "Follow me," and from that moment Matthew became a faithful disciple of Jesus. Afer the ascension of our Lord, Matthew preached to pagan nations. He was martyred (possibly in Persia). His body reposes in the Cathedral of Salerno, Italy.

ENTRANCE ANT.   Mt 28, 19-20

Go and preach to all nations: baptize them and teach them to observe all that I have commanded you, says the Lord.   ➔ No. 2, p. 614

OPENING PRAYER

God of mercy,
you chose a tax collector, St. Matthew,
to share the dignity of the apostles.
By his example and prayers
help us to follow Christ
and remain faithful in your service.
We ask this through our Lord Jesus Christ, your Son,
who lives and reigns with you and the Holy Spirit,
one God, for ever and ever. ℟. **Amen.** ℣

READING I   Eph 4, 1-7. 11-13

God has called his followers to many different roles—each man has his own gifts. But all of these are to be exercised for the common good, to build up the body of Christ into perfect and lasting unity.

A reading from the letter of Paul to the Ephesians

I plead with you, as a prisoner for the Lord, to live a life worthy of the calling you have received, with perfect humility, meekness, and patience, bearing with one another lovingly. Make every effort to preserve the unity which has the Spirit as its origin and peace as its binding force. There is but one body and one Spirit, just as there is but one hope given all of you by your call. There is one Lord, one faith, one baptism; one God and Father of all, who is over all, and works through all, and is in all.

Each of us has received God's favor in the measure in which Christ bestows it.

It is he who gave apostles, prophets, evangelists, pastors, and teachers in roles of service for the faithful to build up the body of Christ, till we become one in faith and in the knowledge of God's Son, and form that perfect man who is Christ come to full stature.—This is the Word of the Lord. ℟. **Thanks be to God.** ℣

Responsorial Psalm Ps 19, 2-3. 4-5

℟. (5) **Their message goes out through all the earth.**

The heavens declare the glory of God,
 and the firmament proclaims his handiwork. — ℟
Day pours out the word to day,
 and night to night imparts knowledge. — ℟
Not a word nor a discourse
 whose voice is not heard;
Through all the earth their voice resounds,
 and to the ends of the world, their message. — ℟ ℣

GOSPEL Mt 9, 9-13

Alleluia

℟. **Alleluia.** We praise you, God; we acknowledge you as Lord;
your glorious band of apostles extols you. ℟. **Alleluia.**

Jesus calls Matthew to be a disciple even though Matthew is a member of the rejected group of tax collectors. Jesus has come to save those who need it most, and the willingness of Matthew's response is answer enough to the selfrighteousness of those who criticize.

℣. The Lord be with you. ℟. **And also with you.**
✠ A reading from the holy gospel according to Matthew. ℟. **Glory to you, Lord.**

As Jesus moved on, he saw a man named Matthew at his post where taxes were collected. He said to him, "Follow me." Matthew got up and followed him. Now it happened that, while Jesus was at table in Matthew's house, many tax collectors and those known as sinners came to join Jesus and his disciples at dinner. The Pharisees saw that and complained to his disciples, "What reason can the Teacher have for eating with tax collectors and those who disregard the law?" Overhearing the remark, he said: "People who are in good health do not need a doctor; sick people do. Go and learn the meaning of the words, 'It is mercy I desire and not sacrifice.' I have come to call, not the self-righteous, but sinners."—This is the gospel of the Lord. ℟. **Praise to you, Lord Jesus Christ.**   ➤ No. 15, p. 623

PRAYER OVER THE GIFTS

Lord,
accept the prayers and gifts we present
on this feast of St. Matthew.
Continue to guide us in your love
as you nourished the faith of your Church
by the preaching of the apostles.
We ask this in the name of Jesus the Lord.
℟. **Amen.**   ➤ No. 21, p. 626 (Pref. P 64-65)

COMMUNION ANT.   Mt 9, 13

I did not come to call the virtuous, but sinners, says the Lord. ℣

PRAYER AFTER COMMUNION

Father,
in this eucharist we have shared the joy of salvation
which St. Matthew knew when he welcomed your
      Son.
May this food renew us in Christ,
who came to call not the just
but sinners to salvation in his kingdom
where he is Lord for ever and ever.
℟. **Amen.**   ➤ No. 32, p. 650

Sept. 26 — STS. COSMAS AND DAMIAN, Martyrs

Optional Memorial

Sts. Cosmas and Damian, two brother physicians, cured many of the faithful who were gravely ill, more by faith in Jesus Christ than by their own natural powers. They suffered martyrdom during the reign of Diocletian about the year 283.

Common of Martyrs, p. 1049.

OPENING PRAYER

Lord,
we honor the memory of Saints Cosmas and Damian.
Accept our grateful praise
for raising them to eternal glory
and for giving us your fatherly care.
We ask this through our Lord Jesus Christ, your Son,
who lives and reigns with you and the Holy Spirit,
one God, for ever and ever. ℟. **Amen.**

Reading I (Wis 3, 1-9), p. 1140, no. 5.
Responsorial Psalm (Ps 126), p. 1145, no. 4.
Gospel (Mt 10, 28-33), p. 1151, no. 2.

PRAYER OVER THE GIFTS

Lord,
we who celebrate the death of your holy martyrs
offer you the sacrifice
which gives all martyrdom its meaning.
Be pleased with our praise.
We ask this through Christ our Lord.
℟. **Amen.**   ➔ No. 21, p. 626 (Pref. P 37-42)

PRAYER AFTER COMMUNION

Lord,
keep your gift ever strong within us.
May the eucharist we receive
in memory of Saints Cosmas and Damian
bring us salvation and peace.
We ask this in the name of Jesus the Lord.
℟. **Amen.**   ➔ No. 32, p. 650

Sept. 27 — ST. VINCENT DE PAUL, Priest

Memorial

Born near Dax, France, St. Vincent, together with Louise de Marillac, founded the Congregation of the Daughters of Charity, and instituted the Congregation of Priests of the Mission, or Lazarists. Leo XIII proclaimed him the special Patron of works of charity. Though honored by the great ones of the world, he remained throughout his life deeply rooted in humility. He died at Paris in 1660.

ENTRANCE ANT.
Lk 4, 18

The Spirit of God is upon me; he has anointed me. He sent me to bring good news to the poor, and to heal the broken-hearted. ➤ No. 2, p. 614

OPENING PRAYER

God our Father,
you gave Vincent de Paul
the courage and holiness of an apostle
for the well-being of the poor
and the formation of the clergy.
Help us to be zealous in continuing his work.
Grant this through our Lord Jesus Christ, your Son,
who lives and reigns with you and the Holy Spirit,
one God, for ever and ever. ℟. **Amen.**

Readings and Intervenient Chants from the Common of Pastors: for Missionaries, p. 1154, or the Common of Holy Men and Women: for Those Who Work for the Underprivileged, p. 1195.

Reading I (1 Cor 1, 26-31), p. 1211, no. 2.
Responsorial Psalm (Ps 112), p. 1209, no. 6
Gospel (Mt 23, 8-12), p. 1171, no. 2.

PRAYER OVER THE GIFTS

Lord,
you helped St. Vincent
to imitate the love he celebrated in these mysteries.
By the power of this sacrifice
may we also become an acceptable gift to you.

We ask this in the name of Jesus the Lord.
℟. **Amen.**   ➔ No 21, p. 626 (Pref. P 37-42)

COMMUNION ANT.   Ps 107, 8-9
**Give praise to the Lord for his kindness, for his
wonderful deeds toward men. He has filled the hungry with good things, he has satisfied the thirsty.** ℣

PRAYER AFTER COMMUNION
Lord,
hear the prayers
of those you have renewed with your sacraments
    from heaven.
May the example and prayers of St. Vincent
help us to imitate your Son
in preaching the good news to the poor.
We ask this in the name of Jesus the Lord.
℟. **Amen.**   ➔ No. 32, p. 650

Sept. 28 — ST. WENCESLAUS, Martyr

Optional Memorial

St. Wenceslaus was Duke of Bohemia during the conversion of the country to Christianity. He suffered
martyrdom at the hands of his own brother, Boleslas,
in 938.

Common of Martyrs, p. 1056.

OPENING PRAYER
Lord,
you taught your martyr Wenceslaus
to prefer the kingdom of heaven
to all that the earth has to offer.
May his prayers free us from our self-seeking
and help us to serve you with all our hearts.
We ask this through our Lord Jesus Christ, your Son,
who lives and reigns with you and the Holy Spirit,
one God, for ever and ever. ℟. **Amen.**

Reading I (1 Pt 3, 14-17), p. 1149, no. 8.
Responsorial Psalm (Ps 126), p. 1145, no. 4.
Gospel (Mt 10, 34-49), p. 1152, no. 3.

Sept. 29 — STS. MICHAEL, GABRIEL AND RAPHAEL,
Archangels

Feast

On September 29 the *Hieronymian Martyrology* records the Dedication of the basilica of St. Michael on the Via Salaria. Mention of this dedication has now been suppressed and to the name of St. Michael have been added the names of St. Gabriel and St. Raphael, whose feasts since 1921 had been celebrated on March 24 and October 24 respectively.

ENTRANCE ANT.   Ps 103, 20

Bless the Lord, all you his angels, mighty in power, you obey his word and heed the sound of his voice.

➔ No. 2, p. 614

OPENING PRAYER

God our Father,
in a wonderful way you guide the work of angels
    and men.
May those who serve you constantly in heaven
keep our lives safe from all harm on earth.
Grant this through our Lord Jesus Christ, your Son,
who lives and reigns with you and the Holy Spirit,
one God, for ever and ever. ℟. **Amen.** ℣

READING I   Dn 7, 9-10. 13-14

Daniel's vision of the Ancient One includes thousands, presumably angels, who are waiting on him. Into their midst comes the glorious son of man, receiving power and dominion from all.

A reading from the book of the prophet Daniel

As Daniel watched:
Thrones were set up
    and the Ancient One took his throne.
His clothing was snow bright,
    and the hair on his head as white as wool;
His throne was flames of fire,
    with wheels of burning fire.
A surging stream of fire
    flowed out from where he sat;

Thousands upon thousands were ministering to him,
 and myriads upon myriads attended him.

The court was convened, and the books were
opened. As the visions during the night continued,
I saw

One like a son of man coming,
 on the clouds of heaven;

When he reached the Ancient One
 and was presented before him,

He received dominion, glory, and kingship;
 nations and peoples of every language serve him.

His dominion is an everlasting dominion
 that shall not be taken away,
 his kingship shall not be destroyed.

This is the Word of the Lord. ℞. **Thanks be to God.** ℣

OR

READING I   Rv 12, 7-12

*The archetypal war between good and evil breaks out between Michael
and the dragon. The powers of good prevail, and the rule of the Lamb
is established—indeed a cause for rejoicing.*

A reading from the book of Revelation

Then war broke out in heaven; Michael and his
angels battled against the dragon. Although the
dragon and his angels fought back, they were overpowered and lost their place in heaven. The huge
dragon, the ancient serpent known as the devil or
Satan, the seducer of the whole world, was driven
out; he was hurled down to earth and his minions
with him.

 Then I heard a loud voice in heaven say:

 "Now have salvation and power come,
 the reign of our God and the authority of his
 Anointed One.

For the accuser of our brothers is cast out,
 who night and day accused them before our
 God.

They defeated him by the blood of the Lamb
and by the word of their testimony;
love for life did not deter them from death.
So rejoice, you heavens,
and you that dwell therein!"

This is the Word of the Lord. ℟. **Thanks be to God.** ♥

Responsorial Psalm   Ps 138, 1-2. 2-3. 4-5

℟. (1) **In the sight of the angels**
I will sing your praises, Lord.

I will give thanks to you, O Lord, with all my heart,
[for you have heard the words of my mouth;]
in the presence of the angels I will sing your
praise;
I will worship at your holy temple
and give thanks to your name, — ℟

Because of your kindness and your truth;
for you have made great above all things
your name and your promise.
When I called, you answered me;
you built up strength within me. — ℟

All the kings of the earth shall give thanks to you,
O Lord,
when they hear the words of your mouth;
And they shall sing of the ways of the Lord:
"Great is the glory of the Lord." — ℟ ♥

GOSPEL   Jn 1, 47-51

Alleluia (Ps 103, 21)

℟. **Alleluia.** Bless the Lord, all you his angels,
his ministers who do his will. ℟. **Alleluia.**

A small sign is sufficient for Nathanael to recognize Jesus as the Son
of God, but Jesus has promised greater things to come. He makes
reference to Daniel's vision of the Son of Man surrounded by angels
and assures that such is to come.

℣. The Lord be with you. ℟. **And also with you.**
✠ A reading from the holy gospel according to John
℟. **Glory to you, Lord.**

When Jesus saw Nathanael coming toward him, he remarked: "This man is a real Israelite. There is no guile in him." "How do you know me?" Nathanael asked him. "Before Philip called you," Jesus answered, "I saw you under the fig tree." "Rabbi," said Nathanael, "you are the Son of God; you are the king of Israel." Jesus responded: "Do you believe just because I told you I saw you under the fig tree? You will see much greater things than that."

He went on to tell them, "I solemnly assure you, you shall see the sky opened and the angels of God ascending and descending on the Son of Man."— This is the gospel of the Lord. ℟. **Praise to you, Lord Jesus Christ.** ➔ No. 15, p. 623

PRAYER OVER THE GIFTS

Lord,
by the ministry of your angels
let our sacrifice of praise come before you.
May it be pleasing to you and helpful to our own
    salvation.
We ask this through Christ our Lord.
℟. **Amen.** ➔ No. 21, p. 626 (Pref. P 60)

COMMUNION ANT. Ps 138, 1

In the sight of the angels I will sing your praises, my God. ℣

PRAYER AFTER COMMUNION

Lord,
hear the prayers of those you renew with the bread
    of life.
Made strong by the courage it gives,
and under the watchful care of the angels,
may we advance along the way of salvation.
We ask this in the name of Jesus the Lord.
℟. **Amen.** ➔ No. 32, p. 650

Sept. 30 — ST. JEROME, Priest and Doctor
Memorial

Father and Doctor of the Latin Church, St. Jerome (about 347-419) is "the man of the Bible." A translator and exegete concerned with the "Hebrew truth," he understood better than his predecessors the importance of the literal sense which he never disassociated from its prolongation or spiritual sense. Pope Damasus, whose secretary he was, commissioned him to revise the Latin text of the Bible. His translation later received the name *Vulgate*. After numerous journeys and a host of activities, the impetuous Jerome whose disputes have remained famous settled for the last 34 years of his life in the Holy Land.

ENTRANCE ANT.   Jos 1, 8

The book of the law must be ever on your lips; reflect on it night and day. Observe and do all that it commands: then you will direct your life with understanding.   ➔ No. 2, p. 614

OPENING PRAYER

Father,
you gave St. Jerome delight
in his study of holy scripture.
May your people find in your word
the food of salvation and the fountain of life.
We ask this through our Lord Jesus Christ, your Son,
who lives and reigns with you and the Holy Spirit,
one God, for ever and ever. ℞. **Amen.**

Readings and Intervenient Chants from the Common of Pastors, p. 1154, or the Common of Doctors of the Church, p. 1177.

READING I   2 Tm 3, 14-17

Paul reminds Timothy to have faith in his teachers. He learned the Scriptures, and they are the inspired word of God.

A reading from the second letter of Paul to Timothy

You, for your part, must remain faithful to what you have learned and believed because you know who

your teachers were. Likewise, from your infancy
you have known the sacred Scriptures, the source
of the wisdom which through faith in Jesus Christ
leads to salvation. All Scripture is inspired of God
and is useful for teaching—for reproof, correction,
and training in holiness so that the man of God may
be fully competent and equipped for every kind of
good work.—This is the Word of the Lord. ℟. **Thanks
be to God.**

Responsorial Psalm (Ps 119), p. 1181, no. 3.
Gospel (Mt 23, 8-12), p. 1186, no. 2.

PRAYER OVER THE GIFTS

Lord,
help us to follow the example of St. Jerome.
In reflecting on your word
may we better prepare ourselves
to offer you this sacrifice of salvation.
We ask this in the name of Jesus the Lord.
℟. **Amen.**   ➔ No 21, p. 626 (Pref. P 37-42)

COMMUNION ANT.   Jer 15, 16

**When I discovered your teaching, I devoured it. Your
words brought me joy and gladness; you have called
me your own, O Lord my God.** ⩣

PRAYER AFTER COMMUNION

Lord,
let this holy eucharist we receive
on the feast of St. Jerome
stir up the hearts of all who believe in you.
By studying your sacred teachings,
may we understand the gospel we follow
and come to eternal life.
Grant this through Christ our Lord.
℟. **Amen.**   ➔ No. 32, p. 650

— OCTOBER —

Oct. 1 — ST. THERESA OF THE CHILD JESUS, Virgin
Memorial

Born in Alencon, Normandy, in 1873, Marie Frances Theresa Martin entered the Carmel of Lisieux at the age of fifteen. She died in the odor of sanctity, Sept. 30, 1897. The rapid growth of devotion to this Saint is one of the greatest phenomena of contemporary religious history. Pope Pius XI canonized her on May 17, 1925.

ENTRANCE ANT. See Dt 32, 10-12

The Lord nurtured and taught her; he guarded her as the apple of his eye. As the eagle spreads its wings to carry its young, he bore her on his shoulders. The Lord alone was her leader.   ➔ No. 2, p. 614

OPENING PRAYER

God our Father,
you have promised your kingdom
to those who are willing to become like little children.
Help us to follow the way of St. Theresa with confidence
so that by her prayers
we may come to know your eternal glory.
Grant this through our Lord Jesus Christ, your Son,
who lives and reigns with you and the Holy Spirit,
one God, for ever and ever. ℟. **Amen.**

Readings and Intervenient Chants from the Common of Virgins, p. 1188, or the Common of Holy Men and Women: for Religious, p. 1195.

READING I Is 66, 10-14

The power of the Lord is manifest to his servants. They are to rejoice and exalt in the fulfillment that he gives them. He will give them wealth and comfort.

A reading from the book of the prophet Isaiah

Rejoice with Jerusalem and be glad because of her,
    all you who love her;
Exult, exult with her,

all you who were mourning over her!
Oh, that you may suck fully
  of the milk of her comfort,
That you may nurse with delight
  at her abundant breasts!
    For thus says the Lord:
Lo, I will spread prosperity over her like a river,
  and the wealth of the nations like an overflowing
    torrent.
As nurslings, you shall be carried in her arms,
  and fondled in her lap;
As a mother comforts her son,
  so will I comfort you;
    in Jerusalem you shall find your comfort.
When you see this, your heart shall rejoice,
  and your bodies flourish like the grass;
The Lord's power shall be known to his servants.
This is the Word of the Lord. ℟. **Thanks be to God.**

Responsorial Psalm (Ps 131), p. 1210, no. 8.

GOSPEL   Mt 18, 1-4

Alleluia (Mt 11, 25)

℟. **Alleluia.** Blessed are you, Father, Lord of heaven
  and earth;
you have revealed to little ones the mysteries of
  the kingdom. ℟. **Alleluia.**

Jesus teaches humility. He says that to enter heaven one must
become like a little child. The lowly are to become great.

℣. The Lord be with you. ℟. **And also with you.**
✠ A reading from the holy gospel according to Matthew. ℟. **Glory to you, Lord.**

The disciples came up to Jesus with the question,
"Who is of greatest importance in the kingdom of
God?" He called a little child over and stood him in
their midst and said: "I assure you, unless you
change and become like little children, you will not
enter the kingdom of God. Whoever makes himself
lowly, becoming like this child, is of greatest im-

portance in that heavenly reign."—This is the gospel of the Lord. ℞. **Praise to you, Lord Jesus Christ.**

➙ No. 15, p. 623

PRAYER OVER THE GIFTS

Lord,
we praise the wonder of your grace in St. Theresa.
As you were pleased with the witness she offered,
be pleased also to accept this service of ours.
We ask this through Christ our Lord.
℞. **Amen.** ➙ No 21, p. 626 (Pref. P 37-42)

COMMUNION ANT. Mt 18, 3

Unless you change and become like little children, says the Lord, you shall not enter the kingdom of heaven. ℣

PRAYER AFTER COMMUNION

Lord,
by the power of your love
St. Theresa offered herself completely to you
and prayed for the salvation of all mankind.
May the sacraments we have received fill us with love
and bring us forgiveness.
We ask this in the name of Jesus the Lord.
℞. **Amen.** ➙ No. 32, p. 650

Oct. 2 — GUARDIAN ANGELS *Memorial*

This feast, kept in Spain since the 16th century, was extended to the whole Church by Paul V in 1608 and assigned by Clement X in 1670 to the first free day after the feast of St. Michael, namely October 2. It is generally thought that in addition to each person having his own guardian angel, kingdoms, provinces, families, dioceses, churches, and religious communities also have one. They are God's messengers whose mission is to serve the future heirs of salvation.

ENTRANCE ANT. Dn 3, 58

Bless the Lord, all you angels of the Lord. Sing his glory and praise for ever. ➙ No. 2, p. 614

OPENING PRAYER

God our Father,
in your loving providence
you send your holy angels to watch over us.
Hear our prayers,
defend us always by their protection
and let us share your life with them for ever.
We ask this through our Lord Jesus Christ, your Son,
who lives and reigns with you and the Holy Spirit,
one God, for ever and ever. ℟. **Amen.** ✝

READING I   Ex 23, 20-23

The Lord promises the guiding force of his angel. He is to be trusted,
and enemies will be conquered.

A reading from the book of Exodus

The Lord said: "See, I am sending an angel before
you, to guard you on the way and bring you to the
place I have prepared. Be attentive to him and heed
his voice. Do not rebel against him, for he will not
forgive your sin. My authority resides in him. If you
heed his voice and carry out all I tell you, I will be
an enemy to your enemies and a foe to your foes.

"My angel will go before you and bring you to
the Amorites, Hittites, Perizzites, Canaanites, Hivites and Jebusites; and I will wipe them out."—This
is the Word of the Lord. ℟. **Thanks be to God.** ✝

Responsorial Psalm   Ps 91, 1-2. 3-4. 5-6. 10-11

℟. (11) **He has put his angels in charge of you,**
    to guard you in all your ways.

You who dwell in the shelter of the Most High,
    who abide in the shadow of the Almighty,
Say to the Lord, "My refuge and my fortress,
    my God, in whom I trust. — ℟

For he will rescue you from the snare of the fowler,
    from the destroying pestilence.
With his pinions he will cover you,
    and under his wings you shall take refuge. — ℟

His faithfulness is a buckler and a shield.
>You shall not fear the terror of the night
>nor the arrow that flies by day;
Not the pestilence that roams in darkness
>nor the devastating plague at noon. — ℟

No evil shall befall you,
>nor shall affliction come near your tent,
For to his angels he has given command about you,
>that they guard you in all your ways. — ℟ ❖

The Gospel is special in this Memorial.

GOSPEL   Mt 18, 1-5. 10

Alleluia (Ps 103, 21)

℟. **Alleluia.** Bless the Lord, all you his angels,
his ministers who do his will. ℟. **Alleluia.**

Only those like little children will enter heaven. He who is of least
account will be considered great.

℣. The Lord be with you. ℟. **And also with you.**
✠ A reading from the holy gospel according to Matthew. ℟. **Glory to you, Lord.**

The disciples came up to Jesus with the question,
"Who is of greatest importance in the kingdom of
God?" He called a little child over and stood him in
their midst and said: "I assure you, unless you change
and become like little children, you will not enter
the kingdom of God. Whoever makes himself lowly,
becoming like this child, is of greatest importance
in that heavenly reign. Whoever welcomes one such
child for my sake welcomes me.

"See that you never despise one of these little
ones. I assure you, their angels in heaven constantly
behold my heavenly Father's face."—This is the gospel of the Lord. ℟. **Praise to you, Lord Jesus Christ.**

➜ No. 15, p. 623

PRAYER OVER THE GIFTS

Father,
accept the gifts we bring you

in honor of your holy angels.
Under their constant care,
keep us free from danger in this life
and bring us to the joy of eternal life,
where Jesus is Lord for ever and ever.
℟. **Amen.**   → No. 21, p. 626 (Pref. P 60)

COMMUNION ANT.   Ps 138, 1

**In the sight of the angels I will sing your praises,
my God.** ℣

PRAYER AFTER COMMUNION

Lord,
you nourish us with the sacraments of eternal life.
By the ministry of your angels
lead us into the way of salvation and peace.
We ask this in the name of Jesus the Lord.
℟. **Amen.**   → No. 32, p. 650

Oct. 4 — ST. FRANCIS OF ASSISI

Memorial

Known as the Seraphic Saint, St. Francis was born at
Assisi, Italy, in 1182. St. Francis in his youth loved
pleasure and fine clothes. He renounced his wealth and
became the most extraordinary Saint of the Middle
Ages. He founded the Order of Friars Minor, the Second Order of the Poor Clares, and the Tertiaries or
Third Order of St. Francis. Our Lord favored him with
the Stigmata. He died in 1226.

ENTRANCE ANT.

**Francis, a man of God, left his home and gave away
his wealth to become poor and in need. But the Lord
cared for him.**   → No. 2, p. 614

OPENING PRAYER

Father,
you helped St. Francis to reflect the image of Christ.
through a life of poverty and humility.
May we follow your Son

by walking in the footsteps of Francis of Assisi,
and by imitating his joyful love.
Grant this through our Lord Jesus Christ, your Son,
who lives and reigns with you and the Holy Spirit,
one God, for ever and ever. ℟. **Amen.**

*Readings and Intervenient Chants from the Common
of Holy Men and Women: for Religious, p. 1195.*

READING I   Gal 6, 14-18
Paul boasts in the cross of Jesus. He bears the marks of Christ. In
this, he is created anew.

A reading from the letter of Paul to the Galatians
May I never boast of anything but the cross of our
Lord Jesus Christ! Through it, the world has been
crucified to me and I to the world. It means nothing
whether one is circumcised or not. All that matters
is that one is created anew. Peace and mercy on all
who follow this rule of life, and on the Israel of
God.

Henceforth, let no man trouble me, for I bear
the brand marks of Jesus in my body.

Brothers, may the favor of our Lord Jesus Christ
be with your spirit. Amen.—This is the Word of the
Lord. ℟. **Thanks be to God.**

Responsorial Psalm (Ps 16), p. 1207, no. 3.
Gospel (Mt 11, 25-30), p. 1221, no. 3.

PRAYER OVER THE GIFTS
Lord,
as we bring you our gifts,
prepare us to celebrate the mystery of the cross,
to which St. Francis adhered with such burning love.
We ask this in the name of Jesus the Lord.
℟. **Amen.**   ➜ No 21, p. 626 (Pref. P 37-42)

COMMUNION ANT.   Mt 5, 3
**Blessed are the poor in spirit; the kingdom of heaven
is theirs.** ℣

PRAYER AFTER COMMUNION

Lord,
by the holy eucharist we have celebrated,
help us to imitate
the apostolic love and zeal of St. Francis.
May we who receive your love
share it for the salvation of all mankind.
We ask this through Christ our Lord.
℞. **Amen.**   → No. 32, p. 650

Oct. 6 — ST. BRUNO, Priest

Optional Memorial

St. Bruno was born in Cologne, Germany. With six of
his friends he retired to one of the desert hills of Dau-
phiny, and there formed the nucleus of the Order of the
Carthusians. He died in 1101.

*Common of Pastors, p. 1071; or Common of Holy Men
and Women: for Religious, p. 1097.*

OPENING PRAYER

Father,
you called St. Bruno to serve you in solitude.
In answer to his prayers
help us to remain faithful to you
amid the changes of this world.
We ask this through our Lord Jesus Christ, your Son,
who lives and reigns with you and the Holy Spirit,
one God, for ever and ever. ℞. **Amen.**

Reading I (Phil 3, 8-14), p. 1214, no. 9.
Responsorial Psalm (Ps 1), p. 1206, no. 1.
Gospel (Lk 9, 57-62), p. 1228, no. 15.

Oct. 7 — OUR LADY OF THE ROSARY

Memorial

The feast of Our Lady of the Rosary was instituted in
1573 as a special commemoration of the victory gained
at Lepanto, on Sunday, October 7, 1571, when the forces

of Islam which were threatening to invade Europe were
hurled back and broken—a favor attributed to the recitation of the Rosary. Prescribed by Gregory XIII for
certain churches, it was introduced into the Roman
Calendar by Clement XI in 1716 and assigned to the
first Sunday of October in thanksgiving for another
triumph over the same enemy in Hungary that year
by the Emperor Charles VI. Leo XIII increased its rank
to obtain our Lady's help amid the present trials of the
Church, and in 1913 it was assigned to October 7.

ENTRANCE ANT.   Lk 1, 28. 42

**Hail, Mary, full of grace, the Lord is with you; blessed
are you among women and blessed is the fruit of
your womb.**   ➔ No. 2, p. 614

OPENING PRAYER

Lord,
fill our hearts with your love,
and as you revealed to us by an angel
the coming of your Son as man,
so lead us through his suffering and death
to the glory of his resurrection,
who lives and reigns with you and the Holy Spirit,
one God, for ever and ever. ℟. **Amen.**

*Readings and Intervenient Chants from the Common
of the Blessed Virgin Mary, p. 1118.*

Reading I (Acts 1, 12-14), p. 1124, no. 1.
Responsorial Psalm (Lk 1), p. 1128, no. 5.
Gospel (Lk 1, 26-28), p. 1133, no. 3.

PRAYER OVER THE GIFTS

Lord,
may these gifts we offer in sacrifice transform our
    lives.
By celebrating the mysteries of your Son,
may we become worthy of the eternal life he prom-
    ises,
for he is Lord for ever and ever.
℟. **Amen.**   ➔ No. 21, p. 626 (Pref. P 56-57)

COMMUNION ANT.   Lk 1, 31

You shall conceive and bear a Son, and you shall call his name Jesus. ℣

PRAYER AFTER COMMUNION

Lord our God,
in this eucharist we have proclaimed
the death and resurrection of Christ.
Make us partners in his suffering
and lead us to share his happiness
and the glory of eternal life,
where he is Lord for ever and ever.
℟. **Amen.**   ➔ No. 32, p. 650

Oct. 9 — STS. DENIS, Bishop and Martyr
AND HIS COMPANIONS, Martyrs

Optional Memorial

St. Denis was the first Bishop of Paris, who together with his friends preached the gospel in what was then Gaul. He and his companions suffered martyrdom in the 3rd century.

Common of Martyrs, p. 1049.

OPENING PRAYER

Father,
you sent St. Denis and his companions
to preach your glory to the nations,
and you gave them the strength
to be steadfast in their sufferings for Christ.
Grant that we may learn from their example
to reject the power and wealth of this world
and to brave all earthly trials.
We ask this through our Lord Jesus Christ, your Son,
who lives and reigns with you and the Holy Spirit,
one God, for ever and ever. ℟. **Amen.**

Reading I (2 Cor 6, 4-10), p. 1147, no. 4.
Responsorial Psalm (Ps 126), p. 1145, no. 4.
Gospel (Mt 5, 13-16), p. 1220, no. 2.

The Same Day, Oct. 9
ST. JOHN LEONARDI, Priest

Optional Memorial

St. John Leonardi was a contemporary of St. Philip Neri and St. John Calasanctius. His whole life was devoted to the redemption of sinners and the restoration of Church discipline in Italy. He died in 1609.

Common of Pastors: for Missionaries, p. 1077; or Common of Holy Men and Women: for Those Who Work for the Underprivileged, p. 1099.

OPENING PRAYER

Father,
giver of all good things,
you proclaimed the good news to countless people
through the ministry of St. John Leonardi.
By the help of his prayers
may the true faith continue to grow.
Grant this through our Lord Jesus Christ, your Son,
who lives and reigns with you and the Holy Spirit,
one God, for ever and ever. ℟. **Amen.**

Reading I (2 Cor 4, 1-2. 5-7), p. 1166, no. 6.
Responsorial Psalm (Ps 96), p. 1162, no. 4.
Gospel (Lk 5, 1-11), p. 1173, no. 6.

Oct. 14 — ST. CALLISTUS I, Pope and Martyr

Optional Memorial

St. Callistus was born in Rome and succeeded St. Zephyrinus as Pope. He provided for the burial of the martyrs in the catacombs and instituted the Ember Day Fasts. He suffered martyrdom in 223 during the reign of Alexander Severus.

Common of Martyrs, p. 1056; or Common of Pastors: for Popes, p. 1066.

OPENING PRAYER

God of mercy,
hear the prayers of your people
that we may be helped by St. Callistus,

whose martyrdom we celebrate with joy.
We ask this through our Lord Jesus Christ, your Son,
who lives and reigns with you and the Holy Spirit,
one God, for ever and ever. ℞. **Amen.**

Reading I (1 Pt 5, 1-4), p. 1169, no. 13.
Responsorial Psalm (Ps 40), p. 236.
Gospel (Lk 22, 24-30), p. 1174, no. 8.

Oct. 15 — ST. TERESA OF AVILA, Virgin and Doctor

Memorial

St. Teresa was born at Avila, Spain, in 1515. At twenty
years of age she entered the Carmelite Order. She was
instrumental in reforming the rule of the Order. She
wrote many books on Mystical Theology considered by
Popes Gregory XV and Urban VII to be equal to those
of a Doctor of the Church. She died at the age of 67. In
1970 Pope Paul VI named her a Doctor of the Church.

ENTRANCE ANT.   Ps 42, 2-3

**Like a deer that longs for running streams, my soul
longs for you, my God. My soul is thirsting for the
living God.**   ➤ No. 2, p. 614

OPENING PRAYER

Father,
by your Spirit you raised up St. Teresa of Avila
to show your Church the way to perfection.
May her inspired teaching
awaken in us a longing for true holiness.
Grant this through our Lord Jesus Christ, your Son,
who lives and reigns with you and the Holy Spirit,
one God, for ever and ever. ℞. **Amen.**

*Readings and Intervenient Chants from the Common
of Virgins, p. 1188, or the Common of Doctors of the
Church, p. 1177.*

READING I   Rom 8, 22-27

All await and hope for redemption. Hope means awaiting what cannot
be seen. The Spirit makes intercession for the followers of Jesus as
God wills.

A reading from the letter of Paul to the Romans

We know that all creation groans and is in agony even until now. Not only that, but we ourselves, although we have the Spirit as first fruits, groan inwardly while we await the redemption of our bodies. In hope we were saved. But hope is not hope if its object is seen; how is it possible for one to hope for what he sees? And hoping for what we cannot see means awaiting it with patient endurance.

The Spirit too helps us in our weakness, for we do not know how to pray as we ought; but the Spirit himself makes intercession for us with groanings which cannot be expressed in speech. He who searches hearts knows what the Spirit means, for the Spirit intercedes for the saints as God himself wills.—This is the Word of the Lord. ℞. **Thanks be to God.**

Responsorial Psalm (Ps 19), p. 1180, no. 1.
Gospel (Jn 15, 1-8), p. 1231, no. 20.

PRAYER OVER THE GIFTS

King of heaven,
accept the gifts we bring in your praise,
as you were pleased with St. Teresa's offering
of her life in your service.
We ask this in the name of Jesus the Lord.
℞. **Amen.**   ➔ No 21, p. 626 (Pref. P 37-42)

COMMUNION ANT.   Ps 89, 2

For ever I will sing the goodness of the Lord; I will proclaim your faithfulness to all generations. ℣

PRAYER AFTER COMMUNION

Lord our God,
watch over the family you nourish
with the bread from heaven.
Help us to follow St. Teresa's example
and sing your merciful love for ever.
We ask this through Christ our Lord.
℞. **Amen.**   ➔ No. 32, p. 650

Oct. 16 — ST. HEDWIG, Religious

Optional Memorial

Having fulfilled all the duties of a wife and mother, St. Hedwig, Duchess of Poland, retired to a Cistercian convent after the death of her husband, where she died in 1243.

Common of Holy Men and Women: for Religious, p. 1097.

OPENING PRAYER

All-powerful God,
may the prayers of St. Hedwig bring us your help
and may her life of remarkable humility
be an example to us all.
We ask this through our Lord Jesus Christ, your Son,
who lives and reigns with you and the Holy Spirit,
one God, for ever and ever. ℟. **Amen.**

Reading I (Sir 26, 1-4. 13-16), p. 1201, no. 14.
Responsorial Psalm (Ps 128), p. 1209, no. 7.
Gospel (Mk 3, 31-35), p. 1226, no. 11.

The Same Day, Oct. 16
ST. MARGARET MARY ALACOQUE, Virgin

Optional Memorial

Born in the diocese of Autun, France, St. Margaret Mary Alacoque consecrated her heart, while yet a child, to the Most Sacred Heart of Jesus. As a Visitation Nun, this Saint was chosen by God to reveal to the Christian World the devotion to the Sacred Heart of Jesus in 1675. She, together with Father de la Colombiere, S.J., was the chief instrument in the institution of the Feast of the Sacred Heart. She died on October 17, 1690.

Common of Virgins, p. 1085; or Common of Holy Men and Women: for Religious, p. 1097.

OPENING PRAYER

Lord,
pour out on us the riches of the Spirit
which you bestowed on St. Margaret Mary.
May we come to know the love of Christ,
which surpasses all human understanding,
and be filled with the fullness of God.
Grant this through our Lord Jesus Christ, your Son,
who lives and reigns with you and the Holy Spirit,
one God, for ever and ever. ℟. **Amen.**

Reading I (Eph 3, 14-19), p. 1213, no. 7.
Responsorial Psalm (Ps 23), p. 1161, no. 2.
Gospel (Mt 11, 25-30), p. 1221, no. 3.

Oct. 17 — ST. IGNATIUS, Bishop and Martyr

Memorial

St. Ignatius second successor of St. Peter at Antioch,
was martyred about 107. "The whole system of Catholic
doctrine may be discovered at least in outline in . . .
his seven epistles" (Cardinal Newman). He was sent in
chains to Rome and being thrown to the beasts exclaimed, "May I become agreeable bread to the Lord."

ENTRANCE ANT.   Gal 2, 19-20

**With Christ I am nailed to the cross. I live now not
with my own life, but Christ lives within me. I live
by faith in the Son of God, who loved me and sacrificed himself for me.**   ➤ No. 2, p. 614

OPENING PRAYER

All-powerful and ever-living God,
you ennoble your Church
with the heroic witness of all
who give their lives for Christ.
Grant that the victory of St. Ignatius of Antioch
may bring us your constant help
as it brought him eternal glory.

We ask this through our Lord Jesus Christ, your Son,
who lives and reigns with you and the Holy Spirit,
one God, for ever and ever. ℟. **Amen.**

*Readings and Intervenient Chants from the Common
of Martyrs, p. 1138, or the Common of Pastors, p. 1154.*

Reading I (Phil 3, 17—4, 1), p. 1001.
Responsorial Psalm (Ps 34), p. 1144, no. 2.
Gospel (Jn 12, 24-26), p. 1152, no. 5.

PRAYER OVER THE GIFTS

Lord,
receive our offering
as you accepted St. Ignatius
when he offered himself to you as the wheat of
  Christ,
formed into pure bread by his death for Christ,
who lives and reigns for ever and ever.
℟. **Amen.**   ➤ No 21, p. 626 (Pref. P 37-42)

COMMUNION ANT.

**I am the wheat of Christ, ground by the teeth of
beasts to become pure bread.** ℣

PRAYER AFTER COMMUNION

Lord,
renew us by the bread of heaven
which we have received on the feast of St. Ignatius.
May it transform us into loyal and true Christians.
Grant this through Christ our Lord.
℟. **Amen.**   ➤ No. 32, p. 650

PROPER OF SAINTS CONTINUES ON p. 695
WITH OCTOBER 18

INTRODUCTION TO THE
ORDER OF MASS

by REV. JOHN C. KERSTEN, S.V.D.

1. CELEBRATIONS

A bicentennial of freedom and self-determination is a reason for celebration. A nation does not want to forget this great event of the past. Likewise, we annually celebrate Thanksgiving Day, Independence Day, Washington's and Lincoln's birthdays. These memorials foster our gratitude and our awareness as a nation under God.

The Jews celebrate their Exodus from bondage in Egypt, which is their birthday as a free nation, with the annual Passover. The remarkable thing is that they attribute their redemption expressly to the intervention of almighty God and celebrate it annually with a detailed ritual. Until the destruction of the Jewish temple in Jerusalem (70 A.D.) this ritual consisted of the Passover sacrifice (offering God a lamb as a symbol of appreciation) and a sacrificial repast (symbolizing both communion with God, to whom the victim was offered, and communion with fellow worshipers). Afterward the Jewish Passover became, what it still is, only a memorial meal.

Nevertheless, this celebration is not just a grateful remembrance of the past; rather past and present coincide. At the Passover, Jews identify themselves with those who actually did leave Egypt. As Jewish

595

tradition has it: "From generation to generation everyone must consider himself as having personally gone out of Egypt. Therefore we must thank him [God] and praise him who led our fathers and us through these wonderful things out of slavery to freedom" (Mishna Pes. 10, 5).

2.   THE CHRISTIAN PASSOVER

As a faithful Jew, Jesus celebrated the annual Passover. In the Gospels, we have detailed information about the last time he celebrated it with his disciples on the night before his death. This event is known as "The Last Supper." After the Passover lamb had been sacrificed to God in the temple, it was brought to the upper room where Jesus and his friends ate it as a sacrificial repast according to Jewish ritual.

At this Last Supper, Jesus did a remarkable thing. He gave this ancient sacrifice and sacred meal (the Jewish Passover) a new meaning. Referring to his cruel death on the cross, he said in other words: "From now on I am that Passover lamb, sacrificed to deliver you figuratively from the slavery in Egypt and actually from all evil. Do this as a memorial of me." In meditating on our Lord's death on the cross, the early Church saw Jesus as a Jewish high priest offering sacrifice to God. This sacrifice, however, was not a lamb; it was his own body and blood, shed to set us free from the bondage of evil (Heb 9, 10).

Following this trend of thought, we understand Paul when he says: "Christ, our Passover, has been sacrificed" (1 Cor 5, 7). Our Eucharistic celebration is a Jewish Passover with a new meaning. The Jews celebrate Passover as a memorial of their redemption from bondage in Egypt, brought about by God's mighty hand. We Christians celebrate the Eucharist as a memorial of our redemption from the slavery of evil, brought about by Christ's death on the cross.

3. HOW TO CELEBRATE

In celebrating the memorial of our redemption, the Eucharist [Mass], we do what our Lord has told us to do: "Do this as a remembrance of me" (Lk 22, 19). Moreover, we look to the early Church of Jerusalem, closest to the source of Christianity. In Acts we read: "The community of believers were of one heart and one mind" (Acts 4, 32). "They devoted themselves to the apostles' instruction and the communal life, to the breaking of the bread and the prayers" (Acts 2, 42). These early Christians were very much aware of our Lord's promise: "Where two or three are gathered in my name, there am I in their midst" (Mt 18, 20).

"In the celebration of Mass, which perpetuates the sacrifice of the cross, Christ is really present in the assembly itself, which is gathered in his name" (General Instruction of the Roman Missal, ch. II, no. 7). All Christians share in Christ's royal priesthood, which is a function of intercession for all fellowmen. Hence, the celebration of the Eucharist is the action of the whole Church. All should participate. However, through the sacrament of orders, some Christians are singled out to exercise a special ministry in this priestly people, whose "spiritual sacrifice to God is accomplished through the ministry of presbyters [priests], in union with the sacrifice of Christ, our one and only Mediator" (Ibid., no. 5).

In summary, "the celebration of Mass is the action of Christ and the people of God hierarchically [in graded order] assembled" (Ibid., ch. I, no. 1), of one heart and mind, each playing his role in the great memorial drama of our redemption, the Eucharist.

4. STRUCTURE

Mass is made up of the Liturgy of the Word (Bible readings and Homily) and the Liturgy of the Eucharist. There are also introductory rites, which prepare us for both the table of God's word and the table of Christ's body and blood, and a concluding rite which consists of a final blessing and dismissal. Assembled "in graded order," we listen to the prayers assigned to the priest, actively take part in the dialogues, sing wholeheartedly, meditatively apply God's word to our own life situation, make Christ's sacrifice, present in the signs of bread and wine, a token of our own self-surrender to God, and make Communion an intimate encounter with our Lord.

There is no time for idle dreaming. If properly understood, participating in the Eucharist is exciting —even without the usual trappings we associate with excitement, such as a swinging band! Music at Mass is meaningful only if it underlines and fosters activities of heart and mind.

5.   THE LANGUAGE OF SYMBOLS

Religious symbolism points to beautiful realities often more effectively than mere words can do. Entering the church, I make the sign of the cross with holy water. It reminds me of my baptism. Likewise, the sprinkling with holy water, which may replace the penitential rite, points to cleansing from sin. Genuflecting is a sign of respect for the Blessed Sacrament, kneeling is a symbol of humility, and standing in prayer expresses respect for Almighty God. (Do we not stand up to shake hands?)

Incense clouds may symbolize my prayers going up to God, and striking one's breast is a confession of sinfulness. The handshake of peace should be a genuine symbol of love and concern for all fellow members. As religious people, we should develop a feeling for symbolism and make it meaningful. Void symbolism is boring.

6. INTRODUCTORY RITES OF THE MASS

The introductory rites consist of songs and prayers which precede the Liturgy of the Word and the Liturgy of the Eucharist.

a) The **Entrance Antiphon** deepens the unity of the people and introduces us to the mystery of the season or feast.

b) Within the sanctuary there stands that which is the very heart of the church—the altar. Since we in the Catholic tradition give high preference to the Liturgy of the Eucharist, the altar is central, not the pulpit. Entering the sanctuary **the priest venerates the altar with a kiss.** The altar bears the gift which Christ will offer to the heavenly Father.

c) The **Penitential Rite** speaks for itself. We should worship with a clean heart. Notice that the "I confess" of the new rite mentions the much overlooked "in what I have failed to do." ("During this past week where have I failed to be the kind of person I should be in the eyes of my Maker?")

d) **Praise to Christ.** The "Lord, Have Mercy" (Kyrie) is an acclamation which praises the Lord and implores his mercy. The "Glory to God" (Gloria) is an ancient hymn in which the Church assembled in the Spirit praises and prays to the Father and the Lamb.

e) **Opening Prayer.** The Introductory Rites conclude with a prayer which expresses the theme of the celebration and addresses a petition in the people's name to God the Father through the mediation of Christ in the Holy Spirit. The people make the prayer their own and give their assent by the acclamation: Amen.

7. LITURGY OF THE WORD

a) First we listen to a reading from the Hebrew Bible, which we call the Old Testament. Since the

Church sees all the aspirations of the ancient Hebrews fulfilled in Christ, we must read the Old Testament in order to understand its Christian interpretation, which is the New Testament. The Hebrew Bible contains a wealth of God-inspired wisdom. We must especially bear in mind that the Bible never tells stories for a story's sake. In telling a story, the sacred writer wants to teach religious values. Hence, the reader should always try to find the point of the story, which is **God's word to us.**

As for the **Responsorial Psalm,** we should become acquainted with the way the Church re-interprets the Psalms and gives them a Christian meaning. Often the refrain indicates how we should adapt a particular psalm in its liturgical setting on Sunday.

b) The second reading is usually taken from **letters composed by the apostles.** As the early Jerusalem Church has done, we devote ourselves to the apostles' instruction. (See no. 3 above.) The Church is apostolic! Both the first and the second reading are usually done by lay members of the congregation.

c) The Liturgy of the Word culminates in **the reading of the Gospel,** which deals directly with God's manifestation in Jesus Christ. Candlelight (Christ is the light of the world!) and incense (sign of respect) can be used to help emphasize the importance of the Gospel reading. Christ is present and speaks to us.

d) As a rule, the **Homily** develops some point of the Bible readings. Indeed, the congregation may rightfully expect that the priest will be well acquainted with Biblical theology and prepare his sermons carefully. On the other hand, the congregation must be realistic. One cannot expect a spectacular performance every Sunday. Neither may we expect that the preacher will say only "nice things." Paul told the young bishop Timothy: "I charge you to preach the word [of God], to stay with this task whether convenient or inconvenient—teaching, reproving, appealing—constantly teaching and never losing patience" (2 Tm 4, 2). The priest has to do his duty and apply the Bible message to the life situation of the congregation.

e) The **Profession of Faith** is our assent to the word of God, which we have heard in the readings and Homily. And exercising our priestly function (see no. 3 above) **we make intercession** for all mankind by saying the petitions and/or underlining them by our response.

8. THE LITURGY OF THE EUCHARIST

At the Last Supper, Christ took bread, gave thanks and praise to the Father, broke it, and gave it to his disciples, saying: "Take this and eat it: this is my body." Then he took the cup, again gave thanks, and gave it to his disciples, saying: "Take this and drink from it: this is the cup of my blood. Do this in memory of me." (See no. 2, above.) Corresponding to these words and actions of our Lord, the Church has ararnged the celebration of the Eucharist as follows.

Preparation of the gifts. Bread, wine and water are brought to the sanctuary.

The Eucharistic prayer (which means "prayer of thanksgiving and sanctification"). It has a preface (introduction), followed by the preface acclamation, the "Holy, holy, . . ." by the congregation. In this framework of thanksgiving, the offerings of bread and wine become the body and blood of Christ and are offered to God in sacrifice.

Communion rite (a sign of the unity of the faithful). In communion all receive the body and blood of Christ as a sacrificial repast. (See nos. 1 and 2, above.)

PREPARATION OF THE GIFTS

Members of the congregation bring the gifts of bread and wine to the altar. We should pay attention to its symbolism. Bread and wine (in Oriental setting, daily food) stand for all of us, who want to offer ourselves as "an everlasting gift to God" (Euch. Pr. III). Other gifts (collection) are added. This money is used for the poor and the support of the church. All of this should be seen as a symbolical giving of self.

The presentation song, prayers, lifting up of the gifts, and incense, if used, underline the idea of self-giving. "Lord God, we ask you to receive us and be pleased with the sacrifice we offer you with humble and contrite hearts" (Prayer by priest). All of this symbolism has only so much meaning as **you** give to it by giving **yourself** to God. You can show this by a heartfelt Amen to the Prayer over the Gifts, which asks the Father's blessing.

EUCHARISTIC PRAYER

At a farewell party for a retiring employee most of the time is taken up by speaking words of thanks and appreciation for services rendered, and only at the end is a token of appreciation offered, a gift which signifies whatever has been said.

The Eucharistic Prayer should be considered in a similar setting. Most of it consists of words of praise and thanksgiving, and in that framework time and again we offer Almighty God a token of our gratitude, namely, the body and blood of Christ (Christ himself in the signs of bread and wine), offered in sacrifice on the altar of the cross "once for all" (Heb 10, 10).

The Roman Missal offers a choice of many Prefaces and four versions of the Eucharistic Prayer proper. All contain the following elements.

a) **Preface.** We should wholeheartedly join in the dialogue, in which we are invited to give thanks to God, and the acclamation, the "Holy, holy . . . ," said/sung in union with all the angels of heaven.

b) **Epiclesis** (Invocation). These are the prayers before the Consecration in which the priest and we with him invoke God's power and ask him that the gifts offered by men may be consecrated, that is, become the body and blood of Christ and source of salvation for those who partake. "[God] let your Spirit come upon these gifts to make them holy, so that they may become for us the body and blood of our Lord, Jesus Christ" (Euch. Pr. II).

c) **Narrative of the Institution and Consecration.** We celebrate the sacrifice which Jesus Christ instituted at the Last Supper when in the signs of bread and wine he offered his body and blood (himself), gave them to the apostles, and told them to do the same "in memory" of him.

d) **Anamnesis** (a calling to mind). Calling to mind our Lord's death, resurrection, and ascension, we offer God in thanksgiving "this holy and living sacrifice," the body and blood of Christ, and in and with him ourselves "as an everlasting gift" to the Almighty (Euch. Pr. III). (See also nos. 2 and 3, above.)

e) **Intercessions,** which we should make our own.

f) **Final Doxology** (hymn of praise), which we should confirm with our acclamation "Amen" (So be it!).

COMMUNION RITE

At a banquet we celebrate togetherness (communion) not only with the host and hostess but also with the fellow guests. Intending not to meet certain people could be a reason to decline an invitation.

The night before his death, our Lord ate the Passover lamb with his disciples as a sacrificial repast.

(See nos. 1 and 2, above.) Traditionally, eating from the lamb which had been offered to God symbolized communion with God and fellow worshipers. We should see "Holy Communion" in a similar vein. We eat "our Passover, which has been sacrificed" (1 Cor 5, 7, see no. 2, above), and should realize that by doing so we signify our oneness not only with God in Jesus Christ, but also with all who partake. This is clearly indicated by the preparatory rites which lead directly to it.

a) **The Lord's Prayer.** This is a petition both for daily food, which for Christians means also the Eucharistic bread, and for forgiveness from sin, "forgive us . . . as we forgive those who trespass against us." Without taking this prayer seriously, signifying communion with Christ and fellowmen would be a void symbolism.

b) **Rite of Peace.** Before we share the table of the Lord, we shake hands as a sign of love for one another. With the priest we ask for peace and unity in Christ's kingdom.

c) **Breaking of Bread.** In early Christianity the Eucharist (Mass) was known as "The Breaking of Bread" (See no. 3, above). Using a loaf of bread, its breaking was a necessity for distributing it, but simultaneously it was seen as a beautiful symbolism: All are one in partaking of the one loaf of bread, Jesus Christ (1 Cor 10, 17). For practical reasons we now use small altar breads and one large one, which is broken when the congregation prays/sings "The Lamb of God." Symbolism is still there. The priest shows the broken bread. Christ was "broken," sacrificed, as a spotless lamb to take away the sin of the world.

d) The **Communion Antiphon** expresses the spiritual union of all who partake in the Eucharistic banquet. Note that in Biblical language the words "flesh, body, blood" do not indicate the things as such but the whole person and the event which they signify, namely, Jesus Christ giving himself in his meritorious death, in which we share when we partake in the Eucharist.

e) **Silent Prayer.** If spontaneous silent prayer does not work too well, meditatively you could pray again the Responsorial Psalm to the first Bible reading or the Communion Psalm in your Missal, and take a thought that strikes you as a starting point for private prayer. Our personal prayer is summed up in a final prayer by the priest (Prayer after Communion). We make it our prayer by our acclamation, Amen—So be it!

9. CONCLUDING RITE

The presiding priest greets us, gives his blessing, and dismisses the congregation with the mission to love and serve the Lord. Partaking in the Eucharist means a renewed commitment to God and fellowmen. We have prayed: "[God] we offer you in thanksgiving this holy and living sacrifice. Look with favor on your Church's offering, and see the Victim [Christ] whose death has reconciled us to yourself. . . . May he [Christ] make us an everlasting gift to you" (Euch. Pr. III). We hope to make this commitment real during the week "strengthened by the bread of heaven." Not even caring enough to try to do so would make our partaking in the Eucharist a void and meaningless symbolism. Symbolize only reality!

COMMUNION PRAYERS

PRAYERS BEFORE HOLY COMMUNION

Act of Faith

Lord Jesus Christ, I firmly believe that you are present in this Blessed Sacrament as true God and true Man, with your Body and Blood, Soul and Divinity. My Redeemer and my Judge, I adore your Divine Majesty together with the angels and saints. I believe, O Lord; increase my faith.

Act of Hope

Good Jesus, in you alone I place all my hope. You are my salvation and my strength, the Source of all good. Through your mercy, through your Passion and Death, I hope to obtain the pardon of my sins, the grace of final perseverance and a happy eternity.

Act of Love

Jesus, my God, I love you with my whole heart and above all things, because you are the one supreme Good and an infinitely perfect Being. You have given your life for me, a poor sinner, and in your mercy you have even offered yourself as food for my soul.

My God, I love you. Inflame my heart so that I may love you more.

Act of Contrition

O my Savior, I am truly sorry for having offended you because you are infinitely good and sin displeases you. I detest all the sins of my life and I desire to atone for them. Through the merits of your Precious Blood, wash from my soul all stain of sin, so that, cleansed in body and soul, I may worthily approach the Most Holy Sacrament of the Altar.

Act of Desire

Jesus, my God and my all, my soul longs for you. My heart yearns to receive you in Holy Communion.

Come, Bread of heaven and Food of angels, to nourish my soul and to rejoice my heart. Come, most lovable Friend of my soul, to inflame me with such love that I may never again be separated from you.

Prayer of St. Thomas Aquinas

Almighty and ever-living God,
I approach the sacrament of your only-begotten Son,
    our Lord Jesus Christ.
I come sick to the doctor of life,
unclean to the fountain of mercy,
blind to the radiance of eternal light,
and poor and needy to the Lord of heaven and earth.
Lord, in your great generosity,
heal my sickness, wash away my defilement,
enlighten my blindness, enrich my poverty,
and clothe my nakedness.
May I receive the bread of angels,
the King of kings and Lord of lords,
with humble reverence,
with the purity and faith,
the repentance and love, and the determined purpose
that will help to bring me to salvation.
May I receive the sacrament of the Lord's body
    and blood,
and its reality and power.
Kind God,
may I receive the body of your only-begotten Son,
    our Lord Jesus Christ,
born from the womb of the Virgin Mary,
and so be received into his mystical body
and numbered among his members.
Loving Father,
as on my earthly pilgrimage
I now receive your beloved Son
under the veil of a sacrament,
may I one day see him face to face in glory,
who lives and reigns with you for ever Amen.

PRAYERS AFTER HOLY COMMUNION

Act of Faith

Jesus, I firmly believe that you are present within me as God and Man, to enrich my soul with graces and to fill my heart with the happiness of the blessed. I believe that you are Christ, the Son of the living God!

Act of Adoration

With deepest humility, I adore you, my Lord and God; you have made my soul your dwelling place. I adore you as my Creator from whose hands I came and with whom I am to be happy forever.

Act of Love

Dear Jesus, I love you with my whole heart, my whole soul, and with all my strength. May the love of your own Sacred Heart fill my soul and purify it so that I may die to the world for love of you, as you died on the Cross for love of me. My God, you are all mine; grant that I may be all yours in time and in eternity.

Act of Thanksgiving

From the depths of my heart I thank you, dear Lord, for your infinite kindness in coming to me. How good you are to me! With your most holy Mother and all the angels, I praise your mercy and generosity toward me, a poor sinner. I thank you for nourishing my soul with your Sacred Body and Precious Blood. I will try to show my gratitude to you in the Sacrament of your love, by obedience to your holy commandments, by fidelity to my duties, by kindness to my neighbor and by an earnest endeavor to become more like you in my daily conduct.

Prayer to Christ the King

O Christ Jesus, I acknowledge you King of the universe. All that has been created has been made for you. Exercise upon me all your rights. I renew my baptismal promises, renouncing Satan and all his works and pomps. I promise to live a good Christian life and to do all in my power to procure the triumph of the rights of God and your Church.

Divine Heart of Jesus, I offer you my poor actions in order to obtain that all hearts may ackowledge your sacred Royalty, and that thus the reign of your peace may be established throughout the universe. Amen.

Prayer of St. Thomas Aquinas

Lord, Father all-powerful and ever-living God,
I thank you,
for even though I am a sinner, your unprofitable
    servant,
not because of my worth but in the kindness of your
    mercy,
you have fed me
with the precious body and blood of your Son, our
    Lord Jesus Christ.
I pray that this holy communion
may not bring me condemnation and punishment
but forgiveness and salvation.
May it be a helmet of faith
and a shield of good will.
May it purify me from evil ways
and put an end to my evil passions.
May it bring me charity and patience,
humility and obedience,
and growth in the power to do good.
May it be my strong defense
against all my enemies, visible and invisible,
and the perfect calming of all my evil impulses,
bodily and spiritual.
May it unite me more closely to you,
the one true God,
and lead me safely through death

and everlasting happiness with you.
And I pray that you will lead me, a sinner,
to the banquet where you,
with your Son and Holy Spirit,
are true and perfect light,
total fulfillment, everlasting joy,
gladness without end,
and perfect happiness to your saints.
Grant this through Christ our Lord. Amen.

Prayer to Our Redeemer

Soul of Christ, make me holy.
Body of Christ, be my salvation.
Blood of Christ, let me drink your wine.
Water flowing from the side of Christ, wash me
    clean.
Passion of Christ, strengthen me.
Kind Jesus, hear my prayer;
hide me within your wounds
and keep me close to you.

Defend me from the evil enemy.
Call me at my death
to the fellowship of your saints,
that I may sing your praise with them
through all eternity. Amen.

Prayer to Jesus Christ Crucified

My good and dear Jesus,
I kneel before you,
asking you most earnestly
to engrave upon my heart
a deep and lively faith, hope, and charity,
with true repentance for my sins,
and a firm resolve to make amends.
As I reflect upon your five wounds,
and dwell upon them with deep compassion and
    grief.

I recall, good Jesus, the words the prophet David
   spoke
long ago concerning yourself:
they have pierced my hands and my feet,
they have counted all my bones!

A *plenary indulgence* is granted on each Friday of Lent
and Passiontide to the faithful, who after Communion
piously recite the above prayer before an image of Christ
crucified; on other days of the year the indulgence is *partial. (No. 22)*

Prayer to Mary

O Jesus living in Mary, come and live in your servants, in the spirit of your holiness, in the fulness of your power, in the perfection of your ways, in the truth of your mysteries. Reign in us over all adverse power by your Holy Spirit, and for the glory of the Father. Amen.

Mary, I come to you with childlike confidence and earnestly beg you to take me under your powerful protection. Grant me a place in your loving motherly Heart. I place my immortal soul into your hands and give you my own poor heart.

Prayer to St. Joseph

Guardian of virgins, and holy father Joseph, to whose faithful custody Christ Jesus, innocence itself, and Mary, Virgin of virgins, were committed; I beg you, by these dear pledges, Jesus and Mary, that, being preserved from all uncleanness, I may with spotless mind, pure heart and chaste body, ever serve Jesus and Mary most chastely all the days of my life. Amen.

PLAN OF THE MASS

INTRODUCTORY RITES

1. Entrance Antiphon **(Proper)**
2. Greeting
3. Rite of Blessing and Sprinkling Holy Water
4. Penitential Rite
5. Kyrie
6. Gloria
7. Opening Prayer **(Proper)**

LITURGY OF THE WORD

8. First Reading **(Proper)**
9. Responsorial Psalm **(Proper)**
10. Second Reading **(Proper)**
11. Alleluia **(Proper)**
12. Gospel **(Proper)**
13. Homily
14. Profession of Faith
15. General Intercessions

LITURGY OF THE EUCHARIST

(Eucharistic Prayer)

16. Offertory Song
17. Preparation of the Bread
18. Preparation of the Wine
19. Invitation to Prayer
20. Prayer over the Gifts **(Proper)**
21. Introductory Dialogue
22. Preface
23. Sanctus

Eucharistic Prayer 1 — p. 628
Eucharistic Prayer 2 — p. 633
Eucharistic Prayer 3 — p. 637
Eucharistic Prayer 4 — p. 641

(Communion Rite)

24. Lord's Prayer
25. Sign of Peace
26. Breaking of the Bread
27. Prayers before Communion
28. Reception of Communion
29. Communion Ant. **(Proper)**
30. Silence after Communion
31. Prayer after Communion **(Proper)**

CONCLUDING RITE

32. Greeting
33. Blessing
34. Dismissal

THE ORDER OF MASS

Options are indicated by A, B, C, D in the margin.

INTRODUCTORY RITES

Acts of prayer and penitence prepare us to meet Christ as he comes in Word and Sacrament. We gather as a worshiping community to celebrate our unity with him and with one another in faith.

1 ENTRANCE ANTIPHON

STAND

If it is not sung, it is recited by all or some of the people.

Joined together as Christ's people, we open the celebration by raising our voices in praise of God who is present among us. This song should deepen our unity as it introduces the Mass we celebrate today.

> Turn to Today's Mass

2 GREETING (3 forms)

When the priest comes to the altar, he makes the customary reverence with the ministers and kisses the altar. Then, with the ministers, he goes to his seat. After the entrance song, all make the sign of the cross:

Priest: In the name of the Father, ✠ and of the Son, and of the Holy Spirit.

PEOPLE: Amen.

614

The priest welcomes us in the name of the Lord. We show our union with God, our neighbor, and the priest by a united response to his greeting.

Priest: The grace of our Lord Jesus Christ and the love of God and the fellowship of the Holy Spirit be with you all.

PEOPLE: And also with you.

———————— OR ————————

Priest: The grace and peace of God our Father and the Lord Jesus Christ be with you.

PEOPLE: Blessed be God, the Father of our Lord Jesus Christ.

or:

And also with you.

———————— OR ————————

Priest: The Lord be with you.

PEOPLE: And also with you.

[Bishop: Peace be with you.

People: **And also with you.**

3 RITE OF BLESSING and SPRINKLING HOLY WATER

The rite of blessing and sprinkling holy water may be celebrated in all churches and chapels at all Sunday Masses celebrated on Sunday or Saturday evening, see p. 652-654.

4 PENITENTIAL RITE (3 forms)

(Omitted when the rite of blessing and sprinkling holy water has taken place or some part of the liturgy of the hours has preceded)

Before we hear God's word, we acknowledge our sins humbly, ask for mercy, and accept his pardon.

Invitation to repent:

After the introduction to the day's Mass, the priest invites the people to recall their sins and to repent of them in silence:

A As we prepare to celebrate the mystery of Christ's love,
let us acknowledge our failures
and ask the Lord for pardon and strength.

B Coming together as God's family,
with confidence let us ask the Father's forgiveness,
for he is full of gentleness and compassion.

C My brothers and sisters,
to prepare ourselves to celebrate the sacred mysteries,
let us call to mind our sins.

Then, after a brief silence, one of the following forms is used.

Priest and **PEOPLE:**

I confess to almighty God,
and to you, my brothers and sisters,
that I have sinned through my own fault

They strike their breast:

in my thoughts and in my words,
in what I have done,

and in what I have failed to do;
and I ask blessed Mary, ever virgin,
all the angels and saints,
and you, my brothers and sisters,
to pray for me to the Lord our God.

———————— OR ————————

B

Priest: Lord, we have sinned against you:
        Lord, have mercy.
PEOPLE: **Lord, have mercy.**
Priest: Lord, show us your mercy and love.
PEOPLE: **And grant us your salvation.**

———————— OR ————————

C

Priest or other minister:

    You were sent to heal the contrite:
    Lord, have mercy.

PEOPLE: **Lord, have mercy.**

Priest or other minister:

    You came to call sinners:
    Christ, have mercy.

PEOPLE: **Christ, have mercy.**

Priest or other minister:

    You plead for us at the right hand of the
    Father:

    Lord, have mercy.

PEOPLE: **Lord, have mercy.**

(Other invocations may be used as on pp. 655-657).

Absolution:

At the end of any of the forms of the penitential rite:

Priest: May almighty God have mercy on us,
              forgive us our sins,
              and bring us to everlasting life.

PEOPLE: Amen.

5 KYRIE

Unless included in the penitential rite, the Kyrie is sung or said by all, with alternating parts for the choir or cantor and for the people:

℣. Lord, have mercy.

℟. **Lord, have mercy.**

℣. Christ, have mercy.

℟. **Christ, have mercy.**

℣. Lord, have mercy.

℟. **Lord, have mercy.**

6 GLORIA

As the Church assembled in the Spirit, we praise and pray to the Father and the Lamb.

When the Gloria is sung or said, the priest or the cantors or everyone together may begin it:

Glory to God in the highest,
    and peace to his people on earth.
Lord God, heavenly King,
almighty God and Father,
    we worship you, we give you thanks,
    we praise you for your glory.

Lord Jesus Christ, only Son of the Father,
Lord God, Lamb of God,
you take away the sin of the world:
  have mercy on us;
you are seated at the right hand of the Father:
  receive our prayer.
For you alone are the Holy One,
you alone are the Lord,
you alone are the Most High,
  Jesus Christ,
  with the Holy Spirit,
  in the glory of God the Father. Amen.

7 OPENING PRAYER

The priest invites us to pray silently for a moment and then, in our name, expresses the theme of the day's celebration and petitions God the Father through the mediation of Christ in the Holy Spirit.

Priest: Let us pray.

> **➤ Turn to Today's Mass**

Priest and people pray silently for a while. Then the priest says the opening prayer and concludes:

Priest: For ever and ever.

PEOPLE: Amen.

LITURGY OF THE WORD

The proclamation of God's Word is always centered on Christ, present through his Word. Old Testament writings prepare for him; New Testament books speak of him directly. All of scripture calls us to believe once more and to follow. After the reading we reflect upon God's words and respond to them.

As in Today's Mass `SIT`

8 FIRST READING

At end of reading: Reader: This is the Word of the Lord.
PEOPLE: Thanks be to God.

9 RESPONSORIAL PSALM

The people repeat the response sung by the cantor the first time and then after each verse.

10 SECOND READING

At end of reading: Reader: This is the Word of the Lord.
PEOPLE: Thanks be to God.

11 ALLELUIA (Gospel Acclamation) `STAND`

Jesus will speak to us in the gospel. We rise now out of respect and prepare for his message with the alleluia.

The people repeat the alleluia after cantor's alleluia and then after the verse.

During Lent one of the following invocations is used as a response instead of the alleluia:

(A) **Praise to you, Lord Jesus Christ, king of endless glory!**
(B) **Praise and honor to you, Lord Jesus Christ!**
(C) **Glory and praise to you, Lord Jesus Christ!**
(D) **Glory to you, Word of God, Lord Jesus Christ!**

12 GOSPEL

Before proclaiming the gospel, the deacon asks the priest: Father, give me your blessing. *The priest says*:

The Lord be in your heart and on your lips
that you may worthily proclaim his gospel.

In the name of the Father, and of the Son, ✠ and
of the Holy Spirit. *The deacon answers:* **Amen.**

If there is no deacon, the priest says quietly:

Almighty God, cleanse my heart and my lips
that I may worthily proclaim your gospel.

Deacon (or priest):

The Lord be with you.

PEOPLE: **And also with you.**

Deacon (or priest):

✠ A reading from the holy gospel according
to N.

PEOPLE: Glory to you, Lord.

At the end:

Deacon (or priest):

This is the gospel of the Lord.

PEOPLE: Praise to you, Lord Jesus Christ.

Then the deacon (or priest) kisses the book, saying quietly: May the words of the gospel wipe away our sins.

13 HOMILY

SIT

God's word is spoken again in the homily. The Holy Spirit speaking through the lips of the preacher explains and applies today's biblical readings to the needs of this particular congregation. He calls us to respond to Christ through the life we lead.

STAND

14 PROFESSION OF FAITH (CREED)

As a people we express our acceptance of God's message in the scriptures and homily. We summarize our faith by proclaiming a creed handed down from the early Church.

All say the profession of faith on Sundays.

We believe in one God,
   the Father, the Almighty,
   maker of heaven and earth,
   of all that is seen and unseen.

We believe in one Lord, Jesus Christ,
   the only Son of God,
   eternally begotten of the Father,
   God from God, Light from Light,
   true God from true God,
   begotten, not made, one in Being with the
      Father.
   Through him all things were made.
   For us men and for our salvation
      he came down from heaven:

All bow at the following words up to: and became man.

   by the power of the Holy Spirit
      he was born of the Virgin Mary, and
      became man.

For our sake he was crucified under Pontius
Pilate;
he suffered, died, and was buried.
On the third day he rose again
in fulfillment of the Scriptures;
he ascended into heaven
and is seated at the right hand of the
Father.
He will come again in glory to judge the
living and the dead,
and his kingdom will have no end.

We believe in the Holy Spirit, the Lord,
the giver of life,
who proceeds from the Father and the Son.
With the Father and the Son he is worshiped
and glorified.
He has spoken through the Prophets.
We believe in one holy catholic and apostolic Church.
We acknowledge one baptism for the forgiveness of sins.
We look for the resurrection of the dead,
and the life of the world to come. Amen.

15 GENERAL INTERCESSIONS

(Prayer of the Faithful)

As a priestly people we unite with one another to pray for
today's needs in the Church and the world.

*After the priest gives the introduction the deacon or
other minister sings or says the invocations.*
PEOPLE: Lord, hear our prayer.

(or other response, according to local custom)
At the end the priest says the concluding prayer:
PEOPLE: Amen.

LITURGY OF THE EUCHARIST

Made ready by reflection on God's Word, we enter now into the eucharistic sacrifice itself, the Supper of the Lord. We celebrate the memorial which the Lord instituted at his Last Supper. We are God's new people, the redeemed brothers of Christ, gathered by him around his table. We are here to bless God and to receive the gift of Jesus' body and blood so that our faith and life may be transformed.

SIT

16 OFFERTORY SONG

The bread and wine for the Eucharist, with our gifts for the Church and the poor, are gathered and brought to the altar. We prepare our hearts by song or in silence as the Lord's table is being set.

While the gifts of the people are brought forward to the priest and are placed on the altar, the offertory song is sung.

17 PREPARATION OF THE BREAD

Before placing the bread on the altar, the priest says quietly:

Blessed are you, Lord, God of all creation.
Through your goodness we have this bread to offer,
which earth has given and human hands have made.
It will become for us the bread of life.

If there is no singing, the priest may say this prayer aloud, and the people may respond:

People: **Blessed be God for ever.**

624

18 PREPARATION OF THE WINE

When he pours wine and a little water into the chalice, the deacon (or the priest) says quietly:

By the mystery of this water and wine
may we come to share in the divinity of Christ,
who humbled himself to share in our humanity.

Before placing the chalice on the altar, he says:

Blessed are you, Lord, God of all creation.
Through your goodness we have this wine to offer,
fruit of the vine and work of human hands.
It will become our spiritual drink.

If there is no singing, the priest may say this prayer aloud, and the people may respond:

People: **Blessed be God for ever.**

The priest says quietly:

Lord God, we ask you to receive us
and be pleased with the sacrifice we offer you
with humble and contrite hearts.

Then he washes his hands, saying:

Lord, wash away my iniquity;
cleanse me from my sin.

19 INVITATION TO PRAYER

Priest: Pray, brethren, that our sacrifice may be
acceptable to God, the almighty Father.

PEOPLE:

**May the Lord accept the sacrifice at your hands,
for the praise and glory of his name,
for our good, and the good of all his Church.**

20 PRAYER OVER THE GIFTS `STAND`

The priest, speaking in our name, asks the Father to bless
and accept these gifts.

> ➤ **Turn to Today's Mass**

At the end, **PEOPLE:** Amen.

EUCHARISTIC PRAYER

We begin the eucharistic service of praise and thanksgiving, the center of the entire celebration, the central prayer of worship. At the priest's invitation we lift our hearts to God and unite with him in the words he addresses to the Father through Jesus Christ. Together we join Christ in his sacrifice, celebrating his memorial in the holy meal and acknowledging with him the wonderful works of God in our lives.

21 INTRODUCTORY DIALOGUE

Priest: The Lord be with you.

PEOPLE: And also with you.

Priest: Lift up your hearts.

PEOPLE: We lift them up to the Lord.

Priest: Let us give thanks to the Lord our God.

PEOPLE: It is right to give him thanks and praise.

22 PREFACE

As indicated in the individual Masses throughout this Missal, the priest may say one of the following Prefaces (listed in numerical order).

No.	Page	No.	Page
P 1: Advent I, **658**		P 8: Lent I, **660**	
P 2: Advent II, **658**		P 9: Lent II, **661**	
		P 10: Lent III, **661**	
P 3: Christmas I, **659**		P 11: Lent IV, **661**	
P 4: Christmas II, **659**			
P 5: Christmas III **659**		P 17: Passion of Lord I, **662**	
		P 18: Passion of Lord II, **662**	
P 6: Epiphany, **660**			

23 ACCLAMATION

Priest and **PEOPLE:**

Holy, holy, holy Lord, God of power and might, heaven and earth are full of your glory.

Hosanna in the highest.

Blessed is he who comes in the name of the Lord.

Hosanna in the highest.

`KNEEL`

Then the priest continues with one of the following Eucharistic Prayers.

EUCHARISTIC PRAYER No. 1

The Roman Canon

(This Eucharistic Prayer is especially suitable for Sundays and Masses with proper "Communicantes" and "Hanc igitur.")

[The words within brackets may be omitted.]

[*Praise to the Father*]

We come to you, Father,
with praise and thanksgiving,
through Jesus Christ your Son.
Through him we ask you to accept and bless
these gifts we offer you in sacrifice.

[*Intercessions: For the Church*]

We offer them for your holy Catholic Church,
watch over it, Lord, and guide it;
grant it peace and unity throughout the world.

We offer them for N. our Pope,
for N. our bishop,
and for all who hold and teach the catholic faith
that comes to us from the apostles.

Remember, Lord, your people,
especially those for whom we now pray, N. and N.

Remember all of us gathered here before you.
You know how firmly we believe in you
and dedicate ourselves to you.
We offer you this sacrifice of praise

for ourselves and those who are dear to us.
We pray to you, our living and true God,
for our well-being and redemption.

[*In Communion with the Saints*]
In union with the whole Church *
we honor Mary,
the ever-virgin mother of Jesus Christ our Lord and
   God.
We honor Joseph, her husband,
the apostles and martyrs
Peter and Paul, Andrew,
[James, John, Thomas,
James, Philip,
Bartholomew, Matthew, Simon and Jude;
we honor Linus, Cletus, Clement, Sixtus,
Cornelius, Cyprian, Lawrence, Chrysogonus,
John and Paul, Cosmas and Damian]
and all the saints.
May their merits and prayers
gain us your constant help and protection.
[Through Christ our Lord. Amen.]
Father, accept this offering *
from your whole family.
Grant us your peace in this life,
save us from final damnation,
and count us among those you have chosen.
[Through Christ our Lord. Amen.]
Bless and approve our offering;
make it acceptable to you,
an offering in spirit and in truth.
Let it become for us
the body and blood of Jesus Christ,
your only Son, our Lord.

* *See page* **684** *for Special Communicantes and Hanc Igitur.*

1

[*The Lord's Supper*]

The day before he suffered
he took bread in his sacred hands
and looking up to heaven,
to you, his almighty Father,
he gave you thanks and praise.
He broke the bread,
gave it to his disciples, and said:

Take this, all of you, and eat it:
this is my body which will be given up for you.

When supper was ended,
he took the cup.
Again he gave you thanks and praise,
gave the cup to his disciples, and said:

Take this, all of you, and drink from it:
this is the cup of my blood,
the blood of the new and everlasting covenant.
It will be shed for you and for all men
so that sins may be forgiven.
Do this in memory of me.

[*Memorial Acclamation*]

Priest: Let us proclaim the mystery of faith.

PEOPLE:

A Christ has died,
Christ is risen,
Christ will come again.

B Dying you destroyed our death,
rising you restored our life.
Lord Jesus, come in glory.

C **When we eat this bread and drink this cup,**]
we proclaim your death, Lord Jesus,
until you come in glory.

D **Lord, by your cross and resurrection**
you have set us free.
You are the Savior of the world.

[*The Memorial Prayer*]

Father, we celebrate the memory of Christ, your Son.
We, your people and your ministers,
recall his passion,
his resurrection from the dead,
and his ascension into glory;
and from the many gifts you have given us
we offer to you, God of glory and majesty,
this holy and perfect sacrifice:
the bread of life
and the cup of eternal salvation.
Look with favor on these offerings
and accept them as once you accepted
the gifts of your servant Abel,
the sacrifice of Abraham, our father in faith,
and the bread and wine offered by your priest
  Melchisedech.
Almighty God,
we pray that your angel may take this sacrifice
to your altar in heaven.
Then, as we receive from this altar
the sacred body and blood of your Son,
let us be filled with every grace and blessing.
[Through Christ our Lord. Amen.]

1

[*For the Dead*]

Remember, Lord, those who have died
and have gone before us marked with the sign of
　faith,
especially those for whom we now pray, *N.* and *N.*
May these, and all who sleep in Christ,
find in your presence
light, happiness, and peace.
[Through Christ our Lord. Amen.]

For ourselves, too, we ask
some share in the fellowship of your apostles and
　martyrs,
with John the Baptist, Stephen, Matthias, Barnabas,
[Ignatius, Alexander, Marcellinus, Peter,
Felicity, Perpetua, Agatha, Lucy,
Agnes, Cecilia, Anastasia]
and all the saints.
Though we are sinners,
we trust in your mercy and love.
Do not consider what we truly deserve,
but grant us your forgiveness.
Through Christ our Lord
you give us all these gifts.
You fill them with life and goodness,
you bless them and make them holy.

Through him,　　　　　[*Concluding Doxology*]
with him,
in him,
in the unity of the Holy Spirit,
all glory and honor is yours,
almighty Father,
for ever and ever.
All reply:　**Amen.**

Continue with the Mass, as on p. 646.

EUCHARISTIC PRAYER No. 2

(This Eucharistic Prayer is particularly suitable on Weekdays or for special circumstances)

℣. The Lord be with you.   **STAND**

℟. **And also with you.**

℣. Lift up your hearts.

℟. **We lift them up to the Lord.**

℣. Let us give thanks to the Lord our God.

℟. **It is right to give him thanks and praise.**

PREFACE   [*Praise to the Father*]

Father, it is our duty and our salvation,
always and everywhere
to give you thanks
through your beloved Son, Jesus Christ.

He is the Word through whom you made the
   universe,
the Savior you sent to redeem us.

By the power of the Holy Spirit
he took flesh and was born of the Virgin Mary.

For our sake he opened his arms on the cross;
he put an end to death
and revealed the resurrection.

In this he fulfilled your will
and won for you a holy people.

And so we join the angels and the saints
in proclaiming your glory
as we sing (say):

2 SANCTUS

[*First Acclamation of the People*]

**Holy, holy, holy Lord, God of power and might,
heaven and earth are full of your glory.
Hosanna in the highest.
Blessed is he who comes in the name of the Lord.
Hosanna in the highest.**

KNEEL

[*Invocation of the Holy Spirit*]

Lord, you are holy indeed,
the fountain of all holiness.

Let your Spirit come upon these gifts to make them
   holy,
so that they may become for us
the body and blood of our Lord, Jesus Christ.

[*The Lord's Supper*]

Before he was given up to death,
a death he freely accepted,
he took bread and gave you thanks.
He broke the bread,
gave it to his disciples, and said:
Take this, all of you, and eat it:
this is my body which will be given up for you.
When supper was ended, he took the cup.
Again he gave you thanks and praise,
gave the cup to his disciples, and said:
Take this, all of you, and drink from it:
this is the cup of my blood,
the blood of the new and everlasting covenant.
It will be shed for you and for all men
so that sins may be forgiven.
Do this in memory of me.

2

[*Memorial Acclamation*]

Priest: Let us proclaim the mystery of faith.

PEOPLE:

A   Christ has died,
Christ is risen,
Christ will come again.

B   Dying you destroyed our death,
rising you restored our life.
Lord Jesus, come in glory.

C   When we eat this bread and drink this cup,
we proclaim your death, Lord Jesus,
until you come in glory.

D   Lord, by your cross and resurrection
you have set us free.
You are the Savior of the world.

[*The Memorial Prayer*]

In memory of his death and resurrection,
we offer you, Father, this life-giving bread,
this saving cup.

We thank you for counting us worthy
to stand in your presence and serve you.

[*Invocation of the Holy Spirit*]

May all of us who share in the body and blood of
   Christ
be brought together in unity by the Holy Spirit.

2

[*Intercessions: For the Church*]

Lord, remember your Church throughout the world;
make us grow in love,
together with N. our Pope,
N. our bishop, and all the clergy.*

[*For the Dead*]

Remember our brothers and sisters
who have gone to their rest
in the hope of rising again;
bring them and all the departed
into †the light of your presence.

[*In Communion with the Saints*]

Have mercy on us all;
make us worthy to share eternal life
with Mary, the virgin mother of God,
with the apostles,
and with all the saints who have done your will
    throughout the ages.

May we praise you in union with them,
and give you glory
through your Son, Jesus Christ.

[*Concluding Doxology*]

Through him,
with him,
in him,
in the unity of the Holy Spirit,
all glory and honor is yours,
almighty Father,
for ever and ever.

All reply: **Amen.**
    Continue with the Mass, as on p. 646.

---

* In Masses for the Dead the following may be added:
Remember N., whom you have called from this life.
In baptism he (she) died with Christ:
may he (she) also share his resurrection.

EUCHARISTIC PRAYER No. 3   **3**

(This Eucharistic Prayer may be used with any Preface and preferably on Sundays and feast days)

KNEEL

[Praise to the Father]

Father, you are holy indeed,
and all creation rightly gives you praise.
All life, all holiness comes from you
through your Son, Jesus Christ our Lord,
by the working of the Holy Spirit.
From age to age you gather a people to yourself,
so that from east to west
a perfect offering may be made
to the glory of your name.

[Invocation of the Holy Spirit]

And so, Father, we bring you these gifts.
We ask you to make them holy by the power of your
    Spirit,
that they may become the body and blood
of your Son, our Lord Jesus Christ,
at whose command we celebrate this eucharist.

[The Lord's Supper]

On the night he was betrayed,
he took bread and gave you thanks and praise.
He broke the bread, gave it to his disciples, and said:

Take this, all of you, and eat it:
this is my body which will be given up for you.

3 When supper was ended, he took the cup.
Again he gave you thanks and praise,
gave the cup to his disciples, and said:

Take this, all of you, and drink from it:
this is the cup of my blood,
the blood of the new and everlasting covenant.
It will be shed for you and for all men
so that sins may be forgiven.
Do this in memory of me.

[*Memorial Acclamation*]

Priest: Let us proclaim the mystery of faith.

PEOPLE:

A   Christ has died,
Christ is risen,
Christ will come again.

B   Dying you destroyed our death,
rising you restored our life.
Lord Jesus, come in glory.

C   When we eat this bread and drink this cup,
we proclaim your death, Lord Jesus,
until you come in glory.

D   Lord, by your cross and resurrection
you have set us free.
You are the Savior of the world.

[*The Memorial Prayer*]

Father, calling to mind the death your Son endured
for our salvation,

his glorious resurrection and ascension into heaven,
and ready to greet him when he comes again,
we offer you in thanksgiving this holy and living
   sacrifice.
Look with favor on your Church's offering,
and see the Victim whose death has reconciled us to
   yourself.

[*Invocation of the Holy Spirit*]

Grant that we, who are nourished by his body and
   blood,
may be filled with his Holy Spirit,
and become one body, one spirit in Christ.

[*Intercessions: In Communion with the Saints*]

May he make us an everlasting gift to you
and enable us to share in the inheritance of your
   saints,
with Mary, the virgin mother of God;
with the apostles, the martyrs,
(Saint *N.*) and all your saints,
on whose constant intercession we rely for help.

[*For the Church*]

Lord, may this sacrifice, which has made our peace
   with you,
advance the peace and salvation of all the world.
Strengthen in faith and love your pilgrim Church on
   earth:
your servant, Pope *N.*, our bishop *N.*,
and all the bishops,
with the clergy and the entire people your Son has
   gained for you.
Father, hear the prayers of the family you have
   gathered here before you.

3 In mercy and love unite all your children
wherever they may be.*

[*For the Dead*]

Welcome into your kingdom our departed brothers
   and sisters,
and all who have left this world in your friendship.

We hope to enjoy for ever the vision of your glory,
through Christ our Lord, from whom all good things
   come.

[*Concluding Doxology*]

Through him,
with him,
in him,
in the unity of the Holy Spirit,
all glory and honor is yours,
almighty Father,
for ever and ever.

All reply: **Amen.**

Continue with the Mass, as on p. 646.

---

* In Masses for the Dead the following is said:
Remember *N*.
In baptism he (she) died with Christ:
may he (she) also share his resurrection,
when Christ will raise our mortal bodies
and make them like his own in glory.
Welcome into your kingdom our departed brothers and
   sisters,
and all who have left this world in your friendship.
There we hope to share in your glory
when every tear will be wiped away.
On that day we shall see you, our God, as you are.
We shall become like you
and praise you for ever through Christ our Lord,
from whom all good things come.
Through him, etc., *as above.*

EUCHARISTIC PRAYER No. 4   4

℣. The Lord be with you.   **STAND**
℟. **And also with you.**
℣. Lift up your hearts.
℟. **We lift them up to the Lord.**
℣. Let us give thanks to the Lord our God.
℟. **It is right to give him thanks and praise.**

PREFACE

Father in heaven, it is right that we should give you
    thanks and glory:
you alone are God, living and true.

Through all eternity you live in unapproachable light.

Source of life and goodness, you have created all
    things, to fill your creatures with every blessing
and lead all men to the joyful vision of your light.

Countless hosts of angels stand before you to do your
    will;
they look upon your splendor
and praise you, night and day.

United with them, and in the name of every creature
    under heaven,
we too praise your glory as we sing (say):

SANCTUS   [*First Acclamation of the People*]

**Holy, holy, holy Lord, God of power and might,
heaven and earth are full of your glory.
    Hosanna in the highest.
Blessed is he who comes in the name of the Lord.
    Hosanna in the highest.**   **KNEEL**

[*Praise to the Father*]

Father, we acknowledge your greatness:
all your actions show your wisdom and love.

641

4 You formed man in your own likeness
and set him over the whole world
to serve you, his creator,
and to rule over all creatures.

Even when he disobeyed you and lost your friendship
you did not abandon him to the power of death,
but helped all men to seek and find you.

Again and again you offered a covenant to man,
and through the prophets taught him to hope for
salvation.

Father, you so loved the world
that in the fullness of time you sent your only Son
to be our Savior.

He was conceived through the power of the Holy
Spirit, and born of the Virgin Mary,
a man like us in all things but sin.

To the poor he proclaimed the good news of salvation,
to prisoners, freedom,
and to those in sorrow, joy.

In fulfillment of your will
he gave himself up to death;
but by rising from the dead,
he destroyed death and restored life.

And that we might live no longer for ourselves but
for him,
he sent the Holy Spirit from you, Father,
as his first gift to those who believe,
to complete his work on earth
and bring us the fullness of grace.

[*Invocation of the Holy Spirit*]

Father, may this Holy Spirit sanctify these offerings.
Let them become the body and blood of Jesus Christ
our Lord

as we celebrate the great mystery
which he left us as an everlasting covenant.

[The Lord's Supper]

He always loved those who were his own in the
world.
When the time came for him to be glorified by you,
his heavenly Father,
he showed the depth of his love.
While they were at supper,
he took bread, said the blessing, broke the bread
and gave it to his disciples, saying:

Take this, all of you, and eat it:
this is my body which will be given up for you.

In the same way, he took the cup, filled with wine.
He gave you thanks, and giving the cup to his disciples, said:

Take this, all of you, and drink from it:
this is the cup of my blood,
the blood of the new and everlasting covenant.
It will be shed for you and for all men
so that sins may be forgiven.
Do this in memory of me.

[Memorial Acclamation]

Priest: Let us proclaim the mystery of faith.

PEOPLE:

A Christ has died,
Christ is risen,
Christ will come again.

B   Dying you destroyed our death,
rising you restored our life.
Lord Jesus, come in glory.

C   When we eat this bread and drink this cup,
we proclaim your death, Lord Jesus,
until you come in glory.

D   Lord, by your cross and resurrection
you have set us free.
You are the Savior of the world.

[The Memorial Prayer]

Father, we now celebrate this memorial of our redemption.

We recall Christ's death, his descent among the dead,
his resurrection, and his ascension to your right
hand;

and, looking forward to his coming in glory, we
offer you his body and blood,

the acceptable sacrifice which brings salvation to
the whole world.

Lord, look upon this sacrifice which you have given
to your Church;

and by your Holy Spirit, gather all who share this
bread and wine

into the one body of Christ, a living sacrifice of
praise.

[Intercessions: For the Church]

Lord, remember those for whom we offer this sacrifice,

especially *N.*, our Pope,
N., our bishop, and bishops and clergy everywhere.

Remember those who take part in this offering,
those here present and all your people,
and all who seek you with a sincere heart.

[*For the Dead*]

Remember those who have died in the peace of
   Christ
and all the dead whose faith is known to you alone.

[*In Communion with the Saints*]

Father, in your mercy grant also to us, your children,
to enter into our heavenly inheritance
in the company of the Virgin Mary, the mother of
   God,
and your apostles and saints.

Then, in your kingdom, freed from the corruption of
   sin and death,
we shall sing your glory with every creature through
   Christ our Lord,
through whom you give us everything that is good.

Through him,   [*Concluding Doxology*]
with him,
in him,
in the unity of the Holy Spirit,
all glory and honor is yours,
almighty Father,
for ever and ever.

All reply: **Amen.**

COMMUNION RITE

To prepare for the paschal meal, to welcome the Lord, we pray for forgiveness and exchange a sign of peace. Before eating Christ's body and drinking his blood, we must be one with him and with all our brothers in the Church.

24 LORD'S PRAYER

STAND

Priest:

A Let us pray with confidence to the Father
in the words our Savior gave us:

B Jesus taught us to call God our Father,
and so we have the courage to say:

C Let us ask our Father to forgive our sins
and to bring us to forgive those who sin against us.

D Let us pray for the coming of the kingdom
as Jesus taught us.

Priest and **PEOPLE:**

> **Our Father, who art in heaven,**
> **hallowed be thy name;**
> **thy kingdom come;**
> **thy will be done on earth as it is in heaven.**
> **Give us this day our daily bread;**
> **and forgive us our trespasses**
> **as we forgive those who trespass against us;**
> **and lead us not into temptation,**
> **but deliver us from evil.**

Priest: Deliver us, Lord, from every evil,
and grant us peace in our day.
In your mercy keep us free from sin

646

and protect us from all anxiety
as we wait in joyful hope
for the coming of our Savior, Jesus Christ.

PEOPLE: For the kingdom, the power, and the glory are yours, now and for ever.

25 SIGN OF PEACE

The Church is a community of Christians joined by the Spirit in love. It needs to express, deepen, and restore its peaceful unity before eating the one Body of the Lord and drinking from the one cup of salvation. We do this by a sign of peace.

The priest says the prayer for peace:

Lord Jesus Christ, you said to your apostles:
I leave you peace, my peace I give you.
Look not on our sins, but on the faith of your Church,
and grant us the peace and unity of your kingdom
where you live for ever and ever.

PEOPLE: Amen.

Priest: The peace of the Lord be with you always.

PEOPLE: And also with you.

Deacon (or priest):

Let us offer each other the sign of peace.

The people exchange a sign of peace and love, according to local custom.

26 BREAKING OF THE BREAD

Christians are gathered for the "breaking of the bread," another name for the Mass. In communion, though many we are made one body in the one bread, which is Christ.

Then the following is sung or said:

PEOPLE:

Lamb of God, you take away the sins of the world:

have mercy on us.

Lamb of God, you take away the sins of the world:

have mercy on us.

Lamb of God, you take away the sins of the world:

grant us peace.

The hymn may be repeated until the breaking of the bread is finished, but the last phrase is always: "Grant us peace."

Meanwhile the priest breaks the host over the paten and places a small piece in the chalice, saying quietly:

May this mingling of the body and blood of our Lord Jesus Christ

bring eternal life to us who receive it.

27 PRAYERS BEFORE COMMUNION

We pray in silence and then voice words of humility and hope as our final preparation before meeting Christ in the Eucharist.

Before communion, the priest says quietly one of the following prayers:

Lord Jesus Christ, Son of the living God, by the will of the Father and the work of the Holy Spirit your death brought life to the world. By your holy body and blood free me from all my sins and from every evil. Keep me faithful to your teaching, and never let me be parted from you.

OR: Lord Jesus Christ, with faith in your love and mercy, I eat your body and drink your blood. Let it not bring me condemnation, but health in mind and body.

28 RECEPTION OF COMMUNION

The priest genuflects. Holding the host elevated slightly over the paten, the priest says:

Priest: This is the Lamb of God
who takes away the sins of the world.
Happy are those who are called to his supper.

Priest and **PEOPLE** (once only):

Lord, I am not worthy to receive you,
but only say the word and I shall be healed.

Before receiving communion, the priest says quietly: May the body of Christ bring me to everlasting life. May the blood of Christ bring me to everlasting life. *He then gives communion to the people.*

Priest: The body of Christ: Communicant. **Amen.**

29 **COMMUNION SONG or ANTIPHON**

The Communion Psalm or other appropriate Song or Hymn is sung while Communion is given to the faithful. If there is no singing, the Communion Antiphon is said:

> **➤ Turn to Today's Mass**

The vessels are cleansed by the priest or deacon. Meanwhile he says quietly:

Lord, may I receive these gifts in purity of heart. May they bring me healing and strength, now and for ever.

30 PERIOD OF SILENCE or Song of Praise

After communion there may be a period of silence, or a song of praise may be sung.

31 PRAYER AFTER COMMUNION ~~STAND~~

The priest prays in our name that we may live the life of faith since we have been strengthened by Christ himself. Our Amen makes his prayer our own.

Priest: Let us pray.

Priest and people may pray silently for a while. Then the priest says the prayer after communion.

→ Turn to Today's Mass

At the end, **PEOPLE:** Amen.

CONCLUDING RITE

We have heard God's Word and eaten the body of Christ. Now it is time for us to leave, to do good works, to praise and bless the Lord in our daily lives.

32 GREETING ~~STAND~~

After any brief announcements (sit), the blessing and dismissal follow:

Priest: The Lord be with you.

PEOPLE: And also with you.

33 BLESSING

A Simple form

Priest: May almighty God bless you, the Father, and the Son, ✠ and the Holy Spirit.

PEOPLE: Amen.

On certain days or occasions another more solemn form of blessing or prayer over the people may be used as the rubrics direct.

B Solemn blessing

Texts of all the solemn blessings are given on pp. 682-689.

Deacon: Bow your heads and pray for God's blessing.

The priest always concludes the solemn blessing by adding:

May almighty God bless you,
the Father, and the Son, ✠ and the Holy Spirit.

PEOPLE: Amen.

C Prayer over the people

Texts of all prayers over the people are given on pp. 689-693.

After the prayer over the people, the priest always adds:

And may the blessing of almighty God,
the Father, and the Son, ✠ and the Holy Spirit,
come upon you and remain with you for ever.

PEOPLE: Amen.

34 DISMISSAL

Deacon (or priest):

A Go in the peace of Christ.

B The Mass is ended, go in peace.

C Go in peace to love and serve the Lord.

PEOPLE: Thanks be to God.

If any liturgical service follows immediately, the rite of dismissal is omitted.

RITE OF BLESSING AND
SPRINKLING HOLY WATER

When this rite is celebrated it takes the place of the penitential rite at the beginning of Mass. The Kyrie is also omitted.

After greeting the people the priest remains standing at his chair. A vessel containing the water to be blessed is placed before him. Facing the people, he invites them to pray, using these or similar words:

Dear friends,
this water will be used
to remind us of our baptism.
Let us ask God to bless it,
and to keep us faithful
to the Spirit he has given us.

After a brief silence, he joins his hands and continues:

A.

God our Father,
your gift of water
brings life and freshness to the earth;
it washes away our sins
and brings us eternal life.

We ask you now
to bless ✝ this water,
and to give us your protection on this day
which you have made your own.
Renew the living spring of your life within us
and protect us in spirit and body,
that we may be free from sin
and come into your presence
to receve your gift of salvation.
We ask this through Christ our Lord. ℟. **Amen.**

B. Or:

Lord God almighty,
creator of all life,
of body and soul,

652

we ask you to bless ✠ this water:
as we use it in faith
forgive our sins
and save us from all illness
and the power of evil.

Lord,
in your mercy
give us living water,
always springing up as a fountain of salvation:
free us, body and soul, from every danger,
and admit us to your presence
in purity of heart.
Grant this through Christ our Lord.

C. Or (during the Easter season):

Lord God almighty,
hear the prayers of your people:
we celebrate our creation and redemption.
Hear our prayers and bless ✠ this water
which gives fruitfulness to the fields,
and refreshment and cleansing to man.
You chose water to show your goodness
when you led your people to freedom
through the Red Sea
and satisfied their thirst in the desert
with water from the rock.
Water was the symbol used by the prophets
to foretell your new covenant with man.
You made the water of baptism holy
by Christ's baptism in the Jordan:
by it you give us a new birth
and renew us in holiness.
May this water remind us of our baptism,
and let us share the joy
of all who have been baptized at Easter.
We ask this through Christ our Lord.

*Where it is customary, salt may be mixed with the holy
water. The priest blesses the salt, saying:*

Almighty God,
we ask you to bless ✝ this salt
as once you blessed the salt scattered over the water
by the prophet Elisha.
Wherever this salt and water are sprinkled,
drive away the power of evil,
and protect us always
by the presence of your Holy Spirit.
Grant this through Christ our Lord.

Then he pours the salt into the water in silence.

Taking the sprinkler, the priest sprinkles himself and his ministers, then the rest of the clergy and people. He may move through the church for the sprinkling of the people. Meanwhile, an antiphon or another appropriate song is sung.

When he returns to his place and the song is finished, the priest faces the people and, with joined hands, says:

May almighty God cleanse us of our sins,
and through the eucharist we celebrate
make us worthy to sit at his table
in his heavenly kingdom.

The people answer: **Amen.**

When it is prescribed, the Gloria *is then sung or said.*

PENITENTIAL RITE

ALTERNATIVE FORMS FOR C p. 617

ii

Priest or other minister:
Lord Jesus, you came to gather the nations
into the peace of God's kingdom:
Lord, have mercy.

People: **Lord, have mercy.**

Priest or other minister:
You come in word and sacrament to strengthen us in
   holiness:
Christ, have mercy.

People: **Christ, have mercy.**

Priest or other minister:
You will come in glory with salvation for your people:
Lord, have mercy.

People: **Lord, have mercy.** (➤ p. 617)

iii

Priest or other minister:
Lord Jesus, you are mighty God and Prince of peace:
Lord, have mercy.

People: **Lord, have mercy.**

Priest or other minister:
Lord Jesus, you are Son of God and Son of Mary:
Christ, have mercy.

People: **Christ, have mercy.**

Priest or other minister:
Lord Jesus, you are Word made flesh and splendor of
   the Father:
Lord, have mercy.

People: **Lord, have mercy.** (➤ p. 617)

iv

Priest or other minister:
Lord Jesus, you came to reconcile us
to one another and to the Father:
Lord, have mercy.

People: **Lord, have mercy.**

Priest or other minister:
Lord Jesus, you heal the wounds of sin and division:
Christ, have mercy.

People: **Christ, have mercy.**

Priest or other minister:
Lord Jesus, you intercede for us with your Father:
Lord, have mercy.

People: **Lord, have mercy.** (➤ p. 617)

v

Priest or other minister:
You raise the dead to life in the Spirit:
Lord, have mercy.

People: **Lord, have mercy.**

Priest or other minister:
You bring pardon and peace to the sinner:
Christ, have mercy.

People: **Christ, have mercy.**

Priest or other minister:
You bring light to those in darkness:
Lord, have mercy.

People: **Lord, have mercy.** (➤ p. 617)

vi

Priest or other minister:
Lord Jesus, you raise us to new life:
Lord, have mercy.

People: **Lord, have mercy.**

Priest or other minister:
Lord Jesus, you forgive us our sins:
Christ, have mercy.

People: **Christ, have mercy.**

Priest or other minister:
Lord Jesus, you feed us with your body and blood:
Lord, have mercy.

People: **Lord, have mercy.** (➤ p. 617)

vii

Priest or other minister:
Lord Jesus, you have shown us the way to the Father:
Lord, have mercy.

People: **Lord, have mercy.**

Priest or other minister:
Lord Jesus, you have given us the consolation of the
truth:
Christ, have mercy.

People: **Christ, have mercy.**

Priest or other minister:
Lord Jesus, you are the Good Shepherd,
leading us into everlasting life:
Lord, have mercy.

People: **Lord, have mercy.** (➤ p. 617)

viii

Priest or other minister:
Lord Jesus, you healed the sick:
Lord, have mercy.

People: **Lord, have mercy.**

Priest or other minister:
Lord Jesus, you forgave sinners:
Christ, have mercy.

People: **Christ, have mercy.**

Priest or other minister:
Lord Jesus, you give us yourself to heal us and bring us
strength:
Lord, have mercy.

People: **Lord, have mercy.** (➤ p. 617)

PREFACES

ADVENT I (P 1)

The Two Comings of Christ
(From the First Sunday of Advent to December 16)

Father, all-powerful and ever-living God,
we do well always and everywhere to give you thanks
through Jesus Christ our Lord.

When he humbled himself to come among us as a man,
he fulfilled the plan you formed long ago
and opened for us the way to salvation.

Now we watch for the day
hoping that the salvation promised us will be ours
when Christ our Lord will come again in his glory.

And so, with all the choirs of angels in heaven
we proclaim your glory
and join in their unending hymn of praise: ➤ No. 23, p. 627

ADVENT II (P 2)

Waiting for the Two Comings of Christ
(From December 17 to December 24)

Father, all-powerful and ever-living God,
we do well always and everywhere to give you thanks
through Jesus Christ our Lord.

His future coming was proclaimed by all the prophets.
The virgin mother bore him in her womb
    with love beyond all telling.
John the Baptist was his herald
and made him known when at last he came.

In his love he has filled us with joy
as we prepare to celebrate his birth,
so that when he comes he may find us watching in prayer,
our hearts filled with wonder and praise.

And so, with all the choirs of angels in heaven
we proclaim your glory
and join in their unending hymn of praise: ➤ No. 23, p. 627

CHRISTMAS I (P 3)
Christ the Light
(From Christmas to Saturday before Epiphany)

Father, all-powerful and ever-living God,
we do well always and everywhere to give you thanks
through Jesus Christ our Lord.

In the wonder of the incarnation
your eternal Word has brought to the eyes of faith
a new and radiant vision of your glory.
In him we see our God made visible
and so are caught up in love of the God we cannot see.

And so, with all the choirs of angels in heaven
we proclaim you glory
and join in the unending hymn of praise:➤ No. 23, p. 627

CHRISTMAS II (P 4)
Christ Restores Unity to All Creation
(From Christmas to Saturday before Epiphany)

Father, all-powerful and ever-living God,
we do well always and everywhere to give you thanks
through Jesus Christ our Lord.

Today you fill our hearts with joy
as we recognize in Christ the revelation of your love.
No eye can see his glory as our God,
yet now he is seen as one like us.

Christ is your Son before all ages,
yet now he is born in time.
He has come to lift up all things to himself,
to restore unity to creation,
and to lead mankind from exile into your heavenly
    kingdom.

With all the angels of heaven
we sing our joyful hymn of praise: ➤ No. 23, p. 627

CHRISTMAS III (P 5)
Divine and Human Exchange in the Incarnation of the Word
(From Christmas to Saturday before Epiphany)

Father, all-powerful and ever-living God,
we do well always and everywhere to give you thanks

through Jesus Christ our Lord.
Today in him a new light has dawned upon the world:
God has become one with man,
and man has become one again with God.

Your eternal Word has taken upon himself our human
    weakness,
giving our mortal nature immortal value.
So marvelous is this oneness between God and man
that in Christ man restores to man the gift of everlasting
    life.

In our joy we sing to your glory
with all the choirs of angels: ➤ No. 23, p. 627

EPIPHANY (P 6)

Christ the Light of the Nations

Father, all-powerful and ever-living God,
we do well always and everywhere to give you thanks.

Today you revealed in Christ your eternal plan of salvation
and showed him as the light of all peoples.
Now that his glory has shone among us
you have renewed humanity in his immortal image.

Now, with angels and archangels,
and the whole company of heaven,
we sing the unending hymn of your praise:
    ➤ No. 23, p. 627

LENT I (P 8)

The Spiritual Meaning of Lent

Father, all-powerful and ever-living God,
we do well always and everywhere to give you thanks
through Jesus Christ our Lord.

Each year you give us this joyful season
when we prepare to celebrate the paschal mystery
with mind and heart renewed.
You give us a spirit of loving reverence for you,
    our Father,
and of willing service to our neighbor.

As we recall the great events that gave us new life in
    Christ,
you bring the image of your Son to perfection within us.

Now, with angels and archangels,
and the whole company of heaven,
we sing the unending hymn of your praise: ➤ No. 23, p. 627

LENT II (P 9)

The Spirit of Penance

Father, all-powerful and ever-living God,
we do well always and everywhere to give you thanks.

This great season of grace is your gift to your family
to renew us in spirit.
You give us strength to purify our hearts,
to control our desires,
and so to serve you in freedom.

You teach us how to live in this passing world
with our heart set on the world that will never end.

Now, with all the saints and angels,
we praise you for ever: ➤ No. 23, p. 627

LENT III (P 10)

The Fruits of Self-denial

Father, all-powerful and ever-living God,
we do well always and everywhere to give you thanks.

You ask us to express our thanks by self-denial.
We are to master our sinfulness and conquer our pride.
We are to show to those in need your goodness to our-
selves.

Now, with all the saints and angels,
we praise you for ever: ➤ No. 23, p. 627

LENT IV (P 11)

The Reward of Fasting

Father, all-powerful and ever-living God,
we do well always and everywhere to give you thanks.

Through our observance of Lent
you correct our faults and raise our minds to you,
you help us grow in holiness,
and offer us the reward of everlasting life
through Jesus Christ our Lord.

Through him the angels and all the choirs of heaven
worship in awe before your presence.
May our voices be one with theirs
as they sing with joy the hymn of your glory:

➤ No. 23, p. 627

PASSION OF THE LORD I (P 17)

The Power of the Cross

Father, all-powerful and ever-living God,
we do well always and everywhere to give you thanks.

The suffering and death of your Son
brought life to the whole world,
moving our hearts to praise your glory.
The power of the cross reveals your judgment on this
    world
and the kingship of Christ crucified.

We praise you, Lord,
with all the angels and saints in their song of joy:

➤ No. 23, p. 627

PASSION OF THE LORD II (P 18)

The Victory of the Passion

Father, all-powerful and ever-living God,
we do well always and everywhere to give you thanks
through Jesus Christ our Lord.

The days of his life-giving death and glorious resurrection
    are approaching.
This is the hour when he triumphed over Satan's pride.
tl.e time when we celebrate the great event of our redemp-
    tion.

Through Christ
the angels of heaven offer their prayer of adoration
as they rejoice in your presence for ever.
May our voices be one with theirs
in their triumphant hymn of praise: ➤ No. 23, p. 627

EASTER I (P 21)

The Paschal Mystery

(Easter Vigil, Easter Sunday and during the octave)

Father, all-powerful and ever-living God,
we do well always and everywhere to give you thanks
through Jesus Christ our Lord.

We praise you with greater joy than ever
on this Easter night (day),
when Christ became our paschal sacrifice.

He is the true Lamb who took away the sins of the world.
By dying he destroyed our death;
by rising he restored our life.

And so, with all the choirs of angels in heaven
we proclaim your glory
and join in their unending hymn of praise: → No. 23, p. 627

EASTER II (P 22)

New Life in Christ

Father, all-powerful and ever-living God,
we do well always and everywhere to give you thanks
through Jesus Christ our Lord.

We praise you with greater joy than ever in this
      Easter season,
when Christ became our paschal sacrifice.

He has made us children of the light,
rising to new and everlasting life.
He has opened the gates of heaven
to receive his faithful people.
His death is our ransom from death;
his resurrection is our rising to life.

The joy of the resurrection renews the whole world,
while the choirs of heaven sing for ever to your glory:

→ No. 23, p. 627

EASTER III (P 23)

Christ Lives and Intercedes for Us For Ever

Father, all-powerful and ever-living God,
we do well always and everywhere to give you thanks
through Jesus Christ our Lord.

We praise you with greater joy than ever in this
    Easter season,
when Christ became our paschal sacrifice.

He is still our priest,
our advocate who always pleads our cause.
Christ is the victim who dies no more,
the Lamb, once slain, who lives for ever.

The joy of the resurrection renews the whole world,
while the choirs of heaven sing for ever to your glory:

➤ No. 23, p. 627

EASTER IV (P 24)

The Restoration of the Universe through the Paschal Mystery

Father, all-powerful and ever-living God,
we do well always and everywhere to give you thanks
through Jesus Christ our Lord.

We praise you with greater joy than ever in this
    Easter season,
when Christ became our paschal sacrifice.

In him a new age has dawned,
the long reign of sin is ended,
a broken world has been renewed,
and man is once again made whole.

The joy of the resurrection renews the whole world,
while the choirs of heaven sing for ever to your glory:

➤ No. 23, p. 627

EASTER V (P 25)

Christ Is Priest and Victim

Father, all-powerful and ever-living God,
we do well always and everywhere to give you thanks
through Jesus Christ our Lord.

We praise you with greater joy than ever in this
    Easter season,
when Christ became our paschal sacrifice.

As he offered his body on the cross,
his perfect sacrifice fulfilled all others.

As he gave himself into your hands for our salvation,
he showed himself to be the priest, the altar, and the lamb
   of sacrifice.

The joy of the resurrection renews the whole world,
while the choirs of heaven sing for ever to your glory:

➤ No. 23, p. 627

ASCENSION I (P 26)

The Mystery of the Ascension

(Ascension to the Saturday before Pentecost inclusive)

Father, all-powerful and ever-living God,
we do well always and everywhere to give you thanks.

[Today] the Lord Jesus, the king of glory,
the conqueror of sin and death,
ascended to heaven while the angels sang his praises.

Christ, the mediator between God and man,
judge of the world and Lord of all,
has passed beyond our sight,
not to abandon us but to be our hope.
Christ is the beginning, the head of the Church;
where he has gone, we hope to follow.

The joy of the resurrection and ascension renews the
   whole world,
while the choirs of heaven sing for ever to your glory:

➤ No. 23, p. 627

ASCENSION II (P 27)

The Mystery of the Ascension

(Ascension to the Saturday before Pentecost inclusive)

Father, all-powerful and ever-living God,
we do well always and everywhere to give you thanks
through Jesus Christ our Lord.

In his risen body he plainly showed himself to his disciples
and was taken up to heaven in their sight
to claim for us a share in his divine life.

And so, with all the choirs of angels in heaven
we proclaim your glory
and join in their unending hymn of praise: ➤ No. 23, p. 627

WEEKDAYS I (P 37)

All Things Made One in Christ

(For Masses without Proper or Seasonal Preface)

Father, all-powerful and ever-living God,
we do well always and everywhere to give you thanks
through Jesus Christ our Lord.

In him you have renewed all things
and you have given us all a share in his riches.

Though his nature was divine,
he stripped himself of glory
and by shedding his blood on the cross
he brought his peace to the world.

Therefore he was exalted above all creation
and became the source of eternal life
to all who serve him.

And so, with all the choirs of angels in heaven
we proclaim your glory
and join in their unending hymn of praise:

➤ No. 23, p. 627

WEEKDAYS II (P 38)

Salvation Through Christ

(For Masses without Proper or Seasonal Preface)

Father, all-powerful and ever-living God,
we do well always and everywhere to give you thanks.

In love you created man,
in justice you condemned him,
but in mercy you redeemed him,
through Jesus Christ our Lord.

Through him the angels and all the choirs of heaven
worship in awe before your presence.
May our voices be one with theirs
as they sing with joy
the hymn of your glory:

➤ No. 23, p. 627

WEEKDAYS III (P 38)

Praise of God in Creation and through the Conversion of Man

(For Masses without Proper or Seasonal Preface)

Father, all-powerful and ever-living God,
we do well always and everywhere to give you thanks.

Through your beloved Son
you created our human family.
Through him you restored us to your likeness.

Therefore it is your right
to receive the obedience of all creation,
the praise of the Church on earth,
the thanksgiving of your saints in heaven.

We too rejoice with the angels
as we proclaim your glory for ever: → No. 23, p. 627

WEEKDAYS IV (P 40)

Praise of God Is His Gift

(For Masses without Proper or Seasonal Preface)

Father, all-powerful and ever-living God,
we do well always and everywhere to give you thanks.

You have no need of our praise,
yet our desire to thank you is itself your gift.
Our prayer of thanksgiving adds nothing to your greatness,
but makes us grow in your grace,
through Jesus Christ our Lord.

In our joy we sing to your glory
with all the choirs of angels:

WEEKDAYS V (P 41)

The Mystery of Christ Is Proclaimed

(For Masses without Proper or Seasonal Preface)

Father, all-powerful and ever-living God,
we do well always and everywhere to give you thanks
through Jesus Christ our Lord.

With love we celebrate his death.
With living faith we proclaim his resurrection.
With unwavering hope we await his return in glory.

Now, with the saints and all the angels
we praise you for ever: ➔ No. 23, p. 627

WEEKDAYS VI (P 42)

Salvation in Christ

(For Masses without Proper or Seasonal Preface)

Father, it is our duty and our salvation,
always and everywhere
to give you thanks
through your beloved Son, Jesus Christ.

He is the Word through whom you made the universe,
the Savior you sent to redeem us.
By the power of the Holy Spirit
he took flesh and was born of the Virgin Mary.

For our sake he opened his arms on the cross;
he put an end to death
and revealed the resurrection.
In this he fulfilled your will
and won for you a holy people.

And so we join the angels and the saints
in proclaiming your glory: ➔ No. 23, p. 627

HOLY EUCHARIST I (P 47)

Father, all-powerful and ever-living God,
we do well always and everywhere to give you thanks
through Jesus Christ our Lord.

He is the true and eternal priest
who established this unending sacrifice.
He offered himself as a victim for our deliverance
and taught us to make this offering in his memory.
As we eat his body which he gave for us.
we grow in strength.
As we drink his blood which he poured out for us,
we are washed clean.

Now, with angels and archangels,
and the whole company of heaven,
we sing the unending hymn of your praise: ➔ No. 23, p. 627

HOLY EUCHARIST II (P 48)

Father, all-powerful and ever-living God,
we do well always and everywhere to give you thanks
through Jesus Christ our Lord.

At the last supper,
as he sat at table with his apostles,
he offered himself to you as the spotless lamb,
the acceptable gift that gives you perfect praise.
Christ has given us this memorial of his passion
to bring us its saving power until the end of time.

In this great sacrament you feed your people
and strengthen them in holiness,
so that the family of mankind
may come to walk in the light of one faith,
in one communion of love.
We come then to this wonderful sacrament
to be fed at your table
and grow into the likeness of the risen Christ.

Earth unites with heaven
to sing the new song of creation
as we adore and praise you for ever: ➤ No. 23, p. 627

DEDICATION OF A CHURCH I (P 52)

In the Dedicated Church

Father, all-powerful and ever-living God,
we do well always and everywhere to give you thanks.

We thank you now for this house of prayer
in which you bless your family
as we come to you on pilgrimage.
Here you reveal your presence
by sacramental signs,
and make us one with you
through the unseen bond of grace.
Here you build your temple of living stones,
and bring the Church to its full stature
as the body of Christ throughout the world,
to reach its perfection at last
in the heavenly city of Jerusalem,

which is the vision of your peace.

In communion with all the angels and saints
we bless and praise your greatness
in the temple of your glory: ➔ No. 23, p. 627

DEDICATION OF A CHURCH II (P 53)

Outside the Dedicated Church

Father, all-powerful and ever-living God,
we do well always and everywhere to give you thanks.

Your house is a house of prayer,
and your presence makes it a place of blessing.
You give us grace upon grace
to build the temple of your Spirit,
creating its beauty from the holiness of our lives.

Your house of prayer
is also the promise of the Church in heaven.
Here your love is always at work.
preparing the Church on earth
for its heavenly glory
as the sinless bride of Christ,
the joyful mother of a great company of saints.

Now, with the saints and all the angels
we praise you for ever: ➔ No. 23, p. 627

HOLY SPIRIT I (P 54)

(For Votive Masses of the Holy Spirit)

Father, all-powerful and ever-living God,
we do well always and everywhere to give you thanks
through Jesus Christ our Lord.

He ascended above all the heavens,
and from his throne at your right hand
poured into the hearts of your adopted children
the Holy Spirit of your promise.

With steadfast love
we sing your unending praise;
we join with the hosts of heaven
in their triumphant song: ➔ No. 23, p. 627

HOLY SPIRIT II (P 55)

(For Votive Masses of the Holy Spirit)

Father, all-powerful and ever-living God,
we do well always and everywhere to give you thanks.
You give your gifts of grace
for every time and season
as you guide the Church
in the marvelous ways of your providence.

You give us your Holy Spirit
to help us always by his power,
so that with loving trust
we may turn to you in all our troubles,
and give you thanks in all our joys,
through Jesus Christ our Lord.

In our joy we sing to your glory
with all the choirs of angels: ➤ No. 23, p. 627

BLESSED VIRGIN MARY I (P 56)

Motherhood of Mary

Father, all-powerful and ever-living God,
we do well always and everywhere to give you thanks
(as we celebrate . . . of the Blessed Virgin Mary).
(as we honor the Blessed Virgin Mary).

Through the power of the Holy Spirit,
she became the virgin mother of your only Son,
our Lord Jesus Christ,
who is for ever the light of the world.

Through him the choirs of angels
and all the powers of heaven
praise and worship your glory.
May our voices blend with theirs
as we join in their unending hymn: ➤ No. 23, p. 627

BLESSED VIRGIN MARY II (P 57)

The Church Echoes Mary's Song of Praise

Father, all-powerful and ever-living God,
we do well always and everywhere to give you thanks,
and to praise you for your gifts
as we contemplate your saints in glory.

In celebrating the memory of the Blessed Virgin Mary,
it is our special joy to echo her song of thanksgiving.
What wonders you have worked throughout the world.
All generations have shared the greatness of your love.
When you looked on Mary your lowly servant,
you raised her to be the mother of Jesus Christ, your
Son, our Lord,
the savior of all mankind.

Through him the angels of heaven
offer their prayer of adoration
as they rejoice in your presence for ever.
May our voices be one with theirs
in their triumphant hymn of praise: ➜ No. 23, p. 627

ANGELS (P 60)

The Glory of God in the Angels

Father, all-powerful and ever-living God,
we do well always and everywhere to give you thanks.

In praising your faithful angels and archangels,
we also praise your glory,
for in honoring them, we honor you, their creator.
Their splendor shows us your greatness,
which surpasses in goodness the whole of creation.

Through Christ our Lord
the great army of angels rejoices in your glory.
In adoration and joy
we make their hymn of praise our own: ➜ No. 23, p. 627

APOSTLES I (P 64)

The Apostles Are Shepherds of God's People
(For Masses of the apostles)

Father, all-powerful and ever-living God,
we do well always and everywhere to give you thanks.

You are the eternal Shepherd
who never leaves his flock untended.
Through the apostles
you watch over us and protect us always.
You made them shepherds of the flock
to share in the work of your Son,
and from their place in heaven they guide us still.

And so, with all the choirs of angels in heaven
we proclaim your glory
and join in their unending hymn of praise: → No. 23, p. 627

APOSTLES II (P 65)

Apostolic Foundation and Witness
(For Masses of the apostles and evangelists)

Father, all-powerful and ever-living God,
we do well always and everywhere to give you thanks.

You founded your Church on the apostles
to stand firm for ever
as the sign on earth of your infinite holiness
and as the living gospel for all men to hear.

With steadfast love
we sing your unending praise:
we join with the hosts of heaven
in their triumphant song: → No. 23, p. 627

MARTYRS (P 66)

The Sign and Example of Martyrdom
(For solemnities and feasts of martyrs)

Father, all-powerful and ever-living God,
we do well always and everywhere to give you thanks.

Your holy martyr N. followed the example of Christ,
and gave his (her) life for the glory of your name.
His (her) death reveals your power
shining through our human weakness.
You choose the weak and make them strong
in bearing witness to you,
through Jesus Christ our Lord.

In our unending joy we echo on earth
the song of the angels in heaven
as they praise your glory for ever: → No. 23, p. 627

PASTORS (P 67)

The Presence of Shepherds in the Church
(For solemnities and feasts of pastors)

Father, all-powerful and ever-living God,
we do well always and everywhere to give you thanks.

You give the Church this feast in honor of Saint N.;
you inspire us by his holy life,
instruct us by his preaching,
and give us your protection in answer to his prayers.

We join the angels and the saints
as they sing their unending hymn of praise:

➔ No. 23, p. 627

VIRGINS AND RELIGIOUS (P 68)

The Sign of a Life Consecrated to God
(For solemnities and feasts of virgins and religious)

Father, all-powerful and ever-living God,
we do well always and everywhere to give you thanks.

Today we honor your saints
who consecrated their lives to Christ
for the sake of the kingdom of heaven.
What love you show us
as you recall mankind to its innocence,
and invite us to taste on earth
the gifts of the world to come!

Now, with the saints and all the angels
we praise you for ever:

➔ No. 23, p. 627

HOLY MEN AND WOMEN I (P 69)

The Glory of the Saints
(For Masses of all saints, patrons, and titulars of churches, and
on the solemnities and feasts of saints which have no Proper Preface)

Father, all-powerful and ever-living God,
we do well always and everywhere to give you thanks.

You are glorified in your saints,
for their glory is the crowning of your gifts.
In their lives on earth
you give us an example.
In our communion with them,
you give us their friendship.
In their prayer for the Church
you give us strength and protection.
This great company of witnesses spurs us on to victory,
to share their prize of everlasting glory,
through Jesus Christ our Lord.

With angels and archangels
and the whole company of saints
we sing our unending hymn of praise: ➤ No. 23, p. 627

HOLY MEN AND WOMEN II (P 70)

The Activity of the Saints

(For Masses of all saints, patrons, and titulars of churches, and on the solemnities and feasts of saints which have no Proper Preface)

Father, all-powerful and ever-living God,
we do well always and everywhere to give you thanks.

You renew the Church in every age
by raising up men and women outstanding in holiness,
living witnesses of your unchanging love.
They inspire us by their heroic lives,
and help us by their constant prayers
to be the living sign of your saving power.

We praise you, Lord, with all the angels and saints
in their song of joy: ➤ No. 23, p. 627

RELIGIOUS PROFESSION (P 75)

Father, all-powerful and ever-living God,
we do well always and everywhere to give you thanks
through Jesus Christ our Lord.

He came, the son of a virgin mother,
named those blessed who were pure of heart,
and taught by his whole life the perfection of chastity.

He chose always to fulfill your holy will,
and became obedient even to dying for us,
offering himself to you as a perfect oblation.

He consecrated more closely to your service
those who leave all things for your sake,
and promised that they would find a heavenly treasure.

And so, with all the angels and saints
we proclaim your glory
and join in their unending hymn of praise: ➤ No. 23, p. 627

CHRISTIAN UNITY (P 76)

Father, all-powerful and ever-living God,
we do well always and everywhere to give you thanks
through Jesus Christ our Lord.
Through Christ you bring us to the knowledge of your
truth,
that we may be united by one faith and one baptism
to become his body.
Through Christ you have given the Holy Spirit to all peoples.
How wonderful are the works of the Spirit,
revealed in so many gifts!
Yet how marvelous is the unity
the Spirit creates from their diversity,
as he dwells in the hearts of your children,
filling the whole Church with his presence
and guiding it with his wisdom!
In our joy we sing to your glory
with all the choirs of angels:
➤ No. 23, p. 627

CHRISTIAN DEATH I (P 77)

Father, all-powerful and ever-living God,
we do all always and everywhere to give you thanks
through Jesus Christ our Lord.
In him, who rose from the dead,
our hope of resurrection dawned.
The sadness of death gives way
to the bright promise of immortality.
Lord, for your faithful people life is changed, not ended.
When the body of our earthly dwelling lies in death
we gain an everlasting dwelling place in heaven.
And so, with all the choirs of angels in heaven
we proclaim your glory
and join in their unending hymn of praise:
➤ No. 23, p. 627

CHRISTIAN DEATH II (P 78)

Father, all-powerful and ever-living God,
we do well always and everywhere to give you thanks
through Jesus Christ our Lord.

He chose to die
that he might free all men from dying.
He gave his life
that we might live to you alone for ever.

In our joy we sing to your glory
with all the choirs of angels:
➤ No. 23, p. 627

CHRISTIAN DEATH III (P 79)

Father, all-powerful and ever-living God,
we do all always and everywhere to give you thanks
through Jesus Christ our Lord.

In him the world is saved,
man is reborn,
and the dead rise again to life.

Through Christ the angels of heaven
offer their prayer of adoration
as they rejoice in your presence for ever.
May our voices be one with theirs
in their triumphant hymn of praise:
➤ No. 23, p. 627

CHRISTIAN DEATH IV (P 80)

Father, all-powerful and ever-living God,
we do well always and everywhere to give you thanks.

By your power you bring us to birth.
By your providence you rule our lives.
By your command you free us at last from sin
as we return to the dust from which we came.
Through the saving death of your Son
we rise at your word to the glory of the resurrection.

Now we join the angels and the saints
as they sing their unending hymn of praise:
➤ No. 23, p. 627

CHRISTIAN DEATH V (P 81)

Father, all-powerful and ever-living God,
we do well always and everywhere to give you thanks
through Jesus Christ our Lord.

Death is the just reward for our sins,
yet, when at last we die,
your loving kindness calls us back to life
in company with Christ
whose victory is our redemption.

Our hearts are joyful,
for we have seen your salvation,
and now with the angels and saints
we praise you for ever: ➤ No. 23, p. 627

INDEPENDENCE DAY AND OTHER CIVIC OBSERVANCES I (P 82)

Father, all-powerful and ever-living God,
we do well to sing your praise for ever,
and to give you thanks in all we do
through Jesus Christ our Lord.

He spoke to men a message of peace
and taught us to live as brothers.
His message took form in the vision of our fathers
as they fashioned a nation
where men might live as one.
This message lives on in our midst
as a task for men today
and a promise for tomorrow.

We thank you, Father, for your blessings in the past
and for all that, with your help, we must yet achieve.
And so, with hearts full of love,
we join the angels today and every day of our lives,
to sing your glory in a hymn of endless praise:
                              ➤ No. 23, p. 627

INDEPENDENCE DAY AND OTHER CIVIC OBSERVANCES II (P 83)

Father, all-powerful and ever-living God,
we praise your oneness and truth.

We praise you as the God of creation,
and the Father of Jesus, the Savior of mankind,
in whose image we seek to live.
He loved the children of the lands he walked
and enriched them with his witness of justice and truth.
He lived and died that we might be reborn in the Spirit
and filled with love of all men.

And so, with hearts full of love,
we join the angels, today and every day of our lives,
to sing your glory in a hymn of endless praise:

➤ No. 23, p. 627

THANKSGIVING DAY (P 84)

Father,
we do well to join all creation,
in heaven and on earth,
in praising you, our mighty God
through Jesus Christ our Lord.

You made man to your own image
and set him over all creation.
Once you chose a people
and gave them a destiny
and, when you brought them out of bondage to freedom,
they carried with them the promise
that all men would be blessed
and all men could be free.

What the prophets pledged
was fulfilled in Jesus Christ,
your Son and our saving Lord.
It has come to pass in every generation
for all men who have believed that Jesus
by his death and resurrection
gave them a new freedom in his Spirit.

It happened to our fathers,
who came to this land as if out of the desert
into a place of promise and hope.
It happens to us still, in our time,
as you lead all men through your Church
to the blessed vision of peace.

And so, with hearts full of love,
we join the angels, today and every day of our lives,
to sing your glory in a hymn of endless praise:

➤ No. 23, p. 627

PROPER COMMUNICANTES
AND HANC IGITUR
FOR EUCHARISTIC PRAYER I

Communicantes for Christmas

In union with the whole Church
we celebrate that day (night)
when Mary without loss of her virginity
gave this world its savior.
We honor her,
the ever-virgin mother of Jesus Christ, our Lord and
  God, etc., p. 629.

Communicantes for the Epiphany

In union with the whole Church
we celebrate that day
when your only Son,
sharing your eternal glory,
showed himself in a human body.
We honor Mary, etc., p. 629.

Communicantes for Easter

In union with the whole Church
we celebrate that day (night)
when Jesus Christ, our Lord,
rose from the dead in his human body.
We honor Mary, etc., p. 629.

Hanc Igitur for Easter

Father, accept this offering
from your whole family
and from those born into the new life
of water and the Holy Spirit,
with all their sins forgiven.
Grant us your peace in this life,
save us from final damnation,
and count us among those you have chosen.
[Through Christ our Lord. Amen.]

➔ Canon, p. 629: Bless, etc.

Communicantes for the Ascension

In union with the whole Church
we celebrate that day
when your only Son, our Lord,
took his place with you
and raised our frail human nature to glory.
We honor Mary, etc., p. 629.

Communicantes for Pentecost

In union with the whole Church
we celebrate the day of Pentecost
when the Holy Spirit appeared to the apostles
in the form of countless tongues.
We honor Mary, etc., p. 629.

SOLEMN BLESSINGS

The following blessings may be used, at the discretion of the priest, at the end of Mass, or after the liturgy of the word, the office, and the celebration of the sacraments.

The deacon, or in his absence the priest himself, gives the invitation: Bow your heads and pray for God's blessing. *Another form of invitation may be used. Then the priest extends his hands over the people while he says or sings the blessings. All respond:* Amen.

I. Celebrations during the Proper of Seasons

1. ADVENT

You believe that the Son of God once came to us;
you look for him to come again.
May his coming bring you the light of his holiness
and free you with his blessing. ℟. **Amen.**

May God make you steadfast in faith,
joyful in hope, and untiring in love
all the days of your life. ℟. **Amen.**

You rejoice that our Redeemer came to live with us as
man.
When he comes again in glory,
may he reward you with endless life. ℟. **Amen.**

May almighty God bless you,
the Father, and the Son, ✠ and the Holy Spirit. ℟. **Amen.**

2.   CHRISTMAS

When he came to us as man,
the Son of God scattered the darkness of this world,
and filled this holy night (day) with his glory.
May the God of infinite goodness
scatter the darkness of sin
and brighten your hearts with holiness. ℟. **Amen.**

God sent his angels to shepherds
to herald the great joy of our Savior's birth.
May he fill you with joy
and make you heralds of his gospel. ℟. **Amen.**

When the Word became man,
earth was joined to heaven.
May he give you his peace and good will,
and fellowship with all the heavenly host. ℟. **Amen.**

May almighty God bless you,
the Father, and the Son, ✛ and the Holy Spirit. ℟. **Amen.**

3. BEGINNING OF THE NEW YEAR

Every good gift comes from the Father of light.
May he grant you his grace and every blessing,
and keep you safe throughout the coming year. ℟. **Amen.**

May he grant you unwavering faith,
constant hope, and love that endures to the end. ℟. **Amen.**

May he order your days and work in his peace,
hear your every prayer,
and lead you to everlasting life and joy. ℟. **Amen.**

May almighty God bless you,
the Father, and the Son, ✛ and the Holy Spirit, ℟. **Amen.**

4. EPIPHANY

God has called you out of darkness
into his wonderful light.
May you experience his kindness and blessings,
and be strong in faith, in hope, and in love. ℟. **Amen.**

Because you are followers of Christ,
who appeared on this day as a light shining in darkness,
may he make you a light to all your sisters and brothers.
℟. **Amen.**

The wise men followed the star,
and found Christ who is light from light.
May you too find the Lord
when your pilgrimage is ended. ℟. **Amen.**

May almighty God bless you,
the Father, and the Son, ✛ and the Holy Spirit. ℟. **Amen.**

5. PASSION OF THE LORD

The Father of mercies has given us an example of unselfish love
in the sufferings of his only Son.
Through your service of God and neighbor
may you receive his countless blessings. ℟. **Amen.**

You believe that by his dying
Christ destroyed death for ever.
May he give you everlasting life. ℟. **Amen.**

He humbled himself for our sakes.
May you follow his example
and share in his resurrection. ℟. **Amen.**

May almighty God bless you,
the Father, and the Son, ✝ and the Holy Spirit. ℟. **Amen.**

6. EASTER VIGIL AND EASTER SUNDAY

May almighty God bless you on this solemn feast of
   Easter,
and may he protect you against all sin. ℟. **Amen.**

Through the resurrection of his Son
God has granted us healing.
May he fulfill his promises,
and bless you with eternal life. ℟. **Amen.**

You have mourned for Christ's sufferings;
now you celebrate the joy of his resurrection.
May you come with joy to the feast which lasts for ever.
   ℟. **Amen.**

May almighty God bless you,
the Father, and the Son, ✝ and the Holy Spirit. ℟. **Amen.**

7. EASTER SEASON

Through the resurrection of his Son
God has redeemed you and made you his children.
May he bless you with joy. ℟. **Amen.**

The Redeemer has given you lasting freedom.
May you inherit his everlasting life. ℟. **Amen.**

By faith you rose with him in baptism.
May your lives be holy,
so that you will be united with him for ever ℟. **Amen.**

May almighty God bless you,
the Father, and the Son, ✝ and the Holy Spirit. ℟. **Amen.**

8. ASCENSION

May almighty God bless you on this day
when his only Son ascended into heaven

to prepare a place for you. ℟. **Amen.**

After his resurrection, Christ was seen by his disciples.
When he appears as judge
may you be pleasing for ever in his sight. ℟. **Amen.**

You believe that Jesus has taken his seat in majesty
at the right hand of the Father.
May you have the joy of experiencing
that he is also with you to the end of time,
according to his promise. ℟. **Amen.**

May almighty God bless you,
the Father, and the Son, ✢ and the Holy Spirit. ℟. **Amen.**

9. HOLY SPIRIT

(This day) the Father of light
has enlightened the minds of the disciples
by the outpouring of the Holy Spirit.
May he bless you
and give you the gifts of the Spirit for ever. ℟. **Amen.**

May that fire which hovered over the disciples
as tongues of flame
burn out all evil from your hearts
and made them glow with pure light. ℟. **Amen.**

God inspired speech in different tongues
to proclaim one faith.
May he strengthen your faith
and fulfill your hope of seeing him face to face. ℟. **Amen.**

May almighty God bless you,
the Father, and the Son, ✢ and the Holy Spirit. ℟. **Amen.**

10. ORDINARY TIME I

Blessing of Aaron (Num 6:24-26)

May the Lord bless you and keep you. ℟. **Amen.**
May his face shine upon you,
and be gracious to you. ℟. **Amen.**

May he look upon you with kindness,
and give you his peace. ℟. **Amen.**

May almighty God bless you,
the Father, and the Son, ✢ and the Holy Spirit. ℟. **Amen.**

11. ORDINARY TIME II (Phil 4:7)

May the peace of God
which is beyond all understanding
keep your hearts and minds
in the knowledge and love of God
and of his Son, our Lord Jesus Christ. ℟. **Amen.**

May almighty God bless you,
the Father, and the Son, ✛ and the Holy Spirit. ℟. **Amen.**

12. ORDINARY TIME III

May almighty God bless you in his mercy,
and make you always aware of his saving wisdom.
    ℟. **Amen.**

May he strengthen your faith with proofs of his love,
so that you will persevere in good works. ℟. **Amen.**

May he direct your steps to himself,
and show you how to walk in charity and peace. ℟. **Amen.**

May almighty God bless you,
the Father, and the Son, ✛ and the Holy Spirit. ℟. **Amen.**

13. ORDINARY TIME IV

May the God of all consolation
bless you in every way
and grant you peace all the days of your life. ℟. **Amen.**

May he free you from all anxiety
and strengthen your hearts in his love. ℟. **Amen.**

May he enrich you with his gifts of faith, hope, and love,
so that what you do in this life
will bring you to the happiness of everlasting life.
    ℟. **Amen.**

May almighty God bless you,
the Father, and the Son, ✛ and the Holy Spirit. ℟. **Amen.**

14. ORDINARY TIME V

May almighty God keep you from all harm
and bless you with every good gift. ℟. **Amen.**

May he set his Word in your heart
and fill you with lasting joy ℟. **Amen.**

May you walk in his ways,

always knowing what is right and good,
until you enter your heavenly inheritance. ℟. **Amen.**

May almighty God bless you,
the Father, and the Son, ✢ and the Holy Spirit. ℟. **Amen.**

II. Celebrations of Saints

15. BLESSED VIRGIN MARY

Born of the Blessed Virgin Mary,
the Son of God redeemed mankind.
May he enrich you with his blessings. ℟. **Amen.**

You received the author of life through Mary.
May you always rejoice in her loving care. ℟. **Amen.**
You have come to rejoice at Mary's feast.
May you be filled with the joys of the Spirit
and the gifts of your eternal home. ℟. **Amen.**

May almighty God bless you,
the Father, and the Son, ✢ and the Holy Spirit. ℟. **Amen.**

16. PETER AND PAUL

The Lord has set you firm within his Church,
which he built upon the rock of Peter's faith.
May he bless you with a faith that never falters. ℟. **Amen.**

The Lord has given you knowledge of the faith
through the labors and preaching of St. Paul.
May his example inspire you to lead others to Christ
by the manner of your life. ℟. **Amen.**

May the keys of Peter, and the words of Paul,
their undying witness and their prayers,
lead you to the joy of that eternal home
which Peter gained by his cross, and Paul by the sword.
℟. **Amen.**

May almighty God bless you,
the Father, and the Son, ✢ and the Holy Spirit. ℟. **Amen.**

17. APOSTLES

May God who founded his Church upon the apostles
bless you through the prayers of St. N. (and St. N.).
℟. **Amen.**

May God inspire you to follow the example of the
  apostles,
and give you witness to the truth before all men.
  ℟. **Amen.**

The teaching of the apostles has strengthened your faith.
May their prayers lead you
to your true and eternal home. ℟. **Amen.**

May almighty God bless you,
the Father, and the Son, ✚ and the Holy Spirit.   **Amen.**

18. ALL SAINTS

God is the glory and joy of all his saints,
whose memory we celebrate today.
May his blessing be with you always. ℟. **Amen.**

May the prayers of the saints deliver you from the present
  evil.
May their example of holy living
turn your thoughts to service of God and neighbor.
  ℟. **Amen.**

God's holy Church rejoices that her saints
have reached their heavenly goal,
and are in lasting peace.
May you come to share all the joys of our Father's house.
  ℟. **Amen.**

May almighty God bless you,
the Father, and the Son, ✚ and the Holy Spirit. ℟. **Amen.**

III. Other Blessings

19. DEDICATION OF A CHURCH

The Lord of earth and heaven
has assembled you before him this day
to dedicate this house of prayer
(to recall the dedication of this church).
May he fill you with the blessings of heaven. ℟. **Amen.**

God the Father wills that all his children
scattered throughout the world
become one family in his Son.
May he make you his temple,
the dwelling-place of his Holy Spirit. ℟. **Amen.**

May God free you from every bond of sin,
dwell within you and give you joy.
May you live with him for ever
in the company of all his saints.
May almighty God bless you,
the Father, and the Son, ✠ and the Holy Spirit. ℟. **Amen.**

20. THE DEAD

In his great love,
the God of all consolation gave man the gift of life.
May he bless you with faith
in the resurrection of his Son,
and with the hope of rising to new life. ℟. **Amen.**

To us who are alive
may he grant forgiveness,
and to all who have died
a place of light and peace. ℟. **Amen.**

As you believe that Jesus rose from the dead,
so may you live with him for ever in joy. ℟. **Amen.**

May almighty God bless you,
the Father, and the Son, ✠ and the Holy Spirit. ℟. **Amen.**

PRAYERS OVER THE PEOPLE

*The following prayers may be used, at the discretion of
the priest, at the end of the Mass, or after the liturgy of
the word, the office, and the celebration of the sacraments.*

*The deacon, or in his absence the priest himself, gives
the invitation:* Bow your heads and pray for God's
blessing. *Another form of invitation may be used. Then
the priest extends his hands over the people while he
says or sings the prayer. All respond:* Amen.
After the prayer, the priest always adds:

And may the blessing of almighty God,
the Father, and the Son, ✠ and the Holy Spirit,
come upon you and remain with you for ever. ℟. **Amen.**

1. Lord,
    have mercy on your people.
    Grant us in this life the good things
    that lead to the everlasting life you prepare for us.
    We ask this through Christ our Lord.

2. Lord,
   grant your people your protection and grace.
   Give them health of mind and body,
   perfect love for one another,
   and make them always faithful to you.
   Grant this through Christ our Lord.

3. Lord,
   may all Christian people both know and cherish
   the heavenly gifts they have received.
   We ask this in the name of Jesus the Lord.

4. Lord,
   bless your people and make them holy
   so that, avoiding evil,
   they may find in you the fulfillment of their longing.
   We ask this through Christ our Lord.

5. Lord,
   bless and strengthen your people.
   May they remain faithful to you
   and always rejoice in your mercy.
   We ask this in the name of Jesus the Lord.

6. Lord,
   you care for your people even when they stray.
   Grant us a complete change of heart,
   so that we may follow you with greater fidelity.
   Grant this through Christ our Lord.

7. Lord,
   send your light upon your family.
   May they continue to enjoy your favor
   and devote themselves to doing good.
   We ask this through Christ our Lord.

8. Lord,
   we rejoice that you are our creator and ruler.
   As we call upon your generosity,
   renew and keep us in your love.
   Grant this through Christ our Lord.

9. Lord,
   we pray for your people who believe in you.
   May they enjoy the gift of your love,

share it with others,
and spread it everywhere.
We ask this in the name of Jesus the Lord.

10. Lord,
bless your people who hope for your mercy.
Grant that they may receive
the things they ask for at your prompting.
Grant this through Christ our Lord.

11. Lord,
bless us with your heavenly gifts,
and in your mercy make us ready to do your will.
We ask this through Christ our Lord.

12. Lord,
protect your people always,
that they may be free from every evil
and serve you with all their hearts.
We ask this through Christ our Lord.

13. Lord,
help your people to seek you with all their hearts
and to deserve what you promise.
Grant this through Christ our Lord.

14. Father,
help your people to rejoice in the mystery of redemption
and to win its reward.
We ask this in the name of Jesus the Lord.

15. Lord,
have pity on your people;
help them each day to avoid what displeases you
and grant that they may serve you with joy.
We ask this through Christ our Lord.

16. Lord,
care for your people and purify them.
Console them in this life
and bring them to the life to come.
We ask this in the name of Jesus the Lord.

17. Father,
look with love upon your people,

the love which our Lord Jesus Christ showed us
when he delivered himself to evil men
and suffered the agony of the cross,
for he is Lord for ever.

18. Lord,
grant that your faithful people
may continually desire to relive the mystery of the
    eucharist
and so be reborn to lead a new life.
We ask this through Christ our Lord.

19. Lord God,
in your great mercy,
enrich your people with your grace
and strengthen them by your blessing
so that they may praise you always.
Grant this through Christ our Lord.

20. May God bless you with every good gift from on high.
May he keep you pure and holy in his sight at all times.
May he bestow the riches of his grace upon you,
bring you the good news of salvation,
and always fill you with love for all men.
We ask this through Christ our Lord.

21. Lord,
make us pure in mind and body,
that we will avoid all evil pleasures
and always delight in you.
We ask this in the name of Jesus the Lord.

22. Lord,
bless your people and fill them with zeal.
Strengthen them by your love to do your will.
We ask this through Christ our Lord.

23. Lord,
come, live in your people
and strengthen them by your grace.
Help them to remain close to you in prayer
and give them a true love for one another.
Grant this through Christ our Lord.

24. Father,
    look kindly on your children who put their trust in you;
    bless them and keep them from all harm,
    strengthen them against the attacks of the devil.
    May they never offend you
    but seek to love you in all they do.
    We ask this through Christ our Lord.

FEASTS OF SAINTS

25. God our Father,
    may all Christian people rejoice in the glory of your
        saints.
    Give us fellowship with them
    and unending joy in your kingdom.
    We ask this in the name of Jesus the Lord.

26. Lord,
    you have given us many friends in heaven.
    Through their prayers we are confident
    that you will watch over us always
    and fill our hearts with your love.
    Grant this through Christ our Lord.

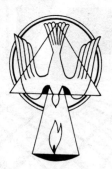

VIRGINIA BRODERICK

PROPER OF SAINTS (Cont'd)

Oct. 18 — ST. LUKE, Evangelist

Feast

St. Luke was born in Antioch and exercised the profession of a doctor. Together with St. Paul, he evangelized Greece and Rome. He wrote the third Gospel and the Acts of the Apostles. He suffered martyrdom toward the end of the 1st century. He is typified by an ox (one of the four living creatures of the vision of Ezekiel), because he begins his Gospel with the history of Zechariah, the priest, offering sacrifice to God, and emphasizes the universal priesthood of Christ.

ENTRANCE ANT. Is 52, 7

How beautiful on the mountains are the feet of the man who brings tidings of peace, joy and salvation.

➜ No. 2, p. 614

OPENING PRAYER

Father,
you chose Luke the evangelist to reveal
by preaching and writing
the mystery of your love for the poor.
Unite in one heart and spirit
all who glory in your name,
and let all nations come to see your salvation.
Grant this through our Lord Jesus Christ, your Son,
who lives and reigns with you and the Holy Spirit,
one God, for ever and ever. ℟. **Amen.** ℣

READING I 2 Tm 4, 9-17

Paul gives the impression of being abandoned by all on whom he has previously depended. The one who remains with him, and particularly in time of trouble, is the Lord.

A reading from the second letter of Paul to Timothy

Do your best to join me soon, for Demas, enamored of the present world, has left me and gone to Thessalonica. Crescens has gone to Galatia and Titus to Dalmatia. I have no one with me but Luke. Get Mark

695

and bring him with you, for he can be of great service to me. Tychicus I have sent to Ephesus. When you come, bring the cloak I left in Troas with Carpus, and the books, especially the parchments.

Alexander the coppersmith did me a great deal of harm; the Lord will repay him according to his deeds. Meanwhile, you too had better be on guard, for he has strongly resisted our preaching. At the first hearing of my case in court, no one took my part. In fact everyone abandoned me. May it not be held against them! But the Lord stood by my side and gave me strength, so that through me the preaching task might be completed and all the nations might hear the gospel.—This is the Word of the Lord. ℞. **Thanks be to God.** ⌄

Responsorial Psalm   Ps 145, 10-11. 12-13. 17-18

℞. (12) **Your friends tell the glory of your kingship, Lord.**

Let all your works give you thanks, O Lord,
    and let your faithful ones bless you.
Let them discourse of the glory of your kingdom
    and speak of your might. — ℞

Making known to men your might
    and the glorious splendor of your kingdom.
Your kingdom is a kingdom for all ages,
    and your dominion endures through all generations. — ℞

The Lord is just in all his ways
    and holy in all his works.
The Lord is near to all who call upon him,
    to all who call upon him in truth. — ℞ ⌄

GOSPEL   Lk 10, 1-9

Alleluia (Jn 15, 16)

℞. **Alleluia.** I have chosen you from the world, says the Lord,
    to go and bear fruit that will last. ℞. **Alleluia.**

Jesus appoints the seventy-two and tells them to be ready to go, to be on their way. Their mission is to preach the word of the Lord. They are not to be concerned over what they will eat or where they will sleep. These things will be provided. Their task is to make the word of the Lord visible.

℣. The Lord be with you. ℞. **And also with you.**

✠ A reading from the holy gospel according to Luke
℞. **Glory to you, Lord.**

The Lord appointed a further seventy-two and sent them in pairs before him to every town and place he intended to visit. He said to them: "The harvest is rich but the workers are few; therefore ask the harvest-master to send workers to his harvest. Be on your way, and remember: I am sending you as lambs in the midst of wolves. Do not carry a walking staff or traveling bag; wear no sandals and greet no one along the way. On entering any house, first say, 'Peace to this house.' If there is a peaceable man there, your peace will rest on him; if not, it will come back to you. Stay in the one house eating and drinking what they have, for the laborer is worth his wage. Do not move from house to house.

"Into whatever city you go, after they welcome you, eat what they set before you, and cure the sick there. Say to them, 'The reign of God is at hand.'"
—This is the gospel of the Lord. ℞. **Praise to you, Lord Jesus Christ.**   ➔ No. 15, p. 623

PRAYER OVER THE GIFTS

Father,
may your gifts from heaven free our hearts to serve you.
May the sacrifice we offer on the feast of St. Luke bring us healing and lead us to eternal glory,
where Jesus is Lord for ever and ever.
℞. **Amen.**   ➔ No. 21, p. 626 (Pref. P 65)

COMMUNION ANT.   See Lk 10, 1. 9
The Lord sent disciples to proclaim to all the towns: the kingdom of God is very near to you.

PRAYER AFTER COMMUNION

All-powerful God,
may the eucharist we have received at your altar
make us holy
and strengthen us in the faith of the gospel
preached by St. Luke.
We ask this in the name of Jesus the Lord.
℟. **Amen.**   ⇢ No. 32, p. 650

————————————

[In the dioceses of the United States, Memorial]

Oct. 19 — STS. ISAAC JOGUES AND JOHN DE BREBEUF, Priests and Martyrs, AND COMPANIONS, Martyrs

Optional Memorial

Isaac Jogues, John de Brebeuf, Charles Garnier, Anthony Daniel, Gabriel Lallemant, Noel Chabanel, John de Lalande, and Rene Goupil, French Jesuits, were among the missionaries who preached the Gospel to Huron and Iroquois Indians in the United States and Canada. They were martyred by the Iroquois Indians in the years 1642, 1648, and 1649. Pope Pius XI beatified them on June 21, 1925, and in 1930 they were canonized by the same Pope.

Common of Martyrs, p. 1049; or Common of Pastors: for Missionaries, p. 1077.

OPENING PRAYER

Father,
you consecrated the first beginnings
of the faith in North America
by the preaching and martyrdom
of Saints John and Isaac and their companions.
By the help of their prayers
may the Christian faith continue to grow
throughout the world.
We ask this through our Lord Jesus Christ, your Son,
who lives and reigns with you and the Holy Spirit,
one God, for ever and ever. ℟. **Amen.**

Reading I (2 Cor 4, 7-15), p. 1147, no. 3.
Responsorial Psalm (Ps 126), p. 1145, no. 4.
Gospel (Mt 28, 16-20), p. 1171, no. 3.

The Same Day, Oct. 19
ST. PAUL OF THE CROSS, Priest

Optional Memorial

This holy Founder of the "Passionists" had always a great love for Christ crucified, and his Congregation has continued to preach "the mystery of the Cross and devotion to the Passion." He died at Rome in 1775.

ENTRANCE ANT.   1 Cor 2, 2

I resolved that while I was with you I would think of nothing but Jesus Christ and him crucified.

➤ No. 2, p. 614

OPENING PRAYER

Father,
you gave your priest St. Paul
a special love for the cross of Christ.
May his example inspire us
to embrace our own cross with courage.
Grant this through our Lord Jesus Christ, your Son,
who lives and reigns with you and the Holy Spirit,
one God, for ever and ever. ℟. **Amen.**

Readings and Intervenient Chants from the Common of Pastors, p. 1154, or the Common of Holy Men and Women: for Religious, p. 1195.

Reading I (1Cor 1, 18-25), p. 1164, no. 2.
Responsorial Psalm (Ps 117), p. 1163, no. 6.
Gospel (Mt 16, 24-27), p. 1222, no. 5.

PRAYER OVER THE GIFTS

All-powerful God,
receive the gifts we offer
in memory of St. Paul of the Cross.
May we who celebrate the mystery
of the Lord's suffering and death

put into effect the self-sacrificing love
we proclaim in this eucharist.
We ask this through Christ our Lord.
℟. **Amen.**   ➔ No 21, p. 626 (Pref. P 37-42)

COMMUNION ANT.   1 Cor 1, 23-24
**We preach a Christ who was crucified; he is the
power and the wisdom of God.** ℣

PRAYER AFTER COMMUNION
Lord,
in the life of St. Paul
you helped us to understand the mystery of the
    cross.
May the sacrifice we have offered strengthen us,
keep us faithful to Christ,
and help us to work in the Church
for the salvation of all mankind.
We ask this in the name of Jesus the Lord.
℟. **Amen.** _____ ➔ No. 32, p. 650

Oct. 23 — ST. JOHN OF CAPISTRANO, Priest

Optional Memorial

St. John was born at Capistrano in 1385. He was ordained a Franciscan priest. He preached a crusade in which
seventy thousand warriors enrolled. These crusades,
with God's assistance, delivered Europe from the Mo-
hammedans. St. John died in 1456.

Common of Pastors: for Missionaries, p. 1077.

OPENING PRAYER
Lord,
you raised up St. John of Capistrano
to give your people comfort in their trials.
May your Church enjoy unending peace
and be secure in your protection.
We ask this through our Lord Jesus Christ, your Son,
who lives and reigns with you and the Holy Spirit,
one God, for ever and ever. ℟. **Amen.**

Reading I (2 Cor 5, 14-20), p. 1166, no. 7.
Responsorial Psalm (Ps 16), p. 1207, no. 3.
Gospel (Lk 9, 57-62), p. 1228, no. 15.

Oct. 24 — ST. ANTHONY CLARET, Bishop

Optional Memorial

Born in Sallent, Spain, St. Anthony labored as a missionary in Catalonia and the Canary Islands. In 1849 he established the *Congregation of the Missionary Sons of the Immaculate Heart of Mary*. Later as Archbishop of Santiago de Cuba, he founded the *Teaching Sisters of Mary Immaculate*. He spread devotion to the Blessed Sacrament and the Immaculate Heart of Mary by his preaching and writings (which also helped revive the Catalan language). He died in 1870.

Common of Pastors: for Missionaries, p. 1077; or for Bishops, p. 1069.

OPENING PRAYER

Father,
you endowed Anthony Claret
with the strength of love and patience
to preach the gospel to many nations.
By the help of his prayers
may we work generously for your kingdom
and gain our brothers and sisters for Christ,
who lives and reigns with you and the Holy Spirit,
one God, for ever and ever. ℟. **Amen.**

Readings and Intervenient Chants may also be taken from the Common of Holy Men and Women: for Religious, p. 1195.

Reading I (Is 52, 7-10), p. 1156, no. 5.
Responsorial Psalm (Ps 96), p. 1162, no. 4.
Gospel (Mk 1, 14-20), p. 1172, no. 4.

Oct. 28 — STS. SIMON AND JUDE, Apostles

Feast

St. Simon, surnamed the Canaanite and also the Zealot, to distinguish him from St. Peter and from St. Simeon, preached in Persia and Babylonia. St. Jude, known as Thaddeus, was the brother of St. James the Less and a relative of Jesus. He is the author of an Epistle to the Eastern Churches. It is said that he preached the gospel in Palestine. Both St. Simon and St. Jude were martyred in the 1st century.

ENTRANCE ANT.

The Lord chose these holy men for their unfeigned love, and gave them eternal glory. ➔ No. 2, p. 614

OPENING PRAYER

Father,
you revealed yourself to us
through the preaching of your apostles Simon and
    Jude.
By their prayers,
give your Church continued growth
and increase the number of those who believe in
    you.
Grant this through our Lord Jesus Christ, your Son,
who lives and reigns with you and the Holy Spirit,
one God, for ever and ever. ℟. **Amen.** ℣

READING I   Eph 2, 19-22

Paul speaks to the Ephesians reminding them that all Christians are part of the building of faith. They are members of the household of God. All become fitted together to become a temple in the Lord.

A reading from the letter of Paul to the Ephesians

You are strangers and aliens no longer. No, you are fellow citizens of the saints and members of the household of God. You form a building which rises on the foundation of the apostles and prophets, with Christ Jesus himself as the capstone. Through him the whole structure is fitted together and takes shape as a holy temple in the Lord; in him you are being built into this temple, to become a dwelling place for God in the Spirit.—This is the Word of the Lord. ℟. **Thanks be to God.** ℣

Responsorial Psalm   Ps 19, 2-3. 4-5

℟. (5) **Their message goes out through all the earth.**

The heavens declare the glory of God,
   and the firmament proclaims his handiwork.
Day pours out the word to day,
   and night to night imparts knowledge. — ℟

Not a word nor a discourse
   whose voice is not heard;
Through all the earth their voice resounds,
   and to the end of the world, their message. — ℟ ℣

GOSPEL   Lk 6, 12-16
Alleluia

℟. **Alleluia.** We praise you, God; we acknowledge
   you as Lord;
your glorious band of apostles extols you. ℟. **Al-leluia.**

After praying for a whole night, Jesus selects twelve to be his apostles. These men are his chosen leaders who are to have a unique mission within the Church.

℣. The Lord be with you. ℟. **And also with you.**
✠ A reading from the holy gospel according to Luke
℟. **Glory to you, Lord.**

Jesus went out to the mountain to pray, spending the night in communion with God. At daybreak he called his disciples and selected twelve of them to be his apostles: Simon, to whom he gave the name Peter, and Andrew his brother, James and John, Philip and Bartholomew, Matthew and Thomas, James son of Alphaeus, and Simon called the Zealot, Judas son of James, and Judas Iscariot, who turned traitor.—This is the gospel of the Lord. ℟. **Praise to you, Lord Jesus Christ.**   ➤ No. 15, p. 623

PRAYER OVER THE GIFTS

Lord,
each year we recall the glory
of your apostles Simon and Jude.
Accept our gifts
and prepare us to celebrate these holy mysteries.
We ask this in the name of Jesus the Lord.
℟. **Amen.**   → No. 21, p. 626 (P 64-65)

COMMUNION ANT.   Jn 14, 23

**If anyone loves me, he will hold to my words, and
my Father will love him, and we will come to him,
and make our home with him.** ℣

PRAYER AFTER COMMUNION

Father,
in your Spirit we pray:
may the sacrament we receive today
keep us in your loving care
as we honor the death of Saints Simon and Jude.
We ask this through Christ our Lord.
℟. **Amen.**   → No. 32, p. 650

— NOVEMBER —

Nov. 1 — ALL SAINTS

See Vol. I (Sunday Missal), p. 1304.

Nov. 2 — ALL SOULS

The commemoration of all the faithful departed, on the
day after the Solemnity of All Saints, was instituted in
the Benedictine Monastery of Cluny by Abbot Odilo in
the year 998. The influence of the monks of Cluny caused
it to spread widely during the 11th century; but it began
to be celebrated at Rome only at the start of the 14th
century.

1

ENTRANCE ANT.   1 Thes 4, 14; 1 Cor 15, 22

Just as Jesus died and rose again, so will the Father bring with him those who have died in Jesus. Just as in Adam all men die, so in Christ all will be made alive.   → No. 2, p. 614

OPENING PRAYER

Let us pray

[for all our departed brothers and sisters]

Merciful Father,

hear our prayers and console us.

As we renew our faith in your Son,

whom you raised from the dead,

strengthen our hope that all our departed brothers

and sisters

will share in his resurrection,

who lives and reigns with you and the Holy Spirit,

one God, for ever and ever. ℟. **Amen.** ℣

The Readings and Intervenient Chants found in Masses 2 and 3 may also be used, as well as those on pp. 715-742.

READING I   Jb 19, 1. 23-27

Job speaks about God's future vindication of the just. This passage is not as clear as later New Testament texts, but it does emphatically proclaim existence after death and the vision of God.

A reading from the book of Job

Job answered and said.

Oh, would that my words were written down!

Would that they were inscribed in a record:

That with an iron chisel and with lead

they were cut in the rock forever!

But as for me, I know that my Vindicator lives,

and that he will at last stand forth upon the dust;

Whom I myself shall see:

my own eyes, not another's, shall behold him,

And from my flesh I shall see God;
   my inmost being is consumed with longing.
This is the Word of the Lord. ℟. **Thanks be to God.** ℣

Responsorial Psalm   Ps 23, 1-3. 3-4. 5. 6

℟. (1) **The Lord is my shepherd;
there is nothing I shall want.**

The Lord is my shepherd; I shall not want.
   In verdant pastures he gives me repose;
Beside restful waters he leads me;
   he refreshes my soul. — ℟

He guides me in right paths
   for his name's sake.
Even though I walk in the dark valley
   I fear no evil; for you are at my side
With your rod and your staff
   that give me courage. — ℟

You spread the table before me
   in the sight of my foes;
You anoint my head with oil;
   my cup overflows. — ℟

Only goodness and kindness follow me
   all the days of my life;
And I shall dwell in the house of the Lord
   for years to come. — ℟ ℣

℟. Or: (4) **Though I walk in the valley of darkness,
I fear no evil, for you are with me.** ℣

READING II   1 Cor 15, 51-57

Paul tells the Corinthians that man's risen body will be a body so
changed by the power of God as to be immortal. Christ died for sin
which is the cause of man's death; he rose from the dead to be the
cause of man's resurrection.

   A reading from the first letter of Paul to the
              Corinthians

I am going to tell you a mystery. Not all of us shall
fall asleep, but all of us are to be changed—in an
instant, in the twinkling of an eye, at the sound of
the last trumpet. The trumpet will sound and the

dead will be raised incorruptible, and we shall be
changed. This corruptible body must be clothed with
incorruptibility, this mortal body with immortality.
When the corruptible frame takes on incorruptibility
and the mortal immortality, then will the saying of
Scripture be fulfilled: "Death is swallowed up in
victory." "O death, where is your victory? O death,
where is your sting?" The sting of death is sin, and
sin gets its power from the law. But thanks be to
God who has given us the victory through our Lord
Jesus Christ.—This is the Word of the Lord. ℟.
Thanks be to God. ℣

GOSPEL   Jn 6, 37-40
Alleluia (Mt 25, 34)

℟. **Alleluia.** Come, you whom my Father has blessed,
      says the Lord;
inherit the kingdom prepared for you since the foun-
      dation of the world. ℟. **Alleluia.**

Jesus teaches the crowd that in doing the will of his Father, he
would never reject anyone who would come to him. God wants all
men to be saved and to have eternal life.

℣. The Lord be with you. ℟. **And also with you.**
✠ A reading from the holy gospel according to John
℟. **Glory to you, Lord.**

Jesus said to the crowd:
      "All that the Father gives me shall come to me;
      no one who comes will I ever reject,
      because it is not to do my own will
      that I have come down from heaven,
      but to do the will of him who sent me.
      It is the will of him who sent me
      that I should lose nothing of what he has given me;
      rather, that I should raise it up on the last day.
      Indeed, this is the will of my Father,
      that everyone who looks upon the Son
      and believes in him
      shall have eternal life.
      Him I will raise up on the last day."

This is the gospel of the Lord. ℞. **Praise to you, Lord Jesus Christ.** ➤ No. 15, p. 623

PRAYER OVER THE GIFTS

Lord,
we are united in this sacrament
by the love of Jesus Christ.
Accept these gifts
and receive our brothers and sisters
into the glory of your Son,
who is Lord for ever and ever.
℞. **Amen.** ➤ No. 21, p. 626 (Pref. P 77-81)

COMMUNION ANT. Jn 11, 25-26

I am the resurrection and the life, says the Lord. If anyone believes in me, even though he dies, he will live. Anyone who lives and believes in me, will not die. ∀

PRAYER AFTER COMMUNION

Lord God,
may the death and resurrection of Christ
which we celebrate in this eucharist
bring the departed faithful to the peace of your
    eternal home.
We ask this in the name of Jesus the Lord.
℞. **Amen.** ➤ No. 32, p. 650

Optional Solemn Blessings, p. 682, and Prayers over the People, p. 689.

2

ENTRANCE ANT. See 4 Ezr 2, 34-35

Give them eternal rest, O Lord, and may your light shine on them for ever. ➤ No. 2, p. 614

OPENING PRAYER

Let us pray
  [for all our departed brothers and sisters]

Lord God,
you are the glory of believers
and the life of the just.
Your Son redeemed us
by dying and rising to life again.
Since our departed brothers and sisters believed in
    the mystery of our resurrection,
let them share the joys and blessings of the life to
    come.
We ask this through our Lord Jesus Christ, your Son,
who lives and reigns with you and the Holy Spirit,
one God, for ever and ever. ℟. **Amen.** ✔

*The Readings and Intervenient Chants found in Masses
1 and 3 may also be used, as well as those on pp. 715-742.*

READING I   Wis 3, 1-9 or 3, 1-6. 9

The souls of the just are in the hands of God. It is a life that is
contrasted with the standards of the world. The life of those who have
known and believed in God is "full of immortality." After being tried
by God they will reap their reward.

(SHORT FORM)

A reading from the book of Wisdom

The souls of the just are in the hand of God,
    and no torment shall touch them.
They seemed, in the view of the foolish, to be dead;
    and their passing away was thought an affliction
    and their going forth from us, utter destruction.
But they are in peace.
For if before me, indeed, they be punished,
    yet is their hope full of immortality;
Chastised a little, they shall be greatly blessed,
    because God tried them
    and found them worthy of himself.
As gold in the furnace, he proved them,
    and as sacrificial offerings he took them to him-
    self.
Because grace and mercy are with his holy ones,
    and his care is with his elect.
This is the Word of the Lord. ℟. **Thanks be to God.** ✔

Responsorial Psalm   Pss 115, 5. 6; 116, 10-11. 15-16

℞. (Ps 115, 9) **I will walk in the presence of the Lord, in the land of the living.**

They have mouths but speak not;
 they have eyes but see not;
They have ears but hear not;
 they have noses but smell not. — ℞

I believed, even when I said,
 "I am greatly afflicted";
I said in my alarm,
 "No man is dependable." — ℞

Precious in the eyes of the Lord
 is the death of his faithful ones.
O Lord, I am your servant;
 you have loosed my bonds. — ℞ ✟

℞. Or: **Alleluia.** ✟

READING II   Phil 3, 20-21

While toiling for the building up of this earth, the Christian knows
that his ultimate citizenship is in heaven. Salvation does not lie in
the body but in Christ who at his second coming will transform the
body of all his faithful to be like his glorious body.

A reading from the letter of Paul to the
Philippians

We have our citizenship in heaven; it is from there
that we eagerly await the coming of our Savior, the
Lord Jesus Christ. He will give a new form to this
lowly body of ours and remake it according to the
pattern of his glorified body, by his power to subject everything to himself.—This is the Word of the
Lord. ℞. **Thanks be to God.** ✟

GOSPEL   Jn 11, 17-27 or 11, 21-27

Alleluia (Jn 11, 25. 26)

℞. **Alleluia.** I am the resurrection and the life, said
 the Lord;
he who believes in me will not die for ever. ℞. **Alleluia.**

Amid man's continuous quest for immortality, there is only one who can impart it to him—Jesus, "the resurrection and the life." And this immortality will be coupled with a joy without end.

℣. The Lord be with you. ℟. **And also with you.**
✠ A reading from the holy gospel according to John
℟. **Glory to you, Lord.**

(SHORT FORM)

Martha said to Jesus, "Lord, if you had been here, my brother would never have died. Even now, I am sure that God will give you whatever you ask of him." "Your brother will rise again," Jesus assured her. "I know he will rise again," Martha replied, "in the resurrection on the last day." Jesus told her:

"I am the resurrection and the life:
whoever believes in me,
though he should die, will come to life;
and whoever is alive and believes in me
will never die.

Do you believe this?" "Yes, Lord," she replied. "I have come to believe that you are the Messiah, the Son of God: he who is to come into the world."— This is the gospel of the Lord. ℟. **Praise to you, Lord Jesus Christ.** ➔ No. 15, p. 623

PRAYER OVER THE GIFTS

All-powerful Father,
may this sacrifice wash away
the sins of our departed brothers and sisters in the
blood of Christ.
You cleansed them in the waters of baptism.
In your loving mercy grant them pardon and peace.
We ask this in the name of Jesus the Lord.
℟. **Amen.** ➔ No. 21, p. 626 (P 77-81)

COMMUNION ANT. See 4 Ezr 2, 35. 34
May eternal light shine on them, O Lord, with all your saints for ever, for you are rich in mercy. Give

them eternal rest, O Lord, and may perpetual light
shine on them for ever, for you are rich in mercy. ℣

PRAYER AFTER COMMUNION

Lord,
in this sacrament you give us your crucified and
    risen Son.
Bring to the glory of the resurrection our departed
    brothers and sisters
who have been purified by this holy mystery.
Grant this through Christ our Lord.
℟. **Amen.**   ➔ No. 32, p. 650

*Optional Solemn Blessings, p. 682, and Prayers over the
People, p. 689.*

3

ENTRANCE ANT.   Rom 8, 11

**God, who raised Jesus from the dead, will give new
life to our own mortal bodies through his Spirit
living in us.**   ➔ No. 2, p. 614

OPENING PRAYER

Let us pray
    [for all our departed brothers and sisters]
God, our creator and redeemer,
by your power Christ conquered death
and returned to you in glory.
May all your people who have gone before us in faith
    share his victory
and enjoy the vision of your glory for ever.
We ask this through our Lord Jesus Christ, your Son,
who lives and reigns with you and the Holy Spirit,
one God, for ever and ever. ℟. **Amen.** ℣

*The Readings and Intervenient Chants found in Masses
1 and 2 may also be used, as well as those on pp. 715-742.*

READING I   2 Mc 12, 43-46

As Judas (the ruler of Israel) makes a collection of goods, he shows a belief in life after death and the need to pray for the dead. It is a holy and pious thought to think of the dead.

A reading from the second book of Maccabees

Judas [the ruler of Israel] then took up a collection among all his soldiers, amounting to two thousand silver drachmas, which he sent to Jerusalem to provide for an expiatory sacrifice. In doing this he acted in a very excellent and noble way, inasmuch as he had the resurrection of the dead in view; for if he were not expecting the fallen to rise again, it would have been useless and foolish to pray for them in death. But if he did this with a view to the splendid reward that awaits those who had gone to rest in godliness, it was a holy and pious thought. Thus he made atonement for the dead that they might be freed from this sin.—This is the Word of the Lord. ℟. **Thanks be to God.** ℣

Responsorial Psalm   Ps 130, 1-2. 3-4. 4-6. 7-8

℟. (1) **Out of the depths, I cry to you, Lord.**

I trust in the Lord;
    my soul trusts in his word.
My soul waits for the Lord
    more than sentinels wait for the dawn.
More than sentinels wait for the dawn,
    let Israel hope in the Lord. — ℟

For with the Lord is kindness
    and with him is plenteous redemption;
And he will redeem Israel
    from all their iniquities. — ℟ ℣

℟. Or: (5) **I hope in the Lord,
I trust in his word.** ℣

READING II   Rv 14, 13

In addition to faith in Jesus, there is also need of good works. These will accompany the doers after death to their advantage. Happy are the dead who die thus in the Lord.

A reading from the book of Revelation

I, John, heard a voice from heaven say to me: "Write this down: Happy now are the dead who die in the Lord!" The Spirit added, "Yes, they shall find rest from their labors, for their good works accompany them."—This is the Word of the Lord. ℟. **Thanks be to God.** ✓

GOSPEL   Jn 14, 1-6

Alleluia (Phil 3, 20)

℟. **Alleluia.** Our true home is in heaven,
and Jesus Christ whose return we long for
will come from heaven to save us. ℟. **Alleluia.**

Jesus is the way, the truth, and the life who has preceded his followers to the Father's heavenly house in order to prepare a place also
for them. Those who trust in him will safely reach their home at
journey's end.

℣. The Lord be with you. ℟. **And also with you.**
✠ A reading from the holy gospel according to John
℟. **Glory to you, Lord.**

Jesus said to his disciples:
   "Do not let your hearts be troubled.
   Have faith in God
   and faith in me.
   In my Father's house there are many dwelling
      places;
   otherwise, how could I have told you
   that I was going to prepare a place for you?
   I am indeed going to prepare a place for you,
   and then I shall come back to take you with me,
   that where I am you also may be.
   You know the way that leads where I go."
   "Lord," said Thomas, "we do not know where
you are going. How can we know the way?" Jesus
told him:
   "I am the way, and the truth, and the life;
   no one comes to the Father but through me."
This is the gospel of the Lord. ℟. **Praise to you, Lord Jesus Christ.**   ➔ No. 15, p. 623

PRAYER OVER THE GIFTS

Lord,
in your kindness accept these gifts for our departed
  brothers and sisters
and for all who sleep in Christ.
May his perfect sacrifice
free them from the power of death
and give them eternal life.
We ask this in the name of Jesus the Lord.
℟. **Amen.** → No. 21, p. 626 (P 77-81)

COMMUNION ANT. Phil 3, 20-21

**We are waiting for our Savior, the Lord Jesus Christ;
he will transfigure our lowly bodies into copies of
his own glorious body.** ℣

PRAYER AFTER COMMUNION

Lord,
may our sacrifice bring peace and forgiveness
to our brothers and sisters who have died.
Bring the new life given to them in baptism
to the fullness of eternal joy.
We ask this through Christ our Lord.
℟. **Amen.** → No. 32, p. 650

*Optional Solemn Blessings, p. 682, and Prayers over the
People, p. 689.*

OTHER POSSIBLE READINGS

OLD TESTAMENT READING

1 Jb 19, 1. 23-27

See p. 705.

---

2 Wis 3, 1-9 or 3, 1-6. 9

See p. 709.

---

3   Wis 4, 7-14

The purpose of life is to live in a way that is pleasing to God. Life, whether long or short, will be judged by God. The just man lives a perfect life and he shall rest in God.

A reading from the book of Wisdom

The just man, though he die early, shall be at rest.
For the age that is honorable comes not with the
    passing of time,
  nor can it be measured in terms of years.
Rather, understanding is the hoary crown for men,
  and an unsullied life, the attainment of old age.
He who pleased God was loved;
  he who lived among sinners was transported—
Snatched away, lest wickedness pervert his mind
  or deceit beguile his soul;
For the witchery of paltry things obscures what is
    right
  and the whirl of desire transforms the innocent
    mind.
Having become perfect in a short while, he reached
    the fullness of a long career;
  for his soul was pleasing to the Lord,
  therefore he sped him out of the midst of wicked-
    ness.
But the people saw and did not understand,
  nor did they take this into account.
This is the Word of the Lord. ℟. **Thanks be to God.**

---

4   Is 25, 6. 7-9

God will care for his people. He will wipe their tears away. He will destroy death forever.

A reading form the book of the prophet Isaiah
On this mountain the Lord of hosts
  will provide for all peoples.

On this mountain he will destroy
    the veil that veils all peoples,
The web that is woven over all nations;
    he will destroy death forever.
The Lord God will wipe away
    the tears from all faces;
The reproach of his people he will remove
    from the whole earth; for the Lord has spoken.
On that day it will be said:
"Behold our God, to whom we looked to save us!
    This is the Lord for whom we looked;
    let us rejoice and be glad that he has saved us!"
This is the Word of the Lord. ℟. **Thanks be to God.**

---

5   Lam 3, 17-26

There is happiness in waiting for the salvation God will bring. Although there is sorrow in life, the Lord knows the needs of his people and his mercies are unlimited.

A reading from the book of Lamentations

My soul is deprived of peace,
    I have forgotten what happiness is;
I tell myself my future is lost,
    all that I hoped for from the Lord.
The thought of my homeless poverty
    is wormwood and gall;
Remembering it over and over
    leaves my soul downcast within me.
But I will call this to mind,
    as my reason to have hope:
The favors of the Lord are not exhausted,
    his mercies are not spent;
They are renewed each morning,
    so great is his faithfulness.
My portion is the Lord, says my soul;
    therefore will I hope in him.
Good is the Lord to one who waits for him,
    to the soul that seeks him;

It is good to hope in silence
    for the saving help of the Lord.
This is the Word of the Lord. ℟. **Thanks be to God.**

---

6   Dn 12, 1-3

Daniel describes the judgment of the Lord. It will be a time of
distress for some and life for others. The saved will be like stars
forever.

A reading from the book of the prophet Daniel

[I, Daniel, mourned and I heard this word of the
Lord:]
"At that time there shall arise
    Michael, the great prince,
    guardian of your people;
It shall be a time unsurpassed in distress
    since nations began until that time.
At that time your people shall escape,
    everyone who is found written in the book.
Many of those who sleep
    in the dust of the earth shall awake;
Some shall live forever,
    others shall be an everlasting horror and disgrace.
But the wise shall shine brightly
    like the splendor of the firmament,
And those who lead the many to justice
    shall be like the stars forever."
This is the Word of the Lord. ℟. **Thanks be to God.**

---

7   2 Mc 12, 43-46

See p. 713.

NEW TESTAMENT READING

1   Acts 10, 34-43 or 10, 34-36. 42-43

Peter teaches that the man who fears God and lives rightly will be pleasing to God. He reviews the life, death, and mandate of Jesus.

[If the "Short Form" is used, the indented text in brackets is omitted.]

A reading from the Acts of the Apostles

Peter proceeded to address the people in these words: "I begin to see how true it is that God shows no partiality. Rather, the man of any nation who fears God and acts uprightly is acceptable to him. This is the message he has sent to the sons of Israel, 'the good news of peace' proclaimed through Jesus Christ who is Lord of all.

[I take it you know what has been reported all over Judea about Jesus of Nazareth, beginning in Galilee with the baptism John preached; of the way God anointed him with the Holy Spirit and power. He went about doing good works and healing all who were in the grip of the devil, and God was with him. We are witnesses to all that he did in the land of the Jews and in Jerusalem. They killed him finally, 'hanging him on a tree,' only to have God raise him up on the third day and grant that he be seen, not by all, but only by such witnesses as had been chosen beforehand by God—by us who ate and drank with him after he rose from the dead.]

He commissioned us to preach to the people and to bear witness that he is the one set apart by God as judge of the living and the dead. To him all the prophets testify, saying that everyone who believes in him has forgiveness of sins through his name."— This is the Word of the Lord. ℞. **Thanks be to God.**

2   Rom 5, 5-11

There is hope in Jesus. He died freely for sinners to reconcile them to his Father. All the more reason after their reconciliation, all may be saved in the life of Jesus.

A reading from the letter of Paul to the Romans

Hope will not leave us disappointed, because the love of God has been poured out in our hearts through the Holy Spirit who has been given to us. At the appointed time, when we were still powerless, Christ died for us godless men. It is rare that anyone should lay down his life for a just man, though it is barely possible that for a good man someone may have the courage to die. It is precisely in this that God proves his love for us: that while we were still sinners, Christ died for us. Now that we have been justified by his blood, it is all the more certain that we shall be saved by him from God's wrath. For if, when we were God's enemies, we were reconciled to him by the death of his Son, it is all the more certain that we who have been reconciled will be saved by his life. Not only that; we go so far as to make God our boast through our Lord Jesus Christ, through whom we have now received reconciliation.—This is the Word of the Lord. ℟. **Thanks be to God.**

---

3   Rom 5, 17-21

Through Adam sin came into the world: through Jesus overflowing grace became available. By this, sin may be forgiven and men may be justified.

A reading from the letter of Paul to the Romans

If death began its reign through one man because of his offense, much more shall those who receive the overflowing grace and gift of justice live and reign through the one man, Jesus Christ.

To sum up, then: just as a single offense brought condemnation to all men, a single righteous act brought all men acquittal and life. Just as through one man's disobedience all became sinners, so through one man's obedience all shall become just.

The law came in order to increase offenses; but despite the increase of sin, grace has far surpassed it, so that, as sin reigned through death, grace may reign by way of justice leading to eternal life, through Jesus Christ our Lord.—This is the Word of the Lord. ℞. **Thanks be to God.**

---

4   Rom 6, 3-9 or 6, 3-4. 8-9

Through baptism a follower of Jesus dies to sin and, being buried, he rises in Jesus through the carrying out of the Paschal Mystery. Death no longer has any power over Jesus.

[If the "Short Form" is used, the indented text in brackets is omitted.]

A reading from the letter of Paul to the Romans

Are you aware that we who were baptized into Christ Jesus were baptized into his death? Through baptism into his death we were buried with him, so that, just as Christ was raised from the dead by the glory of the Father, we too might live a new life.

[If we have been united with him through likeness to his death, so shall we be through a like resurrection. This we know: our old self was crucified with him so that the sinful body might be destroyed and we might be slaves to sin no longer. A man who is dead has been freed from sin.]

If we have died with Christ, we believe that we are also to live with him. We know that Christ, once raised from the dead, will never die again; death has no more power over him.—This is the Word of the Lord. ℞. **Thanks be to God.**

5 Rom 8, 14-23

Life in this world involves suffering, but through the Spirit all may become adopted children of God and heirs with Christ to eternal life. This present life is a prelude to life in heaven.

A reading from the letter of Paul to the Romans

All who are led by the Spirit of God are sons of God. You did not receive a spirit of slavery leading you back into fear, but a spirit of adoption through which we cry out, "Abba!" (that is, "Father"). The Spirit himself gives witness with our spirit that we are children of God. But if we are children, we are heirs as well: heirs of God, heirs with Christ, if only we suffer with him so as to be glorified with him.

I consider the sufferings of the present to be as nothing compared with the glory to be revealed in us. Indeed, the whole created world eagerly awaits the revelation of the sons of God. Creation was made subject to futility, not of its own accord but by him who once subjected it; yet not without hope, because the world itself will be freed from its slavery to corruption and share in the glorious freedom of the children of God. Yes, we know that all creation groans and is in agony even until now. Not only that, but we ourselves, although we have the Spirit as first fruits, groan inwardly while we await the redemption of our bodies.—This is the Word of the Lord. ℟. **Thanks be to God.**

---

6 Rom 8, 31-35. 37-39

God so loved his chosen ones that he sent his Son to die for them. Nothing can separate those who love God from the love that God has for them in Jesus.

A reading from the letter of Paul to the Romans

If God is for us, who can be against us? Is it possible that he who did not spare his own Son but handed him over for the sake of us all will not grant us all things besides? Who shall bring a charge against God's chosen ones? God, who justifies? Who shall condemn them? Christ Jesus, who died or rather was raised up, who is at the right hand of God and who intercedes for us?

Who will separate us from the love of Christ? Trial, or distress, or persecution, or hunger, or nakedness, or danger, or the sword? Yet in all this we are more than conquerors because of him who has loved us. For I am certain that neither death nor life, neither angels nor principalities, neither the present nor the future, nor powers, neither height nor depth nor any other creature, will be able to separate us from the love of God that comes to us in Christ Jesus, our Lord.—This is the Word of the Lord. ℟. **Thanks be to God.**

---

7 Rom 14, 7-9. 10-12

Jesus is Lord of the living and the dead. Everyone will have to give an account of his life before God himself.

A reading from the letter of Paul to the Romans

None of us lives as his own master and none of us dies as his own master. While we live we are responsible to the Lord, and when we die we die as his servants. Both in life and in death we are the Lord's. That is why Christ died and came to life again, that he might be Lord of both the dead and the living. We shall all have to appear before the judgment seat of God. It is written, "As surely as I live, says the Lord, every knee shall bend before me and every tongue shall give praise to God."

Every one of us will have to give an account of himself before God.—This is the Word of the Lord. ℟. **Thanks be to God.**

---

8   1 Cor 15, 20-24. 25-28

Jesus, the God-man, died for sin and rose from the dead. All will come to life again in Jesus who will reign over all. God will be all in all.

A reading from the first letter of Paul to the Corinthians

Christ has been raised from the dead, the first fruits of those who have fallen asleep. Death came through a man; hence the resurrection of the dead comes through a man also. Just as in Adam all die, so in Christ all will come to life again, but each one in proper order: Christ the first fruits and then, at his coming, all those who belong to him. After that will come the end, when, after having destroyed every sovereignty, authority, and power, he will hand over the kingdom to God the Father. Christ must reign until God has put all enemies under his feet, and the last enemy to be destroyed is death. Scripture reads that God "has placed all things under his feet." But when it says that everything has been made subject, it is clear that he who has made everything subject to Christ is excluded. When, finally, all has been subjected to the Son, he will then subject himself to the One who made all things subject to him, so that God may be all in all.—This is the Word of the Lord. ℟. **Thanks be to God.**

_____

9   1 Cor 15, 51-57

See p. 706.

_____

10   2 Cor 5, 1. 6-10

When the body of man dies, another dwelling awaits him. In this life men live trying to be pleasing to God because all must appear before the judgment seat of God.

A reading from the second letter of Paul to the
Corinthians

We know that when the earthly tent in which we
dwell is destroyed we have a dwelling provided for
us by God, a dwelling in the heavens, not made by
hands but to last forever.

Therefore we continue to be confident. We know
that while we dwell in the body we are away from
the Lord. We walk by faith, not by sight. I repeat,
we are full of confidence and would much rather be
away from the body and at home with the Lord.
This being so, we make it our aim to please him
whether we are with him or away from him. The
lives of all of us are to be revealed before the tribunal
of Christ so that each one may receive his recompense, good or bad, according to his life in the body.
—This is the Word of the Lord. ℟. **Thanks be to God.**

---

11   Phil 3, 20-21

See p. 710.

---

12   1 Thes 4, 13-18

See p. 255.

---

13   2 Tm 2, 8-13

See p. 1148 (omit last paragraph).

---

14   1 Jn 3, 1-2

How much God loves his people cannot be understood in this life.
This will be revealed in the life to come.

A reading from the first letter of John

See what love the Father has bestowed on us
in letting us be called children of God!
Yet that in fact is what we are.
The reason the world does not recognize us

is that it never recognized the Son.
Dearly beloved,
we are God's children now;
what we shall later be has not yet come to light.
We know that when it comes to light
we shall be like him,
for we shall see him as he is.
This is the Word of the Lord. ℟. **Thanks be to God.**

---

15   1 Jn 3, 14-16

See p. 1217 (omit last seven lines).

---

16   Rv 14, 13

See p. 713.

---

17   Rv 20, 11—21, 1

John reveals a time at the end of the world when judgment will come.
Each person will be judged according to the life that he lived and
then this world will pass away.

A reading from the book of Revelation

I, John, saw a large white throne and the One who
sat on it. The earth and the sky fled from his presence until they could no longer be seen. I saw the
dead, the great and the lowly, standing before the
throne. Lastly, among the scrolls, the book of the
living was opened. The dead were judged according
to their conduct as recorded on the scrolls. The sea
gave up its dead; then death and the nether world
gave up their dead. Each person was judged according to his conduct. Then death and the nether world
were hurled into the pool of fire which is the second
death; anyone whose name was not found inscribed
in the living was hurled into this pool of fire.
   Then I saw new heavens and a new earth. The
former heavens and the former earth had passed

away, and the sea was no longer there.—This is the
Word of the Lord. ℟. **Thanks be to God.**

---

18 Rv 21, 1-5. 6-7

In his vision John sees a new world most beautiful to behold. Here
God will live with his people. Every pain and tear will be wiped away.

A reading from the book of Revelation

I, John, saw new heavens and a new earth. The
former heavens and the former earth had passed
away, and the sea was no longer. I also saw a new
Jerusalem, the holy city, coming down out of heaven
from God, beautiful as a bride prepared to meet her
husband. I heard a loud voice from the throne cry
out: "This is God's dwelling among men. He shall
dwell with them and they shall be his people, and
he shall be their God who is always with them. He
shall wipe every tear from their eyes, and there shall
be no more death or mourning, crying out or pain,
for the former world has passed away."

The One who sat on the throne said to me, "See, I
make all things new!" I am the Alpha and the Omega,
the Beginning and the End. To anyone who thirsts
I will give to drink without cost from the spring of
life-giving water. He who wins the victory shall inherit these gifts; I will be his God and he shall be my
son."—This is the Word of the Lord. ℟. **Thanks be
to God.**

RESPONSORIAL PSALM

1 Ps 23, 1-3. 3-4. 5. 6

See p. 706.

---

2 Ps 25, 6-7. 17-18. 20-21

℟. (1) **To you, O Lord, I lift my soul.**

Remember that your compassion, O Lord,
and your kindness are from of old.
In your kindness remember me,
because of your goodness, O Lord. — ℟

Relieve the troubles of my heart,
and bring me out of my distress.
Put an end to my affliction and my suffering,
and take away all my sins. — ℟

Preserve my life, and rescue me;
let me not be put to shame, for I take refuge in you.
Let integrity and uprightness preserve me,
because I wait for you, O Lord. — ℟

℟. Or: (3) **No one who waits for you, O Lord,
will ever be put to shame.**

---

3 Ps 27, 1. 4. 7. 8. 9. 13-14

℟. (1) **The Lord is my light and my salvation.**

The Lord is my light and my salvation;
whom should I fear?
The Lord is my life's refuge;
of whom who should I be afraid? — ℟

One thing I ask of the Lord;
this I seek:
To dwell in the house of the Lord
all the days of my life,
That I may gaze on the loveliness of the Lord
and contemplate his temple. — ℟

Hear, O Lord, the sound of my call;
have pity on me, and answer me.
Your presence, O Lord, I seek.
Hide not your face from me. — ℟

I believe that I shall see the bounty of the Lord
in the land of the living.
Wait for the Lord with courage;
be stouthearted, and wait for the Lord. — ℟

℟. Or: (13) **I believe that I shall see the good
things of the Lord in the land of the living.**

---

4 Pss 42, 2. 3. 5; 43, 3. 4. 5

℟. (Ps 42, 3) **My soul is thirsting for the living God:
when shall I see him face to face?**

As the hind longs for the running waters,
  so my soul longs for you, O God. — ℟

Athirst is my soul for God, the living God.
  When shall I go and behold the face of God? — ℟

When I went with the throng
  and led them in procession to the house of God,
Amid loud cries of joy and thanksgiving,
  with the multitude keeping festival. — ℟

Send forth your light and your fidelity;
  they shall lead me on
And bring me to your holy mountain,
  to your dwelling-place. — ℟

Then will I go in to the altar of God,
  the God of my gladness and joy;
Then will I give you thanks upon the harp,
  O God, my God! — ℟

Why are you so downcast, O my soul?
  Why do you sigh within me?
Hope in God! For I shall again be thanking him,
  in the presence of my savior and my God. — ℟

---

5 Ps 63, 2-3. 3-4. 5-6. 8-9

℟. (2) **My soul is thirsting for you, O Lord my God.**

O God, you are my God whom I seek;
  for you my flesh pines and my soul thirsts
  like the earth, parched, lifeless and without
    water. — ℟

Thus have I gazed toward you in the sanctuary
  to see your power and your glory.

For your kindness is a greater good than life;
    my lips shall glorify you. — ℟
Thus will I bless you while I live;
    lifting up my hands, I will call upon your name.
As with the riches of a banquet shall my soul be
      satisfied,
    and with exultant lips my mouth shall praise
    you. — ℟
You are my help,
    and in the shadow of your wings I shout for joy.
My soul clings fast to you;
    your right hand upholds me. — ℟

---

6   Ps 103, 8. 10. 13-14. 15-16. 17-18

℟. (8) **The Lord is kind and merciful.**

Merciful and gracious is the Lord,
    slow to anger and abounding in kindness.
Not according to our sins does he deal with us,
    nor does he requite us according to our crimes.—℟

As a father has compassion on his children,
    so the Lord has compassion on those who fear
    him,
For he knows how we are formed;
    he remembers that we are dust. —℟

Man's days are like those of grass;
    like a flower of the field he blooms;
The wind sweeps over him and he is gone,
    and his place knows him no more. — ℟

But the kindness of the Lord is from eternity
    to eternity toward those who fear him,
And his justice toward children's children
    among those who keep his covenant
    and remember to fulfill his precepts. — ℟

℟. Or: (Ps 37, 39) **The salvation of the just comes
    from the Lord.**

---

7 Pss 115, 5. 6; 116, 10-11. 15-16

See p. 710.

---

8 Ps 122, 1-2. 3-4. 4-5. 6-7. 8-9

℟. (1) **I rejoiced when I heard them say:**
let us go to the house of the Lord.

I rejoiced because they said to me,
"We will go up to the house of the Lord."
And now we have set foot
within your gates, O Jerusalem. — ℟

Jerusalem, built as a city
with compact unity.
To it the tribes go up,
the tribes of the Lord. — ℟

According to the decree for Israel,
to give thanks to the name of the Lord.
In it are set up judgment seats,
seats for the house of David. — ℟

Pray for the peace of Jerusalem!
May those who love you prosper!
May peace be within your walls,
prosperity in your buildings. — ℟

Because of my relatives and friends
I will say, "Peace be within you!"
Because of the house of the Lord, our God,
I will pray for your good. — ℟

℟. Or: **Let us go rejoicing to the house of the Lord.**

---

9 Ps 130, 1-2. 3-4. 4-6. 7-8

See p. 713.

10　　　　　　　　　　　　　　Ps 143, 1-2. 5-6. 7. 8. 10

℟ (1) **O Lord, hear my prayer.**

O Lord, hear my prayer;
　　hearken to my pleading in your faithfulness;
　　in your justice answer me.
And enter not into judgment with your servant,
　　for before you no living man is just. — ℟

I remember the days of old;
　　I meditate on all your doings,
　　the works of your hands I ponder.
I stretch out my hands to you;
　　my soul thirsts for you like parched land. — ℟

Hasten to answer me, O Lord,
　　for my spirit fails me.
At dawn let me hear of your kindness,
　　for in you I trust. — ℟

Teach me to do your will,
　　for you are my God.
May your good spirit guide me
　　on level ground. — ℟

ALLELUIA VERSE AND
VERSE BEFORE THE GOSPEL

1　　　　　　　　　　　　　　　　　　Mt 11, 25

Blessed are you, Father, Lord of heaven and earth;
you have revealed to little ones the mysteries of
　　the kingdom.

2　　　　　　　　　　　　　　　　　　Mt 25, 34

Come, you whom my Father has blessed, says the
　　Lord;
inherit the kingdom prepared for you since the foun-
　　dation of the world.

3　　　　　　　　　　　　　　　　　　Jn 3, 16

God loved the world so much, he gave his only Son,
that all who believe in him might have eternal life.

4   Jn 6, 39

This is the will of my Father, says the Lord,
that I should lose nothing of all that he has given
    to me,
and that I should raise it up on the last day.

5   Jn 6, 10

This is the will of my Father, says the Lord,
all who believe in the Son will have eternal life
and I will raise them to life again on the last day.

6   Jn 11, 25. 26

I am the resurrection and the life, said the Lord:
he who believes in me will not die for ever.

7   Phil 3, 20

Our true home is in heaven,
and Jesus Christ whose return we long for
will come from heaven to save us.

8   2 Tm 2, 11-12

If we die with Christ, we shall live with him,
    and if we are faithful to the end, we shall reign
        with him.

9   Rv 1, 56

Jesus Christ is the firstborn of the dead;
glory and kingship be his for ever and ever. Amen.

10   Rv 14, 13

Happy are those who have died in the Lord;
let them rest from their labors for their good deeds
        go with them.

GOSPEL

1   Mt 5, 1-12

See p. 1220.

---

2   Mt 11, 25-30

See p. 1221.

_____

3   Mt 25, 1-13

See p. 1223.

_____

4   Mt 25, 31-46

See p. 1225.

_____

5   Mk 15, 33-39; 16, 1-6 or 15, 33-39

In midafternoon, after being nailed to the cross, Jesus dies. The temple curtain is torn in two. Jesus is buried, and on Easter when the women come to anoint the body of Jesus, an angel tells them that Jesus has risen from the dead.

[If the "Short Form" is used, the indented text in brackets is omitted.]

℣. The Lord be with you. ℟. **And also with you.**
✠ A reading from the holy gospel according to Mark
℟. **Glory to you, Lord.**
When noon came, darkness fell on the whole countryside and lasted until midafternoon. At that time Jesus cried in a loud voice, **"Eloi, Eloi, lama sabach-thani?"** which means, "My God, my God, why have you forsaken me?" A few of the bystanders who heard it remarked, "Listen! He is calling on Elijah!" Someone ran off, and soaking a sponge in sour wine, stuck it on a reed to try to make him drink. The man said, "Now let's see whether Elijah comes to take him down."

Then Jesus, uttering a loud cry, breathed his last. At that moment the curtain in the sanctuary was torn in two from top to bottom. The centurion who stood guard over him, on seeing the manner of his death, declared, "Clearly this man was the Son of God!"

[When the sabbath was over, Mary Magdalene, Mary the mother of James, and Salome bought perfumed oils with which they intended to go and anoint Jesus. Very early, just after sunrise on the first day of the week, they came to the tomb. They were saying to one another, "Who will roll back the stone for us from the entrance to the tomb?" When they looked, they found that the stone had been rolled back. (It was a huge one.) On entering the tomb they saw a young man sitting at the right, dressed in a white robe. This frightened them thoroughly, but he reassured them: "You need not be amazed! You are looking for Jesus of Nazareth, the one who was crucified. He has been raised up; he is not here. See the place where they laid him."]

This is the gospel of the Lord. ℟. **Praise to you, Lord Jesus Christ.**   → No. 15, p. 623

---

6   Lk 7, 11-17

See p. 284.

---

7   Lk 12, 35-40

See p. 1230.

---

8   Lk 23, 33. 39-43

At Calvary, Jesus is crucified between two criminals. The one mocks Jesus while the other asks for remembrance. Jesus promises him salvation.

℣. The Lord be with you. ℟. **And also with you.**
✠ A reading from the holy gospel according to Luke
℟. **Glory to you, Lord.**

When Jesus and the others came to Skull Place, as it was called, they crucified him there and the criminals as well, one on his right and the other on his left. One of the criminals hanging in crucifixion blasphemed him: "Aren't you the Messiah? Then save yourself and us." But the other one rebuked him: "Have you no fear of God, seeing you are under the same sentence? We deserve it, after all. We are only paying the price for what we've done, but this man has done nothing wrong." He then said, "Jesus, remember me when you enter upon your reign." And Jesus replied, "I assure you: this day you will be with me in paradise."—This is the gospel of the Lord. R̶. **Praise to you, Lord Jesus Christ.**

➤ No. 15, p. 623

---

9   Lk 23, 44-49; 24, 1-6 or 23, 44-49

Amid several phenomena, Jesus dies. The centurion and others admit that Jesus is the Son of God. On Sunday the women come to the tomb to anoint the body of Jesus only to find that he has risen from the dead.

[*If the "Short Form" is used, the indented text in brackets is omitted.*]

V̶. The Lord be with you. R̶. **And also with you.**
✠ A reading from the holy gospel according to Luke
R̶. **Glory to you, Lord.**

It was around midday, and darkness came over the whole land until midafternoon with an eclipse of the sun. The curtain in the sanctuary was torn in two. Jesus uttered a loud cry and said,

"Father, into your hands I commend my spirit." After he had said this, he expired. The centurion, upon seeing what had happened, gave glory to God by saying, "Surely this was an innocent man." After the crowd assembled for this spectacle witnessed what had happened, they returned beating their breasts. All his friends and the women who had accompanied him from Galilee were standing at a distance watching everything.

[On the first day of the week, at dawn, the women came to the tomb bringing the spices

they had prepared. They found the stone rolled
back from the tomb; but when they entered the
tomb, they did not find the body of the Lord
Jesus. While they were still at a loss over what
to think of this, two men in dazzling garments
stood beside them. Terrified, the women bowed
to the ground. The men said to them: "Why do
you search for the Living One among the dead?
He is not here; he has been raised up."]
This is the gospel of the Lord. ℟. **Praise to you,
Lord Jesus Christ.**   ➔ No. 15, p. 623

---

10   Lk 24, 13-35 or 24, 13-16. 28-35
On the way to Emmaus, Jesus meets two of his disciples who are un-
aware of his resurrection. Jesus reviews with them the prophecies
of the Messiah. It is in the breaking of the bread that they recognize
the Master.

*[If the "Short Form" is used, the indented text in
brackets is omitted.]*

℣. The Lord be with you. ℟. **And also with you.**
✠ A reading from the holy gospel according to John
℟. **Glory to you, Lord.**

Two of the disciples of Jesus on that same day (the
first day of the week) were making their way to a
village named Emmaus seven miles distant from Jerusalem, discussing as they went all that had happened. In the course of their lively exchange, Jesus approached and began to walk along with them. However, they were restrained from recognizing him.
[He said to them, "What are you discussing as
you go your way?" They halted in distress and
one of them, Cleopas by name, asked him, "Are
you the only resident of Jerusalem who does
not know the things that went on there these
past few days?" He said to them, "What
things?" They said: "All those that had to do
with Jesus of Nazareth, a prophet powerful in
word and deed in the eyes of God and all the

people; how our chief priests and leaders delivered him up to be condemned to death, and crucified him. We were hoping that he was the one who would set Israel free. Besides all this, today, the third day since these things happened, some women of our group have just brought us some astonishing news. They were at the tomb before dawn and failed to find his body, but returned with the tale that they had seen a vision of angels who declared he was alive. Some of our number went to the tomb and found it to be just as the women said; but him they did not see."

Then he said to them, "What little sense you have! How slow you are to believe all that the prophets have announced! Did not the Messiah have to undergo all this so as to enter into his glory?" Beginning, then, with Moses and all the prophets, he interpreted for them every passage of Scripture which referred to him.]

By now they were near the village to which they were going, and he acted as if he were going farther. But they pressed him: "Stay with us. It is nearly evening—the day is practically over." So he went in to stay with them.

When he had seated himself with them to eat, he took bread, pronounced the blessing, then broke the bread and began to distribute it to them. With that their eyes were opened and they recognized him; whereupon he vanished from their sight. They said to one another, "Were not our hearts burning inside us as he talked to us on the road and explained the Scriptures to us?" They got up immediately and returned to Jerusalem, where they found the Eleven and the rest of the company assembled. They were greeted with, "The Lord has been raised! It is true! He has appeared to Simon." Then they recounted what had happened on the road and how they had come to know him in the breaking of bread.—This is the gospel of the Lord. ℟. **Praise to you, Lord Jesus Christ.**

➤ No. 15, p. 623

---

11 Jn 6, 37-40

See p. 707.

---

12 Jn 6, 51-58

Jesus tells the crowd that he is the living bread and that anyone who eats his flesh and drinks his blood will have life everlasting. Even at this time the people fail to understand; still, Jesus promises that, in him, those who eat will have eternal life.

℣. The Lord be with you. ℟. **And also with you.**
✠ A reading from the holy gospel according to John
℟. **Glory to you, Lord.**

Jesus told the crowd:

"I myself am the living bread
come down from heaven.
If anyone eats this bread
he shall live forever;
the bread I will give
is my flesh, for the life of the world."

At this the Jews quarreled among themselves, saying, "How can he give us his flesh to eat?" Thereupon Jesus said to them:

"Let me solemnly assure you,
if you do not eat the flesh of the Son of Man
and drink his blood,
you have no life in you.
He who feeds on my flesh
and drinks my blood
has life eternal,
and I will raise him up on the last day.
For my flesh is real food
and my blood real drink.
The man who feeds on my flesh
and drinks my blood
remains in me, and I in him.

Just as the Father who has life sent me
and I have life because of the Father,
so the man who feeds on me
will have life because of me.
This is the bread that came down from heaven.
Unlike your ancestors who ate and died none-
     theless,
the man who feeds on this bread shall live for-
     ever."

This is the gospel of the Lord. ℞. **Praise to you, Lord
Jesus Christ.** ➜ No. 15, p. 623

-----

13   Jn 11, 17-27 or 11, 21-27
See p. 710.

-----

14   Jn 11, 32-45
Jesus is summoned by Martha and Mary to the tomb of Lazarus. He is
overcome with emotion, but he directs that the stone be taken from
the tomb. He commands Lazarus to come forth, and Lazarus returns
to life.

℣. The Lord be with you. ℞. **And also with you.**
✠ A reading from the holy gospel according to John
℞. **Glory to you, Lord.**

When Mary the sister of Lazarus came to the place
where Jesus was, seeing him, she fell at his feet
and said to him, "Lord, if you had been here my
brother would never have died." When Jesus saw her
weeping, and the Jewish folk who had accompanied
her also weeping, he was troubled in spirit, moved
by the deepest emotions. "Where have you laid him?"
he asked. "Lord, come and see," they said. Jesus
began to weep, which caused the Jews to remark,
"See how much he loved him!" But some said, "He
opened the eyes of that blind man. Why could he
not have done something to stop this man from
dying?" Once again troubled in spirit, Jesus approached the tomb.

It was a cave with a stone laid across it. "Take away the stone," Jesus directed. Martha, the dead man's sister, said to him, "Lord, it has been four days now; surely there will be a stench!" Jesus replied, "Did I not assure you that if you believed you would see the glory of God?" They then took away the stone and Jesus looked upward and said:

"Father, I thank you for having heard me.
I know that you always hear me
but I have said this for the sake of the crowd,
that they may believe that you sent me."

Having said this, he called loudly, "Lazarus, come out!" The dead man came out, bound hand and foot with linen strips, his face wrapped in a cloth. "Untie him," Jesus told them, "and let him go free."

This caused many of the Jews who had come to visit Mary, and had seen what Jesus did, to put their faith in him.—This is the gospel of the Lord. ℟. **Praise to you, Lord Jesus Christ.**   ➔ No. 15, p. 623

---

15   Jn 12, 23-28 or 12, 23-26

Jesus tells his disciples that unless the grain of wheat dies, it would never produce fruit. Whoever loves his life will lose it. He who hates his life will preserve it for life eternal.

[If the "Short Form" is used, the indented text in brackets is omitted.]

℣. The Lord be with you. ℟. **And also with you.**
✠ A reading from the holy gospel according to John
℟. **Glory to you, Lord.**

Jesus told his disciples:

"The hour has come
for the Son of Man to be glorified.
I solemnly assure you,
unless the grain of wheat falls to the earth and
dies,
it remains just a grain of wheat.
But if it dies,

it produces much fruit.
The man who loves his life
loses it,
while the man who hates his life in this world
preserves it to life eternal.
If anyone would serve me,
let him follow me;
where I am,
there will my servant be.
Anyone who serves me,
the Father will honor.
  [My soul is troubled now,
  yet what should I say—
  Father, save me from this hour?
  But it was for this that I came to this hour.
  Father, glorify your name!"
  Then a voice came from the sky:
    "I have glorified it,
    and will glorify it again."]

This is the gospel of the Lord. ℟. **Praise to you, Lord Jesus Christ.**   ➔ No. 15, p. 623

---

16   Jn 14, 1-6

See p. 714.

---

17   Jn 17, 24-26

See p. 1233 (omit first stanza and start with "Father").

Nov. 3 — ST. MARTIN DE PORRES, Religious

Optional Memorial

St. Martin de Porres died at Lima, Peru, on November 3, 1639. He was canonized in 1962. His cult is very popular and is spread throughout the Americas.

Common of Holy Men and Women: for Religious, p. 1097.

OPENING PRAYER

Lord,
you led Martin de Porres by a life of humility
to eternal glory.
May we follow his example
and be exalted with him in the kingdom of heaven.
Grant this through our Lord Jesus Christ, your Son,
who lives and reigns with you and the Holy Spirit,
one God, for ever and ever. ℞. **Amen.**

Reading I (Col 3, 12-17), p. 274.
Responsorial Psalm (Ps 131), p. 1210, no. 8.
Gospel (Jn 15, 9-17), p. 1232, no. 21.

Nov. 4 — ST. CHARLES BORROMEO, Bishop

Memorial

St. Charles was one of the Reformers of the Church in
the 16th century, according to the norms instituted in
the Council of Trent. He erected many monasteries,
founded many charitable institutions, and was a model
for Bishops. He died in 1584.

Common of Pastors: for Bishops, p. 1069.

OPENING PRAYER

Father,
keep in your people the spirit
which filled Charles Borromeo.
Let your Church be continually renewed
and show the image of Christ to the world
by being conformed to his likeness,
who lives and reigns with you and the Holy Spirit,
one God, for ever and ever. ℞. **Amen.**

Reading I (Rom 12, 3-13), p. 1164, no. 1.
Responsorial Psalm (Ps 96), p. 1162, no. 4.
Gospel (Jn 10, 11-16), p. 1175, no. 9.

PRAYER OVER THE GIFTS

Lord,
look with kindness on the gifts we bring to your
altar

on this feast of St. Charles.
You made him an example of virtue
and concern for the pastoral ministry.
Through the power of this sacrifice
may we abound in good works.
We ask this through Christ our Lord.
℟. **Amen.**   ➤ No 21, p. 626 (Pref. P 37-42)

PRAYER AFTER COMMUNION

Lord,
may the holy mysteries we have received
give us that courage and strength
which made St. Charles faithful in his ministry
and constant in his love.
We ask this in the name of Jesus the Lord.
℟. **Amen.**   ➤ No. 32, p. 650

Nov. 9 — DEDICATION OF ST. JOHN LATERAN

Feast

This basilica is the cathedral of the pope as bishop of
Rome; hence, it is called "Mother and Chief of all
Churches of the City and the World." It was erected
by Constantine on ground belonging to the Laterani
family and was originally known as the Constantinian
basilica. The first religious title given was Basilica of the
Holy Savior, but it was subsequently dedicated to St.
John the Baptizer and is now called the Basilica of St.
John Lateran.

ENTRANCE ANT.   Rv 21, 2

**I saw the holy city, new Jerusalem, coming down
from God out of heaven, like a bride adorned in readiness for her husband.**   ➤ No. 2, p. 614

OPENING PRAYER

God our Father,
from living stones, your chosen people,
you built an eternal temple to your glory.
Increase the spiritual gifts you have given to your
    Church,

so that your faithful people may continue to grow
into the new and eternal Jerusalem.
We ask this through our Lord Jesus Christ, your Son,
who lives and reigns with you and the Holy Spirit,
one God, for ever and ever. ℟. **Amen.** ✟

OR

Father,
you called your people to be your Church.
As we gather together in your name,
may we love, honor, and follow you
to eternal life in the kingdom you promise.
Grant this through our Lord Jesus Christ, your Son
who lives and reigns with you and the Holy Spirit,
one God, for ever and ever. ℟. **Amen.** ✟

*The Readings and Intervenient Chants from the
Common of the Dedication of a Church, p. 1106, may
also be chosen.*

*When this feast occurs apart from Sunday, only one
of the first two readings is read before the Gospel.*

READING I   2 Chr 5, 6-10. 13—6, 2

The cloud of God's Presence, which filled the temple of Solomon, is
a reminder that in order to pray, it is necessary to enter that "cloud"
and put aside all distraction. Solomon says that the Lord will dwell
in his temple.

A reading from the second book of Chronicles

King Solomon and the entire community of Israel
gathered about him before the ark were sacrificing
sheep and oxen so numerous that they could not be
counted or numbered. The priests brought the ark
of the covenant of the Lord to its place beneath the
wings of the cherubim in the sanctuary, the holy of
holies of the temple. The cherubim had their wings
spread out over the place of the ark, sheltering the
ark and its poles from above. The poles were long
enough so that their ends could be seen from that
part of the holy place nearest the sanctuary; however, they could not be seen beyond. The ark has remained there to this day. There was nothing in it but

the two tablets which Moses put there on Horeb, the
tablets of the covenant which the Lord made with
the Israelites at their departure from Egypt.

When the trumpeters and singers were heard as
a single voice praising and giving thanks to the Lord,
and when they raised the sound of the trumpets,
cymbals and other musical instruments to "give
thanks to the Lord, for he is good, for his mercy endures forever," the building of the Lord's temple was
filled with a cloud. The priests could not continue
to minister because of the cloud, since the Lord's
glory filled the house of God.

Then Solomon said: "The Lord intends to dwell
in the dark cloud. I have truly built you a princely
house and dwelling, where you may abide forever."
—This is the Word of the Lord. ℟. **Thanks be to
God.** ℣

Responsorial Psalm   Ps 84, 3. 4. 5-6. 8. 11

℟. (2) **How lovely is your dwelling-place,
    Lord, mighty God!**

My soul yearns and pines
    for the courts of the Lord.
My heart and my flesh
    cry out for the living God. — ℟

Even the sparrow finds a home,
    and the swallow a nest
    in which she puts her young—
Your altars, O Lord of hosts,
    my king and my God! — ℟

Happy they who dwell in your house!
    continually they praise you.
Happy the men whose strength you are!
    They go from strength to strength. — ℟

I had rather one day in your courts
    than a thousand elsewhere;
I had rather lie at the threshold of the house of my
    God

than dwell in the tents of the wicked. — ℟ ℣

℟. Or: (Rv 21, 3) **Here God lives among his people.** ℣

READING II   1 Cor 3, 9-13. 16-17

> Paul elaborates on the temple figure, of which your parish church is a sign. God's people can only be a solid building, in which the Spirit of God dwells, if it is built on the solid foundation that is Christ.

A reading from the first letter of Paul to the Corinthians

You are God's building. Thanks to the favor God showed me I laid a foundation as a wise master-builder might do, and now someone else is building upon it. Everyone, however, must be careful how he builds. No one can lay a foundation other than the one that has been laid, namely Jesus Christ. If different ones build on this foundation with gold, silver, precious stones, wood, hay or straw, the work of each will be made clear. The Day will disclose it. That day will make its appearance with fire, and fire will test the quality of each man's work.

Are you not aware that you are the temple of God, and that the Spirit of God dwells in you? If anyone destroys God's temple, God will destroy him. For the temple of God is holy, and you are that temple.—This is the Word of the Lord. ℟. **Thanks be to God.** ℣

GOSPEL   Lk 19, 1-10

Alleluia (2 Chr 7, 16)

℟. **Alleluia.** I have chosen and sanctified this house, says the Lord,
that my name may remain in it for ever. ℟. **Alleluia.**

Zacchaeus makes a great effort to see Jesus. In turn, Jesus acknowledges Zacchaeus' desire to see him and, after the greeting, goes to Zacchaeus' house. Zacchaeus then makes a formal act of faith.

℣. The Lord be with you. ℟. **And also with you.**
✠ A reading from the holy gospel according to Luke
℟. **Glory to you, Lord.**

Entering Jericho, Jesus passed through the city.
There was a man there named Zacchaeus, the chief
tax collector and a wealthy man. He was trying to see
what Jesus was like, but being small of stature, was
unable to do so because of the crowd. He first ran
on in front, then climbed a sycamore tree which was
along Jesus' route, in order to see him. When Jesus
came to the spot he looked up and said, "Zacchaeus,
hurry down. I mean to stay at your house today." He
quickly descended, and welcomed him with delight.
When this was observed, everyone began to murmur, "He has gone to a sinner's house as a guest."
Zacchaeus stood his ground and said to the Lord: "I
give half my belongings, Lord, to the poor. If I have
defrauded anyone in the least, I pay him back fourfold." Jesus said to him: "Today salvation has come
to this house, for this is what it means to be a son
of Abraham. The Son of Man has come to search out
and save what was lost."—This is the gospel of the
Lord. ℟. **Praise to you, Lord Jesus Christ.**

➤ No. 15, p. 623

PRAYER OVER THE GIFTS

Lord,
receive our gifts.
May we who share this sacrament
experience the life and power it promises,
and hear the answer to our prayers.
We ask this in the name of Jesus the Lord.
℟. **Amen.**   ➤ No. 21, p. 626 (Pref. P 53)

COMMUNION ANT.   1 Pt 2, 5

**Like living stones let yourselves be built on Christ as
a spiritual house, a holy priesthood.** ℣

PRAYER AFTER COMMUNION

Father,
you make your Church on earth
a sign of the new eternal Jerusalem.
By sharing in this sacrament
may we become the temple of your presence
and the home of your glory.
Grant this in the name of Jesus the Lord.
℟. **Amen.**   ➔ No. 32, p. 650

Optional Solemn Blessings, p. 682, and Prayers over the People, p. 689.

Nov. 10 — ST. LEO I, Pope and Doctor

Memorial

St. Leo the Great overcame Attila by his eloquence, defended Papal Primacy, and enriched literature with his profound discourses. He died in 461.

Common of Pastors: for Popes, p. 1066; or Common of Doctors of the Church, p. 1082.

OPENING PRAYER

God our Father,
you will never allow the power of hell
to prevail against your Church,
founded on the rock of the apostle Peter.
Let the prayers of Pope Leo the Great
keep us faithful to your truth
and secure in your peace.
We ask this through our Lord Jesus Christ, your Son,
who lives and reigns with you and the Holy Spirit,
one God, for ever and ever. ℟. **Amen.**

Reading I (Sir 39, 6-11), p. 1178, no. 4.
Responsorial Psalm (Ps 37), p. 1181, no. 2.
Gospel (Mt 16, 13-19), p. 1171, no. 1.

PRAYER OVER THE GIFTS

Lord,
by these gifts we bring,
fill your people with your light.
May your Church continue to grow everywhere under
    your guidance
and under the leadership of shepherds pleasing to
    you.
Grant this through Christ our Lord.
℟. **Amen.**   ➤ No. 21, p. 626 (Pref. P 37-42)

PRAYER AFTER COMMUNION

Lord,
as you nourish your Church with this holy banquet,
govern it always with your love.
Under your powerful guidance
may it grow in freedom
and continue in loyalty to the faith.
We ask this in the name of Jesus the Lord.
℟. **Amen.**   ➤ No. 32, p. 650

Nov. 11 — ST. MARTIN OF TOURS, Bishop

Memorial

St. Martin, Bishop of Tours, was a converted soldier
and then a missioner, admirable for his great love of
poverty. He is one of the greatest Saints of France and
the most celebrated Bishop of the 4th century.

ENTRANCE ANT.   1 Sm 2, 35

**I will raise up for myself a faithful priest; he will
do what is in my heart and in my mind, says the
Lord.**   ➤ No. 2, p. 614

OPENING PRAYER

Father,
by his life and death
Martin of Tours offered you worship and praise.
Renew in our hearts the power of your love,

so that neither death nor life may separate us from
you.
Grant this through our Lord Jesus Christ, your Son,
who lives and reigns with you and the Holy Spirit,
one God, for ever and ever. ℟. **Amen.**

*Readings and Intervenient Chants from the Common
of Pastors, p. 1154, or the Common of Holy Men and
Women: for Religious, p. 1195.*

Reading I (Is 61, 1-3), p. 1157, no. 6.
Responsorial Psalm (Ps 89), p. 1161, no. 3.
Gospel (Mt 25, 31-46), p. 1225, no. 10.

PRAYER OVER THE GIFTS

Lord God,
bless these gifts we present
on this feast of St. Martin.
May this eucharist help us
in joy and sorrow.
We ask this in the name of Jesus the Lord.
℟. **Amen.** → No. 21, p. 626 (Pref. P 37-42)

COMMUNION ANT. Mt 25, 40

**I tell you, anything you did for the least of my broth-
ers, you did for me, says the Lord.** ℣

PRAYER AFTER COMMUNION

Lord,
you have renewed us with the sacrament of unity:
help us to follow your will in all that we do.
As St. Martin gave himself completely to your service,
may we rejoice in belonging to you.
We ask this through Christ our Lord.
℟. **Amen.** → No. 32, p. 650

Nov. 12 — ST. JOSAPHAT, Bishop and Martyr
Memorial

Born in Poland, St. Josaphat entered the Order of St.
Basil. He is noted for his indefatigable efforts in uniting

the schismatic Greek Church with the Roman Church.
He was martyred by the schismatics in 1623.

Common of Martyrs, p. 1056; or Common of Pastors: for Bishops, p. 1069.

OPENING PRAYER

Lord,
fill your Church with the Spirit
that gave St. Josaphat courage
to lay down his life for his people.
By his prayers
may your Spirit make us strong
and willing to offer our lives
for our brothers and sisters.
We ask this through our Lord Jesus Christ, your Son,
who lives and reigns with you and the Holy Spirit,
one God, for ever and ever. ℟. **Amen.**

Reading I (Eph 4, 1-7. 11-13), p. 1167, no. 8.
Responsorial Psalm (Ps 1), p. 1206, no. 1.
Gospel (Jn 17, 20-26), p. 1233, no. 22.

PRAYER OVER THE GIFTS

God of mercy,
pour out your blessing upon these gifts,
and make us strong in the faith
which St. Josaphat professed by shedding his blood.
We ask this in the name of Jesus the Lord.
℟. **Amen.**   → No. 21, p. 626 (Pref. P 37-42)

PRAYER AFTER COMMUNION

Lord,
may this eucharist we have shared
fill us with your Spirit of courage and peace.
Let the example of St. Josaphat
inspire us to spend our lives
working for the honor and unity of your Church.
Grant this through Christ our Lord.
℟. **Amen.**   → No. 32, p. 650

[In the dioceses of the United States]

Nov. 13 — ST. FRANCES XAVIER CABRINI, Virgin

Memorial

St. Frances Xavier Cabrini was born in Lombardi, Italy, in 1850. In 1880 she founded the Missionary Sisters of the Sacred Heart, and in the United States she founded schools, hospitals, and orphanages for the care especially of Italian immigrants and children. She died in Chicago, Dec. 22, 1917, and was canonized by Pope Pius XII on July 7, 1946.

Common of Virgins, p. 1085.

OPENING PRAYER

God our Father,
you called Frances Xavier Cabrini from Italy
to serve the immigrants of America.
By her example teach us concern for the stranger,
the sick, and the frustrated.
By her prayers help us to see Christ
in all the men and women we meet.
Grant this through our Lord Jesus Christ, your Son,
who lives and reigns with you and the Holy Spirit,
one God, for ever and ever. ℟. **Amen.**

Reading I (1 Cor 7, 25-35), p. 1191, no. 1.
Responsorial Psalm (Ps 45), p. 1190, no. 1.
Gospel (Mk 10, 13-16), p. 1227, no. 13.

Nov. 15 — ST. ALBERT THE GREAT,
Bishop and Doctor

Optional Memorial

Born in 1206, St. Albert the Great was the famous teacher of St. Thomas Aquinas. Named to the Bishopric of Ratisbon, he retired to dedicate his talents to writing and teaching. He died in Poland in 1288.

Common of Pastors: for Bishops, p. 1069; *or Common of Doctors of the Church, p.* 1082.

OPENING PRAYER

God our Father,
you endowed St. Albert with the talent
of combining human wisdom with divine faith.
Keep us true to his teachings
that the advance of human knowledge
may deepen our knowledge and love of you.
Grant this through our Lord Jesus Christ, your Son,
who lives and reigns with you and the Holy Spirit,
one God, for ever and ever. ℞. **Amen.**

Reading I (Sir 15, 1-6), p. 1178, no. 3.
Responsorial Psalm (Ps 119), p. 1181, no. 3.
Gospel (Mt 13, 47-53), p. 185.

Nov. 16 — ST. MARGARET OF SCOTLAND

Optional Memorial

St. Margaret, born in Hungary, Queen of Scotland for
30 years, was the personification of heroic virtue. She
introduced the observance of lenten fast, sanctified
Sunday, and abolished superstitious practices. Her acts
of charity were numberless. She died after a long and
serious illness in 1093.

*Common of Holy Men and Women: for Those Who
Work for the Underprivileged, p. 1099.*

OPENING PRAYER

Lord,
you gave St. Margaret of Scotland
a special love for the poor.
Let her example and prayers
help us to become a living sign of your goodness.
We ask this through our Lord Jesus Christ, your Son,
who lives and reigns with you and the Holy Spirit,
one God, for ever and ever. ℞. **Amen.**

Reading I (Is 58, 6-11), p. 1202, no. 15.
Responsorial Psalm (Ps 112), p. 1209, no. 6.
Gospel (Jn 15, 9-17), p. 1232, no. 21.

The Same Day, Nov. 16
ST. GERTRUDE, Virgin

Optional Memorial

A Cistercian Religious, St. Gertrude wrote many works
on Mystical Theology. She was also a devout client of
the Sacred Heart of Jesus. She died in 1334.

*Common of Virgins, p. 1085, or Common of Holy Men
and Women: for Religious, p. 1097.*

OPENING PRAYER

Father,
you filled the heart of St. Gertrude
with the presence of your love.
Bring light into our darkness
and let us experience the joy of your presence
and the power of your grace.
Grant this through our Lord Jesus Christ, your Son,
who lives and reigns with you and the Holy Spirit,
one God, for ever and ever. ℟. **Amen.**

Reading I (Eph 3, 14-19), p. 1213, no. 7.
Responsorial Psalm (Ps 23), p. 1161, no. 2.
Gospel (Jn 15, 1-8), p. 1231, no. 20.

Nov. 17 — ST. ELIZABETH OF HUNGARY, Religious

Memorial

Daughter of the King of Hungary, St. Elizabeth married
Louis IV of Thuringia. After his death, she entered the
Third Order of St. Francis where she practiced heroic
works of charity.

*Common of Holy Men and Women: for Those Who
Work for the Underprivileged, p. 1099.*

OPENING PRAYER

Father,
you helped Elizabeth of Hungary
to recognize and honor Christ
in the poor of this world.
Let her prayers help us to serve our brothers and
sisters

in time of trouble and need.
We ask this through our Lord Jesus Christ, your Son,
who lives and reigns with you and the Holy Spirit,
one God, for ever and ever. ℟. **Amen.**

Reading I (1 Jn 3, 14-18), p. 1217, no. 15.
Responsorial Psalm (Ps 34), p. 1207, no. 4.
Gospel (Lk 6, 27-38), p. 275.

Nov. 18 — DEDICATION OF THE CHURCHES
OF STS. PETER AND PAUL, Apostles

Optional Memorial

The Dedication of the Basilica of Sts. Peter and Paul
has been commemorated on November 18 since the 11th
century. The present Vatican Basilica was consecrated
on November 18, 1626; and the Ostian Basilica on December 10, 1854.

ENTRANCE ANT. Ps 44, 17-18

**You have made them princes over all the earth; they
declared your fame to all generations; for ever will
the nations declare your praise.** → No. 2, p. 614

OPENING PRAYER
Lord,
give your Church the protection of the apostles.
From them it first received the faith of Christ.
May they help your Church to grow in your grace
until the end of time.
Grant this through our Lord Jesus Christ, your Son,
who lives and reigns with you and the Holy Spirit,
one God, for ever and ever. ℟. **Amen.**

The readings are special in this Optional Memorial.

READING I Acts 28, 11-16. 30-31

Paul discusses his travels while under arrest which finally lead him
to Rome. He is met by some of the faithful. Paul is able in a limited
way to continue spreading the gospel.

A reading from the Acts of the Apostles

After three months in Malta we set sail in a ship which had passed the winter at the island. It was an Alexandrian vessel with the "Heavenly Twins" as its figurehead. We put in at Syracuse and spent three days there. Then we sailed around the toe and arrived at Rhegium. A day later a south wind began to blow which enabled us to reach Puteoli in two days. Here we found some of the brothers, who urged us to stay on with them for a week.

This is how we finally came to Rome. Certain brothers from Rome who heard about us came out as far as the Forum of Appius and the Three Taverns to meet us. When Paul saw them, he thanked God and took courage afresh. Upon our entry into Rome Paul was allowed to take a lodging of his own, although a soldier was assigned to keep guard over him.

For two full years Paul stayed on in his rented lodgings, welcoming all who came to him. With full assurance, and without any hindrance whatever, he preached the reign of God and taught about the Lord Jesus Christ.—This is the Word of the Lord. ℟. **Thanks be to God.** ℣

Responsorial Psalm   Ps 98, 1. 2-3. 3-4. 5-6

℟. (2) **The Lord has revealed to the nations his saving power.**

Sing to the Lord a new song,
    for he has done wondrous deeds;
His right hand has won victory for him,
    his holy arm. — ℟

The Lord has made his salvation known:
    in the sight of the nations he has revealed his justice.

He has remembered his kindness and his faithfulness
    toward the house of Israel. — ℟

All the ends of the earth have seen
　the salvation by our God.
Sing joyfully to the Lord, all you lands;
　break into song; sing praise. — ℞

Sing praise to the Lord with the harp,
　with the harp and melodious song.
With trumpets and the sound of the horn
　sing joyfully before the King, the Lord. — ℞ ℣

GOSPEL Mt 14, 22-33

Alleluia

℞. **Alleluia.** We praise you, God; we acknowledge
　　you as Lord;
　your glorious band of apostles extols you. ℞. **Alle-
　luia.**

Jesus appears on the water when the disciples are afraid the boat is
about to capsize in the storm. Peter recognizes Jesus who beckons
him to walk on the water, and Peter does so until he begins to doubt.
All then acknowledge Jesus as the Son of God.

℣. The Lord be with you. ℞. **And also with you.**
✠ A reading from the holy gospel according to Matthew. ℞. **Glory to you, Lord.**

While dismissing the crowds, Jesus insisted that
his disciples get into the boat and precede him to
the other side. When he had sent them away, he
went up on the mountain by himself to pray, remaining there alone as evening drew on. Meanwhile
the boat, already several hundred yards out from
shore, was being tossed about in the waves raised
by strong head winds. At about three in the morning,
he came walking toward them on the lake. When the
disciples saw him walking on the water, they were
terrified. "It is a ghost!" they said, and in their fear
they began to cry out. Jesus hastened to reassure
them: "Get hold of yourselves! It is I. Do not be
afraid!" Peter spoke up and said, "Lord, if it is really
you, tell me to come to you across the water."
"Come!" he said. So Peter got out of the boat and

began to walk on the water, moving toward Jesus. But when he perceived how strong the wind was, becoming frightened he began to sink, and cried out, "Lord, save me!" Jesus at once stretched out his hand and caught him. "How little faith you have!" he exclaimed. "Why did you falter?" Once they had climbed into the boat, the wind died down. Those who were in the boat showed him reverence, declaring, "Beyond doubt you are the Son of God!"— This is the gospel of the Lord. ℟. **Praise to you, Lord Jesus Christ.**
➤ No. 15, p. 623

PRAYER OVER THE GIFTS

Lord,
accept the gift of our worship
and hear our prayers for mercy.
Keep alive in our hearts the truth you gave us
through the ministry of your apostles Peter and
  Paul.
We ask this through Christ our Lord.
℟. **Amen.**
➤ No. 21, p. 626 (Pref. P 64-65)

COMMUNION ANT.
Jn 6, 69-70

Lord, you have the words of everlasting life, and we believe that you are God's Holy One. ℣

PRAYER AFTER COMMUNION

Lord,
you have given us bread from heaven.
May this celebration
in memory of your apostles Peter and Paul
bring us the joy of their constant protection.
We ask this in the name of Jesus the Lord.
℟. **Amen.**
➤ No. 32, p. 650

Nov. 21 — PRESENTATION OF MARY

Memorial

This feast is founded on a pious tradition, originated by three apocryphal gospels, but which is probably authentic, relating that the Blessed Virgin was presented in the temple of Jerusalem at the age of three and that she lived there with other girls and the holy women who had them in their charge. This event was already commemorated in the 6th century in the East. Gregory XI in 1372 heard of that feast, kept in Greece on November 21, and introduced it at Avignon. In 1585 Sixtus V extended it to the universal Church.

Common of the Blessed Virgin Mary, p. 1040.

OPENING PRAYER

Eternal Father,
we honor the holiness and glory of the Virgin Mary.
May her prayers bring us
the fullness of your life and love.
We ask this through our Lord Jesus Christ, your Son,
who lives and reigns with you and the Holy Spirit,
one God, for ever and ever. ℟. **Amen.**

Reading I (Zec 2, 14-17), p. 1124, no. 11.
Respsonorial Psalm (Lk 1), p. 1128, no. 5.
Gospel (Mt 12, 46-50), p. 166.

Nov. 22 — ST. CECILIA, Virgin and Martyr

St. Cecilia, a Roman by birth, was forced to marry Valerian, a pagan. She converted him and Tiburtius, his brother, to the faith. Although married, St. Cecilia preserved her virginity. She died in 230.

Common of Martyrs, p. 1056; or Common of Virgins, p. 1085.

OPENING PRAYER

Lord of mercy,
be close to those who call upon you.
With St. Cecilia to help us
hear and answer our prayers.

Grant this through our Lord Jesus Christ, your Son,
who lives and reigns with you and the Holy Spirit,
one God, for ever and ever. ℟. **Amen.**

Reading I (Lv 19, 1-2. 17-18), p. 1195, no. 2.
Responsorial Psalm (Ps 15), p. 1206, no. 2.
Gospel (Mt 10, 28-23), p. 1151, no. 2.

Nov. 23 — ST. CLEMENT I, Pope and Martyr

Optional Memorial

St. Clement, the third successor of St. Peter to the See
of Rome, suffered martyrdom during the reign of Emperor Trajan in 100.

*Common of Martyrs, p. 1056; or Common of Pastors:
for Popes, p. 1066.*

OPENING PRAYER

All-powerful and ever-living God,
we praise your power and glory
revealed to us in the lives of all your saints.
Give us joy on this feast of St. Clement,
the priest and martyr
who bore witness with his blood to the love he proclaimed
and the gospel he preached.
We ask this through our Lord Jesus Christ, your Son,
who lives and reigns with you and the Holy Spirit,
one God, for ever and ever. ℟. **Amen.**

Reading I (1 Pt 5, 1-4), p. 1169, no. 13.
Responsorial Psalm (Ps 89), p. 1161, no. 3.
Gospel (Lk 5, 1-11), p. 1173, no. 6

The Same Day, Nov. 23
ST. COLUMBAN, Abbot

Optional Memorial

Manuscripts of the *Hieronymian Martyrology* which
are fairly ancient record—on November 23, 615—the
burial of St. Columban at Bobbio in Italy. There is widespread devotion to him in many countries.

Common of Pastors: for Missionaries, p. 1077; or Common of Holy Men and Women: for Religious, p. 1097.

OPENING PRAYER

Lord,
you called St. Columban to live the monastic life
and to preach the gospel with zeal.
May his prayers and example
help us to seek you above all things
and to work with all our hearts
for the spread of the faith.
Grant this through our Lord Jesus Christ, your Son,
who lives and reigns with you and the Holy Spirit,
one God, for ever and ever. ℟. **Amen.**

Reading I (Is 52, 7-10), p. 1156, no. 5.
Responsorial Psalm (Ps 96), p. 1162, no. 4.
Gospel (Lk 9, 57-62), p. 1228, no. 15.

Nov. 30 — ST. ANDREW, Apostle

Feast

St. Andrew, the brother of St. Peter, was a native of the town of Bethsaida in Galilee. A fisherman by profession and a disciple of St. John the Baptist, he and his brother, St. Peter, joined Jesus as members of the Apostolic College. After the dispersion of the Apostles, St. Andrew preached in Greece and several other countries. He suffered martyrdom in Patras, Greece, and according to common opinion, by crucifixion on a cross made in the form of the letter **X**.

ENTRANCE ANT.   See Mt 4, 18-19

By the Sea of Galilee the Lord saw two brothers, Peter and Andrew. He called them: come and follow me, and I will make you fishers of men.

➤ No. 2, p. 614

OPENING PRAYER

Lord,
in your kindness hear our petitions.

You called Andrew the apostle
to preach the gospel and guide your Church in faith.
May he always be our friend in your presence
to help us with his prayers.
We ask this through our Lord Jesus Christ, your Son,
who lives and reigns with you and the Holy Spirit,
one God, for ever and ever. ℟. **Amen.** ✠

READING I   Rom 10, 9-18

An inward faith is demanded that will guide the whole man, but it is
also an assent to an expression of that faith. The man seeking justification and salvation is called on to acknowledge Christ as the risen
Lord.

A reading from the letter of Paul to the Romans

If you confess with your lips that Jesus is Lord, and
believe in your heart that God raised him from the
dead, you will be saved. Faith in the heart leads to
justification, confession on the lips to salvation.
Scripture says, "No one who believes in him will
be put to shame." Here there is no difference between Jew and Greek; all have the same Lord, rich
in mercy toward all who call upon him. "Everyone
who calls on the name of the Lord will be saved."

But how shall they call on him in whom they have
not believed? And how can they believe unless they
have heard of him? And how can they hear unless
there is someone to preach? And how can men
preach unless they are sent? Scripture says, "How
beautiful are the feet of those who announce good
news!" But not all have believed the gospel. Isaiah
asks, "Lord, who has believed what he has heard
from us?" Faith, then, comes through hearing, and
what is heard is the word of Christ. I ask you, have
they not heard? Certainly they have, for "their
voice has sounded over the whole earth, and their
words to the limits of the world."—This is the Word
of the Lord. ℟. **Thanks be to God.** ✠

Responsorial Psalm   Ps 19, 2-3. 4-5

℟. (5) **Their message goes out through all the earth.**

The heavens declare the glory of God,
  and the firmament proclaims his handiwork.
Day pours out the word to day,
  and night to night imparts knowledge. — ℟

Not a word nor a discourse
  whose voice is not heard;
Through all the earth their voice resounds,
  and to the end of the world, their message. — ℟ ℣

GOSPEL   Mt 4, 18-22

Alleluia (Mt 4, 19)

℟. **Alleluia.** Come, follow me, says the Lord,
and I will make you fishers of men. ℟. **Alleluia.**

Peter, Andrew, James and John follow our Lord immediately. They
drop their fishing net, leave their families and become disciples. The
promise of Christ to make them "fishers of men" is an intimation of
the apostolic office.

℣. The Lord be with you. ℟. **And also with you.**
✠ A reading from the holy gospel according to Matthew. ℟. **Glory to you, Lord.**

As Jesus was walking along the Sea of Galilee he
watched two brothers, Simon now known as Peter,
and his brother Andrew, casting a net into the sea.
They were fishermen. He said to them, "Come after
me and I will make you fishers of men." They immediately abandoned their nets and became his followers. He walked along farther and caught sight
of two other brothers, James, Zebedee's son, and
his brother John. They too were in their boat, getting their nets in order with their father Zebedee.
He called them, and immediately they abandoned
boat and father to follow him.—This is the gospel
of the Lord. ℟. **Praise to you, Lord Jesus Christ.**

➤ No. 15, p. 623

PRAYER OVER THE GIFTS

All-powerful God,
may these gifts we bring on the feast of St. Andrew
be pleasing to you
and give life to all who receive them.
We ask this in the name of Jesus the Lord.
℟. **Amen.**   ➤ No. 21, p. 626 (Pref. P 64-65)

COMMUNION ANT.   Jn 1, 41-42

**Andrew told his brother Simon: We have found the
Messiah, the Christ; and he brought him to Jesus.** ℣

PRAYER AFTER COMMUNION

Lord,
may the sacrament we have received give us courage
to follow the example of Andrew the apostle.
By sharing in Christ's suffering
may we live with him for ever in glory,
for he is Lord for ever and ever.
℟. **Amen.**   ➤ No. 32, p. 650

[In the dioceses of the United States]

Fourth Thursday of November
THANKSGIVING DAY

United States citizens have cherished Thanksgiving
Day as a civil and religious festival since its institution
by Governor William Bradford of Plymouth Colony in
1621. This custom spread throughout the British North
American Colonies. During the Revolutionary War the
Continental Congress adopted it, and the states observed the day thereafter. President Abraham Lincoln designated it as a national holiday. A joint resolution of
Congress in 1941 fixed the fourth Thursday of November as the national day of thanksgiving.

ENTRANCE ANT.   Eph 5, 19-20

**Sing and play music in your hearts to the Lord, al-
ways giving thanks for everything to God the Father
in the name of our Lord Jesus Christ.** ➤ No. 2, p. 614

OPENING PRAYER

Let us pray
    [that our gratitude to God may bear fruit
    in loving service to our fellow men and women]
Father all-powerful,
your gifts of love are countless
and your goodness infinite.
On Thanksgiving Day we come before you
with gratitude for your kindness:
open our hearts to concern for our fellow men and
    women,
so that we may share your gifts in loving service.
We ask this through our Lord Jesus Christ, your Son,
who lives and reigns with you and the Holy Spirit,
one God, for ever and ever. ℟. **Amen.** ℣

*The Readings and Intervenient Chants found at the
end of this Mass may also be chosen.*

READING I   Is 63, 7-9

Isaiah sings of God's favors. His mercy and kindness he gives to his
loyal children. God saved his people himself because of his love and
pity for them.

A reading from the book of the prophet Isaiah

The favors of the Lord I will recall,
    the glorious deeds of the Lord,
Because of all he has done for us;
    for he is good to the house of Israel,
He has favored us according to his mercy
    and his great kindness.
He said: They are indeed my people,
    children who are not disloyal;
So he became their savior
    in their every affliction.
It was not a messenger or an angel,
    but he himself who saved them.
Because of his love and pity
    he redeemed them himself,

Lifting them and carrying them
   all the days of old.
This is the Word of the Lord. ℟. **Thanks be to God. ℣**

Responsorial Psalm   Ps 138, 1-2. 2-3. 4-5

℟. (2) **I will give thanks to your name,**
   because of your kindness and your truth.

I will give thanks to you, O Lord, with all my heart,
   [for you have heard the words of my mouth;]
      in the presence of the angels I will sing your
      praise;
I will worship at your holy temple. — ℟

I will give thanks to your name,
   because of your kindness and your truth;
For you have made great above all things
   your name and your promise.
When I called, you answered me;
   you built up strength within me. — ℟

All the kings of the earth shall give thanks to you,
   O Lord,
   when they hear the words of your mouth;
And they shall sing of the ways of the Lord:
   "Great is the glory of the Lord." — ℟ ℣

READING II   1 Cor 1, 3-9

Paul reminds the Corinthians of the favors God has given them, every
gift of knowledge and speech. God is faithful and he will strengthen
his people always.

A reading from the first letter of Paul to the
Corinthians

Grace and peace from God our Father and the Lord
Jesus Christ.
   I continually thank my God for you because of
the favor he has bestowed on you in Christ Jesus,
in whom you have been richly endowed with every
gift of speech and knowledge. Likewise, the witness
I bore to Christ has been so confirmed among you

that you lack no spiritual gift as you wait for the revelation of our Lord Jesus Christ. He will strengthen you to the end, so that you will be blameless on the day of our Lord Jesus [Christ]. God is faithful, and it was he who called you to fellowship with his Son, Jesus Christ our Lord.—This is the Word of the Lord. ℟. **Thanks be to God.** ↓

GOSPEL   Lk 12, 15-21

Alleluia (Eph 1, 3)

℟. **Alleluia.** May the God and Father of our Lord
        Jesus Christ be praised:
God, who has bestowed on us in Christ every spiritual blessing in the heavens! ℟. **Alleluia.**

The security of a man's life does not come from his possessions even when he has them in abundance. Jesus teaches of what little value material possessions really are.

℣. The Lord be with you. ℟. **And also with you.**
✠ A reading from the holy gospel according to Luke
℟. **Glory to you, Lord.**

Jesus said to the crowd, "Avoid greed in all its forms. A man may be wealthy, but his possessions do not guarantee him life." He told them a parable in these words: "There was a rich man who had a good harvest. 'What shall I do?' he asked himself. 'I have no place to store my harvest. I know!' he said. 'I will pull down my grain bins and build larger ones. All my grain and my goods will go there. Then I will say to myself: You have blessings in reserve for years to come. Relax! Eat heartily, drink well. Enjoy yourself.' But God said to him, 'You fool! This very night your life shall be required of you. To whom will all this piled-up wealth of yours go?' That is the way it works with the man who grows rich for himself instead of growing rich in the sight of God."—This is the gospel of the Lord. ℟. **Praise to you, Lord Jesus Christ.** ↓

GENERAL INTERCESSIONS

Priest: Moved to thanksgiving by our hearing of God's word, we turn to the heavenly Father in confident petition.

Deacon (or other minister): For your servants, N. our Pope, N. our bishop, and all the clergy throughout the world,

People: We pray to the Lord.

Deacon: For our civil officials and for all civil servants,

People: We pray to the Lord.

Deacon: That the people of our nation may recognize the needs of other peoples and respond to them,

People: We pray to the Lord.

Deacon: That the wealth and resources of our nation may be a blessing for all Americans,

People: We pray to the Lord.

Deacon: That the Eucharist may always be the source and expression of our thanksgiving,

People: We pray to the Lord.

Priest: God our Father, help us to love creation as you love it, so that we may prepare ourselves to enjoy the feast of everlasting Thanksgiving: through Christ our Lord.

People: Amen. ➤ No. 16, p. 624

PRAYER OVER THE GIFTS

God our Father,
from your hand we have received generous gifts
so that we might learn to share your blessings in gratitude.
Accept these gifts of bread and wine,
and let the perfect sacrifice of Jesus
draw us closer to all our brothers and sisters in the family of man.

Grant this through Christ our Lord.
℟. **Amen.**   → No. 21, p. 626 (P 84)

COMMUNION ANT.   Ps 138, 1
**I will give thanks to you with all my heart, O Lord,
for you have answered me.** ℣

OR   Ps 116, 12-13
**What return can I make to the Lord for all that he
gives to me? I will take the cup of salvation, and call
on the name of the Lord.** ℣

PRAYER AFTER COMMUNION
Lord God,
in this celebration
we have seen the depths of your love for every man
      and woman
and been reminded of our negligence toward others.
Help us to reach out in love to all your people,
so that we may share with them
the goods of time and eternity.
Grant this through Christ our Lord.
℟. **Amen.**   → No. 32, p. 650

_____

OTHER POSSIBLE READINGS

OLD TESTAMENT READING

1   Dt 8, 7-18

Moses reminds the Israelites that God is leading them into a land of
plenty where all their needs will be taken care of. But they must
give praise and thanks to God and keep his commandments. They
must keep the covenant. All good things come from God.

A reading from the book of Deuteronomy

Moses told the people: "The Lord, your God, is
bringing you into a good country, a land with streams
of water, with springs and fountains welling up in
the hills and valleys, a land of wheat and barley,
of vines and fig trees and pomegranates, of olive

trees and of honey, a land where you can eat bread without stint and where you will lack nothing, a land whose stones contain iron and in whose hills you can mine copper. But when you have eaten your fill, you must bless the Lord, your God, for the good country he has given you. Be careful not to forget the Lord, your God, by neglecting his commandments and decrees and statutes which I enjoin on you today: lest, when you have eaten your fill, and have built fine houses and lived in them, and have increased your herds and flocks, your silver and gold, and all your property, you then become haughty of heart and unmindful of the Lord, your God, who brought you out of the land of Egypt, that place of slavery; who guided you through the vast and terrible desert with its saraph serpents and scorpions, its parched and waterless ground; who brought forth water for you from the flinty rock and fed you in the desert with manna, a food unknown to your fathers, that he might afflict you and test you, but also make you prosperous in the end. Otherwise, you might say to yourselves, 'It is my own power and the strength of my own hand that has obtained for me this wealth.' Remember then, it is the Lord, your God, who gives you the power to acquire wealth, by fulfilling, as he has now done, the covenant which he swore to your fathers."—This is is Word of the Lord. ℞. **Thanks be to God.**

---

2   1 Kgs 8, 55-61

Solomon gives praise to God who fulfilled his promise of caring for his people. Solomon prays that God will continue to be with his people as of old. In turn, the people must observe the statutes and commandments of God.

A reading from the first book of Kings

Solomon stood and blessed the whole community of Israel, saying in a loud voice: "Blessed be the

Lord who has given rest to his people Israel, just as he promised. Not a single word has gone unfulfilled of the entire generous promise he made through his servant Moses. May the Lord, our God, be with us as he was with our fathers and may he not forsake us nor cast us off. May he draw our hearts to himself, that we may follow him in everything and keep the commands, statutes, and ordinances which he enjoined on our fathers. May this prayer I have offered to the Lord, our God, be present to him day and night, that he may uphold the cause of his servant and of his people Israel as each day requires, that all the peoples of the earth may know the Lord is God and there is no other. You must be wholly devoted to the Lord, our God, observing his statutes and keeping his commandments, as on this day."
—This is the Word of the Lord. ℟. **Thanks be to God.**

---

3   Sir 50, 22-24

Sirach acknowledges the wondrous deeds of God from giving life and helping man grow. He prays that this goodness of the Lord will continue forever.

A reading from the book of Sirach

And now, bless the God of all,
    who has done wondrous things on earth;
Who fosters men's growth from their mother's womb,
    and fashions them according to his will!
May he grant you joy of heart
    and may peace abide among you;
May his goodness toward us endure in Israel
    as long as the heavens are above.
This is the Word of the Lord. ℟. **Thanks be to God.**

---

4   Is 63, 7-9
See p. 766.

---

5 Jl 2, 21-24. 26-27

Joel notes the great things done by God. He tells the people to rejoice in the Lord who makes the grain grow, gives food, and cares for his people. God is in their midst; there is no other.

A reading from the book of the prophet Joel

Fear not, O land!
exult and rejoice!
for the Lord has done great things.
Fear not, beasts of the field!
for the pastures of the plain are green;
The tree bears its fruit,
the fig tree and the vine give their yield.
And do you, O children of Zion, exult
and rejoice in the Lord, your God!
He has given you the teacher of justice:
he has made the rain come down for you,
the early and the late rain as before.
The threshing floors shall be full of grain
and the vats shall overflow with wine and oil.
You shall eat and be filled,
and shall praise the name of the Lord, your God,
Because he has dealt wondrously with you;
my people shall nevermore be put to shame.
And you shall know that I am in the midst of Israel;
I am the Lord, your God, and there is no other;
My people shall nevermore be put to shame.
This is the Word of the Lord. ℟. **Thanks be to God.**

---

6 Zep 3, 14-15

The prophet Zephaniah tells the people to sing for joy to the Lord who has saved them from their enemies. There is nothing more to fear.

A reading from the book of the prophet Zephaniah

Shout for joy, O daughter Zion!
sing joyfully, O Israel!
Be glad and exult with all your heart,
O daughter Jerusalem!

The Lord has removed the judgment against you!
> he has turned away your enemies;

The King of Israel, the Lord, is in your midst,
> you have no further misfortune to fear.

This is the Word of the Lord. ℟. **Thanks be to God.**

NEW TESTAMENT READING

1   1 Cor 1, 3-9

See p. 767.

---

2   Eph 1, 3-14

God chose his people before the world began. They are adopted through Jesus. Through the blood of Jesus, they are a redeemed people. Jesus is the pledge of everlasting life.

A reading from the letter of Paul to the
Ephesians

Praised be the God and Father of our Lord Jesus Christ, who has bestowed on us in Christ every spiritual blessing in the heavens! God chose us in him before the world began, to be holy and blameless in his sight, to be full of love; he likewise predestined us through Christ Jesus to be his adopted sons—such was his will and pleasure— that all might praise the divine favor he has bestowed on us in his beloved.

It is in Christ and through his blood that we have been redeemed and our sins forgiven, so immeasurably generous is God's favor to us. God has given us the wisdom to understand fully the mystery, the plan he was pleased to decree in Christ, to be carried out in the fullness of time: namely, to bring all things in the heavens and on earth into one under Christ's headship.

In him we were chosen; for in the decree of God, who administers everything according to his will and counsel, we were predestined to praise his glory by being the first to hope in Christ. In him you too were chosen; when you heard the glad tidings of salvation, the word of truth, and believed in it, you were sealed with the Holy Spirit who had been promised. He is the pledge of our inheritance, the first payment against the full redemption of a people God has made his own, to praise his glory.—This is the Word of the Lord. ℞. **Thanks be to God.**

3   Col 3, 12-17

Paul instructs the Colossians to develop all virtues. Forgive one another and put on love which binds all together. The peace of Christ must reign. Whatever work is done, let it be done in the name of Jesus.

A reading from the letter of Paul to the Colossians

Because you are God's chosen ones, holy and beloved, clothe yourselves with heartfelt mercy, with kindness, humility, meekness, and patience. Bear with one another; forgive whatever grievances you have against one another. Forgive as the Lord has forgiven you. Over all these virtues put on love, which binds the rest together and makes them perfect. Christ's peace must reign in your hearts, since as members of the one body you have been called to that peace. Dedicate yourselves to thankfulness. Let the word of Christ, rich as it is, dwell in you. In wisdom made perfect, instruct and admonish one another. Sing gratefully to God from your hearts in psalms, hymns, and inspired songs. Whatever you do, whether in speech or in action, do it in the name of the Lord Jesus. Give thanks to God the Father through him.—This is the Word of the Lord. ℞. **Thanks be to God.**

4   1 Tm 6, 6-11. 17-19

Paul warns Timothy about wealth and how it can lead to corruption. Some even made it a passion. Those of God, however, trust in the Lord. They become rich in virtue doing good works and sharing what they have.

A reading from the first letter of Paul to
Timothy

There is great gain in religion, provided one is content with a sufficiency. We brought nothing into this world, nor have we the power to take anything out. If we have food and clothing we have all that we need. Those who want to be rich are falling into temptation and a trap. They are letting themselves be captured by foolish and harmful desires which drag men down to ruin and destruction. The love of money is the root of all evil. Some men in their passion for it have strayed from the faith and have come to grief amid great pain.

Man of God that you are, flee from all this. Instead, seek after integrity, piety, faith, love, steadfastness and a gentle spirit.

Tell those who are rich in this world's goods not be to proud, and not to rely on so uncertain a thing as wealth. Let them trust in the God who provides us richly with all things for our use. Charge them to do good, to be rich in good works and generous, sharing what they have. Thus will they build a secure foundation for the future, for receiving that life which is life indeed.—This is the Word of the Lord. ℞. **Thanks be to God.**

RESPONSORIAL PSALM

1   Ps 67, 2-3. 5. 7-8

℞. (7) **The earth has yielded its fruits;**
     God, our God, has blessed us.

May God have pity on us and bless us;
     may he let his face shine upon us.
So may your way be known upon earth;
     among all nations, your salvation. — ℞

May the nations be glad and exult
     because you rule the peoples in equity;
     the nations on the earth you guide. — ℞

The earth has yielded its fruits;
  God, our God, has blessed us.
May God bless us,
  and may all the ends of the earth fear him! — ℟

℟. Or: **May the peoples praise you, O God;
  may all the peoples praise you!**

---

2   1 Chr 29, 10-11. 11-12. 12

℟. (13) **We praise the majesty of your name.**

Blessed may you be, O Lord,
  God of Israel our father,
    from eternity to eternity. — ℟

Yours, O Lord, are grandeur and power,
  majesty, splendor, and glory;
For all in heaven and on earth is yours. — ℟

Yours, O Lord, is the sovereignty;
  you are exalted as head over all.
Riches and honor are from you. — ℟

And you have dominion over all.
  In your hand are power and might;
It is yours to give grandeur and strength to all. — ℟

---

3   Ps 113, 1-2. 3-4. 5-6. 7-8

℟. (2) **Blessed be the name of the Lord
  both now and forever.**

Praise, you servants of the Lord,
  praise the name of the Lord.
Blessed be the name of the Lord
  both now and forever. — ℟

From the rising to the setting of the sun
  is the name of the Lord to be praised.
High above all nations is the Lord;
  above the heavens is his glory. — ℟

Who is like the Lord, our God, who is enthroned on
  high
    and looks upon the heavens and the earth be-
      low? — ℟

He raises up the lowly from the dust;
 from the dunghill he lifts up the poor
To seat them with princes,
 with the princes of his own people. — ℟

℟. Or: **Alleluia.**

---

4   Ps 138, 1-2. 2-3. 4-5

See p. 767.

---

5   Ps 145, 2-3. 4-5. 6-7. 8-9. 10-11

℟. (1) **I will bless your name, O Lord, forever and ever.**

Every day I will bless you,
 and I will praise your name forever and ever.
Great is the Lord and highly to be praised;
 his greatness is unsearchable. — ℟

Generation after generation praises your works
 and proclaims your might.
They speak of the splendor of your glorious majesty
 and tell of your wondrous works. — ℟

They discourse of the power of your terrible deeds
 and declare your greatness.
They publish the fame of your abundant goodness
 and joyfully sing of your justice. — ℟

The Lord is gracious and merciful,
 slow to anger and of great kindness.
The Lord is good to all
 and compassionate toward all his works. — ℟

Let all your works give you thanks, O Lord,
 and let your faithful ones bless you.
Let them discourse of the glory of your kingdom
 and speak of your might. — ℟

ALLELUIA VERSE

1   Ps 126, 5

Those that sow in tears
   shall reap rejoicing

---

2   Eph 1, 3

See p. 768.

---

3   1 Thes 5, 18

Rejoice always, never cease praying,
   render constant thanks;
such is God's will for you in Christ Jesus.

---

4   Ambrosian hymn

We praise you, O God, we acclaim you the Lord.
The holy Church throughout the world worships
   you.

GOSPEL

1   Mk 5, 18-20

Jesus directs the man from whom a devil was cast out and who
wanted to stay with the Master to go back to his people and tell them
what the Lord did for him. All who hear are amazed.

℣. The Lord be with you. ℟. **And also with you.**
✠ A reading from the holy gospel according to Mark
℟. **Glory to you, Lord.**

As Jesus was getting into the boat, the man who had
been possessed was pressing to accompany him.
Jesus did not grant his request, but told him instead:
"Go home to your family and make it clear to them
how much the Lord in his mercy has done for you."
At that the man went off and began to proclaim
throughout the Ten Cities what Jesus had done for

him. They were all amazed at what they heard.—
This is the gospel of the Lord. ℟. **Praise to you, Lord
Jesus Christ.**   ➔ No. 15, p. 623

---

2   Lk 12, 15-21

See p. 768.

---

3   Lk 17, 11-19

Ten lepers come to Jesus asking to be cleansed. Jesus sends them
to the priests and on their way they are cured. Only one comes back
to Jesus to give thanks.

℣. The Lord be with you. ℟. **And also with you.**
✠ A reading from the holy gospel according to Luke
℟. **Glory to you, Lord.**

On his journey to Jerusalem Jesus passed along the
borders of Samaria and Galilee. As he was entering
a village, ten lepers met him. Keeping their distance,
they raised their voices and said, "Jesus, Master,
have pity on us!" When he saw them, he responded,
"Go and show yourselves to the priests." On their way
there they were cured. One of them, realizing that
he had been cured, came back praising God in a
loud voice. He threw himself on his face at the feet
of Jesus and spoke his praises. This man was a Samaritan.

Jesus took the occasion to say, "Were not all ten
made whole? Where are the other nine? Was there
no one to return and give thanks to God except this
foreigner?" He said to the man, "Stand up and go
your way; your faith has been your salvation."—
This is the gospel of the Lord. ℟. **Praise to you, Lord
Jesus Christ.**   ➔ No. 15, p. 623

PROPER OF SEASONS

READINGS AND INTERVENIENT CHANTS FOR ORDINARY TIME

(YEAR II)

INTRODUCTION FOR 10th to 14th WEEK

The Prophets—*The prophetic books of the Bible, together with the oral preaching of the prophets, were the result of the institution of prophetism, in which a succession of Israelites chosen by God and appointed by him to be prophets received communications from him and transmitted them to the people in his name (Dt 18, 15-20). The prophets were spokesmen of God, intermediaries between him and his people. The communications they received from God came through visions, dreams, and ecstasies and were transmitted to the people through sermons, writings, and symbolic actions.*

The office of prophet was due to a direct call from God. It was not the result of heredity, just as it was not a permanent gift but a transient one, subject entirely to the divine will. The prophets preserved and developed revealed religion (1 Sm 12, 6-25), denounced idolatry (1 Kgs 14, 1-13), defended the moral law (2 Sm 12, 1-15), gave counsel in political matters (Is 31, 1ff), and often also in matters of private life (1 Sm 9, 6-9). At times miracles confirmed their preaching, and their predictions of the future intensified the expectation of the Messiah and of his kingdom.

The literary form of prophecy uses warning and threat besides exhortation and promise to declare in God's name events of the near and distant future (Is 8—9). Kindly and persuasive tones pervade the promises of reward and even the threats of punishment (Am 5, 14-15). Disregard for exact chronological perspective in the prophecies is another characteristic. Predictions of the immediate and distant future are often interrelated, not on the basis of years separating the events but on the analogy of the pattern joining present with very distant, though similar, conditions and circumstances. This is prophetic compenetration, idealization in which persons and things of the more immediate present, in the prophet's day, fade into a wider and more perfect order of persons and things of the future; the former are figures and types of the latter.

The Book of Kings (Cont'd)—(See *Volume I*, pp. 207-208.) This second part of these books continues the history of the kings of Israel and Judah and interweaves within it the accounts of the activities of the great prophets Elijah and Elisha. Elijah is one of the most important figures in Old Testament history. He was the successful leader in the struggle against the encroaching worship of the pagan Baal.

The Book of Amos—Amos was a shepherd of Tekoa in Judah, who exercised his ministry during the prosperous reign of Jeroboam II (786-746 B.C.). He prophesied in Israel at the great cult center of Bethel, from which he was finally expelled by the priest in charge of this royal sanctuary. Amos is a prophet of divine judgment, and the sovereignty of Yahweh in nature and history dominates his thought. However, in common with the other prophets, Amos knew that divine punishment is never completely destructive; it is part of the hidden plan of God to bring salvation to men. The perversity of the human will may retard, but it cannot totally frustrate, this design of a loving God.

The Book of Hosea—Hosea's ministry to the Northern Kingdom followed closely upon that of Amos.

While the latter had spoken as a southerner to the prosperous Israel enjoying an era of peace, Hosea spoke as a native to his own people who were suffering from war with Assyria and in virtual anarchy. The prophet's personal life is an incarnation of God's redeeming love. He spoke out against the influence of pagan practices and is known as the cantor of God's redeeming love, which is opposed and frustrated by the people's infidelity.

The Gospel of Matthew — *Of all the Gospels that of Matthew gives the most faithful and distinct image of Christ's teaching. However, it would seem that it is not the oldest, for in its present form it uses almost all the material contained in the Gospel of Mark, although inserting a few changes and additions. Scholars today tend to place the definitive date of its composition during the years 80-85, or perhaps even 90.*

Even today readers are struck by its clearness, its pedagogical direction, and the remarkable balance kept between the narrative sections and the five magnificent discourses in ch. 6-7, 10, 13, 18, and 24-25.

While Mark probably addresses himself to the Romans and Luke to the Greeks, Matthew, who is a Jew, writes for the Jews. It is the most Jewish of the Gospels, in its style, its methods of composition, and its way of arguing. Matthew wants to convince his brethren that Jesus is indeed the Messiah who was expected by the Prophets, and thus he tries to show that Jesus has fulfilled the Scriptures. But above all, the theme that is dearest to the heart of any Jewish convert is the drama of Israel, and it is this which is the major theme of the Gospel of Matthew.

For Matthew, Israel is the People of God, for it is to Israel that Jesus was sent and to Israel that Jesus announced the Kingdom of God, that reign which already with Jesus is secretly present among men. But Israel refuses to recognize Jesus. The hostility between Jesus and the scribes, the Pharisees and the high priests increases. Jesus himself hardens his position. He announces that the Kingdom destined for Israel will be taken away and entrusted to a people who will be fruitful, the new Israel, the Church (Mt 21, 43). Henceforth the drama hastens its course and quickly comes to its end with the Crucifixion.

Matthew's Gospel has been called the Gospel of the Church. However, it is even more the Gospel of Jesus. Matthew constantly seeks to bring out the majesty of Jesus, his superhuman greatness, and his power. For Matthew, Jesus is the Lord. This title recurs eighty times in his Gospel, while it appears only eighteen times in the Gospel of Mark. The term itself designates Jesus risen, working mightily, and always present in his Church.

For Matthew, Jesus is also the Christ, the Messiah, a title he gives him as early as in the genealogy (Mt 1, 16-18). But he is above all the Son of God (Mt 3, 17; 8, 29; 17, 5; 26, 63; 27, 34, etc.). In a word, Matthew, professes the divinity of Jesus.

MONDAY OF THE TENTH WEEK
IN ORDINARY TIME

READING I   1 Kgs 17, 1-6

Elijah follows the Lord's directions. He goes to the Wadi Cherith, east of the Jordan, and escapes the famine. Ravens bring him food and drink.

A reading from the first book of Kings

Elijah the Tishbite, from Tishbe in Gilead, said to Ahab: "As the Lord, the God of Israel, lives, whom I serve, during these years there shall be no dew or rain except at my word." The Lord then said to Elijah: "Leave here, go east and hide in the Wadi Cherith, east of the Jordan. You shall drink of the stream, and I have commanded ravens to feed you there." So he left and did as the Lord had commanded. He went and remained by the Wadi Cherith, east of the Jordan. Ravens brought him bread and meat in the morning, and bread and meat in the evening, and he drank from the stream.—This is the Word of the Lord. ℟. **Thanks be to God.** ✣

Responsorial Psalm   Ps 121, 1-2. 3-4. 5-6. 7-8

℟. (2) **Our help is from the Lord
who made heaven and earth.**

I lift up my eyes toward the mountains;
  whence shall help come to me?
My help is from the Lord,
  who made heaven and earth. — ℟

May he not suffer your foot to slip;
  may he slumber not who guards you:
Indeed he neither slumbers nor sleeps,
  the guardian of Israel. — ℟

The Lord is your guardian; the Lord is your shade;
  he is beside you at your right hand.
The sun shall not harm you by day,
  nor the moon by night. — ℟

The Lord will guard you from all evil;
   he will guard your life.
The Lord will guard your coming and your going,
   both now and forever. — ℟ ℣

GOSPEL Mt 5, 1-12

See p. 73.

TUESDAY OF THE TENTH WEEK
IN ORDINARY TIME

READING I 1 Kgs 17, 7-16

The Lord comands Elijah to move to Zarephath. There he meets a widow. She shares her food with Elijah and is rewarded with enough to care for her and her son an entire year. Elijah tells her that the Lord will provide.

A reading from the first book of Kings

The brook [where Elijah was hiding] ran dry, because no rain had fallen in the land. So the Lord said to him: "Move on to Zarephath of Sidon and stay there. I have designated a widow there to provide for you." He left and went to Zarephath. As he arrived at the entrance of the ctiy, a widow was gathering sticks there; he called out to her, "Please bring me a small cupful of water to drink." She left to get it, and he called out after her, "Please bring along a bit of bread." "As the Lord, your God, lives," she answered, "I have nothing baked; there is only a handful of flour in my jar and a little oil in my jug. Just now I was collecting a couple of sticks, to go in and prepare something for myself and my son; when we have eaten it, we shall die." "Do not be afraid," Elijah said to her. "Go and do as you propose. But first make me a little cake and bring it to me. Then you can prepare something for yourself and your son. For the Lord, God of Israel, says, 'The jar of flour shall not go empty, nor the jug of oil run dry, until the day when the Lord sends rain upon the earth.'" She left and did as Elijah had said. She was able to eat for a year, and he and her son as well; the jar of flour did not go empty, nor the jug of oil run dry, as the Lord had foretold through Elijah. —This is the Word of the Lord. ℟. **Thanks be to God.** ↓

Responsorial Psalm   Ps 4, 2-3. 4-5. 7-8

℟. (7) **Lord, let your face shine on us.**

When I call, answer me, O my just God,
  you who relieve me when I am in distress;
  have pity on me, and hear my prayer!
Men of rank, how long will you be dull of heart?
  Why do you love what is vain and seek after
    falsehood? — ℟

Know that the Lord does wonders for his faithful one;
  the Lord will hear me when I call upon him.
Tremble, and sin not;
  reflect, upon your beds, in silence. — ℟

O Lord, let the light of your countenance shine upon
    us!
  You put gladness into my heart,
  more than when grain and wine abound. — ℟ ↓

GOSPEL   Mt 5, 13-16

See p. 75.

WEDNESDAY OF THE TENTH WEEK IN ORDINARY TIME

READING I 1 Kgs 18, 20-39

Elijah appeals to the people to follow the Lord. He proves he is a prophet: he calls upon the Lord. Fire comes down and consumes the holocaust. The people again believe: "The Lord is God."

A reading from the first book of Kings

Ahab sent to all the Israelites and had the prophets assemble on Mount Carmel.

Elijah appealed to all the people and said, "How long will you straddle the issue? If the Lord is God, follow him; if Baal, follow him." The people, however, did not answer him. So Elijah said to the people, "I am the only surviving prophet of the Lord, and there are four hundred and fifty prophets of Baal. Give us two young bulls. Let them choose one, cut it into pieces, and place it on the wood, but start no fire. I shall prepare the other and place it on the wood, but shall start no fire. You shall call on your gods, and I will call on the Lord. The God who answers with fire is God." All the people answered, "Agreed!"

Elijah then said to the prophets of Baal, "Choose one young bull and prepare it first, for there are more of you. Call upon your gods, but do not start the fire." Taking the young bull that was turned over to them, they prepared it and called on Baal from morning to noon, saying, "Answer us, Baal!" But there was no sound, and no one answering. And they hopped around the altar they had prepared. When it was noon, Elijah taunted them: "Call louder, for he is a god and may be meditating, or may have retired, or may be on a journey. Perhaps he is asleep and must be awakened." They called out louder and slashed themselves with swords and spears, as was their custom, until blood gushed over them. Noon passed and they remained in a prophetic state until the time for offering sacrifice. But there was not a sound; no one answered, and no one was listening.

Then Elijah said to all the people, "Come here to me." When they had done so, he repaired the altar of the Lord which had been destroyed. He took twelve stones, for the number of tribes of the sons of Jacob, to whom the Lord had said, "Your name shall be Israel." He built an altar in honor of the Lord with the stones, and made a trench around the altar large enough for two seahs of grain. When he had arranged the wood, he cut up the young bull and laid it on the wood. "Fill four jars with water," he said, "and pour it over the holocaust and over the wood." "Do it again," he said, and they did it again. "Do it a third time," he said, and they did it a third time. The water flowed around the altar, and the trench was filled with the water.

At the time for offering sacrifice, the prophet Elijah came forward and said, "Lord, God of Abraham, Isaac, and Israel, let it be known this day that you are God in Israel and that I am your servant and have done all these things by your command. Answer me, Lord! Answer me, that this people may know that you, Lord, are God and that you have brought them back to their senses." The Lord's fire came down and consumed the holocaust, wood, stones, and dust, and it lapped up the water in the trench. Seeing this, all the people fell prostrate and said, "The Lord is God! The Lord is God!"—This is the Word of the Lord. ℞. **Thanks be to God.** ❧

Responsorial Psalm   Ps 16, 1-2. 4. 5. 8. 11

℞. (1) **Keep me safe, O God;**
    you are my hope.

Keep me, O God, for in you I take refuge;
   I say to the Lord, "My Lord are you." — ℞

They multiply their sorrows
  who court other gods.
Blood libations to them I will not pour out,
  nor will I take their names upon my lips. — ℟

O Lord, my allotted portion and my cup,
  you it is who hold fast my lot.
I set the Lord ever before me;
  with him at my right hand I shall not be disturbed. — ℟

You will show me the path to life,
  fullness of joys in your presence,
    the delights at your right hand forever. — ℟ ℣

GOSPEL   Mt 5, 17-19

See p. 77.

THURSDAY OF THE TENTH WEEK IN ORDINARY TIME

READING I   1 Kgs 18, 41-46

Elijah prays for rain on the top of Mt. Carmel. A small cloud appears, rising from the sea. The sky grows dark and a heavy rain falls. Elijah runs before Ahab to the approaches of Jezreel.

A reading from the first book of Kings

Elijah said to Ahab, "Go up, eat and drink, for there is the sound of a heavy rain." So Ahab went up to eat and drink, while Elijah climbed to the top of Carmel, crouched down to the earth, and put his head between his knees. "Climb up and look out to sea," he directed his servant, who went up and looked, but reported, "There is nothing." Seven times he said, "Go, look again!" And the seventh time the youth reported, "There is a cloud as small as a man's hand rising from the sea." Elijah said, "Go

and say to Ahab, "Harness up and leave the mountain before the rain stops you.'" In a trice, the sky grew dark with clouds and wind, and a heavy rain fell. Ahab mounted his chariot and made for Jezreel. But the hand of the Lord was on Elijah, who girded up his clothing and ran before Ahab as far as the approaches to Jezreel.—This is the Word of the Lord.
℟. **Thanks be to God.** ⩔

Responsorial Psalm   Ps 65, 10. 10-11. 12-13

℟. (2) **It is right to praise you in Zion, O God.**

You have visited the land and watered it;
   greatly have you enriched it.
God's watercourses are filled;
   you have prepared the grain. — ℟

Thus have you prepared the land: drenching its furrows,
   breaking up its clods,
Softening it with showers,
   blessing its yield. — ℟

You have crowned the year with your bounty,
   and your paths overflow with a rich harvest;
The untilled meadows overflow with it,
   and rejoicing clothes the hills. — ℟ ⩔

GOSPEL   Mt 5, 20-26

See p. 79.

FRIDAY OF THE TENTH WEEK
IN ORDINARY TIME

READING I   1 Kgs 19, 9. 11-16

The Lord speaks to Elijah, directing him to stand on the mountain. After a wind, earthquake, and fire, the Lord speaks and sends him to anoint Hazael as king of Aram and Jehu as king of Israel and to name Elisha the next prophet.

A reading from the first book of Kings

Elijah came [from the mountain of God, Horeb] to a cave, where he took shelter. But the word of the Lord came to him and said, "Go outside and stand on the mountain before the Lord; the Lord will be passing by." A strong and heavy wind was rending the mountains and crushing rocks before the Lord —but the Lord was not in the wind. After the wind there was an earthquake—but the Lord was not in the earthquake. After the earthquake there was fire —but the Lord was not in the fire. After the fire there was a tiny whispering sound. When he heard this Elijah hid his face in his cloak and went and stood at the entrance of the cave. A voice said to him, "Elijah, why are you here?" He replied, "I have been most zealous for the Lord, the God of hosts. But the Israelites have forsaken your covenant, torn down your altars, and put your prophets to the sword. I alone am left, and they seek to take my life." "Go, take the road back to the desert near Damascus," the Lord said to him. "When you arrive, you shall anoint Hazael as king of Aram. Then you shall anoint Jehu, son of Nimshi, as king of Israel, and Elisha, son of Shaphat of Abel-meholah, as prophet to succeed you."—This is the Word of the Lord. ℞. **Thanks be to God.** ℣

Responsorial Psalm   Ps 27, 7-8. 8-9. 13-14

℞. (8) **I long to see your face, O Lord.**

Hear, O Lord, the sound of my call;
   have pity on me, and answer me.
Of you my heart speaks; you my glance seeks. — ℞

Your presence, O Lord, I seek.
   Hide not your face from me;
Do not in anger repel your servant.
   You are my helper: cast me not off. — ℞

I believe that I shall see the bounty of the Lord
  in the land of the living.
Wait for the Lord with courage;
  be stouthearted, and wait for the Lord. — ℟ ℣

GOSPEL   Mt 5, 27-32

See p. 81.

SATURDAY OF THE TENTH WEEK
IN ORDINARY TIME

READING I   1 Kgs 19, 19-21

*Elijah finds Elisha working in a field. Elisha slaughters his oxen, uses
his plows for fuel to cook them, and gives the food to his people.
Then he leaves and follows Elijah.*

A reading from the first book of Kings

Elijah set out, and came upon Elisha, son of Shaphat,
as he was plowing with twelve yoke of oxen; he
was following the twelfth. Elijah went over to him
and threw his cloak over him. Elisha left the oxen,
ran after Elijah, and said, "Please, let me kiss my
father and mother goodbye, and I will follow you."
"Go back!" Elijah answered. "Have I done anything
to you?" Elisha left him and, taking the yoke of
oxen, slaughtered them; he used the plowing equipment for fuel to boil their flesh, and gave it to his
people to eat. Then he left and followed Elijah as his
attendant.—This is the Word of the Lord. ℟. **Thanks
be to God. ℣**

Responsorial Psalm   Ps 16, 1-2, 5. 7-8. 9-10
℟. (5) **You are my inheritance, O Lord.**
Keep me, O God, for in you I take refuge;
  I say to the Lord, "My Lord are you."

O Lord, my allotted portion and my cup,
  you it is who hold fast my lot. — ℟

I bless the Lord who counsels me;
  even in the night my heart exhorts me.

I set the Lord ever before me;
  with him at my right hand I shall not be disturbed. — ℟

Therefore my heart is glad and my soul rejoices,
  my body, too, abides in confidence;
Because you will not abandon my soul to the nether
    world,
  nor will you suffer your faithful one to undergo
    corruption. — ℟ ✠

GOSPEL Mt 5, 33-37

See p. 83.

MONDAY OF THE ELEVENTH WEEK
IN ORDINARY TIME

READING I 1 Kgs 21, 1-16

Naboth refuses to trade or sell his vineyard to King Ahab. Ahab becomes
disturbed and confides in Jezebel, his wife. She lays a plot to have
Naboth stoned. After Naboth is killed, Jezebel tells Ahab to go and
take the vineyard.

A reading from the first book of Kings

Naboth the Jezreelite had a vineyard in Jezreel next
to the palace of Ahab, king of Samaria. Ahab said
to Naboth, "Give me your vineyard to be my vege-
table garden, since it is close by, next to my house.
I will give you a better vineyard in exchange, or, if
you prefer, I will give you its value in money." "The
Lord forbid," Naboth answered him, "that I should
give you my ancestral heritage." Ahab went home
disturbed and angry at the answer Naboth the Jezreelite had made to him: "I will not give you my

ancestral heritage." Lying down on his bed, he turned away from food and would not eat.

His wife Jezebel came to him and said to him, "Why are you so angry that you will not eat?" He answered her, "Because I spoke to Naboth the Jezreelite and said to him, 'Sell me your vineyard, or, if you prefer, I will give you a vineyard in exchange.' But he refused to let me have his vineyard." "A fine ruler over Israel you are indeed!" his wife Jezebel said to him. "Get up. Eat and be cheerful. I will obtain the vineyard of Naboth the Jezreelite for you."

So she wrote letters in Ahab's name and, having sealed them with his seal, sent them to the elders and to the nobles who lived in the same city with Naboth. This is what she wrote in the letters: "Proclaim a fast and set Naboth at the head of the people. Next, get two scoundrels to face him and accuse him of having cursed God and king. Then take him out and stone him to death." His fellow citizens— the elders and the nobles who dwelt in his city— did as Jezebel had ordered them in writing, through the letters she had sent them. They proclaimed a fast and placed Naboth at the head of the people. Two scoundrels came in and confronted him with the accusation, "Naboth has cursed God and king." And they led him out of the city and stoned him to death. Then they sent the information to Jezebel that Naboth had been stoned to death.

When Jezebel learned that Naboth had been stoned to death, she said to Ahab, "Go on, take possession of the vineyard of Naboth the Jezreelite which he refused to sell you, because Naboth is not alive, but dead." On hearing that Naboth was dead, Ahab started off on his way down to the vineyard of Naboth the Jezreelite, to take possession of it.—This is the Word of the Lord. ℟. **Thanks be to God.** ⴲ

Responsorial Psalm Ps 5, 2-3. 5-6. 7

℟. (2) **Lord, listen to my groaning.**

Hearken to my words, O Lord,
  attend to my sighing.
Heed my call for help,
  my king and my God! — ℟

At dawn I bring my plea expectantly before you.
  For you, O God, delight not in wickedness;
  no evil man remains with you;
The arrogant may not stand in your sight. — ℟

You hate all evildoers.
  You destroy all who speak falsehood;
The bloodthirsty and the deceitful
  the Lord abhors. — ℟ ℣

GOSPEL Mt 5, 38-42

See p. 85.

TUESDAY OF THE ELEVENTH WEEK
IN ORDINARY TIME

READING I 1 Kgs 21, 17-29

The Lord instructs Elijah to meet Ahab. Because of Naboth's murder,
Elijah tells Ahab that he will be destroyed along with every male in
his line. Jezebel shall be devoured by dogs in the street. Ahab mourns,
and God postpones the punishment.

A reading from the first book of Kings

[After the death of Naboth] the Lord said to Elijah
the Tishbite: "Start down to meet Ahab, king of Israel, who rules in Samaria. He will be in the vineyard of Naboth, of which he has come to take possession. This is what you shall tell him, 'The Lord
says: After murdering, do you also take possession?

For this, the Lord says: In the place where the dogs licked up the blood of Naboth, the dogs shall lick up your blood, too.'" "Have you found me out, my enemy?" Ahab said to Elijah. "Yes," he answered. "Because you have given yourself up to doing evil in the Lord's sight, I am bringing evil upon you: I will destroy you and will cut off every male in Ahab's line, whether slave or freeman, in Israel. I will make your house like that of Jeroboam, son of Nebat, and like that of Baasha, son of Ahijah, because of how you have provoked me by leading Israel into sin." (Against Jezebel, too, the Lord declared, "The dogs shall devour Jezebel in the district of Jezreel.") "When one of Ahab's line dies in the city, dogs will devour him; when one of them dies in the field, the birds of the sky will devour him." Indeed, no one gave himself up to the doing of evil in the sight of the Lord as did Ahab, urged on by his wife Jezebel. He became completely abominable by following idols, just as the Amorites had done, whom the Lord drove out before the Israelites.

When Ahab heard these words, he tore his garments and put on sackcloth over his bare flesh. He fasted, slept in the sackcloth, and went about subdued. Then the Lord said to Elijah the Tishbite, "Have you seen that Ahab has humbled himself before me? Since he has humbled himself before me, I will not bring the evil in his time. I will bring the evil upon his house during the reign of his son."— This is the Word of the Lord. ℞. **Thanks be to God.** ℣

Responsorial Psalm   Ps 51, 3-4. 5-6. 11. 16

℞. (3) **Be merciful, O Lord, for we have sinned.**

Have mercy on me, O God, in your goodness;
  in the greatness of your compassion wipe out my
    offense.
Thoroughly wash me from my guilt
  and of my sin cleanse me. — ℞

For I acknowledge my offense,
    and my sin is before me always:
"Against you only have I sinned,
    and done what is evil in your sight." — ℟

Turn away your face from my sins,
    and blot out all my guilt.

Free me from blood guilt, O God, my saving God;
    then my tongue shall revel in your justice. — ℟ ⅴ

GOSPEL   Mt 5, 43-48

See p. 87.

_____

WEDNESDAY OF THE ELEVENTH WEEK
IN ORDINARY TIME

READING I   2 Kgs 2, 1. 6-14

Elijah is to leave. He is taken up away from Elisha in a flaming chariot
to heaven. Elisha picks up Elijah's mantle and returns over the Jordan
River where it divides for him. He shares in Elijah's spirit.

A reading from the second book of Kings

When the Lord was about to take Elijah up to
heaven in a whirlwind, [they went together to Jeri-
cho]. Elijah said to Elisha, "Please stay here; the
Lord has sent me on the Jordan." "As the Lord
lives, and as you yourself live," Elisha replied, "I
will not leave you." And so the two went on together. Fifty of the guild prophets followed, and
when the two stopped at the Jordan, stood facing
them at a distance. Elijah took his mantle, rolled it
up and struck the water, which divided, and both
crossed over on dry ground.

When they had crossed over, Elijah said to Elisha,
"Ask for whatever I may do for you, before I am
taken from you." Elisha answered, "May I receive
a double portion of your spirit?" "You have asked

something that is not easy," he replied. "Still, if you see me taken up from you, your wish will be granted; otherwise not." As they walked on conversing, a flaming chariot and flaming horses came between them, and Elijah went up to heaven in a whirlwind. When Elisha saw it happen he cried out, "My father! my father! Israel's chariots and drivers!" But when he could no longer see him, Elisha gripped his own garment and tore it in two.

Then he picked up Elijah's mantle which had fallen from him, and went back and stood at the bank of the Jordan. Wielding the mantle which had fallen from Elijah, he struck the water in his turn and said: "Where is the Lord, the God of Elijah?" When Elisha struck the water it divided and he crossed over.—This is the Word of the Lord. ℟. **Thanks be to God.** ℣

Responsorial Psalm   Ps 31, 20. 21. 24

℟. (25) **Let your hearts take comfort,
    all who hope in the Lord.**

How great is the goodness, O Lord,
    which you have in store for those who fear you,
And which, toward those who take refuge in you,
    you show in the sight of men. — ℟

You hide them in the shelter of your presence
    from the plottings of men;
You screen them within your abode
    from the strife of tongues. — ℟

Love the Lord, all you his faithful ones!
    The Lord keeps those who are constant,
    but more than requites those who act
        proudly — ℟ ℣

GOSPEL   Mt 6, 1-6. 16-18

See p. 89.

THURSDAY OF THE ELEVENTH WEEK
IN ORDINARY TIME

READING I　　　　　　　　　　　　Sir 48, 1-14

Elijah's words were like fire. He shut the heavens three times, brought
a dead man back to life, sent kings to destruction, and made a
prophet his successor. Elisha is filled with a twofold portion of his
spirit.

A reading from the book of Sirach

Like a fire there appeared the prophet Elijah
　　whose words were as a flaming furnace.
Their staff of bread he shattered,
　　in his zeal he reduced them to straits;
By God's word he shut up the heavens
　　and three times brought down fire.
How awesome are you, Elijah!
　　Whose glory is equal to yours?
You brought a dead man back to life
　　from the nether world, by the will of the Lord.
You sent kings down to destruction,
　　and nobles, from their beds of sickness.
You heard threats at Sinai,
　　at Horeb avenging judgments.
You anointed kings who should inflict vengeance,
　　and a prophet as your successor.
You were taken aloft in a whirlwind,
　　in a chariot with fiery horses.
You are destined, it is written, in time to come
　　to put an end to wrath before the day of the Lord,
To turn back the hearts of fathers toward their sons,
　　and to re-establish the tribes of Jacob.
Blessed is he who shall have seen you before he dies,
　　O Elijah, enveloped in the whirlwind!
Then Elisha, filled with a twofold portion of his
　　　　spirit,
　　wrought many marvels by his mere word.
During his lifetime he feared no one,
　　nor was any man able to intimidate his will.

Nothing was beyond his power;
　beneath him flesh was brought back into life.
In life he performed wonders,
　and after death, marvelous deeds.
This is the Word of the Lord. ℟. **Thanks be to God.** ✣

Responsorial Psalm　　　Ps 97, 1-2. 3-4. 5-6. 7

℟. (12) **Let good men rejoice in the Lord.**

The Lord is king; let the earth rejoice;
　let the many isles be glad.
Clouds and darkness are round about him,
　justice and judgment are the foundation of his
　　throne. — ℟

Fire goes before him
　and consumes his foes round about.
His lightnings illumine the world;
　the earth sees and trembles. — ℟

The mountains melt like wax before the Lord,
　before the Lord of all the earth.
The heavens proclaim his justice,
　and all peoples see his glory. — ℟

All who worship graven things are put to shame,
　who glory in the things of nought;
　all gods are prostrate before him. — ℟ ✣

GOSPEL　　　　　　　　　　　　　Mt 6, 7-15

See p. 92.

FRIDAY OF THE ELEVENTH WEEK
IN ORDINARY TIME

READING I　　　　　　　　2 Kgs 11, 1-4. 9-18. 20

Jehoash is spared by his nurse. Jehoiada, the priest, prepares the
way for him. Athaliah shouts treason when Jehoash appears, and she
is put to death. The temple of Baal is destroyed, and the people
rejoice.

A reading from the second book of Kings

When Athaliah, the mother of Ahaziah, saw that her son was dead, she began to kill off the whole royal family. But Jehosheba, daughter of King Jehoram and sister of Ahaziah, took Jehoash, his son, and spirited him away, along with his nurse, from the bedroom where the princes were about to be slain. She concealed him from Athaliah, and so he did not die. For six years he remained hidden in the temple of the Lord, while Athaliah ruled the land.

But in the seventh year, Jehoiada summoned the captains of the Carians and of the guards. He had them come to him in the temple of the Lord, exacted from them a sworn commitment, and then showed them the king's son.

The captains did just as Jehoiada the priest commanded. Each one with his men, both those going on duty for the sabbath and those going off duty that week, came to Jehoiada the priest. He gave the captains King David's spears and shields, which were in the temple of the Lord. And the guards, with drawn weapons, lined up from the southern to the northern limit of the enclosure, surrounding the altar and the temple on the king's behalf. Then Jehoiada led out the king's son and put the crown and the insignia upon him. They proclaimed him king and anointed him, clapping their hands and shouting, "Long live the king!"

Athaliah heard the noise made by the people, and appeared before them in the temple of the Lord. When she saw the king standing by the pillar, as was the custom, and the captains and trumpeters near him, with all the people of the land rejoicing and blowing trumpets, she tore her garments and cried out, "Treason, treason!" Then Jehoiada the priest instructed the captains in command of the force: "Bring her outside through the ranks. If anyone follows her," he added, "let him die by the sword." He had given orders that she should not be slain in the temple of the Lord. She was led out forcibly to the horse gate of the royal palace, where she was put to death.

Then Jehoiada made a covenant between the Lord as one party and the king and the people as the other, by which they would be the Lord's people; and another covenant, between the king and the people. Thereupon all the people of the land went to the temple of Baal and demolished it. They shattered its altars and images completely, and slew Mattan, the priest of Baal, before the altars. Jehoiada appointed a detachment for the temple of the Lord. All the people of the land rejoiced and the city was quiet, now that Athaliah had been slain with the sword at the royal palace.—This is the Word of the Lord. ℟. **Thanks be to God.** ℣

Responsorial Psalm   Ps 132, 11. 12. 13-14. 17-18
℟. (33) **The Lord has chosen Zion for his dwelling.**
The Lord swore to David
   a firm promise from which he will not withdraw:
"Your own offspring
   I will set upon your throne." — ℟

If your sons keep my covenant
   and the decrees which I shall teach them,
Their sons, too, forever
   shall sit upon your throne." — ℟

For the Lord has chosen Zion;
   he prefers her for his dwelling.
"Zion is my resting place forever;
   in her will I dwell, for I prefer her. — ℟

In her will I make a horn to sprout forth for David;
   I will place a lamp for my anointed.

His enemies I will clothe with shame,
  but upon him my crown shall shine." — ℟ ♼

GOSPEL Mt 6, 19-23

See p. 94.

_____

SATURDAY OF THE ELEVENTH WEEK IN ORDINARY TIME

READING I 2 Chr 24, 17-25

After Jehoiada dies, again false idols are worshiped. The people ignore the prophets. Zechariah warns the people, and King Joash slays him. Joash falls to the Arameans.

A reading from the second book of Chronicles

After the death of Jehoiada, the princes of Judah came and paid homage to the king, and the king then listened to them. They forsook the temple of the Lord, the God of their fathers, and began to serve the sacred poles and the idols; and because of this crime of theirs, wrath came upon Judah and Jerusalem. Although prophets were sent to them to convert them to the Lord, the people would not listen to their warnings. Then the spirit of God possessed Zechariah, son of Jehoiada the priest. He took his stand above the people and said to them: "God says, 'Why are you transgressing the Lord's commands, so that you cannot prosper? Because you have abandoned the Lord, he has abandoned you.'" But they conspired against him, and at the king's order they stoned him to death in the court of the Lord's temple. Thus King Joash was unmindful of the devotion shown him by Jehoiada, Zechariah's father, and slew his son. And as he was dying, he said, "May the Lord see and avenge."

At the turn of the year a force of Arameans came up against Joash. They invaded Judah and Jerusalem, did away with all the princes of the people, and sent all their spoil to the king of Damascus. Though the Aramean force came with few men, the Lord surrendered a very large force into their power, because Judah had abandoned the Lord, the God of their fathers. So punishment was meted out to Joash.— This is the Word of the Lord. ℟. **Thanks be to God. ⱴ**

Responsorial Psalm   Ps 89, 4-5. 29-30. 31-32. 33-34

℟. (29) **For ever I will keep my love for him.**

I have made a covenant with my chosen one,
  I have sworn to David my servant:
Forever will I confirm your posterity
  and establish your throne for all generations. — ℟

Forever I will maintain my kindness toward him,
  and my covenant with him stands firm.
I will make his posterity endure forever
  and his throne as the days of heaven. — ℟

If his sons forsake my law
  and walk not according to my ordinances,
If they violate my statutes
  and keep not my commands, — ℟

I will punish their crime with a rod
  and their guilt with stripes.
Yet my kindness I will not take from him,
  nor will I belie my faithfulness. — ℟ ⱴ

GOSPEL   Mt 6, 24-34

See p. 96.

MONDAY OF THE TWELFTH WEEK
IN ORDINARY TIME

READING I   2 Kgs 17, 5-8. 13-15. 18

Hoshea, the last king of Israel, is judged more benignly than his predecessors. The Lord had warned Israel and Judah. The people reject God and his covenant. Only Judah remains.

A reading from the second book of Kings

Shalmaneser, king of Assyria, occupied the whole land and attacked Samaria, which he besieged for three years. In the ninth year of Hoshea, the king of Assyria took Samaria, and deported the Israelites to Assyria, setting them in Halah, at the Habor, a river of Gozan, and in the cities of the Medes.

This came about because the Israelites sinned against the Lord, their God, who had brought them up from the land of Egypt, from under the domination of Pharaoh, king of Egypt, and because they venerated other gods. They followed the rites of the nations whom the Lord had cleared out of the way of the Israelites [and the kings of Israel whom they set up].

And though the Lord warned Israel and Judah by every prophet and seer, "Give up your evil ways and keep my commandments and statutes, in accordance with the entire law which I enjoined on your fathers and which I sent you by my servants the prophets," they did not listen, but were as stiff-necked as their fathers, who had not believed in the Lord, their God. They rejected his statutes, the covenant which he had made with their fathers, and the warnings which he had given them, till, in his great anger against Israel, the Lord put them away out of his sight. Only the tribe of Judah was left.—This is the Word of the Lord. ℟. **Thanks be to God. ℣**

Responsorial Psalm   Ps 60, 3. 4-5. 12-13

℟. (7) **Help us with your right hand, O Lord, and answer us.**

O God, you have rejected us and broken our defenses;
 you have been angry; rally us! — ℟

You have rocked the country and split it open;
 repair the cracks in it, for it is tottering.
You have made your people feel hardships;
 you have given us stupefying wine. — ℟

Have not you, O God, rejected us,
 so that you go not forth, O God, with our armies?
Give us aid against the foe,
 for worthless is the help of men. — ℟ ℣

GOSPEL   Mt 7, 1-5

See p. 99.

TUESDAY OF THE TWELFTH WEEK
IN ORDINARY TIME

READING I   2 Kgs 19, 9-11. 14-21. 31-35. 36

Hezekiah receives a letter from Sennacherib which he spreads before the Lord in the temple. This action shows his belief in God's presence in the temple. Because the Lord sent his angels in a plague, Sennacherib is compelled to return to Assyria.

A reading from the second book of Kings

Sennacherib, king of Assyria, sent envoys to Hezekiah, with this message: "Thus shall you say to Hezekiah, king of Judah: 'Do not let your God on whom you rely deceive you by saying that Jerusalem will not be handed over to the king of Assyria. You have heard what the kings of Assyria have done to all other countries: they doomed them! Will you, then, be saved?'"

Hezekiah took the letter from the hand of the messengers and read it; then he went up to the temple of the Lord, and spreading it out before him, he prayed in the Lord's presence: "O Lord, God of Israel, enthroned upon the cherubim! You alone are God over all the kingdoms of the earth. You have made the heavens and the earth. Incline your ear, O Lord, and listen! Open your eyes, O Lord, and see! Hear the words of Sennacherib which he sent to taunt the living God. Truly, O Lord, the kings of Assyria have laid waste the nations and their lands, and cast their gods into the fire; they destroyed them because they were not gods, but the work of human hands, wood and stone. Therefore, O Lord, our God, save us from the power of this man, that all the kingdoms of the earth may know that you alone, O Lord, are God."

Then Isaiah, son of Amoz, sent this message to Hezekiah: "Thus says the Lord, the God of Israel, in answer to your prayer for help against Sennacherib, king of Assyria: I have listened! This is the word the Lord has spoken concerning him:

" 'She despises you, laughs you to scorn,
    the virgin daughter Zion!
Behind you she wags her head,
    daughter Jerusalem.
For out of Jerusalem shall come a remnant,
    and from Mount Zion, survivors.
    The zeal of the Lord of hosts shall do this.'

"Therefore, thus says the Lord concerning the king of Assyria: 'He shall not reach this city, nor shoot an arrow at it, nor come before it with a shield, nor cast up siegeworks against it. He shall return by the same way he came, without entering the city, says the Lord. I will shield and save this city for my own sake, and for the sake of my servant David.' "

That night the angel of the Lord went forth and

struck down one hundred and eighty-five thousand men in the Assyrian camp. So Sennacherib, the king of Assyria, broke camp, and went back home to Nineveh.—This is the Word of the Lord. ℟. **Thanks be to God.** ⅴ

Responsorial Psalm   Ps 48, 2-3. 3-4. 10-11

℟. (9) **God upholds his city for ever.**

Great is the Lord and wholly to be praised
   in the city of our God.
His holy mountain, fairest of heights,
   is the joy of all the earth. — ℟

Mount Zion, "the recesses of the North,"
   is the city of the great King.
God is with her castles;
   renowned is he as a stronghold. — ℟

O God, we ponder your kindness
   within your temple.
As your name, O God, so also your praise
   reaches to the ends of the earth.
Of justice your right hand is full. — ℟ ⅴ

GOSPEL   Mt 7, 6. 12-14

See p. 101.

WEDNESDAY OF THE TWELFTH WEEK IN ORDINARY TIME

READING I   2 Kgs 22, 8-13; 23, 1-3

The king has Hilkiah, the high priest, research the laws of the Lord. He has all the contents of the Law read to the people. The king renews the covenant with the Lord, and all the people stand as participants in it.

A reading from the second book of Kings

The high priest Hilkiah informed the scribe Shaphan,

"I have found the book of the law in the temple of the Lord." Hilkiah gave the book to Shaphan, who read it. Then the scribe Staphan went to the king and reported, "Your servants have smelted down the metals available in the temple and have consigned them to the master workmen in the temple of the Lord." The scribes Shaphan also informed the king that the priest Hilkiah had given him a book, and then read it aloud to the king. When the king had heard the contents of the book of the law, he tore his garments and issued this command to Hilkiah the priest, Ahikam, son of Shaphan, Achbor, son of Micaiah, the scribe Shaphan, and the king's servant Asaiah: "Go, consult the Lord for me, for the people, for all Judah, about the stipulations of this book that has been found, for the anger of the Lord has been set furiously ablaze against us, because our fathers did not obey the stipulations of this book, nor fulfill our written obligations."

The king then had all the elders of Judah and of Jerusalem summoned together before him. The king went up to the temple of the Lord with all the men of Judah and all the inhabitants of Jerusalem: priests, prophets, and all the people, small and great. He had the entire contents of the book of the covenant that had been found in the temple of the Lord, read out to them. Standing by the column, the king made a covenant before the Lord that they would follow him and observe his ordinances, statutes and decrees with their whole hearts and souls, thus reviving the terms of the covenant which were written in this book. And all the people stood as participants in the covenant.—This is the Word of the Lord. ℟. **Thanks be to God.** ⬇

Responsorial Psalm   Ps 119, 33. 34. 35. 36. 37. 40
℟. (33) **Teach me the way of your decrees, O Lord.**

Instruct me, O Lord, in the way of your statutes,
  that I may exactly observe them. — ℟

Give me discernment, that I may observe your law
  and keep it with all my heart. — ℟

Lead me in the path of your commands,
  for in it I delight. — ℟

Incline my heart to your decrees
  and not to gain. — ℟

Turn away my eyes from seeing what is vain:
  by your way give me life. — ℟

Behold, I long for your precepts;
  in your justice give me life. — ℟ ℣

GOSPEL   Mt 7, 15-20

See p. 104.

THURSDAY OF THE TWELFTH WEEK
IN ORDINARY TIME

READING I   2 Kgs 24, 8-17

The Babylonian armies terminate Jehoiachin's brief reign. Nebuchadnezzar takes Jehoiachin to Babylon as a royal hostage. He pillages but does not destroy the temple. The king of Babylon appoints Mattaniah, the third son of Josiah, to reign as king of Judah.

A reading from the second book of Kings

Jehoiachin was eighteen years old when he began to reign, and he reigned three months in Jerusalem. His mother's name was Nehushta, daughter of Elnathan of Jerusalem. He did evil in the sight of the Lord, just as his forebears had done.

At that time the officials of Nebuchadnezzar, king of Babylon, attacked Jerusalem, and the city came under siege. Nebuchadnezzar, king of Babylon, himself arrived at the city while his servants were besieging it. Then Jehoiachin, king of Judah, together with his mother, his ministers, officers, and functionaries, surrendered to the king of Babylon, who, in the eighth year of his reign, took him captive. He carried off all the treasures of the temple of the Lord and those of the palace, and broke up all the gold utensils that Solomon, king of Israel, had provided in the temple of the Lord, as the Lord had foretold. He deported all Jerusalem: all the officers and men of the army, ten thousand in number, and all the craftsmen and smiths. None were left among the people of the land except the poor. He deported Jehoiachin to Babylon, and also led captive from Jerusalem to Babylon the king's mother and wives, his functionaries, and the chief men of the land. The king of Babylon also led captive to Babylon all seven thousand men of the army, and a thousand craftsmen and smiths, all of them trained soldiers. In place of Jehoiachin, the king of Babylon appointed his uncle Mattaniah king, and changed his name to Zedekiah.

—This is the Word of the Lord. ℟. **Thanks be to God.** ℣

Responsorial Psalm   Ps 79, 1-2. 3-5. 8. 9

℟. (9) **For the glory of your name,**
   O Lord, deliver us.

O God, the nations have come into your inheritance;
   they have defiled your holy temple,
   they have laid Jerusalem in ruins.
They have given the corpses of your servants
   as food to the birds of heaven,
   the flesh of your faithful ones to the beasts of
      the earth. — ℟
They have poured out their blood like water
   round about Jerusalem,
   and there is no one to bury them.
We have become the reproach of our neighbors,
   the scorn and derision of those around us.
O Lord, how long? Will you be angry forever?

Will your jealousy burn like fire? — ℟

Remember not against us the iniquities of the past;
  may your compassion quickly come to us,
  for we are brought very low. — ℟

Help us, O God our savior,
  because of the glory of your name;
Deliver us and pardon our sins
  for your name's sake. — ℟ ℣

GOSPEL   Mt 7, 21-29

See p. 107.

FRIDAY OF THE TWELFTH WEEK
IN ORDINARY TIME

READING I   2 Kgs 25, 1-12

The Babylonian armies open the siege of Jerusalem. Zedekiah's sons
are executed. He is taken to Babylon in chains. The land is completely
devastated and the population reduced to a few thousands.

A reading from the second book of Kings

In the tenth month of the ninth year of Zedekiah's
reign, on the tenth day of the month, Nebuchadnezzar, king of Babylon, and his whole army advanced
against Jerusalem, encamped around it, and built
siege walls on every side. The siege of the city continued until the eleventh year of Zedekiah. On the
ninth day of the fourth month, when famine had
gripped the ctiy, and the people had no more bread,
the ctiy walls were breached. Then the king and all
the soldiers left the city by night through the gate
between the two walls which was near the king's
garden. Since the Chaldeans had the city surrounded,
they went in the direction of the Arabah. But the
Chaldean army pursued the king and overtook him
in the desert near Jericho, abandoned by his whole
army.

The king was therefore arrested and brought to Riblah to the king of Babylon, who pronounced sentence on him. He had Zedekiah's sons slain before his eyes. Then he blinded Zedekiah, bound him with fetters, and had him brought to Babylon.

On the seventh day of the fifth month (this was in the nineteenth year of Nebuchadnezzar, king of Babylon), Nebuzaradan, captain of the bodyguard, came to Jerusalem as the representative of the king of Babylon. He burned the house of the Lord, the palace of the king, and all the houses of Jerusalem; every large building was destroyed by fire. Then the Chaldean troops who were with the captain of the guard tore down the walls that surrounded Jerusalem.

Then Nebuzaradan, captain of the guard, led into exile the last of the people remaining in the city, and those who had deserted to the king of Babylon, and the last of the artisans. But some of the country's poor, Nebuzaradan, captain of the guard, left behind as vinedressers and farmers.—This is the Word of the Lord. ℟. **Thanks be to God.** ℣

Responsorial Psalm   Ps 137, 1-2. 3. 4-5. 6

℟. (6) **Let my tongue be silenced,
if I ever forget you!**

By the streams of Babylon
    we sat and wept
    when we remembered Zion.
On the aspens of that land
    we hung up our harps. — ℟

Though there our captors asked of us
    the lyrics of our songs,
And our despoilers urged us to be joyous:
    "Sing for us the songs of Zion!" — ℟

How could we sing a song of the Lord
    in a foreign land?

If I forget you, Jerusalem,
    may my right hand be forgotten! — ℟

May my tongue cleave to my palate
    if I remember you not,

If I place not Jerusalem
    ahead of my joy. — ℟ ♥

GOSPEL   Mt 8, 1-4

See p. 109.

SATURDAY OF THE TWELFTH WEEK
IN ORDINARY TIME

READING I   Lam 2, 2. 10-14. 18-19

The Babylonians destroy fortress towns in the Judean provinces while
besieging Jerusalem. Serious disaster follows upon serious guilt.
Sorrow, pain, and hardships become life without the Lord. The
people are instructed to lift up their hands to the Lord and pray to him.

A reading from the book of Lamentations

The Lord has consumed without pity
    all the dwellings of Jacob;
He has torn down in his anger
    the fortresses of daughter Judah;
He has brought to the ground in dishonor
    her king and her princes.
On the ground in silence sit
    the old men of daughter Zion;
They strew dust on their heads
    and gird themselves with sackcloth;
The maidens of Jerusalem
    bow their heads to the ground.
Worn out from weeping are my eyes,
    within me all is in ferment;
My gall is poured out on the ground
    because of the downfall of the daughter of my
        people,

As child and infant faint away
  in the open spaces of the town.
They ask their mothers,
  "Where is the cereal?"—in vain,
As they faint away like the wounded
  in the streets of the ctiy,
And breathe their last
  in their mothers' arms.
To what can I liken or compare you,
  O daughter Jerusalem?
What example can I show you for your comfort,
  virgin daughter Zion?
For great as the sea is your downfall;
  who can heal you?
Your prophets had for you
  false and specious visions;
They did not lay bare your guilt,
  to avert your fate;
They beheld for you in vision
  false and misleading portents.
Cry out to the Lord;
  moan, O daughter Zion!
Let your tears flow like a torrent
  day and night;
Let there be no respite for you,
  no repose for your eyes.
Rise up, shrill in the night,
  at the beginning of every watch;
Pour out your heart like water
  in the presence of the Lord;
Lift up your hands to him
  for the lives of your little ones
[Who faint from hunger
  at the corner of every street].
This is the Word of the Lord. ℟. **Thanks be to God.** ℣

Responsorial Psalm   Ps 74, 1-2. 3-5. 5-7. 20-21
℟. (19) **Lord, forget not the life of your poor ones.**

Why, O God, have you cast us off forever?
  Why does your anger smolder against the sheep
    of your pasture?
Remember your flock which you built up of old,
  the tribe you redeemed as your inheritance,
    Mount Zion, where you took up your abode. — ℟

Turn your steps toward the utter ruins;
  toward all the damage the enemy has done in
    the sanctuary.
Your foes roar triumphantly in your shrine;
  they have set up their tokens of victory.
They are like men coming up with axes to a clump
    of trees. — ℟

With chisel and hammer they hack at all the panel-
    ing of the sanctuary.
  They set your sanctuary on fire;
The place where your name abides they have razed
    and profaned. — ℟

Look to your covenant,
  for the hiding places in the land and the plains
    are full of violence.
May the humble not retire in confusion;
  may the afflicted and the poor praise your
    name. — ℟

GOSPEL   Mt 8, 5-17

See p. 111.

MONDAY OF THE THIRTEENTH WEEK
IN ORDINARY TIME

READING I   Am 2, 6-10. 13-16

Amos describes how the Lord forgives. The Lord delivered the Is-
raelites from bondage. The Lord brought them to the land of the
Amorites and destroyed the Amorites. The Lord also sends warning
against evil deeds.

A reading from the book of the prophet Amos

Thus says the Lord:

For three crimes of Israel, and for four,
    I will not revoke my word;
Because they sell the just man for silver,
    and the poor man for a pair of sandals.
They trample the heads of the weak
    into the dust of the earth,
    and force the lowly out of the way.
Son and father go to the same prostitute,
    profaning my holy name.
Upon garments taken in pledge
    they recline beside any altar;
And the wine of those who have been fined
    they drink in the house of their god.
Yet it was I who destroyed the Amorites before
        them,
    who were as tall as the cedars,
    and as strong as the oak trees.
I destroyed their fruit above,
    and their roots beneath.
It was I who brought you up from the land of Egypt,
    and who led you through the desert for forty
        years,
    to occupy the land of the Amorites.
Beware, I will crush you into the ground
    as a wagon crushes when laden with sheaves.
Flight shall perish from the swift,
    and the strong man shall not retain his strength;

The warrior shall not save his life,
  nor the bowman stand his ground;
The swift of foot shall not escape,
  nor the horseman save his life.
And the most stouthearted of warriors
  shall flee naked on that day, says the Lord.
This is the Word of the Lord. ℞. **Thanks be to God.** ℣

Responsorial Psalm Ps 50, 16-17. 18-19. 20-21. 22-23
℞. (22) **Remember this, you who never think of God.**

Why do you recite my statutes,
  and profess my covenant with your mouth,
Though you hate discipline
  and cast my words behind you? — ℞

When you see a thief, you keep pace with him,
  and with adulterers you throw in your lot.
To your mouth you give free rein for evil,
  you harness your tongue to deceit. — ℞

You sit speaking against your brother;
  against your mother's son you spread rumors.
When you do these things, shall I be deaf to it?
  Or do you think that I am like yourself?
  I will correct you by drawing them up before
    your eyes. — ℞

Consider this, you who forget God,
  lest I rend you and there be no one to rescue you.
He that offers praise as a sacrifice glorifies me;
  and to him that goes the right way I will show
    the salvation of God. — ℞ ℣

GOSPEL   Mt 8, 18-22
See p. 115.

TUESDAY OF THE THIRTEENTH WEEK
IN ORDINARY TIME

READING I   Am 3, 1-8; 4, 11-12

God's selection of Israel involves responsibility. Because Israel failed to comply, she is to be punished. Their election was for service; it was not merely a guarantee of divine protection. Failure to serve calls for punishment.

A reading from the book of the prophet Amos

Hear this word, O men of Israel, that the Lord pronounces over you, over the whole family that I brought up from the land of Egypt:
You alone have I favored,
    more than all the families of the earth;
Therefore I will punish you
    for all your crimes.
Do two walk together
    unless they have agreed?
Does a lion roar in the forest
    when it has no prey?
Does a young lion cry out from its den
    unless it has seized something?
Is a bird brought to earth by a snare
    when there is no lure for it?
Does a snare spring up from the ground
    without catching anything?
If the trumpet sounds in a city,
    will the people not be frightened?
If evil befall a city,
    has not the Lord caused it?
Indeed, the Lord God does nothing
    without revealing his plan
    to his servants, the prophets.
The lion roars—
    who will not be afraid!
The Lord God speaks—
    who will not prophesy!

I brought upon you such upheaval
　　as when God overthrew Sodom and Gomorrah:
　　you were like a brand plucked from the fire;
Yet you returned not to me,
　　says the Lord.
So now I will deal with you in my own way, O
　　　Israel!
　　and since I will deal thus with you,
　　prepare to meet your God, O Israel.
This is the Word of the Lord. ℟. **Thanks be to God.** ⱽ

Responsorial Psalm　　　　　　Ps 5, 4-6. 6-7. 8

℟. (9) **Lead me in your justice, Lord.**

　　At dawn I bring my plea expectantly before you.
For you, O God, delight not in wickedness;
　　no evil man remains with you;
　　the arrogant may not stand in your sight. — ℟

You hate all evildoers;
　　you destroy all who speak falsehood;
The bloodthirsty and the deceitful
　　the Lord abhors. — ℟

But I, because of your abundant kindness,
　　will enter your house;
I will worship at your holy temple
　　in fear of you, O Lord. — ℟ ⱽ

GOSPEL　　　　　　　　　　　Mt 8, 23-27

See p. 117.

WEDNESDAY OF THE THIRTEENTH WEEK
IN ORDINARY TIME

READING I   Am 5, 14-15. 21-24

The Israelites mistakenly thought that election by Yahweh gave a guarantee of protection, and he tells them to seek the Lord so that they may have life. They are to hate evil and do good.

A reading from the book of the prophet Amos

Seek good and not evil,
    that you may live;
Then truly will the Lord, the God of hosts,
    be with you as you claim!
Hate evil and love good,
    and let justice prevail at the gate;
Then it may be that the Lord, the God of hosts,
    will have pity on the remnant of Joseph.
I hate, I spurn your feasts, says the Lord,
    I take no pleasure in your solemnities;
Your cereal offerings I will not accept,
    nor consider your stall-fed peace offerings.
Away with your noisy songs!
    I will not listen to the melodies of your harps.
But if you would offer me holocausts,
    then let justice surge like water,
    and goodness like an unfailing stream.
Tihs is the Word of the Lord. ℟. **Thanks be to God.** ℣

Responsorial Psalm Ps 50, 7. 8-9. 10-11. 12-13. 16-17

℟. (23) **To the upright I will show the saving power
    of God.**

Hear, my people, and I will speak;
    Israel, I will testify against you;
    God, your God, am I. — ℟

Not for your sacrifices do I rebuke you,
    for your holocausts are before me always.
I take from your house no bullock,
    no goats out of your fold. — ℟

For mine are all the animals of the forests,
  beasts by the thousand on my mountains.
I know all the birds of the air,
  and whatever stirs in the plains, belongs to me.—℟

If I were hungry, I should not tell you,
  for mine are the world and its fullness.
Do I eat the flesh of strong bulls,
  or is the blood of goats my drink? — ℟

Why do you recite my statutes,
  and profess my covenant with your mouth,
Though you hate discipline
  and cast my words behind you? — ℟ ℣

GOSPEL   Mt 8, 28-34

See p. 119.

THURSDAY OF THE THIRTEENTH WEEK
IN ORDINARY TIME

READING I   Am 7, 10-17

Amaziah conspires against Amos. Amos warns that he was selected by
the Lord. He then foretells what is to happen to Amaziah and the unfortunate fate of his family.

A reading from the book of the prophet Amos

Amaziah, the priest of Bethel, sent word to Jeroboam, king of Israel: "Amos has conspired against
you here within Israel; the country cannot endure
all his words. For this is what Amos says:

  Jeroboam shall die by the sword,
    and Israel shall surely be exiled from its land."

To Amos, Amaziah said: "Off with you, visionary,
flee to the land of Judah! There earn your bread
by prophesying, but never again prophesy in Bethel;
for it is the king's sanctuary and a royal temple."

Amos answered Amaziah, "I was no prophet, nor have I belonged to a company of prophets; I was a shepherd and a dresser of sycamores. The Lord took me from following the flock, and said to me, Go, prophesy to my people Israel. Now hear the word of the Lord!"

> You say: prophesy not against Israel,
>   preach not against the house of Isaac.
>   Now thus says the Lord:
> Your wife shall be made a harlot in the city,
>   and your sons and daughters shall fall by
>   the sword;
> Your land shall be divided by measuring line,
>   and you yourself shall die in an unclean land;
> Israel shall be exiled far from its land.

This is the Word of the Lord. ℟. **Thanks be to God.** ℣

Responsorial Psalm   Ps 19, 8. 9. 10. 11

℟. (10) **The judgments of the Lord are true,**
   and all of them are just.

The law of the Lord is perfect,
   refreshing the soul;
The decree of the Lord is trustworthy,
   giving wisdom to the simple. — ℟

The precepts of the Lord are right,
   rejoicing the heart;
The command of the Lord is clear,
   enlightening the eye. — ℟

The fear of the Lord is pure,
   enduring forever;
The ordinances of the Lord are true,
   all of them just. — ℟

They are more precious than gold,
   than a heap of purest gold;
Sweeter also than syrup
   or honey from the comb. — ℟ ℣

GOSPEL   Mt 9, 1-8

See p. 122.

FRIDAY OF THE THIRTEENTH WEEK
IN ORDINARY TIME

READING I   Am 8, 4-6. 9-12

Because of greed, the Israelites wait impatiently to engage in business
and oppress the poor. But Amos warns them. Sackcloth and shaved
heads are a sign of lamentation. The people will search in vain for
a prophet to proclaim the word of God.

A reading from the book of the prophet Amos

Hear this, you who trample upon the needy
    and destroy the poor of the land!
"When will the new moon be over," you ask,
    "that we may sell our grain,
    and the sabbath, that we may display the wheat?
We will diminish the ephah,
    add to the shekel,
    and fix our scales for cheating!
We will buy the lowly man for silver,
    and the poor man for a pair of sandals;
    even the refuse of the wheat we will sell!"
On that day, says the Lord God,
    I will make the sun set at midday
    and cover the earth with darkness in broad day-
        light.
I will turn your feasts into mourning
    and all your songs into lamentations.
I will cover the loins of all with sackcloth
    and make every head bald.
I will make them mourn as for an only son,
    and bring their day to a bitter end.
Yes, days are coming, says the Lord God,
    when I will send famine upon the land:

Not a famine of bread, or thirst for water,
  but for hearing the word of the Lord.
Then shall they wander from sea to sea
  and rove from the north to the east
In search of the word of the Lord,
  but they shall not find it.
This is the Word of the Lord. ℞. **Thanks be to God.** ℣

Responsorial Psalm   Ps 119, 2. 10. 20. 30. 40. 131

℞. (Mt 4, 46) **Man does not live on bread alone,
    but on every word that comes from the mouth of
    God.**

Happy are they who observe his decrees,
  who seek him with all their heart. — ℞

With all my heart I seek you;
  let me not stray from your commands. — ℞

My soul is consumed with longing
  for your ordinances at all times. — ℞

The way of truth I have chosen;
  I have set your ordinances before me. — ℞

Behold, I long for your precepts;
  in your justice give me life. — ℞

I gasp with open mouth
  in my yearning for your commands. — ℞ ℣

GOSPEL   Mt 9, 9-13

See p. 125.

SATURDAY OF THE THIRTEENTH WEEK
IN ORDINARY TIME

READING I   Am 9, 11-15

The prophet Amos anticipates the rebuilding of the Kingdom of David.
Judgment will be followed by Salvation. The Lord indicates that on
that day the restoration of Israel is designated.

A reading from the book of the prophet Amos

Thus says the Lord:
On that day I will raise up
  the fallen hut of David;
I will wall up its breaches,
  raise up its ruins,
  and rebuild it as in the days of old,
That they may conquer what is left of Edom
  and all the nations that shall bear my name,
  say I, the Lord, who will do this.
Yes, days are coming,
  says the Lord,
When the plowman shall overtake the reaper,
  and the vintager, him who sows the seed;
The juice of grapes shall drip down the mountains,
  and all the hills shall run with it.
I will bring about the restoration of my people Israel;
  they shall rebuild and inhabit their ruined cities,
Plant vinyards and drink the wine,
  set out gardens and eat the fruits.
I will plant them upon their own ground;
  never again shall they be plucked
From the land I have given them,
  say I, the Lord, your God.
This is the Word of the Lord. ℟. **Thanks be to God.** ☩

Responsorial Psalm   Ps 85, 9. 11-12. 13-14

℟. (9) **The Lord speaks of peace to his people.**

I will hear what God proclaims;
  the Lord—for he proclaims peace
To his people, and to his faithful ones,
  and to those who put in him their hope. — ℟

Kindness and truth shall meet;
  justice and peace shall kiss.
Truth shall spring out of the earth,
  and justice shall look down from heaven. — ℟

The Lord himself will give his benefits;
    our land shall yield its increase.
Justice shall walk before him,
    and salvation, along the way of his steps. — ℟ ℣

GOSPEL   Mt 9, 14-17

See p. 128.

MONDAY OF THE FOURTEENTH WEEK
IN ORDINARY TIME

READING I   Hos 2, 16. 17-18. 21-22

Israel will return to the desert to reestablish contact with Yahweh.
The desert is an ideal place to seek God. The time of salvation, when
Yahweh saves his people, expresses confidence in the future resto-
ration of Israel.

    A reading from the book of the prophet Hosea

    Thus says the Lord:
I will allure her;
    I will lead her into the desert
    and speak to her heart.
She shall respond there as in the days of her youth,
    when she came up from the land of Egypt.
    On that day, says the Lord,
She shall call me "My husband,"
    and never again "My baal."
I will espouse you to me forever:
    I will espouse you in right and in justice,
    in love and in mercy;
I will espouse you in fidelity,
    and you shall know the Lord.
This is the Word of the Lord. ℟. **Thanks be to God.** ℣

Responsorial Psalm   Ps 145, 2-3. 4-5. 6-7. 8-9

℟. (8) **The Lord is kind and merciful.**

Every day will I bless you,
    and I will praise your name forever and ever.

Great is the Lord and highly to be praised;
  his greatness is unsearchable. — ℟

Generation after generation praises your works
  and proclaims your might.

They speak of the splendor of your glorious majesty
  and tell of your wondrous works. — ℟

They discourse of the power of your terrible deeds
  and declare your greatness.

They publish the fame of your abundant goodness
  and joyfully sing of your justice. — ℟

The Lord is gracious and merciful,
  slow to anger and of great kindness.

The Lord is good to all
  and compassionate toward all his works. — ℟ ✟

GOSPEL   Mt 9, 18-26

See p. 131.

TUESDAY OF THE FOURTEENTH WEEK
IN ORDINARY TIME

READING I   Hos 8, 4-7. 11-13

The appointment of a king and idolatry, especially the setting up of
the golden calves, points to Israel's original break with the Davidic
Kingdom. Israel has built many altars without following Yahweh's
many directions. Hosea condemns their idolatrous misuse. The lawless
sacrifices offend God.

A reading from the book of the prophet Hosea

They made kings [in Israel] but not by my authority;
  they established princes, but without my approval.
With their silver and gold they made
  idols for themselves, to their own destruction.
Cast away your calf, O Samaria!
  my wrath is kindled against them;
How long will they be unable to attain
  innocence in Israel?

The work of an artisan,
    no god at all,
Destined for the flames—
    such is the calf of Samaria!
When they sow the wind,
    they shall reap the whirlwind;
The stalk of grain that forms no ear
    can yield no flour;
Even if it could,
    strangers would swallow it.
When Ephraim made many altars to expiate sin,
    his altars became occasions of sin.
Though I write for him my many ordinances,
    they are considered as a stranger's.
Though they offer sacrifice,
    immolate flesh and eat it,
    the Lord is not pleased with them.
He shall still remember their guilt
    and punish their sins;
    they shall return to Egypt.
This is the Word of the Lord. ℟. **Thanks be to God.** ℣

Responsorial Psalm   Ps 115, 3-4. 5-6. 7-8. 9-10

℟. (9) **The house of Israel trusts in the Lord.**

Our God is in heaven;
    whatever he wills, he does.
Their idols are silver and gold,
    the handiwork of men. — ℟

They have mouths but speak not;
    they have eyes but see not;
They have ears but hear not;
    they have noses but smell not. — ℟

They have hands but feel not;
    they have feet but walk not.
Their makers shall be like them,
    everyone that trusts in them, — ℟ ℣

℟. Or: **Alleluia.** ℣

GOSPEL Mt 9, 32-38

See p. 133.

———————

WEDNESDAY OF THE FOURTEENTH WEEK
IN ORDINARY TIME

READING I Hos 10, 1-3. 7-8. 12

A prosperous Israel has multiplied its cult places, but its religion is false. The picture of devastation is developed; people, leaders, and religion will all disappear. Hosea turns to the hope of Israel's beginning again in justice and piety.

A reading from the book of the prophet Hosea

Israel is a luxuriant vine
  whose fruit matches its growth.
The more abundant his fruit,
  the more altars he built;
The more productive his land,
  the more sacred pillars he set up.
Their heart is false,
  now they pay for their guilt;
God shall break down their altars
  and destroy their sacred pillars.
If they would say,
  "We have no king"—
Since they do not fear the Lord,
  what can the king do for them?
The king of Samaria shall disappear,
  like foam upon the waters.
The high places of Aven shall be destroyed,
  the sin of Israel;
  thorns and thistles shall overgrow their altars.
Then they shall cry out to the mountains, "Cover
    us!"
  and to the hills, "Fall upon us!"

"Sow for yourselves justice,
   reap the fruit of piety;
Break up for yourselves a new field,
   for it is time to seek the Lord,
   till he come and rain down justice upon you."
This is the Word of the Lord. ℞. **Thanks be to God.** ℣

Responsorial Psalm   Ps 105, 2-3. 4-5. 6-7

℞. (4) **Seek always the face of the Lord.**

Sing to him, sing his praise,
   proclaim all his wondrous deeds.
Glory in his holy name;
   rejoice, O hearts that seek the Lord! — ℞

Look to the Lord in his strength;
   seek to serve him constantly.
Recall the wondrous deeds that he has wrought,
   his portents, and the judgments he has uttered.—℞

You descendants of Abraham, his servants,
   sons of Jacob, his chosen ones!
He, the Lord, is our God;
   throughout the earth his judgments prevail.—℞ ℣

℞. Or: **Alleluia.** ℣

GOSPEL   Mt 10, 1-7

See p. 136.

THURSDAY OF THE FOURTEENTH WEEK
IN ORDINARY TIME

READING I   Hos 11, 1. 3-4. 8-9

Hosea reveals God's true nature. Yahweh's fatherly love produces
Israel's redemption. He cannot destroy his beloved people. God's love
does not have any element of selfishness.

   A reading from the book of the prophet Hosea

When Israel was a child I loved him,
   out of Egypt I called my son.

It was I who taught Ephraim to walk,
    who took them in my arms;
I drew them with human cords,
    with bands of love;
I fostered them like one
    who raises an infant to his cheeks;
Yet, though I stooped to feed my child,
    they did not know that I was their healer.
My heart is overwhelmed,
    my pity is stirred.
I will not give vent to my blazing anger,
    I will not destroy Ephraim again;
For I am God and not man,
    the Holy One present among you;
    I will not let the flames consume you.
This is the Word of the Lord. ℟. **Thanks be to God.** ℣

Responsorial Psalm   Ps 80, 2. 3. 15-16

℟. (4) **Let us see your face, Lord,
    and we shall be saved.**

O shepherd of Israel, hearken,
    from your throne upon the cherubim, shine forth,
Rouse your power. — ℟

Once again, O Lord of hosts,
    look down from heaven, and see:
Take care of this vine,
    and protect what your right hand has planted
    [the son of man whom you yourself made
        strong]. — ℟ ℣

GOSPEL   Mt 10, 7-15

See p. 138.

FRIDAY OF THE FOURTEENTH WEEK
IN ORDINARY TIME

READING I   Hos 14, 2-10

Hosea's prophecy closes on a note of hope—hope based on the certainty that Yahweh loves his people. Yahweh's love is described. Israel will flourish in beauty and plenty.

A reading from the book of the prophet Hosea

Return, O Israel, to the Lord, your God;
  you have collapsed through your guilt.
Take with you words,
  and return to the Lord;
Say to him, "Forgive all iniquity,
  and receive what is good, that we may render
  as offerings the bullocks from our stalls.
Assyria will not save us,
  nor shall we have horses to mount;
We shall say no more, 'Our god,'
  to the work of our hands;
  for in you the orphan finds compassion."
I will heal their defection,
  I will love them freely;
  for my wrath is turned away from them.
I will be like the dew for Israel:
  he shall blossom like the lily;
He shall strike root like the Lebanon cedar,
  and put forth his shoots.
His splendor shall be like the olive tree
  and his fragrance like the Lebanon cedar.
Again they shall dwell in his shade
  and raise grain;
They shall blossom like the vine,
  and his fame shall be like the wine of Lebanon.
Ephraim! What more has he to do with idols?
  I have humbled him, but I will prosper him.
"I am like a verdant cypress tree"—
  Because of me you bear fruit!
Let him who is wise understand these things;

let him who is prudent know them.
Straight are the paths of the Lord,
in them the just walk,
but sinners stumble in them.
This is the Word of the Lord. ℞. **Thanks be to God.** ℣

Responsorial Psalm   Ps 51, 3-4. 8-9. 12-13. 14. 17

℞. (17) **My mouth will declare your praise.**

Have mercy on me, O God, in your goodness;
in the greatness of your compassion wipe out my
offense.
Thoroughly wash me from my guilt
and of my sin cleanse me. — ℞

Behold, you are pleased with sincerity of heart,
and in my inmost being you teach me wisdom.
Cleanse me of sin with hyssop, that I may be purified;
wash me, and I shall be whiter than snow. — ℞

A clean heart create for me, O God,
and a steadfast spirit renew within me.
Cast me not out from your presence,
and your holy spirit take not from me. — ℞

Give me back the joy of your salvation,
and a willing spirit sustain in me.
O Lord, open my lips,
and my mouth shall proclaim your praise. — ℞ ℣

GOSPEL   Mt 10, 16-23

See p. 141.

———————————

SATURDAY OF THE FOURTEENTH WEEK
IN ORDINARY TIME

READING I   Is 6, 1-8

Isaiah tells of his overpowering encounter with the Holy One. The
holiness of God is a central theme of Isaiah. Isaiah was aware of his
own unworthiness. One of the seraphim touches his lips with the
ember, and his wickedness is removed and his sin purged.

A reading from the book of the prophet Isaiah

In the year King Uzziah died, I saw the Lord seated on a high and lofty throne, with the train of his garment filling the temple. Seraphim were stationed above; each of them had six wings: with two they veiled their faces, with two they veiled their feet, and with two they hovered aloft.

"Holy, holy, holy is the Lord of hosts!" they cried one to the other. "All the earth is filled with his glory!" At the sound of that cry, the frame of the door shook and the house was filled with smoke.

Then I said, "Woe is me, I am doomed! For I am a man of unclean lips, living among a people of unclean lips; yet my eyes have seen the King, the Lord of hosts!" Then one of the seraphim flew to me, holding an ember which he had taken with tongs from the altar.

He touched my mouth with it. "See," he said, "now that this has touched your lips, your wickedness is removed, your sin purged."

Then I heard the voice of the Lord saying, "Whom shall I send? Who will go for us?" "Here I am," I said; "send me!"—This is the Word of the Lord. ℟. **Thanks be to God.** ℣

Responsorial Psalm Ps 93, 1. 1-2. 5

℟. (1) **The Lord is king;**
he is robed in majesty.

The Lord is king, in splendor robed;
  robed is the Lord and girt about with strength.—℟

And he has made the world firm,
  not to be moved.
Your throne stands firm from of old;
  from everlasting you are, O Lord. — ℟

Your decrees are worthy of trust indeed;
  holiness befits your house,
    O Lord, for length of days. — ℟ ℣

GOSPEL   Mt 10, 24-33

See p. 143.

———————————

INTRODUCTION FOR 15th TO 19th WEEK

The Book of Isaiah—*This magnificent poet (who is read during Advent and beginning with Saturday of the 14th Week) is the greatest of the prophets and one of the major witnesses of the Messianic hope in Israel. His ministry began in the second half of the 8th century B.C. which saw the collapse of the Northern Kingdom (722) and the constant peril of the Southern Kingdom at the hands of her foes. Isaiah was a man of great vision, ability and political influence whose message is stamped by the majesty, holiness, and glory of the Lord and the pettiness and sinfulness of man. His prophecies concerning Immanuel are most important because of their Messianic character and their influence on Christian revelation.*

In the tradition of Amos, Hosea, and Micah, his contemporaries, Isaiah attacks social injustice as that which is most indicative of Judah's tenuous relationship with God. He exhorts his hearers to trust in their omnipotent God and to live accordingly. Thus justice and righteousness, teaching and word, and assurance of divine blessing upon the faithful and punishment upon the faithless are recurrent themes in his message from the Holy One of Israel to a proud and stubborn people.

Chapters 40—55 (called Second Isaiah) are attributed to an anonymous poet who prophesied toward the end of the Babylonian exile. From this section come the great Messianic oracles known as the Songs of the Servant, whose mysterious destiny of suffering and glorification is fulfilled in the passion and glorification of Christ. Chapters 56—66 (Third Isaiah) contain oracles from a later period and were composed by disciples who inherited the spirit and continued the work of the great prophet.

The Book of Micah—*A contemporary of Isaiah from the common people (of an obscure village west of Jerusalem called Moresheth), Micah stands with Amos, Hosea, and Isaiah as a fierce champion of the pure worship of the Lord. Like them, he directs a word of judgment against his people but also proclaims the power of divine forgiveness and the hope of a future restoration. His prediction that a prince of David's house would rule over a reunited Israel was seen by Matthew as fulfilled in Christ's birth in Bethlehem.*

The Book of Jeremiah—*Beginning his career reluctantly in 626 B.C., this "prophet of the eleventh hour" had the unpleasant task of predicting the destruction of the Holy City and the Southern Kingdom, and of witnessing these events. He also foretold the return from the Babylonian Exile, and uttered the great oracle of the "New Covenant" (31, 31-34), sometimes called 'the Gospel before the Gospel." This passage contains his most sublime teaching and is a landmark in Old Testament theology. He continues to urge us today to go beyond a formalistic religion and put in its place a religion of the heart. Because of his many sufferings for his divine mission, Jeremiah is regarded as a type of Jesus Christ.*

The Book of Ezekiel—*Both priest and prophet, Ezekiel ministered to his fellow exiles from 593 to 563; he is the prophet of the temple and the liturgy as well as the absolute majesty of God. Like Jeremiah, Ezekiel denounces the false illusions of his people, their moral corruption, and especially the idolatry of their worship. He preaches a religion of the heart, announces a new covenant, and insists on the personal responsibility of every member of the people. Called the "father of Judaism," Ezekiel announces the restoration of Israel and the coming of God to reign over his people like a shepherd.*

MONDAY OF THE FIFTEENTH WEEK
IN ORDINARY TIME

READING I   Is 1, 10-17

Sacrifice is worthless without the proper interior dispositions. Isaiah notes that "washing yourselves clean" does not mean the purely ritual washing of the Law, but an interior cleansing of the heart.

A reading from the book of the prophet Isaiah

Hear the word of the Lord,
  princes of Sodom!
Listen to the instruction of our God,
  people of Gomorrah!
What care I for the number of your sacrifices?
  says the Lord.
I have had enough of whole-burnt rams
  and fat of fatlings;
In the blood of calves, lambs and goats
  I find no pleasure.
When you come in to visit me,
  who asks these things of you?
Trample my courts no more!
  Bring no more worthless offerings;
  your incense is loathsome to me.
New moon and sabbath, calling of assemblies,
  octaves with wickedness: these I cannot bear.
Your new moons and festivals I detest;
  they weigh me down, I tire of the load.
When you spread out your hands,
  I close my eyes to you;
Though you pray the more,
  I will not listen.
Your hands are full of blood!
  Wash yourselves clean!
Put away your misdeeds from before my eyes;
  cease doing evil; learn to do good.
Make justice your aim: redress the wronged,
  hear the orphan's plea, defend the widow.
This is the Word of the Lord. ℟. **Thanks be to God.** ℣

Responsorial Psalm   Ps 50, 8-9. 16-17. 21. 23

℞. (23) **To the upright I will show the saving power of God.**

Not for your sacrifices do I rebuke you,
  for your holocausts are before me always.
I take from your house no bullock,
  no goats out of your fold. — ℞

Why do you recite my statutes,
  and profess my covenant with your mouth
Though you hate discipline
  and cast my words behind you? — ℞

When you do these things, shall I be deaf to it?
  Or do you think that I am like yourself?
I will correct you by drawing them up before your
  eyes.
He that offers praise as a sacrifice glorifies me;
  and to him that goes the right way I will show
  the salvation of God. — ℞

GOSPEL   Mt 10, 34—11, 1

See p. 148.

TUESDAY OF THE FIFTEENTH WEEK
IN ORDINARY TIME

READING I   Is 7, 1-9

Rezin was the last king of Damascus. The coalition of Aram and Israel threw Judah into a state of emergency. Disaster will come, but some will be saved. The people are as firm as their faith.

A reading from the book of the prophet Isaiah

In the days of Ahaz, king of Judah, son of Jotham, son of Uzziah, Rezin, king of Aram, and Pekah, king of Israel, son of Remaliah, went up to attack Jerusalem, but they were not able to conquer it. When word came to the house of David that Aram was encamped in Ephraim, the heart of the king and the heart of the people trembled, as the trees of the forest tremble in the wind.

Then the Lord said to Isaiah: Go out to meet Ahaz, you and your son Shear-jashub, at the end of the conduit of the upper pool, on the highway of the fuller's field, and say to him: Take care you remain tranquil and do not fear; let not your courage fail before these two stumps of smoldering brands [the blazing anger of Rezin and the Arameans, and of the son of Remaliah], because of the mischief that Aram [Ephraim and the son of Remaliah] plots against you, saying, "Let us go up and tear Judah asunder, make it our own by force, and appoint the son of Tabeel king there."

Thus says the Lord:
This shall not stand, it shall not be!
Damascus is the capital of Aram,
    and Rezin the head of Damascus;
Samaria is the capital of Ephraim,
    and Remaliah's son the head of Samaria,
But within sixty years and five,
    Ephraim shall be crushed, no longer a nation.
Unless your faith is firm
    you shall not be firm!
This is the Word of the Lord. ℟. **Thanks be to God.** ℣

Responsorial Psalm   Ps 48, 2-3. 3-4. 5-6. 7-8
℟. (9) **God upholds his city for ever.**
Great is the Lord and wholly to be praised
    in the city of our God.
His holy mountain, fairest of heights,
    is the joy of all the earth. — ℟

Mount Zion, "the recesses of the North,"
    is the city of the great King.

God is with her castles;
    renowned is he as a stronghold. — ℟

For lo! the kings assemble,
    they come on together;
They also see, and at once are stunned,
    terrified, routed. — ℟

Quaking seizes them there;
    anguish, like a woman's in labor,
As though a wind from the east
    were shattering ships of Tarshish. — ℟ ℣

GOSPEL Mt 11, 20-24

See p. 151.

WEDNESDAY OF THE FIFTEENTH WEEK IN ORDINARY TIME

READING I Is 10, 5-7. 13-16

The Assyrian king has not the faintest notion that a Divine Sovereign is using him to attain his purpose. Isaiah seems to say that the once powerful king shall waste away with a disease.

A reading from the book of the prophet Isaiah

Thus says the Lord:
Woe to Assyria! My rod in anger,
    my staff in wrath.
Against an impious nation I send him,
    and against a people under my wrath I order him
To seize plunder, carry off loot,
    and tread them down like the mud of the streets.
But this is not what he intends,
    nor does he have this in mind;
Rather, it is in his heart to destroy,
    to make an end of nations not a few.
    For he says:

"By my own power I have done it,
  and by my wisdom, for I am shrewd.
I have moved the boundaries of peoples,
  their treasures I have pillaged,
  and, like a giant, I have put down the enthroned.
My hand has seized like a nest
  the riches of nations;
As one takes eggs left alone,
  so I took in all the earth;
No one fluttered a wing,
  or opened a mouth, or chirped!"
Will the axe boast against him who hews with it?
  When will the saw exalt itself above him who
    wields it?
As if a rod could sway him who lifts it,
  or a staff him who is not wood!
Therefore the Lord, the Lord of hosts,
  will send among his fat ones leanness,
And instead of his glory there will be kindling
  like the kindling of fire.
This is the Word of the Lord. ℞. **Thanks be to God.** ℣

Responsorial Psalm   Ps 94, 5-6. 7-8. 9-10. 14-15
℞. (14) **The Lord will not abandon his people.**
Your people, O Lord, they trample down,
  your inheritance they afflict.
Widow and stranger they slay,
  the fatherless they murder. — ℞
And they say, "The Lord sees not;
  the God of Jacob perceives not."
Understand, you senseless ones among the people;
  and, you fools, when will you be wise? — ℞
Shall he who shaped the ear not hear?
  or he who formed the eye not see?
Shall he who instructs nations not chastise,
  he who teaches men knowledge? — ℞
For the Lord will not cast off his people,
  nor abandon his inheritance;

But judgment shall again be with justice,
   and all the upright of heart shall follow it. — ℟ ❣

GOSPEL   Mt 11, 25-27

See p. 153.

———————————

THURSDAY OF THE FIFTEENTH WEEK
IN ORDINARY TIME

READING I   Is 26, 7-9. 12. 16-19

Isaiah encourages the people, speaking to them of justice and peace.
There is an explicit hope in the resurrection of individuals. They
shall awake and sing for joy.

A reading from the book of the prophet Isaiah

The way of the just is smooth;
   the path of the just you make level.
Yes, for your way and your judgments, O Lord,
   we look to you;
Your name and your title
   are the desire of our souls.
My soul yearns for you in the night,
   yes, my spirit within me keeps vigil for you;
When your judgment dawns upon the earth,
   the world's inhabitants learn justice.
O Lord, you mete out peace to us,
   for it is you who have accomplished all we have
      done.
O Lord, oppressed by your punishment,
   we cried out in anguish under your chastising.
As a woman about to give birth
   writhes and cries out in her pains,
   so were we in your presence, O Lord.
We conceived and writhed in pain,
   giving birth to wind;

Salvation we have not achieved for the earth,
  the inhabitants of the world cannot bring it forth.
But your dead shall live, their corpses shall rise;
  awake and sing, you who lie in the dust.
For your dew is a dew of light,
  and the land of shades gives birth.
This is the Word of the Lord. ℟. **Thanks be to God.** ℣

Responsorial Psalm   Ps 102, 13-14. 15. 16-17. 19-21

℟. (20) **From heaven the Lord looks down on the earth.**

You, O Lord, abide forever,
  and your name through all generations.
You will arise and have mercy on Zion,
  for it is time to pity her.
For her stones are dear to your servants,
  and her dust moves them to pity. — ℟

And the nations shall revere your name, O Lord,
  and all the kings of the earth your glory,
When the Lord has rebuilt Zion
  and appeared in his glory;
When he has regarded the prayer of the destitute,
  and not despised their prayer. — ℟

Let this be written for the generation to come,
  and let his future creatures praise the Lord:
"The Lord looked down from his holy height,
  from heaven he beheld the earth,
To hear the groaning of the prisoners,
  to release those doomed to die." — ℟ ℣

GOSPEL   Mt 11, 28-30
See p. 156.

—————————

FRIDAY OF THE FIFTEENTH WEEK
IN ORDINARY TIME

READING I   Is 38, 1-6. 21-22. 7-8

The Lord hears Hezekiah's prayer and directs Isaiah to cure his illness.
Isaiah promises to reverse the forward direction of the sun's shadow
and bring it back the distance it has already traveled.

A reading from the book of the prophet Isaiah

In those days, when Hezekiah was mortally ill, the
prophet Isaiah, son of Amoz, came and said to him:
"Thus says the Lord: Put your house in order, for
you are about to die; you shall not recover." Then
Hezekiah turned his face to the wall and prayed to
the Lord: "O Lord, remember how faithfully and
wholeheartedly I conducted myself in your presence,
doing what was pleasing to you!" And Hezekiah
wept bitterly.

Then the word of the Lord came to Isaiah: "Go,
tell Hezekiah: Thus says the Lord, the God of your
father David: I have heard your prayer and seen your
tears. I will heal you: in three days you shall go
up to the Lord's temple; I will add fifteen years to
your life. I will rescue you and this city from the
hand of the king of Assyria; I will be a shield to this
city."

Isaiah then ordered a poultice of figs to be taken
and applied to the boil, that he might recover. Then
Hezekiah asked, "What is the sign that I shall go
up to the temple of the Lord?"

[Isaiah answered:] "This will be the sign for you
from the Lord that he will do what he has promised:
See, I will make the shadow cast by the sun on the
stairway to the terrace of Ahaz go back the ten steps
it has advanced." So the sun came back the ten steps
it had advanced.—This is the Word of the Lord.
℞. **Thanks be to God.** ⍌

Responsorial Psalm   Is 38, 10. 11. 12. 16

℟. (17) **You saved my life, O Lord;
I shall not die.**

Once I said,
"In the noontime of life I must depart!
To the gates of the nether world I shall be consigned
for the rest of my years." — ℟

I said, "I shall see the Lord no more
in the land of the living.
No longer shall I behold my fellow men
among those who dwell in the world." — ℟

My dwelling, like a shepherd's tent,
is struck down and borne away from me;
You have folded up my life, like a weaver
who severs the last thread. — ℟

Those live whom the Lord protects;
yours is the life of my spirit.
You have given me health and life. — ℟ ✓

GOSPEL   Mt 12, 1-8

See p. 158.

SATURDAY OF THE FIFTEENTH WEEK
IN ORDINARY TIME

READING I   Mi 2, 1-5

Micah attacks the wealthy landowners who have been dispossessing
the poor by illegal means. These unprincipled men plot ways to rob
the underprivileged. The unjust exploiters will themselves be despoiled by the Assyrian invaders.

A reading from the book of the prophet Micah

Woe to those who plan iniquity,
and work out evil on their couches;
In the morning light they accomplish it
when it lies within their power.

They covet fields, and seize them;
　houses, and they take them;
They cheat an owner of his house,
　a man of his inheritance.
　　Therefore thus says the Lord:
Behold, I am planning against this race an evil
　from which you shall not withdraw your necks;
Nor shall you walk with head high,
　for it will be a time of evil.
On that day a satire shall be sung over you,
　and there shall be a plaintive chant:
"Our ruin is complete,
　our fields are portioned out among our captors,
The fields of my people are measured out,
　and no one can get them back!"
Thus you shall have no one
　to mark out boundaries by lot
　in the assembly of the Lord.
This is the Word of the Lord. ℟. **Thanks be to God.** ℣

Responsorial Psalm　　　　Ps 10, 1-2. 3-4. 7-8. 14

℟. (12) **Do not forget the poor, O Lord!**

Why, O Lord, do you stand aloof?
　Why hide in times of distress?
Proudly the wicked harass the afflicted,
　who are caught in the devices the wicked have
　　contrived. — ℟

For the wicked man glories in his greed,
　and the covetous blasphemes, sets the Lord at
　　nought.
The wicked man boasts, "He will not avenge it";
　"There is no God," sums up his thoughts. — ℟

His mouth is full of cursing, guile and deceit;
　under his tongue are mischief and iniquity.
He lurks in ambush near the villages;
　in hiding he murders the innocent;
　his eyes spy upon the unfortunate. — ℟

You do see, for you behold misery and sorrow,
  taking them in your hands.
On you the unfortunate man depends;
  of the fatherless you are the helper. — ℟ ✠

GOSPEL   Mt 12, 14-21

See p. 160.

MONDAY OF THE SIXTEENTH WEEK
IN ORDINARY TIME

READING I   Mi 6, 1-4. 6-8

Micah tells what Yahweh requires of man. Israel, the defendant, is speaking, and the various kinds of sacrifices are discussed. A sacrifice without interior religion is futile.

A reading from the book of the prophet Micah

Hear what the Lord says:
Arise, present your plea before the mountains,
  and let the hills hear your voice!
Hear, O mountains, the plea of the Lord,
  pay attention, O foundations of the earth!
For the Lord has a plea against his people,
  and he enters into trial with Israel.
O my people, what have I done to you,
  or how have I wearied you? Answer me!
For I brought you up from the land of Egypt,
  from the place of slavery I released you;
And I sent before you Moses,
  Aaron, and Miriam.
With what shall I come before the Lord,
  and bow before God most high?
Shall I come before him with holocausts,
  with calves a year old?
Will the Lord be pleased with thousands of rams,
  with myriad streams of oil?

Shall I give my first-born for my crime,
   the fruit of my body for the sin of my soul?
You have been told, O man, what is good,
   and what the Lord requires of you:
Only to do the right and to love goodness,
   and to walk humbly with your God.
This is the Word of the Lord. ℟. **Thanks be to God.** ℣

Responsorial Psalm   Ps 50, 5-6. 8-9. 16-17. 21. 23

℟. (23) **To the upright I will show the saving power
   of God.**

"Gather my faithful ones before me,
   those who have made a covenant with me by sac-
     rifice."
And the heavens proclaim his justice;
   for God himself is the judge. — ℟

Not for your sacrifices do I rebuke you,
   for your holocausts are before me always.
I take from your house no bullock,
   no goats out of your fold. — ℟

"Why do you recite my statutes,
   and profess my covenant with your mouth,
Though you hate discipline
   and cast my words behind you? — ℟

When you do these things, shall I be deaf to it?
   Or do you think that I am like yourself?
   I will correct you by drawing them up before your
     eyes.
He that offers praise as a sacrifice glorifies me;
   and to him that goes the right way I will show
     the salvation of God." — ℟ ℣

GOSPEL   Mt 12, 38-42

See p. 163.

TUESDAY OF THE SIXTEENTH WEEK
IN ORDINARY TIME

READING I   Mi 7, 14-15. 18-20

Micah reflects a perceptible note of nostalgia and loneliness. The
Lord is addressed as the shepherd of his people. They ask him to bring
them out of the forest and into fertile pastures.

A reading from the book of the prophet Micah

Shepherd your people with your staff,
  the flock of your inheritance,
That dwells apart in a woodland,
  in the midst of Carmel.
Let them feed in Bashan and Gilead,
  as in the days of old;
As in the days when you came from the land of
    Egypt,
  show us wonderful signs.
Who is there like you, the God who removes guilt
    and pardons sin for the remnant of his inheritance;
Who does not persist in anger forever,
  but delights rather in clemency,
And will again have compassion on us,
  treading underfoot our guilt?
You will cast into the depths of the sea
  all our sins;
You will show faithfulness to Jacob,
  and grace to Abraham,
As you have sworn to our fathers
  from days of old.
This is the Word of the Lord. ℟. **Thanks be to God.** ℣

Responsorial Psalm   Ps 85, 2-4. 5-6. 7-8

℟. (8) **Lord, let us see your kindness.**

You have favored, O Lord, your land;
  you have restored the well-being of Jacob.
You have forgiven the guilt of your people;
  you have covered all their sins.

You have withdrawn all your wrath;
   you have revoked your burning anger. — ℟

Restore us, O God our savior,
   and abandon your displeasure against us.

Will you be ever angry with us,
   prolonging your anger to all generations? — ℟

Will you not instead give us life;
   and shall not your people rejoice in you?

Show us, O Lord, your kindness,
   and grant us your salvation. — ℟ ℣

GOSPEL   Mt 12, 46-50

See p. 166.

─────────────────────

WEDNESDAY OF THE SIXTEENTH WEEK
IN ORDINARY TIME

READING I   Jer 1, 1. 4-10

Yahweh enters into dialogue with Jeremiah. God knows man and
stands as his unique Master. Jeremiah fears he is too young for his
mission, but Yahweh intimately sustains his messenger.

The beginning of the book of the prophet
Jeremiah

The words of Jeremiah, son of Hilkiah, of a priestly
family in Anathoth, in the land of Benjamin.
The word of the Lord came to me thus:
   Before I formed you in the womb I knew you,
      before you were born I dedicated you,
      a prophet to the nations I appointed you.
   "Ah, Lord God!" I said,
      "I know not how to speak; I am too young."
But the Lord answered me,
   Say not, "I am too young."
      To whomever I send you, you shall go;
      whatever I command you, you shall speak.

Have no fear before them,
    because I am with you to deliver you, says the
        Lord.
Then the Lord extended his hand and touched my
mouth, saying,
    See, I place my words in your mouth!
        This day I set you
            over nations and over kingdoms,
    To root up and to tear down,
        to destroy and to demolish,
            to build and to plant.
This is the Word of the Lord. ℟. **Thanks be to God.** ⩔

Responsorial Psalm   Ps 71, 1-2. 3-4. 5-6. 15. 17

℟. (15) **I will sing of your salvation.**
In you, O Lord, I take refuge;
    let me never be put to shame.
In your justice rescue me, and deliver me;
    incline your ear to me, and save me. — ℟

Be my rock of refuge,
    a stronghold to give me safety,
    for you are my rock and my fortress.
O my God, rescue me from the hand of the
        wicked. — ℟

For you are my hope, O Lord;
    my trust, O God, from my youth.
On you I depend from birth;
    from my mother's womb you are my strength.—℟

My mouth shall declare your justice,
    day by day your salvation.
O God, you have taught me from my youth,
    and till the present I proclaim your wondrous
        deeds. — ℟ ⩔

GOSPEL   Mt 13, 1-9

See p. 168.

THURSDAY OF THE SIXTEENTH WEEK
IN ORDINARY TIME

READING I   Jer 2, 1-3. 7-8. 12-13

Jeremiah's accusations are directed to all the leaders. The priests devoted themselves only to short instructions on particular matters. Jeremiah uses the beautiful image of broken cisterns to depict the futility of foreign alliances.

A reading from the book of the prophet Jeremiah

This word of the Lord came to me: "Go, cry out this message for Jerusalem to hear!
I remember the devotion of your youth,
    how you loved me as a bride,
Following me in the desert,
    in a land unsown.
Sacred to the Lord was Israel,
    the first fruits of his harvest;
Should anyone presume to partake of them,
    evil would befall him, says the Lord.
When I brought you into the garden land
    to eat its goodly fruits,
You entered and defiled my land,
    you made my heritage loathsome.
The priests asked not,
    "Where is the Lord?"
Those who dealt with the law knew me not;
    the shepherds rebelled against me.
The prophets prophesied by Baal,
    and went after useless idols.
Be amazed at this, O heavens,
    and shudder with sheer horror, says the Lord.
Two evils have my people done:
    they have forsaken me, the source of living waters;
They have dug themselves cisterns,
    broken cisterns, that hold no water.
This is the Word of the Lord. ℟. **Thanks be to God.** ℣

Responsorial Psalm   Ps 36, 6-7. 8-9. 10-11

℟. (10) **You are the source of life, O Lord.**

O Lord, your kindness reaches to heaven;
  your faithfulness, to the clouds.
Your justice is like the mountains of God;
  your judgments, like the mighty deep. — ℟

How precious is your kindness, O God!
  The children of men take refuge in the shadow of
    your wings.
They have their fill of the prime gifts of your house;
  from your delightful stream you give them to
    drink. — ℟

For with you is the fountain of life,
  and in your light we see light.
Keep up your kindness toward your friends,
  your just defense of the upright of heart. — ℟ ∀

GOSPEL   Mt 13, 10-17

See p. 170.

FRIDAY OF THE SIXTEENTH WEEK
IN ORDINARY TIME

READING I   Jer 3, 14-17

Jerusalem is already destroyed and the Ark of the Covenant has disappeared, not to be replaced. Jerusalem by its new splendor will
again become the center where all nations gather.

A reading from the book of the prophet Jeremiah

Return, rebellious children, says the Lord,
  for I am your Master;
I will take you, one from a city, two from a clan,
  and bring you to Zion.
I will appoint over you shepherds after my own
    heart,
  who will shepherd you wisely and prudently.

When you multiply and become fruitful in the land,
 says the Lord,
They will in those days no longer say,
 "The ark of the covenant of the Lord!"
They will no longer think of it, or remember it,
 or miss it, or make another.

 At that time they will call Jerusalem the Lord's throne; there all nations will be gathered together to honor the name of the Lord at Jerusalem, and they will walk no longer in their hardhearted wickedness.—This is the Word of the Lord. ℞. **Thanks be to God.** ℣

Responsorial Psalm   Jer 31, 10. 11-12. 13

℞. (10) **The Lord will guard us,**
 like a shepherd guarding his flock.

Hear the word of the Lord, O nations,
 proclaim it on distant coasts, and say:
He who scattered Israel, now gathers them together,
 he guards them as a shepherd his flock. — ℞

The Lord shall ransom Jacob,
 he shall redeem him from the hand of his conqueror.
Shouting, they shall mount the heights of Zion,
 they shall come streaming to the Lord's blessings. — ℞

Then the virgins shall make merry and dance,
 and young men and old as well.
I will turn their mourning into joy,
 I will console and gladden them after their sorrows. — ℞ ℣

GOSPEL   Mt 13, 18-23

See p. 173.

SATURDAY OF THE SIXTEENTH WEEK
IN ORDINARY TIME

READING I   Jer 7, 1-11

The Lord directs Jeremiah to admonish the people to reform. The temple belongs to the Lord. False gods are not to be worshiped. The Lord abhors murder, adultery, and perjury.

A reading from the book of the prophet Jeremiah

The following message came to Jeremiah from the Lord: Stand at the gate of the house of the Lord, and there proclaim this message: Hear the word of the Lord, all you of Judah who enter these gates to worship the Lord! Thus says the Lord of hosts, the God of Israel: Reform your ways and your deeds, so that I may remain with you in this place. Put not your trust in the deceitful words: "This is the temple of the Lord! The temple of the Lord! The temple of the Lord!" Only if you thoroughly reform your ways and your deeds; if each of you deals justly with his neighbor; if you no longer oppress the resident alien, the orphan, and the widow; if you no longer shed innocent blood in this place, or follow strange gods to your own harm, will I remain with you in this place, in the land which I gave your fathers long ago and forever.

But here you are, putting your trust in deceitful words to your own loss! Are you to steal and murder, commit adultery and perjury, burn incense to Baal, go after strange gods that you know not, and yet come to stand before me in this house which bears my name, and say: "We are safe; we can commit all these abominations again"? Has this house which bears my name become in your eyes a den of thieves? I too see what is being done, says the Lord.—This is the Word of the Lord. ℞. **Thanks be to God.** ⅴ

Responsorial Psalm   Ps 84, 3. 4. 5-6. 8. 11

℟. (2) **How lovely is your dwelling-place,
    Lord, mighty God!**

My soul yearns and pines
    for the courts of the Lord.
My heart and my flesh
    cry out for the living God. — ℟

Even the sparrow finds a home,
    and the swallow a nest
    in which she puts her young—
Your altars, O Lord of hosts,
    my king and my God! — ℟

Happy they who dwell in your house!
    continually they praise you.
Happy the men whose strength you are!
    they go from strength to strength. — ℟

I had rather one day in your courts
    than a thousand elsewhere;
I had rather lie at the threshold of the house of my
        God
    than dwell in the tents of the wicked. — ℟ ⍈

GOSPEL   Mt 13, 24-30

See p. 175.

MONDAY OF THE SEVENTEENTH WEEK
IN ORDINARY TIME

READING I   Jer 13, 1-11

The loincloth represents the people of God. The prophet is Yahweh
himself. Previously Jeremiah had denounced the alliances with Mesopotamia as a betrayal of the Covenant.

A reading from the book of the prophet Jeremiah

The Lord said to me: Go buy yourself a linen loincloth; wear it on your loins, but do not put it in

water. I bought the lioncloth, as the Lord commanded, and put it on. A second time the word of the Lord came to me thus: Take the loincloth which you bought and are wearing, and go now to the Parath; there hide it in a cleft of the rock. Obedient to the Lord's command, I went to the Parath and buried the loincloth. After a long interval, he said to me: Go now to the Parath and fetch the loincloth which I told you to hide there. Again I went to the Parath, sought out and took the loincloth from the place where I had hid it. But it was rotted, good for nothing! Then the message came to me from the Lord: Thus says the Lord: So also I will allow the pride of Judah to rot, the great pride of Jerusalem.

This wicked people who refuse to obey my words, who walk in the stubbornness of their hearts, and follow strange gods to serve and adore them shall be like this loincloth which is good for nothing. For, as close as the lioncloth clings to a man's lions, so had I made the whole house of Israel and the whole house of Judah cling to me, says the Lord; to be my people, my renown, my praise, my beauty. But they did not listen.—This is the Word of the Lord. ℟. **Thanks be to God.** ℣

Responsorial Psalm   Dt 32, 18-19. 20. 21

℟. (18) **You have forgotten God who gave you birth.**

You were unmindful of the Rock that begot you.
  You forgot the God who gave you birth.
When the Lord saw this, he was filled with loathing
  and anger toward his sons and daughters. — ℟

"I will hide my face from them," he said.
  "and see what will then become of them.
What a fickle race they are,
  sons with no loyalty in them! — ℟

Since they have provoked me with their 'no-god'
  and angered me with their vain idols,

I will provoke them with a 'no-people';
with a foolish nation I will anger them." — ℟ ♥

GOSPEL   Mt 13, 31-35

See p. 178.

TUESDAY OF THE SEVENTEENTH WEEK
IN ORDINARY TIME

READING I   Jer 14, 17-22

A collective lament here is a description of the plague and Yahweh's
answer. Now a war is shattering Judah. The Canaanite Baal cult
included rites for the rain necessary for the fertility of the fields.

A reading from the book of the prophet Jeremiah

Let my eyes stream with tears
    day and night, without rest,
Over the great destruction which overwhelms
    the virgin daughter of my people,
    over her incurable wound.
If I walk out into the field,
    look! those slain by the sword;
If I enter the city,
    look! those consumed by hunger.
Even the prophet and the priest
    forage in a land they know not.
Have you cast Judah off completely?
    Is Zion loathsome to you?
Why have you struck us a blow
    that cannot be healed?
We wait for peace, to no avail;
    for a time of healing, but terror comes instead.
We recognize, O Lord, our wickedness,
    the guilt of our fathers;
    that we have sinned against you.
For your name's sake spurn us not,
    disgrace not the throne of your glory;

remember your covenant with us, and break it not.
Among the nations' idols is there any that gives rain?
Or can the mere heavens send showers?
Is it not you alone, O Lord,
our God, to whom we look?
You alone have done all these things.
This is the Word of the Lord. ℟. **Thanks be to God.** ℣

Responsorial Psalm   Ps 79, 8. 9. 11. 13

℟. (9) **For the glory of your name,
O Lord, deliver us.**

Remember not against us the iniquities of the past;
may your compassion quickly come to us,
for we are brought very low. — ℟

Help us, O God our savior,
because of the glory of your name;
Deliver us and pardon our sins
for your name's sake. — ℟

Let the prisoners' sighing come before you;
with your great power free those doomed to death.
Then we, your people and the sheep of your pasture,
will give thanks to you forever;
through all generations we will declare your
praise. — ℟ ℣

GOSPEL   Mt 13, 35-43

See p. 181.

WEDNESDAY OF THE SEVENTEENTH WEEK
IN ORDINARY TIME

READING I   Jer 15, 10. 16-21

Jeremiah laments his birth. Yahweh intended him to be "a man of
strife." What brings persecution to him is his message. Yahweh
renews the prophet's mission and confirms it.

A reading from the book of the prophet Jeremiah

Woe to me, mother, that you gave me birth!
a man of strife and contention to all the land!
I neither borrow nor lend,
yet all curse me.
When I found your words, I devoured them;
they became my joy and the happiness of my
heart.
Because I bore your name,
O Lord, God of hosts.
I did not sit celebrating
in the circle of merrymakers;
Under the weight of your hand I sat alone
because you filled me with indignation.
Why is my pain continuous,
my wound incurable, refusing to be healed?
You have indeed become for me a treacherous brook,
whose waters do not abide!
Thus the Lord answered me:
If you repent, so that I restore you,
in my presence you shall stand;
If you bring forth the precious without the vile,
you shall be my mouthpiece.
Then it shall be they who turn to you,
and you shall not turn to them;
And I will make you toward this people
a solid wall of brass.
Though they fight against you,
they shall not prevail,
For I am with you,
to deliver and rescue, says the Lord.
I will free you from the hand of the wicked,
and rescue you from the grasp of the violent.
This is the Word of the Lord. ℟. **Thanks be to God.** ℣

Responsorial Psalm   Ps 59, 2-3. 4. 10-11. 17. 18
℟. (17) **God is my refuge on the day of distress**

Rescue me from my enemies, O my God;
  from my adversaries defend me.
Rescue me from evildoers;
  from bloodthirsty men save me. — ℟

For behold, they lie in wait for my life;
  mighty men come together against me,
Not for any offense or sin of mine, O Lord. — ℟

  O my strength! for you I watch;
    for you, O God, are my stronghold,
    my gracious God!
May God come to my aid. — ℟

But I will sing of your strength
  and revel at dawn in your kindness;
You have been my stronghold,
  my refuge in the day of distress. — ℟

  O my strength! your praise will I sing;
    for you, O God, are my stronghold,
    my gracious God. — ℟ ⋁

GOSPEL   Mt 13, 44-46

See p. 183.

THURSDAY OF THE SEVENTEENTH WEEK
IN ORDINARY TIME

READING I   Jer 18, 1-6

The symbolism emerging from the workmanship of the potter is now
specified. Yahweh is the potter who "shapes" the man. This image
has been used to express the absolute dependence of man on God in
the order of creation.

A reading from the book of the prophet Jeremiah

This word came to Jeremiah from the Lord: Rise
up, be off to the potter's house; there I will give you
my message. I went down to the potter's house and
there he was, working at the wheel. Whenever the
object of clay which he was making turned out

badly in his hand, he tried again, making of the clay another object of whatever sort he pleased. Then the word of the Lord came to me: Can I not do to you, house of Israel, as this potter has done? says the Lord. Indeed, like clay in the hand of the potter, so are you in my hand, house of Israel.—This is the Word of the Lord. ℟. **Thanks be to God.** ℣

Responsorial Psalm Ps 146, 1-2. 2-4. 5-6

℟. (5) **Blest are they whose help is the God of Jacob.**

Praise the Lord, O my soul;
   I will praise the Lord all my life;
   I will sing praise to my God while I live. — ℟

Put not your trust in princes,
   in man, in whom there is no salvation.

When his spirit departs he returns to his earth;
   on that day his plans perish. — ℟

Happy he whose help is the God of Jacob,
   whose hope is in the Lord, his God.

Who made heaven and earth,
   the sea and all that is in them. — ℟ ℣

℟. Or: **Alleluia.** ℣

GOSPEL Mt 13, 47-53

See p. 185.

FRIDAY OF THE SEVENTEENTH WEEK
IN ORDINARY TIME

READING I Jer 26, 1-9

Yahweh will suspend his judgment if the people repent and observe the Law. Yahweh reveals himself only through the true prophets. Jeremiah's words provoke a general scandal and bring a charge against him.

A reading from the book of the prophet Jeremiah

In the beginning of the reign of Jehoiakim, son of Josiah, king of Judah, this message came from the Lord: Thus says the Lord: Stand in the court of the house of the Lord and speak to the people of all the cities of Judah who come to worship in the house of the Lord; whatever I command you, tell them, and omit nothing. Perhaps they will listen and turn back, each from his evil way, so that I may repent of the evil I have planned to inflict upon them for their evil deeds. Say to them: Thus says the Lord: If you disobey me, not living according to the law I placed before you and not listening to the words of my servants the prophets, whom I send you constantly though you do not obey them, I will treat this house like Shiloh, and make this the city which all the nations of the earth shall refer to when cursing another.

Now the priests, the prophets, and all the people heard Jeremiah speak these words in the house of the Lord. When Jeremiah finished speaking all that the Lord bade him speak to all the people, the priests and prophets laid hold of him, crying, "You must be put to death! Why do you prophesy in the name of the Lord: 'This house shall be like Shiloh,' and 'This city shall be desolate and deserted'?" And all the people gathered about Jeremiah in the house of the Lord. — This is the Word of the Lord. ℟. **Thanks be to God.** ℣

Responsorial Psalm   Ps 69, 5. 8-10. 14

℟. (14) **Lord, in your great love, answer me.**

Those outnumber the hairs of my head
    who hate me without cause.
Too many for my strength
    are they who wrongfully are my enemies.
    Must I restore what I did not steal? — ℟

Since for your sake I bear insult,
and shame covers my face.
I have become an outcast to my brothers,
a stranger to my mother's sons,
Because zeal for your house consumes me,
and the insults of those who blaspheme you fall
upon me. — ℟

But I pray to you, O Lord,
for the time of your favor, O God!
In your great kindness answer me
with your constant help. — ℟ ℣

GOSPEL

Mt 13, 54-58

See p. 188.

SATURDAY OF THE SEVENTEENTH WEEK IN ORDINARY TIME

READING I

Jer 26, 11-16. 24

Jeremiah is confronted with the opposition of the priests and leaders for the teaching he has made against the nation: "This man Jeremiah does not deserve death; it is in the name of the Lord, our God, that he speaks to us."

A reading from the book of the prophet Jeremiah

The priests and prophets said to the princes and to all the people, "This man deserves death; he has prophesied against this city, as you have heard with your own ears." Jeremiah gave this answer to the princes and all the people: "It was the Lord who sent me to prophesy against this house and city all that you have heard. Now, therefore, reform your ways and your deeds; listen to the voice of the Lord your God, so that the Lord will repent of the evil with which he threatens you. As for me, I am in your hands; do with me what you think good and right. But mark well: if you put me to death, it is innocent blood you bring on yourselves, on this city and its citizens. For in truth it was the Lord who sent me to you, to speak all these things for you to hear."

Thereupon the princes and all the people said to the priests and the prophets, "This man does not deserve death; it is in the name of the Lord, our God, that he speaks to us." But Ahikam, son of Shaphan, protected Jeremiah, so that he was not handed over to the people to be put to death.—This is the Word of the Lord. ℟. **Thanks be to God.** ℣

Responsorial Psalm   Ps 69, 15-16. 30-31. 33-34

℟. (14) **Lord, in your great love, answer me.**

Rescue me out of the mire; may I not sink!
　　may I be resuced from my foes,
　　and from the watery depths.
Let not the flood-waters overwhelm me,
　　nor the abyss swallow me up,
　　nor the pit close its mouth over me. — ℟

But I am afflicted and in pain;
　　let your saving help, O God, protect me.
I will praise the name of God in song,
　　and I will glorify him with thanksgiving. — ℟

"See, you lowly ones, and be glad;
　　you who seek God, may your hearts be merry!
For the Lord hears the poor,
　　and his own who are in bonds he spurns
　　　　not." — ℟ ℣

GOSPEL   Mt 14, 1-12

See p. 190.

MONDAY OF THE EIGHTEENTH WEEK
IN ORDINARY TIME

READING I Jer 28, 1-17

God wishes to bring to his people a new awareness of what the chosen people of Israel were to make manifest to the world—that the peace which the Lord desires for all men is not earned by human endeavors but is given by the Lord to the heart of man.

A reading from the book of the prophet Jeremiah

In [the beginning of] the reign of Zedekiah, king of Judah, in the fifth month of the fourth year, the prophet Hananiah, son of Azzur, from Gibeon, said to me in the house of the Lord in the presence of the priests and all the people: "Thus says the Lord of hosts, the God of Israel: 'I will break the yoke of the king of Babylon. Within two years I will restore to this place all the vessels of the temple of the Lord which Nebuchadnezzar, king of Babylon, took away from this place to Babylon. And I will bring back to this place Jeconiah, son of Jehoiakim, king of Judah, and all the exiles of Judah who went to Babylon,' says the Lord, 'for I will break the yoke of the king of Babylon.'"

The prophet Jeremiah answered the prophet Hananiah in the presence of the priests and all the people assembled in the house of the Lord, and said: Amen! thus may the Lord do! May he fulfill the things you have prophesied by bringing the vessels of the house of the Lord and all the exiles back from Babylon to this place! But now, listen to what I am about to state in your hearing and the hearing of all the people. From of old, the prophets who were before you and me prophesied war, woe, and pestilence against many lands and mighty kingdoms. But the prophet who prophesies peace is recognized as truly sent by the Lord only when his prophetic prediction is fulfilled.

Thereupon the prophet Hananiah took the yoke from the neck of the prophet Jeremiah, broke it, and said in the presence of all the people: "Thus says the Lord: 'Even so, within two years I will break the yoke of Nebuchadnezzar, king of Babylon, from off the neck of all the nations.'" At that, the prophet Jeremiah went away.

Some time after the prophet Hananiah had broken the yoke from off the neck of the prophet Jeremiah, the word of the Lord came to Jeremiah: Go tell Hananiah this: Thus says the Lord: By breaking a wooden yoke, you forge an iron yoke! For thus says the Lord of hosts, the God of Israel: A yoke of iron I will place on the necks of all these nations serving Nebuchadnezzar, king of Babylon, and they shall serve him; even the beasts of the field I give him.

To the prophet Hananiah the prophet Jeremiah said: Hear this, Hananiah! The Lord has not sent you, and you have raised false confidence in this people. For this, says the Lord, I will dispatch you from the face of the earth; this very year you shall die, because you have preached rebellion against the Lord. That same year, in the seventh month, Hananiah the prophet died.—This is the Word of the Lord. ℟. **Thanks be to God.** ℣

Responsorial Psalm   Ps 119, 29, 43. 79. 80. 95. 102
℟. (68) **Teach me your laws, O Lord.**

Remove from me the way of falsehood,
    and favor me with your law. — ℟

Take not the word of truth from my mouth,
    for in your ordinances is my hope. — ℟

Let those turn to me who fear you
    and acknowledge your decrees. — ℟

Let my heart be perfect in your statutes,
    that I be not put to shame. — ℟

Sinners wait to destroy me,
   but I pay heed to your decrees. — ℞
From your ordinances I turn not away,
   for you have instructed me. — ℞ ℣

GOSPEL   Mt 14, 13-21 (or 22-36)

See p. 192.

TUESDAY OF THE EIGHTEENTH WEEK
IN ORDINARY TIME

READING I   Jer 30, 1-2. 12-15. 18-22

Jeremiah points out the realities of the Israelites' way of living. Man
is caught up in the sickness of hatred, mistrust, envy, war, apathy,
contentions with one another, and the like. Yet the Lord promises hope.

A reading from the book of the prophet Jeremiah

The following message came to Jeremiah from the
Lord: Thus says the Lord, the God of Israel: Write
all the words I have spoken to you in a book.
      Thus says the Lord:
Incurable is your wound,
   grievous your bruise;
There is none to plead your cause,
   no remedy for your running sore,
   no healing for you.
All your lovers have forgotten you,
   they do not seek you.
I struck you as an enemy would strike,
   punished you cruelly;
Why cry out over your wound?
   your pain is without relief.
Because of your great guilt,
   your numerous sins,

I have done this to you.
Thus says the Lord:
See! I will restore the tents of Jacob,
his dwellings I will pity;
City shall be rebuilt upon hill,
and palace restored as it was.
From them will resound songs of praise,
the laughter of happy men.
I will make them not few, but many;
they will not be tiny, for I will glorify them.
His sons shall be as of old,
his assembly before me shall stand firm;
I will punish all his oppressors.
His leader shall be one of his own,
and his rulers shall come from his kin.
When I summon him, he shall approach me;
how else should one take the deadly risk
of approaching me? says the Lord.
You shall be my people,
and I will be your God.
This is the Word of the Lord. ℞. **Thanks be to God.** ℣

Responsorial Psalm Ps 102, 16-18. 19-21. 29. 22-23
℞. (17) **The Lord will build up Zion again,
and appear in all his glory.**
The nations shall revere your name, O Lord,
and all the kings of the earth your glory,
When the Lord has rebuilt Zion
and appeared in his glory;
When he has regarded the prayer of the destitute,
and not despised their prayer. — ℞

Let this be written for the generation to come,
and let his future creatures praise the Lord:
"The Lord looked down from his holy height,
from heaven he beheld the earth,
To hear the groaning of the prisoners,
to release those doomed to die." — ℞

The children of your servants shall abide,
    and their posterity shall continue in your pres-
      ence.
That the name of the Lord may be declared in Zion;
    and his praise, in Jerusalem,
When the peoples gather together,
    and the kingdoms, to serve the Lord. — ℟ ℣

GOSPEL   Mt 14, 22-36 (or 15, 1-2. 10-14)

See p. 196.

WEDNESDAY OF THE EIGHTEENTH WEEK
IN ORDINARY TIME

READING I   Jer 31, 1-7

The Lord loves man with an age-old love and eagerly desires to show his mercy. To be rebuilt by this love and mercy, man has need of baring his mind to what the Lord has revealed. Love and mercy are always renewing and remaking what is loved.

A reading from the book of the prophet Jeremiah

At that time, says the Lord,
I will be the God of all the tribes of Israel,
    and they shall be my people.
        Thus says the Lord:
The people that escaped the sword
    have found favor in the desert.
As Israel comes forward to be given his rest,
    the Lord appears to him from afar:
With age-old love I have loved you;
    so I have kept my mercy toward you.
Again I will restore you, and you shall be rebuilt,
    O virgin Israel;
Carrying your festive tambourines,
    you shall go forth dancing with the merrymakers.
Again you shall plant vineyards
    on the mountains of Samaria;
those who plant them shall enjoy the fruits.

Yes, a day will come when the watchmen
 will call out on Mount Ephraim:
"Rise up, let us go to Zion,
 to the Lord, our God."
For thus says the Lord:
Shout with joy for Jacob,
 exult at the head of the nations;
 proclaim your praise and say:
The Lord has delivered his people,
 the remnant of Israel.
This is the Word of the Lord. ℟. **Thanks be to God. ⱽ**

Responsorial Psalm   Jer 31, 10. 11-12. 13
℟. (10) **The Lord will guard us,**
 like a shepherd guarding his flock.

Hear the word of the Lord, O nations,
 proclaim it on distant coasts, and say:
He who scattered Israel, now gathers them together,
 he guards them as a shepherd his flock. — ℟

The Lord shall ransom Jacob,
 he shall redeem him from the hand of his conqueror.
Shouting, they shall mount the heights of Zion,
 they shall come streaming to the Lord's blessings. — ℟

Then the virgins shall make merry and dance,
 and young men and old as well.
I will turn their mourning into joy,
 I will console and gladden them after their sorrows. — ℟ ⱽ

GOSPEL   Mt 15, 21-28

See p. 200.

THURSDAY OF THE EIGHTEENTH WEEK IN ORDINARY TIME

READING I   Jer 31, 31-34

Jeremiah says that the Lord will make a new Covenant—not like the one that was broken. The Lord will write his law in the hearts of all men, from the least to the greatest.

A reading from the book of the prophet Jeremiah

The days are coming, says the Lord, when I will make a new covenant with the house of Israel and the house of Judah. It will not be like the covenant I made with their fathers the day I took them by the hand to lead them forth from the land of Egypt; for they broke my covenant, and I had to show myself their master, says the Lord. But this is the covenant which I will make with the house of Israel after those days, says the Lord. I will place my law within them, and write it upon their hearts; I will be their God, and they shall be my people. No longer will they have need to teach their friends and kinsmen how to know the Lord. All, from least to greatest, shall know me, says the Lord, for I will forgive their evildoing and remember their sin no more.—This is the Word of the Lord. ℟. **Thanks be to God.** ℣

Responsorial Psalm   Ps 51, 12-13. 14-15. 18-19

℟. (12) **Create a clean heart in me, O God.**

A clean heart create for me, O God,
    and a steadfast spirit renew within me.
Cast me not out from your presence,
    and your holy spirit take not from me. — ℟

Give me back the joy of your salvation,
    and a willing spirit sustain in me.
I will teach transgressors your ways,
    and sinners shall return to you. — ℟

For you are not pleased with sacrifices;
> should I offer a holocaust, you would not accept it,
My sacrifice, O God, is a contrite spirit;
> a heart contrite and humbled, O God, you will
> not spurn. — ℟ ♦

GOSPEL   Mt 16, 13-23

See p. 203.

FRIDAY OF THE EIGHTEENTH WEEK IN ORDINARY TIME

READING I   Na 2, 1. 3; 3, 1-3. 6-7

The Good News of salvation is proclaimed and promised by the Lord.
All strife and perpetrators of strife will be done away with in this age.

A reading from the book of the prophet Nahum

See, upon the mountains there advances
> the bearer of good news, announcing peace!
Celebrate your feast, O Judah,
> fulfill your vows!
For nevermore shall you be invaded
> by the scoundrel; he is completely destroyed.
The Lord will restore the vine of Jacob,
> the pride of Israel,
Though ravagers have ravaged them
> and ruined the tendrils.
Woe to the bloody city, all lies,
> full of plunder, whose looting never stops!
The crack of the whip, the rumbling sound of wheels;
> horses a-gallop, chariots bounding,
Cavalry charging,
The flame of the sword, the flash of the spear,
> the many slain, the heaping corpses,
> the endless bodies to stumble upon!

I will cast filth upon you,
  disgrace you and put you to shame;
Till everyone who sees you runs from you, saying,
  "Nineveh is destroyed; who can pity her?
  Where can one find any to console her?"
This is the Word of the Lord. ℟. **Thanks be to God.** ℣

Responsorial Psalm   Dt 32, 35-36. 39. 41

℟. (39) **It is I who deal death and give life.**

Close at hand is the day of their disaster,
  and their doom is rushing upon them!
Surely, the Lord shall do justice for his people;
  on his servants he shall have pity. — ℟

"Learn then that I, I alone, am God,
  and there is no god besides me.
It is I who bring both death and life,
  I who inflict wounds and heal them. — ℟

I will sharpen my flashing sword,
  and my hand shall lay hold of my quiver.
With vengeance I will repay my foes
  and requite those who hate me." — ℟ ℣

GOSPEL   Mt 16, 24-28

See p. 205.

SATURDAY OF THE EIGHTEENTH WEEK
IN ORDINARY TIME

READING I   Hb 1, 12—2, 4

The Lord's eyes are too pure to look upon evil, and when his eyes
view, they must be purifying. God has certainly determined the course
and action of the world or he would cease looking at it with his
purifying glance.

A reading from the book of the prophet Habakkuk

Are you not from eternity, O Lord,
  my holy God, immortal?
O Lord, you have marked him for judgment,
  O Rock, you have readied him for punishment!
Too pure are your eyes to look upon evil,
  and the sight of misery you cannot endure.
Why, then, do you gaze on the faithless in silence
  while the wicked man devours
  one more just than himself?
You have made man like the fish of the sea,
  like creeping things without a ruler.
He brings them all up with his hook,
  he hauls them away with his net,
He gathers them in his seine;
  and so he rejoices and exults.
Therefore he sacrifices to his net,
  and burns incense to his seine;
For thanks to them his portion is generous,
  and his repast sumptuous.
Shall he, then, keep on brandishing his sword
  to slay peoples without mercy?
I will stand at my guard post,
  and station myself upon the rampart,
And keep watch to see what he will say to me,
  and what answer he will give to my complaint.
Then the Lord answered me and said:
  Write down the vision
Clearly upon the tablets,
  so that one can read it readily.
For the vision still has its time,
  presses on to fulfillment, and will not disappoint;
If it delays, wait for it,
  it will surely come, it will not be late.
The rash man has no integrity;
  but the just man, because of his faith, shall live.
This is the Word of the Lord. ℟. **Thanks be to God.** ℣

Responsorial Psalm   Ps 9, 8-9. 10-11. 12-13

℟. (11) **You will never abandon those who seek you, Lord.**

The Lord sits enthroned forever;
  he has set up his throne for judgment.
He judges the world with justice;
  he governs the peoples with equity. — ℟

The Lord is a stronghold for the oppressed,
  a stronghold in times of distress.
They trust in you who cherish your name,
  for you forsake not those who seek you, O
    Lord. — ℟

Sing praise to the Lord enthroned in Zion;
  proclaim among the nations his deeds;
For the avenger of blood has remembered;
  he has not forgotten the cry of the afflicted.—℟ ℣

GOSPEL   Mt 17, 14-20

See p. 207.

MONDAY OF THE NINETEENTH WEEK
IN ORDINARY TIME

READING I   Ez 1, 2-5. 24-28

Ezekiel has a vision. Upon a throne he sees a figure from the waist
up of a man, surrounded with splendor; beneath is fire. Above in the
firmament is a reflection like sapphire. Such is the awesome glory
of the Lord.

A reading from the book of the prophet Ezekiel

In the fifth month of the fifth year, that is, of King
Jehoiachin's exile, the word of the Lord came to the
priest Ezekiel, the son of Buzi, in the land of the
Chaldeans by the river Chebar.—There the hand of
the Lord came upon me.

As I looked, a stormwind came from the North, a huge cloud with flashing fire [enveloped in brightness], from the midst of which [the midst of the fire] something gleamed like electrum. Within it were figures resembling four living creatures that looked like this: their form was human. Then I heard the sound of their wings, like the roaring of mighty waters, like the voice of the Almighty. When they moved, the sound of the tumult was like the din of an army. [And when they stood still, they lowered their wings.]

Above the firmament over their heads, something like a throne could be seen, looking like sapphire. Upon it was seated, up above, one who had the appearance of a man. Upward from what resembled his waist I saw what gleamed like electrum; downward from what resembled his waist I saw what looked like fire; he was surrounded with splendor. Like the bow which appears in the cloud on a rainy day was the splendor that surrounded him. Such was the vision of the likeness of the glory of the Lord.— This is the Word of the Lord. ℞. **Thanks be to God.** ℣

Responsorial Psalm   Ps 148, 1-2. 11-12. 12-14. 14

℞. **Heaven and earth are filled with your glory.**

Praise the Lord from the heavens,
  praise him in the heights;
Praise him, all you his angels,
  praise him, all you his hosts. — ℞

Let the kings of the earth and all peoples,
  the princes and all the judges of the earth,
Young men too, and maidens,
  old men and boys, — ℞

Praise the name of the Lord,
  for his name alone is exalted;
His majesty is above earth and heaven, — ℞
And he has lifted up the horn of his people.

Be this his praise from all his faithful ones,
from the children of Israel, the people close to
him. Alleluia. — ℟ ℣

℟. Or: **Alleluia.. ℣**

GOSPEL   Mt 17, 22-27

See p. 210.

TUESDAY OF THE NINETEENTH WEEK
IN ORDINARY TIME

READING I   Ez 2, 8—3, 4

Ezekiel is chosen and commissioned by God to be his messenger, his
prophet to the Israelites. The prophets were sent by God to remind
the people of their responsibilities toward God. This is a rewarding
task, but never easy or painless.

A reading from the book of the prophet Ezekiel

The Lord said, "As for you, son of man, obey me
when I speak to you: be not rebellious like this
house of rebellion, but open your mouth and eat
what I shall give you.

It was then I saw a hand stretched out to me, in
which was a written scroll which he unrolled before me. It was covered with writing front and back,
and written on it was: Lamentation and wailing and
woe!

He said to me: Son of man, eat what is before
you; eat this scroll, then go, speak to the house of
Israel. So I opened my mouth and he gave me the
scroll to eat. Son of man, he then said to me, feed
your belly and fill your stomach with this scroll I
am giving you. I ate it, and it was as sweet as honey
in my mouth. He said: Son of man, go now to the
house of Israel, and speak my words to them.—
This is the Word of the Lord. ℟. **Thanks be to God. ℣**

Responsorial Psalm   Ps 119, 14. 24. 72. 103. 111. 131

℟. (103) **How sweet to my taste is your promise!**

In the way of your decrees I rejoice,
   as much as in all riches. — ℟

Yes, your decrees are my delight;
   they are my counselors. — ℟

The law of your mouth is to me more precious
   than thousands of gold and silver pieces. — ℟

How sweet to my palate are your promises,
   sweeter than honey to my mouth! — ℟

Your decrees are my inheritance forever;
   the joy of my heart they are. — ℟

I gasp with open mouth
   in my yearning for your commands. — ℟ ℣

GOSPEL   Mt 18, 1-5. 10. 12-14

See p. 212.

WEDNESDAY OF THE NINETEENTH WEEK IN ORDINARY TIME

READING I   Ez 9, 1-7; 10, 18-22

Ezekiel's work begins to unfold. God wants things to be straightened out; he wants the lines to be drawn. The people will have to make a very fundamental choice—either be faithful to God, or die.

A reading from the book of the prophet Ezekiel

The Lord cried loud for me to hear: Come, you scourges of the city! With that I saw six men coming from the direction of the upper gate which faces the north, each with a destroying weapon in his hand. In their midst was a man dressed in linen, with a writer's case at his waist. They entered and stood beside the bronze altar. Then he called to the man dressed in linen with the writer's case at his waist, saying to him: Pass through the city [through Jerusalem] and mark an X on the foreheads of those who moan and groan over all the abominations that are practiced within it. To the others I heard him say: Pass through the city after him and strike! Do not look on them with pity nor show any mercy! Old men, youths and maidens, women and children —wipe them out! But do not touch any marked with the X; begin at my sanctuary. So they began with the men [the elders] who were in front of the temple. Defile the temple, he said to them, and fill the courts with the slain; then go out and strike in the city.

Then the glory of the Lord left the threshold of the temple and rested upon the cherubim. These lifted their wings, and I saw them rise from the earth, the wheels rising along with them. They stood at the entrance of the eastern gate of the Lord's house, and the glory of the God of Israel was up above them. These were the living creatures I had seen beneath the God of Israel by the river Chebar, whom I now recognized to be cherubim. Each had four faces and four wings; something like human hands were under their wings. Their faces looked just like those I had seen by the river Chebar; each one went straight forward.—This is the Word of the Lord. ℞. **Thanks be to God.** ⍖

Responsorial Psalm   Ps 113, 1-2. 3-4. 5-6

℞. (4) **The glory of the Lord is higher than the skies.**

Praise, you servants of the Lord,
    praise the name of the Lord.
Blessed be the name of the Lord
    both now and forever. — ℞

From the rising to the setting of the sun
    is the name of the Lord to be praised.
High above all nations is the Lord;
    above the heavens is his glory. — ℞

Who is like the Lord, our God, who is enthroned on
  high
  and looks upon the heavens and the earth below — ℟ ✝

℟. Or: **Alleluia.** ✝

GOSPEL   Mt 18, 15-20

See p. 214.

THURSDAY OF THE NINETEENTH WEEK
IN ORDINARY TIME

READING I   Ez 12, 1-2

Ezekiel is reminded by God that his mission as spokesman for God is
to a rebellious people. The prophet can expect to be rebuked by them.

A reading from the book of the prophet Ezekiel

The word of the Lord came to me: Son of man, you
live in the midst of a rebellious house; they have
eyes to see but do not see, and ears to hear but do
not hear, for they are a rebellious house.—This is
the Word of the Lord. ℟. **Thanks be to God.** ✝

Responsorial Psalm   Ps 78, 56-57. 58-59. 61-62

℟. (7) **Do not forget the works of the Lord!**

They tempted and rebelled against God the Most
  High,
  and kept not his decrees.
They turned back and were faithless like their fathers;
  they recoiled like a treacherous bow. — ℟

They angered him with their high places
  and with their idols roused his jealousy.
God heard and was enraged
  and utterly rejected Israel. — ℟

And he surrendered his strength into captivity,
  his glory into the hands of the foe.
He abandoned his people to the sword
  and was enraged against his inheritance. — ℟. ↓

GOSPEL   Mt 18, 21—19, 1

See p. 217.

FRIDAY OF THE NINETEENTH WEEK
IN ORDINARY TIME

READING I   Ez 16, 1-15. 60. 63

Ezekiel tries to point out to the people the extent of God's dedication to them. He uses a lengthy allegory or parable in which the nation
of Israel is described as a lone young girl, ignored and abandoned.
God rescues her from her abandonment. God chooses her, loves her,
saves her.

A reading from the book of the prophet Ezekiel

The word of the Lord came to me: Son of man, make
known to Jerusalem her abominations. Thus says the
Lord God to Jerusalem: By origin of birth you are
of the land of Canaan; your father was an Amorite
and your mother a Hittite. As for your birth, the
day you were born your navel cord was not cut;
you were neither washed with water nor anointed,
nor were you rubbed with salt, nor swathed in
swaddling clothes. No one looked on you with pity
or compassion to do any of these things for you.
Rather, you were thrown out on the ground as something loathsome, the day you were born.

Then I passed by and saw you weltering in your
blood. I said to you: Live in your blood and grow
like a plant in the field. You grew and developed,
you came to the age of puberty; your breasts were
formed, your hair had grown, but you were still
stark naked. Again I passed by you and saw that

you were now old enough for love. So I spread the corner of my cloak over you to cover your nakedness; I swore an oath to you and entered into a covenant with you; you became mine, says the Lord God. Then I bathed you with water, washed away your blood, and anointed you with oil. I clothed you with an embroidered gown, put sandals of fine leather on your feet; I gave you a fine linen sash and silk robes to wear. I adorned you with jewelry: I put bracelets on your arms, a necklace about your neck, a ring in your nose, pendants in your ears, and a glorious diadem upon your head. Thus you were adorned with gold and silver; your garments were of fine linen, silk, and embroidered cloth. Fine flour, honey, and oil were your food. You were exceedingly beautiful, with the dignity of a queen. You were renowned among the nations for your beauty, perfect as it was, because of my splendor which I had bestowed on you, says the Lord God.

But you were captivated by your own beauty, you used your renown to make yourself a harlot, and you lavished your harlotry on every passer-by, whose own you became. Yet I will remember the covenant I made with you when you were a girl, and I will set up an everlasting covenant with you, that you may remember and be covered with confusion, and that you may be utterly silenced for shame when I pardon you for all you have done, says the Lord God.—This is the Word of the Lord. ℟. **Thanks be to God.** ℣

OR

READING I   Ez 16, 59-63

The Lord promises to keep his covenant which was broken by the people. He will reestablish his covenant that the people may know that he is Lord. They will be covered with confusion, but the Lord will pardon.

A reading from the book of the prophet Ezekiel

Thus speaks the Lord God: I will deal with you according to what you have done, you who despised your oath, breaking a covenant. Yet I will remember the covenant I made with you when you were a girl, and I will set up an everlasting covenant with you. Then you shall remember your conduct and be ashamed when I take your sisters, those older and younger than you, and give them to you as daughters, even though I am not bound by my covenant with you. For I will re-establish my covenant with you, that you may know that I am the Lord, that you may remember and be covered with confusion, and that you may be utterly silenced for shame when I pardon you for all you have done, says the Lord God.—This is the Word of the Lord.
℟. **Thanks be to God.** ℣

Responsorial Psalm   Is 12, 2-3. 4. 5-6

℟. **You have turned from your anger to comfort me.**

God indeed is my savior;
    I am confident and unafraid.
My strength and my courage is the Lord,
    and he has been my savior.
With joy you will draw water. —℟

Give thanks to the Lord, acclaim his name;
    among the nations make known his deeds,
    proclaim how exalted is his name. — ℟

Sing praise to the Lord for his glorious achievement;
    let this be known throughout all the earth.
Shout with exultation, O city of Zion,
    for great in your midst
    is the Holy One of Israel! — ℟ ℣

GOSPEL   Mt 19, 3-12

See p. 220.

SATURDAY OF THE NINETEENTH WEEK
IN ORDINARY TIME

READING I   Ez 18, 1-10. 13. 30-32

All life belongs to the Lord. If a man obeys the law and is virtuous, he shall live, and those who sin shall not live. The Lord will judge each one according to his ways.

A reading from the book of the prophet Ezekiel

The word of the Lord came to me: Son of man, what is the meaning of this proverb that you recite in the land of Israel:

"Fathers have eaten green grapes,
    thus their children's teeth are on edge"?

As I live, says the Lord God: I swear that there shall no longer be anyone among you who will repeat this proverb in Israel. For all lives are mine; the life of the father is like the life of the son, both are mine; only the one who sins shall die.

If a man is virtuous—if he does what is right and just, if he does not eat on the mountains, nor raise his eyes to the idols of the house of Israel; if he does not defile his neighbor's wife, nor have relations with a woman in her menstrual period; if he oppresses no one, gives back the pledge received for a debt, commits no robbery; if he gives food to the hungry and clothes the naked; if he does not lend at interest nor exact usury; if he holds off from evildoing, judges fairly between a man and his opponent; if he lives by my statutes and is careful to observe my ordinances, that man is virtuous—he shall surely live, says the Lord God.

But if he begets a son who is a thief, a murderer, or lends at interest and exacts usury—this son certainly shall not live. Because he practiced all these abominations, he shall surely die; his death shall be his own fault.

Therefore I will judge you, house of Israel, each one according to this ways, says the Lord God. Turn

and be converted from all your crimes, that they
may be no cause of guilt for you. Cast away from
you all the crimes you have committed, and make
for yourselves a new heart and a new spirit. Why
should you die, O house of Israel? For I have no
pleasure in the death of anyone who dies, says the
Lord God. Return and live!—This is the Word of the
Lord. ℟. **Thanks be to God.** ⅴ

Responsorial Psalm Ps 51, 12-13. 14-15. 18-19

℟. (12) **Create a clean heart in me, O God.**

A clean heart create for me, O God,
  and a steadfast spirit renew within me.
Cast me not out from your presence,
  and your holy spirit take not from me. — ℟

Give me back the joy of your salvation,
  and a willing spirit sustain in me.
I will teach transgressors your ways,
  and sinners shall return to you. — ℟

For you are not pleased with sacrifices;
  should I offer a holocaust, you would not accept it.
My sacrifice, O God, is a contrite spirit;
  a heart contrite and humbled, O Lord, you will
    not spurn. — ℟ ⅴ

GOSPEL Mt 19, 13-15

See p. 223.

INTRODUCTION FOR 20th TO 24th WEEK

The Second Epistle to the Thessalonians—*The first Epistle (see p. 225) failed to quiet the doubts and fears of the Thessalonians, and so Paul hastened to supply them with fuller information on the subject of the "parousia," or Second Coming of Christ. He informed them that the "parousia" was not at hand. It could not take place until a great apostasy occurred and Antichrist appeared. Some of the Thessalonians who were convinced that the Second Coming of Christ was at hand thought it useless to work, and consequently lived irregularly. Paul condemned this practice, and ordered the offenders to be corrected. He urged all to adhere to his teachings, whether these were given orally or in writing.*

The First Epistle to the Corinthians—*This Epistle was written by Paul about the year 56 to put an end to disorders in the Corinthian Church and to answer questions put to him in a letter from that community. It is invaluable for the light it sheds on Paul's mind and character, its vigorous presentation of the Gospel, and the vivid picture it gives of the actual life of a particular local church in the middle of the 1st century. In large measure, the questions asked of Paul no longer concern us, but Paul deals with each question on a higher level. It is from what constitutes the heart of the Christian message that he seeks to resolve each particular case. Accordingly, what would have been mere cases of conscience or problems concerning liturgical rules become, thanks to Paul's genius, an occasion for profound thoughts concerning true liberty, the sanctification of the body, the primacy of love, union with Christ, etc.*

From one end of the Epistle to the other, we see the new spirit of the Gospel affirmed in all its originality and freedom and placed against the practices of Judaism and the errors of the paganism of its time. *In the hymn in honor of love, the religious thought reaches the height attained by Jesus himself in his exaltation and praise of love—the ideal and most pure form of the love of God.*

The Gospel of Luke—*Many scholars discern in the Lucan Gospel and Acts of the Apostles an apologetic strain presumably directed against unfounded criticisms of Christian teaching. Written after the persecution of Nero that began in 64 A.D. and caused hostility toward Christians throughout the empire, Luke-Acts reveal that Jesus himself was accounted innocent by the Roman governor Pontius Pilate (Lk 23, 4. 15. 22), and that St. Paul, founder of many Christian communities in the empire, was often acquitted by the Roman magistrates of charges against him (Acts 16, 36; 18, 12-17; 25, 26; 26, 32).*

The evangelist portrays Christianity, not as a political movement, nor as a sect organized for an initiated few, but as a religious faith open to all men. His portrait of Jesus, drawn from the Gospel tradition, manifests the Savior's concern for humanity, and his identification with the poor, the outcast, and the criminal. Although the apologetic thought in Luke's writings must be acknowledged, it was nevertheless not his chief purpose to produce an apology for Christianity.

Luke wants to present the history of salvation from the beginnings of the world until the return of Christ. For Luke, this history comprises three great periods which he clearly distinguishes: "The Law and the Prophets were in force until John" (16, 16); the time of Christ, from his coming on earth until his Ascension; finally, the time of the Church whose foundations were laid in the preceding period, and which is unfolding fully from that time on.

In this history it is the coming of Christ that marks the truly decisive turning point; it constitutes the "middle of the times." During the time of expectation

*men had fixed their eyes on the "middle of the times"
that was to come. During the time of the Church, men
look backward with their eyes on Jesus. The life of
Jesus becomes for the Church a sort of prototype
of her own life and a model for every member. It is
a question of realizing, of fulfilling from day to day,
what Jesus has lived and what he has taught (9, 23),
until his final return.*

*Unlike the other evangelists, Luke presents no
main thesis. He is content to let the material of the
gospel narrative speak for itself without any argu-
mentative intrusion of his own. The correct understanding of the importance of the Christian gospel is
delicately introduced into the traditional material.
By aligning Jesus' birth (2, 1ff) and the preaching of
John the Baptizer (3, 1f) with the facts of secular
history, the evangelist indicates that the gospel tradition did not originate in myth about gods, but was
lived out by Jesus of Nazareth in the real world
wherein all men are born, struggle over the meaning
of their existence, and die. He depicts Jesus as reso-
lutely facing the reality which that world had in store
for him (9, 51). Luke also, in harmony with the growing realization of the Christian communities of his
time, removes the concept of the proximate parousia
so prominent in Mark 13. But neither these concepts
nor any particular aspects of Jesus' teaching that
Luke chooses to emphasize are presented in any but
a serene fashion. His reverence extends, not only to
Jesus as God's Son (1, 35), and to the invisible persons
of the Father (11, 2) and the Holy Spirit (11, 13), but
also to humanity itself as the fruitful recipient of
God's word.*

*No other evangelist has placed such emphasis on
the prophetic word of Jesus; no other is so optimistic
over the favorable response it is destined to receive.
Nothing that the divine word enacts in history can
fail (1, 37). The word of Jesus on love of enemies*

(6, 27-42) is seen as the only weapon which the small Christian communities of Luke's time possess to combat the forces of persecution. The word of God is the teaching of Jesus, to be planted in the hearts of men (8, 11). And it is the function of the Christian community (24, 27) to confront humanity with this word, which undergoes vicissitudes but inevitably finds out those who will hear, believe, and act (8, 15. 21; 11, 28).

The parables that are proper to Luke are among the best and most popular passages in Scripture— namely, the Prodigal Son, the Good Samaritan, and the Publican and the Pharisee. If we did not have Luke's prologue, we would know almost nothing about the childhood of Jesus, nor about that of John the Baptizer, and Mary for us would be only a name. His story of the Passion, sometimes closer to that of John than to that of Matthew, gives us important details that are not found elsewhere. Finally, Luke is the only one who mentions certain apparitions of Christ—for example, to the disciples of Emmaus.

If, then, we make a careful examination of the third Gospel, in comparison with those of Matthew and Mark, we cannot help noticing an essential feature of Luke's Gospel that a superficial reading would not reveal—namely, his extraordinary concern about poverty. We could similarly point to a number of other features that justify the titles that have been given to this Gospel, such as the Gospel of Universal Salvation, the Gospel of Philanthropy, the Gospel of Mercy, and the Gospel of Joy.

————————

MONDAY OF THE TWENTIETH WEEK
IN ORDINARY TIME

READING I   Ez 24, 15-24

Ezekiel was a prophet in Babylon for the deported Israelites. The temple will be destroyed; their customs will all be changed; the sons and daughters they left behind will be killed. They are undergoing a long season of dire punishment for sin.

A reading from the book of the prophet Ezekiel

The word of the Lord came to me: Son of man, by a sudden blow I am taking away from you the delight of your eyes, but do not mourn or weep or shed any tears. Groan in silence, make no lament for the dead, bind on your turban, put your sandals on your feet, do not cover your beard, and do not eat the customary bread. That evening my wife died, and the next morning I did as I had been commanded. Then the people asked me, "Will you not tell us what all these things that you are doing mean for us?" I therefore spoke to the people that morning, saying to them: Thus the word of the Lord came to me: Say to the house of Israel: Thus says the Lord God: I will now desecrate my sanctuary, the stronghold of your pride, the delight of your eyes, the desire of your soul. The sons and daughters you left behind shall fall by the sword. Ezekiel shall be a sign for you: all that he did you shall do when it happens. Thus you shall know that I am the Lord. You shall do as I have done, not covering your beards nor eating the customary bread. Your turbans shall remain on your heads, your sandals on your feet. You shall not mourn or weep, but you shall rot away because of your sins and groan one to another.— This is the Word of the Lord. ℟. **Thanks be to God.** ℣

Responsorial Psalm   Dt 32, 18-19. 20. 21

℟. (18) **You have forgotten God who gave you birth.**

You were unmindful of the Rock that begot you.
    You forgot the God who gave you birth.
When the Lord saw this, he was filled with loathing
    and anger toward his sons and daughters. — ℟

"I will hide my face from them," he said,
    "and see what will then become of them.
What a fickle race they are,
    sons with no loyalty in them! — ℟

Since they have provoked me with their 'no-god'
    and angered me with their vain idols,
I will provoke them with a 'no-people';
    with a foolish nation I will anger them." — ℟ ✠

GOSPEL   Mt 19, 16-22

See p. 229.

TUESDAY OF THE TWENTIETH WEEK
IN ORDINARY TIME

READING I   Ez 28, 1-10

Ezekiel has the backing of the Lord and he is afraid of no one, not
even the king of Tyre. The king of Israel, Ahab, had married Jezebel,
the daughter of the king of Tyre, with disastrous effects on the
religion of Israel.

A reading from the book of the prophet Ezekiel

The word of the Lord came to me: Son of man, say
to the prince of Tyre: Thus says the Lord God:
Because you are haughty of heart,
    and say, "A god am I!
I occupy a godly throne
    in the heart of the sea!"—
And yet you are a man, and not a god,
    however you may think yourself like a god.

Oh yes, you are wiser than Daniel,
  there is no secret that is beyond you.
By your wisdom and your intelligence
  you have made riches for yourself;
You have put gold and silver
  into your treasuries.
By your great wisdom applied to your trading
  you have heaped up your riches;
  your heart has grown haughty from your riches—
    therefore thus says the Lord God:
Because you have thought yourself
  to have the mind of a god,
Therefore I will bring against you
  foreigners, the most barbarous of nations.
They shall draw their swords
  against your beauteous wisdom,
  they shall run them through your splendid apparel.
They shall thrust you down to the pit, there to die
  a bloodied corpse, in the heart of the sea.
Will you then say, "I am a god!"
  when you face your murderers?
No, you are a man, not a god,
  handed over to those who will slay you.
You shall die the death of the uncircumcised
  at the hands of foreigners,
  for I have spoken,
    says the Lord God.
This is the Word of the Lord. ℟. **Thanks be to God.** ℣

Responsorial Psalm   Dt 32, 26-27. 27-28. 30. 35-36

℟. (39) **It is I who deal death and give life.**
"I would have said, 'I will make an end of them
  and blot out their name from men's memories,'
Had I not feared the insolence of their enemies,
  feared that these foes would mistakenly boast,—℟
'Our own hand won the victory;
  the Lord had nothing to do with it.'"

For they are a people devoid of reason,
    having no understanding. — ℞

"How could one man rout a thousand,
    or two men put ten thousand to flight,
Unless it was because their Rock sold them
    and the Lord delivered them up?" — ℞

Close at hand is the day of their disaster,
    and their doom is rushing upon them!
Surely, the Lord shall do justice for his people;
    on his servants he shall have pity. — ℞ ℣

GOSPEL   Mt 19, 23-30

See p. 231.

_____

WEDNESDAY OF THE TWENTIETH WEEK
IN ORDINARY TIME

READING I   Ez 34, 1-11

Shepherd was the common biblical term for leaders. Power corrupts.
Here Ezekiel condemns the selfish shepherds. People have to account
for responsibilities.

A reading from the book of the prophet Ezekiel

The word of the Lord came to me: Son of man,
prophesy against the shepherds of Israel, in these
words prophesy to them [to the shepherds]: Thus
says the Lord God: Woe to the shepherds of Israel
who have been pasturing themselves! Should not
shepherds, rather, pasture sheep? You have fed off
their milk, worn their wool, and slaughtered the
fatlings, but the sheep you have not pastured. You
did not strengthen the weak nor heal the sick nor
bind up the injured. You did not bring back the
strayed nor seek the lost, but you lorded it over
them harshly and brutally. So they were scattered
for lack of a shepherd, and became food for all the

wild beasts. My sheep were scattered and wandered over all the mountains and high hills; my sheep were scattered over the whole earth, with no one to look after them or to search for them.

Therefore, shepherds, hear the word of the Lord: As I live, says the Lord God, because my sheep have been given over to pillage, and because my sheep have become food for every wild beast, for lack of a shepherd; because my shepherds did not look after my sheep, but pastured themselves and did not pasture my sheep; because of this, shepherds, hear the word of the Lord: Thus says the Lord God: I swear I am coming against these shepherds. I will claim my sheep from them and put a stop to their shepherding my sheep so that they may no longer pasture themselves. I will save my sheep, that they may no longer be food for their mouths.

For thus says the Lord God: I myself will look after and tend my sheep.—This is the Word of the Lord. ℟. **Thanks be to God.** ℣

Responsorial Psalm   Ps 23, 1-3. 3-4. 5. 6

℟. (1) **The Lord is my shepherd;**
   there is nothing I shall want.

The Lord is my shepherd; I shall not want.
   In verdant pastures he gives me repose;
Beside restful waters he leads me;
   he refreshes my soul. — ℟

He guides me in right paths
   for his name's sake.
Even though I walk in the dark valley
   I fear not evil; for you are at my side
With your rod and your staff
   that give me courage. — ℟

You spread the table before me
   in the sight of my foes;
You anoint my head with oil;
   my cup overflows. — ℟

Only goodness and kindness follow me
 all the days of my life;
And I shall dwell in the house of the Lord
 for years to come. — ℟ ✝

GOSPEL   Mt 20, 1-16

See p. 234.

THURSDAY OF THE TWENTIETH WEEK IN ORDINARY TIME

READING I   Ez 36, 23-28

Ezekiel reminds the people of the ever-present need of regeneration and purification. This desirable change is brought about by God's action in grace and enlightenment. The Lord will cleanse his people.

A reading from the book of the prophet Ezekiel

The Lord said: I will prove the holiness of my great name, profaned among the nations, in whose midst you have profaned it. Thus the nations shall know that I am the Lord, says the Lord God, when in their sight I prove my holiness through you. For I will take you away from among the nations, gather you from all the foreign lands, and bring you back to your own land. I will sprinkle clean water upon you to cleanse you from all your impurities, and from all your idols I will cleanse you. I will give you a new heart and place a new spirit within you, taking from your bodies your stony hearts and giving you natural hearts. I will put my spirit within you and make you live by my statutes, careful to observe my decrees. You shall live in the land I gave your fathers; you shall be my people, and I will be your God.—This is the Word of the Lord. ℟. **Thanks be to God.** ✝

Responsorial Psalm   Ps 51, 12-13. 14-15. 18-19

℞. (Ez 36, 25) **I will pour clean water on you
  and wash away all your sins.**

A clean heart create for me, O God,
  and a steadfast spirit renew within me.
Cast me not out from your presence,
  and your holy spirit take not from me. — ℞

Give me back the joy of your salvation,
  and a willing spirit sustain in me.
I will teach transgressors your ways,
  and sinners shall return to you. — ℞

For you are not pleased with sacrifices;
  should I offer a holocaust, you would not accept it,
My sacrifice, O God, is a contrite spirit;
  a heart contrite and humbled, O God, you will not
    spurn. — ℞ ↓

GOSPEL   Mt 22, 1-14

See p. 236.

FRIDAY OF THE TWENTIETH WEEK
IN ORDINARY TIME

READING I   Ez 37, 1-14

This is Ezekiel's prophecy—the vision of the dry bones. It is aimed
at the Jewish exiles who were losing hope of returning to their
homeland. They assumed they would die where they were and become
nothing but a field of bones.

A reading from the book of the prophet Ezekiel

The hand of the Lord came upon me, and he led me
out in the spirit of the Lord and set me in the center
of the plain, which was now filled with bones. He
made me walk among them in every direction so
that I saw how many they were on the surface of
the plain. How dry they were! He asked me: Son

of man, can these bones come to life? "Lord God," I answered, "you alone know that." Then he said to me: Prophesy over these bones, and say to them: Dry bones, hear the word of the Lord! Thus says the Lord God to these bones: See! I will bring spirit into you, that you may come to life. I will put sinews upon you, make flesh grow over you, cover you with skin, and put spirit in you so that you may come to life and know that I am the Lord. I prophesied as I had been told, and even as I was prophesying I heard a noise; it was a rattling as the bones came together, bone joining bone. I saw the sinews and the flesh come upon them, and the skin cover them, but there was no spirit in them. Then he said to me: Prophesy to the spirit, prophesy, son of man, and say to the spirit: Thus says the Lord God: From the four winds come, O spirit, and breathe into these slain that they may come to life. I prophesied as he told me, and the spirit came into them; they came alive and stood upright, a vast army. Then he said to me: Son of man, these bones are the whole house of Israel. They have been saying, "Our bones are dried up, our hope is lost, and we are cut off." Therefore, prophesy and say to them: Thus says the Lord God: O my people, I will open your graves and have you rise from them, and bring you back to the land of Israel. Then you shall know that I am the Lord, when I open your graves and have you rise from them, O my people! I will put my spirit in you that you may live, and I will settle you upon your land; thus you shall know that I am the Lord. I have promised, and I will do it, says the Lord.— This is the Word of the Lord. ℟. **Thanks be to God.** ℣

Responsorial Psalm　　　　Ps 107, 2-3. 4-5. 6-7. 8-9

℟. (1) **Give thanks to the Lord,**
　his love is everlasting.

Let the redeemed of the Lord say,
  those whom he has redeemed from the hand of the
    foe
And gathered from the lands,
  from the east and the west, from the north and
    the south. — ℞

They went astray in the desert wilderness;
  the way to an inhabited city they did not find.
Hungry and thirsty,
  their life was wasting away within them.—℞.

They cried to the Lord in their distress;
  from their straits he rescued them.
And he led them by a direct way
  to reach an inhabited city. — ℞

Let them give thanks to the Lord for his kindness
  and his wondrous deeds to the children of men,
Because he satisfied the longing soul
  and filled the hungry soul with good things. — ℞ ℣

℞. Or: **Alleluia.** ℣

GOSPEL   Mt 22, 34-40

See p. 239. ———————

SATURDAY OF THE TWENTIETH WEEK
IN ORDINARY TIME

READING I   Ez 43, 1-7

Ezekiel tells of the glorious restoration of the new Israel after the
exile would be over. The Lord enters in all his majesty and promises
to dwell in the rebuilt temple.

A reading from the book of the prophet Ezekiel

The angel led me to the gate which faces the east,
and there I saw the glory of the God of Israel coming from the east. I heard a sound like the roaring
of many waters, and the earth shone with his glory.
The vision was like that which I had seen when he
came to destroy the city, and like that which I had
seen by the river Chebar. I fell prone as the glory

of the Lord entered the temple by way of the gate which faces the east, but spirit lifted me up and brought me to the inner court. And I saw that the temple was filled with the glory of the Lord. Then I heard someone speaking to me from the temple, while the man stood beside me. The voice said to me: Son of man, this is where my throne shall be, this is where I will set the soles of my feet; here I will dwell among the Israelites forever.—This is the Word of the Lord. ℟. **Thanks be to God.** ℣

Responsorial Psalm   Ps 85, 9-10. 11-12. 13-14

℟. (10) **The glory of the Lord will dwell in our land.**

I will hear what God proclaims;
    the Lord—for he proclaims peace.
Near indeed is his salvation to those who fear him,
    glory dwelling in our land. — ℟

Kindness and truth shall meet;
    justice and peace shall kiss.
Truth shall spring out of the earth,
    and justice shall look down from heaven. — ℟

The Lord himself will give his benefits;
    our land shall yield its increase.
Justice shall walk before him,
    and salvation, along the way of his steps. — ℟ ℣

GOSPEL   Mt 23, 1-12

See p. 242.

MONDAY OF THE TWENTY-FIRST WEEK IN ORDINARY TIME

READING I   2 Thes 1, 1-5. 11-12

Paul greets the Thessalonians. He thanks God for their mutual love and especially for their constant faith in spite of persecution and trial. They suffer for the kingdom of God.

The beginning of the second letter of Paul to the Thessalonians

Paul, Silvanus and Timothy, to the church of the Thessalonians, who belong to God our Father and the Lord Jesus Christ. Grace and peace be yours from God the Father and the Lord Jesus Christ. It is no more than right that we thank God unceasingly for you, brothers, because your faith grows apace and your mutual love increases; so much so that in God's communities we can boast of your constancy and your faith in persecution and trial. You endure these as an expression of God's just judgment, in order to be found worthy of his reign—it is for his kingdom you suffer.

We pray for you always that our God may make you worthy of his call, and fulfill by his power ever honest intention and work of faith. In this way the name of our Lord Jesus may be glorified in you and you in him, in accord with the gracious gift of our God and of the Lord Jesus Christ.— This is the Word of the Lord. ℟. **Thanks be to God.** ℣

Responsorial Psalm   Ps 96, 1-2. 2-3. 4-5

℟. (3) **Proclaim his marvelous deeds to all the nations.**

Sing to the Lord a new song;
    sing to the Lord, all you lands;
    sing to the Lord; bless his name. — ℟

Announce his salvation, day after day.
    Tell his glory among the nations;
    among all peoples, his wondrous deeds. —℟

For great is the Lord and highly to be praised;
    awesome is he, beyond all gods.
For all the gods of the nations are things of nought,
    but the Lord made the heavens. — ℟ ℣

GOSPEL Mt 23, 13-22

Sec p. 244.

TUESDAY OF THE TWENTY-FIRST WEEK
IN ORDINARY TIME

READING I 2 Thes 2, 1-3. 14-16

The Thessalonians seem to have misunderstood something Paul said about the return of Christ. Paul tells them to hang on tight to the traditions they received. Evidently the Thessalonians were under pressure from fallen-aways and unbelievers.

A reading from the second letter of Paul to the
Thessalonians

On the question of the coming of our Lord Jesus Christ and our being gathered to him, we beg you, brothers, not to be so easily agitated or terrified, whether by an oracular utterance, or rumor, or a letter alleged to be ours, into believing that the day of the Lord is here.

Let no one seduce you, no matter how.

God called you through our preaching of the good news so that you might achieve the glory of our Lord Jesus Christ. Therefore, brothers, stand firm. Hold fast to the traditions you received from us, either by our word or by letter. May our Lord Jesus Christ himself, may God our Father who loved us and in his mercy gave us eternal consolation and hope, console your hearts and strengthen them for every good work and word.—This is the Word of the Lord. ℟. **Thanks be to God.** ℣

Responsorial Psalm Ps 96, 10. 11-12. 13

℟. (13) **The Lord comes to judge the earth.**

Say among the nations: The Lord is king.
He has made the world firm, not to be moved;
  he governs the peoples with equity. — ℟

Let the heavens be glad and the earth rejoice;
    let the sea and what fills it resound;
    let the plains be joyful and all that is in them!
Then shall all the trees of the forest exult. — ℟

Before the Lord, for he comes;
    for he comes to rule the earth.
He shall rule the world with justice
    and the peoples with his constancy. — ℟ ℣

GOSPEL   Mt 23, 23-26

See p. 246.

WEDNESDAY OF THE TWENTY-FIRST WEEK
IN ORDINARY TIME

READING I   2 Thes 3, 6-10. 16-18

Paul wants the faithful to have nothing to do with those who have
wandered from his teaching and from what he calls tradition. The
apostle also says that anyone who will not work should likewise not
eat.

A reading from the second letter of Paul to the
Thessalonians

We command you, brothers, in the name of the Lord
Jesus Christ, to avoid any brother who wanders
from the straight path and does not follow the tradition you received from us. You know how you
ought to imitate us. We did not live lives of disorder when we were among you, nor depend on anyone for food. Rather, we worked day and night, laboring to the point of exhaustion so as not to impose
on any of you. Not that we had no claim on you,
but that we might present ourselves as an example
for you to imitate. Indeed, when we were with you
we used to lay down the rule that anyone who would
not work should not eat.
    May he who is the Lord of peace give you conti-

nued peace in every possible way. The Lord be with you all.

This greeting is in my own hand—Paul's. I append this signature to every letter I write.

May the grace of our Lord Jesus Christ be with you all.—This is the Word of the Lord. ℟. **Thanks be to God.** ℣

Responsorial Psalm   Ps 128, 1-2. 4-5

℟. (1) **Happy are those who fear the Lord.**

Happy are you who fear the Lord,
    who walk in his ways!
For you shall eat the fruit of your handiwork;
    happy shall you be, and favored. — ℟

Behold, thus is the man blessed
    who fears the Lord.
The Lord bless you from Zion:
    may you see the prosperity of Jerusalem
    all the days of your life. — ℟ ℣

GOSPEL   Mt 23, 27-32

See p. 248.

THURSDAY OF THE TWENTY-FIRST WEEK IN ORDINARY TIME

READING I   1 Cor 1, 1-9

Paul writes his first letter to the Corinthians in answer to several questions. He identifies the Christian and shows his permanent relation to Jesus Christ and to our heavenly Father. This serves as a good premise for anything he will tell them afterward.

The beginning of the first letter of Paul to the Corinthians

Paul, called by God's will to be an apostle of Christ Jesus, and Sosthenes our brother, send greetings to the church of God which is in Corinth; to you who have been consecrated in Christ Jesus and called to be a holy people, as to all those who, wherever they may be, call on the name of our Lord Jesus Christ, their Lord and ours. Grace and peace from God our Father and the Lord Jesus Christ.

I continually thank my God for you because of the favor he has bestowed on you in Christ Jesus, in whom you have been richly endowed with every gift of speech and knowledge. Likewise, the witness I bore to Christ has been so confirmed among you that you lack no spiritual gift as you wait for the revelation of our Lord Jesus Christ. He will strengthen you to the end, so that you will be blameless on the day of our Lord Jesus [Christ]. God is faithful, and it was he who called you to fellowship with his Son, Jesus Christ our Lord.—This is the Word of the Lord. ℟. **Thanks be to God.** ✣

Responsorial Psalm   Ps 145, 2-3. 4-5. 6-7

℟. (1) **I will praise your name for ever, Lord.**

Every day will I bless you,
  and I will praise your name forever and ever.
Great is the Lord and highly to be praised;
  his greatness is unsearchable. —℟

Generation after generation praises your works
  and proclaims your might.
They speak of the splendor of your glorious majesty
  and tell of your wondrous works. — ℟

They discourse of the power of your terrible deeds
  and declare your greatness.
They publish the fame of your abundant goodness
  and joyfully sing your justice. — ℟ ✣

GOSPEL   Mt 24, 42-51

See p. 250.

FRIDAY OF THE TWENTY-FIRST WEEK
IN ORDINARY TIME

READING I   1 Cor 1, 17-25

Paul says that the wisdom of men is foolishness to the world. What does the world know about the cross or eternal life? "God's folly is wiser than men, and his weakness more powerful." He reveals the substance of salvation.

A reading from the first letter of Paul to the
Corinthians

Christ did not send me to baptize but to preach the gospel—not with wordy "wisdom," however, lest the cross of Christ be rendered void of its meaning!

The message of the cross is complete absurdity to those who are headed for ruin, but to us who are experiencing salvation it is the power of God. Scripture says,

"I will destroy the wisdom of the wise,
    and thwart the cleverness of the clever."

Where is the wise man to be found? Where the scribe? Where is the master of worldly argument? Has not God turned the wisdom of this world into folly? Since in God's wisdom the world did not come to know him through its "wisdom," it pleased God to save those who believe through the absurdity of the preaching of the gospel. Yes, Jews demand "signs" and Greeks look for "wisdom," but we preach Christ crucified, a stumbling block to Jews, and an absurdity to Gentiles; but to those who are called, Jews and Greeks alike, Christ the power of God and the wisdom of God. For God's folly is wiser than men, and his weakness more powerful than men.—This is the Word of the Lord. ℟. **Thanks be to God.** ℣

Responsorial Psalm   Ps 33, 1-2. 4-5. 10. 11
℟. (5) **The earth is full of the goodness of the Lord.**
Exult, you just, in the Lord;
    praise from the upright is fitting.

Give thanks to the Lord on the harp;
  with the ten-stringed lyre chant his praises. — ℟
For upright is the word of the Lord,
  and all his works are trustworthy.
He loves justice and right;
  of the kindness of the Lord the earth is full. — ℟
The Lord brings to nought the plans of nations;
  he foils the designs of peoples.
But the plan of the Lord stands forever;
  the design of his heart, through all genera-
    tions. — ℟ ✟

GOSPEL   Mt 25, 1-13

See p. 252.

SATURDAY OF THE TWENTY-FIRST WEEK
IN ORDINARY TIME

READING I   1 Cor 1, 26-31

Paul continues his attempt to discourage vain disputes. God rejects
the wisdom of men and confounds them with the utmost simplicity.
Invariably, God seems to bring success out of failure, strength out
of weakness.

A reading from the first letter of Paul to the
Corinthians

Brothers, you are among those called. Consider your
own situation. Not many of you are wise, as men account wisdom; not many are influential; and surely
not many are well-born. God chose those whom the
world considers absurd to shame the wise; he singled out the weak of this world to shame the strong.
He chose the world's lowborn and despised, those
who count for nothing, to reduce to nothing those
who were something so that mankind can do no

boasting before God. God it is who has given you life in Christ Jesus. He has made him our wisdom and also our justice, our sanctification, and our redemption. This is just as you find it written, "Let him who would boast, boast in the Lord."—This is the Word of the Lord. ℟. **Thanks be to God.** ℣

Responsorial Psalm Ps 33, 12-13. 18-19. 20-21

℟. (12) **Happy the people the Lord has chosen to be his own.**

Happy the nation whose God is the Lord,
  the people he has chosen for his own inheritance.
From heaven the Lord looks down;
  he sees all mankind. — ℟

But see, the eyes of the Lord are upon those who
    fear him,
  upon those who hope for his kindness,
To deliver them from death
  and preserve them in spite of famine. — ℟

Our soul waits for the Lord,
  who is our help and our shield,
For in him our hearts rejoice;
  in his holy name we trust. — ℟ ℣

GOSPEL Mt 25, 14-30
See p. 254.

MONDAY OF THE TWENTY-SECOND WEEK
IN ORDINARY TIME

READING I 1 Cor 2, 1-5

Paul comes out bluntly with his message to the Corinthians: Jesus and him crucified. They must either accept it or reject it. Faith does not rest on the wisdom of men but relies on the power of God.

A reading from the first letter of Paul to the Corinthians

As for myself, brothers, when I came to you I did not come proclaiming God's testimony with any particular eloquence or "wisdom." No, I determined that while I was with you I would speak of nothing but Jesus Christ and him crucified. When I came among you it was in weakness and fear, and with much trepidation. My message and my preaching had none of the persuasive force of "wise" argumentation, but the convincing power of the Spirit. As a consequence, your faith rests not on the wisdom of men but on the power of God.—This is the Word of the Lord. ℞. **Thanks be to God.** ℣

Responsorial Psalm   Ps 119, 97. 98. 99. 100. 101. 102
℞. (97) **Lord, I love your commands.**

How I love your law, O Lord!
  It is my meditation all the day. — ℞

Your command has made me wiser than my enemies,
  for it is ever with me. — ℞.

I have more understanding than all my teachers
  when your decrees are my meditation. — ℞

I have more discernment than the elders,
  because I observe your precepts. — ℞

From every evil way I withhold my feet,
  that I may keep your words. — ℞

From your ordinances I turn not away,
  for you have instructed me. — ℞ ℣

GOSPEL   Lk 4, 16-30

See p. 257.

TUESDAY OF THE TWENTY-SECOND WEEK
IN ORDINARY TIME

READING I   1 Cor 2, 10-16

Paul expresses a truth of constant concern. It is the grace of God alone that should really be held in great respect. His Divine Spirit forms the test and measures the performance and the goal of perfection.

A reading from the first letter of Paul to the
Corinthians

The Spirit scrutinizes all matters, even the deep things of God. Who, for example, knows a man's innermost self but the man's own spirit within him? Similarly, no one knows what lies at the depths of God but the Spirit of God. The Spirit we have received is not the world's spirit but God's Spirit, helping us to recognize the gifts he has given us. We speak of these gifts, not in words of human wisdom but in words taught by the Spirit, thus interpreting spiritual things in spiritual terms. The natural man does not accept what is taught by the Spirit of God. For him, that is absurdity. He cannot come to know such teaching because it must be appraised in a spiritual way. The spiritual man, on the other hand, can appraise everything, though he himself can be appraised by no one. For "Who has known the mind of the Lord so as to instruct him?" But we have the mind of Christ.—This is the Word of the Lord. ℟. **Thanks be to God.** ℣

Responsorial Psalm   Ps 145, 8-9. 10-11. 12-13. 13-14
℟. (17) **The Lord is just in all his ways.**

The Lord is gracious and merciful,
    slow to anger and of great kindness.
The Lord is good to all
    and compassionate toward all his works. — ℟

Let all your works give you thanks, O Lord,
   and let your faithful ones bless you.
Let them discourse of the glory of your kingdom
   and speak of your might, — ℟
Making known to men your might
   and the glorious splendor of your kingdom.
Your kingdom is a kingdom for all ages,
   and your dominion endures through all generations. — ℟
The Lord is faithful in all his words
   and holy in all his works.
The Lord lifts up all who are falling
   and raises up all who are bowed down. — ℟ ⅴ

GOSPEL   Lk 4, 31-37

See p. 259.

WEDNESDAY OF THE TWENTY-SECOND WEEK IN ORDINARY TIME

READING I   1 Cor 3, 1-9

Paul reminds the Corinthians that they are stewards of God, placed
here by him in order to do his work. God is always with them. He is
interested in all that concerns them. They are co-workers with him,
and he gives the increase.

A reading from the first letter of Paul to the
                          Corinthians

Brothers, I could not talk to you as spiritual men
but only as men of flesh, as infants in Christ. I fed
you with milk, and did not give you solid food because you were not ready for it. You are not ready
for it even now, being still very much in a natural
condition. For as long as there are jealousy and
quarrels among you, are you not of the flesh? And
is not your behavior that of ordinary men? When
someone says, "I belong to Paul," and another, "I

belong to Apollos," is it not clear that you are still at the human level?

After all, who is Apollos? And who is Paul? Simply ministers through whom you became believers, each of them doing only what the Lord assigned him. I planted the seed and Apollos watered it, but God made it grow. This means that neither he who plants nor he who waters is of any special account, only God, who gives the growth. He who plants and he who waters work to the same end. Each will receive his wages in proportion to his toil. We are God's co-workers, while you are his cultivation, his building.—This is the Word of the Lord. ℞. **Thanks be to God.** ℣

Responsorial Psalm   Ps 33, 12-13. 14-15. 20-21

℞. (12) **Happy the people the Lord has chosen to be his own.**

Happy the nation whose God is the Lord,
  the people he has chosen for his own inheritance.
From heaven the Lord looks down;
  he sees all mankind. — ℞

From his fixed throne he beholds
  all who dwell on the earth,
He who fashioned the heart of each,
  he who knows all their works. — ℞

Our soul waits for the Lord,
  who is our help and our shield,
For in him our hearts rejoice;
  in his holy name we trust. — ℞ ℣

GOSPEL   Lk 4, 38-44

See p. 261.

THURSDAY OF THE TWENTY-SECOND WEEK IN ORDINARY TIME

READING I   1 Cor 3, 18-23

Those who do wrong know only grief, and woe follows. Paul constantly teaches that all things are for the people of God; still they belong to Christ, and Christ belongs to God.

A reading from the first letter of Paul to the Corinthians

Let no one delude himself. If any one of you thinks he is wise in a worldly way, he had better become a fool. In that way he will really be wise, for the wisdom of this world is absurdity with God. Scripture says, "He catches the wise in their craftiness"; and again, "The Lord knows how empty are the thoughts of the wise." Let there be no boasting about men. All things are yours, whether it be Paul, or Apollos, or Cephas, or the world, or life, or death, or the present, or the future: all these are yours, and you are Christ's and Christ is God's.—This is the Word of the Lord. ℟. **Thanks be to God.** ♥

Responsorial Psalm   Ps 24, 1-2. 3-4. 5-6

℟. (1) **To the Lord belongs the earth and all that fills it.**

The Lord's are the earth and its fullness;
    the world and those who dwell in it.
For he founded it upon the seas
    and established it upon the rivers. — ℟

Who can ascend the mountain of the Lord?
    or who may stand in his holy place?
He whose hands are sinless, whose heart is clean,
    who desires not what is vain. — ℟

He shall receive a blessing from the Lord,
    a reward from God his savior.

Such is the race that seeks for him,
that seeks the face of the God of Jacob. — ℟ ℣

GOSPEL Lk 5, 1-11

See p. 263.

FRIDAY OF THE TWENTY-SECOND WEEK
IN ORDINARY TIME

READING I 1 Cor 4, 1-5

All are stewards of God. In his commandments he has laid down what each must do and what each must avoid. He has implanted in his people an instinctive love of truth and justice. For all this each one must give an account.

A reading from the first letter of Paul to the Corinthians

Men should regard us as servants of Christ and administrators of the mysteries of God. The first requirement of an administrator is that he prove trustworthy. It matters little to me whether you or any human court pass judgment on me. I do not even pass judgment on myself. Mind you, I have nothing on my conscience. But that does not mean that I am declaring myself innocent. The Lord is the one to judge me, so stop passing judgment before the time of his return. He will bring to light what is hidden in darkness and manifest the intentions of hearts. At that time, everyone will receive his praise from God.—This is the Word of the Lord. ℟. **Thanks be to God.** ℣

Responsorial Psalm Ps 37, 3-4. 5-6. 27-28. 39-40

℟. (39) **The salvation of the just comes from the Lord.**

Trust in the Lord and do good,
that you may dwell in the land and enjoy security.

Take delight in the Lord,
  and he will grant you your heart's requests. — R̥
Commit to the Lord your way;
  trust in him, and he will act.
He will make justice dawn for you like the light;
  bright as the noonday shall be your vindication. — R̥

Turn from evil and do good,
  that you may abide forever;
For the Lord loves what is right,
  and forsakes not his faithful ones.
Criminals are destroyed
  and the posterity of the wicked is cut off. — R̥

The salvation of the just is from the Lord;
  he is their refuge in time of distress.
And the Lord helps them and delivers them;
  he delivers them from the wicked and saves them,
  because they take refuge in him. — R̥ ℣

GOSPEL   Lk 5, 33-39

See p. 265.

SATURDAY OF THE TWENTY-SECOND WEEK
IN ORDINARY TIME

READING I   1 Cor 4, 9-15

Paul conveys a truth which is at the very root of all practical Christianity. Humility is at the root of all virtue as pride is of all sin. Humility really consists in being convinced that all men are exactly what God knows them to be.

A reading from the first letter of Paul to the
                    Corinthians

God has put us apostles at the end of the line, like men doomed to die in the arena. We have become a spectacle to the universe, to angels and men alike. We are fools on Christ's account. Ah, but in Christ you are wise! We are the weak ones, you the strong! They honor you, while they sneer at us! Up to this very hour we go hungry and thirsty, poorly clad, roughly treated, wandering about homeless. We work hard at manual labor. When we are insulted we respond with a blessing. Persecution comes our way; we bear it patiently. We are slandered, and we try conciliation. We have become the world's refuse, the scum of all; that is the present state of affairs.

I am writing you in this way not to shame you but to admonish you as my beloved children. Granted you have ten thousand guardians in Christ, you have only one father. It was I who begot you in Christ Jesus through my preaching of the gospel.—This is the Word of the Lord. ℟. **Thanks be to God.** ℣

Responsorial Psalm   Ps 145, 17-18. 19-20. 21

℟. (18) **The Lord is near to all who call him.**

The Lord is just in all his ways
   and holy in all his works.
The Lord is near to all who call upon him,
   to all who call upon him in truth. — ℟

He fulfills the desire of those who fear him,
   he hears their cry and saves them.
The Lord keeps all who love him,
   but all the wicked he will destroy. — ℟

May my mouth speak the praise of the Lord,
   and may all flesh bless his holy name forever and
      ever. — ℟ ℣

GOSPEL   Lk 6, 1-5

See p. 267.

MONDAY OF THE TWENTY-THIRD WEEK IN ORDINARY TIME

READING I   1 Cor 5, 1-8

Christ has carried his cross. He has made it possible for his followers to breathe immortality. Evil is as yeast among the faithful who must purge it out and replace it with sincerity and truth.

A reading from the first letter of Paul to the Corinthians

It is actually reported that there is lewd conduct among you, of a kind not even found among the pagans—a man living with his own father's wife. Still you continue to be self-satisfied, instead of grieving and getting rid of the offender! As for me, though absent in body I am present in spirit, and have already passed sentence in the name of our Lord Jesus Christ on the man who did this deed. United in spirit with you and empowered by our Lord Jesus, I hand him over to Satan for the destruction of his flesh, so that his spirit may be saved on the day of the Lord.

This boasting of yours is an ugly thing. Do you not know that a little yeast has its effect all through the dough? Get rid of the old yeast to make of yourselves fresh dough, unleavened loaves, as it were; Christ our Passover has been sacrificed. Let us celebrate the feast not with the old yeast, that of corruption and wickedness, but with the unleavened bread of sincerity and truth. —This is the Word of the Lord. ℟. **Thanks be to God.** ℣

Responsorial Psalm   Ps 5, 5-6. 7. 12

℟. (9) **Lead me in your justice, Lord.**

For you, O God, delight not in wickedness;
    no evil man remains with you;
    the arrogant may not stand in your sight.
You hate all evildoers; — ℟

You destroy all who speak falsehood;
  the bloodthirsty and the deceitful
  the Lord abhors. — ℟
But let all who take refuge in you
  be glad and exult forever.
Protect them, that you may be the joy
  of those who love your name. — ℟ ⊻

GOSPEL   Lk 6, 6-11

See p. 269.

TUESDAY OF THE TWENTY-THIRD WEEK
IN ORDINARY TIME

READING I   1 Cor 6, 1-11

Paul admonishes the Corinthians about judging one another. He asks
who should judge and what court is competent. Sinners will not inherit the kingdom of heaven. Christians have been washed clean
in the blood of Jesus.

A reading from the first letter of Paul to the
                    Corinthians

How can anyone with a case against another dare
bring it for judgment to the wicked and not to
God's holy people? Do you not know that the believers will judge the world? If the judgment of the
world is to be yours, are you to be thought unworthy of judging in minor matters? Do you not know
that we are to judge angels? Surely, then, we are
up to deciding everyday affairs. If you have such
matters to decide, do you accept as judges those
who have no standing in the church? I say this in
an attempt to shame you. Can it be that there is no
one among you wise enough to settle a case between one member of the church and another? Must
brother drag brother into court, and before unbelievers at that? Why, the very fact that you have

lawsuits against one another is disastrous for you. Why not put up with injustice, and let yourselves be cheated? Instead, you yourselves injure and cheat your very own brothers. Can you not realize that the unholy will not fall heir to the kingdom of God? Do not deceive yourselves: no fornicators, idolators, or adulterers, no sodomites, thieves, misers, or drunkards, no slanderers or robbers will inherit God's kingdom. And such were some of you; but you have been washed, consecrated, justified in the name of our Lord Jesus Christ and in the Spirit of our God. —This is the Word of the Lord. ℟. **Thanks be to God.** ⍒

Responsorial Psalm   Ps 149, 1-2. 3-4. 5-6. 9

℟. (4) **The Lord takes delight in his people.**

Sing to the Lord a new song
   of praise in the assembly of the faithful.
Let Israel be glad in their maker,
   let the children of Zion rejoice in their king. — ℟

Let them praise his name in the festive dance,
   let them sing praise to him with timbrel and harp.
For the Lord loves his people,
   and he adorns the lowly with victory. — ℟

Let the faithful exult in glory;
   let them sing for joy upon their couches;
   let the high praises of God be in their throats.
This is the glory of all his faithful. Alleluia. — ℟ ⍒

℟. Or: **Alleluia.** ⍒

GOSPEL   Lk 6, 12-19

See p. 271.

See p. 271.

WEDNESDAY OF THE TWENTY-THIRD WEEK IN ORDINARY TIME

READING I   1 Cor 7, 25-31

The saints have found in Christ the secret of their holiness. In him they were fed life everlasting. No matter what state of life a Christian has chosen, he belongs to God. Complete happiness in heaven will be the result of absolute union with God and his teachings.

A reading from the first letter of Paul to the
Corinthians

I have not received any commandment from the Lord with respect to virgins, but I give my opinion as one who is trustworthy, thanks to the Lord's mercy. It is this: In the present time of stress it seems good to me for a person to continue as he is. Are you bound to a wife? Then do not seek your freedom. Are you free of a wife? If so, do not go in search of one. Should you marry, however, you will not be committing sin. Neither does a virgin commit a sin if she marries. Such people, however, will have trials in this life, and these I should like to spare you.

I tell you, brothers, the time is short. From now on those with wives should live as though they had none; those who weep should live as though they were not weeping, and those who rejoice as though they were not rejoicing; buyers should conduct themselves as though they owned nothing, and those who make use of the world as though they were not using it, for the world as we know it is passing away.—This is the Word of the Lord. ℟. **Thanks be to God.** ♥

Responsorial Psalm   Ps 45, 11-12. 14-15. 16-17

℟. (11) **Listen to me, daughter;
    see and bend your ear.**

Hear, O daughter, and see; turn your ear,
    forget your people and your father's house.

So shall the king desire your beauty;
  for he is your lord, and you must worship him.—℞

All glorious is the king's daughter as she enters;
  her raiment is threaded with spun gold.

In embroidered apparel she is borne in to the king;
  behind her the virgins of her train are brought
    to you. — ℞

They are borne in with gladness and joy;
  they enter the palace of the king.

The place of your fathers your sons shall have;
  you shall make them princes through all the
    land. — ℞ ℣

GOSPEL   Lk 6, 20-26

See p. 273.

THURSDAY OF THE TWENTY-THIRD WEEK
IN ORDINARY TIME

READING I   1 Cor 8, 1-7. 11-13

Knowledge alone leads to pride. Among the Jews, the law of love was
practiced up to a point. Christ said: "By this all men know you as
my disciples if you have love for one another."

A reading from the first letter of Paul to the
Corinthians

"Knowledge" inflates, but love upbuilds. If a man
thinks he knows something, that means he has never
really known it as he ought. But if anyone loves
God, that man is known by him. So then, about this
matter of eating meats that have been offered to
idols; we know that an idol is really nothing, and
that there is no God but one. Even though there
are so-called gods in the heavens and on the earth
—there are, to be sure, many such "gods" and "lords"
—for us there is one God, the Father, from whom

all things come and for whom we live; and one Lord Jesus Christ, through whom everything was made and through whom we live.

Not all, of course, possess this "knowledge." Because some were so recently devoted to idols, they eat meat, fully aware that it has been sacrificed, and because their conscience is weak, it is defiled by the eating. Because of your "knowledge" the weak one perishes—that brother for whom Christ died. When you sin thus against your brothers and wound their weak consciences, you are sinning against Christ. Therefore, if food causes my brother to sin I will never eat meat again, so that I may not be an occasion of sin to him.—This is the Word of the Lord. ℟. **Thanks be to God.** ℣

Responsorial Psalm   Ps 139, 1-3. 13-14. 23-24

℟. (24) **Guide me, Lord, along the everlasting way.**

O Lord, you have probed me and you know me;
    you know when I sit and when I stand;
    you understand my thoughts from afar.
My journeys and my rest you scrutinize,
    with all my ways you are familiar. — ℟

Truly you have formed my inmost being;
    you knit me in my mother's womb.
I give you thanks that I am fearfully, wonderfully made;
    wonderful are your works. — ℟

Probe me, O God, and know my heart;
    try me, and know my thoughts;
See if my way is crooked,
    and lead me in the way of old. — ℟ ℣

GOSPEL   Lk 6, 27-38

See p. 275.

FRIDAY OF THE TWENTY-THIRD WEEK IN ORDINARY TIME

READING I 1 Cor 9, 16-19. 22-27

The fruits of a Christian are his works, and by them he is to be known. Words may deceive, but works do not. Paul says: "I have made myself all things to all men in order to save at least some. I have made myself the slave of all so as to win over as many as possible."

A reading from the first letter of Paul to the Corinthians

Preaching the gospel is not the subject of a boast; I am under compulsion and have no choice. I am ruined if I do not preach it! If I do it willingly, I have my recompense; if unwillingly, I am nonetheless entrusted with a charge. And this recompense of mine? It is simply this, that when preaching I offer the gospel free of charge and do not make full use of the authority the gospel gives me.

Although I am not bound to anyone, I made my self the slave of all so as to win over as many as possible. To the weak I became a weak person with a view to winning the weak. I have made myself all things to all men in order to save at least some of them. In fact, I do all that I do for the sake of the gospel in the hope of having a share in its blessings.

You know that while all the runners in the stadium take part in the race, the award goes to one man. In that case, run so as to win! Athletes deny themselves all sorts of things. They do this to win a crown of leaves that withers, but we a crown that is imperishable.

I do not run like a man who loses sight of the finish line. I do not fight as if I were shadowboxing. What I do is discipline my own body and master it, for fear that after having preached to others I myself should be rejected.—This is the Word of the Lord. ℟. **Thanks be to God.** ↓

Responsorial Psalm   Ps 84, 3. 4. 5-6. 8. 12

℞. (2) **How lovely is your dwelling-place,
 Lord, mighty God!**

My soul yearns and pines
 for the courts of the Lord.
My heart and my flesh
 cry out for the living God. — ℞

Even the sparrow finds a home,
 and the swallow a nest
 in which she puts her young—
Your altars, O Lord of hosts,
 my king and my God! — ℞

Happy they who dwell in your house!
 continually they praise you.
Happy the men whose strength you are!
They go from strength to strength. — ℞

For a sun and a shield is the Lord God;
 grace and glory he bestows;
The Lord withholds no good thing
 from those who walk in sincerity. — ℞ ↓

GOSPEL   Lk 6, 39-42

See p. 277.

SATURDAY OF THE TWENTY-THIRD WEEK
IN ORDINARY TIME

READING I   1 Cor 10, 14-22

The body of Jesus builds a living, confidential union between the humblest believer and the person of Jesus Christ. He became the food and strength by which men journeying through the wilderness of life shall reach their everlasting home.

A reading from the first letter of Paul to the
Corinthians

I am telling you, whom I love, to shun the worship of idols, and I address you as one addresses sensible people. You may judge for yourselves what I am saying. Is not the cup of blessing we bless a sharing in the blood of Christ? And is not the bread we break a sharing in the body of Christ? Because the loaf of bread is one, we, many though we are, are one body, for we all partake of the one loaf. Look at Israel according to the flesh and see if those who eat the sacrifices do not share in the altar!

What am I saying—that meat offered to an idol is really offered to that idol, or that an idol is a reality? No, I mean that the Gentiles sacrifice to demons and not to God, and I do not want you to become sharers with demons. You cannot drink the cup of the Lord and also the cup of demons. You cannot partake of the table of the Lord and likewise the table of demons. Do we mean to provoke the Lord to jealous angers? Surely we are not stronger than he!—This is the Word of the Lord. ℟. **Thanks to be God.** ☩

Responsorial Psalm   Ps 116, 12-13. 17-18

℟. (17) **To you, Lord, I will offer a sacrifice of praise.**

How shall I make a return to the Lord
    for all the good he has done for me?
The cup of salvation I will take up,
    and I will call upon the name of the Lord. — ℟

To you will I offer sacrifice of thanksgiving,
    and I will call upon the name of the Lord.
My vows to the Lord I will pay
    in the presence of all his people. — ℟ ☩

GOSPEL   Lk 6, 43-49

See p. 279.

MONDAY OF THE TWENTY-FOURTH WEEK
IN ORDINARY TIME

READING I　　　　　　　　　　1 Cor 11, 17-26. 33

Paul chides the Corinthians for the factions that developed in the
Christian community. Some even go hungry at their meetings because
of discrimination. The Eucharist is celebrated to remember Jesus.
This proclaims the death of Jesus until he comes again.

A reading from the first letter of Paul to the
Corinthians

What I now have to say is not said in praise, because your meetings are not profitable but harmful.
First of all, I hear that when you gather for a meeting
there are divisions among you, and I am inclined
to believe it. There may even have to be factions
among you for the tried and true to stand out clearly.
When you assemble it is not to eat the Lord's Supper, for everyone is in haste to eat his own supper.
One person goes hungry while another gets drunk.
Do you not have homes where you can eat and
drink? Would you show contempt for the church of
God, and embarrass those who have nothing? What
can I say to you? Shall I praise you? Certainly not
in this matter!

I received from the Lord what I handed on to you,
namely, that the Lord Jesus on the night in which
he was betrayed took bread, and after he had given
thanks, broke it and said, "This is my body, which
is for you. Do this in remembrance of me." In the
same way, after the supper, he took the cup, saying, "This cup is the new covenant in my blood. Do
this, whenever you drink it, in remembrance of me."
Every time, then, you eat this bread and drink this
cup, you proclaim the death of the Lord until he
comes! Therefore, my brothers, when you assemble
for the meal, wait for one another.—This is the
Word of the Lord. ℟. **Thanks be to God.** ✟

Responsorial Psalm Ps 40, 7-8. 8-9. 10. 17

℟. (1 Cor 11, 26) **Proclaim the death of the Lord until he comes again.**

Sacrifice or oblation you wished not,
 but ears open to obedience you gave me.
Holocausts or sin-offerings you sought not;
 then said I, "Behold I come." — ℟

"In the written scroll it is prescribed for me,
 to do your will, O my God, is my delight,
 and your law is within my heart!" — ℟

I announced your justice in the vast assembly;
 I did not restrain my lips, as you, O Lord,
 know. — ℟

But may all who seek you,
 exult and be glad in you.
And may those who love your salvation
 say ever, "The Lord be glorified." — ℟ ℣

GOSPEL Lk 7, 1-10

See p. 281.

TUESDAY OF THE TWENTY-FOURTH WEEK IN ORDINARY TIME

READING I 1 Cor 12, 12-14. 27-31

In the Body of Jesus all are one regardless of race. All are baptized in Jesus. Everyone in the Body of Christ has a unique work to perform for Jesus.

A reading from the first letter of Paul to the Corinthians

The body is one and has many members, but all the members, many though they are, are one body; and so it is with Christ. It was in one Spirit that all of us, whether Jew or Greek, slave or free, were baptized into one body. All of us have been given to drink of the one Spirit. Now the body is not one member, it is many.

You, then, are the body of Christ. Every one of you is a member of it. Furthermore, God has set up in the church first apostles, second prophets, third teachers, then miracle workers, healers, assistants, administrators, and those who speak in tongues. Are all prophets? Are all teachers? Do all work miracles or have the gift of healing? Do all speak in tongues, all have the gift of interpretation of tongues? Set your hearts on the greater gifts.—This is the Word of the Lord. ℟. **Thanks be to God.** ℣

Responsorial Psalm   Ps 100, 1-2. 3. 4. 5

℟. (3) **We are his people:
the sheep of his flock.**

Sing joyfully to the Lord, all you lands;
    serve the Lord with gladness;
    come before him with joyful song.

Know that the Lord is God;
    he made us, his we are;
    his people, the flock he tends. — ℟

Enter his gates with thanksgiving,
    his courts with praise;
Give thanks to him; bless his name. — ℟

Give thanks to him; bless his name, for he is good:
    the Lord, whose kindness endures forever,
    and his faithfulness, to all generations. — ℟ ℣

GOSPEL   Lk 7, 11-17

See p. 284

WEDNESDAY OF THE TWENTY-FOURTH WEEK
IN ORDINARY TIME

READING I   1 Cor 12, 31—13, 3

Love is not possession of, but participation in the good of the beloved,
Love is the sum and goal of all the virtues. Love is incredible evidence

that God is the "Living God." Paul describes that sublime virtue of love.

A reading from the first letter of Paul to the Corinthians

Set your hearts on the greater gifts.

I will show you the way that surpasses all the others. If I speak with human tongues and angelic as well, but do not have love, I am a noisy gong, a clanging cymbal. If I have the gift of prophecy and, with full knowledge, comprehend all mysteries, but if I have faith great enough to move mountains, but have not love, I am nothing. If I give everything I have to feed the poor and hand over my body to be burned, but have not love, I gain nothing.

Love is patient; love is kind. Love is not jealous, it does not put on airs, it is not snobbish. Love is never rude, it is not self-seeking, it is not prone to anger; neither does it brood over injuries. Love does not rejoice in what is wrong but rejoices with the truth. There is no limit to love's forbearance, to its trust, its hope, its power to endure.

Love never fails. Prophecies will cease, tongues will be silent, knowledge will pass away. Our knowledge is imperfect and our prophesying is imperfect. When the perfect comes, the imperfect will pass away. When I was a child I used to talk like a child, think like a child, reason like a child. When I became a man I put childish ways aside. Now we see indistinctly, as in a mirror; then we shall see face to face. My knowledge is imperfect now; then I shall know even as I am known. There are in the end three things that last: faith, hope, and love, and the greatest of these is love.—This is the Word of the Lord. ℟. **Thanks be to God. ℣**

Responsorial Psalm   Ps 33, 2-3. 4-5. 12. 22

℟. (12) **Happy the people the Lord has chosen to be his own.**

Give thanks to the Lord on the harp;
  with the ten-stringed lyre chant his praises.
Sing to him a new song;
  pluck the strings skillfully, with shouts of glad-
    ness. — ℟

For upright is the word of the Lord,
  and all his works are trustworthy.
He loves justice and right;
  of the kindness of the Lord the earth is full. — ℟

Happy the nation whose God is the Lord,
  the people he has chosen for his own inheritance.
May your kindness, O Lord, be upon us
  who have put our hope in you. — ℟ ℣

GOSPEL   Lk 7, 31-35

See p. 286.

THURSDAY OF THE TWENTY-FOURTH WEEK
IN ORDINARY TIME

READING I   1 Cor 15, 1-11

Paul writes that he is the least of the apostles—but this grace of
his has not proved fruitless. He reviews the doctrines of faith. Christ
died but rose and was seen by the apostles who preach about Christ
raised from the dead.

A reading from the first letter of Paul to the
                    Corinthians

Brothers, I want to remind you of the gospel I
preached to you, which you received and in which
you stand firm. You are being saved by it at this
very moment if you retain it as I preached it to
you. Otherwise you have believed in vain. I handed
on to you first of all what I myself received, that
Christ died for our sins in accord with the Scriptures; that he was buried and, in accord with the
Scriptures, rose on the third day; that he was seen

by Cephas, then by the Twelve. After that he was seen by five hundred brothers at once, most of whom are still alive, although some have fallen asleep. Next he was seen by James; then by all the apostles. Last of all he was seen by me, as one born out of the normal course. I am the least of the apostles; in fact, because I persecuted the church of God, I do not even deserve the name. But by God's favor I am what I am. This favor of his to me has not proved fruitless. Indeed, I have worked harder than all the others, not on my own but through the favor of God. In any case, whether it be I or they, this is what we preach and this is what you believed.—This is the Word of the Lord. ℟.
Thanks be to God. ℣

Responsorial Psalm   Ps 118, 1-2. 16-17. 28

℟. (1) **Give thanks to the Lord, for he is good.**

Give thanks to the Lord, for he is good,
    for his mercy endures forever.
Let the house of Israel say,
    "His mercy endures forever." — ℟

"The right hand of the Lord is exalted;
    the right hand of the Lord has struck with power."
I shall not die, but live,
    and declare the works of the Lord. — ℟

You are my God, and I give thanks to you;
    O my God, I extol you.
I give thanks to you because you heard me,
    and you have been my savior. — ℟ ℣

℟. Or: **Alleluia.** ℣

GOSPEL   Lk 7, 36-50

See p. 287.

FRIDAY OF THE TWENTY-FOURTH WEEK IN ORDINARY TIME

READING I 1 Cor 15, 12-20

Jesus rose from the dead and thereby proved his divine origin and his power to save all men. A faith that does not include this realization can be a mere living of the past.

A reading from the first letter of Paul to the Corinthians

If Christ is preached as raised from the dead, how is it that some of you say there is no resurrection of the dead? If there is no resurrection of the dead, Christ himself has not been raised. And if Christ has not been raised, our preaching is void of content and your faith is empty too. Indeed, we should then be exposed as false witnesses of God, for we have borne witness before him that he raised up Christ; but he certainly did not raise him up if the dead are not raised. Why? Because if the dead are not raised, then Christ was not raised; and if Christ was not raised, your faith is worthless. You are still in your sins, and those who have fallen asleep in Christ are the deadest of the dead. If our hopes in Christ are limited to this life only, we are the most pitiable of men.

But as it is, Christ has been raised from the dead, the first fruits of those who have fallen asleep.— This is the Word of the Lord. ℟. **Thanks be to God.** ℣

Responsorial Psalm Ps 17, 1. 6-7. 8. 15

℟. (15) **Lord, when your glory appears, my joy will be full.**

Hear, O Lord, a just suit;
  attend to my outcry;
    hearken to my prayer from lips without deceit.—℟

I call upon you, for you will answer me, O God;
  incline your ear to me; hear my word.

Show your wondrous kindness,
  O savior of those who hope in you. — ℞

Hide me in the shadow of your wings
  but I in justice shall behold your face;
  on waking, I shall be content in your pres-
    ence. — ℞ ✝

GOSPEL   Lk 8, 1-3

See p. 290.

SATURDAY OF THE TWENTY-FOURTH WEEK IN ORDINARY TIME

READING I   1 Cor 15, 35-37. 42-49

Paul points out that the glory of resurrection is not a matter of body
or soul, but of spirit. In the power of Christ's resurrection, all are
being modeled on the "heavenly man."

A reading from the first letter of Paul to the
Corinthians

Perhaps someone will say, "How are the dead to be
raised up? What kind of body will they have?" A
nonsensical question! The seed you sow does not
germinate unless it dies. When you sow, you do not
sow the full-blown plant, but a kernel of wheat or
some other grain. So is it with the resurrection of
the dead. What is sown in the earth is subject to
decay, what rises is incorruptible. What is sown is
ignoble, what rises is glorious. Weakness is sown,
strength rises up. A natural body is put down and
a spiritual body comes up.

  If there is a natural body, be sure there is also
a spiritual body. Scripture has it that Adam, the
first man, became a living soul; the last Adam has
become a life-giving spirit. Take note, the spiritual
was not first; first came the natural and after that

the spiritual. The first man was of earth, formed from dust, the second is from heaven. Earthly men are like the man of earth, heavenly men are like the man of heaven. Just as we resemble the man from earth, so shall we bear the likeness of the man from heaven.—This is the Word of the Lord. ℟.
Thanks be to God. ℣

Responsorial Psalm   Ps 56, 10-12. 13-14

℟. (14) **I will walk in the presence of God,**
  with the light of the living.

Now I know that God is with me.
  In God, in whose promise I glory,
In God I trust without fear;
  what can flesh do against me? — ℟

I am bound, O God, by vows to you;
  your thank offerings I will fulfill.
For you have rescued me from death,
  my feet, too, from stumbling;
  that I may walk before God in the light of the
    living. — ℟ ℣

GOSPEL   Lk 8, 4-15

See p. 292.

INTRODUCTION FOR 25th TO 29th WEEK

The Wisdom Books—*The wisdom literature of the Bible is the fruit of a movement among ancient oriental people to gather, preserve and express, usually in aphoristic style, the results of human experience as an aid toward understanding and solving the problems of life. In Israel especially, the movement concerned itself with such basic and vital problems as man's origin and destiny, his quest for happiness, the problem of suffering, of good and evil in human conduct, of death, and the state beyond the grave. Originating with oral tradition, these formulations found their way into the historical books of the Old Testament in the shape of proverbs, odes, chants, epigrams, and also into those psalms intended for instruction. All this literature is versified by the skillful use of parallelism, that is, of the balanced and symmetrical phrases peculiar to Hebrew poetry.*

Those who cultivated wisdom were called sages. Men of letters, scribes, skilled in the affairs of government, and counselors to rulers, they were instructors of the people, especially of youth (Sir 51, 13-30). In times of crisis they guided the people by revaluating tradition, thus helping to preserve unity, peace and good will. The most illustrious of the sages, and the originator of wisdom literature in Israel, was Solomon. Because of his fame, some of the wisdom books of which he was not the author bear his name.

Despite numerous resemblances, sometimes exaggerated, between the sapiential literature of pagan nations and the wisdom books of the Bible, the former are often replete with vagaries and abound in polytheistic conceptions; the latter remained profoundly human, universal, fundamentally moral, and essentially religious and monotheistic. Under the influence of the law and the prophets, wisdom became piety and virtue; impiety and vice were folly. The teachers of wisdom were regarded as men of God, and their books were placed beside the law and the prophets. The highest wisdom became identified with the spirit of God through which the world was created and preserved (Prv 8, 22-31), and mankind was enlightened.

The limitations of Old Testament wisdom served to crystallize the problems of human life and destiny, thus preparing for their solution through New Testament revelation.

The Book of Proverbs—*Consisting of maxims stemming from various periods (8th to 5th centuries B.C.), this book deals with various aspects of human wisdom, to guide man in his life toward perfection in accord with God's will. It must be read in the light of the New Testament teaching of Jesus, the Word of God and the personification of wisdom.*

The Book of Ecclesiastes—*Written about the 3rd century B.C., this book examines a wide range of human experience only to conclude that all things are vanity except the fear of the Lord and observance of his commandments, and that God requites man in his own good time. The author's vain search for success and happiness on earth finds its solution in our Lord's assurance of these things to his followers not in this world but in the bliss of heaven.*

The Book of Job—*Composed about the 5th century B.C., this is an artistic dialogue skillfully handling the problem of suffering though only from the standpoint of temporal life. The anxiety of its author over reconciling God's justice and wisdom with the suffering of the innocent is relieved by the Gospel account of the crucified and risen Redeemer.*

The Epistle to the Galatians—*Written about 49 or 50 A.D., this is possibly the most personal and emotional of Paul's Epistles. In it he strongly defends his person and his doctrine. In indignation he asserts the divine origin of his teaching and of his authority; he shows that justification is not through the Mosaic law, but through faith in Jesus Christ, who was crucified and who rose from the dead; he concludes that consequently the Mosaic law was something transient and not permanent, that it is not an essential part of Christianity. Nor does he fail to insist on the necessity of the evangelical virtues, especially love, the offspring of faith.*

The Epistle to the Ephesians—*This is one of the "Captivity Epistles" probably written during Paul's first Roman imprisonment, 61-63 A.D. Very similar in theme and language to the Epistle to the Colossians, but much more abstract, profound and systematic, this Epistle's central thought is the Church regarded as the mystical body of Christ, through which God pours out the divine life of grace in most generous fashion to its members, the Christians, in and through its head, Jesus Christ. The spiritual, organic unity of its members with Christ and with one another is emphasized as the basic principle of the life of the mystical body. Then comes an exhortation to lead the new life that befits those incorporated into the sublime unity of the mystical body.*

MONDAY OF THE TWENTY-FIFTH WEEK IN ORDINARY TIME

READING I   Prv 3, 27-34

To serve one's neighbor immediately means to do what is wholesome. A person should not plot against a neighbor nor be envious of him but rather strive for friendship.

A reading from the book of Proverbs

Refuse no one the good on which he has a claim
  when it is in your power to do it for him.
Say not to your neighbor, "Go, and come again,
  tomorrow I will give," when you can give at once.
Plot no evil against your neighbor,
  against him who lives at peace with you.
Quarrel not with a man without cause,
  with one who has done you no harm.
Envy not the lawless man
  and choose none of his ways:
To the Lord the perverse man is an abomination,
  but with the upright is his friendship.
The curse of the Lord is on the house of the wicked,
  but the dwelling of the just he blesses;
When he is dealing with the arrogant, he is stern,
  but to the humble he shows kindness.
This is the Word of the Lord. ℟. **Thanks be to God.** ℣

Responsorial Psalm   Ps 15, 2-3. 3-4. 5

℟. (1) **He who does justice shall live on the Lord's
  holy mountain.**

He who walks blamelessly and does justice;
  who thinks the truth in his heart
  and slanders not with his tongue; — ℟

Who harms not his fellow man,
  nor takes up a reproach against his neighbor;
By whom the reprobate is despised,
  while he honors those who fear the Lord; — ℟

Who lends not his money at usury
  and accepts no bribe against the innocent.
He who does these things
  shall never be disturbed. — ℟ ℣

GOSPEL   Lk 8, 16-18

See p. 297.

TUESDAY OF THE TWENTY-FIFTH WEEK
IN ORDINARY TIME

READING I   Prv 21, 1-6. 10-13

The reading from Proverbs here is a random collection of disconnected wise sayings and cannot be taken as a whole. To do what is right and just is more acceptable to the Lord than sacrifice. The Lord searches out the heart of man.

A reading from the book of Proverbs

Like a stream is the king's heart in the hand of the
    Lord;
  wherever it pleases him, he directs it.
All the ways of a man may be right in his own eyes,
  but it is the Lord who proves hearts.
To do what is right and just
  is more acceptable to the Lord than sacrifice.
Haughty eyes and a proud heart—
  the tillage of the wicked is sin.
The plans of the diligent are sure of profit,
  but all rash haste leads certainly to poverty.
He who makes a fortune by a lying tongue
  is chasing a bubble over deadly snares.
The soul of the wicked man desires evil;
  his neighbor finds no pity in his eyes.
When the arrogant man is punished, the simple are
    the wiser;
  when the wise man is instructed, he gains knowl-
    edge.
The just man appraises the house of the wicked:
  there is one who brings down the wicked to ruin.
He who shuts his ear to the cry of the poor
  will himself also call and not be heard.
This is the Word of the Lord. ℟. **Thanks be to God.** ℣

Responsorial Psalm   Ps 119, 1. 27. 30. 34. 35. 44

℟. (35) **Guide me, Lord, in the way of your commands.**

Happy are they whose way is blameless,
  who walk in the law of the Lord. — ℟

Make me understand the way of your precepts,
    and I will meditate on your wondrous deeds. — ℟

The way of truth I have chosen;
    I have set your ordinances before me. — ℟

Give me discernment, that I may observe your law
    and keep it with all my heart. — ℟

Lead me in the path of your commands,
    for in it I delight. — ℟

And I will keep your law continually,
    forever and ever. — ℟ ℣

GOSPEL Lk 8, 19-21

See p. 299.

WEDNESDAY OF THE TWENTY-FIFTH WEEK IN ORDINARY TIME

READING I Prv 30, 5-9

A wise man is he who adds nothing to the Lord's word and is provided only with the food he needs, "lest being full, I deny you, saying, 'Who is the Lord?'" Our Lord gives the good that is necessary.

A reading from the book of Proverbs

Every word of God is tested;
    he is a shield to those who take refuge in him.
Add nothing to his words,
    lest he reprove you, and you be exposed as a
      deceiver.
Two things I ask of you,
    deny them not to me before I die:
Put falsehood and lying far from me,
    give me neither poverty nor riches;
    [provide me only with the food I need;]
Lest, being full, I deny you,
    saying, "Who is the Lord?"
Or, being in want, I steal,
    and profane the name of my God.
This is the Word of the Lord. ℟. **Thanks be to God.** ℣

Responsorial Psalm Ps 119, 29. 72. 89. 101. 104. 163

℞. (105) **Your word, O Lord, is a lamp for my feet.**

Remove from me the way of falsehood,
    and favor me with your law. — ℞

The law of your mouth is to me more precious
    than thousands of gold and silver pieces. — ℞

Your word, O Lord, endures forever;
    it is firm as the heavens. — ℞

From every evil way I withhold my feet,
    that I may keep your words. — ℞

Through your precepts I gain discernment;
    therefore I hate every false way. — ℞

Falsehood I hate and abhor;
    your law I love. — ℞ ∨

GOSPEL   Lk 9, 1-6

See p. 301.

THURSDAY OF THE TWENTY-FIFTH WEEK
IN ORDINARY TIME

READING I   Eccl 1, 2-11

Ecclesiastes shows a strong Hellenistic thought. To the Greek poets, human life does not move in any direction or toward any purpose, but only circles in endless tragic and comic repetitions. It views the cycle of nature and nothing is new under the sun.

A reading from the book of Ecclesiastes

Vanity of vanities, says Qoheleth,
    vanity of vanities! All things are vanity.
What profit has man from all the labor
    which he toils at under the sun?
One generation passes and another comes,
    but the world forever stays.
The sun rises and the sun goes down;
    then it presses on to the place where it rises.

Blowing now toward the south, then toward the
north,
   the wind turns again and again, resuming its
   rounds.
All rivers go to the sea,
   yet never does the sea become full.
To the place where they go,
   the rivers keep on going.
All speech is labored;
   there is nothing man can say.
The eye is not satisfied with seeing
   nor is the ear filled with hearing.
What has been, that will be; what has been done,
that will be done. Nothing is new under the sun.
Even the thing of which we say, "See, this is new!"
has already existed in the ages that preceded us.
There is no remembrance of the men of old; nor of
those to come will there be any remembrance among
those who come after them.—This is the Word of
the Lord. ℟. **Thanks be to God.** ℣

Responsorial Psalm   Ps 90, 3-4. 5-6. 12-13. 14. 17
℟. (1) **In every age, O Lord, you have been our
   refuge.**
You turn man back to dust,
   saying, "Return, O children of men."
For a thousand years in your sight
   are as yesterday, now that it is past,
   or as a watch of the night. — ℟

You make an end of them in their sleep;
   the next morning they are like the changing grass,
Which at dawn springs up anew,
   but by evening wilts and fades. — ℟

Teach us to number our days aright,
   that we may gain wisdom of heart.
Return, O Lord! How long?
   Have pity on your servants! — ℟

Fill us at daybreak with your kindness,
that we may shout for joy and gladness all our
days.
And may the gracious care of the Lord our God be
ours;
prosper the work of our hands for us!
[Prosper the work of our hands!] — ℟ ∇

GOSPEL Lk 9, 7-9

See p. 303.

FRIDAY OF THE TWENTY-FIFTH WEEK
IN ORDINARY TIME

READING I Eccl 3, 1-11

This famous and beautiful passage exemplifies the general theme of
Ecclesiastes. There is the right time for everything. Man can never
grasp God's purpose in any particular "time." He should rather accept
each time as a gift.

A reading from the book of Ecclesiastes

There is an appointed time for everything,
and a time for every affair under the heavens.
A time to be born, and a time to die;
a time to plant, and a time to uproot the plant.
A time to kill, and a time to heal;
a time to tear down, and a time to build.
A time to weep, and a time to laugh;
a time to mourn, and a time to dance.
A time to scatter stones, and a time to gather them;
a time to embrace, and a time to be far from
embraces.
A time to seek, and a time to lose;
a time to keep, and a time to cast away.
A time to rend, and a time to sew;
a time to be silent, and a time to speak.
A time to love, and a time to hate;
a time of war, and a time of peace.

What advantage has the worker from his toil? I have considered the task which God has appointed for men to be busied about. He has made everything appropriate to its time, and has put the timeless into their hearts, without men's ever discovering, from beginning to end, the work which God has done.—This is the Word of the Lord. ℟. **Thanks be to God.** ⋎

Responsorial Psalm   Ps 144, 1-2. 3-4

℟. (1) **Blessed be the Lord, my Rock!**

Blessed be the Lord, my rock,
   my refuge and my fortress,
My stronghold, my deliverer,
   my shield, in whom I trust. — ℟

Lord, what is man, that you notice him;
   the son of man, that you take thought of him?
Man is like a breath;
   his days, like a passing shadow. — ℟ ⋎

GOSPEL   Lk 9, 18-22

See p. 305.

SATURDAY OF THE TWENTY-FIFTH WEEK IN ORDINARY TIME

READING I   Eccl 11, 9—12, 8

Ecclesiastes records the vitality of youth, but still God will judge. A man should look into his future. Life belongs to God and will return to him.

A reading from the book of Ecclesiastes

Rejoice, O young man, while you are young
   and let your heart be glad in the days of your
      youth.
Follow the ways of your heart,
   the vision of your eyes;

Yet understand that as regards all this
  God will bring you to judgment.
Ward off grief from your heart
  and put away trouble from your presence,
  though the dawn of youth is fleeting.
Remember your Creator in the days of your youth,
  before the evil days come
And the years approach of which you will say,
  I have no pleasure in them;
Before the sun is darkened,
  and the light, and the moon, and the stars,
  while the clouds return after the rain;
When the guardians of the house tremble,
  and the strong men are bent,
And the grinders are idle because they are few,
  and they who look through the windows grow
    blind;
When the doors to the street are shut,
  and the sound of the mill is low;
When one waits for the chirp of a bird,
  but all the daughters of song are suppressed;
And one fears heights,
  and perils in the street;
When the almond tree blooms,
  and the locust grows sluggish
  and the caper berry is without effect,
Because man goes to his lasting home,
  and mourners go about the streets;
Before the silver cord is snapped
  and the golden bowl is broken,
And the pitcher is shattered at the spring,
  and the broken pulley falls into the well,
And the dust returns to the earth as it once was,
  and the life breath returns to God who gave it.
Vanity of vanities, says Qoheleth,
  all things are vanity!
This is the Word of the Lord. ℟. **Thanks be to God.** ℣

Responsorial Psalm   Ps 90, 3-4. 5-6. 12-13. 14. 17

℟. (1) **In every age, O Lord, you have been our refuge.**

You turn man back to dust,
     saying, "Return, O children of men."
For a thousand years in your sight
     are as yesterday, now that it is past,
     or as a watch of the night. — ℟

You make an end of them in their sleep;
     the next morning they are like the changing grass,
Which at dawn springs up anew,
     but by evening wilts and fades. — ℟

Teach us to number our days aright,
     that we may gain wisdom of heart.
Return, O Lord! How long?
     Have pity on your servants! — ℟

Fill us at daybreak with your kindness,
     that we may shout for joy and gladness all our
          days.
And may the gracious care of the Lord our God be
     ours;
     prosper the work of our hands for us!
     [Prosper the work of our hands!] — ℟ ℣

GOSPEL   Lk 9, 43-45

See p. 307.

MONDAY OF THE TWENTY-SIXTH WEEK
IN ORDINARY TIME

READING I   Jb 1, 6-22

The story of Job is the universal cry of Man in the face of calamity.
Job is faced with not one calamity, but four. He loses his oxen, sheep,
camels, and finally his own family. Job has not done anything to
deserve such treatment.

A reading from the book of Job

One day, when the sons of God came to present
themselves before the Lord, Satan also came among

them. And the Lord said to Satan, "Whence do you come?" Then Satan answered the Lord and said, "From roaming the earth and patrolling it." And the Lord said to Satan, "Have you noticed my servant Job, and that there is no one on earth like him, blameless and upright, fearing God and avoiding evil?" But Satan answered the Lord and said, "Is it for nothing that Job is God-fearing? Have you not surrounded him and his family and all that he has with your protection? You have blessed the work of his hands, and his livestock are spread over the land. But now put forth your hand and touch anything that he has, and surely he will blaspheme you to your face." And the Lord said to Satan, "Behold, all that he has is in your power; only do not lay a hand upon his person." So Satan went forth from the presence of the Lord.

And so one day, while his sons and his daughters were eating and drinking wine in the house of their eldest brother, a messenger came to Job and said, "The oxen were ploughing and the asses grazing beside them, and the Sabeans carried them off in a raid. They put the herdsmen to the sword, and I alone have escaped to tell you." While he was yet speaking, another came and said, "Lightning has fallen from heaven and struck the sheep and their shepherds and consumed them; and I alone have escaped to tell you." While he was yet speaking, another came and said, "The Chaldeans formed three columns, seized the camels, carried them off, and put those tending them to the sword, and I alone have escaped to tell you." While he was yet speaking, another came and said, "Your sons and daughters were eating and drinking wine in the house of their eldest brother, when suddenly a great wind came across the desert and smote the four corners of the house. It fell upon the young people and they are dead; and I alone have escaped to tell you." Then

Job began to tear his cloak and cut off his hair. He cast himself prostrate upon the ground, and said, "Naked I came forth from my mother's womb,
    and naked shall I go back again.
The Lord gave and the Lord has taken away;
    blessed be the name of the Lord!"
In all this Job did not sin, nor did he say anything disrespectful of God.—This is the Word of the Lord.
R⁷. **Thanks be to God.** ↓

Responsorial Psalm   Ps 17, 1. 2-3. 6-7

R⁷. (6) **Lord, bend your ear and hear my prayer.**

Hear, O Lord, a just suit;
    attend to my outcry;
        hearken to my prayer from lips without deceit.—R⁷

From you let my judgment come;
    your eyes behold what is right.
Though you test my heart, searching it in the night,
    though you try me with fire, you shall find no
        malice in me. — R⁷

I call upon you, for you will answer me, O God;
    incline your ear to me; hear my word.
Show your wondrous kindness,
    O savior of those who flee
        from their foes to refuge at your right hand.—R⁷ ↓

GOSPEL   Lk 9, 46-50

See p. 309

TUESDAY OF THE TWENTY-SIXTH WEEK
IN ORDINARY TIME

READING I   Jb 3, 1-3. 11-17. 20-23

Job questions the reason for his life. Why was he even born? Why is life given only for toil and suffering to wait solely for the grave? The path of life is hidden from men and known to God.

A reading from the book of Job

Job opened his mouth and cursed his day. Job spoke
out and said:
Perish the day on which I was born,
    the night when they said, "The child is a boy!"
Why did I not perish at birth,
    come forth from the womb and expire?
Or why was I not buried away like an untimely birth,
    like babes that have never seen light?
Wherefore did the knees receive me?
    or why did I suck at the breasts?
For then I should have lain down and been tranquil;
    had I slept, I should then have been at rest
With kings and counselors of the earth
    who built where now there are ruins,
Or with princes who had gold
    and filled their houses with silver.
There the wicked cease from troubling,
    there the weary are at rest.
Why is light given to the toilers,
    and life to the bitter in spirit?
They wait for death and it comes not;
    they search for it rather than for hidden treasures,
Rejoice in it exultingly,
    and are glad when they reach the grave:
Men whose path is hidden from them,
    and whom God has hemmed in!
This is the Word of the Lord. ℟. **Thanks be to God.** ℣

Responsorial Psalm   Ps 88, 2-3. 4-5. 6. 7-8
℟. (3) **Let my prayer come before you, Lord.**
O Lord, my God, by day I cry out;
    at night I clamor in your presence.
Let my prayer come before you;
    incline your ear to my call for help. — ℟
For my soul is surfeited with troubles
    and my life draws near to the nether world.

I am numbered with those who go down into the pit;
    I am a man without strength. — ℟

My couch is among the dead,
    like the slain who lie in the grave,
Whom you remember no longer
    and who are cut off from your care. — ℟

You have plunged me into the bottom of the pit,
    into the dark abyss.
Upon me your wrath lies heavy,
    and with all your billows you overwhelm
      me. — ℟ ✟

GOSPEL   Lk 9, 51-56

See p. 311.

WEDNESDAY OF THE TWENTY-SIXTH WEEK
IN ORDINARY TIME

READING I   Jb 9, 1-12. 14-16

Job, in trying to explain his feelings to his friends, begins by seeking to establish the relationship that exists between himself and all men with God. Man will always remain in his place in this relationship of Creator and creature.

A reading from the book of Job

Job answered his friends and said:
I know well that it is so;
    but how can a man be justified before God?
Should one wish to contend with him,
    he could not answer him once in a thousand times.
God is wise in heart and mighty in strength;
    who has withstood him and remained unscathed?
He removes the mountains before they know it;
    he overturns them in his anger.
He shakes the earth out of its place,
    and the pillars beneath it tremble.
He commands the sun, and it rises not;
    he seals up the stars.

He alone stretches out the heavens
  and treads upon the crests of the sea.
He made the Bear and Orion,
  the Pleiades and the constellations of the south;
He does great things past finding out,
  marvelous things beyond reckoning.
Should he come near me, I see him not;
  should he pass by, I am not aware of him;
Should he seize me forcibly, who can say him nay?
  Who can say to him, "What are you doing?"
How much less shall I give him any answer,
  or choose out arguments against him!
Even though I were right, I could not answer him,
  but should rather beg for what was due me.
If I appealed to him and he answered my call,
  I could not believe that he would hearken to my
    words.

This is the Word of the Lord. ℞. **Thanks be to God.** ℣

Responsorial Psalm   Ps 88, 10-11. 12-13. 14-15

℞. (3) **Let my prayer come before you, Lord.**

Daily I call upon you, O Lord;
  to you I stretch out my hands.
Will you work wonders for the dead?
  Will the shades arise to give you thanks? — ℞

Do they declare your kindness in the grave,
  your faithfulness among those who have perished?
Are your wonders made known in the darkness,
  or your justice in the land of oblivion? — ℞

But I, O Lord, cry out to you;
  with my morning prayer I wait upon you.
Why, O Lord, do you reject me;
  why hide from me your face? — ℞ ℣

GOSPEL   Lk 9, 57-62

See p. 314.

THURSDAY OF THE TWENTY-SIXTH WEEK IN ORDINARY TIME

READING I   Jb 19, 21-27

God's hand is the instrument of creation, but it also works destruction. Job asks for pity and compassion. Job is utterly alone. From this depth he achieves a deep faith.

A reading from the book of Job

Job said:
Pity me, pity me, O you my friends,
    for the hand of God has struck me!
Why do you hound me as though you were divine,
    and insatiably prey upon me?
Oh, would that my words were written down!
    Would that they were inscribed in a record:
That with an iron chisel and with lead
    they were cut in the rock forever!
But as for me, I know that my Vindicator lives,
    and that he will at last stand forth upon the dust;
Whom I myself shall see:
    my own eyes, not another's, shall behold him.
And from my flesh I shall see God;
    my inmost being is consumed with longing.
This is the Word of the Lord. ℟. **Thanks be to God.** ℣

Responsorial Psalm   Ps 27, 7-8. 8-9. 13-14

℟. (13) **I believe that I shall see the good things of the Lord in the land of the living.**

Hear, O Lord, the sound of my call;
    have pity on me, and answer me.
Of you my heart speaks; you my glance seeks; — ℟

Your presence, O Lord, I seek.
    Hide not your face from me;
    do not in anger repel your servant.
You are my helper: cast me not off. — ℟

I believe that I shall see the bounty of the Lord
    in the land of the living.

Wait for the Lord with courage;
   be stouthearted, and wait for the Lord. — ℞ ℣

GOSPEL   Lk 10, 1-12

See p. 316.

FRIDAY OF THE TWENTY-SIXTH WEEK
IN ORDINARY TIME

READING I   Jb 38, 1. 12-21; 40, 3-5

The divine speech sweeps away all false problems. Yahweh puts to Job a series of unanswerable questions. The explanation of Job's problem must be sought in God. Job knows God is addressing him personally and is concerned with him as his servant.

A reading from the book of Job

The Lord addressed Job out of the storm and said:
Have you ever in your lifetime commanded the
     morning
   and shown the dawn its place
For taking hold of the ends of the earth,
   till the wicked are shaken from its surface?
The earth is changed as is clay by the seal,
   and dyed as though it were a garment;
But from the wicked the light is withheld,
   and the arm of pride is shattered.
Have you entered into the sources of the sea,
   or walked about in the depths of the abyss?
Have the gates of death been shown to you,
   or have you seen the gates of darkness?
Have you comprehended the breadth of the earth?
   Tell me, if you know all:
Which is the way to the dwelling place of light,
   and where is the abode of darkness,
That you may take them to their boundaries
   and set them on their homeward paths
You know, because you were born before them,
   and the number of your years is great!

Then Job answered the Lord and said:
Behold, I am of little account; what can I answer
you?
I put my hand over my mouth.
Though I have spoken once, I will not do so again;
though twice, I will do so no more.
This is the Word of the Lord. ℞. **Thanks be to God.** ℣

Responsorial Psalm   Ps 139, 1-3. 7-8. 9-10. 13-14
℞. (24) **Guide me, Lord, along the everlasting way.**

O Lord, you have probed me and you know me;
you know when I sit and when I stand;
you understand my thoughts from afar.
My journeys and my rest you scrutinize,
with all my ways you are familiar. — ℞

Where can I go from your spirit?
from your presence where can I flee?
If I go up to the heavens, you are there;
if I sink to the nether world, you are present
there. — ℞

If I take the wings of the dawn,
if I settle at the farthest limits of the sea,
Even there your hand shall guide me,
and your right hand hold me fast. — ℞

Truly you have formed my inmost being;
you knit me in my mother's womb.
I give you thanks that I am fearfully, wonderfully
made;
wonderful are your works. — ℞ ℣

GOSPEL   Lk 10, 13-16

See p. 319.

SATURDAY OF THE TWENTY-SIXTH WEEK IN ORDINARY TIME

READING I   Jb 42, 1-3. 5-6. 12-16

Job acknowledges his arrogance and confesses that God's ways and plans are infinitely beyond his understanding. Job's service has been based on faith. God has deigned to let himself be found by Job. Job is rewarded beyond measure.

A reading from the book of Job

Then Job answered the Lord and said:
I know that you can do all things,
    and that no purpose of yours can be hindered.
I have dealt with great things that I do not under-
        stand;
    things too wonderful for me, which I cannot know.
I had heard of you by word of mouth,
    but now my eye has seen you.
Therefore I disown what I have said,
    and repent in dust and ashes.

Thus the Lord blessed the latter days of Job more than his earlier ones. For he had fourteen thousand sheep, six thousand camels, a thousand yoke of oxen, and a thousand she-asses. And he had seven sons and three daughters, of whom he called the first Jemimah, the second Keziah, and the third Keren-happuch. In all the land no other women were as beautiful as the daughters of Job; and their father gave them an inheritance among their brethren. After this, Job lived a hundred and forty years; and he saw his children, his grandchildren, and even his great-grandchildren.—This is the Word of the Lord.
℟. **Thanks be to God.** ❖

Responsorial Psalm   Ps 119, 66. 71. 75. 91. 125. 130

℟. (135) **Lord, let your face shine on me.**

Teach me wisdom and knowledge,
    for in your commands I trust. — ℟

It is good for me that I have been afflicted,
    that I may learn your statutes. — ℟

I know, O Lord, that your ordinances are just,
    and in your faithfulness you have afflicted me.—℟

According to your ordinances they still stand firm:
    all things serve you. — ℟

I am your servant; give me discernment
    that I may know your decrees. — ℟

The revelation of your words sheds light,
    giving understanding to the simple. — ℟ ℣

GOSPEL Lk 10, 17-24

See p. 321.

MONDAY OF THE TWENTY-SEVENTH WEEK IN ORDINARY TIME

READING I Gal 1, 6-12

Paul is amazed at the turn of events in Galatia where defections have occurred so rapidly. New converts are allowing themselves to be turned away from God. Only one gospel can be true—the one gospel of Jesus Christ.

A reading from the letter of Paul to the Galatians

I am amazed that you are so soon deserting him who called you in accord with his gracious design in Christ, and are going over to another gospel. But there is no other. Some who wish to alter the gospel of Christ must have confused you. For if even we or an angel from heaven should preach to you a gospel not in accord with the one we delivered to you, let a curse be upon him! I repeat what I have just said: if anyone preaches a gospel to you other than the one you received, let a curse be upon him!

Whom would you say I am trying to please at this point—men or God? Is this how I seek to ingratiate myself? If I were trying to win man's approval, I would surely not be serving Christ!

I assure you, brothers, the gospel I proclaimed to you is no mere human invention. I did not receive

it from any man, nor was I schooled in it. It came
by revelation from Jesus Christ.—This is the Word
of the Lord. ℟. **Thanks be to God.** ℣

Responsorial Psalm   Ps 11, 1-2. 7-8. 9-10

℟. (5) **The Lord will remember his covenant for ever.**

I will give thanks to the Lord with all my heart
  in the company and assembly of the just.
Great are the works of the Lord,
  exquisite in all their delights. — ℟

The works of his hands are faithful and just;
  sure are all his precepts,
Reliable forever and ever,
  wrought in truth and equity. — ℟

He has sent deliverance to his people;
  he has ratified his covenant forever;
Holy and awesome is his name.
  His praise endures forever. — ℟ ℣

℟. Or: **Alleluia.** ℣

GOSPEL   Lk 10, 25-37

See p. 324.

TUESDAY OF THE TWENTY-SEVENTH WEEK
IN ORDINARY TIME

READING I   Gal 1, 13-24

The Galatians were acquainted with Paul's past. He was deeply rooted
in the Jewish religion. Even as a Christian he speaks with reverence
of "his" people. He wishes to get to know Peter. Apart from Peter,
Paul met only James.

A reading from the letter of Paul to the Galatians

You have heard, I know, the story of my former
way of life in Judaism. You know that I went to
extremes in persecuting the church of God and tried
to destroy it; I made progress in Jewish observance

far beyond most of my contemporaries, in my excess of zeal to live out all the traditions of my ancestors.

But the time came when he who had set me apart before I was born and called me by his favor chose to reveal his Son to me, that I might spread among the Gentiles the good tidings concerning him. Immediately, without seeking human advisers or even going to Jerusalem to see those who were apostles before me, I went off to Arabia; later I returned to Damascus. Three years after that I went up to Jerusalem to get to know Cephas, with whom I stayed fifteen days. I did not meet any other apostles except James, the brother of the Lord. I declare before God that what I have just written is true.

Thereafter I entered the regions of Syria and Cilicia. The communities of Christ in Judea had no idea what I looked like; they had only heard that "he who was formerly persecuting us is now preaching the faith he tried to destroy," and they gave glory to God on my account.—This is the Word of the Lord. ℟. **Thanks be to God.** ℣

Responsorial Psalm   Ps 139, 1-3. 13-14. 14-15

℟. (24) **Guide me, Lord, along the everlasting way.**

O Lord, you have probed me and you know me;
    you know when I sit and when I stand;
    you understand my thoughts from afar.
My journeys and my rest you scrutinize,
    with all my ways you are familiar. — ℟

Truly you have formed my inmost being,
    you knit me in my mother's womb.
I give you thanks that I am fearfully, wonderfully
        made;
    wonderful are your works. — ℟

My soul also you knew full well;
    nor was my frame unknown to you

When I was made in secret,
  when I was fashioned in the depths of the
    earth. — ℟ ⋎

GOSPEL   Lk 10, 38-42

See p. 327.

WEDNESDAY OF THE TWENTY-SEVENTH WEEK
IN ORDINARY TIME

READING I   Gal 2, 1-2. 7-14

Paul had been active among the Gentile converts. He follows the
guidance of the Holy Spirit. Paul withstands Peter in Antioch. Peter's
behavior affects the other Jewish Christians.

A reading from the letter of Paul to the Galatians

After fourteen years, I went up to Jerusalem again
with Barnabas, this time taking Titus with me. I
went prompted by a revelation, and I laid out for
their scrutiny the gospel as I present it to the Gentiles—all this in private conference with the leaders,
to make sure the course I was pursuing, or had pursued, was not useless.

On the contrary, recognizing that I had been entrusted with the gospel for the uncircumcised, just
as Peter was for the circumcised (for he who worked
through Peter as his apostle among the Jews had
been at work in me for the Gentiles), and recognizing, too, the favor bestowed on me, those who were
the acknowledged pillars, James, Cephas, and John,
gave Barnabas and me the handclasp of fellowship,
signifying that we should go to the Gentiles as they
to the Jews. The only stipulation was that we should
be mindful of the poor—the one thing that I was
making every effort to do.

When Cephas came to Antioch I directly withstood him, because he was clearly in the wrong. He

had been taking his meals with the Gentiles before others came who were from James. But when they arrived he drew himself apart to avoid trouble with those who were circumcised. The rest of the Jews joined in his dissembling, till even Barnabas was swept away by their pretense. As soon as I observed that they were not being straightforward about the truth of the gospel, I had this to say to Cephas in the presence of all: "If you who are a Jew are living according to Gentile ways rather than Jewish, by what logic do you force the Gentiles to adopt Jewish ways?"—This is the Word of the Lord. ℟. **Thanks be to God.** ℣

Responsorial Psalm   Ps 117, 1. 2

℟. (Mk 16, 15) **Go out to all the world,
     and tell the Good News.**

Praise the Lord, all you nations,
     glorify him, all you peoples! — ℟

For steadfast is his kindness toward us,
     and the fidelity of the Lord endures forever.—℟ ℣

℟. Or: **Alleluia.** ℣

GOSPEL   Lk 11, 1-4

See p. 329.

THURSDAY OF THE TWENTY-SEVENTH WEEK
IN ORDINARY TIME

READING I   Gal 3, 1-5

Paul calls the Galatians personally to give an accounting. He pays them no compliments. They still have not grasped the fact that Law and faith are two different things. The Spirit is the pledge of perfected righteousness.

A reading from the letter of Paul to the Galatians

My good people of Galatia, have you gone out of your minds? Who has cast a spell over you—you before whose eyes Jesus Christ was displayed to view upon his cross? I want to know only one thing from you: how did you receive the Spirit? Was it through observance of the law or through faith in what you heard? How could you be so stupid? After beginning in the spirit, are you now to end in the flesh? Have you had such remarkable experiences all to no purpose—if indeed they were to no purpose? Is it because you observe the law or because you have faith in what you heard that God lavishes the Spirit on you and works wonders in your midst?—This is the Word of the Lord. ℞. **Thanks be to God.** ℣

Responsorial Psalm   Lk 1, 69-70. 71-72. 73-75

℞. (68) **Blessed be the Lord God of Israel,
for he has visited his people.**

He has raised a horn of saving strength for us
    in the house of David his servant,
As he promised through the mouths of his holy ones
    the prophets of ancient times. — ℞

Salvation from our enemies
    and from the hands of all our foes.
He has dealt mercifully with our fathers
    and remembered the holy covenant he made.—℞

The oath he swore to Abraham our father he would
    grant us:
    that, rid of fear and delivered from the enemy,
We should serve him devoutly and through all our
    days,
    be holy in his sight. — ℞ ℣

GOSPEL   Lk 11, 5-13

See p. 331.

FRIDAY OF THE TWENTY-SEVENTH WEEK
IN ORDINARY TIME

READING I Gal 3, 7-14

*In the Scripture it is noted that God would make the Gentiles righteous.
To live by the accomplishment of laws is to be under a curse. The
apostle finally discloses the positive action of God which renders it
possible to be righteous before God. Christ has ransomed all men.*

A reading from the letter of Paul to the Galatians

Those who believe are sons of Abraham. Because
Scripture saw in advance that God's way of justify-
ing the Gentiles would be through faith, it foretold
this good news to Abraham: "All nations shall be
blessed in you." Thus it is that all who believe are
blessed along with Abraham, the man of faith.

All who depend on observance of the law, on the
other hand, are under a curse. It is written, "Cursed
is he who does not abide by everything written in
the book of the law and carry it out." It should be
obvious that no one is justified in God's sight by
the law, for "the just man shall live by faith." But
the law does not depend on faith. Its terms are:
"Whoever does these things shall live by them."
Christ has delivered us back from the power of the
law's curse by becoming himself a curse for us, as
it is written: "Accursed is anyone who is hanged
on a tree." This has happened so that through Christ
Jesus the blessing bestowed on Abraham might descend on the Gentiles in Christ Jesus, thereby making it possible for us to receive the promised Spirit
through faith.—This is the Word of the Lord. ℟.
Thanks be to God. ℣

Responsorial Psalm Ps 111, 1-2. 3-4. 5-6

℟. (5) **The Lord will remember his covenant for ever.**
I will give thanks to the Lord with all my heart
    in the company and assembly of the just.

Great are the works of the Lord,
  exquisite in all their delights. — ℞

Majesty and glory are his work,
  and his justice endures forever.

He has won renown for his wondrous deeds;
  gracious and merciful is the Lord. — ℞

He has given food to those who fear him;
  he will forever be mindful of his covenant.

He has made known to his people the power of his
    works,
  giving them the inheritance of the nations.—℞ ℣

℞. Or: **Alleluia.** ℣

GOSPEL   Lk 11, 15-26

See p. 333.

SATURDAY OF THE TWENTY-SEVENTH WEEK
IN ORDINARY TIME

READING I   Gal 3,22-29

The Law could not bring righteousness. Faith came with Christ into
the world in the form of faith in Jesus Christ. Freedom came through
faith, which God revealed.

A reading from the letter of Paul to the Galatians

Scripture has locked all things in under the constraint of sin. Why? So that the promise might be fulfilled, in those who believe, in consequence of faith in Jesus Christ.

Before faith came we were under the constraint of the law, locked in until the faith that was coming should be revealed. In other words, the law was our monitor until Christ came to bring about our justification through faith. But now that faith is here, we are no longer in the monitor's charge. Each one of you is a son of God because of your faith in Christ Jesus. All of you who have been baptized into Christ have clothed yourselves with him. There does not exist among you Jew or Greek, slave or freeman, male or female. All are one in Christ Jesus. Furthermore, if you belong to Christ you are the descendants of Abraham, which means you inherit all that was promised.—This is the Word of the Lord. ℟. **Thanks be to God.** ⱽ

Responsorial Psalm   Ps 105, 2-3. 4-5. 6-7

℟. (8) **The Lord remembers his covenant for ever.**
Sing to him, sing his praise.
   proclaim all his wondrous deeds.
Glory in his holy name;
   rejoice, O hearts that seek the Lord! — ℟

Look to the Lord in his strength;
   seek to serve him constantly.
Recall the wondrous deeds that he has wrought,
   his portents, and the judgments he has uttered.—℟

You descendants of Abraham, his servants,
   sons of Jacob, his chosen ones!
He, the Lord, is our God;
   throughout the earth his judgments prevail.—℟ ⱽ

℟. Or: **Alleluia.** ⱽ

GOSPEL   Lk 11, 27-28

See p. 336.

MONDAY OF THE TWENTY-EIGHTH WEEK IN ORDINARY TIME

READING I   Gal 4, 22-24. 26-27. 31—5, 1
Paul reviews the historic figures of the Genesis story. Christians can boast of the real covenant made by God with Abraham, for they are sons of Abraham according to the promise. "Christ freed us" sums up the message of Paul's letter.

A reading from the letter of Paul to the Galatians
It is written that Abraham had two sons, one by the slave girl, the other by his freeborn wife. The son

of the slave girl had been begotten in the course of nature, but the son of the free woman was the fruit of the promise. All this is clearly an allegory: the two women stand for the two covenants. One is from Mount Sinai and she brought forth children to slavery: this is Hagar. But the Jerusalem on high is freeborn, and it is she who is our mother. That is why Scripture says:

"Rejoice, you barren one who bear no children;
  break into song, you stranger to the pains of childbirth!
For many are the children of the wife deserted—
  far more than of her who has a husband!"

Therefore, my brothers, we are not children of a slave girl but of a mother who is free.

It was for liberty that Christ freed us. So stand firm, and do not take on yourselves the yoke of slavery a second time!—This is the Word of the Lord. ℞. **Thanks be to God.** ℣

Responsorial Psalm Ps 113, 1-2. 3-4. 5. 6-7

℞. (2) **Blessed be the name of the Lord for ever.**

Praise, you servants of the Lord,
  praise the name of the Lord.
Blessed be the name of the Lord
  both now and forever. — ℞

From the rising to the setting of the sun
  is the name of the Lord to be praised.
High above all nations is the Lord;
  above the heavens is his glory. — ℞

Who is like the Lord, our God,
  who looks upon the heavens and the earth below?
He raises up the lowly from the dust;
  from the dunghill he lifts up the poor. — ℞ ℣

℞. Or: **Alleluia.** ℣

GOSPEL Lk 11, 29-32
See p. 338.

TUESDAY OF THE TWENTY-EIGHTH WEEK
IN ORDINARY TIME

READING I Gal 5, 1-6

In Christ all have become free. The Galatians must choose one or the other: Christ and freedom, or the Law and slavery. No compromise is possible. The principle of justification is faith working through love.

A reading from the letter of Paul to the Galatians

Christ freed us for liberty. So stand firm, and do not take on yourselves the yoke of slavery a second time! Pay close attention to me, Paul, when I tell you that if you have yourselves circumcised, Christ will be of no use to you! I point out once more to all who receive circumcision that they are bound to the law in its entirety. Any of you who seek your justification in the law have severed yourselves from Christ and fallen from God's favor! It is in the spirit that we eagerly await the justification we hope for, and only faith can yield it. In Christ Jesus neither circumcision nor the lack of it counts for anything; only faith, which expresses itself through love.—This is the Word of the Lord. ℟. **Thanks be to God.** ℣

Responsorial Psalm Ps 119, 41. 43. 44. 45. 47. 48

℟. (41) **Let your loving kindness come to me, O Lord.**

Let your kindness come to me, O Lord,
    your salvation according to your promise. — ℟

Take not the word of truth from my mouth,
    for in your ordinances is my hope. — ℟

And I will keep your law continually,
    forever and ever. — ℟

And I will walk at liberty,
    because I seek your precepts. — ℟

And I will delight in your commands,
    which I love. — ℟

And I will lift up my hands to your commands
and meditate on your statutes. — ℟ ↓

GOSPEL   Lk 11, 37-41

See p. 340.

WEDNESDAY OF THE TWENTY-EIGHTH WEEK
IN ORDINARY TIME

READING I   Gal 5, 18-25

Paul's concrete advice illustrates the love which he stresses. "Good
deeds" are not to be excluded from Christian life. There is no law
against such virtuous actions.

A reading from the letter of Paul to the Galatians

If you are guided by the spirit, you are not under
the law. It is obvious what proceeds from the flesh:
lewd conduct, impurity, licentiousness, idolatry, sor-
cery, hostilities, bickering, jealousy, outbursts of
rage, selfish rivalries, dissensions, factions, envy,
drunkenness, orgies, and the like. I warn you, as I
have warned you before: those who do such things
will not inherit the kingdom of God!

In contrast, the fruit of the spirit is love, joy,
peace, patient endurance, kindness, generosity, faith,
mildness, and chastity. Against such there is no law!
Those who belong to Christ Jesus have crucified
their flesh with its passions and desires. Since we
live by the spirit, let us follow the spirit's lead.—This is
the Word of the Lord. ℟. **Thanks be to God.** ↓

Responsorial Psalm   Ps 1, 1-2. 3. 4. 6

℟. (Jn 8, 12) **Those who follow you, Lord, will have
   the light of life.**

Happy the man who follows not
   the counsel of the wicked

Nor walks in the way of sinners,
    nor sits in the company of the insolent,
But delights in the law of the Lord
    and meditates on his law day and night. — ℞

He is like a tree
    planted near running water,
That yields its fruit in due season,
    and whose leaves never fade.
    [Whatever he does, prospers.] — ℞

Not so the wicked, not so;
    they are like chaff which the wind drives away.
For the Lord watches over the way of the just,
    but the way of the wicked vanishes. — ℞ ℣

GOSPEL   Lk 11, 42-46

See p. 342.

THURSDAY OF THE TWENTY-EIGHTH WEEK
IN ORDINARY TIME

READING I   Eph 1, 3-10

Paul passes directly to the praise of God for revealing his plan of salvation. The hymn has a strong baptismal character in its reference to sonship, forgiveness of sins, incorporation into Christ, and the seal of the Spirit.

The beginning of the letter of Paul to the
Ephesians

Paul, the apostle of Jesus Christ: Praised be the God and Father of our Lord Jesus Christ: God, who has bestowed on us in Christ every spiritual blessing in the heavens! God chose us in him before the world began, to be holy and blameless in his sight, to be full of love; he likewise predestined us through Christ Jesus to be his adopted sons—such was his will and pleasure—that all might praise the divine favor he has bestowed on us in his beloved.

It is in Christ and through his blood that we have been redeemed and our sins forgiven, so immeasurably generous is God's favor to us. God has given us the wisdom to understand fully the mystery, the plan he was pleased to decree in Christ, to be carried out in the fullness of time: namely, to bring all things in the heavens and on earth into one under Christ's headship.—This is the Word of the Lord. ℟. **Thanks be to God.** ℣

Responsorial Psalm   Ps 98, 1. 2-3. 3-4. 5-6

℟. (2) **The Lord has made known his salvation.**

Sing to the Lord a new song,
  for he has done wondrous deeds;
His right hand has won victory for him,
  his holy arm. — ℟

The Lord has made his salvation known:
  in the sight of the nations he has revealed his
    justice.
He has remembered his kindness and his faithfulness
  toward the house of Israel. — ℟

All the ends of the earth have seen,
  the salvation by our God.
Sing joyfully to the Lord, all you lands;
  break into song; sing praise. — ℟

Sing praise to the Lord with the harp,
  with the harp and melodious song.
With trumpets and the sound of the horn
  sing joyfully before the King, the Lord. — ℟ ℣

GOSPEL   Lk 11, 47-54

See p. 344.

FRIDAY OF THE TWENTY-EIGHTH WEEK
IN ORDINARY TIME

READING I   Eph 1, 11-14

For Paul the young Christian Church is divided into two main groups:
"we," the faithful who have come to the faith out of the chosen
people, and "you," the believers from out of the Gentile world. But
there is only one Spirit.

A reading from the letter of Paul to the
Ephesians

In Christ we were chosen; for in the decree of God,
who administers everything according to his will
and counsel, we were predestined to praise his glory
by being the first to hope in Christ. In him you too
were chosen; when you heard the glad tidings of
salvation, the word of truth, and believed in it, you
were sealed with the Holy Spirit who had been promised. He is the pledge of our inheritance, the first
payment against the full redemption of a people
God has made his own to praise his glory.—This is
the Word of the Lord. ℟. **Thanks be to God.** ✔

Responsorial Psalm   Ps 33, 1-2. 4-5. 12-13

℟. (12) **Happy the people the Lord has chosen to be
his own.**

Exult, you just, in the Lord;
    praise from the upright is fitting.
Give thanks to the Lord on the harp;
    with the ten-stringed lyre chant his praises.—℟
For upright is the word of the Lord,
    and all his works are trustworthy.
He loves justice and right;
    of the kindness of the Lord the earth is full. — ℟
Happy the nation whose God is the Lord,
    the people he has chosen for his own inheritance.
From heaven the Lord looks down;
    he sees all mankind. — ℟ ✔

GOSPEL   Lk 12, 1-7

See p. 346.

SATURDAY OF THE TWENTY-EIGHTH WEEK IN ORDINARY TIME

READING I   Eph 1, 15-23

Paul brings out the connection between faith and love. Faith is a commitment to Christ. Paul sees the resurrection, ascension, and glorification of Christ as one great continuous act of the Father.

A reading from the letter of Paul to the Ephesians

From the time I first heard of your faith in the Lord Jesus and your love for all the members of the church, I have never stopped thanking God for you and recommending you in my prayers. May the God of our Lord Jesus Christ, the Father of glory, grant you a spirit of wisdom and insight to know him clearly. May he enlighten your innermost vision that you may know the great hope to which he has called you, the wealth of his glorious heritage to be distributed among the members of the church, and the immeasurable scope of his power in us who believe. It is like the strength he showed in raising Christ from the dead and seating him at his right hand in heaven, high above every principality, power, virtue, and domination, and every name that can be given in this age or in the age to come.

He has put all things under Christ's feet and made him head of the church, which is his body: the fullness of him, who fills the universe in all its parts.— This is the Word of the Lord. ℟. **Thanks be to God. ℣**

Responsorial Psalm Ps 8, 2-3. 4-5. 6-7

℟. (1) **You gave your Son authority over all your creation.**

O Lord, our Lord,
how glorious is your name over all the earth!
You have exalted your majesty above the heavens.
Out of the mouths of babes and sucklings
you have fashioned praise because of your
foes. — ℟

When I behold your heavens, the work of your fingers,
the moon and the stars which you set in place—
What is man that you should be mindful of him,
or the son of man that you should care for
him? —℟

You have made him little less than the angels,
and crowned him with glory and honor.
You have given him rule over the works of your
hands,
putting all things under his feet. — ℟ ❯

GOSPEL Lk 12, 8-12

See p. 348.

MONDAY OF THE TWENTY-NINTH WEEK
IN ORDINARY TIME

READING I Eph 2, 1-10

This chapter is filled with sharp contrasts between human weakness
and the result of the operation of God's mighty power. Paul refers
to the body as the instrument of the desires and longing of a self-
centered life. Faith is a gift from God.

A reading from the letter of Paul to the
Ephesians

You were dead because of your sins and offenses,
as you gave allegiance to the present age and to the

prince of the air, that spirit who is even now at work among the rebellious. All of us were once of their company; we lived at the level of the flesh, following every whim and fancy, and so by nature deserved God's wrath like the rest. But God is rich in mercy; because of his great love for us he brought us to life with Christ when we were dead in sin. By this favor you were saved. Both with and in Christ Jesus he raised us up and gave us a place in the heavens, that in the ages to come he might display the great wealth of his favor, manifested by his kindness to us in Christ Jesus. I repeat, it is owing to his favor that salvation is yours through faith. This is not your own doing, it is God's gift; neither is it a reward for anything you have accomplished, so let no one pride himself on it. We are truly his handiwork, created in Christ Jesus to lead the life of good deeds which God prepared for us in advance. This is the Word of the Lord. ℟. **Thanks be to God.** ⍦

Responsorial Psalm   Ps 100, 2. 3. 4. 5

℟. (3) **The Lord made us, we belong to him.**

Serve the Lord with gladness;
    come before him with joyful song. — ℟

Know that the Lord is God;
    he made us, his we are;
    his people, the flock he tends. — ℟

Enter his gates with thanksgiving,
    his courts with praise. — ℟

Give thanks to him; bless his name, for he is good:
    the Lord, whose kindness endures forever,
    and his faithfulness, to all generations. — ℟ ⍦

GOSPEL   Lk 12, 13-21

See p. 349.

See p. 349.

TUESDAY OF THE TWENTY-NINTH WEEK IN ORDINARY TIME

READING I   Eph 2, 12-22

Paul reminds the Ephesians that formerly they were excluded from the Covenant without hope. By his death Jesus reconciled them with God. Jesus is the cornerstone fitting together the whole structure of salvation.

A reading from the letter of Paul to the Ephesians

In former times, you had no part in Christ and were excluded from the community of Israel. You were strangers to the covenant and its promise; you were without hope and without God in the world. But now in Christ Jesus you who once were far off have been brought near through the blood of Christ. It is he who is our peace, and who made the two of us one by breaking down the barrier of hostility that kept us apart. In his own flesh he abolished the law with its commands and precepts, to create in himself one new man from us who had been two, and to make peace, reconciling both of us to God in one body through his cross which put that enmity to death. He came and "announced the good news of peace to you who were far off, and to those who were near"; through him we both have access in one Spirit to the Father.

This means that you are strangers and aliens no longer. No, you are fellow citizens of the saints and members of the household of God. You form a building which rises on the foundation of the apostles and prophets, with Christ Jesus himself as the capstone. Through him the whole structure is fitted together and takes shape as a holy temple in the Lord; in him you are being built into this temple, to become a dwelling place for God in the Spirit.—This is the Word of the Lord. ℞. **Thanks be to God.** ℣

Responsorial Psalm   Ps 85, 9-10. 11-12. 13-14

℟. (9) **The Lord speaks of peace to his people.**

I will hear what God proclaims;
   the Lord—for he proclaims peace.
Near indeed is his salvation to those who fear him,
   glory dwelling in our land. — ℟

Kindness and truth shall meet;
   justice and peace shall kiss.
Truth shall spring out of the earth,
   and justice shall look down from heaven. — ℟

The Lord himself will give his benefits;
   our land shall yield its increase.
Justice shall walk before him,
   and salvation, along the way of his steps. — ℟ ↓

GOSPEL   Lk 12, 35-38

See p. 351.

WEDNESDAY OF THE TWENTY-NINTH WEEK
IN ORDINARY TIME

READING I   Eph 3, 2-12

Paul is writing from prison. He points to his own call as an example
of the grace and favor of God. God foreordained his work of restoring
the universe in the Church.

A reading from the letter of Paul to the
Ephesians

I am sure you have heard of the ministry which God
in his goodness gave me in your regard. That is why
to me, Paul, a prisoner for Christ Jesus on behalf of
you Gentiles, God's secret plan as I have briefly
described it was revealed. When you read what I
have said, you will realize that I know what I am
talking about in speaking of the mystery of Christ,
unknown to men in former ages but now revealed

by the Spirit to the holy apostles and prophets. It is no less than this: in Christ Jesus the Gentiles are now co-heirs with the Jews, members of the same body and sharers of the promise through the preaching of the gospel.

Through the gift God in his goodness bestowed on me by the exercise of his power, I became a minister of the gospel. To me, the least of all believers, was given the grace to preach to the Gentiles the unfathomable riches of Christ and to enlighten all men on the mysterious design which for ages was hidden in God, the Creator of all. Now, therefore, through the church, God's manifold wisdom is made known to the principalities and powers of heaven, in accord with his age-old purpose, carried out in Christ Jesus our Lord. In Christ and through faith in him we can speak freely to God, drawing near him with confidence.—This is the Word of the Lord. ℟. **Thanks be to God.** ℣

Responsorial Psalm   Is 12, 2-3. 4. 5-6

℟. (3) **You will draw water joyfully from the springs of salvation.**

God indeed is my savior;
    I am confident and unafraid.
My strength and my courage is the Lord,
    and he has been my savior.
With joy you will draw water
    at the fountain of salvation. — ℟

Give thanks to the Lord, acclaim his name;
    among the nations make known his deeds,
    proclaim how exalted is his name. — ℟

Sing praise to the Lord for his glorious achievement;
    let this be known throughout all the earth.
Shout with exultation, O city of Zion,
    for great in your midst
    is the Holy One of Israel! — ℟ ℣

GOSPEL Lk 39-48

See p. 353.

THURSDAY OF THE TWENTY-NINTH WEEK
IN ORDINARY TIME

READING I Eph 3, 14-21

It is through Christ that men become true sons of God. Only the believer reaches the fullness of God's nature and all its transforming power. The Church and Christ are necessary complements of each other.

A reading from the letter of Paul to the
Ephesians

That is why I kneel before the Father from whom every family in heaven and on earth takes its name; and I pray that he will bestow on you gifts in keeping with the riches of his glory. May he strengthen you inwardly through the workings of his Spirit. May Christ dwell in your hearts through faith, and may charity be the root and foundation of your life. Thus you will be able to grasp fully, with all the holy ones, the breadth and length and height and depth of Christ's love, and experience this love which surpasses all knowledge, so that you may attain to the fullness of God himself.

To him whose power now at work in us can do immeasurably more than we ask or imagine—to him be glory in the church and in Christ Jesus through all generations, world without end. Amen.—This is the Word of the Lord. ℟. **Thanks be to God.** ℣

Responsorial Psalm Ps 33, 12. 4-5. 11-12. 18-19
℟. (5) **The earth is full of the goodness of the Lord.**
Exult, you just, in the Lord;
    praise from the upright is fitting.

Give thanks to the Lord on the harp;
  with the ten-stringed lyre chant his praises. — ℟

For upright is the word of the Lord,
  and all his works are trustworthy.

He loves justice and right;
  of the kindness of the Lord the earth is full. — ℟

But the plan of the Lord stands forever;
  the design of his heart, through all generations.

Happy the nation whose God is the Lord,
  the people he has chosen for his own inheri-
    tance. — ℟

But see, the eyes of the Lord are upon those who
    fear him,
  upon those who hope for his kindness,

To deliver them from death
  and preserve them in spite of famine. — ℟ ℣

GOSPEL   Lk 12, 49-53

See p. 356.

FRIDAY OF THE TWENTY-NINTH WEEK
IN ORDINARY TIME

READING I   Eph 4, 1-6

Paul's great interest, that of unity of the Church, is evident in all his
writings. Those who are called to partake of the Christian life must
live a life worthy of that calling.

A reading from the letter of Paul to the
Ephesians

I plead with you as a prisoner for the Lord, to live
a life worthy of the calling you have received, with
perfect humility, meekness, and patience, bearing
with one another lovingly. Make every effort to preserve the unity which has the Spirit as its origin and

peace as its binding force. There is but one body and one Spirit, just as there is but one hope given all of you by your call. There is one Lord, one faith, one baptism; one God and Father of all, who is over all, and works through all, and is in all.—This is the Word of the Lord. ℟. **Thanks be to God.** ✟

Responsorial Psalm   Ps 24, 1-2. 3-4. 5-6

℟. (6) **Lord, this is the people that longs to see your face.**

The Lord's are the earth and its fullness;
    the world and those who dwell in it.
For he founded it upon the seas
    and established it upon the rivers. — ℟

Who can ascend the mountain of the Lord?
    or who may stand in his holy place?
He whose hands are sinless, whose heart is clean,
    who desires not what is vain. — ℟

He shall receive a blessing from the Lord,
    a reward from God his savior.
Such is the race that seeks for him,
    that seeks the face of the God of Jacob. — ℟ ✟

GOSPEL   Lk 12, 54-59

See p. 357.

SATURDAY OF THE TWENTY-NINTH WEEK IN ORDINARY TIME

READING I   Eph 4, 7-16

Paul explains that within the basic unity of the Church there are diverse gifts from the Risen Christ. Each member, exercising his gift and function for the benefit of all, will contribute to the up-building of the whole Body of Christ.

A reading from the letter of Paul to the
Ephesians

Each of us has received God's favor in the measure
in which Christ bestows it. Thus you find Scripture
saying:

"When he ascended on high, he took a host of
captives
and gave gifts to men."

"He ascended"—what does this mean but that he
had first descended into the lower regions of the
earth? He who descended is the very one who ascended high above the heavens, that he might fill all
men with his gifts.

It is he who gave apostles, prophets, evangelists,
pastors and teachers in roles of service for the faithful to build up the body of Christ, till we become one
in faith and in the knowledge of God's Son and form
that perfect man who is Christ come to full stature.

Let us, then, be children no longer, tossed here
and there, carried about by every wind of doctrine
that originates in human trickery and skill in pro-
posing error. Rather, let us profess to the truth in
love and grow to the full maturity of Christ the head.
Through him the whole body grows, and with the
proper functioning of the members joined firmly
together by each supporting ligament, builds itself
up in love.—This is the Word of the Lord. ℟. **Thanks
be to God.** ✠

Responsorial Psalm   Ps 122, 1-2. 3-4. 4-5

℟. (1) **I rejoiced when I heard them say:
let us go to the house of the Lord.**

I rejoiced because they said to me,
   "We will go up to the house of the Lord."
And now we have set foot
   within your gates, O Jerusalem. — ℟

Jerusalem, built as a city
  with compact unity.
To it the tribes go up,
  the tribes of the Lord. — ℟

According to the decree for Israel,
  to give thanks to the name of the Lord.
In it are set up judgment seats,
  seats for the house of David. — ℟ ⩔

GOSPEL   Lk 13, 1-9

See p. 359.

INTRODUCTION FOR 30th TO 34th WEEK

The Epistle to the Philippians—*Learning that St. Paul had been cast into prison, the church at Philippi, in order to assist him, sent Epaphroditus with a sum of money and with instructions to remain beside the Apostle as his companion and servant. While thus employed, Epaphroditus fell sick and nearly died. Upon his recovery, St. Paul decided to send him back to Philippi. The Epistle (written in 63 A.D.) expresses gratitude to the church for its gift and commends the service rendered by Epaphroditus. At the same time Paul takes the opportunity of exhorting the faithful to compose their dissensions, and he warns them against Jewish converts who wished to make Old Testament practices obligatory for Christians.*

Paul recalls the example of Christ who—in contrast with Adam who sought to assert himself and assure his life by his unaided efforts—wholly "emptied" himself, renouncing all self-will and submitting entirely to the will of his Father (2, 6-11). This hymn, which in all probability antedates Paul, and which he makes his own, is one of the most extraordinary texts of the ancient Church. Christ's lot is exemplary. He who lives in and by Christ must, like him, renounce his own interests, his will to power, and expect praise and glory from God alone.

The Epistle to Titus—*One of the "Pastoral Epistles" written between 63 and 67 A.D., this Epistle gives instructions to Titus similar to those given in the First Epistle to Timothy.*

It instructs Titus about the character of the men he is to choose in view of the pastoral difficulties peculiar to Crete. It suggests the special individual and social virtues which the various age groups and classes in the Christian community should be encouraged to acquire. The motives for improving one's personal character are to be found preeminently in the mysteries of the incarnation and the second coming of Christ. The community is to be fashioned into a leaven for Christianizing the social world about it. Good works are to be the evidence of their faith in God; those who engage in religious controversy are, after suitable warning, to be ignored.

The Epistle to Philemon—*During his first Roman imprisonment (61-63 A.D.), St. Paul came to know a slave named Onesimus, who had deserted his master Philemon, a wealthy Christian of Colossae in Phrygia. After the apostle had won the fugitive over to Christianity, he looked for a favorable opportunity to send him back to his master. This opportunity offered itself when he was dispatching a letter to the Colossians in the year 63 A.D. Onesimus accompanied St. Paul's messenger Tychicus. To Philemon the apostle addressed a touching appeal, entreating his friend to deal kindly with the runaway.*

The Second Epistle of John—*Writing toward the end of the 1st century A.D., John commends the recipients of the letter for their steadfastness in the true faith, and exhorts them to persevere, lest they lose the reward of their labors. He exhorts them to love one another, but warns them to have no fellowship with heretics, and not even to greet them.*

The Third Epistle of John—*Though brief, this Epistle vividly portrays certain features in the life of the early Church. Gaius is praised for his hospitality and for walking in the truth. Diotrephes, on the contrary, is censured for his ambition and lack of hospitality. A certain Demetrius is also commended for his virtue.*

The Book of Revelation—*Written about 95 A.D., this book is the most mysterious of all the books of the Bible. It cannot be adequately comprehended except against the historical background which occasioned its writing. Like the Book of Daniel and* other apocalypses, it was composed as resistance literature to meet a crisis. The book itself suggests that the crisis was ruthless persecution of the early church by the Roman authorities; the harlot Babylon symbolizes pagan Rome, the city on seven hills. The book is, then, an exhortation and admonition to the Christian to stand firm in the faith and to avoid compromise with paganism, despite the threat of adversity and martyrdom; he is to await patiently the fulfillment of God's mighty promises. The triumph of God in the world of men remains a mystery, to be accepted in faith and longed for in hope. It is a triumph that unfolded in the history of Jesus of Nazareth, and continues to unfold in the history of the individual Christian who follows the way of the cross, even, if necessary, to a martyr's death.

Though the perspective is eschatological—ultimate salvation and victory are said to take place at the end of the present age when Christ will come in glory at the parousia—the book presents the decisive struggle of Christ and his followers against Satan and his cohorts as already over. Christ's overwhelming defeat of the kingdom of Satan has ushered in the everlasting reign of God. Even the forces of evil unwittingly carry out the divine plan for God is the sovereign Lord of history.

MONDAY OF THE THIRTIETH WEEK
IN ORDINARY TIME

READING I   Eph 4, 32—5, 8

Paul admonishes the Ephesians to suffer irritations with patience and love and to "bear all things" with kindness and forgiveness. Paul stresses here the main vices which beset human weakness.

A reading from the letter of Paul to the Ephesians

Be kind to one another, compassionate, and mutually forgiving, just as God has forgiven you in Christ.

Be imitators of God as his dear children. Follow the way of love, even as Christ loved you. He gave himself for us as an offering to God, a gift of pleasing fragrance.

As for lewd conduct or promiscuousness or lust of any sort, let them not even be mentioned among you; your holiness forbids this. Nor should there be any obscene, silly, or suggestive talk; all that is out of place. Instead, give thanks. Make no mistake about this: no fornicator, no unclean or lustful person—in effect an idolator—has any inheritance in the kingdom of Christ and of God. Let no one deceive you with worthless arguments. These are sins that bring God's wrath down on the disobedient; therefore have nothing to do with them. There was a time when you were darkness, but now you are light in the Lord.—This is the Word of the Lord. ℟. **Thanks be to God.** ℣

Responsorial Psalm   Ps 1, 1-2. 3. 4. 6

℟. (Eph 5, 1) **Behave like God as his very dear children.**

Happy the man who follows not
   the counsel of the wicked,
Nor walks in the way of sinners,
   nor sits in the company of the insolent,

But delights in the law of the Lord
    and meditates on his law day and night. — ℟.
He is like a tree
    planted near running water,
That yields its fruit in due season,
    and whose leaves never fade.
    [Whatever he does, prospers.] — ℟
Not so the wicked, not so;
    they are like the chaff which the wind drives away.
For the Lord watches over the way of the just,
    but the way of the wicked vanishes. — ℟ ▼

GOSPEL Lk 13, 10-17

See p. 363.

TUESDAY OF THE THIRTIETH WEEK
IN ORDINARY TIME

READING I Eph 5, 21-33

Here the relationship of Christ to the Church is paralleled with the
bond between a man and his wife. Paul sees the leading role in
marriage to be the husband's. But he excludes any idea of self-will,
self-seeking, and abuse.

A reading from the letter of Paul to the Ephesians

Defer to one another out of reverence for Christ.
Wives should be submissive to their husbands as if
to the Lord because the husband is head of his wife
just as Christ is head of his body, the church, as well
as its savior. As the church submits to Christ, so
wives should submit to their husbands in everything.

Husbands, love your wives, as Christ loved the
church. He gave himself up for her to make her holy,
purifying her in the bath of water by the power of
the word, to present to himself a glorious church,
holy and immaculate, without stain or wrinkle or

anything of that sort. Husbands should love their wives as they do their own bodies. He who loves his wife loves himself. Observe that no one ever hates his own flesh; no, he nourishes it and takes care of it as Christ cares for the church—for we are members of his body.

> "For this reason a man shall leave his father and mother,
> and shall cling to his wife,
> and the two shall be made into one."

This is a great foreshadowing; I mean that it refers to Christ and the church. In any case, each one should love his wife as he loves himself, the wife for her part showing respect for her husband.—This is the Word of the Lord. ℞. **Thanks be to God.** ℣

Responsorial Psalm   Ps 128, 1-2. 3. 4-5

℞. (1) **Happy are those who fear the Lord.**

Happy are you who fear the Lord,
  who walk in his ways!
For you shall eat the fruit of your handiwork;
  happy shall you be, and favored. — ℞

Your wife shall be like a fruitful vine
  in the recesses of your home;
Your children like olive plants
  around your table. — ℞

Behold, thus is the man blessed
  who fears the Lord.
The Lòrd bless you from Zion:
  may you see the prosperity of Jerusalem
  all the days of your life. — ℞ ℣

GOSPEL   Lk 13, 18-21

See p. 366.

WEDNESDAY OF THE THIRTIETH WEEK
IN ORDINARY TIME

READING I   Eph 6, 1-9

Children are to obey their parents since all authority comes from
God. Fathers are to love and train their children. Slaves are to obey
their masters. God, who is all-just, will be the judge.

A reading from the letter of Paul to the
Ephesians

Children, obey your parents in the Lord, for that is
what is expected of you. "Honor your father and
mother" is the first commandment to carry a promise with it—"that it may go well with you, and that
you may have long life on earth."

Fathers, do not anger your children. Bring them
up with the training and instruction befitting the
Lord.

Slaves, obey your human masters with the reverence, the awe, and the sincerity you owe to Christ.
Do not render service for appearance only and to
please men, but do God's will with your whole heart
as slaves of Christ. Give your service willingly, doing
it for the Lord rather than men. You know that each
one, whether slave or free, will be repaid by the
Lord for whatever good he does.

Masters, act in a similar way toward your slaves.
Stop threatening them. Remember that you and they
have a Master in heaven who plays no favorites.—
This is the Word of the Lord. ℟. **Thanks be to God.** ℣

Responsorial Psalm   Ps 145, 10-11. 12-13. 13-14

℟. (13) **The Lord is faithful in all his words.**

Let all your works give you thanks, O Lord,
    and let your faithful ones bless you.
Let them discourse of the glory of your kingdom
    and speak of your might. — ℟

Making known to men your might
and the glorious splendor of your kingdom.
Your kingdom is a kingdom of all ages,
and your dominion endures through all generations. — ℟

The Lord is faithful in all his words
and holy in all his works.
The Lord lifts up all who are falling
and raises up all who are bowed down. — ℟ ℣

GOSPEL   Lk 13, 22-30

See p. 367.

THURSDAY OF THE THIRTIETH WEEK
IN ORDINARY TIME

READING I   Eph 6, 10-20

Paul stresses the Christian source of power and strength in the face
of opposition. The standard equipment of the Christian is the truth
of his faith and the word of God. Paul asks for prayers.

A reading from the letter of Paul to the
Ephesians

Draw your strength from the Lord and his mighty
power. Put on the armor of God so that you may be
able to stand firm against the tactics of the devil.
Our battle ultimately is not against human forces
but against the principalities and powers, the rulers
of this world of darkness, the evil spirits in regions
above. You must put on the armor of God if you are
to resist on the evil day; do all that your duty requires, and hold your ground. Stand fast, with the
truth as the belt around your waist, justice as your
breastplate, and zeal to propagate the gospel of peace
as your footgear. In all circumstances hold faith up
before you as your shield; it will help you extinguish

the fiery darts of the evil one. Take the helmet of salvation and the sword of the spirit, the word of God.

At every opportunity pray in the Spirit, using prayers and petitions of every sort. Pray constantly and attentively for all in the holy company. Pray for me that God may put his word on my lips, that I may courageously make known the mystery of the gospel—that mystery for which I am an ambassador in chains. Pray that I may have courage to proclaim it as I ought.—This is the Word of the Lord. ℟. **Thanks be to God.** ℣

Responsorial Psalm   Ps 144, 1. 2. 9-10

℟. (1) **Blessed be the Lord, my Rock!**

Blessed be the Lord, my rock,
   who trains my hands for battle, my fingers for
      war. — ℟

My refuge and my fortress,
   my stronghold, my deliverer,
My shield, in whom I trust,
   who subdues peoples under me. — ℟

O God, I will sing a new song to you;
   with a ten-stringed lyre I will chant your praise,
You who give victory to kings,
   and deliver David, your servant. — ℟ ℣

GOSPEL   Lk 13, 31-35

See p. 369.

FRIDAY OF THE THIRTIETH WEEK
IN ORDINARY TIME

READING I   Phil 1, 1-11

Paul invokes a blessing coming both from the Father and from the Lord Jesus Christ. A note of joy is struck that runs throughout the letter. The "good work" so begun and continued will be rewarded with the glorious destiny of the Christian: to be with the Lord.

The beginning of the letter of Paul to the Philippians

Paul and Timothy, servants of Christ Jesus, to all the holy ones at Philippi, with their bishops and deacons in Christ Jesus. Grace and peace be yours from God our Father and from the Lord Jesus Christ!

I give thanks to my God every time I think of you —which is constantly, in every prayer I utter—rejoicing, as I plead on your behalf, at the way you have all continually helped promote the gospel from the very first day.

I am sure of this much: that he who has begun the good work in you will carry it through to completion, right up to the day of Christ Jesus. It is only right that I should entertain such expectations in your regard since I hold all of you dear—you who, to a man, are sharers of my gracious lot when I lie in prison or am summoned to defend the solid grounds on which the gospel rests. God himself can testify how much I long for each of you with the affection of Christ Jesus! My prayer is that your love may more and more abound, both in understanding and wealth of experience, so that with a clear conscience and blameless conduct you may learn to value the things that really matter, up to the very day of Christ. It is my wish that you may be found rich in the harvest of justice which Jesus Christ has ripened in you, to the glory and praise of God.—This is the Word of the Lord. ℟. **Thanks be to God.** ℣

Responsorial Psalm Ps 111, 1-2. 3-4. 5-6

℞. (2) **How great are the works of the Lord!**

I will give thanks to the Lord with all my heart
in the company and assembly of the just.
Great are the works of the Lord,
exquisite in all their delights. — ℞

Majesty and glory are his work,
and his justice endures forever.
He has won renown for his wondrous deeds;
gracious and merciful is the Lord. — ℞

He has given food to those who fear him;
he will forever be mindful of his covenant.
He has made known to his people the power of his
works,
giving them the inheritance of the nations. — ℞ ⅴ

℞. Or: **Alleluia.** ⅴ

GOSPEL Lk 14, 1-6

See p. 371.

SATURDAY OF THE THIRTIETH WEEK
IN ORDINARY TIME

READING I Phil 1, 18-26

Paul rejoices in the growth of the Christian faith. He ponders the
alternatives of his living and dying. Paul is aware that the culmination of physical existence is ultimately to be "with Christ," and that
is why to die is a gain.

A reading from the letter of Paul to the
Philippians

All that matters is that in any and every way, whether from specious motives or genuine ones, Christ
is being proclaimed! That is what brings me joy.
Indeed, I shall continue to rejoice in the conviction
that "this will turn out to my salvation," thanks to

your prayers and the support I receive from the
Spirit of Jesus Christ. I firmly trust and anticipate
that I shall never be put to shame for my hopes; I
have full confidence that now as always Christ will
be exalted through me, whether I live or die. For, to
me, "life" means Christ; hence dying is so much
gain. If, on the other hand, I am to go on living in
the flesh, that means productive toil for me—and I
do not know which to prefer. I am strongly attracted
by both: I long to be freed from this life and to be
with Christ, for that is the far better thing; yet it is
more urgent that I remain alive for your sakes. This
fills me with confidence that I will stay with you,
and persevere with you all, for your joy and your
progress in the faith. My being with you once again
should make you even prouder of me in Christ.—
This is the Word of the Lord. ℞. **Thanks be to God.** ℣

Responsorial Psalm   Ps 42, 2. 3. 5

℞. (3) **My soul is thirsting for the living God.**

As the hind longs for the running waters,
   so my soul longs for you, O God. — ℞
Athirst is my soul for God, the living God.
   When shall I go and behold the face of God? — ℞
I went with the throng
   and led them in procession to the house of God,
Amid loud cries of joy and thanksgiving,
   with the multitude keeping festival. — ℞ ℣

GOSPEL   Lk 14, 1. 7-11

See p. 373.

MONDAY OF THE THIRTY-FIRST WEEK IN ORDINARY TIME

READING I   Phil 2, 1-4

Paul asks the Philippians to be of one mind and heart, never to be envious or to act out of pride or contempt but rather to be humble. This will bring him joy and happiness.

A reading from the letter of Paul to the Philippians

In the name of the encouragement you owe me in Christ, in the name of the solace that love can give, of fellowship in spirit, compassion, and pity, I beg you: make my joy complete by your unanimity, possessing the one love, united in spirit and ideals. Never act out of rivalry or conceit; rather, let all parties think humbly of others as superior to themselves, each of you looking to others' interests rather than his own.—This is the Word of the Lord. ℟. **Thanks be to God.** ⬧

Responsorial Psalm   Ps 131, 1. 2. 3

℟. **In you, Lord, I have found my peace.**

O Lord, my heart is not proud,
   nor are my eyes haughty;
I busy not myself with great things,
   nor with things too sublime for me. — ℟

Nay rather, I have stilled and quieted
   my soul like a weaned child.
Like a weaned child on its mother's lap,
   [so is my soul within me.] — ℟

O Israel, hope in the Lord,
   both now and forever. — ℟ ⬧

GOSPEL   Lk 14, 12-14

See p. 375.

TUESDAY OF THE THIRTY-FIRST WEEK
IN ORDINARY TIME

READING I   Phil 2, 5-11

Paul exhorts the Philippians to imitate Christ. This humility and abasement should be the model for their conduct. Jesus did not stand on his dignity, but at Jesus' name every knee should bend.

A reading from the letter of Paul to the Philippians

Your attitude must be Christ's:
Though he was in the form of God,
    he did not deem equality with God
    something to be grasped at.
Rather, he emptied himself
    and took the form of a slave,
    being born in the likeness of men.
He was known to be of human estate
    and it was thus that he humbled himself,
    obediently accepting even death,
    death on a cross!
Because of this,
    God highly exalted him
    and bestowed on him the name
    above every other name,
So that at Jesus' name
    every knee must bend
    in the heavens, on the earth,
    and under the earth,
    and every tongue proclaim
    to the glory of God the Father:
    JESUS CHRIST IS LORD!
This is the Word of the Lord. ℟. **Thanks be to God.** ℣

Responsorial Psalm   Ps 22, 26-27. 28-30. 31-32
℟. (26) **I will praise you, Lord, in the assembly of
    your people.**
I will fulfill my vows before those who fear him.
The lowly shall eat their fill;

they who seek the Lord shall praise him:
"May your hearts be ever merry!" — ℟

All the ends of the earth
   shall remember and turn to the Lord;

All the families of the nations
   shall bow down before him.

For dominion is the Lord's,
   and he rules the nations.

To him alone shall bow down
   all who sleep in the earth. — ℟

To him my soul shall live;
   my descendants shall serve him.

Let the coming generation be told of the Lord
   that they may proclaim to a people yet to be born
   the justice he has shown. — ℟ ℣

GOSPEL   Lk 14, 15-24

See p. 377.

WEDNESDAY OF THE THIRTY-FIRST WEEK IN ORDINARY TIME

READING I   Phil 2, 12-18

The eschatological fulfillment of Christian hope depends on the moral conduct of the individual. Christians should not argue. They should rejoice in their sufferings, being poured out like Christ.

A reading from the letter of Paul to the Philippians

My dearly beloved, obedient as always to my urging, work with anxious concern to achieve your salvation, not only when I happen to be with you but all the more now that I am absent. It is God who, in his good will toward you, begets in you any measure of desire or achievement. In everything you do, act without grumbling or arguing; prove yourselves innocent and straightforward, children of God beyond reproach in the midst of a twisted and depraved generation—among whom you shine like the stars in the sky while holding fast to the word of life. As I look to the day of Christ, you give me cause to boast that I did not run the race in vain or work to no purpose. Even if my life is to be poured out as a libation over the sacrificial service of your faith, I am glad of it and rejoice with all of you. May you be glad on the same score, and rejoice with me!—This is the Word of the Lord. ℟. **Thanks be to God. ℣**

Responsorial Psalm   Ps 27, 1. 4. 13-14

℟. (1) **The Lord is my light and my salvation.**

The Lord is my light and my salvation;
  whom should I fear?
The Lord is my life's refuge;
  of whom should I be afraid? — ℟

One thing I ask of the Lord;
  this I seek:
To dwell in the house of the Lord
  all the days of my life,
That I may gaze on the loveliness of the Lord
  and contemplate his temple. — ℟

I believe that I shall see the bounty of the Lord
  in the land of the living.
Wait for the Lord with courage;
  be stouthearted, and wait for the Lord. — ℟ ℣

GOSPEL   Lk 14, 25-33

See p. 379.

THURSDAY OF THE THIRTY-FIRST WEEK
IN ORDINARY TIME

READING I   Phil 3, 3-8

The Spirit is the dynamic source of Christian life. Through it the Christian is enabled to pray to the Father. Paul describes his communion with Christ as a goal to be attained—in a race still to be run.

A reading from the letter of Paul to the Philippians

It is we who are the circumcision, who worship in the spirit of God and glory in Christ Jesus rather than putting our trust in the flesh—though I can be confident even there. If anyone thinks he has a right to put his trust in external evidence, all the more can I! I was circumcised on the eighth day, being of the stock of Israel and the tribe of Benjamin, a Hebrew of Hebrew origins; in legal observance I was a Pharisee, and so zealous that I persecuted the church. I was above reproach when it came to justice based on the law.

But those things I used to consider gain I have now reappraised as loss in the light of Christ. I have come to rate all as loss in the light of the surpassing knowledge of my Lord Jesus Christ.—This is the Word of the Lord. ℟. **Thanks be to God.** ⱱ

Responsorial Psalm   Ps 105, 2-3. 4-5. 6-7

℟. (3) **Let hearts rejoice who search for the Lord.**

Sing to him, sing his praise,
    proclaim all his wondrous deeds.
Glory in his holy name;
    rejoice, O hearts that seek the Lord! — ℟

Look to the Lord in his strength;
    seek to serve him constantly.
Recall the wondrous deeds that he has wrought,
    his portents, and the judgments he has uttered.—℟

You descendants of Abraham, his servants,
  sons of Jacob, his chosen ones!
He, the Lord, is our God;
  throughout the earth his judgments prevail.—℟ ℣

℟. Or: **Alleluia.** ℣

GOSPEL Lk 15, 1-10

See p. 381.

FRIDAY OF THE THIRTY-FIRST WEEK
IN ORDINARY TIME

READING I Phil 3, 17—4, 1

Paul does not hesitate to propose himself for imitation, since he
himself is an imitator of Christ Jesus. He uses strong words of reproach and exhorts a firm stand in following Jesus.

A reading from the letter of Paul to the
Philippians

Be imitators of me, my brothers. Take as your guide
those who follow the example that we set. Unfortu-
nately, many go about in a way which shows them
to be enemies of the cross of Christ. I have often
said this to you before; this time I say it with tears.
Such as these will end in disaster! Their only god is
their belly, and their glory is in their shame. I am
talking about those who are set upon the things of
this world. As you well know, we have our citizenship in heaven; it is from there that we eagerly await
the coming of our savior, the Lord Jesus Christ. He
will give a new form to this lowly body of ours and
remake it according to the pattern of his glorified
body, by his power to subject everything to himself.
  For these reasons, my brothers, you whom I so
love and long for, you who are my joy and my crown,
continue, my dear ones, to stand firm in the Lord.—
This is the Word of the Lord. ℟. **Thanks be to God.** ℣

Responsorial Psalm Ps 122, 1-2. 3-4. 4-5

℟. (1) **I rejoiced when I heard them say:
let us go to the house of the Lord.**

I rejoiced because they said to me,
  "We will go up to the house of the Lord."
And now we have set foot
  within your gates, O Jerusalem. — ℟

Jerusalem, built as a city
  with compact unity.
To it the tribes go up,
  the tribes of the Lord. — ℟

According to the decree for Israel,
  to give thanks to the name of the Lord.
In it are set up judgment seats,
  seats for the house of David. — ℟ ℣

GOSPEL Lk 16, 1-8

See p. 383.

SATURDAY OF THE THIRTY-FIRST WEEK
IN ORDINARY TIME

READING I Phil 4, 10-19

Paul expresses his gratitude for the aid sent by the Philippians because of their concern for him. Above all, he is encouraged by the sentiment that it manifests.

A reading from the letter of Paul to the
Philippians

It gave me great joy in the Lord that your concern for me bore fruit once more. You had been concerned all along, of course, but lacked the opportunity to show it. I do not say this because I am in want, for whatever the situation I find myself in I have learned to be self-sufficient. I am experienced in being brought low, yet I know what it is to have an abundance. I have learned how to cope with every circumstance—how to eat well or go hungry, to be well provided for or do without. In him who is the source of my strength I have strength for everything.

Nonetheless, it was kind of you to want to share in my hardships. You yourselves know, my dear Philippians, that at the start of my evangelizing, when I left Macedonia, not a single congregation except yourselves shared with me by giving me something for what it had received. Even when I was at Thessalonica you sent something for my needs, not once but twice. It is not that I am eager for the gift; rather, my concern is for the ever-growing balance in your account. Herewith is my receipt which says that I have been fully paid, and more. I am well supplied because of what I received from you through Epaphroditus, a fragrant offering, a sacrifice acceptable and pleasing to God.

My God in turn will supply your needs fully, in a way worthy of his magnificent riches in Christ Jesus. —This is the Word of the Lord. ℞. **Thanks be to God.** ℣

Responsorial Psalm Ps 112, 1-2. 5-6. 8. 9

℞. (1) **Happy the man who fears the Lord.**

Happy the man who fears the Lord,
   who greatly delights in his commands.
His posterity shall be mighty upon the earth;
   the upright generation shall be blessed. — ℞

Well for the man who is gracious and lends,
   who conducts his affairs with justice;
He shall never be moved;
   the just man shall be in everlasting remembrance. — ℞

His heart is steadfast; he shall not fear.
Lavishly he gives to the poor;
　his generosity shall endure forever;
　his horn shall be exalted in glory. — ℟ ❧

℟. Or: **Alleluia.** ❧

GOSPEL　　　　　　　　　　　　　　Lk 16, 9-15

See p. 386.

MONDAY OF THE THIRTY-SECOND WEEK IN ORDINARY TIME

READING I　　　　　　　　　　　　　Ti 1, 1-9

God has chosen his special time to reveal the gospel message. Paul reminds Titus of his role and further describes the qualities expected in the first leader of a Christian community.

The beginning of the letter of Paul to Titus

Paul, a servant of God, sent as an apostle of Jesus Christ for the sake of the faith of those whom God has chosen, and to promote their knowledge of the truth as our religion embodies it, in the hope of that eternal life which God, who cannot lie, promised in endless ages past. This he has now manifested in his own good time as his word, in the preaching entrusted to me by the command of God our Savior. Paul to Titus, my own true child in our common faith: May grace and peace from God our Father, and Christ Jesus our Savior, be with you.

My purpose in leaving you in Crete was that you might accomplish what had been left undone, especially the appointment of presbyters in every town. As I instructed you, a presbyter must be irreproachable, married only once, the father of children who are believers and are known not to be wild and insubordinate. The bishop as God's steward must be blameless. He may not be self-willed or arrogant, a drunkard, a violent or greedy man. He should, on the contrary, be hospitable and a lover of goodness; steady, just, holy, and self-controlled. In his teaching he must hold fast to the authentic message, so that he will be able both to encourage men to follow sound doctrine and to refute those who contradict it.—This is the Word of the Lord. ℟. **Thanks be to God.** ℣

Responsorial Psalm   Ps 24, 1-2. 3-4. 5-6
℟. (6) **Lord, this is the people that longs to see your face.**

The Lord's are the earth and its fullness;
  the world and those who dwell in it.
For he founded it upon the seas
  and established it upon the rivers. — ℟

Who can ascend the mountain of the Lord?
  or who may stand in his holy place?
He whose hands are sinless, whose heart is clean,
  who desires not what is vain. — ℟

He shall receive a blessing from the Lord,
  a reward from God his savior.
Such is the race that seeks for him,
  that seeks the face of the God of Jacob. — ℟ ℣

GOSPEL   Lk 17, 1-6

See p. 388.

TUESDAY OF THE THIRTY-SECOND WEEK
IN ORDINARY TIME

READING I   Ti 2, 1-8. 11-14

Paul tells Titus to direct the men and women to live the full Christian life. Paul means to emphasize that the Christian teaching is in accord with intellectual and moral soundness.

A reading from the letter of Paul to Titus

As for yourself, let your speech be consistent with sound doctrine. Tell the older men that they must be temperate, serious-minded, and self-controlled; likewise sound in the faith, loving, and steadfast. Similarly, the older women must behave in ways that befit those who belong to God. They must not be slanderous gossips or slaves to drink. By their good example they must teach the younger women to love their husbands and children, to be sensible, chaste, busy at home, kindly, submissive to their husbands. Thus the word of God will not fall into disrepute. Tell the young men to keep themselves completely under control—nor may you yourself fail to set them good example. Your teaching must have the integrity of serious, sound words to which no one can take exception. If it does, no opponent will be able to find anything bad to say about us, and hostility will yield to shame.

The grace of God has appeared, offering salvation to all men. It trains us to reject godless ways and worldly desires, and live temperately, justly, and devoutly in this age as we await our blessed hope, the appearing of the glory of the great God and of our Savior Christ Jesus. It was he who sacrificed himself for us, to redeem us from all unrighteousness and to cleanse for himself a people of his own, eager to do what is right.—This is the Word of the Lord. ℟. **Thanks be to God.** ℣

Responsorial Psalm   Ps 37, 3-4. 18. 23. 27. 29

℞. **The salvation of the just comes from the Lord.**

Trust in the Lord and do good,
    that you may dwell in the land and enjoy security.
Take delight in the Lord,
    and he will grant you your heart's requests. — ℞

The Lord watches over the lives of the wholehearted;
    their inheritance lasts forever.
By the Lord are the steps of a man made firm,
    and he approves his way. — ℞

Turn from evil and do good,
    that you may abide forever;
The just shall possess the land
    and dwell in it forever. — ℞ ⅴ

GOSPEL   Lk 17, 7-10

See p. 390.

WEDNESDAY OF THE THIRTY-SECOND WEEK
IN ORDINARY TIME

READING I   Ti 3, 1-7

Paul directs Titus to exhort the Christians to be obedient to the
civil authorities, reminding them that these authorities are established
by God. Regeneration in the Holy Spirit indicates baptism which
brings about a new life through water and the Holy Spirit.

A reading from the letter of Paul to Titus

Remind people to be loyally subject to the government and its officials, to obey the laws, to be ready
to take on any honest employment. Tell them not to
speak evil of anyone or be quarrelsome. They must
be forbearing and display a perfect courtesy toward
all men. We ourselves were once foolish, disobedient,
and far from true faith; we were the slaves of our

passions and of pleasures of various kinds. We went our way in malice and envy, hateful ourselves and hating one another. But when the kindness and love of God our Savior appeared, he saved us, not because of any righteous deeds we had done, but because of his mercy. He saved us through the baptism of new birth and renewal by the Holy Spirit. This Spirit he lavished on us through Jesus Christ our Savior, that we might be justified by his grace and become heirs, in hope, of eternal life.—This is the Word of the Lord. ℟. **Thanks be to God.** ⍊

Responsorial Psalm   Ps 23, 1-3. 3-4. 5. 6

℟. (1) **The Lord is my shepherd;**
   there is nothing I shall want.

The Lord is my shepherd; I shall not want.
   In verdant pastures he gives me repose;
Beside restful waters he leads me;
   he refreshes my soul. — ℟

He guides me in right paths
   for his name's sake.
Even though I walk in the dark valley
   I fear no evil; for you are at my side
With your rod and your staff
   that give me courage. — ℟

You spread the table before me
   in the sight of my foes;
You anoint my head with oil;
   my cup overflows. — ℟

Only goodness and kindness follow me
   all the days of my life;
And I shall dwell in the house of the Lord
   for years to come. — ℟ ⍊

GOSPEL   Lk 17, 11-19

See p. 392.

THURSDAY OF THE THIRTY-SECOND WEEK IN ORDINARY TIME

READING I

Phlm 7-20

Paul prays that a sense of solidarity with Philemon in faith in Christ will be productive of a deeper knowledge of all the good that comes to the saints.

A reading from the letter of Paul to Philemon

I find great joy and comfort in your love, because through you the hearts of God's people have been refreshed.

Therefore, although I feel that I have every right to command you to do what ought to be done, I prefer to appeal in the name of love. Yes, I, Paul, ambassador of Christ and now a prisoner for him, appeal to you for my child whom I have begotten during my imprisonment. He has become in truth Onesimus [Useful], for he who was formerly useless to you is now useful indeed both to you and to me. It is he I am sending you—and that means I am sending my heart!

I had wanted to keep him with me, that he might serve me in your place while I am in prison for the gospel; but I did not want to do anything without your consent, that kindness might not be forced on you but might be freely bestowed. Perhaps he was separated from you for a while for this reason: that you might possess him forever, no longer as a slave but as more than a slave, a beloved brother, especially dear to me; and how much more than a brother to you, since now you will know him both as a man and in the Lord.

If then you regard me as a partner, welcome him as you would me. If he has done you an injury or owes you anything, charge it to me. I, Paul, write this in my own hand: I agree to pay—not to mention that you owe me your very self! You see, brother, I want to make you "useful" to me in the Lord. Refresh this heart of mine in Christ.—This is the Word of the Lord. ℟. **Thanks be to God.** ℣

Responsorial Psalm   Ps 146, 7. 8-9. 9-10

℟. (5) **Blest are they whose help is the God of Jacob.**

Happy is he who
    secures justice for the oppressed,
    gives food to the hungry.
The Lord sets captives free. — ℟

The Lord gives sight to the blind.
The Lord raises up those that were bowed down;
    the Lord loves the just.
The Lord protects strangers. — ℟

The fatherless and the widow he sustains,
    but the way of the wicked he thwarts.
The Lord shall reign forever;
    your God, O Zion, through all generations. Alleluia. — ℟ ℣

GOSPEL   Lk 17, 20-25

See p. 395.

FRIDAY OF THE THIRTY-SECOND WEEK IN ORDINARY TIME

READING I   2 Jn 4-9

The church to which John's epistle is addressed has been exposed to false doctrine. The safeguard against every evil is in fulfilling the commandment of love, which includes every other commandment. Fellowship with God is achieved by adhering to the true doctrine of Christ.

A reading from the second letter of John

It has given me great joy to find some of your children walking in the path of truth, just as we were commanded by the Father. But now, my Lady, I

would make this request of you (not as if I were
writing you some new commandment; rather, it is
a commandment we have had from the start): let us
love one another. This love involves our walking according to the commandments, and as you have heard
from the beginning, the commandment is the way
in which you should walk.

Many deceitful men have gone out into the world,
men who do not acknowledge Jesus Christ as coming
in the flesh. Such is the deceitful one! This is the antichrist! Look out that you yourselves do not lose what
you have worked for; you must receive your reward
in full. Anyone who is so "progressive" that he does
not remain rooted in the teaching of Christ does not
possess God, while anyone who remains rooted in the
teaching possesses both the Father and the Son.—
This is the Word of the Lord. ℟. **Thanks be to God. ℣**

Responsorial Psalm   Ps 119, 1. 2. 10. 11. 17. 18

℟. (1) **Happy are they who follow the law of the
      Lord!**

Happy are they whose way is blameless,
    who walk in the law of the Lord. — ℟

Happy are they who observe his decrees,
    who seek him with all their heart. — ℟

With all my heart I seek you;
    let me not stray from your commands. — ℟

Within my heart I treasure your promise,
    that I may not sin against you. — ℟

Be good to your servant, that I may live
    and keep your words. — ℟

Open my eyes, that I may consider
    the wonders of your law. — ℟ ℣

GOSPEL   Lk 17, 26-37

See p. 397.

SATURDAY OF THE THIRTY-SECOND WEEK IN ORDINARY TIME

READING I   3 Jn 5-8

John writes to commend Gaius for receiving Christian missionaries in true charity and to encourage continuance of this action. Jews spoke of "the Name" rather than pronounce the sacred name, Yahweh.

A reading from the third letter of John

Beloved, you demonstrate fidelity by all that you do for the brothers even though they are strangers; indeed, they have testified to your love before the church. And you will do a good thing if, in a way that pleases God, you help them to continue their journey. It was for the sake of the Name that they set out, and they are accepting nothing from the pagans. Therefore, we owe it to such men to support them and thus to have our share in the work of truth.— This is the Word of the Lord. ℟. **Thanks be to God.** ℣

Responsorial Psalm   Ps 112, 1-2. 3-4. 5-6

℟. (1) **Happy the man who fears the Lord.**

Happy the man who fears the Lord,
   who greatly delights in his commands.
His posterity shall be mighty upon the earth;
   the upright generation shall be blessed. — ℟

Wealth and riches shall be in his house;
   his generosity shall endure forever.
He dawns through the darkness, a light for the upright;
   he is gracious and merciful and just. — ℟

Well for the man who is gracious and lends,
   who conducts his affairs with justice;
He shall never be moved;
   the just man shall be in everlasting remembrance. — ℟ ℣

℟. Or: **Alleluia.** ℣

GOSPEL   Lk 18, 1-8

See p. 399.

MONDAY OF THE THIRTY-THIRD WEEK IN ORDINARY TIME

READING I   Rv 1, 1-4; 2, 1-5

The book of Revelation announced the unveiling of the mystery of history and the inauguration of the Kingdom of God. The necessary mediation of Christ is a major doctrine of John.

The beginning of the book of Revelation

This is the revelation God gave to Jesus Christ, that he might show his servants what must happen very soon. He made it known by sending his angel to his servant John, who in reporting all he saw bears witness to the word of God and the testimony of Jesus Christ. Happy is the man who reads this prophetic message, and happy are those who hear it and heed what is written in it, for the appointed time is near!

To the seven churches in the province of Asia: John wishes you grace and peace—from him who is and who was and who is to come, and from the seven spirits before his throne.

I heard the Lord saying to me:

"To the presiding spirit of the church in Ephesus, write this:

"'The One who holds the seven stars in his right hand and walks among the seven lampstands of gold has this to say: I know your deeds, your labors, and your patient endurance. I know you cannot tolerate wicked men; you have tested those self-styled apostles, who are nothing of the sort, and discovered that they are impostors. You are patient and endure hardships for my cause. Moreover, you do not become discouraged. I hold this against you, though: you have turned aside from your early love. Keep firmly in mind the heights from which you have fallen. Repent, and return to your former deeds.' "—This is the Word of the Lord. ℞. **Thanks be to God.** ℣

Responsorial Psalm   Ps 1, 1-2. 3. 4. 6

℞. (Rv 2, 7) **Those who are victorious I will feed from the tree of life.**

Happy the man who follows not
    the counsel of the wicked
Nor walks in the way of sinners,
    nor sits in the company of the insolent,
But delights in the law of the Lord
    and meditates on his law day and night. — ℞

He is like a tree
    planted near running water,
That yields its fruit in due season,
    and whose leaves never fade.
[Whatever he does, prospers.] — ℞

Not so the wicked, not so;
    they are like chaff which the wind drives away.
For the Lord watches over the way of the just,
    but the way of the wicked vanishes. — ℞ ℣

GOSPEL   Lk 18, 35-43

See p. 402.

TUESDAY OF THE THIRTY-THIRD WEEK
IN ORDINARY TIME

READING I Rv 3, 1-6. 14-22

Sardis had the reputation of living luxuriously. This community had fallen back into spiritual death. To be watchful is the attitude necessary for Christians. Laodicea also receives a most severe reprimand.

A reading from the book of Revelation

I, John, heard the Lord say to me: "To the presiding spirit of the church in Sardis, write this:

" 'The One who holds the seven spirits of God, the seven stars, has this to say: I know your conduct; I know the reputation you have of being alive, when in fact you are dead! Wake up, and strengthen what remains before it dies. I find that the sum of your deeds is less than complete in the sight of my God. Call to mind how you accepted what you heard; keep to it, and repent. If you do not rouse yourselves, I will come upon you like a thief, at a time you cannot know. I realize that you have in Sardis a few persons who have not soiled their garments; these shall walk with me in white because they are worthy.

" 'The victor shall go clothed in white. I will never erase his name from the book of the living, but will acknowledge him in the presence of my Father and his angels.

" 'Let him who has ears to hear heed the Spirit's word to the churches!

" 'To the presiding spirit of the church in Laodicea, write this:

" 'The Amen, the Witness faithful and true, the Source of God's creation, has this to say: I know your deeds; I know you are neither cold nor hot. How I wish you were one or the other—hot or cold! But because you are lukewarm, neither hot nor cold, I will spew you out of my mouth! You keep saying, "I am so rich and secure that I want for nothing." Little do you realize how wretched you are, how pitiable and poor, how blind and naked! Take my advice. Buy from me gold refined by fire if you would be truly rich. Buy white garments in which to be clothed, if the shame of your nakedness is to be covered. Buy ointment to smear on your eyes, if you would see once more. Whoever is dear to me I reprove and chastise. Be earnest about it, therefore. Repent!

" 'Here I stand, knocking at the door. If anyone hears me calling and opens the door, I will enter his house and have supper with him, and he with me. I will give the victor the right to sit with me on my throne, as I myself won the victory and took my seat beside my Father on his throne.

" 'Let him who has ears to hear heed the Spirit's word to the churches.' "—This is the Word of the Lord. ℟. **Thanks be to God.** ℣

Responsorial Psalm   Ps 15, 2-3. 3-4. 5

℟. (Rv 3, 21) **Him who is victorious I will sit beside me on my throne.**

He who walks blamelessly and does justice;
　　who thinks the truth in his heart
　　and slanders not with his tongue; — ℟

Who harms not his fellow man,
　　nor takes up a reproach against his neighbor;
By whom the reprobate is despised,
　　while he honors those who fear the Lord; — ℟

Who lends not his money at usury
　　and accepts no bribe against the innocent.
He who does these things
　　shall never be disturbed. — ℟ ℣

GOSPEL   Lk 19, 1-10

See p. 404.

WEDNESDAY OF THE THIRTY-THIRD WEEK
IN ORDINARY TIME

READING I   Rv 4, 1-11

John glimpses the court of heaven where God sits enthroned and rules the universe. John alone is admitted to the transcendental world. He describes in detail the glorious Son of Man, the Mediator who reveals God to us.

A reading from the book of Revelation

After this I, John, had another vision: above me there was an open door to heaven, and I heard the trumpetlike voice which had spoken to me before. It said, "Come up here and I will show you what must take place in time to come." At once I was caught up in esctasy. A throne was standing there in heaven, and on the throne was seated One whose appearance had a gemlike sparkle as of jasper and carnelian. Around the throne was a rainbow as brilliant as emerald. Surrounding this throne were twenty-four other thrones upon which were seated twenty-four elders; they were clothed in white garments and had crowns of gold on their heads. From the throne came flashes of lightning and peals of thunder; before it burned seven flaming torches, the seven spirits of God. The floor around the throne was like a sea of glass that was crystal-clear.

At the very center, around the throne itself, stood four living creatures covered with eyes front and back. The first creature resembled a lion, the second an ox; the third had the face of a man, while the fourth looked like an eagle in flight. Each of the four living creatures had six wings and eyes all over, inside and out.

Day and night, without pause, they sing:
"Holy, holy, holy, is the Lord God Almighty,
 He who was, and who is, and who is to come!"

Whenever these creatures give glory and honor and praise to the One seated on the throne, who lives forever and ever, the twenty-four elders fall down before the One seated on the throne, and worship him who lives forever and ever. They throw down their crowns before the throne and sing:
"O Lord our God, you are worthy
   to receive glory and honor and power!
For you have created all things;
   by your will they came to be and were made!"
This is the Word of the Lord. ℟. **Thanks be to God.** ℣

Responsorial Psalm   Ps 150, 1-2. 3-4. 5-6

℟. (Rv 4, 8) **Holy, holy, holy Lord, mighty God!**

Praise the Lord in his sanctuary,
   praise him in the firmament of his strength.
Praise him for his mighty deeds,
   praise him for his sovereign majesty. — ℟

Praise him with the blast of the trumpet,
   praise him with lyre and harp,
Praise him with timbrel and dance,
   praise him with strings and pipe. — ℟

Praise him with sounding cymbals,
   praise him with clanging cymbals.
Let everything that has breath
   praise the Lord! Alleluia. — ℟ ℣

GOSPEL   Lk 19, 11-28

See p. 407.

THURSDAY OF THE THIRTY-THIRD WEEK
IN ORDINARY TIME

READING I   Rv 5, 1-10

John describes the Lamb by whom redemption came about through the death of Jesus. Christ has brought about victory by his sacrifice. John also writes about the sealed scroll.

A reading from the book of Revelation

I, John, saw in the right hand of the One who sat on the throne a scroll. It had writing on both sides and was sealed with seven seals. Then I saw a mighty angel who proclaimed in a loud voice: "Who is worthy to open the scroll and break its seals?" But no one in heaven or on earth or under the earth could be found to open the scroll or examine its contents. I wept bitterly because no one could be found worthy to open or examine the scroll. One of the elders said to me: "Do not weep. The Lion of the tribe of Judah, the Root of David, has won the right by his victory to open the scroll with the seven seals."

Then, between the throne with the four living creatures and the elders, I saw a Lamb standing, a Lamb that had been slain. He had seven horns and seven eyes; these eyes are the seven spirits of God, sent to all parts of the world. The Lamb came and received the scroll from the right hand of the One who sat on the throne. When he had taken the scroll, the four living creatures and the twenty-four elders fell down before the Lamb. Along with their harps, the elders were holding vessels of gold filled with aromatic spices, which were the prayers of God's holy people. This is the hymn they sang:
"Worthy are you to receive the scroll
    and break open its seals,
    for you were slain.
With your blood you purchased for God

men of every race and tongue,
of every people and nation.
You made of them a kingdom,
and priests to serve our God,
and they shall reign on the earth."
This is the Word of the Lord. ℞. **Thanks be to God.** ℣

Responsorial Psalm   Ps 149, 1-2. 3-4. 5-6. 9

℞. (Rv 5, 10) **The Lamb has made us a kingdom of
priests to serve our God.**

Sing to the Lord a new song
of praise in the assembly of the faithful.
Let Israel be glad in their maker,
let the children of Zion rejoice in their king. — ℞

Let them praise his name in the festive dance,
let them sing praise to him with timbrel and harp.
For the Lord loves his people,
and he adorns the lowly with victory. — ℞

Let the faithful exult in glory;
let them sing for joy upon their couches;
let the high praises of God be in their throats.
This is the glory of all his faithful. Alleluia. — ℞ ℣

℞. Or: **Alleluia.** ℣

GOSPEL   Lk 19, 41-44

See p. 410.

FRIDAY OF THE THIRTY-THIRD WEEK
IN ORDINARY TIME

READING I   Rv 10, 8-11

John is directed to take the scroll and eat it. The action of eating
symbolizes John's complete assimilation of the contents of the
scroll which tasted like honey but turned sour in his stomach.

A reading from the book of Revelation

The voice which I, John, heard from heaven spoke to me again and said, "Go, take the open scroll from the hand of the angel standing on the sea and on the land." I went up to the angel and said to him, "Give me the little scroll." He said to me, "Here, take it and eat it! It will be sour in your stomach, but in your mouth it will taste as sweet as honey." I took the little scroll from the angel's hand and ate it. In my mouth it tasted as sweet as honey, but when I swallowed it my stomach turned sour. Then someone said to me, "You must prophesy again for many peoples, nations, languages and kings."—This is the Word of the Lord. ℟. **Thanks be to God.** ℣

Responsorial Psalm   Ps 119, 14. 24. 72. 103. 111. 131

℟. (103) **How sweet to my taste is your promise!**

In the way of your decrees I rejoice,
    as much as in all riches. — ℟

Yes, your decrees are my delight;
    they are my counselors. — ℟

The law of your mouth is to me more precious
    than thousands of gold and silver pieces. — ℟

How sweet to my palate are your promises,
    sweeter than honey to my mouth! — ℟

Your decrees are my inheritance forever;
    the joy of my heart they are. — ℟

I gasp with open mouth
    in my yearning for your commands. — ℟ ℣

GOSPEL   Lk 19, 45-48

See p. 412.

SATURDAY OF THE THIRTY-THIRD WEEK IN ORDINARY TIME

READING I   Rv 11, 4-12

The two witnesses fit Moses and Elijah. In particular, Moses and Elijah represent the Law and the prophets bearing witness to Christ. These two personages would represent the entire Church which must bear living witness to Christ.

A reading from the book of Revelation

To me, John, it was said: See my two witnesses; these are the two olive trees and the two lampstands which stand in the presence of the Lord of the earth. If anyone tries to harm them, fire will come out of the mouths of these witnesses to devour their enemies. Anyone attempting to harm them will surely be slain in this way. These witnesses have power to close up the sky so that no rain will fall during the time of their mission. They also have power to turn water into blood and to afflict the earth at will with any kind of plague.

When they have finished giving their testimony, the wild beast that comes up from the abyss will wage war against them and conquer and kill them. Their corpses will lie in the streets of the great city, which has the symbolic name "Sodom" or "Egypt," where also their Lord was crucified. Men from every people and race, language and nation, stare at their corpses for three and a half days but refuse to bury them. The earth's inhabitants gloat over them and in their merriment exchange gifts, because these two prophets harassed everyone on earth. But after the three and a half days, the breath of life which comes from God returned to them. When they stood on their feet sheer terror gripped those who saw them. The two prophets heard a loud voice from heaven say to them, "Come up here!" So they went up to heaven in a cloud as their enemies looked on.— This is the Word of the Lord. ℟. **Thanks be to God.** ℣

Responsorial Psalm   Ps 144, 1. 2. 9-10

℟. (1) **Blessed be the Lord, my Rock!**

Blessed be the Lord, my rock,
   who trains my hands for battle, my fingers for
   war. — ℟

My refuge and my fortress,
   my stronghold, my deliverer,
My shield, in whom I trust,
   who subdues peoples under me. — ℟

O God, I will sing a new song to you;
   with a ten-stringed lyre I will chant your praise,
You who give victory to kings,
   and deliver David, your servant. — ℟ ℣

GOSPEL   Lk 20, 27-40

See p. 415.

MONDAY OF THE THIRTY-FOURTH WEEK
IN ORDINARY TIME

READING I   Rv 14, 1-3. 4-5

The Church of God will survive the fury of brutal and hostile powers. God's name upon the forehead signifies that one is consecrated to his service. Only the 144,000—an unlimited number—so marked with God's name can learn the powerful and melodious heavenly song.

A reading from the book of Revelation

I, John, saw the Lamb appear in my vision. He was standing on Mount Zion, and with him were the hundred and forty-four thousand who had his name and the name of his Father written on their foreheads. I heard a sound from heaven which resembled the roaring of the deep, or loud peals of thunder; the sound I heard was like the melody of harpists playing on their harps. They were singing a new hymn before the throne in the presence of the four living creatures and the elders. This hymn no one could learn except the hundred and forty-four thousand who had been ransomed from the world. They are pure and follow the Lamb wherever he goes. They have been ransomed as the first fruits of mankind for God and the Lamb. On their lips no deceit has been found; they are indeed without flaw.—This is the Word of the Lord. ℟. **Thanks be to God. ꝟ**

Responsorial Psalm   Ps 24, 1-2. 3-4. 5-6

℟. (6) **Lord, this is the people that longs to see your face.**

The Lord's are the earth and its fullness;
    the world and those who dwell in it.
For he founded it upon the seas
    and established it upon the rivers. — ℟

Who can ascend the mountain of the Lord?
    or who may stand in his holy place?
He whose hands are sinless, whose heart is clean,
    who desires not what is vain. — ℟

He shall receive a blessing from the Lord,
    a reward from God his savior.
Such is the race that seeks for him,
    that seeks the face of the God of Jacob. — ℟ ꝟ

GOSPEL   Lk 21, 1-4

See p. 418.

TUESDAY OF THE THIRTY-FOURTH WEEK
IN ORDINARY TIME

READING I   Rv 14, 14-19

Christ wears the crown of the conqueror, but the sickle shows that he comes now in his role of Judge. The universal harvest coincides with the Parousia of the Son of Man. The Father is Master of the harvest.

A reading from the book of Revelation

As I, John, watched, a white cloud appeared, and on the cloud sat One like a Son of Man wearing a gold crown on his head and holding a sharp sickle in his hand. Another angel came out of the temple and in a loud voice cried out to him who sat on the cloud, "Use your sickle and cut down the harvest, for now is the time to reap; the earth's harvest is fully ripe." So the one sitting on the cloud wielded his sickle over all the earth and reaped the earth's harvest.

Then out of the temple in heaven came another angel, who likewise held a sharp sickle. A second angel, who was in charge of the fire at the altar of incense, cried out in a loud voice to the one who held the sharp sickle, "Use your sharp sickle and gather the grapes from the vines of the earth, for the clusters are ripe." So the angel wielded his sickle over the earth and gathered the grapes of the earth. He threw them into the huge winepress of God's wrath.
—This is the Word of the Lord. ℞. **Thanks be to God.** ℣

Responsorial Psalm   Ps 96, 10. 11-12. 13

℞. (13) **The Lord comes to judge the earth.**

Say among the nations: The Lord is king.
He has made the world firm, not to be moved;
   he governs the peoples with equity. — ℞

Let the heavens be glad and the earth rejoice;
   let the sea and what fills it resound;

let the plains be joyful and all that is in them!
Then shall the trees of the forest exult. — ℟

Before the Lord, for he comes;
   for he comes to rule the earth.
He shall rule the world with justice
   and the peoples with his constancy. — ℟ ⩣

GOSPEL   Lk 21, 5-11

See p. 421.

WEDNESDAY OF THE THIRTY-FOURTH WEEK
IN ORDINARY TIME

READING I   Rv 15, 1-4

John reveals calamities that surround the final judgment upon the
world and its inhabitants. The plagues are the manifestation of God's
anger. The distance that separates God from all of creation indicates
that God demands sanctity. The victory of the redeeming "Lamb"
is the apex and the goal of salvation history.

A reading from the book of Revelation

I, John, saw in heaven another sign, great and awe-
inspiring: seven angels holding the seven final plagues which would bring God's wrath to a climax.

   I then saw something like a sea of glass mingled
with fire. On the sea of glass were standing those
who had won the victory over the beast and its image, and the number that signified its name. They
were holding the harps used in worshiping God, and
they sang the song of Moses, the servant of God, and
the song of the Lamb:

"Mighty and wonderful are your works,
   Lord God Almighty!
Righteous and true are your ways,
   O King of the nations!
Who would dare refuse you honor,
   or the glory due your name, O Lord?

Since you alone are holy,
   all nations shall come
   and worship in your presence.
Your mighty deeds are clearly seen."
This is the Word of the Lord. ℟. **Thanks be to God.** ✣

Responsorial Psalm   Ps 98, 1. 2-3. 7-8. 9

℟. (Rv 15, 3) **Great and wonderful are all your works,
   Lord, mighty God!**

Sing to the Lord a new song,
   for he has done wondrous deeds;
His right hand has won victory for him,
   his holy arm. — ℟

The Lord has made his salvation known:
   in the sight of the nations he has revealed his
      justice.
He has remembered his kindness and his faithfulness
   toward the house of Israel. — ℟

Let the sea and what fills it resound,
   the world and those who dwell in it;
Let the rivers clap their hands,
   the mountains shout with them for joy. — ℟

Before the Lord, for he comes,
   for he comes to rule the earth;
He will rule the world with justice
   and the peoples with equity. — ℟ ✣

GOSPEL   Lk 21, 12-19

See p. 423.

———————

THURSDAY OF THE THIRTY-FOURTH WEEK
IN ORDINARY TIME

READING I   Rv 18, 1-2. 21-23; 19, 1-3. 9

John sees the fall of mighty Babylon from its past majesty. A great concourse sings Alleluia, expressing the joy and happiness of those joined with their bridegroom at the celestial wedding feast—the feast of the Lamb.

A reading from the book of Revelation

I, John, saw another angel coming down from heaven. His authority was so great that all the earth was lighted up by his glory. He cried out in a strong voice:
"Fallen, fallen is Babylon the great!
    She has become a dwelling place for demons.
She is a cage for every unclean spirit,
    a cage for every filthy and disgusting bird."
    A powerful angel picked up a stone like a huge millstone and hurled it into the sea, and said:
"Babylon the great city
    shall be cast down like this with violence,
    and nevermore be found!
No tunes of harpists and minstrels,
    of flutists and trumpeters,
    shall ever again be heard in you!
No craftsmen in any trade
    shall ever again be found in you!
No sound of the millstone
    shall ever again be heard in you!
No light from a burning lamp
    shall ever again shine out in you!
No voices of bride and groom
    shall ever again be heard in you!
Because your merchants were the world's nobility,
    you led all nations astray by your sorcery."

After this I heard what sounded lke the loud song
of a great assembly in heaven. They were singing:
"Alleluia!
Salvation, glory, and might belong to our God,
   for his judgments are true and just!
He has condemned the great harlot
   who corrupted the earth with her harlotry.
He has avenged the blood of his servants
   which was shed by her hand."
Once more they sang, "Alleluia!" The angel then said
to me: "Write this down: Happy are they who have
been invited to the wedding feast of the Lamb."—
This is the Word of the Lord. ℟. **Thanks be to God.** ✓

Responsorial Psalm   Ps 100, 2. 3. 4. 5

℟. (Rv 19, 9) **Blessed are they who are called to the
   wedding feast of the Lamb.**

Sing joyfully to the Lord, all you lands;
   serve the Lord with gladness;
   come before him with joyful song. — ℟

Know that the Lord is God;
   he made us, his we are;
   his people, the flock he tends. — ℟

Enter his gates with thanksgiving,
   his courts with praise.
Give thanks to him; bless his name. — ℟

For the Lord is good:
   the Lord, whose kindness endures forever,
   and his faithfulness, to all generations. — ℟ ✓

GOSPEL   Lk 21, 20-28

See p. 426.

See p. 426.

FRIDAY OF THE THIRTY-FOURTH WEEK
IN ORDINARY TIME

READING I   Rv 20, 1-4. 11—21, 2

Satan has already been driven from heaven. The resurrection of the dead and the last judgment follow upon the intermediate reign of Christ. The single white throne symbolizes God's absolute dominion; nothing can thwart his will.

A reading from the book of Revelation

I, John, saw an angel come down from heaven, holding the key to the abyss and a huge chain in his hand. He seized the dragon, the ancient serpent, who is the devil or Satan, and chained him up for a thousand years. The angel hurled him into the abyss, which he closed and sealed over him. He did this so that the dragon might not lead the nations astray until the thousand years are over. After this, the dragon is to be released for a short time.

Then I saw some thrones. Those who were sitting on them were empowered to pass judgment. I also saw the spirits of those who had been beheaded for their witness to Jesus and the word of God, those who had never worshiped the beast or its image nor accepted its mark on their foreheads or their hands. They came to life again and reigned with Christ for a thousand years.

Next I saw a large white throne and the One who sat on it. The earth and the sky fled from his presence until they could no longer be seen. I saw the dead, the great and the lowly, standing before the throne. Lastly, among the scrolls, the book of the living was opened. The dead were judged according to their conduct as recorded on the scrolls. The sea gave up its dead; then death and the nether world gave up their

dead. Each person was judged according to his conduct. Then death and the nether world were hurled
into the pool of fire, which is the second death; anyone whose name was not found inscribed in the book
of the living was hurled into this pool of fire.

Then I saw new heavens and a new earth. The
former heavens and the former earth had passed
away, and the sea was no longer. I also saw a new
Jerusalem, the holy city, coming down out of heaven
from God, beautiful as a bride prepared to meet her
husband.—This is the Word of the Lord. ℟. **Thanks
be to God.** ℣

Responsorial Psalm   Ps 84, 3. 4. 5-6. 8

℟. (Rv 21, 3) **Here God lives among his people.**

My soul yearns and pines
  for the courts of the Lord.
My heart and my flesh
  cry out for the living God. — ℟

Even the sparrow finds a home,
  and the swallow a nest
  in which she puts her young—
Your altars, O Lord of hosts,
  my king and my God! — ℟

Happy they who dwell in your house!
  continually they praise you.
Happy the men whose strength you are!
  They go from strength to strength. — ℟ ℣

GOSPEL   Lk 21, 29-33

See p. 429.

SATURDAY OF THE THIRTY-FOURTH WEEK
IN ORDINARY TIME

READING I   Rv 22, 1-7

Finally, John describes the heavenly Jerusalem as the abode of the divine life. Here flows the river of life. On its bank flowers the tree of life-giving fruit. The Throne of God is the center of the Divine Presence, replacing the Temple.

A reading from the book of Revelation

The angel then showed me, John, the river of life-giving water, clear as crystal, which issued from the throne of God and of the Lamb and flowed down the middle of the streets. On either side of the river grew the trees of life which produce fruit twelve times a year, once each month; their leaves serve as medicine for the nations. Nothing deserving a curse shall be found there. The throne of God and of the Lamb shall be there, and his servants shall serve him faithfully. They shall see him face to face and bear his name on their foreheads. The night shall be no more. They will need no light from lamps or the sun, for the Lord God shall give them light, and they shall reign forever.

The angel said to me: "These words are trustworthy and true; the Lord, the God of prophetic spirits, has sent his angel to show his servants what must happen very soon.

"Remember, I am coming soon! Happy the man who heeds the prophetic message of this book!"—This is the Word of the Lord. ℞. **Thanks be to God.** ℣

Responsorial Psalm   Ps 95, 1-2. 3-5. 6-7

℞. (1 Cor 16, 22; Rv 22, 20) **Marana tha! Come, Lord Jesus!**

Come, let us sing joyfully to the Lord;
    let us acclaim the Rock of our salvation.
Let us greet him with thanksgiving;
    let us joyfully sing psalms to him. — ℞

For the Lord is a great God,
  and a great king above all gods;
In his hands are the depths of the earth,
  and the tops of the mountains are his.
His is the sea, for he has made it,
  and the dry land, which his hands have formed.—℟

Come, let us bow down in worship;
  let us kneel before the Lord who made us.
For he is our God,
  and we are the people he shepherds, the flock he
    guides. — ℟ ▼

GOSPEL   Lk 21, 34-36

See p. 432.

COMMON OF SAINTS
ANTIPHONS AND PRAYERS

1) The following Mass formularies are used for all Masses of Saints who have no complete formulary in the Proper of Saints. In each case, an appropriate rubric gives the page number of the specific Common or Commons that may be used.

2) In the individual Commons, several Mass formularies, with antiphons and prayers, are arranged for convenience.

The priest, however, may interchange antiphons and prayers of the same Common choosing according to the circumstances those texts which seem pastorally appropriate.

In addition, for Masses of Memorial, the Prayer over the Gifts and the Prayer after Communion may be taken from the weekdays of the current liturgical season as well as from the Commons.

3) In the Common of Martyrs and in the Common of Holy Men and Women, all the prayers may be used of men or women with the necessary change of gender.

4) In the individual Commons, texts in the singular may be changed to the plural and vice versa.

5) Certain Masses which are given for specific seasons and circumstances should be used for those seasons and circumstances.

6) During the Easter Season an alleluia should be added at the end of the Entrance and Communion Antiphons.

7) In accord with the rules given in the Introduction to the Proper of Saints, the Readings and Intervenient Chants in the Common of Saints may always be used in any individual celebration in honor of the Saints when there are pastoral reasons for doing so.

COMMON OF THE DEDICATION OF A CHURCH

The Common of the Dedication of a Church comprises three formularies. The first is said on the day of the dedication. The others are used on the anniversary of the dedication: the second in the dedicated church itself, for example, the parish church; and the third outside the dedicated church, for example on the feast of St. John Lateran (Nov. 9) or of the Cathedral of the local diocese.

1. ON THE DAY OF DEDICATION

ENTRANCE ANT.   See Gn 28, 17

This is a place of awe; this is God's house, the gate of heaven, and it shall be called the royal court of God.   → No. 2, p. 614

OPENING PRAYER

All powerful and ever-living God,
fill this church with your love
and give your help to all who call on you in faith.
May the power of your word and sacraments in this place
bring strength to the people gathered here.
We . . . for ever and ever. ℟. **Amen.** ↓

READINGS AND INTERVENIENT CHANTS

See pp. 1106-1118.

PRAYER OVER THE GIFTS

Lord,
accept the gifts of your Church
which we offer with joy.
May all your people gathered in this holy place
come to eternal salvation by these mysteries.
Grant this in the name of Jesus the Lord.
℟. **Amen.**   → No. 21, p. 626 (Pref. P 52)

COMMUNION ANT.   Mt 21, 13; Lk 11, 19

My house shall be called a house of prayer, says the Lord; ask here and you shall receive, seek and you shall find, knock and the door will open. ↓

PRAYER AFTER COMMUNION

Lord,
may your truth grow in our hearts
by the holy gifts we receive.
May we worship you always in your holy temple
and come to rejoice with all the saints in your presence.
We ask this through Christ our Lord.
℟. **Amen.** → No. 32, p. 650

2. ANNIVERSARY OF DEDICATION

A. IN THE DEDICATED CHURCH

ENTRANCE ANT Ps 68, 36

Greatly to be feared is God in his sanctuary; he, the God of Israel, gives power and strength to his people. Blessed be God! → No. 2, p. 614

OPENING PRAYER

Father,
each year we recall the dedication of this church
to your service.
Let our worship always be sincere
and help us to find your saving love in this church.
Grant this through our Lord Jesus Christ, your Son,
who lives and reigns with you and the Holy Spirit,
one God, for ever and ever. ℟. **Amen.** ↓

READINGS AND INTERVENIENT CHANTS

See pp. 1106-1118.

PRAYER OVER THE GIFTS

Lord,
as we recall the day you filled this church
with your glory and holiness,
may our lives also become an acceptable offering
to you.
Grant this in the name of Jesus the Lord.
℟. **Amen.** → No. 21, p. 626 (Pref. P 52)

COMMUNION ANT.   1 Cor 3, 16-17

You are the temple of God, and God's Spirit dwells in you. The temple of God is holy; you are that temple. ℣

PRAYER AFTER COMMUNION

Lord,
we know the joy and power of your blessing in our
    lives.
As we celebrate the dedication of this church,
may we give ourselves once more to your service.
Grant this through Christ our Lord.
℟. **Amen.**   ➔ No. 32, p. 650

─────────────

B. OUTSIDE THE DEDICATED CHURCH

ENTRANCE ANT.   Rv 21, 2

I saw the holy city, new Jerusalem, coming down from God out of heaven, like a bride adorned in readiness for her husband.   ➔ No. 2, p. 614

OPENING PRAYER

God our Father,
from living stones, your chosen people,
you built an eternal temple to your glory.
Increase the spiritual gifts you have given to your
    Church,
so that your faithful people may continue to grow
into the new and eternal Jerusalem.
We ask this through our Lord Jesus Christ, your Son,
who lives and reigns with you and the Holy Spirit,
one God, for ever and ever. ℟. **Amen.** ℣

OR

Father,
you called your people to be your Church.
As we gather together in your name,
may we love, honor, and follow you
to eternal life in the kingdom you promise.

Grant this through our Lord Jesus Christ, your Son,
who lives and reigns with you and the Holy Spirit,
one God, for ever and ever. ℟. **Amen.** ✟

READINGS AND INTERVENIENT CHANTS
See pp. 1106-1118.

PRAYER OVER THE GIFTS
Lord,
receive our gifts.
May we who share this sacrament
experience the life and power it promises,
and hear the answer to our prayers.
We ask this in the name of Jesus the Lord.
℟. **Amen.**   ➔ No. 21, p. 626 (Pref. P 53)

COMMUNION ANT.   1 Pt 2, 5
**Like living stones let yourselves be built on Christ
as a spiritual house, a holy priesthood.** ✟

PRAYER AFTER COMMUNION
Father,
you make your Church on earth
a sign of the new and eternal Jerusalem.
By sharing in this sacrament
may we become the temple of your presence
and the home of your glory.
Grant this in the name of Jesus the Lord.
℟. **Amen.**   ➔ No. 32, p. 650

COMMON OF THE BLESSED
VIRGIN MARY

The Common of the Blessed Virgin Mary comprises six Mass formularies and one Prayer formulary. These are used on feasts of the Virgin Mary during the year as indicated in the Missal. They are also utilized for the Mass of the Blessed Virgin Mary on Saturday in Ordinary Time when there is no feast higher than an optional Memorial.

These Masses are also used for the Saturday celebrations of the Blessed Virgin Mary and for votive Masses of the Blessed Virgin Mary.

1

ENTRANCE ANT. Sedulius
Hail, holy Mother! The child to whom you gave birth is the King of heaven and earth for ever.

→ No. 2, p. 614

OPENING PRAYER

Lord, God,
give to your people the joy
of continual health in mind and body.
With the prayers of the Virgin Mary to help us,
guide us through the sorrows of this life
to eternal happiness in the life to come.
Grant this through our Lord Jesus Christ, your Son,
who lives and reigns with you and the Holy Spirit,
one God, for ever and ever. ℟. **Amen.** ✟

OR

Lord,
take away the sins of your people.
May the prayers of Mary the mother of your Son
help us,
for alone and unaided we cannot hope to please you.
We ask this through our Lord Jesus Christ, your Son,
who lives and reigns with you and the Holy Spirit,
one God, for ever and ever. ℟. **Amen.** ✟

READINGS AND INTERVENIENT CHANTS

See pp. 1118-1137.

PRAYER OVER THE GIFTS

Father,
the birth of Christ your Son
deepened the virgin mother's love for you,
and increased her holiness.
May the humanity of Christ
give us courage in our weakness;
may it free us from our sins,
and make our offering acceptable.
We ask this through Christ our Lord.
℞. **Amen.** ➤ No. 21, p. 626 (Pref. P 56-57)

COMMUNION ANT. See Lk 11, 27

Blessed is the womb of the Virgin Mary; she carried the Son of the eternal Father. ℣

PRAYER AFTER COMMUNION

Lord,
we rejoice in your sacraments and ask your mercy
as we honor the memory of the Virgin Mary.
May her faith and love
inspire us to serve you more faithfully
in the work of salvation.
Grant this in the name of Jesus the Lord.
℞. **Amen.** ➤ No. 32, p. 650

2

ENTRANCE ANT.

Blessed are you, Virgin Mary, who carried the creator of all things in your womb; you gave birth to your maker, and remain for ever a virgin.

➤ No. 2, p. 614

OPENING PRAYER

God of mercy,
give us strength.
May we who honor the memory of the Mother of
God

rise above our sins and failings with the help of her
prayers.
Grant this through our Lord Jesus Christ, your Son,
who lives and reigns with you and the Holy Spirit,
one God, for ever and ever. ℟. **Amen.** ✣

OR

Lord,
may the prayers of the Virgin Mary
bring us protection from danger
and freedom from sin
that we may come to the joy of your peace.
We ask this through our Lord Jesus Christ, your Son,
who lives and reigns with you and the Holy Spirit,
one God, for ever and ever. ℟. **Amen.** ✣

READINGS AND INTERVENIENT CHANTS

See pp. 1118-1137.

PRAYER OVER THE GIFTS

Lord,
we honor the memory of the mother of your Son.
May the sacrifice we share
make of us an everlasting gift to you.
Grant this through Christ our Lord.
℟. **Amen.**   ➔ No. 21, p. 626 (Pref. P 56-57)

COMMUNION ANT.   Lk 1, 49

**The Almighty has done great things for me. Holy
is his name.** ✣

PRAYER AFTER COMMUNION

Lord,
you give us the sacraments of eternal redemption.
May we who honor the memory of the mother of
your Son
rejoice in the abundance of your grace
and experience your unfailing help.
We ask this through Christ our Lord.
℟. **Amen.**   ➔ No. 32, p. 650

3

ENTRANCE ANT. See Jdt 13, 23. 25

You have been blessed, O Virgin Mary, above all other women on earth by the Lord the most high God; he has so exalted your name that your praises shall never fade from the mouths of men.

➤ No. 2, p. 614

OPENING PRAYER

Lord,
as we honor the glorious memory of the Virgin Mary,
we ask that by the help of her prayers
we too may come to share the fullness of your grace.
Grant this through our Lord Jesus Christ, your Son,
who lives and reigns with you and the Holy Spirit,
one God, for ever and ever. ℟. **Amen.** ✠

OR

Lord Jesus Christ,
you chose the Virgin Mary to be your mother,
a worthy home in which to dwell.
By her prayers keep us 'from danger
and bring us to the joy of heaven,
where you live and reign with the Father and the
    Holy Spirit,
one God, for ever and ever. ℟. **Amen.** ✠

READINGS AND INTERVENIENT CHANTS

See pp. 1118-1137.

PRAYER OVER THE GIFTS

Lord,
we bring you our sacrifice of praise
at this celebration in honor of Mary, the mother of
    your Son.
May this holy exchange of gifts
help us on our way to eternal salvation.
We ask this in the name of Jesus the Lord.
℟. **Amen.** ➤ No. 21, p. 626 (Pref. P 56-57)

COMMUNION ANT.   See Lk 1, 48

All generations will call me blessed, because God has looked upon his lowly handmaid. ℣

PRAYER AFTER COMMUNION

Lord,
we eat the bread of heaven.
May we who honor the memory of the Virgin Mary
come one day to your banquet of eternal life.
Grant this through Christ our Lord.
℟. **Amen.**   ➤ No. 32, p. 650

---

4. ADVENT SEASON

ENTRANCE ANT.   Is 45, 8

Let the clouds rain down the Just One, and the earth bring forth a Savior.

OR   Lk 1, 30-32

The angel said to Mary: You have won God's favor. You will conceive and bear a Son, and he will be called Son of the Most High.   ➤ No. 2, p. 614

OPENING PRAYER

Father,
in your plan for our salvation
your Word became man,
announced by an angel and born of the Virgin Mary.
May we who believe that she is the Mother of God
receive the help of her prayers.
We ask this through our Lord Jesus Christ, your Son,
who lives and reigns with you and the Holy Spirit,
one God, for ever and ever. ℟. **Amen.** ℣

READINGS AND INTERVENIENT CHANTS

See pp. 1118-1137.

PRAYER OVER THE GIFTS

Lord,
may the power of your Spirit,
which sanctified Mary the mother of your Son,
make holy the gifts we place upon this altar.
We ask this through Christ our Lord.
℟. **Amen.** ➤ No. 21, p. 626 (Pref. P 56-57 or P 2)

COMMUNION ANT. Is 7, 14

The Virgin is with child and shall bear a son, and she will call him Emmanuel. ℣

PRAYER AFTER COMMUNION

Lord our God,
may the sacraments we receive
show us your forgiveness and love.
May we who honor the mother of your Son
be saved by his coming among us as man,
for he is Lord for ever and ever.
℟. **Amen.** ➤ No. 32, p. 650

---

5. CHRISTMAS SEASON

ENTRANCE ANT.

Giving birth to the King whose reign is unending, Mary knows the joys of motherhood together with a virgin's honor; none like her before, and there shall be none hereafter.

OR

O virgin Mother of God, the universe cannot hold him, and yet, becoming man, he confined himself in your womb. ➤ No. 2, p. 614

OPENING PRAYER

Father,
you gave the human race eternal salvation
through the motherhood of the Virgin Mary.

May we experience the help of her prayers in our
    lives,
for through her we received the very source of life,
your Son, our Lord Jesus Christ,
who lives and reigns with you and the Holy Spirit,
one God, for ever and ever. ℟. **Amen.** ↓

READINGS AND INTERVENIENT CHANTS

See pp. 1118-1137.

PRAYER OVER THE GIFTS

Lord,
accept our gifts and prayers
and fill our hearts with the light of your Holy Spirit.
Help us to follow the example of the Virgin Mary:
to seek you in all things
and to do your will with gladness.
We ask this in the name of Jesus the Lord.
℟. **Amen.**   ➤ No. 21, p. 626 (Pref. P 56-57)

COMMUNION ANT.   Jn 1, 14

**The Word of God became man, and lived among us,
full of grace and truth.** ↓

PRAYER AFTER COMMUNION

Lord,
as we celebrate this feast of the Blessed Virgin Mary,
you renew us with the body and blood of Christ your
    Son.
May this sacrament give us a share in his life,
for he is Lord for ever and ever.
℟. **Amen.**   ➤ No. 32, p. 650

_____

6. EASTER SEASON

ENTRANCE ANT.   See Acts 1, 14

**The disciples were constantly at prayer together,
with Mary the mother of Jesus, alleluia.**

                                          ➤ No. 2, p. 614

OPENING PRAYER

God our Father,
you give joy to the world
by your resurrection of your Son, our Lord Jesus
    Christ.
Through the prayers of his mother, the Virgin Mary,
bring us to the happiness of eternal life.
We ask this through our Lord Jesus Christ, your Son,
who lives and reigns with you and the Holy Spirit,
one God, for ever and ever. ℟. **Amen.** ✠

OR

God our Father,
you gave the Holy Spirit to your apostles
as they joined in prayer with Mary, the mother of
    Jesus.
By the help of her prayers
keep us faithful in your service
and let our words and actions be so inspired
as to bring glory to your name.
Grant this through our Lord Jesus Christ, your Son,
who lives and reigns with you and the Holy Spirit,
one God, for ever and ever. ℟. **Amen.** ✠

READINGS AND INTERVENIENT CHANTS
See pp. 1118-1137.

PRAYER OVER THE GIFTS

Father,
as we celebrate the memory of the Virgin Mary,
we offer you our gifts and prayers.
Sustain us by the love of Christ,
who offered himself as a perfect sacrifice on the
    cross,
and is Lord for ever and ever.

℟. **Amen.**   ➔ No. 21, p. 626 (Pref. P 56-57)

COMMUNION ANT.

Rejoice, virgin mother, for Christ has arisen from his grave, alleluia. ℣

PRAYER AFTER COMMUNION

Lord,
may this sacrament strengthen the faith in our
    hearts.
May Mary's Son, Jesus Christ,
whom we proclaim to be God and man,
bring us to eternal life
by the saving power of his resurrection,
for he is Lord for ever and ever.
℟. **Amen.**   ➔ No. 32, p. 650

OTHER PRAYERS FOR MASSES OF THE
BLESSED VIRGIN MARY

OPENING PRAYER

All-powerful God,
we rejoice in the protection of the holy Virgin Mary.
May her prayers help to free us from all evils here
    on earth
and lead us to eternal joy in heaven.
Grant this through our Lord Jesus Christ, your Son,
who lives and reigns with you and the Holy Spirit,
one God, for ever and ever. ℟. **Amen.** ℣

READINGS AND INTERVENIENT CHANTS

See pp. 1118-1137.

PRAYER OVER THE GIFTS

Lord,
accept the prayers and gifts we present today
as we honor Mary, the Mother of God.
May they please you
and bring us your forgiveness and help.
We ask this in the name of Jesus the Lord.
℟. **Amen.**   ➔ No. 21, p. 626

PRAYER AFTER COMMUNION
Lord,
we are renewed with the sacraments of salvation.
May we who celebrate the memory of the Mother
   of God
come to realize the eternal redemption you promise.
We ask this through . . . ℟. **Amen.**   ➤ No. 32, p. 650

COMMON OF MARTYRS

The Common of Martyrs comprises ten Mass formularies and three Prayer formularies. Since the Martyrs were associated in a very special way with the mystery of Christ's death and resurrection, their worship takes on special significance when it is celebrated during the Easter Season. That is why the formularies are separated into those for Martyrs "outside the Easter Season" and "in the Easter Season."

1. FOR SEVERAL MARTYRS, OUTSIDE THE EASTER SEASON

ENTRANCE ANT.
The saints are happy in heaven because they followed Christ. They rejoice with him for ever because they shed their blood for love of him.   ➤ No. 2, p. 614

OPENING PRAYER
Father,
we celebrate the memory of Saints N. and N.
who died for their faithful witnessing to Christ.
Give us the strength to follow their example,
loyal and faithful to the end.
We ask this through our Lord Jesus Christ, your Son,
who lives and reigns with you and the Holy Spirit,
one God, for ever and ever. ℟. **Amen.** ▼

READINGS AND INTERVENIENT CHANTS
See pp. 1138-1154.

PRAYER OVER THE GIFTS
Father,
receive the gifts we bring

in memory of your holy martyrs.
Keep us strong in our faith
and in our witness to you.
Grant this through Christ our Lord.
℟. **Amen.**   → No. 21, p. 626

COMMUNION ANT.   Lk 22, 28-30

**You are the men who have stood by me faithfully
in my trials, and now I confer a kingdom on you,
says the Lord. You will eat and drink at my table
in my kingdom.** ℣

PRAYER AFTER COMMUNION
God our Father,
in your holy martyrs you show us the glory of the
    cross.
Through this sacrifice, strengthen our resolution
to follow Christ faithfully
and to work in your Church for the salvation of all.
We ask this through Christ our Lord.
℟. **Amen.**   → No. 32, p. 650

2. FOR SEVERAL MARTYRS, OUTSIDE THE EASTER SEASON

ENTRANCE ANT.   Ps 34, 20-21

**Many are the sufferings of the just, and from them
all the Lord has delivered them; the Lord preserves
all their bones, not one of them shall be broken.**
    → No. 2, p. 614

OPENING PRAYER
All-powerful, ever-living God,
turn our weakness into strength.
As you gave your martyrs N. and N.
the courage to suffer death for Christ,
give us the courage to live in faithful witness to you.
Grant this through our Lord Jesus Christ, your Son,

who lives and reigns with you and the Holy Spirit,
one God, for ever and ever. ℟. **Amen.** ✓

READINGS AND INTERVENIENT CHANTS
See pp. 1138-1154.

PRAYER OVER THE GIFTS
Lord,
accept the gifts we bring
to celebrate the feast of your martyrs.
May this sacrifice free us from sin
and make our service pleasing to you.
We ask this through Christ our Lord.
℟. **Amen.** ➤ No. 21, p. 626

COMMUNION ANT. Jn 15, 13

**No one has greater love, says the Lord, than the man
who lays down his life for his friends.** ✓

PRAYER AFTER COMMUNION
Lord,
we eat the bread from heaven
and become one body in Christ.
Never let us be separated from his love
and help us to follow your martyrs N. and N.
by having the courage to overcome all things through
    Christ,
who loved us all,
and lives and reigns with you for ever and ever.
℟. **Amen.** ➤ No. 32, p. 650

---

3. FOR SEVERAL MARTYRS, OUTSIDE THE EASTER SEASON

ENTRANCE ANT. Ps 40, 39

**The salvation of the just comes from the Lord. He
is their strength in time of need.** ➤ No. 2, p. 614

OPENING PRAYER

Lord,
may the victory of your martyrs give us joy.
May their example strengthen our faith,
and their prayers give us renewed courage.
We ask this through our Lord Jesus Christ, your Son,
who lives and reigns with you and the Holy Spirit,
one God, for ever and ever. ℟. **Amen.** ↓

OR

Lord,
hear the prayers of the martyrs N. and N.
and give us courage to bear witness to your truth.
Grant this through our Lord Jesus Christ, your Son,
who lives and reigns with you and the Holy Spirit,
one God, for ever and ever. ℟. **Amen.** ↓

READINGS AND INTERVENIENT CHANTS

See pp. 1138-1154.

PRAYER OVER THE GIFTS

Lord,
accept the gifts of your people
as we honor the suffering and death
of your martyrs N. and N.
As the eucharist gave them strength in persecution
may it keep us faithful in every difficulty.
We ask this through Christ our Lord.
℟. **Amen.** ➔ No. 21, p. 626

COMMUNION ANT. Mk 8, 35

Whoever loses his life for my sake and the gospel, says the Lord, will save it. ↓

PRAYER AFTER COMMUNION

Lord,
keep this eucharist effective within us.
May the gift we receive
on this feast of the martyrs N. and N.

bring us salvation and peace.
Grant this in the name of Jesus the Lord.
℟. **Amen.** → No. 32, p. 650

---

4. FOR SEVERAL MARTYRS, OUTSIDE THE EASTER SEASON

ENTRANCE ANT. Ps 34, 18
The Lord will hear the just when they cry out, from all their afflictions he will deliver them.

→ No. 2, p. 614

OPENING PRAYER
God our Father,
every year you give us the joy
of celebrating this feast of Saints N. and N.
May we who recall their birth to eternal life
imitate their courage in suffering for you.
Grant this through our Lord Jesus Christ, your Son,
who lives and reigns with you and the Holy Spirit,
one God, for ever and ever. ℟. **Amen.** ▼

OR

God our Father,
your generous gift of love
brought Saints N. and N. to unending glory.
Through the prayers of your martyrs
forgive our sins and free us from every danger.
We ask this through our Lord Jesus Christ, your Son,
who lives and reigns with you and the Holy Spirit,
one God, for ever and ever. ℟. **Amen.** ▼

READINGS AND INTERVENIENT CHANTS
See pp. 1138-1154.

PRAYER OVER THE GIFTS
Lord,
you gave Saints N. and N. the fulfillment of their
    faith

in the vision of your glory.
May the gifts we bring to honor their memory
gain us your pardon and peace.
We ask this in the name of Jesus the Lord.
℟. **Amen.** ➔ No. 21, p. 626

COMMUNION ANT. 2 Cor 4, 11

**We are given over to death for Jesus, that the life
of Jesus may be revealed in our dying flesh.** ℣

PRAYER AFTER COMMUNION

Lord,
may this food of heaven
bring us a share in the grace you gave the martyrs
N. and N.
From their bitter sufferings may we learn to become
strong
and by patient endurance earn the victory of rejoicing in your holiness.
Grant this through Christ our Lord.
℟. **Amen.** ➔ No. 32, p. 650

5. FOR SEVERAL MARTYRS, OUTSIDE THE EASTER SEASON

ENTRANCE ANT.

**The holy martyrs shed their blood on earth for
Christ; therefore they have received an everlasting
reward.** ➔ No. 2, p. 614

OPENING PRAYER

Lord,
we honor your martyrs N. and N.
who were faithful to Christ
even to the point of shedding their blood for him.
Increase our own faith and free us from our sins,
and help us to follow their example of love.
We ask this through our Lord Jesus Christ, your Son,

who lives and reigns with you and the Holy Spirit,
one God, for ever and ever. ℞. **Amen.** ✠

READINGS AND INTERVENIENT CHANTS

See pp. 1138-1154.

PRAYER OVER THE GIFTS

Lord,
be pleased with the gifts we bring.
May we who celebrate the mystery of the passion
   of your Son
make this mystery part of our lives
by the inspiration of the martyrs N. and N.
Grant this through Christ our Lord. ℞. **Amen.**

OR

Lord,
may these gifts which we bring you in sacrifice
to celebrate the victory of Saints N. and N.
fill our hearts with your love
and prepare us for the reward you promise
to those who are faithful.
We ask this in the name of Jesus the Lord. ℞. **Amen.**

➜ No. 21, p. 626

COMMUNION ANT.   See Rom 8, 38-39

**Neither death nor life nor anything in all creation
can come between us and Christ's love for us.** ✠

PRAYER AFTER COMMUNION

Lord,
you give us the body and blood of Christ your only
   Son
on this feast of your martyrs N. and N.
By being faithful to your love
may we live in you,
receive life from you,
and always be true to your inspiration.
We ask this in the name of Jesus the Lord.
℞. **Amen.**   ➜ No. 32, p. 650

---

6. FOR ONE MARTYR, OUTSIDE THE EASTER SEASON

ENTRANCE ANT.

This holy man fought to the death for the law of his God, never cowed by the threats of the wicked; his house was built on solid rock.   → No. 2, p. 614

OPENING PRAYER

God of power and mercy,
you gave N., your martyr, victory over pain and suffering.
Strengthen us who celebrate this day of his triumph
and help us to be victorious over the evils that
  threaten us.
Grant this through our Lord Jesus Christ, your Son,
who lives and reigns with you and the Holy Spirit,
one God, for ever and ever. ℞. **Amen.** ▼

READINGS AND INTERVENIENT CHANTS

See pp. 1138-1154.

PRAYER OVER THE GIFTS

Lord,
bless our offerings and make them holy.
May these gifts fill our hearts
with the love which gave St. N. victory
over all his suffering.
We ask this through Christ our Lord. ℞. **Amen.**

OR

Lord,
accept the gifts we offer in memory of the martyr N.
May they be pleasing to you
as was the shedding of his blood for the faith.
Grant this through Christ our Lord. ℞. **Amen.**

→ No. 21, p. 626

COMMUNION ANT. Mt 16, 24

If anyone wishes to come after me, he must renounce himself, take up his cross, and follow me, says the Lord. ℣

PRAYER AFTER COMMUNION

Lord,
may the mysteries we receive
give us the spiritual courage which made your martyr N.
faithful in your service and victorious in his suffering.
Grant this in the name of Jesus the Lord.
℟. **Amen.** ➔ No. 32, p. 650

---

7. FOR ONE MARTYR, OUTSIDE THE EASTER SEASON

ENTRANCE ANT.

Here is a true martyr who shed his blood for Christ; his judges could not shake him by their menaces, and so he won through to the kingdom of heaven.

➔ No. 2, p. 614

OPENING PRAYER

All-powerful, ever-living God,
you gave St. N. the courage to witness to the gospel of Christ
even to the point of giving his life for it.
By his prayers help us to endure all suffering for love of you
and to seek you with all our hearts,
for you alone are the source of life.
Grant this through our Lord Jesus Christ, your Son,
who lives and reigns with you and the Holy Spirit,
one God, for ever and ever. ℟. **Amen.** ℣

READINGS AND INTERVENIENT CHANTS
See pp. 1138-1154.

PRAYER OVER THE GIFTS
God of love,
pour out your blessing on our gifts
and make our faith strong,
the faith which St. N. professed by shedding his
blood.
We ask this through Christ our Lord. ℞. **Amen.**

OR
Lord,
accept these gifts we present in memory of St. N.,
for no temptation could turn him away from you.
We ask this through Christ our Lord. ℞. **Amen.**

➤ No. 21, p. 626

COMMUNION ANT. Jn 15, 5

**I am the vine and you are the branches, says the
Lord; he who lives in me, and I in him, will bear
much fruit.** ℣

PRAYER AFTER COMMUNION
Lord,
we are renewed by the mystery of the eucharist.
By imitating the fidelity of St. N. and by your
patience
may we come to share the eternal life you have
promised.
We ask this in the name of Jesus the Lord.
℞. **Amen.**

➤ No. 32, p. 650

8.　**FOR SEVERAL MARTYRS, IN THE EASTER SEASON**

ENTRANCE ANT.　　　　　　Mt 25, 34

Come, you whom my Father has blessed; inherit the kingdom prepared for you since the foundation of the world, alleluia.　　　➜ No. 2, p. 614

OPENING PRAYER

Father,
you gave your martyrs N. and N.
the courage to die in witness to Christ and the gospel.
By the power of your Holy Spirit,
give us the humility to believe
and the courage to profess
the faith for which they gave their lives.
We ask this through our Lord Jesus Christ, your Son,
who lives and reigns with you and the Holy Spirit,
one God, for ever and ever. ℟. **Amen.** ▼

OR

God our all-powerful Father,
you strengthen our faith
and take away our weakness.
Let the prayers and example of your martyrs N. and
　　N. help us
to share in the passion and resurrection of Christ
and bring us to eternal joy with all your saints.
We ask this through our Lord Jesus Christ, your Son,
who lives and reigns with you and the Holy Spirit,
one God, for ever and ever. ℟. **Amen.** ▼

READINGS AND INTERVENIENT CHANTS
See pp. 1138-1154.

PRAYER OVER THE GIFTS
Lord,
we celebrate the death of your holy martyrs.

May we offer the sacrifice which gives all martyr-
  dom its meaning.
Grant this through Christ our Lord.
℟. **Amen.**   ➔ No. 21, p. 626

COMMUNION ANT.   Rv 2, 7
**Those who are victorious I will feed from the tree
of life, which grows in the paradise of my God, alleluia.** ⓥ

PRAYER AFTER COMMUNION
Lord,
at this holy meal
we celebrate the heavenly victory of your martyrs
  N. and N.
May this bread of life
give us the courage to conquer evil,
so that we may come to share the fruit of the tree
  of life in paradise.
We ask this through Christ our Lord.
℟. **Amen.**   ➔ No. 32, p. 650

---

9. FOR SEVERAL MARTYRS, IN THE
EASTER SEASON

ENTRANCE ANT.   Rv 12, 11
**These are the saints who were victorious in the blood
of the Lamb, and in the face of death they did not
cling to life; therefore they are reigning with Christ
for ever, alleluia.**   ➔ No. 2, p. 614

OPENING PRAYER
Lord,
you gave your martyrs N. and N.
the privilege of shedding their blood
for boldly proclaiming the death and resurrection
  of your Son.

May this celebration of their victory give them
  honor among your people.
We ask this through our Lord Jesus Christ, your Son,
who lives and reigns with you and the Holy Spirit,
one God, for ever and ever. ℟. **Amen.** ↓

READINGS AND INTERVENIENT CHANTS
See pp. 1138-1154.

PRAYER OVER THE GIFTS
Lord,
fill these gifts with the blessing of your Holy Spirit
and fill our hearts with the love
which gave victory to Saints N. and N.
in dying for the faith.
We ask this through Christ our Lord.
℟. **Amen.**   → No. 21, p. 626

COMMUNION ANT.   2 Tm 2, 11-12
**If we die with Christ, we shall live with him, and if
we are faithful to the end, we shall reign with him,
alleluia.** ↓

PRAYER AFTER COMMUNION
Lord,
we are renewed by the breaking of one bread
in honor of the martyrs N. and N.
Keep us in your love
and help us to live the new life Christ won for us.
Grant this in the name of Jesus the Lord.
℟. **Amen.**   → No. 32, p. 650

---

10. FOR ONE MARTYR, IN THE EASTER SEASON

ENTRANCE ANT.   See 4 Ezr 2, 35
**Light for ever will shine on your saints, O Lord, al-
leluia.**   → No. 2, p. 614

OPENING PRAYER

God our Father,
you have honored the Church with the victorious
    witness of St. N.,
who died for his faith.
As he imitated the sufferings and death of the Lord,
may we follow in his footsteps and come to eternal
    joy.
We ask this through our Lord Jesus Christ, your Son,
who lives and reigns with you and the Holy Spirit,
one God, for ever and ever. ℟. **Amen.** ⍒

READINGS AND INTERVENIENT CHANTS

See pp. 1138-1154.

PRAYER OVER THE GIFTS

Lord,
accept this offering of praise and peace
in memory of your martyr N.
May it bring us your forgiveness
and inspire us to give you thanks now and for ever.
Grant this in the name of Jesus the Lord.
℟. **Amen.**   ➔ No. 21, p. 626

COMMUNION ANT.   Jn 12, 24-25

**I tell you solemnly: Unless a grain of wheat falls on
the ground and dies, it remains a single grain; but
if it dies, it yields a rich harvest, alleluia.** ⍒

PRAYER AFTER COMMUNION

Lord,
we receive your gifts from heaven
at this joyful feast.
May we who proclaim at this holy table
the death and resurrection of your Son
come to share his glory with all your holy martyrs.
Grant this through Christ our Lord.
℟. **Amen.**   ➔ No. 32, p. 650

OTHER PRAYERS FOR MARTYRS

FOR MISSIONARY MARTYRS

OPENING PRAYER

God of mercy and love,
through the preaching of your martyrs N. and N.
you brought the good news of Christ
to people who had not known him.
May the prayers of Saints N. and N.
make our own faith grow stronger.
We ask this through our Lord Jesus Christ, your Son,
who lives and reigns with you and the Holy Spirit,
one God, for ever and ever. R̞. **Amen.** ▼

READINGS AND INTERVENIENT CHANTS

See pp. 1138-1154.

PRAYER OVER THE GIFTS

Lord,
at this celebration of the eucharist
we honor the suffering and death of your martyrs
N. and N.
In offering this sacrifice
may we proclaim the death of your Son
who gave these martyrs courage not only by his
words
but also by the example of his own passion,
for he is Lord for ever and ever.
R̞. **Amen.**
➔ No. 21, p. 626

PRAYER AFTER COMMUNION

Lord,
may we who eat at your holy table
be inspired by the example of Saints N. and N.
May we keep before us the loving sacrifice of your
Son,
and come to the unending peace of your kingdom.
We ask this in the name of Jesus the Lord.
R̞. **Amen.**
➔ No. 32, p. 650

FOR A VIRGIN MARTYR

OPENING PRAYER

God our Father,
you give us joy each year
in honoring the memory of St. N.
May her prayers be a source of help for us,
and may her example of courage and chastity be
    our inspiration.
Grant this through our Lord Jesus Christ, your Son,
who lives and reigns with you and the Holy Spirit,
one God, for ever and ever. ℟. **Amen.** ℣

READINGS AND INTERVENIENT CHANTS

See pp. 1138-1154.

PRAYER OVER THE GIFTS

Lord,
receive our gifts
as you accepted the suffering and death of St. N.
in whose honor we celebrate this eucharist.
We ask this through Christ our Lord.
℟. **Amen.**   ➔ No. 21, p. 626

PRAYER AFTER COMMUNION

Lord God,
you gave St. N. the crown of eternal joy
because she gave her life
rather than renounce the virginity she had promised
in witness to Christ.
With the courage this eucharist brings
help us to rise out of the bondage of our earthly
    desires
and attain to the glory of your kingdom.
Grant this through Christ our Lord.
℟. **Amen.**   ➔ No. 32, p. 650

FOR A HOLY WOMAN MARTYR

OPENING PRAYER
Father,
in our weakness your power reaches perfection.
You gave St. N. the strength
to defeat the power of sin and evil.
May we who celebrate her glory share in her
    triumph.
We ask this through our Lord Jesus Christ, your Son,
who lives and reigns with you and the Holy Spirit,
one God, for ever and ever. ℟. **Amen.** ⍌

READINGS AND INTERVENIENT CHANTS
See pp. 1138-1154.

PRAYER OVER THE GIFTS
Lord,
today we offer this sacrifice in joy
as we recall the victory of St. N.
May we proclaim to others the great things
you have done for us
and rejoice in the constant help of your martyr's
    prayers.
Grant this through Christ our Lord.
℟. **Amen.** ➔ No. 21, p. 626

PRAYER AFTER COMMUNION
Lord,
by this sacrament you give us eternal joys
as we recall the memory of St. N.
May we always embrace the gift of life
we celebrate at this eucharist.
We ask this in the name of Jesus the Lord.
℟. **Amen.** ➔ No. 32, p. 650

COMMON OF PASTORS

The Common of Pastors comprises twelve Mass formularies: two for a Pope or Bishop (nos. 1-2); two for a Bishop (nos. 3-4); one for a Pastor (no. 5); two for several Pastors (nos. 6-7); one for a Founder of Churches (no. 8); one for several Founders of Churches (no. 9); and three for a Missionary Pastor (nos. 10-12).

1. FOR POPES OR BISHOPS

ENTRANCE ANT.

The Lord chose him to be his high priest; he opened his treasures and made him rich in all goodness.

➔ No. 2, p. 614

OPENING PRAYER

(for popes)

All-powerful and ever-living God,
you called St. N. to guide your people
by his word and example.
With him we pray to you:
watch over the pastors of your Church
with the people entrusted to their care,
and lead them to salvation.
We ask this through our Lord Jesus Christ, your Son,
who lives and reigns with you and the Holy Spirit,
one God, for ever and ever. ℟. **Amen.** ✣

OR (for bishops)

Father,
you gave St. N. to your Church
as an example of a good shepherd.
May his prayers help us on our way to eternal life.
Grant this through our Lord Jesus Christ, your Son,
who lives and reigns with you and the Holy Spirit,
one God, for ever and ever. ℟. **Amen.** ✣

READINGS AND INTERVENIENT CHANTS

See pp. 1154-1176.

PRAYER OVER THE GIFTS

Lord,
we offer you this sacrifice of praise
in memory of your saints.

May their prayers keep us from evil
now and in the future.
Grant this through Christ our Lord.
℟. **Amen.**   → No. 21, p. 626

COMMUNION ANT.   See Jn 10, 11
The good shepherd gives his life for his sheep. ⍌

PRAYER AFTER COMMUNION
Lord God,
St. N. loved you
and gave himself completely in the service of your
    Church.
May the eucharist awaken in us that same love.
We ask this in the name of Jesus the Lord.
℟. **Amen.**   → No. 32, p. 650

_____

2. FOR POPES OR BISHOPS

ENTRANCE ANT.   See Sir 45, 30
**The Lord sealed a covenant of peace with him, and
made him a prince, bestowing the priestly dignity
upon him for ever.**   → No. 2, p. 614

OPENING PRAYER
(for popes)
Father,
you made St. N. shepherd of the whole Church
and gave to us the witness of his virtue and teaching.
Today as we honor this outstanding bishop,
we ask that our light may shine before men
and that our love for you may be sincere.
Grant this through our Lord Jesus Christ, your Son,
who lives and reigns with you and the Holy Spirit,
one God, for ever and ever. ℟. **Amen.** ⍌

OR (for bishops)

All-powerful God,
you made St. N. a bishop and leader of the Church
to inspire your people with his teaching and example.
May we give fitting honor to his memory
and always have the assistance of his prayers.
We ask this through our Lord Jesus Christ, your Son,
who lives and reigns with you and the Holy Spirit,
one God, for ever and ever. ℟. **Amen.** ⤷

READINGS AND INTERVENIENT CHANTS
See pp. 1154-1176.

PRAYER OVER THE GIFTS
Lord,
may the sacrifice which wipes away the sins of all
   the world
bring us your forgiveness.
Help us as we offer it
on this yearly feast in honor of St. N.
Grant this through Christ our Lord.
℟. **Amen.**   ➔ No. 21, p. 626

COMMUNION ANT.   Jn 21, 17
**Lord, you know all things: you know that I love
you.** ⤷

PRAYER AFTER COMMUNION
Lord God,
let the power of the gifts we receive
on this feast of St. N.
take full effect within us.
May this eucharist bring us your help in this life
and lead us to happiness in the unending life to
   come.
We ask this through Christ our Lord.
℟. **Amen.**   ➔ No. 32, p. 650

3. FOR BISHOPS

ENTRANCE ANT.   Ez 34, 11. 23-24

I will look after my sheep, says the Lord, and I will raise up one shepherd who will pasture them. I, the Lord, will be their God.   ➤ No. 2, p. 614

OPENING PRAYER

All-powerful, ever-living God,
you made St. N. bishop and leader of your people.
May his prayers help to bring us your forgiveness
    and love.
We ask this through our Lord Jesus Christ, your Son,
who lives and reigns with you and the Holy Spirit,
one God, for ever and ever. ℟. **Amen.** ▼

READINGS AND INTERVENIENT CHANTS
See pp. 1154-1176.

PRAYER OVER THE GIFTS

Lord,
accept the gifts we bring to your holy altar
on this feast of St. N.
May our offering bring honor to your name
and pardon to your people.
We ask this through Christ our Lord.
℟. **Amen.**   ➤ No. 21, p. 626

COMMUNION ANT.   Jn 15, 16

You have not chosen me; I have chosen you. Go and bear fruit that will last. ▼

PRAYER AFTER COMMUNION

Lord,
may we who receive this sacrament
be inspired by the example of St. N.
May we learn to proclaim what he believed
and put his teaching into action.
We ask this in the name of Jesus the Lord.
℟. **Amen.**   ➤ No. 32, p. 650

4. FOR BISHOPS

ENTRANCE ANT.   1 Sm 2, 35
I will raise up for myself a faithful priest; he will do what is in my heart and in my mind, says the Lord.
➔ No. 2, p. 614

OPENING PRAYER
Lord God,
you counted St. N. among your holy pastors,
renowned for faith and love which conquered evil
    in this world.
By the help of his prayers
keep us strong in faith and love
and let us come to share his glory.
Grant this through our Lord Jesus Christ, your Son,
who lives and reigns with you and the Holy Spirit,
one God, for ever and ever. ℟. **Amen.** ▼

READINGS AND INTERVENIENT CHANTS
See pp. 1154-1176.

PRAYER OVER THE GIFTS
Lord,
accept the gifts your people offer you
on this feast of St. N.
May these gifts bring us
your help for which we long.
We ask this through Christ our Lord.
℟. **Amen.**   ➔ No. 21, p. 626

COMMUNION ANT.   Jn 10, 10
I came that men may have life, and have it to the full, says the Lord.

PRAYER AFTER COMMUNION
Lord our God,
you give us the holy body and blood
of your Son.

May the salvation we celebrate
be our undying hope.
Grant this through Christ our Lord.
℞. **Amen.**   ➔ No. 32, p. 650

_____

5. FOR PASTORS

ENTRANCE ANT.   Lk 4, 18
**The Spirit of God is upon me; he has anointed me.
He sent me to bring good news to the poor, and to
heal the broken-hearted.**   ➔ No. 2, p. 614

OPENING PRAYER
God our Father,
in St. (bishop) N. you gave
a light to your faithful people.
You made him a pastor of the Church
to feed your sheep with his word
and to teach them by his example.
Help us by his prayers to keep the faith he taught
and follow the way of life he showed us.
Grant this through our Lord Jesus Christ, your Son,
who lives and reigns with you and the Holy Spirit,
one God, for ever and ever. ℞. **Amen.** ▼

READINGS AND INTERVENIENT CHANTS
See pp. 1154-1176.

PRAYER OVER THE GIFTS
Father of mercy,
we have these gifts to offer in honor of your saints
who bore witness to your mighty power.
May the power of the eucharist
bring us your salvation.
Grant this through Christ our Lord.
℞. **Amen.**   ➔ No. 21, p. 626

COMMUNION ANT.   Mt 28, 20
**I, the Lord, am with you always, until the end of the
world. ▼**

PRAYER AFTER COMMUNION

Lord,
may the mysteries we receive
prepare us for the eternal joys
St. N. won by his faithful ministry.
We ask this in the name of Jesus the Lord.
℟. **Amen.** ℣

OR

All-powerful God,
by our love and worship
may we who share this holy meal
always follow the example of St. N.
Grant this in the name of Jesus the Lord. ℟. **Amen.**

➤ No. 32, p. 650

6.   FOR PASTORS

ENTRANCE ANT.   Jer 3, 15

**I will give you shepherds after my own heart, and
they shall feed you on knowledge and sound teaching.**

OR   Dan 3, 84. 87

**Priests of God, bless the Lord; praise God, all you
that are holy and humble of heart.**

➤ No. 2, p. 614

OPENING PRAYER

Lord God,
you gave your Saints (bishops) N. and N.
the spirit of truth and love
to shepherd your people.
May we who honor them on this feast
learn from their example
and be helped by their prayers.
We ask this through our Lord Jesus Christ, your Son,

who lives and reigns with you and the Holy Spirit,
one God, for ever and ever. ℟. **Amen.** ↓

READINGS AND INTERVENIENT CHANTS
See pp. 1154-1176.

PRAYER OVER THE GIFTS
Lord,
accept these gifts from your people.
May the eucharist we offer to your glory
in honor of Saints N. and N.
help us on our way to salvation.
Grant this in the name of Jesus the Lord.
℟. **Amen.** ➜ No. 21, p. 626

COMMUNION ANT. Mt 20, 28
**The Son of Man did not come to be served, but to
serve, and to give his life as a ransom for many.** ↓

PRAYER AFTER COMMUNION
Lord,
we receive the bread of heaven
as we honor the memory of your Saints N. and N.
May the eucharist we now celebrate
lead us to eternal joys.
Grant this in the name of Jesus the Lord.
℟. **Amen.** ➜ No. 32, p. 650

---

7. FOR PASTORS

ENTRANCE ANT. Ps 131, 9
**Lord, may your priests be clothed in justice, and
your holy ones leap for joy.** ➜ No. 2, p. 614

OPENING PRAYER
All-powerful God,
hear the prayers of Saints N. and N.
Increase your gifts within us
and give us peace in our days.

We ask this through our Lord Jesus Christ, your Son,
who lives and reigns with you and the Holy Spirit,
one God, for ever and ever. ℟. **Amen.** ↓

READINGS AND INTERVENIENT CHANTS
See pp. 1154-1176.

PRAYER OVER THE GIFTS
Lord,
accept the gifts we bring to your altar
in memory of your Saints N. and N.
As you led them to glory through these mysteries,
grant us also your pardon and love.
We ask this in the name of Jesus the Lord.
℟. **Amen.**   → No. 21, p. 626

COMMUNION ANT.   Mt 24, 46-47
**Blessed is the servant whom the Lord finds watching
when he comes; truly I tell you, he will set him over
all his possessions.** ↓

OR   Lk 12, 42
**The Lord has put his faithful servant in charge of his
household, to give them their share of bread at the
proper time.** ↓

PRAYER AFTER COMMUNION
All-powerful God,
by the eucharist we share at your holy table
on this feast of Saints N. and N.
increase our strength of character and love for you.
May we guard from every danger the faith you have
    given us
and walk always in the way that leads to salvation.
Grant this in the name of Jesus the Lord.
℟. **Amen.**   → No. 32, p. 650

8. FOR FOUNDERS OF CHURCHES

ENTRANCE ANT.   Is 59, 21; 56, 7

My words that I have put in your mouth, says the Lord, will never be absent from your lips, and your gifts will be accepted on my altar. → No. 2, p. 614

OPENING PRAYER

God of mercy,
you gave our fathers the light of faith
through the preaching of St. N.
May we who glory in the Christian name
show in our lives the faith we profess.
We ask this through our Lord Jesus Christ, your Son,
who lives and reigns with you and the Holy Spirit,
one God, for ever and ever. ℟. **Amen.** ⍙

OR

Lord,
look upon the family whom your St. (bishop) N.
  brought to life
with the word of truth
and nourished with the sacrament of life.
By his ministry you gave us the faith;
by his prayers help us grow in love.
Grant this through our Lord Jesus Christ, your Son,
who lives and reigns with you and the Holy Spirit,
one God, for ever and ever. ℟. **Amen.** ⍙

READINGS AND INTERVENIENT CHANTS
See pp 1154-1176.

PRAYER OVER THE GIFTS

Lord,
may the gifts your people bring
in memory of St. N.
bring us your gifts from heaven.
We ask this in the name of Jesus the Lord.
℟. **Amen.**   → No. 21, p. 626

COMMUNION ANT.   Mk 10, 45

The Son of Man came to give his life as a ransom for many. ↓

PRAYER AFTER COMMUNION

Lord,
may this pledge of our eternal salvation
which we receive on this feast of St. N.
be our help now and always.
Grant this through Christ our Lord.
R̴. **Amen.**   → No. 32, p. 650

---

9. FOR FOUNDERS OF CHURCHES

ENTRANCE ANT.

The Lord chose these holy men for their unfeigned love, and gave them eternal glory. The Church has light by their teaching.   → No. 2, p. 614

OPENING PRAYER

Lord,
look with love on the church of N.
Through the apostolic zeal of Saints N. and N.
you gave us the beginnings of our faith:
through their prayers keep alive our Christian love.
We ask this through our Lord Jesus Christ, your Son,
who lives and reigns with you and the Holy Spirit,
one God, for ever and ever. R̴. **Amen.** ↓

OR

God,
you called our fathers to the light of the gospel
by the preaching of your bishop N.
By his prayers help us to grow in the love and
    knowledge
of your Son, our Lord Jesus Christ,
who lives and reigns with you and the Holy Spirit,
one God, for ever and ever. R̴. **Amen.** ↓

READINGS AND INTERVENIENT CHANTS
See pp. 1154-1176.

PRAYER OVER THE GIFTS
Lord,
accept the gifts your people bring
on this feast of Saints N. and N.
Give us purity of heart
and make us pleasing to you.
We ask this through Christ our Lord.
℟. **Amen.** → No. 21, p. 626

COMMUNION ANT. Jn 15, 15
No longer shall I call you servants, for a servant knows not what his master does. Now I shall call you friends, for I have revealed to you all that I have heard from my Father. ℣

PRAYER AFTER COMMUNION
Lord,
as we share in your gifts,
we celebrate this feast of Saints N. and N.
We honor the beginnings of our faith
and proclaim your glory in the saints.
May the salvation we receive from your altar
be our unending joy.
Grant this through Christ our Lord.
℟. **Amen.** → No. 32, p. 650

---

10.   FOR MISSIONARIES

ENTRANCE ANT.
These are holy men who became God's friends and glorious heralds of his truth. → No. 2, p. 614

OPENING PRAYER
Father,
through your St. (bishop) N.
you brought those who had no faith

out of darkness into the light of truth.
By the help of his prayers,
keep us strong in our faith
and firm in the hope of the gospel he preached.
Grant this through our Lord Jesus Christ, your Son,
who lives and reigns with you and the Holy Spirit,
one God, for ever and ever. ℞. **Amen.** ✣

OR

All-powerful and ever-living God,
you made this day holy
by welcoming St. N. into the the glory of your king-
    dom.
Keep us true to the faith he professed with untiring
    zeal,
and help us to bring it to perfection by acting in love.
We ask this through our Lord Jesus Christ, your Son,
who lives and reigns with you and the Holy Spirit,
one God, for ever and ever. ℞. **Amen.** ✣

READINGS AND INTERVENIENT CHANTS
See pp. 1154-1176.

PRAYER OVER THE GIFTS
All-powerful God,
look upon the gifts we bring on this feast
in honor of St. N.
May we who celebrate the mystery of the death of
    the Lord
imitate the love we celebrate.
We ask this through Christ our Lord.
℞. **Amen.**   ➔ No. 21, p. 626

COMMUNION ANT.   Ez 34, 15
**I will feed my sheep, says the Lord, and give them
repose.** ✣

PRAYER AFTER COMMUNION
Lord,
St. N. worked tirelessly for the faith,

spending his life in its service.
With the power this eucharist gives
make your people strong in the same true faith
and help us to proclaim it everywhere
by all we say and do.
℟. **Amen.**   ➔ No. 32, p. 650

11. FOR MISSIONARIES

ENTRANCE ANT.   Is 52, 7
**How beautiful on the mountains are the feet of the
man who brings tidings of peace, joy and salvation.**
                                        ➔ No. 2, p. 614

OPENING PRAYER
Father,
you made your Church grow
through the Christian zeal and apostolic work of
   St. N.
By the help of his prayers
give your Church continued growth in holiness and
   faith.
Grant this through our Lord Jesus Christ, your Son,
who lives and reigns with you and the Holy Spirit,
one God, for ever and ever. ℟. **Amen.** ▼

READINGS AND INTERVENIENT CHANTS
See pp. 1154-1176.

PRAYER OVER THE GIFTS
Lord,
be pleased with our prayers
and free us from all guilt.
In your love, wash away our sins
that we may celebrate the mysteries which set us
   free.
Grant this in the name of Jesus the Lord.
℟. **Amen.**   ➔ No. 21, p. 626

COMMUNION ANT.   Mk 16, 15; Mt 28, 20

Go out to all the world, and tell the good news: I am with you always, says the Lord. ℣

OR   Jn 15, 4-5

Live in me and let me live in you, says the Lord; he who lives in me, and I in him, will bear much fruit. ℣

PRAYER AFTER COMMUNION

Lord our God,
by these mysteries help our faith grow to maturity
in the faith the apostles preached and taught,
and the faith which St. N. watched over with such
   care.
We ask this through Christ our Lord.
℟. **Amen.**   ➜ No. 32, p. 650

---

12. FOR MISSIONARIES

ENTRANCE ANT.   Ps 95, 3-4

Proclaim his glory among the nations, his marvelous deeds to all the peoples; great is the Lord and worthy of all praise.   ➜ No. 2, p. 614

OPENING PRAYER

God of mercy,
you gave us St. N. to proclaim the riches of Christ.
By the help of his prayers
may we grow in knowledge of you,
be eager to do good,
and learn to walk before you
by living the truth of the gospel.
Grant this through our Lord Jesus Christ, your Son,
who lives and reigns with you and the Holy Spirit,
one God, for ever and ever. ℟. **Amen.** ℣

OR (for martyrs)

All-powerful God,
help us to imitate with steadfast love
the faith of Saints N. and N.
who won the crown of martyrdom
by giving their lives in the service of the gospel.
We ask this through our Lord Jesus Christ, your Son,
who lives and reigns with you and the Holy Spirit,
one God, for ever and ever. ℟. **Amen.** ✟

READINGS AND INTERVENIENT CHANTS
See pp. 1154-1176.

PRAYER OVER THE GIFTS
Lord,
we who honor the memory of St. N.
ask you to send your blessing on these gifts.
By receiving them may we be freed from all guilt
and share in the food from the heavenly table.
We ask this through Christ our Lord.
℟. **Amen.** → No. 21, p. 626

COMMUNION ANT.
See Lk 10, 1. 9

**The Lord sent disciples to proclaim to all the towns:
the kingdom of God is very near to you.** ✟

PRAYER AFTER COMMUNION
Lord,
let the holy gifts we receive fill us with life
so that we who rejoice in honoring the memory of
    St. N.
may also benefit from his example of apostolic zeal.
Grant this through Christ our Lord.
℟. **Amen.** → No. 32, p. 650

COMMON OF DOCTORS OF
THE CHURCH

The Common of Doctors of the Church comprises only
two Mass formularies. One of the reasons for this is
that the relatively few saints who fit into this category
also fall into another—for example, pastors or religious.
Thus a combination of the texts of these categories
offers ample opportunity for the desired variety.

1

ENTRANCE ANT.   Sir 15, 5

**The Lord opened his mouth in the assembly, and
filled him with the spirit of wisdom and understanding, and clothed him in a robe of glory.**

OR   Ps 37, 30-31

**The mouth of the just man utters wisdom, and his
tongue speaks what is right; the law of his God is in
his heart.**   ➔ No. 2, p. 614

OPENING PRAYER

God our Father,
you made your St. (bishop) N. a teacher in your
   Church.
By the power of the Holy Spirit
establish his teaching in our hearts.
As you give him to us as a patron,
may we have the protection of his prayers.
Grant this through our Lord Jesus Christ, your Son,
who lives and reigns with you and the Holy Spirit,
one God, for ever and ever. ℟. **Amen.** ∀

READINGS AND INTERVENIENT CHANTS
See pp. 1177-1187.

PRAYER OVER THE GIFTS

Lord,
accept our sacrifice on this feast of St. N.,
and following his example
may we give you our praise
and offer you all we have.
Grant this in the name of Jesus the Lord.
℟. **Amen.**   ➔ No. 21, p. 626

COMMUNION ANT.   Lk 12, 42

The Lord has put his faithful servant in charge of his household, to give them their share of bread at the proper time. ℣

PRAYER AFTER COMMUNION

God our Father,
Christ the living bread renews us.
Let Christ our teacher instruct us
that on this feast of St. N.
we may learn your truth
and practice it in love.
We ask this through Christ our Lord.
℟. **Amen.**   ➤ No. 32, p. 650

2

ENTRANCE ANT.   Dn 12, 3

The learned will shine like the brilliance of the firmament, and those who train many in the ways of justice will sparkle like the stars for all eternity.

OR   See Sir 44, 15. 14

Let the peoples declare the wisdom of the saints and the Church proclaim their praises; their names shall live for ever.   ➤ No. 2, p. 614

OPENING PRAYER

Lord God,
you filled St. N. with heavenly wisdom.
By his help may we remain true to his teaching
and put it into practice.
We ask this through our Lord Jesus Christ, your Son,
who lives and reigns with you and the Holy Spirit,
one God, for ever and ever. ℟. **Amen.** ℣

READINGS AND INTERVENIENT CHANTS
See pp. 1177-1187.

PRAYER OVER THE GIFTS

Lord,
by this celebration,
may your Spirit fill us with the same light of faith
that shines in the teaching of St. N.
We ask this through Christ our Lord.
℟. **Amen.** ➔ No. 21, p. 626

COMMUNION ANT. 1 Cor 1, 23-24
**We preach a Christ who was crucified; he is the
power and the wisdom of God.** ⋎

PRAYER AFTER COMMUNION

Lord,
you renew us with the food of heaven.
May St. N. remain our teacher and example
and keep us thankful for all we have received.
Grant this in the name of Jesus the Lord.
℟. **Amen.** ➔ No. 32, p. 650

COMMON OF VIRGINS

The Common of Virgins comprises four Mass formularies, three for one Virgin and the last for several Virgins. The saint who is a Virgin in many cases also fits into another category. One may thus use both categories in choosing the texts for each celebration.

ENTRANCE ANT.

Here is a wise and faithful virgin who went with lighted lamp to meet her Lord. ➔ No. 2, p. 614

OPENING PRAYER

God our Savior,
as we celebrate with joy the memory of the virgin N.,
may we learn from her example of faithfulness and love.
We ask this through our Lord Jesus Christ, your Son,
who lives and reigns with you and the Holy Spirit,
one God, for ever and ever. ℟. **Amen.** ✟

READINGS AND INTERVENIENT CHANTS

See pp. 1188-1194.

PRAYER OVER THE GIFTS

Lord,
we see the wonder of your love
in the life of the virgin N.
and her witness to Christ.
Accept our gifts of praise
and make our offering pleasing to you.
Grant this through Christ our Lord.
℟. **Amen.** ➔ No. 21, p. 626

COMMUNION ANT. Mt 25, 5

The bridegroom is here; let us go out to meet Christ the Lord. ✟

PRAYER AFTER COMMUNION

Lord God,
may this eucharist renew our courage and strength.
May we remain close to you, like St. N.,

by accepting in our lives
a share in the suffering of Jesus Christ,
who lives and reigns with you for ever and ever.
℟. **Amen.**   ➜ No. 32, p. 650

2

ENTRANCE ANT.

**Let us rejoice and shout for joy, because the Lord
of all things has favored this holy and glorious virgin
with his love.**   ➜ No. 2, p. 614

OPENING PRAYER

Lord God,
you endowed the virgin N. with gifts from heaven.
By imitating her goodness here on earth
may we come to share her joy in eternal life.
We ask this through our Lord Jesus Christ, your Son,
who lives and reigns with you and the Holy Spirit,
one God, for ever and ever. ℟. **Amen.** ⍗
OR (for a virgin foundress)

Lord our God,
may the witness of your faithful bride the virgin N.
awaken the fire of divine love in our hearts.
May it inspire other young women to give their lives
to the service of Christ and his Church.
Grant this through our Lord Jesus Christ, your Son,
who lives and reigns with you and the Holy Spirit,
one God, for ever and ever. ℟. **Amen.** ⍗

READINGS AND INTERVENIENT CHANTS
See pp. 1188-1194.

PRAYER OVER THE GIFTS

Lord,
may the gifts we bring you
help us follow the example of St. N.
Cleanse us from our earthly way of life,
and teach us to live the new life of your kingdom.
We ask this through Christ our Lord.
℟. **Amen.**   ➜ No. 21, p. 626

COMMUNION ANT.   Mt 25, 4. 6
**The five sensible virgins took flasks of oil as well as
their lamps. At midnight a cry was heard: the bridegroom is here; let us go out to meet Christ the Lord.** ℣

PRAYER AFTER COMMUNION
Lord,
may our reception of the body and blood of your
    Son
keep us from harmful things.
Help us by the example of St. N.
to grow in your love on earth
that we may rejoice for ever in heaven.
We ask this in the name of Jesus the Lord.
℟. **Amen.**   ➙ No. 32, p. 650

──────────────

3

ENTRANCE ANT.
**Come, bride of Christ, and receive the crown, which
the Lord has prepared for you for ever.**
                              ➙ No. 2, p. 614

OPENING PRAYER
Lord,
you have told us that you live for ever
in the hearts of the chaste.
By the prayers of the virgin N.,
help us to live by your grace
and to become a temple of your Spirit.
Grant this through our Lord Jesus Christ, your Son,
who lives and reigns with you and the Holy Spirit,
one God, for ever and ever. ℟. **Amen.** ℣

OR
Lord,
hear the prayers of those who recall the devoted
    life of the virgin N.

Guide us on our way and help us to grow
in love and devotion as long as we live.
We ask this through our Lord Jesus Christ, your Son,
who lives and reigns with you and the Holy Spirit,
one God, for ever and ever. ℟. **Amen.** ⍒

READINGS AND INTERVENIENT CHANTS
See pp. 1188-1194.

PRAYER OVER THE GIFTS
Lord,
receive our worship in memory of N. the virgin.
By this perfect sacrifice
make us grow in unselfish love for you
and for our brothers.
We ask this through Christ our Lord.
℟. **Amen.**   ➔ No. 21, p. 626

COMMUNION ANT.   See Lk 10, 42
**The wise virgin chose the better part for herself,
and it shall not be taken away from her.** ⍒

PRAYER AFTER COMMUNION
God of mercy,
we rejoice that on this feast of St. N.
you give us the bread of heaven.
May it bring us pardon for our sins,
health of body,
your grace in this life,
and glory in heaven.
Grant this through Christ our Lord.
℟. **Amen.**   ➔ No. 32, p. 650

4

ENTRANCE ANT.   Ps 148, 12-14
**Let virgins praise the name of the Lord, for his name
alone is supreme; its majesty outshines both earth
and heaven.**   ➔ No. 2, p. 614

OPENING PRAYER

Lord,
increase in us your gifts of mercy and forgiveness.
May we who rejoice at this celebration
in honor of the virgins N. and N.
receive the joy of sharing eternal life with them.
We ask this through our Lord Jesus Christ, your Son,
who lives and reigns with you and the Holy Spirit,
one God, for ever and ever. R̶. **Amen.** ▼

READINGS AND INTERVENIENT CHANTS
See pp. 1188-1194.

PRAYER OVER THE GIFTS

Lord,
we bring you our gifts and prayers.
We praise your glory on this feast of the virgins
  N. and N.,
whose witness to Christ was pleasing to you.
Be pleased also with the eucharist we now offer.
Grant this through Christ our Lord.
R̶. **Amen.** ➜ No. 21, p. 626

COMMUNION ANT. Mt 25, 10
**The bridegroom has come, and the virgins who were
ready have gone in with him to the wedding.** ▼

OR Jn 14, 21. 23
**Whoever loves me will be loved by my Father.
We shall come to him and make our home with him.** ▼

PRAYER AFTER COMMUNION

Lord,
may the mysteries we receive
on this feast of the virgins N. and N.
keep us alert and ready to welcome your Son at his
  return,
that he may welcome us to the feast of eternal life.
Grant this through Christ our Lord.
R̶. **Amen.** ➜ No. 32, p. 650

COMMON OF HOLY MEN AND WOMEN

The Common of Holy Men and Women comprises twelve Mass formularies. The first six refer to the saints in general: the first to one (no. 1) and the others to several (nos. 2-6). The other six refer to some specific state and field of endeavor: religious (nos. 7-8), those who worked for the underprivileged (no. 9), teachers (no. 10), and those who were especially noteworthy for holiness (nos. 11-12).

The following Masses, if indicated for a particular rank of saints, are used for saints of that rank. If no indication is given, the Masses may be used for saints of any rank.

1

ENTRANCE ANT.   Ps 145, 10-11

May all your works praise you, Lord, and your saints bless you; they will tell of the glory of your kingdom and proclaim your power.   ➔ No. 2, p. 614

OPENING PRAYER

Ever-living God,
the signs of your love are manifest
in the honor you give your saints.
May their prayers and their example encourage us
to follow your Son more faithfully.
We ask this through our Lord Jesus Christ, your Son,
who lives and reigns with you and the Holy Spirit,
one God, for ever and ever. ℟. **Amen.** ℣

READINGS AND INTERVENIENT CHANTS

See pp. 1195-1233.

PRAYER OVER THE GIFTS

Lord, in your kindness hear our prayers
and the prayers which the saints offer on our behalf.
Watch over us that we may offer fitting service
    at your altar.
Grant this in the name of Jesus the Lord.
℟. **Amen.**   ➔ No. 21, p. 626

COMMUNION ANT.   Ps 68, 4

May the just rejoice as they feast in God's presence, and delight in gladness of heart. ℣

OR Lk 12, 37

Blessed are those servants whom the Lord finds watching when he comes; truly I tell you, he will seat them at his table and wait on them. ℣

PRAYER AFTER COMMUNION

Father, our comfort and peace,
we have gathered as your family
to praise your name and honor your saints.
Let the sacrament we have received
be the sign and pledge of our salvation.
We ask this through Christ our Lord.
℟. **Amen.** ➜ No. 32, p. 650

2

ENTRANCE ANT. Ps 64, 11

The just man will rejoice in the Lord and hope in him, and all the upright of heart will be praised.
➜ No. 2, p. 614

OPENING PRAYER

God our Father,
you alone are holy;
without you nothing is good.
Trusting in the prayers of St. N.
we ask you to help us
to become the holy people you call us to be.
Never let us be found undeserving
of the glory you have prepared for us.
We ask this through our Lord Jesus Christ, your Son,
who lives and reigns with you and the Holy Spirit,
one God, for ever and ever. ℟. **Amen.** ℣

READINGS AND INTERVENIENT CHANTS
See pp. 1195-1233.

PRAYER OVER THE GIFTS

All-powerful God,
may the gifts we present
bring honor to your saints,
and free us from sin in mind and body.
We ask this in the name of Jesus the Lord.
℞. **Amen.**   ➜ No. 21, p. 626

COMMUNION ANT.   Jn 12, 26

**He who serves me, follows me, says the Lord; and
where I am, my servant will also be.** ℣

PRAYER AFTER COMMUNION

Lord,
your sacramental gifts renew us
at this celebration of the birth of your saints to
    glory.
May the good things you give us
lead us to the joy of your kingdom.
We ask this through Christ our Lord.
℞. **Amen.**   ➜ No. 32, p. 650

3

ENTRANCE ANT.   Ps 21, 2-3

**Lord, your strength gives joy to the just; they greatly
delight in your saving help. You have granted them
their heart's desire.**   ➜ No. 2, p. 614

OPENING PRAYER

Father,
your saints guide us when in our weakness we tend
    to stray.
Help us who celebrate the birth of St. N. to glory
grow closer to you by following his (her) example.
We ask this through our Lord Jesus Christ, your Son,
who lives and reigns with you and the Holy Spirit,
one God, for ever and ever. ℞. **Amen.** ℣

READINGS AND INTERVENIENT CHANTS
See pp. 1195-1233.

PRAYER OVER THE GIFTS
Lord,
let the sacrifice we offer
in memory of St. N.
bring to your people the gifts of unity and peace.
Grant this in the name of Jesus the Lord.
℟. **Amen.**   ➤ No. 21, p. 626

COMMUNION ANT.   Mt 16, 24
If anyone wishes to come after me, he must renounce himself, take up his cross, and follow me, says the Lord. ℣

PRAYER AFTER COMMUNION
Lord,
may the sacraments we receive
on this feast in honor of N.
give us holiness of mind and body
and bring us into your divine life.
We ask this through Christ our Lord.
℟. **Amen.**   ➤ No. 32, p. 650

4

ENTRANCE ANT.   Mal 2, 6
The teaching of truth was in his mouth, and no wrong was found on his lips; he walked with me in peace and justice, and turned many away from wickedness.   ➤ No. 2, p. 614

OPENING PRAYER
Merciful Father,
we fail because of our weakness.
Restore us to your love
through the example of your saints.

We ask this through our Lord Jesus Christ, your Son, who lives and reigns with you and the Holy Spirit, one God, for ever and ever. ℟. **Amen.** ℣

READINGS AND INTERVENIENT CHANTS
See pp. 1195-1233.

PRAYER OVER THE GIFTS
Lord,
may this sacrifice we share
on the feast of your St. N.
give you praise
and help us on our way to salvation.
Grant this in the name of Jesus the Lord.
℟. **Amen.**   ➤ No. 21, p. 626

COMMUNION ANT.   Mt 5, 8-9
Happy are the pure of heart for they shall see God. Happy the peacemakers; they shall be called the sons of God. Happy are they who suffer persecution for justice' sake; the kingdom of heaven is theirs. ℣

PRAYER AFTER COMMUNION
Lord,
our hunger is satisfied by your holy gift.
May we who have celebrated this eucharist
experience in our lives the salvation which it brings.
We ask this in the name of Jesus the Lord.
℟. **Amen.**   ➤ No. 32, p. 650

5

ENTRANCE ANT.   Ps 92, 13-14
The just man will flourish like the palm tree. Planted in the courts of God's house, he will grow great like the cedars of Lebanon.   ➤ No. 2, p. 614

OPENING PRAYER

Lord,
may the prayers of the saints
bring help to your people.
Give to us who celebrate the memory of your saints
a share in their eternal joy.
Grant this through our Lord Jesus Christ, your Son,
who lives and reigns with you and the Holy Spirit,
one God, for ever and ever. ℟. **Amen.** ⅴ

READINGS AND INTERVENIENT CHANTS

See pp. 1195-1233.

PRAYER OVER THE GIFTS

Lord,
give to us who offer these gifts at your altar
the same spirit of love that filled St. N.
By celebrating this sacred eucharist with pure minds
  and loving hearts
may we offer a sacrifice that pleases you,
and brings salvation to us.
Grant this through Christ our Lord.
℟. **Amen.** → No. 21, p. 626

COMMUNION ANT. Mt 11, 28

**Come to me, all you that labor and are burdened, and
I will give you rest, says the Lord.** ⅴ

PRAYER AFTER COMMUNION

Lord,
may the sacrament of holy communion which we
  receive
bring us health and strengthen us
in the light of your truth.
We ask this in the name of Jesus the Lord.
℟. **Amen.** → No. 32, p. 650

6

ENTRANCE ANT.   Jer 17, 7-8

Blessed is the man who puts his trust in the Lord; he will be like a tree planted by the waters, sinking its roots into the moist earth; he will have nothing to fear in time of drought.   ➤ No. 2, p. 614

OPENING PRAYER

All-powerful God,
help us who celebrate the memory of St. N.
to imitate his (her) way of life.
May the example of your saints
be our challenge to live holier lives.
Grant this through our Lord Jesus Christ, your Son,
who lives and reigns with you and the Holy Spirit,
one God, for ever and ever. ℞. **Amen.** ↓

READINGS AND INTERVENIENT CHANTS

See pp. 1195-1233.

PRAYER OVER THE GFTS

Lord,
we bring our gifts to your holy altar
on this feast of your saints.
In your mercy let this eucharist
give you glory
and bring us to the fullness of your love.
Grant this through Christ our Lord.
℞. **Amen.**   ➤ No. 21, p. 626

COMMUNION ANT.   Jn 15, 9

As the Father has loved me, so have I loved you; remain in my love. ↓

PRAYER AFTER COMMUNION

Lord our God,
may the divine mysteries we celebrate
in memory of your saint

fill us with eternal peace and salvation.
We ask this in the name of Jesus the Lord.
℞. **Amen.**   ➙ No. 32, p. 650

_____

7. FOR RELIGIOUS

ENTRANCE ANT.   Ps 16, 5-6
**The Lord is my inheritance and my cup; he alone
will give me my reward. The measuring line has
marked a lovely place for me; my inheritance is my
great delight.**   ➙ No. 2, p. 614

OPENING PRAYER
Lord God,
you kept St. N. faithful to Christ's pattern of poverty
   and humility.
May his (her) prayers help us to live in fidelity to
   our calling
and bring us to the perfection you have shown us
   in your Son,
who lives and reigns with you and the Holy Spirit,
one God, for ever and ever. ℞. **Amen.** ✠

OR (for an abbot)
Lord,
in your abbot N.
you give an example of the gospel lived to perfection.
Help us to follow him
by keeping before us the things of heaven
amid all the changes of this world.
Grant this through our Lord Jesus Christ, your Son,
who lives and reigns with you and the Holy Spirit,
one God, for ever and ever. ℞. **Amen.** ✠

READINGS AND INTERVENIENT CHANTS
See pp. 1195-1233.

PRAYER OVER THE GFTS

God of all mercy,
you transformed St. N.
and made him (her) a new creature in your image.
Renew us in the same way
by making our gifts of peace acceptable to you.
We ask this in the name of Jesus the Lord.
R̸. **Amen.**   ➤ No. 21, p. 626

COMMUNION ANT.   See Mt 19, 27-29

**I solemnly tell you: those who have left everything
and followed me will be repaid a hundredfold and
will gain eternal life.** ℣

PRAYER AFTER COMMUNION

All-powerful God,
may we who are strengthened by the power of this
    sacrament
learn from the example of St. N.
to seek you above all things
and to live in this world as your new creation.
We ask this through Christ our Lord.
R̸. **Amen.**   ➤ No. 32, p. 650

---

8. FOR RELIGIOUS

ENTRANCE ANT.   See Ps 24, 5-6

**These are the saints who received blessings from
the Lord, a prize from God their Savior. They are
the people that long to see his face.** ➤ No. 2, p. 614

OPENING PRAYER

God our Father,
you called St. N. to seek your kingdom in this world
by striving to live in perfect charity.
With his (her) prayers to give us courage,
help us to move forward with joyful hearts in the
    way of love.

We ask this through our Lord Jesus Christ, your Son,
who lives and reigns with you and the Holy Spirit,
one God, for ever and ever. ℟. **Amen.** ✟

READINGS AND INTERVENIENT CHANTS
See pp. 1195-1233.

PRAYER OVER THE GFTS
Lord,
may the gifts we bring to your altar
in memory of St. N.
be acceptable to you.
Free us from the things that keep us from you
and teach us to seek you as our only good.
We ask this through Christ our Lord.
℟. **Amen.**   → No. 21, p. 626

COMMUNION ANT.   Ps 33, 9
**Taste and see the goodness of the Lord; blessed is
he who hopes in God.** ✟

PRAYER AFTER COMMUNION
Lord,
by the power of this sacrament and the example of
   St. N.
guide us always in your love.
May the good work you have begun in us
reach perfection in the day of Christ Jesus
who is Lord for ever and ever.
℟. **Amen.**   → No. 32, p. 650

---

9. FOR THOSE WHO WORK FOR THE UNDERPRIVILEGED

ENTRANCE ANT.   Mt 25, 34. 36. 40
**Come, you whom my Father has blessed, says the
Lord: I was ill and you comforted me. I tell you,
anything you did for one of my brothers, you did
for me.**   → No. 2, p. 614

OPENING PRAYER

Lord God,
you teach us that the commandments of heaven
are summarized in love of you and love of our
    neighbor.
By following the example of St. N.
in practicing works of charity
may we be counted among the blessed in your king-
    dom.
Grant this through our Lord Jesus Christ, your Son,
who lives and reigns with you and the Holy Spirit,
one God, for ever and ever. ℟. **Amen.** ℣

READINGS AND INTERVENIENT CHANTS
See pp. 1195-1233.

PRAYER OVER THE GIFTS

Lord,
accept the gifts of your people.
May we who celebrate the love of your Son
also follow the example of your saints
and grow in love for you and for one another.
We ask this through Christ our Lord.
℟. **Amen.**   → No. 21, p. 626

COMMUNION ANT.   Jn 15, 13

**No one has greater love, says the Lord, than the man
who lays down his life for his friends.** ℣

OR   Jn 13, 35

**By the love you have for one another, says the Lord,
everyone will know that you are my disciples.** ℣

PRAYER AFTER COMMUNION

Lord,
may we who are renewed by these mysteries
follow the example of St. N.
who worshiped you with love
and served your people with generosity.
We ask this through Christ our Lord. ℟. **Amen.**

OR

Lord,

we who receive the sacrament of salvation ask your
  mercy.

Help us to imitate the love of St. N.

and give to us a share in his (her) glory.

Grant this through Christ our Lord. ℟. **Amen.**

➔ No. 32, p. 650

---

10. FOR TEACHERS

ENTRANCE ANT. Mk 10, 14

**Let the children come to me, and do not stop them,
says the Lord; to such belongs the kingdom of God.**

OR Mt 5, 19

**The man that keeps these commandments and teach-
es them, he is the one who will be called great in
the kingdom of heaven, says the Lord.**

➔ No. 2, p. 614

OPENING PRAYER

Lord God,

you called St. N. to serve you in the Church

by teaching his (her) fellow man the way of salvation.

Inspire us by his (her) example:

help us to follow Christ our teacher,

and lead us to our brothers and sisters in heaven.

We ask this through our Lord Jesus Christ, your Son,

who lives and reigns with you and the Holy Spirit,

one God, for ever and ever. ℟. **Amen.** ℣

READINGS AND INTERVENIENT CHANTS

See pp. 1195-1233.

PRAYER OVER THE GIFTS

Lord,

accept the gifts your people bring

in memory of your saints.

May our sharing in this mystery
help us to live the example of love you give us.
Grant this in the name of Jesus the Lord.
℟. **Amen.**   ➜ No. 21, p. 626

COMMUNION ANT.   Mt 18, 3

**Unless you change, and become like little children,
says the Lord, you shall not enter the kingdom of
heaven.** ↓

OR   Jn 8, 12

**I am the light of the world, says the Lord; the man
who follows me will have the light of life.** ↓

PRAYER AFTER COMMUNION
All-powerful God,
may this holy meal help us
to follow the example of your saints
by showing in our lives
the light of truth and love for our brothers.
We ask this in the name of Jesus the Lord.
℟. **Amen.**   ➜ No. 32, p. 650

----

11. FOR HOLY WOMEN

ENTRANCE ANT.   See Prv 31, 30. 28

**Honor the woman who fears the Lord. Her sons will
bless her, and her husband praise her.**
                                          ➜ No. 2, p. 614

OPENING PRAYER
God our Father,
every year you give us joy on this feast of St. N.
As we honor her memory by this celebration,
may we follow the example of her holy life.
We ask this through our Lord Jesus Christ, your Son,
who lives and reigns with you and the Holy Spirit,
one God for ever and ever. ℟. **Amen.** ↓

OR (for several)

All-powerful God,

may the prayers of Saints N. and N. bring us help
  from heaven

as their lives have already given us

an example of holiness.

We ask this through our Lord Jesus Christ, your Son,

who lives and reigns with you and the Holy Spirit,

one God for ever and ever. ℟. **Amen.** ↓

READINGS AND INTERVENIENT CHANTS
See pp. 1195-1233.

PRAYER OVER THE GIFTS

Lord,

may the gifts we present in memory of St. N.

bring us your forgiveness and salvation.

We ask this in the name of Jesus the Lord.

℟. **Amen.** ➜ No. 21, p. 626

COMMUNION ANT. Mt 13, 45-46

**The kingdom of heaven is like a merchant in search
of fine pearls; on finding one rare pearl he sells
everything he has and buys it.** ↓

PRAYER AFTER COMMUNION

All-powerful God,

fill us with your light and love

by the sacrament we receive on the feast of St. N.

May we burn with love for your kingdom

and let our light shine before men.

We ask this through Christ our Lord.

℟. **Amen.** ➜ No. 32, p. 650

---

12. FOR HOLY WOMEN

ENTRANCE ANT. See Prv 14, 1-2

**Praise to the holy woman whose home is built on
faithful love and whose pathway leads to God.**

➜ No. 2, p. 614

OPENING PRAYER
Father,
rewarder of the humble,
you blessed St. N. with charity and patience.
May her prayers help us, and her example inspire us
to carry our cross and to love you always.
We ask this through our Lord Jesus Christ, your Son,
who lives and reigns with you and the Holy Spirit,
one God for ever and ever. ℟. **Amen.** ℣

OR
Lord,
pour upon us the spirit of wisdom and love
with which you filled your servant St. N.
By serving you as she did,
may we please you with our faith and our actions.
Grant this through our Lord Jesus Christ, your Son,
who lives and reigns with you and the Holy Spirit,
one God for ever and ever. ℟. **Amen.** ℣

READINGS AND INTERVENIENT CHANTS
See pp. 1195-1233.

PRAYER OVER THE GIFTS
Lord,
receive the gifts your people bring to you
in honor of your saints.
By the eucharist we celebrate
may we progress toward salvation.
Grant this in the name of Jesus the Lord.
℟. **Amen.**   → No. 21, p. 626

COMMUNION ANT.   Mt 12, 50
**Whoever does the will of my Father in heaven is my
brother and sister and mother, says the Lord.** ℣

PRAYER AFTER COMMUNION
Lord,
we receive your gifts

at this celebration in honor of St. N.
May they free us from sin
and strengthen us by your grace.
We ask this in the name of Jesus the Lord.
℞. **Amen.**   ➔ No. 32, p. 650

OPTIONAL ANTIPHONS FOR SOLEMNITIES AND FEASTS

1. **Let us rejoice in the Lord, and keep a festival in honor of the holy (martyr, pastor) N. Let us join with the angels in joyful praise to the Son of God.**

2. **Let us all rejoice in the Lord as we honor St. N., our protector. On this day this faithful friend of God entered heaven to reign with Christ for ever.**

3. **Let us rejoice in celebrating the victory of our patron saint. On earth he proclaimed Christ's love for us. Now Christ leads him to a place of honor before his Father in heaven.**

4. **Let us rejoice in celebrating the feast of the blessed martyr N. He fought for the law of God on earth; now Christ has granted him an everlasting crown of glory.**

5. **All his saints and all who fear the Lord, sing your praises to our God; for the Lord our almighty God is King of all creation. Let us rejoice and give him glory.**

6. **We celebrate the day when blessed N. received his reward; with all the saints he is seated at the heavenly banquet in glory.**

COMMON OF SAINTS

READINGS AND INTERVENIENT CHANTS

DEDICATION OF A CHURCH

READING I

OUTSIDE THE EASTER SEASON

1   Gn 28, 11-18

A reading from the book of Genesis

When Jacob came upon a certain shrine, as the sun had already set, he stopped there for the night. Taking one of the stones at the shrine, he put it under his head and lay down to sleep at that spot. Then he had a dream: a stairway rested on the ground, with its top reaching to the heavens; and God's messengers were going up and down on it. And there was the Lord standing beside him and saying:

"I, the Lord, am the God of your forefather Abraham and the God of Isaac; the land on which you are lying I will give to you and your descendants. These shall be as plentiful as the dust of the earth, and through them you shall spread out east and west, north and south. In you and your descendants all the nations of the earth shall find blessing. Know that I am with you; I will protect you wherever you go, and bring you back to this land. I will never leave you until I have done what I promised you."

When Jacob awoke from his sleep, he exclaimed, "Truly, the Lord is in this spot, although I did not know it!" In solemn wonder he cried out: "How awesome is this shrine! This is nothing else but an abode of God, and that is the gateway to heaven!" Early the next morning Jacob took the stone that he had put under his head, set it up as a memorial stone, and poured oil on top of it.

2

1 Kgs 8, 22-23. 27-30

A reading from the first book of Kings

Solomon stood before the altar of the Lord in the presence of the whole community of Israel, and stretching forth his hands toward heaven, he said, "Lord, God of Israel, there is no God like you in heaven above or on earth below; you keep your covenant of kindness with your servants who are faithful to you with their whole heart.

"Can it indeed be that God dwells among men on earth? If the heavens and the highest heavens cannot contain you, how much less this temple which I have built! Look kindly on the prayer and petition of your servant, O Lord, my God, and listen to the cry of supplication which I, your servant, utter before you this day. May your eyes watch night and day over this temple, the place where you have decreed you shall be honored; may you heed the prayer which I, your servant, offer in this place. Listen to the petitions of your servant and of your people Israel which they offer in this place. Listen from your heavenly dwelling and grant pardon."

3

2 Chr 5, 6-10. 13—6, 2

A reading from the second book of Chronicles

King Solomon and the entire community of Israel gathered about him before the ark were sacrificing sheep and oxen so numerous that they could not be counted or numbered. The priests brought the ark of the covenant of the Lord to its place beneath the wings of the cherubim in the sanctuary, the holy of holies of the temple. The cherubim had their wings spread out over the place of the ark, sheltering the ark and its poles from above. The poles were long enough so that their ends could be seen from that part of the holy place nearest the sanctuary; however, they could not be seen beyond. The ark has remained there to this day. There was nothing in it but the two tablets which Moses put there on Horeb, the tablets of the covenant which the Lord made with the Israelites at their departure from Egypt.

When the trumpeters and singers were heard as a single voice praising and giving thanks to the Lord, and when they raised the sound of the trumpets, cymbals and other musical instruments to "give thanks to the Lord, for he is good, for his mercy endures forever," the building of the Lord's temple was filled with a cloud. The priests could not continue to minister because of the cloud, since the Lord's glory filled the house of God.

Then Solomon said: "The Lord intends to dwell in the dark cloud. I have truly built you a princely house and dwelling, where you may abide forever."

4
                                 1 Mc 4, 52-59

[For the consecration of an altar]

A reading from the first book of Maccabees

Early in the morning on the twenty-fifth day of the ninth month, that is, the month of Chislev, in the year one hundred and forty-eight, they arose and offered sacrifice according to the law on the new altar of holocausts that they had made. On the anniversary of the day on which the Gentiles had defiled it, on that very day it was reconsecrated with songs, harps, flutes, and cymbals. All the people prostrated themselves and adored and praised Heaven, who had given them success.

For eight days they celebrated the dedication of the altar and joyfully offered holocausts and sacrifices of deliverance and praise. They ornamented the façade of the temple with gold crowns and shields; they repaired the gates and the priests' chambers and furnished them with doors. There was great joy among the people now that the disgrace of the Gentiles was removed. Then Judas and his brothers and the entire congregation of Israel decreed that the days of the dedication of the altar should be observed with joy and gladness on the anniversary every year for eight days from the twenty-fifth day of the month Chislev.

5
                                     Is 56, 1. 6-7

A reading from the book of the prophet Isaiah

Thus says the Lord:
Observe what is right, do what is just;
  for my salvation is about to come,
  my justice, about to be revealed.

And the foreigners who join themselves to the Lord,
   ministering to him,
Loving the name of the Lord,
   and becoming his servants—
All who keep the sabbath free from profanation
   and hold to my covenant,
Them I will bring to my holy mountain
   and make joyful in my house of prayer;
Their holocausts and sacrifices
   will be acceptable on my altar,
For my house shall be called
   a house of prayer for all peoples.

6

Ez 43, 1-2. 4-7

A reading from the book of the prophet Ezekiel

The angel led me to the gate which faces the east, and
there I saw the glory of the God of Israel coming from the
east. I heard a sound like the roaring of many waters, and
the earth shone with his glory. I fell prone as the glory of
the Lord entered the temple by way of the gate which
faces the east, but spirit lifted me up and brought me to
the inner court. And I saw that the temple was filled with
the glory of the Lord. Then I heard someone speaking to
me from the temple, while the man stood beside me. The
voice said to me: Son of man, this is where my throne shall
be, this is where I will set the soles of my feet; here I will
dwell among the Israelites forever.

READING I

IN THE EASTER SEASON

1

Acts 7, 44-50

A reading from the Acts of the Apostles

[Stephen spoke to the people, the elders and the scribes:]
"Our fathers in the desert had the meeting tent as God
prescribed it when he spoke to Moses, ordering him to
make it according to the pattern he had seen. The next
generation of our fathers inherited it. Under Joshua, they

brought it into the land during the conquest of those peoples whom God drove out to make room for our fathers. So it was until the time of David, who found favor with God and begged that he might 'find a dwelling place for' the house of 'Jacob.' It was Solomon who ultimately constructed the building for that house. Yet the Most High does not dwell in buildings made by human hands, for as the prophet says:

'The heavens are my throne,
    the earth is my footstool;
What kind of house can you build me?
    asks the Lord.
    What is my resting-place to be like?
Did not my hand make all these things?' "

---

2   Rv 8, 3-4

[For the consecration of an altar]

A reading from the book of Revelation

I, John saw another angel come in holding a censer of gold. He took his place at the altar of incense and was given large amounts of incense to deposit on the altar of gold in front of the throne, together with the prayers of all God's holy ones. From the angel's hand the smoke of the incense went up before God, and with it the prayers of God's people.

---

3   Rv 21, 1-5

A reading from the book of Revelation

I, John, saw new heavens and a new earth. The former heavens and the former earth had passed away, and the sea was no longer. I also saw a new Jerusalem, the holy city, coming down out of heaven from God, beautiful as a bride prepared to meet her husband. I heard a loud voice from the throne cry out: "This is God's dwelling among men. He shall dwell with them and they shall be his people, and he shall be their God who is always with them. He shall wipe every tear from their eyes, and there shall be no more death or mourning, crying out or pain, for the former world has passed away."

The One who sat on the throne said to me, "See, I make all things new!"

4

Rv 21, 9-14

A reading from the book of Revelation

The angel said to me, "Come, I will show you the woman who is the bride of the Lamb." He carried me away in spirit to the top of a very high mountain and showed me the holy city Jerusalem coming down out of heaven from God. It gleamed with the splendor of God. The city had the radiance of a precious jewel that sparkled like a diamond. Its wall, massive and high, had twelve gates at which twelve angels were stationed. Twelve names were written on the gates, the names of the twelve tribes of Israel. There were three gates facing east, three north, three south, and three west. The wall of the city had twelve courses of stones as its foundation, on which were written the names of the twelve apostles of the Lamb.

RESPONSORIAL PSALM

1

1 Chr 29, 10. 11. 11-12. 12

℟. (13) **We praise your glorious name, O mighty God.**
Blessed may you be, O Lord,
   God of Israel our father,
   from eternity to eternity.
℟. **We praise your glorious name, O mighty God.**
Yours, O Lord, are grandeur and power,
   majesty, splendor, and glory.
   For all in heaven and on earth is yours.
℟. **We praise your glorious name, O mighty God.**
Yours, O Lord, is the sovereignty;
   you are exalted as head over all.
   Riches and honor are from you.
℟. **We praise your glorious name, O mighty God.**
You have dominion over all.
   In your hand are power and might;
   it is yours to give grandeur and strength to all.
℟. **We praise your glorious name, O mighty God.**

---

2   Ps 84, 3. 4. 5-6. 8. 11

℟. (2) **How lovely is your dwelling-place,
    Lord, mighty God!**
My soul yearns and pines
    for the courts of the Lord.
My heart and my flesh
    cry out for the living God.
℟. **How lovely is your dwelling-place, Lord, mighty God!**
Even the sparrow finds a home,
    and the swallow a nest
    in which she puts her young—
Your altars, O Lord of hosts,
    my king and my God!
℟. **How lovely is your dwelling-place, Lord, mighty God!**
Happy they who dwell in your house!
    continually they praise you.
Happy the men whose strength you are!
    They go from strength to strength.
℟. **How lovely is your dwelling-place, Lord, mighty God!**
I had rather one day in your courts
    than a thousand elsewhere;
I had rather lie at the threshold of the house of my God
    than dwell in the tents of the wicked.
℟. **How lovely is your dwelling-place, Lord, mighty God!**
℟. Or: (Rv 21, 3) **Here God lives among his people.**

———————————

3   Ps 95, 1-2. 3-5. 6-7

℟. (2) **Let us come before the Lord and praise him.**
Come, let us sing joyfully to the Lord;
    let us acclaim the Rock of our salvation.
Let us greet him with thanksgiving;
    let us joyfully sing psalms to him.
℟. **Let us come before the Lord and praise him.**
For the Lord is a great God,
    and a great king above all gods;
In his hands are the depths of the earth,
    and the tops of the mountains are his.
His is the sea, for he has made it,
    and the dry land, which his hands have formed.
℟. **Let us come before the Lord and praise him.**

Come, let us bow down in worship;
  let us kneel before the Lord who made us.
For he is our God,
  and we are the people he shepherds, the flock he guides.
℟. **Let us come before the Lord and praise him.**

---

4   Ps 122, 1-2. 3-4. 4-5. 8-9

℟. (1) **I rejoiced when I heard them say:**
  let us go to the house of the Lord.
I rejoiced because they said to me,
  "We will go up to the house of the Lord."
And now we have set foot
  within your gates, O Jerusalem—
℟. **I rejoiced when I heard them say:**
  let us go to the house of the Lord.
Jerusalem, built as a city
  with compact unity.
To it the tribes go up,
  the tribes of the Lord.
℟. **I rejoiced when I heard them say:**
  let us go to the house of the Lord.
According to the decree for Israel,
  to give thanks to the name of the Lord.
In it are set up judgment seats,
  seats for the house of David.
℟. **I rejoiced when I heard them say:**
  let us go to the house of the Lord.
Because of my relatives and friends
  I will say, "Peace be within you!"
Because of the house of the Lord, our God,
  I will pray for your good.
℟. **I rejoiced when I heard them say:**
  let us go to the house of the Lord.
℟. Or: **Let us go rejoicing to the house of the Lord.**

READING II

1   1 Cor 3, 9-13. 16-17
A reading from the first letter of Paul to the Corinthians
You are God's building. Thanks to the favor God showed
me I laid a foundation as a wise master-builder might do,

and now someone else is building upon it. Everyone, however, must be careful how he builds. No one can lay a foundation other than the one that has been laid, namely Jesus Christ. If different ones build on this foundation with gold, silver, precious stones, wood, hay or straw, the work of each will be made clear. The Day will disclose it. That day will make its appearance with fire, and fire will test the quality of each man's work.

Are you not aware that you are the temple of God, and that the Spirit of God dwells in you? If anyone destroys God's temple, God will destroy him. For the temple of God is holy, and you are that temple.

---

2   Eph 2, 19-22

A reading from the letter of Paul to the Ephesians

You are strangers and aliens no longer. No, you are fellow citizens of the saints and members of the household of God. You form a building which rises on the foundation of the apostles and prophets, with Christ Jesus himself as the capstone. Through him the whole structure is fitted together and takes shape as a holy temple in the Lord; in him you are being built into this temple, to become a dwelling place for God in the Spirit.

---

3   Heb 12, 18-19. 22-24

A reading from the letter to the Hebrews

You have not drawn near to an untouchable mountain and a blazing fire, and gloomy darkness and storm and trumpet blast, and a voice speaking words such that those who heard begged that they be not addressed to them. No, you have drawn near to Mount Zion and the city of the living God, the heavenly Jerusalem, to myriads of angels in festal gathering, to the assembly of the first-born enrolled in heaven, to God the judge of all, to the spirits of just men made perfect, to Jesus, the mediator of a new covenant, and to the sprinkled blood which speaks more eloquently than that of Abel.

4　　　　　　　　　　　　　　　　　　　1 Pt 2, 4-9

A reading from the first letter of Peter

Come to the Lord, a living stone, rejected by men but approved, nonetheless, and precious in God's eyes. You too are living stones, built as an edifice of spirit, into a holy priesthood, offering spiritual sacrifices acceptable to God through Jesus Christ. For Scripture has it:

"See, I am laying a cornerstone in Zion,
　　an approved stone, and precious.
He who puts his faith in it shall not be shaken."

The stone is of value for you who have faith. For those without faith, it is rather

"A stone which the builders rejected,
　　that became a cornerstone."

It is likewise "an obstacle and a stumbling stone." Those who stumble and fall are the disbelievers in God's word; it belongs to their destiny to do so.

You, however, are "a chosen race, a royal priesthood, a consecrated nation, a people he claims for his own to proclaim the glorious works" of the One who called you from darkness into his marvelous light.

ALLELUIA VERSE AND

VERSE BEFORE THE GOSPEL

1　　　　　　　　　　　　　　　　　　　2 Chr 7, 16

I have chosen and sanctified this house, says the Lord,
that my name may remain in it for all time.

2　　　　　　　　　　　　　　　　　　　Is 66, 1

Heaven is my throne and earth is my footstool, says the
　　Lord;
what is the house that you would build for me?

3　　　　　　　　　　　　　　　　　　　Ez 37, 27

My dwelling-place shall be with them, says the Lord,
and I will be their God and they will be my people.

4   See Mt 7, 8

In my house, says the Lord, everyone who asks will
    receive;
whoever seeks shall find; and to him who knocks it shall
    be opened.

GOSPEL

1   Mt 5, 23-24

✠ A reading from the holy gospel according to Matthew

Jesus said to his disciples: "If you bring your gift to the
altar and there recall that your brother has anything
against you, leave your gift at the altar, go first to be reconciled with your brother, and then come and offer your
gift."

2   Lk 19, 1-10

✠ A reading from the holy gospel according to Luke

Entering Jericho, Jesus passed through the city. There
was a man there named Zacchaeus, the chief tax collector
and a wealthy man. He was trying to see what Jesus was
like, but being small of stature, was unable to do so because of the crowd. He first ran on in front, then climbed
a sycamore tree which was along Jesus' route, in order to
see him. When Jesus came to the spot he looked up and
said, "Zacchaeus, hurry down. I mean to stay at your
house today." He quickly descended, and welcomed him
with delight. When this was observed, everyone began
to murmur, "He has gone to a sinner's house as a guest."
Zacchaeus stood his ground and said to the Lord: "I
give half my belongings, Lord, to the poor. If I have
defrauded anyone in the least, I pay him back fourfold."
Jesus said to him: "Today salvation has come to this house,
for this is what it means to be a son of Abraham. The Son
of Man has come to search out and save what was lost."

3   Jn 2, 13-22

☩ A reading from the holy gospel according to John

As the Jewish Passover was near, Jesus went up to Jerusalem. In the temple precincts he came upon people engaged in selling oxen, sheep and doves, and others seated changing coins. He made a [kind of] whip of cords and drove them all out of the temple area, sheep and oxen alike, and knocked over the moneychangers' tables, spilling their coins. He told those who were selling doves: "Get them out of here! Stop turning my Father's house into a marketplace!" His disciples recalled the words of Scripture: "Zeal for your house consumes me."

At this the Jews responded, "What sign can you show us authorizing you to do these things?" "Destroy this temple," was Jesus' answer, "and in three days I will raise it up." They retorted, "This temple took forty-six years to build, and you are going to 'raise it up in three days'!" Actually he was talking about the temple of his body. Only after Jesus had been raised from the dead did his disciples recall that he had said this, and come to believe the Scripture and the word he had spoken.

---

4   Jn 4, 19-24

☩ A reading from the holy gospel according to John

The [Samaritan] woman said to Jesus: "Sir, I can see you are a prophet. Our ancestors worshiped on this mountain, but you people claim that Jerusalem is the place where men ought to worship God." Jesus told her:

"Believe me, woman,
an hour is coming
when you will worship the Father
neither on this mountain
nor in Jerusalem.
You people worship what you do not understand,
while we understand what we worship;
after all, salvation is from the Jews.
Yet an hour is coming, and is already here,
when authentic worshipers
will worship the Father in Spirit and truth.

Indeed, it is just such worshipers
the Father seeks.
God is Spirit,
and those who worship him
must worship in Spirit and truth."

COMMON OF THE

BLESSED VIRGIN MARY

READING I

OUTSIDE THE EASTER SEASON

1   Gn 3, 9-15. 20

A reading from the book of Genesis

[After Adam had eaten of the fruit of the tree,] the Lord
God then called to the man and asked him, "Where are
you?" He answered, "I heard you in the garden; but I was
afraid, because I was naked, so I hid myself." Then he
asked, "Who told you that you were naked? You have
eaten, then, from the tree of which I had forbidden you to
eat!" The man replied, "The woman whom you put here
with me—she gave me fruit from the tree, and so I ate it."
The Lord God then asked the woman, "Why did you do
such a thing?" The woman answered,

"The serpent tricked me into it, so I ate it."

Then the Lord God said to the serpent:

"Because you have done this, you shall be banned
    from all the animals
    and from all the wild creatures;
On your belly shall you crawl,
    and dirt shall you eat
    all the days of your life.
I will put enmity between you and the woman,
    and between your offspring and hers;
He will strike at your head,
    while you strike at his heel."

The man called his wife Eve, because she became the
mother of all the living.

2

A reading from the book of Genesis

The Lord said to Abram: "Go forth from the land of your kinsfolk and from your father's house to a land that I will show you.

"I will make of you a great nation,
 and I will bless you;
I will make your name great,
 so that you will be a blessing.

"I will bless those who bless you
 and curse those who curse you.
All the communities of the earth
 shall find blessing in you."

Abram went as the Lord directed him, and Lot went with him. Abram was seventy-five years old when he left Haran. Abram took his wife Sarai, his brother's son Lot, all the possessions that they had accumulated, and the persons they had acquired in Haran, and they set out for the land of Canaan. When they came to the land of Canaan, Abram passed through the land as far as the sacred place at Shechem, by the terebinth of Moreh. (The Canaanites were then in the land.)

The Lord appeared to Abram and said, "To your descendants I will give this land." So Abram built an altar there to the Lord who had appeared to him.

3

A reading from the second book of Samuel

When King David was settled in his palace, and the Lord had given him rest from his enemies on every side, he said to Nathan the prophet, "Here I am living in a house of cedar, while the ark of God dwells in a tent!" Nathan answered the king, "Go, do whatever you have in mind, for the Lord is with you." But that night the Lord spoke to Nathan and said: "Go, tell my servant David, 'Thus says the Lord: Should you build me a house to dwell in? It was I who took you from the pasture and from the care of the flock to be commander of my people Israel. I have been with you wherever you went, and I have destroyed all your enemies before you. And I will make you famous like the great ones of the earth. I will fix a place for my people Israel; I will plant them so that they may dwell in their place without further disturbance. Neither shall the wicked continue to afflict them as they did of old, since the time I first appointed judges over my people Israel. I will give you rest from all your enemies. The Lord also reveals to you that he will establish a house for you. Your house and your kingdom shall endure forever before me; your throne shall stand firm forever.'"

---

4   1 Chr 15, 3-4. 15-16; 16, 1-2

A reading from the first book of Chronicles

David assembled all Israel in Jerusalem to bring the ark of the Lord to the place which he had prepared for it. David also called together the sons of Aaron and the Levites. The Levites bore the ark of God on their shoulders with poles, as Moses had ordained according to the word of the Lord.

David commanded the chiefs of the Levites to appoint their brethren as chanters, to play on musical instruments, harps, lyres, and cymbals to make a loud sound of rejoicing.

They brought in the ark of God and set it within the tent which David had pitched for it. Then they offered up holocausts and peace offerings to God. When David had finished offering up the holocausts and peace offerings, he blessed the people in the name of the Lord.

---

5   Prv 8, 22-31

A reading from the book of Proverbs

[Thus speaks the Wisdom of God:]
"The Lord begot me, the firstborn of his ways,
   the forerunner of his prodigies of long ago;
From of old I was poured forth,
   at the first, before the earth.
When there were no depths I was brought forth,
   when there were no fountains or springs of water;
Before the mountains were settled into place,
   before the hills, I was brought forth;

While as yet the earth and the fields were not made,
    nor the first clods of the world.
"When he established the heavens I was there,
    when he marked out the vault over the face of the deep;
When he made firm the skies above,
    when he fixed fast the foundations of the earth;
When he set for the sea its limit,
    so that the waters should not transgress his command;
Then was I beside him as his craftsman,
    and I was his delight day by day,
Playing before him all the while,
    playing on the surface of his earth;
    [and I found delight in the sons of men.]"

---

6   Sir 24, 1. 3-4. 8-12. 19-21

A reading from the book of Sirach

Wisdom sings her own praises,
    before her own people she proclaims her glory.
"From the mouth of the Most High I came forth,
    and mistlike covered the earth.
In the highest heavens did I dwell,
    my throne on a pillar of cloud.
"Then the Creator of all gave me his command,
    and he who formed me chose the spot for my tent,
Saying, 'In Jacob make your dwelling,
    in Israel your inheritance.'
Before all ages, in the beginning, he created me,
    and through all ages I shall not cease to be.
In the holy tent I ministered before him,
    and in Zion I fixed my abode.
Thus in the chosen city he has given me rest,
    in Jerusalem is my domain.
I have struck root among the glorious people,
    in the portion of the Lord, his heritage.
"You will remember me as sweeter than honey,
    better to have than the honey comb.
He who eats of me will hunger still,
    he who drinks of me will thirst for more;
He who obeys me will not be put to shame,
    he who serves me will never fail."

---

7   Is 7, 10-14

A reading from the book of the prophet Isaiah

The Lord spoke to Ahaz: Ask for a sign from the Lord, your God; let it be deep as the nether world, or high as the sky! But Ahaz answered, "I will not ask! I will not tempt the Lord!" Then he said: Listen, O house of David! Is it not enough for you to weary men, must you also weary my God? Therefore the Lord himself will give you this sign: the virgin shall be with child, and bear a son, and shall name him Immanuel.

---

8   Is 9, 1-6

A reading from the book of the prophet Isaiah

The people who walked in darkness
  have seen a great light;
Upon those who dwelt in the land of gloom
  a light has shone.
You have brought them abundant joy
  and great rejoicing,
As they rejoice before you as at the harvest,
  as men make merry when dividing spoils.
For the yoke that burdened them,
  the pole on their shoulder,
And the rod of their taskmaster
  you have smashed, as on the day of Midian.
For every boot that tramped in battle,
  every cloak rolled in blood,
  will be burned as fuel for flames.
For a child is born to us, a son is given us;
  upon his shoulder dominion rests.
They name him Wonder-Counselor, God-Hero,
  Father-Forever, Prince of Peace.
His dominion is vast
  and forever peaceful,
From David's throne, and over his kingdom,
  which he confirms and sustains
By judgment and justice,
  both now and forever.
The zeal of the Lord of hosts will do this!

---

9 Is 61, 9-11

A reading from the book of the prophet Isaiah

The descendants of my people shall be renowned among
the nations,
and their offspring among the peoples;
All who see them shall acknowledge them
as a race the Lord has blessed.

I rejoice heartily in the Lord,
in my God is the joy of my soul;
For he has clothed me with a robe of salvation,
and wrapped me in a mantle of justice,
Like a bridegroom adorned with a diadem,
like a bride bedecked with her jewels.
As the earth brings forth its plants,
and a garden makes its growth spring up,
So will the Lord God make justice and praise
spring up before all the nations.

---

10 Mi 5, 1-4

A reading from the book of the prophet Micah

You, Bethlehem-Ephrathah,
too small to be among the clans of Judah,
From you shall come forth for me
one who is to be ruler in Israel;
Whose origin is from of old,
from ancient times.
(Therefore the Lord will give them up, until the time
when she who is to give birth has borne,
And the rest of his brethren shall return
to the children of Israel.)
He shall stand firm and shepherd his flock
by the strength of the Lord,
in the majestic name of the Lord, his God;
And they shall remain, for now his greatness
shall reach to the ends of the earth;
he shall be peace.

---

11   Zec 2, 14-17

A reading from the book of the prophet Zechariah

Sing and rejoice, O daughter Zion! See, I am coming to dwell among you, says the Lord. Many nations shall join themselves to the Lord on that day, and they shall be his people, and he will dwell among you, and you shall know that the Lord of hosts has sent me to you. The Lord will possess Judah as his portion in the holy land, and he will again choose Jerusalem. Silence, all mankind, in the presence of the Lord! for he stirs forth from his holy dwelling.

READING I

IN THE EASTER SEASON

1   Acts 1, 12-14

A reading from the Acts of the Apostles

[After Jesus had ascended to heaven,] the apostles returned to Jerusalem from the mount called Olivet near Jerusalem—a mere sabbath's journey away. Entering the city, they went to the upstairs room where they were staying: Peter and John and James and Andrew; Philip and Thomas, Bartholomew and Matthew; James son of Alpheus; Simon, the Zealot party member, and Judas son of James. Together they devoted themselves to constant prayer. There were some women in their company, and Mary the mother of Jesus, and his brothers.

2   Rv 11, 19; 12, 1-6. 10

A reading from the book of Revelation

God's temple in heaven opened and in the temple could be seen the ark of his covenant.

A great sign appeared in the sky, a woman clothed with the sun, with the moon under her feet, and on her head a crown of twelve stars. Because she was with child, she wailed aloud in pain as she labored to give birth. Then another sign appeared in the sky: it was a huge dragon, flaming red, with seven heads and ten horns; on his heads were seven diadems. His tail swept a third of the stars from the sky and hurled them down to the earth. Then the dragon stood before the woman about to give birth, ready to devour her child when it should be born. She gave birth to a son—a boy destined to shepherd all the nations with an iron rod. Her child was snatched up to God and to his throne. The woman herself fled into the desert, where a special place had been prepared for her by God.

Then I heard a loud voice in heaven say:

"Now have salvation and power come,
the reign of our God and the authority of his Anointed One."

---

3   Rv 21, 1-5

A reading from the book of Revelation

I, John, saw new heavens and a new earth. The former heavens and the former earth had passed away, and the sea was no longer. I also saw a new Jerusalem, the holy city, coming down out of heaven from God, beautiful as a bride prepared to meet her husband. I heard a loud voice from the throne cry out: "This is God's dwelling among men. He shall dwell with them and they shall be his people, and he shall be their God who is always with them. He shall wipe every tear from their eyes, and there shall be no more death or mourning, crying out or pain, for the former world has passed away."

The One who sat on the throne said to me, "See, I make all things new!"

RESPONSORIAL PSALM

1   1 Sm 2, 1. 4-5. 6-7. 8

℟. (1) **My heart rejoices in the Lord, my Savior.**
As Hannah worshiped the Lord, she said:
"My heart exults in the Lord,
my horn is exalted in my God.
I have swallowed up my enemies;
I rejoice in my victory.

℟. **My heart rejoices in the Lord, my Savior.**
The bows of the mighty are broken,
   while the tottering gird on strength.
The well-fed hire themselves out for bread,
   while the hungry fatten on spoil.
The barren wife bears seven sons,
   while the mother of many languishes.
℟. **My heart rejoices in the Lord, my Savior.**
The Lord puts to death and gives life;
   he casts down to the nether world;
   he raises up again.
The Lord makes poor and makes rich,
   he humbles, he also exalts.
℟. **My heart rejoices in the Lord, my Savior.**
He raises the needy from the dust;
   from the ash heap he lifts up the poor,
To seat them with nobles
   and make a glorious throne their heritage."
℟. **My heart rejoices in the Lord, my Savior.**

———————

2   Jdt 13, 18. 19. 20

℟. (9) **You are the highest honor of our race.**
Blessed are you, daughter, by the Most High God, above
all the women on earth; and blessed be the Lord God, the
creator of heaven and earth.
℟. **You are the highest honor of our race.**
Your deed of hope will never be forgotten by those who
tell of the might of God.
℟. **You are the highest honor of our race.**
May God make this redound to your everlasting honor,
rewarding you with blessings, because you risked your
life when your people were being oppressed, and you
averted our disaster, walking uprightly before our God.
And all the people answered, "Amen! Amen!"
℟. **You are the highest honor of our race.**

———————

3   Ps 45, 11-12. 14-15. 16-17

℟. (11) **Listen to me, daughter;**
   see and bend your ear.

Hear, O daughter, and see; turn your ear,
  forget your people and your father's house.
So shall the king desire your beauty;
  for he is your lord, and you must worship him.
R̷. **Listen to me, daughter;**
  see and bend your ear.
All glorious is the king's daughter as she enters;
  her raiment is threaded with spun gold.
In embroidered apparel she is borne in to the king;
  behind her the virgins of her train are brought to you.
R̷. **Listen to me, daughter;**
  see and bend your ear.
They are borne in with gladness and joy;
  they enter the palace of the king.
The place of your fathers your sons shall have;
  you shall make them princes through all the land.
R̷. **Listen to me, daughter;**
  see and bend your ear.

---

4   Ps 113, 1-2. 3-4. 5-6. 7-8

R̷. (2) **Blessed be the name of the Lord for ever.**
Praise, you servants of the Lord,
  praise the name of the Lord.
Blessed be the name of the Lord
  both now and forever.
R̷. **Blessed be the name of the Lord for ever.**
From the rising to the setting of the sun
  is the name of the Lord to be praised.
High above all nations is the Lord;
  above the heavens is his glory.
R̷. **Blessed be the name of the Lord for ever.**
Who is like the Lord, our God, who is enthroned on high
  and looks upon the heavens and the earth below?
R̷. **Blessed be the name of the Lord for ever.**
He raises up the lowly from the dust;
  from the dunghill he lifts up the poor
To seat them with princes,
  with the princes of his own people.
R̷. **Blessed be the name of the Lord for ever.**
R̷. Or: **Alleluia.**

---

5   Lk 1, 46-47. 48-49. 50-51. 52-53. 54-55

℟. (49) **The Almighty has done great things for me and holy**
   is his name.

Mary said:

"My being proclaims the greatness of the Lord,
   my spirit finds joy in God my savior.

℟. **The Almighty has done great things for me and holy**
   is his name.

For he has looked upon his servant in her lowliness;
   all ages to come shall call me blessed.

God who is mighty has done great things for me,
   holy is his name.

℟. **The Almighty has done great things for me and holy**
   is his name.

His mercy is from age to age
   on those who fear him.

He has shown might with his arm;
   he has confused the proud in their inmost thoughts.

℟. **The Almighty has done great things for me and holy**
   is his name.

He has deposed the mighty from their thrones
   and raised the lowly to high places.

The hungry he has given every good thing,
   while the rich he has sent empty away.

℟. **The Almighty has done great things for me and holy**
   is his name.

He has upheld Israel his servant,
   ever mindful of his mercy;

Even as he promised our fathers,
   promised Abraham and his descendants forever."

℟. **The Almighty has done great things for me and holy**
   is his name.

℟. Or: **O Blessed Virgin Mary, you carried the Son of the**
   eternal Father.

READING II

1

Rom 5, 12. 17-19

A reading from the letter of Paul to the Romans

Just as through one man sin entered the world and with sin death, so death came to all men inasmuch as all sinned. If death began its reign through one man because of his offense, much more shall those who receive the overflowing grace and gift of justice live and reign through the one man, Jesus Christ.

To sum up, then: just as a single offense brought condemnation to all men, a single righteous act brought all men acquittal and life. Just as through one man's disobedience all became sinners, so through one man's obedience all shall become just.

2

Rom 8, 28-30

A reading from the letter of Paul to the Romans

We know that God makes all things work together for the good of those who have been called according to his decree. Those whom he foreknew he predestined to share the image of his Son, that the Son might be the first-born of many brothers. Those he predestined he likewise called; those he called he also justified; and those he justified he in turn glorified.

3

Gal 4, 4-7

A reading from the letter of Paul to the Galatians

When the designated time had come, God sent forth his Son born of a woman, born under the law, to deliver from the law those who were subjected to it, so that we might receive our status as adopted sons. The proof that you are sons is the fact that God has sent forth into our hearts the spirit of his Son which cries out "Abba!" ("Father!") You are no longer a slave but a son! And the fact that you are a son makes you an heir, by God's design.

---

4   Eph 1, 3-6. 11-12

A reading from the letter of Paul to the Ephesians

Praised be the God and Father of our Lord Jesus Christ, who has bestowed on us in Christ every spiritual blessing in the heavens! God chose us in him before the world began, to be holy and blameless in his sight, to be full of love; he likewise predestined us through Christ Jesus to be his adopted sons—such was his will and pleasure—that all might praise the divine favor he has bestowed on us in his beloved.

In him we were chosen; for in the decree of God, who administers everything according to his will and counsel, we were predestined to praise his glory by being the first to hope in Christ.

ALLELUIA VERSE AND
VERSE BEFORE THE GOSPEL

1   Lk 1, 28

Hail, Mary, full of grace, the Lord is with you;
blessed are you among women.

2   Lk 1, 45

Blessed are you, O Virgin Mary, for your firm believing,
that the promises of the Lord would be fulfilled.

3   See Lk 2, 19

Blessed is the Virgin Mary who kept the word of God,
and pondered it in her heart.

4

Happy are you, holy Virgin Mary, deserving of all praise;
from you rose the sun of justice, Christ the Lord.

GOSPEL

1   Mt 1, 1-16. 18-23 or 1, 18-23

[If the "Short Form" is used, the indented text in brackets is omitted.]

✠ The beginning (or: A reading) of the holy gospel according to Matthew

[A family record of Jesus Christ, son of David, son of Abraham. Abraham was the father of Isaac, Isaac the father of Jacob, Jacob the father of Judah and his brothers.

Judah was the father of Perez and Zerah, whose mother was Tamar.

Perez was the father of Hezron,

Hezron the father of Ram.

Ram was the father of Amminadab,

Amminadab the father of Nahshon,

Nahshon the father of Salmon.

Salmon was the father of Boaz, whose mother was Rahab,

Boaz was the father of Obed, whose mother was Ruth.

Obed was the father of Jesse,

Jesse the father of King David.

David was the father of Solomon, whose mother had been the wife of Uriah.

Solomon was the father of Rehoboam,

Rehoboam the father of Abijah,

Abijah the father of Asa.

Asa was the father of Jehoshaphat,

Jehoshaphat the father of Joram,

Joram the father of Uzziah.

Uzziah was the father of Jotham,

Jotham the father of Ahaz,

Ahaz the father of Hezekiah.

Hezekiah was the father of Manasseh,

Manasseh the father of Amos,

Amos the father of Josiah.

Josiah became the father of Jechoniah and his broth-
ers at the time of the Babylonian exile.
After the Babylonian exile
Jechoniah was the father of Shealtiel,
Shealtiel the father of Zerubbabel.
Zerubbabel was the father of Abiud,
Abiud the father of Eliakim,
Eliakim the father of Azor.
Azor was the father of Zadok,
Zadok the father of Achim,
Achim the father of Eliud.
Eliud was the father of Eleazar,
Eleazar the father of Matthan,
Matthan the father of Jacob.
Jacob was the father of Joseph the husband of Mary.
It was of her that Jesus who is called the Messiah
was born.]

Now this is how the birth of Jesus Christ came about.
When his mother Mary was engaged to Joseph, but before
they lived together, she was found with child through the
power of the Holy Spirit. Joseph her husband, an upright
man unwilling to expose her to the law, decided to divorce
her quietly. Such was his intention when suddenly the
angel of the Lord appeared in a dream and said to him:
"Joseph, son of David, have no fear about taking Mary
as your wife. It is by the Holy Spirit that she has conceived
this child. She is to have a son and you are to name him
Jesus because he will save his people from their sins." All
this happened to fulfill what the Lord had said through
the prophet:

"The virgin shall be with child
and give birth to a son,
and they shall call him Emmanuel,"
a name which means "God is with us."

---

2   Mt 2, 13-15. 19-23

✠ A reading from the holy gospel according to Matthew

After the astrologers had departed from Bethlehem, the
angel of the Lord suddenly appeared in a dream to Joseph
with the command: "Get up, take the child and his mother,
and flee to Egypt. Stay there until I tell you otherwise.

Herod is searching for the child to destroy him." Joseph got up and took the child and his mother and left that night for Egypt. He stayed there until the death of Herod, to fulfill what the Lord had said through the prophet:

"Our of Egypt I have called my son."

But after Herod's death, the angel of the Lord appeared in a dream to Joseph in Egypt with the command: "Get up, take the child and his mother, and set out for the land of Israel. Those who had designs on the life of the child are dead." He got up, took the child and his mother, and returned to the land of Israel. He heard, however, that Archelaus had succeeded his father Herod as king of Judea, and he was afraid to go back there. Instead, because of a warning received in a dream, Joseph went to the region of Galilee. There he settled in a town called Nazareth. In this way what was said through the prophets was fulfilled:

"He shall be called a Nazorean."

---

3   Lk 1, 26-38

✠ A reading from the holy gospel according to Luke

The angel Gabriel was sent from God to a town of Galilee named Nazareth, to a virgin betrothed to a man named Joseph, of the house of David. The virgin's name was Mary. Upon arriving, the angel said to her: "Rejoice, O highly favored daughter! The Lord is with you. Blessed are you among women." She was deeply troubled by his words, and wondered what his greeting meant. The angel went on to say to her: "Do not fear, Mary. You have found favor with God. You shall conceive and bear a son and give him the name Jesus. Great will be his dignity and he will rule over the house of Jacob forever and his reign will be without end."

Mary said to the angel, "How can this be since I do not know man?" The angel answered her: "The Holy Spirit will come upon you and the power of the Most High will overshadow you; hence, the holy offspring to be born will be called Son of God. Know that Elizabeth your kinswoman has conceived a son in her old age; she who was thought to be sterile is now in her sixth month, for nothing is impossible with God."

Mary said: "I am the maidservant of the Lord. Let it be done to me as you say." With that the angel left her.

---

4 Lk 1, 39-47

✠ A reading from the holy gospel according to Luke

Mary set out, proceeding in haste into the hill country to a town of Judah, where she entered Zechariah's house and greeted Elizabeth. When Elizabeth heard Mary's greeting, the baby stirred in her womb. Elizabeth was filled with the Holy Spirit and cried out in a loud voice: "Blessed are you among women and blessed is the fruit of your womb. But who am I that the mother of my Lord should come to me? The moment your greeting sounded in my ears, the baby stirred in my womb for joy. Blessed is she who trusted that the Lord's words to her would be fulfilled."

Then Mary said:

"My being proclaims the greatness of the Lord,
my spirit finds joy in God my savior."

---

5 Lk 2, 1-14

✠ A reading from the holy gospel according to Luke

In those days Caesar Augustus published a decree ordering a census of the whole world. This first census took place while Quirinius was governor of Syria. Everyone went to register, each to his own town. And so Joseph went from the town of Nazareth in Galilee to Judea, to David's town of Bethlehem—because he was of the house and lineage of David—to register with Mary, his espoused wife, who was with child.

While they were there the days of her confinement were completed. She gave birth to her first-born son and wrapped him in swaddling clothes and laid him in a manger, because there was no room for them in the place where travelers lodged.

There were shepherds in the locality, living in the fields and keeping night watch by turns over their flocks. The angel of the Lord appeared to them as the glory of the Lord shone around them, and they were very much afraid. The angel said to them: "You have nothing to fear! I come to proclaim good news to you— tidings of great joy to be shared by the whole people. This day in David's city a savior has been born to you, the Messiah and Lord. Let this be a sign to you: in a manger you will find an infant wrapped in swaddling clothes." Suddenly, there was with the angel a multitude of the heavenly host, praising God and saying,

"Glory to God in high heaven,
peace on earth to those on whom his favor rests."

---

6 Lk 2, 15-19

✠ A reading from the holy gospel according to Luke

The shepherds said to one another: "Let us go over to Bethlehem and see this event which the Lord has made known to us." They went in haste and found Mary and Joseph, and the baby lying in the manger; once they saw, they understood what had been told them concerning this child. All who heard of it were astonished at the report given them by the shepherds.

Mary treasured all these things and reflected on them in her heart.

---

7 Lk 2, 27-35

✠ A reading from the holy gospel according to Luke

Simeon came to the temple, inspired by the Spirit; and when the parents brought in the child Jesus to perform for him the customary ritual of the law, he took him in his arms and blessed God in these words:

"Now, Master, you can dismiss your servant in peace;
you have fulfilled your word.
For my eyes have witnessed your saving deed
displayed for all the peoples to see:
A revealing light to the Gentiles,
the glory of your people Israel."

The child's father and mother were marveling at what was being said about him. Simeon blessed them and said to Mary his mother: "This child is destined to be the downfall and the rise of many in Israel, a sign that will be opposed—and you yourself shall be pierced with a sword—so that the thoughts of many hearts may be laid bare."

---

8   Lk 2, 41-52

✠ A reading from the holy gospel according to Luke

The parents of Jesus used to go every year to Jerusalem
for the feast of the Passover, and when he was twelve they
went up for the celebration as was their custom. As they
were returning at the end of the feast, the child Jesus
remained behind unknown to his parents. Thinking he was
in the party, they continued their journey for a day, looking for him among their relatives and acquaintances.

Not finding him, they returned to Jerusalem in search of
him. On the third day they came upon him in the temple sitting in the midst of the teachers, listening to them and
asking them questions. All who heard him were amazed
at his intelligence and his answers.

When his parents saw him they were astonished, and
his mother said to him: "Son, why have you done this to
us? You see that your father and I have been searching for
you in sorrow." He said to them: "Why did you search for
me? Did you not know I had to be in my Father's house?"
But they did not grasp what he said to them.

He went down with them then, and came to Nazareth,
and was obedient to them. His mother meanwhile kept all
these things in memory. Jesus, for his part, progressed
steadily in wisdom and age and grace before God and men.

---

9   Lk 11, 27-28

✠ A reading from the holy gospel according to Luke

While Jesus was speaking to the crowd a woman called
out, "Blest is the womb that bore you and the breasts that
nursed you!" "Rather," he replied, "blest are they who hear
the word of God and keep it."

---

10   Jn 2, 1-11

✠ A reading from the holy gospel according to John

There was a wedding at Cana in Galilee, and the mother of
Jesus was there. Jesus and his disciples had likewise been
invited to the celebration. At a certain point the wine ran
out, and Jesus' mother told him, "They have no more wine."

Jesus replied, "Woman, how does this concern of yours involve me? My hour has not yet come." His mother instructed those waiting on table, "Do whatever he tells you." As prescribed for Jewish ceremonial washings, there were at hand six stone water jars, each one holding fifteen to twenty-five gallons. "Fill those jars with water," Jesus ordered, at which they filled them to the brim. "Now," he said, "draw some out and take it to the waiter in charge." They did as he instructed them. The waiter in charge tasted the water made wine, without knowing where it had come from; only the waiters knew, since they had drawn the water. Then the waiter in charge called the groom over and remarked to him: "People usually serve the choice wine first; then when the guests have been drinking a while, a lesser vintage. What you have done is keep the choice wine until now." Jesus performed this first of his signs at Cana in Galilee. Thus did he reveal his glory, and his disciples believed in him.

11   Jn 19, 25-27

✠ A reading from the holy gospel according to John

Near the cross of Jesus there stood his mother, his mother's sister, Mary the wife of Clopas, and Mary Magdalene. Seeing his mother there with the disciple whom he loved, Jesus said to his mother, "Woman, there is your son." In turn he said to the disciple, "There is your mother." From that hour onward, the disciple took her into his care.

COMMON OF MARTYRS

READING I

OUTSIDE THE EASTER SEASON

1   2 Chr 24, 18-22

A reading from the second book of Chronicles

The princes of Judah forsook the temple of the Lord, the God of their fathers, and began to serve the sacred poles and the idols; and because of this crime of theirs, wrath came upon Judah and Jerusalem. Although prophets were sent to them to convert them to the Lord, the people would not listen to their warnings. Then the spirit of God possessed Zechariah, son of Jehoiada the priest. He took his stand above the people and said to them: "God says, 'Why are you transgressing the Lord's commands, so that you cannot prosper? Because you have abandoned the Lord, he has abandoned you.'" But they conspired against him, and at the king's order they stoned him to death in the court of the Lord's temple. Thus King Joash was unmindful of the devotion shown him by Jehoiada, Zechariah's father, and slew his son. And as he was dying, he said, "May the Lord see and avenge."

----

2   2 Mc 6, 18. 21. 24-31

A reading from the second book of Maccabees

Eleazar, one of the foremost scribes, a man of advanced age and noble appearance, was being forced to open his mouth to eat pork. Those in charge of that unlawful ritual meal took the man aside privately because of their long acquaintance with him and urged him to bring meat of his own providing such as he could legitimately eat, and to pretend to be eating some of the meat of the sacrifice prescribed by the king. He told them: "At our age it would be unbecoming to make such a pretense; many young men would think the ninety-year-old Eleazar had gone over to an alien religion. Should I thus dissimulate for the sake of a brief moment of life, they would be led astray by me, while I would bring shame and dishonor on my old age.

Even if, for the time being, I avoid the punishment of men, I shall never, whether alive or dead, escape the hands of the Almighty. Therefore, by manfully giving up my life now, I will prove myself worthy of my old age, and I will leave to the young a noble example of how to die willingly and generously for the revered and holy laws."

He spoke thus, and went immediately to the instrument of torture. Those who shortly before had been kindly disposed, now became hostile toward him because what he had said seemed to them utter madness. When he was about to die under the blows, he groaned and said: "The Lord in his holy knowledge knows full well that, although I could have escaped death, I am not only enduring terrible pain in my body from this scourging, but also suffering it with joy in my soul because of my devotion to him." This is how he died, leaving in his death a model of courage and an unforgettable example of virtue not only for the young but for the whole nation.

----

3   2 Mc 7, 1-2. 9-14

A reading from the second book of Maccabees

It happened that seven brothers with their mother were arrested and tortured with whips and scourges by the king, to force them to eat pork in violation of God's law. One of the brothers, speaking for the others, said: "What do you expect to achieve by questioning us? We are ready to die rather than transgress the laws of our ancestors."

[The second brother] at the point of death said: "You accursed fiend, you are depriving us of this present life, but the King of the world will raise us up to live again forever. It is for his laws that we are dying."

After him the third suffered their cruel sport. He put out his tongue at once when told to do so, and bravely held out his hands, as he spoke these noble words: "It was from Heaven that I received these; for the sake of his laws I disdain them; from him I hope to receive them again." Even the king and his attendants marveled at the young man's courage, because he regarded his sufferings as nothing.

After he had died, they tortured and maltreated the fourth brother in the same way. When he was near death, he said, "It is my choice to die at the hands of men with

the God-given hope of being restored to life by him; but
for you, there will be no resurrection to life."

4　　　　　　　　　　　　　　　　2 Mc 7, 1. 20-23. 27-29

A reading from the second book of Maccabees

It happened that seven brothers with their mother were
arrested and tortured with whips and scourges by the king,
to force them to eat pork in violation of God's law.

Most admirable and worthy of everlasting remembrance
was the mother, who saw her seven sons perish in a single
day, yet bore it courageously because of her hope in the
Lord. Filled with a noble spirit that stirred her womanly
heart with manly courage, she exhorted each of them in
the language of their forefathers with these words: "I do
not know how you came into existence in my womb; it
was not I who gave you the breath of life, nor was it I who
set in order the elements of which each of you is composed. Therefore, since it is the Creator of the universe
who shapes each man's beginning, as he brings about the
origin of everything, he, in his mercy, will give you back
both breath and life, because you now disregard yourselves for the sake of his law.

"Son, have pity on me, who carried you in my womb for
nine months, nursed you for three years, brought you up,
educated and supported you to your present age. I beg
you, child, to look at the heavens and the earth and see all
that is in them; then you will know that God did not make
them out of existing things; and in the same way the human race came into existence. Do not be afraid of this
executioner, but be worthy of your brothers and accept
death, so that in the time of mercy I may receive you again
with them."

5　　　　　　　　　　　　　　　　　　　Wis 3, 1-9

A reading from the book of Wisdom

The souls of the just are in the hand of God,
　　and no torment shall touch them.
They seemed, in the view of the foolish, to be dead:
　　and their passing away was thought an affliction
　　and their going forth from us, utter destruction.

But they are in peace.
For if before men, indeed, they be punished,
    yet is their hope full of immortality;
Chastised a little, they shall be greatly blessed,
    because God tried them
    and found them worthy of himself.
As gold in the furnace, he proved them,
    and as sacrificial offerings he took them to himself.
In the time of their visitation they shall shine,
    and shall dart about as sparks through stubble;
They shall judge nations and rule over people,
    and the Lord shall be their King forever.
Those who trust in him shall understand truth,
    and the faithful shall abide with him in love:
Because grace and mercy are with his holy ones,
    and his care is with his elect.

---

6   Sir 51, 1-8

A reading from the book of Sirach

I give you thanks, O God of my father;
    I praise you, O God my savior!
I will make known your name, refuge of my life;
    you have been my helper against my adversaries.
You have saved me from death,
    and kept back my body from the pit.
From the clutches of the nether world you have snatched
        my feet;
    you have delivered me, in your great mercy
From the scourge of a slanderous tongue,
    and from lips that went over to falsehood;
From the snare of those who watched for my downfall,
    and from the power of those who sought my life;
From many a danger you have saved me,
    from flames that hemmed me in on every side;
From the midst of unremitting fire,
    from the deep belly of the nether world;
From deceiving lips and painters of lies,
    from the arrows of dishonest tongues.
I was at the point of death,
    my soul was nearing the depths of the nether world;
I turned every way, but there was no one to help me,
    I looked for one to sustain me, but could find no one.

But then I remembered the mercies of the Lord,
  his kindness through ages past;
For he saves those who take refuge in him,
  and rescues them from every evil.

READING I

IN THE EASTER SEASON

1   Acts 7, 55-60

A reading from the Acts of the Apostles

Stephen, filled with the Holy Spirit, looked to the sky
above and saw the glory of God, and Jesus standing at
God's right hand. "Look!" he exclaimed, "I see an opening
in the sky, and the Son of Man standing at God's right
hand." The onlookers were shouting aloud, holding their
hands over their ears as they did so. Then they rushed at
him as one man, dragged him out of the city, and began
to stone him. The witnesses meanwhile were piling their
cloaks at the feet of a young man named Saul. As Stephen
was being stoned he could be heard praying, "Lord Jesus,
receive my spirit." He fell to his knees and cried out in a
loud voice, "Lord, do not hold this sin against them." And
with that he died.

---

2   Rv 7, 9-17

A reading from the book of Revelation

I, John, saw before me a huge crowd which no one could
count from every nation and race, people and tongue.
They stood before the throne and the Lamb, dressed in
long white robes and holding palm branches in their hands.
They cried out in a loud voice, "Salvation is from our God,
who is seated on the throne, and from the Lamb!" All
the angels who were standing around the throne and the
elders and the four living creatures fell down before the
throne to worship God. They said: "Amen! Praise and
glory, wisdom, thanksgiving, and honor, power and might
to our God forever and ever. Amen!"

Then one of the elders asked me, "Who are these, all dressed in white? And where have they come from?" I said to him, "Sir, you should know better than I." He then told me, "These are the ones who have survived the great period of trial; they have washed their robes and made them white in the blood of the Lamb.

"It was this that brought them before God's throne:
    day and night they minister to him in his temple;
    he who sits on the throne will give them shelter.
Never again shall they know hunger or thirst,
    nor shall the sun or its heat beat down on them,
    for the Lamb on the throne will shepherd them.
He will lead them to springs of life-giving water,
    and God will wipe every tear from their eyes."

---

3   Rv 12, 10-12

A reading from the book of Revelation

I, John, heard a loud voice in heaven say:
"Now have salvation and power come,
    the reign of our God and the authority of his Anointed
        One.
For the accuser of our brothers is cast out,
    who night and day accused them before our God.
They defeated him by the blood of the Lamb
    and by the word of their testimony;
    love for life did not deter them from death.
So rejoice, you heavens,
    and you that dwell therein!"

---

4   Rv 21, 5-7

A reading from the book of Revelation

The One who sat on the throne said to me, "See, I make all things new!" Then he said, "Write these matters down, for the words are trustworthy and true!" He went on to say: "These words are already fulfilled! I am the Alpha and the Omega, the Beginning and the End. To anyone who thirsts I will give to drink without cost from the spring of life-giving water. He who wins the victory shall inherit these gifts; I will be his God and he shall be my son."

RESPONSORIAL PSALM

1   Ps 31, 3-4. 6. 7. 8. 17. 21

R̼. (6) **Into your hands, O Lord,**
    I entrust my spirit.
Be my rock of refuge,
    a stronghold to give me safety.
You are my rock and my fortress;
    for your name's sake you will lead and guide me.

R̼. **Into your hands, O Lord,**
    I entrust my spirit.
into your hands I commend my spirit;
    you will redeem me, O Lord, O faithful God.
My trust is in the Lord.
    I will rejoice and be glad of your kindness.

R̼. **Into your hands, O Lord,**
    I entrust my spirit.
Let your face shine upon your servant;
    save me in your kindness.
You hide them in the shelter of your presence
    from the plottings of men.

R̼. **Into your hands, O Lord,**
    I entrust my spirit.

---

2   Ps 34, 2-3. 4-5. 6-7. 8-9

R̼. (5) **The Lord set me free from all my fears.**
I will bless the Lord at all times;
    his praise shall be ever in my mouth.
Let my soul glory in the Lord;
    the lowly will hear me and be glad.

R̼. **The Lord set me free from all my fears.**
Glorify the Lord with me,
    let us together extol his name.
I sought the Lord, and he answered me
    and delivered me from all my fears.

R̼. **The Lord set me free from all my fears.**
Look to him that you may be radiant with joy,
    and your faces may not blush with shame.
When the afflicted man called out, the Lord heard,
    and from all his distress he saved him.

℞. **The Lord set me free from all my fears.**
The angel of the Lord encamps
  around those who fear him, and delivers them.
Taste and see how good the Lord is;
  happy the man who takes refuge in him.
℞. **The Lord set me free from all my fears.**

---

3   Ps 124, 2-3. 4-5. 7-8

℞. (3) **Our soul has escaped like a bird from the hunter's net.**

Had not the Lord been with us—
  when men rose up against us,
Then would they have swallowed us alive,
  when their fury was inflamed against us.
℞. **Our soul has escaped like a bird from the hunter's net.**
Then would the waters have overwhelmed us;
  the torrent would have swept over us;
Over us then would have swept
  the raging waters.
℞. **Our soul has escaped like a bird from the hunter's net.**
Broken was the snare,
  and we were freed.
Our help is in the name of the Lord,
  Who made heaven and earth.
℞. **Our soul has escaped like a bird from the hunter's net.**

---

4   Ps 126, 1-2. 2-3 4-5. 6.

℞. (5) **Those who sow in tears, shall reap with shouts of joy.**
When the Lord brought back the captives of Zion,
  we were like men dreaming.
Then our mouth was filled with laughter,
  and our tongue with rejoicing.
℞. **Those who sow in tears, shall reap with shouts of joy.**
Then they said among the nations,
  "The Lord has done great things for them."
The Lord has done great things for us;
  we are glad indeed.
℞. **Those who sow in tears, shall reap with shouts of joy.**

Restore our fortunes, O, Lord,
  like the torrents in the southern desert.
Those that sow in tears
  shall reap rejoicing.

℟. **Those who sow in tears, shall reap with shouts of joy.**

Although they go forth weeping,
  carrying the seed to be sown,
They shall come back rejoicing,
  carrying their sheaves.

℟. **Those who sow in tears, shall reap with shouts of joy.**

READING II

1   Rom 5, 1-5

A reading from the letter of Paul to the Romans

Now that we have been justified by faith, we are at peace
with God through our Lord Jesus Christ. Through him we
have gained access by faith to the grace in which we
now stand, and we boast of our hope for the glory of God.
But not only that—we even boast of our afflictions! We
know that affliction makes for endurance, and endurance
for tested virtue, and tested virtue for hope. And this hope
will not leave us disappointed, because the love of God
has been poured out in our hearts through the Holy Spirit
who has been given to us.

2   Rom 8, 31-39

A reading from the letter of Paul to the Romans

If God is for us, who can be against us? Is it possible that
he who did not spare his own Son but handed him over
for the sake of us all will not grant us all things besides?
Who shall bring a charge against God's chosen ones? God,
who justifies? Who shall condemn them? Christ Jesus, who
died or rather was raised up, who is at the right hand of
God and who intercedes for us?

Who will separate us from the love of Christ? Trial, or
distress, or persecution, or hunger, or nakedness, or danger, or the sword? As Scripture says; "For your sake we

are being slain all the day long; we are looked upon as sheep to be slaughtered." Yet in all this we are more than conquerors because of him who has loved us. For I am certain that neither death nor life, neither angels nor principalities, neither the present nor the future, nor powers, neither height nor depth nor any other creature, will be able to separate us from the love of God that comes to us in Christ Jesus, our Lord.

---

3   2 Cor 4, 7-15

A reading from the second letter of Paul to the Corinthians

We possess our treasure in earthen vessels to make it clear that its surpassing power comes from God and not from us. We are afflicted in every way possible, but we are not crushed; full of doubts, we never despair. We are persecuted but never abandoned; we are struck down but never destroyed. Continually we carry about in our bodies the dying of Jesus, so that in our bodies the life of Jesus may also be revealed. While we live we are constantly being delivered to death for Jesus' sake, so that the life of Jesus may be revealed in our mortal flesh. Death is at work in us, but life in you. We have that spirit of faith of which Scripture says, "Because I believed, I spoke out." We believed and so we speak, knowing that he who raised up the Lord Jesus will raise us up along with Jesus and place both us and you in his presence. Indeed, everything is ordered to your benefit, so that the grace bestowed in abundance may bring greater glory to God because they who give thanks are many.

---

4   2 Cor 6, 4-10

A reading from the second letter of Paul to the Corinthians

In all that we do we strive to present ourselves as ministers of God, acting with patient endurance amid trials, difficulties, distresses, beatings, imprisonments and riots; as men familiar with hard work, sleepless nights, and fastings; conducting themselves with innocence, knowledge, and patience, in the Holy Spirit, in sincere love; as men with the message of truth and the power of God; wielding the weapons of righteousness with right hand and left, whether honored or dishonored, spoken of well or ill. We are called imposters, yet we are truthful; nobodies who in fact are well known; dead, yet here we are, alive; punished, but not put to death; sorrowful, though we are always rejoicing; poor, yet we enrich many. We seem to have nothing, yet everything is ours!

———————

5 2 Tm 2, 8-13; 3, 10-12

A reading from the second letter of Paul to Timothy

Remember that the Lord Jesus Christ, a descendant of David, was raised from the dead. This is the gospel I preach; in preaching it I suffer as a criminal, even to the point of being thrown into chains—but there is no chaining the word of God! Therefore I bear with all of this for the sake of those whom God has chosen, in order that they may obtain the salvation to be found in Christ Jesus and with it eternal glory.

You can depend on this:
If we have died with him
we shall also live with him;
If we hold out to the end
we shall reign with him.
But if we deny him he will deny us. If we are unfaithful he will still remain faithful for he cannot deny himself.

You have followed closely my teaching and my conduct. You have observed my resolution, fidelity, patience, love, and endurance, through persecutions and sufferings in Antioch, Iconium, and Lystra. You know what persecutions I had to bear, and you know how the Lord saved me from them all. Anyone who wants to live a godly life in Christ Jesus can expect to be persecuted.

———————

6 Heb 10, 32-36

A reading from the letter to the Hebrews

Recall the days gone by when, after you had been enlightened, you endured a great contest of suffering. At times you were publicly exposed to insult and trial; at other times you associated yourselves with those who were being so dealt with. You even joined in the sufferings of those who were in prison and joyfully assented to the confiscation of your goods, knowing that you had better and more permanent possessions. Do not, then, surrender your confidence; it will have great reward. You need patience to do God's will and receive what he has promised.

7
Jas 1, 2-4. 12

A reading from the letter of James

My brothers, count it pure joy when you are involved in every sort of trial. Realize that when your faith is tested this makes for endurance. Let endurance come to its perfection so that you may be fully mature and lacking in nothing.

Happy the man who holds out to the end through trial! Once he has been proved, he will receive the crown of life the Lord has promised to those who love him.

8
1 Pt 3, 14-17

A reading from the first letter of Peter

Even if you should have to suffer for justice' sake, happy will you be. "Fear not and do not stand in awe of what this people fears. Venerate the Lord," that is, Christ, in your hearts. Should anyone ask you the reason for this hope of yours, be ever ready to reply, but speak gently and respectfully. Keep your conscience clear so that, whenever you are defamed, those who libel your way of life in Christ may be disappointed. If it should be God's will that you suffer, it is better to do so for good deeds than for evil ones.

9
1 Pt 4, 12-19

A reading from the first letter of Peter

Do not be surprised, beloved, that a trial by fire is occurring in your midst. It is a test for you, but it should not catch you off guard. Rejoice, instead, insofar as you share Christ's sufferings. When his glory is revealed, you will rejoice exultantly. Happy are you when you are insulted for the sake of Christ, for then God's Spirit in its glory has come to rest on you. See to it that none of you suffers for being a murderer, a thief, a malefactor, or a destroyer of another's rights. If anyone suffers for being a Christian, however, he ought not to be ashamed. He should rather glorify God in virtue of that name. The season of judgment has begun, and begun with God's own household. If it begins this way with us, what must be the end for those who refuse obedience to the gospel of God? And if "the just man is saved only with difficulty, what is to become of the godless and the sinner?" Accordingly, let those who suffer as God's will requires continue in good deeds and entrust their lives to a faithful Creator.

10 1 Jn 5, 1-5

A reading from the first letter of John

Everyone who believes that Jesus is the Christ
has been begotten by God.
Now, everyone who loves the father
loves the child he has begotten.
We can be sure that we love God's children
when we love God
and do what he has commanded.
The love of God consists in this:
that we keep his commandments —
and his commandments are not burdensome.
Everyone begotten of God conquers the world,
and the power that has conquered the world
is this faith of ours.
Who, then, is conqueror of the world?
The one who believes that Jesus is the Son of God.

ALLELUIA VERSE AND

VERSE BEFORE THE GOSPEL

1 Mt 5, 10

Happy are they who suffer persecution for justice' sake;
the kingdom of heaven is theirs.

2 2 Cor 1, 3-4

Blessed be the Father of mercies and the God of all comfort,
who consoles us in all our afflictions.

3   Jas 1, 12

Happy the man who stands firm when trials come;
he has proved himself, and will win the crown of life.

4   1 Pt 4, 14

If you are insulted for the name of Christ, blessed are you,
for the Spirit of God rests upon you.

5

We praise you, God; we acknowledge you as Lord;
the radiant army of martyrs acclaims you.

GOSPEL

1   Mt 10, 17-22

✠ A reading from the holy gospel according to Matthew

Jesus said to his apostles: "Be on your guard with respect
to others. They will hale you into court, they will flog you
in their synagogues. You will be brought to trial before
rulers and kings, to give witness before them and before
the Gentiles on my account. When they hand you over, do
not worry about what you will say or how you will say it.
When the hour comes, you will be given what you are to
say. You yourselves will not be the speakers; the Spirit of
your Father will be speaking in you.

"Brother will hand over brother to death, and the father
his child; children will turn against parents and have them
put to death. You will be hated by all on account of me.
But whoever holds out till the end will escape death."

---

2   Mt 10, 28-33

✠ A reading from the holy gospel according to Matthew

Jesus said to his disciples: "Do not fear those who deprive
the body of life but cannot destroy the soul. Rather, fear
him who can destroy both body and soul in Gehenna. Are
not two sparrows sold for next to nothing? Yet not a single
sparrow falls to the ground without your Father's consent.
As for you, every hair of your head has been counted; so
do not be afraid of anything. You are worth more than an

entire flock of sparrows. Whoever acknowledges me before men I will acknowledge before my Father in heaven. Whoever disowns me before men I will disown before my Father in heaven."

---

3 Mt 10, 34-39

✠ A reading from the holy gospel according to Matthew

Jesus said to his disciples: "Do not suppose that my mission on earth is to spread peace. My mission is to spread, not peace, but division. I have come to set a man at odds with his father, a daughter with her mother, a daughter-in-law with her mother-in-law: in short, to make a man's enemies those of his own household. Whoever loves father or mother, son or daughter more than me is not worthy of me. He who will not take up his cross and come after me is not worthy of me. He who seeks only himself brings himself to ruin, whereas he who brings himself to nought for me discovers who he is."

---

4 Lk 9, 23-26

✠ A reading from the holy gospel according to Luke

Jesus said to all: "Whoever wishes to be my follower must deny his very self, take up his cross each day, and follow in my steps. Whoever would save his life will lose it, and whoever loses his life for my sake will save it. What profit does he show who gains the whole world and destroys himself in the process? If a man is ashamed of me and my doctrine, the Son of Man will be ashamed of him when he comes in his glory and that of his Father and his holy angels."

---

5 Jn 12, 24-26

✠ A reading from the holy gospel according to John

Jesus said to his disciples:

"I solemnly assure you,
    unless the grain of wheat falls to the earth and dies,
    it remains just a grain of wheat.
But if it dies,
    it produces much fruit.

The man who loves his life
loses it,
while the man who hates his life in this world
preserves it to life eternal.
If anyone would serve me,
let him follow me;
where I am,
there will my servant be.
Anyone who serves me,
the Father will honor."

6

Jn 15, 18-21

✠ A reading from the holy gospel according to John

Jesus said to his disciples:

"If you find that the world hates you,
know it has hated me before you.
If you belonged to the world,
it would love you as its own;
the reason it hates you
is that you do not belong to the world.
But I chose you out of the world.
Remember what I told you:
no slave is greater than his master.
They will harry you
as they harried me.
They will respect your words
as much as they respected mine.
All this they will do to you because of my name,
for they know nothing of him who sent me."

7

Jn 17, 11-19

✠ A reading from the holy gospel according to John

Jesus looked up to heaven and prayed:

"O Father most holy,
protect them with your name which you have given
me,
[that they may be one, even as we are one.]
As long as I was with them,
I guarded them with your name which you gave me.
I kept careful watch,

and not one of them was lost,
none but him who was destined to be lost—
in fulfillment of Scripture.
Now, however, I come to you;
I say all this while I am still in the world
that they may share my joy completely.
I gave them your word,
and the world has hated them for it;
they do not belong to the world,
[any more than I belong to the world].
I do not ask you to take them out of the world,
but to guard them from the evil one.
They are not of the world,
any more than I am of the world.
Consecrate them by means of truth—
'Your word is truth,'
As you have sent me into the world,
so I have sent them into the world;
I consecrate myself for their sakes now,
that they may be consecrated in truth."

COMMON OF PASTORS

READING I

OUTSIDE THE EASTER SEASON

1   Ex 32, 7-14

A reading from the book of Exodus

The Lord said to Moses, "Go down at once to your people,
whom you brought out of the land of Egypt, for they have
become depraved. They have soon turned aside from the
way I pointed out to them, making for themselves a molten
calf and worshiping it, sacrificing to it and crying out,
'This is your God, O Israel, who brought you out of the
land of Egypt!' I see how stiff-necked this people is," continued the Lord to Moses. "Let me alone, then, that my
wrath may blaze up against them to consume them. Then
I will make of you a great nation."

But Moses implored the Lord, his God, saying, "Why, O Lord, should your wrath blaze up against your own people, whom you brought out of the land of Egypt with such great power and with so strong a hand? Why should the Egyptians say, 'With evil intent he brought them out, that he might kill them in the mountains and exterminate them from the face of the earth'? Let your blazing wrath die down; relent in punishing your people. Remember your servants Abraham, Isaac and Israel, and how you swore to them by your own self, saying, 'I will make your descendants as numerous as the stars in the sky; and all this land that I promised, I will give your descendants as their perpetual heritage.' " So the Lord relented in the punishment he had threatened to inflict on his people.

2

Dt 10, 8-9

A reading from the book of Deuteronomy

Moses said to the people: "At that time the Lord set apart the tribe of Levi to carry the ark of the covenant of the Lord, to be in attendance before the Lord and minister to him, and to give blessings in his name, as they have done to this day. For this reason, Levi has no share in the heritage with his brothers; the Lord himself is his heritage, as the Lord, your God, has told him."

3

1 Sm 16, 1. 6-13

A reading from the first book of Samuel

The Lord said to Samuel: "Fill your horn with oil, and be on your way. I am sending you to Jesse of Bethlehem, for I have chosen my king from among his sons." As Jesse and his sons came, he looked at Eliab and thought, "Surely the Lord's anointed is here before him." But the Lord said to Samuel: "Do not judge from his appearance or from his lofty stature, because I have rejected him. Not as man sees does God see, because man sees the appearance but the Lord looks into the heart." Then Jesse called Abinadab and presented him before Samuel, who said, "The Lord has not chosen him." Next Jesse presented Shammah, but Samuel said, "The Lord has not chosen this one either." In the same way Jesse presented seven sons before Samuel, but Samuel said to Jesse, "The Lord has not chosen any one of these." Then Samuel asked Jesse, "Are these all the sons you have?" Jesse replied, "There is still the youngest, who is tending the sheep." Samuel said to Jesse, "Send for him; we will not begin the sacrificial banquet until he arrives here." Jesse sent and had the young man brought to them. He was ruddy, a youth handsome to behold and making a splendid appearance. The Lord said, "There— anoint him, for this is he!" Then Samuel, with the horn of oil in hand, anointed him in the midst of his brothers; and from that day on, the spirit of the Lord rushed upon David.

4   Is 6, 1-8

A reading from the book of the prophet Isaiah

In the year King Uzziah died, I saw the Lord seated on a high and lofty throne, with the train of his garment filling the temple. Seraphim were stationed above; each of them had six wings: with two they veiled their faces, with two they veiled their feet, and with two they hovered aloft.

"Holy, holy, holy is the Lord of hosts!" they cried one to the other. "All the earth is filled with his glory!" At the sound of that cry, the frame of the door shook and the house was filled with smoke.

Then I said, "Woe is me, I am doomed! For I am a man of unclean lips, living among a people of unclean lips; yet my eyes have seen the King, the Lord of hosts!" Then one of the seraphim flew to me, holding an ember which he had taken with tongs from the altar.

He touched my mouth with it. "See," he said, "now that this has touched your lips, your wickedness is removed, your sin purged."

Then I heard the voice of the Lord saying, 'Whom shall I send? Who will go for us?" "Here I am," I said; "send me!"

5   Is 52, 7-10

[For missionaries]

A reading from the book of the prophet Isaiah

How beautiful upon the mountains
    are the feet of him who brings glad tidings,

Announcing peace, bearing good news,
  announcing salvation, and saying to Zion,
   "Your God is King!'"
Hark! Your watchmen raise a cry,
  together they shout for joy,
For they see directly, before their eyes,
  the Lord restoring Zion.
Break out together in song,
  O ruins of Jerusalem!
For the Lord comforts his people,
  he redeems Jerusalem.
The Lord has bared his holy arm
  in the sight of all the nations;
All the ends of the earth will behold
  the salvation of our God.

---

6   Is 61, 1-3

A reading from the book of the prophet Isaiah

The spirit of the Lord is upon me,
  because the Lord has anointed me;
He has sent me to bring glad tidings to the lowly,
  to heal the brokenhearted,
To proclaim liberty to the captives
  and release to the prisoners,
To announce a year of favor from the Lord
  and a day of vindication by our God,
  to comfort all who mourn;
To place on those who mourn in Zion
  a diadem instead of ashes,
To give them oil of gladness in place of mourning,
  a glorious mantle instead of a listless spirit.

---

7   Jer 1, 4-9

A reading from the book of the prophet Jeremiah

The word of the Lord came to me thus:
Before I formed you in the womb I knew you,
  before you were born I dedicated you,
  a prophet to the nations I appointed you.
  "Ah, Lord God!" I said,
"I know not how to speak; I am too young."

But the Lord answered me,
  Say not, "I am too young."
    To whomever I send you, you shall go;
      whatever I command you, you shall speak.
Have no fear before them,
  because I am with you to deliver you, says the Lord.
Then the Lord extended his hand and touched my mouth,
  saying,
See, I place my words in your mouth!

------

8   Ez 3, 17-21

A reading from the book of the prophet Ezekiel

The word of the Lord came to me: Son of man, I have appointed you a watchman for the house of Israel. When you hear a word from my mouth, you shall warn them for me.

If I say to the wicked man, You shall surely die; and you do not warn him or speak out to dissuade him from his wicked conduct so that he may live: that wicked man shall die for his sin, but I will hold you responsible for his death. If, on the other hand, you have warned the wicked man, yet he has not turned away from his evil nor from his wicked conduct, then he shall die for his sin, but you shall save your life.

If a virtuous man turns away from virtue and does wrong when I place a stumbling block before him, he shall die. He shall die for his sin, and his virtuous deeds shall not be remembered; but I will hold you responsible for his death if you did not warn him. When, on the other hand, you have warned a virtuous man not to sin, and he has in fact not sinned, he shall surely live because of the warning, and you shall save your own life.

------

9   Ez 34, 11-16

A reading from the book of the prophet Ezekiel

Thus says the Lord God: I myself will look after and tend my sheep. As a shepherd tends his flock when he finds himself among his scattered sheep, so will I tend my sheep. I will rescue them from every place where they were scattered when it was cloudy and dark. I will lead them out from among the peoples and gather them from the foreign lands; I will bring them back to their own country and pasture them upon the mountains of Israel [in the land's ravines and all its inhabited places]. In good pastures will I pasture them, and on the mountain heights of Israel shall be their grazing ground. There they shall lie down on good grazing ground, and in rich pastures shall they be pastured on the mountains of Israel. I myself will pasture my sheep; I myself will give them rest, says the Lord God. The lost I will seek out, the strayed I will bring back, the injured I will bind up, the sick I will heal [but the sleek and the strong I will destroy], shepherding them rightly.

READING I

IN THE EASTER SEASON

1   Acts 13, 46-49

[For missionaries]

A reading from the Acts of the Apostles

Paul and Barnabas said to the Jews: "The word of God has to be declared to you first of all; but since you reject it and thus convict yourselves as unworthy of everlasting life, we now turn to the Gentiles. For thus were we instructed by the Lord: 'I have made you a light to the nations, a means of salvation to the ends of the earth.'" The Gentiles were delighted when they heard this and responded to the word of the Lord with praise. All who were destined for life everlasting believed in it. Thus the word of the Lord was carried throughout that area.

---

2   Acts 20, 17-18. 28-32. 36

A reading from the Acts of the Apostles

Paul sent word from Miletus to Ephesus, summoning the elders of that church. When they came to him he delivered this address: "Keep watch over yourselves, and over the whole flock the Holy Spirit has given you to guard. Shepherd the church of God, which he has acquired at the price of his own blood. I know that when I am gone, savage wolves will come among you who will not spare the flock. From your own number, men will present themselves distorting the truth and leading astray any who follow them.

Be on guard, therefore. Do not forget that for three years, night and day, I never ceased warning you individually even to the point of tears. I commend you now to the Lord, and to that gracious word of his which can enlarge you, and give you a share among all who are consecrated to him."

After this discourse, Paul knelt down with them all and prayed.

---

3   Acts 26, 19-23

[For missionaries]

A reading from the Acts of the Apostles

Paul said: "King Agrippa, I could not disobey that heavenly vision. I preached a message of reform and of conversion to God, first to the people of Damascus, then to the people of Jerusalem and all the country of Judea; yes, even to the Gentiles. I urged them to act in conformity with their change of heart. That is why the Jews seized me in the temple court and tried to murder me. But I have had God's help to this very day, and so I stand here to testify to great and small alike. Nothing that I say differs from what the prophets and Moses foretold: namely, that the Messiah must suffer, and that, as the first to rise from the dead, he will proclaim light to our people and to the Gentiles."

RESPONSORIAL PSALM

1   Ps 16, 1-2. 5. 7-8. 11

℟. (5) **You are my inheritance, O Lord.**
Keep me, O God, for in you I take refuge;
   I say to the Lord, "My Lord are you."
O Lord, my allotted portion and my cup,
   you it is who hold fast my lot.
℟. **You are my inheritance, O Lord.**
I bless the Lord who counsels me;
   even in the night my heart exhorts me.
I set the Lord ever before me;
   with him at my right hand I shall not be disturbed.
℟. **You are my inheritance, O Lord.**

You will show me the path to life,
   fullness of joys in your presence,
   the delights at your right hand forever.
℟. **You are my inheritance, O Lord.**

---

2   Ps 23, 1-3. 3-4. 5. 6

℟. (1) **The Lord is my shepherd;**
   there is nothing I shall want.
The Lord is my shepherd; I shall not want.
   In verdant pastures he gives me repose;
Beside restful waters he leads me;
   he refreshes my soul.

℟. **The Lord is my shepherd;**
   there is nothing I shall want.
He guides me in right paths
   for his name's sake.
Even though I walk in the dark valley
   I fear no evil; for you are at my side
With your rod and your staff
   that give me courage.

℟. **The Lord is my shepherd;**
   there is nothing I shall want.
You spread the table before me
   in the sight of my foes;
You anoint my head with oil;
   my cup overflows.

℟. **The Lord is my shepherd;**
   there is nothing I shall want.
Only goodness and kindness follow me
   all the days of my life;
And I shall dwell in the house of the Lord
   for years to come.

℟. **The Lord is my shepherd;**
   there is nothing I shall want.

---

3   Ps 89, 2-3. 4-5. 21-22. 25. 27

℟. (2) **For ever I will sing the goodness of the Lord.**
The favors of the Lord I will sing forever;
   through all generations my mouth shall proclaim your
   faithfulness.

For you have said, "My kindness is established forever";
in heaven you have confirmed your faithfulness.
℟. **For ever I will sing the goodness of the Lord.**
"I have made a covenant with my chosen one,
I have sworn to David my servant:
Forever will I confirm your posterity
and establish your throne for all generations."
℟. **For ever I will sing the goodness of the Lord.**
I have found David, my servant;
with my holy oil I have anointed him,
That my hand may be always with him,
and that my arm may make him strong.
℟. **For ever I will sing the goodness of the Lord.**
My faithfulness and my kindness shall be with him,
and through my name shall his horn be exalted.
He shall say of me, "You are my father,
my God, the Rock, my savior."
℟. **For ever I will sing the goodness of the Lord.**

---

4   Ps 96, 1-2. 2-3. 7-8. 10

℟. (3) **Proclaim his marvelous deeds to all the nations.**
Sing to the Lord a new song;
sing to the Lord, all you lands.
Sing to the Lord; bless his name.
℟. **Proclaim his marvelous deeds to all the nations.**
Announce his salvation, day after day.
Tell his glory among the nations;
Among all peoples, his wondrous deeds.
℟. **Proclaim his marvelous deeds to all the nations.**
Give to the Lord, you families of nations,
give to the Lord glory and praise;
give to the Lord the glory due his name!
℟. **Proclaim his marvelous deeds to all the nations.**
Say among the nations: The Lord is king.
He has made the world firm, not to be moved;
He governs the people with equity.
℟. **Proclaim his marvelous deeds to all the nations.**

---

5   Ps 110, 1. 2. 3. 4

℟. (4) **You are a priest for ever,**
   in the line of Melchizedek.
The Lord said to my Lord: "Sit at my right hand
   till I make your enemies your footstool."
℟. **You are a priest for ever,**
   in the line of Melchizedek.
The scepter of your power the Lord will stretch forth
      from Zion:
"Rule in the midst of your enemies.
℟. **You are a priest for ever,**
   in the line of Melchizedek.
Yours is princely power in the day of your birth, in holy
      splendor;
before the daystar, like the dew, I have begotten you."
℟. **You are a priest for ever,**
   in the line of Melchizedek.
The Lord has sworn, and he will not repent:
   "You are a priest forever, according to the order of
   Melchizedek."
℟. **You are a priest for ever,**
   in the line of Melchizedek.

---

6   Ps 117, 1. 2

℟. (Mk 16, 15) **Go out to all the world,**
   and tell the Good News.
Praise the Lord, all you nations;
   glorify him, all you peoples!
℟. **Go out to all the world,**
   and tell the Good News.
For steadfast is his kindness toward us,
   and the fidelity of the Lord endures forever.
℟. **Go out to all the world,**
   and tell the Good News.
℟. Or: **Alleluia.**

READING II

1   Rom 12, 3-13

A reading from the letter of Paul to the Romans

In virtue of the favor given to me, I warn each of you not to think more highly of himself than he ought. Let him estimate himself soberly, in keeping with the measure of faith that God has apportioned him. Just as each of us has one body with many members, and not all the members have the same function, so too we, though many, are one body in Christ and individually members one of another. We have gifts that differ according to the favor bestowed on each of us. One's gift may be prophecy; its use should be in proportion to his faith. It may be the gift of ministry; it should be used for service. One who is a teacher should use his gift for teaching; one with the power of exhortation should exhort. He who gives alms should do so generously; he who rules should exercise his authority with care; he who performs works of mercy should do so cheerfully.

Your love must be sincere. Detest what is evil, cling to what is good. Love one another with the affection of brothers. Anticipate each other in showing respect. Do not grow slack but be fervent in spirit; he whom you serve is the Lord. Rejoice in hope, be patient under trial, persevere in prayer. Look on the needs of the saints as your own; be generous in offering hospitality.

---

2   [For missionaries]   1 Cor 1, 18-25

A reading from the first letter of Paul to the Corinthians

The message of the cross is complete absurdity to those who are headed for ruin, but to us who are experiencing salvation it is the power of God. Scripture says,

"I will destroy the wisdom of the wise,
    and thwart the cleverness of the clever."

Where is the wise man to be found? Where the scribe? Where the master of worldly argument? Has not God turned the wisdom of this world into folly? Since in God's wisdom the world did not come to know him through its wisdom, it pleased God to save those who believe through the absurdity of the preaching of the gospel. Yes, Jews demand "signs" and Greeks look for "wisdom," but we preach Christ crucified, a stumbling block to Jews and an absurdity to Gentiles, but to those who are called, Jews and Greeks alike, Christ the power of God and the wisdom of God. For God's folly is wiser than men, and his weakness more powerful than men.

3   1 Cor 4, 1-5

A reading from the first letter of Paul to the Corinthians

Men should regard us as servants of Christ and administrators of the mysteries of God. The first requirement of an administrator is that he prove trustworthy. It matters little to me whether you or any human court pass judgment on me. I do not even pass judgment on myself. Mind you, I have nothing on my conscience. But that does not mean that I am declaring myself innocent. The Lord is the one to judge me, so stop passing judgment before the time of his return. He will bring to light what is hidden in darkness and manifest the intentions of hearts. At that time, everyone will receive his praise from God.

---

4   1 Cor 9, 16-19. 22-23

A reading from the first letter of Paul to the Corinthians

Preaching the gospel is not the subject of a boast; I am under compulsion and have no choice. I am ruined if I do not preach it! If I do it willingly, I have my recompense; if unwillingly, I am nonetheless entrusted with a charge. And this recompense of mine? It is simply this, that when preaching I offer the gospel free of charge and do not make full use of the authority the gospel gives me.

Although I am not bound to anyone, I made myself the slave of all so as to win over as many as possible. To the weak I became a weak person with a view to winning the weak. I have made myself all things to all men in order to save at least some of them. In fact, I do all that I do for the sake of the gospel in the hope of having a share in its blessings.

5   2 Cor 3, 1-6

A reading from the second letter of Paul to the Corinthians

Am I beginning to speak well of myself again? Or do I
need letters of recommendation to you or from you as
others might? You are my letter, known and read by all
men, written on your hearts. Clearly you are a letter of
Christ which I have delivered, a letter written not with
ink but by the Spirit of the living God, not on tablets of
stone but on tablets of flesh in the heart.

This great confidence in God is ours, through Christ. It
is not that we are entitled of ourselves to take credit for
anything. Our sole credit is from God, who has made us
qualified ministers of a new covenant, a covenant not of
a written law but of spirit.

_____

6   2 Cor 4, 1-2. 5-7

A reading from the second letter of Paul to the Corinthians

Because we possess the ministry through God's mercy,
we do not give in to discouragement. Rather, we repudiate
shameful, underhanded practices. We do not resort to
trickery or falsify the word of God. We proclaim the
truth openly and commend ourselves to every man's
conscience before God. It is not ourselves we preach but
Christ Jesus as Lord, and ourselves as your servants for
Jesus' sake. For God, who said, "Let light shine out of
darkness," has shone in our hearts, that we in turn might
make known the glory of God shining on the face of
Christ. This treasure we possess in earthen vessels to make
it clear that its surpassing power comes from God and
not from us.

_____

7   2 Cor 5, 14-20

A reading from the second letter of Paul to the Corinthians

The love of Christ impels us who have reached the conviction that since one died for all, all died. He died for all so
that those who live might live no longer for themselves,
but for him who for their sakes died and was raised up.

Because of this we no longer look on anyone in terms of mere human judgment. If at one time we so regarded Christ, we no longer know him by this standard. This means that if anyone is in Christ, he is a new creation. The old order has passed away; now all is new! All this has been done by God, who has reconciled us to himself through Christ and has given us the ministry of reconciliation. I mean that God, in Christ, was reconciling the world to himself, not counting men's transgressions against them, and that he has entrusted the message of reconciliation to us. This makes us ambassadors for Christ, God as it were appealing through us. We implore you, in Christ's name: be reconciled to God!

---

8   Eph 4, 1-7. 11-13

A reading from the letter of Paul to the Ephesians

I plead with you as a prisoner for the Lord, to live a life worthy of the calling you have received, with perfect humility, meekness, and patience, bearing with one another lovingly. Make every effort to preserve the unity which has the Spirit as its origin and peace as its binding force. There is but one body and one Spirit, just as there is but one hope given all of you by your call. There is one Lord, one faith, one baptism; one God and Father of all, who is over all, and works through all, and is in all.

Each of us has received God's favor in the measure in which Christ bestows it.

It is he who gave apostles, prophets, evangelists, pastors and teachers in roles of service for the faithful to build up the body of Christ, till we become one in faith and in the knowledge of God's Son, and form that perfect man who is Christ come to full stature.

---

9   Col 1, 24-29

A reading from the letter of Paul to the Colossians

Even now I find my joy in the suffering I endure for you. In my own flesh I fill up what is lacking in the sufferings of Christ for the sake of his body, the church. I became a minister of this church through the commission God gave me to preach among you his word in its fullness, that mystery hidden from ages and generations past but now revealed to his holy ones. God has willed to make known to them the glory beyond price which this mystery brings to the Gentiles — the mystery of Christ in you, your hope of glory. This is the Christ we proclaim while we admonish all men and teach them in the full measure of wisdom, hoping to make every man complete in Christ. For this I work and struggle, impelled by that energy of his which is so powerful a force within me.

10   1 Thes 2, 2-8

A reading from the first letter of Paul to the Thessalonians

We drew courage from our God to preach his good tidings to you in the face of great opposition. The exhortation we deliver does not spring from deceit or impure motives or any sort of trickery; rather, having met the test imposed on us by God, as men entrusted with the good tidings, we speak like those who strive to please God, "the tester of our hearts," rather than men.

We were not guilty, as you well know, of flattering words or greed under any pretext, as God is our witness! Neither did we seek glory from men, you or any others, even though we could have insisted on our own importance as apostles of Christ.

On the contrary, while we were among you we were as gentle as any nursing mother fondling her little ones. So well disposed were we to you, in fact, that we wanted to share with you not only God's tidings but our very lives so dear had you become to us.

11   2 Tm 1, 13-14; 2, 1-3

A reading from the second letter of Paul to Timothy

Take as a model of sound teaching what you have heard me say, in faith and love in Christ Jesus. Guard the rich deposit of faith with the help of the Holy Spirit who dwells within us.

So you, my son, must be strong in the grace which is

ours in Christ Jesus. The things which you have heard from me through many witnesses you must hand on to trustworthy men who will be able to teach others. Bear hardship along with me as a good soldier of Christ Jesus.

------

12   2 Tm 4, 1-5

A reading from the second letter of Paul to Timothy

In the presence of God and of Christ Jesus, who is coming to judge the living and the dead, and by his appearing and his kingly power, I charge you to preach the word, to stay with this task, whether convenient or inconvenient —correcting, reproving, appealing—constantly teaching and never losing patience. For the time will come when people will not tolerate sound doctrine, but, following their own desires, will surround themselves with teachers who tickle their ears. They will stop listening to the truth and will wander off to fables. As for you, be steady and self-possessed; put up with hardship, perform your work as an evangelist, fulfill your ministry.

------

13   1 Pt 5, 1-4

A reading from the first letter of Peter

To the elders among you I, a fellow elder, a witness of Christ's sufferings and sharer in the glory that is to be revealed, make this appeal. God's flock is in your midst; give it a shepherd's care. Watch over it willingly as God would have you do, not under coercion; and not for shameful profit either, but generously. Be examples to the flock, not lording it over those assigned to you, so that when the chief Shepherd appears you will win for yourselves the unfading crown of glory.

ALLELUIA VERSE AND
VERSE BEFORE THE GOSPEL

1   Mt 28, 19-20

Go and teach all people my gospel.
I am with you always, until the end of the world.

2   Mk 1, 17

Come, follow me, says the Lord,
and I will make you fishers of men.

3   Lk 4, 18-19

The Lord sent me to bring Good News to the poor,
and freedom to prisoners.

4   Jn 10, 14

I am the good shepherd, says the Lord;
I know my sheep, and mine know me.

5   Jn 15, 15

I call you my friends, says the Lord,
for I have made known to you all that the Father has told
    me.

6   2 Cor 5, 19

God was in Christ, to reconcile the world to himself;
and the Good News of reconciliation he has entrusted to us.

GOSPEL

1   Mt 16, 13-19

[For a pope]

✠ A reading from the holy gospel according to Matthew

When Jesus came to the neighborhood of Caesarea Philippi, he asked his disciples this question: "Who do people say that the Son of Man is?" They replied, "Some say John the Baptizer, others Elijah, still others Jeremiah or one of the prophets." "And you," he said to them, "who do you say that I am?" "You are the Messiah," Simon Peter answered, "the Son of the living God!" Jesus replied, "Blest are you, Simon son of John! No mere man has revealed this to you, but my heavenly Father. I for my part declare to you, you are 'Rock,' and on this rock I will build my church, and the jaws of death shall not prevail against it. I will entrust to you the keys of the kingdom of heaven. Whatever you declare bound on earth shall be bound in heaven; whatever you declare loosed on earth shall be loosed in heaven."

---

2   Mt 23, 8-12

✠ A reading from the holy gospel according to Matthew

Jesus said to his disciples: "Avoid the title 'Rabbi.' One among you is your teacher, the rest are learners. Do not call anyone on earth your father. Only one is your father, the One in heaven. Avoid being called teachers. Only one is your teacher, the Messiah. The greatest among you will be the one who serves the rest. Whoever exalts himself shall be humbled, but whoever humbles himself shall be exalted."

---

3   Mt 28, 16-20

[For missionaries]

✠ A reading from the holy gospel according to Matthew

The eleven disciples made their way to Galilee, to the mountain to which Jesus had summoned them. At the sight of him, those who had entertained doubts fell down in homage. Jesus came forward and addressed them in these words:

"Full authority has been given to me
both in heaven and on earth;
go, therefore, and make disciples of all the nations.
Baptize them in the name
'of the Father,
and of the Son,
and of the Holy Spirit.'
Teach them to carry out everything I have commanded
you.
And know that I am with you always, until the end of
the world!"

---

4   Mk 1, 14-20

✠ A reading from the holy gospel according to Mark

After John's arrest, Jesus appeared in Galilee proclaiming God's good news: "This is the time of fulfillment. The reign of God is at hand! Reform your lives and believe in the good news!"

As he made his way along the Sea of Galilee, he observed Simon and his brother Andrew casting their nets into the sea; they were fishermen. Jesus said to them, "Come after me; I will make you fishers of men." They immediately abandoned their nets and became his followers. Proceeding a little farther along, he caught sight of James, Zebedee's son, and his brother John. They too were in their boat putting their nets in order. He summoned them on the spot. They abandoned their father Zebedee, who was in the boat with the hired men, and went off in his company.

---

5   Mk 16, 15-20

[For missionaries]

✠ A reading from the holy gospel according to Mark

Jesus appeared to the Eleven and said to them: "Go into the whole world and proclaim the good news to all creation. The man who believes in it and accepts baptism will be saved; the man who refuses to believe in it will be condemned. Signs like these will accompany those who have professed their faith: they will use my name to expel demons, they will speak entirely new languages, they will be able to handle serpents, they will be able to drink deadly poison without harm, and the sick upon whom they lay their hands will recover." Then, after speaking to them, the Lord Jesus was taken up into heaven and took his seat at God's right hand. The Eleven went forth and preached everywhere. The Lord continued to work with them throughout and confirm the message through the signs which accompanied them.

---

6 Lk 5, 1-11

[For missionaries]

✠ A reading from the holy gospel according to Luke

As Jesus stood by the Lake of Gennesaret, and the crowd pressed in on him to hear the word of God, he saw two boats moored by the side of the lake; the fishermen had disembarked and were washing their nets. He got into one of the boats, the one belonging to Simon, and asked him to pull out a short distance from the shore; then, remaining seated, he continued to teach the crowds from the boat. When he had finished speaking he said to Simon, "Put out into deep water and lower your nets for a catch." Simon answered, "Master, we have been hard at it all night long and have caught nothing; but if you say so, I will lower the nets." Upon doing this they caught such a great number of fish that their nets were at the breaking point. They signaled to their mates in the other boat to come and help them. These came, and together they filled the two boats until they nearly sank.

At the sight of this, Simon Peter fell at the knees of Jesus saying, "Leave me, Lord. I am a sinful man." For indeed, amazement at the catch they had made seized him and all his shipmates, as well as James and John, Zebedee's sons, who were partners with Simon. Jesus said to Simon, "Do not be afraid. From now on you will be catching men." With that they brought their boats to land, left everything, and became his followers.

---

7 Lk 10-1-9

✠ A reading from the holy gospel according to Luke
The Lord appointed a further seventy-two and sent them
in pairs before him to every town and place he intended
to visit. He said to them: "The harvest is rich but the workers are few; therefore ask the harvest-master to send workers to his harvest. Be on your way, and remember: I am
sending you as lambs in the midst of wolves. Do not carry
a walking staff or traveling bag; wear no sandals and greet
no one along the way. On entering any house, first say,
'Peace to this house.' If there is a peaceable man there, your
peace will rest on him; if not, it will come back to you. Stay
in the one house eating and drinking what they have, for
the laborer is worth his wage. Do not move from house to
house.

"Into whatever city you go, after they welcome you, eat
what they set before you, and cure the sick there. Say to
them, 'The reign of God is at hand.' "

---

8 Lk 22, 24-30

✠ A reading from the holy gospel according to Luke
A dispute arose among the apostles about who should be
regarded as the greatest. Jesus said: "Earthly kings lord it
over their people. Those who exercise authority over them
are called their benefactors. Yet it cannot be that way with
you. Let the greater among you be as the junior, the leader
as the servant. Who, in fact, is the greater—he who re-
clines at table or he who serves the meal? Is it not those who
recline at table? Yet I am in your midst as the one who serves
you. You are the ones who have stood loyally by me in my
temptations. I for my part assign to you the dominion my
Father has assigned to me. In my kingdom you will eat and
drink at my table, and you will sit on thrones judging the
twelve tribes of Israel."

✠ A reading from the holy gospel according to John

Jesus said:

"I am the good shepherd;
the good shepherd lays down his life for the sheep.
The hired hand—who is no shepherd,
    nor owner of the sheep—
catches sight of the wolf coming
and runs away, leaving the sheep
to be snatched and scattered by the wolf.
That is because he works for pay;
he has no concern for the sheep.

"I am the good shepherd.
I know my sheep
and my sheep know me
in the same way that the Father knows me
and I know the Father;
for these sheep I will give my life.
I have other sheep
that do not belong to this fold.
I must lead them, too,
and they shall hear my voice.
There shall be one flock then, one shepherd."

_____

✠ A reading from the holy gospel according to John

Jesus said to his disciples:

"As the Father has loved me,
so I have loved you.
Live on in my love.
You will live in my love
if you keep my commandments,
even as I have kept my Father's commandments,
and live in his love.
All this I tell you
that my joy may be yours
and your joy may be complete.

This is my commandment:
love one another
as I have loved you.
There is no greater love than this:
to lay down one's life for one's friends.
You are my friends
if you do what I command you.
I no longer speak of you as slaves,
for a slave does not know what his master is about.
Instead, I call you friends,
since I have made known to you all that I heard from my
    Father.
It was not you who chose me,
it was I who chose you
to go forth and bear fruit.
Your fruit must endure,
so that all you ask the Father in my name
he will give you.
The command I give you is this:
that you love one another."

11   Jn 21, 15-17

[For a pope]

✠ A reading from the holy gospel according to John

Jesus appeared to his disciples again and when they had
eaten their meal, he said to Simon Peter, "Simon, son of
John, do you love me more than these?" "Yes, Lord," Peter
said, "you know that I love you." At which Jesus said,
"Feed my lambs."

A second time he put his question, "Simon, son of John,
do you love me?" "Yes, Lord," Peter said, "you know that I
love you." Jesus replied, "Tend my sheep."

A third time Jesus asked him, "Simon, son of John, do
you love me?" Peter was hurt because he had asked a third
time, "Do you love me?" So he said to him: "Lord, you
know everything. You know well that I love you." Jesus
told him, "Feed my sheep."

COMMON OF DOCTORS
OF THE CHURCH

READING I

OUTSIDE THE EASTER SEASON

1   1 Kgs 3, 11-14

A reading from the first book of Kings

The Lord said to Solomon: "Because you have asked—not for a long life for yourself, nor for riches, nor for the life of your enemies, but for understanding so that you may know what is right—I do as you requested. I give you a heart so wise and understanding that there has never been anyone like you up to now, and after you there will come no one to equal you. In addition, I give you what you have not asked for, such riches and glory that among kings there is not your like. And if you follow me by keeping my statutes and commandments, as your father David did, I will give you a long life."

---

2   Wis 7, 7-10. 15-16

A reading from the book of Wisdom

I prayed, and prudence was given me;
    I pleaded, and the spirit of Wisdom came to me.
I preferred her to scepter and throne,
And deemed riches nothing in comparison with her,
    nor did I liken any priceless gem to her;
Because all gold, in view of her, is a little sand,
    and before her silver is to be accounted mire.
Beyond health and comeliness I loved her,
And I chose to have her rather than the light,
    because the splendor of her never yields to sleep.
Now God grant I speak suitably
    and value these endowments at their worth:
For he is the guide of Wisdom
    and the director of the wise.

For both we and our words are in his hand,
    as well as all prudence and knowledge of crafts.

---

3 Sir 15, 1-6

A reading from the book of Sirach

He who fears the Lord will do this;
    he who is practiced in the law will come to wisdom.
Motherlike she will meet him,
    like a young bride she will embrace him,
Nourish him with the bread of understanding,
    and give him the water of learning to drink.
He will lean upon her and not fall,
    he will trust in her and not be put to shame.
She will exalt him above his fellows;
    in the assembly she will make him eloquent.
Joy and gladness he will find,
    an everlasting name inherit.

---

4 Sir 39, 6-11

A reading from the book of Sirach

If it pleases the Lord Almighty,
    he will be filled with the spirit of understanding;
He will pour forth his words of wisdom
    and in prayer give thanks to the Lord,
Who will direct his knowledge and his counsel,
    as he meditates upon his mysteries.
He will show the wisdom of what he has learned
    and glory in the law of the Lord's covenant.
Many will praise his understanding;
    his fame can never be effaced;
Unfading will be his memory,
    through all generations his name will live;
Peoples will speak of his wisdom,
    and in assembly sing his praises.
While he lives he is one out of a thousand,
    and when he dies his renown will not cease.

READING I

IN THE EASTER SEASON

1 Acts, 2, 14. 22-24. 32-36

A reading from the Acts of the Apostles

[On the day of Pentecost] Peter stood up with the Eleven, raised his voice, and addressed them: "Men of Israel, listen to me! Jesus the Nazorean was a man whom God sent to you with miracles, wonders and signs as his credentials. These God worked through him in your midst, as you well know. He was delivered up by the set purpose and plan of God; you even made use of pagans to crucify and kill him. God freed him from death's bitter pangs, however, and raised him up again, for it was impossible that death should keep its hold on him.

"This is the Jesus God has raised up, and we are his witnesses. Exalted at God's right hand, he first received the promised Holy Spirit from the Father, then poured this Spirit out on us. This is what you now see and hear. David did not go up to heaven, yet David says,

'The Lord said to my Lord,
  Sit at my right hand
  until I make your enemies your footstool.'

Therefore let the whole house of Israel know beyond any doubt that God has made both Lord and Messiah this Jesus whom you crucified."

---

2 Acts 13, 26-33

A reading from the Acts of the Apostles

When Paul came to Antioch in Pisidia, he spoke in the synagogue and said: "My brothers, children of the family of Abraham and you others who reverence our God, it was to us that this message of salvation was sent forth. The inhabitants of Jerusalem and their rulers failed to recognize him, and in condemning him they fulfilled the words of the prophets which we read sabbath after sabbath. Even though they found no charge against him which deserved death, they begged Pilate to have him executed. Once they had thus brought about all that had been written of him, they took him down from the tree and laid him in a tomb. Yet God raised him from the dead, and for many days thereafter Jesus appeared to those who had come up with him from Galilee to Jerusalem. These are his witnesses now before the people.

"We ourselves announce to you the good news that what God promised our fathers he has fulfilled for us, their children, in raising up Jesus, according to what is written in the second psalm, 'You are my son; this day I have begotten you.'"

RESPONSORIAL PSALM

1   Ps 19, 8. 9. 10. 11

℟. (10) **The judgments of the Lord are true,**
    and all of them are just.
The law of the Lord is perfect,
    refreshing the soul;
The decree of the Lord is trustworthy,
    giving wisdom to the simple.

℟. **The judgments of the Lord are true,**
    and all of them are just.
The precepts of the Lord are right,
    rejoicing the heart;
The command of the Lord is clear,
    enlightening the eye.

℟. **The judgments of the Lord are true,**
    and all of them are just.
The fear of the Lord is pure,
    enduring forever;
The ordinances of the Lord are true,
    all of them just.

℟. **The judgments of the Lord are true,**
    and all of them are just.
They are more precious than gold,
    than a heap of purest gold;
Sweeter also than syrup
    or honey from the comb.

℞. **The judgments of the Lord are true,**
  and all of them are just.
℞. Or: **Your words, Lord are spirit and life.**

---

2   Ps 37, 3-4. 5-6. 30-31

℞. (30) **The mouth of the just man murmurs wisdom.**
Trust in the Lord and do good,
  that you may dwell in the land and enjoy security.
Take delight in the Lord,
  and he will grant you your heart's requests.
℞. **The mouth of the just man murmurs wisdom.**
Commit to the Lord your way;
  trust in him, and he will act.
He will make justice dawn for you like the light;
  bright as the noonday shall be your vindication.
℞. **The mouth of the just man murmurs wisdom.**
The mouth of the just man tells of wisdom
  and his tongue utters what is right.
The law of his God is in his heart,
  and his steps do not falter.
℞. **The mouth of the just man murmurs wisdom.**

---

3   Ps 119, 9. 10. 11. 12. 13. 14

℞. (12) **Lord, teach me your decrees.**
How shall a young man be faultless in his way?
  By keeping to your words.
℞. **Lord, teach me your decrees.**
With all my heart I seek you;
  let me not stray from your commands.
℞. **Lord, teach me your decrees.**
Within my heart I treasure your promise,
  that I may not sin against you.
℞. **Lord, teach me your decrees.**
Blessed are you, O Lord;
  teach me your statutes.
℞. **Lord, teach me your decrees.**
With my lips I declare
  all the ordinances of your mouth.
℞. **Lord, teach me your decrees.**

In the way of your decrees I rejoice,
   as much as in all riches.
℟. **Lord, teach me your decrees.**

READING II

1   1 Cor 1, 18-25

A reading from the first letter of Paul to the Corinthians
The message of the cross is complete absurdity to those
who are headed for ruin, but to us who are experiencing
salvation it is the power of God. Scripture says,
   "I will destroy the wisdom of the wise,
   and thwart the cleverness of the clever."
Where is the wise man to be found? Where the scribe?
Where is the master of worldly argument? Has not God
turned the wisdom of this world into folly. Since in God's
wisdom the world did not come to know him through
wisdom, it pleased God to save those who believe through
the absurdity of the preaching of the gospel. Yes, Jews demand "signs" and Greeks look for "wisdom," but we preach
Christ crucified, a stumbling block to Jews and an absurdity to Gentiles, but to those who are called, Jews and
Greeks alike, Christ the power of God and the wisdom of
God. For God's folly is wiser than men, and his weakness
more powerful than men.

---

2   1 Cor 2, 1-10

A reading from the first letter of Paul to the Corinthians
Brothers, when I came to you I did not come proclaiming
God's testimony with any particular eloquence or "wisdom." No, I determined that while I was with you I would
speak of nothing but Jesus Christ and him crucified. When
I came among you it was in weakness and fear, and with
much trepidation. My message and my preaching had none
of the persuasive force of "wise" argumentation, but the
convincing power of the Spirit. As a consequence, your

faith rests not on the wisdom of men but on the power of God.

There is, to be sure, a certain wisdom which we express among the spiritually mature. It is not a wisdom of this age, however, nor of the rulers of this age, who are men headed for destruction. No, what we utter is God's wisdom: a mysterious, a hidden wisdom. God planned it before all ages for our glory. None of the rulers of this age knew the mystery; if they had known it, they would never have crucified the Lord of glory. Of this wisdom it is written:

"Eye has not seen, ear has not heard,
   nor has it so much as dawned on man
   what God has prepared for those who love him."

Yet God has revealed this wisdom to us through the Spirit.

3   1 Cor 2, 10-16

A reading from the first letter of Paul to the Corinthians

The spirit scrutinizes all matters, even the deep things of God. Who, for example, knows a man's innermost self but the man's own spirit within him? Similarly, no one knows what lies at the depths of God but the Spirit of God. The Spirit we have received is not the world's spirit but God's Spirit, helping us to recognize the gifts he has given us. We speak of these, not in words of human wisdom but in words taught by the Spirit, thus interpreting spiritual things in spiritual terms. The natural man does not accept what is taught by the Spirit of God. For him, that is absurdity. He cannot come to know such teaching because it must be appraised in a spiritual way. The spiritual man, on the other hand, can appraise everything, though he himself can be appraised by no one. For, "Who has known the mind of the Lord so as to instruct him?" But we have the mind of Christ.

4   Eph 3, 8-12

A reading from the letter of Paul to the Ephesians

To me, the least of all believers, was given the grace to preach to the Gentiles the unfathomable riches of Christ and to enlighten all men on the mysterious design which for ages was hidden in God, the Creator of all. Now, therefore, through the church, God's manifold wisdom is made known to the principalities and powers of heaven, in accord with his age-old purpose, carried out in Christ Jesus our Lord. In Christ and through faith in him we can speak freely to God, drawing near him with confidence.

---

5   Eph 4, 1-7. 11-13

A reading from the letter of Paul to the Ephesians

I plead with you, as a prisoner for the Lord, to live a life worthy of the calling you have received, with perfect humility, meekness, and patience, bearing with one another lovingly. Make every effort to preserve the unity which has the Spirit as its origin and peace as its binding force. There is but one body and one Spirit, just as there is but one hope given all of you by your call. There is one Lord, one faith, one baptism; one God and Father of all, who is over all, and works through all, and is in all.

Each of us has received God's favor in the measure in which Christ bestows it. It is he who gave apostles, prophets, evangelists, pastors, and teachers in roles of service for the faithful to build up the body of Christ, till we become one in faith and in the knowledge of God's Son, and form that perfect man who is Christ come to full stature.

---

6   2 Tm 1, 13-14; 2, 1-3

A reading from the second letter of Paul to Timothy

Take as a model of sound teaching what you have heard me say, in faith and love in Christ Jesus. Guard the rich deposit of faith with the help of the Holy Spirit who dwells within us.

So you, my son, must be strong in the grace which is ours in Christ Jesus. The things which you have heard from me through many witnesses you must hand on to trustworthy men who will be able to teach others. Bear hardship along with me as a good soldier of Christ Jesus.

---

7   2 Tm 4, 1-5

A reading from the second letter of Paul to Timothy

In the presence of God and of Christ Jesus, who is coming to judge the living and the dead, and by his appearing and his kingly power, I charge you to preach the word, to stay with this task whether convenient or inconvenient—correcting, reproving, appealing—constantly teaching and never losing patience. For the time will come when people will not tolerate sound doctrine, but, following their own desires, will surround themselves with teachers who tickle their ears. They will stop listening to the truth and will wander off to fables. As for you, be steady and self-possessed; put up with hardship, perform your work as an evangelist, fulfill your ministry.

ALLELUIA VERSE AND
VERSE BEFORE THE GOSPEL

1   Mt 5, 16

Let your light shine before men,
that they may see your good works and glorify your
    Father.

2   1Cor 1, 18

The message of the cross is folly to those who turn away,
but to those who are saved it is the power of God.

3   1 Cor 2, 7

We teach a secret and hidden wisdom of God,
which he decreed for our glory before time began.

4

The seed is the word of God, Christ is the sower;
all who come to him will live for ever.

GOSPEL

1 Mt 5, 13-16

✠ A reading from the holy gospel according to Matthew

Jesus said to his disciples: "You are the salt of the earth. But what if salt goes flat? How can you restore its flavor? Then it is good for nothing but to be thrown out and trampled underfoot.

"You are the light of the world. A city set on a hill cannot be hidden. Men do not light a lamp and then put it under a bushel basket. They set it on a stand where it gives light to all in the house. In the same way, your light must shine before men so that they may see goodness in your acts and give praise to your heavenly Father"

---

2 Mt 23, 8-12

✠ A reading from the holy gospel according to Matthew

Jesus said to his disciples: "Avoid the title 'Rabbi.' One among you is your teacher, the rest are learners. Do not call anyone on earth your father. Only one is your father, the One in heaven. Avoid being called teachers. Only one is your teacher, the Messiah. The greatest among you will be the one who serves the rest. Whoever exalts himself shall be humbled, but whoever humbles himself shall be exalted."

---

3 Mk 4, 1-10. 13-20 or 4, 1-9

[If the "Short Form" is used, the indented text in brackets is omitted.]

✠ A reading from the holy gospel according to Mark

[Jesus began to teach beside the lake. Such a huge crowd gathered around him that he went and sat in a boat on the water, while the crowd remained on the shore nearby. He began to instruct them at great length, by the use of parables, and in the course of his teaching said: "Listen carefully to this. A farmer went out sowing. Some of what he sowed landed on the footpath, where the birds came along and ate it. Some of the seed landed on rocky ground where it had little soil; it sprouted immediately because the soil had no depth. Then, when the sun rose and scorched it, it began to wither for lack of roots. Again, some landed among thorns, which grew up and choked it off, and there was no yield of grain. Some seed, finally, landed on good soil and yielded grain that sprang up to produce at a rate of thirty- and sixty- and a hundredfold." Having spoken this parable, he added: "Let him who has ears to hear me, hear!"]

Now when he was away from the crowd, those present with the Twelve questioned him about the parables. He said to them: "You do not understand this parable? How then are you going to understand other figures like it? What the sower is sowing is the word. Those on the path are the ones to whom, as soon as they hear the word, Satan comes to carry off what was sown in them. Similarly, those sown on rocky ground are people who on listening to the word accept it joyfully at the outset. Being rootless, they last only a while. When some pressure or persecution overtakes them, because of the word, they falter. Those sown among thorns are another class. They have listened to the word, but anxieties over life's demands, and the desire for wealth and cravings of other sorts come to choke it off; it bears no yield. But those sown on good soil are the ones who listen to the word, take it to heart, and yield at thirty- and sixty- and a hundred-fold."

COMMONS OF VIRGINS

READING I

OUTSIDE THE EASTER SEASON

1   Sg 8, 6-7

A reading from the Song of Solomon

Set me as a seal on your heart,
 as a seal on your arm;
For stern as death is love,
 relentless as the nether world is devotion;
 its flames are a blazing fire.
Deep waters cannot quench love,
 nor floods sweep it away.
Were one to offer all he owns to purchase love,
 he would be roundly mocked.

---

2   Hos 2, 16. 17. 21-22

A reading from the book of the prophet Hosea

I will lead her into the desert
 and speak to her heart.
She shall respond there as in the days of her youth,
 when she came up from the land of Egypt.

I will espouse you to me forever:
 I will espouse you in right and in justice,
 in love and in mercy;
I will espouse you in fidelity,
 and you shall know the Lord.

READING I

DURING THE EASTER SEASON

1   Rv 19, 1. 5-9

A reading from the book of Revelation

I, John, heard what sounded like the loud song of a great
assembly in heaven. They were singing:

"Alleluia!
Salvation, glory, and might belong to our God."
A voice coming from the throne cried out:
"Praise our God, all you his servants,
the small and the great, who revere him!"

Then I heard what sounded like the shouts of a great
crowd, or the roaring of the deep, or mighty peals of thunder, as they cried:

"Alleluia!
The Lord is king,
our God, the Almighty!
Let us rejoice and be glad,
and give him glory!
For this is the wedding day of the Lamb;
his bride has prepared herself for the wedding.
She has been given a dress to wear
made of finest linen, brilliant white."

(The linen dress is the virtuous deeds of God's saints.)

The angel then said to me: "Write this down: Happy are
they who have been invited to the wedding feast of the
Lamb."

----

2   Rv 21, 1-5

A reading from the book of Revelation

I, John, saw new heavens and a new earth. The former
heavens and the former earth had passed away, and the
sea was no longer. I also saw a new Jeruslem, the holy city,
coming down out of heaven from God, beautiful as a bride
prepared to meet her husband. I heard a loud voice from
the throne cry out: "This is God's dwelling among men. He

shall dwell with them and they shall be his people, and he shall be their God who is always with them. He shall wipe every tear from their eyes, and there shall be no more death or mourning, crying out or pain, for the former world has passed away."

The One who sat on the throne said to me, "See, I make all things new!"

RESPONSORIAL PSALM

1   Ps 45, 11-12. 14-15. 16-17

℟. (11) **Listen to me, daughter;**
    see and bend your ear.

Hear, O daughter, and see; turn your ear,
    forget your people and your father's house.
So shall the king desire your beauty;
    for he is your lord, and you must worship him.

℟. **Listen to me, daughter;**
    see and bend your ear.

All glorious is the king's daughter as she enters;
    her raiment is threaded with spun gold.
In embroidered apparel she is borne in to the king;
    behind her the virgins of her train are brought to you.

℟. **Listen to me, daughter;**
    see and bend your ear.

They are borne in with gladness and joy;
    they enter the palace of the king.
The place of your fathers your sons shall have;
    you shall make them princes through all the land.

℟. **Listen to me, daughter;**
    see and bend your ear.

℟. Or: (Mt 25, 6) **The bridegroom is here;**
    let us go out to meet Christ the Lord.

2 Ps 148, 1-2. 11-12. 13-14. 14

℟. **Alleluia.**

Praise the Lord from the heavens,
  praise him in the heights;
Praise him, all you his angels,
  praise him, all you his hosts.

℟. **Alleluia.**

Let the kings of the earth and all peoples,
  the princes and all the judges of the earth,
Young men too, and maidens,
  old men and boys.

℟. **Alleluia.**

Praise the name of the Lord,
  for his name alone is exalted;
His majesty is above earth and heaven.

℟. **Alleluia.**

He has lifted up the horn of his people.
  Be this his praise from all his faithful ones;
From the children of Israel, the people close to him.
  Alleluia.

℟. **Alleluia.**

READING II

1 1 Cor 7, 25-35

A reading from the first letter of Paul to the Corinthians

With respect to virgins, I have not received any commandment from the Lord, but I give my opinion as one who is trustworthy, thanks to the Lord's mercy. It is this: In the present time of stress it seems good to me for a person to continue as he is. Are you bound to a wife? Then do not seek your freedom. Are you free of a wife? If so, do not go in search of one. Should you marry, however, you will not be committing sin. Neither does a virgin commit a sin if she marries. Such people, however, will have trials in this life, and these I should like to spare you.

I tell you, brothers, the time is short. From now on those with wives should live as though they had none; those who weep should live as though they were not weeping, and those who rejoice as though they were not rejoicing; buyers should conduct themselves as though they owned nothing, and those who make use of the world as though they were not using it, for the world as we know it is passing away.

I should like you to be free of all worries. The unmarried man is busy with the Lord's affairs, concerned with pleasing the Lord; but the married man is busy with this world's demands and occupied with pleasing his wife. This means he is divided. The virgin—indeed, any unmarried woman—is concerned with things of the Lord, in pursuit of holiness in body and spirit. The married woman, on the other hand, has the cares of this world to absorb her and is concerned with pleasing her husband. I am going into this with you for your own good. I have no desire to place restrictions on you, but I do want to promote what is good, what will help you to devote yourselves entirely to the Lord.

2   2 Cor 10, 17—11, 2

A reading from the second letter of Paul to the Corinthians

"Let him who would boast, boast in the Lord." It is not the man who recommends himself who is approved but the man whom the Lord recommends.

You must endure a little of my folly. Put up with me, I beg you! I am jealous of you with the jealousy of God himself, since I have given you in marriage to one husband, presenting you as a chaste virgin to Christ.

ALLELUIA VERSE AND

VERSE BEFORE THE GOSPEL

1

This is the wise bridesmaid, whom the Lord found waiting; at his coming, she went in with him to the wedding feast.

2

Come, bride of Christ, and receive the crown,
which the Lord has prepared for you for ever.

GOSPEL

1   Mt 19, 3-12

✠ A reading from the holy gospel according to Matthew

Some of the Pharisees came up to Jesus and said, to test him, "May a man divorce his wife for any reason whatever?" He replied, "Have you not read that at the beginning the Creator made them male and female and declared, 'For this reason a man shall leave his father and mother and cling to his wife, and the two shall become as one'? Thus they are no longer two but one flesh. Therefore, let no man separate what God has joined." They said to him, "Then why did Moses command divorce and the promulgation of a divorce decree?" "Because of your stubbornness Moses let you divorce your wives," he replied: "but at the beginning it was not that way. I now say to you, whoever divorces his wife (lewd conduct is a separate case) and marries another commits adultery, and the man who marries a divorced woman commits adultery."

His disciples said to him, "If that is the case between man and wife, it is better not to marry." He said, "Not everyone can accept this teaching, only those to whom it is given to do so. Some men are incapable of sexual activity from birth; some have been deliberately made so; and some there are who have freely renounced sex for the sake of God's reign. Let him accept this teaching who can."

---

2   Mt 25, 1-13

✠ A reading of the holy gospel according to Matthew

Jesus told this parable to his disciples; "The reign of God can be likened to ten bridesmaids who took their torches and went out to welcome the groom. Five of them were foolish, while the other five were sensible. The foolish ones, in taking their torches, brought no oil along, but the sensible ones took flasks of oil as well as their torches. The groom delayed his coming, so they all began to nod, then to fall asleep. At midnight someone shouted, 'The groom is here! Come out and greet him!' At the outcry all the virgins woke up and got their torches ready. The foolish ones said to the sensible, 'Give us some of your oil. Our torches are going out.' But the sensible ones replied, 'No, there may not be enough for you and us. You had better go to the dealers and buy yourselves some.' While they went off to buy it the groom arrived, and the ones who were ready went in to the wedding with him. Then the door was barred. Later the other bridesmaids came back. 'Master, master!' they cried. 'Open the door for us.' But he answered, 'I tell you, I do not know you.' The moral is: keep your eyes open, for you know not the day or the hour."

---

3   Lk 10, 38-42

✠ A reading of the holy gospel according to Luke

Jesus entered a village where a woman named Martha welcomed him to her home. She had a sister named Mary, who seated herself at the Lord's feet and listened to his words. Martha, who was busy with all the details of hospitality, came to him and said, "Lord, are you not concerned that my sister has left me all alone to do the household tasks? Tell her to help me."

The Lord in reply said to her: "Martha, Martha, you are anxious and upset about many things; one thing only is required. Mary has chosen the better portion and she shall not be deprived of it."

COMMON OF HOLY MEN AND WOMEN

OUTSIDE THE EASTER SEASON

1   Gn 12, 1-4

A reading from the book of Genesis

The Lord said to Abram: "Go forth from the land of your kinsfolk and from your father's house to a land that I will show you.

"I will make of you a great nation,
    and I will bless you;
I will make your name great,
    so that you will be a blessing.
I will bless those who bless you
    and curse those who curse you.
All the communities of the earth
    shall find blessing in you."

Abram went as the Lord directed him.

———————————

2   Lv 19, 1-2. 17-18

A reading from the book of Leviticus

The Lord said to Moses, "Speak to the whole Israelite community and tell them: Be holy, for I, the Lord, your God, am holy.

"You shall not bear hatred for your brother in your heart. Though you may have to reprove your fellow man, do not incur sin because of him. Take no revenge and cherish no grudge against your fellow countrymen. You shall love your neighbor as yourself. I am the Lord."

———————————

3   Dt 6, 3-9

A reading from the book of Deuteronomy

Moses said to the people: "Hear, Israel, and be careful to observe the commandments, that you may grow and prosper the more, in keeping with the promise of the Lord, the God of your fathers, to give you a land flowing with milk and honey.

"Hear, O Israel! The Lord is our God, the Lord alone! Therefore, you shall love the Lord, your God, with all your heart, and with all your soul, and with all your strength. Take to heart these words which I enjoin on you today. Drill them into your children. Speak of them at home and abroad, whether you are busy or at rest. Bind them at your wrist as a sign and let them be as a pendant on your forehead. Write them on the doorposts of your houses and on your gates."

----

4   Dt 10, 8-9

[For religious]

A reading from the book of Deuteronomy

Moses said to the people: "At that time the Lord set apart the tribe of Levi to carry the ark of the covenant of the Lord, to be in attendance before the Lord and minister to him, and to give blessings in his name, as they have done to this day. For this reason, Levi has no share in the heritage with his brothers; the Lord himself is his heritage, as the Lord, your God, has told him."

----

5   1 Kgs 19, 4-9. 11-15

[For religious]

A reading from the first book of Kings

Elijah went a day's journey into the desert, until he came to a broom tree and sat beneath it. He prayed for death: "This is enough, O Lord! Take my life, for I am no better than my fathers." He lay down and fell asleep under the broom tree, but then an angel touched him and ordered him to get up and eat. He looked and there at his head was a hearth cake and a jug of water. After he ate and drank, he lay down again, but the angel of the Lord came back a second time, touched him, and ordered, "Get up and eat, else the journey will be too long for you!" He got up, ate and drank; then, strengthened by that food, he walked forty nights to the mountain of God, Horeb.

There he came to a cave, where he took shelter. Then the Lord said, "Go outside and stand on the mountain before the Lord; the Lord will be passing by." A strong and heavy wind was rending the mountains and crushing rocks before the Lord—but the Lord was not in the wind. After the wind there was an earthquake—but the Lord was not in the earthquake. After the earthquake there was fire—but the Lord was not in the fire. After the fire there was a tiny whispering sound. When he heard this, Elijah hid his face in his cloak and went and stood at the entrance of the cave. A voice said to him, "Elijah, why are you here?" He replied, "I have been most zealous for the Lord, the God of hosts. But the Israelites have forsaken your covenant, torn down your altars, and put your prophets to the sword. I alone am left, and they seek to take my life." "Go, take the road back to the desert near Damascus," the Lord said to him.

6

1 Kgs 19, 16. 19-21

[For religious]

A reading from the first book of Kings

The Lord said to Elijah: "You shall anoint Elisha, son of Shaphat of Abel-meholah, as prophet to succeed you.

Elijah set out, and came upon Elisha, son of Shaphat, as he was plowing with twelve yoke of oxen; he was following the twelfth. Elijah went over to him and threw his cloak over him. Elisha left the oxen, ran after Elijah, and said, "Please, let me kiss my father and mother goodbye, and I will follow you." "Go back!" Elijah answered. "Have I done anything to you?" Elisha left him and, taking the yoke of oxen, slaughtered them; he used the plowing equipment for fuel to boil their flesh, and gave it to his people to eat. Then he left and followed Elijah as his attendant.

----

7   Tb 8, 5-7

A reading from the book of Tobit

On their wedding night Sarah got up, and she and Tobiah
started to pray and beg that deliverance might be theirs.
He began with these words:

"Blessed are you, O God of our fathers;
   praised be your name forever and ever.
Let the heavens and all your creation
   praise you forever.
You made Adam and you gave him his wife Eve
   to be his help and support;
   and from these two the human race descended.
You said, 'It is not good for the man to be alone;
   let us make him a partner like himself.'
Now, Lord, you know that I take this wife of mine
   not because of lust
   but for a noble purpose.
Call down your mercy on me and on her,
   and allow us to live together to a happy old age."

---

8   Tb 12, 6-13

[For those who work for the underprivileged]

A reading from the book of Tobit

The angel said to Tobit and his son: "Thank God! Give him
the praise and the glory. Before all the living, acknowledge
the many good things he has done for you, by blessing and
extolling his name in song. Before all men, honor and proclaim God's deeds, and do not be slack in praising him. A
king's secret it is prudent to keep, but the works of God
are to be declared and made known. Praise them with due
honor. Do good, and evil will not find its way to you. Prayer
and fasting are good, but better than either is almsgiving
accompanied by righteousness. A little with righteousness
is better than abundance with wickedness. It is better to
give alms than store up gold; for almsgiving saves one
from death and expiates every sin. Those who regularly
give alms shall enjoy a full life; but those habitually guilty
of sin are their own worst enemies.

"I will now tell you the whole truth; I will conceal nothing at all from you. I have already said to you, 'A king's secret it is prudent to keep, but the works of God are to be made known with due honor.' I can now tell you that when you, Tobit, and Sarah prayed, it was I who presented and read the record of your prayer before the Glory of the Lord; and I did the same thing when you used to bury the dead. When you did not hesitate to get up and leave your dinner in order to go and bury the dead, I was sent to put you to the test."

---

9   Jdt 8, 2-8

[For widows]

A reading from the book of Judith

Judith's husband, Manasseh, of her own tribe and clan, had died at the time of the barley harvest. While he was in the field supervising those who bound the sheaves, he suffered sunstroke; and he died of this illness in Bethulia, his native city. He was buried with his forefathers in the field between Dothan and Balamon. The widowed Judith remained three years and four months at home, where she set up a tent for herself on the roof of her house. She put sackcloth about her loins and wore widow's weeds. She fasted all the days of her widowhood, except sabbath eves and sabbaths, new moon eves and new moons, feastdays and holidays of the house of Israel. She was beautifully formed and lovely to behold. Her husband, Manasseh, had left her gold and silver, servants and maids, livestock and fields, which she was maintaining. No one had a bad word to say about her, for she was a very God-fearing woman.

---

10   Est C, 1-7. 10

A reading from the book of Esther

Mordecai recalled all that the Lord had done and he prayed to him and said: "O Lord God, almighty King, all things are in your power, and there is no one to oppose you in your will to save Israel. You made heaven and earth and every wonderful thing under the heavens. You are Lord of all, and there is no one who can resist you, Lord. You know all things. You know, O Lord, that it was not out of insolence or pride or desire for fame that I acted thus in not bowing down to the proud Haman. Gladly would I have kissed the soles of his feet for the salvation of Israel. But I acted as I did so as not to place the honor of man above that of God. I will not bow down to anyone but you, my Lord. It is not out of pride that I am acting thus. Hear my prayer; have pity on your inheritance and turn our sorrow into joy: thus we shall live to sing praise to your name, O Lord. Do not silence those who praise you."

---

11   Prv 31, 10-13. 19-20. 30-31

A reading from the book of Proverbs

When one finds a worthy wife,
  her value is far beyond pearls.
Her husband, entrusting his heart to her,
  has an unfailing prize.
She brings him good, and not evil,
  all the days of her life.
She obtains wool and flax
  and makes cloth with skillful hands.
She puts her hands to the distaff,
  and her fingers ply the spindle.
She reaches out her hands to the poor,
  and extends her arms to the needy.
Charm is deceptive and beauty fleeting;
  the woman who fears the Lord is to be praised.
Give her a reward of her labors,
  and let her works praise her at the city gates.

---

12   Sir 2, 7-11

A reading from the book of Sirach

You who fear the Lord, wait for his mercy,
  turn not away lest you fall.
You who fear the Lord, trust him,
  and your reward will not be lost.

You who fear the Lord, hope for good things,
    for lasting joy and mercy.
Study the generations long past and understand;
    has anyone hoped in the Lord and been disappointed?
Has anyone persevered in his fear and been forsaken?
    has anyone called upon him and been rebuffed?
Compassionate and merciful is the Lord;
    he forgives sins, he saves in time of trouble.

---

13   Sir 3, 17-24

A reading from the book of Sirach

My son, conduct your affairs with humility,
    and you will be loved more than a giver of gifts.
Humble yourself the more, the greater you are,
    and you will find favor with God.
For great is the power of God;
    by the humble he is glorified.
What is too sublime for you, seek not,
    into things beyond your strength search not.
What is committed to you, attend to;
    for what is hidden is not your concern.
With what is too much for you meddle not,
    when shown things beyond human understanding.
Their own opinion has misled many,
    and false reasoning unbalanced their judgment.
Where the pupil of the eye is missing, there is no light,
    and where there is no knowledge, there is no wisdom.

---

14   Sir 26, 1-4. 13-16

A reading from the book of Sirach

Happy the husband of a good wife,
    twice-lengthened are his days;
A worthy wife brings joy to her husband,
    peaceful and full is his life.
A good wife is a generous gift
    bestowed upon him who fears the Lord;
Be he rich or poor, his heart is content,
    and a smile is ever on his face.

A gracious wife delights her husband,
  her thoughtfulness puts flesh on his bones;
A gift from the Lord is her governed speech,
  and her firm virtue is of surpassing worth.
Choicest of blessings is a modest wife,
  priceless her chaste person.
Like the sun rising in the Lord's heavens,
  the beauty of a virtuous wife is the radiance of her home.

---

15   Is 58, 6-11

[For those who work for the underprivileged]

A reading from the book of the prophet Isaiah
  Thus says the Lord:
This is the fasting that I wish:
  releasing those bound unjustly,
  untying the thongs of the yoke;
Setting free the oppressed,
  breaking every yoke;
Sharing your bread with the hungry,
  sheltering the oppressed and the homeless;
Clothing the naked when you see them,
  and not turning your back on your own.

Then your light shall break forth like the dawn,
  and your wound shall quickly be healed;
Your vindication shall go before you,
  and the glory of the Lord shall be your rear guard.
Then you shall call, and the Lord will answer,
  you shall cry for help, and he will say: Here I am!
If you remove from your midst oppression,
  false accusation and malicious speech;
If you bestow your bread on the hungry
  and satisfy the afflicted;
Then light shall rise for you in darkness,
  and the gloom shall become for you like midday;
Then the Lord will guide you always
  and give you plenty even on the parched land.
He will renew your strength,
  and you shall be like a watered garden,
  like a spring whose water never fails.

---

16   Jer 20, 7-9

A reading from the book of the prophet Jeremiah

You duped me, O Lord, and I let myself be duped;
  you were too strong for me, and you triumphed.
All the day I am an object of laughter;
  everyone mocks me.
Whenever I speak, I must cry out,
  violence and outrage is my message;
The word of the Lord has brought me
  derision and reproach all the day.
I say to myself, I will not mention him,
  I will speak in his name no more.
But then it becomes like fire burning in my heart,
  imprisoned in my bones;
I grow weary holding it in,
  I cannot endure it.

---

17   Mi 6, 6-8

A reading from the book of the prophet Micah

With what shall I come before the Lord,
  and bow before God most high?
Shall I come before him with holocausts,
  with calves a year old?
Will the Lord be pleased with thousands of rams,
  with myriad streams of oil?
Shall I give my first-born for my crime,
  the fruit of my body for the sin of my soul?
You have been told, O man, what is good,
  and what the Lord requires of you:
Only to do the right and to love goodness,
  and to walk humbly with your God.

---

18   Zep 2, 3; 3, 12-13

A reading from the book of the prophet Zephaniah

Seek the Lord, all you humble of the earth,
  who have observed his law;

Seek justice, seek humility;
  perhaps you may be sheltered
  on the day of the Lord's anger.
But I will leave as a remnant in your midst
  a people humble and lowly,
Who shall take refuge in the name of the Lord:
  the remnant of Israel.
They shall do no wrong
  and speak no lies;
Nor shall there be found in their mouths
  a deceitful tongue;
They shall pasture and couch their flocks
  with none to disturb them.

READING I

IN THE EASTER SEASON

1   Acts 4, 32-35

[For religious]

A reading from the Acts of the Apostles

The community of believers were of one heart and one
mind. None of them ever claimed anything as his own;
rather, everything was held in common. With power the
apostles bore witness to the resurrection of the Lord Jesus,
and great respect was paid to them all; nor was there anyone needy among them, for all who owned property or
houses sold them and donated the proceeds. They used to
lay them at the feet of the apostles to be distributed to
everyone according to his need.

---

2   Rv 3, 14. 20-22

A reading from the book of Revelation

The Amen, the faithful Witness and true, the Source of
God's creation, has this to say: "Here I stand, knocking at
the door. If anyone hears me calling and opens the door,

I will enter his house and have supper with him, and he with me. I will give the victor the right to sit with me on my throne, as I myself won the victory and took my seat beside my Father on his throne.

"Let him who has ears to hear heed the Spirit's word to the churches."

---

3   Rv 19, 1. 5-9

A reading from the book of Revelation

I, John, heard what sounded like the loud song of a great assembly in heaven. They were singing:

"Alleluia!

Salvation, glory, and might belong to our God."

A voice coming from the throne cried out:

"Praise our God, all you his servants,

the small and the great, who revere him!"

Then I heard what sounded like the shouts of a great crowd, or the roaring of the deep, or mighty peals of thunder, as they cried:

"Alleluia!

The Lord is king,

our God, the Almighty!

Let us rejoice and be glad,

and give him glory!

For this is the wedding day of the Lamb,

his bride has prepared herself for the wedding.

She has been given a dress to wear

made of finest linen, brilliant white."

(The linen dress is the virtuous deeds of God's saints.)

The angel then said to me: "Write this down: Happy are they who have been invited to the wedding feast of the Lamb."

---

4   Rv 21, 5-7

A reading from the book of Revelation

The One who sat on the throne said to me, "See, I make all things new!" Then he said, "Write these matters down, for the words are trustworthy and true!" He went on to

say: "These words are already fulfilled! I am the Alpha
and the Omega, the Beginning and the End. To anyone
who thirsts I will give drink without cost from the spring
of life-giving water. He who wins the victory shall inherit
these gifts; I will be his God and he shall be my son."

RESPONSORIAL PSALM

1 Ps 1, 1-2. 3. 4. 6

℟. (Ps 40, 5) **Happy are they who hope in the Lord.**
Happy the man who follows not
    the counsel of the wicked
Nor walks in the way of sinners,
    nor sits in the company of the insolent,
But delights in the law of the Lord.
    and meditates on his law day and night.
℟. **Happy are they who hope in the Lord.**
He is like a tree
    planted near running water,
That yields its fruit in due season,
    and whose leaves never fade.
    [Whatever he does, prospers.]
℟. **Happy are they who hope in the Lord.**
Not so the wicked, not so;
    they are like chaff which the wind drives away.
For the Lord watches over the way of the just,
    but the way of the wicked vanishes.
℟. **Happy are they who hope in the Lord.**
℟. Or: (Ps 92, 13-14) **The just man will flourish like a
    palm tree
  in the garden of the Lord.**

---

2 Ps 15, 2-3. 3-4. 5

℟. (1) **He who does justice shall live on the Lord's holy
    mountain.**
He who walks blamelessly and does justice;
    who thinks the truth in his heart
    and slanders not with his tongue;
℟. **He who does justice shall live on the Lord's holy
    mountain.**

Who harms not his fellow man,
nor takes up a reproach against his neighbor;
By whom the reprobate is despised,
while he honors those who fear the Lord.

℞. **He who does justice shall live on the Lord's holy mountain.**

Who lends not his money at usury
and accepts no bribe against the innocent.
He who does these things
shall never be disturbed.

℞. **He who does justice shall live on the Lord's holy mountain.**

---

3   Ps 16, 1-2. 5. 7-8. 11

℞. (5) **You are my inheritance, O Lord.**
Keep me, O God, for in you I take refuge;
I say to the Lord, "My Lord are you."
O Lord, my allotted portion and my cup,
you it is who hold fast my lot.

℞. **You are my inheritance, O Lord.**

I bless the Lord who counsels me;
even in the night my heart exhorts me.
I set the Lord ever before me;
with him at my right hand I shall not be disturbed.

℞. **You are my inheritance, O Lord.**

You will show me the path to life,
fullness of joys in your presence,
the delights at your right hand forever.

℞. **You are my inheritance, O Lord.**

---

4   Ps 34, 2-3. 4-5. 6-7. 8-9. 10-11

℞. (2) **I will bless the Lord at all times.**
I will bless the Lord at all times;
his praise shall be ever in my mouth.
Let my soul glory in the Lord;
the lowly will hear me and be glad.

℞. **I will bless the Lord at all times.**

Glorify the Lord with me,
let us together extol his name.

I sought the Lord, and he answered me
  and delivered me from all my fears.
℟. **I will bless the Lord at all times.**
Look to him that you may be radiant with joy,
  and your faces may not blush with shame.
When the afflicted man called out, the Lord heard,
  and from all his distress he saved him.
℟. **I will bless the Lord at all times.**
The angel of the Lord encamps
  around those who fear him, and delivers them.
Taste and see how good the Lord is;
  happy the man who takes refuge in him.
℟. **I will bless the Lord at all times.**
Fear the Lord, you his holy ones,
  for nought is lacking to those who fear him.
The great grow poor and hungry;
  but those who seek the Lord want for no good thing.

℟. **I will bless the Lord at all times.**
℟. Or: (9) **Taste and see the goodness of the Lord.**

---

5   Ps 103, 1-2. 3-4. 8-9. 13-14. 17-18

℟. (1) **Oh, bless the Lord, my soul.**
Bless the Lord, O my soul;
  and all my being, bless his holy name.
Bless the Lord, O my soul;
  and forget not all his benefits.
℟. **Oh, bless the Lord, my soul.**
He pardons all your iniquities,
  he heals all your ills.
He redeems your life from destruction,
  he crowns you with kindness and compassion.
℟. **Oh, bless the Lord, my soul.**
Merciful and gracious is the Lord,
  slow to anger and abounding in kindness.
He will not always chide,
  nor does he keep his wrath forever.
℟. **Oh, bless the Lord, my soul.**
As a father has compassion on his children,
  so the Lord has compassion on those who fear him,
For he knows how we are formed;
  he remembers that we are dust.

℟. **Oh, bless the Lord, my soul.**
But the kindness of the Lord is from eternity
   to eternity toward those who fear him,
And his justice toward children's children
   among those who keep his covenant.
℟. **Oh, bless the Lord, my soul.**

----

6   Ps 112, 1-2. 3-4. 5-6. 7-8. 9

℟. (1) **Happy the man who fears the Lord.**
Happy the man who fears the Lord,
   who greatly delights in his commands.
His posterity shall be mighty upon the earth;
   the upright generation shall be blessed.
℟. **Happy the man who fears the Lord.**
Wealth and riches shall be in his house;
   his generosity shall endure forever.
He dawns through the darkness, a light for the upright;
   he is gracious and merciful and just.
℟. **Happy the man who fears the Lord.**
Well for the man who is gracious and lends,
   who conducts his affairs with justice;
He shall never be moved;
   the just man shall be in everlasting remembrance.
℟. **Happy the man who fears the Lord.**
An evil report he shall not fear;
   his heart is firm, trusting in the Lord.
His heart is steadfast; he shall not fear
Till he looks down upon his foes.
℟. **Happy the man who fears the Lord.**
Lavishly he gives to the poor;
   his generosity shall endure forever;
   his horn shall be exalted in glory.
℟. **Happy the man who fears the Lord.**
℟. Or: **Alleluia.**

----

7   Ps 128, 1-2. 3. 4-5

℟. (1) **Happy are those who fear the Lord.**
Happy are you who fear the Lord,
   who walk in his ways!
For you shall eat the fruit of your handiwork;
   happy shall you be, and favored.

℞. **Happy are those who fear the Lord.**
Your wife shall be like a fruitful vine
    in the recesses of your home;
Your children like olive plants
    around your table.
℞. **Happy are those who fear the Lord.**
Behold, thus is the man blessed
    who fears the Lord.
The Lord bless you from Zion:
    may you see the prosperity of Jerusalem
    all the days of your life.
℞. **Happy are those who fear the Lord.**

---

8   Ps 131, 1. 2. 3

℞. **In you, Lord, I have found my peace.**
O Lord, my heart is not proud,
    nor are my eyes haughty;
I busy not myself with great things,
    nor with things too sublime for me.
℞. **In you, Lord, I have found my peace.**
Nay rather, I have stilled and quieted
    my soul like a weaned child.
Like a weaned child on its mother's lap,
    [so is my soul within me.]
℞. **In you, Lord, I have found my peace.**
O Israel, hope in the Lord,
    both now and forever.
℞. **In you, Lord, I have found my peace.**

READING II

1   Rom 8, 26-30

A reading from the letter of Paul to the Romans
The Spirit too helps us in our weakness, for we do not
know how to pray as we ought; but the Spirit himself
makes intercession for us with groanings which cannot
be expressed in speech. He who searches hearts knows
what the Spirit means, for the Spirit intercedes for the
saints as God himself wills.

We know that God makes all things work together for the good of those who have been called according to his decree. Those whom he foreknew he predestined to share the image of his Son, that the Son might be the first-born of many brothers. Those he predestined he likewise called; those he called he also justified; and those he justified he in turn glorified.

2   1 Cor 1, 26-31

A reading from the first letter of Paul to the Corinthians
Brothers, you are among those called. Consider your own situation. Not many of you are wise, as men account wisdom; not many are influential; and surely not many are well-born. God chose these whom the world considers absurd to shame the wise; he singled out the weak of this world to shame the strong. He chose the world's low-born and despised, those who count for nothing, to reduce to nothing those who were something; so that mankind can do no boasting before God. God it is who has given you life in Christ Jesus. He has made him our wisdom and also our justice, our sanctification, and our redemption. This is just as you find it written, "Let him who would boast, boast in the Lord."

3   1 Cor 12, 31— 13, 13 or 13, 4-13

[If the "Short Form" is used, the indented text in brackets is omitted.]

A reading from the first letter of Paul to the Corinthians
[Set your hearts on the greater gifts.
    Now I will show you the way which surpasses all the others. If I speak with human tongues and angelic as well, but not have love, I am a noisy gong, a clanging cymbal. If I have the gift of prophecy and, with full knowledge, comprehend all mysteries, if I have faith great enough to move mountains, but have not love, I am nothing. If I give everything I have to feed the poor and hand over my body to be burned, but have not love, I gain nothing.]

Love is patient; love is kind. Love is not jealous, it does not put on airs, it is not snobbish. Love is never rude, it is not self-seeking, it is not prone to anger; neither does it brood over injuries. Love does not rejoice in what is wrong but rejoices with the truth. There is no limit to love's forbearance, to its trust, its hope, its power to endure.

Love never fails. Prophecies will cease, tongues will be silent, knowledge will pass away. Our knowledge is imperfect and our prophesying is imperfect. When the perfect comes, the imperfect will pass away. When I was a child I used to talk like a child, think like a child, reason like a child. When I became a man I put childish ways aside. Now we see indistinctly, as in a miror; then we shall see face to face. My knowledge is imperfect now; then I shall know even as I am known. These are in the end three things that last: faith, hope, and love, and the greatest of these is love.

---

4 2 Cor 10, 17—11, 2

A reading from the second letter of Paul to the Corinthians
"Let him who would boast, boast in the Lord." It is not the man who recommends himself who is approved but the man whom the Lord recommends.

You must endure a little of my folly. Put up with me, I beg you! I am jealous of you with the jealousy of God himself, since I have given you in marriage to one husband, presenting you as a chaste virgin to Christ.

---

5 Gal 2, 19-20

A reading from the letter of Paul to the Galatians
It was through the law that I died to the law, to live for God. I have been crucified with Christ, and the life I live now is not my own; Christ is living in me. I still live my human life, but it is a life of faith in the Son of God, who loved me and gave himself for me.

6   Gal 6, 14-16

A reading from the letter of Paul to the Galatians

May I never boast of anything but the cross of our Lord
Jesus Christ! Through it, the world has been crucified to
me and I to the world. It means nothing whether one is
circumcised or not. All that matters is that one is created
anew. Peace and mercy on all who follow this rule of life,
and on the Israel of God.

7   Eph 3, 14-19

A reading from the letter of Paul to the Ephesians

I kneel before the Father from whom every family in
heaven and on earth takes its name; and I pray that he
will bestow on you gifts in keeping with the riches of
his glory. May he strengthen you inwardly through the
working of his Spirit. May Christ dwell in your hearts
through faith, and may charity be the root and foundation
of your life. Thus you will be able to grasp fully, with all
the holy ones, the breadth and length and height and
depth of Christ's love, and experience this love which
surpasses all knowledge, so that you may attain to the
fullness of God himself.

------

8   Eph 6, 10-13. 18

A reading from the letter of Paul to the Ephesians

Draw your strength from the Lord and his mighty power.
Put on the armor of God so that you may be able to stand
firm against the tactics of the devil. Our battle ultimately
is not against human forces but against the principalities
and powers, the rulers of this world of darkness, the evil
spirits in regions above. You must put on the armor of
God if you are to resist on the evil day; do all that your
duty requires, and hold your ground.

At every opportunity pray in the Spirit, using prayers
and petitions of every sort. Pray constantly and attentively for all in the holy company.

------

9   Phil 3, 8-14

A reading from the letter of Paul to the Philippians

I have come to rate all as loss in the light of the surpassing knowledge of my Lord Jesus Christ. For his sake
I have forfeited everything; I have accounted all else
rubbish so that Christ may be my wealth and I may be
in him, not having any justice of my own based on observance of the law. The justice I possess is that which
comes through faith in Christ. It has its origin in God
and is based on faith. I wish to know Christ and the power
flowing from his resurrection; likewise to know how to
share in his sufferings by being formed into the pattern
of his death. Thus do I hope that I may arrive at resurrection from the dead.

It is not that I have reached it yet, or have already
finished my course; but I am racing to grasp the prize if
possible, since I have been grasped by Christ [Jesus].
Brothers, I do not think of myself as having reached the
finish line. I give no thought to what lies behind but push
on to what is ahead. My entire attention is on the finish
line as I run toward the prize to which God calls me —
life on high in Christ Jesus.

———————

10   Phil 4, 4-9

A reading from the letter of Paul to the Philippians

Rejoice in the Lord always! I say it again. Rejoice! Everyone should see how unselfish you are. The Lord himself
is near. Dismiss all anxiety from your minds. Present your
needs to God in every form of prayer and in petitions full
of gratitude. Then God's own peace, which is beyond all
understanding, will stand guard over your hearts and
minds, in Christ Jesus.

Finally, my brothers, your thoughts should be wholly
directed to all that is true, all that deserves respect, all
that is honest, pure, admirable, decent, virtuous, or worthy
of praise. Live according to what you have learned and
accepted, what you have heard me say and seen me do.
Then will the God of peace be with you.

———————

11   1 Tm 5, 3-10

[For widows]

A reading from the first letter of Paul to Timothy

Honor the claims of widows who are real widows — that is, who are alone and bereft. If a widow has any children or grandchildren, let these learn that piety begins at home and that they should fittingly support their parents and grandparents; this is the way God wants it to be. The real widow, left destitute, is one who has set her hope on God and continues night and day in supplications and prayers. A widow who gives herself up to selfish indulgence, however, leads a life of living death.

Make the following rules about widows, so that no one may incur blame. If anyone does not provide for his own relatives and especially for members of his immediate family, he has denied the faith; he is worse than an unbeliever. To be on the church's roll of widows, a widow should be not less than sixty years of age. She must have been married only once. Her good character will be attested to by her good deeds. Has she brought up children? Has she been hospitable to strangers? Has she washed the feet of Christian visitors? Has she given help to those in distress? In a word, has she been eager to do every possible good work?

----

12   Jas 2, 14-17

A reading from the letter of James

My brothers, what good is it to profess faith without practicing it? Such faith has no power to save one, has it? If a brother or sister has nothing to wear and no food for the day, and you say to them, "Good-bye and good luck! Keep warm and well fed," but do not meet their bodily needs, what good is that? So it is with the faith that does nothing in practice. It is thoroughly lifeless.

----

13 1 Pt 3, 1-9

A reading from the first letter of Peter

You married women must obey your husbands, so that any of them who do not believe in the word of the gospel may be won over apart from preaching, through their wives' conduct. They have only to observe the reverent purity of your way of life. The affectation of an elaborate hairdress, the wearing of golden jewelry, or the donning of rich robes is not for you. Your adornment is rather the hidden character of the heart, expressed in the unfading beauty of a calm and gentle disposition. This is precious in God's eyes. The holy women of past ages used to adorn themselves in this way, reliant on God and obedient to their husbands — for example, Sarah, who was subject to Abraham and called him her master. You are her children when you do what is right and let no fears alarm you.

You husbands, too, must show consideration for those who share your lives. Treat women with respect as the weaker sex, heirs just as much as you to the gracious gift of life. If you do so, nothing will keep your prayers from being answered.

In summary, then, all of you should be like-minded, sympathetic, loving toward one another, kindly disposed, and humble. Do not return evil for evil or insult for insult. Return a blessing instead. This you have been called to do, that you may receive a blessing as your inheritance.

---

14 1 Pt 4, 7-11

A reading from the first letter of Peter

Remain calm so that you will be able to pray. Above all, let your love for one another be constant, for love covers a multitude of sins. Be mutually hospitable without complaining. As generous distributors of God's manifold grace, put your gifts at the service of one another, each in the measure he has received. The one who speaks is to deliver God's message. The one who serves is to do it with the strength provided by God. Thus, in all of you God is to be glorified through Jesus Christ: to him be glory and dominion throughout the ages. Amen.

---

15   **1 Jn 3, 14-28**

[For those who work for the underprivileged]

A reading from the first letter of John

That we have passed from death to life we know
because we love the brothers.
The man who does not love is among the living dead.
Anyone who hates his brother is a murderer,
and you know that eternal life
abides in no murderer's heart.
The way we came to understand love
was that he laid down his life for us;
we too must lay down our lives for our brothers.
I ask you, how can God's love survive in a man
who has enough of this world's goods
yet closes his heart to his brother
when he sees him in need?
Little children,
let us love in deed
and not merely talk about it.

---

16   **1 Jn 4, 7-16**

A reading from the first letter of John

Beloved,
let us love one another
because love is of God;
everyone who loves is begotten of God
and has knowledge of God.
The man without love has known nothing of God,
for God is love.
God's love was revealed in our midst in this way:
he sent his only Son to the world
that we might have life through him.
Love, then, consists in this:

not that we have loved God
but that he has loved us
and has sent his Son as an offering for our sins.
Beloved,
if God has loved us so,
we must have the same love for one another.
No one has ever seen God.
Yet if we love one another
God dwells in us,
and his love is brought to perfection in us.
The way we know we remain in him
and he in us
is that he has given us of his Spirit.
We have seen for ourselves, and can testify,
that the Father has sent the Son as savior of the
    world.
When anyone acknowledges that Jesus is the Son
    of God,
God dwells in him
and he in God
We have come to know and to believe in
the love God has for us.
God is love,
and he who abides in love
abides in God,
and God in him.

---

17   1 Jn 5, 1-5

A reading from the first letter of John

Everyone who believes that Jesus is the Christ
has been begotten of God.
Now, everyone who loves the father
loves the child he has begotten.
We can be sure that we love God's children
when we love God
and do what he has commanded.
The love of God consists in this:
that we keep his commandments—
and his commandments are not burdensome.
Everyone begotten of God conquers the world,

and the power that has conquered the world
is this faith of ours.
Who, then, is conqueror of the world?
The one who believes that Jesus is the Son of God.

ALLELUIA VERSE AND

VERSE BEFORE THE GOSPEL

1 Mt 5, 3

Happy the poor in spirit;
the kingdom of heaven is theirs!

2 Mt 5, 6

Happy those who hunger and thirst for what is right;
they shall be satisfied.

3 Mt 5, 8

Happy are the pure of heart, for they shall see God.

4 Mt 11, 25

Blessed are you, Father, Lord of heaven and earth;
you have revealed to little ones the mysteries of the
   kingdom.

5 Mt 11, 28

Come to me, all you that labor and are burdened,
and I will give you rest, says the Lord.

6 Jn 8, 12

I am the light of the world, says the Lord;
the man who follows me will have the light of life.

7 Jn 8, 31-32

If you stay in my word, you will indeed be my disciples,
and you will know the truth, says the Lord.

8 Jn 13, 34

I give you a new commandment:
love one another as I have loved you.

9   Jn 14, 23

If anyone loves me, he will hold to my words,
and my Father will love him, and we will come to him.

10   Jn 15, 4-5

Live in me and let me live in you, says the Lord;
my branches bear much fruit.

GOSPEL

1   Mt 5, 1-12

✠ A reading from the holy gospel according to Matthew

When Jesus saw the crowds he went up on the mountainside. After he had sat down his disciples gathered around
him, and he began to teach them:

"How blest are the poor in spirit: the reign of God is
  theirs.

Blest too are the sorrowing; they shall be consoled.

[Blest are the lowly; they shall inherit the land.]

Blest are they who hunger and thirst for holiness;
  they shall have their fill.

Blest are they who show mercy; mercy shall be theirs.

Blest are the single-hearted for they shall see God.

Blest too the peacemakers; they shall be called sons
  of God.

Blest are those persecuted for holiness' sake; the
  reign of God is theirs.

Blest are you when they insult you and persecute you
  and utter every kind of slander against you because
  of me.

Be glad and rejoice, for your reward in heaven is
  great."

---

2   Mt 5, 13-16

✠ A reading from the holy gospel according to Matthew

Jesus said to his disciples: "You are the salt of the earth.
But what if salt goes flat? How can you restore its flavor?

Then it is good for nothing but to be thrown out and trampled underfoot.

"You are the light of the world. A city set on a hill cannot be hidden. Men do not light a lamp and then put it under a bushel basket. They set it on a stand where it gives light to all in the house. In the same way, your light must shine before men so that they may see goodness in your acts and give praise to your heavenly Father."

3   Mt 11, 25-30

✠ A reading from the holy gospel according to Matthew

On one occasion Jesus said: "Father, Lord of heaven and earth, to you I offer praise; for what you have hidden from the learned and the clever you have revealed to the merest children. Father, it is true. You have graciously willed it so. Everything has been given over to me by my Father. No one knows the Son but the Father, and no one knows the Father but the Son—and anyone to whom the Son wishes to reveal him.

"Come to me, all you who are weary and find life burdensome, and I will refresh you. Take my yoke upon your shoulders and learn from me, for I am gentle and humble of heart. Your souls will find rest, for my yoke is easy and my burden light."

4   Mt 13, 44-46

✠ A reading from the holy gospel according to Matthew

Jesus said to the crowds: "The reign of God is like buried treasure which a man found in a field. He hid it again, and rejoicing at his find went and sold all he had and bought that field. Or again, the kingdom of heaven is like a merchant's search for fine pearls. When he found one really valuable pearl, he went back and put up for sale all that he had and bought it."

5

Mt 16, 24-27

✠ A reading from the holy gospel according to Matthew
Jesus said to his disciples: "If a man wishes to come after
me, he must deny his very self, take up his cross, and begin
to follow in my footsteps. Whoever would save his life
will lose it, but whoever loses his life for my sake will
find it. What profit would a man show if he were to gain
the whole world and ruin himself in the process? What
can a man offer in exchange for his very self? The Son
of Man will come with his Father's glory accompanied
by his angels. When he does, he will repay each man
according to his conduct."

6

Mt 18, 1-4

✠ A reading from the holy gospel according to Matthew
The disciples came up to Jesus with the question, "Who
is of greatest importance in the kingdom of God?" He
called a little child over and stood him in their midst and
said: "I assure you, unless you change and become like
little children, you will not enter the kingdom of God.
Whoever makes himself lowly, becoming like this child,
is of greatest importance in that heavenly reign."

7

Mt 19, 3-12

[For religious]

✠ A reading from the holy gospel according to Matthew
Some Pharisees came up to Jesus and said, to test him,
"May a man divorce his wife for any reason whatever?"
He replied, "Have you not read that at the beginning the
Creator made them male and female and declared, 'For
this reason a man shall leave his father and mother and
cling to his wife, and the two shall become as one'? Thus
they are no longer two but one flesh. Therefore, let no
man separate what God has joined." They said to him,
"Then why did Moses command divorce and the promulgation of a divorce decree?" "Because of your stubbornness

Moses let you divorce your wives," he replied; "but at the beginning it was not that way. I now say to you, whoever divorces his wife (lewd conduct is a separate case) and marries another commits adultery, and the man who marries a divorced woman commits adultery."

His disciples said to him, "If that is the case between man and wife, it is better not to marry." He said, "Not everyone can accept this teaching, only those to whom it is given to do so. Some men are incapable of sexual activity from birth; some have been deliberately made so; and some there are who have freely renounced sex for the sake of God's reign. Let him accept this teaching who can."

---

8   Mt 25, 1-13

✠ A reading from the holy gospel according to Matthew

Jesus told this parable to his disciples: "The reign of God can be likened to ten bridesmaids who took their torches and went out to welcome the groom. Five of them were foolish, while the other five were sensible. The foolish ones, in taking their torches, brought no oil along, but the sensible ones took flasks of oil as well as their torches. The groom delayed his coming, so they all began to nod, then to fall asleep. At midnight someone shouted, 'The groom is here! Come out and greet him!' At the outcry all the virgins woke up and got their torches ready. The foolish ones said to the sensible, 'Give us some of your oil. Our torches are going out.' But the sensible ones replied, 'No, there may not be enough for you and us. You had better go to the dealers and buy yourselves some.' While they went off to buy it the groom arrived, and the ones who were ready went in to the wedding with him. Then the door was barred. Later the other bridesmaids came back. 'Master, master!' they cried. 'Open the door for us.' But he answered, 'I tell you, I do not know you.' The moral is: keep your eyes open, for you know not the day or the hour."

---

9   Mt 25, 14-30 or 25, 14-23

[If the "Short Form" is used, the indented text in brackets is omitted.]

✠ A reading from the holy gospel according to Matthew
Jesus told his disciples this parable: "It is the case of a man who was going on a journey. He called in his servants and handed his funds over to them according to each man's abilities. To one he disbursed five thousand silver pieces, to a second two thousand, and to a third a thousand. Then he went away. Immediately the man who received the five thousand went to invest it and made another five. In the same way, the man who received the two thousand doubled his figure. The man who received the thousand went off instead and dug a hole in the ground, where he buried his master's money. After a long absence, the master of those servants came home and settled accounts with them. The man who had received the five thousand came forward bringing the additional five. 'My lord,' he said, 'you let me have five thousand. See, I have made five thousand more.' His master said to him, 'Well done! You are an industrious and reliable servant. Since you were dependable in a small matter I will put you in charge of larger affairs. Come, share your master's joy!' The man who had received the two thousand then stepped forward. 'My lord,' he said, 'you entrusted me with two thousand and I have made two thousand more.' His master said to him, 'Cleverly done! You too are an industrious and reliable servant. Since you were dependable in a small matter I will put you in charge of larger affairs. Come, share your master's joy!'

   ["Finally the man who had received the thousand
   stepped forward. 'My lord,' he said, 'I knew you
   were a hard man. You reap where you did not sow
   and gather where you did not scatter, so out of fear
   I went off and buried your thousand silver pieces
   in the ground. Here is your money back.' His master
   exclaimed: 'You worthless, lazy lout! You know I
   reap where I did not sow and gather where I did not
   scatter. All the more reason to deposit my money
   with the bankers, so that on my return I could have

had it back with interest. You, there! Take the thousand away from him and give it to the man with the ten thousand. Those who have, will get more until they grow rich, while those who have not, will lose even the little they have. Throw this worthless servant into the darkness outside, where he can wail and grind his teeth.' "]

---

10   Mt 25, 31-46 or 25, 31-40

[**For those who work for the underprivileged**]

[If the "Short Form" is used, the indented text in brackets is omitted.]

✠ A reading from the holy gospel according to Matthew

Jesus said to his disciples: "When the Son of Man comes in his glory, escorted by all the angels of heaven, he will sit upon his royal throne, and all the nations will be assembled before him. Then he will separate them into two groups, as a shepherd separates sheep from goats. The sheep he will place on his right hand, the goats on his left. The king will say to those on his right: 'Come. You have my Father's blessing! Inherit the kingdom prepared for you from the creation of the world. For I was hungry and you gave me food, I was thirsty and you gave me drink. I was a stranger and you welcomed me, naked and you clothed me. I was ill and you comforted me, in prison and you came to visit me.' Then the just will ask him: 'Lord, when did we see you hungry and feed you or see you thirsty and give you drink? When did we welcome you away from home or clothe you in your nakedness? When did we visit you when you were ill or in prison?' The king will answer them: 'I assure you, as often as you did it for one of my least brothers, you did it for me.'

["Then he will say to those on his left: 'Out of my sight, you condemned, into that everlasting fire prepared for the devil and his angels! I was hungry and you gave me no food, I was thirsty and you gave me no drink. I was away from home and you gave me no welcome, naked and you gave me no clothing. I was ill and in prison and you did not come to comfort me.' Then they in turn will ask: 'Lord, when did we see you hungry or thirsty or away from home or naked or ill or in prison and not attend you in your needs?' He will answer them: 'I assure you, as often as you neglected to do it to one of these least ones, you neglected to do it to me.' These will go off to eternal punishment and the just to eternal life."]

----

11   Mk 3, 31-35

✠ A reading from the holy gospel according to Mark

The mother of Jesus and his brothers arrived, and as they stood outside [the house] they sent word to Jesus to come out. The crowd seated around him told him, "Your mother and your brothers and sisters are outside asking for you." He said in reply, "Who are my mother and my brothers?" And gazing around him at those seated in the circle he continued, "These are my mother and my brothers. Whoever does the will of God is brother and sister and mother to me."

----

12   Mk 9, 34-37

[For teachers]

✠ A reading from the holy gospel according to Mark

The disciples of Jesus had been arguing along the way about who was the most important. So he sat down and called the Twelve around him and said, "If anyone wishes to rank first, he must remain the last one of all and the servant of all." Then he took a little child, stood him in their midst, and putting his arms around him, said to them, "Whoever welcomes a child such as this for my sake welcomes me. And whoever welcomes me welcomes, not me, but him who sent me."

---

13   Mk 10, 13-16

[For teachers]

✠ A reading from the holy gospel according to Mark

People were bringing their little children to Jesus to have him touch them, but the disciples were scolding them for this. Jesus became indignant when he noticed it and said to them: "Let the children come to me and do not hinder them. It is to just such as these that the kingdom of God belongs. I assure you that whoever does not accept the kingdom of God like a little child shall not enter into it." Then he embraced them and blessed them, placing his hands on them.

---

14   Mk 10, 17-30 or 10, 17-27

[If the "Short Form" is used, the indented text in brackets is omitted.]

[For religious]

✠ A reading from the holy gospel according to Mark

As Jesus was setting out on a journey a man came running up, knelt down before him and asked, "Good Teacher, what must I do to share in everlasting life?" Jesus answered, "Why do you call me good? No one is good but God alone. You know the commandments:

'You shall not kill;
You shall not commit adultery;
You shall not steal;
You shall not bear false witness;
You shall not defraud;
Honor your father and your mother.' "

He replied, "Teacher, I have kept all these since my childhood." Then Jesus looked at him with love and told him,
"There is one thing more you must do. Go and sell what
you have and give to the poor; you will then have treasure
in heaven. After that come and follow me." At these words
the man's face fell. He went away sad, for he had many
possessions. Jesus looked around and said to his disciples,
"How hard it is for the rich to enter the kingdom of God!"
The disciples could only marvel at his words. So Jesus repeated what he had said: "My sons, how hard it is to enter
the kingdom of God! It is easier for a camel to pass through
a needle's eye than for a rich man to enter the kingdom of
God."

They were completely overwhelmed at this, and exclaimed to one another, "Then who can be saved?" Jesus
fixed his gaze on them and said, "For man it is impossible
but not for God. With God all things are possible."

> [Peter was moved to say to him: "We have put
> aside everything to follow you!" Jesus answered: "I
> give you my word, there is no one who has given up
> home, brothers or sisters, mother or father, children
> or property, for me and for the gospel who will not
> receive in this present age a hundred times as many
> homes, brothers and sisters, mothers, children and
> property—and persecution besides—and in the age
> to come, everlasting life."]

15

Lk 9, 57-62

[For religious]

✠ A reading from the holy gospel according to Luke
As Jesus and his disciples were making their way along,
someone said to him, "I will be your follower wherever you

go." Jesus said to him, "The foxes have lairs, the birds of the sky have nests, but the Son of Man has nowhere to lay his head." To another he said, "Come after me." The man replied, "Let me bury my father first." Jesus said to him, "Let the dead bury their dead; come away and proclaim the kingdom of God." Yet another said to him, "I will be your follower, Lord, but first let me take leave of my people at home." Jesus answered him, "Whoever puts his hand to the plow but keeps looking back is unfit for the reign of God."

16   Lk 10, 38-42

✠ A reading from the holy gospel according to Mark

Jesus entered a village where a woman named Martha welcomed him to her home. She had a sister named Mary, who seated herself at the Lord's feet and listened to his words. Martha, who was busy with all the details of hospitality, came to him and said, "Lord, are you not concerned that my sister has left me all alone to do the household tasks? Tell her to help me."

The Lord in reply said to her: "Martha, Martha, you are anxious and upset about many things; one thing only is required. Mary has chosen the better portion and she shall not be deprived of it."

17   Lk 12, 32-34

[For religious]

✠ A reading from the holy gospel according to Luke

Jesus said to his disciples: "Do not live in fear, little flock. It has pleased your Father to give you the kingdom. Sell what you have and give alms. Get purses for yourselves that do not wear out, a never-failing treasure with the Lord which no thief comes near nor any moth destroys. Wherever your treasure lies, there your heart will be."

18 Lk 12, 35-40

✠ A reading from the holy gospel according to Luke

Jesus said to his disciples: "Let your belts be fastened around your waists and your lamps be burning ready. Be like men awaiting their master's return from a wedding, so that when he arrives and knocks, you will open for him without delay. It will go well with those servants whom the master finds wide-awake on his return. I tell you, he will put on an apron, seat them at table, and proceed to wait on them. Should he happen to come at midnight or before sunrise and find them prepared, it will go well with them. You know as well as I that if the head of the house knew when the thief was coming he would not let him break into his house. Be on guard, therefore. The Son of Man will come when you least expect him."

19 Lk 14, 25-33

[For religious]

✠ A reading from the holy gospel according to Luke

On one occasion when a great crowd was with Jesus, he turned to them and said, "If anyone comes to me without turning his back on his father and mother, his wife and his children, his brothers and sisters, indeed his very self, he cannot be my follower. Anyone who does not take up his cross and follow me cannot be my disciple. If one of you decides to build a tower, will he not first sit down and calculate the outlay to see if he has enough money to complete the project? He will do that for fear of laying the foundation and then not being able to complete the work; at which all who saw it would then jeer at him, saying, 'That man began to build what he could not finish.'

"Or if a king is about to march on another king to do battle with him, will he not sit down first and consider whether, with ten thousand men, he can withstand an enemy coming against him with twenty thousand? If he cannot, he will send a delegation while the enemy is still at a distance, asking for terms of peace. In the same way, none of you can be my disciple if he does not renounce all his possessions."

————————

20   Jn 15, 1-8

✠ A reading from the holy gospel according to John

Jesus said to his disciples:
    "I am the true vine
    and my Father is the vinegrower.
    He prunes away
    every barren branch,
    but the fruitful ones
    he trims clean
    to increase their yield.
    You are clean already,
    thanks to the word I have spoken to you.
    Live on in me, as I do in you.
    No more than a branch can bear fruit of itself
    apart from the vine
    can you bear fruit
    apart from me.
    I am the vine, you are the branches.
    He who lives in me and I in him,
    will produce abundantly,
    for apart from me you can do nothing.

    A man who does not live in me
    is like a withered, rejected branch,
    picked up to be thrown in the fire and burnt.
    If you live in me,
    and my words stay a part of you,
    you may ask what you will—
    it will be done for you.
    My Father has been glorified
    in your bearing much fruit
    and becoming my disciples."

————————

21   Jn 15, 9-17

✠ A reading from the holy gospel according to John

Jesus said to his disciples:
  "As the Father has loved me,
    so I have loved you.
  Live on in my love.
  You will live in my love
  if you keep my commandments,
    even as I have kept my Father's commandments,
  and live in his love.
  All this I tell you
  that my joy may be yours
  and your joy may be complete.
  This is my commandment:
  love one another
    as I have loved you.
  There is no greater love than this:
  to lay down one's life for one's friends.
  You are my friends
  if you do what I command you.
  I no longer speak of you as slaves,
  for a slave does not know what his master is about.
  Instead, I call you friends,
  since I have made known to you all that I heard from
    my Father.
  It was not you who chose me,
  it was I who chose you
  to go forth and to bear fruit.
  Your fruit must endure
  so that all you ask the Father in my name
  he will give you.
  The command I give you is this,
  that you love one another."

✠ A reading from the holy gospel according to John

Jesus looked up to heaven and prayed:

"Holy Father,
I do not pray for my disciples alone.
I pray also for those who will believe in me through
    their word,
that all may be one
as you, Father, are in me, and I in you;
I pray that they may be [one] in us,
that the world may believe that you sent me.
I have given them the glory you gave me
that they may be one as we are one—
I living in them, you living in me—
that their unity may be complete.
So shall the world know that you sent me,
and that you loved them as you loved me.

"Father,
all those you gave me
I would have in my company
where I am,
to see this glory of mine
which is your gift to me,
because of the love you bore me before the world
    began.
Just Father,
the world has not known you,
but I have known you;
and these men have known that you sent me.
To them I have revealed your name,
and I will continue to reveal it
so that your love for me may live in them,
and I may live in them."

APPENDIX I:
SELECTED MASSES AND PRAYERS

This section contains excerpts of selected Masses and Prayers that the celebrant may use on certain days of low rank. (See Tables of Choices of Masses and Texts, pp. [18]-[19].) For convenient reference the numbers attached to these Masses and Prayers in the Sacramentary have been retained. The complete series of Masses and Prayers (including the Readings) for Various Needs and Occasions, Votive Masses, and Masses for the Dead will be found in the last volume of this Weekday Missal. It is always preferable to use *weekday* Readings, as indicated herein.

MASSES AND PRAYERS FOR VARIOUS NEEDS AND OCCASIONS

On Weekdays of Ordinary Time and certain other occasions, the complete Mass formulary found in the Sacramentary (processional chants and presidential prayers) or only the Opening Prayer may be taken from the following Masses and Prayers for Various Needs and Occasions. (See Introduction to Proper of Saints, pp. 917ff and the Tables of Choices of Masses and Texts, pp. [18]-[19].)

1. FOR THE UNIVERSAL CHURCH

OPENING PRAYER

God our Father,
in your care and wisdom
you extend the kingdom of Christ to embrace the
    world
to give all men redemption.
May the Catholic Church be the sign of our salvation,
may it reveal for us the mystery of your love,
and may that love become effective in our lives.
Grant this . . . for ever and ever. ℟. **Amen.**

PRAYER OVER THE GIFTS

God of mercy,
look on our offering,

and by the power of this sacrament
help all who believe in you
to become the holy people you have called to be
    your own.
We ask this in the name of Jesus the Lord. ℟. **Amen.**

PRAYER AFTER COMMUNION

God our Father,
we are sustained by your sacraments;
we are renewed by this pledge of love at your altar.
May we live by the promises of your love which we
    receive,
and become a leaven in the world
to bring salvation to mankind.
Grant this through Christ our Lord. ℟. **Amen.**

---

2. FOR THE POPE

OPENING PRAYER

Father of providence,
look with love on N. our Pope,
your appointed successor to St. Peter
on whom you built your Church.
May he be the visible center and foundation
of our unity in faith and love.
Grant this . . . for ever and ever. ℟. **Amen.**

PRAYER OVER THE GIFTS

Lord,
be pleased with our gifts
and give guidance to your holy Church
together with N. our Pope,
to whom you have entrusted the care of your flock.
We ask this in the name of Jesus the Lord. ℟. **Amen.**

PRAYER AFTER COMMUNION

God our Father,
we have eaten at your holy table.
By the power of this sacrament,

make your Church firm in unity and love,
and grant strength and salvation
to your servant N.,
together with the flock you have entrusted to his
care.
Grant this through Christ our Lord. ℟. **Amen.**

---

3. FOR THE BISHOP

OPENING PRAYER

God, eternal shepherd,
you tend your Church in many ways,
and rule us with love.
Help your chosen servant N.
as pastor for Christ,
to watch over your flock.
Help him to be a faithful teacher,
a wise administrator, and a holy priest.
We ask this . . . for ever and ever. ℟. **Amen.**

PRAYER OVER THE GIFTS

Lord,
accept these gifts which we offer for your servant
N., your chosen priest.
Enrich him with the gifts and virtues of a true apostle
for the good of your people.
We ask this through Christ our Lord. ℟. **Amen.**

PRAYER AFTER COMMUNION

Lord,
by the power of these holy mysteries
increase in our bishop N. your gifts of wisdom and
love.
May he fulfill his pastoral ministry
and receive the eternal rewards
you promise to your faithful servants.
Grant this through Christ our Lord. ℟. **Amen.**

---

4. ON THE ANNIVERSARY OF ORDINATION

OPENING PRAYER

Father,
unworthy as I am, you have chosen me
to share in the eternal priesthood of Christ
and the ministry of your Church.
May I be an ardent but gentle servant
of your gospel and your sacraments.
Grant this . . . for ever and ever. ℞. **Amen.**

PRAYER OVER THE GIFTS

Lord,
in your mercy, accept our offering
and help me to fulfill the ministry you have given me
in spite of my unworthiness.
Grant this through Christ our Lord. ℞. **Amen.**

PRAYER AFTER COMMUNION

Lord,
on this anniversary of my ordination
I have celebrated the mystery of faith
to the glory of your name.
May I always live in truth
the mysteries I handle at your altar.
Grant this in the name of Jesus the Lord. ℞. **Amen.**

---

9. FOR PRIESTLY VOCATIONS

ENTRANCE ANT. Mt 9, 38

**Jesus says to his disciples: ask the Lord to send
workers into his harvest.** ➔ No. 2, p. 614

OPENING PRAYER

Father,
in your plan for our salvation you provide shepherds
for your people.
Fill your Church with the spirit of courage and love.
Raise up worthy ministers for your altars

and ardent but gentle servants of the gospel.
Grant this . . . for ever and ever. ℟. **Amen.**

READINGS AND INTERVENIENT CHANTS

The current weekday *readings and intervenient chants
are used.*

PRAYER OVER THE GIFTS

Lord,
accept our prayers and gifts.
Give the Church more priests
and keep them faithful in their love and service.
Grant this in the name of Jesus the Lord.
℟. **Amen.**   ➜ No. 21, p. 626

COMMUNION ANT.   1 Jn 3, 16

**This is how we know what love is: Christ gave up his
life for us; and we too must give up our lives for our
brothers.** ↓

PRAYER AFTER COMMUNION

Lord,
hear the prayers of those who are renewed
with the bread of life at your holy table.
By this sacrament of love
bring to maturity
the seeds you have sown
in the field of your Church;
may many of your people choose to serve you
by devoting themselves to the service of their bro-
    thers and sisters.
We ask this through Christ our Lord.
℟. **Amen.**   ➜ No. 32, p. 650

---

11. FOR RELIGIOUS VOCATIONS

ENTRANCE ANT.   Mt 19, 21

**If you want to be perfect, go, sell what you own,
give it all to the poor, then come, follow me.**
                                        ➜ No. 2, p. 614

OPENING PRAYER

Father,
you call all who believe in you to grow perfect in love
by following in the footsteps of Christ your Son.
May those whom you have chosen to serve you as
   religious
provide by their way of life
a convincing sign of your kingdom
for the Church and the whole world.
We ask this . . . for ever and ever. ℟. **Amen.** ✟

READINGS AND INTERVENIENT CHANTS

The current weekday *readings and intervenient chants
are used.*

PRAYER OVER THE GIFTS

Father,
in your love accept the gifts we offer you,
and watch over those who wish to follow your Son
   more closely,
and to serve you joyfully in religious life.
Give them spiritual freedom
and love for their brothers and sisters.
We ask this through Christ our Lord.

℟. **Amen.** → No. 21, p. 626

COMMUNION ANT. See Mt 19, 27-29

**I solemnly tell you: those who have left everything
and followed me will be repaid a hundredfold and
will gain eternal life.** ✟

PRAYER AFTER COMMUNION

Father, make your people grow strong
by sharing this spiritual food and drink.
Keep them faithful to the call of the gospel
that the world may see in them
the living image of your Son, Jesus Christ,
who is Lord for ever and ever.

℟. **Amen.** → No. 32, p. 650

12. FOR THE LAITY

OPENING PRAYER

God our Father,
you send the power of the gospel into the world
as a life-giving leaven.
Fill with the Spirit of Christ
those whom you call to live in the midst of the
    world
and its concerns;
help them by their work on earth
to build up your eternal kingdom.
We ask this . . . for ever and ever. ℟. **Amen.**

PRAYER OVER THE GIFTS

Father, you gave given your Son
to save the whole world by his sacrifice.
By the power of this offering,
help all your people
to fill the world with the Spirit of Christ.
Grant this through Christ our Lord. ℟. **Amen.**

PRAYER AFTER COMMUNION

Lord,
you share with us the fullness of your love,
and give us new courage at this eucharistic feast.
May the people you call to work in the world
be effective witnesses to the truth of the gospel
and make your Church a living presence
in the midst of that world.
We ask this through Christ our Lord. ℟. **Amen.**

13. FOR UNITY OF CHRISTIANS

ENTRANCE ANT.   Jn 10, 14-15

I am the Good Shepherd. I know my sheep, and mine
know me, says the Lord, just as the Father knows
me and I know the Father. I give my life for my
sheep.   ➜ No. 2, p. 614

OPENING PRAYER

Almighty and eternal God,
keep together those you have united.
Look kindly on all who follow Jesus your Son.
We are all consecrated to you by our common baptism;
make us one in the fullness of faith
and keep us one in the fellowship of love.
We ask this . . . for ever and ever. ℟. **Amen.** ↓

READINGS AND INTERVENIENT CHANTS

The current weekday *readings and intervenient chants are used.*

PRAYER OVER THE GIFTS

Lord,
by one perfect sacrifice
you gained us as your people.
Bless us and all your Church
with gifts of unity and peace.
We ask this in the name of Jesus the Lord.
℟. **Amen.** → No. 21, p. 626 (P 76)

COMMUNION ANT. See 1 Cor 10, 17

Because there is one bread, we, though many, are one body, for we all share in the one loaf and in the one cup. ↓

PRAYER AFTER COMMUNION

Lord,
may this holy communion,
the sign and promise of our unity in you,
make that unity a reality in your Church.
We ask this through Christ our Lord.
℟. **Amen.** → No. 32, p. 650

14. FOR THE SPREAD OF THE GOSPEL

OPENING PRAYER
God our Father,
you will all men to be saved
and come to the knowledge of your truth.
Send workers into your great harvest
that the gospel may be preached to every creature
and your people, gathered together by the word of
life
and srengthened by the power of the sacraments,
may advance in the way of salvation and love.
We ask this . . . for ever and ever. ℟. **Amen.**

PRAYER OVER THE GIFTS
Lord,
look upon the face of Christ your Son
who gave up his life to set all men free.
Through him may your name be praised
among all peoples from East to West,
and everywhere may one sacrifice be offered to give
you glory.
We ask this through Christ our Lord. ℟. **Amen.**

PRAYER AFTER COMMUNION
Lord,
you renew our life with this gift of redemption.
Through this help to eternal salvation
may the true faith continue to grow throughout the
world.
We ask this in the name of Jesus the Lord. ℟. **Amen.**

---

16. FOR PASTORAL OR SPIRITUAL MEETINGS

ENTRANCE ANT.   Mt 18, 20
**Where two or three are gathered together in my
name, says the Lord, I am there among them.**

➤ No. 2, p. 614

OPENING PRAYER

Lord,
pour out on us the spirit of understanding, truth,
    and peace.
Help us to strive with all our hearts
to know what is pleasing to you,
and when we know your will
make us determined to do it.
We ask this . . . for ever and ever. ℟. **Amen.** ▼

READINGS AND INTERVENIENT CHANTS

The current weekday *readings and intervenient chants
are used.*

PRAYER OVER THE GIFTS

God our Father,
look with love on the gifts of your people.
Help us to understand what is right and good in
    your sight
and to proclaim it faithfully to our brothers and
    sisters.
We ask this through Christ our Lord.
℟. **Amen.** ➔ No. 21, p. 626

COMMUNION ANT.

**Where charity and love are found, God is there.
The love of Christ has gathered us together.** ▼

PRAYER AFTER COMMUNION

God of mercy,
may the holy gifts we receive
give us strength in doing your will,
and make us effective witnesses of your truth
to all whose lives we touch.
We ask this in the name of Jesus the Lord.
℟. **Amen.** ➔ No. 32, p. 650

17. FOR THE NATION, (STATE,) OR CITY

OPENING PRAYER

God our Father,
you guide everything in wisdom and love.
Accept the prayers we offer for our nation;
by the wisdom of our leaders and integrity of our
    citizens,
may harmony and justice be secured
and may there be lasting prosperity and peace.
We ask this . . . for ever and ever. ℟. **Amen.**

18. FOR THOSE WHO SERVE IN PUBLIC OFFICE

OPENING PRAYER

Almighty and eternal God,
you know the longings of men's hearts
and you protect their rights.
In your goodness,
watch over those in authority,
so that people everywhere may enjoy
freedom, security, and peace.
We ask this . . . for ever and ever. ℟. **Amen.** ℣

19. FOR THE ASSEMBLY OF NATIONAL LEADERS

OPENING PRAYER

Father,
you guide and govern everything with order and love.
Look upon the assembly of our national leaders
and fill them with the spirit of your wisdom.
May they always act in accordance with your will
and their decisions be for the peace and well-being
    of all.
We ask this . . . for ever and ever. ℟. **Amen.**

22. FOR PEACE AND JUSTICE

ENTRANCE ANT. See Sir 36, 18-19

Give peace, Lord, to those who wait for you; listen to the prayers of your servants, and guide us in the way of justice. ➤ No. 2, p. 614

OPENING PRAYER

God our Father,
you revealed that those who work for peace
will be called your sons.
Help us to work without ceasing
for that justice
which brings true and lasting peace.
We ask this . . . for ever and ever. ℟. **Amen.**

READINGS AND INTERVENIENT CHANTS

The current weekday *readings and intervenient chants are used.*

PRAYER OVER THE GIFTS

Lord,
may the saving sacrifice of your Son, our King and
    peacemaker,
which we offer through these sacramental signs of
    unity and peace,
bring harmony and concord to all your children.
We ask this through Christ our Lord.
℟. **Amen.** ➤ No. 21, p. 626

COMMUNION ANT. Jn 14, 27

Peace I leave with you, my own peace I give you, says the Lord. ℣

PRAYER AFTER COMMUNION

Lord, you give us the body and blood of your Son
and renew our strength.
Fill us with the spirit of love
that we may work effectively to establish among
    men

Christ's farewell gift of peace.
We ask this through Christ our Lord.
℟. **Amen.**   ➜ No. 32, p. 650

25. FOR THE BLESSING OF MAN'S LABOR

OPENING PRAYER

God our Creator,
it is your will that man accept the duty of work.
In your kindness may the work we begin
bring us growth in this life
and help to extend the kingdom of Christ.
We ask this . . . for ever and ever. ℟. **Amen.**

PRAYER OVER THE GIFTS

God our Father,
you provide the human race with food for strength
and with the eucharist for its renewal;
may these gifts which we offer
always bring us health of mind and body.
Grant this through Christ our Lord. ℟. **Amen.**

PRAYER AFTER COMMUNION

Lord,
hear the prayers
of those who gather at your table of unity and love.
By doing the work you have entrusted to us
may we sustain our life on earth
and build up your kingdom in faith.
Grant this through Christ our Lord. ℟. **Amen.**

28A. FOR THOSE WHO SUFFER FROM FAMINE

OPENING PRAYER

All-powerful Father,
God of goodness,
you provide for all your creation.

Give us an effective love for our brothers and sisters
who suffer from lack of food.
Help us do all we can to relieve their hunger,
that they may serve you with carefree hearts.
We ask this . . . for ever and ever. R̀. **Amen.**

PRAYER OVER THE GIFTS

Lord,
look upon this offering which we make to you
from the many good things you have given us.
This eucharist is the sign of your abundant life
and the unity of all men in your love.
May it keep us aware of our Christian duty
We ask this through Christ our Lord. R̀. **Amen.**

PRAYER AFTER COMMUNION

God, all-powerful Father,
may the living bread from heaven
give us the courage and strength
to go to the aid of our hungry brothers and sisters.
We ask this through Christ our Lord. R̀. **Amen.**

---

32. FOR THE SICK

ENTRANCE ANT. Ps 6, 3
**Have mercy on me, God, for I am sick; heal me, Lord,
my bones are racked with pain.**

OR See Is 53, 4
**The Lord has truly borne our sufferings; he has
carried all our sorrows.** ➤ No. 2, p. 614

OPENING PRAYER

Father,
to teach us the virtue of patience in human illness.
your Son accepted our sufferings
Hear the prayers we offer for our sick brothers and
    sisters.
May all who suffer pain, illness or disease

realize that they are chosen to be saints,
and know that they are joined to Christ
in his suffering for the salvation of the world,
who lives and reigns with you and the Holy Spirit,
one God, for ever and ever. ℟. **Amen.** ♥

OR

All-powerful and ever-living God,
the lasting health of all who believe in you,
hear us as we ask your loving help for the sick;
restore their health,
that they may again offer joyful thanks in your
    Church.
Grant this . . . for ever and ever. ℟. **Amen.** ♥

READINGS AND INTERVENIENT CHANTS

The current weekday *readings and intervenient chants
are used.*

PRAYER OVER THE GIFTS

God our Father,
your love guides every moment of our lives.
Accept the prayers and gifts we offer
for our sick brothers and sisters;
restore them to health
and turn our anxiety for them into joy.
We ask this in the name of Jesus the Lord.
℟. **Amen.**   ➔ No. 21, p. 626

COMMUNION ANT.   Col 1, 24

**I will make up in my own body what is lacking in
the suffering of Christ, for the sake of his body, the
Church.** ♥

PRAYER AFTER COMMUNION

God our Father,
our help in human weakness,
show our sick brothers and sisters
the power of your loving care.
In your kindness make them well

and restore them to your Church.
We ask this through Christ our Lord.
℟. **Amen.** ➤ No. 32, p. 650

---

33. FOR THE DYING

Mass for the Sick, p. 1247, with the following prayers:

OPENING PRAYER

God of power and mercy,
you have made death itself
the gateway to eternal life.
Look with love on our dying brother (sister),
and make him (her) one with your Son in his suffering and death,
that, sealed with the blood of Christ,
he (she) may come before you free from sin.
We ask this . . . for ever and ever. ℟. **Amen.**

PRAYER OVER THE GIFTS

Father, accept this sacrifice we offer
for our dying brother (sister),
and by it free him (her) from all his (her) sins.
As he (she) accepted the sufferings you asked him (her) to bear in this life,
may he (she) enjoy happiness and peace for ever in the life to come.
We ask this through Christ our Lord.
℟. **Amen.** ➤ No. 21, p. 626

PRAYER AFTER COMMUNION

Lord, by the power of this sacrament,
keep your servant safe in your love.
Do not let evil conquer him (her) at the hour of death,
but let him (her) go in the company of your angels
to the joy of eternal life.
We ask this through Christ our Lord.
℟. **Amen.** ➤ No. 32, p. 650

34. IN TIME OF EARTHQUAKE

OPENING PRAYER

God our Father,
you set the earth on its foundation.
Keep us safe from the danger of earthquakes
and let us always feel the presence of your love.
May we be secure in your protection
and serve you with grateful hearts.
We ask this . . . for ever and ever. ℟. **Amen.**

---

35. FOR RAIN

OPENING PRAYER

Lord God,
in you we live and move and have our being.
Help us in our present time of trouble,
send us the rain we need,
and teach us to seek your lasting help
on the way to eternal life.
We ask this . . . for ever and ever. ℟. **Amen.**

---

36. FOR FINE WEATHER

OPENING PRAYER

All-powerful and ever-living God,
we find security in your forgiveness.
Give us the fine weather we pray for
and use them always for your glory and our good.
We ask this . . . for ever and ever. ℟. **Amen.**

---

38. FOR ANY NEED

ENTRANCE ANT.

I am the Savior of all people, says the Lord. Whatever their troubles, I will answer their cry, and I will always be their Lord. ➜ No. 2, p. 614

OPENING PRAYER

God our Father,
our strength in adversity,
our health in weakness,
our comfort in sorrow,
be merciful to your people.
As you have given us the punishment we deserve,
give us also new life and hope as we rest in your
    kindness.
We ask this . . . for ever and ever. ℞. **Amen.**

READINGS AND INTERVENIENT CHANTS

The current weekday *readings and intervenient chants
are used.*

PRAYER OVER THE GIFTS

Lord,
receive the prayers and gifts we offer:
may your merciful love set us free from the punish-
    ment we receive for our sins.
We ask this in the name of Jesus the Lord.
℞. **Amen.**   ➤ No. 21, p. 626

COMMUNION ANT.   Mt 11, 28

**Come to me, all you that labor and are burdened,
and I will give you rest, says the Lord.** ⅴ

PRAYER AFTER COMMUNION

Lord, look kindly on us in our sufferings,
and by the death your Son endured for us
turn away from us your anger
and the punishment our sins deserve.
We ask this through Christ our Lord.
℞. **Amen.**   ➤ No. 32, p. 650

---

39. IN THANKSGIVING

ENTRANCE ANT.   Eph 5, 19-20

Sing and play music in your hearts to the Lord,

always giving thanks for everything to God the
Father in the name of our Lord Jesus Christ.

➤ No. 2, p. 614

OPENING PRAYER

Father of mercy,
you always answer your people in their sufferings.
We thank you for your kindness
and ask you to free us from all evil,
that we may serve you in happiness all our days.
We ask this . . . for ever and ever. ℞. **Amen.** ℣

READINGS AND INTERVENIENT CHANTS

The current weekday *readings and intervenient chants
are used.*

PRAYER OVER THE GIFTS

Lord,
you gave us your only Son
to free us from death and from every evil.
Mercifully accept this sacrifice
in gratitude for saving us from our distress.
We ask this through Christ our Lord.
℞. **Amen.**

➤ No. 21, p. 626 (P 40)

COMMUNION ANT.   Ps 138, 1

**I will give thanks to you with all my heart, O Lord,
for you have answered me.** ℣

OR   Ps 116, 12-13

**What return can I make to the Lord for all that he
gives to me? I will take the cup of salvation, and call
on the name of the Lord.** ℣

PRAYER AFTER COMMUNION

All-powerful God,
by this bread of life
you free your people from the power of sin
and in your love renew their strength.

Help us grow constantly in the hope of eternal glory.
Grant this through Christ our Lord.
℞. **Amen.** → No. 32, p. 650

----

44. FOR RELATIVES AND FRIENDS

OPENING PRAYER
Father,
by the power of your Spirit
you have filled the hearts of your faithful people
with gifts of love for one another.
Hear the prayers we offer for our relatives and
friends.
Give them health of mind and body
that they may do your will with perfect love.
We ask this . . . for ever and ever. ℞. **Amen.**

PRAYER OVER THE GIFTS
Lord,
have mercy on our relatives and friends
for whom we offer this sacrifice of praise.
May these holy gifts gain them the help of your
blessing
and bring them to the joy of eternal glory.
We ask this through Christ our Lord. ℞. **Amen.**

PRAYER AFTER COMMUNION
Lord,
we who receive these holy mysteries
pray for the relatives and friends you have given us
in love.
Pardon their sins.
Give them your constant encouragement
and guide them throughout their lives,
until the day when we, with all who have served you,
will rejoice in your presence for ever.
Grant this through Christ our Lord. ℞. **Amen.**

VOTIVE MASSES

(For rules governing these Masses, see p. 1234)

2. HOLY CROSS

ENTRANCE ANT. See Gal 6, 14

We should glory in the cross of our Lord Jesus Christ, for he is our salvation, our life and our resurrection; through him we are saved and made free.

➤ No. 2, p. 614

OPENING PRAYER

God our Father,
in obedience to you
your only Son accepted death on the cross
for the salvation of mankind.
We acknowledge the mystery of the cross on earth.
May we receive the gift of redemption in heaven.
We ask this . . . for ever and ever. ℟. **Amen.** ▼

READINGS AND INTERVENIENT CHANTS

The current weekday readings and intervenient chants are used.

PRAYER OVER THE GIFTS

Lord,
may this sacrifice once offered on the cross
to take away the sins of the world
now free us from our sins.
We ask this through Christ our Lord.
℟. **Amen.** ➤ No. 21, p. 626 (Pref. P 17)

COMMUNION ANT. Jn 12, 32

When I am lifted up from the earth, I will draw all men to myself, says the Lord. ▼

PRAYER AFTER COMMUNION

Lord Jesus Christ,
you are the holy bread of life.
Bring to the glory of the resurrection

the people you have redeemed by the wood of the
cross.

We ask this through Christ our Lord.

℟. **Amen.** ➔ No. 32, p. 650

3B. HOLY EUCHARIST
JESUS THE HIGH PRIEST

ENTRANCE ANT. Ps 109, 4

**The Lord has sworn an oath and he will not retract:
you are a priest for ever, in the line of Melchisedech.**

➔ No. 2, p. 614

OPENING PRAYER

Father,

for your glory and our salvation

you appointed Jesus Christ eternal High Priest.

May the people he gained for you by his blood

come to share in the power of his cross and resurrection

by celebrating his memorial in this eucharist,

for he lives and reigns with you and the Holy Spirit,

one God, for ever and ever. ℟. **Amen.** ℣

READINGS AND INTERVENIENT CHANTS

The current weekday *readings and intervenient chants
are used.*

PRAYER OVER THE GIFTS

Lord,

may we offer these mysteries worthily and often,

for whenever this memorial sacrifice is celebrated

the work of our redemption is renewed.

We ask this through Christ our Lord.

℟. **Amen.** ➔ No. 21, p. 626 (Pref. P 47-48)

COMMUNION ANT. 1 Cor 11, 24-25

This body will be given for you. This is the cup of

the new covenant in my blood; whenever you receive them, do so in remembrance of me. ℣

PRAYER AFTER COMMUNION

Lord,
by sharing in this sacrifice
which your Son commanded us to offer as his memorial,
may we become, with him, an everlasting gift to you.
We ask this through Christ our Lord.
℟. **Amen.**　　　　　　　　　　　　→ No. 32, p. 650

5. PRECIOUS BLOOD

ENTRANCE ANT.　　　　　　　　　　　　Rv 5, 9-10
By your blood, O Lord, you have redeemed us from every tribe and tongue, from every nation and people: you have made us into the kingdom of God.
　　　　　　　　　　　　　　　　　→ No. 2, p. 614

OPENING PRAYER

Father,
by the blood of your own Son
you have set all men free and saved us from death.
Continue your work of love within us,
that by constantly celebrating the mystery of our salvation
we may reach the eternal life it promises.
We ask this . . . for ever and ever. ℟. **Amen.** ℣

READINGS AND INTERVENIENT CHANTS

The current weekday *readings and intervenient chants are used.*

PRAYER OVER THE GIFTS

Lord,
by offering these gifts in this eucharist
may we come to Jesus, the mediator of the new covenant,

find salvation in the sprinkling of his blood
and draw closer to the kingdom
where he is Lord for ever and ever.
℟. **Amen.** ➔ No. 21, p. 626 (Pref. P 17)

COMMUNION ANT. See 1 Cor 10, 10

**The cup that we bless is a communion with the blood
of Christ; and the bread that we break is a communion with the body of the Lord.** ℣

PRAYER AFTER COMMUNION

Lord,
you renew us with the food and drink of salvation.
May the blood of our Savior
be for us a fountain of water
springing up to eternal life.
We ask this through Christ our Lord.
℟. **Amen.** ➔ No. 32, p. 650

6. THE SACRED HEART OF JESUS

ENTRANCE ANT. Ps 33, 11. 19

**The thoughts of his heart last through every genera-
tion, that he will rescue them from death and feed
them in time of famine.** ➔ No. 2, p. 614

OPENING PRAYER

Lord God,
give us the strength and love of the heart of your
  Son
that, by becoming one with him,
we may have eternal salvation.
We ask this . . . for ever and ever. ℟. **Amen.** ℣

READINGS AND INTERVENIENT CHANTS

The current weekday *readings and intervenient chants
are used.*

PRAYER OVER THE GIFTS

Father of mercy,
in your great love for us
you have given us your only Son.
May he take us up into his own perfect sacrifice,
that we may offer you fitting worship.
We ask this through Christ our Lord. ℞. **Amen.** ⅴ

PREFACE (P 45)

Father, all-powerful and ever-living God,
we do well always and everywhere to give you
    thanks
through Jesus Christ our Lord.

Lifted high on the cross,
Christ gave his life for us,
so much did he love us.
From his wounded side flowed blood and water,
the fountain of sacramental life in the Church.
To his open heart the Savior invites all men,
to draw water in joy from the springs of salvation.

Now, with all the saints and angels,
we praise you for ever: ➔ No. 23, p. 627

COMMUNION ANT.   Jn 7, 37-38

**The Lord says: If anyone is thirsty, let him come to
me; whoever believes in me, let him drink. Streams
of living water shall flow out from within him.** ⅴ

OR   Jn 19, 34

**One of the soldiers pierced Jesus' side with a lance,
and at once there flowed out blood and water.** ⅴ

PRAYER AFTER COMMUNION

Lord,
we have received your sacrament of love.
By becoming more like Christ on earth
may we share his glory in heaven,
where he lives and reigns for ever and ever.
℞. **Amen.**   ➔ No. 32, p. 650

———————————

7B. HOLY SPIRIT

ENTRANCE ANT. Jn 16, 13

When the Spirit of truth comes, says the Lord, he will lead you to the whole truth. ➤ No. 2, p. 614

OPENING PRAYER

Lord,
may the Helper, the Spirit who comes from you,
fill our hearts with light
and lead us to all truth
as your Son promised,
for he lives and reigns with you and the Holy Spirit,
one God, for ever and ever. ℞. **Amen.** ✠

READINGS AND INTERVENIENT CHANTS

The current weekday *readings and intervenient chants are used.*

PRAYER OVER THE GIFTS

Father, look with kindness
on the gifts we bring to your altar.
May we worship you in spirit and truth:
give us the humility and faith
to make our offering pleasing to you.
We ask this through Christ our Lord.
℞. **Amen.** ➤ No. 21, p. 626 (Pref. P 55)

COMMUNION ANT. Jn 15, 26; 16, 14

The Lord says, the Spirit who comes from the Father will glorify me. ✠

PRAYER AFTER COMMUNION

Lord our God,
you renew us with food from heaven;
fill our hearts with the gentle love of your Spirit.
May the gifts we have received in this life
lead us to the gift of eternal joy.
We ask this through Christ our Lord.
℞. **Amen.** ➤ No. 32, p. 650

8. BLESSED VIRGIN MARY
MASS OF THE IMMACULATE HEART OF MARY

See p. 1023.

DAILY MASSES FOR THE DEAD

These Masses may be celebrated according to the rules given on p. 1234.

C. FOR MORE THAN ONE PERSON OR FOR ALL THE DEAD

ENTRANCE ANT.
Give them eternal rest, O Lord, and let them share your glory. ➤ No. 2, p. 614

OPENING PRAYER
God, our creator and redeemer,
by your power Christ conquered death
and returned to you in glory.
May all your people who have gone before us in faith
share his victory
and enjoy the vision of your glory for ever,
where Christ lives and reigns with you and the Holy
    Spirit,
one God, for ever and ever. ℟. **Amen.** ✣

READINGS AND INTERVENIENT CHANTS

The current weekday readings and intervenient chants are used.

PRAYER OVER THE GIFTS

Lord,
receive this sacrifice
for our brothers and sisters.
On earth you gave them the privilege of believing in
  Christ:
grant them the eternal life promised by that faith.
We ask this through Christ our Lord.
℟. **Amen.**   ➤ No. 21, p. 626 (Pref. P 77-81)

COMMUNION ANT.   1 Jn 4, 9

**God sent his only Son into the world so that we
could have life through him.** ℣

PRAYER AFTER COMMUNION

Lord,
may our sacrifice bring peace and forgiveness
to our brothers and sisters who have died.
Bring the new life given to them in baptism
to the fullness of eternal joy.
We ask this through Christ our Lord.
℟. **Amen.**   ➤ No. 32, p. 650

VARIOUS PRAYERS FOR THE DEAD

1A. FOR A POPE

OPENING PRAYER

God our Father,
you reward all who believe in you.
May your servant, N. our Pope, vicar of Peter, and
  shepherd of your Church,
who faithfully administered the mysteries of your
  forgiveness and love on earth,

rejoice with you for ever in heaven.
We ask this . . . for ever and ever. ℟. **Amen.**

PRAYER OVER THE GIFTS

Lord,
by this sacrifice which brings us peace,
give your servant, N. our Pope,
the reward of eternal happiness
and let your mercy win for us
the gift of your life and love.
We ask this through Christ our Lord. ℟. **Amen.**

PRAYER AFTER COMMUNION

Lord,
you renew us with the sacraments of your divine
  life.
Hear our prayers for your servant, N. our Pope.
You made him the center of the unity of your Church
  on earth,
count him now among the flock of the blessed in your
  kingdom.
Grant this through Christ our Lord. ℟. **Amen.**

2A. FOR THE DIOCESAN BISHOP

OPENING PRAYER

All-powerful God,
you made N. your servant
the guide of your family.
May he enjoy the reward of all his work
and share the eternal joy of his Lord.
We ask this . . . for ever and ever. ℟. **Amen.**

PRAYER OVER THE GIFTS

Merciful God,
may this sacrifice,
which N. your servant offered during his life
for the salvation of the faithful,
help him now to find pardon and peace.
We ask this through Christ our Lord. ℟. **Amen.**

PRAYER AFTER COMMUNION

Lord,
give your mercy and love to N. your servant.
He hoped in Christ and preached Christ.
By this sacrifice may he share with Christ
the joy of eternal life.
We ask this through Christ our Lord. ℟. **Amen.**

3A. FOR A PRIEST

OPENING PRAYER

Lord,
you gave N. your servant and priest
the privilege of a holy ministry in this world.
May he rejoice for ever in the glory of your kingdom.
We ask this . . . for ever and ever. ℟. **Amen.**

PRAYER OVER THE GIFTS

All-powerful God,
by this eucharist may N. your servant and priest
rejoice for ever in the vision of the mysteries
which he faithfully ministered here on earth.
We ask this through Christ our Lord. ℟. **Amen.**

PRAYER AFTER COMMUNION

God of mercy,
we who receive the sacraments of salvation
pray for N. your servant and priest.
You made him a minister of your mysteries on earth.
May he rejoice in the full knowledge of your truth
   in heaven.
We ask this through Christ our Lord. ℟. **Amen.**

6A. FOR ONE PERSON

OPENING PRAYER

Lord,
those who die still live in your presence
and your saints rejoice in complete happiness.

Listen to our prayers for N. your son (daughter)
who has passed from the light of this world,
and bring him (her) to the joy of eternal radiance.
We ask this . . . for ever and ever. ℟. **Amen.**

PRAYER OVER THE GIFTS

Lord,
be pleased with this sacrifice we offer for N. your
   servant.
May he (she) find in your presence
the forgiveness he (she) always longed for
and come to praise your glory for ever
in the joyful fellowship of your saints.
We ask this through Christ our Lord. ℟. **Amen.**

PRAYER AFTER COMMUNION

Lord,
we thank you for the holy gifts we receive
and pray for N. our brother (sister).
By the suffering and death of your Son
free him (her) from the bonds of his (her) sins
and bring him (her) to endless joy in your presence.
We ask this through Christ our Lord. ℟. **Amen.**

11A. FOR SEVERAL PERSONS

OPENING PRAYER

Lord,
be merciful to your servants N. and N.
You cleansed them from sin in the fountain of new
   birth.
Bring them now to the happiness of life in your kingdom.
We ask this . . . for ever and ever. ℟. **Amen.**

PRAYER OVER THE GIFTS

Lord,
we offer you this sacrifice.
Hear our prayers for N. and N.,

and through this offering
grant our brothers (sisters) your everlasting forgiveness.
We ask this through Christ our Lord. ℟. **Amen.**

PRAYER AFTER COMMUNION

Lord,
we who receive your sacraments
ask your mercy and love.
By sharing in the power of this eucharist
may our brothers (sisters) win forgiveness of their
sins,
enter your kingdom,
and praise your for all eternity.
We ask this through Christ our Lord. ℟. **Amen.**

_____

13. FOR PARENTS

OPENING PRAYER

Almighty God,
you command us to honor father and mother.
In your mercy forgive the sins of my (our) parents
and let me (us) one day see them again
in the radiance of eternal joy.
We ask this . . . for ever and ever. ℟. **Amen.**

PRAYER OVER THE GIFTS

Lord,
receive the sacrifice we offer for my (our) parents.
Give them eternal joy in the land of the living,
and let me (us) join them one day in the happiness of
the saints.
We ask this through Christ our Lord. ℟. **Amen.**

PRAYER AFTER COMMUNION

Lord,
may this sharing in the sacrament of heaven
win eternal rest and light for my (our) parents

and prepare me (us) to share eternal glory with
them.
We ask this through Christ our Lord. ℟. **Amen.**

---

14. FOR RELATIVES, FRIENDS, AND BENEFACTORS

OPENING PRAYER

Father,
source of forgiveness and salvation for all mankind,
hear our prayer.
By the prayers of the ever-virgin Mary,
may our friends, relatives, and benefactors
who have gone from this world
come to share eternal happiness with all your saints.
We ask this . . . for ever and ever. ℟. **Amen.**

PRAYER OVER THE GIFTS

God of infinite mercy,
hear our prayers
and by this sacrament of our salvation
forgive all the sins of our relatives, friends, and
benefactors.
We ask this through Christ our Lord. ℟. **Amen.**

PRAYER AFTER COMMUNION

Father all-powerful, God of mercy,
we have offered you this sacrifice of praise
for our relatives, friends, and benefactors.
By the power of this sacrament
free them from all their sins
and give them the joy of eternal light.
We ask this through Christ our Lord. ℟. **Amen.**

APPENDIX II

ALLELUIA VERSE
FOR WEEKDAYS OF THE YEAR

DECEMBER 1 TO DECEMBER 16

1   See Ps 79, 4
℟. **Alleluia.** Come and save us, Lord our God;
let us see your face, and we shall be saved. ℟. **Alleluia.**

2   Ps 85, 8
℟. **Alleluia.** Lord, let us see your kindness,
and grant us your salvation. ℟. **Alleluia.**

3   Is 33, 22
℟. **Alleluia.** The Lord will judge us by his law;
he is our King and Savior. ℟. **Alleluia.**

4   Is 40, 9. 10
℟. **Alleluia.** Raise your voice and tell the Good News:
the Lord our God comes in strength. ℟. **Alleluia.**

5   Is 45, 8
℟. **Alleluia.** Let the clouds rain down the Just One, and the earth bring forth a Savior. ℟. **Alleluia.**

6   Is 55, 6
℟. **Alleluia.** Seek the Lord while he can be found. Call on him while he is near. ℟. **Alleluia.**

7   Lk 3, 4. 6
℟. **Alleluia.** Prepare the way for the Lord, make straight his paths:
all mankind shall see the salvation of God. ℟. **Alleluia.**

8
℟. **Alleluia.** Come, O Lord, do not delay:
forgive the sins of your people. ℟. **Alleluia.**

9
℟. **Alleluia.** Behold, our Lord shall come with power,
he will enlighten the eyes of his servants. ℟. **Alleluia.**

10
℟. **Alleluia.** Come, Lord, bring to us your peace;
let us rejoice before you with a perfect heart. ℟. **Alleluia.**

11
℟. **Alleluia.** Behold, the king will come, the Lord of earth:
and he will set us free. ℟. **Alleluia.**

12
℟. **Alleluia.** The day of the Lord is near:
he comes to save us. ℟. **Alleluia.**

13
℟. **Alleluia.** The Lord will come; go out to meet him!
He is the prince of peace. ℟. **Alleluia.**

14
℟. **Alleluia.** The Lord is coming to save his people;
happy are those prepared to meet him. ℟. **Alleluia.**

DECEMBER 17 TO DECEMBER 24

1
℟. **Alleluia.** Come, Wisdom of our God Most High,
guiding creation with power and love:
teach us to walk in the paths of knowledge: ℟. **Alleluia.**

2
℟. **Alleluia.** Come, Leader of ancient Israel,
giver of the Law to Moses on Sinai:
rescue us with your mighty power. ℟. **Alleluia.**

3
℟. **Alleluia.** Come, Flower of Jesse's stem,
sign of God's love for all his people:
save us without delay. ℟. **Alleluia.**

4
℟. **Alleluia.** Come, Key of David,
opening the gates of God's eternal Kingdom:
free the prisoners of darkness! ℟. **Alleluia.**

5
℟. **Alleluia.** Come, Radiant Dawn,
splendor of eternal light, sun of justice:
shine on those lost in the darkness of death! ℟. **Alleluia.**

6
℟. **Alleluia.** Come, King of all nations,
source of your Church's unity and faith:
save all mankind, your own creation! ℟. **Alleluia.**

7
℟. **Alleluia.** Come, Emmanuel,
God's presence among us, our King, our Judge:
save us, Lord our God! ℟. **Alleluia.**

BEFORE EPIPHANY

1   Jn 1, 14. 12
℟. **Alleluia.** The Word of God became a man and lived among us.
He enabled those who accepted him
to become the children of God. ℟. **Alleluia.**

2   Heb 1, 1-2

℟. **Alleluia.** In the past God spoke to our fathers through the prophets; now he speaks to us through his Son. ℟. **Alleluia.**

3

℟. **Alleluia.** A holy day has dawned upon us.
Today a great light has come upon the earth.
Come you nations and adore the Lord. ℟. **Alleluia.**

AFTER EPIPHANY

1   Mt 4, 16

℟. **Alleluia.** A people in darkness have seen a great light;
a radiant dawn shines on those lost in death. ℟. **Alleluia.**

2   Mt 4, 23

℟. **Alleluia.** Jesus preached the Good News of the Kingdom
and healed all who were sick. ℟. **Alleluia.**

3   Lk 4, 18-19

℟. **Alleluia.** The Lord sent me to bring Good News to the poor,
and freedom to prisoners. ℟. **Alleluia.**

4   Lk 7, 16

℟. **Alleluia.** A great prophet has risen among us;
God has visited his people. ℟. **Alleluia.**

5   See 1 Tm 3, 16

℟. **Alleluia.** Glory to Christ who is proclaimed to the world;
glory from all who believe in him! ℟. **Alleluia.**

VERSES BEFORE THE GOSPEL
FOR THE WEEKDAYS OF LENT

See p. 620 for the various responses before and after each verse.

1   Ps 51, 12. 14

Create a clean heart in me, O God;
give back to me the joy of your salvation.

2   Ps 95, 8

If today you hear his voice, harden not your hearts.

3   Ps 130, 5. 7

I hope in the Lord, I trust in his word;
with him there is mercy and fullness of redemption.

4   Ex 18, 31

Rid yourselves of all your sins;

and make a new heart and
a new spirit.

5   Ez 33, 11
I do not wish the sinner to
die, says the Lord,
but to turn to me and live.

6   Jl 2, 12-13
With all your heart turn
to me
for I am tender and com-
passionate.

7   Am 5, 14
Seek good and not evil
so that you may live,
and the Lord will be with
you.

8   Mt 4, 4
Man does not live on bread
alone,
but on every word that
comes from the mouth of
God.

9   Mt 4, 17
Repent, says the Lord,
the kingdom of heaven is at
hand.

10   See Lk 8, 15
Happy are they who have
kept the word with a
generous heart,
and yield a harvest through
perseverance.

11   Lk 15, 18
I will rise and go to my

Father and tell him:
Father, I have sinned
against heaven and
against you.

12   Jn 3, 16
God loved the world so
much, he gave us his only
Son,
that all who believe in him
might have eternal life.

13   Jn 6, 64. 69
Your words, Lord, are spir-
it and life;
you have the message of
eternal life.

14   Jn 8, 12
I am the light of the world,
says the Lord:
he who follows me will have
the light of life.

15   Jn 11, 26. 26
I am the resurrection and
the life, said the Lord:
he who believes in me will
not die for ever.

16   2 Cor 6, 2
This is the favorable time,
this is the day of salvation.

17
The seed is the word of God,
Christ is the sower;
all who come to him will
live for ever.

EASTER SEASON UP TO THE ASCENSION

1   Lk 24, 46
R̸. **Alleluia.** Christ had to
suffer and to rise from
the dead,

and so enter into his glory.
R̸. **Alleluia.**

2   Jn 10, 14
R̸. **Alleluia.** I am the good

shepherd, says the Lord;
I know my sheep and mine
know me. ℟. **Alleluia.**

3 Jn 10, 27
℟. **Alleluia.** My sheep listen
to my voice, says the
Lord;
I know them and they fol-
low me. ℟. **Alleluia.**

4 Jn 20, 29
℟. **Alleluia.** You believe in
me, Thomas, because you
have seen me;
happy those who have not
seen me, but still believe!
℟. **Alleluia.**

5 Rom 6, 9
℟. **Alleluia.** Christ now
raised from the dead will
never die again;
death no longer has power
over him. ℟. **Alleluia.**

6 Col 3, 1
℟. **Alleluia.** If then you
have been raised with
Christ, seek the things
that are above,
where Christ is seated at
the right hand of God.
℟. **Alleluia.**

7 Rv 1, 5
℟. **Alleluia.** Jesus Christ,
you are the faithful wit-
ness, first-born from the
death;
you have loved us and
washed away our sins in
your blood. ℟. **Alleluia.**

8
℟. **Alleluia.** Christ has risen
and shines upon us,
whom he has redeemed by
his blood. ℟. **Alleluia.**

9
℟. **Alleluia.** Nailed to the
cross for our sake,
the Lord is now risen from
the grave. ℟. **Alleluia.**

10
℟. **Alleluia.** Christ is risen,
and makes all things new;
he has shown pity to all
mankind. ℟. **Alleluia.**

11
℟. **Alleluia.** We know that
Christ is truly risen from
the dead;
victorious king, deal kindly
with us. ℟. **Alleluia.**

EASTER SEASON AFTER THE ASCENSION

1 Mt 28, 19. 20
℟. **Alleluia.** Go and teach
all people my gospel;
I am with you always, until
the end of the world. ℟.
Alleluia.

2 Jn 14, 16
℟. **Alleluia.** The Father will
send you the Holy Spirit,
says the Lord,
to be with you for ever.
℟. **Alleluia.**

3 Jn 14, 18

℟. **Alleluia.** The Lord said: I will not leave you orphans.
I will come back to you, and your hearts will rejoice. ℟. **Alleluia.**

4 Jn 14, 26

℟. **Alleluia.** The Holy Spirit will teach you all things, and remind you of all I have said to you. ℟. **Alleluia.**

5 Jn 16, 7. 13

℟. **Alleluia.** I will send you the Spirit of truth, says the Lord;

he will lead you to the whole truth. ℟. **Alleluia.**

6 Jn 16, 28

℟. **Alleluia.** I went from the Father and came into the world;
and now I leave the world to return to the Father. ℟. **Alleluia.**

7 Col 3, 1

℟. **Alleluia.** If then you have been raised with Christ, seek the things that are above,
where Christ is seated at the right hand of God. ℟. **Alleluia.**

ORDINARY TIME

1 1 Sm 3, 9; Jn 6, 69

℟. **Alleluia.** Speak, O Lord, your servant is listening; you have the words of everlasting life. ℟. **Alleluia.**

2 Ps 19, 9

℟. **Alleluia.** Your words, O Lord, give joy to my heart,
your teaching is light to my eyes. ℟. **Alleluia.**

3 Ps 25, 4. 5

℟. **Alleluia.** Teach me your paths, my God, and lead me in your truth. ℟. **Alleluia.**

4 Ps 27, 11

℟. **Alleluia.** Teach me your way, O Lord,
and lead me on a straight road. ℟. **Alleluia.**

5 Ps 95, 8

℟. **Alleluia.** If today you hear his voice, harden not your hearts. ℟. **Alleluia.**

6 Ps 111, 8

℟. **Alleluia.** Your laws are all made firm, O Lord, established for ever more. ℟. **Alleluia.**

7 Ps 119, 18

℟. **Alleluia.** Unveil my eyes, O Lord,
and I will see the marvels of your law. ℟. **Alleluia.**

8 Ps 119, 27

℟. **Alleluia.** Instruct me in the way of your rules, and I will reflect on all your wonders. ℟. **Alleluia.**

9   Ps 119, 34

℟. **Alleluia.** Teach me the
meaning of your law, O
Lord,
and I will guard it with all
my heart. ℟. **Alleluia.**

10   Ps 119, 35. 29

℟. **Alleluia.** Turn my heart
to do your will;
teach me your law, O God.
℟. **Alleluia.**

11   Ps 119, 88

℟. **Alleluia.** Give me life,
O Lord,
and I will do your com-
mands. ℟. **Alleluia.**

12   Ps 119, 105

℟. **Alleluia.** Your word is a
lamp for my feet,
and a light on my path.
℟. **Alleluia.**

13   Ps 119, 135

℟. **Alleluia.** Let your face
shine on your servant,
and teach me your laws.
℟. **Alleluia.**

14   Ps 130, 5

℟. **Alleluia.** I hope in the
Lord,
I trust in his word. ℟. **Al-
leluia.**

15   Ps 145, 13

℟. **Alleluia.** The Lord is
faithful in all his words
and holy in his deeds. ℟.
Alleluia.

16   Ps 147, 2. 15

℟. **Alleluia.** O praise the
Lord, Jerusalem;
he sends out his word to the
earth. ℟. **Alleluia.**

17   Mt 4, 4

℟. **Alleluia.** Man does not
live on bread alone,
but on every word that
comes from the mouth of
God. ℟. **Alleluia.**

18   Mt 11, 25

℟. **Alleluia.** Blessed are
you, Father, Lord of
heaven and earth;
you have revealed to little
ones the mysteries of the
kingdom. ℟. **Alleluia.**

19   See Lk 8, 15

℟. **Alleluia.** Happy are
they who have kept the
word with a generous
heart,
and yield a harvest through
perseverance. ℟. **Alle-
luia.**

20   Jn 6, 64. 69

℟. **Alleluia.** Your words,
Lord, are spirit and life,
you have the words of everlasting life. ℟. **Alleluia.**

21   Jn 10, 27

℟. **Alleluia.** My sheep listen
to my voice, says the
Lord;
I know them, and they follow me. ℟. **Alleluia.**

23   Jn 14, 5

℟. **Alleluia.** I am the way,
the truth, and the life,
says the Lord;
no one comes to the Father,
except through me. ℟.
Alleluia.

24   Jn 14, 23

℟. **Alleluia.** If anyone loves

me, he will hold to my words,
and my Father will love him, and we will come to him. ℟. **Alleluia.**

25 Jn 15, 15
℟. **Alleluia.** I call you my friends, says the Lord,
for I have made known to you all that Father has told me. ℟. **Alleluia.**

26 Jn 17, 17
℟. **Alleluia.** Your word, O Lord, is truth;
make us holy in the truth. ℟. **Alleluia.**

27 See Acts 16, 14
℟. **Alleluia.** Open our hearts, O Lord,
to listen to the words of your Son. ℟. **Alleluia.**

28 2 Cor 5, 19
℟. **Alleluia.** God was in Christ, to reconcile the world to himself;
and the Good News of reconciliation he has entrusted to us. ℟. **Alleluia.**

29 See Eph 1, 17-18
℟. **Alleluia.** May the Father of our Lord Jesus Christ enlighten the eyes of our heart
that we might see how great is the hope
to which we are called. ℟. **Alleluia.**

30 Phil 2, 15-16
℟. **Alleluia.** Shine on the world like bright stars;

you are offering it the word of life. ℟. **Alleluia.**

31 Col 3, 16. 17
℟. **Alleluia.** Give thanks to God our Father through Jesus Christ our Lord,
and may the fullness of his message live within you. ℟. **Alleluia.**

32 1 Thes 2, 13
℟. **Alleluia.** Receive this message not as the words of man,
but as truly the word of God. ℟. **Alleluia.**

33 2 Thes 2, 14
℟. **Alleluia.** God has called us with the gospel;
the people won for him by Jesus Christ our Lord. ℟. **Alleluia.**

34. 2 Tm 1, 10
℟. **Alleluia.** Our Savior Jesus Christ has done away with death,
and brought us life through his gospel. ℟. **Alleluia.**

35 Heb 4, 12
℟. **Alleluia.** The word of God is living and active;
it probes the thoughts and motives of our heart. ℟. **Alleluia.**

36 Jas 1, 18
℟. **Alleluia.** The Father gave us birth by his message of truth,
that we might be as the first fruits of his creation. ℟. **Alleluia.**

37   Jas 1, 21

℟. **Alleluia.** Receive and submit to the word planted in you;

it can save your souls. ℟. **Alleluia.**

38   1 Pt 1, 25

℟. **Alleluia.** The word of the Lord stands for ever;

it is the word given to you, the Good News. ℟. **Alleluia.**

39   1 Jn 2, 5

℟. **Alleluia.** He who keeps the word of Christ,

grows perfect in the love of God. ℟. **Alleluia.**

For the Last Week

1   Mt 24, 42. 44

℟. **Alleluia.** Be watchful and ready;

you know not when the Son of Man is coming. ℟. **Alleluia.**

2   Lk 21, 28

℟. **Alleluia.** Lift up your heads and see;

your redemption is near at hand. ℟. **Alleluia.**

3   Lk 21, 36

℟. **Alleluia.** Be watchful, pray constantly,

that you may be worthy to stand before the Son of Man. ℟. **Alleluia.**

4   Rv 2, 10

℟. **Alleluia.** Be faithful until death, says the Lord, and I will give you the crown of life. ℟. **Alleluia.**

TREASURY OF PRAYERS

MORNING PRAYERS

Most holy and adorable Trinity, one God in three Persons, I praise you and give you thanks for all the favors you have bestowed upon me. Your goodness has preserved me until now. I offer you my whole being and in particular all my thoughts, words and deeds, together with all the trials I may undergo this day. Give them your blessing. May your Divine Love animate them and may they serve your greater glory.

I make this morning offering in union with the Divine intentions of Jesus Christ who offers himself daily in the holy Sacrifice of the Mass, and in union with Mary, his Virgin Mother and our Mother, who was always the faithful handmaid of the Lord.

Glory be to the Father, and to the Son, and to the Holy Spirit. Amen.

Prayer for Divine Guidance through the Day

Partial indulgence (No. 21) *

Lord, God Almighty, you have brought us safely to the beginning of this day. Defend us today by your mighty power, that we may not fall into any sin, but that all our words may so proceed and all our thoughts and actions be so directed, as to be always just in your sight. Through Christ our Lord. Amen.

---

* The indulgences quoted in this Missal are taken from the 1968 Vatican edition of the "Enchiridion Indulgentiarum" (published by Catholic Book Publishing Co.).

Partial indulgence (No. 1)

Direct, we beg you, O Lord, our actions by your holy inspirations, and carry them on by your gracious assistance, that every prayer and work of ours may begin always with you, and through you be happily ended. Amen.

NIGHT PRAYERS

I adore you, my God, and thank you for having created me, for having made me a Christian and preserved me this day. I love you with all my heart and I am sorry for having sinned against you, because you are infinite Love and infinite Goodness. Protect me during my rest and may your love be always with me. Amen.

Eternal Father, I offer you the Precious Blood of Jesus Christ in atonement for my sins and for all the intentions of our Holy Church.

Holy Spirit, Love of the Father and the Son, purify my heart and fill it with the fire of your Love, so that I may be a chaste Temple of the Holy Trinity and be always pleasing to you in all things. Amen.

Plea for Divine Help

Partial indulgence (No. 24)

Hear us, Lord, holy Father, almighty and eternal God; and graciously send your holy angel from heaven to watch over, to cherish, to protect, to abide with, and to defend all who dwell in this house. Through Christ our Lord. Amen.

CONFESSION PRAYERS

Prayer before Confession

O Holy Spirit, enlighten my mind that I may know my sins, and inspire true sorrow for them. Make me firmly resolve not to commit them again.

Most loving Savior, Lamb of God, you freely gave your life for sinners. Help me to make an act of contrition that is animated by perfect love of God.

Immaculate Virgin Mary, refuge of sinners, help me to fulfill my resolution of henceforth accepting and fulfilling God's Holy Will, as you have done. Amen.

Helpful Suggestions for Confession

1. It is well to personalize our confession by identifying ourselves, e.g., "I am a married woman and have three children," or "I am a widower," or "I am a teacher," etc. This reveals us to the Celebrant as a real person, living in a real situation and serving God in a particular vocation. It helps the Celebrant to judge our service to Christ and to direct us in conforming ourselves to Him.

2. The Sacrament of Penance is a means of Christian perfection. We should use it in a manner that will help us to grow more like Christ. We could refer to the progress, or lack of it, that we think we have made since our last visit to this Sacrament, e.g., "In my last confession I resolved to love Christ more in the people with whom I work; since then, I have improved, but still I have failed many times." Again, this personalizes our confession and avoids automatic listing of sins.

3. Our sorrow and purpose of amendment should be expressed before we receive the Sacrament, and is evidenced by our "Amen" in response to the principal prayer of absolution. It can also be expressed in the very confession of our sins. For example, we could say "In the past month I was irritable many times with my wife and family, hurting the spirit of our home. This month I really want to correct this."

4. How often should I meet the Lord in this Sacrament?
If we have consciously chosen against the Lord in our life,
in some serious matter, we should promptly seek his mercy
in this Sacrament, as long as we are truly repentant. If
there is no question of a turning away from God in this
way, Confession is not necessary for us, regardless of how
long it may be since our last Confession. However, received
with the proper dispositions, it will help us to grow in the
Christian life. If we receive the Sacrament often, but without necessity, the burden is on us to receive it fruitfully.
The Christian's life is one of constant conversion, of a
continually renewed commitment. If our regular confession is made in that light, and with that purpose, the
Lord's grace will effect things in our spiritual life.

Examination of Conscience

How long has it been since my last confession?

Did I conceal any sin?

Did I say my penance?

Have I neglected my home and my family duties?

Have I been lazy, neglectful, or willfully distracted during my prayers or at Mass?

Have I used God's name irreverently, or taken false or
needless oaths?

Have I missed Mass through my own fault on Sundays or
holydays, or worked unnecessarily on Sunday?

Have I disobeyed, angered, or been disrespectful toward
my parents, teachers, employers, or other superiors?

Have I been unjust and unkind to those over whom I have
authority?

Have I quarreled with or willfully hurt anyone?

Have I refused to forgive?

Have I been guilty of cruelty, mental or physical, toward
anyone?

Have I caused another to commit sin?

Have I offended in any way by thought, word, or deed
against the holy virtue of purity?

Have I led others into sin?

Have I stolen or destroyed property belonging to any other
person, or company?

Have I neglected my home and my family duties?

Have I given a bad example to the members of my family or others?

Have I knowingly accepted stolen goods?

Have I paid all my just debts?

Have I told lies, repeated gossip, or injured another person's character?

Have I been angry, greedy, proud, envious, jealous, lazy, immodest; or intemperate in eating or drinking?

Have I willfully broken any of the Church laws concerning fast or abstinence?

Have I failed to support my Church?

Have I received Communion during Easter Time?

For married people.

Have I failed to show love, respect, and good example towards my partner?

Have I neglected my duty to my children in regard to their religious instruction, to their training in good habits, and to their schooling?

Have I sinned against the duties of married life?

We must confess the number of our grave sins.

The Penitent's Formula for the Sacrament of Penance

Penitent: Bless me Father, for I have sinned.

Celebrant: The Lord be on your lips and in your heart that you may properly confess all your sins, in the Name of the Father, ✠ and of the Son, and of the Holy Spirit.

Penitent: It is . . . . . . since my last confession . . . . . .
(The penitent confesses)

Penitent: For these and all my sins I am truly sorry.
(The Celebrant instructs and gives the penance)

Celebrant: Now absolves the Penitent, who does not say the Act of Contrition but reverently listens, and answers "Amen" to the principal prayer of absolution. Our "Amen" is a sign of our acceptance of God's mercy, and an evidence of our sorrow.

"May Our Lord Jesus Christ absolve you, and by his authority I absolve you, [from every bond of excommunication and interdict to the extent of my power and your need. And finally, I absolve you]from your sins, in the Name of the Father, ✠ and of the Son, and of the Holy Spirit."

Penitent: Amen

After Confession

My dearest Jesus, I have told all my sins as well as I could. I have tried hard to make a good confession. I feel sure that you have forgiven me. I thank you. It is only because of all your sufferings that I can go to confession and free myself from my sins. Your Heart is full of love and mercy for poor sinners. I love you because you are so good to me.

My loving Savior, I shall try to keep from sin and to love you more each day. My dear Mother Mary, pray for me and help me to keep my promises. Protect me and do not let me fall back into sin.

COMMUNION PRAYERS

See p. 606.

BENEDICTION OF THE MOST BLESSED SACRAMENT

At the opening of Benediction any Eucharistic Hymn may be sung.

Hymn: Down in adoration falling,
    Lo! The sacred Host we hail;
Lo! O'er ancient forms departing
    Newer rites of grace prevail;
Faith for all defects supplying
    Where the feeble senses fail.

To the everlasting Father
    And the Son who reigns on high,
With the Spirit blest proceeding,
    Forth from each eternally,
Be salvation, honor, blessing,
    Might, and endless majesty. Amen.

℣. You have given them bread from heaven. (P.T. Alleluia.)

℟. Having all sweetness with it. (P.T. Alleluia.)

Celebrant: Let us pray: O God, who in this wonderful sacrament left us a memorial of your passion, grant, we implore you, that we may so venerate the sacred mysteries of your Body and Blood as always to be conscious of the fruit of your redemption. You who live and reign, forever and ever. ℟. Amen.

Partial indulgence (No. 59)

The Divine Praises

Blessed be God. * Blessed be his holy name. * Blessed be Jesus Christ, true God and true man. * Blessed be the name of Jesus. * Blessed be his most Sacred Heart. * Blessed be his most Precious Blood. * Blessed be Jesus in the most Holy Sacrament of the Altar. * Blessed be the Holy Spirit, the Paraclete. * Blessed be the great Mother of God, Mary most holy. * Blessed be her holy and Immaculate Conception. * Blessed be her glorious Assumption. * Blessed be the name of Mary, Virgin and Mother. * Blessed be St. Joseph, her most chaste spouse. * Blessed be God in his angels and in his saints.

THE STATIONS OF THE CROSS

THE Stations of the Cross is a devotion in which we accompany, in spirit, our Blessed Lord in His sorrowful journey to Calvary, and devoutly meditate on His sufferings and death.

1. Jesus Is Condemned to Death
Dear Jesus, help me to sin no more and to be very obedient.

4. Jesus Meets His Mother
Dear Jesus, may Your Mother console me and all who are sad.

2. Jesus Bears His Cross
Dear Jesus, let me suffer for sinners in union with You.

5. Jesus Is Helped by Simon
Dear Jesus, may I do all things to please You all day long.

3. Jesus Falls the First Time
Dear Jesus, help those who sin to rise and to be truly sorry

6. Veronica Wipes His Face
Dear Jesus, give me courage and generosity to help others.

7. Jesus Falls a Second Time
Dear Jesus, teach us to be sorry for all our many sins.

11. Jesus Is Nailed to the Cross
Dear Jesus, keep me close to You from this moment until I die.

8. Jesus Speaks to the Women
Dear Jesus, comfort those who have no one to comfort them.

12. Jesus Dies on the Cross
Dear Jesus, be with me when I die and take me to heaven.

9. Jesus Falls a Third Time
Dear Jesus, show me how to be obedient and to be very kind.

13. He Is Taken from the Cross
Dear Jesus, teach me to place all my trust in Your holy Love.

10. Stripped of His Garments
Dear Jesus, teach me to be pure in thought, word and deed.

14. He Is Laid in the Tomb
Dear Jesus, help me to keep the commandments You have given.

THE HOLY ROSARY OF THE
BLESSED VIRGIN MARY

THE Rosary calls to mind the five Joyful, the five Sorrowful, and the five Glorious Mysteries in the life of Christ and His Blessed Mother. It is composed of fifteen decades, each decade consisting of one "Our Father," ten "Hail Marys," and one "Glory be to the Father."

How to Say the Rosary

The Apostles' Creed is said on the Crucifix; the Our Father is said on each of the Large Beads; the Hail Mary on each of the Small Beads; the Glory Be to the Father after the three Hail Marys at the beginning of the Rosary, and after each group of Small Beads.

When the hands are occupied (driving a car, etc.) the indulgences for saying the Rosary may be gained as long as the beads are on one's person.

The Five

Joyful

Mysteries

1. The Annunciation
For love of humility.

2. The Visitation
For charity.

3. The Nativity
For poverty.

4. The Presentation
For obedience.

5. Finding in Temple
For piety.

1. Agony in Garden
For true contrition

2. Scourging at Pillar
For purity.

3. Crowned with Thorns
For moral courage.

4. Carrying of Cross
For patience.

5. The Crucifixion
For final perseverance.

The Five
Glorious
Mysteries

1. The Resurrection
For faith.

2. The Ascension
For hope.

3. Descent of Holy Spirit
For love of God.

4. Assumption of B.V.M.
For devotion to Mary.

5. Crowning of B.V.M.
For eternal happiness.

INDICES
GENERAL INDEX

PROPER OF SEASONS (Cont'd)
Ordinary Time

PROPER OF SAINTS ..

ORDER OF MASS

PROPER OF SAINTS (Cont'd)

PROPER OF SEASONS (Cont'd)

COMMON OF SAINTS
(Antiphons and Prayers)

COMMON OF SAINTS
(Readings and Intervenient Chants)

APPENDICES

TREASURY OF PRAYERS

INDICES

INDEX OF SAINTS

INDEX OF BIBLICAL READINGS

GENESIS

INDEX OF PSALMS

INDEX OF PREFACES

See pp. 626-627.